W9-BNN-579

Encyclopedia of
IMMIGRATION
AND
MIGRATION
IN THE
AMERICAN WEST

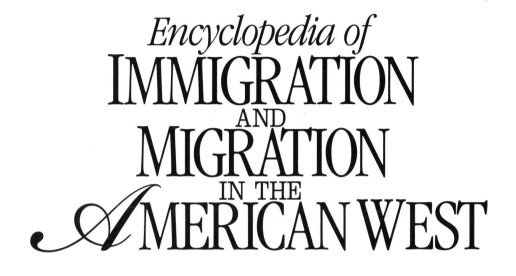

To
Ocean Chi Kiang Bakken
of Bozeman, Montana
and
the memory of
Susan Ellsworth

Encyclopedia of
IMMIGRATION
AND
MIGRATION
IN THE
AMERICAN WEST

VOLUME 1

EDITED BY

GORDON MORRIS BAKKEN & ALEXANDRA KINDELL
California State University, Fullerton   *Iowa State University*

A SAGE Reference Publication

SAGE Publications
Thousand Oaks ▪ London ▪ New Delhi

For information:

Sage Publications, Inc.
2455 Teller Road
Thousand Oaks, California 91320
E-mail: order@sagepub.com

Sage Publications Ltd.
1 Oliver's Yard
55 City Road
London EC1Y 1SP
United Kingdom

Sage Publications India Pvt. Ltd.
B-42, Panchsheel Enclave
Post Box 4109
New Delhi 110 017 India

Printed in the United States of America.

Library of Congress Cataloging-in-Publication Data

Encyclopedia of immigration and migration in the American West / editors Gordon Morris Bakken, Alexandra Kindell.
    p. cm.
Includes bibliographical references and index.
ISBN 1-4129-0550-8 (cloth : alk. paper)
   1. Migration, Internal—West (U.S.)—History—Encyclopedias. 2. West (U.S.)—Emigration
and immigration—Encyclopedias. 3. Indians of North America—West (U.S.)—Encyclopedias.
4. African Americans—West (U.S.)—Encyclopedias. 5. Immigrants—West (U.S.)—Encyclopedias.
6. Ethnology—West (U.S.) 7. Pioneers—West (U.S.)—Encyclopedias. I. Bakken, Gordon Morris.
II. Kindell, Alexandra.
HB1965.E53 2006
304.8'78003—dc22   2005025714

This book is printed on acid-free paper.

06 07 08 09 10 11 9 8 7 6 5 4 3 2 1

Publisher:	Rolf Janke
Acquisitions Editor:	Jerry Westby
Reference Systems Coordinator:	Leticia Gutierrez
Project Editor:	Tracy Alpern
Copy Editors:	Stacey Shimizu
	Catherine Chilton
	Cate Huisman
Typesetter:	C&M Digitals (P) Ltd.
Indexer:	David Luljak
Cover Designer:	Michelle Lee Kenny

CONTENTS

LIST OF ENTRIES

Reader's Guide

To give the reader a quick sense of the topics contained in this work, we have arranged most of the entries in the following topical guide. Broad topical entries for cities contain substantial information on the ethnic migrations through those urban areas. American Indian tribes have tribal histories telling some of their experiences with migration. Ethnic groups have limited entries, and some of them are stories of places. Immigration laws and the history of the Immigration and Nationalization Service give readers detailed public policy information on how federal law affected immigration. Libraries were very much a part of the migration matrix in the American West. Economic change and war were the push and pull of migration. Natural resources laws and events are an important part of the western experience, going far beyond the gold rush to California. Biographies tell personal stories of people in places giving life to the immigration and migration experiences of Americans. We hope you find this topical guide useful, but we remind you to also use the index as a search tool. This is particularly important because so much of the migration and immigration experience takes place in cities.

AMERICAN INDIANS

American Indian Migration to Phoenix, Arizona
Apache
Arapaho
Assiniboine
Blackfoot Nation
Bureau of Indian Affairs
Cahuilla Nation
California Indians of the North Coast and
    Northwestern Coast
California Indians of the Northern Mountains
California Indians of the Northern Valley
Chemehuevi
Cheyennes
Creek Nation
Crow Nation
Cupeños
Gabrielino
Gros Ventre
Hopi
Juaneños
Kumeyaay (Diegueño, I'ipay, and Tipai)

Lakotas
Luiseño
Maidu
Mojave
Nez Perce
Northern Pueblo
Palouse Indians
Trail of Tears
Upland Yumans
Utes
Washoe
Yakama
Yokuts

BIOGRAPHY

Austin, Stephen Fuller
Bartleson, John
Bass, Charlotta A. Spear(s)
Bidwell, John
Bloom, Jessie S.
Brent, Joseph Lancaster
Carr, Jeanne Carver Smith

CITIES AND TOWNS

ECONOMIC CHANGE AND WAR

Defense Industry
Dry Farming
Farming Families on the Oregon Frontier
Iran-Iraq War and the Migration of Iranian
    Youth to California
Military Base Closures
United States Marine Corps Recruit Depot
    San Diego
World War I Americanization Programs
    in California
World War II Defense Industries
World War II–Postwar Effects on
    Western Migration

ETHNIC AND RACIAL GROUPS

African American Communities in California
Anglo Migration to Southern California Before
    the Depression
Basque Americans
Chileans and the California Gold Rush
Chinese Immigration
Czechs and Swedes in Saunders
    County, Nebraska
Euro-American Migration on the Overland Trails
French Basques of Bakersfield, California
Frisians
Irish in the West
Koreatown
Little Italy
Little Tokyo and Japantown
Mexican Migration to California
Okies
Pacific Islanders
Slaves in California
Vietnamese American Women

IMMIGRATION LAWS AND POLICIES

Asian Immigration Law
Chinese Exclusion Act
Forced Migration of Anarchists
Forced Migration of Italians During World War II
Gentleman's Agreement
German and Italian Internment

Immigration Act of 1965
Immigration and Naturalization Service (INS)
Immigration Reform and Control Act of 1986
Indian Removal Act of 1830
Japanese Internment
Lawyers and Legislation
Operation Wetback
Proposition 187
War Brides of Montana
World War II Relocation Program

LIBRARIES

California Libraries
Libraries and the Immigrant
Public Libraries in Utah

NATURAL RESOURCES
EVENTS AND LAWS

Alien Land Law of 1913
Arizona Copper Discoveries
Black Hills Gold Rush of 1874
Comstock Lode, 1859
Enlarged Homestead Act of 1909
Fraser River Gold Rush of 1858
Frisco Mine, Beaver County, Utah
Helena's Exploited Resources
Homestead Act
Idaho Silver Strikes
Logging
Mineral Land Policy
Nevada's Mining Discoveries of the
    20th Century
Nineteenth-Century Land Policy
Pick-Sloan Plan of 1944
Pike's Peak Rush
Rexburg, Idaho, and the Minidoka Project

THE WAY WEST

Men on Emigrant Trails
Mormon Colonization of Utah
Route 66
Rowland-Workman Expedition of 1841
Women on Emigrant Trails

ABOUT THE EDITORS

Gordon Morris Bakken is Professor of History at California State University, Fullerton; Past President of Phi Alpha Theta, the national honor society in history; Founding Vice President and a Director of the California Supreme Court Historical Society; former Parliamentarian of the Organization of American Historians; Series Editor of *The Legal History of North America* for the University of Oklahoma Press, Editor of *Law in the Western United States* (2000) for the University of Oklahoma Press, and a member of the editorial boards of *Western Legal History* and *Montana: The Magazine of Western History.* He is also Editor of *California Legal History,* the journal of the California Supreme Court Historical Society.

Professor Bakken earned his BS (1966), MS (1967), PhD (1970), and JD (1973) at the University of Wisconsin. He is the author or editor of sixteen books, forty-one articles, sixteen book chapters and encyclopedia entries, and numerous reviews. With Brenda Farrington, he coauthored *Learning California History* (1999) and the six-volume work *The American West* (2000). He has held twelve research grants, including the Russell Sage Residency Fellowship in Law; two American Bar Foundation Fellowships; and the Bradley Fellowship at the Montana Historical Society.

Professor Bakken has been the faculty advisor for the Theta Pi chapter of Phi Alpha Theta on the California State University, Fullerton, campus since 1982. He teaches Westward Movement, Women of the American West, Women and American Law, American Legal and Constitutional History, Development of American Law, American Military Heritage, Historical Thinking, Historical Writing, Historical Editing, California History, Real Estate and Land Use Law, Principles of Real Estate, Environmental Law, Administrative Law, and Collective Bargaining, as well as survey courses in American History.

Alexandra Kindell is a doctoral candidate at Iowa State University, in residence at the Huntington Library in San Marino, California. She teaches California History at Vanguard University and California State University, Fullerton, as well as Historical Writing at California State University, Fullerton. She previously served as Assistant Editor of *Agricultural History,* the journal of record for the field of agricultural and rural history. She is actively involved with the history section of the Southwestern Social Science Association.

She is the recipient of the Phi Alpha Theta Doctoral Scholarship (2004), the Garst Dissertation Fellowship (2004), the Colonial Dames Scholarship (2002), the Carmen Bayati Memorial Scholarship (1997), and the Warren Beck Memorial Scholarship (1996). Her scholarship has been recognized twice with the Procter Prize in American History at the Southwestern Historical Association (1999 and 2002). Her most recent publication, "Women and Veterinary Medicine," appeared in the *Encyclopedia of Women in the American West* (2003).

Kindell received her BA (1997) and MA (2001) from California State University, Fullerton, and expects to receive her PhD from Iowa State University in May 2006.

CONTRIBUTORS

Richard Aarstad
Montana Historical Society

Elwood Bakken
Independent Scholar

Gordon Morris Bakken
California State University, Fullerton

Eduardo Barrios
California State University, Fullerton

Ellen B. Baumler
Montana Historical Society

Scott M. Behen
California State University, Fullerton

Barbara Berglund
University of South Florida

Peggy Park Bernal
Huntington Library

Catherine M. Bilanchone
California State University, Fullerton

Megan Birk
Purdue University

Timothy Braatz
Saddleback College

Gilbert J. Bradshaw
Brigham Young University

Lincoln Bramwell
University of New Mexico

Kathleen Brosnan
University of Houston

Patrick K. Brown
Attorney at Law, Los Angeles

Dino E. Buenviaje
University of California, Riverside

Ann Butterfield
Pioneer Museum of Bozeman

Daniel Cady
Fresno State University

Ian Chambers
University of California, Riverside

Cynthia Culver
California State University, Channel Islands

Brandon Davis
California State University, Fullerton

Lawrence de Graaf
California State University, Fullerton

Susan Badger Doyle
Independent Scholar

Wendy Elliott-Scheinberg
California State University, Fullerton

Lisa E. Emmerich
California State University, Chico

Tracy Smith Falk
Independent Scholar

Mateo Mohammad Farzaneh
University of California, Riverside

Jody Foley
Montana Historical Society

Natalie Fousekis
California State University, Fullerton

Kellin D. Francis
Independent Scholar

G. W. Franck
Iowa State University

Brian Frehner
University of Oklahoma

Susanne Gaskins
California State University, Fullerton

Victor W. Geraci
University of California, Berkeley

Douglas Gibb
California State University, Fullerton

Patrick Gibson
California State University, Fullerton

Matt Sakiestewa Gilbert
University of California, Riverside

Debra L. Gold Hansen
San Jose State University

Vanessa Ann Gunther
California State University, Fullerton

David Harmon
Finger Lakes Community College

Matthew Adam Henderson
California State University, Fullerton

Paul T. Hietter
Mesa Community College

Laurie Hinck
University of New Mexico

Hal Hoffman
Mount San Antonio College

Paivi Hoikkala
California State Polytechnic University at Pomona

Joel R. Hyer
Chadron State College

Jon Ille
University of California, Riverside

Robin Jensen
Brigham Young University

Suzzanne Kelley
North Dakota State University

Scott Keys
California State University, Fullerton

Alexandra Kindell
Iowa State University

Rebecca Kugel
University of California, Riverside

Renee M. Laegreid
Hastings College

Janne Lahti
University of Helsinki

Patricia Loughlin
University of Central Oklahoma

Leleua Loupe
University of California, Riverside

Neal Lynch
Independent Scholar

Steve C. Lyon
California State University, Fullerton

Matthew S. Makley
Arizona State University

Mary Marki
Long Beach City College

Thomas de Martino
Independent Scholar

Sandra K. Mathews-Lamb
Nebraska Wesleyan University

Thomas Maxwell-Long
California State University, San Bernardino

Rob McCoy
Washington State University

Robert McLain
California State University, Fullerton

Kenneth McMullen
California State University, Fullerton

Cindy Mediavilla
University of California, Los Angeles

Susan Meier
Riverside Community College

Robert Miller
California State University, Fullerton

Melody Miyamoto
Arizona State University

Jennifer Mizzell
Louisiana State University

Linda Molno
California State Polytechnic University at Pomona

Danelle Moon
San Jose State University

Paul Nienkamp
Iowa State University

Derek Oden
Iowa State University

Caroline Owen
California State University, Fullerton

J'Nell Pate
Tarleton State University

Sally Pierotti
California State University, Fullerton

Charlene Porsild
Montana Historical Society Library

Heather R. Puckett
Registered Professional Archaeologist

Ion Puschila
Garey High School, Pomona, California

Karen C. Rosa
California State University, Fullerton

Susan Sanchez-Barnett
Baltimore County, Maryland Public Schools

Raymond D. Screws
Nebraska Humanities Council

Charles Joseph Sedey
Don Lugo High School, Chino, California

Brian Shovers
Montana Historical Society

Christopher Small
Claremont Graduate School

Jeff Smith
U.S. Forest Service

Kimberly Sorenson
California State University, Fullerton

Paul R. Spitzzeri
Homestead Museum, Industry, California

Daniel Stackhouse
Claremont Graduate School

George Stantis
California State University, Fullerton

Suzanne M. Stauffer
University of California, Los Angeles

Timothy A. Strand
Claremont Graduate School

Jacquelyn Sundstrand
University of Nevada–Reno

Nancy Taniguchi
California State University, Stanislaus

Hank Thayer
Independent Scholar

Rhonda Tintle
Oklahoma State University

Clifford E. Trafzer
University of California, Riverside

Trangdai Tranguyen
Stanford University

Susan Tschabrun
California State University, Fullerton

Leland Turner
Texas Tech University

Lonnie Wilson
FBI, Joint Terrorism Task Force

Kelly A. Woestman
Pittsburg State University, Kansas

Ronald C. Woolsey
Citrus College

Tony Yang
California State University, Fullerton

ACKNOWLEDGMENTS

This encyclopedia was made possible by the willingness of many scholars to write, revise, edit, and ponder the meaning of immigration and migration in the American West. The subject matter was far more than ethnic groups crossing the plains, landing at ports, or crossing borders. The story of people in places, often many places, dominates this work. It has been no mean task to bring this information and the research guides to print.

The professionals at Sage Reference made this work possible. We owe a great debt to Rolf A. Janke, Jerry Westby, and Leticia Gutierrez for their support of this project, patience, and guidance. Working with the Sage team is a wonderful scholarly life experience. The Sage copy editors substantially improved the entries and made the editors ruminate language and meaning.

We also thank all of the librarians who made this research possible. Our author-librarians were particularly helpful. Dr. Debra Gold Hansen at San Jose State University produced an exceptional entry and guided us to other librarians working on important projects. Danelle Moon of Yale University started on her entry in New Haven and migrated to San Jose State University as Director SJSU Special Collections and Archives at the Dr. Martin Luther King, Jr. Library in the midst of the project. Dr. Susan Tschabrun at California State University, Fullerton, produced three important research guides and worked with numerous graduate students on their entry projects. Jacqueline K. Sundstrand of the University of Nevada wrote two research guides on special collections at her university. Dr. Cindy Mediavilla at the University of California, Los Angeles, wrote from a rich research background. Dr. Suzanne M. Stauffer contributed an insightful entry on Utah's libraries and migrants. The librarians at the Huntington Library in San Marino, California, and at the Pollock Library at California State University, Fullerton, helped many of our scholars with their projects.

The professional staff of the Montana Historical Society was particularly generous with their time and expertise. Charlene Porsild, Director of the Research Center; Jodie Foley, Oral Historian; Dr. Ellen Baumler, Interpretative Historian; Rich Aarstad, Reference Historian; and Brian Shovers, Senior Reference Historian, all contributed to this work and helped others give shape to their research.

We hope this work will bring the subject matter to life and provide sufficient examples of scholarship to stimulate others in helping the public understand how important the history of the American West is in the American experience.

PREFACE

The American West is a vast landscape, larger than Western Europe and ranging across geographic variations from deserts and mountains to fertile valleys and swift rivers. This great and varied landmass became home to successive waves of immigrants who, over ten thousand years, shaped it and were shaped by it. The immigrant groups were as varied as the landscape in which they came to live. Indian peoples were the first, moving steadily south and west over generations, changing as the landscape they encountered challenged and then supported them. Soon after the opening of the 16th century, representatives of several European nations appeared, at first singly and then in small groups. Although initially few in numbers, they made their homes across the West; interacted with Indian peoples through trade, missions, and sometimes alliances; and publicized the new (for Europe) land. This connection with Indian peoples would lead to a great exchange that profoundly affected both groups. Europeans received knowledge of new agricultural crops (principally corn, but also beans, squash, and chili peppers), the wildlife that would form the basis of their sustenance, and soon trade and the lore associated with survival in this vast landscape. Indian peoples received the horse (a gift that would refashion the lives and cultures of those Indian groups on the plains), European iron tools, and diseases. The last would become significant in reshaping Indian populations for the next three hundred years.

The horse allowed the Indian peoples of the plains to remain sovereign over their great grass land, but elsewhere across the West, representatives of European nations and large trading companies began to penetrate into the distant reaches of the landscape, initially in motion and then in permanent settlements. By the middle of the 18th century, as the colonies on the East

Coast fought a war for independence, in the West, Russians had moved down from the north into what would become California, the Spanish had established missions in Texas and California, and British trading ships and naval vessels cruised the waters off the Pacific coast. Within three generations, the rise of the now-independent United States changed the political landscape of the West, and soon, its human habitations as well. In a series of diplomatic and military triumphs, America annexed Texas, acquired the Oregon Country by treaty, and immediately thereafter, California, Arizona, and New Mexico by conquest. By the middle of the 19th century, European nations—so significant in the West's history for more than three hundred years—had been reduced to bystanders. Thereafter, the United States would lay sole claim to sovereignty.

The discovery of gold in California in 1848 brought immigrants from all over the world in response to the fever occasioned by the news. Within a few months, they came from Hawaii to the west; Peru and Chile to the south; Mexico to the southwest; and, within a year, Americans and Europeans added large numbers to the total. Soon, Chinese and Australians had joined the flood of immigrants. With the arrival of these varied peoples, California became the most ethnically diverse place in the world. This was only the beginning of the great immigration that would change the face of the West and its peoples. By the opening of the 20th century, the West was home to Germans and Russians (North Dakota), Basques (Nevada), Chinese (in railroad and mining towns), Irish miners (Montana), Mexican agricultural laborers (interior valleys of California), and a dozen other groups from the plains and across the mountains to the shores of the Pacific.

From the beginnings of European occupation, with its missions and fur trading posts, the West has been a place of urban centers. In the 20th century, these have become great cities. For some five hundred years of European presence, the West has become a place of hope and opportunity. The enumerations of the decennial census note that the West is the most rapidly growing part of the nation and the most rapidly urbanizing. Large groups of new immigrants from around the world have come to Los Angeles, San Francisco, and Seattle, among other places. Questions of the relationship of the nation to its new arrivals have been posed and answered more than in any other places. Its story and the story of its people continue to unfold into the 21st century. The editors begin in these volumes to document the past and raise questions for the next generation of readers interested in the topic of the American West.

—Malcolm Rohrbough
Department of History
University of Iowa

INTRODUCTION

The American West, in myth and in reality, became so only after vast migrations and periods of massive immigration. The original inhabitants established migratory and settled communities from the Pacific coast to the 90th meridian centuries before the first European, Pacific Islander, or Asian set foot on its soil. Eventually, the Spanish and Russian explorations, Spanish colonization, and gradual American settlement of the West pushed American Indians off ancestral lands. In the narrative of the American West, this is the beginning of the American Story, rhetorically marked by the end of the Indian's role in the historian's narrative. American Indians become invisible on history's pages after 1890, yet their story also is one of migration, often forced but sometimes motivated by personal and economic reasons. This work represents many of the tribes and bands that constitute our native heritage, in an attempt to reintegrate the significance of their migrations with those of later arrivals. Migration in and out of the West was a periodic affair for most inhabitants.

The periods of migration are clear. The 19th century witnessed the highest levels, with the gold rush constituting the single greatest migration of Americans, one joined by numerous individuals from China, Germany, and a variety of other countries. In the late 19th century, migration declined until World War II, when thousands came west in search of work and homes in the urban defense industry and suburban, semipastoral neighborhoods in the emerging Sun Belt. The West was a place of opportunity, and people moved to grasp farms, ranches, and small business opportunities in the 19th century. Some opportunities were more ephemeral: For example, African Americans moved west searching for freedom from the discrimination they faced in eastern and southern states. Despite the Jim Crow laws and attitudes brought by

southern migrants, especially in places such as southern California, African Americans created neighborhoods and towns in which they hoped to better their lives. So, too, Mexican, Italian, Vietnamese, and countless other ethnic groups moved west for new opportunities and better lives.

To give the reader a sense of what immigration and migration involved in the public sphere, our authors have provided specific entries on immigration law. In addition to discussions of the general federal provisions, this encyclopedia contains specific entries on actions taken to discriminate against Asian immigrants. Officials used the open spaces in western areas to build internment camps for Japanese and Italians forced from their homes during World War II. Moreover, Americans moving into the West pushed others out, particularly American Indians and Mexicans, so that they would need to find new homes in a region they had known as home before the arrival of Americans.

To put the forced migrations of American Indians in perspective, our authors have addressed well-known incidents such as the Trail of Tears, the forced migration of American Indians from the Southeast to Indian Territory in what is now Oklahoma. They have also provided select tribal histories: Readers will find entries on the Apache, Arapaho, Blackfoot, Cahuilla, Chemehuevi, Cheyenne, Creek, Crow, Cupeño, Gros Ventre, Hopi, Juaneño, Kumeyaay, Lakota, Luiseño, Maidu, Mojave, Nez Perce, Northern Pueblo, Palouse, Upland Yuman, Ute, Washo, Yakama, and Yokut. In a broader perspective, some authors discuss American Indians regionally, as in the entries on tribes in California's northern coast, mountains, and valleys. One author focused on Phoenix, Arizona, and brought to light the many American Indian migrations to that city, giving a geographical context to the people as well as a human context to the city. In addition, an entry on the Bureau of Indian Affairs puts the administration of Indian reservations in perspective. Readers will come to understand that a vast number of internal and external forces influenced tribal migrations.

Migrations and immigration in the American West followed specific economic opportunities, especially mineral exploitation. Our authors explain mineral land policies in several entries and discuss specific mining rushes in others. The gold rush to California, Arizona copper discoveries, Idaho silver strikes, Last Chance Gulch, Pike's Peak, the Black Hills, and other mining events are covered in several entries. Many of these mineral rushes resulted in "instant cities," built to serve the miners and to funnel profit from their enterprise into the community and the country at large. Our authors produced entries on Bisbee, Arizona; Butte, Montana; Cripple Creek, Colorado; Goldfield, Nevada; Grass Valley, California; Helena, Montana; Inyo County, California; Julian, California; Leadville, Colorado; Libby, Montana; Price, Utah; Rawhide, Nevada; Rhyolite, Nevada; Tombstone, Arizona; Tonopah, Nevada; Tucson, Arizona; and Virginia City, Montana, to name only a few. Men and women arrived in these towns for the mining rushes and moved on to the next discovery of minerals or stayed to establish permanent communities with more varied economies, especially agricultural.

Land seekers and former miners established farms and ranches throughout the West. Families arriving via the emigrant trails brought stability to certain areas, building churches, schools, and other American institutions as they broke the soil for farming. African Americans came to California first for the gold but soon also sought out land on which to form communities based in agriculture. They established the noted communities of Nicodemus, Kansas, and Dearfield, Colorado. Farms, ranches, and the railroad had a great deal to do with community formation and location. Our authors explored these relationships in entries on Billings, Montana; Bozeman, Montana; Cody, Wyoming; Fort Worth, Texas; Fresno, California; Great Falls, Montana; Jackson, Wyoming; Lincoln, Nebraska; Northwood, North Dakota; Omaha, Nebraska; Park City, Utah; Salt Lake City, Utah; San Diego, California; San Dimas, California; Santa Ana,

California; Tacoma, Washington; and Wichita, Kansas, to name a few. Other authors provide a view of farming in Oregon in broad brush for regional context. One author explains the significance of dry farming techniques to the migration of farmers to the Great Plains. These areas retained their populations due to agriculture and stock raising, even if their economies eventually shifted to industry, commerce, or recreation and tourism.

Within the study of migration and immigration, certain individuals stand out as examples of the ordinary as well as the extraordinary efforts it took to populate the region. To provide the reader with a personal perspective, our authors have focused on the experiences of people in motion in the American West. Biographies include Stephen F. Austin, John Bartleson, Jessie Bloom, Joseph Brent, Joseph Chapman, Cottrell Dellums, Abigail Duniway, Edith Feldenheimer, Ray Frank, Greg Gianforte, William Hartnell, David Jacks, Olive May Percival, John T. Reed, Ben Singleton, Levi Strauss, William Thrall, and Benjamin Wilson. Hundreds of other individuals are included in more general entries, and some of our authors provide a gendered perspective on immigration and migration. One explores the lives of Vietnamese American women and another discusses war brides in Montana. These immigration stories put people in their temporal context and highlight the relationship between migrants and the distinct places making up the heterogeneous region we call the West.

In the process of researching the assigned topics, several of our authors found surprising historical evidence, forcing them to rethink their topics in new light. Professor Lawrence de Graaf, known for his pioneering work on African American communities in the West, has reevaluated interpretations of African American communities in his entry, based on extensive primary source research. The authors examining the relationship of libraries to immigrants also bring new insight on the subject. Authors produced entries on California's libraries, libraries and their immigrant users, and public libraries in Utah. In addition, our librarian authors also produced a most useful section of research guides. We suspect that many of the entries in this encyclopedia will stimulate research on these subjects, and we invite scholars to answer new questions raised within the entries. The history of the American West is an open field for scholars interested in approaching the region in new ways. The research guides will spur researchers on their way to greater knowledge and insight.

In this encyclopedia, we called on authors to present the tapestry of the West and its population in sweeping entries, focused biographies, community histories, economic enterprise analysis, and demographic studies. It is our hope that you will find this work informative and stimulating for further inquiry into the many facets of our history.

—Gordon Morris Bakken
California State University, Fullerton
—Alexandra Kindell
Iowa State University

A

⊞ ACJACHEMEN

See JUANEÑOS

⊞ AFRICAN AMERICAN COMMUNITIES IN CALIFORNIA

From their time in slavery, African Americans have sought refuge and opportunity by migrating to places populated solely by their race. Various towns have been labeled *all-black towns*. Scholars have tried to distinguish areas that merit that label by establishing definitions for a black town as "a separate community containing a population at least 90 percent black in which the residents attempted to determine their own political destiny." While the earliest all-black towns were set up during Reconstruction in the South, those in the West began with the migration of blacks from that region to Kansas in the 1870s. Other towns were efforts to secure remaining open land in the West, especially in Oklahoma in the late 1880s and 1890s. Behind some settlements were race leaders who envisioned all-black towns bringing political and economic independence and a chance for their race to prove its worth. In other cases, such "race men" were entrepreneurial promoters who used the desire for social equality for personal profit. In yet other cases, the main promoters were white men who often sold blacks marginal land. Finally, some communities that were in fact nearly all black became so without design, usually from black workers concentrating in

a place where they could obtain employment. Most 19th-century black towns were agricultural communities, and their leaders often agreed with Booker T. Washington's view that African Americans could progress if they "cast their buckets where they were" occupationally in separate social settings.

Blacks sought California as a place of freedom and opportunity, but some associated that promise with separate race communities. The earliest concentrations of African Americans were several experiments at importing them as farm workers. Proposals to set up plantations with slaves before the Civil War never materialized, but at the end of the war, the idea was revived, and at least one small colony was set up in Tulare County. The most ambitious effort coincided with the establishment of cotton growing in the Bakersfield area in the late 1880s. A cotton growers' association imported a colony of African American workers from the South and set up cabins for them. But many workers soon found better jobs elsewhere and left the colony. Within a short time, the whole plan had failed, as did a similar plan to import blacks to pick grapes around Fresno. Both of these were responses to the shortage of farm labor following the Chinese Exclusion Act of 1882. With the arrival of Japanese and other immigrant farm labor, interest among white farmers in importing blacks ended for the rest of the century.

Efforts by African Americans to establish black settlements were also largely in agricultural areas, especially the San Joaquin Valley. Black farmers set up a colony in Fowler in 1890, and by the early 1900s, that town had between 30 and 40 black families. Most

1

were landowners and prospered into the 20th century. Four miles away was the small town of Bowles, where a "colored settlement" was established in the early 1900s. In the early 1920s, it was one of four California towns cited as "populated and governed entirely or almost entirely by Negroes." Substantial numbers of black farmers also resided in Visalia, Hanford, and other valley cities. While none of these could be called a black town, their residents established churches, social clubs, even a black baseball team in Visalia. A different type of black community lived in Wasco, where white landowners formed a colony of black farm workers in 1907. That colony continued at least through the 1930s. In Yolo County, west of Sacramento, a group of blacks made one of the first uses of state homestead land, following the repeal of the restriction of such grants to white citizens. The area came to be known as "Nigger Hill," and it attracted black ranchers from other parts of northern California. It eventually disappeared as a community, though it would be considered—and ultimately rejected—as the site of a state historic park in the 1970s.

While conditions in most of these towns were primitive in terms of technology, black newspapers emphasized the progress and prosperity of the "energetic class" of farmers who lived there and held them up as an example of the promise of rural life and land ownership. Isolated black rural settlements were also set up in the early 1900s in Paso Robles and the northern California community of Weed. The latter was a company lumber town established in 1907, and in 1916 the company offered to ship black workers there. By 1920, Weed had 447 blacks; by 1930, 541, nearly all clustered in one part of the town with separate businesses and social institutions that they set up.

Southern California was also the site of all-black communities. In the early 1900s, the black Los Angeles Forum learned that the federal government had opened homesteads in Sidewinder Valley, near the community of Victorville. A substantial colony, including prominent Los Angeles residents and Southern migrants, moved to the area, setting up farms and homes. By 1914, they had claimed 20,000 acres and were filing claims for more in nearby Victor Valley. But by 1920, many of the original settlers had left, discouraged by the shortage of water and the difficulty

of converting desert into profitable cropland. Other blacks were attracted to the colony through the 1910s by appeals from race newspapers to seize the opportunity for free land and ads from black realtors. Their numbers sustained chapters of both the National Association for the Advancement of Colored People (NAACP) and the Garveyite United Negro Improvement Association (UNIA) into the early 1920s. By the end of that decade, the distinct black colony had ended, and blacks simply became a portion of the population of Victorville.

Each of the other agricultural communities also became a black enclave within a predominantly non-black community. In none of them did African American settlers establish a framework of government or economy uniquely their own. Such informal black towns thus stand in contrast to the more long-lived effort to establish a formal all-black agricultural town: Allensworth. This colony was the vision of Colonel Allen Allensworth, an army chaplain who believed that inculcating moral values and economic self-sufficiency in black troops would lead to racial progress. When he retired in 1906, he envisioned establishing an agricultural colony that would be "a model colored community" and a "center for moral and civic education." These ideals reflected those of Booker T. Washington, a friend of the colonel, and the colony was envisioned as a Tuskegee of the West. These goals took tangible form in 1908 when Allensworth, along with William Payne and other prominent blacks in Los Angeles, formed the California Colony and Home Promoting Association. Its purpose was to acquire land for an all-black colony, which would demonstrate blacks' abilities at self-sufficiency and government and refute then widespread views of innate inferiority.

Colonel Allensworth and associates were unable to acquire land for their visions until a company run by white land speculators, Pacific Farming Company, entered the scene. This firm had already established the town of Alpaugh, in Tulare County, and offered 4,000 acres nearby at $100 per acre (triple what it had charged whites for Alpaugh) on terms of $5 per month. The site, renamed Allensworth, was arid, windswept, and alkaline in places. But it straddled a main rail line, raising hopes that it would be a center of local commerce. Initially, the colony association promoted the land, but when it procured few buyers, Pacific Farming took over. It solicited black veterans with the idea of a home for themselves and their families. Two other white-run companies linked to Pacific Farming promised to develop water resources. By 1912, Colonel Allensworth hailed the officials of Pacific Farming for rescuing the colony when it seemed it might fail. But such praise soon turned sour, as these companies failed to provide water equipment, invited the Santa Fe railroad to build a line through Alpaugh that left Allensworth a mere whistle-stop, and tried to end sales of local land to blacks. After 1913, these companies faded from the scene.

Allensworth by the early 1910s had developed from an experimental colony to an apparently prosperous all-black town. Its legal status was recognized by Tulare County in 1910, when it helped settlers set up a public school. By 1914, the school population needed a larger building, and the original school became a branch of the Tulare County Library. These two institutions became hubs of town activity, serving as meeting halls for local civic groups. The town also became part of a new Justice of the Peace district, which in 1914 elected Oscar Overr as the first black justice west of the Rocky Mountains. The hope of making Allensworth a model of black government was implemented by setting up an advisory council of administrators consisting of seven departments and subsequently a board of trade that acted like a city council. The Allensworth Realty Company took over all sales of land on the argument that "a Negro community with a white man at the money end was not nor ever would be a success." Allensworth had two established congregations, Baptist and AME, and one church building.

This town grew slowly through its first six years. In 1912, it had 85 families, all black and over one third of them veterans from the North and Midwest. The remaining two thirds were about equally from California or other states. By 1914, the population had grown to about 200. Thereafter, while new families continued to come to Allensworth, they were offset by a steady exodus of earlier residents. Most observers in the 1910s depicted these settlers as happy and prosperous. Several had established farms in alfalfa, sugar beets, grain, and poultry. Some worked in nearby businesses; some hired out to white-owned ranches and farms in the area. Businesses were established in the town, including a

hotel, grain warehouses, and storage bins, and a variety of artisans pursued their trades. These impressions of prosperity were reinforced in 1916, when Allensworth products nearly swept the prizes for both home and farm exhibits at the county fair. The school employed two black teachers—among the few hired anywhere in the state—and offered classes into high school.

Beneath appearances of prosperity, however, Allensworth had serious economic problems. Its population never grew to the critical mass needed to sustain an economic community. As a result, owning and managing personal farms became a secondary occupation for many. They gained their main income from working in white-owned enterprises, often as farm laborers. Professionals and artisans found insufficient work in Allensworth and were obliged to join the ranks of the laborers. This type of work often involved travel and weeks away from home. The consequent low amount of money in the community left its retail stores struggling. The largest businesses, such as the grain warehouse, were white-owned. All of these conditions ran counter to the ideals of Allensworth as a model of black self-sufficiency and community structure. Nor was the colony a haven from discrimination. Residents seeking work in other towns encountered signs stating "NO negroes, filipinos, mexicans, dogs," much as they did elsewhere. The Santa Fe railroad hired almost no blacks. These conditions, coupled with the shortage of good water and the diversion of rail trade to Alpaugh left the community by the mid-1910s with one hope for developing into a prosperous community: becoming a center for black education.

Education was a central activity of some all-black towns and one of the most important to residents of Allensworth. They supported a local bond to construct the larger schoolhouse, supplemented state and county funds for teachers, and offered classes beyond the age limits required by state law. The idea of an industrial school was an ideal of many black educators and a growing movement in California. The state had mandated public high schools and opened the first state polytechnic school at San Luis Obispo at the turn of the century. Similar technical schools were established in other communities. Therefore, when in 1914, a state industrial school was proposed in Allensworth, it seemed to be a timely idea.

The racial composition of this school was ambiguous. Initially, town leaders proposed an agricultural and manual training school modeled after Tuskegee, where black students could secure technical training without the racially hostile climate of integrated schools. They emphasized that it would be the only industrial school for blacks west of the Rockies. Also race-oriented was the contention that California had more than 50,000 blacks who deserved such a school. But they also gained the support of local white school officials, who viewed the endeavor as training the general population in agriculture. The hope that private funds would cover most costs was dashed in 1914 by a recession, opposition from black leaders in urban communities, and the death of Colonel Allensworth, who was hit by a motorcycle in Los Angeles. Thereafter, the school was pursued as a state-sponsored institution. The bill to establish Allensworth Polytechnic Institute stated it would furnish manual arts education to "young people of both sexes" to fit them for "non-professional walks of life." While the bill made no mention of race, it became a major test of basic principles of separate black communities.

Black leaders in Los Angeles feared that the establishment of such a school even implicitly for blacks would lead school districts to suggest they not attend other public schools, especially local polytechnic schools. Some were leery of the bill's support in Tulare County, the scene of the last court suit against formal school segregation in California in 1890. This fear was underscored by a San Francisco newspaper story that the bill's sponsor had stated that segregated schools might do more for blacks in California than the current system. Proponents of the school noted that state law forbade segregated schools, and they contrasted the difficulty proponents of integration had finding employment with Allensworth having the only black principal in the state. In the end, however, the school issue was settled not on lofty arguments of race policy but on mundane considerations of funding. The bill's appropriation of $50,000 was more than the Assembly Ways and Means Committee was willing to accept, and it killed the bill. With its death went hopes that Allensworth might become a vibrant community.

In the 1920s, the colony declined to the point of disintegration. The death of Colonel Allensworth took away its most inspiring leader. Its agriculture had declined to a few hundred acres, and its population became so small that it was in danger of losing its post office. Water shortages became acute as the area suffered a multiyear drought. Its school, library, and some social groups remained, but its NAACP chapter was closed for lack of anyone to serve as its president. By mid-decade, the remaining residents were describing their stay as a "sacrifice" and pleading for other blacks to come to the town to keep its ideal alive. As residents moved away, many homes and buildings were occupied by itinerant workers, and the town became "sort of a camping ground." This decline was especially striking because it was unique to the all-black town, not the whole area. The number of African Americans in Tulare County increased more than fourfold between 1910 and 1930 to 819, but only 44 of these resided in Allensworth.

The town made a partial recovery after World War II, largely by adopting new ways of farming. Most buildings remained standing, though many were abandoned. The problem of scarce water was worsened by discovery of unhealthful amounts of arsenic in the local supply. Only donations of water from federal agencies and neighboring communities enabled residents to remain. The town also began to lose its racial exclusiveness, as Mexican Americans moved in. By the 1960s, they constituted half of the students in the Allensworth school. The place seemed destined to become a ghost town until a state worker, Ed Pope, proposed making it a state historic park in 1969. This idea was formally adopted by the state legislature two years later, and in 1976, the state approved plans to develop Allensworth Historic Park and restore its buildings. The project proved costly and proceeded slowly, but today it is open as a monument to both its pioneer settlers and to the idea of all-black towns in California.

In sheer numbers, the most significant set of virtually all of the all-black communities sprang up in the Imperial Valley. Cotton became a popular crop there, spreading to 20,000 acres by 1912. Growers initially associated that crop with Southerners, particularly African Americans, so growers' associations and labor contractors advertised for pickers in the South, particularly Texas. Wages rose to $1.75 per hundred pounds by 1916, much above those in the South, so black workers began streaming into the valley. Railroad agents encouraged the migration by using railroad facilities for job announcements and facilitating train travel. The onset of the "Great Migration" to northern cities slowed the black movement to the Imperial Valley. By the entry of the United States into World War I, Mexican and Filipino workers were providing most of the labor on Imperial Valley farms.

Because the earliest cotton ranches were mostly around the towns of Imperial and El Centro, black migrants concentrated in these communities. Their Southern culture, coupled with a similar background among many growers, established racial segregation as the norm, and those policies created de facto black communities in these towns. Black newspapers in Los Angeles periodically encouraged readers facing unemployment in that city to seek opportunities in the Imperial Valley. The greatest attraction of this area, as in other agricultural colonies, was the hope of becoming landowners and establishing farms. A black company, Calexico Investment Company, was formed in 1918 to organize blacks in the valley into a colony by acquiring land and establishing businesses. Los Angeles black employment agencies made special arrangements to procure cotton workers. By the 1920s, El Centro was being seen as a successor to Allensworth in the openings it offered to blacks, especially black teachers. This was epitomized by the move of William Payne from Allensworth to become principal of the all-black school in El Centro. Other prominent Los Angeles blacks would be drawn to that town to set up businesses or social and cultural organizations. A concentration of blacks begun by an influx of common laborers was molded into a community by a migration of elite blacks.

For many residents, however, these black communities were less than idyllic. The laborers were essentially transients, living in tents or nondescript shelters with dirt floors. Housing eventually improved to wooden shacks, with little in the way of improvements to their setting. Some black visitors to Imperial were struck by the proximity of houses of prostitution to homes with children, often with black women imported to work as prostitutes. Such conditions clashed with the ideal of blacks realizing moral and economic progress by going back to the land, and this discouraged migration to Imperial Valley. Though the population in some towns grew through the 1920s, only El Centro had over 500 blacks by 1930. The deportation of many Mexicans in the 1930s rekindled demand for black workers, but that faded after the cotton workers strike of 1934. By the end of that decade, Imperial Valley towns had ceased to be regarded as distinctive African American communities.

As with Allensworth, black communities in the Imperial Valley became associated with school segregation. In this case, however, it was initially white prejudice rather than black visions that raised the issue. In 1913, the El Centro Elementary School District created a separate school for its black students. The initial rationale was that other schools were crowded, but school officials openly professed their belief in black inferiority. Imperial set up a separate school for blacks in 1923. In other towns with smaller black populations, school boundaries were drawn around the residential concentrations of blacks and Mexicans to produce separate schools from those attended by whites. As in the South, such "separate but equal" schools were notably inferior. The whole valley had no high school open to blacks until a makeshift addition was put on their elementary school in El Centro in 1924. That city's elementary school was next to houses of prostitution until the early 1920s. Black parents in Imperial protested the imposition of segregation and briefly reactivated the valley NAACP chapter. But this failed to change the policy of segregation, which remained intact through the 1930s.

That this separate school system drew praise from some African Americans illustrates one of the appeals of separate black towns. El Centro adopted a policy of hiring black teachers for its segregated school, and it became one of the few markets they had. Until the 1950s, California required teachers to have one year of experience in the state before securing a regular teaching appointment. With no major urban districts hiring blacks until the early 1920s (and then only a token number in elementary schools), El Centro and Imperial had two of the state's three black principals and all four of its high school teachers in 1925. This practice also mollified protests against Jim Crow schools. When William Payne tried to get his daughter into El Centro's general high school, that school board set up a separate black high and named him its teacher. The transition of black teachers from one all-black town to another was completed when Margaret Prince left Allensworth to join Payne in El Centro.

These agricultural communities were promoted by the belief that they were an escape from racism and discrimination and that land ownership was the path to prosperity. Both of these hopes culminated south of the international border in the effort to establish an all-black colony in Baja California. In the period of the Mexican Revolution, southern California investors had shown great interest in that area, and blacks had historically viewed Mexico as a haven. This colony was the brainchild of a group of Los Angeles black businessmen and attorney Hugh Macbeth. They set up the Lower California Mexican Land and Development Company, which issued 250,000 shares of stock, bought 21,800 acres of land in the Santa Clara Valley, and in 1918 began a multiyear campaign to entice other African Americans to buy lots of 40 acres in what was called "Little Liberia." Their appeal was directed toward blacks who had been successful in business, not common laborers. It soon attracted people from several other black farming communities, especially Imperial Valley, Fowler, and Bowles, due to lower land costs and opportunities for acquiring substantial acreage. By 1922, wealthy residents of all-black towns in Oklahoma were also visiting the colony and considering investing in it.

The promoters of Little Liberia resembled those of Allensworth in their linking the colony to racial uplift. Blacks must become producers, and agriculture was the key to becoming self-supporting. But they could only do this in a country that respected all races. Mexico offered blacks a chance to get out of menial and service jobs and become landlords of the soil. A few leaders set themselves up in the colony in 1918, and by 1920 some began building houses and preparing to farm the land. While the colony initially was planned for only about 200 families, Hugh Macbeth made lofty predictions that Baja California would become the breadbasket of Los Angeles and the colony might evolve into a state of 20,000 within a decade.

These visions turned to dust in 1923, when the Mexican government halted any possibility of large-scale migration to the colony. Concerned that blacks would aggravate the "ethnic problem" in Mexico and perhaps bothered by Macbeth's predictions, President Alvaro Obregon issued an order barring most African Americans from entering Mexico. The U.S. Department of the Interior circulated this order to its border offices, and a suit by the NAACP demanding that U.S. agencies reverse this action was rejected. The hope that blacks would go back to the soil also was unfulfilled. Only a handful of black families settled in the colony. The final blow came when an audit revealed that Hugh Macbeth was running up large debts and the colony was raising more drinking parties than crops. This led to suspicions that the company did not hold clear title to the land, which was borne out in 1928, when the Mexican government demanded the land be repatriated and most investors lost their holdings. These events ended the idea of settling Baja California and the era of black agricultural colonies.

Primarily black communities were also being formed in California's urban centers, especially Los Angeles, before their black residents were largely confined to ghettoes. The earliest of these was Abila, located south of Watts. Originally a rancho of the Avila family, the area attracted blacks in the 1890s. Sometimes referred to as "Mudtown," this area attracted migrants who recreated traditional Southern life with small farms along dirt paths. Abila continued to be recognized as a distinct black town through the 1910s. In 1908, the first black old-folks home in the Los Angeles area was relocated there, and an enlarged building was erected in 1917. But Abila was soon overshadowed and semantically absorbed into a larger community of Watts. This area developed in 1902, when Charles Watts donated 10 acres to the Pacific Electric (PE) Company for a junction of its Los Angeles–San Pedro and Venice–Santa Ana lines. This site was called both Watts Junction and Abila Junction, adding to the ambiguity over their respective boundaries. Initially, it was a community of Mexican track workers. But their 1903 strike led PE to import blacks, and many of these settled in the Ramsaur Tract just south of the junction, creating a nearly all-black subdivision. Watts grew rapidly to an incorporated town in 1907, but its multiethnic population remained roughly divided into communities of blacks in the southwest,

Mexicans in the southeast, and whites to the north of the Watts Junction station.

Neither Abila nor Watts was promoted by African American companies or colonizers. But 12 of its 37 tracts, all in the southern area of the city, were open to blacks, and that, combined with lots as low as $90 on terms of $1 down and $1 a week, attracted them. In 1914, a white Progressive lawyer, who believed that home ownership would uplift blacks, opened Dunbar Park in the northern part of Abila and advertised for buyers through black Realtors. By 1920, Watts alone had the seventh largest black population of any city in California—652 residents—and the highest percentage of its population composed of African Americans—14.4 percent.

Watts and Abila remained a mix of rural and suburban life. Some blacks accumulated farms of one or two acres, with hundreds of animals as well as crops. Most residential lots had generous backyards designated for chickens or agriculture. Besides various race businesses, Watts had a UNIA chapter, and Abila was the site of a proposed baseball and amusement park in the 1920s. In 1916, blacks in both communities organized a Colored Voters Independent League. This last organization illustrates considerable political activity on the part of blacks, inspired by the fact that Watts was an independent city in which they might be significant. Such activity in a city marked by political turmoil and frequent elections, coupled with the steady influx of African Americans into the city, has led to the view that the annexation of Watts into Los Angeles in 1926 was engineered by the Ku Klux Klan or other race-conscious groups to deny blacks a chance to govern a California city. However, Watts was only one of 34 areas that Los Angeles acquired in the 1920s, largely because it offered Owens Valley water. Blacks favored annexation by more than two to one in the election. They would continue to become a growing percentage of that area's population through the 1930s but remained heavily concentrated in its southwest section and excluded from schools outside it. Watts' future notoriety would come after World War II as the epitome of impoverished areas of the Los Angeles ghetto, though it was then more nearly all black than when Abila was cited as a distinctive black town.

Another separate African American community in Los Angeles was formed in 1905, the Furlong Tract.

An Irish landowner, James Furlong, sold acreage south of Los Angeles to black families, augmenting some who had already moved in. Most early residents were businessmen or sufficiently well off to own homes. In 1910, the Holmes Avenue Elementary School was built, and the following year it hired the first black teacher in the Los Angeles school system. It also had a black principal of the evening school and was long the only public school in the city to hire blacks. Furlong Tract also was the site of the city's first black baseball and amusement park. By the 1920s, this once isolated community became linked with the growing black population along Central Avenue, and both its elite population and its distinctiveness as a community disappeared. By the 1930s, it was a slum, inhabited largely by poorer blacks.

The last effort at a separate all-black town was Val Verde, a community near present-day Valencia. It was established in the 1920s at a time when housing restrictions were confining blacks to a few areas of Los Angeles and they were increasingly excluded from public recreational facilities such as beaches and swimming pools. African Americans tried to establish separate recreational centers at Manhattan Beach, Huntington Beach, and Lake Elsinore, but the first two were thwarted, and the third proved too remote for extensive use. So, in 1924 a group of prominent Los Angeles blacks led by Realtor Sidney P. Dones secured 30 acres of land in the Santa Clarita Valley to form the colony of Eureka Villa, though part of it was always known as Val Verde. It was to become the "black Palm Springs," a place where African Americans could escape for a day or a week and enjoy various recreational facilities, or in some cases live permanently.

The Eureka Villa Improvement Association offered 700 lots early in 1925 and promoted them by parades and exhortations that investment in this "race community center" was a way of showing pride in being black. By the end of that year, however, lowered prices and efforts to lease some of the land to oil companies suggest that only a small number of people bought lots. The area did become a favorite vacation place for middle-class blacks who had the means to make the 100 mile round trip for the next three decades. In 1939, it received a boost when a white businessman donated 50 acres adjacent to it to Los Angeles County, and Works' Progress Administration workers built a clubhouse and park, which were christened Val Verde. The community center developed churches, a beauty contest, and a wide range of activities into the 1950s. But when recreational facilities were opened up in the 1960s, most blacks abandoned the long drive to Val Verde, and many of its homes were taken over by whites and Mexicans, ending the community's ethnic uniqueness.

California's separate black communities did not attract a large number of migrants, and in many cases the black residents were from other parts of California. The economic pursuits of these communities' black residents and their transition to multiethnic towns reflected the fallacy of the idea that a race could completely separate its activities from the broader world around it. Despite promotions that these colonies would be models of black progress, the rapid turnover in their populations suggests that the vast majority of African Americans found life in large heterogeneous cities much more attractive.

All-black towns failed to attract African Americans because most were located in rural areas and centered on agriculture. Both of these features were contrary to trends from the late 19th through the 20th centuries, when millions of families left farms. For African Americans, farms carried memories of life in the South, especially in California, where most employment was as transient laborers. Rural life remained primitive and hard compared to the dazzling technology in cities. By 1930, more than 38,000 blacks lived in Los Angeles, less than 50 in Allensworth, testimony that dusty, dry fields were a sorry substitute for night clubs and jazz bands, especially when the latter seemed more indicative of black contributions to society than the former.

All-black towns also suffered from the efforts to promote them. Most rural colonies were located in remote places that had been regarded as undesirable. The realities of trying to make a living there contradicted the glowing images that black promoters had painted of these colonies. Because several towns were basically real estate ventures, investors came to suspect that only the promoters made money from them. In several places, the African American organizers had obtained the land from whites; in other cases, whites set up the residences or jobs. In both cases,

black residents sensed they were being exploited. These problems caused many prosperous blacks who had supported these ventures to become skeptical of such promotions, and the major dynamic for anything but a part-time getaway like Val Verde died.

The significance of California's all-black towns to migration in the American West lies in the appreciation that migration is more than the movement of people and the social, economic, and political factors that impel such movement. It is also appreciating the visions and ideals that can lead people to go to other places, the history of hopes and dreams, and why they are often dashed. California's earliest black colonies reflected the image of the Golden State as a haven from oppression and a land of opportunity; the ideals of Booker T. Washington that social separation and self-sufficiency in traditional occupations were the prescription for racial progress; and the populist view that agrarian life was a morally uplifting culture in contrast to the vices of urban society. By the 1920s, some of these ideals had lost their appeal, as rural areas became depressed and California became as much a reservoir of racial prejudice as many other areas. As blacks flocked into restricted areas in major cities during and after World War II, these ghettoes became virtually all-black cities in themselves. Many African Americans then became less interested in creating black towns than in getting out of them.

—*Lawrence B. de Graaf*

See also Huntington Beach, California; Los Angeles, California; Pittman, Tarea Hall; Slaves in California

Suggested Reading

Adler, Patricia. "Watts: From Suburb to Black Ghetto." Ph.D. Dissertation, University of Southern California, 1977.

Beasley, Delilah. *Negro Trail Blazers of California.* Los Angeles, 1919. (Reprinted New York: Negro Universities Press, 1969)

Flamming, Douglas. *Bound for Freedom: Black Los Angeles in Jim Crow America.* Berkeley: University of California Press, 2005.

Hamilton, Kenneth M. *Black Towns and Profit: Promotion and Development in the Trans-Appalachian West.* Urbana: University of Illinois Press, 1991.

McBroome, Delores N. "African American Boosterism, Agriculture, and Investment in Allensworth and Little Liberia." In *Seeking El Dorado: African Americans in California,* edited by Lawrence B. de Graaf, Kevin Mulroy, and Quintard Taylor. Seattle: University of Washington Press & Autry Museum of Western Heritage, 2001.

Ramsey, Eleanor M. "Allensworth: A Study in Social Change." Ph.D. Dissertation, University of California, Berkeley, 1977.

Ramsey, Eleanor M., and Janice S. Lewis. "Black Americans in California." In *Five Views: An Ethnic Sites Survey for California.* Sacramento, CA: Office of Historic Preservation, 1988.

Sides, Josh. *L.A. City Limits: African American Los Angeles From the Great Depression to the Present.* Berkeley: University of California Press, 2003.

Wheeler, B. Gordon. "Allensworth: California's All-Black Community." *Wild West*, February 2000. Available from http://www.historynet.com/we/blallensworth

AFRICAN AMERICAN MIGRATION PATTERNS

See GOLDFIELD, NEVADA; HELENA, MONTANA; NICODEMUS, KANSAS; TOPEKA, KANSAS; WICHITA, KANSAS

ALIEN LAND LAW OF 1913

The Alien Land Law of 1913 made it illegal for aliens (immigrants), who were not eligible for citizenship, to own land in California. In addition, the aliens could not lease any agricultural land for more than three years. Although the language of the law applied to all such aliens, Japanese immigrants were the targeted group. Governor Hiram Johnson signed the bill into law on May 19, 1913.

The impetus for the bill resulted from the prejudice against the Japanese that started in the 1880s. The intensity increased after 1907, as the Japanese began to move from being farm laborers to farm owners. This shift brought the Japanese into a more direct conflict with the white growers. Also, more Japanese were immigrating to California. Before 1900, there were few Japanese immigrants, but by 1920, there were approximately 72,000 Japanese in California.

Many white Californians expressed fears that the Japanese would not assimilate due to their style of clothing, their religion, the fact that they spoke a non-European language, and generally did not blend into society.

As an example of Californian's prejudice against the Japanese, in 1906 the San Francisco school board passed rules segregating the Japanese students (some of whom were born in the United States) from the rest of the students. This in spite of the fact the city of San Francisco had received $100,000 from the government of Japan in earthquake-emergency aid. The Japanese government lodged a formal complaint against this discrimination. The severity of the diplomatic note caused a brief war scare in Washington and led to the intervention of the federal government into the school situation. The U.S. government caused the San Francisco school board to modify its policies to readmit Japanese children so long as they could speak some English and were not too old. As a follow-up to this incident, the United States and Japan entered into a gentleman's agreement whereby Japan agreed to only issue passports to nonlaborers.

To circumvent the Alien Land Law of 1913, many Japanese immigrants bought land and placed it in the names of their native-born children. The Japanese devised this and other ingenious mechanisms to artfully maneuver around the repressive law.

Anti-Japanese forces came to view the 1913 act as ineffective and submitted a ballot proposition during the 1920 elections. This measure, the Webb-Haney Act, passed by a three-to-one margin. The provisions of the 1920 act denied aliens ineligible for citizenship the right to lease farmland or even to sharecrop.

In 1952, the U.S. Supreme Court, in *Fujii Sei v. State of California,* found the Alien Land Law to be unconstitutional.

—*Kenneth McMullen*

See also GENTLEMAN'S AGREEMENT

Suggested Reading

"Alien Land Laws." Available from http://www.santacruzpl .org/history/ww2/9066/land.shtml

Chuman, Frank F. *The Bamboo People: The Law and Japanese-Americans.* Del Mar, CA: Publisher's Inc., 1976.

Matsumoto, Valarie. *Farming the Home Place: A Japanese American Community in California, 1919–1982.* Ithaca, NY: Cornell University Press, 1993.

Morris, Edmund. *Theodore Rex.* New York: Random House, 2001.

Niiya, Brian, ed. *Encyclopedia of Japanese-American History: An A-to-Z Reference From 1868 to Present.* Rev. ed. Los Angeles: Japanese American National Museum, 2000.

Sackman, David Cazaux. *Orange Empire: California and the Fruits of Eden.* Berkeley: University of California Press, 2005.

⊞ ALIEN REGISTRATION ACT OF 1940

See FORCED MIGRATION OF ITALIANS DURING WORLD WAR II

⊞ AMERICAN INDIAN MIGRATION TO PHOENIX, ARIZONA

"Everything is connected to the past," says Tohono O'odham Daniel Preston of the link of his people to the Huhugam. The Huhugam, Piman for "those who are gone," inhabited the Salt River Valley in central Arizona long before the founding of Phoenix in 1870. They lived along major drainages, pioneering the building of extensive canal networks to irrigate their fields of corn, squash, beans, cotton, agave, and other native plants. Archaeological excavations reveal the story of a rich culture and complex social structure that peaked between 1150 and 1350. By 1400, the Huhugam had vacated their homes in the Phoenix Basin, but other Native peoples have made the area their home since the founding of the city of Phoenix in 1870.

Throughout the city's history, Native people have represented only a small segment of the total population of Phoenix. In 2002, American Indians, Eskimos, and Aleuts numbered 57,498 persons, making up 1.8 percent of the population of the greater Phoenix area. Yet Phoenix is an "Indian city." There are four reservations in the vicinity of Phoenix. It has also developed into a major administrative center for Indian Affairs. Besides the Bureau of Indian Affairs (BIA) and the Indian Health Service (IHS), the city houses the offices of several statewide Native American organizations. These agencies draw reservation residents to town on tribal business and provide employment opportunities. The Phoenix Indian High School contributed to the city's profile until its closure in 1990. Other educational facilities in the metropolitan area continue to bring Indian youth into the urban setting. Phoenix is also a focal point for southwestern Native culture. The nearby reservation communities and local Indian groups organize powwows and other cultural events throughout the year. The Heard Museum and the Pueblo Grande Museum not only promote Native arts and history, but they sponsor annual Indian markets, attracting artists and craftsmen from around the nation. In addition, there are numerous galleries specializing in Indian arts and crafts.

Early Phoenix was far less tolerant of Indian peoples and cultures. Local Pima and Maricopa people often traveled to the city to sell their handicrafts and firewood, to deliver grains to local mills, to acquire supplies on which they had come to depend, and occasionally to look for employment. Contemporary newspaper accounts suggest the aversion of local residents for Indians appearing in the city; especially offensive was their "scant" clothing and occasional intoxication. To regulate these visits and the behavior of Native Americans while in town, the city passed a series of ordinances requiring that Indians wear "proper" clothing and leave town before sundown, unless employed by a white person. Violators were subject to fines, even hard labor.

The presence of Native Americans in the city began to increase when the Phoenix Indian School opened its doors in 1891 with an initial class of 41 local Pima and Maricopa boys. When two leading citizens had suggested that the BIA establish its school in Phoenix, instead of the proposed site at Fort McDowell, they had more than the civilization of Indian children in mind. The building of the school would not only inject federal dollars into the economy and boost the growth of the city, it would also provide local businesses with a cheap labor force. Indian parents, on their part, often supported the education of their children, understanding its significance to their future livelihood. The school also started an active recruitment campaign, and by the end of the decade, over 700 pupils were enrolled at the school—almost all of them from tribes outside of central Arizona.

As the number of students at the school increased, so did their involvement in the local community when

Superintendent Wellington Rich decided to experiment with the outing system in 1893. Promoted as a way to accelerate the Americanization of Indian students by placing them in an Anglo work and living environment, the outing system quickly evolved into a method of providing local businesses with cheap labor. As Superintendent Harwood Hall noted in 1894, "The hiring of an Indian youth is not looked upon by the people of this valley from a philanthropic standpoint. It is simply a matter of business." Indian boys worked as laborers and field hands and in other menial jobs while the use of Indian girls as domestic help was even more widespread. By the late 1890s, nearly 200 young women had been placed with Phoenix families as domestics. Although these employment relationships were not permanent, they undoubtedly facilitated the integration of Native Americans into the city's workforce and encouraged further Indian migrations to Phoenix.

Phoenicians also came to see the value of the Indian School as a tourist attraction. With two major railroads and a favorable winter climate, the city attracted tourists in search of the "Wild West." At the core of this vision was the "vanishing" American Indian. Phoenix catered to this interest by incorporating "Native" elements to its parades, fairs, and carnivals. In this context, Phoenicians also developed more tolerance to reservation residents in their midst, as they seemed to represent the "wild" Indians better than the "civilized" Indian School children. "Quaint" Indians thus became a selling point for the emerging tourism industry. Without doubt, Indian people themselves realized the potential for income in the tourist trade as Native households increasingly faced the need to participate in the cash economy. Proximity to Phoenix—and its tourist trade—offered an opportunity to supplement their meager livelihood on reservations.

The BIA presence in Phoenix was also augmented when a sanatorium was established on the Indian School grounds in 1909. By the end of World War I, the sanatorium was caring for over 100 Indian patients from around the nation annually. Yet the number of Native Americans who permanently resided in the city remained small. The goal of Indian education was to turn Native children into Americans who would willingly leave their reservations and move into mainstream America. Accordingly, the Phoenix Indian School encouraged students to establish homes and look for jobs in the city, but with little success. In 1910, only 10 Indian couples maintained households, totaling 43 persons, in the Phoenix area. At the same time, increasing numbers of reservation residents participated in the workforce as the growing urban center looked for cheap labor for its various construction projects. These projects reflected what became a pattern of labor force participation for Native American men. Because of low educational attainment, they performed mostly unskilled, seasonal labor in construction and agriculture. The irregular nature of employment further resulted in a back-and-forth migration pattern between the reservation and the city.

By the 1920 census, the number of Native Americans permanently residing in Phoenix had more than doubled to 105. The participation of Indian men in World War I undoubtedly influenced their decision to move to the city, while women stayed after completing their schooling to take advantage of employment opportunities. Prospects for men also increased when local agriculture began to recover from its postwar slump, prompting a demand for field hands and other laborers. In 1922, the Indian School began to coordinate the Native workforce in Phoenix, practically serving as an employment agency. Meanwhile, the depressed reservation economies boosted Indian enrollment in these efforts to locate—and eventually assimilate—in the city.

When the Institute for Government Research surveyed the conditions of the nation's Native population in 1926, the numbers of urban, or "migrated," Indians had grown sufficient enough to merit a chapter in the commission's final report. This document, known as the Meriam Report, estimated the number of Indians in Phoenix at 250. Pimas clearly constituted the largest group among the 42 Native families, while a few permanent Indian residents came from outside the state. Compared with those in Albuquerque and Santa Fe, the other major southwestern cities included in the report, Phoenix Indian households maintained the highest standard of living, owing to greater opportunities and the availability of reasonably priced housing. There was also greater occupational diversity in Phoenix than in the other two cities. These factors, coupled with Indian educational and health service facilities, helped establish the foundation of Indian Phoenix even though the Native population represented less than 1 percent of the city's total population. Further evidence of the permanence of Native Americans in the city was the emergence of Indian-oriented social and recreational activities, mainly in connection with the Young Women's Christian Association, the Cook Christian Bible School, and the Central Presbyterian Church. The latter became the key in creating a sense of community for the city's Indian population while maintaining connections to nearby reservations.

During the Great Depression, as jobs became scarce and employers favored Anglo workers, Phoenix reflected the national decline in Indian urban populations with a nearly 17 percent decrease by 1940. The Roosevelt administration provided a further incentive for back migration when it established the Indian Emergency Conservation Work Program, better known as the Indian CCC. This congressional appropriation funded conservation projects on 33 reservations, including those in Arizona; one of the five district field offices was also located in Phoenix. At the same time, the administration of the Wheeler-Howard Act, or the Indian New Deal, reinforced the BIA presence in the city. Together with the already existing institutions, the Indian New Deal thus helped create opportunities for educated Indians while reservations beckoned the less-skilled workers.

American entry into World War II had a profound impact in Native American communities, as it did the nation as a whole. A higher percentage of Indian people served in the military during the war than any other ethnic group; 4,500 Navajos alone signed up for military service. The Navajo code talkers and Ira B. Hayes, a Pima from Gila River in Arizona who helped raise the flag on Iwo Jima, have become lasting symbols of Indian participation in the war effort. In addition, the war years witnessed the first large-scale exodus of women and men from reservations as they sought wartime employment. The western states benefited disproportionately as the federal government spent more than $40 billion in the region, establishing new factories and awarding contracts for war materiel. While the war industries first drew on local sources of labor, they also attracted a flood of new migrants, including ethnic minorities who, for the first time, found opportunities on a large scale in the industrial workforce. By 1943, some 46,000 Native Americans, approximately one fourth of them women, had left their reservations for work in agriculture and the war industries.

In Phoenix, World War II triggered an economic and population boom without precedent. The activation of military installations and the opening of several airfields were followed by the establishment of defense industries. Pushed by depressed reservation economies and pulled by these wartime prospects, many Arizona Indians recognized the opportunity for advancing their economic fortunes by moving to Phoenix and Tucson. Agriculture and other war projects in the rural areas also drew large numbers of Indian workers. For example, more than 10,000 Navajos engaged in off-reservation employment, including defense work as well as positions with railroads, construction companies, and agricultural operations.

While men continued to toil in unskilled jobs, census records from 1940 and 1950 reveal a significant occupational redistribution among urban Indian women in Arizona. Domestic and other service work certainly dominated Native women's employment patterns, but there was a noteworthy shift toward clerical and sales work as well as professional employment. These changes tell the story of wartime opportunity while they also reflect the growth of BIA bureaucracy during the war years. Women specifically were able to find employment in the reorganized BIA as they had acquired necessary skills in clerical work while in school.

The optimism about the future, created by positive Indian experiences during the war, quickly subsided in the postwar era. Demobilization abated the need for labor, while the returning veterans, especially Anglo men, received priority in hiring. Among the last hired, Native American war workers often became the first fired and returned to reservations where they encountered a stark reality of diminishing land bases, growing populations, housing shortages, lack of services, and few economic opportunities. Returning to the city seemed the logical solution to reservation poverty. In the years between 1940 and 1950, Indian urban populations nationwide nearly doubled. Phoenix experienced an even more phenomenal growth as the number of Native residents increased from 249 in 1940 to 789 in 1950.

The Navajo and Hopi case best illustrates the postwar economic crisis on reservations that prompted so many to leave and served as an impetus for a new federal policy of assimilation, labeled *relocation*. In the winter of 1947, severe weather compounded the dire economies on the reservations and threatened the Navajos and Hopis with starvation, prompting Congress to act. As part of the solution, the BIA initiated a job placement service in 1948 to ease pressure on reservation resources and create opportunity by assisting Navajos and Hopis to find employment off the reservation. This assistance became part of the 1950 Navajo-Hopi Rehabilitation Act, and served as the model for the national relocation program that gained full force under Commissioner of Indian Affairs Dillon S. Myer. He created the Branch of Placement and Relocation within the BIA in 1951, and the first relocatees moved in February 1952.

Commissioner Glenn Emmons continued to vigorously support and expand the relocation program. Yet the low educational levels and lack of specific skills hampered the employment program as the demand for unskilled labor steadily declined in the economic growth years of the Cold War. Vocational training thus assumed importance as part of relocation. In 1956, Congress passed legislation to assist Indians between the ages of 18 and 35 to attend vocational institutions and to participate in on-the-job training or apprenticeship programs. By the end of the decade, the BIA replaced the term *relocation* with *employment assistance* to reflect this new emphasis. The new terminology also sought to shift attention away from the negative connotations of relocation as part of the policy of termination.

While Phoenix was not a destination city for relocation, BIA employment assistance and vocational training programs did influence Indian migrations to the city. The Arizona State Employment Service (ASES) stepped up its efforts, in collaboration with the BIA, to place Phoenix Indian High School students as early as 1949. Adult vocational training in the city began in 1958, with ASES assuming major responsibility for trainee selection. Although not as successful as anticipated, these programs brought young Indian people, especially single women, to the Phoenix area to participate in popular courses in welding, nursing, beauty and barber work, and business administration. Graduates and dropouts alike often opted to stay in Phoenix or another urban area. Their stories traveled back home and attracted new migrants, while the perennial economic problems on reservations served as the major push factor. Meanwhile, the explosive growth of Phoenix in the 1950s provided increasing opportunities in the workforce.

The BIA's efforts on reservations to encourage urban relocation undoubtedly played a role in many a decision to move to Phoenix. The city offered the same opportunities as the major relocation centers of San Francisco, Los Angeles, and Chicago. An added advantage was the city's proximity to home. Relocation often meant a radical severing of ties to the home reservation. The move to Phoenix, however, allowed for families and individuals to return to their reservation communities for weekends and holidays, resulting in frequent travel back and forth. Such ties guaranteed the persistence of cultural practices in the urban environment and served as an important mechanism of adjustment.

Educational opportunities in the Phoenix area served as an important pull factor for Indian youth. The extensive Native involvement in the war effort had prompted recognition of the value of education, and many tribes began to set aside funds for scholarships. The National Indian Education Center, founded in 1948 at Arizona State University, brought in youth for teacher training while providing increasing opportunities for professional employment. Native American students also attended the region's community colleges. Phoenix College especially drew a large number of Indian students, helping them adjust to the demands of higher education. The ASES continued to facilitate the transfer of Indian High School students into the world of higher education and employment.

While educational opportunities widened, so did openings in the workforce for educated Indians. The 1949 reorganization of the BIA, its relocation activities, and Indian preference in hiring increased the number of Native Americans working for the Phoenix-area BIA office. In 1955, the Public Health Service assumed responsibility for Indian health care, and operations in the Phoenix area were streamlined. The Phoenix Indian hospital also cared for an increasing number of reservation residents, creating new jobs.

The net result of all these changes—training, education, and employment—was an increase in the Indian population. By 1960, 1,164 American Indians declared Phoenix their permanent residence and 1,337 Native Americans lived in the metropolitan area. It is, of course, worth noting that the 1960 census was the first to use self-identification in determining ethnicity.

Because Phoenix was not a relocation center, the BIA did not keep records of who moved there. However, the relocation records prove helpful in constructing a profile of who tended to leave a reservation and move to an urban area. It appears that men were more likely to leave than women. The BIA recruitment campaigns emphasized "traditional" family households and focused on male employment, recruiting both single and married men. Yet there were few guarantees of success, and heads of families often relocated alone and only sent for their families once they had established themselves in the city. Because Phoenix is situated so close to many reservation communities, it is also likely that many Indian men worked in the city during the week and traveled home to their families for the weekends and holidays. Indeed, most of the Native American population in the metropolitan area consisted of members of Arizona tribes.

Reports of the ASES on assistance to reservation Indians also helps shed light on the occupational patterns of these urban migrants. During the calendar year 1960, for instance, ASES placed over 24,000 Arizona Indians in employment. This figure represented an all-time high, reflecting the changing economic conditions on reservations and the growing significance of wage labor in Native American communities. The majority of these workers still found employment in the agricultural sector, with 48 percent placed in nonagricultural positions. Of these workers, the vast majority were employed in the service sector or in private households, accounting for 42 percent of the total nonagricultural placements. The growth of the tourism industry in Arizona undoubtedly influenced this high figure. Resorts and hotels employed especially women as maids and kitchen help while others worked as domestics. Government emerged as the second largest nonagricultural employer, with 31 percent of the ASES placements; yet the percentage of Indian employees in state agencies remained disproportionately small and concentrated in the lower salary ranges. In fact, in all sectors of the economy, Indians continued to occupy the lowest skill levels.

Income statistics speak to the tangible result of these occupational patterns: persistent poverty. Although migration often translated into economic improvement over the reservation, urban life also meant added costs, including housing, transportation, and health care. Furthermore, Indian incomes lagged behind the national average. The 1970 census reveals that Native American incomes in Phoenix were even lower than the national average for the group. By now, 5,893 Indians lived in Phoenix proper, constituting less than 1 percent of the city's population; the metropolitan area population had reached a total of 7,957 Native Americans. More than 30 percent of all Indian persons and 25 percent of families had incomes below the poverty level as compared to an 11.7 percent poverty rate for the county. Nearly 40 percent of the total Native population lived in the low-income inner-city area, while a cluster of middle-class residences had developed near the Indian High School. However, the school campus constituted the only area in the city with Indians as the numerical majority, housing nearly 1,000 students and staff. Its student body consisted largely of Arizona Indians, with Navajos, Apaches, and Hopis in the majority.

Arizona tribes also made up 71 percent of the city's total Native American population, while nearly three fourths of the out-of-state population came from southern and western states. Census information further suggests that the population was overwhelmingly young, with 83 percent under 40 years of age. Forty-five percent of all Indians older than 25 years of age held high school diplomas, but only 16 percent had attended college, while less than 3 percent had more than four years of higher education. These statistics translated into an unemployment rate for inner-city Indian men higher than any other ethnic group in the city: 13.5 percent.

Although not specifically targeting Native American communities, President Johnson's War on Poverty provided an opportunity to address some of the challenges facing inner-city Indians in Phoenix. The first efforts emerged from within the Central Presbyterian Church, which had come to be identified as the religious and social center of the Phoenix Indian community; it also had a strong commitment to addressing the physical needs of its congregation. The city, too, took advantage of the poverty programs, but Native Americans remained less vocal than other ethnic groups about their specific concerns, resulting in less engagement by the city in improving Indian neighborhoods.

In the 1970s, the Phoenix Native American population clearly began to develop a sense of identity as members of an urban community. National Indian activism provided a backdrop to this emerging "sense of belonging," while local advocates helped secure visibility for Native concerns in city politics. Funding from the municipal and federal governments propelled the Phoenix Indian Center to the forefront of promoting Indian welfare. The city also responded to the political energy in the community, expanding its funding to include a variety of Indian-oriented programs. The proliferation of such programs offered further opportunities for work, while federal educational initiatives brought new Indian students to the area. These new arrivals found a focus in a number of Indian student clubs, which, in addition to their social function, increasingly assumed political goals in the context of local leadership development and against the backdrop of national activism. The American Indian Movement (AIM) also established a chapter in Phoenix, although it never reached a very strong active following in the city. Yet AIM certainly played a role in raising consciousness of Indian affairs and concerns among Phoenicians—Indian and non-Indian alike.

By 1980, the U.S. Census Bureau reported that more than half of all American Indians in the nation lived in urban areas. Although this number certainly reflects the urbanization of reservations themselves, the change to a large degree resulted from the continuing out-migration of reservation residents. The Phoenix Indian community now amounted to 10,808 people; the number of metropolitan-area Indian residents had reached 16,781. Although tribal ties remained strong for many of these urban residents, the emergence of intertribal networks and Indian-oriented programs nurtured a sense of commonality that served as an adaptive mechanism in the urban environment. This sense of unity was undoubtedly strengthened by the fact that 61 percent of the population still consisted of

Arizona tribes; approximately one half of the out-of-state population came from western and southern states. Native Americans also remained a relatively young group, with median age at 21.6 years. Educational levels had increased considerably from a decade earlier: 65 percent of those over 25 now held high school diplomas while 9.5 percent had more than four years of college. These educational levels reflect the active recruiting of students and the increasing emphasis in Indian communities on education as the key to economic and social improvement.

Income statistics to some degree mirror these rising educational levels. Median incomes had increased among the Indian population as a whole, although women lagged behind men, earning only about one half of the average male income. This disparity also shows in the poverty rates. Indian families remained the least advantaged, with nearly 24 percent living below the poverty level; female-headed households made up nearly one half of these low-income families. Although almost 15 percent of Indian women in Phoenix now held managerial and professional positions, the overwhelming majority concentrated in low-paying jobs in the clerical and service sectors of the economy.

In the two decades since 1980, the Phoenix metropolitan area has experienced phenomenal population and economic growth. At the same time, employment has expanded along transportation corridors away from the central city, spurring the growth of the suburbs and the nearby cities. Between 1980 and 1990, the population grew by 39.9 percent to 2.2 million; the 1990s experienced an even more dramatic growth of 45.3 percent to a total of 3.2 million, making Phoenix the second-fastest growing metropolitan area in the nation after Las Vegas, Nevada. Furthermore, migrations account for more than two thirds of this growth.

As the city has grown, so has its Native American population. By the 2000 census, the greater Phoenix metropolitan area housed a total of 58,122 American Indians and Alaska Natives. The city of Phoenix had an Indian population of 35,093, or 2.7 percent of the total population. In analyzing these figures and comparing them to previous census data, however, it is important to keep in mind that the Census Bureau changed the definition on race for the 2000 census. Respondents were now asked to report *one or more* races they considered themselves to be. Yet, even if we only consider the 26,696 people who listed themselves as "American Indian or Alaska Native alone," the growth of this population has been significant in these last two decades. Nationally, Phoenix ranks third in the size of its Native population; only New York and Los Angeles have higher actual numbers of Indian residents.

The U.S. Equal Employment Opportunity Commission 2000 census data for Maricopa County—although inclusive of several reservation communities—also provides important insights into the economic profile of the growing urban Indian population. The evidence points to increasing educational levels and improved access to higher-paying jobs. More than 11 percent of the American Indian and Alaska Native population over 16 years of age in the civilian labor force held a bachelor's, graduate, or other professional degree, while nearly another 40 percent had at least some college education. At the same time, however, 20 percent of the Native population had not finished high school. Occupationally, nearly one half of the American Indian labor force still concentrated in the lower-paying categories of service workers, laborers, operatives, administrative support personnel, and craft workers, but significant improvement had occurred in professional employment. Approximately 17 percent now found employment as health care practitioners; science, engineering, and computer professionals; management, business, and financial workers; and as other professionals. Clearly, though, Native Americans are underrepresented in each of these areas of employment vis-à-vis their percentage of the total population. Furthermore, unemployment remains high. While 4.7 percent of the Maricopa County population was unemployed, the percentage of Native Americans was 10.1. Even more alarming is the female unemployment rate: 11.3 percent among Native women as opposed to the 4 percent in the total workforce. These figures seem to suggest the continuing trend of female and child poverty.

The story of the United States is one of immigration and migration. The 2000 census figures clearly demonstrate that Native Americans increasingly participate in this larger story as they have, in the words of Zuni tribal member Cal Seciwa, Director of the American Indian Institute at Arizona State University, "grown and been able to navigate the dominant society in areas such as education and employment." Phoenix provides only one example of this trend. Yet, as more Indian people move to urban areas, learn trades, and become professionals, they also choose to only partially assimilate in the mainstream culture. "Our loyalties and our hearts are back home, where we have family, religious and other cultural ties," continues Seciwa. Frequent visits to their homelands reinforce these cultural ties, while urban institutions, like the Phoenix Indian Center, provide venues to navigate the city environment. Everything continues to be connected to the past.

—*Paivi Hoikkala*

See also Bureau of Indian Affairs; Indian Removal Act of 1830; Phoenix, Arizona; World War II Defense Industries

Suggested Reading

Chaudhuri, Joyotpaul. *Urban Indians of Arizona: Phoenix, Tucson, and Flagstaff.* Tucson: University of Arizona Press, 1974.

Clark, Blue. "Bury My Heart in Smog: Urban Indians." In *"They Made Us Many Promises": The American Indian Experience 1524 to the Present.* 2nd ed., edited by Philip Weeks. Wheeling, IL: Harlan Davidson, 2002.

Fixico, Donald L. *The Urban Indian Experience in America.* Albuquerque: University of New Mexico Press, 2000.

Lobo, Susan, and Kurt Peters, eds. *American Indians and the Urban Experience.* Walnut Creek, CA: AltaMira, 2001.

Weibel-Orlando, Joan. *Indian Country, L.A.: Maintaining Ethnic Community in Complex Society.* Urbana: University of Illinois Press, 1991.

ANGLO MIGRATION TO SOUTHERN CALIFORNIA BEFORE THE DEPRESSION

Between 1880 and 1930, southern California experienced a massive influx of white Protestant, interregional migrants. In that period, residents of the Midwest particularly chose to relocate to Los Angeles—the principal city in southern California—and the surrounding area over any other location west of the Rocky Mountains. Overwhelming in their numbers, midwestern migrants dwarfed other interregional transplants. Although northeasterners initially accounted for the white population in southern California, their numbers dropped just after the turn of the century. Other regional migrants, such as those from the American South, made little numerical impact prior to the end of World War I. While many have attributed this significant flow of native midwesterners to the notion of an American proclivity toward westward movement, in real terms, multiple factors spurred this specific voluminous human stream. Some left the Midwest to escape the bitterly cold winters and take advantage of southern California's salubrious climate. Other midwesterners simply desired to break away from the farm and looked to Los Angeles as a place of greater leisure. Yet much of the story of Los Angeles and its unprecedented development is really the story of a small group of like-minded businessmen and women who advertised the virtues of the city and region in a series of massive but targeted advertising campaigns. Thus, in order to understand the pull of white migrants to southern California, it is necessary to acknowledge the role of those who initially advertised the region as a land of mild climate, healthy convalescence, and limited toil. In a number of ways, the success of Los Angeles as a population center was contingent upon the success of these regional boosters.

The growth of the area itself was astounding. From 1880 to 1930, the population of Los Angeles alone jumped from 11,183 to 1,238,048. In that period, the largest single interregional migrant group represented the states of the American Midwest. By 1930, there were nearly 370,000 former midwesterners in the city of Los Angeles alone, and twice as many in the entire county. Yet this growth and population composition was hardly an act of providence, but rather the result of a competition for white, midwestern migrants, and the want of regional development. Far from being blown by the wind to the Pacific, midwesterners were indeed lured to the West by promises of health, wealth, and leisure, as advertised by Los Angeles's boosters. Generally, boosters were businesspeople who invested in a city's potential for development and consequently profited in periods of growth or suffered in times of decline. Thus, boosters worked tirelessly to advertise their cities to the nation while at the same time attempting to bolster regional commerce. While

other far western cities, such as Seattle and Portland, attempted to lure the same midwesterners, Los Angeles succeeded to a much greater extent. Southern California's ambitious boosters (who were often principle figures in real estate, tourism, agriculture, and heavy industry) laid the foundation for a profitable metropolis. But in this region, as in many others, boosters also wanted to create a certain *type* of city, a city of character rather than just a large city of monetary returns. During the late 19th and early 20th centuries, these boosters explicitly attempted to draw hardworking, conservative white migrants away from their small towns in the Midwest to southern California in order to build an orderly Anglo-Saxon haven on the shores of the Pacific Ocean.

Southern California boosterism as it relates to the peopling of the region evolved in successive stages. During the initial phase of Los Angeles boosterism in the late 19th and early 20th centuries, businessmen attempted to attract white farmers (often using tourism as a lure) by advertising the agricultural abundance, natural beauty, and health benefits associated with southern California's mild but sunny climate. One 1888 publication proclaimed, "Los Angeles is THE MOST COMFORTABLE SUMMER RESORT IN THE WORLD. Sunstroke is unknown. There are no hot nights. In the shade it is always cool." Another pamphlet in 1904 effusively addressed the litany of the reasons migrants should consider relocating to the Los Angeles area:

> May [this book's] message also pass to the seeker of health, of pleasure or an ideal home place and embody the invitation and welcome which is ever bespoken for those who journey to this glowing southland. . . . Here may be found picturesque old missions founded by the fathers; the varied mountain and ocean scenery; broad cultivated acres; orchards and vineyards burdened with rich harvests; gardens and parks of tropical luxuriance, while last and best, are the homes of our people—builded here where, amid smiling, fruitful valleys, the snow-capped mountains meet the peaceful sea and the glorious sunshine is an ever-present inspiration.

And, while many migrants responded to this style of advertising, most chose to abandon farming upon arrival.

Soon after the turn of the 20th century, one particular booster organization rose to undisputed prominence and abandoned the relocation of white agriculturalists in favor of a more cosmopolitan campaign.

The next phase of boosterism coincides with the newfound prominence of the Los Angeles Chamber of Commerce. The chamber, which was composed of leading area businessmen and local politicians, had worked for a number of years promoting the region, but gained real clout by 1910, when it was informally incorporated into the realm of city and county governments and given public funds to promote greater Los Angeles's social and industrial development. Concentrating on leisure and economic opportunity rather than health and farming, the chamber by the 1920s had saturated the nation with tens of millions of pamphlets and brochures aimed at tourists and would-be migrants looking to both relax and work.

By all indications, the chamber succeeded during the period at both drawing new residents and siphoning migrants from other potential western destinations. While the other emerging cities on the West Coast, such as Seattle and Portland, experienced rapid growth from 1900 to 1910, Los Angeles clearly outpaced them in its ability to attract a steady stream of migrants. For instance, Portland began the 20th century with a mere 10,000 people fewer than Los Angeles, but by 1920, that gap had risen to nearly 320,000. Though not quite as dramatically, this is also true of Seattle. By 1910, Seattle was the most populated city in the Pacific Northwest, and, although it held 80 percent of Los Angeles's total population at the turn of the century, by the next census Los Angeles outpaced Seattle by 82,000, and by 262,000 in 1920. From 1910, Los Angeles's population grew at a rate three times as high as Portland's and well over twice Seattle's rate. By 1920, Los Angeles surpassed San Francisco as the most populated city in the West. Additionally, while those other cities' rate of midwestern in-migration stagnated, Los Angeles's continued to grow.

Empowered by the city and county governments, Los Angeles boosters went far beyond simply trying to populate the region. They believed that they could design the region as an Anglo-Saxon haven and thus, in their opinion, control the character of the city itself. The Chamber of Commerce made no secret of its desire to lure whites over other minorities, and it often contrasted southern California to the ghettoized cities of the eastern seaboard, with their foreign influences and immigrant masses. The chamber even went to the extent of studying the immigration and developing measures, if necessary, to reduce its impact. For example, in 1912, concerned about the ease with which immigrants might reach the area after the opening of the Panama Canal, the chamber commissioned a study to assess the adverse affects of eastern European immigrants on southern California. According to the report, the chamber wanted "to ascertain the best means of keeping out the undesirable aliens and attract the industrious and more desirable class of immigrants." In another chamber report, the group announced that it was "not in sympathy with the great throngs of Southern Europeans who of late years have formed the majority of our immigrants."

The Chamber of Commerce invested most of its energy not in keeping undesirables out, but in the courting of native-born white Americans. With the black, Latino, Asian, and eastern European population rapidly rising in the city despite efforts to dissuade immigration, area boosters were still able to maintain a steady midwestern white plurality. To ensure this statistical dominance, the organization deliberately targeted the white, middle-class, Protestant Midwest. This group was clearly the most valued demographic. The reasons for the particular midwestern preference are varied but rather straightforward. The Midwest represented the center of the country's population; its inhabitants were mobile, had benefited financially from the solid grain prices, and could contribute to southern California's economy. So, for these boosters, according to Carey McWilliams, "Every consideration was subordinated to the paramount concern of attracting church-going Middle Westerners to Southern California."

But there were also other cultural considerations. City boosters recognized midwesterners as similar to themselves; that is, the Midwest audience they wanted to appeal to was predominantly white, Protestant (but not southern Baptist or southern Methodist), and— more often than not—Republican. Often couched in terms of "class," boosters wanted to limit their promotional scope as to exclude people that they believed could not meet a minimum moral standard, and thus they focused on this particular audience. For example, in 1910 the Chamber of Commerce participated in the Omaha Corn Show because it would be well attended by "a class of people desirable for us to reach." The notion of a migrant's "character" so intrigued the chamber that they even promoted southern California–topical lectures in Esperanto, in the hope that they might engender the migration of a more "intelligent class of people." In its use of the term *class,* the chamber meant to attract not only a group that rose above a minimum economic standard, but to lure people with a similar worldview.

In practical terms, the Chamber of Commerce developed a promotional strategy that targeted particular areas in an effort to move white, middle-class residents into southern California. For example, the chamber extensively campaigned in Chicago, the entire state of Iowa, and Detroit and in the first two decades of the 20th century. Recognizing Chicago as the rail hub of the nation, the chamber committee on promotion saturated the area with brochures and other promotional materials. They also noted that the state of Illinois was the population center of the nation. As one Los Angeles booster claimed in 1909, "Immigration practically radiates from Chicago, and I am equally satisfied we will have to fight most of our battles there."

Yet the attempt to transplant Illinois' whites to the West also demanded a more interactive campaign, one modeled after national and international world's fairs. Exceedingly popular in the 19th and early 20th centuries, these expositions pulled in mass audiences for brief but often spectacular occasions. From world's fairs to industrial expos, these spectacles drew middle-class whites away from their small towns and afforded them the experience of witnessing the products of the globe in a single tent. Generally a method of advancing interregional commerce, expositions were funded by businesspeople and boosters and were for a decidedly middle-class audience. Boosters in their own regions, these promoters invited other cities and regions to display goods and information in an effort to form commercial relationships. For the Chamber of Commerce, the purpose of the expositions was to import a vision of southern California products to states and cities in certain regions not only to promote trade, but middle-class migration as well. The displays

of southern California agricultural abundance were a visual spectacle that included such sights as a life-size model of an elephant covered entirely in walnuts, or a 25-foot tower. These displays, however, were not intended for the working-class people who might find entertainment at places like Coney Island, but for the education and edification of the middle-class spectator.

Illinois, and Chicago in particular, became the exposition epicenter. As the chamber's promotional efforts grew, so did its emphasis of expositions in the Midwest in general, and Chicago in particular. Early on, Los Angeles boosters specifically targeted the Midwest in their choice of expositions. Although the chamber occasionally engaged in expositions in outside of the Midwest in the first decade of the 20th century, by 1910 it focused exclusively on midwestern states, particularly Illinois. In the space of three years, the chamber participated in nine expositions. Of those, seven were held in the Midwest, with three in Chicago alone. The chamber's desire for the model migrant limited its scope to an area where class and geography aligned in a manner that invited focused promotional saturation.

The same was true of Iowa. As one historian has shown, Los Angeles boosters made a special effort to draw Iowans off of their farms and out of their small towns to the shores of the Pacific. As a result, Iowa consistently ranked in the top 10 states contributing to Los Angeles's population from 1910 to 1930. By 1930, there were over 40,000 Iowans in the city of Los Angeles alone. And, like the Chamber of Commerce itself, Iowa was a Republican stronghold where northern Protestantism dominated religious expression, and a state whose residents were overwhelmingly white. So successful was this push for Iowans in southern California that the region was nicknamed "Iowa by the Sea" and "Caliowa."

Always uncomfortable with a Mexican, Chinese, Japanese nonagricultural workforce, Chamber of Commerce officials also sought to compel white midwestern industrial worker migration. Shortly after the implementation of an exclusively Midwest-focused strategy, the chamber targeted industrial workers and investors in Detroit by publishing a pamphlet specifically for distribution in that city entitled "Oil in California." Three months later, it printed its annual "Los Angeles Today," for distribution at expositions and on train cars. The pamphlet illustrated the superiority of Los Angeles climate and working conditions relative to major midwestern cites. Indianapolis, Ft. Wayne, Chicago, Springfield, Detroit, Cleveland, Toledo, Columbus, and Dayton were all significantly colder, more difficult to navigate, and did not have the natural advantages that Los Angeles possessed. Only in Los Angeles, it appeared, could one toil less and enjoy the weather throughout the year. In one promotional tract, the chamber quoted a vacationing worker from Detroit who visited the Hotpoint appliance manufacturing plant in Ontario, California. The astonished midwesterner proclaimed that he had "never dreamt of finding, in the heart of fragrant orange groves, a thoroughly modern, splendidly equipped factory turning out goods with a national reputation."

Overall, the strategy of the Los Angeles Chamber of Commerce appears to have (in the short term) succeeded. The principal targets of the promotional campaign responded to the publicity blitz. By 1920, midwestern states filled the ranks of states contributing to migrants to Los Angeles. Illinois, with 38,064, was followed by New York (the only non-midwestern state in the top five with 26,958), Ohio (25,511), Missouri (24,104), and Iowa (19,968). Other states with similar out-migration patterns as these midwestern states—such as Tennessee—but outside of the chamber's promotional realm contributed far fewer migrants.

There is also evidence to suggest that the Chamber of Commerce's goal of a white, socially conservative population was temporarily achieved. In 1915, writer Willard Huntington Wright observed that "the inhabitants of Los Angeles are culled largely from the smaller cities of the Midwest." He went on to claim that the transplantation of "militant moralists" and their midwestern values had transformed southern California from a small pueblo to an oversized puritanical village in a brief but formative period. After the publication of Wright's essay, a respondent in the Los Angeles *Examiner* claimed that Los Angeles "deliberately chooses to be dubbed 'Puritan,' 'Middle-West Farmer,' 'Provincial,' etc., and glories in the fact that she has been able to sweep away many of the flaunting indecencies that still disgrace older and more vice-complacent communities." The sum of these assessments concerning midwestern cultural contribution to southern California suggests that the Chamber of Commerce was indeed successful in its effort to import regionally influenced middle-class values.

—Dan Cady

See also Los Angeles, California; Okies

Suggested Reading

Davis, Clark. *Company Men: White Collar Life and Corporate Cultures in Los Angeles, 1892–1941.* Baltimore, MD: Johns Hopkins University Press, 2000.

Fogelson, Robert. *The Fragmented Metropolis, Los Angeles, 1850–1930.* Berkeley: University of California Press, 1967.

Mayo, Morrow. *Los Angeles.* New York: Knopf, 1933.

McWilliams, Carey. *Southern California Country: An Island on the Land.* New York: Duell, Sloan, & Pearce. (Reprinted Santa Barbara, CA: Peregrine Smith, 1973)

Nicolaides, Becky M. *My Blue Heaven: Life and Politics in the Working-Class Suburb of Los Angeles, 1920–1965.* Chicago: University of Chicago Press, 2002.

Pitt, Leonard. "The Midwesternization of a Cowtown." *California History* 60 (Spring 1981).

Spooner, Denise. "A New Perspective on the Dream: Midwestern Images of Southern California in the Post–World War Decades." *California History* 76 (Spring 1997).

Starr, Kevin. *Material Dreams: Southern California through the 1920s.* New York: Oxford University Press, 1990.

Woehlke, Walter V. "Angels in Overalls: Being a True and Veracious Account of Workaday Life in the Angelic Region, Together with a Exposition of the Manners and Methods by Which the Inhabitants of the Angel City Boosted the Demand for Junipers and Jeans, and an Attempt to Show That Bellboys, Millionaires, Hotel Clerks and Tourists Have No Exclusive Entry into the Aforesaid Realm." *Sunset Magazine* (March 1912).

Wright, Willard Huntington. "Los Angeles—The Chemically Pure." In *The Smart Set Anthology*, edited by Burton Roscoe and Geoff Couklin. New York: Reynal and Hitchcock, 1934.

Zimmerman, Tom. "Paradise Promoted: Boosterism and the Los Angeles Chamber of Commerce." *California History* 64 (Winter 1985).

APACHE

The Apache people of today are a confederation of seven Athabascan- or Apachean-speaking tribes who once shared a common ancestor. Modern Apache people include the Chiricahua, Jicarilla, Mescalero, Navajo, Lipan, Western Apache, and the Kiowa-Apache. Because the Kiowa-Apache are culturally related to the Plains Indians and especially the Kiowa people, they will not be included in this study.

Linguistic evidence indicates the original group formed as a distinct tribe or related group of tribes while living in the Mackenzie Basin of Canada. Within this region, the ancient Apache were linked to other linguistic groups that occupied the northern Pacific coast from Alaska to Oregon and inland to the basin. This would indicate an initial migratory history that crossed the Bering Strait and then divided into several groupings, some of which followed the west coast of America, while others moved inland. Around 1,000 years ago, the Apachean dialect broke from these related languages and for the next 300 years developed independently. Approximately 700–800 years ago, these ancient Apache people began to move south into what is now the United States. Questions abound as to whether the Apache people traveled into the Southwest via a western or an eastern route. Because the Apache have traditionally been a hunter-gatherer society, archaeological evidence of their passage through any region would be scant, if any evidence remained at all.

There is some question as to whether the ancient Apache lived for a time in the Salt Lake Basin, occupying caves in the region before continuing their southward journey. However, this presumption is not well accepted. The journey of more than 1,500 miles from the Mackenzie Basin to the Southwestern region of the United States ended for the Apache around 1300–1400. The reason for their move from Canada to the arid Southwest cannot be ascertained. Archeological evidence in the Gobernador Largo Canyon of southern Colorado and northern New Mexico would place the Navajo—who built more permanent structures than their brethren—in the latter years of the 15th century. However, even this tantalizing information about the ancient Apache is scant. Additional archeological evidence has been found in the Dismal River region of New Mexico, but this does not antedate 1650. Once the ancient Apache reached the Southwest, the linguistic and political differences that would come to characterize the seven distinct tribes would proceed rapidly, so that within 400 years of reaching the region they had formed into distinct tribes.

The ancestors of the Navajo, Western Apache, Mescalero, and Chiricahua were the first to move south and westward, followed by the Lipan and Jicarilla. The Kiowa-Apache likely diverged from the Lipan and Jicarilla around 1500 and became more closely related to the plains culture than the Pueblo culture that would impact all other Apache tribes. Also, around the year 1500, the Navajo and Western Apache drifted further south and west until by 1600 the Lipan and Jicarilla no longer had any contact with either group. By the following century, even the Lipan and Jicarilla, who had remained a single band until this time, had become culturally and linguistically distinct from each other.

Eventually, each tribe would come to claim distinct lands that would further shape its worldview and culture. The Chiricahua established themselves west of the Rio Grande River in southwest New Mexico, southeast Arizona and into northern Mexico. The Mescalero held territory along the east of the Rio Grande River to the Pecos River in northwest Texas. The Lipan held land in central and southwest Texas, while the Jicarilla established themselves in northern New Mexico and southern Colorado. The Western Apache likely preceded the Navajo into the San Juan Basin of Arizona, New Mexico, and Utah. Eventually, they would settle further south than the Navajo. Lastly, the Kiowa-Apache would eventually establish themselves in the southern plains.

Within their separate territories, the Apache people thrived and developed their own individual traits as cultural groups. However, their common ancestry provided for more similarities than dissimilarities. Central to Apache existence was the "family cluster," a cohesive group of extended family whose members were dictated by matrilineal relationships. Each family within this cluster was related by marriage or blood but also had their own separate dwelling. Beyond the cluster, extended families lived in similar groups and together they constituted a band. Because of the vast territories among the Apache bands, no formal political authority developed. Among some Apache groups, such as the Mescalero and Lipan, band consciousness was weak, with the filial awareness diverted instead to the family cluster. Within the family groupings, no formal political authority existed, but a respected elder of the tribe served as spokesman for the group, and often the group was referred to by the name of this spokesman.

Female membership in the family cluster was decided by birth; as such, a woman was a lifetime member of the band. Unlike women, men gained their positions within the family cluster only through marriage. Once a man entered this matrilineal grouping, he was expected to work with the other members of the cluster to acquire food and to provide protection. The Apache were once thought to have had an agricultural tradition, but by the time they reached the U.S. Southwest, the aridity of the region made this tradition difficult to continue. Only the Navajo engaged in any significant form of planting and cultivating. At the opposite of this spectrum, the Kiowa-Apache refused to engage in any form of agriculture. Other Apache bands engaged in a passive form of planting, but primarily relied on hunting and gathering for their sustenance.

Cooperative work effort was so important to the continued survival of the group that when a man and woman divorced, if the man had been a good worker, other family members would attempt to reconcile the couple. Conversely, a man who was lazy could be run out of the family group by his wife's relatives. While work was most often divided along gender lines, the Apache culture still allowed for sufficient flexibility. At times women would assist in the hunt for small- or medium-sized game, and men—especially grandfathers and uncles—would assist in some child-rearing tasks or hide processing. Each man or woman owned the implements they used to meet the labor expectations of the group, and when a member of the band died, these implements would be destroyed so as not to encourage the dead to return.

In the Apache cosmology, the world was created from competing good and evil forces, many of which assumed the form of familiar animals, such as the coyote or owl. When an individual died, they traveled to a land of abundance or scarcity, depending on whether the person had been good or bad. In the Navajo religion, the dead returned to the original place where man had first appeared on the earth—an opening that led to a subterranean world where the ancients still lived. In a world where reminders of creation and good and evil abounded, Apache religious practice, as with those of all Native peoples, was expressed in daily rituals even though, to many, it may not have appeared to be formal worship.

In the harsh environment of the Southwest, food was often difficult to come by and defending resources was necessary. Often, groups engaged in raiding to acquire scarce goods. While raiding was preferable to war, bands would fight to avenge the loss of a family member or to defend territory. For the Apache, however, the practice of counting coup was not important as a means of distinguishing a warrior's bravery. Most Apache, rather pragmatically, felt it was better to kill an enemy than leave him alive. The fierce warrior of the Apache was likely the first individual Europeans met when they attempted to colonize the Southwest.

However, the first European to enter the territory of the Apache was Father Marcos de Niza in 1539. In the journals he left, no mention of an aboriginal people appears. Because of this, the possibility that the Apache had not yet permanently settled into the land has been considered. It would be difficult to counter this contention because the Apache, as a nomadic tribe, have left few archaeological remnants. However, it is equally possible that explorers and the Apache simply did not encounter each other on the vast landscape. Greater weight must be given to the latter assumption, as in 1540–1541 Francisco Vasquez de Coronado in his exploration of the Southwest reported encountering what were most likely bands of Chiricahua Apache hunters. Coronado referred to the bands he encountered as Querechos and Tejas Indians, which might have added to the confusion as to when the Apache permanently took up residence in the region.

Regardless of whether the Apache arrived before de Niza or soon after, the Apache were solidly entrenched in the region by the time Spanish exploration evolved into settlement. Whereas previous encounters had passed with few difficulties, as the number of foreigners in their land increased, so did the hostility exhibited by the Apache. In 1583, attempts to explore the mountains near Acoma, New Mexico, for minerals was met with pitched resistance from numerous Indians—likely the Chiricahua. When the Spanish sought to establish permanent settlements in Apache territory, the resistance exhibited by the Indians accelerated. In 1598, Juan de Onate attempted to establish a capital for the territory of New Mexico at the confluence of the Chama and Rio Grande Rivers, but the Apache launched so many attacks that the original settlement of San Gabriel had to be moved to modern-day Santa Fe in 1610.

For the rest of the 17th century, the Apache and the Spanish settled into an uneasy existence. The Apache continued to staunchly defend their territory against incursions by Europeans, who sought land, slaves, or converts. The contact that did occur between these two factions, besides identifying a clash of cultures, also provides a further summation of the migratory pattern of the Apache. As the Spanish priests scoured the region in search of converts and laborers, many noted the similarities and distinctions among the bands they encountered. In 1626, Father Alonzo de Benavides identified the distinction between the Chiricahua Apache, who lived west of the Rio Grande, and the Mescalero Apache, who lived to the east of the river. Benavides would also later note the similarities in their languages, which would imply that these two bands of Apache had only recently divided into their distinct tribes. The migratory patterns of the Apache people were aided immeasurably by the coming of the Spanish. As the Spanish established missions and presidios in the Southwest, they imported livestock, cattle, sheep, and especially horses. Like all native cultures that adopted the horse, the acquisition would forever change their culture and their previous migratory and settlement patterns.

By the end of the 17th century, Spanish reports record Apache warriors riding into battles on horseback, in some cases on horses that wore Spanish armor. The Indians became so proficient in using the horse to attack the Spanish that by the middle of the 17th century the Chiricahua were routinely attacking Sonora from a stronghold in the Datil Mountains 125 miles to the north. The Western Apache may have also aided the Chiricahua in these attacks. By 1718, San Antonio, Texas, was founded; almost from the inception of the settlement, the Lipan Apache repeated the same pattern of raiding the horse herds and randomly attacking the colonists. As the settlement pattern of the Spanish slowed by the 18th century, the territorial boundaries of the Apache were fixed, and the individual tribes refused to yield ground to the Spanish upstarts. Because most of the Spanish settlement centered around the Rio Grande, the tribes most often encountered by the Europeans were the Chiricahua

and the Mescalero. Holding the central position within the territory claimed by all the Apache, they retained contact with the other bands the longest and undoubtedly enlisted the aid of those tribes that were geographically closest to them.

By the 19th century, the war for control of the Spanish crown and her possessions resulted in an open revolt in Mexico and eventually culminated in Mexico's independence in 1821. Faced with trouble at home, Spain focused the attention of her military might on subduing rebellion, not on attacking the Apache. Through a series of treaties, a fractured peace settled over the region. That peace would be broken when the United States and Mexico went to war in 1846. By the time this lopsided war was over, most of Mexico's possessions in the Southwest had been annexed by the United States. Texas, which had proclaimed its independence from Mexico a decade earlier, had this declaration formalized in the treaty that ended the hostilities and established much of the territorial boundaries that still exist between the United States and Mexico. The change from Mexican to American ownership would have a profound impact on the Apache.

The brunt of the initial action against the Apache people was borne by the Navajo. By the turn of the 19th century, the Navajo had completed their 300-year exodus, breaking from the Chiricahua along the San Juan Mountains in New Mexico and moving toward the Colorado River. When Mexico broke off relations with Spain, the Navajo held territory from the Chama River in New Mexico to the Colorado and San Juan Rivers in Arizona. Like their Apache brethren, the Navajo fiercely protected their lands from incursion. Unfortunately, the transition from Mexican to American control would infuse the region with a larger and more determined military force than the Apache had previously encountered.

Conflict with the new settlers initially followed the same pattern previously established by the Spanish. The Navajo fought any who claimed their lands or attempted to steal their women and children to sell as slaves. So fierce was their opposition that, by 1850, the United States had entered into three peace treaties with the Navajo. Army forts were established within the Navajo's land, and Indian agents were called upon to ensure peace. Theirs would be a futile effort. As settlers into the Southwest increased, violence between the whites and the Apache accelerated. To keep the peace, the army patrolled the region, but instead of keeping peace, the soldiers were often the instigators of the violence. Additional attacks against Indian strongholds came from slave traders, who scoured the Southwest attacking villages and seizing Apache women and children. The military did little to curtail this activity. The army also did little to prevent settlers from running off or killing the livestock owned by the Indians. Finally, the discovery of gold and silver on Apache lands resulted in further encroachment. These attacks against the Navajo and other Apache bands reached their peak in 1858, when the U.S. Army declared war on the Navajo.

Only half-hearted attempts to negotiate peace were attempted, and the depredations continued on both sides. In 1859, some consideration was given to establishing a reservation for the Mescalero and the Lipan in northern New Mexico, but the government preferred instead to deal with the Apache with violence. In 1862, the secretary of war formalized the army's war declaration and ordered the army to strike and subdue the Navajo. A plan was devised to attack first the Mescalero Apache and by extension the Lipan, who were closely allied but lived in the mountains to their north, and then the Navajo. From 1862 to 1863, the Mescalero withered under the brunt of the army's forces, and after a campaign that lasted less than half a year, they were defeated. The army created a reserve for the Mescalero near Fort Sumner and named it Bosque Redondo; there, they installed the remaining Mescalero and Lipan Apache before turning their attention to the Navajo.

While the Navajo were attacked next, their defeat was not achieved as quickly as that of the Mescalero. Their numbers were larger and they were able to rely on this strength and the agricultural stores they had accumulated. These advantages, however, would not last indefinitely. The army, led by Colonel Christopher Carson, embarked on a scorched-earth campaign, killing Navajo livestock, burning crops, and allowing other groups to continue their harassment of the tribe. By 1864, most of the Navajo were starving, dead, or had been captured. Those captured Navajos were moved to the Bosque Redondo Reservation, but their

numbers quickly overwhelmed the limited resources of the reserve. In May 1868, another treaty was negotiated with the Navajo, and they were provided lands back in their original territory. Since that time, the Navajo Reservation has expanded several times to accommodate the growing tribe, and they are now the largest tribe in the Southwest.

With the Navajo and the Mescalero subdued, the U.S. Army was able to turn its attention to the remaining bands of the Apache. The Chiricahua would prove to be one of the most intractable to remove from their native lands. In 1852, copper mines were reopened in eastern Chiricahua territory, and then later gold was discovered in Pinos Altos; both areas are near Santa Rita, in western New Mexico. The discovery of mineral wealth accelerated the number of settlers to the region, and the Chiricahua were forced to defend their homeland. For the next 35 years, government treatment of the Chiricahua would vary dramatically. Military conquests alternated with attempts to settle the Chiricahua on a reservation that had been established in the foothills of the Mogollon Mountains along the Gila River in 1860. This attempt was met with little success. While the Apache acted in good faith, the U.S. Army often broke its agreements and assassinated tribal leaders who had come in peacefully to talk. It would take another decade of fighting before tribal members agreed in any number to settle on reservation lands. While the Chiricahua insisted on remaining on lands that had traditionally been theirs, settlers to the region prevented this from happening, and land was set aside along the Arizona–New Mexico border. By 1872, the Chiricahua began to settle into the new Tularosa Valley Reservation and a second Chiricahua Reservation further south along the border between Arizona and Mexico. By 1874, these reservations would be abandoned in preference for the Hot Springs Reservation, which was established along the Rio Grande River in southeastern New Mexico. However, complaints of theft from across the border in Mexico and raiding in the region resulted in the forced removal of the Chiricahua from the Hot Springs Reservation in 1877 to the San Carlos Reservation in southeastern Arizona.

At this new reservation, the Chiricahua were forced to live with bands of the Western Apache; despite their common ancestry, each tribe felt the other was an intrusion. Many fled the San Carlos Reserve and either joined other bands of Apache on established reservations or fled back into the mountains that had been their home. Attempts to resettle the Chiricahua were hampered by the continued aggression of the military and new hostilities between the Western Apache and the army. By 1882, the Chiricahua had decided to remove themselves to Mexico and established a village in the Sierra Madre Mountains in northern Mexico. The U.S. Army pursued the Chiricahua, and in 1883 they were persuaded to return to the San Carlos Reservation. The unhappy conditions on the reservation eventually resulted in a small exodus led by Geronimo back to the Sierra Madre Mountains in 1885. Relentlessly pursued by both U.S. and Mexican forces, this tiny band eventually surrendered in 1886 but were not allowed to return to the reservation as had been promised. Instead, they were arrested and most sent to Fort Marion in Florida. Geronimo and about half the men of the band were incarcerated at Fort Pickens, which was also in Florida. Living conditions rapidly deteriorated, and within a year 20 percent of the Chiricahua were dead. The army determined to move the tribe to improve conditions, and by 1888 both groups of captives had been moved to the Mount Vernon Barracks in Alabama. Despite the move, the Chiricahua continued to perish at an alarming rate, and in 1894 they were again moved to a new location, this time to the Fort Sill Reservation in Oklahoma, where they continued to be considered prisoners of the U.S. Army until 1913. In 1913, the Chiricahua Apache were granted amnesty and given the choice of returning to the Mescalero Reservation in southeast New Mexico or accepting allotments of land in Oklahoma. Eighty-four Chiricahua Apache chose to accept the allotments; that area still is inhabited by the band today. The remaining 187 members of the band moved to the Mescalero Reservation. By the late 20th century, the Mescalero, Lipan, and Chiricahua Apache Indians assimilated to each other's culture and an amalgamated group now lives in the same reserve that they have occupied for almost 100 years.

The Jicarilla band of Apache fared better than the Chiricahua during the early American period. In part,

this is likely because the Jicarilla were a smaller band and occupied lands less favored by whites. However, the same pattern of raiding and retribution that characterized American contact with the Apache was evident. In 1851, the Jicarilla entered into an agreement with the U.S. government in which they agreed to observe territorial boundaries and cease all hostilities, but the U.S. Senate never ratified this treaty. By the following year, the territorial government in New Mexico, independent of federal oversight, began encouraging the Jicarilla to settle on lands west of the Rio Grande River in order to quell the escalating violence between the Apache and settlers. Their effort was not supported by the federal government and within two years was ordered shut down. The Jicarilla left the makeshift reservation and returned to raiding. Instead of reestablishing the reservation, the army declared war on the tribe. By 1855, the Jicarilla sued for peace and another agreement was reached whereby the Indians agreed to occupy a set territory and cease all hostility. As with the previous treaty, this one was not ratified by the U.S. Senate, which left the status of the Jicarilla in limbo. Several Indian agencies were created over the years and food rations were distributed, but no land was set aside for the Jicarilla to occupy. While all other Indian tribes in the New Mexico territory had been provided with land, only the Jicarilla were denied this basic provision. Twenty years after agreeing to cease hostilities with white settlers in their territory and after signing two treaties, neither of which was honored by the federal government, the Jicarilla were finally provided with a permanent reservation.

In 1874, the Jicarilla Apache Reservation was established along the San Juan River in northwest New Mexico. However, the life of the reservation would be short lived, and two years later it was abandoned in favor of white settlement. Bureaucratic bungling continued for another decade before the Jicarilla were finally settled on the Mescalero Apache Reservation in 1883. Forced into inadequate and unfamiliar territory, the Jicarilla Apache petitioned the federal government for a reservation of their own in territory familiar to their people. By 1887, now more than 30 years since they had agreed to cease all hostility with the whites, the Jicarilla had their reservation. Located west of the

Charma River in the San Juan Mountains, the reserve initially encompassed more than 400,000 acres at an altitude of between 6,000 and 8,000 feet. Unfortunately, for the Jicarilla, many whites had already homesteaded the land and title disputes would not be resolved until the first decade of the 20th century. Additionally, the elevation of the land made agriculture nearly impossible and livestock raising tenuous at best because of the lack of winter pasturage at lower elevations.

Despite these hardships, the federal government did not act to relieve the living conditions of the Jicarilla. Funds that had been earmarked for livestock purchases often sat in accounts that were mismanaged or ignored by the Bureau of Indian Affairs. Unable to sustain themselves, the Jicarilla Apache population dropped by more than 20 percent from 1900 to 1920, from 815 to 588 members. Their deaths were largely attributed to disease, especially tuberculosis and malnutrition. By 1920, with the tribe on the brink of extinction, the federal government acted. It began to provide health care and distributed livestock to tribal members. This change in policy assisted the Jicarilla in reestablishing their tribe as a viable culture. By the following decade, their population increased to 647 members and the incidence of disease declined. The Indian Reorganization Act of 1934 allowed the tribe to officially form its own government and oversee the affairs of the tribe. The Jicarilla took advantage of this provision, and in 1937 established a formal Jicarilla tribal government to oversee the affairs of the tribe. The result was an improvement in the lives of the Jicarilla Apache and continued growth of the tribe.

The Western Apache engaged in the same raiding and retaliation warfare that their brethren in the east prosecuted during the Spanish and Mexican periods. However, the relative equality among foes would change following the Mexican War. Sporadic incidents of violence continued between white settlers and the Western Apache through the first decade of U.S. control, but accelerated wildly after Arizona became a territory in 1863 and gold was discovered in the San Francisco Mountains. The rush of gold seekers into their territory was followed by the U.S. military. In 1864, the Western Apache agreed to a treaty of peace with the army, but no reserves were established

for their exclusive use. As the white population increased and pressures on the limited resources of the land were exhausted, raiding and retaliation increased on both sides. The federal government designated three reservations for the Western Apache between 1871 and 1872: Fort Apache Reservation, Camp Verde Reservation, and the San Carlos Apache Reservation.

Despite the creation of the reserves, raiding continued, and the army launched a campaign to subdue the Western Apache. Faced with a seemingly inexhaustible foe with extensive resources at their command, the Western Apache withered against the onslaught and most were removed to the reservations. However, by 1874, the federal government decided to close Camp Verde, the northernmost of the reservations, and concentrate all the Apache in one central location—the San Carlos Reservation. The unfortunate outcome of this policy was to overtax the limited resources of the land and to mix divergent groups of Apache, including several bands of the Western Apache and the Chiricahua. Many of these tribes did not see eye to eye. The result was mass evacuations from the reservation and a sharp increase in hostility between settlers and the Apache. By 1884, the decision to close Camp Verde had been reversed and calm had been restored to the region in large part because of the aid offered by Western Apache Indians, who assisted in the defeat of truculent Chiricahua Indians such as Geronimo. Because of the aid provided by the Indian scouts, the Western Apache were able to remain principally on the lands they had traditionally claimed. The northern bands suffered the greatest displacement when they were relocated into central Arizona reservations of Fort Apache or San Carlos. The Western Apache continued their relationship with the army into the 20th century as guides and laborers. Eventually, livestock raising and lumber harvesting would serve as the economic mainstays of the tribe. Despite the relative wealth associated with these industries, they are not enough to sustain the growing needs of the Western Apache people and many have been forced to abandon the lands of their ancestors in order to find work off the reservation.

Today, the Apache Indians continue to be as fiercely independent as the bands that first encountered the Spanish colonists 400 years ago. While some social disintegration has occurred, especially among the Lipan, the Apache continue to support viable, cohesive cultures that represent a worldview that is not governed by the accumulation of possessions. Tribal unity and cultural preservation form the core beliefs of the tribal governments, beliefs that will undoubtedly serve the Apache people far into the future.

—Vanessa Ann Gunther

See also Santa Fe, New Mexico

Suggested Reading

Benedek, Emily. *The Wind Won't Know Me: A History of the Navajo-Hopi Land Dispute.* Norman: University of Oklahoma Press, 1992.

Griffen, William B. *Apaches at War and Peace: The Janos Presidio, 1750–1858.* Norman: University of Oklahoma Press, 1988.

Ogle, Ralph H. *Federal Control of the Western Apaches, 1848–1886.* Albuquerque: University of New Mexico Press, 1970.

Roberts, David. *Once They Moved Like the Wind: Cochise, Geronimo and the Apache Wars.* New York: Simon & Schuster, 1993.

Sonnichsen, C. L. *The Mescalero Apaches.* 2nd ed. Norman: University of Oklahoma Press, 1973.

Steele, Ian K. *Warpaths: Invasions of North America.* New York: Oxford University Press, 1994.

Sweeny, Edwin R. *Cochise: Chiricahua Apache Chief.* Norman: University of Oklahoma Press, 1995.

Worcester, Donald E. *The Apache: Eagles of the Southwest.* Norman: University of Oklahoma Press, 1979.

⌗ APACHE PASS TRAIL

See Euro-American Migration on the Overland Trails

⌗ ARAPAHO

The Arapaho originated in what is now the northeastern United States before immigrating onto the Great Plains in the 1600s and 1700s. Although pressure from English and French settlers forced them west, it was through trade with Europeans that many tribes were able to acquire firearms, and this combined with horses obtained directly or indirectly from the Spanish helped create the nomadic lifestyle of the plains. This also enabled newly arriving tribes to drive preexisting plains tribes such as the Shoshone farther toward the Rocky Mountains. After reaching the plains, the Arapaho divided into two main groups: the Northern Arapaho remaining near the North Platte River in Wyoming and the Southern Arapaho settling near the Arkansas River in Colorado.

In the middle of the 1800s, the Arapaho abandoned their homelands and traditional nomadic way of life for two reasons. The first was the near extinction of the buffalo. As Arapaho elder Dr. Pius Moss recounts,

Indians depended on the buffalo that roamed the vast North American plains area. That was his way of life . . . the buffalo. Complete dependency on this animal. Wherever the animal was, that's where the Arapaho was. If the animal moved, he moved. . . . Because of the buffalo's migration, the Arapaho had to be nomadic, in quest of the buffalo from time to time. Now, the Arapahos moved all over the plains area, eastern slope of the Rockies, into Canada, . . . east to the Mississippi River and south to the Mexican border, . . . wherever the grass allowed the buffalo to roam in. . . . Now, after the animal was annihilated—rubbed off by the buffalo hunters from the face of the plains area—the Arapahos and the Plains Indians were at a loss. Their area of living, . . . their way of life . . . was taken away. They had to go into another area to find a way of life that would take care of them and when that began, there were changes coming in quite regular.

Led by Chief Black Coal, the Northern Arapaho began moving through Wyoming, South Dakota, Nebraska, and Kansas partly in search of buffalo and partly to avoid being forced into the Oklahoma territory by the U.S. Army. After concluding that his people needed a home, Chief Black Coal decided to meet with the Shoshone Chief Washakie in Wyoming to see if the Arapaho could live there. The two chiefs were friends, but their tribes were anything but, according to Dr. Moss:

He [Chief Black Coal] left his gun, he left his knife, everything that concerned being on the warpath. . . . He went down to the camp clean. He walked down. He left his horse. When he got to the camp, very close no one noticed him. When he got within the bounds of the camp, that's when the young people noticed him . . . that he was not one of them. So right away they got around him and they wanted to kill him. But he kept making the sign that meant, "I want to see my friend the Chief." So one of the young people took note of that and summoned Chief Washakie. About that time, the [threat] to Chief Black Coal was just about to be exercised . . . to kill him. Chief Washakie, realizing this, told the young people, "Whoever touches this man will have to answer to me." So then, the young people, hearing that, dispersed. That's when the treaty began between these two friends . . . two Chiefs.

According to the agreement, the Shoshone would occupy the part of the reservation that was west of the spring, and the Arapaho would occupy the eastern portion. Members of either tribe were free to go into the other's territory. Thus, in 1876, the Northern Arapaho began living near Yellowstone National Park on the Wind River Reservation in Wyoming, where they remain today alongside the Shoshone.

The Sand Creek Massacre of 1864 was the other cause for Arapaho migration. The Arapaho, along with the Comanche, Kiowa, Cheyenne, and some Sioux had been making emigration difficult for pioneers over the route to Denver and further south along the Santa Fe Trail. Colonel J. M. Chivington led a state militia of Colorado Volunteers in a retaliatory strike that became a massacre at Sand Creek. The Arapaho left Colorado, because of their custom that "wherever death occurs, they do not go back." Again, in the words of Arapaho elder Dr. Moss,

Asfar as history tells us and what the Arapahos say, . . . the women, children old men and those men that were in camp were just about completely wiped out. The U.S. Army opening fire on a camp that had the American flag and flag of truce flying in camp. Now, just whatever happened, why it happened that way has not been actually or really determined. Because of that happening, the Arapahos did leave and never return . . . but that was their home country.

War resulted for the next few years until the Arapaho and the United States signed treaties in 1867 and 1869. One of these, the Medicine Lodge Treaty was signed near Fort Dodge, Kansas, in October of 1867 and included among the signers the Arapaho

Chief Little Raven. Attacks on pioneers stopped for a time, but intertribal warfare continued as the Arapaho and Cheyenne fought the Osage and Kaw tribes. Eventually, the Arapaho were forced onto the Indian Territory, where several other tribes had been removed. The Indian Territory later became the state of Oklahoma, where the Southern Arapaho now reside with the Cheyenne. A third Arapaho group, the Gros Ventre, calls Fort Belknap, Montana, home and shares it with the Assiniboine.

Life on the Wind River Reservation brought Christianity, farming, ranching, log cabins, mission schools, and private property to the Northern Arapaho in the late 1800s and early 1900s. The Bureau of Indian Affairs replaced the traditional leadership of chiefs with tribal councils. During World War II, many Arapaho served in the armed forces, and as a result of this integration, assimilation, including the increased use of English, intensified. The introduction and influence of television beginning in the 1950s was also significant. A natural reaction against these changes occurred in the 1960s and 1970s as the Arapaho created schools to teach traditional language and culture, and in 1999 the tribe started the Wind River Tribal College. The Arapaho have also established Tribal Resource Centers and Language and Cultural Commissions that seek to preserve and pass on Arapaho traditions. Despite these efforts, a loss of linguistic and cultural identity among the younger Arapaho remains a problem. A lack of elders who speak Arapaho as well as limited funds for teachers and programs are among the causes. Historic and cultural traditions such as storytelling are becoming extinct, and even those such as the Sun Dance that are still performed are done in English.

The tribal headquarters of the Northern Arapaho is in Fort Washakie on the Wind River Reservation in Wyoming. A council headed by Chairman Burton Hutchinson and Co-Chairman Carlton Underwood— and including Samuel J. Dresser, Theodore "Lionel" Bell, Allison Sage, Jr., and Dean Goggles—currently governs the tribe.

The Northern Arapaho tribe has recently been involved in numerous activities intended to not only preserve the past but also improve reservation life by adapting to modern times. The tribe has undertaken an

Arapaho-language revitalization program, which emphasizes immersion to help young tribal members learn the language of their ancestors. In addition, the Wind River Tribal College awarded bilingual certificates to 13 students in June of 2004. The tribe has also recently started an information technology department, and construction of a $7.2 million casino with 400 gaming machines began in June of 2004.

The Southern Arapaho in Oklahoma are governed by a constitution that they share with the Cheyenne. The constitution, which was ratified in 1975, states,

> We, the Cheyenne-Arapaho Tribes of Oklahoma, in order to promote more unified tribal economic progress, to better transact our tribal business and industrial affairs, to protect our religious rights, . . . to negotiate with the representatives of federal, state, and local governments in regard to all matters affecting the tribes now or in the future, and to further the general welfare of ourselves and our posterity, do hereby adopt the following constitution and by-laws pursuant to the Thomas-Rogers Oklahoma Indian Welfare Act of June 26, 1936, which shall replace as our governing document that constitution and by-laws ratified September 18, 1937, and all amendments thereto.

A tribal council governs the Southern Arapaho and Cheyenne and is made up of all tribal members who are 18 years of age or older. A Cheyenne-Arapaho business committee made up of eight members acts for the tribe and oversees expenditures. The proportion of Cheyenne-Arapaho Indian blood one possesses determines membership in the tribe. The usual requirement is that a person has at least one-fourth blood of the Cheyenne-Arapaho Tribes of Oklahoma.

The influence of western concepts such as individual rights and private property can be seen in the tribal constitution, which bears several similarities to the American Constitution. Article 3, Section 1 of the Constitution of the Cheyenne and Arapaho Tribes of Oklahoma states,

> No person shall be denied by the tribes . . . those rights . . . including freedom of speech, conscience, worship and assembly. . . . Individual rights in allotted and inherited lands shall not be disturbed by anything contained in this constitution and by-laws.

An election board sets elections for business committee members. Each committee member has a four-year term, but there is a term limit: no member may serve more than three terms consecutively. Tribal members who are 21 or older are eligible to serve on the committee.

In recent years, the Arapaho have had to revisit one of the worst events in their history. Colorado Senator Ben Nighthorse Campbell introduced legislation in 1998 to authorize the Sand Creek Massacre National Historic Site Study Act. A location study subsequently identified the exact location and size of a potential historic site using "oral history, archived sources and other historical documentation, archeology and remote imagery, geomorphology, aerial photography, and traditional tribal methods." This involved a collaboration of the National Park Service, the Colorado Historical Society, property owners, volunteers, the Cheyenne and Arapaho Tribes in Oklahoma, the Northern Cheyenne Tribe in Montana, and the Northern Arapaho Tribe in Wyoming.

After two years of site study, Congress issued the Sand Creek Massacre National Historic Site Act in 2000. According to the Sand Creek Massacre National Historic Site Web site, the law authorizes the National Park Service to buy as much property as possible

> to adequately protect, interpret, memorialize, and commemorate the site, . . . [and it] confirms the site's national significance, and provides an opportunity for tribes, the State of Colorado, and other entities to be involved in its support and development . . . [as well as] provides enhanced cultural understanding and defines the conditions of descendant and tribal access for traditional, cultural, or historical observance.

The new historic site also includes several specific locations related to the Sand Creek Massacre. The site's Web page includes the following catalog:

> the location of the Cheyenne village and several Arapaho lodges; the point(s) from which the Colorado Regiments first spotted the encampment; the location of Indian pony herds; the area of flight, bordering Sand Creek, that the Indians took during and after the initial attack; the general path of battalion advancements, individual skirmishing and other collateral action; the military bivouac area for the nights of

November 29 and 30; spots in the creek and along it's [*sic*] banks where the Cheyenne dug sandpits/survival pits, and the points from which battery salvoes were launched into the camp and later into the sandpits.

Another recent issue facing the Arapaho is Indian gaming in the form of casinos on reservation land. While the Arapaho have had casinos for years on the reservation that they share with the Cheyenne in Oklahoma, the effort to create a reservation and build casinos on ancestral Arapaho land in Colorado has brought promise and controversy. Council Tree Communications, an investment group, calls the proposal the "Cheyenne-Arapaho Homecoming Project." The project would include purchasing land near Denver and then having it declared a reservation, which would then be donated to the tribes along with any casino profits. In this way, the Cheyenne and Arapaho would be compensated for the Sand Creek Massacre of 1864. The group says the $100 million casino would result in various benefits for the tribes, including money ($2 million of which would go to help establish the Sand Creek Memorial at the National Park Site in the southeastern part of the state), jobs, and a Plains Indian Cultural & Media Center.

As in other states with Indian casinos, Colorado could potentially benefit from gaming. Council Tree Communications estimates billions could flow into the state as well as 3,000-plus jobs and more than 50,000 visitors. Polling sponsored by Council Tree shows broad bipartisan support among Colorado voters for both the reservation and the casino. However, support for the proposal is not unanimous. Besides Coloradoans in rural areas who are opposed to the development and traffic that would inevitably come as a result of the casino, some members of the Cheyenne and Arapaho are opposed despite the financial benefits. In addition to Colorado being the homeland of the Cheyenne and Arapaho, tribe members visit the Sand Creek site to pray. Colorado Governor Bill Owens and Senator Campbell also oppose the casino, but for different reasons. Owens does not want gaming to be expanded in the state because it takes money from families. The governor has said that he will not give his permission, as federal law requires, to create the reservation and casino. Campbell considers it sacrilege to include the

Sand Creek Memorial in the project, but will not support the casino even if it is not connected to the historic site for which he has been working. However, the chairman of the Cheyenne-Arapaho business committee, James Pedro, supports the project in part because it will clear up confusion about conflicting ownership claims in the 27 million acres of the proposed site. In addition, the Cheyenne-Arapaho Tribal Council believes the project will lead to a return to ancestral lands and numerous economic opportunities.

In June of 2004, the representative of Colorado's Fourth Congressional District, Congresswoman Marilyn Musgrave, issued a press release in which she urged Congress to not approve the new reservation. Citing past voter and legislative action, Musgrave asked Speaker of the House Dennis Hastert to respect the will of the people of Colorado. The federal Indian Gaming Regulatory Act requires approval by either the governor of a state, the secretary of the Department of the Interior, or Congress. Nevertheless, Musgrave argued that the federal law should not take precedence over state and local will. She added that the *Oklahoman* newspaper had reported that the Cheyenne-Arapaho Tribes of Oklahoma were being investigated for illegal use of casino profits by the federal government and expressed concern at the prospect of expanding their gaming activities into Colorado.

Today, the Arapaho people face the uphill challenge of preserving their history, language, and culture. They are divided across several states; live among an overwhelming majority in America that is unaware and in many cases uninterested in its own past, let alone anyone else's; and struggle with how to adapt a traditional way of life to a seemingly incompatible modern one. Inevitably, some of the old ways have had to be abandoned, but through education and opportunity, the past can be remembered while providing for the future.

—Daniel S. Stackhouse, Jr.

See also GROS VENTRE

Suggested Reading

"Arapaho." *Columbia Encyclopedia.* 6th ed. New York: Columbia University Press, 2004.
"Cheyenne and Arapaho Tribes of Oklahoma Constitution and By-Laws." Available from http://thorpe.ou.edu/constitution/Chyn_aph.html

Frazier, Deborah. "Reservation, Casino in Works Near DIA." *Rocky Mountain News,* December 31, 2003. Available from http://www.rockymountainnews.com

"Montana-Wyoming Tribal Leaders Council." Available from http://tlc.wtp.net

Moss, Pius. "The Story of the Origin of the Arapaho People." A transcript of stories told by Dr. Pius Moss, as Elder of the Arapaho Tribe on the Wind River Reservation. *The Wyoming Companion.* Laramie, WY: High Country, 1994–2004. Available from http://www.wyomingcompanion.com/wcwrr.html

Musgrave, Marilyn. "Musgrave Urges Congress to Honor Colo Voters on Gaming." Press release, June 18, 2004. Available from http://wwwc.house.gov

National Park Service. "Sand Creek Massacre National Historic Site." Available from http://www.nps.gov/sand/sitestudy.htm

Northern Arapaho Tribal Web Site. Available from http://www.northernarapaho.com

Taylor, Colin F. *The American Indian.* London: Salamander Books, 2004.

"Tribe Will Deal for Casino." *Fort Collins Coloradoan* Online, January 16, 2004. Available from http://www.coloradoan.com

"Tribe's Casino Delayed, but Still on Track." *Casper Star Tribune,* May 20, 2004. Available from http://www.casperstartribune.net

University of Colorado at Boulder. "The Arapaho Project." Boulder: Colorado University Regents, 2000. Available from http://www.colorado.edu/csilw/arapahoproject/index.html

⊞ ARIZONA COPPER DISCOVERIES

Copper discoveries never created a rush, as did gold or silver strikes. World suppliers of this utilitarian metal concentrated in Cornwall, England, and Andalusia, Spain, but these places gave way to Michigan, Montana, and Arizona. Copper, employed in kitchenware and roofing materials, gained value with the advent of electricity. Antonio Espejo noted copper's presence near Jerome in 1582. Areas richest in copper concentrations were Mexican until after the Gadsden Purchase of 1854. Lack of cheap rail transportation for importing needed supplies and exporting metal made copper mining unprofitable until the 1870s. Apache presence compounded the problems of mining southern Arizona. Ultimately, the presence of copper brought a steady flow of different peoples into this arid region.

An early venture into copper extraction occurred during 1854 in Ajo, an area of southern Arizona that Mexico disputed as possessing. Surface copper removed and carted by mule from Ajo across to San Diego was shipped to Swansea, Wales, for smelting. The copper then sold at $360 a ton. Crude extraction methods left most subterranean copper behind, but mining resumed in the early 20th century. Ajo had high numbers of Mexican laborers due to its proximity to the border. Ajo busted and now is a small town of 1,700 people with over half its population being white, a third Hispanic, and about 10 percent Indian.

The first successful region to extract copper was Clifton-Morenci. In July of 1870, Jim and Bob Metcalf discovered two major deposits at Clifton and Morenci. Apache hostility prevented the Metcalfs from laying claim to these deposits until 1872. Fear of Apache raids kept labor away. This prompted the Arizona Copper Company at Clifton to import both Chinese and Mexican labor. In the 1870s, Clifton Camp was only about 200 workers strong, mostly Mexican. Transportation problems lost the company money, but the company managed to stay afloat by employing a store system to sell supplies to the miners. The Arizona Company sold out to Scottish investors. They added transportation rails to this mining region. Fuel and market accessibility drove down production and transportation costs. By 1883, Clifton had a significantly larger labor force, including 400 Chinese. Mexicans and Anglo workers drove out the Chinese that year, making it a "white man's camp."

The Detroit Copper Company claimed Morenci. Morenci mirrored adjacent Clifton in its working force and problems. In 1882, this site suffered an Apache raid, forcing smelters near the San Francisco River to be relocated to Morenci. Though not as large as the Clifton site, these sites, combined, by 1911 had 3,500 miners, the second highest region in output, the lowest accident rate, and a workforce that was half Mexican.

Copper discoveries continued through the 1870s, as seen in Globe and Jerome. Globe, known for its silver "rush" in the 1870s, ignored copper until the Old Dominion Copper Mining Company operated in 1881. The Globe-Miami region by the 20th century hardly had any Mexican labor, but the Globe region had received immigrants from mining communities since its inception. People from regions with mining history, such as Germany, Scotland, Ireland, Spain, and England, traveled to Michigan, Montana, and Arizona as their highly specialized mining skills were needed. Mining techniques simplified by machines allowed an influx of semiskilled labor in the form of Czechs, Serbs, Italians, Montenegrins, and Bohemians. Balkan encroachment by Austria forced some Slavic migration. Mining towns were melting pots for Europeans, though often camps were segregated.

Morris Andrew Ruffner first found copper deposits in Jerome in 1878. James S. Douglas, for whom the city of Douglas, Arizona, is named, told Ruffner the two rich sites at Jerome were worthless. A distance of 180 miles separated the great ore bodies and, without transportation, extraction seemed costly. In 1884, it had only 75 employees, some of whom were imported Chinese laborers. The coupling of low copper prices and high transportation costs shut this site down from 1885 to 1887. In 1890, the population grew to 250 and railroads brought in families, almost quadrupling the population to 800 by 1900. James Douglas proved his father wrong at Jerome with brief success: In 1917, a great deposit was found, which sprouted the town to 7,000 people, but by 1920 it dwindled to 4,000 miners. Jerome now contains roughly 330 people, 87 percent of whom are white.

Bisbee and Douglas, both just north of the Mexican border, developed a powerful copper extracting force. In 1877, Hugh Jones located the Copper Queen Mine but abandoned it after not finding silver. Edward Reilly wanted to investigate the Copper Queen without capital; he turned to Louis Zeckendorf and Albert Steinfeld, Tucson merchants. Reilly traveled to San Francisco to enlist metallurgists and mine developers. The first advanced smelters were standard in the Bisbee regions. The labor pool in Bisbee was largely Mexican, but also contained English, Irish, Finnish, Austrian, and Serbian workers, with Italians, Germans Swedes, and Swiss coming later.

In the fall of 1880, James Douglas urged the Copper Queen owners to buy the adjacent Atlanta mine claim; they did not listen, though the Phelps Dodge Company did. Unsuccessful at first, after investing $80,000 in exploration, the company eventually found rich ore at 210 feet. The new finds assured mine success, but to avoid litigation with the Copper Queen property, the Phelps Dodge Company bought the Copper Queen. Douglas turned into a smelting district, and transportation facilitated copper processing, which made this region dominant into the latter part of the 20th century.

Arizona produced half of the U.S. total of copper by 1920, with about a third of that produced by the old finds. All newer finds concentrated in these same regions. The 20th century saw the Mexican revolution, which drove labor into Arizona. Legislation to limit Mexican immigration arose during the early part of the 20th century, but copper companies fought this. In 1920, quota restrictions limiting Mexican workers to 20 percent of the workforce would have destroyed copper operations in the state where more than 60 percent of smeltermen were of Mexican origin. Mining persists in Arizona, though it is very limited. Most mining towns are virtual ghost towns, though some, such as Bisbee and Jerome, are now tourist attractions. Mining helped the population of Arizona expand from 88,000 people to more than 100,000 American-born residents by 1900. Now Arizona has a population of 5 million, mostly white but with Hispanic origin making up a quarter of the population.

—Eduardo Barrios

See also BISBEE AND DOUGLAS, ARIZONA

Suggested Reading

Clements, Eric, L. *After the Boom in Tombstone and Jerome, Arizona.* Reno: University of Nevada Press, 2003.

Hyde, Charles. *Copper for America: The United States Copper Industry From Colonial Times to the 1990s.* Tucson: University of Arizona Press, 1998.

Nugent, Walter. *Into the West: The Story of Its People.* New York: Knopf, 1999.

Schwantes, Carlos. *Bisbee: Urban Outpost on the Frontier.* Tucson: University of Arizona Press, 1992.

Sheridan, Thomas. *Arizona: A History.* Tucson: University of Arizona Press, 1996.

Trimble, Marshall. *Roadside History of Arizona.* Missoula, MT: Mountain Press, 1986.

⊞ ASIAN IMMIGRATION LAW

The advent of immigration from China and other parts of Asia that began in 1849 with the California gold rush resulted in increased hostility by native-born Americans and immigrants from different cultural backgrounds. The hostility translated into significant legal efforts to curb or eliminate Asian immigration. In response to these legal attacks, Asians fought back in federal court. The resulting body of laws and legal decisions influenced more than just immigration law in the United States; many areas of American law have felt the touch of civil rights cases brought by Asian victims of abuse.

During the 1870s, a number of states began to adopt their own laws regulating immigration. The enactments came in response to public hostility to immigration brought on by economic troubles within the United States. However, in *Henderson v. Mayor of City of New York,* the Supreme Court of the United States decided that only Congress could regulate immigration. The decision struck down immigration laws in California, Louisiana, and New York. The Supreme Court had ruled in a similar manner in 1849 with the *Passenger Cases* that the federal government of the United States had sole authority to regulate immigration.

California, in particular, generated the greatest hostility toward Chinese immigration and, by no coincidence, had the greatest number of Chinese immigrants living within it. By 1879, the majority of Californians decided to rewrite the state's constitution in order to correct the "social problems" within the state, including the "Chinese Problem." In California, antipathy toward Asians exceeded that for Mexicans, another source of non-European labor, in large part because Mexicans were not perceived as a threat to the status quo. An inextricable link existed between the issue of Chinese immigrants and the primary source of "pull" for Chinese labor, the railroads. The two issues in combination bore the greatest responsibility for social violence at the time. Both of these issues, railroads and Chinese immigration, spurred specific measures within the new constitution. The economic dominance and the political favor shown to the railroads in the form of land grants along right of ways would lead to numerous conflicts between the railroads and settlers competing for the same lands, and a special provision in the new constitution creating a railroad commission. The conflict between the domineering railroads and

the settlers manifested itself most violently in the bloody Mussel Slough gunfight of May 11, 1880.

The friction over the issue of the Chinese residents of California had existed since the 1849 gold rush. The perpetration of several depredations against the Chinese occurred with the enactment of discriminatory taxes, codes, and regulations that were directed specifically at the Chinese. The enactment of racist legislation reached an acme of justification with the adoption of Section XIX of the California Constitution of 1879, which specifically authorized discriminatory legislation against Chinese. This section admonished the state government to deter the immigration of Chinese, prohibited the employment of Chinese by corporations or public entities, and empowered local authorities to enact ordinances to remove Chinese from within city limits.

Initial restrictions on immigration were not aimed specifically at Chinese but at people generally found to be socially undesirable. In 1882, restrictions became law and therefore prohibited the immigration of "idiots," lunatics, criminals, and public charges and authorized a $0.50 head tax. An 1891 amendment expanded the list of undesirables to include anarchists and polygamists.

The Chinese Exclusion Act of 1882 came to Congress from California. John F. Miller, senator from California, referred to Chinese immigration as the "Chinese evil" and "Chinese invasion." Senator Miller, in describing the sentiment in California supporting the exclusion of Chinese, cited a vote taken in the state overwhelmingly supporting exclusion and stated that Californians were "the people of all others in the United States who know most of the Chinese evil." During the debate, Senator George F. Hoar of Massachusetts opposed Chinese exclusion and denied any ill effects of Chinese immigration. Senator Hoar used census figures to show negligible numbers of Chinese living in most of the United States, such as the five recorded in Massachusetts. On the other hand, Senator Hoar's figures also indicated nearly 80,000 Chinese in California and similarly disproportionately high numbers in other western states.

The Chinese community, in response to the hostility and legal attack, fought back in the courts. The first victory for the Chinese in court came with an

1862 case regarding taxes. A special police tax was imposed on the Chinese, and the ensuing court case decided in California Supreme Court, *Lin Sing v. Washburn,* overturned the tax. The decision relied heavily on *Brown v. Maryland* for precedent and on the commerce clause and federal jurisdiction over commerce to void the tax.

The railroads, also under attack by the 1879 California constitution, defended themselves by legal action at the same time as the Chinese. The case of *Southern Pacific Railroad Co. v. Orton,* pending at the time of the gunfight at Mussel Slough, affected both the railroads directly and the Chinese indirectly. The significance to the Chinese arose from the acceptance and application of substantive due process in the decision. Substantive due process, derived from the Fourteenth Amendment's due process clause, was first argued in the dissent of Justices Stephen J. Field and Joseph P. Bradley in *The Slaughterhouse Cases* in 1873. The constitutional theory of substantive due process held that issues of personal liberty were subject to judicial review. In American jurisprudence, personal liberty and personal property are closely related; substantive due process implied judicial review of regulations related to personal property and hence of economic regulations. The majority opinion for *Munn v. Illinois,* written by Chief Justice Morrison R. Waite, also conceded that regulatory statutes might impinge on due process and thereby implied recognition of substantive due process.

Further reinforcement of Orton came with the decisions in *Southern Pacific Railroad Co. v. Doyle, Southern Pacific Railroad Co. v. Phillips,* and *Southern Pacific Railroad v. Cox.* All of these cases originated from the Ninth Circuit Court of Appeals, and demonstrated a pattern and disposition by the Ninth Circuit Court of exercising judicial review in accordance with the principle of substantive due process. These cases also constituted a body of jurisprudence that could be used later to support the application of substantive due process.

The first significant application of the Equal Protection Clause and substantive due process occurred in a Chinese civil rights case, *Ho Ah Kow v. Nunan,* also known as the "Queue Case." The decision came shortly after the adoption of the California Constitution of 1879. San Francisco passed an ordinance allowing for, as a

form of punishment, the cutting off of the queue of hair worn by Chinese, another manifestation of hostility toward Chinese. The ordinance was overturned pursuant to the equal protection clause of the Fourteenth Amendment. The court recognized that the ordinance was directed solely at the Chinese and was therefore discriminatory. The court interpreted the language of the equal protection clause to be broad in meaning, the use of "person" in the clause to include Chinese.

The next significant decision would come the following year, 1880. This case directly attacked Section XIX of the California Constitution of 1879 and further defined the meaning of the equal protection clause of the Fourteenth Amendment. *In re Tiburcio Parrot,* also referred to as "the Parrot Case," overturned the prohibition on the employment of Chinese included in Section XIX of the California constitution. In addition to the reference to the equal protection clause, the Parrot Case decision by Justice Lorenzo Sawyer included the determination of the right of a person to contract to work. This case began the process of establishing the connection between substantive due process, contract law in relation to labor, and the status of Chinese immigrants.

The process continued with the 1882 case *In re Quong Woo* and the 1886 case *In re Wo Lee.* Both cases derived from San Francisco ordinances regarding the operation of laundries. *In re Quong Woo* determined that Chinese had freedom to apply their labor where they wished. *In re Wo Lee* found that the ordinance in question intended to drive the Chinese laundries out of business and therefore violated the equal protection clause of the Fourteenth Amendment and, of equal importance, applied the term "person" not only to Chinese but also to a business entity. This allowed the application of civil liberty protection to business entities. Yet another San Francisco laundry case, *Yick Wo v. Hopkins,* decided by the U.S. Supreme Court, firmly established the broad definition of the equal protection clause and the equally broad use of substantive due process. In its decision, the Supreme Court relied on the precedent set in the earlier decisions relating to the Chinese in California.

Finally, the Supreme Court ended the depredations of Section XIX of the California Constitution of 1879 with its *In re Lee Sing* ruling. In yet another attack on its Chinese population, San Francisco attempted to expel all Chinese from its city limits. The Court found Section XIX unconstitutional and explicitly ruled that corporations held the same rights under the Fourteenth Amendment as individuals.

In 1905, substantive due process established by these precedents, the relationship of substantive due process to contract law and labor law, and subsequent reinforcement by additional railroad cases provided the legal justification in the majority decision by the U.S. Supreme Court in *Lochner v. New York* to restrict the ability of government to regulate a particular form of commerce in regards to labor, a cornerstone of laissez-faire constitutionalism. The Court reserved the ultimate determination of public need and the right to limit police authority as it related to commerce to the judiciary.

All of the litigation success by Chinese utilizing the Fourteenth Amendment and substantive due process provided a useful weapon in legally opposing the Chinese Exclusion Act. Many Chinese seeking admittance to the United States appealed their cases to the federal courts, almost all of the cases occurring within the Ninth Circuit Court. Of those Chinese who attempted to land and appealed to the courts, 85 percent succeeded in gaining admission during the 1880s and 1890s. Their success owed much to the courts allowing exceptions not provided for in the law, such as alternative proofs of prior residence or membership in other classes of exempted Chinese. These exceptions opened the door to fraud, only partially constrained by subsequent amendments.

In addition, the federal courts offered supplicants advantages not available during administrative exclusion proceedings. The first and foremost of these consisted of the availability and access to lawyers. Chinese contesting their cases could also call witnesses, the federal courts being far more tolerant and less critical of witnesses than the administrators handling exclusion proceedings. Finally, the judges and the lawyers handling the Chinese cases shared a commonality of procedural abilities and rules. Consequently, the formal nature of federal court resulted in the burden on the government in federal court greatly exceeding the burden necessary in an administrative hearing.

The litigation in the Chinese cases of the 19th century provided a foundation for immigration cases in subsequent decades and up to the present. Strategy consisted of forcing the case into federal court. After going to court, government attorneys might choose to drop the case if they found they lacked resources or failed to meet the higher standard of judicial scrutiny in district court than that which exists in administrative proceedings.

A simple fraud took advantage of the exempted classes contained within the Chinese Exclusion Act, as noted above. A far more elaborate scheme developed later, referred to as the "Paper Sons" fraud. Children of legal resident Chinese could still immigrate to the United States. This scheme utilized altered documents to establish proof of birth with parentage connected to a legal Chinese resident of the United States. The scheme developed after the 1906 San Francisco earthquake and fire, which consumed the county birth records to that date.

Beginning in the 1890s and gaining momentum in the first decade of the 20th century, the government of the United States began to undermine and resist the efforts of Chinese to use substantive due process to force their cases into federal court. The success of the Chinese in court, as described above, directly contributed to the greater emphasis of the authority of the Bureau of Immigration. *In re Chae Chan Ping* helped establish that the United States had inherent sovereign powers to regulate immigration. In 1894, a rider to an appropriations bill established that exclusion cases did not require review in federal court. The Supreme Court affirmed the authority of the Bureau of Immigration in the case of Nishimura Ekiu, a Japanese facing expulsion for being a public charge. The Court deferred jurisdiction to the administrative procedure. By doing so, the Supreme Court essentially stated that substantive due process did not apply to immigration matters. The Supreme Court also rejected a direct attack on the constitutionality of the Chinese Exclusion Act. Interestingly, Justice Stephen J. Field wrote the majority opinion, the same justice who had championed substantive due process that had worked so well in favor of the Chinese community.

By 1924, other sources of immigration, primarily people from eastern and southern Europe, joined the Chinese in being severely restricted. In fact, the 1924 Immigration Act served to restrict all immigration to the United States. The act provided the basic structure for all immigration, including Chinese, until 1965. The 1924 act established quotas with a heavy bias favoring immigration from northern European nations. The 1965 Immigration Act shifted the emphasis of immigration to the United States from adherence to the quotas to "family unity." This policy granted priority status to applications for immigration to relatives of American citizens or legal resident aliens.

The final legal act that shifted Chinese immigration into mainstream immigration came in 1943 when Congress repealed the Chinese Exclusion Act. This change in the law came about in the midst of World War II. The United States found itself discriminating against an allied nation, China, in favor of immigrants from an enemy nation, Germany. Consequently, the United States repealed the law.

Likewise, the prohibition of Chinese naturalization was repealed in 1952. Some of the impetus to removing the bar to Chinese naturalization came from the recent communist takeover of China in 1947. Republicans, wishing to show support for Chinese nationalists and eliminate communist propaganda regarding American racism and hypocrisy, supported the repeal of the restriction. Democrats, beginning to show a nascent interest in civil rights and antidiscrimination legislation, also supported the repeal. The subsequent consensus resulted in removing the last exceptional legal differences between Chinese immigration and immigration from other parts of the world.

The repeal of the naturalization restrictions for Chinese in 1952 signaled the triumph of a legal struggle that began 80 years earlier as Chinese immigrants sought refuge from discrimination in American courts of law. Their efforts in protecting their own civil rights provided the legal foundation for the civil rights law that would follow in the 20th century. Not only did the Chinese reap the benefits of their struggle, but also American society has greatly benefited in the improvement in civil rights that owes so much to these earlier victims of discrimination.

—*Lonnie Wilson*

See also CHINESE EXCLUSION ACT, CHINESE IMMIGRATION, IMMIGRATION ACT OF 1965, IMMIGRATION AND NATURALIZATION SERVICE (INS), IMMIGRATION REFORM AND CONTROL ACT OF 1986

Suggested Reading

Bodnar, John. *The Transplanted: A History of Immigrants in Urban America.* Bloomington: Indiana University Press, 1985.

Daniels, Roger. *Not Like Us: Immigrants and Minorities in America, 1890–1924.* Chicago: Ivan R. Dee, 1997.

Gyory, Andrew. *Closing the Gate: Race, Politics, and the Chinese Exclusion Act.* Chapel Hill: University of North Carolina Press, 1998.

Handlin, Oscar. *The Uprooted: The Epic Story of the Great Migration That Made the American People.* 2nd ed. Boston: Little, Brown, 1979.

Hays, Samuel P. *The Response to Industrialism, 1885–1914.* Chicago: University of Chicago Press, 1957.

Lee, Erika. *At America's Gates: Chinese Immigration During the Exclusion Era, 1882–1943.* Chapel Hill: University of North Carolina Press, 2003.

Salyer, Lucy E. *Laws Harsh as Tigers: Chinese Immigrants and the Shaping of Modern Immigration Law.* Chapel Hill: University of North Carolina Press, 1995.

Yans-McLaughlin, Virginia, ed. *Immigration Reconsidered: History, Sociology, and Politics.* New York: Oxford University Press, 1990.

ⵌ ASSINIBOINE

Like many Native peoples, the Assiniboine or Nakota population straddles both sides of the international border between the United States and Canada, making a discussion of their history only in the American West problematic. To truly appreciate the Assiniboine's westward migration, it is essential to consider their presence in both nations, as international borders were a European concept. Attempts to stem the fluidity of movement across this arbitrary line had little to do with Assiniboine history until the establishment of the reservations and reserves in the latter 19th century.

Many anthropologists conjecture that during the 16th century the Assiniboine split from the Yanktonai Sioux and became the northern vanguard of the large Siouan westward migration out of what is now the American Midwest. This division forced the Assiniboine to move in a northwesterly direction and in the process facilitated their long-term alliance with the Cree. The position of their traditional territory forced them into confrontations with numerous tribes, especially the Blackfoot, Ojibwe, and Dakota, and coupled with smallpox outbreaks in 1737, 1780–1781, and 1837–1838 caused a dramatic reduction in their numbers forcing their population to diffuse over a large geographic area. Despite all of these difficulties, Assiniboine communities continued to support one another and maintained their cultural integrity. Over time, 31 bands developed, which today live in the American state of Montana on federally recognized reservations at Fort Belknap and Fort Peck. In Canada, Assiniboine live on various reserves in the provinces Saskatchewan and Alberta. More recent migrations have led many Assiniboine to settle in communities away from reservations and reserves.

The Assiniboine's ongoing movement across the prairie created a cultural dynamic emphasizing mobility. The root of most Native cultures is the creation story, which details not only a physical beginning, but also the outline for a total worldview. The Assiniboine's creation story emphasizes movement. After Ik-tomi, a legendary character, created the universe, animals, and seven men and seven women, he determined that this land was not appropriate for them. Ordering various animals, such as fowls, muskrats, mink, beaver, and the fisher, to bring mud from the bottom of a lake, he finally created a new land for the Assiniboine. Ik-tomi ordered the seven human couples to migrate to this new land and multiply. The Assiniboine creation story parallels the Earthdiver tradition of other Native peoples, illustrating the interconnectedness of those who settled on the plains. Unique to the Assiniboine was an emphasis on the number seven and the diversity of wildlife used in the final creation of their homeland.

The human movement prevalent in the creation story carries through to Assiniboine spiritual practices, in which entire bands would come together from long distances to participate in ceremonies, dances, and social gatherings. Especially important events, such as the longstanding Medicine Lodge Dance (Sun Dance), at times brought hundreds to thousands of participants and spectators together. Through fasting and piercing their breasts, male participants in the Medicine Lodge Dance induced visions in which they would travel in a hypnotic state and see future war glory or other positive life outcomes. When the ceremonies concluded, the Assiniboine bands would pack up their lodges and return home. An example of a dance that came into vogue after European contact was the Grass Dance, a pan-Indian ceremony originating with the Lakota that taught traditional values and discipline. The Grass Dance illustrates the long-term contact through movement among diverse Native peoples of the Great Plains. The continuation of the Grass Dance among the Assiniboine to the present illustrates the strength of traditional culture despite living in disparate locations in two countries, while modifications of the costume demonstrate the continued interaction between Native peoples in the region.

The Assiniboine saw no difference between the spiritual and material worlds, which meant that daily movements for game or other commodities took on extreme importance and led to ritualization. Setting up and taking down camp provides one example into this phenomenon, where a precise ritual developed in order to maximize efficiency in movement. Once an Assiniboine band had made the decision to move its camp, women quickly prepared travois that were pulled by two dogs prior to the arrival of the horse. By necessity, Assiniboine teepee construction enabled a speedy dismantlement and a quick setup. Elders and children unable to walk rested on a travois until the day's journey ended. The inability of dogs to pull heavy loads with any speed hampered the Assiniboine economically and militarily, especially after other Native peoples on the northern plains began acquiring horses in the early 18th century.

The arrival of the horse enhanced the Assiniboine's ability to hunt game and rapidly move their camps. The first notation of the Assiniboine with horses occurred in 1754, when fur trader Anthony Hendry found a western band with horses. These horses had probably been stolen from the Blackfoot and enabled this particular band to compete economically and militarily with their neighbors in the area. The method of loading a horse travois followed the same pattern as when dogs had been used, but with the ability to ride a horse a band could move up to four times faster. Those Assiniboine with horses began hunting buffalo with bows, arrows, and rifles. Some Assiniboine that lacked horses continued to trap buffalo or drive them off buffalo jumps, while the northernmost bands lived beyond the bison's range. Despite the arrival of horses in the region, the Assiniboine, geographically distant from centers of trade, often lacked the large horse herds found among the Crow, Lakota, and Cheyenne.

While the stereotype of Native Americans on the Great Plains after 1800 was that they were always on horseback, at times the terrain necessitated other means of transportation. When the Assiniboine traveled on rivers or streams, they used a bull boat constructed in a semicircular shape with a tree branch frame and lined with a buffalo hide. An individual could sit comfortably in the boat with a few necessities and watch the terrain unveil itself as it floated down the waterway. Much like drift boats seen on streams across the American West today, bull boats proved incredibly buoyant and, when constructed properly, were unlikely to capsize. When moving across perilous terrain, the Assiniboine proved highly adaptable at maximizing their chances of reaching their destination by using the material in their environment efficiently.

Even prior to the arrival of the horse, the Assiniboine's migration had led them over a great distance, and by the 17th century they had broken with the Yanktonai living in close proximity with the Cree in what would become the prairie provinces of Canada. Evidence of the early commencement of this split comes from the Jesuits, who considered the Assiniboine a distinct tribe by 1640. The Assiniboine quickly adapted to this new home territory by creating an alliance with the western Cree, who arrived shortly after them. This alliance began after a brief period of hostilities. Alexander McKenzie and other early traders during the 18th and 19th centuries believed the Cree migrated with the Assiniboine due to their close relationship. However, the oral tradition and recent archaeology disprove this assessment. The strength of this bond between these two Native peoples can be seen by the long duration of their alliance and the propensity for intermarriage that further cemented this friendship. Also, the farther north an Assiniboine band migrated, the closer their culture appeared to the Cree, while those whose migration stopped to the south took on cultural patterns closer to Plains Indians. Wherever the Assiniboine settled, their alliance with the Cree proved propitious, as nascent capitalism, through fur trading, entered their home territories during the 17th century. Working in conjunction with the Cree, the Assiniboine maximized their yields and created a niche in this ultracompetitive environment.

The fur trade revolutionized Native societies by introducing European tools, along with firearms and alcohol, which would have both negative and positive consequences. When permanent trading commenced at Hudson Bay through the Hudson Bay Company in 1682, the Assiniboine entered into relationships with fur traders immediately and entered the English sphere of influence. Fur traders and Jesuit missionaries began noting that their home territory centered in an area from Lake Winnipeg toward Saskatchewan and many had already participated in the fur trade prior to the establishment of permanent forts. The probability exists that the Assiniboine cut their teeth in the fur trade by traveling east to trade with individual French trappers on the northern bank of Lake Superior. The important Jesuit missionary Father Allouez recognized the imprint of the fur trade on the Assiniboine in 1656 by noting they had already been "discovered" by the French. Among the tribes that eventually resided in Montana, the Assiniboine had the longest relationship with Europeans because of their northerly migration. However, members of the large fur trading La Verendrye family commented in the 1740s that eastern Assiniboine bands who lived near woodlands knew how to trap, while their plains brethren had to be taught. The La Verendryes' statement illustrates that most Assiniboine participated in the fur trade to some degree during the 18th century. The wide geographic distribution of the Assiniboine explains different cultural and economic traits, accounting for seasonal wild rice cultivation among the eastern most bands and buffalo hunting among the western bands.

Once ensconced in the fur trade, mobility during trapping and visiting forts became exceedingly important to the economic well-being of the Assiniboine. The initial use of dog travois proved slow, placing Assiniboine trappers at risk as they moved to the north to trade with the Hudson Bay Company. After an initial period of hegemony against their Blackfoot and Ojibwe rivals, the Cree and Assiniboine began to face grave dangers as these two groups began to assert their own dominance. Attacks by Blackfoot or Ojibwe could prove cataclysmic because the loss of valuable furs, as well as young men in the prime of life, could prove devastating economically. Another threat came from the Dakota to the south, who in alliance with the French chased a large number of English-allied Assiniboine in 1729 from southern Manitoba possibly as far north as the Churchill River. Southern bands that traveled farthest to trading posts faced the gravest threat due to the long distances traveled. Southern and western Assiniboine bands that acquired horses first could move to their destinations rapidly, forestalling many attacks that may have occurred in the past.

Goods acquired through trade to the north with the French and English facilitated annual movements to the south to trade with the Mandan each summer during the late 17th century and into the 18th. The Assiniboine received corn and other vegetables, while the Mandan received guns, axes, and tobacco. Southern trade with the Mandan corresponded with hunting and other activities that necessitated summer movement. The fur trade created wide-ranging movements by the Assiniboine from Hudson Bay in northern Canada to the Mandan Villages in North Dakota.

The 19th century introduced new power relations in the region as the United States emerged as the dominant power on the Great Plains. The Lewis and Clark expedition of 1804–1806 soon ushered in American fur traders, including individual trappers such as John Coulter. Small enterprises controlled by the likes of Manuel Lisa also existed during the early 19th century. These early forays into the fur trade lured some Assiniboine south, but John Jacob Astor and the American Fur Company consolidated American domination of the fur and hide trade by 1830. The construction of Fort Union at the confluence of the Yellowstone and Missouri Rivers in 1829 enabled numerous Native peoples from around the Great Plains to trade at one central location. Until its closure in 1861, Assiniboine regularly traded and visited other Native people at Fort Union. As a result of American economic dominance in the region, many Assiniboine joined southern bands living along the Missouri, swelling their American population. This phase of Assiniboine migration dramatically altered the population distribution, because previously a majority lived in Canada. However, from the 1840s onward a majority hunted, camped, and traded in the United States. The Assiniboine had primarily become a plains people and could be found hunting buffalo and warring

with the Crow, Blackfoot, and Gros Ventre along the upper Yellowstone and Missouri Rivers in Montana and North Dakota.

The United States first placed an agent among the Assiniboine in 1826, but little governmental interference existed due to the isolation of the upper Missouri region. From the 1850s onward, the Assiniboine began to feel the pernicious hand of government on both sides of the international border, as settlers and economic pressures necessitated the seclusion of Native peoples on reservations. The Fort Laramie Treaty of 1851 proved a watershed moment in Native American history on the Great Plains as, from this point forward, boundaries existed delineating tribal homelands. Chiefs First Fly and Crazy Bear negotiated and signed the treaty on behalf of all Assiniboine living in the United States creating a defined territory, soon called the Milk River Reservation, that included most of Northeastern Montana. The 1855 Isaac Stevens Treaty with the Blackfoot stipulated the establishment of a common hunting ground near the present-day Montana community of Havre. This dynamic area, located between the Assiniboine and Gros Ventre reservation to the east and the Blackfoot Reservation to the west, caused increasing conflict over resources. Not only the Assiniboine, but the Blackfoot, Gros Ventre, and River Crow prowled the area in pursuit of game.

The Fort Laramie and Isaac Stevens treaties initially did little to stop the migration and movements of the Assiniboine living in the United States, because they could still freely hunt, visit neighbors in Canada, and fight with rivals as they had for generations. However, the decades of the 1860s and 1870s saw dramatic changes that wrought havoc on Native peoples across the Northern Plains. The closure of Fort Union in 1861 eliminated the prime source of trade goods in the region, while the conclusion of the Civil War redirected American attention westward. Slowly, the U.S. government carved up Assiniboine territory into smaller parcels and forced a nomadic people to take up the plow.

The U.S. government subdivided the Milk River Reservation into two parts in 1873, creating the Fort Peck Reservation out of the eastern portion and the Fort Belknap from the western. Assiniboine who lived at Fort Peck now shared a reservation with the

Yanktonai Sioux, bringing the two back together after three centuries apart, while those at Fort Belknap cohabitated with their implacable enemy the Gros Ventre. These two reservations were many times smaller than the Milk River Reservation, and by the end of the decade the few remaining buffalo ventured too far south to hunt. The 1880s saw further land sales, particularly in 1888 when the U.S. government compelled tribal leaders to sell half of the Fort Belknap Reservation to enable white settlers to enter the region. By the end of the 1880s, traditional forms of annual migration, hunting, and even horse stealing had ceased, and the Assiniboine had become wards of the American government with their land largely leased to large cattle operators. Allotment did not occur until 1909 on Fort Peck and 1921 at Fort Belknap, leaving reservation residents in economic limbo for nearly 40 years.

Unlike the Southern Assiniboine living in the United States, little governmental attention had been paid the Northern Assiniboine by the Canadian government. It was not until the Cypress Hills Massacre in 1873, where whiskey runners and other ruffians massacred Assiniboine led by Little Soldier, that the Canadian government negotiated a series of treaties that gave them fixed territories in the area. Negotiated among bands from central Saskatchewan, southern Saskatchewan, and Alberta at Forts Carleton, Pitt, and McLeon, the treaties established a series of reserves for the Assiniboine in Saskatchewan and Alberta. However, during the 1890s the Canadians' desire to settle the prairies led to a constriction in the size of these reserves. Eventually, the Canadian Assiniboine scattered to numerous reserves including Carry the Kettle, Pheasant Rump, and Ocean Man in Saskatchewan and the Alexis, Paul, Wesley, Big Horn, and Eden Valley reserves in Alberta. While on each of these reserves the Assiniboine constitute a majority, on other reserves in both provinces their populations exist as a minority. With no reserves in Manitoba, the long migration westward left their traditional heartland around Lake Winnipeg largely devoid of an Assiniboine population.

By the beginning of the 20th century, the Assiniboine population had plummeted from 28,000 in 1823 to 1,217 in the United States and 873 in Canada by 1908.

Corralled on reservations, the surviving Assiniboine seemed to have completed their ceaseless migration, but in fact their movement continued throughout the 20th century. Young Assiniboine attended boarding schools from Carlisle in Carlisle, Pennsylvania, to Sherman Indian Institute in Riverside, California. When Assiniboine students returned to their reservations, they brought a pan-Indian identity that integrated cultural elements from across "Indian Country."

Assiniboine moved frequently back and forth to various reserves and reservations, regardless of national borders, illustrating the strong bond between the American and Canadian bands. Movement also took place to towns, such as Havre and Glasgow, Montana, located near the Fort Peck and Fort Belknap reservations. Longer migrations to cities in Montana and Alberta, occurring primarily for wage labor and educational opportunities, eventually created lasting Assiniboine communities in Billings, Great Falls, and Lethbridge. Finally, the relocation project undertaken by the Bureau of Indian Affairs during the 1950s sent Assiniboine as far as the East Coast and California. The constant migrations by the Assiniboine over centuries created a resiliency that enabled them to survive in an environment where they faced hostile neighbors and an uncertain climate. Although the Assiniboine diffused over an immense geographic area and developed different economic pursuits, the strong cultural affiliation among the bands never diminished.

—Jon Ille

See also BLACKFOOT NATION, GROS VENTRE

Suggested Reading

Fort Belknap Curriculum Development Project. *Assiniboine Memories: Legends of the Nakota People.* Hays, MT: Fort Belknap Education Department, 1983.

Long, James L. *Land of Nakoda: The Story of the Assiniboine Indian.* Helena: Montana Historical Society Press, 2004.

Lowie, Robert H. *The Assiniboine.* New York: American Museum of Natural History, 1909.

Rodnick, David. *The Fort Belknap Assiniboine of Montana: A Study in Culture Change.* Brooklyn, NY: AMS Press, 1978.

Russell, Dale R. *The Eighteenth Century Western Cree and Their Neighbors.* Hull, Quebec: Canadian Museum of Civilization, 1991.

⏣ ATCHISON, TOPEKA AND SANTA FE RAILWAY

See HARVEY, FREDERICK HENRY

⏣ AUSTIN, STEPHEN FULLER (1793–1836)

Whenever the term *father* is used to describe a man's contributions to society, invention, or country, one can be assured that the namesake has been applied in glowing recognition for the various achievements that have been accomplished. This moniker has been aptly applied to one such "father," Stephen Fuller Austin, also known as the Father of Texas. Throughout Austin's life, he was able to provide intense leadership in the face of dreaded opposition, which resulted in the successful launch of a nation. Without the vision of Stephen Austin, the state of Texas might never have been born as a republic and subsequently as an addition to the United States of America.

Stephen Fuller Austin was born on November 3, 1793, in present day Wythe County in southwestern Virginia, to Moses and Maria Brown Austin. Moses owned and operated a smelter in the lead mine region of Virginia and could be evaluated as generally successful. A few years after Stephen was born, the lead mines in Virginia had all but been bled dry, and Moses had to pull up stakes and look elsewhere for business. A few speculators had claimed that there were new and untapped deposits in the upper Louisiana region, also known as Missouri, and Moses decided to brave the unknown and ended up creating the first permanent settlement in Washington County, Missouri. As the furnaces were built and the lead extracted, the Austins found themselves doing quite well, and Moses became one of the founders of the First Bank of St. Louis.

Tragic times would soon befall the Austins, for in 1818 speculative land values crashed, causing the Bank of St. Louis to fail and all of Moses Austin's dreams to fail with it. With virtually nothing, Moses decided to brave the frontier again in search of wealth and traveled to Texas, entering San Antonio in August of 1820. During this time, his son Stephen served as a circuit judge in Arkansas, followed by a trip to New Orleans to study law, where he became well attuned to frontier life and the various challenges associated with it. At 27 years of age, Stephen would have to take over the reigns of exploration from his father. As Moses was traveling back to Missouri from San Antonio with a Royal Commission in hand to settle 300 families in Texas, he was robbed and developed a bad cold. He died upon his return to Washington County, but Stephen was fully prepared to carry on his father's legacy.

Because his family had been ruined by land speculation on land purchased from the U.S. government, Stephen Austin felt that he had a significantly better chance of success on Spanish land as opposed to American soil. When he received the official papers from Monterrey, Mexico, and the Spanish commissioners, he was well aware that the resolution required "faith to the Catholic Church and to the King, as well as the new immigrants [will] introduce agriculture, industry, and arts." Austin and the Spanish commissioners realized that the colonists were Protestant, but as long as they were law-abiding and productive, a blind eye was turned.

As Austin was surveying possible territory for his colony, many factors had to be considered before deciding upon a permanent location. First and foremost was the incursion of hostile Indian tribes. Up and down the El Camino Real, or Royal Road, there existed many dangerous regions. After a lengthy journey, Austin concluded that the Brazos bottomland, with access to the Gulf of Mexico, would be just fine for the plantation model of the American economic system to thrive, plus it lay outside the region of dangerous Indian country. With the settlement in place, the next goal would be to attract settlers. Stephen Austin found that the second step would be much easier than the first.

When Austin returned to Louisiana, many letters and requests for settlement were waiting for him. Each prospective colonist was required to pay $0.12 an acre and guaranteed 4,500 acres per family or 1,500 acres per man. All government was local and self-governing, with Austin as the acting head with the title of *empresario*. Whereas many settlers could not afford the sum for the entire 4,500 acres, Austin was unwilling to turn away anyone based upon their ability to pay. Nevertheless, Stephen Austin was taking quite a substantial risk with this endeavor. After all was said and done, the "Old Three Hundred," as the original settlers would come to be known, embarked upon their journey with some of the best farmland in all of Texas. With nothing but river bottoms, endless grass-covered prairies, and dreams these 300 men, women, and children braved the elements in the hope that their hard labor would soon, and hopefully very soon, pay off.

At this time, Stephen Austin realized that he was not going to become rich during the development of Texas; nevertheless, the colony was the most important thing in the world to him. Times were difficult in the first year of the colony, 1822–1823, as a severe drought hit the region and bands of Karankawa Indians raided many settlers' homes. A number of frustrated families made the trek back to their points of origin. As far as law was concerned, all colonists were subject to the governance of Spain, then independent Mexico, and finally to the settlement itself. The economy developed upon the barter system, with a cow and calf equaling $10. Cotton provided the basis for the Texas export system, and in 1825 the proportion of whites to slaves was 3 to 1.

As the colony began to grow at a rapid rate, Austin realized that he would have to separate governmental decisions to spread responsibility. The entirety of the colony was divided into two distinct districts, the Colorado and the Brazos, which each elected an *alcalde,* or magistrate, to handle matters of law within the district. While this may have seemed to present possible problems in interpreting the law, it did not, for there was little if any crime committed within the districts. In reality, it was Austin himself who possessed virtually all of the power within the colony. Essentially, Stephen Austin was the acting dictator of Texas, yet few would ever call him such or label him thus. He had the power of all appointments and the colony was exempt from all taxes, for its sole purpose in the eyes of Mexico was to defend the area and fend for itself. Austin acted as the executive, legislative, and judicial branches of the Texas government, all rolled into one, and he would essentially control all aspects of both "national" and local government until 1832.

As the years passed, the number of settlers increased in Texas. By 1825, 500 families were present,

another 100 more by 1827, and by 1828 more than 1,000 families and 1,200 homes had sprouted in the new colony. Something very special was happening in Texas, and many in the United States realized this as well, evidenced by an increasing movement to annex Texas and take advantage of its geography and vision. Presidents John Quincy Adams and Andrew Jackson offered Mexico $1 million and $5 million, respectively, for Texas, only to be soundly turned down both times.

During the 1820s, many other *empresarios* attempted to follow the sound foundation set down by Stephen Austin, and additional colonies were settled in and around Austin's Colorado and Brazos regions. In 1825, immigration and the number of colonies grew, and in that year alone 25 *empresario* commissions were granted. In addition to American settlers, Mexicans began to get in on the action as well. While Mexicans could acquire land with a bit more ease than Americans, the greater proportion of settlers continued to arrive from the United States, with even a handful making the journey from Europe. This massive influx would cause the Mexican government to issues a few new laws to eventually hinder the great increase in population. A general colonization law was implemented in August of 1824, which stated that public lands be administered by the Mexican states, no person could possess more than 48,708 acres, and all immigrants were required to become Mexican citizens. Nevertheless, the population in and around the colony continued to increase, and Austin understood that when the population of Texas grew sufficiently, statehood status would not be that far behind.

Things changed dramatically for Stephen Austin and Texas in the year 1830. At this time, the Mexican government forbade any further immigration from the United States, hoping to seal off the ballooning American population. In order to enforce this, Mexico sent a number of troops north of the Rio Grande to stop all future settlers from crossing into Mexican territory. Austin was incensed and felt that the overall stability of Mexico was in question. It was then that Stephen Austin realized that a move of secession and independence might be more favorable than being annexed by the United States. After getting into an argument with the vice president of Mexico and claiming that Texas would gain self-government with or without his help, Stephen Austin found himself in solitary confinement, charged with high treason. For three months, Austin could neither see nor speak to anyone, after which he was moved to a prison that allowed him visitors, where he would remain for another two years. Ironically, it was General Antonio Lopez de Santa Anna, the future president of Mexico and commander in chief of Mexican forces who defeated the Texan rebels at the Alamo, who set Austin free in 1832.

In a sense, the imprisonment of Stephen Austin provided the spark for Texan independence. For many years, the fundamental differences between white American settlers and those who lived south of the Rio Grande were simmering, eventually to boil over in a series of power struggles between the infant colonial settlements and the incompetent Mexican government. When Mexico flatly refused to grant Texas statehood status and imprisoned Austin, things were starting to spiral out of control. When Austin returned to Texas from prison, he and the colony witnessed a new set of leaders, ready to take up the flag of independence with a fury that would be impressive.

Leading the pack was the former governor of Tennessee, Sam Houston, who arrived in Texas in 1832 and would become commander in chief of the army in November of 1835. Next was James Bowie, a famous fighter and legendary personality in Louisiana and Mississippi who was known for his skill with the Bowie knife he made famous. Bowie arrived in Texas in 1828 and married into a wealthy Spanish family in Bexar, only to join the Texans a few years later. William B. Travis, William Wharton, Branch Archer, and a number of others would be included among the new breed in Texas, young lovers of self-government who settled for nothing less than either separation from the state of Coahuila or secession.

As the turbulent situation became more so, the new dictator of Mexico, Antonio Lopez de Santa Anna, readied troops for the march northward to deal with the troublesome Texas contingent with the hope of quieting the simmering cauldron. Before his imprisonment, Stephen Austin was convinced that his Texas colony should remain a part of Mexico in order to foster continuous beneficial treatment, as well as an important cooperative spirit between the two nations. Upon his

return to Texas, those past feelings changed dramatically. Austin understood that in order for Texas to further exist, it must secede from Mexico, and at this time Stephen Austin joined up with the likes of Houston, Bowie, and Travis.

In December of 1835, Austin traveled to Washington, DC, to ask for credit, loans, and sympathy from the Jackson administration for their upcoming battle against the Mexican government. Unbeknown to him, Austin was beginning to be upstaged by the other revolutionaries, most notably, Sam Houston. Stephen Austin was not the rabble-rousing type; rather, he focused on steadfast leadership of the simple mold—persuasion, discussion, and agreement. However, now it was time for Texas to experience some good, old-fashioned action in its struggle for independence.

Slowly but surely, the upstart band of Texans compiled victory after small victory against tremendous odds fighting the heavily armed and vastly superior Mexican army. Not all battles were victories, for Santa Anna overwhelmed a small Texan contingent at the Alamo in March of 1836, a story with which many are familiar. Nevertheless, after a series of advances and retreats, culminating with Houston's victory at the Battle of San Jacinto, the Texans would emerge victorious in their search for a truly independent identity.

Stephen Austin did not participate in any of the battles for independence, for it was Sam Houston who raised the torch as the new leader of the Texas people. Austin had been relegated to backup to the more revolutionary Houston. It seemed as if Houston had taken the groundwork that had been laid by Austin. After his return from Washington, DC, Austin realized that Houston had taken the spotlight, ready to bask in the glory of an independent Texas. There were still many Texans who appreciated and respected Austin for all the work he had done in the past, but it was evident that his time had passed, and it was now someone else's show.

During Texas's first presidential election in 1836, Austin was persuaded to run, but all knew he would be soundly defeated by the ever-popular Sam Houston, which he was. As a concession, Houston asked Austin to be his secretary of state, to which he agreed. Stephen Austin would fit perfectly in the role of diplomat, for diplomacy was his game, one at which he was extremely skilled. Austin finished his career the way he started it, working toward the ultimate goal of cooperation between adversaries and ending with benefits to both.

Very shortly after the election, Stephen Austin fell ill, which developed into pneumonia. Austin's constitution was not able to handle the severe drain upon his system, and on December 28, 1836, at the age of 43, Austin passed away. Many Texans were truly shocked at his death, for Austin had paved the way for Texas's road to independence. Sam Houston would immortalize Austin by bequeathing the title "Father of Texas" upon him, and this moniker remains to this day. Austin was memorialized in a number of different ways, most notably as one of the state statues placed in Statuary Hall of the U.S. Capitol. Each state is allowed two statues to represent it in the hall, and the state of Texas chose Stephen Austin and Sam Houston.

Sculptor Elisabet Ney was commissioned to produce the marble statue of Austin, and when asked why Austin was such a deserving candidate for the honor, she replied that while Austin was not the aggressive warrior that Houston was, his deeds, his courage, his sufferings, and his love for others entitled him to equal recognition. Perhaps no better qualities are possible for a father, most importantly a father of a republic.

—*Charles Sedey*

Suggested Reading

Barker, Eugene. *The Life of Stephen F. Austin, Founder of Texas, 1793–1836. A Chapter of the Westward Movement of the Anglo-American People*. New York: Da Capo Press, 1968.

Bechdolt, Frederick. *Giants of the Old West*. Freeport, NY: Books for Libraries Press, 1930.

Cantrell, Greg. *Stephen F. Austin, Empresario of Texas*. New Haven, CT: Yale University Press, 1968.

Fehrenbach, T. R. *Lone Star: A History of Texas and the Texans*. New York: Macmillan, 1968.

⊞ AUSTRALIAN IMMIGRANTS

See IDAHO SILVER STRIKES

B

See FRENCH BASQUES OF BAKERSFIELD, CALIFORNIA

⊞ BAKERSFIELD, CALIFORNIA

⊞ BARTLESON, JOHN
(1786–1848)

In early 1840, in frontier Missouri, the Western Emigration Society formed to explore emigration to Mexican California. Glowing reports from Antoine Robidoux, a trader and trapper who had already traveled to California via a southerly route; the correspondence of a former Independence, Missouri, resident-turned-Californian, Dr. John Marsh; and regular publicity in the St. Louis and frontier presses combined to increase the desirability of emigration. The society quickly grew to more than 500 who agreed to head west to California.

However, the extensive interest in the expedition faltered when local newspapers printed the letters of Thomas J. Farnham. These letters excoriated the Mexican authorities in California, who meted out harsh punishments for the Englishmen and Americans whom they suspected of revolutionary activities in April of 1840. At the time, Farnham was heading east from the conclusion of his travels as a member of the Peoria party—who had traveled to Oregon in 1839—and was in California during the unrest. Interest in emigrating to California imploded and, when the May 9, 1841, deadline for the rendezvous at Sapling Grove, Missouri, arrived, only John Bidwell and his immediate

companions kept the date. Eventually, approximately 60 people arrived, including Dr. Marsh's acquaintances William Baldridge, Elias Barnett, Michael C. Nye, and John Bartleson.

Marsh, who became acquainted with Bartleson while he was a storekeeper before immigrating to Santa Fe and eventually California, played a significant part in the path chosen by the party. His correspondences to several friends who remained in Missouri—including two eventual Bidwell-Bartleson party members, Baldridge and Nye—included details for a suggested overland route to California. The route relied upon the experiences of Jedediah S. Smith, an American fur trader; Peter S. Ogden, an explorer and trader for the Hudson Bay Company; and Joseph R. Walker, all of whom made similar journeys in the decades prior to the Bidwell-Bartleson trek.

The party officially formed on May 18, 1841, next to the Kansas River and elected "Colonel" John Bartleson as its leader. Bartleson strong-armed the election when he threatened to pull out of the party, along with seven or eight men in his contingent, if not voted captain. Bidwell claimed that Bartleson was not "the best man for the position," and the accounts of his fellow travelers depicted a man not truly fit, or experienced enough, to lead this party. The party was fortunate to discover a missionary group whose path coincided with theirs as far as Soda Springs on the Bear River in what would become Idaho along what became known as the Oregon Trail. The Catholic missionaries had Captain Thomas Fitzpatrick, an experienced mountaineer, as their guide, which provided the inexperienced

Bidwell-Bartleson party a chance to travel more securely, with a proven leader, than it could have otherwise. The mixed party of horses, mules, oxen, and wagons departed on the morning of May 19.

Bartleson was an ill-suited leader more concerned for his own well being than that of the party. Father Nicholas Point, one of the missionaries who illustrated much of the journey, described Bartleson as "calm in temperament but enterprising in character," and he was likely speaking of an event before the separation of the parties at Soda Springs. Nicholas "Cheyenne" Dawson wrote in his narratives of a meeting that occurred on July 23, 1841, with some trappers and traders in which a barter trade was set up. While Dawson mentions a trade in garments and ammunition, his account is notably silent regarding the trade of secreted alcohol that Bidwell claimed was stored in some of the wagons, including Captain Bartleson's. In fact, Bidwell wrote that the meeting with the traders was sought after to benefit Bartleson and the other members who had secreted the alcohol, presumably members of his cohort. This was merely the first evidence of the selfish and inexperienced nature of Bartleson's leadership; confirmation became evident after the parties separated at Soda Springs.

On August 10, 1841, at Soda Springs, the groups split and the Bidwell-Bartleson party shrank to 32 California-bound members. A series of events and near mishaps involving Indians, lost oxen, and members left behind culminated in an event that resulted in the de facto removal of Bartleson as the party's captain. On October 6, after being berated by Bidwell for abandoning him while rushing the party ahead, Bartleson persuaded the party to give him, along with eight of his companions, twice their share of meat from a freshly slaughtered ox, and then he abandoned them. He admonished the party that he had been "found fault with long enough, and we are going to California. If you can keep up with us, all right, if you cannot, you may go to hell," as he and his followers left camp. Almost 10 days later, the party welcomed the nine deserters, starving and sick from dysentery, back into the party with a much-needed meal from two of the last remaining oxen. During his absence, Benjamin Kelsey, due to his knack for finding the way, became the de facto leader and remained so for the duration of the trek.

Though it was not the first to travel overland to California, the Bidwell-Bartleson party is significant because it is recognized as the first *planned* overland emigration with California as the ultimate destination for settlement. Though some historians often refer to the emigrant party as the Bidwell party due to the successes of Bidwell and his publicized accounts of the westward journey, Bartleson was in fact the leader of the party and earned his billing as such. The Bidwell-Bartleson party was John Bartleson's lone, yet significant, contribution to the history of westward migration in the United States. Several members of the party reported that after his return on October 16, 1841, Bartleson exclaimed that if he ever got back to Missouri, he would never leave and would be happy enough to eat out of the trough with his animals. He was back in Missouri in 1842 after traveling nearly 4,000 miles with a dozen men, including Joseph Chiles. Bartleson died in Washington Township, Missouri, almost exactly seven years after his desertion of the Bidwell-Bartleson party, on October 7, 1841.

—*Scott M. Behen*

See also BIDWELL, JOHN

Suggested Reading

Bancroft, Hubert Howe. *The Works, Vol. 4: History of California.* San Francisco: A. L. Bancroft, 1885.

Bidwell, General John. *Echoes of the Past.* New York: Citadel, 1962.

Gillis, Michael J., and Michael F. Magliari. *John Bidwell and California: The Life and Writings of a Pioneer 1841–1900.* Spokane, WA: Arthur H. Clark, 2003.

Hafen, Leroy R. *The Mountain Men and the Fur Trade of the Far West: Biographical Sketches of the Participants by Scholars of the Subject and with Introductions by the Editor. Vol. 2, The Far West and the Rockies Historical Series.* Glendale, CA: Arthur H. Clark, 1965.

Hafen, Leroy R., and Ann W. Hafen, eds. *To the Rockies and Oregon 1839–1842: With Diaries and Accounts by Sidney Smith, Amos Cook, Joseph Holman, E. Willard Smith, Francis Fletcher, Joseph Williams, Obadiah Oakley, Robert Shortess, T. J. Farnham. Vol. 3, The Far West and the Rockies Historical Series 1820–1875.* Glendale, CA: Arthur H. Clark, 1955.

Lyman, George D. *John Marsh, Pioneer: The Life Story of a Trail-Blazer on Six Frontiers.* Chautauqua, NY: Chautauqua Press, 1931.

McLynn, Frank. *Wagons West: The Epic Story of America's Overland Trails.* New York: Grove, 2002.

Nugent, Walter. *Into the West: The Story of Its People.* New York: Knopf, 1999.

Nunis, Doyce B., Jr., ed. *The Bidwell-Bartleson Party: 1841 California Emigrant Adventure, the Documents and Memoirs of the Overland Pioneers.* Santa Cruz, CA: Western Tanager Press, 1991.

White, David A. *News of the Plains and Rockies, 1803–1865: Original Narratives of Overland Travel and Adventure Selected From the Wagner-Camp and Becker Bibliography of Western Americana. Vol. 2, C: Santa Fe Adventurers, 1818–1843, and D: Settlers, 1819–1865.* Spokane, WA: Arthur H. Clark, 1996.

⊞ BASQUE AMERICANS

Basque people were originally from the western Pyrenees region of Spain. Some of the first Basques entered the United States to mine gold in California during the Gold Rush. Many of these Basques came not from Spain but from Argentina, Chile, and France. They came in the hundreds hoping to attain a good deal of wealth and return home better off. After the first wave of Basques reached California, they wrote home and sent for friends and relatives, which in turn brought many more Basques to the American West. Some Basques continued to mine, but many opted to try their hand at raising livestock and grazing. The tending of sheep proved to be a favorable business for the Basque community, for there was a great deal of open land on which sheep could graze.

By the 1860s, the Basques coming to the United States came mainly from Spain rather than from South America. Many of these Basques left their homes, crossed the Atlantic Ocean, traveled across the United States, and settled somewhere in the western United States. Prior to coming to America, the longest trip for many Spanish Basques would have consisted of a trip of around 50 miles. It is not known exactly how many Basques came to the United States, as most Basques were labeled citizens of Spain. Like many immigrants from other lands, many Basques came seeking to earn money and return home, and like many other groups, they chose to stay rather than return home. Basques were pulled by economic opportunities or pushed by economic hardships. Basques in Spain continued to use a form of primogeniture, in which the oldest child often inherited the bulk of their parents' property, leaving the younger children with little hope or chance of economic advancement.

The Basque language proved to be a barrier for assimilation, so when offered jobs as sheepherders, these foreigners took the opportunity. Sheepherding required little education. Basque herders proved to be sturdy and honest in their work. As a result, Basque newcomers replaced Indian and Mexican sheepherders. Many of the first Basque sheepherders wrote home about the opportunity of working with sheep, and many Basques back home responded by leaving Spain in search of work.

Basques thrived at their new occupation. They often would agree to tend to a herd in exchange for a few head of the flock at year's end. The owner of a flock of sheep did not have to own land; instead, the sheep could graze on public lands. Because sheep have a strong herd mentality, all that was often needed to look after the sheep was a herder and a dog or two. Sheepherding also proved ideal for Basques because, with their inability to speak English, they did not have to interact much with native residents. The late 1880s to the 1920s was a time of large migration to the American Northwest. Basques settled in northern Nevada, northeastern Oregon, and southern Idaho.

The newly arrived Basques were strongly Roman Catholic and in several places built Roman Catholic churches. In Boise, Idaho, a Basque Roman Catholic priest came from Spain to preach to the growing Basque population. The priest, Father Bernardo Arregui, arrived in 1911 and ministered to the Basques in southern Idaho and northern Oregon. The Basques of Idaho also created a mutual aid society for those who needed help. By World War I, Boise was the center of Basque culture in the Pacific Northwest.

Other occupations that many Basques participated in were agriculture, working in lumber mills, and opening and working in boardinghouses. Boardinghouses were significant in the Basque community. A number of Basque boardinghouses were opened in Boise and northern Oregon. Many a sheepherder would spend his off-time residing in a boardinghouse where there were other people to interact with. Many Basque young women found employment working in boardinghouses and often met their future husbands there. The boardinghouse was a place for socializing, and for many a place where traditional Basque foods were served. Dances and other social gatherings were held at boardinghouses. The boardinghouse was also significant as a place where newly arrived immigrants could go for help in getting established in the new country. The competition between the various houses was often fierce, and customers often formed attachments to particular Basque establishments.

For many Basque Americans, the years of 1900–1920 marked a time in which a significant number of these people gave up the goal of returning to Spain. It also marked a time in which many of the second-generation Basque Americans were raised. A common trait for the second generation was to speak the Basque language at home but speak English outside the home, particularly at school. Many of the second generation began to see themselves as Basque Americans and not just Basque. Second-generation Basques who had been educated in the United States no longer were content to take the same jobs as their parents; they began to enter new professions and open up business establishments.

—*Timothy A. Strand*

See also Boise, Idaho; Chileans and the California Gold Rush; French Basques of Bakersfield, California

Suggested Reading

Douglas, William A., and Richard Etulain. *Basque Americans: A Guide to Information Sources.* Detroit, MI: Gale Research, 1981.

Etulain, Richard W., ed. *Basques of the Pacific Northwest.* Pocatello: Idaho State University Press, 1991.

Lane, Richard H., and William A. Douglas. *Basque Sheepherders of the American West.* Reno: University of Nevada Press, 1985.

McCullough, Flavia Maria. *The Basques in the Northwest.* San Francisco: R. and E. Research Associates, 1974.

Paris, Beltran, as told to William A. Douglas. *Beltran, Basque Sheepman of the American West.* Reno: University of Nevada Press, 1979.

Peterson, Frank Ross. *Idaho, a Bicentennial History.* New York: Norton, 1976.

⌗ BASS, CHARLOTTA A. SPEAR(S)
(? –1969)

Charlotta A. Spear (or Spears) Bass was an early advocate of gender equality and social and economic egalitarianism for all minorities. As the editor of the African American periodical the *California Eagle* for almost 40 years, she used journalism as her public platform to challenge local employment practices and restrictive covenants, become a local and national political activist, and promote women's agency. As a female editor and politician, she transcended many racial and gender barriers of her generation. Her attempt to liberalize American racial ideologies on a local and national level contributed toward Los Angeles's demographic diversity, and improved racial and gender relations in the 21st century.

Despite the proliferation of documents regarding her adult life, Charlotta A. Spear's childhood remains elusive. Various sources including legal documents and her autobiography record the birth of Charlotta A. Spear in either 1874, 1879, or 1880 to Hiram and Kate Spears in either Ohio; Little Compton, Rhode Island; or Sumter, South Carolina. Even the spelling of her maiden name, Spear or Spears, has been contested. Charlotta's writings indicate that she had four siblings, yet other sources claim that she was the sixth of 11 children. As a young woman, Charlotta was inspired by Edward Bellamy's 1888 visionary work *Looking Backward,* which prophesized that by the year 2000 America would be a utopia with a nationalized industry and equal distributions of wealth that eliminated class divisions. This nationalist philosophy emphasized that evolutionary not revolutionary tactics lead by an educated elite would be the harbinger of social change. Although Bellamy's egalitarian ideals were inspirational, Charlotta's subsequent activism to secure economic and social impartiality for all minorities more closely aligned with W. E. B. DuBois's methods of confrontational political activism.

In 1910, Charlotta moved to Los Angeles, California. John J. Neimore, who in 1879 founded the *California Eagle,* the oldest African American newspaper, hired Charlotta at $5.00 per week, thus beginning her career as a voice of reform. Charlotta shouldered the editing, publishing, distributing, and bookkeeping duties with the death of Mr. Neimore in 1912. Needing assistance in 1913, she hired and eventually married Joseph Blackburn (J. B.) Bass, an experienced editor. Working as a team, which in itself promoted women's equality in marriage and the workplace, the Basses continued to address myriad issues including race, class, and gender.

Charlotta and her husband's efforts to assure civil rights for the paper's African American readers and other minorities alike included coverage of labor strikes, boycotts, riots, peaceful demonstrations, as well as individual battles against the courts or landlords. Besides these efforts, Charlotta lobbied the Los Angeles City Council and County Board of Supervisors regarding employment and housing equality and became the president of the Marcus Garvey United Negro Improvement Association's (UNIA) 156th Division, which promoted Black separatism. She also joined the Los Angeles chapter of the National Association for the Advancement of Colored People (NAACP), which conversely supported integration, where she met and worked alongside her source of early inspiration, W. E. B. DuBois. During her tenure at the UNIA, however, Charlotta continued to support integration despite the organization's official prosegregation platform. Charlotta also organized and was elected president of the Industrial Business Council, an organization that battled employment discrimination. Charlotta and the *California Eagle* became an institution of reform in the African American community, which prepared her for the subsequent events that dramatically changed the social and physical landscape of Los Angeles.

The value of the arid San Fernando Valley appreciated from the newly constructed aqueduct, the building of a harbor, and the era's largest interurban and streetcar network called the Pacific Electric Red and Yellow Cars. These developments resulted in a significant growth in the population after 1910. Up until this point, African Americans were not subjected to residential covenants and had a high home ownership rate of 36 percent. Although the African American population increased by approximately 80 percent between 1910 and 1930, they remained a mere 3–4 percent of the city's total population. Despite the influx of African Americans in the community over that 20-year period, Charlotta believed that the increasingly discriminatory practices resulted from the heightened migration of white Southern workers after 1910.

Charlotta and her husband continuously publicized and rallied support for victims of discrimination in the *California Eagle* on a local, national, and international level. For a local family imprisoned for allegedly breaking restrictive covenant regulations, Charlotta organized a picket line exceeding 1,000 protesters outside their home. Because the national publicity of the event mustered public support, the family secured ownership of the property and the Supreme Court subsequently ruled the covenants "unenforceable" in 1948. Besides local crusades, Charlotta wrote articles that featured women's scholastic or professional achievements in nontraditional jobs. National pursuits included a case in Alabama, where Charlotta and her husband raised money for legal fees and orchestrated a march. On an international level, Charlotta discussed "nationalist" independence movements in Africa that reflected her continued hope for Bellamy's utopia. In 1925, she battled and won a libel court case against the Ku Klux Klan, launched campaigns against the White Citizen's Council, and helped defeat racist politicians such as prospective City Councilman Harry F. Burke, who chaired the White Home Owners Protective Organization.

By that time, the *California Eagle* had a constituency ranged from 5,000 and 10,000 readers, averaged between 12 to 20 pages, and sold for a nickel. Two years before her husband J. B. Bass's death in 1934, Charlotta hired Loren Miller. Like other black periodicals, the *California Eagle*'s focus changed from community uplift in the 1920s to the predominant concerns regarding employment and discrimination in the 1930s, as exemplified by the paper's promotion of the national "Don't Buy Where You Can't Work" campaign. Other national issues raised by the paper included segregation, lynching, and black politician's platforms.

Certain national and international factors that arose in 1941 altered the social and political landscape. Examples included the passage of the Fair Employment Practices Commission (FEPC), the emergence of wartime industries, and the creation of federally subsidized public housing that legally eliminated restrictive housing policies. However, de facto discriminatory practices continued, as did cutbacks in public services, housing, and welfare benefits, and restrictive zoning ordinances eventually emerged.

Charlotta served as the first African American participant on the Los Angeles Grand Jury in 1943.

This momentary improvement in racial relations was overshadowed by her frustration with and subsequent protest against police and military brutality that targeted Mexican American youths in the Zoot Suit Riots of 1943. Her platform continued to radicalize during World War II, a position that seemed to solidify after the death of her nephew in Nazi Germany. For instance, she promoted the "Double V for Victory" program and likened the international fight against fascism with American racism. In 1945, she ran an unsuccessful campaign as an Independent for the City Council. Until the end of the decade, Charlotta remained within the parameters of mainstream African American political ideologies. Frustrated by her party's racial schisms and the lack of Democratic support for civil rights, Charlotta joined the Progressive party, aided the establishment of the Independent Progressive party in California, and supported Henry Wallace's presidential campaign. Because of her increasingly radical political ideologies, the Tenney Committee, which resembled the federal House Un-American Activities Committee, labeled her a "commie," and many attempts were made to discredit her in the late 1940s. Unthwarted, Charlotta ran for the House of Representatives in 1950 representing the predominantly black Fourteenth Congressional District by promoting issues such as world peace, neighborly compassion, and civil rights. Indifferent to defeat, she sold the *California Eagle* to Loren Miller the year before she made the unprecedented decision in 1952 to run for the vice presidency under Progressive presidential candidate Vincent W. Hallinan, whose ideologies similarly reflected socialist positions on domestic and foreign affairs. National support dwindled as the campaign only won 0.23 percent of the vote, therefore reflecting the increase in anticommunist sentiment with the rise of McCarthyism. Her autobiography, self-published in 1959, demonstrated that, despite unfavorable sentiments, Charlotta remained impervious to the threats and controversy she faced, and she vigilantly continued her crusade until her death in 1969.

Throughout Charlotta's career, which exceeded 40 years, she highlighted the juxtaposition between American democratic values and the inequities of discrimination. Through the *California Eagle* or the politician's podium, Charlotta urged Americans to challenge the status quo. Today, the demographic diversity, greater economic equality, and improved racial and gender relations in Los Angeles County and across the nation are a tribute to the dedication of Charlotta A. Spear Bass.

—Catherine M. Bilanchone

See also AFRICAN AMERICAN COMMUNITIES IN CALIFORNIA; LOS ANGELES, CALIFORNIA

Suggested Reading

Abajian, James. *Blacks and Their Contribution to the American West: A Bibliography and Union List of Library Holdings through 1970.* Boston: G. K. Hall, 1974.

Bass, Charlotta A. *Forty Years: Memoirs From the Pages of a Newspaper.* Los Angeles: Charlotta A. Bass, 1960.

Cairns, Kathleen A. *Front-Page Women Journalists, 1920–1950.* Lincoln: University of Nebraska Press, 2003.

Charlotta A. Bass Papers and Manuscript Collection. Los Angeles: Southern California Library for Social Studies and Research.

Danky, James P., ed. *The African-American Newspapers and Periodicals: A National Bibliography and Union List.* Cambridge, MA: Harvard University Press, 1999.

Davis, Marianna W., ed. *Contributions of Black Women to America.* 2 vols. Columbia, SC: Kenday Press, 1982.

De Graaf, Lawrence B. "Negro Migration to Los Angeles, 1930–1950." Ph.D. Dissertation, University of California–Los Angeles, 1962.

Jeter, James Phillip. "Rough Flying: The *California Eagle* (1879–1965)." Presentation to 12th Annual Conference of the American Journalism Historians Association, Salt Lake City, Utah, 1993.

Smith, Jessie Carney, ed. *Notable Black American Women.* Detroit, MI: Gale Research, 1992.

Thomas, June Manning, and Marsha Ritzdorf, eds. *Urban Planning and the African American Community in the Shadows.* Thousand Oaks, CA: Sage, 1997.

Vose, Clement E. *Caucasians Only: The Supreme Court, the NAACP, and the Restrictive Covenant Cases.* Berkeley: University of California Press, 1959.

BASS, JOSEPH BLACKBURN (J. B.)

See BASS, CHARLOTTA A. SPEAR(S)

BEAR FLAG REVOLT

See FREMONT, JOHN CHARLES; ROWLAND-WORKMAN EXPEDITION OF 1841

⊞ BIDWELL, JOHN
(1819–1900)

John Bidwell was born in Ripley, New York, the second child of Abram and Clarissa Griggs Bidwell, on August 5, 1819. Young Bidwell's family moved often; when he was 10, the family migrated first to Erie, Pennsylvania, later to Ashtabula County, Ohio, and at 15 to the western part of Ohio in the vicinity of Greenville. During his teen years, he found work at various jobs in the ubiquitous timber industry, such as hauling lumber and sawmill tender. After attending school back in Ashtabula County, he returned home to the western part of Ohio where, at the age of 18, Bidwell became the unusually young principal of the Kingsville Academy. His biographer, Rockwell D. Hunt, claimed that Bidwell, in his brief stint as a teacher, brought the "first modern teaching" to that region of Ohio. Though he exhibited a high degree of interest in education, both in learning and teaching, during his formative years, it was John Bidwell's journey west as one of the early American pioneers of California and the life he subsequently created there for which he is best known.

In the spring of 1939, Bidwell set out to move further west. He traveled 90 miles south to Cincinnati, mostly by wagon, and then to the new territorial capitol of the Iowa Territory, Burlington, via the Ohio and Mississippi Rivers. After a failed claim on a 160-acre plot near the Iowa River, he traveled south and west across Iowa and into Missouri. Upon arriving across the river from Fort Leavenworth, he laid claim to another 160-acre parcel, which he lost to a squatter while on a trip to St. Louis the following summer. Following these reverses, a series of events unfolded in 1840 that led Bidwell down the path to settling in California.

An encounter with a fur trader recently returned from California and letters from a recent settler to friends in Independence, Missouri, spark a keen interest in migrating further west. Bidwell met Antoine Robidoux, an experienced fur trader just returned from California via Santa Fe, in late 1840. According to Bidwell, Robidoux described California as "one of perennial spring and boundless fertility" while waxing poetically about the abundance of oranges, wild horses, and cattle. At about the same time as these discussions with Robidoux occurred, favorable letters from former Independence resident turned northern California emigrant Dr. John Marsh were published in the local Independence newspaper. This confluence of events led to the establishment of the Western Emigration Society, of which Bidwell was one of the original members, each of whom pledged to meet at Sapling Grove, Missouri, on May 9, 1841 for an overland trip to California via a route suggested by the letters of Dr. Marsh. Within one month, according to Bidwell, more than 500 people had pledged to journey west. He also wrote that letters from interested parties arrived regularly from all parts of Missouri and even included inquiries from as far away as Illinois, Kentucky, and Arkansas.

Bad press about California and the concerted effort of local merchants to keep residents from heading west almost ended the migration before it began. Thomas Farnham, a New York lawyer, published a letter in the New York papers about his time in Monterey on his way back to New York in April of 1840. Farnham witnessed the rough treatment of some Americans during what is known as the Graham Affair and reported in his letter the oppressiveness of the local Californians, warning that it was a dangerous place for Americans to travel. Farnham's letter gained local notoriety when reprinted in the local papers in Missouri. Membership in the Western Emigration Society dropped so precipitously that Bidwell described himself as the only one of the original 500 members who pledged to immigrate to California that actually followed through on the pledge to meet at Sapling Grove.

On May 19, 1841, the Bidwell-Bartleson party departed Sapling Grove, headed initially along the Oregon Trail towards Fort Laramie, and were destined to become the first group of American settlers to travel overland to California. The lesser-known Bartleson blackmailed his way into the captaincy of the party by threatening to pull out of the expedition, along with the eight men he had brought, before the party left Sapling Grove. With less than 70 emigrants committed to going even after waiting 10 additional days, the loss of Bartleson and his men would have been unthinkable. Ultimately, Bartleson's poor leadership and the fact that he returned to Missouri and obscurity the following year relegated him to the lists of the all-but-forgotten pioneers of the American West. Fortunately for the Bidwell-Bartleson party, Thomas

Fitzpatrick, an experienced fur trader, guided the missionaries and thus the party as a whole until they went their separate ways at Soda Springs, in what would become Idaho, in late August.

A fixed accounting of the number of settlers that departed that spring day for various points west is unattainable. Doyce B. Nunis, Jr., determined that the original Bidwell-Bartleson company included 61 persons with the possibility of three, or more, additional children. Nunis also demonstrates that Father Pierre Jean De Smet's Jesuit missionary party, who led the way to Soda Springs, began with 17 people and lost seven members before reaching that waypoint. Ultimately, the party split into three different groups at Soda Springs, with 34 heading to California, at least 23 to Oregon, and the remaining missionaries on to Fort Hall. By the time the group had reached Soda Springs, four members of the original Bidwell-Bartleson group had turned back or stopped at Fort Laramie, and one—George Shotwell—died of an accidental self-inflicted gunshot wound. The party also added an Indian family at Fort Laramie who had departed by the time they had reached the Green River. Meanwhile, Richard Phelan, who had also joined at Fort Laramie, departed with the Oregon-bound contingent at Soda Springs.

The Bidwell-Bartleson party established a new overland trail to California. Leaving Sapling Grove on May 19, 1841, Fitzpatrick led the group north and west, first along the Kansas River, then the Little Blue River, and next into present-day Wyoming along the Platte River arriving at the foot of the Black Hills arriving at Fort Laramie on June 22. With Fitzpatrick still acting as guide, the party, with some slight personnel changes, continued along the Platte River reaching Independence Rock on July 5 and then followed the Sweetwater River until crossing the Green River on July 23. On August 10, the party arrived at Soda Springs along the Bear River. At this point, only 34 people continued with Bidwell on to California. Admonished by fur trappers from Fort Hall to not go too far north for fear of being endlessly lost in the mazelike canyons nor to go too far south for fear of disappearing in the desert country there, the party headed southwest, going around the northern part of the Great Salt Lake. The party scouted ahead and found the Humboldt River, though not before having to abandon their wagons on September 16 due to a lack of feed for and near exhaustion of the hard-working oxen. By following river drainages, the party generally avoided the need to constantly climb the mountains of the Sierra Nevada range that they had reached by October 15, 1841. The party overcame water and food shortages, physical exhaustion, difficult and worn out animals, lost and separated members (including Bidwell), their only violent confrontation with Indians, and the poor leadership of its captain-in-name-only Bartleson before finally descending into the San Joaquin Valley in early November. On November 4, 1841, the Bidwell-Bartleson party concluded its journey, having arrived at Dr. Marsh's settlement just 15 miles east of San Francisco.

Bidwell began working for Johann Sutter within a month of entering California. Beginning in January of 1842, Bidwell oversaw the dismantling of Fort Ross—purchased from the Russian American Company—and the removal of its weaponry to the fort Sutter was constructing at New Helvetia. Over the remainder of his eight years with Sutter, Bidwell performed a wide variety of work. At times, he was a bookkeeper, manager, explorer, mapmaker, farm supervisor, census taker, and homebuilder, and was even in charge of settling people in the Sacramento Valley. By 1844, he became a naturalized Mexican citizen and received two land grants that he sold.

Though the Bear Flag Revolt and Mexican War found Bidwell in the thick of things in California, it was the discovery of gold that led Bidwell to riches and fame. Unlike Sutter and Marshall, Bidwell struck it rich during the gold rush because he was able to keep his own strike secret long enough to work it thoroughly before news of the find spread. He was then able to open up a store and supply the prospectors who did flock to the area when it became publicized. By 1849, Bidwell's Bar was considered a boomtown with more than 600 miners prospecting the land. Though the mining town served as the county seat of Butte during the early and mid-1850s, it did not survive the cyclical boom and bust of the gold mining towns. Shortly after its gold fields dried up, Bidwell's Bar succumbed to fires and it became another ghost town. Bidwell, who stopped mining for gold in 1949, parlayed his considerable fortune into his newly purchased Rancho Chico.

Rancho Chico was transformed into a thriving agricultural business to meet the rising needs for farm produce in the state. It took Bidwell two years to purchase the remaining half of the Rancho from his business partner and another 17 years to actually gain the title. During this time, he fought squatters and legal bureaucracy as California's population swelled from 15,000 in 1845 to nearly 400,000 in 1860. Though he was the owner of many heads of cattle and sheep, Bidwell staunchly fought for new fence laws to end the open-range system that existed in the state. Initially, Rancho Chico's primary income was in winter wheat—which thrived in California's climate so well that it became a boom crop and was exported to England shortly after the end of the Civil War. During the remainder of the 19th century, more and more farmers migrated to California and contributed to it becoming a leading American producer of wheat and subsequently of specialty crops.

Rancho Chico's workers reflected the diversity found on farms throughout California in the last half of the 19th century. By 1857, Bidwell had as many as 25 Indians employed full time while at the same time he had as many as 20 white hands. By 1891, there were 100 people employed year round; white Americans, Mechoopda Indians, and Chinese immigrants. During the peak summer months, Rancho Chico had as many as 500 employees working its produce. Colonel Charles Royce was hired to be the administrator of the farm, and in 1894, in a controversial move, Royce leased the fruit orchards to Chinese immigrants.

Bidwell had a complex relationship with his Indian workers. During the many periods of Indian and settler disturbances in and around Butte County, Bidwell was a strong advocate for restraint in the treatment of Indians. Upon purchasing Rancho Chico, Bidwell invited the local Mechoopda Indians to relocate their village onto his property. The reasoning behind this was twofold: First, he could virtually guarantee a labor force for growing agricultural products; second, he was able to afford the natives protection from the incoming waves of settlers. Though he was initially against the reservation system, events such as the Knoll Tree Massacre in August of 1865 and the reality

that the Indians would never be left with enough land to sustain their traditional ways of life forced him to accept this as the only way to protect the Indians from the ever-present waves of new settlers to the region. However, the relocated Indian village remained sheltered on his estate until well past his death in 1900.

Rancho Chico and Bidwell were never far from the contentious subject of the so-called Chinese question. He continuously employed Chinese immigrant labor and, under Colonel Royce's administration, was one of the first to offer land for lease to Chinese for farming. In the last half of the 19th century, an influx of almost a quarter of a million Chinese immigrants, predominantly to California for its gold mountains, gave rise to a dangerous anti-Chinese sentiment in California. In Butte County, the 3,793 Chinese immigrants made up nearly 20 percent of the population in 1880, causing much of the anti-Chinese sentiment to focus upon Bidwell and his Rancho Chico, where Chinese had been continuously employed since the 1869. It is significant to note that the major crises the erupted around Chinese farm laborers were due to prolonged depression caused by the financial panic of 1873. Records show that, prior to the depression, Chinese labor barely constituted 13 percent of Rancho Chico's workforce. Regardless of the periodic threats, violence, and even anti-Chinese boycotts over the next three decades, Chinese labor remained an important part of Rancho Chico throughout the remainder of Bidwell's life.

Bidwell boasted a 40-year long political career that began with promise and ended with a fizzle. Though he did not learn of his selection until after the event occurred, Bidwell was elected as a representative to the California founding state constitutional convention. In November of 1849, he was elected to the state senate, where he helped organize the system of state and local governments. After choosing not to run for reelection, Bidwell helped to organize California's Democratic party. The bid for a seat on Butte County's first board of supervisors and subsequent run for his prior senate seat both fail miserably in 1855, as the Know-Nothings swept the Democratic ticket. Bidwell was the only California delegate at the 1860 Democratic national convention to vote for Douglas. His prounionist beliefs caused him to flee the Democratic party. This led to his appointment to the Union party's state executive committee and subsequently to be appointed brigadier general in the state militia by the then Republican governor. His ardent support of pro-Union policies to suppress copperhead activism within the state led to his nomination to the Third Congressional District, which he won in 1864 with 56 percent of the vote. The one-term congressman secured the chairmanship of the House Committee on Agriculture, where he succeeded in introducing several bills aimed squarely at helping farmers in California. He chose to run for governor instead of reelection to Congress and lost on the first ballot at the Unionist state convention in 1867. Subsequently, Bidwell ran as an Independent and lost every election, including bids for governor and one hopeless attempt at the presidency.

Bidwell remained a figure in state politics for the remainder of his life. In 1872, he was elected president at the founding meeting of the California Farmers' Union. This organization merged a year later with the national organization, the Patrons of Husbandry, more commonly referred to as the Grange. The Grangers formed the People's Independent party in 1873 and elected Bidwell to their state central committee. The Grangers California state political wing won eight seats in congress and 34 in the senate and later nominated Bidwell to run for governor in 1875. Four years later, Bidwell broke with the Grange over its anti-Chinese allies during the rewriting of the state constitution. The independent Bidwell, who now was an antimonopoly, Jeffersonian agrarian, Jacksonian principled, prosuffrage farmer and prohibitionist, never joined the Farmers' Alliance or Populists party. His decision to call for Chinese exclusion and steady retreat on this position later confirmed him as a nativist. Supported by the Prohibitionist and American parties, Bidwell failed miserably in one last bid for governor in 1890. Two years later, as the Prohibitionist candidate, Bidwell finished a distant fourth in his bid for the nation's highest office.

Referred to by his biographer as the "Prince of California Pioneers," Bidwell maintained a powerful presence in the first several decades of California's history as an American state. Had he been present at just one or two prominent events in California history, he may have existed merely as a footnote in some obscure text on overland migration. Bidwell was in the first overland emigrant train to California, which now bears his namesake. He was involved in the Bear Flag Revolt and received a commission in the Army as it evolved into the Mexican War. Bidwell was one of California's first state senators and played an important part in the creation of its state and local governments. He was at the nexus of the California gold rush and parlayed the wealth he gained into a stable future at Rancho Chico. He was commissioned a brigadier general in the state militia during the Civil War and also served a term in the U.S. Congress. Though he fought in no battles and fathered no significant legislation while in Washington, he did constantly work to promote the state of California and the well-being of all of its citizens, whether they were indigenous, immigrants, or migrants.

—*Scott M. Behen*

See also BARTLESON, JOHN; SUTTER, JOHANN AUGUST

Suggested Reading

Gillis, Michael J., and Michael F. Magliari. *John Bidwell and California: The Life and Writings of a Pioneer 1841–1900*. Spokane, WA: Arthur H. Clark, 2003.

Hoopes, Chad L. *What Makes a Man: The Annie E. Kennedy and John Bidwell Letters 1866–1868*. Fresno, CA: Valley Publishers, 1973.

Hunt, Rockwell D. *John Bidwell: Prince of California Pioneers*. Caldwell, ID: The Caxton Printers, 1942.

Nunis, Doyce B., Jr., ed. *The Bidwell-Bartleson Party: 1841 California Emigrant Adventure, the Documents and Memoirs of the Overland Pioneers*. Santa Cruz, CA: Western Tanager Press, 1991.

⊞ BIDWELL–BARTLESON PARTY

See BARTLESON, JOHN; BIDWELL, JOHN

⊞ BILLINGS, MONTANA

The history of Montana's largest city begins in the 1860s. An increasing tide of immigrants crossed the Yellowstone Valley headed for the gold fields of southwestern Montana via the Bozeman Trail. This did not sit well with the Sioux and Cheyenne Indians, who also inhabited the area. Neither tribe wanted to lose additional land and resources to the increasing number of white settlers pushing into the northern plains. Another Indian tribe, the Crows, also valued the area that came to be known as Billings as a traditional hunting and gathering site because of its abundant game. Over the next few months, the Sioux and Cheyenne attacked and killed many settlers in this area and set fire to government forts. Finally, in 1868, the Fort Laramie Treaty officially closed the Bozeman Trail and reserved the Native Americans' seasonal hunting rights throughout the Powder, Tongue, and Bighorn drainages. With this closure, settlement along the Yellowstone screeched to a halt. For the next decade, settlers avoided the area south of the Yellowstone and used steamships on the upper Missouri to travel to such places as Fort Benton and Helena.

Perry W. McAdow, an entrepreneur from Bozeman, became the man that helped develop the Yellowstone Valley. He believed that transportation industry was the key to the settlement and development of the valley. He traveled to the area and noticed that settlers had already begun to use the fertile grounds to grow crops. Settlers moving east from the Gallatin Valley had farmed the flats around the Yellowstone Valley since 1877 and rejoiced at the news that the railroad was coming their way.

In 1882, the Northern Pacific Railroad surveyed the area and began preparations for the coming of the railroad. As the railroad approached the Yellowstone Valley, capitalists linked to the Northern Pacific Railroad Company controlled and profited from the development of town sites. The Northern Pacific sold two sections of land to the Montana and Minnesota Land & Improvement Company. With its prime geographic area, the company established the Billings Townsite Company. They did this to sell plots of land for the building of the town of Billings. Not surprisingly, the largest stockholders of the Montana and Minnesota Land & Improvement Company were the leaders of the Northern Pacific Railroad. These leaders included Heman Clark, general contractor for and president of the Northern Pacific; Frederick Billings, former Northern Pacific president; and Thomas Oakes, Northern Pacific vice president.

Heman Clark eventually became the first president of the Billings Townsite Company.

By May 1882, there were three buildings used as the headquarters to lodge railroad survey crews. The railroad's location at the navigable part of the Yellowstone River made Billings an early trading and shipping point. By the end of 1883, the newspaper reported some 400 buildings and a population of 1,500. Billings was finally incorporated as a city in 1885.

Today, Billings enjoys the title of "Montana's largest city." With an area population of well over 100,000, tourists head to Billings all times of the year. Many historical and cultural points lie within a days drive, including Little Bighorn Battlefield National Monument, Yellowstone National Park, and Pompey's Pillar. Outdoor enthusiasts can backpack in the nearby Beartooth-Absaroka Wilderness and Custer and Gallatin National Forests. Fly-fishing is popular along Rock Creek, Boulder River, Stillwater River, and Yellowstone River. Billings is also home to the Montana Zoo and both a professional hockey and arena football team. Billings has enjoyed a rapid growth rate, supported by various economies, including energy (oil, natural gas, and coal), agriculture (grains such as wheat, barley, and corn; sugar beets; beef and dairy cattle), and transportation (air, rail, and trucking).

—Brandon Davis

Suggested Reading

Van West, Carroll. *Capitalism on the Frontier.* Lincoln: University of Nebraska Press. 1993.

⊞ BISBEE AND DOUGLAS, ARIZONA

Bisbee and Douglas, Arizona, both cities just north of the Mexican border in Arizona, produced roughly 8 billion pounds of copper by 1981 and owe their existence to 19th-century miners. Jack Dunn, a civilian scout accompanying the Sixth U.S. Cavalry, located copper deposits near the Mule Gulch in May of 1877. In December of that year, Hugh Jones, with George Warren, located the mine that came to be named Copper Queen, but Jones abandoned it after not finding silver. Warren lost his one-ninth share during a drunken incident, wagering his share on a foot race against a horse.

Edward Reilly, wanting to investigate the Copper Queen mine but lacking capital, turned to Louis Zeckendorf and Albert Steinfeld. These Tucson merchants loaned Reilly $16,000, enabling him to purchase the rights to the Copper Queen. Reilly went to San Francisco and enlisted John Williams and DeWitt Bisbee, metallurgists and mine developers, and the Martin and Ballard construction firm. Williams and his sons, experienced in copper smelting in South Wales and Michigan, invested $20,000 into the venture and received seven tenths interest in the Copper Queen, while Zeckendorf and Steinfeld retained the rest.

Bisbee started out as a male-dominated camp. One hundred Americans created the open trenches of the first mines. By mid-July 1880, the first furnace arrived; Mexicans worked in smelting, preparing charcoal with Welsh coke for fuel. The town rapidly grew to about 500 people within the first year. A post office was erected; restaurants, mercantile stores, a brewery, and saloons followed. By the turn of the century, families started to arrive, giving the mining district a sense of lasting beyond mining. By 1913, the number of workers of the Bisbee-Douglas region reached 6,000. Bisbee had a cornucopia of peoples, though Chinese were barred by unwritten law or open hostility. Visible class hierarchies existed; Slavic, Serbian, Irish, Welsh, Cornish, Italian, and Hispanic camps were divided from the northern European and American camp. Southern and eastern Europeans had their own camp, while Hispanics had their camp, "tin town." The Calumet and Arizona Company created a planned community in the Warren district, southeast of old Bisbee.

In the fall of 1880, James Douglas urged Zeckendorf and other Copper Queen owners to buy the adjacent Atlanta mine claim. They did not listen, and William E. Dodge, Jr., and D. Willis James, of Phelps, Dodge and Company, bought the Atlanta claim over modern-day Douglas. Unsuccessful at first and investing $80,000 in exploration, the company eventually found rich deposits at 210 feet, assuring the mine's success. To avoid litigation, due to the ore being on part of the Copper Queen property, the Phelps, Dodge and Company bought out the Copper Queen, thinking it had exhausted its ore. Huge investments to improve transportation made this region dominant through the turn of the century under the firm the Copper Queen Consolidated Mining Company. Rails investment connected Douglas and Bisbee, under the Phelps Dodge Corporation. All smelters shifted out to Douglas by the turn of the century.

In 1901, Black Water, Arizona, became Douglass, named after James Douglas. This site eventually became home to the all smelters in the region because of the presence of water. Water also allowed for small-scale ranching in Douglas. By 1904, smelting ended at Bisbee, and newer, more efficient smelters refined the copper of Bisbee and Mexico. These newer smelters came at a cost of $2.5 million. All focus in Bisbee concentrated on mining; rails connected Douglas to Bisbee, facilitating copper smelting and copper transportation. In 1904, a saloon, five hotels, and a street railway filled Douglas. Calumet and Arizona, a new dominating firm, emerged in southern Bisbee and it, too, placed smelters at Douglas. Calumet and Arizona eventually was absorbed during the Depression in order to strengthen Bisbee's Phelps, Dodge and Company. The year 1987 saw the closing of smelters in Douglas. The smelters did not meet air pollution standards, and rather than wasting resources to refit them in a region not mining heavily, Phelps and Dodge shut down permanently.

By 1902, Bisbee's population was 8,000 and Douglas had about 1,000 people. By 1918, the region contained 25,000. One third of the population in Bisbee was English, Irish, Mexican, Finish, Austrian, and Serbian; the rest was American born. Later on, Italian, Germans, Swedes, and Swiss came and joined the population. Mexicans and Italians were at the bottom of the wage scale, working on the surface of mining camps, either smelting or laboring for $1.25 a day. Northern Europeans and American Anglos, on the other hand, earned $3.50 a day in the mines. Bisbee had a small, segregated black community that faced racism. Slovenians, too, faced ostracism as some pushed for labor unions. 1917 was the worst in Bisbee history, as white miners illegally deported almost 2,000 foreign-born miners to New Mexico.

In 1954, the last great pit, the Lavender Pit, opened, but by 1974 its costly nature forced it to shut down. Similar to mining in England and Michigan, cheaper copper from other places forced this operation to cease. To this day, millions of pounds of copper are present, but current techniques make it expensive to extract. In the mid-1960s, half the population disappeared, though mining continued to slow down and stop into the 1980s. The large retirement community in Bisbee is a relic from its mining past. Today, Bisbee's attraction stems from its old buildings and artist village; the economy relies primarily on tourism and supports a population of 6,000.

Douglas, unlike its sister city, still thrives. It is still a ranching center and border station that filters migrants through regularly. Small manufacturing, such as electrical transformers and electronic component production, occurs there. The city is, for the most part, Hispanic (86 percent) and white (12 percent), with a small American Indian population of almost 1.2 percent. Though, in fact, 13 percent of the population are retirement age and another 20 percent are approaching retirement age, it has a diverse population in regard to age. Douglas supports a population of 14,000 and has not diminished but grown, unlike the city that gave it its birth.

—*Eduardo Barrios*

See also ARIZONA COPPER DISCOVERIES

Suggested Reading

Hyde, Charles. *Copper for America: The United States Copper Industry From Colonial Times to the 1990s.* Tucson: University of Arizona Press, 1998.

Nugent, Walter. *Into the West: The Story of Its People.* New York: Knopf, 1999.

Schwantes, Carlos. *Bisbee: Urban Outpost on the Frontier.* Tucson: University of Arizona Press, 1992.

Sheridan, Thomas. *Arizona: A History.* Tucson: University of Arizona Press, 1996.

⌗ BLACK HILLS GOLD RUSH OF 1874

In the fall of 1873, General Philip Sheridan, commander of the Western Division of the Missouri, discussed with President Grant the advisability of establishing a new fort somewhere in the Black Hills of Dakota Territory. The purpose of the fort would be to hold in check the dissident Indian bands located at the Red Cloud and Spotted Tail Agencies. These bands were still reveling in their apparent victory over the whites as symbolized by the Fort Laramie Treaty of 1868. This treaty effectively closed the Bozeman Trail—a *cause célèbre* among the Sioux, which in turn had led to Red Cloud's War and the Fetterman Massacre. With the closure of the Bozeman Trail forts, the Indians felt empowered to dare continued forays against the whites by using the aforementioned agencies as their base of operations for raids as far southeast as Nebraska. Placing a fort in their path might curtail further hostile activity.

Unfortunately for Sheridan, two obstacles must be overcome to see his plan to fruition. First, the Black Hills were nearly dead center in the newly created Great Sioux Reservation and the whole area was not cartographically well known to the U.S. Army surveyors. Second, the Black Hills were incredibly sacred to the Sioux.

Created by the same geologic upheaval that spawned the Rocky Mountains, the limestone and granite cliffs of the Black Hills, with their densely wooded ridges set against the treeless surrounding prairie, were a source of mystery and wonder to the Sioux who first discovered them in the 1770s. Offering wood for teepee poles, clear streams of fresh mountain water, deep canyons where the tribes could withstand the coldest of winters, and abundant game, the Black Hills soon became the center of the Sioux earth, the holy *Paha Sapa*. For whites to trespass on this land would be an act of infamy. Additionally, the whites had officially acknowledged the importance of the Black Hills by ceding the land to the Sioux "for as long as the grass grows and the rivers flow" in the Fort Laramie Treaty.

Not that this mattered much to Sheridan, of "the only good Indian is a dead Indian" fame. Finding the right person to send on this mapping and fact-finding expedition to the heart of Sioux territory was the question. Finally, Sheridan decided to assign the task to George Armstrong Custer.

The golden-haired boy general of the Civil War was an obvious choice. Brash and bold, with a flair for theatricality and an eye for publicity, Custer was the most famous Indian fighter of the era. He had already distinguished himself to Sheridan and won public acclaim for his victory over Black Kettle at the Washita in 1868. Although not actually doing much more than inflicting damage on a sleeping Cheyenne village, Custer had parlayed the "battle" into an epic affair, which now helped him to land this plum assignment. Sheridan may well have banked upon "Yellow Hair's" notoriety to keep the otherwise mercurial Sioux on a low simmer.

In addition to exploring and mapping the area for the army, Custer may well have planned a couple of personal agendas. Always on the lookout for "good press," Custer made sure the expedition was colorful, lighthearted, and newsworthy enough for a write up in the New York *World*. Further, Ben Holladay, the "Stagecoach King," was looking for a way to exploit the Black Hills area in order to set up stage depots, sutler's posts, an Indian agency distribution center for the Department of the Interior, and, as a by-product, towns. In conjunction with Custer and Quartermaster General Rufus Ingalls, Holladay hoped to conveniently be the first person on the spot if *only* the opportunity arose. Could Custer supply such an opportunity?

Indeed, he could, since Custer also pursued a hidden agenda of Sheridan's. Since 1833, rumors had repeatedly surfaced of the presence of gold in the Black Hills. As early as 1861, a group of determined whites had formed the Black Hills Mining and Exploration Association. This band of would-be gold seekers had to be forcibly detained by the army from entering Indian lands for the next decade. However, by 1872, Dakotans were clamoring for the Department of the Interior to remove the Sioux to the eastern side of the Great Reservation—thus leaving the Black Hills open for mining, industry, and town development. Sheridan sought to either confirm or permanently lay to rest the growing gold fever by using the popular Custer as his agent.

Consequently, in the summer of 1874, Custer left Fort Abraham Lincoln, North Dakota, at the head of a two-column expedition composed of nearly 1,000 soldiers, 60 Indian scouts, 2,000 horses, 100 wagons, a 16-piece brass band, 3 Gatling guns, 3 newspaper reporters, and 2 prospector/geologists. Two weeks' march brought them to the Black Hills, where the beauty of the area, the abundance of game, and the timidity of the Sioux tribes encountered turned the assignment into a grandiose picnic. Custer captured specimens of wildlife to generously bequeath to New York's Central Park Zoo. He also downed his first grizzly (with more than a little help from his Indian scouts) and made sure to pose for a photograph taken by one of the newspapermen. Finally, on July 30, 1874, while the troops strolled through a particularly extensive Black Hills glade, which they had nicknamed "Custer Park," one of the geologists, Horatio Nelson Ross, panned a hint of gold out of French Creek. Thus began a drama that played out with all the fatal finality of a Greek tragedy.

The gold rush started with Custer's troops quite literally rushing to the creek, abandoning their rifles, and beginning a frenzied search for wealth. Custer lost no time in sending his scout "Lonesome Charley" Reynolds to Fort Laramie to trumpet the news of gold discovered in the Black Hills. Upon his return to Fort Lincoln, Custer himself told reporters that the reality of his gold find far exceeded all the previous rumors, and actually suggested that would-be gold seekers use nearby Bismarck, North Dakota, as the "jumping off" place for future expeditions.

The consequent invasion of the Black Hills was something of a feeding frenzy. Lured by the myth of instantaneous success rewarding individual effort—a myth fostered, however briefly, by California's gold rush in the 1840s and Nevada's gold and silver rush in the early 1860s—miners ringed the Dakota Territory like hungry wolves. They were barely held at bay by a U.S. Army upholding the letter of the Fort Laramie Treaty while frankly sympathizing with those they kept out. As the number of incidents involving miners slipping through the lines, only to be cautiously escorted out of the area by pursuing troops, increased, the U.S. government was called upon to rescind that portion of the Fort Laramie Treaty which protected the Black Hills.

Red Cloud and Spotted Tail were brought back to Washington, DC, in early 1875 to discuss the possibility of selling the Black Hills to the United States. The Sioux chiefs resolutely refused to give up the *Paha Sapa* and returned home. A commission from Washington was then sent westward to the Dakota Territory to investigate the possibility of either buying outright or at least leasing the Black Hills from the Lakota. The commission met with an assembly of 20,000 Sioux in September of 1875 and attempted to wrangle the Black Hills away from them peacefully. However, the government was in an untenable position. Since the Department of the Interior now handed out rations to some 30,000 Sioux on government agencies operating within the Sioux Reservation, it technically had a duty to protect the Indians as its wards. But since the government also had a duty to protect U.S. citizens now trying to injure U.S. wards by taking away a portion of those wards' property, the government was suffering from a severe conflict of interest.

At any rate, the Indians were not willing to sell, but figured on at least playing the game by *offering* to sell the Black Hills to the United States for the phenomenal (and hopefully impossible) figure of $70 million. The commission balked, but counter-offered the Sioux a lease of the land at $400,000 per year or an outright $6 million purchase payable in 15 installments. After a good laugh, the Sioux flatly refused to either sell or lease the *Paha Sapa*.

The Grant administration threw up its hands in despair and ordered the army to back off on policing the intruding miners. Henceforth, miners would be allowed to enter the Black Hills at their own risk. This action opened the floodgates, and 15,000 miners poured into the area. Miner Alfred Gay founded the town of Gayville in the winter months of early 1876 in an ore-rich Black Hills gulch called Deadwood. By April of the same year, his town had merged with others in the area, and the famed town of Deadwood came into being with a combined population of 7,000. Among the eminent citizens of this boisterous community was former sheriff and sharpshooter James Butler ("Wild Bill") Hickok, who ended his days with a bullet in the back of the head while playing cards in a local saloon. As unofficial center of the Black Hills goldfields, Deadwood contained banks that handled up to $100,000 on a daily basis and boardinghouses that gouged miners $1 a night for the use of a cot.

As the armada of miners increased, so did the likelihood of conflict with hostile Sioux. The U.S. government found itself in the unenviable position of having to protect U.S. citizens illegally trespassing on Indian land, which the U.S. government had, in turn,

promised the Indian it would protect. Since *someone* was bound to lose in this farce, the United States decided to let it be the Sioux. Assuming that most of the depredations against the miners would probably come from the 3,000 or so Sioux under Sitting Bull, Crazy Horse, and Gall, who had not signed the Fort Laramie Treaty of 1868, Washington ordered that these "non-treaty" Lakota come in to the agencies by January 31, 1876, or face military consequences.

The fact that this ultimatum was not prepared for delivery to the hostiles until late in 1875, and never reached them, made little difference. The hostiles would never have come in anyway, and the fact that they did not excused the government from dreaming up another reason for armed engagement.

The tragedy, of course, reached its climax with the army's summer campaign of 1876. Three columns of government troops were assigned to sweep the hostiles back into the agencies by converging on them from the east, west, and south of the valley of the Little Bighorn in southern Montana. The southern column, under George Crook, never made it to the valley. Having engaged the Sioux at the Rosebud on June 17 and, having been repulsed with 28 men killed and 56 wounded, Crook retreated back towards Fort Fetterman and never made the rendezvous with the other columns. The western column, under John Gibbon, stood fast at the Yellowstone River while the eastern column, under Alfred Terry and George Custer, circled south around the hostiles. Custer and Terry were to drive the Sioux northward into Gibbon's waiting clutches. However, the plan backfired. Terry mistakenly allowed Custer and his Seventh Cavalry to reconnoiter the Indian village camped by the Little Bighorn, and Custer, fearing to lose the element of surprise, decided on an attack. Considering his success at the Washita against the Cheyenne, Custer assumed that bravado would once again carry the day. Unfortunately for Custer and the contingent of 225 troopers under his command, he was wrong. On June 25, 1876, some 2,000 combined Sioux and Cheyenne warriors swept over Custer's tiny force and annihilated them to the last man. It was a stunning Indian victory, which the Sioux immediately realized would cost them dearly. Many of the hostiles, including Sitting Bull, headed towards Canada to avoid the U.S.

government's reprisals. The Indians on the reservation were not so lucky.

A new group of commissioners left Washington in the fall of 1876 and, in the wake of the Custer disaster, insisted that the Sioux cede the Black Hills to the United States or lose their winter rations. In the face of threatened starvation, the cowed Lakota gave up their sacred land. Although illegal, since 75 percent of the reservation Indians had not been polled per the terms of the Fort Laramie Treaty, the *Paha Sapa* now belonged to the whites.

By early 1877, another 7,000 miners were scrambling through the Black Hills. Having found a promising lead of quartz in a vein three miles south of Deadwood, Moses and Fred Manuel founded the Homestake Mine and then sold it in 1877 to the San Francisco financial triumvirate of George Hearst, Lloyd Tevis, and James Ben Ali Haggin for $150,000. The California capitalists soon moved to control all the mining and milling in the area and helped to convert the Black Hills gold rush from an individual to a collective industrial effort. As the solitary wildcatting miners died out, so did the boomtowns they created. The colorful prospectors drifted away, to be replaced by a smaller number of wage-earning professionals as the Homestake Mine continued to crank out more bullion than any other American strike. In the century following 1877, the Homestake produced $720 million in gold.

Of all the migrations engendered by the Black Hills gold rush, perhaps the most far-reaching and the most tragic was the migration of the Sioux themselves. In the denouement of the drama created by the gold rush, the Lakota lost their beloved *Paha Sapa*, the majority of the Great Sioux Reservation, and their freedom. As of 1889, they were confined to five agencies—the Standing Rock, Cheyenne River, Pine Ridge, Rosebud, and Lower Brule/Crow Creek—which represented less than half of the original lands ceded to them by the Fort Laramie Treaty. Immigrants from Scandinavia, Russia, and Germany moved into the former Sioux lands to farm and raise cattle where once the buffalo had grazed.

Belatedly, the U.S. Supreme Court offered some measure of apology to the Lakota. In its ruling on *United States v. Sioux Nation of Indians* (1980), the court acknowledged that the U.S. government had acted in bad faith with the Sioux following the Black

Hills gold rush of 1874. By a majority of 8 to 1, the Court voted to award the Sioux nation $17.5 million plus interest, or $106 million, in compensation for its loss. However, in light of the $18 billion in mineral resources extracted from the Black Hills since they were taken from the Sioux, the compensation was still a pittance. In actuality, the most the United States had done was to finally admit before the tribunal of the law and public opinion the extent to which it had allowed a gold rush to influence its policies.

—*Thomas de Martino*

Suggested Reading

Andrist, Ralph. *The Long Death.* New York: Macmillan, 1974.

Barnett, Louise. *Touched by Fire.* New York: Henry Holt, 1996.

Hughes, Richard B. *Pioneer Years in the Black Hills.* Glendale, CA: Arthur H. Clarke, 1957.

Jackson, Donald. *Custer's Gold.* New Haven, CT: Yale University Press, 1966.

Lazarus, Edward. *Black Hills White Justice.* New York: HarperCollins, 1991.

Milner, Clyde A., II, Carol A. O'Connor, and Martha A. Sandweiss, eds. *The Oxford History of the American West.* New York: Oxford University Press, 1994.

Parker, Watson. *Gold in the Black Hills.* Norman: University of Oklahoma Press, 1966.

Stewart, Edgar L. *Custer's Luck.* Norman: University of Oklahoma Press, 1971.

Utley, Robert M. *Cavalier in Buckskin.* Norman: University of Oklahoma Press, 1988.

Wallace, Robert. *The Miners.* Alexandria, VA: Time-Life Books, 1976.

Ward, Geoffrey C. *The West.* Boston: Little, Brown, 1996.

White, Richard. *It's Your Misfortune and None of My Own.* Norman: University of Oklahoma Press, 1991.

⌗ BLACKFOOT NATION

The Blackfoot Indians are a confederation of tribes who, for centuries, lived a nomadic existence on the Great Plains of America and Canada until the coming of white men. According to Blackfoot creation stories, the original people were formed by the Sun Creator and lived near the North Saskatchewan River and the Rocky Mountains. From here, the people prospered, multiplied, and eventually came to populate all of the earth. As the population increased, people began to leave the bands in order to find food; the farther afield they traveled, the more diverse the population became. Eventually, the languages of the people began to change until they no longer spoke the same language, but they found a way to communicate via sign language. Despite this diffusion of their original population, the food provided by the earth was not sufficient. Concerned that his people did not have enough food to eat, the Sun Creator made the buffalo and the lesser animals of the plains to sustain them. From that day forward, the Blackfoot lived a nomadic existence following the herds of buffalo that would soon become central to all aspects of their lives. Eventually, the Blackfoot would come to occupy the land from the North Saskatchewan River in the north, to the Rocky Mountains in the west, to the Milk River in the south, and to the Vermillion River in the east.

Some scholars believe that the Blackfoot, so named because their moccasins were colored black by the ash of their fires, once lived in the woodlands near Eagle Hills, Saskatchewan. Much of this speculation is based on linguistics, as the Blackfoot people are the westernmost of the Algonquin-speaking tribes. According to this tradition, early in the 18th century, immediately before European contact, they moved into the plains in response to pressure exerted by eastern tribes. However, Blackfoot oral tradition does not support this move, and by the time the Blackfoot came into contact with Europeans, no discernable influence of the eastern woodland cultures was noted in their culture. To further erode this tradition, archeological evidence traces the use of Head-Smashed-In Buffalo Jump, in which Indians would drive buffalo herds over a cliff and harvest from the broken remains, in southwest Alberta to 3,000 BCE, while further oral traditions names Old Woman Buffalo Jump, also in southwest Alberta as the place where the marriage between the first man and woman occurred.

The Blackfoot Indians compose a confederacy of three tribes, the Blackfoot or *Siksika,* the Blood or *Kaina,* and the Piegan or *Pikuni.* In the modern day, the Piegan are divided into northern and southern bands, with each band separated from the other by the United States–Canada border. The Southern Piegan are also known in the United States as the Blackfeet.

At the time of European contact, the Blackfoot population was estimated to have between 9,000 to 15,000. Among these diverse yet allied peoples, the buffalo played a central role. Called *ni-ta prowahsini,* or real food, the buffalo was used to make the teepees that the Indians lived in. Its flesh provided the meat that would sustain them through the winter, and its presence would provide them with a comforting reminder of the Sun Creator's favor in providing for his children. All other food was considered inferior to this one staple. Understandably, the Blackfoot existence centered on the tracking, killing, and processing of the buffalo. Whenever possible, tribal bands would stay together while the hunting was good, but just as often would revert back to smaller bands to engage in hunting.

Each band consisted of approximately 50 people, mostly small family groupings whose membership was primarily determined through the father. Each band recognized a civil leader who demonstrated his ability to lead by resolving disputes, maintaining social order, and caring for the poor within the band. Often, this individual had the assistance of a council. While chieftainship was not hereditary, leadership positions often passed from a chief to a close male relative. A leader who did not hold the confidence of his people would be replaced. The Blackfoot also had war chiefs whose leadership was limited to wartime and who relinquished any authority back to the civil leadership when the fighting concluded. Because of the importance buffalo held in their culture, protecting territory was a life and death situation and required constant vigilance. War was not uncommon for the Blackfoot, and their ferocity in battle earned them the respect of tribes who invaded their territory. To further promote stability within their society, the Blackfoot developed war and secret societies. Each society consisted of varying degrees or divisions of rank within the group and had a particular role to play in the preservation of crafts, ceremonies, or tribal order. In this way, the Blackfoot shared equally in the maintenance and stability of their society. By the early 18th century, the world the Blackfoot knew was about to change dramatically.

The first change would impact their nomadic traditions. Prior to European contact, the Blackfoot were dependent on dogs as beasts of burden. By attaching a travois to a dog, the tribes could scour the plains for buffalo. This process limited the number of possessions they could carry and the distance they could travel in a single day. All that changed during an early morning attack around 1731. A party of Shoshone warriors attacked a Piegan camp and won a decisive victory against their traditional enemies while sitting astride what the Piegan assumed were "big dogs." Since the Blackfoot had never seen horses and had not yet had direct contact with Europeans, they identified the horses the Shoshone rode through their own worldview. Concerned that this new animal of the Shoshone would challenge the balance of power on the plains, the Blackfoot enlisted the aid of the eastern Assiniboine and Cree to seek retribution. This alliance introduced another item that would revolutionize life among the plains Indians: the gun. The eastern Assiniboine and Cree had begun recently trading with the European fur traders, providing them with furs in exchange for muskets and household items. For the Plains Indians, the gun would prove to be a significant asset in hunting both their enemies and furs for white men. Armed with these new weapons, the combined forces of the Piegan, Assiniboine, and Cree returned to the Shoshone and routed them, killing at least 50 of the Shoshone warriors.

For the Blackfoot, that early morning raid in 1731 placed them at the confluence of the old and new worlds. Realizing the potential of the goods the Europeans brought, they quickly learned to exploit them. From the west, they obtained horses from those tribes who had stolen them from the Spanish, and from the east they obtained guns from those tribes who had been trading with the English and French. By the middle of the 18th century, the Blackfoot had fully adopted the horse and gun into their culture. This adoption would ensure their survival in the new world of the Europeans, but would also change the culture of all the Plains Indians.

Through trade with the Europeans, the Plains Indians could acquire better weapons and technology to assist them in their daily lives. While the horse allowed them to carry the additional goods they obtained, it also allowed them to move faster to defend their territory or to chase the buffalo. The musket allowed them to forgo the dangerous tradition of running buffalo off cliffs or surrounding them with warriors on foot; instead, they could use their horses to keep pace with the buffalo and shoot at it without exposing themselves to danger.

As the century progressed, the once friendly Cree and Assiniboine began to push into Blackfoot territory in search of more furs to supply the ever-increasing demands of the Europeans. Their incursions forced the Blackfoot to push back against their former friends. In the south, the Shoshone and Crow tribes, and in the west the Kootenai and Flathead had obtained guns, which added a new element of violence to the plains. By the last decades of the 18th century, the Blackfoot no longer relied on intertribal trading for their guns and other European goods and started trading directly with the Hudson's Bay Company, which had constructed a fort on the North Saskatchewan River in 1780. The Blackfoot did not wholly engage in this trade, but did trade horses, buffalo meat and hides, and some furs to the company. Because of their limited participation in the fur trade, the Blackfoot were not encouraged, like the Cree and Assiniboine, to exhaust the game in their territory or to radically alter their subsistence pattern. Blackfoot culture did not encourage the wanton killing of animals; hunting was pursued only to provide sustenance for the tribe.

While they were able to resist the seemingly endless demands of the Europeans to exhaust their land for furs, the Blackfoot were defenseless against the diseases that whites brought with them to the New World. In 1781, a Piegan war party came upon a Shoshone village with seemingly no defenses. At dawn, the Piegan attacked, but instead of being repulsed by the Shoshone warriors, they were greeted with little resistance. The Shoshone camp had already been attacked by smallpox, and the Piegan warriors had arrived to witness the death throes of the village. Undaunted, the Piegan collected war trophies and returned to their village, spreading the disease. By the time the smallpox epidemic had finished ravaging the Blackfoot, an estimated one half of their people had died. Because of their limited contact with the Europeans, the Blackfoot recovered from the epidemic while other Plains tribes struggled. Seizing this advantage, the Blackfoot attacked their traditional enemies, the Shoshone, and forced them further south. They also attacked the Kootenai and Flathead, forcing them to retreat to the west of the Rocky Mountains. By the turn of the 19th century, the Blackfoot, according to trapper Alexander Henry, were "the most independent and happy people of all the tribes E. [east] of the Rocky Mountains."

The happiness the Blackfoot enjoyed would soon be tempered by the continued encroachment of the Europeans. In the spring of 1804, Meriwether Lewis and William Clark were dispatched by President Jefferson to explore the new lands that had been acquired in the Louisiana Purchase in 1803. By July 1806, the Corps of Discovery had completed the bulk of their exploration and were nearing home when they encountered a band of eight Piegan warriors who were herding approximately 30 horses back to their camp. Lewis took this chance meeting as an opportunity to explain who they were and that they had made peace treaties with the Shoshone and the Nez Perce. In exchange, these tribes would be provided weapons and the support of the United States. Since the Shoshone were traditional enemies of the Blackfoot people, Lewis's declaration, although intended to encourage the Blackfoot to also sign a peace treaty, instead had the opposite effect. The United States had allied itself with the Blackfoot's enemies; therefore, they became an enemy of the Blackfoot. Later that evening, to prevent weapons from falling into the hands of their enemies, the Blackfoot braves tried to steal the corps' weapons and run off their horses. A battle ensued, and two of the warriors were killed. Lewis's naiveté regarding the relationships between the Indians of the plains and their neighbors would have a prolonged, negative effect on relations between the Blackfoot Indians and the Americans for the next 20 years. From that day forward, any attempt by an American to move into Blackfoot territory was met with hostility.

The importance of the encounter between the Lewis and Clark expedition and the Blackfoot underscores the growing importance of European technology and goods to the evolving cultures of the plains. The goods the Europeans brought were a double-edged sword for the Blackfoot. While the horse and the gun allowed them to enjoy a new authority in the region, they also led to increased hostility among once friendly tribes over territorial claims. For those who had been traditional enemies, war became more frequent and bloodier. By the early 19th century, pressure from the once friendly Cree and Assiniboine Indians had forced the Piegan to the foothills of the Rocky Mountains and along the Missouri River.

For the most part, the Blackfoot Indians tried to retain the advantages they had gained as one of the few tribes that had adopted the gun and the horse at the same time. Aware of the significant advantage these new innovations gave them, the tribes attempted to stop the British from giving guns to other Indians in the region by blocking those tribes from crossing their territory to get to the trading forts. However, the profits to be made in the fur trade, both by Indian and European alike, rendered this attempt moot. New routes were blazed, and by the first decade of the 19th century the Flathead Indians—traditional enemies of the Blackfoot—had obtained muskets. In 1810, they attacked the Blackfoot and enjoyed a rare victory over their enemy. For the Flathead, it would be a Pyrrhic victory; the Blackfoot ruthlessly pursued a campaign to exterminate the Flathead to keep them from gaining a foothold in their territory. By the 1830s, the Blackfoot had almost succeeded in their goal.

The year 1810 would also mark the permanent settlement of whites in Blackfoot territory when American fur traders built a fort on the Missouri River. Still smarting from their earlier contact with Lewis and Clark, the Blackfoot did not passively accept this incursion into their land, and attacked the fort. By 1823, the Blackfoot were successful in forcing a group of trappers from the Missouri Fur Company to abandon their activities along the Missouri River. It appeared the Blackfoot would be successful in keeping others out of their territory. However, in 1831, the transgressions of the Americans were mollified when Kenneth McKenzie of the American Fur Company made peace with the Blackfoot and was allowed to build a fort on the upper Missouri River. The fort could provide the weapons and goods that the Blackfoot now depended on. In return, McKenzie agreed to keep the white men out of Blackfoot territory in return for the rights to buy buffalo hides and sell alcohol to the Indians. McKenzie's strategy weaned the Blackfoot from trading with the British, who still had their fort on the Saskatchewan River, and introduced alcohol to the Indians. McKenzie's fort also reintroduced smallpox to the Blackfoot. In 1837, a cargo vessel headed to the fort brought the disease back to a susceptible population. By the time the epidemic was over, approximately two thirds of the Blackfoot, or about 6,000 people had died.

With their numbers decimated by disease, once more the Blackfoot were unable to withstand the next challenge to their territory. By the middle of the 19th century, the trade in buffalo hides had increased and white hunters began entering Blackfoot territory. The introduction of more whites to their land resulted in another smallpox epidemic in 1849. Their population dwindling, the Blackfoot began to engage in a significant number of intermarriages between trappers and women of the Southern Piegan and the Blood tribes. By 1855, undoubtedly due to the influence of these newcomers and the assault on their population, the Blackfoot Indians entered into their first treaty with the United States government. They agreed to set the boundaries of their territory so whites could build a railroad. In return, they were guaranteed access to their hunting grounds and annuity payments to compensate them for the loss of their lands. However, the promises made by the federal government would prove to be hollow ones. Realizing that they would not make a profit unless settlers could purchase lands near the rail lines, the railroad company encouraged settlement on the lands that had been promised to the Blackfoot. The federal government did not move to stop them.

By 1864, Montana had been granted territorial status and settlers began to cross its borders. With the influx of new settlers, another epidemic, this time of measles struck the Blackfoot. This incursion was made worse when, in 1866, gold was discovered in the mountains, which provoked an all-out war with the Blackfoot. Settlers petitioned the government to redraft the treaties in order to gain additional territorial concessions, and in 1865 and again in 1869 new agreements were made with the Blackfoot regarding territorial designations, but neither treaty was ratified. In an attempt to control the continuing hostility between whites and Indians, the first Blackfoot agency was created at Fort Benton. However, its inception coincided with another smallpox epidemic that struck the Blackfoot in 1869. According to the first census taken by the agency, from the once vast numbers of the

Blackfoot, now only 15 bands of Piegan, nine bands of Blood, and nine bands of Blackfoot Indians remained. With the Blackfoot population decimated, whites began to demand more land concessions and, in some cases, the eradication of the tribe. Their demands merged with President Ulysses Grant's "Peace Policy," an ill-conceived policy that allowed the Indians to be educated and civilized by religious groups with the intention that they would eventually abandon their native culture and embrace white ways. Predictably, the Indians were not consulted regarding this plan and reacted with some hostility toward it.

The year 1869 also marked the year many of the Blackfoot people, decimated by disease, corralled on a squalid reservation, or attacked by whites simply because of who they were, reached their breaking point. A band of warriors led by a Piegan war chief named Mountain Chief killed a white trader in Blackfoot territory. When word of the killing reached the U.S. Army command, Philip Sheridan dispatched Major Eugene Baker to either capture or kill Mountain Chief. When word reached Baker that the Piegan had camped along the Marias River, they set off to fulfill their mission. However, by the time they arrived, Mountain Chief and his band had already moved on. Instead of pursuing Mountain Chief, Baker and his men set their sights on another band of Piegan Indians who had camped at Willow Rounds, also along the Marias River. On January 23, 1870, Baker and his men attacked a camp led by Heavy Runner. It could not have been a more one-sided battle. Heavy Runner's band consisted mostly of women and children and had been severely weakened by the recent smallpox outbreak. Despite the obvious absence of Indian men in the encampment, Baker ordered his troops to attack. By the time the gunfire ended, 173 Indians lay dead and 140 more had been taken captive. Predictably, most of the victims were women and children. The reckless slaughter of so many innocents and the seemingly redundant epidemics that followed the advancement of whites into their territory caused many of the Blackfoot to withdraw from territory they held in the United States in preference for settlements in Canada. With many of the Blackfoot abandoning their territory in Montana, the U.S. government moved to take advantage of their migration. In 1873 and again in 1874, President Grant issued an executive order reducing the territorial claims of the Blackfoot people. Driven from their homes, the Blackfoot should have been safe from further incursions by Americans, but they were not.

Aware that the land the Blackfoot had retreated to was almost wholly lacking in oversight by the Canadian government, Americans traders followed the Blackfoot and established trading posts in their territory where they exchanged furs for alcohol. With an approximate population of 10,000, considerable money was still to be made from this once venerable enemy. So prolific was this business that, by 1873, an estimated 25 percent of the surviving Blackfoot tribe had died as a result of alcohol. At this rate, the Indians would be extinct before the turn of the new century. In 1874, the Canadian government moved to regain control of their territory from the Americans by establishing the Northwest Mounted Police. Within a few years, the trade in alcohol had been largely stopped and the Blackfoot people began to recover again from their contact with the whites. So profound was the change that, in 1877, the Canadian government approached the Blackfoot with a treaty proposal in which they would abandon their claims to land south of the forty-ninth parallel in return for lands in Canada. Without negotiations, the treaty was accepted and the Blackfoot chose a reserve on the Bow River, while the Blood settled on the Belly River and the Northern Piegan in the Porcupine Hills. Only the Southern Piegan refused to relinquish their land in the United States. While bands of Blackfoot continued to move freely over the border between the United States and Canada, the treaty had effectively reduced the number of Indians in the Great Plains; this demographic shift led to further calls to reduce the lands still claimed by native people.

The reduction in the human population was not the only significant change in the region. By the last decades of the 19th century, the Great Plains of the United States were largely void of the herds of buffalo that had once roamed the land. Their demise, the concerted effort of the government to annihilate the one common food source of the Plains Indians, would almost result in the destruction of the Southern Piegan. In 1883, 600 Piegan reportedly starved to death because there were no buffalo left to hunt. Since previous

treaties with the United States gave the Blackfoot and the Flathead most of western Montana, their newly reduced numbers again made them a likely choice for further land concessions. In 1884, Congress attempted to officially determine the extent of the Southern Piegan Reservation; failing this, in 1888 they ratified another agreement that provided the Southern Piegan with a reduced reservation. However, these concessions were still not enough. In 1895, the Southern Piegan numbered only 1,400 members, with their numbers continuing to contract, Congress again looked to reduce their territory. By 1896, an agreement was reached with the tribe to relinquish their western territory in exchange for $1.5 million. The land that they relinquished would eventually become Glacier National Park.

The most devastating method of forcing territorial concessions, however, was not from congressional fiat. It came with the Dawes Allotment Act in 1887 (also known as the General Allotment Act). Intended as a way of saving the Indian from extinction, the act proposed the division of Indian reservations into individual allotments. Each Indian would be given an allotment and encouraged to abandon their nomadic traditions by either farming or ranching. To prevent Indians from falling victim to unscrupulous whites, the allotee would be unable to sell the land for 25 years, during which time he would presumably learn to husband the land. Whatever lands had not been allotted would then be sold to whites. In this way, the rapidly dwindling numbers of Indians could be assimilated into white culture, and through that adoption, the remnants of their race would be saved. In reality, the Dawes Allotment Act was little more than a land grab. It made no provisions for the expansion of the native people in America and its eventual goal was the total destruction of native culture either by complete assimilation into white culture or through the demise of the native people. From 1907 to 1912, the allotment of lands that had previously been held in common with the Southern Piegan, or Blackfeet, began. Not satisfied with the rapidity of the land change, in 1918, the almost 2,200 Blackfeet Indians who had been granted allotments were allowed to dispose of their allotments before they had reached their 25-year mark.

In Canada, the allotment of native lands did not occur, but the generous provisions of the treaty the government made with the Blackfoot in 1877 came under fire as more whites moved into Alberta. In 1907, 1911, and again in 1918, the Blackfoot were forced to make territorial concession to the Canadian government, and in 1909 the Northern Piegan were also forced to relinquish some of their land to incoming whites. Only the Blood Indians have been able to retain the territory originally set aside for them in the 1877 treaty.

The miserable conditions the Blackfoot were forced to withstand only got worse with World War I. While the war had initially increased the cost of food products and livestock—and subsequently profits—the postwar recession that followed stole what little success the Blackfoot had earned. Coupled with a persistent drought and severe winters from 1917 to 1920, the profits that the farmers in the north once enjoyed evaporated. As the Blackfoot farmers struggled, many were forced to sell their allotments. It appeared that the land that had been theirs for centuries would eventually pass from the hands of the remaining Blackfoot into the hands of the whites. What the Indians needed was a champion; they found that champion in John Collier, the newly appointed head of the Bureau of Indian Affairs.

In 1934, Collier succeeded in getting legislation passed that would halt the further division of Indian land for allotment and stop any pending land sales. Additionally, native people were encouraged to form their own governments to determine how their tribes would be administered and to take pride in their cultural heritage by learning their native language and resurrecting traditional practices that had been discouraged under the whites. Called the Indian Reorganization Act (IRA), Collier's controversial plan was met with resistance by both Indian and white alike. While the merits of the IRA have been debated since it was passed, its primary benefit was to stop the further erosion of Native lands. While many Native peoples refused to organize a tribal government under the provisions set up by the IRA, the Blackfoot people adopted a tribal constitution and elected a governing council.

The next great challenge that faced the Blackfoot people was the same that faced the nation as a whole, World War II. Imbued with a warrior heritage, members of the Blackfoot nation entered the war in numbers disproportionate to their numbers in society and distinguished themselves as brave and able fighters. In the north, few of the Canadian Blackfoot chose to enter the war, as they were more isolated on their reservations than their brethren in the United States. However, for the Blackfoot, as with all encounters with white society, what initially seemed like a good idea would have negative ramifications for the tribe as a whole. As Blackfoot warriors returned to the United States, they came with training that would allow them to escape the poverty of the reservation and enjoy some of the benefits of white society. The GI Bill of Rights granted them funds for housing and an education, something that would be difficult to obtain had they remained on the reservation. To encourage Indians to leave their reservations, the U.S. government provided financial and employment assistance for Indians. What it did not provide was assistance for those wishing to return. This policy would eventually be formalized in 1953 in Public Law 108, which called for the termination of federal custodianship of tribes.

The unfortunate provisions of PL 108 called for the termination of federal oversight in the management of tribal lands and industries. Prior to 1953, Indians had not been given the opportunity to learn to manage their assets. The new law was tantamount to another Dawes Act. If tribes were unable to manage their assets, they would be lost without hope for assistance from the government. Many of the provisions of PL 108 were not put into effect, and the paternalistic behavior of the government continued.

By 1969, a review of the housing on the Blackfoot Reservation revealed that only 32 percent of the housing was up to modern standards. It reflected the degraded conditions of all aspects of Blackfoot life. Indians who lived on the reservation were significantly more likely to suffer poor health, in part because of alcoholism, poor nutrition, or lack of access to healthcare. Life expectancy by extension was considerably shorter than for the average white American. Educational and employment opportunities were almost nonexistent. To combat the neglect by the government and to care for their own people, the Blackfoot began to bring small industries onto the reservation in the 1960s. This provided employment and hope to the tribal members, and gave more of them a reason to stay on the reservation, which further preserved their traditional culture. By the 1970s, classes in the Blackfoot language and traditions were being held on the reservations and, in 1976, the

Blackfeet Community College opened its doors to educate a new generation. Since that time, the Red Crow College on the Blood Reservation and the Old Sun Campus of the Mount Royal College in Calgary opened on the Blackfoot Reservation in Canada. Through the education of their members, the Blackfoot culture has reemerged. Today, the Blackfoot population is approximately 32,000 people, with almost 15,000 of those counted living in the United States. The hope of the Blackfoot people in both Canada and the United States is to continue to explore all aspects of their traditional history and culture while still living in a modern world.

—*Vanessa Ann Gunther*

See also ASSINIBOINE; GALLATIN VALLEY, MONTANA; GROS VENTRE

Suggested Reading

Bullchild, Percy. *The Sun Came Down: The History of the World as My Blackfeet Elders Told It.* San Francisco: Harper & Row, 1985.

Carlson, Paul H. *The Plains Indians.* College Station: Texas A & M University Press, 1998.

Ewers, John Canfield. *The Blackfeet Raiders on the Northwest Plains.* Norman: University of Oklahoma Press, 1983.

Hungry Wolf, Beverly. *The Ways of My Grandmothers.* New York: Quill, 1982.

McClintock, Walter. *Old Indian Trails: An Authentic Look at Native American Life and Culture by the Adopted Son of a Blackfoot Chief.* New York: Houghton Mifflin, 1923.

Rosier, Paul C. *Rebirth of the Blackfeet Nation, 1912–1954.* Lincoln: University of Nebraska Press, 2001.

Utley, Robert M. *The Indian Frontier of the American West 1846–1890.* Albuquerque: University of New Mexico Press, 1984.

Wissler, Clark, and D. C. Duvall. *Mythology of the Blackfoot Indians.* Lincoln: University of Nebraska Press, 1995.

⊞ BLOOM, JESSIE S.
(1887–1980)

Jessie Spiro Bloom was born on December 17, 1887, in Dublin, Ireland, to Leon and Olga Spiro. At the age of 21, she left home to begin work as a secretary in London, England, the first of her many adventures. While in London, Bloom became involved in the growing women's suffrage movement—participating in rallies and distributing prosuffrage newspapers. In 1909, she joined the Women's Suffrage League (WSL) in working towards passage of a suffrage law. Her advocacy for women became a life-long passion.

In 1910, Jessie met Robert L. Bloom, a second cousin, while both were vacationing in Dublin. Two years later, the couple married and soon after immigrated to Alaska. Robert was born on October 15, 1878, in Siaulie, Lithuania. His family moved to Dublin when he was eight years old. At the age of 19, he joined the gold rush in Alaska, and like so many unfortunate prospectors, had little success. Subsequently, he traveled to Seattle, Washington, in search of work to earn funds to be able to return to Alaska. He managed to save enough to return to Fairbanks in 1904, and established a general merchandise and hardware store. Robert was successful enough to afford a vacation back to Dublin, where he met his future wife, and subsequently brought her back to Alaska.

Once they had immigrated to Alaska, the couple succeeded in contributing to and enriching their local community. The couple cofounded the Fairbanks Airplane Company and in 1925 Jessie became one of the first women in Alaska ever to ride in an airplane. She also established the first kindergarten in Fairbanks in 1918. Jessie organized Alaska's first Girl Scout Troop in 1926, and the Girl Scout Training Center located there is named in her honor. The couple was also well known for their conservation efforts in Alaska. They were passionate supporters of campaigns to set aside wildlife preserves and opposed projects that could pose a threat to the state's natural environment

The Blooms also played an integral role in building and promoting Alaska's Jewish community. Robert served as chairman of the Jewish Welfare Board, and the couple served as unofficial chaplains for Jewish servicemen stationed in Alaska during World War II. Later, Robert was a member of an advisory board that helped raise support for an air force base in Alaska.

The Blooms also raised a family in Alaska. They had four daughters: Meta Buttnick, Dr. Olga Bloom Backer, Dr. Deborah Kaplan, and Ruth Ibbetson. Following World War II, the family—Jessie Bloom, her husband, and their four children—finally settled in Seattle. Robert died there in April of 1974 at the age of 95. Jessie remained in Seattle, in close contact with the friends, activities, and causes she had left behind in Alaska, until her death in December of 1980 at the age of 92.

—*Scott M. Behen*

Suggested Reading

Congregation Or HaTzafon. "Temple History Or HaTzafon: A Profile." Available from http://www.mosquitonet.com/~orhatzafon/history.htm#temple

Girl Scouts USA. "Farthest North Girl Scout Council, Council History." Available from http://home.gci.net/~fngsc/TLM_Council_History.htm

Jacob Rader Marcus Center of the American Jewish Archives. "An Inventory to the Robert and Jessie Bloom Papers, Manuscript Collection No. 93 1897–1980. 5.2 Linear Ft." Available from http://www.huc.edu/aja/Bloom.htm

Jewish Women's Archive. "Personal Information for Jessie S. Bloom." Available from http://www.jwa.org/archive/jsp/perInfo.jsp?personID=338

⌗ BOISE, IDAHO

After prospectors discovered gold in the Boise Basin in the summer of 1862, thousands of miners rushed to the area that fall to prepare for operations the following year. Some entrepreneurs realized that the miners needed supplies and sought to develop a community to meet the miners' requirements in southwestern Idaho. Many of these early inhabitants were from California or Oregon, with lesser numbers from Nevada, Colorado, and British Columbia. Simultaneously, wagon trains continued their journey westward through southern Idaho on their way to the Pacific coast. Some of these families remained in Idaho, as they realized that the numerous miners provided a ready market for farmers. The military helped spur the growth of the city by finally approving the construction of Fort Boise in 1863, which also determined the site of the new town. Fort Boise later helped sustain the town during years in which dropping mineral prices devastated the mining industry.

Boise soon took on an aura of permanence, as by the end of 1863, 135 women and 74 children lived in the town. Only Lewiston possessed a similar proportion of families at this early stage. Boise sought to expand its influence beyond that as a regional supply center. Consequently, city leaders sought to transfer the territory's capital from Lewiston to Boise. Lewiston's position continued to grow weaker as its mining industry declined, giving Boise an opportunity. Much to the chagrin of Lewiston's residents, an 1864 resolution moved the capital to Boise. Refugees from Missouri helped give the town Confederate sympathies. Many of these refugees made their home in or near Boise because their supplies ran out, preventing them from continuing their westward flight.

Given the relatively small size of the town, Boise had difficulty attracting railroads. The city wanted the railroad to bring in more people and to expand its trade. However, Boise had to wait until September of 1887 to receive rail service. The expanded service helped Boise increase its population to around 6,000 after 1890.

While some Chinese came to Boise around 1865, completion of the transcontinental railroad created a large number of Chinese in search of work. Many found their way to Idaho. By the 1880s, Boise's Chinatown was the largest in the intermountain region. Idaho's first federal census of 1870 found 4,274 Chinese in the territory, with the majority located in the Boise Basin. The 1882 Chinese Exclusion Act prevented additional Chinese from entering the United States. Some of the Chinese worked as laundrymen, while others worked as truck gardeners. Other Chinese worked as cooks, and by the 1890s some even opened their own restaurants. Regardless of the discrimination that the Chinese faced from white workers, Boise's merchants, landlords, and county officials often supported the Chinese and sought to bring in even more of them to stimulate business and collect additional tax revenue.

After 1870, Basques began arriving in Boise. Though few had experience in shepherding in their homeland in the Pyrenees, many found work in this industry and won a reputation as excellent herders. The Basques could excel at sheepherding, as it did not require any knowledge of English. The Spanish government's increased repression of the Basques after they supported the Carlists in the war of 1872–1876 drove emigration. While many Basques eventually returned home, others remained, and some purchased sheep of their own or moved into other occupations. This was especially true for the second-generation Basques. Consequently, the government started to reduce the Basques' autonomy after the war. The Basques faced similar persecution from Franco in the 20th century, as he wanted to impose Castilian Spanish on all Spaniards to ensure unity.

A number of German immigrants also made Boise their home. The Germans were also among the earliest settlers in the region. Many of these Germans did not come directly to Idaho. Instead, they usually stopped in midwestern states before moving to Idaho. While the height of Germany immigration to the United States came in 1882, this trend did not make itself apparent in Idaho until around 1910. At this point, the opening of the state's Indian reservations provided additional land and probably helped attract German-born immigrants residing in other parts of the country. By World War I, the Germans made up the largest ethnic group in Boise, but wartime fears led to distrust of the immigrants. These fears prompted the Germans to disband their *Turnverein,* a club that promoted physical activity and patriotism.

Idaho also hosted a small Jewish community as evidenced by the opening of its first synagogue in 1895. Boise's Jewish community originally contained immigrants largely from Western Europe, but as more Eastern European immigrants came to the United States, the composition of Boise's Jewish population also changed.

Few African Americans made their way to Boise during the mining rushes. A combination of legislation and discrimination kept them away. However, the availability of jobs eventually created a small African American community in Boise in the early decades of the 20th century. Interestingly, the city's population of African American females outnumbered the males in 1920, even though the state itself had two black males for every female. Even after the arrival of additional blacks in the Northwest during the 1940s, Idaho's black population doubled to only around 1,000 people around 1950, but most of this growth took place in Pocatello.

During the 1960s, Boise received additional growth as young people moved off of family farms and into medium-sized cities. By the late 1970s and early 1980s, the population experienced further growth. In the closing decades of the 20th century, about one third of Boise's new citizens came from California. The city brought in additional jobs and people with its lower cost of homes, minimal taxes, and low crime rate. While the city held 34,000 people in 1960, it surpassed 215,000 by the early 1990s. During the years 1990 through 1996, Boise was the fourth fastest-growing metropolitan area in the United States. The influx of Californians did not bring much, if any, cultural diversity to Idaho. Instead, many of the new arrivals held conservative views, reinforcing rather than challenging Boise's political and cultural makeup. However, Boise also saw the growth of a gay community, as some believed that its urban setting would allow for greater tolerance than the towns they came from. Finally, the presence of Vietnamese and Asian Indians indicates that immigrants continue to choose Boise as their destination.

—*Robert Miller*

See also BASQUE AMERICANS; CHINESE EXCLUSION ACT; LEWISTON AND COEUR D'ALENE, IDAHO

Suggested Reading

Hart, Arthur A. *The Boiseans: At Home.* Boise: Historic Idaho, 1992.

Hart, Arthur A. *Chinatown: Boise, Idaho, 1870–1970.* Boise: Historic Idaho, 2002.

Mercier, Laurie, and Carole Simon-Smolinski, eds. *Idaho's Ethnic Heritage: Historical Overviews.* 2 vols. Boise: Idaho Ethnic Heritage Project, 1990.

Nugent, Walter. *Into the West: The Story of Its People.* New York: Knopf, 1999.

Wells, Merle. *Boise: An Illustrated History.* Woodland Hills, CA: Windsor, 1982.

Zhu, Liping. *A Chinaman's Chance: The Chinese on the Rocky Mountain Mining Frontier.* Niwot: University Press of Colorado, 1997.

BORDER PATROL

See IMMIGRATION AND NATURALIZATION SERVICE (INS)

BOYLE HEIGHTS, CALIFORNIA

Boyle Heights constitutes an area on the southeastern edge of Los Angeles within the city's original boundaries. Inspired by the arrival of a railroad in Los Angeles and its transcontinental connection and prompted by potential profit resulting from subdivision, an early Los Angeles resident began efforts to develop a community on the eastside. Subsequently, the rail nexus generated a real estate and population "boom" that established Boyle Heights as a community within, yet somewhat separate from, the city of Los Angeles.

By 1920, its residents included natives from 42 nations, 48 states, and the territory of Hawaii, encompassing an eclectic socioeconomic neighborhood of peddlers, merchants, laborers, professionals, and capitalists. Contradicting experiences in other major U.S. cities with large immigrant populations, in Boyle Heights most residents lived in single-family homes with a negligible number of lodgers, roomers, or boarders. With few exceptions, children did not work and attended local, unsegregated schools whose pupils reflected a mosaic of ethnically and socially diverse backgrounds.

The physical location of Boyle Heights provided defined boundaries, initially and throughout the first several decades of its existence, which contributed to the neighborhood's uniqueness. Dated 1849, Los Angeles City Map No. 1 shows the "Plan de la Ciudad de Los Angeles" and depicts the area east of the Los Angeles River as totally barren, without indication of a single building or area of cultivation. One hundred years later, man-made commercial and residential structures and developments dotted the neighborhood's landscape, but its defined boundaries maintained the separateness of Boyle Heights from Los Angeles and surrounding communities.

Beginning late in the 19th century along its northern border, the neighborhood of Lincoln Park evolved; later still, builders constructed Ascot Speedway and the California Zoological Gardens just north of the Southern Pacific Railroad tracks. Over time, the eastern boundary of Los Angeles remained unchanged and thus established the limits of the eastward expansion of Boyle Heights. The completion of the Atchison, Topeka, and Santa Fe Railway (AT&SF) into Los Angeles in March 1886 established another barrier, as its lines followed the Los Angeles riverbed along the neighborhood's western edge. At the southern city limits of Los Angeles and boundary of Boyle Heights, the Southern Pacific (SP) and the Los Angeles and Salt Lake (LASL) Railroads followed an east-west route while a separate SP line followed a north-south direction. Dividing the two, the AT&SF covered a southeast-northwest trajectory into Whittier and beyond.

At its western and eastern edges, street angles changed markedly but uniformly along the river and Indiana Street, further establishing the neighborhood's boundaries. Also helping to maintain the community's distinct perimeters, the separate communities of Belvedere and the short-lived Shorb precinct developed beyond Indiana Street on the east. Presently, a grid of streets in Boyle Heights retains a noticeable bend at its edges.

Today, as before, the surrounding neighborhoods of downtown on the west, Lincoln Heights on the north, Belvedere on the east, and Vernon on the south serve to maintain a sense of separateness for residents of Boyle Heights. Adjoining the city and Boyle Heights at the southern boundary, the town of Vernon incorporated in 1905. Built on property that had originally belonged to the Lugo family, Vernon abutted the southeastern edge of the original boundaries of Los Angeles. It never became a heavily populated community, but it developed a concentration of industry with various types of manufacturing establishments, differentiating it from adjacent neighborhoods. The paucity of population and its industrialized build up, with lumberyards and packinghouses, more than anything else, contributed to the demarcation of Vernon from the neighboring community of Boyle Heights.

On the eastern border of Boyle Heights, Belvedere Gardens originated during the first decade of the 20th century. Its population swelled by the late 1920s with thousands of Mexican Americans and immigrant Mexicans, which made it the most densely populated Latino neighborhood in Los Angeles County. Nevertheless, over time, the perimeters of Boyle Heights remained unchanged, setting it apart and contributing to the unification of its neighborhood.

Today's Boyle Heights can further be described as the area west of the Los Angeles riverbed, bisected by several freeways: Santa Ana and Golden State Freeway (5), Hollywood Freeway (101), San Bernardino Freeway (10), and Pomona Freeway (60). East of present-day Boyle Heights, the Long Beach Freeway (710) divides the neighborhood of City Terrace from the city of Monterey Park. Today's intersection of Indiana Street and Olympic Boulevard mark the southeast corner of the original Los Angeles city limits. Indiana Street divided Boyle Heights from Belvedere; Washington and Olympic Boulevards separated Boyle Heights from Vernon, and Alhambra Avenue isolated Boyle Heights from Lincoln Heights. Community life centered around Hollenbeck Park, although later freeway construction decisively marred the community when the Golden State freeway was built through the neighborhood.

Contrary to a popular image of Boyle Heights as a Jewish community during the first half of the 20th century, Los Angeles's eastside neighborhood developed from a multicultural beginning and continued to remain ethnically diverse throughout the first 100 years of its existence. Eastside residents and land speculators, many of whom held instrumental positions on Los Angeles City boards, initiated infrastructure construction, which spurred the growth and expansion of Boyle Heights simultaneous with the population booms. Initial plans for the community to become an affluent residential area deteriorated after the first few years of subdivisions and property promotions, resulting in a neighborhood that by 1920 welcomed a host of migrants and immigrants from across the globe.

The eastside area remained unsettled for several years after American control in 1848 and statehood for California in 1850 because of its position on the bluffs above the Los Angeles River and lack of access due to its location on the east side of the river. Nevertheless, this situation changed in 1857 when an Irish immigrant, Andrew Boyle, took interest in the area and purchased land along the bluffs and built a residence there. Boyle's American son-in-law, William Workman, also moved to the east side of the river and named the area for Boyle. Workman worked in downtown Los Angeles, so he realized the need for easy access. Because he also served on the Los Angeles City Council, his connections enabled development. Although he, at first, envisioned an upscale neighborhood, Workman's subdivisions drew both rich and poor, American and immigrant.

From its beginning, the neighborhood reflected a diverse population, partly because many of its wealthier land owners employed household and agricultural laborers—most of whom came from China, Europe, and Mexico. In the early years, circumstances forced the laborers to reside within the neighborhood because of its isolation. This seclusion developed because no bridge or transportation facility connected Boyle Heights with downtown. This situation caused laborers and the city's elite to live side-by-side and prompted the multicultural neighborhood that developed.

In a 1973 publication, journalist Carey McWilliams commented that in 1880 Boyle Heights provided a "fashionable" address for its residents. The John Hollenbeck mansion on Boyle Avenue validates Williams' assessment. William Hayes Perry's luxurious home on Pleasant Avenue also supports this contention. Perry and a partner owned a lumber company; in 1880, his household included a wife, four children, and a Chinese cook. Herman Betts Benedict, a native of New York, also resided in Boyle Heights in 1880; a merchant, he served as mayor of Booneville, Missouri, for two terms prior to migrating to Los Angeles where he retired. He purchased considerable acreage in the neighborhood as a real estate investment and built an impressive residence on New York (later East Third) Avenue.

However, the 1880 U.S. census manuscript population schedules permit another observation, as these demonstrate that members of all social classes resided in the neighborhood. Day laborers and capitalists contributed not only to the varied social framework, but also constituted an entrenched multicultural standing. A census enumerator listed 40 families in Boyle Heights in 1880; these families include Chinese, California- and Mexican-born Hispanics, transplanted Americans, and European immigrants. They lived scattered throughout the neighborhood. Occupations of the residents also varied. For instance, on Boyle Avenue resided the family of Jose Valencia, a native of Mexico, who worked as a dairyman; five Chinese male gardeners; orchardist and city councilman William Henry Workman, along with his family and servants; and the retired merchant Felix Mancho, a native of Spain, who resided with his Cuba-born wife, his Nicaragua-born daughter, and a Nicaragua-born servant.

Additional listings reveal that, in the Boyle Heights section of Los Angeles, neither native-born nor ethnic immigrants clannishly isolated themselves. Rather, they scattered loosely throughout the neighborhood.

This circumstance continued over the next few decades. Thus, the social and cultural intermingling was much greater than previously realized.

Earlier federal census enumerations also depict Latino families living in the eastside area as early as the 1860s: in the district along Gallardo and Mission Road, upon the bluffs near Andrew Boyle's residence, and along the east side of the Los Angeles River. These were not separate Hispanic settlements in any decade between 1860 and 1930. During this time, in the midst of several Latino families, non-Hispanic, native-born Americans and immigrants also resided. Not only did these residents' ethnic backgrounds vary, but their occupations also ranged from professional to unskilled labor.

Between the 1880s and the 1920s, immigrants to America increased the nation's population by millions; the majority came from southern and eastern European countries, but others arrived from Asian nations. They settled throughout the United States. Some migrated directly to Boyle Heights, but most first settled in eastern cities and later migrated west to join those who had arrived earlier. For instance, Jews from several nations as well as Armenian and Yugoslavian immigrants scattered throughout the neighborhood during the early years of the 20th century; so did Mexicans, Japanese, and African Americans. Although others from these same groups lived in more concentrated areas, they, too, lived among residents from other ethnic backgrounds. The area became culturally mixed from its earliest settlements and retained that environment for more than half a century.

In 1900, paralleling the prior two decades, Boyle Heights continued to reflect an intermixed social and ethnic neighborhood. The federal census for that year shows that Hispanics and immigrants lived among native-born residents as well as members of other ethnic groups. Their occupations included physicians, teachers, dentists, photographers, business owners, and artists; others resided among these professionals, including the skilled, unskilled, and unemployed. Skilled occupations included a watchmaker, brick masons, milliners, and house carpenters, while most of the unskilled classed themselves as day laborers.

Several Boyle Heights residents had intermarried before 1900; thus, their children represented blends of cultural or national backgrounds. Representative of these intermarried couples in the neighborhood were Dolores Dawes, a recent emigrant from Mexico, who married an Irishman; another couple, who came from France and Mexico; and a German whose spouse migrated from Missouri. A Frenchman married a California native whose Hispanic mother also claimed nativity in California. Max Schwed, a grain merchant, his wife, and two children resided on East First Street; a Jewish emigrant from Germany, he married a California-born Hispanic wife whose parents had migrated from Mexico. Minnie Hebinger, a Russian, married an American from Indiana.

By 1910, large numbers of Jews in Los Angeles, estimated at more than 15,000, began to move into Boyle Heights. Many Jewish families had moved to Boyle Heights from either Central Avenue or Temple Street. They joined other Jews who had first moved into the neighborhood prior to 1900. About this time, Louis Lewin and Charles Jacoby purchased land and developed the Pioneer Lot Association, which they subdivided into small parcels and sold inexpensively. Jews from eastern and midwestern cities flocked into the neighborhood. By 1926, only 3 percent of the Jews living in Los Angeles remained in the downtown section; presumably, most had moved east of the railroad yards; low rents drew many into Boyle Heights.

During the early decades of the 20th century, thousands of Russians—mostly Jews fleeing persecution in Europe—flocked into Boyle Heights. These immigrants developed a high-profile commercial and religious ambiance, with numerous synagogues, Orthodox dress, and hundreds of small Jewish business enterprises scattered along the major streets. Many of the neighborhood's Jews joined unions and became leaders of labor organizations, which also contributed to the perception of Boyle Heights as a Jewish enclave. Yet the neighborhood retained its multicultural nature.

Jews formed the largest minority group of residents of Boyle Heights during the 1920s, 1930s, and 1940s; however, they also represented diverse groups. Many Orthodox Jews lived among others who embraced conservative, Reform, and even secular ideologies. Their native lands also contributed distinctive differences among the thousands of Jews who resided in the eastside community. Immigrant Jews arrived from at least

10 different nations, including Russia, Germany, Poland, Czechoslovakia, France, Romania, Lithuania, Latvia, Estonia, and Hungary. The synagogues and community-based organizations, such as the Hebrew Sheltering Home and Jewish Home for the Aged, knew no national differences.

By the 1920s and 1930s, the large number of Jews in Boyle Heights contributed to an atmosphere that many referred to as a *shtetl*. Children played games in the streets; parents shopped at Jewish-owned businesses, such as Canter's Deli, Zellman's Men's Wear, Ginsberg's Vegetarian Cafeteria, Warsaw Bakery, Wolf's Dry Goods, and any number of businesses along Brooklyn Avenue and Wabash Avenue. Jews owned or managed the majority of the economic enterprises and social-political organizations, and most of the shops and stores catered to the Jewish community. The tendency of Jews to meet on street corners speaking in Yiddish also added to the perception of Boyle Heights as a predominantly Jewish community. The dress of Orthodox Jews contributed a third factor that helped build a Jewish immigrant ambiance.

Certainly another factor was the number of synagogues within the community. The most renowned of these was that of Congregation Talmud Torah, called the Breed Street Shul. Its congregation moved from downtown to the eastside community in 1923, and within a few short years claimed the distinction of having the largest congregation west of Chicago. It continued to serve the Jewish community through the 1980s.

Non-Jews from the same countries named above also established homes in Boyle Heights, which contributed to camaraderie among neighbors. For instance, Russian Molokans, who also fled their homeland during the first decade of the 20th century due to religious persecution and military conscription, formed a large community within Boyle Heights. They shared similar dietary restrictions with their Jewish neighbors, so Molokans purchased goods from Jewish peddlers and shopped at kosher stores owned by Jews. They also shared a common homeland and native tongue, although most immigrant Jews spoke Yiddish as their primary language. Jewish residents lived among, worked with, attended school with, and socialized with their neighbors, while non-Jewish residents contributed significantly to the population mix in Boyle Heights.

In Boyle Heights, union movements first swept the neighborhood in the 1890s and by the 1930s and 1940s achieved success. During the early 20th century, the neighborhood became the center of Jewish unions in Los Angeles. The first two unions served Jewish hat makers (International Hat and Capmakers' Union, Local 26) and Jewish carpenters (a local established on Brooklyn Avenue). Local 52 of the Independent Ladies Garment Worker Union organized in 1919, and in 1921 men organized a local chapter of the Amalgamated Clothing Workers.

Jews formed the core of most socialist/left wing groups that met in the neighborhood, including the *Arbeiter Ring* (Workmen's Circle) and the *Folkschul* (Folk School). Some belonged to the Communist party. Many met on the southwest corner of Brooklyn and Soto Streets to offer solutions to the world's ills in their debates in Yiddish. Others, men and women, met at Center Cafeteria on Brooklyn and Mott Streets; their discussions seemed less argumentative and more intellectual to some observers. In 1938, many gathered in a parade to protest against Hitler. Many families became active in one of the three workman's circles, which met to provide cultural activities and secular education. Some joined a *landmanschaftin* (country/nation) group and the Jewish Community Center.

New Deal programs instituted during the Great Depression included the National Recovery Administration, which worked with both labor and industry to regulate hours of work and wages and establish production expectations. Section 7a of the National Industrial Recovery Act (NIRA) established the right of workers to join unions and participate in collective bargaining. These programs undermined the left-wing movement in Boyle Heights, and during the late 1930s and during World War II, residents became less inclined to support socialist and communist organizations.

During the first decades of the 20th century, the Los Angeles school system, which included all public schools in Boyle Heights, underwent significant changes and adopted Progressive reforms. The city's Civic Association also promoted or endorsed reform issues. Progressive reforms achieved in the system included not only the penny lunch program, but supervised after-hours playgrounds, day-care centers, and kindergartens. In 1916, Macy Street School also inaugurated a program that provided clothing for its students. Curricula of the city's elementary school system during these decades targeted enhancing the particular talents of each child and leaned toward a focus on the social and emotional needs of the child. High schools in the city presented speakers to instruct students in social and civic responsibilities. Thus, the schools in Boyle Heights became a prototype of the progressive education ideas of John Dewey and Roswell Gilpatrick.

Professionals stressed the importance of making Americanization a "process of neighborization" in order to make it "serve constructive purposes." Some even emphasized that it was two-way process and that native-born Americans should incorporate socially valuable cultural practices of immigrants as well as try to raise the group consciousness of newcomers. School principals led in the Americanization effort for students whose parents did not. Education provided the means of achieving the goal.

Synagogues and a variety of religious organizations provided identity and self-help for Jewish immigrants in the assimilation process. Cooperation provided the key for these disparate groups. As in other communities throughout the nation where immigrant Jews settled in the same community as well-established Jews, cultural and theological dialogues between Jewish community members helped the process.

None of the schools in Boyle Heights were segregated, although some Los Angeles city schools practiced a high degree of racial discrimination. One historian asserted that, in the 1920s, 80 percent of Mexican school children in Los Angeles attended segregated schools and received a poor education. She added, schools for Mexicans aimed at Americanization, English language instruction, and vocational training, but failed to prepare Mexican students for college. There is little doubt that educational pursuits included assimilation objectives. However, a 1937 Roosevelt High School graduate, Mary Xotchel (Ortiz) Garcia, provided a different perspective. She stated that, in Boyle Heights, she had attended three different elementary schools during the 1920s and early 1930s, graduating from the eighth grade in 1933. Garcia described each of the schools, with its most prominent ethnic groups, and asserted that all were racially mixed. Ethnic students at Utah Street School in Boyle Heights

included "English," Russian, Armenian, Italian, Japanese, and Mexican backgrounds. At Evergreen Street School in Boyle Heights, where she attended third and fourth grades, she encountered other students from Italian, Greek, Japanese, and Russian backgrounds. She then attended Bridge Street School, also in Boyle Heights, in what she described as an Italian neighborhood.

Since most children attended neighborhood schools, restrictive covenants governing real estate provided a means of maintaining segregated schools in Los Angeles, but in Boyle Heights no residential restrictions regulated housing, and neither Asian American nor African American schoolchildren were segregated or required to attend separate schools. Although some Los Angeles city schools and playgrounds were segregated prior to 1930, none in Boyle Heights were. According to former residents, grade school annuals, census enumerations, voting registers, and high school yearbooks from 1926 through 1939, segregationist policies did not affect either housing or education in Boyle Heights. Student bodies included members from numerous ethnic groups, which in turn represented the neighborhood at large. Certainly, then, it can be argued that in Boyle Heights students attended unsegregated schools throughout the neighborhood's existence.

During the 1930s, Jews comprised a majority of the students at many of the Boyle Heights schools, but the majority of the teachers were non-Jewish; one former Roosevelt student identified only two Jewish teachers at the high school in the 1930s and early 1940s. Some Jewish students reported a lack of understanding on the part of their instructors, particularly in respect to Christian-based holidays. During the interview with Mary Garcia, noted previously, she insightfully stated that at Roosevelt High students felt separated more by religion than by nationality.

Throughout the city's history, Boyle Heights' schools remained unsegregated, and they seemingly thrived upon their diverse student bodies. Actually, school boundary lines divided Boyle Heights; for instance, Evergreen Avenue—a major street in the eastern section of the neighborhood—separated Belvedere and Hollenbeck Junior High Schools. Students who lived west of Evergreen attended Hollenbeck; this included those students who had attended Harrison

Elementary. After completion of the ninth grade, many of these students then attended Roosevelt High School, but some lived within the Garfield High School district. Other Boyle Heights elementary schools, whose student bodies fed Roosevelt High, included Malabar, Sheridan, Breed Street, and Soto Street grammar schools.

The diversity of ethnic groups, races, and religions at Roosevelt High reflects the multicultural neighborhood it represented. Former students recall more camaraderie than antagonism, and this seems to be an accurate appraisal, as indicated by the multicultural make-up of the student councils for Roosevelt High School in the 1920s and 1930s. Numerous ethnic groups constituted the student body of Roosevelt High School although the proportions varied over time. Over time, the school's number of represented nationalities varied from 30 to 40, and the school's administration boasted that was the only school west of Chicago with such a varied student body.

Roosevelt High School served as another solidifying aspect of the community. Only one high school served the entire neighborhood, and its student body reflected the multicultural community that surrounded it. Indubitably, students attended classes together, but more important, they played sports, joined clubs, and participated in school events and activities together. This atmosphere also produced a sense of connection that solidified the neighborhood both during and after students' years of schooling.

One way of ascertaining the racial and cultural blending of the Boyle Heights neighborhood is through the window of yearbooks for the community's only high school. Roosevelt High School opened in Boyle Heights in the fall of 1923; the first class to complete three full years at the new school was the class that graduated in the summer of 1926.

The publication of yearbooks for Roosevelt High School began that year. The first, as well as those that followed, provide the viewer with an unusual historical window into the multicultural community the school served and easily disproves the charges that all Los Angeles schools were segregated. At times, assigning a specific nationality to a surname can be questionable due to its commonality in the United States or usage among two or more ethnic groups.

Another factor is that many families residing in Boyle Heights through 1930 and later were not themselves immigrants but descendants from families long in America—people who had migrated from other parts of the nation to Los Angeles. Thus, while the conclusions may deviate slightly from actuality, it is assumed that overall variations are minor.

Between 1926 and 1966, Roosevelt High School's annuals depict separate graduating classes for winter (January) and summer (June). Based upon appearance and/or surname of graduating seniors, it can be ascertained that the school's population represented several ethnic groups among its combined classes in 1926. Of the 251 graduates, by far the largest number were Jews, religious and secular, who totaled approximately 30 percent (73 students); next, the two most populous groups, the Irish and Polish/Russians, represented about 15 percent (36 students) and 12 percent (30 students), respectively. It should also be noted that some of the Polish/Russians may also be Jewish, but a significant number of Russians in Boyle Heights were Molokans, and another smaller group were called "white Russians."

Other cultural groups represented smaller percentages; those included eight African Americans, four Armenians, two Dutch, eight Greeks, three Italians, one Japanese, two Mexican, seven Scandinavians, and five Welsh. Many of the surnames could represent students of a number of ethnicities, for example, Elbert Johnson, a member of the 1926 Roosevelt High School senior class, was 10 when the 1920 census was enumerated in Boyle Heights; this enumeration shows that although he was born in California, his parents, Samuel and Minnie, were born in Denmark and apparently Anglicized their surname. Ida Miller, another California-born 1926 graduate, was the daughter of Harry and Mollie, both natives of Russia with Yiddish their native tongue; their surname, too, was Anglicized. Therefore, in some cases, unless the family can be identified in naturalization or immigration records, federal census, or voting registers (which list each individual's birthplace by country), a few may be identified incorrectly.

More importantly, perhaps, elected student body leaders and class officers included both men and women from several ethnic groups during the winter and summer terms. They included Alex Yahwis, student body president and class president; Robert

McElvy, student body president and vice president; Robert Cooke, student body vice president; Theodore Ginsburg, student body vice president; Fannie Ginsburg, student body secretary; Elthea Kohler, student body secretary; Dave Covalerchek, class president for two terms; Evelyn Trout, class vice president; George Schaffer, class vice president; Louise Maxwell, class vice president for two terms; William Gnash, class secretary and treasurer; Sam Dilman, class treasurer; and David Kadish, class treasurer.

The most prestigious school awards were also allotted diversely. Seniors in the Optimist Club, the second largest student organization on campus, included Russians, Jews, Irish, Americans of native-born parents, Welsh, Scandinavians, African American, Italians, and Greeks. Other student groups, such as the History Club, also included individuals from numerous ethnicities. Whites, blacks, and Hispanics belonged to the Spanish Club (*La Cadena de Oro*), while seniors who joined the French Club (*Le Cercle Français*) included a mix of cultures. The Young Men's Christian Association (YMCA) club for teenagers is the Hi-Y; Roosevelt High School senior members included those from various ethnic backgrounds. Although, some years later, Jews also joined the Hi-Y clubs on the school's campus, in 1926 none belonged.

Ten years later, the 1936 yearbook from Roosevelt High School also depicts a highly diversified student body and leadership. Members of the school's 22-member Student Council and 15 student leaders on the Citizenship Court include men and women of Irish, Japanese, Jewish, and Mexican heritage, as well as others not readily identifiable by name. Leaders of other organizations, such as the Reserve Officers Training Corps (ROTC) and Girls Rifle Club also depict a collage of students. The ROTC's 21 Graduating Officers consisted of men of Mexican, Irish, Jewish, Polish, Armenian, Japanese, and other backgrounds; while those who belonged to the 90-member Women's Rifle Teams represented Irish, German, Russian (Molokan), Polish, Dutch, Jewish, Mexican, and other cultural backgrounds. Names of senior class officers in 1938 show a similar cross-cultural constituency.

Membership in student clubs provides another gauge of the intermingling multiculturalness of Roosevelt High School, as students belonged due to interest in the association's focus, goals, or activities. One example is the Aldebaran Society, which was a popular club on campus: From 1926 through 1966, its membership always included representatives of numerous ethnic groups.

In-migration, technological changes, and Progressive reforms changed the urban scene and its educational institutions during the early years of the 20th century. The social and physical environment of Boyle Heights also altered tremendously during these years. An increased number of schools and public transportation schedules posted in Boyle Heights acknowledged the neighborhood's commitment to the Progressive emphasis on education and the clock and their demands. The multicultural community formed a sense of pride and commitment to success through its schools and social organizations. Neighborhood solidarity existed despite the differences of cultures and religion, and Boyle Heights residents seemed happy to maintain their integrated schools, contrary to elsewhere in Los Angeles.

During the second half of the 20th century, development and demographics in Boyle Heights changed. The state constructed five freeways through various parts of Boyle Heights. Consequently, many families were forced to move away. Some moved into adjacent communities and into Orange County. Many Jews moved into westside areas, such as Fairfax and Culver City, and into cities in the San Fernando Valley.

As early settlers moved out, numerous Mexican immigrant families settled there, buying homes and businesses. Mexican culture and stores began to dominate the community and schools by 1960. As the Mexican immigrants' American-born children grew up, many also moved out of the neighborhood into other areas of southern California.

As Mexicans left the eastside community, Latinos from South and Central America migrated into Boyle Heights. Although the neighborhood today reflects a Hispanic aura, it remains culturally diverse, with its immigrants from numerous nations. Student bodies at the various schools, including Roosevelt High, consist of students from a variety of countries throughout the Western Hemisphere. At times, social conflicts and gang warfare occurs; however, like earlier residents, the neighbors and schools still support the neighborhood's multicultural heritage. Its teachers encourage today's students to learn the history of their unique community through various classroom and community projects.

Boyle Heights never attained an upper-class neighborhood status, although in its early development several individuals built mansions and huge homes there. Today, most of these homes show the wear of years, and many provide housing for several families who combine resources to make ends meet.

Many sources provide documentation of this unique neighborhood. Federal census records for 1880 through 1930 and school yearbooks for 1923 through 1966 provide an overview of this ethnically mixed community, showing conclusively that every block, street, and school contained a culturally diverse blend of residents. Many maps of the area indicate the cultural diversity of the community. For example, the Works Progress Administration (WPA) and the Information Division of Los Angeles County Coordinating Councils prepared area maps of Boyle Heights during the 1930s: These maps also show conclusively the mixed ethnicity of the neighborhood. Oral histories of former residents—of several different cultural backgrounds—illuminate the camaraderie they experienced. Even 50 or more years after they moved from the neighborhood, offspring of the immigrants recall their formative years with appreciation and positive reflections on their culturally diverse experiences in Boyle Heights.

No barrio, ghetto, or Chinatown existed in Boyle Heights between 1857 and 1950; the neighborhood remained diverse—ethnically, socially, and culturally. During the second half of the 20th century and the beginning of the 21st century, however, Boyle Heights presents a vision of a barrio, but within it remain a few from earlier years who retain their ties to the community and its history.

—*Wendy Elliott-Scheinberg*

See also LOS ANGELES, CALIFORNIA

Suggested Reading

Elliott-Scheinberg, Wendy. *Boyle Heights: Jewish Ambiance in a Multi-Cultural Neighborhood.* Ph.D. Dissertation, Claremont Graduate School, 2001.

Prado, Mary S. *Mexican American Women Activists.* Philadelphia: Temple University Press, 1998.

Sanchez, George, and Arthur A. Hansen. *The Boyle Heights Oral History Project.* Los Angeles: Japanese American National Museum, 2002.

⌗ BOZEMAN, MONTANA

Like a good recipe that mixes different ingredients to create a flavor all its own is one way to describe Bozeman. Towns and cities do the same thing, and people will migrate to certain areas because of the flavor of the town. Bozeman's recipe is a mix of agriculture, tourism, education, recreation, and culture. The town's close proximity to Yellowstone National Park, the role of Montana State University, the attraction of thousands of acres of wilderness, and the city's symphonies, opera companies, and museums mark Bozeman as unique in many minds. Bozeman dishes up a taste that has any palette so enthralled that eating it everyday is a necessity.

Bozeman is located in the eastern end of the Gallatin Valley. The valley is part of the northern end of the Rocky Mountain chain. Northeast of Bozeman is the Bridger Range, named after the guide and trapper Jim Bridger. Its highest point is Sacajawea Peak at 9,670 feet. Southeast is the Madison range, named after James Madison, U.S. Secretary of State in 1804; its highest point is Gallatin Peak at 11,015 feet. The Gallatin Range lies south of town and its highest point is Mount Chisholm at 10,333 feet. These mountains surround the town with panoramic views, a feast for the eyes.

Early inhabitants of southwestern Montana referred to the valley as the Valley of Flowers. Prairie grass and sagebrush dominate the lower elevations, along with cottonwoods and willow trees. As elevation increases, conifers such as pine, spruce, and fir texture the area, with islands of aspen intermingled. Wildlife is abundant and diverse. Around Bozeman, one can encounter deer, elk, moose, big horn sheep, wolf, coyote, and bear. The area is also home to many birds and is a major migratory stopping point.

There are many rivers that traverse the area: The Gallatin, Jefferson, and Madison all join together to

Early picture of Main Street, Bozeman, Montana (circa 1860s).

Source: Used with permission of the Pioneer Museum, Bozeman, Montana.

form the Missouri River near Three Forks, Montana. A labyrinth of tributaries supplies these rivers. Fed by snow slowly melting high above the valley floor, these waterways feed the brilliant flora and fauna of the area. Not only are they the source of water, but they also provide easy transportation and recreation to local inhabitants.

The beauty and fertility of the valley caught the attention of early immigrants. The rich river bottom-land and timber resources that surrounded them told early pioneers that this valley could be used to supply the mines of Virginia City and Helena and anybody else who chose to settle in the area. On August 9, 1864, a group of men met to formalize a town with the intent of protecting their interests in the area. The minutes of the meeting record that John M. Bozeman was elected chairmen and recorder of land claims. On nomination by Reverend William White Alderson, the town was named Bozeman. The cost of filing a claim was $1 and required the claimant to become a resident within 10 days in order to hold the claim. The next day, there were seven claims recorded and more followed that autumn. The meeting also established the town boundaries in order to organize land claims. The

town was not formally platted until 1870 and was then incorporated by the state legislature in 1874.

To encourage settlement, it was made known that town lots were made free if a person took up residence. William J. Beall and Daniel E. Rouse built the first two homes. With the addition of W. W. Alderson's ranch just south of town, a measure of permanence was added. During the fall and summer of 1864, six or seven additional houses were built in Bozeman, with others added in the surrounding area. In the first year, Bozeman saw its first hotel, general store, and saloon. The following year, the first grist and flour-mill opened for business north of town. Reverend Alderson gave the first sermon in the valley, but the first church building did not open its doors for service until July 28, 1867. By 1869, Bozeman had its own jail and several schools with a teacher paid with public funds.

John Bozeman's name will forever be connected to the town. However, Bozeman's time in the town was brief. Indians killed Bozeman three years after the founding of the town. Thomas Cover, the gentleman who shared Bozeman's company that fateful day of April 18, 1867, reported they had been attacked by Indians while camped on the banks of the Yellowstone River. The details of Cover's story about the day's events could never be confirmed. Some people found evidence that suggested that Cover had committed the killing. The conflicting details of the day's events, however, did not come to light until many years later, when most the participants had passed away. Bozeman's death at the supposed hands of Indians was significant in that it created a seemingly tangible threat to settlers. Bozeman's death was an instrumental factor in the U.S. government's decision to build a military garrison outside the town of Bozeman. The events surrounding and conflicting accounts of Bozeman's death still draw a lot of attention in local historical circles.

The arrival of the army was a staple ingredient in Bozeman recipe for immigration. Stories of John Bozeman's death in Montana papers caused a so-called general panic of settlers in the area. In response, the federal government approved a fort south of Bozeman. This thrilled local residents, not only for the protection the fort would provide, but also for the money that would come with it. Furthermore, a stationed army garrison now dispelled any doubts about the longevity of Bozeman.

The U.S. Army arrived in the Gallatin Valley on August 27, 1867. One hundred ninety-five men of the 13th Infantry under the command of Captain Robert S. Lamotte immediately started to construct a stockade for the protection of local inhabitants. The fort was named after Colonel Augustus Van Horne Ellis, who died at the battle of Gettysburg on July 2, 1863. In the next couple of years, the infantry would be joined by four companies of the 2nd Regiment of the U.S. Cavalry. The fort proved to be a boom for businessmen, who traded directly with the fort and for Bozeman's main street merchants. Bozeman residents would supply the fort, and the soldiers would spend their pay in the town.

With the addition of a military garrison, the town's growth was exponential. By the 1880s, Bozeman had hotels, boardinghouses, banks, general stores, a milliner, a tailor, boot shops, watchmakers, a jeweler, blacksmiths, wagon shops, liveries, carpenters, a gunsmith, a brickyard, tin shops, a paint shop, a printer, and a photographer. Along with supporting the development of the private sector, Bozeman also supported religion: Catholic, Episcopalian, Methodist, and Presbyterian churches had all formally organized.

The creation of Yellowstone Park by the federal government on March 1, 1872, further supplemented the flow of people and money into the city. Only 90 miles from Bozeman, Yellowstone was sure to benefit from the tourist season. Often referred to as Colter's Hell, the park soon demonstrated its wonders to the people who came. The early tourists also came on hunting and photography expeditions.

In conjunction with the opening of America's first national park, the arrival of the Northern Pacific Railroad to Bozeman had a profound impact on migration to the area. On March 14, 1883, the first locomotive rolled into town. The railroad shrunk travel time greatly, making it possible for people to travel great distances in a few days. This was very important for tourism in Yellowstone Park and Bozeman. Easterners could now take vacations and visit the park without being gone for weeks. In addition, the railroad enabled Bozeman producers to ship their products east, increasing their markets and profits. Tourism would become the butter for Bozeman, but the opening of the state college would be the bread.

In 1862, the U.S. Congress passed the Morrill Land Grant Act, giving states 6.2 million acres of federal land to create and support not less than one college per state in order to promote the educational fields of science, classical studies, agriculture, and engineering. Bozeman had to fight hard for the honor of having a college. After a legendary battle in the legislature, Bozeman won the honor. The Montana State College of Agriculture and Mechanic Arts was founded on February 16, 1893. At first, Montana State College was far from what one sees today. The first 14 students attended classes in an old high school building. As it gained more students, the institution would continually move from one location to another until in 1896 the cornerstone of College Hall was laid and other construction projects were under way. The next year, Montana State College graduated their first four students. The campus continued to grow, offering classes to men and women. By 1911, it had a Greek organization. In the late 1940s, enrollment skyrocketed. Returning veterans of World War II caused the student population to increase by 50 percent. During this period of growth, more buildings and land holdings were added to the college. Even today, with enrollment above 12,000 students, Montana State University (MSU) makes up a large percentage of the population of Bozeman. MSU offers baccalaureate degrees in 51 fields, master's degrees in 40 fields and doctorates in 17 fields.

Furthermore, MSU is one of the most popular reasons for people to immigrate to the town. MSU touts itself as having "a national and international reputation for excellence. . . . It is routinely listed by *U.S.*

Aerial view of Bozeman with Montana State University in the foreground and Bridger Mountains in the background.

Source: Used with permission of the Pioneer Museum, Bozeman, Montana.

News and World Report as one of Americas best buys." MSU's slogan today is "Mountains and Minds," which represents the other reason for migration to the town of Bozeman: recreation.

The surrounding mountains and rivers provide recreational opportunities year-round. The two most popular activities are fishing in the summer and skiing and snowboarding in the winter months. With three rivers in the valley, not to mention the tributaries that feed these rivers, the fishing opportunities are everywhere. In addition to fishing, there is white-water rafting and kayaking. Excellent white water is located within an hour from town. Bozeman also is located amid three ski resorts: Bridger Bowl, 16 miles from town in Bridger Canyon; Big Sky Resort, 45 miles

from Bozeman in the Madison Range; and Moonlight Basin, 47 miles from town and 1.2 miles from Big Sky Village. Since 1955, Bridger Bowl has operated as a nonprofit operation serving the residents of the Gallatin Valley. Big Sky Resort offers all the amenities of a world-class facility. In 2003, Moonlight Basin started operation on the north face of Lone Mountain. Skiing has clearly caught on in the area.

The most impressive feature, and maybe the most unexpected, is the number of cultural organizations in Bozeman. So surprising is this number that the town has grabbed national media attention. Bozeman was the subject of the network television program *Sunday Morning*, which tried to answer the question of how a small cow town in the West could be home to so much culture. It is very impressive that Bozeman, with a population of a little more than 29,000, hosts symphonies, an opera company, theater groups, and a ballet. The town also hosts The Emerson Center for the Arts and Culture and Beall Park Art Center. In addition, Bozeman hosts a plethora of museums.

MSU supports an orchestra, but in 1968 it was felt that it was time to create an independent orchestra that would encourage more community involvement and outreach to more of the population of Bozeman. The mission of the Bozeman Symphony Society is "to support the performance of symphonic and choral music by a resident orchestra and choir for the benefit of audiences, students and musicians residing in south-central Montana."

Bozeman is an all-you-can-eat buffet of performing arts. The Bozeman Intermountain Opera Company performs yearly in town. Montana Shakespeare in the Parks performs in Bozeman at least twice a year. The Equinox Theatre also does performances in town. The Emerson Center holds class for aspiring thespians and a summer camp for kids. The Montana Ballet Company has multiple performances yearly, including the Christmas classic, *The Nutcracker,* and has an outreach program that has whet the palate for dance in thousands of rural kids. The company's mission statement sums up the collective attitude in Bozeman: "The Montana Ballet Company operates under the belief the arts, in all their forms, have the capacity to enrich the lives of those living in the rural mountain west."

The Emerson Center not only is the home for many artist studios, but also has galleries, performance groups, and other professionals. Their 700-seat theater plays host to many concerts, slide shows, and lectures. Together with the Beal Park Art Center, they also offer art education and outreach programs. The Emerson is a community institution and the nucleus for all that goes on in the town.

Housed in the old county jail, the Pioneer Museum conserves and expands a collection of local history. The museum's attractions range from Fort Ellis artifacts and early firearms to jail cells and a hanging gallows. There is a replica of a log cabin and collections of farm implements, old cars, and donated personal possessions. They have one of the best photo archives outside of the State Historical Society in Helena.

Focusing on much broader topics in history is the Museum of the Rockies, Montana's premiere natural history museum. Its collections not only contain the first freestanding full-size Tyrannosaurus Rex and the Taylor Planetarium, but also include collections on geology, Ice Age mammals, Native Americans, and Montana history. The Museum of the Rockies also has a living history farm that is a wonderful representation of life in Montana 100 years ago. Jumping into the modern era is the Compuseum, the American Computer Museum, which is a renowned collection of microprocessors, radio televisions, and other electrical inventions that so many cannot live without. Bozeman also has a children's museum, which stimulates the young population with hands on activities and exhibits.

Bozeman was also featured in a May 9, 1993, *New York Times* article titled "Montana's Cow Town with Charm." In it, Dan O'Brian describes Bozeman as "a place where the Old West meets the New West and the local economy meets the world economy. It's a place where solid old saddle horses encounter titanium mountain bikes." The article goes on to say that Bozeman is not generally friendly to new migration trends, but once you visit, it is very hard not to migrate to the town.

Bozeman's recipe is a unique balance of tradition and change. Traditionally, Bozeman attracted people to settle the land and reap its harvest. Today, you can still see and feel that agricultural presence. MSU attracts people challenged to stimulate their intellectual growth and enjoy the recreation supplied by the surrounding environment. The university also ensures the annual ebb and flow of new ideas and town population with the beginning and ending of every academic calendar. The mountains and their stunning beauty are the most profound characteristic of the town. This will be the main taste that will continue to attract people for the weekend, a few years, or a lifetime.

—*Elwood Bakken*

See also GALLATIN VALLEY, MONTANA; GIANFORTE, GREG

Suggested Reading

Boyne, U.S.A. "Big Sky Resort." Available from http://www.bigskyresort.com

Bozeman Area Chamber of Commerce. *1995 Visitors' Guide.* Bozeman, MT: Bozeman Area Chamber of Commerce, 1995.

Bozeman Area Chamber of Commerce. *2004 Visitors' Guide.* Bozeman, MT: Bozeman Area Chamber of Commerce, 2004.

Montana Ballet Company Web Site. Available from http://www.montanaballet.com

Montana State University. "Mountains and Minds." Available from http://www.montana.edu/msu/history

Pioneer Museum vertical files. Pioneer Museum. Bozeman, MT.

Smith, Phyllis. *Bozeman and the Gallatin Valley a History.* Helena, MT: Falcon, 1996.

⊞ BOZEMAN TRAIL

See Bozeman, Montana; Crow Nation

⊞ BRACERO PROGRAM

See Immigration and Naturalization Service (INS), Mexican Migration to California, Operation Wetback

⊞ BRENT, JOSEPH LANCASTER
(1820–1905)

From the time of the Lewis and Clark expedition, the westward movement had gained momentum, bringing a variety of pioneers from all parts of the nation. In turn, the California gold rush quickened the pace of migration to the Far West. As historian John Walton Caughey observed, the rush to California ignited "an orgy of gold gathering that ranks as the greatest of all mining rushes." Yet many argonauts were ill prepared for the disappointments and arduous work of the diggings. Southern California became a refuge for the displaced and forgotten—those with broken dreams who were determined to make a new life in the Far West.

Joseph Lancaster Brent's journey West represented this circuitous migration to southern California. He stayed for a decade, during which time he became a central figure in the political and social life of Los Angeles. As an influential politician, Brent saw the inside workings of a decade, living in a frontier struggling with problems of race, politics, and commerce. His experiences reveal a diverse society, underlying the contrasts between the fading rancho era and the emerging rough-hewn character of Anglo-American frontier settlement. It was the rush for gold that brought Brent to the West, but it was in southern California that he would leave his imprint as a central figure in local politics.

Born in Maryland and later a resident of Louisiana, at 23 Brent was attracted by the "wonders and riches of California" and fascinated by the stories of fortunes made in the mining camps along the Kern River. For months, Louisiana had been the southern gateway to the California, as gold fever raged from Shreveport to the Gulf of Mexico. The *New Orleans Daily Picayune* warned returning prospectors to hide their booty because "ravenous rogues who infest our cities are on the watch for them in almost every public place."

In late spring of 1850, Brent left for California via the Panama route, which included an overland crossing of the isthmus and a final seafaring leg to San Francisco. This route was far less arduous than an overland expedition, with the prospect of favorable weather and easy access to steamers on the Pacific shore, and was faster than the long voyage around the Horn.

Brent boarded a vessel at New Orleans with all of his possessions, including his father's extensive law library. Once he arrived in California, Brent thought he might practice law, perhaps join the mining camps, or start a commercial venture. In any event, the confident young man who thought himself "as good as any Englishman" sailed to Panama aboard a crowded ship filled with Europeans and Americans, artisans and unskilled laborers, speculators, gamblers, and idealists. In July of 1850, Brent landed at San Francisco harbor, a crowded port filled with steamers and clippers, many of them abandoned offshore. The discarded vessels had brought thousands of people to California, including an exhausted Margaret Hereford (the future Margaret Wilson) only a month before.

Brent found gold rush San Francisco a disagreeable place. The rapid influx of immigrants created unexpected demands, and the fledgling city was unable to provide even basic services, leading to slumlike conditions and unforeseen hazards. Also, food and housing costs were high; Brent found a small room for an exorbitant rate of $16 per day. Adding to the city's problems, during 1850 and 1851 a beleaguered San Francisco suffered a half a dozen fires, including one hotel fire that partially destroyed Brent's law library. The rain, fog, and bitter wind were an unwelcome mix to a Southerner accustomed to the warmly damp and soft air of the Deep South. Brent would have surely agreed with Missourian Mark Twain, who once reportedly said that the coldest winter he ever spent was a summer in San Francisco. Encouraged by his physician-cousin, Thomas Brent, who preceded Brent west, he decided to move to the more temperate environs of Los Angeles, where, he hoped, he might begin a successful law practice.

Brent found rural Los Angeles much like the agrarian South, a pleasant contrast with the bustling intensity of San Francisco. Sprawling ranchos, undulating valleys, and emerald fields dotted with cattle drew Brent as much as he was repelled by the urban nature of tenement dwelling in San Francisco. Brent soon fell in love with the romantic ambience of the pueblo. His spirits soared; invigorated by the land and climate, he declared that "this [environ] in itself made me like the place."

Southern California also fit into the young Brent's image of the Far West, which he envisioned as a wilderness rather than the boomtown-style settlement of the northern mining camps and centers. A wilderness offered adventure, and men who could not only survive but also tame it fascinated the adventuresome Brent. In his early days in Los Angeles, he would spend hours at the local saloons listening to the trappers and journeymen recount their pioneering exploits. Brent would sit until dawn at the Bella Union Hotel, enthralled by the stories as such legendary men as William Wolfskill described the Taos trade, William Workman reminisced about the rancho era, or Benjamin Wilson recalled facing a Mexican firing squad during the recent war. Danger fascinated him, and he noted that these trailblazers "spent most of their lives on the war path, fighting the Indians, fighting the Mexicans, fighting each other." They were a diverse lot. "Strong, original characters," he admiringly observed, "some of them rough, wild men, perhaps

desperadoes and bandits." To Brent, these early residents were icons, the sort of rugged individualists who had survived in the Far West.

Brent was surprised and disappointed that "there seemed to be so little business or trade going on" in Los Angeles. A lack of hard currency retarded investment, and slow commercial growth also meant a small tax base for municipal improvements. The city itself conducted business out of rented homes. Benjamin Hayes' home even served as a courtroom. Local officials enlisted a volunteer police force, and the pueblo had no permanent school, hospital, or jail. "The dearth of capital," Robert Glass Cleland would later explain, "was unquestionably one of southern California's greatest handicaps."

The slow economy, tight money, and few emigrants added up to a difficult first year for the young Brent. He found work as a carpenter's apprentice, carrying bricks and mortar to build the first brick structures in the downtown section. With a meager savings gained from hard labor, he bravely opened his legal practice near the courthouse, across from the Stearns home on Main Street. But four lawyers had already begun practicing before Brent's arrival, which meant that too many attorneys and too few cases made the courtroom a highly competitive place. In a small town, a lawyer's personal reputation often determined whether his law firm would succeed or fail, so a relatively unknown newcomer was at a disadvantage.

Brent had only a few dollars and even fewer clients to sustain his legal practice. Within three months, he had exhausted his savings. Undaunted, either from overconfidence or naiveté, he whimsically declared that his predicament was "a joke" and promptly borrowed $300 from Benjamin Wilson to continue his practice. Over the next few years, he steadily built a reputation and law practice. By 1853, Brent was licensed by the state supreme court and had developed expertise in land title cases, including a successful award of the city's claims to land. He was an "able lawyer [and] one of California's most brilliant men," acknowledged historian W. W. Robinson.

Brent made the best of a limited marketplace, and his success is indicative of both the man and the era. Legal references and law books were scarce, a major drawback in a profession based on written precedent.

"Probably more lawyers than law books," quipped one pundit. Brent's library, although partially destroyed in the San Francisco fire, became an invaluable reference resource. He added Hugo Reid's Indian library to his collection—Reid's way of repaying Brent for defending his claim to mission lands in San Gabriel.

The small community of lawyers and judges shared resources and debated points of law. Brent quickly developed a network of professional and personal friends, many of who were Southerners, including Dr. John Griffin, who had come to Los Angeles at the same time as Brent, and Jonathan Scott, a prominent Missouri attorney who arrived in Los Angeles the year before Brent. Other early Los Angeles lawyers were Albert Clark and William C. Ferrill. Though competitors, the tiny group of barristers nevertheless shared legal advice and reference materials. In 1853, Brent served as a school commissioner with Lewis Granger, another attorney.

Brent made many friends, an invaluable asset in a distant land where brotherhood ranked in value equal to gold. He admired hard workers and the Jacksonian ideals of the common man. Brent was an egalitarian, and the American West seemed to highlight this virtue within the spirit of frontier life. To his clients, many of whom were laborers, men of "rough" manner, he embodied "a higher and gentler civilization." His network of associates and contacts among the community included traders, politicians, businessmen, and soldiers. He almost forgot his Southern roots, so comfortably had they transplanted into the California's world of fandango and rodeo. By 1854, Brent proudly considered himself a Westerner, and a Californian in particular. "[I am] estranged from all ties of family and former friendship," and he recalled that he was "entirely out of the world as I had known it."

Brent developed close ties to the Hispanic elites. The rancheros still had an unmistakable influence in American California's everyday affairs, serving as overseers to an extended family of relatives, employees, and compadres. The pueblo served as a weekend social spot for the dons, vaqueros, and ranch hirelings. Rodeos were held in the town center, along with horse races, cockfights, and dances. The rancheros' large adobe homes in the plaza center served as guest residences. Indeed, the rancho lifestyle still dominated southern California, with land symbolizing wealth equivalent to the northern mining town's gold. When statehood brought disputes over Mexican land titles and grants, Brent became a spokesman for the underdog, those rancheros and dons who argued for legitimacy before indifferent courts. Dividing his time between San Francisco and Los Angeles, Brent represented claimants before the Land Commission. He defended the claims of the Lugo family and Manuel Nieto, and became a close friend of the Del Valle clan. Considered honest and forthright, Brent exercised considerable influence among the Californio elite.

Although Brent benefited from his grateful ranchero clientele, he sincerely enjoyed the romance and charm of Hispanic culture. In 1850, the old pueblo offered little entertainment beyond the heavy drinking and male conversation found in the gaming rooms. Anglo women were few and, as a bachelor with a confident manner, Brent soon became acquainted with the senoritas of the upper echelon. He appreciated the charm of Antonio Coronal's dark-eyed daughters, who wore bright-colored *riboses* knotted in their long flowing hair. He observed the submissive demeanor of Hispanic women in a male-dominated society. Hispanic women served meals, often did not converse at the same table, and, according to Brent, "were not disinclined to marry the American men, who treated their wives with greater consideration." He loved their delicacy, particularly at dances where they played festive games, such as the *coscarones,* a breaking of eggshells filled with colored paper that produced a shower of gold and silver over the ballroom dancers. Brent led a carefree life in those pioneer days, with no responsibilities and "nothing to arrest the flow of spirits, which had been generously bestowed by Nature and encouraged by health."

Many rancheros embraced Brent's courtroom talents with open arms: Here was a man of their stripe who also could deal with incomprehensible Anglo laws and courts. The legal entanglements over land grants created tension among competing Anglo and Hispanic interests. American justice seemed unfair to the proud dons, many of whom felt they were not obliged to prove their claims. Honest legal representation within a system they strongly distrusted proved invaluable. Brent had a reputation for sound advice and shrewd logic. In 1851, he tried his first important case, successfully defending members of the Lugo family accused of murder. The grateful don reportedly paid Brent $20,000 for his services. Professional success led to new friendships, and Joseph Lancaster Brent soon became a confidante of the Californio elite. He frequented Abel Stearns's home and socialized with members of influential families, such as the Alvarado, Pico, and Bandini families. The Del Valle clan adopted him as one of their own, and the eldest children affectionately called him *padrino*. Brent valued his friends and their hospitality, and would converse for hours with Ignacio Del Valle, polishing his Spanish while exchanging lively ideas on life, business, and politics. "Nothing disturbed his calm," wrote Brent of his compadre Don Ignacio. "When you got through his shell, he was warm hearted and had a good deal of humour."

Brent became a prominent civic leader during the 1850s. Politics was a natural arena for him: As a successful attorney, popular, respected by the community elite, Brent had solid leadership qualities. He "stood high as a lawyer and Statesman," read one contemporary account. Ever the diplomat, the affable Brent bolstered his political fortunes by consciously promoting good will with "everyone with whom [he] was brought in contact." Most important, the great issues of the day electrified party politics and piqued Brent's sense of civic activism. He was sensitive to the race issues that threatened the slaveholding society of his birthplace. The legal-minded Brent understood the Constitutional questions regarding states' rights and popular sovereignty, and he could not ignore the sectional questions that threatened to divide his party.

Brent became an integral force among southern California Democrats. Like a puppeteer manipulating events from behind the scenes, he planned strategy, created alliances, counted enemies, and elicited support for upcoming elections. "I have always preferred to put other men forward," he recalled, "and have them carry out my political ideas." The men Brent supported were individualists themselves, capable leaders and loyal Democrats. Throughout the 1850s, Brent supported the political ambitions of many friends: Jack Watson, I. S. K. Ogier, and Benjamin Wilson. William Gwin, a powerful party leader of the Chivalry wing, was one of Brent's close friends who urged him to retain a visible role in state and local politics. Brent could rely on a strong Hispanic bloc and, in turn, he

rallied political support behind Hispanic candidates such as Antonio Coronel and Agustin Olvera. Because of their regard for and trust in him, Brent virtually controlled the large ranchero families' votes, a potent political force. Of the Verdugo family, it was said that Brent could distribute ballots for instant tabulation. Harris Newmark recalled that Brent's "political influence with the old man was supreme."

Control of the powerful Hispanic vote coupled with his Democratic allies among the Anglo populace allowed Brent to dominate county legislation and dictate local elections. By the mid-1850s, he could boast that Los Angeles was "in his vest pocket." Newmark believed that the invincible Brent could nominate candidates "at will." As a delegate to the 1856 Democratic national convention at Cincinnati, Brent dutifully supported the convention nominee, James Buchanan. During the next two years, Brent served in the California legislature and sat on the Judiciary and Ways and Means Committees.

Brent's hold on local party machinery was damaged somewhat by the rise of *bandidos* such as Juan Flores and a corresponding increase of xenophobia within the pueblo. Brent's political opponents targeted Hispanics and other ethnic peoples as responsible for the rise in crime. Though Brent supported tough law enforcement as a member of the Los Angeles Rangers, he felt the rise in crime was a result of the gold rush gone bust, producing transients and displaced miners. "After the emigration into California became larger and the number of desperate men increased," Brent claimed, "the towns were visited by lawless characters." His Hispanic loyalties weakened his credibility, and several rivals emerged within the pueblo: Sheriff Bill Getman, who defended the city against a mob attempt to lynch his deputy, William Jenkins, after the wrongful shooting of a Spanish-speaking citizen, Antonio Ruis; Columbus Sims, a fellow Southerner and proponent of vigilante justice; and Jonathan Scott, Brent's friend and a hanging judge at odds with him on the use of vigilante justice.

Still, Brent won a few political battles in the years preceding the Civil War. He supported Benjamin Wilson's state senate bid as a tactical move to thwart a Know-Nothing candidacy. He delivered Los Angeles for James Buchanan in the 1856 presidential election and championed the Southern rights candidacy of

John C. Breckinridge in the 1860 election. Yet his most satisfying victory may have been his last. In 1860, he vigorously campaigned for Tomas Sanchez in the election for sheriff. With law and order a persistent concern, the sheriff was considered a powerful city official, and prejudices surfaced during the election. Explained Brent, "Many Americans bitterly opposed him, owing to their race and prejudices." Sanchez narrowly won. Brent felt that the election was a personal vindication of past battles and a rebuke to the xenophobia he had opposed in the mid-1850s.

Nevertheless, Brent suffered his share of political setbacks, mainly because of party realignments on the state and national level. In 1859, Brent and rival John G. Downey led a divided Los Angeles Democrat delegation to the nominating convention for governor. When Brent supported the reelection of Governor John B. Weller, the convention rejected Brent and other Weller supporters, denying them a slate. Brent led a walkout of delegates, while Downey remained at the convention in support of the party favorite, Milton Latham. The Democrats eventually nominated Downey for lieutenant governor, perhaps in a show of gratitude for his party loyalty. Brent believed that Downey's motives were self-serving, a blatant power move to gain control of the Los Angeles delegation, and pressed an unsuccessful challenge against the Latham-Downey ticket in the general election. The Brent-Downey feud divided Democrats statewide. "Before it was over," summarized historian David A. Williams, "new dimensions of political vituperation had been reached, the system of democratic politics seriously damaged, and the political issues buried in an avalanche of invective."

The Democrats' failure suggested that political trends had passed Brent by, or at the very least were moving too quickly for him to control. Brent, increasingly an outsider within his own party, conceded that many Angelenos wanted to "break up the political influence which had governed the county for so many years." The city population had doubled by the end of the decade, bringing settlers with new ideas and new ambitions. Los Angeles slowly evolved from a rancho community into a growing Anglo-American settlement; a larger city with broader issues made politics a more sophisticated venture than the uncomplicated era of barroom deals and stump rhetoric. A weary Joseph Lancaster Brent, disillusioned with his inability

to control events, interpreted local opposition as a negative aspect of the westering process. As the pueblo grew, Brent simply reasoned, those who took control were a "rougher element and men who looked upon politics as a money-making business."

In October 1861, 11 years after he had landed at San Francisco, Joseph Lancaster Brent went east to fight for the Confederacy. He opposed abolition and felt the federal government had an obligation to protect the slave owner's property in the territories, but he was not a secessionist at first, enlisting only after the war had started. Nor was he optimistic about the South's prospects for victory. He has the distinction of being the last Confederate general—of eight total—commissioned from the state of California.

Brent's decision to leave southern California and fight in a distant war was painful for him. He had accumulated properties throughout southern California, including nearly 75,000 acres in Los Angeles and the Tejon mountains. In 1859, he purchased the Morengo ranch, a modest estate located two miles from Benjamin Wilson's residence at Lake Vineyard. Fearing that the Union would seize his holdings when he enlisted with the Confederacy, he knew that he would have to liquidate these properties, a slow process that would be left to his friends, with the risk that his properties would be sold at a loss.

Brent also left behind cherished friends, including his neighbor Henry Rice Myles, "a Kentuckian and a very great friend"; Tennessee-born Benjamin Wilson, a confidant Brent admired for his devotion to family and children; James Watson, his political ally and a "Don Quixote," in Brent's words, someone Brent respected as a peacemaker who used force only when necessary; and Tomas Sanchez, a trusted ally with whom he had fought several political battles. To Sanchez, he said his goodbyes with "tears streaming down his cheeks." He also respected some of the loyalists of the Northern cause, men like Winfield Hancock, commissioned in the Union Army, and Phineas Banning, a Republican adversary whom Brent admired for his frank and friendly demeanor. In his mid-30s, this brief chapter in Brent's life was analogous to a shooting star across a dark sky, never to be repeated, "at the time of life when we form our warmest and most enduring friendships."

Brent never returned to southern California. He fought in several campaigns in Louisiana and

Mississippi. After the war, Brent returned to Maryland and later operated a sugar plantation at New River, Louisiana, where he stayed until his death in 1905. Always a man of energy and verve, he remained active in politics most of his life. He wrote political commentaries, delivered public addresses on foreign policy and domestic issues, and participated in several Democratic conventions throughout the century. He always missed Los Angeles; when Brent's final properties at Morengo were sold in 1868, he wrote his longtime friend Benjamin Wilson that he felt the sadness of this passing chapter. The war years planted the seeds for a new beginning in an old homeland. "If I was able to reconcile a sense of duty, I would long since have returned."

Although he never returned, Joseph Lancaster Brent left a distinctive imprint on the pueblo in law and politics and perhaps saved the region from disaster by forestalling rebellion. He participated in a volatile period in local and national history when questions of violence and race were as hotly debated on the frontier as in Washington or Richmond. Most importantly, Brent was torn between his roots and dreams of a future on the frontier. In the end, Joseph Lancaster Brent went east out of familial duty, never to return to the Far West.

—*Ronald C. Woolsey*

See also LAWYERS AND LEGISLATION; LOS ANGELES, CALIFORNIA; SAN FRANCISCO, CALIFORNIA

Suggested Reading

Woolsey, Ronald C. *Migrants West: Toward the Southern California Frontier.* Claremont, CA: Grizzly Bear Publishing, 1996.
Woolsey, Ronald C. "The Politics of a Lost Cause: 'Seceshers' and Democrats in Southern California during the Civil War," *California History* 69, no. 4 (Winter 1990–1991): 372–383.

BRIGHAM CITY, UTAH

William Davis and Simeon Carter, Mormon pioneer settlers, explored the area surrounding Box Elder Creek in 1850. They selected a site on which to build homes. They returned to Salt Lake City for the winter. Davis, James Brooks, and Thomas Pierce returned the following year with their families to take up permanent residence. They built a row of log rooms known as the Davis Fort, which were located in the northwest of town.

Henry G. Sherwood surveyed land, consisting of 40–80 acres each, for farms at the Box Elder settlement. The lots were extra large because the rocky nature of the soil meant larger plots were required to sustain a family. Families were glad to move from the cramped and bedbug-infested fort and began building cabins and farming their plots. This took place in the spring of 1852. By the fall of 1853, eight families with a total of 24 people lived in the settlement.

Brigham Young ordered the settlers to move into forts due to the increasing Indian hostilities in some areas of the territory. A second fort was built at Box Elder.

The first Latter-day Saints immigration company, composed entirely of Scandinavians, arrived in Utah in 1853. John Forsgren, whose wife was the daughter of William Davis, led them. Most of these immigrants would settle in Brigham City.

Church president Brigham Young directed Lorenzo Snow, an apostle in the church, to take 50 families to the Box Elder area and develop a cooperative system in which the community would become self-sufficient, producing all that they consumed. This was directed during the Mormon general conference of 1853. Snow selected artisans skilled in trades important to the development of a pioneer community. Most were Mormon converts from Denmark.

Snow developed into the political and ecclesiastical leader of the community. In 1855, he had the town plat surveyed and renamed the settlement Brigham City after church president Brigham Young. He encouraged the people to build permanent homes. Several small businesses were established during the 1850s. Snow wanted Brigham City to be a model Mormon village. In order to achieve this, he directed Territorial Surveyor Jesse W. Fox to divide the large farms into smaller parcels. This was to make room for the newcomers. The smaller parcels would be five acres each.

The Box Elder County Courthouse was used for city and county business, theatrical productions, and religious meetings until church buildings could be built. The courthouse was constructed from 1855 to 1857. The original adobe structure still forms the foundation of the present courthouse, making it the oldest remaining courthouse in Utah. It was a distinguished federal-style square building, updated in 1887 with an attractive Italianate style cornice, window heads, and a clock/bell tower.

Snow was ready to execute his plans for a cooperative community in 1864. A mercantile store, established in 1864, was the first cooperative business, but soon many different types of industries and services were added. Workers were paid in scrip, which could be used for trade in any of the departments of the cooperative. By the mid-1870s, the cooperative association was producing all the commodities necessary for preservation of the community. Snow had accomplished his goal of making the people of Brigham City independent of the outside world. His cooperative became a prototype for similar ventures in Mormon settlements throughout Utah. It was highly praised as the first and most thriving of the Mormon cooperative organizations. However, a series of financial disasters between 1876 and 1879 crippled the organization. Grasshoppers and drought destroyed crops; the woolen mill burned and was rebuilt at great expense. In 1878, a tax was levied on the scrip issued by the cooperative. These disasters forced the association to begin selling its industries to private businessmen. The Supreme Court ruled on the tax case, favoring the Brigham City co-op in 1884. The money was returned and constructed an amazing new store in the center of town. The co-op went into receivership in 1895.

The Box Elder Tabernacle was lost to a devastating fire that burned to the stone walls within one hour in February 1896. The residents raised money and dedicated a new tabernacle the next year. Peach Day, Utah's oldest continuous harvest celebration, was a turn-of-the-century creation. It was established in 1904 and is practiced annually.

After the demise of the co-op, private enterprise in the area flourished. By 1910, Brigham City's population was 4,000 and its residents were running local industries and retail businesses as well as operating farms. In the 1920s and 1930s, Brigham City essentially remained a small Mormon agricultural town specializing in fruit production.

A great influx of newcomers into the community began during World War II. Local soldiers and sailors were leaving and, at the same time, war-wounded men were arriving on incoming trains for treatment at Bushnell General Hospital. The hospital changed the quiet community. Built on 235 acres in 1942 to minister to soldiers wounded in World War II, the 60-building facility produced a major boost to the economy. Bushnell provided new jobs for local people from the beginning of its construction until it closed in 1946. City fathers agreed to purchase a huge plot of land in the southwest part of town to attract faculty for the hospital. Farmers sold produce to the hospital, and businesses on Main Street increased with the influx of the hospital staff and patients. The facility housed the Intermountain Indian School, a boarding school for young Indian students, from 1950 until 1984. This school integrated students from almost 100 tribes.

Brigham City's growth rate increased quickly in 1957 with the construction of Thiokol Chemical Corporation's Wasatch Division, the largest manufacturing enterprise in Box Elder County's history. Brigham's population of 6,790 in 1950 increased to 11,720 in 1960, to 14,000 in 1970, and to 15,596 in 1980 as both Thiokol's solid-fuel motor production and number of employees expanded. By 1990, Brigham City's population was 20,000.

—*Patrick Gibson*

See also Mormon Colonization of Utah

Suggested Reading

Daughters of Utah Pioneers. *Pioneers Mills and Milling.* Grand County: Daughters of Utah Pioneers, 1983.

Forsgren, Lydia Walker. *History of Box Elder Stake.* Grand County: Daughters of Utah Pioneers, 1937.

Pawar, Sheelwant Bapurao. "An Environmental Study of the Development of the Utah Labor Movement: 1860–1935." Ph.D. Dissertation, University of Utah, 1968.

Powell, Allan Kent, ed. *Utah History Encyclopedia.* Salt Lake City: University of Utah Press, 1994.

⊞ BUREAU OF IMMIGRATION

See Immigration and Naturalization Service (INS)

⊞ BUREAU OF INDIAN AFFAIRS

Since its founding in 1824 the Bureau of Indian Affairs (BIA) has played a central role in shaping the lives and living conditions of the numerous and diverse American Indian tribes living within the borders of the United States. As the federal agency responsible for implementing the policies and legislation concerning American Indians, the BIA quickly became the face of the U.S. government for native peoples. Initially responsible for the provisioning of services, including health, welfare, education, and economic development of Native North Americans, the BIA structured all aspects of American Indian lives. Unfortunately, for many American Indians this presence has been overwhelmingly negative; the BIA has historically acted in a corrupt and paternalistic fashion, initially operating under the goal of assimilation, which has been destructive, if not devastating, to Native peoples, their sacred lands, and their traditional cultures. From official federal policies of removal and relocation to the creation of the reservation system, and beyond, the BIA has played the most visible federal role in the colonization of Native peoples. In addition to contributing to the dismal social, economic, and health conditions prevalent on reservations, the historically underfunded bureau failed repeatedly to effectively secure the money needed to create any meaningful and long-lasting social and economic change for American Indians. The bureau failed to acknowledge the primacy of land to the development of any effective program of social and economic justice for American Indians. Despite these challenges, American Indians have remained remarkably resilient, preserving their cultures and customs in the face of seemingly insurmountable obstacles.

Originally called the Office of Indian Affairs (OIA), the bureau did not actually become the Bureau of Indian Affairs until 1947. Established on March 11, 1824, the OIA was originally conceived as a division of the War Department. Prior to this time, Indian affairs were supervised by the secretary of war and, for a brief time, the Office of Indian Trade. In 1849, the OIA was reassigned to the Department of the Interior, becoming the BIA nearly 100 years later.

With its initial creation in 1824, the OIA was primarily responsible for American Indians living east of the Mississippi River, but this quickly changed. The federal government began unofficially encouraging Indian relocation westward in the early 19th century, despite official assurances that native lands would not be coercively taken. With the 1828 election of Andrew Jackson to the presidency, however, official policy shifted to one of removal and relocation, formalizing the government's westward push. On May 28, 1830, Congress passed the Indian Removal Act authorizing the removal of East Coast–based Indians to the West. Throughout the 1830s and 1840s, this deadly policy of removal and relocation was carried out. The Cherokee, Choctaw, Chickasaw, and Creek Indians were among those removed from their eastern homelands and relocated in distant and unfamiliar western lands. The Cherokee removal in 1838 came to be known as the "Trail of Tears" because of the brutality of the journey in which several thousands died. By 1843, with the relocation largely finished, the OIA, headquartered in Washington, DC, became increasingly influential in the West.

In the 1840s, the OIA restructured its agencies and superintendencies to accommodate newly relocated tribes; such changes and agency additions would continue as westward expansion progressed and increasing numbers of American Indian tribes were involuntarily brought into contact with the federal government. Several tribes living in what is now California that were previously untouched by European-American contact were now brought under the supervision of the OIA. In 1832, the position of Commissioner of Indian Affairs was created, thus centralizing federal power and authority over Indian Affairs within the OIA.

Throughout the 19th century, American Indian tribes were assigned reservation lands by the OIA. Frequently encompassing land deemed undesirable by the federal government, reservation assignments ignored American Indian cultural differences; in many cases, tribes that had historically been foes were placed on the same reservation lands. Overlooking the immense diversity of hundreds of Native American tribes, the OIA treated American Indians as a homogenous group. Additionally, the reservation system disrupted traditional customs. For instance, the reservation assignments ended the mobility of tribes, such as the Yakama of the Pacific Northwest, whose economies depended upon seasonal migration. Many American Indian tribes lost sacred lands, which undermined not only religious customs, but healing customs as well. The sacred land of the Black Hills in what is now South Dakota was taken from the Lakota Sioux, who continue their struggle to have these lands returned.

Reservations changed the nature of the relationships between American Indian tribes and the federal government. Federally appointed land assignments placed tribes in guardian-ward relationships, thus diminishing tribal autonomy. This, combined with the destruction of Native economies, left most tribes impoverished and lacking access to traditional coping mechanisms, such as religious and healing ceremonies. Living in a system of internal colonization, American Indians became dependent upon the federal government for their physical and economic survival.

For at least the first century of its regulation of Indian Affairs, assimilation through "civilization" guided the OIA's interactions with American Indians. In 1887, the Dawes Act (also known as the General Allotment Act or the Dawes Severalty Act) required that tribal land held in common be broken up into parcels that would be allotted to each nuclear Indian family. Hopeful that individual land ownership would "civilize" American Indians, the federal government viewed the Dawes Act as an important means of assimilation. General allotment opened up reservation lands to non-Indians, which meant that whites increasingly began moving onto and buying up previously untouchable reservation lands. In the process, American Indian tribes lost land held in common, and many American Indian individuals lost their parcels to corrupt land dealings. The Dawes Act not only resulted in theft of Indian land, it contributed to the breakdown of the traditional social structures and supports of many native tribes.

The Dawes Act was but one piece in a larger program of assimilation embarked upon by the OIA in the mid- to late 19th century. Guided by assimilation, the OIA set out on an active campaign to "civilize," and initially even Christianize, Native peoples whom it considered to be in desperate need of both. The federal government, as well as missionaries, viewed native religious beliefs and practices as superstitious and pagan, an affront to a "civilized" nation whose own Victorian values rested upon a strong belief in enlightened Christianity. Up through the 1920s, missionaries and OIA agents alike attacked Native religious leaders, restricted American Indian dancing,

and interfered with the free practice of other religious ceremonies.

Guided by assimilation, the OIA set out on an active campaign to Christianize Native peoples. From 1869 to 1882, the OIA operated under the guidance of President Ulysses S. Grant's Indian Peace Policy. Responding to well-publicized abuses of power by federal Indian agents, President Grant instituted the Peace Policy in an effort to remedy these abuses and satisfy the call for Indian reform. The Peace Policy in effect turned over the nomination of federal Indian agents as well as the administration of reservations to Christian churches. The Peace Policy operated on the principle that the leadership of Indian affairs by Christian men and women would end all forms of abuse and corruption within the OIA. Under the Peace Policy, church missions and schools on Indian reservations received federal money and support. Christian churches from a variety of denominations became intimately tied to the OIA, holding and wielding a considerable amount of influence over federal Indian policy, particularly with regard to its goals of assimilation and civilization.

Government and mission boarding schools became a widespread method of achieving the OIA's goals of assimilation. Throughout the 19th and early 20th centuries, American Indian children were separated from their families and placed in these boarding schools to be taught the dominant values of white, middle-class society. American Indian participation in government and mission boarding schools was not always voluntary. On the contrary, parents were often coerced, threatened, and or bribed into allowing their children to leave home for the boarding schools. In many cases, American Indian children were even taken or stolen from their reservation homes by federal agents. By the 1930s, this practice had become so common that it was known among at least one tribe as "kid-catching," and American Indian parents were known to hide their children when federal agents appeared.

At boarding schools, American Indian children were expected to adopt white, middle-class values and speak English only. Threatened, punished, or beaten for speaking their Native languages, American Indian children were also denied their traditional religious practices, clothing, and appearance. The Protestant work ethic, Victorian-inspired gender roles, and white, middle-class standards of health and hygiene replaced tribal customs and practices. American Indian children in boarding schools spent much of their days doing chores; boys and girls were separated, with boys being expected to do the "male" work of farming, and girls expected to perform the "female" work of domestic chores. Not surprisingly, at mission schools, Christianity played a central role in this assimilation process, but even at government boarding schools, students were required to sing Protestant hymns and pray Christian prayers. At both types of boarding schools, American Indian children were frequently converted to Christianity during their attendance. It was believed that this "civilization" process would result not only in the assimilation of the younger generation of American Indians into white society, but future generations as well.

HEALTH CARE AND CIVILIZATION POLICIES

Originally responsible for providing health care services to American Indians, the OIA delivered these services in conjunction with its goals of assimilation. Several federal tribal treaties promised health care to specific American Indian tribes, but it was not until 1832 that the OIA specifically assumed responsibility for Indian health. Even then, however, health care was treated as a benefit provided at the generosity of Congress. Because of this, funding for health care services in both the 19th and 20th centuries fluctuated dramatically from year to year, depending upon congressional budgetary approval.

In the beginning, provisioning of health care services was inconsistent at best. Lacking any comprehensive health care program, the OIA failed to provide the physicians, nurses, hospitals, and other health care facilities promised under certain treaty agreements. Instead, the OIA merely responded in a reactive way to epidemics, such as small pox outbreaks among American Indians. These early health care responses were motivated by a desire to contain epidemics in order to protect the neighboring white populations, rather than out of concern for American Indian health and well-being.

Christian evangelization offered another motivation for providing health care to American Indians. In the 19th century, the OIA turned over much of the responsibility for providing health care services to Christian missionary and church groups receiving federal funding under the provisions of the Peace Policy. These health care services, too, were inadequate and inconsistent, and they were typically infused with evangelical efforts as well. Believing that American Indians successfully receiving Western medical care would be predisposed to accept the Christian religions of those who were providing that care, missionaries viewed Western medicine as an effective evangelical tool. Again, this meant that genuine concern for the health and well-being of Indian individuals and communities was a lost priority.

While attempting to attract American Indian converts through Western medicine, missionaries also actively campaigned against tribal medicine men and women. Missionaries, in conjunction with the OIA, regularly attacked local medicine men and women, imposing restrictions on traditional dancing ceremonies and labeling Native religious and healing practices "superstitious." Additionally, many medicine men and women increasingly identified certain illnesses, such as tuberculosis, as "white diseases" in need of "white medicine." Despite their need, access to Western medical health care facilities and providers was woefully insufficient for American Indians. Attempting to eliminate Native healing and religious practices while simultaneously failing to provide adequate Western medical services, the OIA failed American Indians on two levels.

In one of its first attempts at providing a comprehensive program of health care for American Indians, the OIA turned to the recently created field matron program. Begun in 1886 at the behest of the Society of Friends (Quakers), the field matron program's twin goals of assimilation and civilization relied upon the prejudicial assumption that American Indian women were responsible for keeping entire tribes mired in the past. The field matron program operated on the belief that if American Indian women could be taught to accept the values of white middle class domesticity, they would lead not only their families but entire tribes into "civilization." Field matrons visited the reservation homes of American Indian families and instructed women in the mechanics of proper cooking, nutrition, cleaning, health, hygiene, and parenting. In defining "proper," field matrons relied upon the dominant norms of white, middle-class society. This meant, among other things, replacing Native foods and food preparation practices with European-American inspired diets. Like other health care workers, field matrons were typically selected by and from among the pious missionary community, and they endeavored to instruct American Indian women in Christian principles and values.

As the ever-increasing health care needs of American Indians suffering from tuberculosis, trachoma (a painful eye disease that left many victims blind), and exceptionally high infant and maternal mortality rates became more blatant, the OIA employed agency and contract physicians on reservations. Unfortunately, however, their numbers were inadequate for responding to the urgent health care needs of American Indians. By the beginning of the 20th century, the OIA had failed to address the myriad health problems that threatened American Indian survival.

In the first three decades of the new century, several surveys and studies, including a 1912 Congressional Report, a 1922 Red Cross study, and the 1928 Meriam Report, all found health conditions on American Indian reservations to be appalling. The Red Cross Study, which had been conducted and written by public health nurses, provided the impetus to replace the dwindling field matron program with more highly trained and professionalized public health nurses, thus instituting the field nurse program. Six years later, the Meriam Report, undertaken by the Brookings Institute and authored by Lewis Meriam, excoriated the OIA for its failure to meet the health care needs of American Indians. The Meriam Report, which found that Native economies had been devastated and linked the resulting poverty to the poor health and rampant disease on reservations, blamed the OIA for the economic, social, and physical ruin on the reservations.

Pressured by the national negative attention garnered by the Meriam Report, the OIA began funding an expanded field-nursing program to meet health care needs on reservations; the Meriam Report praised the field-nursing program as the only promising element of Indian health care services. Riding the coattails of the progressive era public health nursing movement,

the OIA hoped that these field nurses—professionally trained in public health—could teach preventive health care on reservations and thereby improve the devastating health conditions among American Indians. In reality, field nurses frequently found themselves not only teaching health education, but also diagnosing and treating patients as well. While an adequately staffed and funded field-nursing program may have held great promise, the reality was that structural issues underlying poor health continued to go unaddressed.

JOHN COLLIER AND THE INDIAN NEW DEAL

In 1933, Indian reform advocate John Collier became the Commissioner of Indian Affairs and instituted the Indian New Deal. Dramatically altering federal Indian policy during his tenure as commissioner (1933–1945), Collier focused on respecting and rebuilding native communities. Influenced by his own social reform background, Collier moved the bureau away from assimilation and towards cultural preservation. This new philosophy took shape in the implementation of the Indian Reorganization Act.

The 1934 passage of the Indian Reorganization Act, also known as the Wheeler-Howard Act, ended general allotment. For the first time since the OIA's inception, the commissioner of Indian Affairs attempted to cultivate the cultures, economies, and religions of Native tribes. In its move away from assimilation, the Indian Reorganization Act prohibited the sale of tribal land to non-Indians without the full consent of the tribe in question. It persuaded tribes to incorporate themselves as corporate entities and to adopt tribal constitutions, created a revolving credit fund for use by tribes, and established Indian hiring preferences within the OIA. For the first time since the initial European contact, American Indians actually increased (rather than lost) their landholdings.

Despite these significant changes, however, many American Indians continued to distrust the OIA. Though its stated intention was to create more freedom for American Indians through self-government, not all tribes were equally impressed by the new legislation; 181 tribes voted to accept the Wheeler-Howard Act, while 77 more rejected it. Even within tribes, the Indian Reorganization Act prompted new factions and exacerbated existing ones as well. Some American Indians distrusted any type of federal intervention, while others felt the Indian Reorganization Act's homogenous plan perpetuated the OIA's long history of neglecting the diversity and thereby the different needs of hundreds of tribes. The formulaic prescription required for participation in the Indian Reorganization Act seemed to some yet another attempt at assimilation.

While the Indian Reorganization Act was contentious among American Indians and did not necessarily create any long-term change, it did in the short run represent a radical shift in the OIA's official policy with regard to Indian affairs. During the years of the Indian New Deal, Commissioner Collier was able to secure funds to help improve services on reservations. One such improvement could be seen in health care. The 1930s saw advancements in the numbers of health care facilities and personnel (particularly field nurses) available to American Indians on reservations. Additionally, during the Indian New Deal, American Indians were encouraged to take part in Western health care by becoming health aides, nurse's assistants, and field nurses. For the first time, too, official policy required noninterference with the practice of tribal medicine men and women. This window of tolerance allowed some cross-cultural health alliances to begin to form.

Unfortunately, however, the advancements made by the Indian New Deal were limited and short-lived. The post–World War II era ushered in a new philosophy and goal within the newly renamed BIA, that of termination. In 1950, President Eisenhower appointed Dillon S. Meyer as Commissioner of Indian Affairs. Meyer's tenure brought about an immediate departure from the policies of the New Deal administration. Marking a regressive return to earlier OIA goals of assimilation, American Indian freedoms were again restricted in the postwar period, as many of the gains of the New Deal era were lost. As the 1950s began, American Indians faced the new challenge of termination.

TERMINATION POLICY

In 1947, the OIA's name changed to the Bureau of Indian Affairs. Soon after, the bureau embarked on a new course of termination. Premised on the belief that

the federal government needed to extricate itself from Indian affairs by ending its services to American Indian tribes, termination threatened the very existence of the BIA, but, more significantly, it threatened the existence of American Indian tribes themselves. In 1953, under Commissioner Meyer's tenure, House Concurrent Resolution 108 officially ushered in termination. The new policy ended the trust relationship between the federal government and Native peoples, and certain American Indian tribes deemed to be "advanced" in their progress towards assimilation were slated for termination. A terminated tribe held land, but not as a reservation, and the tribe itself was no longer under federal regulation or welfare: it was on its own. During the 1950s, the Klamath of Oregon and the Menominee of Wisconsin were terminated with tragic results. Federal reports and follow-up studies found termination to be devastating for members of these two tribes. Termination meant the arbitrary loss of identity in addition to the end of reservations and governmental services. Loss of health care services and facilities, such as Indian hospitals and clinics, proved particularly traumatic for terminated American Indians. Both the Klamath and the Menominee tribes were eventually reinstated many years later due to the efforts of Indian activists like Ada Deer (Menominee), who fought for federal re-recognition of their tribes. Although many American Indians believed the BIA to be corrupt and patronizing, regularly interfering with tribal self-determination, few felt that termination would fix the economic, health, and social problems they faced as tribes; and, indeed, it did not.

Even tribes that did not directly suffer the experience and consequences of termination felt the implications of termination policy. For instance, one element of the termination policy that passed into legislation, Public Law 83–568, authorized the transfer of the Indian Health Services from the BIA to the Public Health Service (PHS), Department of Health, Education, and Welfare. Taking effect in 1955, this law officially removed responsibility for Indian health from the BIA. Initially opposed by many American Indians, because it was viewed as yet another attempt by the federal government to assimilate Native peoples, federal policymakers expected the transfer of Indian Health Services to improve the poor health conditions prevalent among American Indians. At the time of the transfer, Native populations continued to lag far behind the general population in disease and mortality rates. Supporters of the transfer believed that the shift would provide American Indians with the same standards of health care as the general population served by the PHS.

Unfortunately, reports on Indian health in the 10-year period after the transfer proved these expectations wrong. Instead, American Indian life expectancy remained woefully low at 44 years, 16 years less than the 70-year life expectancy for white Americans. Twenty years after the transfer, some health improvements were noted: Tuberculosis, for instance, decreased among American Indians by 91 percent. Yet it is difficult to assess how much of this improvement was a direct result of the transfer itself. Other factors, such as the Sanitation and Facilities Services Act of 1958, which brought running water and sewer services to American Indian homes for the first time, certainly played a role in improving health. And despite any improvements, by 1976, American Indians continued to suffer from tuberculosis at a rate of 4.6 times that of the general U.S. population while the mortality rate for influenza and pneumonia remained more than twice as high as for that of the general population. This, combined with a dramatic increase in American Indian deaths by suicide and accidents, meant that by the mid-1970s American Indian health remained in grave danger.

AMERICAN INDIAN ACTIVISM

Influenced in part by the civil rights movement, young American Indian activists in the 1960s and 1970s began a struggle for their own civil rights. Motivated by a long history of BIA interference with tribal authority as well as BIA corruption, these activists sought social and economic justice for their communities. American Indian activists recognized a need for the federal government to extricate itself from Indian affairs, but rather than accomplishing this through termination, these activists wanted the government to provide the funding and services it owed and had promised to tribes while allowing them autonomy in creating and implementing these services. Recognizing the primacy of land rights to their struggle for

independence, activists sought, among other things, the return of stolen lands. Many American Indians linked land issues with the overall welfare of native economies, religion, and health.

As early as the 1950s, Pacific Northwest tribes engaged in struggles to preserve their fishing rights. Staging "fish-ins," these Indian activists protested the BIA's failure to live up to the 1854–1855 treaty agreements that promised protection of Indian fishing rights to Pacific Northwest tribes. These early struggles motivated Indians across the country to mobilize for civil rights. In 1964, a group of Sioux Indians first seized the island of Alcatraz off the coast of San Francisco, claiming their right to use vacant land as promised by the 1868 Treaty of Fort Laramie. Although the original group was escorted out by federal agents, several hundred Indians from many different tribes calling themselves Indians of all Nations began a second occupation of Alcatraz in 1969, this one lasting until 1971. In 1968, urban Indians in Minnesota formed the American Indian Movement (AIM). In 1972, members of AIM caravanned to Washington, DC, the site of the centralized control of the BIA, with a list of demands in hand. Receiving no response, the group seized the BIA offices. The BIA takeover ended with the Nixon administration agreeing to take their demands under advisement. In a strongly symbolic gesture, American Indians highlighted their disapproval of the BIA, demonstrating the need for the BIA to actually represent and act upon Indian needs and perspectives. The following year, having seen no changes in the economic, health, and social situation, AIM activists occupied Wounded Knee in South Dakota, and the resulting standoff lasted for months, ending in two Indian fatalities and one FBI casualty. Through these militant protests, American Indian activists brought the ongoing injustices perpetrated against American Indians into the national spotlight.

Although the demands of AIM activists in particular were never met, American Indian activism continued into the 1980s and beyond in many different forms. Throughout the 1980s, Pacific Northwest women and men continued their fight for fishing rights. American Indian women from diverse tribes formed Women of All Red Nations (WARN) to, among other things, counter sterilization abuse of Indian women that occurred at Indian Health Services Hospitals throughout the 1970s. More recently, Indian leaders and activists have organized to resist excavation, mining, and corporate building on sacred land sites; have spoken out against the cooptation of Native spiritual and healing practices by the New Age Movement; and have engaged in protests to have offensive mascots removed from sports teams. Additionally American Indian activists continue to struggle for quality health care services, particularly in off-reservation and urban areas where an increasingly large portion of the American Indian population now lives.

THE BIA TODAY

Today, the BIA operates within a conflicted reality. While still the governmental agency responsible for the management and administration of Indian lands held in trust (including providing services to the 1.8 million American Indians and Alaska natives who are members of the 562 federally recognized tribes), the BIA continues to struggle with the paternalistic aspects of those functions. Positive changes have occurred in the recent past in an effort to make the bureau more responsive to American Indian needs and perspectives, yet the BIA continues to suffer from a legacy of corruption and abusive practices that have fostered feelings of mistrust and antagonism among many American Indians.

In the wake of termination, the BIA lost even more credibility with American Indians, than it had previously. The post-termination Commissioner of Indian Affairs, Philleo Nash (1961–1966), worked to convince American Indians that termination was indeed over; his efforts resulted in rebuilding some degree of trust between native peoples and the federal government. Nash's successor, Robert L. Bennett (1966–1969), an Oneida Indian, was only the second American Indian to hold the position of Commissioner of Indian Affairs (Ely Parker, a Seneca Indian, had held the post in 1869–1871). Bennett's tenure marked the beginning of the shift to American Indian leadership within the bureau. In 1973, one year after the takeover of the BIA, the new commissioner, Morris Thompson, an Athabascan Indian from Alaska, helped move the

BIA toward a philosophy of tribal self-determination, with passage of the Indian Self-Determination and Education Assistance Act in 1975. While transferring operating power of federal programs to tribes, the act required the federal government to continue funding those programs, thus distinguishing it from termination legislation. Nonetheless, many tribes remained reluctant to embrace the act, fearing that it was at heart just another attempt at termination. In 1978, Congress passed the American Indian Religious Freedom Act, guaranteeing the rights of Native religious practice for the first time.

Today, while the BIA continues to wrestle with its conflicted past, greater numbers of American Indians have taken up leadership roles within the bureau in an effort to make it both representative of Native perspectives and responsive to real issues of social and economic justice for American Indians. While in the 1930s, nearly two thirds of BIA employee positions were occupied by non-Natives, the past 30 years have witnessed a dramatic increase in the numbers of Native staff, with American Indians making up about 89 percent of personnel today. In 1977, the position of Assistant Secretary of Indian Affairs was created as the top leadership position within the bureau. Since its inception, the position has been held by American Indians, with Ada E. Deer (Menominee) becoming the first American Indian woman to fill this role in 1993. David Anderson (Ojibwa), who took office in February 2004, is the current Assistant Secretary.

Thus, the bureau's recent history is a mixed one. While the BIA's mission has officially changed from the early days of assimilation and evangelization of native populations to today's focus on tribal self-determination, in practice the bureau continues to carry with it a legacy of mistrust. As recently as 1992, the BIA was criticized for its mishandling of Indian land-holdings in trust. Although the BIA is no longer directly responsible for Indian Health Services, its policies regarding land and economic development continue to play a role in American Indian health. American Indians living in the West continue to fight for the return of stolen land, for self-determination, and for the resources to rebuild their economies. American Indian health and health care services, both on and off reservations, lag behind that of the general

U.S. population. Yet American Indian gains of leadership roles within the BIA points to the possibility of continued change and perhaps a more hopeful future for the American Indians of the Western United States.

—Christin Hancock

See also CALIFORNIA INDIANS OF THE NORTH COAST AND NORTHWESTERN COAST, INDIAN REMOVAL ACT OF 1830, LAKOTAS, TRAIL OF TEARS, YAKAMA

Suggested Reading

Benson, Todd. *Race, Health, and Power: The Federal Government and American Indian Health, 1909–1955*. Ph.D. Dissertation, Stanford University, 1993.

Emmerich, Lisa. "'Right in the Midst of My Own People:' Native American Women and the Field Matron Program." *American Indian Quarterly* 15 (Spring 1991): 201–216.

Fixico, Donald L. *Termination and Relocation: Federal Indian Policy, 1945–1960*. Albuquerque: University of New Mexico Press, 1986.

Johnson, Troy, et al. *American Indian Activism: Alcatraz to the Longest Walk*. Urbana: University of Illinois Press, 1997.

Keller, Robert. *American Protestantism and United States Indian Policy, 1869–1882*. Lincoln: University of Nebraska Press, 1983.

Kvasnicka, Robert M., and Herman J. Viola, eds. *The Commissioners of Indian Affairs, 1824–1977*. Lincoln: University of Nebraska Press, 1979.

Perdue, Theda, ed. *Sifters: Native American Women's Lives*. New York: Oxford University Press, 2000.

Prucha, Francis Paul. *The Great Father: The United States Government and the American Indians*. Lincoln: University of Nebraska Press, 1984.

Trafzer, Clifford, and Diane Weiner, eds. *Medicine Ways: Disease, Health, and Survival Among Native Americans*. Walnut Creek, CA: AltaMira Press, 2001.

⊞ BURLINGAME TREATY

See CHINESE EXCLUSION ACT, CHINESE IMMIGRATION

⊞ BUTTE, MONTANA

Between 1890 and 1930, Butte achieved recognition as having the most ethnically diverse population in the intermountain West and being the largest city between Spokane, Minneapolis, and Salt Lake City. As of 1910, 70 percent of Butte's population claimed foreign heritage. These facts defy a common misperception of the American West as predominantly home to native-born cattle ranchers and homesteaders. The Butte city directory of 1888 trumpeted Butte's ascendancy in the world of mining and smelting, which would remain with the city far into the 20th century: "Butte is to-day beyond any question the greatest mining camp on earth."

Shortly after 1887, when Butte was ranked as the leading producer of copper in the world (surpassing Michigan's Calumet & Hecla mining company and Spain's Rio Tinto), Butte promoters coined the moniker, "The richest hill on earth," which stuck until the demise of the Anaconda Company in the 1970s. From the beginning, Butte's industrial economy attracted a wide range of immigrants. Butte began as a rather unsuccessful gold mining camp in 1864, reflected by population figures in the 1870 Montana census, which counts 98 Chinese out of a total of 241 persons (40 percent), a familiar statistic in western placer mining camps where Chinese miners were allowed to work the placer gravels after white miners had abandoned their claims.

Silver mining represented the next phase of Butte's industrial development, beginning with William Farlin's filing on the Asteroid claim and construction of the Dexter Mill with financial backing from William Andrews Clark, a Butte pioneer who parlayed early investments into a vast empire of mines, railroads, and real estate. The 1880 Montana census demonstrated the continual growth of a foreign-born population: Of a population numbering 5,374, there were 3,502 foreign-born residents, including 501 from England and Wales; 972 from Ireland; and 710 Chinese (these figures are for Deer Lodge County; there was no separate entry for Butte). Silver brought Irishman Marcus Daly to Butte in 1876 as an agent of the Walker Brothers of Utah to investigate the Alice Mine. Six years later, Daly discovered a rich vein of copper in the Anaconda Mine, launching the creation of the world's largest copper mining and metallurgical company. Daly's discovery would signal the beginning of a mass migration of European immigrants to Butte during the next 40 years.

By 1888, Butte claimed more than 300 operating mines, four smelters, and three transcontinental railroads that connected the mining city to world copper markets, goods from the nation and the world, and a labor force representing nations from all corners of the globe. Immigration patterns in the mining city mirrored those of the nation at large: Between 1860 and 1930, the United States absorbed approximately 35 million immigrants, with the largest numbers coming from the United Kingdom, Germany, Canada, Scandinavia, and finally southern and eastern Europe. By 1900, 26 percent of the Butte population claimed Irish ancestry, a higher percentage of Irish residents than any other American city. Two out of three working-class Irishmen worked in the mines of Butte. An examination of the Butte city directories for the years 1886–1914 points to County Cork as the most popular place of origin for Butte Irish, along with others from counties Kerry, Tipperary, Limerick, Galway, and Mayo. And the town of Castletownbere in western Cork, near the copper mines at Hungry Hill, dominated the place of origin for Butte miners. Marcus Daly, who left County Cavan, Ireland, in the 1850s for California and Nevada where he learned the mining trade, constituted a magnet for prospective Irish immigrants seeking a better life in America. The Daly mines including the Anaconda, the Neversweat, the St. Lawrence, and the Mountain Consolidated (Mountain Con) employed an exceptional number of Irish miners, and Daly constructed handball courts (a popular Irish sport) next to the miner's change house at the Mountain Con Mine and posted job notices in Gaelic. Word of Daly's preference for Irish miners, the well-established support system provided by Irish Catholic parishes in Butte and such fraternal organizations as the Hibernians or the Robert Emmet Literary Association, and the Butte Miners' Union all encouraged Irish immigration to Butte.

The diversity of Butte's ethnic population was reflected in the creation of ethnic neighborhoods, an anomaly in mostly rural, sparsely populated Montana. Town Gulch, surrounded by Butte's most prominent copper mines, in short order became known as Dublin Gulch, with St. Mary's Catholic Church at its center. The neighborhood supported Irish-owned groceries and saloons, such as J. H. Lynch's Nevada Saloon and Pat Driscoll's Silver Palace. One could play handball at McCarthy's gym or attend a speech rallying for Irish independence from England up the hill at the Hibernian Hall. News of Ireland came to residents of Dublin Gulch and Corktown through the *Butte Independent,* published by Irish immigrant, James B. Mulcahy. Up the hill from the St. Mary's parish was the St. Lawrence O'Toole Church, serving the miners who lived and worked nearby at the Mountain Con and the Green Mountain Mines. The five Catholic parishes in Butte claimed more than 25,000 members by 1901, while no Protestant denomination had more than 800 members. In Butte, unlike other Irish-American communities, such as Boston and New York, the Irish came first and soon dominated the managerial and mercantile classes, as well as local politics. Only 10 years after its incorporation, Butte had its first Democratic Irish mayor, and between 1893 and 1919, there would be seven more. In 1905, Mayor Patrick Mullins oversaw a city council that was 75 percent Irish and police and fire departments dominated by his fellow immigrants. That pattern continued late into the 20th century.

During the mid-1880s, large numbers of experienced Cornish miners left the Comstock in Nevada for the copper mines of Butte, congregating up the hill from Dublin Gulch in Centerville and Walkerville. The Cornish were predominantly conservative—Republican in their politics and Methodist in their religion. In the 1900 Butte census, the Cornish represented the third largest contingent of immigrants after the Canadians and came to dominate the payrolls of the W. A. Clark mines and those not controlled by Marcus Daly. The Cornishmen brought pasties (meat pies) with them from the tin mining region of southwestern England, as well as their sports of greyhound racing and wrestling. The immigrants from Cornwall joined the American Protective Association (APA), a nativist, anti-Catholic organization that claimed 2,000 members in Butte by 1894. On July 4, 1894, several saloons on West Broadway displayed APA shields in their windows, setting off a riot featuring a hailstorm of paving stones, fire hoses, dynamite blasts, and the death of a policeman. Butte was not immune to conflicts between the British and Irish across the Atlantic.

By 1910, more than 1,000 Italians took up residence in Silver Bow County, congregating on the east side of Butte Hill in a suburb called Meaderville. As early as 1890, saloons operated by Sebastian Palagi, Joseph Bona, and Dominick Gionola appeared in Meaderville, and by 1916 Italian bakeries and boardinghouses could be found in Meaderville and

Walkerville. With prohibition, Meaderville became known for its restaurants, speakeasies, and nightclubs such as the Rocky Mountain Café.

Even as late as 1880, the Chinese remained a significant enclave in the Montana Territory and in Butte, moving from the abandoned placer mines into the laundry and restaurant businesses. They numbered 710 individuals in Deer Lodge County, which included Butte. Butte's Chinatown continued to grow, even after Congress passed the Chinese Exclusion Act in 1882. Organized labor in Butte made several dramatic assaults against the Chinese population, first in 1884 with a circular ordering Chinese to leave town, and then with a boycott organized against Chinese businesses in 1891–1892. However, this initial hostility had little effect on Chinatown; an 1890 Polk's City Directory documented Chinese ownership of 19 of the 20 laundries in Butte. But in 1897, the Silver Bow Trades and Labor Assembly launched another boycott of Chinese businesses, in part prompted by the economic downturn of 1893, which lingered on in the mining community. Organized labor directed its anger at Chinese laundries, stores, and restaurants and at those non-Chinese businesses that employed Asians. The Chinese merchants fought back, hiring Wilbur F. Sanders, one of Montana's most prominent jurists, and bringing a successful injunction against the labor unions in U.S. District Court in 1897. The court victory proved inconsequential, however, since the Chinese population diminished to 280 by 1900. Chinatown was rocked by internal strife in 1917, when the most bitter and longest Tong War in the United States erupted after members of the Bing Kung Tong were murdered by the rival Hip Sing Tong. Violence did not end until 1924. During the economic depression of the 1930s, the Butte Chinatown suffered another blow, with a significant drop in the demand for services they provided, cutting the population to 88 Chinese by 1940.

Scandinavians constituted another significant segment of the Butte population in 1900, led by more than 700 Swedes, more than 300 Norwegians, and 600 Finns. By 1910, the Finnish population had grown to more than 1,300, due in part to the increased demand for skilled timber men in the Butte underground. This massive influx of Finns resulted in the establishment of Finntown, a neighborhood of steam baths and boardinghouses adjacent to some of the major mines east of

Main Street. Finntown was home to the Big Ship, a Finnish boardinghouse that fed and roomed 500 single miners on rotating eight-hour shifts. Butte supported four separate Lutheran congregations: one each for the Swedes, the Norwegians, the Finns, and the Germans. By 1900, more than 1,200 Germans made Butte their home, settling in the southern suburb of Williamsburg, in the vicinity of Butte's breweries and railroad district. German immigrants formed a Butte *Liederkranz* Singing Society in the 1880s, and immigrants of German origin were found scattered in neighborhoods throughout the city throughout the early 20th century.

With copper mining booming between 1910 and 1916, thousands of southeastern European immigrants found their way to Butte. Approximately 2,000 Serbs, Croatians, Slovenes, and Montenegrins settled along the edges of Dublin Gulch, Corktown, the eastside, and McQueen by 1910; there was as well as an enclave of Lebanese known in Butte as Syrians. In 1908, Butte Syrians organized the Syrian Peace Society, the first fraternal society of its type in the country. The Serbs worshiped at a Serbian Orthodox church and the Catholic Croatians celebrated Mesopust, a pre-Lenten festival of drinking and dancing. Butte labor felt threatened by the influx of these immigrants, referring to them as "Bohunks," warning that these "dark invaders" would drive white men from their jobs. The Slavic community banded together in lodges like the Serb-Yugoslav Unity Lodge and the Serbian Montenegrin Federation—and, in fact, the Serbian Orthodox church persists even today.

In 1879, a Jewish merchant named Henry Jacobs became the first mayor of Butte, signaling the arrival of an enclave of German Jewish merchants. In 1881, the Hebrew Benevolent Association organized the first Jewish High Holy Day services, and four years later a Reformed congregation appeared under the name of B'nai Israel. In short order, an influx of Jews from Russia, Romania, Hungary, Poland, and the Ukraine fostered the establishment of an Orthodox congregation, Adath Israel. By 1900, 400 Jewish families made their home in Butte, which increased to 600 families by 1908. These immigrants dominated the mercantile class, managing dry goods, clothing, jewelry, grocery, and furniture stores. Jews also worked as tailors, peddlers, junk dealers, and all of Butte's pawnbrokers were Jewish according to the 1890 Polk directory. By the end of World War I, the ground that the Orthodox Synagogue sat on was sold to the Anaconda Company, but the B'nai Israel Synagogue, erected in 1903, remains across the street from St. Patrick's Church, maintained by only 20 Butte families. The decline in the Butte Jewish population was repeated in other western mining towns with the decline in the mining economy.

Immigration and ethnic persistence were linked inextricably to the fortunes of the mining industry. The decade beginning in 1910 constituted a period of extraordinary upheaval within the Butte Miners' Union and the Anaconda Copper Mining Company. Peaceful relations between workers and management deteriorated with the consolidation of all Butte mining and smelting operations by Anaconda, bringing

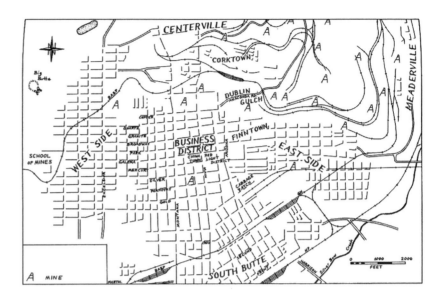

Neighborhoods on the Butte Hill in 1939.

Source: Murphy, Mary. *Mining Cultures: Men, Women, and Leisure in Butte, 1914–41.* Copyright 1997 by the Board of Trustees of the University of Illinois Press. Used with permission of the University of Illinois Press.

with it a new confrontational corporate management style, and a union rocked by dissension from within. Labor strife throughout the war period ultimately led to the dissolution of industrial unionism in Butte by 1920 until its reemergence in 1934. Although there were periodic upswings in the Butte mines during the 1940s and again in the 1960s, a general economic malaise settled over the city from 1920 forward, substantially diminishing Butte's ethnic communities. In an effort to revive the struggling mining industry, Anaconda embarked on a departure from 75 years of underground copper mining with its development of the Berkeley Pit in 1955. The open-pit mining technology had an immediate effect on Butte's ethnic neighborhoods: The Berkeley Pit, located in the heart of the city, expanded in size, forcing the relocation of ethnic enclaves in Meaderville, McQueen, and Finntown. But the Berkeley Pit would not be sufficient to save Butte from world competition and low-grade ore reserves. In 1977, the Anaconda Company was forced to sell its mining and mineral processing empire to Atlantic Richfield Company (ARCO), and six years later ARCO announced the suspension of all

mine operations in Butte after a century of Butte dominance in world metal production. The decline in Butte's population has been dramatic, from a thriving regional metropolis of 85,000 residents at the height of copper production in 1916 to a struggling postindustrial shadow of its former self at 35,000 in 2004.

Just as Butte was the domain of the Irish immigrant in the 1870s with the arrival of native son Marcus Daly, it remains so today. Since 1890, Butte has celebrated St. Patrick's Day with a parade and pints of Guinness, attracting tens of thousands of revelers. In 2003, the Montana Gaelic Society moved its annual *An Ri' Ra'* Irish Festival to Butte, attracting several thousand people to a celebration of Irish history, music, and dance. In the Butte telephone directory, the surnames of Sullivan, Murphy, Kelly, and Harrington still fill pages, and a real estate developer named Harrington from Menlo Park, California, just purchased the historic Silver Bow Club with plans for transforming it into a Celtic-Irish Heritage Center. The imprint of the Irish on Butte has endured. Folklorist Wayland Hand documented the significance of Butte to Irish sojourners in a story recounted in

Butte in the 1940s, when Pat in Butte wrote back to Mike in Ireland at the turn of the century: "Don't stop in the United States; come right on out to Butte."

—*Brian Shovers*

Suggested Reading

Coleman, Julie. *Golden Opportunities: A Biographical History of Montana's Jewish Communities*. Helena, MT: Skyhouse, 1994.

Emmons, David. *The Butte Irish: Class and Ethnicity in an American Mining Town, 1875–1925*. Urbana: University of Illinois Press, 1990.

Lee, Rose Hum. *The Growth and Decline of Chinese Communities in the Rocky Mountain Region*. New York: Arno, 1978.

Malone, Michael. *The Battle for Butte: Mining and Politics on the Northern Frontier, 1864–1906*. Seattle: University of Washington Press, 1981.

Murphy, Mary. *Mining Cultures: Men, Women, and Leisure in Butte, 1914–41*. Urbana: University of Illinois Press, 1997.

C

⊞ CAHUILLA NATION

From creation time into the 21st century, the social, political, religious, and economic organization of the Cahuilla people has been based on movement and migration. One of the largest groups of original people of southern California, the Cahuilla moved on a seasonal basis among winter, summer, and spring homes, gathering the available and managed foods while also hunting and visiting with kin and friends. The people migrated from one destination to the next continuing their socioreligious practices and the lifeways given to them by their creator, Mukat, at creation time. The Cahuilla managed a large territory, living in the deserts, mountains, and mountain passes of southern California. In addition to migrating through their lands procuring food and materials for tools, the Cahuilla traded and interacted extensively with other indigenous nations, intermarrying to maintain social and economic relationships. Yet the Cahuilla nation experienced significant changes after 1846. Having adjusted to the influences of the Spanish mission system in the 1770s–1830s, the war with Mexico and the Treaty of Guadalupe Hidalgo ushered in a new era of American invasion. This invasion had a severe impact on the Cahuilla population, health, lifeway, and economy, disrupting a migratory life cycle that had endured since creation. In spite of the disruptions, the Cahuilla survived the violent invasion and adapted to the new European economies while maintaining their migratory nature.

The Cahuilla story of genesis and tradition of bird singing describes the Cahuilla migrations and movement since creation time. The Cahuilla began their migrations as their creator, Mukat, provided laws that guided their social, religious, economic, and political practices, which directed their movements into the 19th century. In the beginning, during the time of "vast darkness," the two primordial beings of the Cahuilla, Tukmiat, the night, and Amnaha, the greatness of all things, attempted three times to create the first beings. On the third trial, they succeeded in creating the twin god brothers, Mukat and Tamaioit, who quarreled over which was the eldest. The brothers each created the first beings, the first a race of people, or *Mukitum,* and then humans. Mukat created the superior of the beings, winning the quarrel, so Tamaioit migrated to the underworld, taking his creations with him. Mukat provided for the Cahuilla people all they needed to survive, including instructions and tools to live, and the social structure and laws to govern the people. Mukat also caused hardship, and so some people conspired to kill him through poisoning or "witching." Upon his death, the people performed funerary rights and burned his body, from which sprang foods and medicines, such as the tobacco plant he gifted to the people. Though Mukat died and his brother, Tamaioit, migrated away, their influence remains. Spirit bestowed the *Kishamnawhet,* or ceremonial house, where he explained his spirit would dwell and instructed them to perform ceremonies.

Upon the death of Mukat, the people were lost and began to disperse, embarking on their initial migrations, which would take them to their lands in present-day southern California. Movement throughout their territory is a central theme of Cahuilla history, culture, and lifeway. A ceremonial leader picked up the ceremonial headdress and staff and instructed the first people to journey until they found the place they should settle.

Through the tradition of the bird songs and dances, the creation story is remembered and the migrations of the people retold. Navajo scholar Paul Apodaca described the Cahuilla culture as a complex song culture. He explains, "Traditionally singers and songs were present in every aspect of society and all segments of the community," and the culture included song cycles referred to as bird songs, deer songs, turtle songs, and *tangliveve* songs. *Hauinik* (ceremonial singers), *puls* (spiritual leaders), medicine people, and others trained in the tradition sang these songs. The last recognized hauinik, Joe Patencio of Palm Springs (Desert Cahuilla), passed away in 1947. The people sang certain songs for birth and naming ceremonies; initiation ceremonies for manhood and womanhood; first fruit offerings; change in adult status; eagle, rain and curing ceremonies; subsistence; defense for individuals and lineages; and funerary rights. In addition to ceremonial songs, there were also songs for work and basket making, clan songs, social songs, challenge songs, and those songs sung while playing the game called *peon*. People migrated annually throughout southern California to these sings and peon games and to attend other social and religious gatherings of different families and villages.

The bird songs retell the creation and migrations of Cahuilla people. They serve a popular and social function as entertainment and may close rituals to correct anything that may have been performed incorrectly. Bird singing is often accompanied by dancing, creating a social event in which men and women meet and affirm cultural identity. After singing about the creation, the song cycles tell of the people's journey over the lands three times before settling in the lands designated by Mukat to be their rightful living place. The songs describe the animals and plants observed by the people in their migrations, as well as the mountains, valleys, and water sources. Volcanoes described include the dormant craters of Pischa and Amboy. One song describes the origin of the colorful stripes of indigenous frogs and rattlesnakes and reminds the people how *Man-el,* the moon maiden, divided the

first people into their respective moieties of *tuktum* (coyote) and *istam* (wildcat). The songs reaffirm the people's connection with the creator and land.

The Cahuilla established permanent communities in three major areas of the southern California landscape: the mountains, mountain passes, and deserts. Cahuilla lands encompassed the territory marked by San Bernardino Peak on the north, to Borrego Springs on the south, and the San Jacinto plains and Palomar Mountain on the west to the east of the Orocopia Mountains. The people established villages near canyons during warmer seasons and in the deserts during the winter. People traveled and migrated seasonally to utilize food resources in various locations. Avenues for hunting and travel included trails that led from Chino Canyon to San Jacinto Peak, from Palomar Canyon to the Santa Rosa Mountains, Tahquitz Canyon to the San Jacintos and from Andreas Canyon to San Jacinto Peak.

The Pass Cahuilla lived within Banning Pass between Mount San Gorgonio and Mount San Jacinto. The pass leads east to the Colorado Desert and west to Los Angeles and the Pacific, and it linked the extensive trade network in which the Cahuilla participated during their migrations. Palm Springs lies to the east and San Bernardino to the west. Today, Morongo Reservation continues to exist within the Banning Pass. The Desert Cahuilla lived within the east base of Mount San Jacinto and reached into the Colorado Desert. The reservations that exist today include Agua Caliente, Cabazon, Augustine, and Torres-Martinez. The Mountain Cahuilla managed the territory marked by Mount San Jacinto and the neighboring southwest hillsides and valleys, including Gardiner Valley, and southeast to the Santa Rosa Mountains.

The Cahuilla established a large community in the San Jacinto Valley that included Casa Loma and at least seven other villages. Villages included Ivah, located in Massacre Canyon at the present site of Gilman Hot Springs, and Huachippan, the cultural center for the Cahuilla and gathering place for villages and kin groups, where the city of San Jacinto now stands. The village of Corova, or "cool place," was located in Castile Canyon, and Pahsitnah was the largest village on the south hills of what is now known as Big Springs Ranch, just west of the Ramona Bowl. One Cahuilla band located their village of Ararah in a canyon north of Valle Vista on the road to Idyllwild. Soboba village continues to exist today as Soboba Reservation.

Today, the Cahuilla live principally on Agua Caliente, Morongo, Cabazon, Torres-Martinez, Cahuilla, Santa Rosa, Los Coyotes, Ramona, and San Manuel Reservations. The Cahuilla Reservation is located in Anza, California; the Soboba Reservation is located southwest from San Jacinto, California; and Los Coyotes Reservation is located in the San Ysidro Mountains of San Diego County.

The various leaders of the sovereign Cahuilla Nation organized their communities in a way that enabled them to maintain a migratory lifestyle. Prior to invasion, the Cahuilla lived in small villages estimated to include 200 people. Renowned anthropologist Lowell Bean explains that these small villages recognized themselves as being part of a larger political group comprising several villages considered to be related and to share a common territory. The social laws divided clans into the wildcat and coyote moieties to prevent intermarriage of relatives. The moieties intermarried and maintained economic and social alliances. The largest political entity included about 2,000 people and was referred to as a *sib.* Sibs included several lineages, composed of nuclear and extended families that maintained their own food gathering and hunting areas and villages. Others could hunt and gather only with permission or an invitation on those lands. Families and villages migrated on a seasonal basis to hunt and gather natural resources, manage stands of various food crops, and gather for social and religious purposes. Village leaders, such as the *net* and *paha,* organized seasonal migrations to harvest food resources from the land or to hunt and to engage in social and or religious functions with other clans and nations.

Social, religious, and economic leaders decided when and where economic tasks or religious and social events would take place. For each lineage, a *net,* or headman, acted as a ceremonial leader, economic administrator, and political leader assisted by a *paha.* Ultimately, men and women of the community made decisions together concerning the welfare of the whole group; the value of the opinions expressed was based on the individual's standing depending on his or her knowledge, wisdom, and experience in relevant matters, in addition to oratory skill. Respected and gifted speakers traveled between communities and other Native nations to negotiate social and political events and issues. This is a practice of communal leadership that continues to exist today. Together, the community hosted visiting families or kinship groups who had migrated to visit and participate in certain events or prepared to travel or migrate themselves to particular destinations. A *pul* fulfilled the role of a medicine person, using medicinal plants to heal the body and providing counseling and curing ceremonies to heal psychological or social stresses and illness. Particularly talented medicine people traveled extensively, sharing their skill and knowledge. Ultimately, villages and sibs acted autonomously, cooperating with other villages and sibs to maintain social, economic, and political alliances or to reach larger goals. They were related or united internationally by customs and a common language, though dialects varied from region to region and even sib to sib.

Cahuilla people migrated through their territory to utilize a variety of resources and to visit sacred landscapes. The lands of Cahuilla territory provided an abundance of foods and resources that the people managed with a complex and extensive knowledge of agriculture and land and resource management. In addition to their scientific knowledge of the environment, they also maintained a strong spiritual connection and understanding that translated as respect of their natural and managed environment. People took responsibility for maintaining equilibrium with their environment, recognizing all the elements—wind, rain, thunder—and all the flora and fauna as beings that possessed a spirit and power just as humans. At creation, Mukat instructed the Cahuilla how to provide for themselves; what structures to build for living, storage and ceremonial purposes; and how to create works of art for utilitarian and ceremonial purposes.

People gathered foods and medicines from the various life zones from the Colorado Desert Basin to the Piñon Range of the San Jacinto Mountains. Some Cahuilla migrated a good portion of every year. They traveled to the lower desert, which provided mesquite and screw bean, and moved up in elevation to gather agave, yucca, acorns, and piñon nuts. Animals utilized by the Cahuilla included rabbit, deer, mountain sheep, antelope, quail, wood rats, and other small game. Cahuilla lived in a *kish,* a circular brush shelter built over scooped hallow ground and thatched with willow and grasses. *Ramadas*, or shade arbors, provided cool shelters in the summer that consisted of a roof of foliage supported by poles. The people constructed the *Hoyachat,* or sweathouse, of timber and mud up to 12 feet high for cleansing and ceremonial purposes. Southern California also possessed an abundant supply of mineral and hot springs that the people used for bathing, washing, entertainment, medicinal purposes, and, with European contact, as business ventures. One of the most important ceremonial structures was the creator's house, Kishamnahwhet, or big house, a circular structure with a sunken floor and a roof that slanted upward from the side walls, was supported by four forked posts, and was thatched with arrow weed, palm fronds, and willow. Cahuilla-Serrano elder Pauline Murillo, of San Manuel, explains that the Kishamnahwhet is the ceremonial house of the Cahuilla people where important matters and issues concerning the health of the people are addressed. The big house is used for all purposes concerning family and community, for gatherings and celebrations, as well as for healing and memorials.

In addition to the natural resources of their given environment and migratory patterns, the Cahuilla also enjoyed an extensive trade network. Trade with other nations reached to the coast and included the Chumash and Tongva, or Gabrielino. San Gorgonio Pass connected the Cahuilla with tribes east of their territory that included the Yavapai, Hopi, Navajo, Apache, and Quechans of present-day central Arizona. People traded for luxury items, foods, shells, and animal and mineral products. Archaeological studies that recovered California stone materials provide evidence that the trade network reached south to Mexico City in the ancient city of Tenochtitlan of the Aztec empire. Prior to European invasion, the Cahuilla enjoyed the wealth their territory and trade networks provided and the autonomy of truly sovereign bands, connected as a nation through language and culture. Since the beginning of creation, they maintained a complex social, religious, and economic lifestyle rich in art, music, and ceremony that Spanish invasion threatened and American invasion severely degraded. While adapting

to economies introduced by the Spanish and American empires, the migratory nature of Cahuilla labor and lifeways endured.

Until the late 1700s, the Cahuilla lived in the San Jacinto Valley, the mountains, and mountain passes unmolested by European invasions that were taking place in many other parts of the Americas. The Cahuilla had most likely been hearing of foreign invaders through their seasonal migrations and trade with other Native peoples long before actual contact. The Spanish gentry, mission agents, and Anglo settlers in Cahuilla lands introduced changes that altered their traditional migratory practices of food procurement and socioreligious practices. Invasion displaced people from their homes, lands, and resources, upsetting the yearly routines of traveling, food procurement, and seasonal rounds. In 1769, Spanish occupation of southern California began in San Diego by Gaspar de Portola, six years before the beginning of the American Revolution. In 1772, military commander Pedro Fages arrived in the San Jacinto Valley in pursuit of deserted soldiers. Between 1774 and 1776, Juan Bautista de Anza opened a land route for Spanish immigrant settlers, merchants, and soldiers from Sonora in Mexico to Monterey, California. It was during this expedition that he crossed into Riverside County and the Cahuilla Valley. Initially, the Cahuilla acted as mountain guides for Spanish explorers and helped Spanish and Mexican military expeditions whose reconnaissance of the San Jacinto Mountains enabled the ultimate establishment of transit routes for trade and colonization. Spanish exploration signified a historical turning point for the Cahuilla: the invasion of their ancestral lands. The diseases that arrived with European invasion had a dramatic impact on Native peoples of southern California. Smallpox and tuberculosis, among others diseases, devastated Native bands and scattered survivors to other clans and Native nations. Missionary settlements further disrupted the surviving peoples.

The mission system introduced a new, intensive, labor-based agricultural and ranching economy that exploited indigenous labor and redistributed their populations, changing and often inhibiting normal migration patterns. The influence of missions began with the establishment of Mission San Luis Rey by

Fray Antonio Peyri in 1798 at present day Oceanside, California. In the early 1800s, Fray Peyri established Casa Loma, an *assistencia* of San Luis Rey Mission on Rancho San Jacinto, the furthermost rancho located in the San Jacinto Valley. Cahuilla families continued traditional migratory practices while adapting to the new economy as seasonal agricultural and domestic labor. Some worked year-round for employers while traveling periodically to visit family or participate in social, economic, and religious gatherings. The missions forced converts to labor year-round for the missions and to give up completely their former migration cycles and lifeways. Mission padres established stations on or near villages to ensure converts. Many Cahuilla and Luiseño *vaqueros,* or cowboys, stayed to manage the vast herds of cattle and sheep, integrating themselves into the new economy. Migration patterns changed when Cahuilla vaqueros migrated to round up herds, take them to markets and to trade. It is through these ranchos that the missions and the soldiers of the presidios had the most influence over the Cahuilla, especially the Pass Cahuilla. Mission padres brought Cahuilla, Luiseño, Juaneño, and Serrano peoples out to the San Jacinto Rancho as labor.

During the 1820s, the padres of Mission San Luis Rey appointed Juan Antonio, a Mountain Cahuilla, as captain of Rancho San Jacinto. Juan Antonio, with the family name of Costo, was born in the Anza Valley into the *Coos-woot-na* clan around 1783. The mid-1800s were a violent and turbulent period in southern California history, and Juan Antonio is renowned by indigenous and nonindigenous peoples for being a powerful Cahuilla leader who mediated white-Indian relations. Antonio had many villages and migrated between them, and he traveled throughout Cahuilla territory mediating between various Cahuilla bands and many white immigrants. The Lugo family, one of the largest landowners in San Bernardino, hired Antonio as the guardian of their estate to protect the land and livestock from the raids of eastern indigenous nations. Juan Antonio hired other Mountain Cahuilla and established them at Politana, near present-day Colton, to protect the Lugo ranch. By 1824, the missions of San Luis Rey, San Juan Capistrano, San Diego, and San Gabriel exerted influence over present-day Riverside County. Spanish invasion and

the enslavement of Cahuilla and others by the missions introduced disease that heavily impacted the population and the economic, social, political, and religious structure of the Cahuilla lifeways.

In 1822, Alta California became Mexican territory after revolting against Spanish rule. In 1833, the Mexican government secularized the missions, opening lands to private ownership. Secularization ushered in the Californio, or rancho, period in which a few landowners owned large tracts of land. The Cahuilla continued to integrate themselves into this economy as laborers and domestic servants while maintaining their autonomy.

Some Natives remained near the mission, while many others took their skills as vaqueros to work on new ranchos. It was a common practice, if not policy, of ranch owners during the rancho period and later during the Anglo conquest period to hire Cahuilla and Luiseño families to manage their livestock herds. Native families became very skilled in ranch and livestock management. Many others fulfilled the demand for domestic labor. The aboriginal population, now an integral part of European economy, interacted with the Anglo population on a daily basis. Cahuilla people adjusted to the Spanish presence yet maintained both a degree of autonomy and their traditionally migratory lifestyle. The Cahuilla worked for little or no wages and chose their course of livelihood, some living completely apart form mission and ranchos, continuing old lifeways unmolested.

By 1846, Americans began to immigrate to the territory of the Cahuilla and surrounding indigenous nations. Matters worsened in 1848 with the onset of the gold rush following the discovery of gold in the Maidu village of Koloma in northern California. Initially, Californios such as James Marshall took their native ranch hands to the goldfields to pan placer deposits. And by 1850, half the miners were California Indians. Soon, non-Natives from Oregon began murdering California miners and then killing indiscriminately, hunting down Native men, women, and children to kill or enslave. This period of intense violence forced indigenous peoples to move away from foreign settlements, either to escape contact or due to enslavement, and that altered their traditional migratory cycles. Killings significantly reduced the Native population from an estimated 250,000 in 1800 to 100,000 at the eve of the gold rush, and to 20,000 by 1900. Aware that Americans claimed their lands, the Cahuilla people reacted in a variety of ways, that included accommodation through agreeing to treaties while living unchanged; attacking and rebelling; moving away from non-Native towns and travel routes; and dealing with circumstances to the best of their ability.

In 1848, the United States won the war with Mexico, ushering in the American invasion that would further disrupt Cahuilla migrations and lifeways. The war concluded with the signing of the Treaty of Guadalupe Hidalgo, which ceded Spanish- and Mexican-claimed Cahuilla lands to the United States. The American government instituted the reservation system and instituted laws that prohibited traditional migratory patterns. In September of 1850, Congress authorized President Zachary Taylor to appoint three commissioners—Redick McKee, George W. Barbour, and Oliver M. Wozencraft—to negotiate treaties with the Cahuilla, Serrano, and neighboring nations. Anglos began to arrive en masse in Cahuilla lands and exploited natural resources on a grand scale through grazing, mining, deforestation, and development. And as with the mission padres, Spanish military, and Mexican-California families, the Anglo immigrants abused, exploited, and murdered the Cahuilla and other indigenous peoples of southern California. Cahuilla elder Manuel Medina, who has spent his life living throughout southern California, recalled through oral histories that leaders in frontier communities gave monetary incentives to murder aboriginal people. City government officials and the aristocracy awarded Spanish or Anglo vigilantes for presenting the scalp of a Native boy or girl. Medina explained that girls or women, less of a threat than boys, were sometimes married off into Irish or German families. More often, slavers sold girls and women into slavery and prostitution.

The greed for land and resources by non-Native populations and the resulting oppression and murder of Natives continued into statehood. These events fragmented Cahuilla communities, marginalizing them, hindering the social and religious practices, and further inhibiting the traditional patterns of migration. Many individuals who married into European families for survival were unable to continue to participate or organize in many traditional activities. Still others did

continue old traditions, succeeding in their avoidance of white settlements until the American government instituted laws that would reach farther in their influence over Cahuilla life as whites outnumbered the ravaged indigenous populations.

On September 9, 1850, California became a state. On April 22, 1850, Congress passed Statute Chapter 133, the Act for the Government and Protection of Indians. The statute established 22 laws similar to the Jim Crow laws of the south. The laws discriminated against and oppressed indigenous peoples and essentially legalized slavery. In addition, Congress created a board of land commissioners to segregate privately owned land from public domain. Laws banned Native land management practices, such as burning, and removed access to lands and resources, greatly restricting Cahuilla mobility. Following government approval and an official survey, the federal government issued individual patents to each rancho owner. The California and U.S. governments refused to recognize Cahuilla farms and villages and evicted the Cahuilla people, allowing white settlers to claim them as their own. Families were moved from place to place, pushed farther and farther off their lands and grew more destitute as Americans stole the lands they worked to produce food and resources. In addition, Europeans introduced livestock and plant species that destroyed the natural resource base that the Cahuilla managed and depended on for their livelihood, further disrupting their seasonal migrations to manage and gather food resources. Refugees in their own country, the Cahuilla were hindered by American laws from practicing their migration cycles.

Some Cahuilla continued to resist white settlement and traveled throughout southern California visiting with other leaders and encouraging and organizing political and military resistance. But the attack on Warner's Ranch on November 21, 1851, and the final battle in Coyote Canyon on December 20 known as the Garra Revolt, or Garra Uprising, marked the end of overt military Indian resistance in the region. Cahuilla-Cupeño Antonio Garra organized a confederacy and advocated the defeat of the Americans. It was short lived and concentrated in area, but represented the feelings of many first-nation peoples. Cahuilla leader Juan Antonio turned Garra over to the

Americans, leading to Garra's execution as a warning not to oppose American hegemony. People continued to resist, but few chose outright rebellion.

California gold continued to attract thieves and murderers. John Irving, a former captain in the U.S. Cavalry, entered California with his band of desperadoes, which included Australian convicts. His gang traveled through Los Angeles and Cahuilla territory, raping, murdering, stealing, and harassing people, including the Lugo family. While the Irving gang planned to rob a silver train in Mexico and continued to raid the Lugo ranch, Juan Antonio brought the criminal activities of the gang to a halt. Antonio and his partners trapped the Irving gang in Live Oak Canyon where it crossed San Timoteo Canyon and killed all but one of the men. The authorities initially wanted to hang Antonio for killing whites but eventually awarded him and his band for their heroics. In spite of the aid of Antonio and his band, the majority of non-Indians continued to perceive indigenous people as a problem to be remedied and the general livelihood of indigenous peoples continued to worsen. American citizens and the government conceived of new ways to bring an end to Cahuilla lifeways and movement. Americans wanted to confine the movement of indigenous people while usurping their land and natural resources.

Commissioners McKee, Barbour, and Wozencraft, in an effort to solve the "Indian problem," began drawing up treaties to create reservations. The Anglo settlers, legislature, and Congress rejected all the treaties in 1852. Juan Antonio, bitterly disappointed, refused to leave San Timoteo Canyon in spite of further encroachment of lands by Anglos. In 1856, Antonio watched as Americans squatted on his lands, stole his natural resources, and killed his livestock. In 1852, the superintendent of Indian Affairs for California, Edward F. Beale, unsuccessfully proposed another series of reservations. White settlers, successful in their attempts to remove the Cahuilla from their lands, forced Manuel Largo, a net of the Pass Cahuilla, in 1874 to move his band to the old village site of Paui on the west side of Cahuilla Valley. Recognizing the desperation of Cahuilla people for protected lands, President Ulysses S. Grant in 1875 set aside nine small reservations in San Diego County by executive order. Unsurveyed and unprotected by federal law,

white settlers continued to encroach on Native lands and take control of water resources. Without water for agriculture, and with hunting and gathering lands being stolen by settlers, the mission Indians became more desperate and sought ways to survive in their changing environment.

Many Cahuilla had participated in the economies introduced by the missions and ranchos, and many younger Cahuilla turned to low-paying wage and subsistence jobs generated by the American economy. Cahuilla people continued to migrate throughout their territory in search of livelihood. Once traveling to hunt and gather or participate in social events, Cahuilla youth sought work on American ranches, farms, and businesses. Mountain Cahuilla cowboys tended the herds of Charles Thomas, Manuel Arnaiz, and the Tripp family. Some sought seasonal and migratory work on fruit ranches. Living in temporary camps, men, women, and children picked produce for white farmers and migrated from job to job. Cahuilla sheepshearers worked seasonally on ranches and became the best in the business while Cahuilla women sought employment in urban centers as domestic laborers. Women left their children with relatives to move into the larger cities to live with white families and care for employer's homes and children, visiting their own children on holidays and vacations or between jobs. This pattern of migratory wage labor persisted for most of the first half of the 20th century.

During the 19th and 20th centuries, after being ravaged by invasion, the Cahuilla nation continued to endure poverty and ill health. Leaders of various bands continued to travel throughout California to organize politically in an effort to alleviate the suffering of the communities. During the 1920s and 1930s, the Mission Indian Federation demanded destruction of the Office of Indian Affairs in an effort to exercise full tribal sovereignty and improve the general conditions of indigenous California peoples. In the 1930s, many nations, including the Cahuilla, agreed to join the Indian new deal under the Indian Reorganization Act (IRA) passed by Congress in 1934. The IRA sought to improve Indian education and health, extend freedom of religion, and establish the right to maintain language and culture. In many ways, it promised to enable and encourage Indian peoples to renew social, religious, and economic seasonal migrations in new forms with clans and other nations. It acted to form tribal business corporations to acquire business loans from the government for economic development with the theme of conserving the Native American environment. The IRA benefited most Native peoples and changed the course of Indian policies, leading the way for greater self-determination. Having recovered some lands, natural resources, and political sovereignty, Cahuilla bands began to recover some mobility economically, politically, and culturally.

With the legal status of sovereign nation and a federal policy supporting self-determination, the Cahuilla and other sovereign nations of southern California have been rebuilding their nations after 300 years of invasion and oppression. Leaders and government officials of various bands have traveled throughout California and the United States, building relationships with various tribal governments, individual U.S. officials, and many other associations and organizations in an effort to begin economic development and cultural revitalization projects. The Cahuilla have begun developing their economies in an effort to relieve the unemployment, poverty, and ill health on many reservations.

In the 1980s, Cahuilla living on Cabazon and Morongo Reservations began operating bingo parlors that increased the economic well-being and standard of living on several reservations. Many others followed suit, and by the 1990s the California state government and U.S. government attempted to shut down Indian gaming, resentful that Indian tribes brought in revenue the government was unable to control. In 1998, California citizens voted in favor of Proposition 5, which supported Indian gaming. Since the opening of bingo parlors, the Cahuilla have also opened gaming halls. Of the 107 recognized tribes of California, 54 operate casinos. A few of those casinos bring in considerable revenue and bring up the standard of living of surrounding communities as well as their own. Most reservations have not become rich and many more remain impoverished. Indian gaming has provided the resources needed to build tribal government and improve health services and education. Cahuilla in such places as Soboba and Cabazon have instituted scholarship programs for their youth and increased the number attending and graduating colleges and universities. More and more Cahuilla youth are migrating to other cities and states to seek a college education that will serve future generations. In addition, gaming has provided the income to diversify Cahuilla economies, institute cultural revitalization projects, and share income with impoverished nongaming tribes.

As a result of Indian gaming, the Cahuilla have been able to rebuild their governments and communities by organizing language and culture programs and revitalizing ceremonies. Once again, various families and bands of Cahuilla are migrating to gather for social, ceremonial, and religious purposes on a seasonal basis. Vanessa Odom, Juan Antonio's great-great granddaughter, met with Indian youth from southern California and around the country at the Future Leaders of Native Nations Conference, 2004, hosted and created by Christopher Sandoval of the Acjacamen Nation of southern California. She traveled from Torres Martinez to Serrano Territory above Redlands to facilitate leadership training of tomorrow's Native leaders and assume the leadership position her great-great grandfather did in the 1800s. The Cahuilla have adapted to the American economy while maintaining their migratory and complex sociopolitical life way. Members of the community continue to travel around California, the United States, and Mexico as well as other countries to develop and maintain economic and social alliances with other communities, just as they did prior to invasion.

—*Leleua L. Loupe*

See also Gabrielino, Indian Removal Act of 1830, Juaneños, Luiseño

Suggested Reading

Apodaca, Paul. "Tradition, Myth, and Performance of Cahuilla Bird Songs." Ph.D. Dissertation, University of California–Los Angeles, 1999.

Bean, Lowell. *Mukat's People: The Cahuilla Indians of Southern California.* Los Angeles: University of California Press, 1972.

Bean, Lowell, and Harry Lawton. *The Cahuilla Indians of Southern California.* Banning, CA: Malki Museum Press, 1989.

Beattie, G. W., and H. P. Beattie. *Heritage of the Valley: San Bernardino First Century.* Pasadena, CA: San Pasqual Press, 1939.

Bolton, H. E. "The Mission as a Frontier Institution in the Spanish American Colonies." *The American Historical Review* 23, no. 1 (1917–1918): 43–61.

Bolton, H. E. *Anza's California Expeditions*. Berkeley: University of California Press, 1930.

Brigandi, Phil. *Temecula: At the Crossroads of History*. Encinitas, CA: Heritage Media, 1998.

Brumgardt, John R., and Larry L. Bowles. *People of the Magic Waters: The Cahuilla of Palm Springs*. Palm Springs, CA: ETC, 1981.

Caldwell, George W. *Legends of Southern California*. San Francisco: Phillips and Van Orden, 1919.

Coues, E. *On the Trail of a Spanish Pioneer: The Diary of Francisco Garces*. New York: Harper, 1900.

Elliot, Wallace B. *History of San Bernardino and San Diego Counties*. San Francisco: W. W. Elliott, 1883. (Reprinted Riverside, CA: Riverside Museum Press, 1965)

Engelhardt, Zephyrin. *Missions and Missionaries of California, Vol. 8. Upper California*. San Francisco: James H. Barry, 1913.

Fisher, M. F. K. *Spirits of the Valley*. New York: Targ Editions, 1985.

Hanson, Barry, and Bill Jennings. *San Jacinto Valley Railway California Southern–Santa Fe*. Hemet, CA: Save Our Station, 1991.

Hemet Land Company. *Hemet Southern California: Its Homes and Scenes*. Hemet, CA: Hemet Land Co., 1902.

Hemet News. *Down Memory Lane: A Historical Record of People and Events in California*. Hemet, CA: The Hemet News, 1960.

Hemet–San Jacinto Genealogical Society. *San Jacinto Valley: Past and Present*. Dallas, TX: Curtis Media, 1989.

Hudson, Roy F., ed. *Desert Hours with Chief Patencio: As Told to Kate Collins by Chief Francisco Patencio*. Palm Springs, CA: Palm Springs Desert Museum, 1971.

Hyer, Joel R. *We Are Not Savages: Native Americans in Southern California and the Pala Reservation, 1840–1920*. East Lansing: Michigan State University Press, 2001.

James, George Wharton. *Old Missions and Mission Indians of California*. Los Angeles: B. R. Baumgardt, 1895.

James, Harry C. *The Cahuilla Indians*. Banning, CA: Malki Museum Press, 1969.

Madrigal, Anthony. "Ramona and Cahuilla Indian Bird Songs: Contrasting Visions of Southern California." Unpublished paper, University of California–Riverside, 2001.

McWilliams, Carey. *Southern California Country: An Island on the Land*. New York: Duell, Sloan, & Pearce, 1946. (Reprinted Santa Barbara, CA: Peregrine Smith, 1973)

Medina, Manuel. Oral history conducted by Leleua Loupe. May 19, 2001. Riverside, California.

Murillo, Pauline. *Living in Two Worlds*. Highland, CA: Dimples Press, 2001.

Oxendine, Joan. *The Luiseño Village during the Late Prehistoric Era*. Ph.D. Dissertation, University of California–Riverside, 1983.

Pourade, Richard F. *Anza Conquers the Desert: The Anza Expeditions From Mexico to California and the Founding of San Francisco 1774 to 1776*. San Diego, CA: Copley Books, 1971.

Quimby, Garfield M. *History of the Potrero Ranch and Its Neighbors*. Fresno, CA: California History Books, 1975.

Robinson, W. John, and Bruce Risher. *The San Jacintos: The Mountain Country from Banning to Borrego*. Arcadia, CA: Big Santa Anita Historical Society, 1993.

Robinson, W. W. *The Story of Riverside County*. Riverside, CA: Riverside Title, 1957.

Simpson, R. J. "California Mineral Deposits of the San Jacinto Quadrangle, Mining in California." *California Journal of Mining and Geology* 28 (1932): 3–11.

Simpson, R. J. "Historical Mineral Resources of a Portion of the Perns Block." *Journal of Mines and Geology* 31 (1935): 507–521.

Tac, Pablo. *Indian Life and Customs at Mission San Luis Rey: A Record of California Mission Life by Pablo, an Indian Neophyte (1835)*. San Luis Rey, CA: Old Mission, 1958.

Tapper, Violet, and Nellie Lolmaugh. *The Friendliest Valley: Memories of the Hemet San Jacinto Area*. Hemet, CA: Hungry Eye Books, 1979.

Underhill, Ruth. *Indians of Southern California*. Washington, DC: United States Department of the Interior, Bureau of Indian Affairs, 1941.

U.S. Department of Interior. Mission Indian Agency Allotment Schedules and Plates, Including Public Domain Allotments and Homesteads. Records of the Soboba Indian Agency, CA.

Weber, Francis, ed. *King of the Missions: A Documentary History of San Luis Rey de Francia*. Los Angeles: Archdiocese of Los Angeles Archives, 1980.

Whitney, Mary E. *Valley, River, Mountain: Revisiting Fortune Favors the Brave: A History of Lake Hemet Water Company*. Hemet, CA: Hemet Area Museum Association, 1982.

Whittington, Roberta E. *Hemet-San Jacinto: A Geographic Survey of an Agricultural Valley*. M.A. Thesis, University of California–Los Angeles, 1987.

Wright, Gloria. Oral interview conducted by Leleua Loupe. January, April, and November, 2001. Soboba Reservation, San Jacinto, California.

Van Fleet, C. M., and Lucile Hooper. "The Cahuilla Indians." *American Archaeology and Ethnology* 16 (1920): 318–380.

✠ *CALIFORNIA EAGLE*, THE

See BASS, CHARLOTTA SPEAR(S)

✠ CALIFORNIA INDIANS OF THE NORTH COAST AND NORTHWESTERN COAST

Traveling north from San Francisco along the legendary Highway 1, visitors to this region find themselves in a world of dramatic vistas to both the west and the east. This long piece of land, caught between the ocean and the coastal range, runs from the Marin Headlands north to Del Norte County at the present-day California-Oregon border. Looking to the west, out to sea, travelers have miles of rocky, fogbound coast to enchant and enthrall them. The world of the giant redwood trees, among the largest living things on Earth, is located to the east. This was, and remains, the world of the northwestern and the northwestern coastal Indians of California. The Coast Miwok, the Pomo, the Tolowa, the Yurok, the Wiyot, the Mattole, the Nongatl, the Sinkyone, the Lassik, and the Wailaki lived hard by the ocean. Farther inland, but still residing in regions largely shaped by the maritime weather patterns and geography, were the Hupa, the Chilula, the Whilkut, the Karuk, the Cahto, and the Chimariko. Blending the lifeways of the northwestern Indians and the California culture area, these communities adapted themselves to their physical surroundings. In this world of mist and forest, river and redwoods, salmon and whales, these Native nations created some of the most complex and highly stratified cultures in indigenous California.

The spectacular scenery of the northern California coast has been the home, for thousands of years, of Native peoples who fit themselves into their rugged surroundings. Attempts to determine the origins of the indigenous population of the Western Hemisphere have spawned a number of widely divergent theories that have come to coexist uneasily in contemporary America. Passage from northeast Asia via the Bering Straits land bridge, once the dominant theory for the peopling of the Americas, now has competition from those who argue the likelihood of migration from Polynesia, Africa, and even China. Similarly, there is substantial disagreement on when these first migrants arrived. Conventional wisdom dictates that habitation of the Americas began 14,000 to 20,000 BP (years before present) as Asian hunters gradually moved into the Western Hemisphere. Evidence in California suggests that there may have been some human habitation during this period. There is, however, a much stronger archeological record to support settlement during the Paleo-Indian era, dating from 14,000 to 11,000 BP. Certainly, by the later date, substantial populations

were in evidence in the most resource-rich areas of present-day California. In some areas of the northwestern coastal region, there is archaeological evidence that indicates inhabitation from 5,000 BP. Population estimates for this region, as in all of precontact California, differ greatly. Nonetheless, demographers agree that this area was equal to the northern central valley in terms of population density. Perhaps 70,000 or more Native people lived in this area prior to the invasions of their homelands.

There is greater certainty about the cultural affiliations of the Natives living in this region of precontact California. It was a mixed bag of peoples and lifeways. The Coast Miwok living just north of San Francisco Bay spoke a variant dialect belonging to the Utian family. The Karuk living along the Klamath River, the Pomo along the coast near Bodega Bay, and the Chimariko whose sliver of land fell along the Trinity River all shared linguistic ties to the Hokan languages. The Yuki, whose territory was just northeast of Pomo country, spoke their own unique language. So, too, did the Wiyot and the Yurok of the very far northwest. The remainder of northern coast Indians spoke languages derived from the Athapaskan family. The Tolowa, the Hupa, Chilula-Whilkut, the Mattole, and the Wailaki-Nongatl-Lassik-Sinkyone-Cahto languages dominated the far northwestern coastal and riverine areas of this region.

This pastiche of dialects was echoed by the indigenous cultural patterns of the zone. Some tribes, such as the Tolowa, the Hupa, and the Karuk, had very loosely organized societies. The Yurok, on the other hand, had a highly organized and highly stratified society that included both an aristocracy and a form of debt peonage. Despite their sometimes profound differences, their common use of and trade in the area's superabundance of natural resources linked these disparate communities. For those tribes living right along the ocean, the typical California aboriginal diet of salmon, deer, and acorns was augmented by shell fish, surf fish, seals, mussels, clams, and sea lions. The occasional beached whale also contributed to this diet. Those Indian communities located farther inland also relied heavily on the usual subsistence fares of salmon, deer, and acorn. Their diets were varied by the use of steelhead (another anadromous fish), sturgeon, eels, elk, tubers, bulbs, and seeds. Migratory waterfowl often figured in seasonal diets. And wherever its growth could be encouraged, wild tobacco also was a part of the subsistence resources used in this area. In sum, the happy accident of proximity to the ocean, to richly stocked rivers, and to heavily forested foothills and mountain slopes afforded the Natives opportunities to create sedentary villages with substantial dwellings. Though individual and communal survival required the contributions of all, this area was one of plenty where food was not usually a contested item.

Despite this natural largesse, the northern and northwestern coastal areas were, by no means, a utopian Eden. Some communities lived in relative harmony with their neighbors; others did not. Diplomatic relationships defined certain neighbors as friends to welcome and others as enemies to fear. The Yurok, Hupa, Tolowa, Chilula, Whilkut, Chimariko, Karuk, and the Wiyot all apparently fought among themselves. Motives for warfare among these tribes typically included homicides, personal grievances, and the belief that one had been "poisoned" through supernatural means. The Pomo fought among themselves as well as with neighboring nations like the Yuki, Patwin, Wintu, and Wappo. Among these groups, many of the conflicts seem to have been economically motivated. Boundary disputes, theft of personal property, and violation of hunting or gathering areas was enough to set off a round of organized engagements that were either intratribal or intertribal in nature. The settlement of disputes through negotiation and restitution was a strategy successfully employed within and among these tribes. But, that method of resolution did not always stave off hostilities. While pitched battles were rare, deaths were not uncommon. Wholesale warfare to inflict maximum casualties was a foreign concept to these Indians. The arrival of and settlement by the outsiders—Russians, Spanish, Mexicans, English, and Americans—would lead to that hard lesson.

Non-Indians came to the northern coastal areas of California in search of the very same natural resources that facilitated the growth and specialization of these indigenous cultures. Though Sir Francis Drake may have made landfall in Bodega Bay in 1759, the Spanish became the first colonial overlords of Alta California. With the extension of the mission system

northward in the late 18th and early 19th centuries, the southern and eastern Pomo suffered the effects of proximity to the missions' religious and physical demands. Pomo Indians, either by choice or because of coercion, became residents of the San Francisco de Asís (Dolores), San Rafael, and San Francisco Solano (Sonoma) missions. Removal to these centers of assimilation separated the Pomo from their homelands, their languages, and their religious beliefs. It also weakened the ability of the remaining population to independently sustain the community.

The arrival of the Russians in California was roughly simultaneous with this series of events. In 1812, the Russian-America Fur Company established an agricultural station and trading outpost at Bodega Bay. Fort Ross was located in territory shared by the Kashaya Pomo and the Coast Miwok. The Russian-American Fur Company used a combination of methods to secure the labor of the local Indians: some were paid to work as farm laborers; others were coerced into facilitating different aspects of the seal and sea otter trade. Both strategies occasioned resistance by the Pomo, who were unable to dislodge the outsiders. The Russian presence between 1812 and 1825 introduced the Pomo and their neighbors to Eastern Orthodox Christianity, epidemic diseases, and alcohol. It also virtually destroyed the sea otter population. A combination of reasons persuaded the Russians to leave Pomo territory in the mid-1820s. The decimation of the sea otter population and increasing Pomo resistance made the continued occupation of Fort Ross untenable. Their departure did not, however, end the movement of newcomers into the homelands of the northern and northwestern coastal Indians.

The assumption of Mexican independence in the 1820s led to a greater non-Indian presence in Alta California and brought substantial woe to a number of these communities. Land grants carved up the northern reaches of the state, forcing Indians to assimilate into the colonial culture and economy or flee their territories. These land-grant ranches, which extended from the coast inland to the area surrounding Clear Lake, incorporated huge swaths of Pomo and Coast Miwok land. The increasing demand for laborers occasioned slave raids into the coastal and interior regions, decimating tribal communities. The raiders also carried along the seeds of a smallpox epidemic that further eroded the population base. By the late 1830s, all of southern and central Pomo and Coast Miwok lands were under the control of the Mexican government and much of the Native population had been forced into debt peonage. At the same time, farther north and inland, fur traders from the Hudson's Bay Company made contact with the Tolowa, the Yurok, the Karuk, and the Chimariko. As in other parts of northern California, the traders brought the Indians desirable material goods and exposed them to malaria. This caused another wave of deaths in these already vulnerable communities.

The troubles of the 1830s proved a grim precursor to the catastrophic changes that took place during the 1840s and 1850s. With the onset of the gold rush, the lives of the indigenous peoples of northern California changed in terrifying ways. The so-called Argonauts who sought their fortunes away from the Mother Lode mining districts turned to the northern regions of California in search of gold. Thousands of miners and settlers flocked to land along the Klamath, the Trinity, and the Smith Rivers when word of gold spread. As violent as their counterparts in the Sierra mining districts, they looked upon the Native population as another obstacle separating them from great wealth. The tribes of this area had the same kind of vicious warfare turned against them as was inflicted on the Indians of the Sacramento Valley and the northeastern mountains. Newspapers from San Francisco north to Crescent City carried horrifying tales of raids and massacres. At Clear Lake in 1850, Pomo Indians who had defended themselves against two vicious settlers were slaughtered at a place since known as Bloody Island. The Wiyot were virtually wiped out in 1860 on Indian Island in Humboldt Bay. Militia groups like the Coast Rangers (Humboldt County), the Crescent Rifles (Crescent City), and the Humboldt Volunteers (Eureka) ruthlessly tracked down and killed hundreds of Indians from San Francisco to the Oregon border. Greed for gold coupled with a desire to exploit the bountiful natural resources of the region certainly motivated these settlers and miners. So too, unfortunately, did racism and a determination to dehumanize the local Native communities. Together, these forces proved devastating.

Federal officials, while supporting the policy of Indian extermination in California, also attempted to create recognized homelands for those tribal people who did survive the onslaught. Between 1850 and 1852, three federal commissioners negotiated 18 treaties of "friendship and peace" with more than 100 different tribes. The commissioners guaranteed property set asides that totaled approximately 7.5 million acres (11,700 square miles) of land. These reservations, as they were called, would provide some protection to California Indians. At least, that was the plan. Only the most charitable assessment of the 1850–1851 treaty process would describe it as anything other than a swindle of gargantuan proportions. The decision by more than 100 Indian communities to accept these fire-sale terms speaks volumes to their understanding of the new world order occasioned by the Americanization of California. A faint shadow of traditional life might continue, but only in locales that served the best interests of the newcomers. Although the agreements set aside less that 10 percent of the entire state for the tribes, that was still too much. Outraged citizens lobbied furiously against any move to ratify the treaties. Mining interests protested the possible donation of lands that might contain gold. Others bemoaned the loss of potential farm and ranch land to Natives seen as too backward and too indolent to use it profitably. State politicians encouraged the federal government to remove Indians east of the Sierra Nevada, south to the Mexican border, north to Oregon—anywhere but California. Barring that, they demanded that the federal government refrain from ratifying the treaties.

Had the Senate ratified the treaties negotiated with California Indian nations, the Native communities of the northern valley would have been afforded some access to traditional homelands and familiar resources. The decision in 1852 to reject the treaties effectively sentenced the state's indigenous population to landlessness. So, too, did subsequent congressional actions that granted preemption rights to settlers and defined all land in the state as public lands. The only land available for California Indians was property located in the military reservations established in 1853 and 1855. For those Indians of the northern coast and northwestern coastal regions, that meant the Mendocino Indian Reserve near Fort Bragg, the Nome Cult Farm (later the Round Valley Reservation), and other small reserves scattered along the Smith, Klamath, and Salmon Rivers. Typically, these sites were barely adequate for settlement. Most were surrounded by a hostile American population, they rarely had the resources necessary for subsistence, and they had no real legal weight as Indian lands. Nonetheless, federal authorities rounded up hundreds of Indian survivors and forced them to relocate to these reservations. Contemporary elders from Native nations throughout northern and northwestern California recall stories handed down through the generations of "death marches" to Nome Cult during the 1850s and 1860s.

For other tribal groups, nothing of consequence occurred until the early 20th century. In 1905, the missing 18 treaties mysteriously reappeared and prompted the California state government into belated action on behalf of the Indians. The federal government authorized the creation of 61 rancherias, totaling some 7,422 acres, in isolated areas of the central and northern parts of the state. The landless Indians of California ultimately received only a fraction—0.1 percent—of the reservation property set aside under the 1851–1852 treaties.

Slowly, the Natives of this region received trust lands for their inhabitation and use. The Pomo acquired land in more than 20 rancherias scattered throughout their traditional territory. Many of the more inland nations were relocated to Round Valley Reservation in Mendocino County. The other tribal communities also either received rancherias of their own or were combined with other Native groups. Even with these lands, cultural continuity was not assured. Because few rancherias had any usable resource base, more and more Indians found themselves leaving their homes and families to seek employment elsewhere. Certainly, the dearth of federal services provided to the tribes would offer little encouragement to remain in these isolated and poverty-stricken enclaves. Thus, even though the indigenous population had begun its rebound from the 19th century's historic lows, Native people often lived away from their home communities. Some took up work on the farms and ranches owned by nearby Americans; others moved to the urban areas of northern California, hoping to find economic security there. World War II served as another centrifugal force,

drawing younger Native men and women into military service and allied war projects. It was often difficult to persuade those who had left to return to their rancherias.

Postwar federal policies certainly accelerated the dissolution of remaining cultural continuity. In the 1950s, Congress instituted termination policy as a means to complete the assimilation of American Indians into mainstream society. In 1958, Congress passed the California Rancheria Act, legislation intended to prompt the detribalization of selected Native communities. Eventually, 41 rancherias—many of which were located in northern California—voted to accept termination for financial reasons. Among those affected by this policy were the Tolowa in Del Norte County, the Wiyot in Humboldt County, and the Pomo in Mendocino, Sonoma, and Lake Counties. Litigation culminating with a favorable judgment in *Tillie Hardwick et al. v. U.S.* (1983) allowed these and other communities to seek redress from the federal government for their termination. Most of those eligible for reinstatement have regained their legal status as tribal entities. But even those victories have not been able to guarantee the complete reconstitution of traditional rancheria landholdings. Some former tribal lands, such as Pomo territory near Clear Lake, are now private property. Lake Mendocino, a lake created by the U.S. Army Corps of Engineers' construction of a dam, now covers the original Coyote Valley Rancheria. The hundreds of thousands of acres that were once the homes of the indigenous peoples from Bodega Bay to the Oregon border are now mostly the property of non-Indians.

Since the late 1980s, members of these northeastern Native nations have taken advantage of the federal government's support for Indian gaming and developed casinos. Many of the Pomo rancherias now boast casinos, as do the reservations of the far northwestern part of coastal California. Revenues generated by the thousands of visitors who come every year to seek their fortunes are used to augment the existing tribal health, education, and welfare programs. They are also used to support tribal efforts at cultural reclamation. These communities, like other Native groups in California, are trying to revive traditional customs, languages, and religious observances.

The world of the northern coastal and northwestern coastal Indians has changed profoundly in little more than 150 years. Tourism now brings outsiders into areas once considered the especial territory of the Native nations. Environmental degradation has taken its toll on the acorns, the salmon, and the redwood. Nonetheless, the traditions of the Coast Miwok, the Pomo, the Tolowa, the Yurok, the Wiyot, the Mattole, the Nongatl, the Sinkyone, the Lassik, the Wailaki, the Hupa, the Chilula, the Whilkut, the Karuk, the Cahto, and the Chimariko are still very much alive in the people of this extraordinary region.

—*Lisa Emmerich*

See also Bureau of Indian Affairs

Suggested Reading

Blackburn, T. C., and Kat Anderson, eds. *Before the Wilderness: Environmental Management by Native Californians.* Menlo Park, CA: Ballena Press, 1993.

Cook, Sherburne F. *The Population of California Indians, 1769–1970.* Berkeley: University of California Press, 1976.

Costo, Rupert, and Jeanette H. Costo. *Natives of the Golden State: The California Indians.* San Francisco: The Indian Historian Press, 1995.

Heizer, Robert F., ed. *The Destruction of the California Indians.* Lincoln: University of Nebraska Press, 1993.

Margolin, Malcolm. *The Way We Lived: California Indian Stories, Songs, and Reminiscences.* 2nd ed. Berkeley, CA: Heyday Books, 2001.

Thompson, Lucy. *To the American Indian: Reminiscences of a Yurok Woman.* Foreword by Peter Palmquist. Berkeley, CA: Heyday Books, 1991.

Washburn, Wilcomb E., ed. *Handbook of North American Indians, California.* Vol. 8. Washington, DC: U.S. Government Printing Office, 1978.

⊞ CALIFORNIA INDIANS OF THE NORTHERN MOUNTAINS

Looming majestically above the northern Sacramento Valley stands Mount Shasta, rising more than 14,162 above the surrounding countryside. This impressive volcanic peak is the second tallest in the Cascade Range. It is a place of great significance to many people, but not for the same reasons. Outdoor enthusiasts know Mount Shasta as the site of great recreational prospects throughout the year. To those living in this region, the mountain and its attendant landscape provide both scenic beauty and economic opportunities. Travelers heading north or south on Interstate Highway 5 recognize it as the sentinel marker of the Oregon-California border. And for the Native populations of this area, Mount Shasta is a place of great power and cultural importance. Members of the Shastan, the Achumawi, the Atsugewi, and the Modoc nations all regarded the mountain's springs, forests, and upper reaches as sacred spaces. Regardless of the new identities Mount Shasta has taken on during the last 150 years, it will always be one of the most important places to the Indians of California's northern mountains.

The spectacular scenery of north central and northeastern California has been the home, for thousands of years, of Native peoples who adapted themselves to their rugged surroundings. Attempts to determine the origins of the indigenous population of the Western Hemisphere have spawned a number of widely divergent theories that have come to coexist uneasily in contemporary America. The Bering Straits land bridge, once the dominant theory for the peopling of the Americas, now has competition from those who argue the likelihood of migration from Polynesia, Africa, and even China. Similarly, there is substantial disagreement on when these first migrants arrived. Conventional wisdom dictates that habitation of the Americas began 14,000 to 20,000 BP (years before present) as Asian hunters gradually moved into the Western Hemisphere. Evidence in California suggests that there may have been some human habitation during this period. There is, however, a much stronger archeological record to support settlement during the Paleo-Indian era, dating from 14,000 to 11,000 BP. Certainly, by the later date, substantial populations were in evidence in the most resource-rich areas of present-day California. In the area of the northeastern mountains, there is archaeological evidence that indicates inhabitation from 6,500 BP. Though population density in this area increased slightly over the next several millennia, it would never approach the numbers for the valleys or coastal areas. Estimates for the population of the mountainous northeast suggest that there were likely no more than 10,000 Indians prior to European contact.

There is far more certainty about the cultural affiliations of the Natives living in this region of California. Four distinct groups, all speaking variations of the Hokan language stock, constituted the Shastan Indian nation and dominated the northern central mountain area. The largest single community, the Shasta, lived in the Shasta and Scott River valleys and also held territory along the upper Klamath River. Their northernmost boundaries extended into southern Oregon and the Wintu were their southern neighbors. The New River Shasta held a tiny piece of land along the Salmon River to the southeast of the main Shasta homeland. The Konomihu lands were to the west and south of the New River communities, stretching along the Salmon River and its north and south forks. To the southeast of all of these groups lived the Okwanuchu, whose territory encompassed the northern forks of the McCloud River and the upper reaches of the Sacramento River.

The Achumawi resembled the Shasta in that they, too, were a similarly substantial and equally amalgamated population. They are often referred to simply as the Pit River Indians, after the waterway of the same name that bisects their land base. Within their territory, extending north to Goose Lake, west to Mount Shasta, south to Mount Lassen, and east to the Warner Mountain Range, lived 10 discrete communities who also spoke languages from the Hokan family. To their immediate southwest were the Atsugewi, who shared lands with the Achumawi between present-day Burney and Eagle Lake to the east. The Modoc, who spoke a derivation of the Lutuamian language, lived in the far northeastern corner of California, in lands bounded to the west by the Shasta and the south by the Achumawi. Like their western neighbors, the Modoc also had boundaries that extended into southern Oregon.

Whether the world was water-born, as the Achumawi believed, whether the stars viewed by the Shasta Indians were arranged by Coyote and Raccoon, whether the world was named by Kumash, as the Modoc believed, each nation saw itself residing in a unique cultural and spiritual landscape that was essential to their survival. This region was one of sharp contrasts, where snowcapped mountains covered with pines and firs cast a rain shadow over high desert lands with little vegetation. Most of the Indian communities in northeastern California lived above the elevation of 2,500 feet. The area has several active volcanoes and considerable evidence of historic eruptions in lava flows, basalt, and mud flows. This juncture point of the granite Sierra Nevada and the volcanic Cascades has given northeastern California its unique blend of basin and range habitats. Sage, Jeffrey pines, manzanita, bitter brush, alders, and sedges all abound in their respective zones. The rivers and lakes form a home to a variety of fish including salmon and a vast number of waterfowl species. Here, given the comparative scarceness of acorns, the yampa root became one of the primary food supplies. Large game animals such as pronghorn antelope and deer along with such smaller animals as rabbit served as other edible resources. Seeds, tubers, and insects rounded out the foods available to the indigenous inhabitants.

Given their location at the periphery of the classic California culture area and their proximity to the Great Basin culture area, it is not surprising that the Natives of northeastern California merged disparate subsistence patterns and cultural materials into coherent systems that were distinct for each group. Members of the Shastan nation, for example, traded obsidian obtained from the Achumawi for acorns harvested by the Wintu. They traded juniper and Wintu-made beads with their western neighbors, the Karuk and the Hupa, who brought dentalia and other shells inland. The Modoc occasionally traded foodstuffs with those living farther west in Achumawi and Atsugewi country. The Atsugewi traded for clamshell beads with Achumawi, Maidu, and Yana people. By adapting themselves to the combination of river, lake, foothill, and desert conditions that could be found surrounding them, these nations were able to make the best of a sometimes limited resource base and ensure their continued existence as communities.

However tenuous life once may have been, the arrival of non-Indians into northeastern California transformed daily life for many of the area's indigenous people into a struggle for survival. Unlike much of the rest of California's indigenous populations, those living in this area did not have contact with Spanish settlers or missionaries. Their first encounters came with the arrival of fur trappers and traders who moved into the area in the late 1820s. In 1827, Peter Skene Ogden gave the Pit River its name as a comment on the number of pits dug by the Achumawi to trap game animals. Men from the Hudson Bay Company trapped throughout the region in the 1830s and established a permanent trail along the Pit River that allowed them to reach the Sacramento River valley. In addition to providing an English name for the river and trade goods to the local Natives, the Hudson Bay trappers brought along two other "gifts," each of which would profoundly affect the Indians. Malaria seemed to follow the trappers wherever they went. As in the Sacramento River valley, this disease wreaked havoc on the tribes of northeastern California. The spread of virgin soil epidemics in this region eroded the strength of the tribes, making it more difficult for them to keep their communities intact and fend off threats. One of those threats, thanks to the arrival of horse culture, was slavery. The Modoc apparently adopted horses as a tool for economic advantage in the late 17th and early 18th centuries. They used them to convey captives taken from local tribes north to the great trade center along the Columbia River at the Dalles. Not surprisingly, this did little to endear them to their neighbors. Thus, the arrival of foreigners, their diseases, their domesticated animals, and their desire to exploit the natural resource base made life hazardous for the Natives of northeastern California.

The gold rush era only increased the dangers facing the indigenous inhabitants of this region. The Applegate, Nobles, and Lassen trails brought emigrants and prospective miners alike through the mountains and into northern California. More domestic animals to consume scarce forage, more chances for exposure to epidemic disease, and more opportunities for conflict with the incoming settlers and miners—these were the by-products of the three trails. As more and more outsiders flooded through and into their territory, the Natives of the northern mountains learned that Americanization meant the loss of lands, culture, and lives. The only option left to the Indians was armed resistance against this encroachment into their communities. Hindsight may be clear on the futility of these actions, but at the time fighting seemed to be the only way to remind the emigrants that they were the interlopers.

The 1850s gold rush in this area, second only to the mother lode in terms of quantity and value, set in motion a spiral of violence that lasted for more than two decades. Inspired by the legend of a lost "gold lake," thousands moved into the region. The Achumawi

and the Modoc regularly tangled with incoming miners and emigrant trains, hoping to dissuade others from traveling through their lands. This, in turn, led those coming into the region to take their revenge against the Indians they contemptuously referred to as "diggers." The Plumas Rangers, the Kibbe Guard, the Siskiyou Guard, and the Kibbe Rangers were all organized in the late 1850s as detachments of the California militia. These groups were charged with protecting the settlers and controlling the Natives of the northeastern mountains. Avenging attacks, real and imagined, the militia regularly returned from campaigns with strings of Indian ears or heads, saved for the cash rewards offered by the state. Not surprisingly, this brutality pushed the indigenous population to even greater extremes in their attempts to fight back.

The most spectacular of these efforts was the Modoc War of 1872–1873. Natives led by Kientpoos ("Captain Jack") rejected reservation life with the Klamath in Oregon in 1870 and returned to California seeking their homelands. Settlers pressured local authorities and the U.S. government to remove the Indians permanently. Hostilities erupted in the fall of 1872 and lasted until well into the summer of 1873. Kientpoos led his band into the lava bed country and successfully withstood the subsequent siege. After several attempts at negotiation, one of which ended in a surprise attack and the deaths of several American peace commissioners, the U.S. Army resorted to the use of Indian informants to finally capture the leaders of the Modoc resistance. Because of their determined and costly stand against the Americans, the Modoc who had followed Kientpoos were relocated to Indian Territory. Today, there are still Modoc living in Oklahoma as well as in Oregon.

For the other Indian nations of the northeastern mountains, the extension of American control over the whole of their traditional territories meant accommodating entirely new ways of life. They, like other California tribes, participated in the federal treaty-making process of the early 1850s. The commissioners guaranteed property set-asides that totaled approximately 7.5 million acres (11,700 square miles) of land. These reservations, as they were called, would provide some protection to California Indians. At least, that was the plan. Only the most charitable assessment of the 1850–1851 treaty process would describe it as anything other than a swindle of gargantuan proportions. The decision by more than 100 Indian communities to accept these "fire sale" terms speaks volumes to their understanding of the new world order occasioned by the Americanization of California. A faint shadow of traditional life might continue, but only in locales that served the best interests of the newcomers.

Like their other tribal counterparts, the indigenous population of the northeastern mountains discovered that public outrage over the amount of lands set aside for Indian use—less than 10 percent of the entire state—doomed the agreements. And it doomed them to landlessness. The Shastan remnants, the Achumawi, and the Atsugewi would not receive lands set aside for their exclusive use until after the turn of the 20th century. And even then, the 12 rancherias established for their use were mostly small and without water. Small wonder that many of the tribal survivors opted to move into or near the small towns dotting this area to seek work. This exodus was heightened by World War II, as many young Native men and women left the area to seek war-related jobs that paid well.

Since the late 1980s, members of these northeastern Native nations have taken advantage of the federal government's support for Indian gaming and developed casinos. The Diamond Mountain Casino, operated by the Pit River Indians of the Susanville Rancheria is located in Susanville. Two other casinos, the Desert Rose in Alturas and the Pit River Casino in Burney, are also operated by this tribe. Revenues from the casinos are used to augment the existing tribal health, education, and welfare programs. They are also used to support tribal efforts at cultural reclamation. These communities, like other Native groups in California, are trying to stem the loss of traditional customs, languages, and religious observances. To that end, every year, members of the Achumawi and Shasta Indians return to Panther Meadows on Mount Shasta to conduct ceremonies. As they have done for thousands of years, they pray for the healing of their communities and for the renewal of the Earth. But the mountain that hosts and hears these appeals is no longer theirs. Tourist resorts and ski runs now claim space that, only a century and a half ago, used to be the sole province of the Indians of northeastern California.

—*Lisa Emmerich*

See also California Indians of the North Coast and Northwestern Coast, California Indians of the Northern Valley

Suggested Reading

Blackburn, T. C., and M. Kat Anderson. *Before Wilderness: Environmental Management by Native Californians.* Menlo Park, CA: Ballena, 1993.

Heizer, Robert F., ed. *Handbook of North American Indians, California, Vol. 8.* Washington, DC: Smithsonian Institution, 1978.

Hurtado, Albert. *Indian Survival on the California Frontier.* New Haven, CT: Yale University Press, 1988.

Margolin, Malcolm, ed. *The Way We Lived: California Indian Reminiscences, Stories, and Songs.* Berkeley, CA: Heyday Press, 1981.

⌗ CALIFORNIA INDIANS OF THE NORTHERN VALLEY

Situated between the high jagged peaks of the Sierra Nevada and mixed mountainous terrain of the coastal ranges, the Sacramento Valley is the northern segment of California's extraordinarily rich central plain. Today this area, extending some 450 miles on a northwest-southeast axis, is the most important farming area west of the Rocky Mountains. Together with the San Joaquin Valley to the south, the Sacramento Valley constitutes nearly 60 percent of the state's productive farmland. Agriculture has played a dominant role in the development of this part of the state for nearly 150 years. Depending upon the season, travelers driving north from Sacramento toward any of the valley's largest population centers—Marysville, Yuba City, Chico, Red Bluff, or Redding—might see enormous fields of rice, acres of orchards, and substantial grazing lands. Though the original Mexican land grants have long since given way to smaller land holdings, more than a century of farming and ranching have profoundly changed the natural and the human landscapes of this region.

For all their impact on the Sacramento Valley, Americans were not the first to claim this place of remarkable abundance as their own. Long before the rows of almond, orange, and cherry trees began their march across the valley, long before the farmers and engineers conceived of irrigation projects that would tame the flood-prone Sacramento River and bring water to thousands of acres, long before cattle and sheep began to outnumber deer and antelope, thousands of Native Californians called this place their home. To the Nisenan, the Konkow, the Miwok, the Nomlaki, the Patwin, the Yana, and the Wintu, the Sacramento Valley was shaped by the uncontrollable forces of nature and the unknowable forces of the spiritual world. Members of these nations lived, like their ancestors before them for thousands of years, in synch with the seasonal rhythms of heat and cold, floods and drought, fire and rain. Though the gold rush era torrent of settlers displaced many of these Indians, theirs is the first human history of the Sacramento Valley.

Attempts to determine the origins of the indigenous population of the Western Hemisphere have spawned a number of widely divergent theories that have come to coexist uneasily in contemporary America. Passage from northeast Asia via the Bering Straits land bridge, once the dominant theory for the peopling of the Americas, now has competition from those who argue the likelihood of migration from Polynesia, Africa, and even China. Similarly, there is substantial disagreement on when these first migrants arrived. Conventional wisdom dictates that habitation of the Americas began 14,000 to 20,000 BP (years before present) as Asian hunters gradually moved into the Western Hemisphere. Evidence in California suggests that there may have been some human habitation during this period. There is, however, a much stronger archeological record to support settlement during the Paleo-Indian era, dating from 14,000 to 11,000 BP. Certainly, by the later date, substantial populations were in evidence in the most resource-rich areas of present-day California. In the area of the central valley, there is archaeological evidence that indicates probable inhabitation some 11,500 to 7,500 BP. Population density increased over the next three millennia, quite possibly because a flood of Penutian language speaking peoples moved into the Sacramento Valley. These groups, which included the Nisenan, Konkow, Patwin, and Nomlaki, joined the Yana and other Hokan speaking peoples already living in this region.

Though science offers one version of the story behind the presence of humans in the Americas, it is an explanation that has little credence among American Indian intellectuals and in tribal communities. In California, as in every other locale around the world with an extant aboriginal population, there are Native explanations for the development of human society. Histories from indigenous communities in the northern Sacramento Valley rely upon the accounts handed down over generations from religious leaders who received their knowledge through direct contact with the spiritual world. Traditional histories of the world's creation could and did differ, but one commonality linked all of them. Whether created by Old Man Coyote or Earth Maker, or produced by a cataclysmic flood, their homelands were their true place on Earth. For the Nisenan, this meant a connection to the land encompassed by the drainages of the Yuba, Bear, and American Rivers, stretching west to the Sacramento and Feather Rivers and east into the Sierra Nevada. Just north of the Nisenan, the Konkow-Maidu established communities along the Sacramento and Feather Rivers and held territory south toward the Sutter Buttes and east into the Sierra foothills. The Yana, the northern neighbors to the Konkow, inhabited the upper Sacramento River valley and the foothills east of the valley between present-day Chico and Redding. The Wintu occupied the northernmost reaches of the Sacramento Valley and held territory between the Trinity Alps to the west and the Sierra Nevada to the east. To their south, some Nomlaki lived on the eastern shore of the Sacramento River but most of the nation inhabited the far western reaches of the Sacramento Valley well into the Coast Range. The Patwin, southern neighbors to the Nomlaki, established communities along the western shores of the Sacramento River from the Sutter Buttes area down to San Pablo Bay. In every case, regardless of location, these nations lived in cultural and spiritual landscapes in which they, as individuals and communities, belonged to the Earth.

The tremendous abundance of resources in their homelands certainly promoted this felt sense of connection to the Sacramento River, to the foothills of the Coast Range and the Sierra Nevada, and to the broad plains of the northern valley. Archaeological data suggest that the earliest inhabitants of this area relied mostly on hunting for their subsistence. But approximately 4,000 BP, a profound set of changes began to occur. A clear shift away from subsistence patterns that relied almost exclusively on hunting marked the transition of these early, more migratory peoples into more sophisticated, and sedentary, residents of their respective homelands. As groups became increasingly knowledgeable about the resource base around them, more differentiation in use patterns emerged. Seed collection, plant gathering, the harvesting of acorns, and the growing importance of fishing are all hallmarks of this extended period. Each of the nations living in the northern Sacramento Valley enjoyed the benefits of their proximity to distinctly different bioregions.

The northern valley's subsistence "cafeteria" offered a stunning variety of foods for the indigenous population. To take advantage of this, Natives developed hunting, fishing, and gathering rituals along with tools to assist them in their work. They also created migration patterns within their home territories to efficiently monitor and utilize their resource base. Riverine fishers utilized fish weirs, fishing platforms, baskets, and nets during annual salmon and steelhead runs. These tools also came in handy for the harvesting of the permanent population of freshwater clams and mussels, sturgeon, eels, and suckerfish. Waterfowl, especially plentiful during migration, would also have been available and taken using decoys and snares. Valley and plains hunters and gatherers could add game animals like antelope and deer as well as seeds, tubers, and insects to their diet. Here, the inhabitants used fire as a tool to manipulate the landscape, making it more attractive to game animals and enhancing the productivity of native plants. Foothill hunters and gatherers took advantage of many of the same food sources as well as pine nuts harvested from trees in the higher elevations. All of these groups, regardless of location, relied heavily on the California staff of life—acorns. Seven species of oaks produced millions of pounds of acorns, a high-fat food easily stored in their ready-made containers (shells) every autumn. Though regular seasonal changes and occasional natural fluctuations like floods or forest fires could disrupt subsistence patterns, the original residents of the northern valley mostly enjoyed a remarkably secure resource base.

The wide assortment and reliability of the native food supply afforded the Indians much more than a pleasantly varied diet. The exceptional carrying capacity of the Sacramento Valley allowed for the growth of substantial populations that were mainly sedentary. Certainly, the dearth of epidemic diseases that beleaguered Europeans and Asians made for improved life circumstances. So, too, did the extensive trade networks that moved coastal foodstuffs and material goods from California as well as Oregon inland and took valley resources into the Sierra Nevada and beyond. All of these factors combined to help create sizeable communities where societal complexity and economic strata were the norm, not the exception. While a precise determination of California's precontact demography remains elusive, evidence from a number of different ethnographic, archaeological, and historical sources indicates that the long-held estimate of approximately 300,000 inhabitants falls far short of the actual number. Of that traditional number, best estimates place the precontact population of the northern Sacramento Valley area at 76,000. The size and social organization of Valley Indian communities allowed for an even greater manipulation of the rich landscape and distribution of its varied resources.

Despite this natural largesse, the Sacramento Valley was, by no means, a utopian Eden. While most communities lived in relative harmony with their neighbors, some did not. Diplomatic relationships defined some neighbors as friends to welcome and others as enemies to fear. The Maidu and the Konkow sometimes battled the Yana as well as two nations in their northeast, the Washo and Achumawi. The Yana apparently was a nation composed of querulous peoples who were rarely on good terms with most of their neighbors. The southern Yana (the southernmost Yahi) had a tense relationship with the northern Maidu. The Maidu, the Wintu, and the Achumawi disliked the northern Yana. The Nomlaki apparently concentrated their rivalries within the boundaries of their communities. And the Patwin sometimes experienced tensions with the Nisenan. Large-group, organized intertribal violence was uncommon. Random feuds that escalated into raids and surprise attacks were the more typical modes of conflict. And even then, alliances and trade relationships might dictate the prosecution of hostilities.

In sum, the precontact world of the northern Sacramento Valley Indian nations was a place of relative prosperity and stability, a region where the geography, climate, flora, and fauna made life much less of an ongoing struggle for the indigenous residents than in many other areas of North America. Unfortunately, those same blessings would also lead to the unraveling of the rich tapestry of life woven by these California Natives. Bent on the exploitation of the landscape and the indigenous population, the outsiders set in motion a series of changes that could neither be ignored nor halted. Almost unimaginable human and environmental devastation followed the arrival of Spanish, Mexican, and American settlers in the northern valley.

For many California Indians, the beginning of the end of the familiar rhythms of life came with the arrival of Spanish explorers, soldiers, and missionaries. While the relative isolation of Natives of the northern Sacramento Valley protected them from much of the ensuing devastation, it could not do so forever. The Spanish settlements in Sonoma and the San Francisco Bay region meant, at the minimum, disturbing news about the newcomers' treatment of other Indians. Certainly, the Nisenan and the Nomlaki had some slight contact with Spanish explorers in the early 19th century. But most of the northern valley escaped the heavy hand of the Spanish. The Patwins, however, experienced more directly the colonists' determination to "civilize" what to them seemed a wilderness. By the early 19th century, Patwin neophytes had—willingly or otherwise—relocated to Mission Dolores (San Francisco de Asís) and Mission San José. After the construction of Mission San Francisco Solano (located in present-day Sonoma) in 1823, Patwin living in the peripheral areas found themselves living well within the realm of Spanish influence.

With independence, the Mexican colonists of Alta California developed their own patterns of interaction with the Native inhabitants. The secularization of the missions in the 1830s shifted power and influence over to wealthy Mexican landowners in the mid-1830s. Their acquisition of lands that once composed the missions forced Indian residents into landlessness. Some moved into settled areas to seek work; others tried to return to their home communities to escape the settlers and their incessant demands. The creation of large rancheros in northern California brought more and more Natives of the Sacramento Valley into contact, and conflict, with Mexican colonial culture. The hacienda-peon system found a new home in

California as landowners looked to the indigenous population to supply the labor necessary to run their neofeudal fiefdoms. Mariano Vallejo, John Bidwell, Pearson Reading, Peter Lassen, and John Sutter were but a few of those Mexicans and Americans fortunate enough to receive land grants entitling them to huge swathes of "open" land from the Sacramento delta northward. Considerably less lucky were those Native communities who found their homelands now the property of outsiders who viewed them as potential laborers.

This loss of land to colonists was accompanied by the arrival of epidemic diseases in the northern Sacramento Valley. Beginning in the late 1820s, fur trappers from the Hudson's Bay Company moved down the Sacramento Valley, trapping fur bearing animals in Nisenan, Konkow-Maidu, Yana, Wintu, Nomlaki, and Patwin territory. Whatever disruption these men, their trapping techniques, and their trade goods brought to the Indians paled in comparison to the malaria that accompanied their progress through tribal lands in the 1830s. The destructive impact of this event on communities and tribal cultures can only be hinted at in mortality estimates. The trappers themselves recorded the sad details of the population collapse that accompanied the epidemics; so, too, did the survivors who introduced these events into the oral histories of their respective nations. Scholars utilizing these and other contemporary sources speculate that mortality rates among those living closest to the river may have exceeded 75 percent. If not a full-scale demographic collapse, this period certainly witnessed a profound demographic stagger. These waves of disease, whatever their death tolls, eroded the Indian population base and, consequently, compromised control over traditional landholdings.

The immediate devastation wrought by the epidemics and movement of colonists into Native land gave way to a prolonged period of chaos as California Indians struggled to cope with the changing circumstances of their lives. Mexican and American settlers tried persuasion but readily resorted to coercion to ensure a steady labor supply for their ranchos. Every land grant made by the Mexican government further complicated the lives of the Sacramento Valley's indigenous population by threatening them with the loss of personal freedom and subsistence resources. The military policing Alta California participated in impressment raids on Native communities to supply workers to the rancho owners. Expeditions into the southern Sacramento Valley led to substantial Indian resistance that, in turn, led to harsher treatment by the military and civilian militias. Those Natives who evaded capture found themselves struggling to survive on continually shrinking land bases where once plentiful supplies of food now seemed less certain. Even those who lived farther to the north, and had less contact with the outsiders, understood that a process of transformation had been set in motion.

The troubles of the 1830s proved a grim precursor of the catastrophic changes that took place during the 1840s. The first half of the decade saw increasing numbers of American settlers moving inland, bringing their demands for land and labor to the valley Indians. John Sutter, a Swiss émigré, built a commercial post that he grandly named New Helvetia near the confluence of the Sacramento and American Rivers. A shrewd and single-minded businessman who had once participated in the lucrative Santa Fe trade, Sutter was determined to establish a centrally located trade center that would profit from its proximity to the fur trade, emigrant routes, and the emerging agricultural sector. He regarded the region's indigenous population as potential laborers, potential customers, and—most disturbingly—potential trade "goods." The local Nisenan became Sutter's workforce, a makeshift militia to fend off attacks from less hospitable Indians, and his patrons. The rich abundance of the Sacramento Valley, worked and harvested by these inexpensive tribal workers, helped him realize tremendous profits.

Sutter's early influence on the Natives of the Sacramento Valley from his adobe fortress in present-day Sacramento was substantial. But it could not compare to the impact of the discovery of gold. On January 24, 1848—just 10 days before the Treaty of Guadalupe-Hidalgo ended the Mexican War—John Marshall pulled a handful of gold-bearing gravel up from the millrace at Sutter's sawmill in Coloma. This incredible news, when it reached the East, seemed to bear out the possibilities inherent in manifest destiny and promise a rich future for those Americans ready to head west. It invited them, and other fortune seekers from around the world imbued with a similar spirit of adventure, to succumb to a wholly new disease—gold fever. The only treatment for this irrational contagion was immediate relocation to the Mother Lode, where those stricken could try for the imagined cure—the bonanza strike.

The flood of miners into the Sierra Nevada doomed the indigenous cultures and peoples of California to an extended period of turbulence and destruction. As the miners crowded along the routes into the mining districts, they brought with them a host of epidemic diseases that would take a terrible toll on tribal communities. That was, however, just the start. The Yana, the Patwin, the Wintu, the Konkow-Maidu, the Nisenan, and the Nomlaki soon learned that these new neighbors would not countenance any interference, natural or human, in their quest for wealth. Ignoring property rights guaranteed under the terms of the Treaty of Guadalupe-Hidalgo, the miners set about remaking Indian lands into their own. They established claims that voided indigenous boundaries. They logged the Sierra slopes bare, needing wood for sluice boxes and catch dams as well as supports for mining shafts. They rerouted water courses to facilitate hydraulic mining. They hunted the local game animal populations into scarcity. Their placer mining operations fouled the creeks and rivers that once carried thousands of salmon upstream to their spawning grounds. They hunted predatory animals like wolves and bears into oblivion. The so-called Argonauts remade the California environment to suit their needs with little concern for the long-term impact of this transformation.

California Natives responded to this invasion of the Sacramento River valley and its environs in several ways. Some Patwin, Nisenan, Konkow-Maidu, and Nomlaki worked for miners at the various Mother Lode diggings. Like the rancho owners before them, the miners shamelessly exploited their workers. For their part, these Indians used the jobs as a source for food to augment their own dwindling resources and as a means to ingratiate themselves with the newcomers who increasingly dominated the landscape. Unfortunately, this involvement in the gold rush also took Native peoples away from their homes and communities. Not surprisingly, this economic removal had a significant long-term cultural impact. Other members of the Sacramento Valley tribes sought work in the homes and on the farms of the newcomers, also hoping to find a safe niche for themselves. Also seeking safe niches were those Indians who tried to avoid contact with the miners as much as possible.

Whatever their response to the miners, the indigenous populations affected by the gold rush quickly learned that safety in the midst of this chaotic situation was nonexistent. Violent behavior became a fact of life for the Natives shortly after miners started to inundate the Sierra Nevada and valley tribal territories. The valley Indians began to experience a kind of focused, persistent brutality that was unlike anything in their own history of conflict. During the 1850s and 1860s, the state of California sponsored policies that encouraged and legitimized the wholesale murder of Indian men, women, and children. What began as independent guerilla actions by miners, farmers, and ranchers over time became genocide. Almost any non-Indian could muster and outfit a volunteer force, go Indian hunting, and receive reimbursement from the state government (sometimes with funds paid by the federal government). Each of the Indian nations in the northern Sacramento Valley witnessed and experienced this kind of frenzied slaughter. The Wintu were invited to a friendship feast in 1850 where the hosts served poisoned food that killed 100 of the Natives. Still other Wintu were forcibly removed to open lands for farming. Settlers and miners roared through Nisenan and Patwin territory, displacing them from their homelands. The Nomlaki, the Konkow-Maidu, and the Yana all suffered similar fates during this era. The state's indigenous population plummeted from a pre–gold rush (1845) census estimate of 150,000 to fewer than 21,000 in 1880. The decade from 1845 to 1855 was the worst period, with the number of Native inhabitants declining from 150,000 to 50,000. While starvation and diseases certainly played a role in occasioning this carnage, human actions are responsible for the majority of these deaths.

Federal officials, while supporting the policy of Indian extermination in California, also attempted to create recognized homelands for those tribal people who did survive the onslaught. Between 1850 and 1852, three federal commissioners negotiated 18 treaties of "friendship and peace" with more than 100 different tribes. The commissioners guaranteed property set-asides that totaled approximately 7.5 million acres (11,700 square miles) of land. These reservations, as they were called, would provide some protection to California Indians. At least, that was the plan. Only the most charitable assessment of the 1850–1851 treaty process would describe it as anything other than a swindle of gargantuan proportions. The decision by more than 100 Indian communities to accept these fire-sale terms speaks volumes to their understanding of the new world order occasioned by the Americanization of California. A faint shadow of traditional life might continue, but only in locales that served the best interests of the newcomers. Although the agreements set aside less that 10 percent of the entire state for the tribes, that was still too much. Outraged citizens lobbied furiously against any move to ratify the treaties. Mining interests protested the possible donation of lands that might contain gold. Others bemoaned the loss of potential farm and ranch land to Natives seen as too backward and too indolent to use it profitably. State politicians encouraged the federal government to remove Indians east of the Sierra Nevada, south to the Mexican border, north to Oregon—anywhere but California. Barring that, they demanded that the federal government refrain from ratifying the treaties.

Had the Senate ratified the treaties negotiated with California Indian nations, the Native communities of the northern valley would have been afforded some access to traditional homelands and familiar resources. The decision in 1852 to reject the treaties effectively sentenced the state's indigenous population to landlessness. So, too, did subsequent congressional actions that granted preemption rights to settlers and defined all land in the state as public lands. The only land available for California Indians was property located in the military reservations established in 1853 and 1855. For those Indians of the Sacramento Valley, that meant the Nome Lackee Reservation in present-day Tehama County and the Nome Cult Farm (later the Round Valley Reservation) in present-day Mendocino County. Neither of these sites was adequate for settlement for a variety of reasons. Surrounded by a hostile American population, they both lacked water and game. Nonetheless, federal authorities rounded up hundreds of Indians from throughout the central part of northern

California and forced them to relocate to these reservations. The Yuki, original inhabitants of the Nome Cult Farm, quickly found themselves unwilling hosts to Nomlaki, Konkow-Maidu, Wintu, and Yana Indians along with the occasional Pomo, Achumawi, Modoc, and Wailaki. Because many of these groups had once been enemies, it is hardly surprising that hostilities among the removed would erupt. The Nome Lackee Reservation became another destination for valley Indians pushed out of their homes, usually at gunpoint, by Americans. The removals to both reservations were brutal affairs. Men, women, and children were forced to walk for days to their destinations through communities of unsympathetic non-Indians. Those who could not complete the journey because of illness or exhaustion were left behind or sometimes killed by the militias supervising the relocations. The infamous Chico-to-Round-Valley "Trail of Tears" in 1863 is but one example of the ethnic cleansing efforts undertaken against the indigenous peoples of the Sacramento Valley during this era.

For the remainder of the 19th century, northern valley Indians had little respite from the personal and communal havoc visited on them by the Americans. While some attempts were made to provide land bases for the surviving Natives, nothing of consequence occurred until the early 20th century. In 1905, the missing 18 treaties mysteriously reappeared and prompted the California state government into belated action on behalf of the Indians. The federal government authorized the creation of 61 rancherias, totaling some 7,422 acres, in isolated areas of the central and northern parts of the state. The landless Indians of California ultimately received only a fraction—0.1 percent—of the reservation property set aside under the 1851–1852 treaties. The remaining Konkow-Maidu Indians made their homes at the Greenville, Berry Creek, Enterprise, Mooretown, and Chico Rancherias. The Nisenan survivors received land at the Auburn Rancheria. The Nomlaki had land at Round Valley Reservation, Paskenta, and Grindstone Creek Rancherias. The Patwin were scattered among the Cortina, Colusa, and Rumsey Rancherias. And the Wintu and the remnant Yana populations were assigned to the Redding and Rumsey Rancherias. These small communities, some no larger than 25 acres, were all that the Indians could legally claim of their former homelands.

Because few rancherias had any usable resource base, more and more Indians found themselves leaving their homes and families to seek employment elsewhere in the northern Sacramento Valley. Certainly, the dearth of federal services provided to the tribes would offer little encouragement to remain in these isolated and poverty-stricken enclaves. Thus, even though the indigenous population had begun its rebound from the 19th century's historic lows, Native people often lived away from their home communities. Some took up work on the farms and ranches owned by nearby Americans; others moved to the urban areas of northern California, hoping to find economic security there. World War II served as another centrifugal force, drawing younger Native men and women into military service and allied war projects. It was often difficult to persuade those who had left to return to their rancherias.

Postwar federal policies certainly accelerated the dissolution of remaining cultural continuity. In the 1950s, Congress instituted termination policy as a means to complete the assimilation of American Indians into mainstream society. In 1958, Congress passed the California Rancheria Act, legislation intended to prompt the detribalization of selected Native communities. Eventually, 41 rancherias—many of which were located in northern central California—voted to accept termination for financial reasons. Wintu, Nisenan, Konkow-Maidu, and Nomlaki Indians were particularly affected by this policy, losing what little property they had. Litigation culminating with a favorable judgment in *Tillie Hardwick et al. v. U.S.* (1983) allowed these and other communities to seek redress from the federal government for their termination. Most of those eligible for reinstatement have regained their legal status as tribal entities. But even those victories have not been able to guarantee the complete reconstitution of traditional rancheria landholdings. Some, like the Mooretown and Redding Rancherias, have been able to parlay their restored land base into economic success by developing tribal gaming enterprises. Others, like the Mechoopda of the Konkow-Maidu, are still attempting to reconstitute rancheria property. The struggle to reunify once-scattered populations and recreate a communal social space in the aftermath of termination is ongoing. Despite myriad legal, political, and economic hurdles, the Indians of the northern Sacramento Valley continue the fight to retain their cultures and carry on their unique connection to this special place.

—Lisa Emmerich

See also CALIFORNIA INDIANS OF THE NORTH COAST AND NORTHWESTERN COAST; CALIFORNIA INDIANS OF THE NORTHERN MOUNTAINS; SUTTER, JOHANN AUGUST

Suggested Reading

Blackburn, T. C., and Kat Anderson, eds. *Before the Wilderness: Environmental Management by Native Californians.* Menlo Park, CA: Ballena Press, 1993.

Cook, Sherburne F. *The Population of California Indians, 1769–1970.* Berkeley: University of California Press, 1976.

Heizer, Robert F., ed. *The Destruction of the California Indians.* Lincoln: University of Nebraska Press, 1993.

Hurtado, Albert. *Indian Survival on the California Frontier.* New Haven, CT: Yale University Press, 1988.

Jackson, Robert H., and Edward Castillo. *Indians, Franciscans, and Spanish Colonization: The Impact of the Missions on California Indians.* Albuquerque: University of New Mexico Press, 1995.

Margolin, Malcolm. *The Way We Lived: California Indian Stories, Songs, and Reminiscences.* 2nd ed. Berkeley, CA: Heyday Books, 2001.

Phillips, George H. *Indians and Indian Agents: The Origins of the Reservation System in California, 1849–1852.* Norman: University of Oklahoma Press, 1997.

Rawls, James. *Indians of California: The Changing Image.* Reprint edition. Norman: University of Oklahoma Press, 1986.

Washburn, Wilcomb E., ed. *Handbook of North American Indians, California.* Vol. 8. Washington, DC: U.S. Government Printing Office, 1978.

⊞ CALIFORNIA LIBRARIES IN THE POST–WORLD WAR II ERA

With the defense industry booming during World War II, some two million people moved to California seeking jobs during the early 1940s. Another one million arrived during the two years directly following the war. By 1950, California's population had exploded by 54 percent, growing to 10.6 million from 6.9 million in 1940. The impact on local jurisdictions was tremendous. As Governor Earl Warren reported in 1948,

> The stampede has visited us with unprecedented civic problems. . . . We have an appalling housing shortage, our schools are packed to suffocation, and our highways are inadequate and dangerous. We are short of water and short of power, and our sanitation and transportation systems are overtaxed. Our hospitals and our corrective institutions are bursting at the seams.

The state's libraries were also proving inadequate, as thousands of new residents poured into public library facilities for services and books to read. In Los Angeles alone, the number of library card holders increased by 21 percent, growing from 378,000 in 1940 to 459,000 only 10 years later. The increase was even more dramatic in defense industry towns like Burbank, National City, and Santa Monica, where the public libraries served more than double the number of users in 1950 than they had before the war. "All the cities of the State have grown beyond their boundaries," library professor Frederic Mosher wrote in 1951. "The libraries have not been able to keep up. . . . The urgency of the situation demands immediate action."

PAST GLORY

The condition of California's libraries had not always been so desperate. In fact, the state's public library infrastructure set the standard for the rest of the country when California's county library law was passed in 1909 and then revised in 1911. The brainchild of then State Librarian James L. Gillis, the county library law, allowed county supervisors to establish libraries within their jurisdictions, guaranteeing service to even the most remote parts of the state. Many cities that were not required to join the newly formed units did so anyway in hopes of providing better service to their constituents. By 1918, 40 county libraries were created throughout the state, drawing zealous librarians from around the country to come work in California. State library employee Laura Steffen Suggett called California's county libraries the "best library system in the world."

Mabel Gillis continued her father's legacy when she became state librarian in 1930. Tightly embracing the county library concept, she took great interest in the goings-on at the local level. But as she admitted herself, Miss Gillis did not like change and so, instead of encouraging libraries to grow along with the population, she held on to what one librarian later called "an awful lot of little chicken-coop-type branch libraries." Moreover, California's professional library association was deeply divided as librarians bickered over the pros and cons of pursuing state aid. Librarians especially feared that state funding would result in loss of autonomy as well as half-hearted financial support from local governing bodies.

CHANGE IN DIRECTION

As soon as Mabel Gillis announced her impending retirement in 1951, Washington State Librarian Carma Zimmerman was recruited to succeed her. Zimmerman, who was originally from Oklahoma, graduated from the University of California–Berkeley School of Librarianship in 1930 and worked in California libraries until 1945, when she moved north to Washington. There she helped create legislation to establish intercounty libraries, which allowed jurisdictions to partner with neighboring counties to provide widespread and more comprehensive library service. Because of these innovations, Zimmerman was nationally renowned in the library world.

Zimmerman returned to California in September 1951 fully aware of the problems that plagued the state and its libraries. She immediately met with constituents to discuss ways to strengthen services throughout the state. One year later, she published a plan, called "Ideas Toward Library Development," for improving what she considered the "weaknesses" in California's library infrastructure. In particular, she blamed overpopulation, fixed tax rates, and insufficiently trained librarians for eroding public library service throughout the state. She also pointed to needless duplication of services, inadequate facilities, overly emphasized specialization, and lack of interlibrary cooperation. Finally, she called for a grassroots approach to building better library services by urging the profession to define statewide standards that reflected the ever-changing needs of California's population.

Working with the California Library Association, the State Library held a five-day conference, in early 1953, to develop service standards based on quality rather than efficiency. Together, a group of 45 librarians defined a list of benchmarks related to library facilities, personnel, materials, collection management, and equipment. In addition, they recommended the creation of joint library jurisdictions to serve populations of 100,000 or more people.

The state legislature responded by creating an interim assembly committee on education to study the statewide library crisis. In 1957, legislation was passed to create a California Public Library Commission tasked with investigating the organizational structure and operation of libraries throughout the state. Not surprisingly, their findings, which were gathered through a survey conducted by library researcher Ed Wight, corroborated the deficiencies already outlined by the State Library. To eliminate these shortcomings, Wight recommended the creation of multijurisdictional library systems to serve a combined population base of at least 100,000 people. He also recommended that these systems be supported through state funding and that the governor appoint a board to oversee administration of the new infrastructure.

Although library leaders statewide readily accepted the report, many others continued to resist the idea of state-funded multijurisdictional systems. Local government officials were dubious, as well, voicing concerns that the state would provide assistance to only those communities that did not already have a library tax in place. To assuage fears, Governor Pat Brown held a conference on public library service in 1960. Some 500 librarians, library trustees, and city and county officials discussed ways to effectively serve California's exploding population. The governor then held a follow-up conference in the next year. Eventually, thanks to the combined efforts of the State Library and the California Library Association, a statewide master plan for public libraries was adopted, clearly defining the distinct roles of local library jurisdictions and joint library systems. In 1963, the concepts behind the master plan became law when, after several attempts, the Public Library Services Bill was finally passed by the state legislature.

Now called the Public Library Development Act, it allowed independent public libraries to work together cooperatively to serve their combined population base.

Pooling their resources, librarians began to work with nearby jurisdictions to complement their service strengths and weaknesses. In some libraries, the acquisition and cataloging of materials became centralized; while in others interlibrary communication was enhanced through teletype and teletypewriter exchange (TWX) machines purchased with state monies. A study conducted in the late 1960s found that the single greatest advantage to belonging to cooperative library systems was the public's access to larger and stronger library collections. By 1972, 21 public library systems had been established in California.

FEDERAL FUNDING

While California librarians wrestled with the ramifications of state-sponsored systems, library leaders nationwide had joined forces to lobby for federal funding of public libraries. Even as World War II raged on, federal officials began preparing for the future by appointing a National Resources Planning Board (NRPB), which was tasked with projecting the impact of transitioning to a peacetime economy. Of foremost importance was providing the American people with full employment and security, including equitable educational opportunities.

In response to the NRPB's mandate, the American Library Association developed a set of postwar standards for public libraries in 1943. These standards recommended the consolidation of smaller library jurisdictions into larger cooperative ventures, similar to those eventually realized in California. In conjunction with these standards, Congresswoman Emily Taft Douglas introduced a bill in 1946 to provide federal aid to public libraries. Although the bill was quickly defeated, the library community rallied and finally, in 1956, encouraged the passage of the Library Services Act (LSA). For the first time in U.S. history, federal monies were allocated specifically to support public library services.

The legislation, targeted at rural areas unable to otherwise extend library service, provided California with some much-needed fiscal relief. The first LSA-funded project in the state was a bookmobile, which brought materials to more than 2,000 residents in Butte County. This proved so successful that a second

bookmobile was purchased in 1958 to serve the rapidly expanding population of San Diego County. In northern California, federal monies were used to establish a center for acquiring and processing materials for 16 library jurisdictions. More professional librarians were also hired statewide.

The LSA was reauthorized as the Library Services and Construction Act (LSCA) in 1964. The expanded law provided funding for building projects as well as for improved urban library services. With the bill's passage, federal funding expanded nationwide from $7.5 million to $25 million a year. In California, federal funding increased from $250,000 to $3.2 million a year. The impact statewide was staggering, with 21 LSCA-funded library buildings constructed by the end of 1966. Many of these still stand today.

CHANGING POPULATION

During the last quarter of the 20th century, hundreds of thousands of people continued to migrate to California. Many were from neighboring states, but many more had begun to arrive from other countries. In particular, thousands of people began immigrating from Asia and Latin America. Not only were librarians faced, once again, with serving unprecedented numbers of visitors, but also many of these new library users did not read or even speak English. Providing library services to multilingual and ethnically diverse communities became a statewide priority.

In 1987, the California State Library commissioned the RAND Corporation to study the potential impact of international immigrants on the state's libraries. According to their findings, the RAND researchers predicted that Hispanics, Asians, and African Americans would constitute 48 percent of California's population by the year 2000 and that, in some counties, Anglos would actually represent a minority of the population by the turn of the century. Indeed, 51 percent of immigrants moving to large metropolitan areas chose to live in California, with more than 88,000 settling in Los Angeles in just one year.

To meet the needs of these dramatically changing demographics, RAND suggested that librarians work more closely with their communities to decide library service priorities. As a result, the State Library initiated a series of three-year LSCA grants called "Partnerships for Change" (PFC). The PFC program, which lasted between 1988 and 1995, targeted libraries serving ethnically and racially diverse populations and required that community members be included in the planning process. PFC libraries conducted community-based needs assessment, forged community coalitions, expanded their collections, restructured their services, and experimented with culturally responsive public relations to better serve their changing populations. Successful projects were implemented in Alameda County, Berkeley, Carlsbad, Contra Costa County, Fresno County, Fullerton, Kern County, Long Beach, Los Angeles, Mendocino County, Oceanside, the city of Orange, Riverside, San Diego, San Francisco, San Jose, Santa Ana, Stockton/San Joaquin County, Sunnyvale, and Whittier.

According to a survey conducted in 1999, 100 percent of the responding PFC libraries still valued diversity and practiced cultural responsiveness. As a result of PFC, libraries have hired more bilingual employees, have purchased more non-English materials, are more involved with their ethnic communities, and continue to conduct public relations efforts in multiple languages.

—*Cindy Mediavilla*

See also LIBRARIES AND THE IMMIGRANT

Suggested Reading

Kellor, Shelly, and Patty Wong. *Cultivating Change: Redesigning Library Services Using the Partnership for Change Approach.* Available from http://www.library.ca.gov/html/lds.cfm

Mediavilla, Cynthia L. *Carma Russell (Zimmerman) Leigh—An Historical Look at a Woman of Vision and Influence.* Ph.D. Dissertation. University of California–Los Angeles, 2000.

Mosher, Frederic J. "State Aid—A Challenge to California Librarians." *California Librarian* 12 (June 1951), 206.

Payne, Judith. *Public Libraries Face California's Ethnic and Racial Diversity.* Santa Monica, CA: RAND, 1998.

Warren, Earl. "California's Biggest Headache." *Saturday Evening Post* 221 (August 7, 1948), 20.

⊞ CAMPBELL, HARDY WEBSTER

See DRY FARMING

⊞ CARR, JEANNE CARVER SMITH (1825–1903)

Jeanne Carver Smith Carr is perhaps best known as a close friend and correspondent of the famous naturalist John Muir. In her own right, she was a prolific writer, educator, and expert in the fields of botany and horticulture. Her early writings focused on temperance, housework, and women's health, while the subjects of nature, botany, and plants characterized her later work. Her articles appeared in such publications as *Wisconsin Farmer, Wisconsin State Journal, Western Farmer, California Teacher, California Horticulturist, Illustrated Press, Home Journal, Pacific Rural Press, Pasadena and Valley Union,* and *Los Angeles Daily Times,* among other publications.

She was born in 1825 in Castleton, Vermont, the eldest child of Dr. Albert Gallatin and Caroline Carver Smith. Her great-grandfather, Colonel Noah Lee, was one of the founders of the town and an associate of Ethan Allen and Benedict Arnold. She attended Castleton Seminary, where she developed her lifelong interest in botany and met her husband, Ezra Slocum Carr, a professor of chemistry, pharmacy, and natural history at Castleton Medical College and a lecturer at the seminary.

The two were married in 1844 and raised four sons. In 1853, the family moved to Madison, where her husband was a member of the faculty at the University of Wisconsin for 13 years. The move was fortuitous for Jeanne Carr, who met and developed an instant rapport with John Muir, then a student at the university. Their relationship began with her acting as Muir's mentor and matured into a lasting friendship based on their shared love of nature. She also befriended Ralph Waldo Emerson while he was in Madison for his 1867 lecture tour.

The Carrs moved to California in 1868, influenced by the climate and agricultural prospects and the fact that they had family there. Dr. Carr was appointed professor of agriculture, agricultural chemistry, and horticulture at the newly opened University of California and in 1875 was elected California superintendent of public instruction. He appointed his wife deputy superintendent, making her one of the first women to hold public office in California. She combined these duties with her teaching assignments at the Normal School in San Francisco and at Mills Seminary in Oakland and with her responsibilities with the Grange. The Carrs were ardent advocates of the California chapter of the Grange (The Order of the Patrons of Husbandry, an organization for farmers modeled after the Masonic Order), often holding leadership roles in the association.

A disagreement in 1874 between the Carrs, who wanted the University of California to emphasize agriculture and the mechanical arts, and the university administration, who preferred the liberal arts, led to Dr. Carr's dismissal.

Two years later, the couple purchased 42 acres of undeveloped land in Pasadena, encouraged by a student of Dr. Carr's from Wisconsin who was a member of Pasadena's founding association. The Carrs moved to Pasadena in 1880 and became fully involved in the community. Jeanne Carr even gave a paper on horticulture that year at the opening of Pasadena's first citrus fair. She was also active on the Pasadena Free Library and Village Improvement Association and was a trustee of Throop Polytechnic Institute, which later became the California Institute of Technology.

Jeanne Carr became known as "the outstanding woman gardener of the last decades of the [19th] century," according to Victoria Padilla in *Southern California Gardens*. With little help because of limited financial means, she transformed the property, which she named Carmelita ("little grove"), into one of the most beautiful estates in southern California. She implored her friends to send her seeds and cuttings from their travels. At one time, Carmelita had more than 150 species of trees and shrubs, including an English yew tree planted by Sir Joseph Hooker, curator of London's Kew Botanic Gardens. The garden also featured native plants from the nearby San Gabriel Mountains brought into cultivation for the first time by Jeanne Carr.

Many distinguished visitors, including close friends Helen Hunt Jackson and John Muir, made pilgrimages to Carmelita, drawn not only by the reputation of the plantings but also by the warm hospitality of the Carrs.

An advocate of women's independence, Jeanne Carr outlined her ideas in an 1887 article in the *Overland Monthly* entitled "Agriculture as an Occupation for Women in California." She long held a dream of creating a school of horticulture for women in Pasadena to be financed with the income gained from selling the fruit from the Carrs' extensive groves. Frosts and other circumstances conspired against them and the couple had difficulty meeting their living expenses. Eventually they began accepting boarders to enhance their income.

Dr. Carr died in 1894. A few years later, Jeanne Carr moved to a home for women and later settled down on her brother-in-law's ranch in Santa Paula, where she passed away in 1903.

—*Peggy Bernal*

Suggested Reading

Gisel, Bonnie Johanna, ed. *Kindred and Related Spirits: The Letters of John Muir and Jeanne C. Carr*. Salt Lake City: University of Utah Press, 2001.

Muir, John. *Letters to a Friend, Written to Mrs. Ezra S. Carr, 1866–1879*. Dunwoody, GA: Berg, 1973.

Padilla, Victoria. *Southern California Gardens*. Berkeley: University of California Press, 1961.

Pomeroy, Elizabeth. *John Muir, A Naturalist in Southern California*. Pasadena, CA: Many Moons Press, 2001.

⌗ CHAPMAN, JOSEPH (1784–1849)

Joseph Chapman was born in Maine in 1784, though he is at times mentioned as a New Englander or as being from Boston. Pressed by the French privateer Captain Hippolyte Bouchard in Hawaii, Chapman was captured by Spanish soldiers during subsequent raids by Bouchard's ships in Santa Rosa, California, in 1818. Chapman's claim that Bouchard forced him into piracy conflicts with reports that he served as second in command to the privateer, an unusual position for an impressed sailor. Spanish authorities soon released him from prison after his refusal to rejoin Bouchard in an arranged prisoner parole.

A carpenter, blacksmith, and jack-of-all-trades, Chapman was one of the first Americans to settle in California. Stephen C. Foster described Chapman in his book *First American in Los Angeles*, but Hubert Howe Bancroft lists Chapman as the third American pioneer in Spanish California. In 1820, the Santa Ines mission employed him, and in 1821 he built a fulling mill, which cleansed, shrank, and thickened wool cloth by heat, moisture, and pressure. This mill, along with a gristmill previously erected, still exists to this day and a plaque at the historic mission credits Chapman with building one of the first industrial sites in California.

The following year, 1822, was an eventful year for Chapman. He received an amnesty given by the Spanish king to Anglo-American prisoners and was subsequently ordered by Governor Pablo Vicente Sola to the Mission at San Gabriel to construct another mill. During this same year, he received his baptism as a Catholic and wedded Guadalupe Ortega in Santa Ines. Ortega was one of four daughters of an established family whose ranch had graciously hosted him upon his release from capture. This marriage cemented his social recognition among the leading families of the area. The Chapmans eventually had five children, whose descendants still inhabited the region more than 60 years later.

Chapman's exploits and popularity grew as the years passed. Sometime between 1824 and 1826, he purchased a house and some land. He planted thousands of grape vines and is credited by the Sanford Winery in Santa Ynez Valley with being the first American to plant a vineyard in California. He eventually, in 1831, became a naturalized Mexican citizen based partly on his own reputation and his connections to the Ortega family. He continued his business activities in California as a shipbuilder and a surgeon. He framed the 60-ton schooner *Guadalupe* in San Gabriel and carted it to San Pedro, where it was launched upon completion. During the revolution of 1831, he tended to the badly wounded Governor Manuel Victoria. Finally, in 1838, the Mexican government bestowed a grant for the San Pedro rancho upon him, which his wife claimed upon his death in 1849.

Bancroft characterized Chapman as a popular, useful, and most interesting character. It is a considerable understatement to consider this former New Englander-turned-Californio, pirate, blacksmith, carpenter, vineyard-planter, father, shipbuilder, amateur surgeon, and early American pioneer as merely popular, useful, and interesting.

—*Scott M. Behen*

Suggested Reading

Bancroft, Hubert Howe. *The Works of Hubert Howe Bancroft. Vol. 19. History of California, 1801–1824.* San Francisco: A. L. Bancroft, 1885.

Bancroft, Hubert Howe. *The Works of Hubert Howe Bancroft. Vol. 20. History of California, 1825–1840.* San Francisco: A. L. Bancroft, 1885.

Mission Tour. "A Virtual Tour of the California Missions, Lavanderia." Available from http://missiontour.org/santaines/tour06.htm

Nugent, Walter. *Into the West: The Story of Its People.* New York: Knopf, 1999.

CHEMEHUEVI

The only tribe to migrate into California during recorded history was the little-known Chemehuevi. The Chemehuevi are a group of the Ute-Chemehuevi branch of the Shoshonean linguistic family. Their territory encompassed the Great Basin, and several Shoshonean tribes migrated westward prior to the arrival of the Spanish. Shoshonean movement into California took place through several cycles of migration, and the entrance of the Chemehuevi occurred during one of the more recent incursions. The Chemehuevi are an offshoot of the Southern Paiute that occupied the region of southern Nevada below Las Vegas. As the Chemehuevi migrated south, they continued to differentiate from their Southern Paiute origin. The Chemehuevi language over time became unique, so it was unintelligible to other Shoshonean tribes, and their language became dissimilar from other Colorado River tribes as early as the 18th century. The Chemehuevi called themselves *Nüwü*, which means "the people." The Mojave (Mohave) Indians referred to them as *Tcamuweiva* (Chemehuevi), and derivatives of this name became the cognomen originally recorded by early Spanish contacts.

The Chemehuevi migrated into California during the 18th century near Blythe and the Colorado River region, shifting west to the Little and Big San Bernardino Mountains. The Chemehuevi range continued south as far as the Whipple Mountains. The Chemehuevi were not present by the Colorado River below Eldorado Canyon during this time; the Yuman continued to occupy the California side of the Colorado River. The Chemehuevi occupied Chemehuevi Valley

Figure 1   Chemehuevi Migration Since 1775

and later spread south along the Colorado River, occupying the region left vacant by the Halchidhoma. The greater portion of this land could not support intensive agriculture. A component of Chemehuevi territory was mountainous, and water was in scarce supply, especially in the central and northwestern regions. Springs, water holes, and other usable water sources were familiar to the Chemehuevi. They subsisted mainly on products from the desert, but farmed on a small scale when possible. The Chemehuevi subsisted in small groups in order to utilize their environment to the best potential. As the Chemehuevi moved further from their Southern Paiute origins, they began to adopt some custom and speech patterns of the Mojave. Their differentiation became more pronounced the further south the Chemehuevi progressed.

Between 1769 and 1774, the Spaniards established the mission system along the California coastline. In 1771, an expedition presided over by Father Francisco Garcés left Mission San Xavier del Bac near Tucson, proceeding north to the Gila River and its convergence with the Colorado River. Garcés anticipated a possible land route west to the California coast and encouraged Captain Juan Bautista de Anza to initiate a trail from Primeria Alta to California. In 1774, de Anza and Garcés crossed the Colorado Desert from Sonora to

California, halting at Quechan villages encountered along their route. The following year, Anza traveled this same direction with 240 Spanish settlers headed for San Francisco Bay. Garcés sojourned in the Quechan villages and afterwards trekked north along the Colorado River. He encountered the "Chemebets" in 1775 during this journey north and noted their presence in western Arizona and eastern California. Garcés recorded that the Chemehuevi inhabited the territory between the Beneme Indians and the Colorado River as far north as the Ute Nation. It would be three quarters of a century before the next mention of the Chemehuevi would again be recorded, this time by American explorers.

The Chemehuevi were primarily a desert people until the beginning of the 19th century and continued to become further differentiated from their Southern Paiute origin. After the Garcés expedition in 1774, the Yuman and Mojave tribes drove the remnants of the Halchidhoma and Kohauna tribes eastward. They allowed the Chemehuevi to settle along the Colorado River sometime around 1828. The Chemehuevi settled along the Colorado River and developed an agricultural mode of existence, supplemented with traditional hunting and gathering practices on both sides of the river. The Mojave did not object to these Chemehuevi communities and continued to retain the right of passage through their lands. The Mojave recognized Chemehuevi ownership of both sides of the Colorado River and respected their right to farm and live there.

The Chemehuevi continued to expand their territory southward during the early 19th century throughout the sparsely settled desert regions. By the 1850s, there were numerous accounts of the Chemehuevi living in Chemehuevi Valley and other southern areas. The Chemehuevi continued to migrate along the Colorado River below Parker. The Chemehuevi were not reported in this area until the mid-19th century—even the journals of trappers James Pattie and Jedidiah Smith in the 1820s do not mention their inhabitation of this region. The Chemehuevi also expanded to Cottonwood Island, located above the present-day Davis Dam, where they remained until later conflict with the Mojave in the 1860s. Some Chemehuevi chose to continue migrating eastward to reside in Mojave Valley alongside their Mojave allies.

In 1853, the army's Topographic Bureau was instructed by Congress to conduct surveys along several possible routes for a transcontinental railroad. Lieutenant A. W. Whipple headed one of these expeditions and followed the thirty-fifth parallel from Fort Smith, Arkansas, to the Mojave Desert. By 1854, Whipple's expedition had traversed the desert and reached the Colorado River near the Bill Williams Fork. The party detected several Mojaves there and continued north until they arrived at Chemehuevi Valley. Whipple noted that more than 200 Chemehuevi inhabited their valley in various villages. While in the villages, one of the Chemehuevi headmen sketched a map for Whipple of the tribes dwelling along the Colorado River. The Chemehuevi map illustrated several villages that Whipple's expedition might possibly encounter along their journey. This coincided with a report the previous year by Major Samuel P. Heintzelman, stationed at Fort Yuma, who had noted that the "Chi-mi-hua-hua" tribe occupied the right side of the Colorado River 60 miles above the fort. Whipple continued his journey up the Colorado River until he reached the Mojave Desert.

One member of the Whipple expedition, Joseph Christmas Ives, returned to the Colorado River three years later. Ives commanded the Colorado River Exploring Expedition via the steamboat "Explorer" in 1857 with the goal to investigate the Colorado River as far north as they could travel. Their excursion started from Yuma, and they encountered the Chemehuevi along the river near Blythe. Ives' expedition mainly encamped on the eastern side of the river, noting that the Chemehuevi resided on both sides of the river. Chemehuevi farms and settlements were mainly located on the California side, but Chemehuevi territory extended far eastward into Arizona. Ives noted they were present in Chemehuevi Valley, but were different from other Colorado River tribes they encountered. The Chemehuevi settlements noted by the Ives expedition were identical to those mapped by Whipple four years earlier. Ives also wrote about the native utilization of the eastern shore of the Colorado River, recording that the Chemehuevi were firmly established there. Ives and his party continued in a small skiff that eventually brought them to the Las Vegas Wash, near the area in which the Chemehuevi originated.

The Chemehuevi continued to expand their territory along the western side of the Colorado River during the mid-19th century. The influx of American immigrants into Chemehuevi territory during the 1860s was detrimental to native subsistence. Indian Superintendent Charles Poston reported in 1864 that incoming settlers reduced Chemehuevi resources and that it was becoming dangerous for them to visit their hunting grounds. The Chemehuevi ranged a greater distance from their usual habitations near the Colorado River, which increased U.S. anxiety over their wanderings removed from Indian agents. Superintendent Poston recommended a Chemehuevi reservation in 1863, but one was not established at this time. The Chemehuevi Indians did not aspire to reside on the Colorado River Indian Reservation created in 1865.

Chemehuevi dwelling.

Source: Picture from Edward S. Curtis, *The North American Indian*. Courtesy of the Library of Congress.

In the mid-1860s, war broke out between the Chemehuevi and the Mojave, who had previously lived in peace. The Chemehuevi had adapted portions of Mojave customs and language into their culture after they migrated into several sectors previously under Mojave influence. This war was the catalyst for another major Chemehuevi migration, away from their Colorado River settlements and farther southwest into California. As hostilities escalated among the two tribes, the Chemehuevi began migrating beyond the river, off Cottonwood Island and out of Chemehuevi Valley into other sections of southern California. In 1866, a representative from the Chemehuevi traveled to Fort Mojave to request assistance from the United States in creating peace between them. Some Chemehuevi had returned to their homes in Chemehuevi Valley, but Mojave attacks continued against them. A peace treaty was finally agreed to in 1867, but several Chemehuevi groups that had migrated to other locations remained in their new settlements. One group relocated south to the eastern side of the Colorado River near Parker, Arizona. Other Chemehuevi returned near their place of origin in Nevada, while several groups began to dwell near unused desert oases. One group of Chemehuevi shifted to the oasis of Twenty-Nine Palms that was originally inhabited by the Serrano. The Serrano returned to their oasis at Twenty-Nine Palms in 1867–1868, found several Chemehuevi dwelling there, and resided with them in peace. Several Chemehuevi families resided with the Cahuilla near Banning and Beaumont. A few traveled into the San Bernardino Valley and allied themselves with other Native peoples. The Chemehuevi at the end of the 1860s inhabited a large desert region in southeastern California with communities along the Colorado River.

The Chemehuevi continued their migration in the 1860s over southern California in several directions. Chemehuevi survival depended on their ingenuity, and they began to explore new venues for subsistence. Military confrontations with the federal government in the mid-19th century compelled the Chemehuevi to withdraw to isolated locales. In the 1880s, over 100 Chemehuevi resided in different mountainous areas of southern California; sometimes several bands or groups inhabited the same locales. The Chemehuevi at this time ranged as far north as the outskirts of Pasadena, near the north fork of the San Gabriel River and Tehunga Canyon.

President Ulysses S. Grant directed the Office of Indian Affairs to create several new agencies to administer specific native groups. One of the new organizations was the Mission Indian Agency established in 1877. This bureau divided the tribes of southern California into several assemblages, renaming these groups in the process. In their zealousness to organize the Native peoples, the federal government designated many tribes that had never experienced missionization under the Spanish as "mission Indians." One Native group classified as mission Indians were the Chemehuevi living at the oasis of Twenty-Nine Palms. The majority of Chemehuevi did not reside at Twenty-Nine Palms during the latter half of the 19th century, but along the Colorado River. The Mission Agency acknowledged that the native peoples at Twenty-Nine Palms were under their jurisdiction that included this band of Chemehuevi. In 1890 the Mission Indian Agency resolved to create a reservation for the Twenty-Nine Palms Indians. Land had been set aside for a reservation since 1856, but delayed because of confusion over land title between the Natives and the Southern Pacific Railroad.

As early as 1864, Charles Poston, superintendent of Indian affairs in Arizona Territory, had selected an area of the Colorado River for a reservation. Poston proposed this reservation for several tribes that inhabited land along the Colorado River. A reservation was created for the Colorado River Indians on March 3, 1865. Initially, only the Mojave lived on this reservation, having occupied this sector for centuries. The majority of Chemehuevi did not reside on this reservation until the mid-1870s, when many were coerced to live there. Indian Agent J. A. Tormer noted in his report that the Chemehuevi raised their own crops, yet he urged their transfer to the reservation. A group of Chemehuevi continues to reside on this reservation presently, one of four major tribes that constitute the Colorado River Reservation.

By the 1880s, the Chemehuevi occupied an immense area throughout southern California. One Chemehuevi group, after the war between the Mojave and Chemehuevi, returned to Chemehuevi Valley, where they lived for more than 50 years. In 1887, Congress passed the Dawes Allotment Act (also known as the General

Allotment Act), which allowed reservations to be surveyed and divided into individual allotments. The Chemehuevi had never been granted a reservation solely for themselves, but shared reservations with other tribes. In 1910, the federal government added an additional 640-acre tract at Twenty-Nine Palms to be held jointly by the Chemehuevi and the Cahuilla living there. Four hundred of these acres were allotted between the two groups, but only two allotments went to Chemehuevi. Some Chemehuevi that originally inhabited Twenty-Nine Palms during the later half of the 19th century relocated to live with the Paiute in Nevada, joined relatives on the Colorado River or Aqua Caliente Reservations, or continued to inhabit their ancestral lands.

The largest assemblage of Chemehuevi at the beginning of the 20th century continued to populate Chemehuevi Valley. By 1903, only 75 Chemehuevi remained at Fort Mojave, while 225 Chemehuevi were recorded as living in Chemehuevi Valley. Special Agent C. E. Kelsey in 1906–1907 wrote two reports on the conditions of the California Indians for the United States government that included the Chemehuevi. Kelsey submitted a second report the following year, and suggested that Chemehuevi Valley be reserved solely for the Chemehuevi. In 1907, the federal government set aside the land of Chemehuevi Valley solely for Chemehuevi settlement. In 1910, additional lands in Chemehuevi Valley were allotted to several Chemehuevi families. Thirty-nine individuals filed for this valley to be allotted to them, consolidating their tracts side by side to retain their traditional land. This was accomplished under the seldom-used section 4 of the Dawes Allotment Act, which permitted nonreservation Indians to register their lands.

By the 20th century, 10 different tribes occupied Native lands with claimed or vested water rights to the Colorado River: One of these tribes was the Chemehuevi. In 1922, the Colorado River Compact was enacted, which allocated waters of the Colorado River and the neighboring states. This act was passed in anticipation of a future series of dams that would be constructed along the river to harness its energy and distribute water resources to urban centers. The compact was written to include the United States' obligation to the tribes along the Colorado River. Congress authorized the creation of Parker Dam and a reservoir

in California for this project. Numerous acres of fertile lands in Chemehuevi Valley were condemned and the Native populace located off their allotted lands for the erection of the dam and creation of Lake Havasu.

The Chemehuevi Tribe received federal recognition in 1970, and the Chemehuevi Indian Tribe Reservation was established by Executive Order in 1971. The reservation comprises 30,600 acres of Chemehuevi ancestral lands. Current tribal enrollment is around 500 persons, 300 of whom live on or near Havasu Lake. Other groups of Chemehuevi live on the Agua Caliente, Cabazon, Colorado River Indian Tribes, and Morongo Reservations. Economic livelihood derives from retail businesses, tourism, land leases, and gaming.

—Susan Sanchez-Barnett

See also CAHUILLA NATION; LAKE HAVASU CITY, ARIZONA; MOJAVE

Suggested Reading

Miller, Ronald Dean, and Peggy Jean Miller. *The Chemehuevi Indians of Southern California.* Banning, CA: Malki Museum Press, 1967.
Trafzer, Clifford E., Luke Madrigal, and Anthony Madrigal. *Chemehuevi People of the Coachella Valley.* Coachella, CA: Chemehuevi Press, 1997.

CHEROKEE NATION

See TRAIL OF TEARS

CHEYENNES

During the 17th century, Cheyennes started their gradual migrations from the Great Lakes region of the upper Mississippi Valley into the Great Plains of the Trans-Mississippi West. Change from pedestrian gardener-hunters to equestrian buffalo hunters and horse pastoralists, in conjunction with plains trade networking, intertribal warfare, colonial conquest, and reservation confinement characterize Cheyenne migrations. By the early 19th century, Cheyennes established their position in the midst of Native American and colonial conquest and competition as the dominant force of the

Central Plains. However, after mid-century, American conquest, in addition to indigenous competition and ecological limitations of mounted buffalo hunting, brought a collapse and reservation confinement. Throughout their history in the American West, some Cheyenne movements have been voluntary, others pressured by geopolitical rivalries and economic necessities or directly forced by outside powers. Overall, these migrations entail a rich and complex history of change and adaptation in economic, cultural, and social lifeways. Today, approximately 15,000 Cheyennes still live in the West, most of them in Montana and Oklahoma.

When tracing early Cheyenne migrations to the Great Plains, one of the key tasks is to identify who, when, and where Cheyennes really were. The Cheyenne nation is a product of history, an alliance of bands that have interacted and integrated through time. Historical evidence places the origin of Cheyenne peoples north of the Great Lakes, toward the Hudson Bay area. These Algonquian people were frequently known by different names by their different neighbors, and their self-identification, group cohesion, and group composition changed through time and place. Separate Cheyenne groups migrated at different times and along various routes, embracing dissimilar economic adaptations. The word "Cheyenne" is an approximate spelling of the term applied by the Dakota people for "red talkers," meaning "people of alien speech." Cheyennes themselves use the term *Tsistsistas*, strictly translated as "people" but imbedded with meanings such as related to another, similarly bred, like us, our people, or us. Adding to the confusion, outsiders, individually or in groups, were incorporated into the Cheyenne tribe. Most significant incorporation took place when Tsistsistas in the late 1700s encountered Sutaio, strangers from the north speaking an Algonquin language similar to theirs, and merged with them. Despite the merge, Sutaio retained their customs, distinct dialect, and social organization well into the 19th century, and even today it is a matter of distinction, many families being aware of variations in vocabulary as well as the lineage of their own ancestors.

In general, Cheyennes traversed from the woodlands of the Great Lakes region to the Minnesota River by approximately 1700. From there, they migrated to modern-day North Dakota, on the Sheyenne River, concentrating on the Missouri River near the boundary of the Dakotas. Gradually, during the 18th century, migrations continued southwest into the Black Hills region, and from there Cheyennes moved to dominate the Central Plains south of the Black Hills and north of the Arkansas River during the 19th century.

Cheyenne economy in Minnesota revolved around collecting wild rice and, to a lesser extent, hunting buffalo. Villages were relatively large and life semi-sedentary. Pressure from the Assiniboine and the Chippewas, in combination with fears of devastating imported diseases that accompanied and preceded Euro-American conquest, pushed Cheyennes west. In conjunction, visions of economic wealth and affluence offered by the horse and the bison in the plains pulled them out of their homes. By 1800, the bison population east of the Mississippi River was shrinking drastically, but the animal still lived in great numbers on the plains.

In the 1700s, a portion of Cheyennes had established a horticultural lifestyle near the Missouri River that involved farming and living in earthen lodges surrounded by fortifications. Gardening of maize, squash, sunflowers, beans, and other foods had significant roles in their subsistence. Some of these villages were still occupied near the end of the 18th century. Several Cheyennes also lived in skin-covered tipis for at least part of the year and were making transitions to a lifestyle that was more mobile and emphasized buffalo hunting. This would suggest that migrations and changes in lifeways for various Cheyenne groups during this period took place gradually.

For a significant period in the late 1700s and early 1800s, Cheyennes inhabited the plains east of the Black Hills. It was here, with the Black Hills as the center of their world, where they reinvented their universe and culture toward equestrian buffalo hunting. Bear Butte (Noahvose), the "Teaching Hill" and lodge of All Being, Maheo, became the holiest site in the Cheyenne world with the generous essence of Maheo, the people's spiritual substance, flowing forth from the sacred mountain. At Noahvose, Sweet Medicine, Cheyennes' guide and prophet on their trek westward, was called inside the mountain through a great door by Maheo. Sweet Medicine stayed in for four years, guided by Maheo with the help of four sacred powers and four sacred persons in codes of law and behavior. The prophet received four sacred arrows, which conveyed power over enemies and the buffalo in the country surrounding Noahvose. Re-created Cheyenne political and spiritual map of the world placed Noahvose at the center, with its edges roughly at the Missouri, Arkansas, and Yellowstone Rivers and at the Rocky Mountains.

A historical reinterpretation by Karl H. Schlesier places this episode much earlier. Possibly Cheyenne ancestors already migrated to the Northeastern Plains in 500 BCE and during the next two centuries arrived to the area around Noahvose. Centuries later they moved to eastern woodlands near the Great Lakes. Thus the migration to the plains in the late 18th century would be a return to old homelands.

The decades-long westward movement demanded many changes in lifestyle and economy, but it was the push to the Central Plains that initiated the greatest adjustments. Imagined lifestyles of wealth, affluence, freedom, and power as buffalo hunting equestrian nomads proved irresistible, and sometime during the late 18th and early 19th century, Cheyenne bands, probably not all at the same time, decided to put farming behind them and indulge in a more nomadic lifestyle. In fact, Cheyennes were among the few villagers who made a successful transition into mounted nomadism. Several groups, such as Mandans and Hidatsas, continued to rely on farming and trading in permanent villages on the Missouri River, while others, such as Pawnees, chose accommodated equestrian buffalo hunting with living in permanent villages on the Eastern Plains for a part of the year. Cheyennes instead made a life-changing and permanent leap. A central ingredient in this choice, other than the abundance of buffalo and lure of plains commerce, was the horse.

It is unclear when and from whom Cheyennes first obtained the horses that became a vital part of their lives. It seems that they encountered the horse frontier first on the Sheyenne River in the 1750s but that a steady supply of animals was secured only two decades later when they built farming villages on the Missouri River. Northern Cheyennes claim that the horses were first acquired from the Arapahos, but Southern Cheyennes state that the Apaches were the source. Both accounts are probably correct. Cheyennes even have two different words for "horse," which would indicate that different bands obtained them at different times and places.

Horses suddenly expanded the possibilities of hunting bison. Mounted hunters could range much farther, kill more efficiently, and transport the results more easily. Also, now hunters were able to follow the buffalo herds in all seasons if necessary. As a society counting no more than 3,000 people, Cheyennes were able to take their whole population to the hunt, allowing not only a maximum number of hunters but also the maximum number of women in camp nearby to cut and dry large quantity of meat quickly to prevent spoilage. Soon Cheyennes became extremely dependent on these huge animals for virtually every need, from food and clothing to shelter, tools, and even sacred objects. This one resource, buffalo hunting, could provide almost all of the needs of the people in addition to leaving a surplus for trading. It was the mobility brought by the horse and riches of the buffalo economy that transformed Cheyennes into a formidable power of the Central Plains of the early 1800s. Their position, however, proved very precarious.

In the highly contested plains, the position and power of any group depended greatly on geographic location, population resources, production capabilities, and access to trade. Indigenous invasions of Cheyennes, Comanches, and Lakotas in conjunction with increased Euro-American presence reshaped the region. Bison wealth, desire to acquire large herds of horses, increased intertribal and cross-cultural trading opportunities, and economic and territorial competition characterized Cheyenne lives. On the plains, Cheyennes had the opportunity to play a significant role in an old but expanding economic system being reinvigorated by new products and new traders, both Native American and Euro-American. Cheyennes made alliances, some more permanent than others, with Lakotas and Arapahos, and forged wars of economic and territorial control over the rich hunting grounds and important trade routes, in the process carving themselves space among Utes, Shoshonis, and Crows in the west; Lakotas and Plains villagers in the north; the Pawnees in the east; and Kiowas and Comanches to the south. Cheyenne strategy was to secure a power position as middlemen in the rich trade of the plains and to keep other competing tribes at bay. It was an explosive mix, no one truly controlling the rich hunting grounds of the Central Plains, no one willing to give them up. Although the peace of 1840, which significantly lessened territorial warfare among Cheyennes, Comanches, Kiowas, Plains Apaches, and Arapahos, provided some stability, the increased incursions by Euro-Americans, as well as shrinking buffalo herds due to overhunting, disease, and depletion of grasses, kept the situation volatile.

The networks of trade in the plains were complex and the number and variety of goods exchanged substantial. Usually horses went from the southwest toward the north and east. Guns came from the French and the British in the east, and later increasingly from the Americans, and were traded toward the west and south. Buffalo robes and hides, which originated on the plains, were traded in all directions.

When Cheyennes started to gain power in the plains, they took a central position between the poles of trade in the Southern Plains and the middle Missouri. The southern end of plains trade was controlled by the Comanches, who had established extensive networks of high-volume commerce, most importantly as horse raiders, raisers, and traders. In the north, the Missouri villages of the Mandan, Hidatsa, and Arikara were the focal point of trading activities. However, this system gradually changed during the 1820s and 1830s as diseases and Lakota invasion hammered the Missouri villages and Comanches were subjected to increasing American competition. Trading posts of the American Fur Company and Bent's Fort on the Upper Arkansas River reshuffled plains trade, replacing indigenous trade networks with a new order where the Euro-Americans overwhelmingly dictated what was exchanged and where. Increasingly, the plains were drawn into the global capitalistic economy as a distant outpost that supplied raw materials for world consumption. The extraction of plains resources into capitalistic world system drew the indigenous peoples into increasing dependency as they lost control of the trade routes and exchanges.

First Cheyennes acquired wealth in the plains like they never experienced before. Their tipis grew larger and well furnished, horse herds were expanding, and they became feared and respected by their neighbors. When Euro-American traders increased their presence,

Cheyennes adopted an economic survival strategy of marrying their women to white hunters and traders. Thus vital trade links were more secure, for a while at least. Still, changes in trading systems and life as hunter-pastoralists had a shattering effect on Cheyenne society. Often it was wise for Cheyenne bands to specialize economically. Some were horse-catchers and raiders, while others put more emphasis on making buffalo robes or acquiring guns. For Cheyenne society at large the quintessential factor was pasture, wood, shelter, and water during the sternest winter, under the heaviest use, and when the droughts were the worst. No large group of people could fulfill these requirements in the plains environment. Annual cycles of the buffalo kept the people separated much of the year. It was practical to divide into smaller groups that could successfully and economically follow the buffalo. Also, the need for horses and the needs of horses quickly established practical limits on the size of Cheyenne groups. Mostly for trade and prestige reasons (horses were important symbols of wealth and power), Cheyennes had more horses than was needed for effective mounted nomadism.

In sum, cycles and demands of equestrianism and buffalo hunting, with the environmental strains that accompanied these lifeways in the plains grasslands, required living in ever smaller units. Earlier in the river villages, large numbers of Cheyennes could live close together throughout the year. Then many people were actually a necessity for successful harvest or to defend sprawling gardens and permanent villages from enemy attacks. Now, in the plains, Cheyennes were forced to scatter and divide.

Ecological strains caused by horse pastoralism, changing trade balance epitomized by rising outside demand of buffalo hides, and dangers and disturbances caused by white overland traffic undermined the solidarity of Cheyennes and caused them to split into three major groups between 1840 and 1860. This split was more a result of geography and economics than any cultural distinction between the groups. Some bands were drawn by the economic opportunities of Bent's Fort. Established in the 1830s, the fort boasted an annual trade of 15,000 hides and large quantities of horses, thus opening new economic opportunities for Plains Indians while at the same time marking a significant change in power balance of plains commerce. When Bent's Fort replaced Comanches as paramount trades of the Southern Plains, it intensified the change in trade relations, pushing Native tribes increasingly to a role of cheap labor in an economy dominated by Euro-American fur companies.

In the decades following the split, the largest Cheyenne group were Southern Cheyennes who continued to be deeply involved in the production of buffalo robes and trading of horses. They lived south and east of what would become Denver, where there still was plenty of buffalo. Northern Cheyennes resided around the Black Hills and drew into closer alliance with the Lakota bands. A third group, the Dog Soldiers, were originally a military society but had developed into a fully fledged band, heavily intermarried with the most southerly Lakota bands. First the Dog Soldiers were considered outlaws and renegades, but as the white conquest intensified, Dog Soldiers' resistance brought them increasing respect and admiration, as well as more followers.

By the 1860s, the Cheyenne economy was under constant threat, struggling to cope. Overland migration severely disturbed their living space, but it was the Colorado gold rush in 1859 that opened the floodgates of white immigration. A tidal wave of people, animals, goods, and cash flowed into the Central Plains. Cheyenne lands were conquered by anxious town promoters, buffalo hunters, miners, ranchers, and farmers in their search of living space and riches. Transcontinental railroad and subsequent lines cut the Cheyenne heartland into pieces in the late 1860s and early 1870s.

Several treaties initiated by the federal government functioned as the legal justification for the United States to capture Cheyenne lands. With treaties began the process of Cheyenne confinement in reservations and steadfast assault on their culture. In 1851, the Treaty of Fort Laramie gave Cheyennes and Arapahos ownership of the lands between the North Platte and Arkansas Rivers and from the Rocky Mountains some 300 miles east. The Fort Wise Treaty of 1861 stripped them out of this land to a small triangular tract of land anchored on the Arkansas River in south-central Colorado. Subsequent treaties, such as the Treaty of Medicine Lodge Creek in 1867, which restricted Cheyenne movement north of the Arkansas River,

further narrowed Cheyenne living space, established segregated reservations, and exposed Indians to increasing poverty. Life as buffalo hunting equestrians was about to end.

Especially after the Civil War, warfare with the U.S. Army brought increasing destruction into Cheyenne lives. U.S. soldiers, although individually no match for mobile Cheyennes, brought total war to the plains. Winter campaigns with converging columns aimed to strike at indigenous villages, destroy their commissary, capture women and children, and drive indigenous societies into desperate poverty. Massacres at Sand Creek in 1864 and Washita in 1868 epitomize this destructive method of war. At Sand Creek, Colorado, volunteers rushed into a Cheyenne village that was composed mostly of the "peace-faction" of the tribe and engaged in a brutal rampage of murder and pillaging, killing mostly women and children. At Washita, regular troops under Colonel George Armstrong Custer engaged in similar destruction. In both instances, it was Black Kettle's Southern Cheyennes who bore the brunt of the assault. Black Kettle, killed by white troops in Washita, had next to his tipi an American flag as a symbol of friendship. He was among the strongest advocates for peaceful accommodation.

The army's rough tactics drove a portion of Cheyennes into reservations while others increased their resistance, and some fled north to join Northern Cheyennes and Lakotas. The army's warfare of submission, however, erupted in the Northern Plains as well. The victories of the late 1860s that resulted in the abandonment of the Bozeman Trail proved only temporary relief for the Lakota-Cheyenne-Arapaho alliance. Discovery of gold in the Black Hills triggered white invasion into Northern Cheyenne lands. After the government ultimatum that considered every Indian outside the reservation by March 1876 hostile failed, the Great Sioux War of 1876–1877 broke out. Despite famous victories at Rosebud and Little Big Horn, the Indians were subjugated into reservations through actions of total war by 1881. Similarly, Southern Cheyenne bands and the Dog Soldiers were harassed by the U.S. Army. The Battle of Summit Springs in July 1869, where Dog Soldiers clashed with the 5th Cavalry and Pawnee Scouts, resulted in irreplaceable Cheyenne losses. The remnants of armed Cheyenne resistance in the Southern Plains were broken in the Red River War of 1874–1875.

By spring 1877, Northern Cheyennes divided into four major groups, surrendering to white authorities. Some under the leadership of Two Moon journeyed to Fort Keogh, near Miles City, Montana, where they surrendered to the U.S. Army and subsequently were employed by the military as scouts. The main body surrendered at the Red Cloud agency in northwestern Nebraska. The third group went south and joined Southern Cheyennes in the Indian Territory. The fourth group had close ties with Northern Arapahoes and joined them at Wind River Agency in Wyoming. Militarily scarred, homelands occupied, and buffalo economy in ruins, Cheyennes' next migrations were controlled by the United States. Cheyennes struggled to retain cultural cohesion and remnants of the lands where they, just a few generations before, had envisioned a new lifestyle of ample wealth as equestrian buffalo hunters. The first steps of federal juggling occurred when the main body of Northern Cheyennes were sent against their wishes to the Cheyenne-Arapaho Reservation in Indian Territory to join their southern kin.

Many of the Northerners experienced open hostility upon arrival in Indian Territory. Strained relations between the two main Cheyenne divisions became obvious, although there were groups that had retained stronger ties and were thus more welcomed. Different climate, disease, hunger, homesickness, and inadequate medical attention intensified alienation among several Northerners. On September 9, 1878, approximately 300 Northern Cheyennes under the leadership of Dull Knife and Little Wolf left the reservation and headed north. This acclaimed odyssey that spurred national attention and aroused the U.S. Army in vigorous pursuit ended when Cheyennes under Dull Knife surrendered at Fort Robinson, Nebraska, in October 1878. The government imprisoned Dull Knife's people at the fort, aiming to send them back to Indian Territory. When Cheyennes refused, the military cut off food and firewood, thus making the situation extremely desperate. During a cold January night, the impoverished Cheyennes escaped, but the soldiers intercepted and shot down many of them. In February, 58 survivors of Dull Knife's band were taken to Pine Ridge Reservation,

and in the fall of 1879 they were allowed to move to Fort Keogh. The more than 100 followers of Little Wolf had separated from Dull Knife's group, avoided the soldiers around Fort Robinson, and later surrendered in Montana to Cheyenne scouts. Shortly afterward they were employed by the army and thus allowed to remain in Montana.

While Dull Knife and Little Wolf were making their way north in 1878, Little Chief's Northern Cheyennes were forced to relocate south. The two columns, however, did not meet. The newest arrivals soon grew to dislike the region and wanted to return north. In 1881 they were allowed to move to Pine Ridge, South Dakota. Still, more than 600 Northern Cheyennes remained south. Of them, approximately half expressed desire to move north, while others hoped to stay with Southern Cheyennes because of close family and marriage ties. Voluntarily, fewer than 400 Northerners were allowed to migrate to Pine Ridge in 1883; the rest stayed south. At this point, there were nearly 1,000 Northern Cheyennes at Pine Ridge, waiting for the next seemingly arbitrary move of the federal government. Some Northern Cheyennes under Two Moon and White Bull had lived at Fort Keogh since 1877, where they worked in the army. In 1882 the army resettled them 90 miles south on Rosebud Creek and Tongue River. From there, Northern Cheyennes aimed to reunite their people who were scattered in Oklahoma, South Dakota, and Wyoming. In 1891 the army removed the majority of Northern Cheyennes at Pine Ridge to Montana.

During this period of constant forced migration, relocation, and government indecisiveness, Cheyennes were pushed around by the United States, which obviously had no coherent policy or even consistent plans as to where it would allow Northern Cheyennes to live. In fact, American policies developed in undecided chaos as presidential changes brought inconsistency and disruption at the local level of Indian policy management. Cheyennes themselves actively tried to influence their future locale, lobbying for assistance from government officials and humanitarian agencies and succeeded, after years of uncertainty, to claim space for themselves in Montana by the end of the 19th century. A series of executive orders and Interior Department directives provided Northern Cheyennes with a legal claim to the Tongue River country. President Chester A. Arthur had signed an executive order in 1884 that created a small reserve on Rosebud Creek. In 1886, the Interior Department issued additional land for Cheyennes, and in 1900 another executive order confirmed and enlarged the reservation.

Pressure from local settlers, economic interests, and politicians combined with the ambiguities of government policies kept Cheyennes' fate uncertain in the Tongue River country for many years. Stock growers in Montana engineered periodic assaults against them in local newspapers and agitated local and federal politicians. Cheyennes were seen as threats to the success of local cattle industry. Allegations that the Indians stole cattle for their own consumption and disrupted foraging advanced the cattle ranchers' cause. Overall, Cheyennes showed strong determination to remain in Montana, and despite pressures by white ranchers and fears of removal they persevered, did not resort to violence, and managed to retain a foothold on the Northern Plains. In fact, Northern Cheyennes emerged from the years of allotment policies with an enlarged reservation. Their southern kin, however, lost most of their land.

Many Southern Cheyennes in their Oklahoma reserve (which they shared with their Arapaho allies) were not enthusiastic about farming, sending their children to white schools, becoming devoted Christians, or working like the dominant society expected them to. These revolutions in lifeways were imposed on Cheyennes by the white colonizers, resulting in various forms of visible or invisible resistance but also to accommodation. Diseases, maladministration of policies, lack of financial resources, insufficient language skills, and antagonism of white neighbors all ravaged Cheyenne life. White cattlemen intruded the reservation in search of grazing lands for their animals before being ejected by the government. The application of the Dawes Act of 1887 for allotment in severalty evaporated the Cheyenne land base. Aimed to shatter communal ownership and tribalism, this act was enforced amidst Southern Cheyennes in April 1892. Poorly prepared or unwilling to handle the individual plots of land assigned to them, the Indians soon were cheated out of more land by the unscrupulous whites who occupied the "surplus lands" that had been sold after allotments

were issued. In a few hours during 1892, Cheyennes had become a minority in the six counties that were formed out of the Cheyenne-Arapaho Reservation.

The reservation history of the Cheyenne Nation can be divided into two phases. During the early period, preceding the Indian Reorganization Act (IRA) of 1934, Cheyennes were treated like prisoners, living where they were ordered by the government, dependent on rations, and subject to harsh acculturation programs that aimed to break tribal structures and Cheyenne lifeways. After the IRA and Oklahoma Indian Welfare Act of 1936, Cheyennes were gradually given more autonomy to run their own lives, establish tribal governments, and preserve their cultural heritage. Still, the Bureau of Indian Affairs has the right to veto any action of the tribal government or any transaction of privately owned Cheyenne land that is in trust.

During the 1930s, employment became available outside reservations by New Deal programs and other projects. Many people left their extended families to join these programs and ventured to towns. World War II also called a large number of Cheyenne men into service. Many who moved to Los Angeles, Seattle, Chicago, Dallas, or Denver to work in war industries or relocation programs never returned. Rivalries over mineral rights, disputes over the Black Hills and Bear Butte, among other occurrences, have shaped Cheyenne life in recent decades amid postindustrial society. Northern Cheyenne Reservation land, of which most is communally owned by the tribe, is rich in natural resources, such as oil, coal, and timber, and has some good grazing land. Among Southern Cheyennes the land base is much thinner. Of the 3.5 million acres originally owned in Oklahoma in 2000, about 70,000 acres remain in trust and the tribal government owns an additional 10,000 acres. The most pressing concern is heirship as most trust land and most mineral rights are co-owned by 5 to 400 people. Cheyennes have earned income by leasing grazing lands and mineral rights. Northern Cheyennes have, however, decided not to allow any development of their coal reserves, saving the coal for the future. Often, government jobs have formed the core of Cheyenne employment during the last hundred years, but unemployment has remained high and was about 30 percent in 1999 for Northern Cheyennes. Today Cheyennes can get a full education at their reservation through the establishment of Dull Knife Memorial College at Lame Deer in 1975. After a low of 2,500 in the 1930s, the Cheyenne population has increased dramatically. The recorded number for the 1990 U.S. census was almost 11,500, and in 2000 there were approximately 15,000 Cheyennes.

The intercultural situation of the Northerners and Southerners today is significantly different. Northern Cheyennes have managed to retain their reservation pretty much intact and have few non-Cheyennes living there. Their interactions with non-Indians occur largely at surrounding off-reservation towns. Southern Cheyennes live among and around large numbers of non-Indians. Indians constitute only about 6 percent of the population in the seven-county area where they live. Contacts with non-Indians are consequently constant. Interestingly, Northerners and Southerners together have bought land at their sacred site of Bear Butte for religious purposes.

Cheyenne migrations into and in the Trans-Mississippi West form one the most intriguing and complicated human histories in North America. From pedestrian gardener-hunters of the Great Lakes region, Cheyennes gradually migrated into the Central Plains, reformulating their lifeway into equestrian bison hunters and important plains trade middlemen. Through internal division, Euro-American trade dominance, and conquest by the United States, Cheyennes saw control of their life slipping to outsiders. Despite harsh attacks on their culture, sometimes devastating poverty, and hostile attitudes of the surrounding society, the Tsistsistas retain their presence in the Great Plains of the American West.

—Janne Lahti

See also Santa Fe, New Mexico

Suggested Reading

Berthrong, Donald J. *The Cheyenne and Arapaho Ordeal: Reservation and Agency Life in the Indian Territory.* Norman: University of Oklahoma Press, 1976.

Boye, Alan. *Holding Stone Hands: On the Trail of the Cheyenne Exodus.* Lincoln and London: University of Nebraska Press, 1999.

Grinnell, George Bird. *The Cheyenne Indians,* 2 vols. Lincoln: University of Nebraska Press, 1972.

Hämäläinen, Pekka. "The Rise and Fall of Plains Indian Horse Cultures." *The Journal of American History* 90 (December 2003): 833–862.

Moore, John H. *The Cheyenne Nation: A Social and Demographic History.* Lincoln: University of Nebraska Press, 1988.

Moore, John H. *The Cheyenne.* Cambridge, MA: Blackwell Publishers, 1996.

Monnett, John H. *Tell Them We Are Going Home: The Odyssey of the Northern Cheyennes.* Norman: University of Oklahoma Press, 2001.

Schlesier, Karl H. *The Wolves of Heaven: Cheyenne Shamanism, Ceremonies, and Prehistoric Origins.* Norman: University of Oklahoma Press, 1987.

Svingen, Orlan J. *The Northern Cheyenne Indian Reservation, 1877–1900.* Niwot: University Press of Colorado, 1993.

West, Elliott. "Called Out People: The Cheyennes and the Central Plains." *Montana: The Magazine of Western History* 48 (Summer 1998): 2–15.

West, Elliott. *The Contested Plains: Indians, Goldseekers, and the Rush to Colorado.* Lawrence: University Press of Kansas, 1998.

⊞ CHILEANS AND THE CALIFORNIA GOLD RUSH

The discovery of gold in Sutter's Creek in January of 1848 altered the development of California as well as the lives of emigrants who came from around the world lured to the region by "gold fever." These individuals risked everything to take their chances in the goldfields to find fortune and a better life. Once they arrived, many found a very different reality in California. Chilean argonauts were among the first foreign adventurers filled with hopes and aspirations to arrive in San Francisco Bay. However, because of the massive influx of miners and the enormous overcrowding, Chileans were also among the non-Natives targeted by growing antiforeign sentiment. Their fantasy of wealth rapidly became a nightmare as whites viciously attacked Chilean settlements and the relationship between the two groups deteriorated into violence. Chileans were taxed and then expelled from the gold mines. Although a few Chileans chose to remain, most, fearful of the hostile environment and disillusioned by their experiences in California, returned to their homeland.

THE MANIA FOR WEALTH

The 1849 gold rush was touched off by an opportunist attempting to capitalize off of the important discovery.

After purchasing every available axe, pan, and shovel in the city, Samuel Brannan ran wildly through the bustling streets of San Francisco dramatically waving a vile of gold and hollering, "Gold! Gold found in the American River!"

These words echoed through San Francisco, and within months sent shockwaves throughout the world. "California" became synonymous with fortune. Rumors of "inexhaustible gold mines" traveled as far as South America, Europe, and China, and a mania for wealth ensued. Tens of thousands of dream seekers, their minds filled with images of wealth and prosperity, abandoned their humdrum lives to try their luck in California, where they believed the precious metal was so plentiful that "all you had to do was bend over and pick it up."

Before long, gold fever afflicted the world's adventurous spirits who sought a better life in a foreign land. Perhaps as many as 50,000 South Americans migrated to California between 1848 and 1852. Many of them were Chileans. It is difficult to estimate their numbers because documentation from Chile is not readily available. However, the Chilean Foreign Office issued more than 6,000 passports in the first six months of 1849. Realizing that over half of the travelers to California were not bothering to obtain passports, the Chilean Congress passed legislation allowing citizens to travel to California without official documentation.

NEWS OF GOLD REACHES CHILE

Chileans traveling to California came from all regions and social classes. Most of them departed from the strategically positioned port of Valparaiso and nearly all were filled with illusions. They had heard tall tales written in newspaper accounts, trumpeted in local theaters, or spread through town gossip. The stories described not only the gold in California, but also "the endless pine trees in the San Joaquin Valley, the thousands of cows that roamed the vast plains without owners, and the fields which had an eternal supply of vegetables." To Chileans, California was the embodiment of the Garden of Eden, and America was the land of opportunity and equality, beckoning industrious men and women to wealth.

The port of Valparaiso, Chile, was one of the first in South America to send gold seekers to California. Not only were they first, but Chileans left other nations far behind. The Peruvian argonauts set sail 79 days later than the first Chilean ships bound for California's gold.

News of the gold rush arrived in the trading port of Valparaiso on August 18, 1848, when a ship by the name of *JRS* entered the harbor and the captain reported that nearly half of his men had deserted their duties as sailors in San Francisco due to rumors of gold. Ten days later, his report was confirmed when the vessel *Adelaida* arrived with more than $2,500 in California gold dust aboard. Suddenly, gold fever struck the local populous with great force.

The journey from Valparaiso to San Francisco is about 6,700 miles and usually took less than two months. Travelers departing from Valparaiso enjoyed an advantage because they were perched on the Pacific Ocean. Their journey was considerably shorter and easier than that of people traveling around Cape Horn, via the Isthmus of Panama, or overland using the Oregon and California trails. The shorter voyage gave Chileans the benefit of an early arrival and spurred the first Chilean gold seekers to travel to California. A mere two weeks after the arrival of *Adelaida*, the frigate *Virginia* departed from Valparaiso destined for California. The majority of passengers were English-speaking businessmen who had been living and conducting trade in Valparaiso. After their departure, boatloads of gold-seeking Chileans soon followed. The first were the professional miners and experienced tunnel and shaft diggers, followed by individuals from all walks of life, ranging from the aristocrat to the prostitute.

The mass exodus of Chileans evoked mixed reactions from those who remained. In 1849, a local newspaper, *El Mecurio,* sought to present a more realistic view of the *el dorado* of upper California. It described the reality of what awaited gold seekers, but it was too late. The gold fever had struck, and no one wanted to hear the sobering news. A Spanish playwright in Chile wrote a play entitled *I Am Not Going to California* criticizing the abandonment of Valparaiso and the illusions of the gold rush. It was not appreciated by the local populous, and angry crowds gathered at the Theater of the Republic on opening night, December 18, 1848. The demonstrators fiercely protested the play and nearly incited a riot, causing local officials to cancel the performance.

VICENTE PEREZ ROSALES

One famous Chilean who recorded his odyssey to California was Vicente Perez Rosales, the son of a wealthy family. A victim of gold fever and one of the thousands of Chileans to seek adventure in California, Rosales returned to Chile only a few years later completely disillusioned. After he had abandoned his fantasies of wealth in the goldfields and returned home, he published an account of his experiences in California and became a prominent Chilean politician, journalist, and internationally acclaimed literary figure.

Rosales and his group of adventurers, which included his four brothers, a brother-in-law, and two servants, willingly relinquished their wealth in Chile to seek fortune in California. According to Rosales, they confronted an unknown and hostile land, facing deserts, diseases, thieves, and violence, "where justice is found at the end of a pointed gun," because these dangers appeared insignificant compared to the chance of getting their hands on glittering gold.

Travelers faced hardships journeying by sea as they navigated their way to San Francisco Bay. Rosales' description makes it clear that none of the travelers understood the magnitude of their decision to depart their familiar homeland. The troubles his party encountered mounted rapidly. Due to overcrowding, their supplies could not accompany them and followed on another ship. Once they set sail on December 10, 1848, a myriad of incidents plagued them, ranging from the captain's attempt to throw a woman overboard to the depletion of their food sources. Rationing resulted, and the inequitable distribution of food led to a near mutiny on board. Despite hardships, negative feelings dissipated as their ship pulled into San Francisco Bay. Their optimism soared once a San Franciscan boarded the ship and confirmed the high expectations of the eager passengers with the news that gold was indeed everywhere. The travelers on board were both anxious and resolute about carving out their share of fortune in California.

CHILEAN MINERS IN CALIFORNIA

Many Chileans prospered in California. Chile had a history of mining, and the nearly depleted gold mines at home prompted many miners to search for more lucrative diggings in California. The Chilean miners were among the first foreigners to arrive in California, only preceded by the Mexicans from Sonora who had traveled overland. Many Chilean newcomers were shocked to see the crude and rudimentary methods used for mining by the Californians. The local populous lacked mining experience and often employed spoons and knives in an attempt to extract the gold. Chileans, like the Mexican argonauts, had a history of mining and instructed other would-be miners in digging shafts and effectively panning for gold. Chileans utilized the techniques and skills they had developed in their homeland and adopted these methods in California. One such device was the "Chili Mill," so named because of its origins. California gold seekers adopted many words commonly used in Chile and other Spanish-speaking countries. For example, the word *placer,* which derived from *plaza,* had been used in Chile for gold-bearing sand since 1757.

CHILEAN SETTLEMENTS

In the gold country, as well as in towns such as Stockton and San Francisco, Chileans, like other foreigners, grouped themselves in small colonies. The largest colony, Chileto or "Little Chile" was in San Francisco and sat at the foot of Telegraph Hill. It consisted of small wooden huts and makeshift tent dwellings, which appeared filthy and overcrowded. Journalists criticized the settlement, observing that one half of the colony "was a slimy bog" and the other half was full of garbage heaps and broken glass. Not only did writers portray the colony as undesirable, but Anglo Americans often remarked unfavorably on the work ethic of the male Chileans. An observer wrote that the women of Little Chile "always appeared to be washing, but the vocation of the men was a puzzle to the passer-by." Despite contemporary critics, the spirit of the community was undeniable. Many outsiders observed that Little Chile was transformed on Sundays, with men emerging from their homes wearing their best clean shirts, women clothed in bright dresses, and children running around smiling as they all celebrated the Lord's day.

IMPRESSIONS OF CALIFORNIA

Chileans described California as a kind of Babylon of foreign villages, where one could hear every language and view every type of attire. Chileans complimented Yankee ingenuity in settling land acquired from Mexico. Rosales states that the Yankees did more in a few years to improve the land than the Spanish settlers had done in centuries. He further credits American spirit with transforming neglected land into an immense commercial enterprise, pointing out that once the Americans annexed the territory, California emerged as a powerful state both economically and intellectually. Money flowed into schools and building projects, promoting organization and literacy. Rosales contends that, "With the canons of conquest, the Americans also rolled in the printing press."

ANTI-CHILEAN SENTIMENT

As competition increased and gold was depleted, Anglo Americans sought to regulate foreigners and harass them out of California. They were especially desirous of forcing out the Chileans and Mexicans who had benefited from early arrival and the best selection of claims. Spanish speakers referred to the Yankee miners as *gringos envidiosos* or "jealous white men." Rosales describes the relationship between the Americans and Chileans as strained due to the similarity of their character and to the fact that Chileans were ready to fight back when challenged by the Yankees.

Rosales observed the deterioration of relations between Americans and Chileans during his stay in California. Problems between the races were exacerbated by the lawlessness that existed between 1848 and 1850. Vigilante groups, which claimed to curb local crime, emerged in various cities. San Francisco had its own vigilante groups, many of which utilized their newfound authority to torment and harass foreigners. One such group, the Regulators, was commonly called "the Hounds" because of their vow to "hound" out the Mexicans and other foreigners from Californian soil. The antiforeigner sentiment culminated in an attack on Little Chile on July 15, 1849, in which a drunken mob, led by the Hounds, rampaged through the streets crying, "Down with the Chileans! Death to all of them!" The mob tore down tents, stole possessions, and set fire to the remaining ruins. During the chaos and pandemonium, a Chilean mother was murdered and her daughter sexually assaulted. The following day, as news of the atrocities circulated, crowds sympathized with the inhabitants of Little Chile, and San Franciscans collected a charitable fund on behalf of the victims. By nightfall, 19 of the Hounds were captured and imprisoned for the assault, and nine men were convicted of crimes.

As time passed, however, animosity and tensions did not subside. Anglo miners continued to feel antagonism toward foreigners, whom they felt had no right to profit from American soil. Another incident occurred in Calaveras County in December of 1849. A group of Anglo American miners attempted to drive off Spanish speakers from their claim. The hostilities escalated when the Spanish miners attacked the Americans, killing two and wounding four others. As word spread, the Americans stormed the area, vowing to get revenge. The violence culminated in the murder of three Chileans and the beating of several others. Spanish speakers took the brunt of the blame and the wave of violence resulted in the banishment of all Spanish-speaking miners from the region. By 1850, Senator Thomas Jefferson Green helped enact a foreign miners' tax, which required all noncitizens to pay a tax of $20 a month. When Spanish speakers gathered in protest, they were met by a band of heavily armed Anglo Americans, many of whom donned their uniforms from the Mexican War to remind the foreigners who dominated the region.

DISILLUSIONMENT: TO LEAVE OR NOT TO LEAVE

Driven from their claims, many Chileans returned to Little Chile in San Francisco. Unable to find employment, they found little solace in the small colony, which reeked of garbage and offered little more than makeshift tents for homes. Chileans never forgot the denigration they had received: discrimination in the goldfields, expulsions from their claims, and the haunting images of the July riot. Deciding it was time to relinquish their dreams of gold, at least half of them returned to Chile. Few had fulfilled their dreams of wealth and the majority returned home as paupers.

It must be noted that anti-Chilean sentiment failed to force many Chileans to leave their adopted home. According to the U.S. census of 1852, at least 5,571 Chileans remained in California. Moreover, these numbers are conservative, because thousands of Chileans refused to give their names, unwilling to be identified given the anti-Chilean sentiment prevalent at that time.

Many Chileans were undeterred by the hostile climate and became established Californian businessmen. Initially, they formed close-knit communities and maintained a connection with their roots in Chile. After any major event in California, including the great fire of December 24, 1849, they wrote home to inform relatives and friends of their survival in California. They published a Chilean newspaper in San Francisco between 1863 and 1883, and when Chile was threatened by Spain in 1865, they formed patriotic clubs to collect funds to help their motherland. Gradually, however, Chileans were assimilated into American life and were absorbed into the population.

—Mary Marki

Suggested Reading

Hernandez, Robert C. *Los Chilenos en San Francisco: Recuerdos historicos de la emigracion por los descubrimientos del oro, iniciada en 1848.* 2 vols. Valparaiso: Imprenta San Rafael, 1930.

Lopez, Carlos U. "Chilenos in California: A study of the 1850, 1852 and 1860 Censuses." Saratoga, CA: R and E Research, 1973.

Monaghan, Jay. *Chile, Peru, and the California Gold Rush of 1849.* Berkeley: University of California Press, 1973.

Oyarzun, Luis. "El Oro de California y la Vida Chilena." Santiago, Chile: Editorial Universitaria, 1967.

Rawls, James, and Walton Bean. *California, an Interpretive History.* New York: McGraw, 2003.

Rosales, Vicente Perez. "Oro en California." Santiago, Chile: Editorial Nascimento, 1974.

Whitaker, Arthur P. *The United States and the Southern Cone: Argentina, Chile, and Uruguay.* Cambridge, MA: Harvard University Press, 1976.

⌗ CHINA LAKE, INYOKERN, AND RIDGECREST, CALIFORNIA

CHINA LAKE

In 1943, the U.S. Navy's air-to-ground rocket development program, based at the California Technical Institute in Pasadena, California, had trouble obtaining suitable empty land near an underused airfield for testing the rockets. In August 1943, a naval officer and one of the scientists flew in a private plane over the upper Mojave Desert looking for land not being used by the U.S. Army Air Corps in its bomb testing programs, when they spotted the Inyokern airport. Next, a small party explored the valley on the ground. They reported they had encountered no one and saw very little cattle—only about one per square mile. The ground party also reported the presence of mercury mines in the area. Recognizing that the relatively empty land and the basically unused airfield were what they needed, the navy negotiated with the air corps for wartime rights to the airfield at Inyokern. (The U.S. Army Air Corps felt it had first rights to the Inyokern airfield because of its base at Edwards Dry Lake, a little to the south.)

In October of 1943, meetings were held at the headquarters of the Fourth Air Force, San Francisco, where an agreement was reached that gave the navy rights to the area respective to wartime testing. With this agreement in hand, the navy was able to obtain a contract with Kern County for use of the Inyokern airfield and began immediate operations. The navy liked the area for a test station because, although located in the middle of a desert, it was near major resources on the west side of the valley: water (the Los Angeles Aqueduct at the foot of the Sierra Nevada Mountains), power (the 88,000-volt lines of the California Electric Company), telephone (lines of the Inter-State Telegraph Company), and rail (the Southern Pacific tracks). The site also offered clear skies and an expectation of a high number of good flying days per year. It is also recorded that some naval officers felt the distance from Washington, DC, was an advantage in itself, as it would reduce the temptation for detailed management from the Naval Bureau of Ordnance.

The navy established the headquarters at Inyokern because the first test flights used the airfield. The ground-based test ranges were established to the east at China Lake, a playa at the foot of the Argus Range. (The playa's name is derived from Chinese laborers who did brine mining of borax there in the late 1870s.) Permanent base headquarters and the community village were supposed to be built at Inyokern, but were moved when the navy shifted the future center of activity to the China Lake area. The naval air facility at China Lake became active in May of 1945, and all flight operations were moved from Inyokern to Armitage Field, which was named after a naval aviator who died during a test flight at China Lake. The first name of the station was the U.S. Naval Ordnance Test Station (NOTS), Inyokern. After the base's headquarters moved to China Lake, the name changed to USNOTS, China Lake. Later, in 1967, the station designation changed again, this time to Naval Weapons Center; currently, the station designation is Naval Air Weapon Station.

During the life of the station, it has assisted in the development and/or testing of many weapons systems for naval air, including the aircraft-mounted rockets used in World War II (also used by the Eighth Air Force in Europe), the Sidewinder missile, the Shrike missile, the Sparrow missile, the high-speed antiradiation missile (HARM), laser-guided bombs, and the Redeye, a shoulder antitank weapon used by the U.S. Marines. Naval sea weapons development used China Lake as a designated target area for the Tomahawk cruise missile test firings. In addition, China Lake helped develop and test the lunar landing mechanism for the Apollo flights to the moon. The National Aeronautics and Space Administration also used the rugged north area of the base to test the lunar rovers. Among its many laboratories and test facilities is Michelson Laboratory, named for Albert Michelson, a naval officer, who was the first American to receive the Nobel Prize for Physics in 1907.

Originally, the navy claimed 650 square miles, most of which were public domain lands. Twenty-seven people were removed as a result of the condemnations. The Department of the Interior did not always acquiesce when the navy requested parcels of public domain be transferred to navy control. Many thought the new China Lake facility would only be a wartime installation, while some of the naval and civilian personnel who were establishing the base saw it as a permanent facility. Later, in 1944, the navy requested another 363 square miles to be added to the northern side of the base. The navy felt such space was needed to keep the local population safe, as the navy was now testing various bomb configurations to determine such critical factors as aerodynamic characteristics and ground penetration. In addition, more land to the north was needed because rockets with a longer ranger were being tested.

At the same time as the northern land addition was being requested, the navy also asked for additional land to the west and the south. The western extension would place the western boundary of the base near Route 6, now Highway 14. This extension encompassed 6,460 acres, of which 4,570 acres were patented. The southern extension (actually southern and eastern) moved the boundary down to the Trona Road, Route 178, and some land extending eastward along the road. The navy did not reveal one of the key reasons for the need for additional land: It was building the nonnuclear shaped charges for the first U.S. atomic bombs at the China Lake base in the Salt Wells area, which is inside the southern land extension.

In all, the land the navy requisitioned included more than 200 mining properties, more than 1,000 mining claims, and more than 2,800 acres of patented land. In taking control of such a vast area, the navy unintentionally made sure the land remained in its natural state. Inside its borders, China Lake preserves the ranges of wild horses, free-roaming burros, mountain lions, and bighorn sheep. In addition, China Lake contains more than 14,000 different petroglyph images. These images, chipped into stone by Native peoples more than 3,000 years ago, can be viewed on tours arranged through the Maturango Museum in Ridgecrest, California. Finally, during the infrequent years when the rainfall has been sufficient for runoff to gather in the China Lake playa and at the adjacent Mirror Lake playa, fairy shrimp hatch and are active for the short life of the watery lake.

At China Lake, the navy first began constructing rocket test ranges and, a little further west, a naval airfield. The location of the station and the primitive living conditions (wooden barracks, no air conditioning or air coolers) for workers caused a shortage of labor. Although a large number of workers were hired, many only stayed a few days before returning to the Los Angeles area. During an eight-month period in 1944, the navy and its construction contractors hired 24,000 workers, yet the highest number of people actually working on the base at any one time was 7,200. At one time, the navy brought a group of Navajo construction workers to the site. After a couple of months of clashes with the white workers, the Navajos were returned to their homes. In January of 1944, the total base population, including both construction workers and those involved with the weapons development, was 10,000. By October of that year, the population at China Lake was approximately 8,000. Original planning, done mainly in Washington, DC, Pasadena, and San Diego (the headquarters of the Eleventh Naval District), gave little thought to the need of building a total community in the desert as an important part of the navy installation. Future years would show that the development of a high level of living conditions would be required to attract the high-caliber civilian staff necessary to the China Lake technical programs. The executive officer of the stations, in the post–World War II years, felt the civilian employees were not of the highest caliber. Personnel turnover became very high in the post–World War II years. There were more than 2,000 terminations in 1947 when the maximum number of civilian employees was limited to 3,650. The main issue was the lack of adequate housing.

During World War II, "temporary" prefabricated housing was sent to the station; it remained in use until the 1970s. In 1944, the naval officers at China Lake concerned with civilian housing requested that the temporary housing available through the Federal Housing Authority not be used. The navy planners in November of 1943 underestimated what was needed for the base community. One early report talked of a base population of 1,000 when discussing the proposed layout of the community. By February of 1944, the commanding officer estimated a wartime population of 2,000 permanent people, plus 2,000 construction people during the 18 months necessary for the building of the base. Housing in early 1944 was so limited that some families lived in Trona, about 25 miles east of what is now Ridgecrest, until housing could be found for them or built. Part of the planning problem flowed from the unknown future of the station. When first conceived, it was to be a test station. The naval officers and chief civilians involved saw a need for a permanent, development-oriented station. All their efforts were toward that end, and they eventually succeeded. Private developers were slow to buy land for housing when the future of the base remained in doubt. But as the permanence of the station became evident, some developers invested in the area and the off-base housing options began to grow. By 1948, approximately 10,000 people lived on the base, making China Lake the largest community in all of the Mojave Desert.

During the military base closures of the late 1990s and early 2000s, navy air weapons development programs were moved to China Lake when the original parent base closed. Over the years since 1943, the movement of all the scientists, technicians, and naval personnel to the station created a need for housing. This need for housing fueled the growth of what was to become the hamlet of Ridgecrest, located just outside the main gate of China Lake.

INYOKERN

The Indian Wells Valley, home to the China Lake Naval Air Weapons Station and the communities of Inyokern and Ridgecrest, is located approximately 150 miles northeast of Los Angeles, California, in the northern part of the Mojave Desert. Indian Wells Valley derives its name from the Indian Wells springs located at the base of the Sierra Nevada Mountains midway down the western side of the valley. The valley is bordered on the west by the Sierra Nevada Mountains, on the north by the Coso Range, on the east by the Argus Range, and on the south by the Rademacher Hills and the El Paso Mountains. The elevation of the valley floor is 2,300 feet. Average annual rainfall is between two to three inches, although, in an El Niño year, the valley can receive up to 10 inches of rain. In its early years, the population consisted of very small bands of Shoshone Indians. The area had minimal population until the Los Angeles Metropolitan Water District (LAMWD) began building the aqueduct to bring water from the Owens Valley to Los Angeles.

In 1909, Robert R. Thompson, originally from Illinois, moved to the Indian Wells Valley and claimed a homestead near the Inyo County and Kern County border. When the Southern Pacific Railroad built the transfer point known as Magnolia (or Number 16) near his land, he recognized a business opportunity. Thompson and David Shanks, another local landowner, formed the Inyo-Kern Company and built a 12-story hotel, a restaurant, and a general store. By 1912, the company and the area had grown sufficiently that the men formed the Inyokern Land and Water Company, drew a town map, and filed it with the Kern County

Recorder. The resulting town of Inyokern was established in 1914. The Inyokern Land and Water Company drilled wells (water was found at 50 feet) and started farming alfalfa and planted orchards. The company also formed an Irrigation District in 1919, petitioned for the water rights for Mono Lake, and asked for federal monetary grants to bring the water to the area. However, the LAMWD used its clout in Washington, DC, and the company received neither the water rights nor the grants. This doomed any expansion of the city. The small town survived by servicing the needs of the small number of farmers and ranchers in the area, frequently as a shipping point for local produce and cattle to Los Angeles. In the 1920s, the Inyokern airfield consisted of two graded, dirt strips.

In 1933, due to the start of air passenger service from Fresno, California, to Phoenix, Arizona, the Civil Aeronautics Authority built a two-runway airfield in Inyokern as a Kern County emergency field, but it had little use. In 1943, Inyokern had a population of 25 and there were few farms and ranches in the valley. But the needs of the U.S. Navy in World War II brought immense change to the Inyokern area.

RIDGECREST

The first permanent settlers, the George Robertson family, of what eventually became Ridgecrest were homesteaders who filed a claim for land in 1912. The next claim occurred in 1913 and was filed by Grant Bowman. The Robertson homestead made up much of what is the northern part of Ridgecrest, while the Bowman homestead now makes up much of southern Ridgecrest. John McNeil purchased the Robertson property and started a dairy. The Crum brothers purchased the dairy. Other Crum family members settled in the area, and the grouping of six to eight dwellings became known as Crumville.

In the 1920s and the 1930s, a few more farms were started and some additional people, servicing Trona's brine-mining activity, moved into the area. In 1939, the first gas station opened. Due to the lack of trees locally, some homes were built with tufa stone from the Searles Lake area, now designated the Trona Pinnacles National Natural Landmark. Some dwellings from abandoned farms and ranches in the Indian Wells Valley were moved to Crumville for use as rental homes for the workers in Trona. By the early 1940s, the area had farms, two dairies, and an egg ranch. Farmers sold their produce to the mining towns in the general area.

In 1940, the residents petitioned the U.S. Post Office for the name "Sierra View." The post office rejected the name, because it felt there were too many post offices with "Sierra" in the name. The community held a vote and the name "Ridgecrest" won by one vote over "Gilmore." The hamlet was so unimposing, a collection of scattered farmers and a general store, that the first ground examination by the navy did not record the existence of Ridgecrest on its map.

When the navy began building the China Lake base, some of the base personnel built dwellings for the families in Ridgecrest because, at first, there was no housing available for families on the base. Many of the initial homes were built with whatever material could be found, including material that had been "liberated" from the construction materials used on the base. Some of those who lived in Ridgecrest at this time recall how a few dwellings had to use railroad ties for part of the walls. Such dwellings had drifting sand blown into them every day.

As the base grew, so did Ridgecrest. Businesses were started to service the needs of the workers, the personnel stationed at China Lake, and their families. Residents could travel to Los Angeles by rail from Inyokern or to San Bernadino by bus. The valley is now serviced by commercial airlines at the Inyokern Airport for air travel through Los Angeles International Airport. Ridgecrest became an incorporated city on November 29, 1963.

Initially, the school system located all the schools on the base. As the population outside of the base grew, more schools were located in Ridgecrest. In 2004, only one elementary school remained on the China Lake base, and it was slated to be closed and its students placed in newer, off-base schools. The local high school, Burroughs High School, is named for the first commanding officer of NOTS, Captain Sherman E. Burroughs. By the 1960s, community college classes, through the Kern Community College District, were offered at Ridgecrest. These classes continued until the establishment in 1973 of Cerro Coso Community College. Cerro Coso has five instructional sites—the

Eastern Sierra Centers at Bishop and Mammoth, Kern River Valley, South Kern, and Ridgecrest—which together form the largest geographical area (18,000 square miles) served by any community college in California. Cerro Coso has an enrollment at the Ridgecrest campus of more than 2,000 full-time students. In 2004, the college went online with a solar photovoltaic generation plant to help decrease its power expenditures.

Over the years, especially starting in the late 1960s, the navy encouraged the civilian population of the station to find housing off the base. Eventually, all civilian families left the station, and the housing for those families was torn down, although some dwellings were moved off the base and sold to individuals for homes.

Even with the completion of some projects and the cancellation of others, the valley's population has continued to grow. Besides the people moving to the area to work on the station, older residents are attracted to Ridgecrest because of the lower housing costs. The 2000 census of Ridgecrest places the population at 24,927, while Inyokern had a population of 954. The current estimated population for the valley, including the base, is more than 30,000.

—Kenneth McMullen

See also WORLD WAR II DEFENSE INDUSTRIES

Suggested Reading

Christman, Albert B. *Sailors, Scientists, and Rockets—Origins of the Navy Rocket Program and the Naval Ordnance Test Station, Inyokern.* Vol. 1 of *History of the Naval Weapons Center, China Lake, California.* Washington, DC: U.S. Government Printing Office, Navy History Division, 1971.

Gerrard-Gough, J. D., and Albert B. Christman. *Grand Experiment at Inyokern: Narrative of the Naval Ordnance Test Station During the Second World War & the Immediate Postwar Years.* Vol. 2 of *History of the Naval Weapons Center, China Lake, California.* Washington, DC: United States Government Printing Office, Navy History Division, 1978.

Weals, Frederick H. *How It Was: Some Memories by Early Settlers of the Indian Wells Valley and Vicinity.* Rev. ed. Ridgecrest, CA: Historical Society of the Upper Mojave Desert, 1994.

Weals, Frederick H. *Indian Wells Valley: How It Grew.* Ridgecrest, CA: Historical Society of the Upper Mojave Desert, 2001.

⊞ CHINATOWNS

Spurred by the lure of the California gold rush as well as other employment opportunities in the developing American West, significant numbers of Chinese from Guangdong Province made the journey across the Pacific in the middle of the 19th century and joined the flow of pioneers from all over the world descending on the region. Between 1849 and 1882, the year the Chinese Exclusion Act halted most Chinese immigration, nearly 300,000 Chinese entered the United States. More than 90 percent of these immigrants were adult males. The majority settled along the West Coast, especially in California, but Chinese could also be found throughout the West, particularly in areas undergoing intense economic activity—such as railroad building, mining, agriculture, and manufacturing—as well as in pockets of industrializing New England and the plantation economies of the South. Like other new immigrants to America, the Chinese often settled together. The places where they settled and the communities they formed became known as Chinatowns.

While the Chinese established segregated living spaces and work environments that followed patterns similar to those of other immigrant groups, the racial politics within which their experience as newcomers took place set them and their communities apart. Wherever they went, they faced especially virulent forms of hostility and persecution. Despite the fact that many American capitalists looked upon Chinese as an attractive source of cheap labor, other workers in the increasingly insecure industrial labor market felt threatened by Chinese competition. In addition, nativists, drawing on stereotypes about Chinese foreignness, racial difference, and unassimilability, stirred up fears about what it would mean for the nation to include the Chinese as members of the body politic.

These forces fueled the powerful anti-Chinese movement of the 1870s, which unleashed violence against Chinese immigrants in many areas of the American West. They also propelled a far-reaching array of discriminatory legislation that sought to regulate and limit such basic aspects of life as where Chinese could work and live, the kind of property they could own, and who they could marry. Ultimately, such anti-Chinese sentiment culminated in the passage of the Chinese Exclusion Act that, although it initially restricted only the immigration of Chinese laborers, was broadened in 1888 to include all Chinese immigrants with the exception of officials, teachers, students, tourists, and merchants. Renewed in 1892, the act was extended indefinitely in 1902. Because of the anxieties their presence generated, in the West the Chinese often occupied the lowest rung on the racial hierarchy—a position that legitimated these and other actions like them.

The racial hostility that the Chinese encountered not only limited their political and economic rights, it also had a profound impact on the way their communities—Chinatowns—developed. Unfriendly pressures from the outside world made staying with other Chinese safer, was sometimes required by law, and also reinforced cultural preferences for living in the familiar environment of predominantly Chinese communities. As a result, Chinatowns tended to be much longer lasting than the segregated settlements of other immigrant groups. In addition, while the Chinese were like other immigrant groups in their tendency to be sojourners who did not intend to remain in the United States long term, they were unlike other groups in that so many Chinese did, in fact, return to China in the second half of the 19th century.

Because of legislation passed after 1875 that restricted the immigration of Chinese women right at the time when men might otherwise have begun sending for their family members, many Chinese did not have the opportunity to form the kinds of family ties in the United States that kept immigrants from other nations from leaving. A further complicating factor was that a significant proportion of Chinese immigrant women had been brought to the United States to work as prostitutes in a system in which Chinese men sold the bodies of lower-class Chinese women for profit. Continuing unbalanced sex ratios, the sad reality that few prostituted women lived out their indentures, and the depopulation of Chinese communities that followed the passage of the Chinese Exclusion Act delayed the transition from bachelor to family-centered societies. Chinatowns thus continued to exist as truncated communities made up mostly of working-age men with few women, children, or elderly people

long after these skewed social conditions had ceased in the rest of the West. Moreover, while anti-Chinese sentiment contributed to the enduring nature of many Chinatowns, in areas of the West outside the Pacific slope, increasing hostility and the boom and bust cycles typical to frontier economies meant that after 1880 many Chinese communities dramatically contracted and some essentially disappeared. Some of the refugees from Chinatowns in places such as Deadwood, South Dakota; Rock Springs, Wyoming; and Butte, Montana, settled in the established California communities of San Francisco, Stockton, and Sacramento. Others migrated east. By the end of the 19th century, nearly 15,000, or 16 percent, lived in the North Atlantic. Their arrival helped establish Chinatowns in places such as New York City and Boston.

As a result of its position as the initial point of disembarkation for many Chinese immigrants, in the second half of the 19th century, San Francisco's Chinatown emerged as the preeminent Chinatown in the nation, both in size and significance, a position it maintains to this day. It functioned as the center of Chinese America, channeling flows of goods, services, information, and people between China and the United States as well as between Chinese in various parts of America. Reflective of this importance, Chinese immigrants called San Francisco *dabu* or "first city." Like other Chinatowns in the West, it was shaped by the realities of racial hostility, economic exigencies, and the needs of the Chinese community.

From 1849 until 1869, the year that marked the completion of the transcontinental railroad, San Francisco's Chinatown took the form of a way station rather than a major residential settlement for the overwhelmingly male population of Chinese immigrants en route to work in mining, agriculture, or on the railroads. Living where these enterprises were centered, the Chinese were initially a rural population, with only about 8 percent of California's Chinese living in San Francisco's Chinatown as full-time residents in the 1850s and 1860s. By 1850, the Chinese quarter comprised a five-block area not far from the wharves where Chinese immigrants had initially landed. Its hub was Sacramento Street, between Dupont (now called Grant Avenue) and Kearny Streets. Stores selling Chinese wares spread down Dupont Street, between Kearny and Stockton Streets. Ten years later, reflecting the increasing needs of the growing Chinese immigrant population, the Chinese quarter had expanded into a 10-block area, bordered by Kearny, Pacific, Stockton, and Sacramento Streets.

In Chinatown, in addition to being able to acquire a wide variety of goods and services, Chinese immigrants could interact with the district and family associations that were particularly important given the lack of traditional family ties and skewed demographics. These associations functioned in many respects like other 19th-century immigrant benevolent associations—offering services to their members but also exerting a certain amount of social control. Family and district associations provided a dizzying array of assistance: They met incoming ships, provided temporary housing in the buildings they owned, supplied miners and other workers with essential gear, arbitrated disputes, provided credit, sent letters and money back to China, cared for the sick and indigent, maintained altars and temples for religious practices, and even took care of the burial needs of the dead.

While family associations were composed of people with the same surname, district associations (*huigans*), the most important associational forms in American Chinatowns, were made up of people from the same districts in China who also often spoke the same dialects. Merchants formed the first district associations in San Francisco in 1851. Although merchants were not part of China's traditional elite, their skills in navigating the non-Chinese world made them leaders in Chinese American communities. In 1882, in the wake of the Chinese Exclusion Act, the six huigans in California—already joined in a loose federation since 1862—formed a formal and quite powerful organization that became known as the Chinese Consolidated Benevolent Organization or the Chinese Six Companies, which, among other things, hired lawyers to fight discriminatory legislation and exerted control within the community over who would be eligible for return immigration to China. Other associations prominent in Chinatown included *tongs*—originally fraternal organizations that cut across geographic origin and kinship but that became increasingly involved in profiting from underworld activities—and occupational guilds, which came into existence in San

Francisco by the late 1860s and, like American labor unions, organized laundrymen, shoemakers, and cigar makers to protect their economic interests. Throughout Chinatown, men congregated in the backrooms of the district's many stores that served as gathering places for socializing and relaxation.

By 1870, San Francisco's Chinatown had been transformed from a way station to a segregated ghetto—a characterization that would remain apt through the mid-20th century. The escalation of the anti-Chinese movement in the last quarter of the 19th century resulted in the return to Chinatown of many laborers who had been employed throughout the outlying areas of the state. Under these conditions, Chinatown emerged as a sanctuary for those fleeing violence and discrimination. For example, when the transcontinental railroad was completed in 1869, Chinese railroad workers who tried to settle in towns near the railroad's end frequently met with hostility. Large numbers returned to the safety of San Francisco's Chinatown. Similarly, despite the fact that Chinese workers played a critical role in transforming swamplands into arable lands in California's central valleys, farm owners replaced Chinese with white workers in the face of growing anti-Chinese pressures. Many of these displaced Chinese also found refuge in Chinatown. Moreover, just as Chinese from outside the city were pushed toward San Francisco, once in the city Chinese were further pushed toward Chinatown by increasingly widespread residential segregation that made living outside of Chinatown virtually impossible.

Under such circumstances, the population of Chinatown increased from 1,747 in 1860 to 8,128 by 1870, then to 14,688 by 1880, and reaching 25,833 in 1890. As the Chinese became an increasingly urban population throughout the West, especially in California, such growth was echoed in other Chinatowns in places such as Sacramento, Stockton, Marysville, and Los Angeles. While this growth strengthened and enlivened many Chinatown communities by increasing residential settlement and economic activity, this was a double-edged sword in that these developments were products, at least in part, of the hostility of the world outside. Largely relegated to a Chinese-specific ethnic labor market, the growing numbers of Chinese immigrants in San Francisco often found work in the city's light manufacturing industries, in the garment industry, in laundries, in restaurants, and in domestic service. As a result of this rapid and dramatic migration, Chinatown's available housing, designed for a transient labor force, quickly became insufficient to hold this larger, more permanent population. Even though new housing was built and the physical space of Chinatown expanded to an area of 12 city blocks in 1890 and then to 15 blocks by 1906, overcrowding became a part of life. Because of the poverty in which many of Chinatown's residents lived and the refusal of city officials to provide the kind of sanitation services and police protection that was common in other parts of San Francisco, areas of Chinatown descended into blighted, slumlike conditions. It was during this period that tourism—at times both exploitative and invasive—became a part of Chinatown's economy as the district began to appeal to visitors eager to see the exotic as well as the racially abject and as both Chinese and white entrepreneurs discovered they could profit from this desire.

When the Chinese Exclusion Act became law, it—and the numerous measures passed in the succeeding decade to tighten it—effectively reversed the trend of population growth in San Francisco's Chinatown and represented a crushing blow to many Chinese who had hoped to thrive and settle in the United States. As a result, by 1900, Chinatown's population had fallen to 11,000. Then, in 1906, when earthquake and fire ravaged San Francisco, nearly all of Chinatown burned to the ground. The Chinese Six Companies not only helped finance Chinatown's rebuilding, but also succeeded in foiling attempts to relocate the Chinese in order to open up the valuable real estate occupied by Chinatown to development. Chinese men also discovered an inadvertent benefit to the disaster: Because the fires destroyed almost all of San Francisco's municipal records, they found they could more easily claim citizenship and the right to bring their wives to the United States that came with it. As a result, approximately 10,000 Chinese women immigrated between 1907 and 1924, providing the basis for family formation that Chinatowns had lacked up to this point. Also fueling a resurgence in Chinatown's population were children fathered by Chinese Americans while visiting China—and their many impersonators, known as "paper sons"—who were entitled to American citizenship and thus also eligible for immigration. San Francisco's new Chinatown, although in some ways more modern and American in its outlook, suffered from the same kind of overcrowding and blight as the old one. And the cherished second-generation children of Chinese immigrants, although educated in local public schools and universities, still faced considerable employment discrimination outside of Chinatown's boundaries.

The loosening of immigration restrictions that began in 1943 as a result of China's role as an ally in World War II and culminated in the Immigration Act of 1965 not only reopened the United States to Chinese immigration but also allowed the entry of family members on a nonquota basis. This shift in policy marked a watershed moment in the history of the Chinese in American society. It also rejuvenated and reconfigured existing Chinatowns and precipitated the emergence of new ones. As a result of the new wave of immigration that followed, the Chinese population grew from 237,000 in 1960 to 812,200 in 1980 and, in the process, underwent a dramatic shift back to a majority immigrant population. California and New York took in 60 percent of these new immigrants, sending New York's Chinatown population soaring from 15,000 in 1965 to 100,000 twenty years later. In addition, new suburban Chinatowns appeared—often in cities that already had an older, urban Chinatown—organized around Chinese supermarkets and strip malls and often catering to more recent immigrants. Examples of these kinds of Chinatowns include Monterey Park outside of Los Angeles and the Richmond and Sunset districts in San Francisco.

Also, within communities, new kinds of tensions arose between working-class and professional, middle-class Chinese. The old Chinatowns not only tended to be more tourist oriented but also to be the workplaces of large numbers of recent immigrants employed in low-wage menial work. Still plagued by poverty and overcrowding, old Chinatowns became less appealing to middle-class Chinese who were no longer restricted to living in Chinatown and could afford to live elsewhere. Today, although the Chinese remain the largest Asian American population, it is not unusual for Chinatowns to actually be pan-Asian business districts and for some cities to have, in addition to Chinatowns, Filipinotowns, Japantowns, Little Indias, Koreatowns, and Little Saigons.

—Barbara Berglund

See also ASIAN IMMIGRATION LAW, CHINESE EXCLUSION ACT, CHINESE IMMIGRATION, IMMIGRATION ACT OF 1965

Suggested Reading

Chan, Sucheng. *Asian Americans: An Interpretative History.* New York: Twayne, 1991.

Chen, Yong. *Chinese San Francisco, 1850–1943: A Trans-Pacific Community.* Stanford, CA: Stanford University Press, 2000.

Daniels, Roger. *Asian America: Chinese and Japanese in the United States Since 1850.* Seattle: University of Washington Press, 1988.

Dirlik, Arlif, ed. *Chinese on the American Frontier.* New York: Rowman & Littlefield, 2001.

Lee, Erika. *At America's Gates: Chinese Immigration During the Exclusion Era, 1882–1943.* Chapel Hill: University of North Carolina Press, 2003.

Loo, Chalsa. *Chinatown: Most Time, Hard Time.* New York: Praeger, 1991.

Takaki, Ronald. *Strangers From a Different Shore: A History of Asian Americans.* Boston: Little, Brown, 1989.

Yung, Judy. *Unbound Feet: A Social History of Chinese Women in San Francisco.* Berkeley: University of California Press, 1995.

⊞ CHINESE EXCLUSION ACT

The Chinese Exclusion Act was passed in 1882, which excluded Chinese immigrants from entering the United States. The act prohibited Chinese immigration into the United States and disqualified the Chinese already residing in the United States from naturalization and voting. The Chinese Exclusion Act was passed during a time of anti-immigration sentiment in the United States, expressed by organized labor and most notably felt in California.

Chinese immigrants first entered the United States from southern China in 1848. There were three groups of Chinese who immigrated to California. The first was the merchant class. Though considered of low status in China, the merchants served as the leaders of the Chinese community. The great majority of Chinese who emigrated from China were laborers, who had very little education, if any, and who did not interact often with the larger society. The third group allowed to immigrate consisted of the wives of merchants. Few women came to America because Chinese culture generally prohibited women from leaving the home.

There were a variety of factors that prompted Chinese immigration. One reason was the California gold rush, through which they hoped to get rich. Most Chinese who came to California considered themselves sojourners whose intent was to stay long enough to accumulate savings and then return home. The overcrowded living conditions, high taxes, and the chaos and destruction from the Taiping Rebellion in China also drove many Chinese immigrants to the United States. Another reason was that Fujien and Guangdong Provinces, the regions from which many Chinese immigrants hailed, had considerable contact with the outside world, and thus their inhabitants were more willing to traverse the oceans than their inland counterparts.

The numbers of Chinese immigrants arriving in the United States grew at an increasing rate. In 1852 alone, 30,000 Chinese arrived in San Francisco, where many sought employment as servants and laundrymen. The 1860 census reported 34,933 Chinese immigrants living in California. In 1870, the number had grown to 49,277, and by 1880, the Chinese population had grown to 75,132. Chinese immigration filled the demand for cheap labor in California. During the 1860s, cheap labor provided by Chinese immigrants facilitated in the construction of the transcontinental railroad. As many as 10,000 Chinese laborers were on the payroll of the Central Pacific Railroad. However, after the completion of the transcontinental railroad in 1869 and with the outbreak of a financial collapse in 1873, thousands of Chinese workers found themselves unemployed and subject to growing anti-Chinese sentiment.

Hostility toward Chinese immigration was evident as early as the 1850s, but the need for cheap labor won out. Violence against the Chinese population erupted frequently, as early as 1856, with Chinese being subjected to lynching and rioting. The most common objection to Chinese immigration was its threat to the existing labor force. Chinese immigrants were said to be unassimilable, unable to accept American customs and values. Chinese immigrants were resented by native-born Americans for their willingness to work for lower wages, which nativists feared would drag down the wages of all Americans. Another objection to Chinese immigration was that they lived in unsanitary and overcrowded conditions. During the 1870s, there were claims that Chinatowns in San Francisco and other large cities were havens for venereal disease, smallpox, and leprosy. Perhaps the most fundamental reason for anti-Chinese animosity rested on racial and cultural prejudices toward a people who looked and worshipped differently. This hostility would manifest itself through legislative measures.

The movement to discriminate against and exclude Chinese immigration had its roots during the California gold rush. In 1850, the California legislature passed the Chinese Capitation Tax, which targeted Chinese laborers. During the 1870s, the movement to end Chinese immigration to the United States accelerated. Labor unions worked closely with anti-Chinese immigration out of fear that Chinese immigration was setting back the cause of reforming working conditions. The most prominent anti-Chinese group was the short-lived California Workingmen's Party headed by Denis Kearney, who saw ending Chinese immigration as the solution to California's problems.

Anti-Chinese immigration became part of the national agenda when Congress passed the Fifteen Passenger Bill in 1879 prohibiting ships from carrying more than 15 Chinese passengers. President Rutherford B. Hayes vetoed the bill because it violated the Burlingame Treaty signed in 1868, which encouraged Chinese immigration. However, in 1880, the Burlingame Treaty was modified, allowing the United States to "regulate, limit . . . but may not absolutely prohibit" immigration. Anti-Chinese groups throughout the country joined together and lobbied Congress to pass a bill in early 1882 suspending Chinese immigration for 25 years, but it was vetoed by President Chester A. Arthur. The growing influence of the anti-Chinese lobby, however, compelled President Arthur to pass an amended version of the Chinese Exclusion Act in 1882, the first law written that restricted the immigration of an entire ethnic group.

The Chinese Exclusion Act passed in on May 6, 1882, with 32 votes to 15 in the Senate (with 32 not voting) and 201 to 37 in the House of Representatives (with 53 not voting). The act originally was meant to suspend Chinese immigration for 10 years and to exclude both skilled and unskilled laborers. The naturalization of Chinese immigrants by state and federal governments was forbidden. However, anti-Chinese violence continued, most notably in September of 1885 when a riot in Rock Springs, Wyoming, resulted in the killing of 20 Chinese residents. Soon afterward, such incidents were repeated throughout the West Coast. Calls to strengthen the Chinese Exclusion Act soon followed. For the next 20 years, six other acts were passed to further restrict Chinese immigration. In 1892, the Geary Act required Chinese living in the United States to register and obtain a certificate verifying proof of residence. By 1904, the restriction on Chinese immigration was complete. All Chinese laborers were forbidden from entering the United States and its territories. Those already residing in the United States could leave and return only through proper documentation and registration. Only under strict regulations could merchants, teachers, students, and travelers enter the country. The Chinese Exclusion Act, and the laws resulting there from, remained in force for 60 years and thus became the model for anti-immigration legislation.

—*Dino E. Buenviaje*

See also ASIAN IMMIGRATION LAW, CHINATOWNS, CHINESE IMMIGRATION, IMMIGRATION ACT OF 1965, IMMIGRATION AND NATURALIZATION SERVICE

Suggested Reading

Cohen, Warren I. *America's Response to China: A History of Sino-American Relations.* 4th ed. New York: Columbia University Press, 2000.

Gyory, Andrew. *Closing the Gate: Race, Politics, and the Chinese Exclusion Act.* Chapel Hill: University of North Carolina Press, 1998.

Kitts, Charles R. *The United States Odyssey in China, 1784–1990.* Lanham, MD: University Press of America, 1991.

McKee, Delber R. *Chinese Exclusion Versus the Open Door Policy 1900–1906: Clashes Over China Policy in the Roosevelt Era.* Detroit, MI: Wayne State University Press, 1997.

Riccards, Michael P. *The Presidency and the Middle Kingdom: China, the United States, and Executive Leadership.* Lanham, MD: Lexington Books, 2001.

Sandmeyer, Elmer Clarence. *The Anti-Chinese Movement in California,* Urbana: University of Illinois Press, 1991.

Saxton, Alexander. *The Indispensable Enemy: Labor and the Anti-Chinese Movement in California.* Berkeley: University of California Press, 1971.

⊞ CHINESE IMMIGRATION

The 1849 gold rush brought Chinese to the United States in large numbers and set in motion a pattern of immigration by Chinese that would eventually result in the passage of the first restrictionist immigration laws aimed at voluntary immigration to the United States. Most of the early Chinese immigrants consisted of merchants and skilled artisans seeking opportunity. These Chinese did not intend to stay, though many did of necessity. The intent of these immigrants can be surmised by the Chinese term for these early immigrants, *gamsaanhaak*, or "gold mountain guest." This refers to the literal translation of the Chinese writing symbol for California, "Gold Mountain." When the placer mining played out in California, many of the "gold mountain guests" returned to China, and some remained in the United States. Those that followed consisted primarily of laborers, or "coolies."

The coolie trade began in 1806 when the British started importing Chinese laborers to work their sugar plantations. Not coincidentally, the British passed a ban on the slave trade in 1807. The timing of the two events helps illustrate the real nature of the coolie trade. It served as a replacement for black slave labor, contracting impoverished Chinese laborers, or in many cases kidnapping Chinese laborers, to do arduous labor without the social baggage of enslavement. In the United States, Chinese coolies became equated with slaves. The ending of slavery and the future unavailability of black slaves as a labor source stimulated efforts to import Chinese in place of blacks.

Railroad construction provided the initial primary occupation for imported Chinese labor. The Republican Party, enmeshed in a Civil War and desirous to open the western frontier of the United States to settlement, passed several acts to spur railroad construction and encouraged the construction of a transcontinental railroad. In 1864, the Republican campaign platform also advocated encouragement of foreign immigration to facilitate the building of these railroads. That same year, an Act to Encourage Immigration, better known as the Contract Labor Act, became law. This act allowed employers to recruit immigrants for jobs in the United States. Labor organizations opposed the law, and this opposition resulted in its eventual repeal in 1868. By that year, the Republican-controlled government further facilitated the importation of Chinese labor through the Burlingame Treaty, wherein the United States agreed to reciprocal immigration rights with the government of China. Anson Burlingame was a Republican representative in Congress from Massachusetts. In 1861, he became United States minister to China, and resigned that post in 1867. Burlingame then accepted an appointment by the Chinese Emperor as Chinese minister to the United States. As the new Chinese minister, he returned to Washington in a state visit in 1868 and, using old inside political connections, negotiated the treaty that bears his name, which opened immigration with China beyond what had already existed by removing and, at least temporarily, preventing obstructions to immigrants passing from one signatory country to the other.

Time was not on the side of the Burlingame Treaty, however. The completion of the transcontinental railroad in 1869 created a surplus of laborers of both Chinese and European origin. Large numbers of unemployed workers led to labor unrest. An economic downturn in the 1870s further exacerbated the problem. Industrialists and other employers—such as Nathan Bedford Forrest, former Confederate General and Southern war hero as well as founder of the original Ku Klux Klan—generated widespread publicity for their plans to import Chinese laborers to break strikes. Such threats, and the actual employment of Chinese as scabs, drew hot resentment from laborers of European descent. The striking laborers, in increasing proportions, were immigrants themselves. The hostility to the Chinese workers did not stem from the immigrant status of the Chinese, but instead it originated from plainly visible racial and cultural differences and from being on opposite sides of the labor conflict. The hostility to Chinese grew to the point that violent massacres of Chinese began to occur in regions with large communities of Chinese, primarily in the western states. For instance, massacres of Chinese occurred in Los Angeles, California, in 1871; Rock Springs, Wyoming, in 1885; Eureka, California, in 1885; Seattle and Tacoma, Washington, in 1885; and Snake River, Oregon, in 1887.

The friction over the issue of the Chinese residents of California had existed since the 1849 gold rush. The perpetration of several depredations against the Chinese occurred with the enactment of discriminatory taxes, codes, and regulations directed specifically at the Chinese. The enactment of racist legislation reached its acme with the adoption of Section XIX of the California Constitution of 1879, which specifically authorized discriminatory legislation against Chinese. This section admonished the state government to deter the immigration of Chinese, prohibited the employment of Chinese by corporations or public entities, and empowered local authorities to enact ordinances to remove Chinese from within city limits.

In addition to California's constitutional changes, anti-Chinese sentiment in the 1870s led to attempts to restrict Chinese immigration as well. However, such restrictions did not occur until 1882 for a number of reasons. First of all, the Burlingame Treaty prevented the implementation of legal restrictions to Chinese immigration. Political opposition to restriction of immigration provided the second obstacle to stopping Chinese immigration. Political opposition consisted of an improbable alliance of religious groups and industrialists, one closely resembling the same alliance that opposed the slave trade. However, in this case, the coalition supported open immigration, not restriction.

Political opposition to restriction of Chinese immigration crumbled first. Industrialists had perceived Chinese labor, as described above, as a docile, controllable labor force much like slave labor had been before the Civil War. However, in October of 1877 the cigar makers union staged a strike, dragging their union leader, Samuel Gompers, and their union, the Cigar Makers' International Union, along with them. Chinese laborers, expected by employers to be reliable strikebreakers, took common cause with the strikers and also refused to work. This undermined threats to import more Chinese to break the strike, and the strike ultimately succeeded. The business community no longer could trust Chinese workers to behave as a docile work force, and now both sides of the labor issue could blame Chinese laborers for civil disorder. This eroded the opposition to restrictions on Chinese immigration, leaving primarily religious groups in opposition. By 1880, with diminished business opposition and significant popular demand, the United States reached an agreement with China that allowed the United States to regulate or stop Chinese immigration. The year 1882 marked the end of significant railroad construction and the beginning of severe restrictions on immigration by Chinese.

In all, approximately 250,000 Chinese immigrated to America from 1849 to 1882, and males constituted 90 percent of the total. An indeterminate number of sojourners returned to China. Senator George F. Hoar accused the supporters of the Chinese Exclusion Act of fear of the superiority of Chinese immigrants, as opposed to the claims of Chinese cultural inferiority made by proponents of the act.

Contrary to popular belief, the act did not exclude all Chinese, only laborers. The law exempted merchants, teachers, students, "travelers," and anyone able to prove they were already in the United States at the time of the passage of the act. The law also constituted the clear evidence of the beginning of restrictionist sentiment within the United States. The Chinese became the first targets because of the most obvious physical differences, but more significantly because of their cultural differences with Americans of European descent. European immigrants had cultural differences with American natives, but those differences paled in comparison with the cultural differences experienced with Chinese immigrants.

The absence of female immigrants in large numbers contributed to the unsavory reputation of Chinese immigrant communities. The Chinese immigrants could not "settle down" and establish families, and any effort to intermarry with local girls would only inflame the situation. Furthermore, Chinese workers became "the enemy" when business used them as scabs in labor disputes, making a bad situation worse. This perception did not change after the Chinese immigrants felt established enough to join with organize labor in disputes with business. Doing so only alienated the business community that had previously protected Chinese immigration. Consensus became easy to build in the restrictionist mood, and opposition dissipated.

After the passage of the Chinese Exclusion Act, many Chinese seeking admittance to the United States appealed their cases to the federal courts, almost all of the cases occurring within the Ninth Circuit Court. Of those Chinese who attempted to land and appealed to the courts, 85 percent succeeded in gaining admission during the 1880s and 1890s. Their success owed much to the courts allowing exceptions not provided for in the law, such as alternative proofs of prior residence or membership in other classes of exempted Chinese. These exceptions opened the door to fraud, only partially constrained by subsequent amendments.

In addition, the federal courts offered suppliants advantages not available during administrative exclusion proceedings. The first and foremost of these consisted of the availability of and access to lawyers. Chinese contesting their cases could also call witnesses, the federal courts being far more tolerant and less critical of witness than the administrators handling exclusion proceedings. Finally, the judges and the lawyers handling the Chinese cases shared a commonality of procedural abilities and rules. Consequently, the formal nature of federal court meant that the burden on the government was greater there than in an administrative hearing.

If, as many observers claim, the motivation for immigration came from a desire for economic improvement, then how could the average impoverished immigrant obtain and pay for a lawyer to fight his case? Networking provided the answer. Groups of Chinese inside the United States with connections to China provided support to those intending to immigrate. This included prepaid tickets. Most immigrants learned of opportunities for work through agents of American employers looking for cheap labor. Additionally, steamship companies and railroads, seeking passengers and purchasers of western lands, encouraged immigration and subsidized efforts to enter the United States. The vast majority of 19th century Chinese immigrants came from the Pearl River Delta region of Guangdong Province in southern China, giving cultural commonality with one another and adding to the corporate networking of the Chinese community. These elements constitute the primary difference between the continued immigration of Chinese after their exclusion and the continued importation of slaves after the abolition of the slave trade. Chinese wanted to come here, and the Chinese already here helped in the process.

Additionally, the Chinese Six Companies, an advocacy group for Chinese immigrants, also assisted. One tactic of the Chinese Six Companies consisted of agitating for the government to spend more of the limited resources available to the government to go after convicted felons, other criminals, and social miscreants rather than harass and exclude honest, hard-working Chinese immigrants, the theory being to overwhelm the government's ability to cope with the problem. Another effort by the Chinese Six Companies involved organized opposition to compliance with the registration requirements of the 1882 Chinese Exclusion Act for those Chinese who immigrated prior to its enactment. The effort was successful and provided the basis

for the legal arguments that led to court-ruled exemptions to the law, as noted above.

Chinese immigrants did not rely solely on legal means to enter the United States. The Chinese Exclusion Act forced much of the Chinese immigration to go underground. Illegal immigration flourished, with prostitutes being the most profitable. Actually, most of the female Chinese that immigrated during this period did so as prostitutes. Many immigrants resorted to fraud. Yet many other Chinese otherwise barred from entry to the United States simply jumped ship, disappearing into established Chinese communities, supported by the networks cited above. They also found illegal entry through the land borders with Canada and Mexico.

A simple fraud took advantage of the exempted classes contained within the Chinese Exclusion Act. A far more elaborate scheme developed later, referred to as the "paper sons" fraud. Children of legal resident Chinese could still immigrate to the United States. This scheme utilized altered documents to establish proof of birth with parentage connected to a legal Chinese resident of the United States. The scheme developed after the 1906 San Francisco earthquake and fire, which consumed the county birth records to that date. In addition to the legal attacks and unlawful means of entry, Chinese would also enter through Hawaii, a United States possession in 1898 and not subject to the same restrictions as the United States proper.

But for all the means available to thwart the law, the lack of enforcement contributed the most to the ability of Chinese to continue immigrating to the United States. At the time of enactment, no federal agency existed for the enforcement of the new immigration law. The Bureau of Immigration did not exist until 1891. Until that time, the federal government contracted with states to provide enforcement of immigration laws. Typically, the collector of customs at the port enforced the Chinese Exclusion Act. This alone accounts for the facility of simply jumping ship. Officials with only a secondary responsibility for enforcing a law will allocate their efforts accordingly. In fact, when a case started, the local U.S. attorney obtained warrants and passed them to the Treasury Department to execute. Often treasury officials claimed they had no authority to enforce the warrants.

However, Congress did act to strengthen the law and provided for an agency to enforce it. In 1891, Congress created the Bureau of Immigration with sole responsibility to enforce U.S. immigration laws. Unfortunately, it only had 28 employees, tasked not only with keeping out the thousands of Chinese attempting to immigrate by the many subterfuges mentioned above, but also to screen the millions of European immigrants for the social undesirables also legally excludable, such as lunatics and criminals.

The new bureau did begin to make itself felt with Chinese immigration and proved successful in court. During the period 1893–1894, the Bureau of Immigration managed to have 75 percent of its Chinese deportation and exclusion cases upheld. However, criminal convictions within the "crimes involving moral turpitude" provisions of the law and not the Chinese Exclusion Act provided the primary basis of removal from the United States.

Significant changes in the manner and nature of Chinese immigration did not occur until World War II. Illegal immigration through Mexico became more difficult after 1924 due to the creation of the Border Patrol. However, Chinese remained legally excluded from immigration, with the exceptions noted previously, until the United States entered World War II subsequent to the Japanese attack on Pearl Harbor in 1941.

Hostilities between China and Japan predated Pearl Harbor by four years. Japan invaded and occupied the coastal area of China in 1937. Subsequent to the United States' entry into the war, American national leadership realized the embarrassing inequity of excluding immigration from an allied nation such as China, while having far more open immigration from enemy countries such as Germany and Italy. Consequently, in 1943, Congress repealed the Chinese Exclusion Act, and the differences between Chinese immigration and immigration from the rest of the world ended.

However, the pattern of illegal immigration that began with the exclusion of Chinese continues to the present. Chinese continue to enter the United States illegally by fraud, smuggling directly into American ports or by way of third countries such as Canada or Mexico. Many of the criminal organizations that organized the smuggling of Chinese during the period of exclusion are the same organizations providing the same services today.

The Chinese Exclusion Act notwithstanding, Chinese immigration to the United States has been a steady source of immigrants since 1849. The stigma of exclusion having been removed, Chinese immigration now has the same overall character as immigration from any other part of the world. The only possible exception is that the long period of exclusion provided an early impetus to create a support network for illegal immigration that continues to circumvent immigration law.

—Lonnie Wilson

See also ASIAN IMMIGRATION LAW; CHINATOWNS; CHINESE EXCLUSION ACT; HELENA, MONTANA; IDAHO SILVER STRIKES; INYO COUNTY, CALIFORNIA; LEWISTON AND COEUR D'ALENE, IDAHO

Suggested Reading

Bodnar, John. *The Transplanted: A History of Immigrants in Urban America.* Bloomington: Indiana University Press, 1985.

Daniels, Roger. *Not Like Us: Immigrants and Minorities in America, 1890–1924.* Chicago: Ivan R. Dee, 1997.

Gyory, Andrew. *Closing the Gate: Race, Politics, and the Chinese Exclusion Act.* Chapel Hill: University of North Carolina Press, 1998.

Handlin, Oscar. *The Uprooted: The Epic Story of the Great Migration That Made the American People.* 2nd ed. New York: Little, Brown, 1979.

Hays, Samuel P. *The Response to Industrialism, 1885–1914.* Chicago: University of Chicago Press, 1957.

Lee, Erika. *At America's Gates: Chinese Immigration During the Exclusion Era, 1882–1943.* Chapel Hill: University of North Carolina Press, 2003.

Salyer, Lucy E. *Laws Harsh as Tigers: Chinese Immigrants and the Shaping of Modern Immigration Law.* Chapel Hill: University of North Carolina Press, 1995.

Yans-McLaughlin, Virginia, ed. *Immigration Reconsidered: History, Sociology, and Politics.* New York: Oxford University Press, 1990.

⊞ CHIRICAHUA

See APACHE

⊞ CHUMASH

See GABRIELINO

⊞ CODY, WYOMING

The area that eventually became the town of Cody, Wyoming, sits on the west central border of the broad Bighorn Basin in present-day northwestern Wyoming.

The basin is a 12,000-square-foot arid rolling plain with an annual precipitation of 8 inches (the overall average rainfall west of the Mississippi is 12 inches). It lies between a series of phenomenal mountain ranges with peaks rising more than 13,000 feet: the Big Horn Mountains to the east, the Absaroka and Beartooth Mountains to the west, and the Owl Creeks and Wind River to the south. The Yellowstone River and the Clark's Fork of the Yellowstone form the basin's northern boundary. Cody is situated just east of the confluence of the north and south fork's of the Shoshone River, which flow into the Bighorn and then the Yellowstone Rivers.

EARLY HABITATION

A gap between mountain ranges at the basin's northern end provided trail and trade routes for the first inhabitants of the American West beginning at least 11,200 years ago. Three important archeological sites in the Bighorn Basin, each excavated in the late 20th century, indicate the presence of long-standing cultural networks in the Cody area before white settlement.

Intermittent occupation of Shoshone Canyon, 10 miles toward present-day Yellowstone National Park from Cody, began 10,000 years ago. The objects found there show that cultural interactions between Rocky Mountain highlands and plains cultures were common. By the early 1800s, the Bighorn Basin was the center of Crow territory. Many other Native Americans also migrated through the basin. Early travelers followed game trails, which later became major roads. The Bannock trail, one of the Yellowstone region's earliest Indian thoroughfares, had a connecting trail up the Shoshone Valley through what became Cody. Shoshone, Arapaho, and Bannock (often referred to as Sheepeater) Indians traveled the Bannock on seasonal migrations. Trade fairs at places such as the Mandan and Hidatsa villages along the Missouri river in present-day North Dakota and on the Green River in Wyoming brought the Shoshone, Blackfoot, Arapaho, and Crow into contact with each other and, later, with European fur trappers. After the introduction of the horse in the early 18th century (the Shoshone probably acquired the horse from the Comanche on the Green River), travel and migration became easier and encouraged the

expansion of tribes who achieved great wealth in horses. As the Shoshone expanded, for instance, other groups such as the Blackfoot and Kiowa adjusted and moved north and east.

AMERICAN EXPLORATION

When President Thomas Jefferson sent Meriwether Lewis and William Clark up the Missouri River in 1804, he hoped to create viable American trade networks with Indians of the area. Though the Americans did not visit the Bighorn Basin on that trip, one of their explorers, John Colter, later did. After leaving the Lewis and Clark expedition on their return, Colter explored and trapped in the Bighorn Basin, spending the winter of 1806–1807 in the vicinity of the Clark's Fork Canyon within about 60 miles of present-day Cody. In 1807, from Fort Raymond at the mouth of the Big Horn River, Colter traveled to what he named the Stinking Water (later known as the Shoshone), the river that flowed through the heart of Cody. From this exploration, Colter made a map of Shoshone Canyon that Captain Clark later published in the 1820s.

The map facilitated a flood of Anglo American migrants; trappers, hunters, and gold miners came on the heels of explorers. Their journeys were directly tied to the deterioration of Native American migration and power in the Bighorn Basin. By the spring of 1868, government officials used the Fort Laramie Treaty to create a Crow reservation in Montana Territory. Not realizing that Bighorn Basin was being taken from the Crow, Crow Chief Blackfoot later expressed the misunderstanding and his malcontent at having lost access to the Bighorn Valley (Cook et al. 1996):

> The treaty of 1868 is all lies. . . . Neither my white friends, nor the Indian chiefs said yes to what was in that treaty. We owned Horse Creek, Stinking Water and Heart Mountain [landmarks in the Bighorn region]. Many of these Indians were born there.

Wyoming's only reservation, the Wind River, confined Shoshone and later Arapaho Indians. The Wind River Reservation was established in 1868 with the Fort Bridger Treaty for eastern Shoshone and Bannock tribes. By the mid-1870s, the Bannock Indians left for a reservation in Idaho, but by the mid-1870s, the northern Arapaho had joined the reservation and have shared 2,268,000 acres with the Eastern Shoshone since 1878. The 1860s and 1870s were characterized by Indian decline as the reservation system took hold. Between 1881 and 1930, the Crow population dropped from 3,500 to 1,679 before it increased again in the late 20th century.

SETTLEMENT

By the 1870s, hunting, mining, and trapping migrants were augmented by a settled population in the Bighorn region. Cattle ranchers were the primary population base of Wyoming between 1879 and 1896. French investors provided major capital in this early group. To supply large ranchers, Victor Arland, an immigrant from France, created Cody's first trading post in 1880. Arland had moved to the United States from Vincennes, France, in 1870. Facilitating trade and travel to his post, he built the first bridge over the Shoshone River in 1883, contributing to the possibility of a more viable town in the vicinity. Arland's presence might have contributed to other French people settling in the area, such as Charles DeMarris who settled in the Canyon in 1883. He developed a spa and resort on the site of hot springs along the Shoshone River. George Marquette became another prominent figure among the growing population of ranchers in the area. Marquette came to the canyon in 1878, constructing log buildings and operating a store and post office in the first town in the valley, Marquette, named after him. By 1903, when the last cattle drive took place in the Bighorn Valley, infrastructure for the town was firmly in place.

The town of Cody was founded in 1896 when Buffalo Bill Cody, for whom it is named, was 50 years old and had long since established his rank as a western American showman. Cody founded the town with the help of George Beck, a prospector from the Sheridan, Wyoming, area. Beck became interested in the idea of creating an irrigation system for the valley out of the Shoshone River. On Beck's first survey party to determine the feasibility of such a project, Cody's son-in-law, also from Sheridan, accompanied the team. When Cody was told about what the young man had witnessed, he became interested in the project. Beck and his partner,

Horace Alger, concluded that Cody would aid the project immensely because he was "the best advertised man in the world." Together with some of Bill Cody's investors out of Buffalo, New York, the group founded the Shoshone Land and Irrigation Company in 1895.

Cody was founded on its present site in 1896. Two primary elements affected Cody's settlement and the character of its population: access to water and global tourist promotion. Irrigation went hand in glove with the creation of the town. It was only after the Cody Canal, under the Shoshone Land and Irrigation Company, first delivered water on April 30, 1897, that the town began to attract any substantial population. The town of Marquette, founded by George Marquette just west of Cody, in fact thrived more than Cody until the Bighorn Basin's second irrigation project engulfed it in what became an enormous reservoir holding 82,900 cubic yards of water.

The creation of the Shoshone Dam began in 1904 at the confluence of the north and south forks of the Shoshone; it was the first federally funded venture under the Newlands Reclamation Act of 1902. The project was built in stages as various contractors gave into the enormity of the risk. Labor strife followed most companies. In 1907, for instance, Italian workers went on strike and achieved higher wages, until the contractor went bankrupt and could not pay anything. When the contract transferred to another company, Italian laborers struck again in 1909 but were instead replaced with Bulgarians. When the dam was finally completed, it had cost many immigrant workers dearly. Twenty-eight workers were crippled, three people died, and three people were blinded from their work on the project.

Bill Cody's global promotional network, along with the Shoshone and Cody canal projects, affected the nature of people's movements in and through the town as well. From its roots, part of the region's appeal to Bill Cody and his investors was its proximity to Yellowstone and its potential, because of its hot springs, for becoming a popular tourist spa town. The area's viability as a tourist attraction grew in 1901 when the railroad arrived and construction began on a road to the east entrance of Yellowstone Park, 50 miles northeast of Cody. When the road opened in 1903, 310 people entered the park through the east gate. Bill Cody supported the influx of tourists into Cody every year, creating a strong infrastructure for travelers with three hotels on the road from Cody to Yellowstone. The Irma was the centerpiece of Cody; the Wapiti Inn was located about halfway between Cody and Yellowstone; and Pahaska Tepee, fashioned as a hunting lodge, stood just outside the east entrance.

Bill Cody's promotional talents affected the town's first settlers as well its early tourists. Just after the initial canal was finished in 1896, 70 Russian Germans from Chicago moved to Irma Flat, on the outskirts of present-day Cody after witnessing the promotional power of Cody's show, in which he fervently encouraged migration to his town. The immigrants traveled from Chicago to Billings, Montana, and then to Cody with new Studebaker wagons that Cody had purchased to aid in their trip. In May of 1896, the group arrived in the valley, but by September, Cody's first European settlers had moved elsewhere, leaving only one German citizen, Joe Vogel, in Cody. Vogel eventually became one of the town's most prominent citizens, running a beer garden during prohibition. His relatives later migrated to Cody and started a successful furniture store. By the mid-1900s, German ancestry was (and continues to be) more common than any other European background in Cody despite the initial colony's failure. In general, however, Wyoming citizens fit within the greater national population who feared most immigrant groups, such as the Chinese and Irish. In 1895, for instance, the Wyoming legislature petitioned the U.S. Congress to restrict Eastern European and Asian immigration to the United States, even though the state was, and continues to be, more than 90 percent white.

In the early 20th century, when America entered World War I, Cody's residents continued to follow national trends with regards to immigrants. By 1917, Cody's local newspaper shifted its focus from narrow regional issues to highly patriotic concerns with an anti-German tone, like much of the rest of the country. Between Christmas of 1917 and late January of 1918, for instance, three German and Austrian men were arrested, jailed, and condemned by the Cody newspaper. According to one story, S. F. Altmark was arrested for expressing a "German view" in the lobby of the Irma hotel that was "decidedly out of place." The *Cody Enterprise* advocated that "such fellows either must keep their mouths shut or take the consequences.

Internal strife is caused by such agitators and that is a part of the German program in this country." Within the same time frame, Cody citizens created a Home Defense Society and a One Hundred Percent American Club while President Woodrow Wilson's national organizations, such as the Committee on Public Information, took an active role in local propaganda campaigns.

After World War I, Cody's citizens with German ancestry probably had an easier time as attention shifted from international conflict back to tourism and Yellowstone. Cody's Roaring Twenties saw the implementation of further tourist infrastructure, such as dude ranches and summer homes, while overall private ownership of Wyoming land increased. Yellowstone's roads were paved in 1927 with Cody's own streets asphalted in 1929. By 1935, the Cody airport had opened. In 1938, Cody acquired a more consistent economic mainstay when Husky Oil was founded; it remains, as Marathon Oil, in Cody today.

By the early 1940s, the Cody area accommodated yet another influx of people, neither permanent town settlers nor tourists. On August 12, 1942, 292 American citizens of Japanese ancestry arrived from Pomona, California, at Heart Mountain detention facility, located about 10 miles outside Cody. One hundred and twenty-five military police guarded the complex to "protect" the community. With an eventual population of 11,000, there were more citizens at Heart Mountain between 1942 and 1945 than in Cody itself—more, in fact, than in any town in Park County. The camp actually became, for a time, the third largest town in Wyoming. Prevented from ever owning property or voting by the Wyoming legislature, camp prisoners were only allowed to leave the camp with temporary permits to help with local crop harvests or to go to Europe to fight in the war. Many volunteered for duty: Nine hundred men from Heart Mountain served the United States in World War II and 20 were killed. The remaining 8,663 prisoners of Heart Mountain left the Bighorn Basin on November 10, 1945, with $25, train fare home, and $3 per day for meals on route.

The late 20th century brought more tourist and town growth in Cody as its economy exploded with the rest of the country's. Cody's oil industries boomed and its upscale art and summer home population thrived. The Buffalo Bill Historical Center, which opened in 1917, the year Bill Cody died, created its Whitney Museum of Art in 1959 and added the Winchester Arms and Plains Indian museums in 1979. Visitors now come from all over the globe to the center, which houses a total of five museums under one roof. In 1970, a golf course opened in the heart of Cody. Tourism continued to be a mainstay as retail sales in Park County reached $10,573 per capita by 1997. Throughout the 20th century, the minority population stayed extremely limited in Park County. Out of 8,835 people counted in the 2000 U.S. census of Cody, 8,727 identified themselves as white, with only 9 blacks, 37 Native Americans, and 51 Asians counted. Nonetheless, the small community still sees diverse crowds from May to September as tourists hope to find the spirit of one of America's most energetic western advertisers, whose irrigation and promotional work forever changed the Shoshone Canyon and its valley.

—Laurie Hinck

See also CROW NATION, JAPANESE INTERNMENT

Suggested Reading

"Aliens Must Register First Week in February." *Cody Enterprise,* January 23, 1918.

Blevins, Bruce H. *Park County, Wyoming: Facts and Maps Through Time.* Powell, WY: WIM, 1999.

Churchill, Gail Beryl. *Dams, Ditches and Water.* Cody, WY: Rustler, 1979.

Cook, Jeannie, Johnson Lynn Houze, Bob Edgar, and Paul Fees. *Buffalo Bill's Town in the Rockies: A Pictorial History of Cody, Wyoming,* 27. Virginia Beach, VA: Donning, 1996.

Fowler, Laura. *American Indians of the Great Plains.* New York: Columbia University Press, 2003.

"German Hide Buyer of Billings Too Much a Friend of Germany, He Criticized U.S. Government, Now Rests in County Jail Awaiting Federal Officers—Undoubtedly Will Be Place in Detention Camp." *Cody Enterprise,* January 16, 1918, p. 1.

"German Is Jailed for Seditious Remarks." *Cody Enterprise,* December 26, 1917.

Haines, Aubrey. *Bannock Indian Trail.* Yellowstone, WY: Library and Museum Association, 1964.

"Home Defense Club Formed." *Cody Enterprise,* January 23, 1918.

Inouye, Mamoru. *The Heart Mountain Story.* Park County Archives, Cody, Wyoming, 1997.

Kessell, Hudson. *Pahaska Tepee: Buffalo Bill's Old Hunting Lodge and Hotel: A History.* Cody, WY: Buffalo Bill Historical Center, 1987.

Kessell, Velma Berryman. *Behind Barbed Wire: Heart Mountain Relocation Camp.* Billings, MT: Topel, 1992.

Larson, T. A. *History of Wyoming.* 2nd ed. Lincoln: University of Wyoming Press, 1978.

McCracken, Harold. *The Mummy Cave Project in Northwestern Wyoming.* Cody, WY: Buffalo Bill Historical Center, 1978.

Murray, Ester Johansson. *A History of the North Fork of the Shoshone River.* Cody, WY: Lone Eagle Multi Media, 1996.

Nelson, Douglas W. *Heart Mountain: The History of an American Concentration Camp.* Madison: University of Wisconsin, State Historical Society of Wisconsin for the Department of History, 1976.

Patrick, Lucille Nichols. *Best Little Town by a Dam Site: Or Cody's First 20 Years.* Cheyenne, WY: Flintlock, 1968.

"Two Trainloads of Japanese at Camp." *Cody Enterprise,* August 17, 1942.

⌗ COEUR D'ALENE, IDAHO

See LEWISTON AND COEUR D'ALENE, IDAHO

⌗ COLLIER, JOHN

See BUREAU OF INDIAN AFFAIRS

⌗ COMSTOCK LODE, 1859

The Comstock Lode did not actually begin with Henry T. P. Comstock, who vastly underestimated the worth of what he found and who, along with his cronies, was something of a late player in the game.

On their way to the California mines, Mormon prospectors, as early as 1848, had discovered a quartz vein containing gold in the Washoe Mountains east of the Sierra Nevada. As the gold appeared to be of inferior quality and small in quantity, the Mormons continued their trek to the Golden State. They did however take with them tales of their miniscule find, which began to permeate the California goldfields as the placer mining started to die out and the possibility of individual strikes gave way to corporate mining successes. The so-called old sourdoughs wistfully dreamed of recreating the heyday of 1849, when anyone could make a fortune overnight with the right mixture of skill and luck in nearby Nevada—if only the opportunity presented itself.

However, through the mid-1850s, Nevada kept its secret locked underground in an immense vein of variegated ores located some 6,500 feet above sea level on Mount Davidson and extending from Gold Canyon to Six-Mile Canyon. Some placer miners who eked out a minimal living had staked nearly 100 claims in the area without much result.

In 1859, however, the situation changed radically when Henry Comstock and James "Old Virginny" Finney staked two 50- by 400-foot claims at Gold Hill near the head of Gold Canyon. Simultaneously, two Irishmen, Peter O'Reilly and Patrick McLaughlin, staked claims at the head of Six-Mile Canyon. Because the spring that watered the Irishmen's claims emanated from Comstock's holdings (or so he said), Comstock claimed a portion of anything the Irishmen found and invited a friend, Emanuel Penrod, to join in the partnership. The combined claims were eventually christened the Ophir Mine—mentioned in the Bible as the source of King Solomon's wealth. The claims did indeed yield gold, but of a tainted quality. A bluish-black substance was intermixed with the gold, and the five miners routinely separated the unwanted mineral from the yellow ore and tossed it away. Although none of the group was ever interested enough to investigate the composition of the blue material, a prospector from Truckee carted a sack of it to an Assay Office in Grass Valley, California.

The samples assayed turned out to be 75 percent pure silver, worth $3,876 per ton, and 25 percent gold, worth $876 per ton. When the results became known, a good portion of Grass Valley pulled up stakes and headed across the Sierra Nevada toward the Washoe diggings.

The original Ophir Mine owners, realizing that the gold and silver vein extended deeper than the mere placer surface mining they were performing, had by this time already filed lode claims. Consequently, when the California gold seekers arrived, they found that all of the valuable land was firmly in the control of Comstock and his partners.

Unfortunately, all of the Ophir's initial creators, as also chronicled in the Bible, sold their birthrights for a "mess of pottage." Each assumed that the Ophir would play out fairly quickly, as had all the other mines in the area, and each decided to sell his share as soon as possible to the newcomers. The aggregate total of what they received for their shares was $26,000. The Ophir eventually yielded more than $11 million.

Thus, however briefly, Nevada *did* mirror the old California gold rush, where fortunes were made and lost in an instant. Henry T. P. Comstock eventually dribbled away the entire $11,000 he was paid for his portion of the claim and shot himself a decade later. Ironically, the Comstock Lode was named for a man who, dollar for dollar, barely made a dime out of it.

One of the new investors, George Hearst of San Francisco, had a good deal more luck than Comstock. After two months' digging, Hearst and his associates hauled 38 tons of ore back to San Francisco at a profit of $90,000 and enjoyed the notoriety of exhibiting the bars of silver before an astonished citizenry. Assured that the Comstock Lode was more than a will-'o-the-wisp, erstwhile mineral magnates headed to Nevada in droves, with 10,000 miners crossing the mountains and 17,000 claims staked the first year.

Virginia City, Nevada, the boomtown that straddled the Comstock Lode, supposedly got its name from "Old Virginny" Finney, a hopeless drunk who christened the ground on which he spilled a bottle of whiskey with his name. Though an apocryphal story, it suited the town, which eventually contained more than 100 barrooms but only four churches. The disproportionate number of gin mills stemmed from the fact that Nevada was a fairly boring place in comparison to California—boring, cold, and lonely. In two years, Virginia City had grown to house 15,000 people. However, men outnumbered women by 70 to 1 in 1860 and, 10 years later, still outnumbered them by 2 to 1. More often than not, the miner's only companion was the bottle—as much as a quart of whiskey per day, in some cases. In view of the circumstances, it is hardly surprising that during 1863 alone one third of the town was arrested at various times for drunk and disorderly conduct. Samuel Clemens, a Missouri-born resident of the city and writer for the local *Territorial Enterprise,* may have developed his pen name not from the Mississippi riverboat jargon of his youth but, rather, from the bar tabs that he kept running at the local saloons. When out of pocket for a couple of drinks, he simply asked the bartender to "mark twain."

Eventually, some $400 million in precious metals was extracted from the Comstock Lode. Of more wonder than this final figure, however, was the method in which the ore was obtained—a method that created a new type of mining not heretofore seen in the West. This method also created a new social order based on the type of miner qualified to do the job.

The vast majority of the Comstock's wealth was not above ground, but below, in silver veins of phenomenal size—10 to 20 times larger than the ordinary 3-foot-wide vein. However, most of these veins ran to depths of 1,000–3,000 feet below the surface. As the miners descended, both the ambient temperature and the water levels in the tunnels rose. At 1,000 feet, the miner toiled in 100-degree heat. At 3,000 feet, the temperature rose to an unbearable 150 degrees and the subterranean water investing the rocks began to boil and steam. In addition, the pressure on the tunnel walls and the softness of the ore created continual danger of cave-ins. The Comstock challenged its intruders to create miracles of modern engineering.

The challenges faced on the Comstock spelled the death of the solitary miner. Working at such depths, hauling ore thousands of feet to the surface, counteracting water levels and preventing cave-ins at these pressure-intense stress points required machinery and expertise beyond the pocketbook of the individual and tenable only by conglomerate corporations, usually composed of San Francisco financiers.

In 1864, San Franciscan William Ralston organized the Bank of California and immediately established a branch in Virginia City. As the bank loaned money to desperate miners and then foreclosed on their claims when the miners defaulted, the bank came to own a major share of the Comstock Lode mining operations through a holding company called Union Mine and Milling. In competition with the bank, another group of San Francisco investors—John Mackay, James Flood, William O'Brien, and James Fair—bought out the Consolidated Virginia Company and began excavating an area 1,167 feet below the surface of Washoe in 1873. The resulting discovery was a massive vein of silver and gold 54 feet wide, which was appropriately christened "The Big Bonanza."

Hence, the investors became known as the Bonanza Kings. But the question of how to tap the vein remained. The problem was eventually solved through engineering created specifically for the Comstock and financed by corporations like Consolidated Virginia and the Bank of California.

The first task was to prevent cave-ins. Ordinary mines only required a post-and-lintel construction like a doorway to brace the tunnel walls. Depths such as those of the Big Bonanza required something more sturdy. German Philipp Deidesheimer of the Freiberg School of Mines was hired to provide the solution. His proposal was "square sets" of mortised timber 6 feet long and 14 inches square, which created cubes that could, in turn, be locked together like a honeycomb. Deidesheimer's concept allowed for deeper excavation and helped increase the number of mines in the area to more than 100. Eventually, Virginia City rested on ground riddled with a beehive network of timbers. Because the Washoe was nearly treeless, the eastern side of the Sierra Nevada was raided for wood and stripped bare for 100 miles along its base.

Machinery of immense proportions became the norm for the Comstock: single-cylinder, 1,000-horsepower hoisting engines; boilers 16 feet long and 54 inches in diameter; double-cylinder, 2,000-horsepower hoisting engines; and steam pumps with 40-foot flywheels capable of draining 2 million gallons of tunnel water per day from a depth of 1,100 feet. In addition, ore brought out of the mines had to be processed through stamping mills and then reprocessed through panning mills—not to mention the transportation necessary to cart the ore to such mills in the first place. All of this required the capital available only from large corporations. As the Comstock became more mechanized, mines and their adjacent support industries, milling and transportation, became more centralized.

Intricate machinery and hard-rock mining required expertise the placer miner could not provide. So, the corporations looked abroad for workers with the technical skill or stamina necessary to do the job. In 1880, of the 2,770 men listed as hard-rock miners, only 770 were American. The rest were an international mingling of Germans, Mexicans, Irishmen, and Cornishmen. Immigrants from Cornwall had worked the English tin mines for hundreds of years and were used to the danger and hard labor of sledge driving or single and double jacking at extreme depths. Often called "Cousin Jacks," their nickname derived from their continual reply to the foreman's request for more Cornish laborers: "Well, there's me Cousin Jack at 'ome." The Irish and Cornish composed two thirds of the labor force used in the Comstock mines. On Saturdays, when not working in the mines, they tended to brawl with one another and with the German workers after drinking in Virginia City saloons. However, everyone fought the Chinese who, as in the California gold rush, represented the lowest rung on the social ladder. The other groups apparently feared that the Chinese might take their jobs.

The life of a deep-tunnel miner was never less than one step away from injury or death. Descending to depths of 2,000 feet, where temperatures reached the aforementioned 150 degrees, workers stripped down to briefs or worked totally naked, except for the thick-soled shoes necessary to keep their feet from burning. As the heat tore at their lungs, the miners ran to suck fresh air from ventilating tubes. They doused themselves with cold water to replenish what they had lost in sweat. Miner's lung, silicosis, and tuberculosis were rampant, as was pneumonia, caused by sudden ascents from steaming-hot to ice-cold air. In addition, gas leaks, floods, explosions, and lethal failures of equipment, including mineshaft elevators, rounded out the terrors hard-rock miners experienced in their daily routine while the Bonanza Kings made money hand over fist.

Eventually the corporations had to deal with labor. From 1863 onward, Comstock miners moved toward effective unionization as a means of guaranteeing wages, securing benefits, and protecting jobs. In 1863, 300 miners met in Virginia City to form the Miners' Protective Association. Because the aims of the association were not specific enough to gain the attention of management, the association soon dissolved. Shortly thereafter, an economic depression struck the area due to speculation and worthless stocks floated on the market in San Francisco. To recoup their losses, San Francisco corporate heads ordered wage cuts for miners on the Comstock. In response, the miners at Gold Hill organized a strike and vowed to shut down the mines rather than accept wages of less than $4 per day. Calling themselves the Miners' League of Storey County, the miners marched into Virginia City and intimidated local corporate representatives to rescind the wage decrease. However, as the depression continued from late 1864 through 1866, the league lost a good deal of its membership as the corporations began

forming anti-union organizations like the Citizens' Protective Association. When the Miners' League dissolved, it appeared that the corporations had defeated the cause of workers' rights until a new group, the Miners' Union of the Town of Gold Hill, took up the banner in 1866. With clearly defined goals and extensive membership, the union was the emulated example of effective worker solidarity for the entire West and became the cornerstone for the Western Federation of Miners in 1893.

The catalyst that had brought the miners together to finally form an effective union was once again the Chinese. Once the Central Pacific completed its work in 1869, Chinese tracklayers found themselves out of a job and stranded on the Nevada side of the Sierra range. When work was offered to them to grade a roadbed on the Virginia and Truckee line from Virginia City to Carson, Chinese appeared in droves. However, rather than allow the Chinese any type of foothold in the Comstock, the Miners' Union of the Town of Gold Hill marched out of Virginia City with a force of 359 workers and drove the Chinese from the job. Consequently, the union was able to totally expunge Chinese from the local workforce and by 1875 had created a closed shop on the Comstock.

With the coming of the corporations and the final unionization of the workers to balance the equation, the Comstock Lode had fairly run its course. It had passed very rapidly through the phase where miners believed they could recapture the glory days of California and, out of necessity to effectively extract the deep-laid veins of silver and gold, had shifted to the more pragmatic view of mining as an industry rather than a pastime.

Along the way, the Comstock had lured men from around the world and finally taught them the value of working together for common causes. Some of the causes, like standing up to management, were righteous. Other causes, such as the exclusion of the Chinese and the obvious bigotry it cloaked, were not so praiseworthy. However, the lessons learned and the methods devised to make the Washoe ore a success created new standards of industry, management techniques, and labor solidarity that bypassed the demise of Virginia City in the 1890s and headed American business in a direction that still reflects the heritage of

H. T. P. Comstock's lode. Along the way, the business activity generated by the Comstock created 280 towns to serve its consumption. The mine generated far more than legend.

—Thomas de Martino

See also INYO COUNTY, CALIFORNIA; NEVADA MINING DISCOVERIES OF THE 20TH CENTURY

Suggested Reading

DeQuille, Dan. *The Big Bonanza.* New York: Knopf, 1947.

Johnson, David Alan. *Founding the Far West.* Berkeley: University of California Press, 1992.

Lingenfelter, Richard E. *The Hardrock Miners.* Berkeley: University of California Press, 1974.

Lyman, George D. *The Saga of the Comstock Lode.* New York: Scribner, 1934.

Milner, Clyde A., Carol A. O'Connor, and Martha A. Sandweiss, eds. *The Oxford History of the American West.* New York: Oxford University Press, 1994.

Moehring, Eugene. "The Comstock Urban Network." *Pacific Historical Review* 66 (August 1997): 337–362.

Paul, Rodman Wilson. *Mining Frontiers of the Far West 1848–1880.* Albuquerque: University of New Mexico Press, 1974.

Wallace, Robert. *The Miners.* Alexandria: Time-Life, 1976.

Ward, Geoffrey C. *The West.* Boston: Little, Brown, 1996.

White, Richard. *It's Your Misfortune and None of My Own.* Norman: University of Oklahoma Press, 1991.

Young, Otis E. *Western Mining.* Norman: University of Oklahoma Press, 1970.

⌗ CONFEDERATE VETERANS IN SOUTHERN CALIFORNIA

At the close of the American Civil War, former Confederates faced the dismantling of their political and social foundations, and eventually they needed to reconstitute their states to gain readmission to the union. Eleven states in total—South Carolina, Mississippi, Florida, Alabama, Georgia, Louisiana, Texas, Virginia, Arkansas, Tennessee, and North Carolina—awaited reentry; some, as in the case of Texas, until March 1870.

On December 8, 1863, during his annual address to Congress, President Abraham Lincoln issued a Proclamation of Amnesty and Reconstruction.

Acknowledging various congressional legislation and laws bent on the confiscation of Confederate property, including slaves, Lincoln asserted his position as a national leader and, with optimism, as a national healer. To the former Confederates, the president extended "a full pardon . . . with restoration of all rights of property, except as to slaves, and upon the condition that every such person shall take and subscribe an oath." Within this proclamation, Lincoln also issued his well-known "ten percent" plan for reconstructing the government, which allowed the restoration of republican governments in states avowing the loyalty of one tenth of the electorate who voted in 1860. The president closed by assuring both legislators and states in question that his plan was reconciliatory "and while the mode presented is the best the executive can suggest, with his present impressions, it must not be understood that no other possible mode would be acceptable."

At the time of Lincoln's death in 1865, the president and Congress were in a deadlock over the preferred process for Reconstruction. Presidential successor Andrew Johnson issued his first Proclamation of Amnesty and Pardon on May 29, 1865, which was far more austere than the plan introduced by his predecessor. Johnson argued that too many had ignored the generosity of Lincoln's offer of amnesty and that those who had been excluded from amnesty by previous legislation now wished to pursue general reprieve. Unlike Lincoln's proclamation, Johnson's exempted 14 classes from amnesty, 8 more than the late president had proposed in 1863. From the right to amnesty Johnson excepted diplomatic agents, renegade judges, high-ranking military officers, rebel governors, as well as those aiding the rebellion either by taking refuge in Confederate lines or pirating upon the high seas. One of the most telling exceptions, however, was against rebellious individuals whose property held a taxable worth of more than $20,000. This move implied that Johnson hoped to realign the Southern wealth and political clout, primarily by deconstructing the planter aristocracy. Between April and December of 1865, Johnson's plan was enacted.

The Union plans for Reconstruction continued to flounder between Congress and the executive branch, a battle that was fueled by the head-hunting sentiment toward the former rebels. In 1867, the Reconstruction Acts were ratified, dividing the South, sans Tennessee, into five military districts. These acts, opposed by Johnson, eventually led to the president's impeachment.

Within this new environment, at once infused with a combination of patriotic reconciliation and political divergence, Southerners began to rebuild their society. Plagued by what they termed "carpetbaggers" and "scalawags," Southern leaders and citizens sought through bitterness and uncertainty a legitimate foundation for their renewed roles as citizens of the United States. This period in history is often and understandably identified with the southeastern section of the United States. Yet a significant number of former Confederates immigrated west to states such as New Mexico, Texas, and, least recognized, California.

Ironically, although California seems to be the last locale on the minds of historians when recounting Southern history during and after the Civil War, the state is not without a significant Confederate heritage.

During the 1860 election, Lincoln earned a slim California victory, thanks in part to a fractured Democratic Party. Divided over Kansas-Nebraska, the Democrats confronted several split party candidates on the 1860 ballot. Although Democrats remained strong in southern counties of California, Republican cohesion won the state for Lincoln. Despite their loss on the national level, however, Democrats did manage to secure legislative seats in Los Angeles, San Diego, and San Bernardino. According to Ronald C. Woolsey, Lincoln received a 20 percent total in Los Angeles County, a statistic Woolsey credits as indicative of regional Southern sympathy.

The state's political division erupted over various issues, including construction of the transcontinental railroad and slavery. Although slavery was not permitted in California, many immigrants from Confederate states aligned themselves with the radical candidate John C. Breckinridge of Kentucky.

After the 1860 election and firing on Fort Sumter, California followed the rest of the country through a regional split. Woolsey points out that El Monte residents marching through the streets in protest. The Bella Union, Los Angeles' first hotel, located on Main Street between Commercial and Arcadia, became a Confederate support base. When California received word that the country had separated, a portrait of Confederate general P. G. T. Beauregard was displayed

in the hotel's saloon. The Bella Union's Confederate sympathizing lasted until 1862, when it was sold to a new proprietor. Yet the hotel made enough sectional impact to compel Brigadier General Edwin V. Sumner of the Department of the Pacific to proclaim of Los Angeles, "There is more danger of disaffection at this place than any other in the State."

Despite the implication of the votes, small pockets of secessionist sentiment existed in the northern counties as well, with people organizing small, short-lived clubs at the start of the war and advocating compromise. The majority of secessionist secret societies existed in the southern portion of the state, however. In 1911, historian Charles Mial Daul estimated Confederate societies, such as the Knights of the Golden Circle and the Knights of the Columbian Star, to have reached 100,000 in numbers. Although Daul's estimate may have been inflated, the factions' objectives were authentic; according to Karen Sue Hockemeyer, they sought "to capture the Presidio, Mint, and Custom House at Mare Island, and the Arsenal at Benicia."

Many Confederate sympathizers also formed into guerrilla bands, both on land and by sea. The appearance of guerrillas and privateers encouraged the Union army to establish a camp on Santa Catalina Island in 1863. The guerilla bands, for the most part, targeted California gold shipments. Captain Rufus Henry Ingram's partisan rangers and George Belt's guerilla band are primary examples of related insurrectionist activity.

The threat of secessionist insurrection in the southern counties led to a federal military presence, particularly near San Pedro, Baldwin Hills, and Los Angeles. According to Woolsey, the real danger for secessionist sabotage in the southern counties was exaggerated. For this misassumption, Woolsey blames the irregularity of government information during the war. Yet the mere existence of these groups and the seriousness with which they were regarded implies that in contemporary thought the reality of secessionist insurrection in the southern counties was not far-fetched.

During the war, California secessionist newspapers struggled to maintain circulation. The *Visalia Equal Rights Expositor, Stockton Democrat, Stockton Argus, Placerville Mountain Democrat,* and *San Jose Tribune* were all denied access to mailings. The mischievous editor of the *Expositor* eventually led to the building of Camp Babbit near Visalia in an effort to curb secessionist activity. Brandishing the Confederate flag was also curbed in California on April 20, 1863, when it became an offense punishable by a $300 fine or 60 days' jail time.

Thus it is fair to say that, although California was not directly involved in the Civil War, it definitely was not excluded. The state endured its own anxieties over secession and essentially waged its own small-scale war, north and south.

At the end of the war, many Confederate sympathizers chose to abandon the state and to migrate south into Mexico and South America. Likewise, some Confederate veterans and their families in the East chose to migrate west in search of a new land, profit, and the frontier's promise of individual liberty. Many, it may be speculated, fled the harsh edifice of Reconstruction, realizing that successful readmission to the Union not only required their personal acquiescence, but also a willingness to reestablish their lives.

According to Paul Gillette, preservation officer of the Civil War Roundtable of Orange County, Civil War veterans began to migrate west as early as 1870, and by 1900 Santa Ana boasted a higher percentage of Civil War veterans than any other California city. Although, as Gillette notes, Union veterans outnumbered Confederate veterans six to one, the former secessionists were able to make equally significant contributions as their Union counterparts to their new environments. For example, during the 1880s, lawyer Victor Montgomery and state assemblyman Dr. Henry Head, both former Confederates, assisted in the move to secede from Los Angeles County. Gillette, in his paper "The Civil War Legacy of Orange County," lists two other prominent civic leaders with Confederate heritage: the second county treasurer, who "was a Confederate veteran from Virginia who rode for three years with Jeb Stuart's cavalry," and "the first man to survey what became the town of Orange, who "had been a Captain in the Confederate Navy." Another was William Walker, a lawyer, editor, preacher, and doctor whom the *Los Angeles Times*, in September 4, 1891, said "had more grit and composure to the square inch than any man I ever saw."

A record of Confederate veterans and their wives, by the Emma Sansom Chapter of the United Daughters of Confederate Veterans (UDC), lists numerous prominent ex-Confederates who settled in the Orange County area. The record includes J. Y. Anderson of the Fourteenth Virginia Cavalry, who arrived in Anaheim in 1869 and built the first house in Westminster in 1870; Dr. J. S. Gardiner of the Thirty-Seventh Tennessee Volunteers, who performed the first caesarean operation in Orange County, done by candlelight and for a fee of $25; and Josiah Joplin of the Second Virginia Cavalry, who promoted education, was elected county treasurer in 1898, and presented his exhibit of Orange County–related products at the World's Fair in St. Louis, 1904. Victor Montgomery, according to the UDC account, was not only a county lawyer, but was also the first president of the board of education and president of the bar association. In addition to law, Montgomery also pursued a study of the fruit industry and horticulture, with a specialization in the citrus industry. Montgomery's wife, Charlie Louis, was the president of the California division of the UDC from 1903 to 1905 and helped organize the Emma Sansom Chapter, of which she was president for 15 years.

The political influence of ex-Confederates continued to raise concerns into the 1880s. In a letter to the *Los Angeles Times,* September 29, 1882, a Salinas reader warned the citizens of Los Angeles of an upcoming campaign stop by Democratic candidate for congressman-at-large, Charles A. Sumner. Appealing to Republicans to assist the Democratic Party, Sumner confessed to having been "a 'Black' himself in the days when the party was fighting for principles." The unhappy reader added, "He did not explain why a Republican should leave his party and abandon his principles to support a party which has sacrificed its principles to get control of the public mind." As for Sumner's contemporary status as a politician, according to the irate reader, "He [Sumner] stated that one-fourth of the Democratic Convention were ex-Confederates.... Many of our Northern Democrats are disgusted with him, on account of his praise of the ex-Confederates and his expression against old Democratic doctrines."

In August of 1882, the *Sacramento Bee* ran a story, reprinted by the *Los Angeles Times,* condemning

Confederate veteran societies nationwide. After a rebuttal by an "ex-Confederate," the *Los Angeles Times* editor responded,

> Well, we did not expect the healthy sentiments in question to suit the ex-Confederate aforesaid. He appears to be one of those narrow-brained and sour-minded disappointees who are perpetually flying into an uncontrollable rage at the imaginary sight of the "bloody shirt"—whatever that may be.

Within the same editorial, the *Los Angeles Times* writer delivered a second blow against former Confederates, noting that four of the state Democratic nominees were ex-Confederate soldiers:

> "You must let these things die out," said our Democratic friends, "or there will never be perfect harmony and brotherly feeling again." Yet, if any or all these four gentleman had been in the East or South this week, he or they would have been present at the Sedalis (Mo.) reunion as an active participant.

These sentiments were undoubtedly fueled in part by political fervor for the upcoming election. Yet it is apparent that the influence of ex-Confederate sympathies was still a powerful weapon in both northern and southern California.

Confederate memorialization groups also became active in California after the war. On September 10, 1895, approximately 25 "veterans of the 'Lost Cause'" were present at the St. Elmo Hotel in Los Angeles for a meeting of the Confederate Veterans Association. During the meeting, the local organization established a constitution and bylaws and set a date for officer elections. Three years later, on May 19, 1898, all ex-Confederate and ex-Union veterans were invited, on behalf of the National Veterans Reserve, to attend a memorial service at Church of the Unity in Los Angeles. This event, according to the *Los Angeles Times*, was "the first instance since the close of the war that ex-Union and ex-Confederate veterans, as a united fraternal society, [had] ever attended a memorial service."

Reunions continued to increase and expanded outside of the major cities. In Orange County, on May 10, 1899, the first reunion of "Hi" Bledsoe Camp 1201 was held in the County Park, Santiago Canyon. Among the speakers at the reunion was Victor Montgomery,

who commended the soldier of the South for battling on behalf of his beliefs. Also present were Major Spencer R. Thorpe, who spoke on the war's consequences from a Confederate viewpoint, and Commander Peabody, member of the camp, who honored the Confederate veterans as being as brave and as loyal as any veteran who marched into battle. It should be noted, however, that not all Confederate veterans meetings were characterized by nostalgic speeches and solemn ceremony. In October of 1901, the United Confederate Veterans hosted a party that involved "instrumental music, plantation singing, and character songs." The dancing, according to the *Los Angeles Times* reporter, lasted until midnight.

In 1905, at the Temple Auditorium in Los Angeles, thousands of veterans united for a Sunday Memorial Day service. The building filled with veterans from varying wars, including those who fought for both North and South. "Not to be forgotten on the list either," the *Los Angeles Times* reported, "are the Confederate soldiers and the Sons of Veterans, who, though not so strong in numbers, were to be seen everywhere throughout the great building."

Commemoration of Confederate veteran heroes continued far into the 20th century when Kappa Alpha fraternity members at the University of Southern California and the University of California–Los Angeles joined with 700 local alumni to honor the 141st birthday of General Robert E. Lee. The organization, meeting to honor Lee in 1939, was established to preserve the ideals of the general.

Women were also involved in the memorialization of the Confederate cause. At a June 1902 meeting of the United Confederate Veterans, 11 girls, representative of the Confederate states, gave speeches in honor of Confederate generals from their respective locales. The gala was led by Mrs. Victor Montgomery, who in addition to the presentation also gave a poem titled "Cross of Honor."

In the spring of 1916, 19-year-old Santa Monica High School graduate Martha L. Westbrook was sent to Birmingham, Alabama, as a representative of the United Confederate Veterans of California at the national reunion of Confederate Veterans. Westbrook was the granddaughter of Major Albert S. Harris, of General Tyree Bell's brigade, and Dr. J. R. Westbrook, who served under General Nathan Bedford Forrest. A member of the Bay District UDC, Westbrook was chosen by a committee to serve as a sponsor for the California Confederates.

Passing out of the 19th century and into the 20th, the number of veterans began to decline and the pockets of ex-Confederates grew smaller. As one *Santa Ana Morning Dispatch* writer lamented, "One by one they are leaving us—these old heroes of the sixties, and our hearts ache at the realization of how rapidly they are joining their comrades on the other shore." In 1939, the *Morning Dispatch* reported on the ailing health of James H. Campbell, the last surviving veteran of Dixie Manor, a home for Confederate soldiers in San Gabriel. The home, founded in 1929 by a former member of Jefferson Davis's honor guard and soldier under General Robert E. Lee, was set to close after the death of Campbell.

According to Paul Gillette, as of March 2002, 727 Civil War veterans were identified as being interred in southern California cemeteries, including those in Santa Ana, Huntington Beach, San Juan Capistrano, and Fullerton.

The legacy of the Civil War in both northern and southern California can be traced by state delineation. Much like the rest of the country, California reacted strongly to the national divide. Following the war, the state became home for both Unionists and former Confederates, essentially a test case for reuniting national sentiment without the rigor of Reconstruction. The involvement of ex-Confederates in the expansion of southern California and creation of Orange County should not be underestimated or overlooked. These were individuals with strong political and social foundations who, traveling west in search of land, democracy, and individualism, rebuilt lives and established careers in a locale far removed from their personal histories.

—Jennifer Mizzell

See also SANTA ANA, CALIFORNIA

Suggested Reading

Armor, Samuel. *History of Orange County, California: With Biographical Sketches of the Leading Men and Women of the County, Who Have Been Identified With the Growth and Development From the Early Days to the Present Time.* Los Angeles: Historic Record, 1911.

Clendenen, Clarence C. "Dan Showalter—California Secessionist." *California Historical Society Quarterly* 40, no. 4 (1961): 309–326.

Fitzgibbons, Margaret M. *History of the United Daughters of the Confederacy in California: Centennial Edition, 1896–1996.* Mesa, AZ: Blue Bird, 1997.

Gilbert, Benjamin Franklin. "California and the Civil War." *California Historical Society Quarterly* 40, no. 4 (1961): 289–308.

Gillette, Paul. "The Civil War Legacy of Orange County." Civil War Round Table of Orange County Web Site. Available from http://www.cwrtorangecounty-ca.org/

Hockemeyer, Karen Sue. *The Southern Minority?: The Strength of the Confederate and the Copperhead Sentiment in Santa Clara County, California.* M.A. Thesis, San Jose State University, 1988.

"Record of Confederate Veterans and Their Wives, Who Were Pioneers in Orange County, California." 1938–1939 Scrapbook of Emma Sansom Chapter 449, United Daughters of the Confederacy, Santa Ana, CA.

Woolsey, Ronald C. "The Politics of a Lost Cause: 'Seceshers' and Democrats in Southern California during the Civil War." *California History* 69, no. 4 (Winter 1990–1991): 372–383.

COPPER QUEEN MINE

See ARIZONA COPPER DISCOVERIES; BISBEE AND DOUGLAS, ARIZONA

CORNISH IMMIGRANTS

See GRASS VALLEY, CALIFORNIA; IDAHO SILVER STRIKES

CREEK NATION

In the beginning, the Muscogee people were born out of the earth itself. A thick fog sent by Esakitaummesee, the Master of Breath, covered the entire area and separated the people from one another. The people could not see and wandered aimlessly throughout the land, and, fearing isolation, called out to one another. They became lost and drifted apart. The people became separated into small groups, which clung together for fear of being entirely alone.

The Master of Breath took pity on the people and, from the eastern edge of the land, began to blow away the fog until it was completely gone. The people, thankful to the Master of Breath, celebrated with song and swore allegiance to each other. They promised from that day that the groups would be like large families and the members of each family would care for the others.

The group closest to the eastern edge of the land praised the wind that blew the fog away. They named themselves the Wind Clan. As the wind moved west, clearing the fog as it passed, the other groups named themselves after the first animal they saw. They in turn became the Bear, Deer, Alligator, Raccoon, and Bird Clans. The Master of Breath told them, "You are the beginning of each of your families and clans. Live up to your name. When you forget, your clans will die as people."

For thousands of years, indigenous peoples have moved from place to place in what has come to be called North America. Early migrations were a necessity for survival. The hunters and gatherers had to adapt to diverse climates, making certain types of agriculture prohibitive. Natural wildlife migrations resulted in a mobile dinner table and therefore a mobile society. These people had to follow the game for a continuous supply of food, clothing, and shelter. A consequence of the nomadic nature of these people was the relocation of their villages to different locations with some frequency. When the town moved, they took the name of the town with them—it was their identity. With no written language, it is difficult to trace tribal origins other than through oral histories passed down through generations.

Beginning in the late 15th century, Europeans from England, Spain, France, and the Netherlands continued their own migrations, making their way west to explore the so-called New World and claim its wealth and abundance for their respective royalty. What they discovered upon their arrival were scores of indigenous tribes inhabiting the land. What follows is a brief look at the Muscogee (Creek) people and how their lives were impacted by this European invasion.

The Creeks were not one tribe, but rather a loose confederation made up of many tribes within the Muskhogean linguistic group. One of the many myths surrounding the Creek people is the origin of their name. The simplistic version is that the English colonists gave them the name because of the abundant creeks and streams that meandered through their lands. In fact, that geographic area was scattered with a profusion of waterways and tributaries along which the people settled. It was common for the English to name a waterway after the tribe that occupied the land adjacent. Thus the section of the Ocmulgee River in Georgia inhabited by the Ocheese tribe was called Ocheese Creek and the people Ocheese Creek Indians. Over time, the name was abbreviated to simply *Creek* and was applied to the many tribes of the surrounding area. Maskoki, another common spelling for the tribe, is also a derivative. The Native word for "water" is *oki,* and *muskhoge* means "dwellers in the swamps."

Tribes were referred to as *towns,* or *fires,* and were individual unto themselves, with a unique culture, dialect, and government. This alliance of separate and independent towns gradually became a single political organization. The Creek Confederacy maintained peace between its constituents and provided a defensive security and a potential offensive alliance against a common enemy.

These collected towns were further divided into factions. The Upper Creeks dwelled along the Alabama, Coosa, and Tallapoosa Rivers in central Alabama, and the Lower Creeks along the Flint, Ocmulgee, and Chattahoochee Rivers of Georgia. Both Upper and Lower Creek towns were divided into red (war) towns and white (peace) towns. The peace towns dealt with matters relating to peace treaties and were responsible for internal tribal affairs, such as making and regulating laws and the adoption of children. It was customary for Creeks to assimilate any surviving defeated enemies into the tribe, although in many cases only children were adopted, because adults were summarily killed. Red towns dealt with external affairs, such as diplomatic councils and matters of war.

Creek towns were laid out in a square pattern, all including a great house, a council house, and a playground. The great house was actually a group of four structures facing north, south, east, and west. The west building, facing east, housed the chief, or *miko,* of the town. The north was reserved for warriors; the south and east for beloved men and the youth of the town. In the center of the four structures was maintained a perpetual fire in which four logs were continuously burning. All public town meetings and ceremonies took place at the great house.

The council house was circular measuring around 30 feet in diameter. With no openings other than the main entrance, the fire burning in the center area created much heat and smoke. The council house was used for many of the same events as the great house when the weather turned foul and for meetings of a private nature.

The playground was located in the northwest section of the town. A variety of sport took place here, including target shooting and diverse stick-and-ball games, as well as ceremonial dances during the summer season. It was also a place to exact punishment and execution.

Annual ceremonial events acted to strengthen the alliance between the Upper and Lower Creek factions. The annual busk, or *puskita* (Dance of the Green Corn), was—and is—held to celebrate the beginning of the new year, which coincides with the new corn harvest. It is a celebration of renewal. The significance of the ceremony, held over a four- to eight-day period, is the extinguishing of the old fire and the kindling of a new one. It is a time when the clans converge to sing, dance, and tell stories. It is also a time of amnesty, when all grievances save murder were forgiven and never spoken of again.

Creek people were bound together in clans, which were social as well as political organizations. The clan society was matrilineal; that is, the genealogical line descends through the woman's family. Ancestry was traced through the mother's line because the father's line was often obscure. Single groups descending from the same female line formed a clan. They were considered family regardless of whether they were actually related, and for this reason interclan marriage was forbidden. The clan was the strongest bond among the people. Loyalty to tribe and loyalty to town were not as important as loyalty to the clan.

The clan name, given to them by the Master of Breath, was chosen from characteristics of the people. Descendants of the clan ultimately go back to the animal for which the clan was named, so it is considered offensive for a member of the Bear Clan, for example, to hunt and eat a bear.

Children born into the clan were given names based on a significant event or on something they did or said. It was not uncommon for a Creek to be given as many as two or three names over the course of a lifetime. The father had little to do with raising the child. This obligation fell to men in the mother's line, typically an uncle. Child rearing was largely to do with preparing the male child to be a warrior—to exhibit bravery, toughness, and a lack of aversion to blood and pain. There was no formal education for children, nor was there mucn discipline. The child learned by imitating adult behavior.

Although their prehistoric roots were from nomadic bands in the west, migration legends suggest that the Creeks were of Aztec origin and migrated to what are now Alabama and Georgia from northwest Mexico at the time of Cortez. The early to mid-1500s brought the first Europeans to the Eastern shore of the future United States with the expeditions of Hernando de Soto. De Soto was none too friendly to his hosts. It was a typical pattern of operation to befriend the Natives only to ultimately exploit and enslave them, burning their towns in the wake of Spanish exploration.

Among the discoveries of de Soto's early gold-seeking expeditions were a variety of ailments, which had a negative impact on European exploration and discovery. Not only did more than half of de Soto's sailors succumb to indigenous disease, but the North American natives died by the thousands as a result of smallpox, bubonic plague, measles, and other unknown afflictions carried by their new guests. The drastic decline in Native population—an estimated 90 percent in the first 200 years after European contact—caused entire tribes to disappear. The people had to move to safer lands and join forces with other tribes. This forced migration was a necessity for their survival.

The 17th century brought thousands of European settlers to the New World, challenging the land rights of all Native tribes. As the European pressure grew, many Creeks sought escape to the south and crossed the border into Spanish-held Florida. This migration and colonization established the people known as Seminoles, the newest member of the Creek Confederacy. Seminole is derived from the Spanish word *cimarrone,* which means "savage" or "runaway slave."

The founding of the Georgia Colony in 1733 proved to be another challenge for the Creeks. Georgia was a crown colony intended to provide a home for England's "worthy poor," such as debtors and the homeless. Thus, it was established as a garrison province with a strong local militia to protect against hostile Native tribes and Spanish Florida to the south. Colony founder James Oglethorpe negotiated a deal with the Creeks for a section of land along the Savannah River, the border of which gradually and inevitably moved farther and farther west. As with the de Soto expeditions, Natives were displaced and enslaved along the way. Ultimately, the Creeks settled far inland in what is now Alabama.

The Creeks gradually established trade with their new neighbors and were introduced to things never before imagined. Prior to European immigration, Creeks did not have the horse, firearms, a variety of tools, or alcohol. The introduction of these items created a character change in the tribe. They eventually abandoned their agriculture in favor of hunting to provide sought-after skins and pelts; they discarded their craftsmanship in favor of new European-manufactured goods; the men became drunks, the women prostitutes, and crime in the Creek towns generally increased. Indians were taken as slaves when unable to repay debts. Entire villages were forced out of their homes and off their land by the onrushing of the white man.

The French and Indian War, or Seven Years War, although fought primarily further north, significantly impacted the Creek people in the south. The English, French, and Spanish had long clashed over land in the southern country. Spain controlled Florida, France the Louisiana Territory, and England had her colonies along the eastern seaboard. Of the three, the Creeks had the strongest relationship with the French.

Unfortunately, as a result of the Treaty of Paris in 1763, France ceded all North American lands to the British and Spain lost Florida. The western boundary of British-held territory now extended to the Mississippi River. Consequently, more forts were constructed in the western lands, and millions of acres were opened to European settlement. Royal policy established the territory between the Appalachian Mountains and the Mississippi River as Indian country for their exclusive use. However, a Declaration of Independence by the 13 British colonies brought a new war to North America before England's new policy could take effect.

The coming of the American Revolution gave the Creeks a choice. Both sides of the conflict wanted the allegiance of the Natives. The colonists remembered 25 years back when Indians allied with the French. The debate on both sides reflected pro and con arguments, from "the merciless cannibal, thirsting for the blood of man, woman and child! To send forth the infidel savage . . . against your Protestant brethren" to "I think they may be made of excellent use, as scouts and light troops."

Both the British and the Americans offered inducements, from powder and shot to clothing and provisions, to secure loyalties. British agents recruiting Creeks and others from the Five Civilized Tribes cited the rapid expansion of American settlements from the north, which had already entered Tennessee and Kentucky. A British victory in the war, they said, would save their native lands. In the end, most chose to support the British—a choice that proved unwise.

At the conclusion of the American Revolution, the British abandoned the Creeks, leaving them to their own devices and a lot of angry Americans. The British conditioned them to a new way of life, but did not prepare them to survive alone. They drove off all other treading partners only to desert them. The defeated British ceded the land that once belonged to the Natives to the Americans, who immediately drew their own designs for its use.

In 1790, an assembly of Creek headmen visited the capital city of New York. The Washington administration, through Secretary of War Henry Knox, negotiated a treaty with the Creeks resulting in the cession of disputed lands in Georgia in return for protected hunting rights further west. This agreement caused a rift between the Upper and Lower Creeks, which would last beyond the Civil War. The land gained from Britain and the "restlessness of the American frontiersmen" was to make way for the westward expansion of a rapidly growing country hungry for space. The Creeks would soon be on the move again.

Even after the Treaty of Paris in 1783, there was a British presence in North America, and much of this presence was engaged in trading activities with Native tribes. The Spanish to the south and the French to the west also had an interest in cultivating the Creeks as a trading ally. The British worked to gain the friendship of the Creeks by in part acknowledging their rights to land ownership, thereby turning them against the Americans, who only wanted to steal their land.

European pressure was countered by pressure from within the Creek tribe to restore traditional identity to the people. Inspired by the Shawnee Tecumseh and his Religion of the Dancing Lakes, many Creek towns were in favor of rising against the British and taking back their land and culture. This was not so much an alliance with the United States as it was the desire to be removed from all "foreign" influences. This controversy began to split the nation into two factions, each with prominent tribal leadership guiding them.

Ultimately, the Upper and Lower Creeks were on opposite sides of the issue. The Upper Creeks, resolved to return to their native roots, became known as Red Sticks because of their warlike attitude and because their war clubs were covered with red paint. The French called them *baton rouge*.

Skirmishes and raids against the frontier homesteaders in Tennessee and Alabama coincided with the escalating hostilities between the United States and England at the start of the War of 1812. A Tennessee militia was formed, commanded by General Andrew Jackson, with orders to exterminate the Creeks. With superior numbers and advanced weapons (the Creeks, in their desire for tribal culture, chose to fight with bow, arrow, and tomahawk instead of musket), Jackson's militia defeated the Creek nation.

The Treaty of Fort Jackson signed on August 9, 1814, stripped the Creeks of more than 20 million acres of land, including that belonging to the Creek faction that remained loyal to the United States, forcing them to move further west. On what land that was remaining to the Creeks, the United States was permitted to construct roads, have use of waterways, and build military facilities. Some Creeks decided to sail to the Bahamas and seek the protection of the British, while others went to Cuba to find safety with the Spanish.

With Jackson's rise to power over the following 15 years, the future security of the Creek people was continually in doubt. *Jacksa Chula Harjo,* "Jackson, old and fierce," was determined to eliminate the Creek people. In 1829, during his run for the presidency, he made Indian removal a campaign issue. After all, it

was commonly believed that the Creeks infested the land, not utilizing it for farming and other useful purposes, and with land at $0.37 per acre, there were substantial profits to be made.

Jackson's goal to "harass, persecute, and force out . . . Indian populations" was realized with the passage by the Twenty-First Congress of the Indian Removal Act on May 28, 1830, by a vote of 28 to 19 in the Senate and 102 to 97 in the House of Representatives. The act reads as follows:

> Be it enacted by the Senate and the House of Representatives of the United States of America, in Congress assembled, that it shall and may be lawful for the President of the United States to cause so much of any territory belonging to the United States, west of the river Mississippi . . . to which the Indian title has been extinguished . . . to be divided into a suitable number of districts for the reception of such tribes or nations of Indians . . . provided always, that such lands shall revert to the United States if the Indians become extinct or abandon the same.

In his First Annual Message to Congress on December 8, 1830, President Jackson justified Indian removal by outlining the benefits to the American people while assuming the advantages to the Native tribes. By sending Indians "to a land where their existence may be prolonged and *perhaps* made perpetual," the United States was making it possible for them to now be able to "pursue happiness in their own way and under their own rude institutions." However, the provisions of the act guaranteeing land forever were in doubt less than seven months after ratification. To the American people, Jackson promised a republic "studded with cities, towns, and prosperous farms, . . . occupied by more than 12,000,000 happy people" and obtained "by a speedy removal to relieve [the Indians] from all the evils, real or imaginary . . . with which they may be supposed to be threatened." It was the prelude to manifest destiny and the preamble to the Trail of Tears.

Secretary of War Lewis Cass (known as "Big Belly") negotiated a treaty with the Creeks for the cession of their lands in compliance with the Indian Removal Act. The treaty was intended to give the Creeks an option to remove to the Indian Territory or stay on allotments, which they could then sell after a five-year period. This, in addition to a solemn agreement of freedom in the Indian Territory, was the basis of the Treaty of Washington in 1832. It would not take long for the provisions of the treaty to fall apart. The U.S. government's inability and unwillingness to enforce the document led to massive intrusion by countless settlers and rampant fraud by unscrupulous land speculators perpetrated against Indians ignorant of the workings of business.

A contract was granted to J. W. A. Sanford and Company, among others, to provide transportation and sustenance for those Creeks traveling to their new home in the Indian Territory, located in what is now Oklahoma and Kansas. The Indian Territory was composed of just less than 20 million acres, of which the Creeks received just more than 3 million acres. In addition, the tribe received the sum of $2,275,000.

Sanford received $20 for each Indian relocated, with a prorated amount allocated for those that died or by necessity had to be abandoned along the way. The company typically traveled from 12 to 15 miles per day, depending on conditions, at roughly two miles per hour. The Indians carried with them coals or ashes from their town fires to be rekindled at their new home. Foul weather slowed progress and increased the hardship experienced by the people. Because of the generally mild climate of Alabama, the Creeks had only fair-weather clothing with them. Falling temperatures in an unknown land resulted in more deaths from the cold. An estimated 3,500 Creeks died along the trail, including nearly all infants and many elderly.

Throughout it all, life went on, including childbirth and death. Those who died along the trail were often covered with brush and left to be consumed by wolves. Food was scarce due in part to the emigrating company's failure to provide the necessary rations. The daily ration was supposed to be one pound of fresh beef, three fourths of a quart of corn, and four quarts of salt per 100 rations. Horses and oxen received eight quarts of corn per day. But profit was more important than sustenance: What supplies did exist were sold at exorbitant prices.

Of the many trails west from Alabama, most passed through the Arkansas Territory. After a time,

local residents grew more and more resentful of their presence, temporary though it was. The food and provisions that the Creeks were forced to buy at elevated prices depleted the inventories that were available to the townspeople. The increased traffic deteriorated the roads to the point of needing repair. There were allegations of theft of livestock and fears of violence. The territorial governor was called upon to control the situation. Arkansans were relieved at their departure.

Adaptation to new surroundings in the Indian Territory proved a difficult challenge. The past decades had created a widening chasm between the Upper and Lower Creeks. Some wished to embrace the modern era and others longed for their roots. Thousands of Creek people died on the journey west, and thousands more died within a year of their arrival in the Indian Territory.

The Indian Territory was established by the U.S. government for the exclusive use of the numerous Indian tribes that were scattered throughout the country. The Choctaw first used the term *oklahoma* in the middle 1860s; *okla* meaning "people" and *homma* meaning "red." The Indian Territory extended as far north as the Platte River in Nebraska and as far south as the Red River in Texas. Referred to as a territory, it never had territorial status with the federal government, although there were several congressional proposals.

The Creeks made the Indian Territory home. Governments were formed, schools were established, and farms were producing with slave labor. They built transportation systems, founded towns, published newspapers, and generally assimilated into a western way of life. All this, in spite of the increasing gap between the Creek factions and the fact that those responsible for supplying provisions to the tribes were cheating them. Food, clothing, and other essentials supposed to be delivered by the government ended up on the black market and sold at outrageous prices. Farm tools and other equipment never arrived, forcing the Indians to use makeshift tools to plant their crops.

In spite of all this, the Creek people began to flourish. Notwithstanding their progress, the Creeks were still looked upon as unwanted intruders and confrontations were common. The discovery of gold in the West lured thousands of fortune seekers across

Creek land and the army was called in to quash skirmishes with some frequency.

Still, the Creeks fought for their independence and sovereignty. The Upper and Lower Creeks periodically met in a general council to discuss common issues, and in one such meeting, they adopted a constitution. The most singular provision to be included in the Constitution of 1860 was the abolishment of the two-faction system and the adoption of one central body, referred to as the Muscogee Nation. This new dominion was to be led by a principal chief and a second chief elected by the entire unified nation, and the constitution provided for a police force (called Light Horse), judicial districts, a high court, and a national council.

It is not surprising that, at the start of the Civil War, the Confederate government took an interest in the Indian Territory. The area's strategic position was obvious on an open map. Many Creeks felt the U.S. government had abandoned them to the Indian Territory, and the Confederates, eager to ally themselves with the several tribes, opened negotiations to secure their fealty. Confederate Commissioner Albert Pike promised the Creeks protection against Union aggression "so long as grass shall grow and water run," recognizing them as wards and accepting all rights and privileges granted them under U.S. treaties in exchange for military assistance against the Union army. They could also keep their slaves.

In the 16th and 17th centuries, Indians of all tribes were subjected to enslavement by their conquerors. In the early 18th century, the emphasis turned more to Africans rather than Indians. The New World was not new to the Natives. This was their home, and they were intimately familiar with the surrounding areas. They could easily disappear into the wilderness, never to be found again. Africans, on the other hand, were in a foreign land. They had nowhere to hide, and their unique color made them easy to identify.

Runaway black slaves were often captured by the Creeks, but in most cases were returned to their owners. Up until the Revolutionary War, the Creeks had no desire to keep blacks as slaves for themselves, but that was to change. The Creeks began taking in runaways during that war due, in part, to the growing number of mixed blood families whose European side was more familiar with the concept of slavery. The Treaty of Paris in 1783 ceded all previously held British lands to the United States, thereby ending all trade with the vanquished, but the Americans found it difficult to recover their property from the Creeks.

Slaves were not treated as harshly by the Creeks as they were by the British and Americans. They were treated more as brethren. They had freedom of movement throughout the land, were permitted to own property, and were expected to support themselves. There were inequalities, however. The Creeks had their own form of slave codes, one stating that, "if a Negro kill an Indian, the Negro shall suffer death. And if an Indian kill a Negro he shall pay the owner to the value." There was also an aversion to teaching blacks Christianity. Ultimately, some 1,600 black slaves settled with the Creek people after removal to the Indian Territory.

Not all Creeks were in favor of joining the Confederacy. There still existed a division between the Upper and Lower Creek factions and, as in the past, they could not ally themselves against a common enemy. Upper Creeks loyal to Chief Opothleyaholo wished to remain neutral, but ended up fighting a different kind of Civil War against the Confederate First Creek Regiment under Colonel Chilly McIntosh in the Indian Territory. The battles that ensued were not so much Confederate versus Union as they were Confederate versus independent nation. In the end, Confederate forces defeated Opothleyaholo's small band, but the Union prevailed with the victory at the Battle of Pea Ridge in March of 1862.

In the aftermath of the Civil War, the Creeks were made to pay for their allegiance with the Confederacy. Reconstruction in the Indian Territory meant the seizure and redistribution of lands as a penalty for violating the treaties struck with the United States. The Treaty of 1866 compelled the Creeks to live in peace with the United States and with their Indian neighbors, to abolish slavery in the Indian Territory, to relinquish a portion of their land to tribes from other areas, and to agree to a policy of unification into one consolidated government among all the tribes. In addition, the United States was permitted to build railroads through the land. As a result, the Creeks were forced to sell 200,000 acres to the Seminoles for $0.50 per acre and to sell 3,250,000 acres to the federal government for $0.30 per acre. The Creek nation was cut in half and forced to move again.

The effort to consolidate all Indian tribes into one government resulted in the passage of the Dawes Act of 1887, also known as the General Allotment Act. The purpose of the Dawes Act was to assign specific tracts of land to each individual and open up huge parcels of excess land to outside settlers. It also abolished tribal courts and gave the United States legal jurisdiction over the people. The Creeks were exempt from the 1887 act, but were made subject to its provisions in 1893 by the Dawes Commission, which was empowered to negotiate for the "extinguishment of the national or tribal title to any lands now held." This again forced the Creeks to relocate their homes.

The vote in Congress on the Dawes Allotment Act was far from unanimous. A report prepared by the House Committee on Indian Affairs states, "The real aim of this bill is to get at the Indian lands and open them to settlement. . . . If this were done in the name of greed, it would be bad enough; but to do it in the name of humanity . . . is infinitely worse."

Under the Dawes Allotment Act, 160 acres would be allotted to the head of a family, 80 acres to a single person over the age of 18, and 40 acres to single people under the age of 18. This included black freedmen. In addition, U.S. citizenship was granted all those who signed the Dawes roll. Two million acres of land not allotted to individuals, the so-called unassigned lands, were purchased from the Creeks and opened to white settlement. Restrictions were attached to ensure Indian rights were preserved, but in 1907, when Oklahoma achieved statehood, these restrictions were lifted in favor of the endless emigration of white settlers to the western lands.

Other acts of Congress further reduced the size of Creek holdings and diminished the sovereignty over their own land. The Curtis Act in 1906 diminished the roll of tribal government, dissolving tribal courts and laws. The Burke Act, also in 1906, abolished the 25-year trust established by the Dawes Act to assure Native management of their land. A proposed act to establish the state of Sequoyah was replaced in Congress by the act to combine the Indian Territory and the Oklahoma Territory into one state, Oklahoma, which was admitted into the union in 1907. By 1908, all documents relating to the Creek nation were turned over to the U.S. Indian Agency and all property transferred to the direction of the secretary of the interior.

With the closing of the Dawes rolls in 1906, all those who enrolled were officially citizens of the United States. And with the dissolution of the tribal system, the Creeks were once again assimilating into a new culture. They embraced their citizenship to the point of fighting their new country's wars. Creek participation in the colonial, Revolutionary, and Civil Wars was largely calculated for their own preservation. Allying with the winning side brought about more hope of freedom than not. As citizens of the United States, fighting for one's country took on a whole new meaning.

As citizens, the Creeks were subject to the draft, as well as to the consequences of avoiding it. Creeks not holding American citizenship volunteered. The entrance of American soldiers in World War I included some 13,000 American Indians (about 25 percent of all adult Indian men, as opposed to 15 percent of all other adult American men), including 600 in the Thirty-Sixth Division of the American Expeditionary Forces from the state of Oklahoma. Unlike black soldiers sent to fight, the Indians were not segregated, but dispersed throughout the army. Any noncitizen who returned from the war with an honorable discharge was automatically granted American citizenship.

The Creek home front was not to be undone, as seen in acts of patriotism and violence. In 1918, a gang of some 200 Creeks reportedly attacked and killed three Oklahoma citizens protesting the drafting of their sons into the army, and Tsianina Redfeather volunteered to go to France and entertain the troops at the front.

World War II had its share of Creek Indian participation, including First Sergeant Ernest "Chief" Childers of the Forty-Fifth Infantry Division, U.S. Army (formed in 1920), who earned the Medal of Honor for bravery in Italy in 1943. And, although the Navaho tribe is spoken of more frequently, the Creeks were active as code talkers in the Pacific Theater.

Through the years, the Creek Indians have struggled in Oklahoma. Census records show a gradual decrease in population through the first half of the 20th century. At the close of the 18th century, the Creek population was estimated at between 25,000 and 30,000 people. In the early 1830s, prior to removal, census records reported a little more than 21,000, and about 15,000 Creeks survived removal in the late 1830s. The Office of Indian Affairs took a census in 1857 that included 14,888 Creeks. By 1915, that number had fallen to 11,967, and in 1944 to 9,900.

In the meantime, the population of whites in Oklahoma was on the rise. In 1890, the white population of Oklahoma was 109,393, and by 1907 had increased to 538,512. The period after allotment was a time of chaos and abuse within the Creek nation. Restrictions in the Dawes Act prevented Creeks from selling their land for a period of 25 years, but they were permitted to lease it. After Oklahoma statehood, these restrictions were lifted, and many Creeks elected to sell their land to white speculators. Others who did not want to sell were often cheated out of it through their ignorance of the law. The discovery of oil on Creek property only intensified the efforts to move the Creeks off their land.

The period of the 1930s brought more hardships to the Creek people. They were not immune to the Great Depression and the droughts that brought about the Dust Bowl further hindered their survival. It was not until after World War II that fortunes began to turn: Many Creeks who returned from serving their country migrated to the cities to begin their lives anew. But in the period between 1907 and 1970, the Creeks lost an additional 2 million acres of land to whites.

In 1957, the U.S. government instituted a program to educate American Indians and send them to work in major cities around the country. This relocation program offered Creeks an opportunity to live beyond their known boundaries. Many people have been taught trades at schools such as the Haskell Indian Nations University in Lawrence, Kansas. Originally opened to 22 students as the United States Indian Industrial Training School in 1884, Haskell taught boys such subjects as tailoring, wagon making, blacksmithing, and farming, while girls learned cooking, sewing, and homemaking. Today, the university is open to 1,000 students each semester and offers a curriculum in business administration, environmental science, elementary teacher education, and American Indian studies.

In 1971, Congress granted the Creek people the right to elect their own principal chief and govern their own affairs. Prior to this time, as established in the Oklahoma Indian Welfare Act of 1936, the President of the United States appointed the principal chief, who was nothing more than a figurehead. A new Creek constitution was written establishing a form of government including executive, legislative, and judicial branches. By 1980, Creek citizenship was in excess of 28,000, and the 1990 census recorded 45,872 Creeks.

Today the Creek nation is a thriving community of 59,000 scattered throughout the world. The annual Green Corn Ceremony still takes place during the late summer corn harvest in Oklahoma. It continues to be a time of reflection and renewal among the clans of the 16 fires still burning within the nation (initially 44 Tribal Towns, or fires, were established in Oklahoma after resettlement in the 1830s). The nation offers its members a range of community service departments, including social services, children and family services, food distribution program, child care, employment and training, and cultural preservation. A Creek language archive is maintained to teach and reinforce the Creek natural language and that of others in the Muskhogean linguistic dialects. Anyone can go online and learn the language.

The Division of Tribal Affairs looks to the future by seeking out business ventures and development opportunities. The Housing Authority Board of Commissioners helps the membership with lease and purchase programs, affordable housing, and maintenance programs.

The Creek nation publishes the *Muscogee Nation News* on a monthly basis. In addition to national and tribal news, the *News* spotlights messages from the principal and second chiefs, and runs features on education, health, housing, culture, government, job opportunities, sports, and tribal history.

Outside Oklahoma, Creek heritage is kept alive by organizations and groups of Creek citizens. The Southern California Indian Center was chartered in

1969 to promote social and economic self-sufficiency for all tribes. The center focuses on general welfare programs, education, Indian culture, and the elimination of discrimination. The California Creek Association meets monthly and is attended by Creek citizens two and three generations after removal. The meetings are social in nature, always including a potluck lunch, and designed to be educational as well as practical. The association is an outlet for tribal information important to Creek citizens.

Members of the California Creek Association receive help in obtaining information from the Dawes rolls and are encouraged to obtain their Creek citizenship. Citizens are distributed polls and surveys that come from the Creek nation headquarters on topics such as constitutional amendments. They receive monthly lessons on a Creek historical topic and are offered assistance in Creek nation and U.S. voter registration.

Creek history is one of perpetual motion. Since before the coming of the European, the Creeks have voluntarily, by necessity, or forcibly been moved throughout North America and the world. They have been attacked from the outside by foreign invaders and they have fought each other in civil war. Through it all, the Creeks as a people have built and sustained their culture and heritage and always found a way to survive. The annual busk is celebrated and their fire is renewed. In the end, the Creeks remain faithful to the Master of Breath, and stay together as a family and never forget.

—*Neal Lynch*

See also INDIAN REMOVAL ACT OF 1830, TRAIL OF TEARS

Suggested Reading

"The American Indian in the Great War: Real and Imagined." Available from http://raven.cc.ukans.edu/~ww_one/comment/camurat1.html

"Before Creek and Cherokee: The Colonial Transformation of Prehistoric Georgia." Available from http://members.aol.com/jeworth.gbotxt.htm

"The Bluejacket." Available from http://www.nsamidsouth.navy.mil/publications/bluejacket/2002/bj021128.htm

Calloway, Colin G. *The American Revolution in Indian Country.* Cambridge, UK: Cambridge University Press, 1995.

Caughey, John Walton. *McGillivray of the Creeks.* Norman: University of Oklahoma Press, 1959.

"Census Report." Available from http://www.census.gov/population/socdemo/race/indian/ailang1.txt

Corkran, David H. *The Creek Frontier, 1540–1783.* Norman: University of Oklahoma Press, 1967.

"Creek Indians." Available from http://www.rra.dst.txt.us/c_t/indians/CREEK%20INDIANS.cfm

Debo, Angie. *The Road to Disappearance.* Norman: University of Oklahoma Press. 1941.

Ethridge, Robbie. *Creek Country: The Creek Indians and Their World.* Chapel Hill: University of North Carolina Press, 2003.

Gatschet, Albert S. *A Migration Legend of the Creek Indians.* Philadelphia: D. G. Brinton, 1884.

Green, Michael D. *The Creeks: A Critical Bibliography.* Bloomington: Indiana University Press, 1979.

Green, Michael D. *The Politics of Indian Removal: Creek Government and Society in Crisis.* Lincoln: University of Nebraska Press, 1982.

Gibson, Arrell Morgan. *The American Indian: Prehistory to the Present.* Lexington, MA: D. C. Heath, 1980.

Hahn, Steven C. *The Invention of the Creek Nation, 1670–1763.* Lincoln: University of Nebraska Press, 2004.

Haskell Indian Nations University Web Site. Available from http://www.haskell.edu/haskell/about.asp

"How the Clans Came to Be." Available from http://www.indianlegend.com/cdreek/creek_001.htm

"The Indian Removal Act of 1830." Available from http://www.thebearbyte.com/NAResource/RemovalAct.htm

"Indian Territory." Available from http://www.nativeamericanrhymes.com/library/territory.htm

Jahoda, Gloria. *The Trail of Tears.* New York: Wings Books, 1975.

Lewis, David, Jr., and Ann T. Jordan. *Creek Indian Medicine Ways: The Enduring Power of Muskoke Religion.* Albuquerque: University of New Mexico Press, 2002.

Littlefield, Daniel F., Jr. *Africans and Creeks: From the Colonial Period to the Civil War.* Westport, CT: Greenwood, 1979.

Muscogee (Creek) Nation of Oklahoma Web Site. Available from http://www.muscogeenation-nsn.gov

Piker, Joshua. *Okfuskee: A Creek Town in Colonial America.* Cambridge, MA: Harvard University Press, 2004.

"President Andrew Jackson's Case for The Removal Act, First Annual Message to Congress, 8 December 1830." Available from http://www.mtholyoke.edu/acad/intrel/andrew.htm

Prucha, Francis Paul. *American Indian Treaties: The History of a Political Anomaly.* Berkeley: University of California Press, 1994.

Saunt, Claudio. *Black, White, and Indian: Race and the Unmaking of an American Family.* New York: Oxford University Press, 2005.

Saunt, Claudio. *A New Order of Things: Property, Power, and the Transformation of the Creek Indians, 1733–1816.* New York: Cambridge University Press, 1999.

Southern California Indian Center Web Site. Available from http://www.indiancenter.org

Speck, Frank G. *The Creek Indians of Taskigi Town.* Washington, DC: Bureau of American Ethnology, 1904.

Tebbel, John, and Keith Jennison. *The American Indian Wars.* London: Phoenix Press, 2001.

Todd, Helen. *Mary Musgrove: Georgia Indian Princess.* Chicago: Adams Press, 1981.

"Traditions of the Creeks: Story of Their Trek from Mexico More Than Three Centuries Ago." Available from http://anpa.ualr .edu/digital_library/jrg_1/1.htm

"The Trail of Tears: A Chronicle, 1830–1849." Available from http://anpa.ualr.edu/trail_of_tears/indian_removal_project/ a_chronicle/a_chronicle.htm

Weatherford, Jack. *Indian Givers: How the Indians of the Americas Transformed the World.* New York: Fawcett Columbine, 1988.

Wright, J. Leitch, Jr. *Creeks and Seminoles: The Destruction and Regeneration of the Muscogulge People.* Lincoln: University of Nebraska Press, 1986.

Wright, Muriel. *A Guide to the Indian Tribes of Oklahoma.* Norman: University of Oklahoma Press, 1951.

CRIPPLE CREEK, COLORADO

The reputations of most boomtowns are based on hyperbole. Butte, Montana, was the "richest hill on earth." Dawson City in the Yukon was the site of the "Last, Best Gold Rush." Cripple Creek, Colorado, was both the "Greatest Gold Camp on Earth" and "the White Man's Gold Camp." While the former is debatable, the latter was never an exaggeration.

Although rumors of gold had abounded since 1873, gold was not discovered in amounts large enough to pay until April 1891. Even then, because of an earlier hoax, it took a good deal of evidence to convince people that Cripple Creek had any kind of mining future. Rancher Bob Womack, not dissuaded by the area's dubious reputation and difficult topography, prospected the area around Mount Pisgah, just west of Pike's Peak, through the late 1880s. During the winter of 1890–1891, he discovered a large ore deposit and the next spring and summer witnessed a small influx of prospectors. That year, production reached about $200,000, but it was enough that soon thousands more miners headed to the new high-altitude gold camp (most of the mines were situated at 10,000 feet or more above sea level). One new arrival was Winfield

Scott Stratton, who developed what became one of the richest mines in the area, the Independence Mine. Two others, James Burns and Irving Howbert, owned the Portland Mine, which eventually produced nearly $3 million in gold, making it Colorado's most prosperous gold mine. The fame and fortunes of Stratton, Burns, and Howbert attracted others, and soon there was enough gold production in Cripple Creek to support a local stock exchange. In 1893–1894 alone, mines in the Cripple Creek district produced $2 million in gold.

The town of Cripple Creek was established officially in 1893 when the towns of Fremont and Hayden Placer merged. Fremont had been established two years earlier on Horace Bennett's and Julius Myers' Broken Box Ranch, near Womack's original claim. Hayden Placer, as the name suggests, was a town platted on a former placer mine. Soon after, the towns of Victor, Goldfield, Independence, and Anaconda were established, all within the Cripple Creek mining district.

The population of the Cripple Creek district mushroomed in a way similar to other mining areas. In 1890, there were 450 people in the area. Three years later, there were 8,000. By 1900, there were 13,000 in Cripple Creek proper and 32,000 people in the district. When the boom waned in 1910, the population of the district dropped to 19,000 then to 7,000 in 1920. By 1930, Teller County numbered 4,000 residents. As the century wore on, Cripple Creek's population steadily declined to 2,000 by 1950, then 1,300 in 1960, and leveling out to 1,100 people in 2000.

Unlike many other gold towns across the western states, however, Cripple Creek was never a multiethnic place. From its inception, citizens envisioned a town where labor would not be divided by racial and ethnic tensions, and so they worked hard to live up to the pseudonym "The White Man's Gold Camp." And they were largely successful. In 1900, nearly 80 percent of the population of the Cripple Creek district was born in the United States. The few who reported foreign birth were mostly natives of Ireland, Canada, England, Sweden, Germany, Scotland, Wales, and France. By 1910, there was a small group of Finns as well. Like ethnic groups in other western communities, they established local chapters of societies like the Irish Ancient Order of Hibernians, the Scottish Lodge of the Royal Highlanders, and the Swedish Belmont Club.

They planned celebrations for St. Patrick's Day and Robert Burns' Day, but these immigrant groups were all small enough that none of them formed a separate enclave. They were immigrants, to be sure, but immigrants of a very particular "complexion." To put it another way, the census shows a 90 to 95 percent Caucasian population throughout Cripple Creek's history.

In part, this racial homogeneity was due to the efforts of the unions. The Western Federation of Miners, the United Mine Workers, and the Western Labor Union relentlessly preached about the dangers of foreign labor on wages and working conditions. Union leaders encouraged union activists to exclude foreign-born ethnic groups and immigrant labor to prevent labor competition and to protect wages. As a result Chinese, Greeks, Italians, Slavs, and Mexicans were prohibited from moving into Cripple Creek by miners forming blockades in the streets to prevent them from entering town. Individuals who were (or who were perceived to be) of those ethnic groups were turned around and escorted back to the depot, where they were ordered to take the next train back over the pass to Colorado Springs. At national union meetings, Cripple Creek labor leaders boasted that they did not have trouble with foreign labor because there was none in the district.

There were exceptions of course. Joseph and Alexander Gandolpho were fruit candy merchants who were naturalized Americans of Italian birth. They established a small store in Cripple Creek in 1895. The historical record is silent on how this Italian immigrant family was received, but within three years, Joseph left Colorado to join the Klondike gold rush, taking with him a stock of eight tons of oranges, lemons, bananas, and cucumbers that he sold to fruit-starved miners for $1 apiece. Alexander kept the original store going in Cripple Creek until he joined his brother in the Yukon in 1900, taking the remaining inventory of the Cripple Creek store with him.

Union activists may not have bothered the Gandolphos because they were clearly not interested in mining, although there are many stories of Chinese, Mexicans, and African American businesses being boycotted by local residents to discourage them from settling in town. Italians, Greeks, Mexican, and Asians were also barred from union admittance and were therefore unable to work in the mines except as scabs during strikes. This effectively maintained the ethnic complexion of "The White Man's Gold Camp." Most southern Europeans, Mexicans, and Asians looked for more hospitable environs in which to establish themselves and their families, much as the unions had hoped they would.

The one part of town that the unions did little to interfere with was the red-light district, and it was there that a wider variety of ethnic groups lived and worked. While American-born residents like Kitty Henry (who like the Gandolphos, soon left for the Klondike) were the majority, Mexican, Chinese, Japanese, French, British, and African American women worked as prostitutes and dance hall performers to "mine the miners" in Cripple Creek. Male African American, Mexican, Japanese, and Chinese musicians, bartenders, waiters, and procurers migrated in and out of Cripple Creek making their living in conjunction with their female ethnic counterparts.

Given Cripple Creek's overtly nativist climate, it is perhaps not surprising that the largest non-white ethnic group was African American—more than 300 in 1900. As the largest visible minority, and relegated almost exclusively to the demimonde, this group was often in the news. The May 16, 1899, issue of the *Cripple Creek Weekly Tribune* reported, for example, "a colored free-for-all on Myers Avenue last night between 4th and 5th Streets in which even some women were mixed." Likewise, stories of the nefarious activities of Chinese opium den operators abounded in the period.

After the boom waned, and despite the need for more economic diversity, ethnic and racial groups that persisted were expected to work within prescribed fields. For African American men, this meant barbering, bartending, waiting, and other similar positions. For African American women, it continued to mean prostitution and domestic service. According to the *Cripple Creek Weekly Tribune* in April of 1911, "'Aunt Jane' the aged colored lady, well known to the police here, got in bad again. She was found guilty in police court yesterday of drunkenness and disorderly conduct and was fined $1.00 and costs. She will be permitted to work out her fine in cleaning up the jail. At this she is said to be first class."

The census supports the anecdotal evidence. In 1900, there were 310 African Americans living in

Cripple Creek and a grand total of 5 Asians, almost all of whom lived and worked in the red-light district. By 1910, most African Americans had moved on to bigger cities in the West, but the census showed 32 Greeks, 3 Italians, and 13 Asians and "others." By 1930, not a single native of Greece, Italy, Japan, or China appeared on the Cripple Creek census.

Nor did the complexion of Cripple Creek or the attitude of locals change once the heyday of the mining boom ended. A small community of Hispanic families settled on the fringes of the community after World War II. This small enclave lived in several abandoned railway cars on the mountainside between Cripple Creek and Victor in the 1950s. These families were "allowed" to come into town to sell tamales and other food as well as to take in laundry from local families. Residents remember that Mexicans were not welcome in town after dark. Because no one would rent to them, they squatted in the railcars on the abandoned rail line well above town.

Native Americans, African Americans, Mexicans, Chinese, and Japanese people were not just excluded from working in the mines; they were prevented from working in other local businesses and from establishing their own enterprises in Cripple Creek. Even today, townsfolk remember that people of color were unable to sustain their businesses in town because locals refused to patronize their businesses.

At the turn of the 20th century, that "White Man's Camp" called Cripple Creek was hardly what most people would consider a camp at all. Almost from its inception, it had a railway line that boasted more than 10 trains a day. A half-day journey from Colorado Springs and a day's journey from Denver, Cripple Creek enjoyed all the modern amenities and conveniences of the day. It boasted electric lights and telephones almost from its incorporation. Electric interurban cars soon tied Cripple Creek to its neighboring mining cities of Victor and Independence. It was an industrial city, with mine owners and mine workers, kings of industry and knights of labor. Its industrial structure, with owners and workers, rich and poor, scabs and union workers, accounted for its fiercely protected, American-born majority. Local residents were—and are—proud of its "white" complexion. They worked hard to create it and even harder to maintain it.

The trains stopped running in and out of Cripple Creek in 1949. Four years later, the depot reopened as a museum, and it remains in operation today. The population dropped through the post–World War II years, and soon the empty storefronts and Victorian mansions made Cripple Creek a tourist attraction as a ghost town. It remained so until October of 1991, when limited-stakes gambling became legal in Cripple Creek, ushering in a new era for the local economy. The gold mines have continued to operate, on and off, when the price of gold has been high, and gold production continues to be an integral part of the local economy today. Interestingly, according to the 2000 census, the population of Cripple Creek (1,115 individuals) is almost exactly the same as it was a century earlier: 92.29 percent white.

—*Charlene Porsild*

See also Denver, Pueblo, Boulder, Fort Collins, and Colorado Springs, Colorado

Suggested Reading

Abbott, Carl, Stephen J. Leonard, and David McComb. *Colorado: A History of the Centennial State.* Boulder: Colorado Associate University Press, 1982.

Jameson, Elizabeth. *All That Glitters: Class, Conflict, and Community in Cripple Creek.* Urbana: University of Illinois, 1998.

Lee, Mabel Barbee. *Cripple Creek Days.* Lincoln: University of Nebraska Press, 1958.

Levine, Brian. *Cripple Creek-Victor Mining District.* Colorado Springs: Century One, 1987.

MacKell, Jan. *Cripple Creek District: Last of Colorado's Gold Booms.* Charleston, NC: Arcadia, 2003.

Sprague, Marshall. *Money Mountain.* Lincoln: University of Nebraska Press, 1953.

CROW NATION

The Crow Indian tribe originated in the southeastern United States. As with numerous other tribes, the Crow moved west onto the Great Plains in the 1600s and 1700s due to pressure from English and other European settlers. After first living with the Hidatsa on the upper Missouri River, conflict with that tribe led them to migrate further west to Canada, Utah, and Oklahoma before eventually reaching the Rocky Mountains. By 1700, they had finally settled in the Yellowstone River region in what is today Montana. One of their chiefs had had a vision in which the Great Spirit gave him sacred seeds and told him to head to the big mountains and plant them. This would allow his people to grow in population and strength. By 1800, the Crow had adopted the nomadic and warlike Plains Indian way of life, which was created in part because of the acquisition of guns from French and English settlers to the east and horses from Spanish settlers to the south.

As the United States expanded west, an inevitable clash took place between American settlers and nomadic Plains Indians such as the Crow. Pioneer trails before the Civil War and railroads after began cutting across the Great Plains. However, it was the lure of gold that led to the opening of the Bozeman Trail through Wyoming and into Montana in 1864. The trail was dotted with forts at locations such as Fort Laramie and Fort Phil Kearney in order to protect pioneers and gold seekers. Nevertheless, it was around this time that the Crow made a strategic decision to ally with the Americans against larger and better-armed tribes, such as the westward-expanding Sioux and Blackfoot, in order to preserve their homeland and way of life to the extent that they could. By 1865, the Crow had been pushed about as far west as possible without being driven off the plains completely. The following year, 81 soldiers who had left Fort Phil Kearney to defend a wood train under attack by the Sioux were killed in what became known as the Fetterman Massacre.

The possibility that the United States would abandon the Bozeman Trail as a result of the massacre helped further drive the Crow into an alliance with the Americans. Captain Nathaniel C. Kinney, commander of Fort C. F. Smith along the Bozeman Trail, hired 10 Crows as scouts and spies in January of 1867. In February, Long Horse, The Bear in the Water, The Dog That Bats His Eye, and Iron Bull agreed to work as Crow army couriers for $33 per month. A Crow delegation attended peace talks at Fort Laramie in November of 1867. Crow leaders like Bear's Tooth and Blackfoot expressed concern about U.S. presence on the Bozeman Trail and subsequent actions, such as cutting down trees and the killing and wasting of wild game. The delegation did not mention the previous main concern of removing the Sioux from the area. The Crow had come to believe that preserving their way of life and not moving on to a reservation were at least as important as being rid of their tribal enemies. The Americans refused to abandon the Bozeman Trail and nothing was accomplished in 1867. However, in February of 1868, the U.S. government did abandon the trail. The Sioux, Arapaho, and Crow later signed the 1868 Treaty of Fort Laramie. The Crow surrendered all of their land in Wyoming and in parts of Montana. They received a reservation in southeast Montana, as well as doctors, teachers, provisions, and the assistance essential in converting to a settled way of life. Land sales eventually reduced the reservation and left it in several pieces.

In 1910, the first Crow Business Committee was formed and included future reservation superintendent Robert Yellowtail. He served as an interpreter between the Crow and Congress during visits to Washington, DC, in 1915, 1916, and 1917 in an effort to stop Montana politicians from opening the Crow Indian Reservation to homestead farming. Yellowtail was also instrumental in the passage of the Crow Act of 1920, which divided nonallotted Crow land among mostly Crow tribe members. In 1920 coal mining, and in 1930 gas production, started on the reservation. Income from natural resources such as these and oil leasing would eventually become primary sources of income for the Crow people.

In 1934, Commissioner of Indian Affairs John Collier appointed Yellowtail superintendent of the Crow Indian Reservation. As superintendent, he brought in new breeds of livestock and transplanted bison and elk onto the reservation. Among other changes to the reservation under Yellowtail were the building of reservoirs, roads, and mountain trails as well as the introduction of logging, improvements in health care, and increased agricultural activities and ranching. He resigned as superintendent in 1945, but was later involved in the writing and passage of the 1948 Crow tribal constitution and then elected tribal chairman in 1952.

The biggest challenge of his career was a fight over building a dam on the Bighorn River. The controversy began in 1944 when Congress authorized a dam for irrigation and hydroelectric power. Many of the Crow were concerned about environmental damage from flooding. Ironically, the proposal became known as the Yellowtail Dam, even though the Crow tribal chairman was against it. There were members of the Crow people who supported the idea, however, and who were known as the River Crows, while those opposed were called the Mountain Crows. The River Crows wanted to sell the site for $5 million, but the Mountain Crows favored leasing the site for 50 years. Eventually, the River Crow plan was passed in the tribal council and Congress authorized payment, but President Eisenhower vetoed the bill in 1956. Eisenhower signed a subsequent bill with a payment of only $2.5 million in 1958. The Yellowtail Dam was completed six years later.

Women have had an important role in recent Crow leadership. Although the Crow have been self-governing with a constitution and tribal council for decades, it was not until the 1980s and the efforts of Janine Pease Pretty on Top that they won the right to serve in local government beyond the reservation in Montana. In 1986, she was the lead plaintiff in a lawsuit brought before the Federal District Court in Billings against Bighorn County in Montana. The resulting decision caused a reorganization of county commissioner and school district trustee zones, allowing Crow Indian candidates to win election to these posts. Meanwhile, Clara Nomee was the first woman to hold the office of chair of the tribal council and served an unprecedented five terms.

As with other tribes, the Crow have attempted to maintain their traditional language and culture. The majority of people on the Crow Indian Reservation spoke only the Crow language until the 1930s. Today, however, the majority speaks only English. Documenting Crow place names on the reservation, in Montana, and across the United States as well as the stories behind them is one way to preserve the ancestral tongue. Working with Timothy McCleary, a Little Big Horn College general studies instructor, 20 Crow elders have come up with 500 Crow place names since the late 1990s. In contrast to English names, which usually emphasize people or events, Crow names typically reflect physical characteristics of a particular place. Crow elders Barney Old Coyote, Phil Beaumont, Joe

Medicine Crow, and Mickey Old Coyote were instrumental in recalling and documenting numerous Crow stories. Dates are not as important in the stories as details of what happened at a certain butte or stream.

While alcohol addiction has been a persistent problem on many reservations for years, on the Crow Reservation, dependency on methamphetamines, or "crank," has become an epidemic. A program called Crow Detox in Crow Agency, Montana, uses both traditional and modern techniques to deal with drug abuse. Funded by the Crow tribe, Crow Detox also works with Indian Health Services and public health services. However, the number of successful recoveries has been minimal. There are several reasons for methamphetamine addiction on the Crow Indian Reservation. First, the drug can be made with household kitchen products that are easily accessible. Second, due to the small and spread-out population of Montana, dealers of more expensive narcotics do not view the state and its reservations as a lucrative market. However, the readily available ingredients of methamphetamines make it the drug of choice. Fast, easy, and potentially big profits are also attractive to people without many educational or economic opportunities (the government is the largest employer of the Crow people).

In 2001, the Crow tribe ratified a new constitution, the preamble of which states,

> We, the adult members of the Crow Tribe of Indians located on the Crow Indian Reservation as established by the Fort Laramie Treaties of 1851 and 1866, in an effort to enforce and exercise our treaty rights, our inherent sovereign rights, to secure certain privileges and retain inherent powers do hereby adopt this Constitution to create a governing body to represent the members of the Crow Tribe of Indians, to promote the general welfare of the Crow Tribe and to provide for the lawful operation of government.

Enrollment in the tribe is limited to those with at least one Crow grandparent, and membership in any other tribe must be given up in writing. The new constitution emphasizes direct democracy, as all adult enrolled members of the tribe 18 years of age or older and entitled to vote are part of the governing Crow Tribal General Council. The council meets twice a year to receive information from the executive and legislative branches and to vote on initiatives, referendums, and removing officials. The executive branch is currently made up of Chairman Carl Venne; Vice Chairman Vincent Goes Ahead, Jr.; Secretary Larney Little Owl; and Vice Secretary Hubert Two Leggins. All executive branch office holders are limited to two four-year terms. The legislative branch is composed of three members elected by the council from each of the six Crow Indian Reservation districts. Legislative terms are also for four years. Article XI of the constitution is a bill of rights very similar to that in the U.S. Constitution and includes protections for freedom of worship, speech, the press, association, and individual property. There is no protection of the right to bear arms, however. Amendments are passed by a two thirds vote of the Crow Tribal General Council, as long as at least 30 percent of the council participated in an election called to amend the constitution.

For years, one of the most famous and historically significant locations in the American West has been the Custer Battlefield on the Crow Indian Reservation. In the 1990s, the name of the Custer Battlefield was changed to the Little Bighorn Battlefield in order to honor war dead on both sides. The site commemorates the Sioux rout of George Armstrong Custer, his U.S. Army Seventh Cavalry, and their Crow scouts on June 25, 1876. Both sides violated the Fort Laramie Treaty of 1868 and helped cause the battle. Americans moved into Sioux territory to explore for gold and survey possible railroad paths. The Sioux settled on non-ceded hunting grounds near the Little Bighorn River. The American reaction to the greatest Indian victory on the Great Plains resulted in intensified efforts to clear the plains for settlement. This was accomplished largely by the destruction of the buffalo on the Great Plains. Although the number of buffalo had been declining drastically in previous decades as Indians slaughtered large herds in order to trade with settlers in the East, the U.S. Army commenced with a policy that would bring the buffalo to near extinction. The Crow and other plains tribes depended on the buffalo for food, shelter, fuel, and weaponry. With the buffalo gone, the nomadic lifestyle they practiced became unviable, making retreat to reservations the only option for Plains Indians.

In 2003, the National Park Service added the nation's first Indian memorial to the Little Bighorn Battlefield to further recognize Crow, Sioux, Cheyenne, Arapaho, and other tribes who fought there. Colorado Senator Ben Nighthorse Campbell and the Montana congressional delegation supported legislation to build the memorial. Tourism to the grassy hills of the Little Bighorn National Historic Site now brings income to the Crow and visitors to a memorial honoring warriors of two different peoples fighting for two incompatible ways of life.

The Crow Indian Reservation government meets with the Montana state government annually to discuss, among other issues, economic development. The 2003 meeting with Governor Judy Martz included a proposed wind power facility on the reservation. Crow Chairman Carl Venne has sought state and federal government assistance in building and modernizing the Crow home, and the tribe received a $250,000 grant from the Department of the Interior to build its 250- to 500-megawatt power plant. The Crow hope to sell power in the state and then market it outside of Montana. The plant would be located at Dry Creek near Hardin, which is owned by the Crow. In 2004, tribal leaders continued looking for investors by enticing them with tax breaks and other incentives. The tribe owns natural resources such as coal, water, natural gas, timber, and gravel and can therefore keep costs low. This will enable them to produce inexpensive power and be competitive with other power producers.

Recently, Crow Indian tribal historian Joe Medicine Crow received an honorary doctorate in anthropology from the University of Southern California (USC). He had already earned a bachelor's degree in sociology from Linfield College in Oregon in 1937. Two years later, he completed his master's in anthropology at USC. He was the first male from the Crow Indian tribe to ever seek a graduate degree. His thesis, "The Effects of European Culture Upon the Economic, Social, and Religious Life of the Crow Indians," was written without sources because there were virtually none on his subject. Joe Medicine Crow mostly used oral history that had been passed down over the generations. He finished all of the coursework for his doctorate at USC by 1941, but then left the program to serve in World War II. Crow was elected tribal historian in 1948 and has focused on research of Crow history including interviewing 100 prereservation tribal elders. *In the Heart of Crow Country, The Crow Indian's Own Stories* is the first book written by Crow and is the culmination of years of research and collecting stories and anecdotes.

Joe Medicine Crow has lectured at high schools, Little Bighorn College, and other colleges, and in 1999 addressed the United Nations. He was also present at the dedication of the "Peace Through Unity" Indian Memorial at the Little Bighorn Battlefield, where his words are carved on a peace monument. Crow, who is the grandson of Custer's last scout, Whiteman Runs Him, performs a one-man drama revisiting Crow history, including the Little Bighorn battle. He worked on the script for an early Custer movie, *They Died With Their Boots on,* and has ever since wanted to tell his own version. He began doing so in 1964 at the Montana Territorial Centennial celebration and continues to do so today.

—*Daniel S. Stackhouse, Jr.*

Suggested Reading

Agnew, Meaghan. "As the Crow Flies." *USC Trojan Family Magazine* (Summer 2002). Available from http://www.usc.edu

"Crow." *Columbia Encyclopedia.* 6th ed. New York: Columbia University Press, 2004.

"Crow Seek Investors for Power Plant." *Billings Gazette,* June 22, 2004. Available from http://www.billingsgazette.com

"Crow Tribal Constitution." Available from http://www.tribal resourcecenter.org

"Crow Tribal Government Today." *Library@Little Big Horn College.* Little Big Horn College, 2002. Available from http://lib.lbhc.cc.mt.us

Crow Tribe Official Web Site. Available from http://tlc.wtp.net/crow.htm

"Crow Tribe of Montana." FEMA Region VIII Tribal Lands Web Page. Available from http://www.fema.gov/regions/viii/tribal/crowbg.shtm

Farrell, Allison. "Tribes Seek Funds; Martz Balks." *Billings Gazette,* October 11, 2003. Available from http://www.billingsgazette.com

Hedren, Paul L., ed. *The Great Sioux War 1876–77.* Helena: Montana Historical Society Press, 1991.

McCleary, Carrie Moran. "Giving Voice to Crow Country— The Crow Place Name Project." *The Tribal College Journal* 12 (Winter 2000). Available from http://www.tribalcollege journal.org

Miller, John J. "Buffaloed." *National Review,* October 9, 2000, p. 28.

Montana–Wyoming Tribal Leaders Council Web Site. Available from http://tlc.wtp.net

Mullen, T. *Rivers of Change–Trailing the Waterways of Lewis and Clark.* Malibu, CA: Roundwood Press, 2004. Available from http://www.riversofchange.com

Russell, Jeremy. "Medicine Crow to Receive Honorary Degree from USC." *The Custer Museum Gazette,* May 10, 2003. Available from http://www.custermuseum.org/medicine crow.htm

Rzeczkowski, Frank. "The Crow Indians and the Bozeman Trail." Available from http://www.hist.state.mt.us/education/cirguides/transrzeczkowski.asp

Sharette, Maxine. "Links to Poverty." *The Prevention Connection Newsletter* 5 (Fall 2001): 1, 3.

Tall Bear, Neva. "Crank on the Crow Reservation." *AIRO (American Indian Research Opportunities) Reporter* (Summer 1999). Available from http://www.montana.edu/wwwai/imsd/rezmeth/crankoncrow.htm

Taylor, Colin F. *The American Indian.* London: Salamander Books, 2004.

Thackeray, Lorna. "Thousands See Dedication of Indian Memorial at Little Bighorn." *Billings Gazette,* June 26, 2003. Available from http://www.billingsgazette.com

"Yellowtail." In *Encyclopedia of North American Indians,* edited by Frederick Hoxie. New York: Houghton Mifflin, 1996.

⸎ CUPEÑOS

It was deserted

The earth was deserted

First they appeared

First they came out

First Mukat

First Temayawit

First the chiefs

First the ancients.

—Cupeño creation song

Like other Native peoples, the Cupeños of southern California possess rich oral traditions. For them, these stories are records of their past. Cupeños have passed down these narratives for generations, thereby explaining their cultural beliefs, relationships to divine beings, and migration patterns. One account in particular recalls the Cupeño settlement of their homeland. Long ago in the mists of time, Mukat, a deity, guided his people, the Cupeños, from the north into a mountain valley in what is now northern San Diego County. This was sometime after Temayawit, another god, had an argument with Mukat and departed for the underworld. Mukat told the people that the land was theirs and that they should care for it and be happy. The fact that Mukat led the Cupeños to their homelands near modern-day Warner Springs, California, is highly important. It reveals that Cupeños could claim their lands by divine sanction. Mukat himself approved this first migration in Cupeño memory.

As far as can be determined, the Cupeños are actually the descendants of at least three Native peoples in southern California. Jane H. Hill, noted expert on Cupeño language and culture, asserts that the first Cupeños "were a lineage of the Mountain Cahuilla who had moved south from the area around Soboba, [California]." The Cupeño language belongs to the Cupan group of the Takic subfamily of the Uto-Aztecan linguistic family, the same group to which the Cahuilla language belongs. These early Cahuilla peoples migrated into northern San Diego County and eventually intermarried with members of two other local indigenous groups, the Kumeyaays and Luiseños. The Spanish eventually called them *Cupeños,* meaning "the people who live at Cupa," the name of their main village. However, the Cupeños referred to themselves as *Kuupangaxwichem,* or "the people who slept here."

The location of their primary community, Cupa, is significant. Cupa lay near some of the indigenous trade routes that crisscrossed Native California. These trails linked Cupeños commercially to their neighboring relatives, the Cahuilla, Kumeyaays, and Luiseños, as well as to various societies along the Colorado River and other Native Americans in California. As a result of trade, Cupeños obtained such items as dried fish, otter skins, shell beads, salt, pottery, and corn. In addition to trade, these roads served other purposes. Along these routes, Cupeños interacted and intermarried with other local populations, received news and other information, exchanged cultural ideas, and occasionally fought. One of the major results of these associations is that Cupeños developed into a sharp and savvy business people.

The lives of Cupeños changed forever after the Spanish invasion of California in 1769. Cupeños first viewed a Spanish exploring party in 1795. According to one oral tradition, they eventually heard that Spaniards "came from the water, and it is said that for that reason they named them Ocean People." These fair-complected foreigners soon established a mission system along the California coast. Some Cupeños visited the San Luis Rey and San Diego missions, likely out of curiosity or perhaps to conduct trade. Once missionaries baptized Cupeños and other local Native Americans, they refused to permit them to leave the missions. Cupeños living in the missions encountered unfamiliar animals and learned new skills, but they also suffered untold atrocities, abuse, and exposure to deadly diseases. After the secularization of the missions during the 1830s, those Cupeños who survived, almost without exception, returned to their homelands.

By the 1840s, American citizens began moving into California in ever-increasing numbers. Hundreds of Americans passed through the Cupeño villages of Cupa (renamed *Agua Caliente* by the Spanish) and Wilakalpa. Visitors noted that the Cupeños were industrious entrepreneurs and merchants who sought to profit from American immigration to southern California. They sold food and supplies, washed clothes, and provided other services. One American migrant, Jonathan Trumbull Warner of Connecticut, recognized the potential of the Cupeños' mountain home. After contacting Mexican authorities and filling out the necessary paperwork, Warner secured a portion of Cupeño lands for a private rancho. Although several Cupeños eventually worked for Warner, they found him to be menacing and untrustworthy, and decided to evict him from their lands.

By 1851, at least two additional issues deepened Cupeño resentment toward Warner and other non-Native peoples. First, San Diego County forcefully collected from tribal members approximately $600 in cash and livestock for taxes. Second, substantial numbers of American migrants traveled through Cupeño territory, killing local game and allowing their livestock to graze on grasses and other plant life on which Cupeños depended for food. One Cupeño leader, Antonio Garra, concluded that all Americans, including Warner, had to be killed or expelled from California. While participants in the Garra Uprising failed to achieve their primary goal, they did succeed in driving Warner away and seizing almost $59,000 of the intruder's property.

From the commencement of California statehood in 1850, the relationship between the Cupeños and the

U.S. federal government was uncertain and tenuous. During the early 1850s, federal officials visited the Cupeños and dozens of other Native groups throughout the Golden State and conducted treaty negotiations. For instance, Cupeños and their Native neighbors signed the Treaty of Temecula in January 1852. The U.S. Senate never ratified this and other treaties with California's indigenous peoples, thus leaving Cupeños and others in a state of diplomatic limbo. However, in 1875, President Ulysses S. Grant signed an executive order that created nine reservations in southern California, including one at the Cupeño village of Agua Caliente. Cupeños must have been encouraged by the possibility of retaining their homelands forever. Unfortunately, just five years later in 1880, President Rutherford B. Hayes canceled the 1,120-acre Agua Caliente Reservation because John G. Downey, a former governor of California who owned a portion of the Cupeños' territory, claimed that the reserve lay on his lands.

In 1892, ex-governor Downey filed his complaint in hope of evicting the Cupeños from their homeland. The next year, the lawsuit came before the superior court of San Diego County. Referred to initially as *John G. Downey v. Allejandro Barker, et al.,* the case was later designated *Allejandro Barker, et al. v. J. Downey Harvey* after the former governor died in 1894. The court in San Diego based its ruling on the actions of a Board of Land Commissioners, which allegedly visited the Cupeños during the 1850s and informed them of the need to file a land claim within two years. Assuming that the land commission fulfilled these two duties and that the Cupeños failed to file a land claim, the superior court awarded Agua Caliente and surrounding Cupeño lands to Downey's descendents. What is more disturbing about the decision is that the court never located the commission's record of its visit to the Cupeños; that is, the court did not have indisputable evidence that the commission ever alerted this Native people of the necessity of filing a land claim. Between 1899 and 1901, both the supreme court of California and the U.S. Supreme Court upheld the ruling of the court in San Diego.

As a consequence of this lawsuit, the Cupeños had little choice but to migrate elsewhere. The federal government established the Warner's Ranch Indian Commission in order to locate suitable lands for the Cupeños. After considering several sites, the commission recommended lands around Pala, California, approximately 25 miles west of the Cupeño homeland. Shortly thereafter, the federal government agreed to the commission's recommendation and purchased the site. During this period, Cupeños did all that they could to thwart their removal. For instance, they wrote letters of protest to Commissioner of Indian Affairs W. A. Jones, sent one of their own to Washington, DC, to plead their cause before federal officials, hired a lawyer, and even conferred briefly with President Theodore Roosevelt in San Bernardino, California. Unfortunately, all of these attempts to prevent their removal failed.

May 12, 1903, is a sad day in Cupeño history. On this day, the Cupeños' forced migration from their precious homelands to the Pala Indian Reservation commenced. It was extremely difficult for this Native people to leave the lands that they believe Mukat entrusted to their care. According to one eyewitness account, "Sounds of wailing came from the adobe homes of the Indians" during their last few nights at Agua Caliente. In the early hours of May 12, many went into their adobe chapel to pray. Several also gathered at their cemetery to mourn over the graves of their ancestors. Escorted by an Indian agent and hired teamsters, the Cupeños began their own trail of tears, a 55-mile journey that wound through northern San Diego County. Two days later, on May 14, the exhausted group of men, women, and children arrived at Pala, their new home.

Since 1903, the Cupeños have remained at Pala. As Diana Meyers Bahr has aptly pointed out, some Cupeños have migrated to other communities, including Los Angeles, and have taken fundamental elements of their culture with them. Since their arrival at Pala, much has changed for the Cupeños, yet much has stayed the same. Cupeño children entered what became known as the Pala Indian School. There, they learned history, math, English, and other subjects. As was true at other Indian schools, administrators and teachers strived to transform American Indians into Indian Americans. Despite pressure from school officials, Cupeño children continued to speak their Native language on the school playground, between classes, and on the way home. Elders and parents continued to teach their oral traditions and cultural beliefs to the children. Even in the 21st century, Cupeño children still learn their Native language and listen to the stories.

The pressures of Americanization, however, cannot be underestimated. Between 1903 and 1920, Cupeños began to adopt non-Native forms of protest, including labor strikes. Most children learned how to read and write in English. Many women developed an interest in sewing, baking cakes and pies, and American modes of childrearing. Cupeños of all ages purchased liberty bonds during World War I and appear to have exhibited genuine feelings of patriotism toward the United States. Perhaps most significantly, English replaced Cupeño as the primary language of the Cupeños sometime during the 1920s.

Yet, despite what must seem to be almost suffocating influences from American society, Cupeño culture persists and thrives to this day, albeit in modified form. As noted earlier, many Cupeños still speak their Native language, either partially or fluently. They continue to participate in some of their indigenous ceremonies and dances, sing their ancient songs, and play their cherished games, including shinny and peon. What is most important is that Cupeños continue to view themselves as a tribal entity, as a people.

They also continue to remember their removal from their homeland. During the first weekend of May, Cupeños hold their Cupa Day Celebration, a traditional festival in honor of Mukat, their primary deity. They return with their children to Warner's Springs, near Agua Caliente, where they recount their oral traditions as well as the story of their removal. At this site, Cupeños form a circle and offer prayers in the four sacred directions—north, south, east, and west. Their traditional homeland is so important to them that the tribe purchased 240 acres of their former lands in 1994. They acquired some of their most sacred sites, including the cemetery that contains the remains of their ancestors and loved ones. In 2003, during the centennial commemoration of their removal, some 200 Cupeños rented a 41-unit block of the Warner Springs Ranch Resort. Angela Ortega, one tribal member, said during the experience, "I've got goose bumps. I don't feel like I'm just visiting. I feel like I'm home."

One of the more significant developments in recent Cupeño history was the construction of the Cupa Cultural Center at Pala. In 1974, the building formally opened its doors. The center serves as a museum, housing maps, photographs, beautiful baskets, and other artifacts associated with Cupeño history and culture. The curator of the facility, Leroy Miranda, has explained, "It's a place to come and be educated." Mr. Miranda and others have a deep understanding and knowledge of their history and are willing to share it with others. Perhaps the greatest use of the center is to educate Cupeño children about their rich history, culture, and language. In this sense, the Cupa Cultural Center functions as a means to promote education, literacy, and unity among the Cupeño people.

Cupeños have also asserted themselves in other ways, including economically. They have worked in an assortment of occupations, including teachers, manual laborers, construction workers, nurses, and business owners. Tribal members have also successfully cultivated and sold avocados, and owned a gravel pit. Ever since this Native nation was born on the indigenous trade routes centuries ago, they have been a people expert in business pursuits and commerce. Even before their removal from Warner's Ranch, the Cupeños operated a series of bathhouses, spas, and restaurants, catering to the many Anglos passing through their territory.

This entrepreneurial spirit manifested itself again in April of 2001 as the Cupeños opened a $10-million gaming casino. Five years before, in 1996, at the Cupeños' request, Governor Pete Wilson and Cupeño representatives began negotiating a gaming agreement. As pointed out on the tribe's official Web site, Cupeños "patiently waited and sought the right to operate a casino through diplomatic means." That patience has truly borne fruit. By 2004, they had expanded their casino into a $100-million-plus resort, arguably one of the most elegant gaming facilities in the state of California. The Cupeños and Luiseños of Pala maintain the casino, along with business partner Anchor Gaming of Las Vegas. It currently employs 1,500 people and has 2,000 slot machines and tables, 77 table games, 8 restaurants, 4 entertainment venues, a 10,000-square-foot day spa, and a 507-room, 10-story, four-star hotel. When visiting the Pala Casino, it is not uncommon to see tourists from all over the United States and from countries around the world, particularly from nations along the Pacific Rim. It should not be surprising that the Cupeños would became involved in business ventures similar to those they had at Warner's Ranch prior to their removal. Some of their primary strengths as a people include adaptability, ingenuity, and a willingness to meet the needs of their patrons.

The Cupeños recognize that they will determine their own future, as they have always sought to do. Generally, they lead happy and prosperous lives. Cupeños, together with some of their Luiseño neighbors who also reside at Pala, are now known as the Pala Band of Mission Indians. Robert Smith, a competent and wise leader, is currently serving as their tribal chairman. Today, the total population of Cupeños and Luiseños affiliated with Pala numbers more than 850, of which approximately 600 still reside on the reservation. The size of the Pala Reservation is about 11,800 acres, not including the 240 acres Cupeños own at Warner Springs. Indeed, Mukat is pleased with and continues to watch over his people, the Cupeños.

—*Joel R. Hyer*

See also Cahuilla Nation, Luiseño

Suggested Reading

Bahr, Diana Meyers. *From Mission to Metropolis: Cupeño Indian Women in Los Angeles.* Norman: University of Oklahoma Press, 1993.

Hyer, Joel R. *"We Are Not Savages": Native Americans in Southern California and the Pala Reservation, 1840–1920.* East Lansing: Michigan State University Press, 2001.

Pala Casino Web Site. Available from http://www.pala casino.com

Pala Indians Web Site. Available from http://www.pala indians.com

⊞ CUSTER, GEORGE ARMSTRONG

See Black Hills Gold Rush of 1874, Crow Nation

⊞ CZECHS AND SWEDES IN SAUNDERS COUNTY, NEBRASKA

As with many areas of the Great Plains, eastern Nebraska was a magnet for European immigrants during the late 19th and early 20th centuries. Usually, immigrants settled within their own clustered areas. And while this was true for Saunders County, Nebraska, it also possessed a unique settlement circumstance. Saunders was the only county in Nebraska where large numbers of Czechs and Swedes settled in close proximity to each other. Despite this, both groups still carved out their own clustered and homogenous rural ethnic neighborhoods, where assimilation was slow and strong ethnic identity prevailed.

According to the 1910 federal census, roughly 46 percent of the population in Saunders County was the combination of Czechs and Swedes and their descendents. The majority of them were first and second generation, with a few third-generation immigrants. Saunders County ranked fourth in Nebraska in the percentage of first-generation Czechs and fifth in first-generation Swedes. Together, Czechs and Swedes born abroad constituted about 15 percent of the county's population in 1910. No other county in Nebraska approached this percentage. In fact, the only county in Nebraska where more Czechs and Swedes lived in combination was Douglas, which was dominated by the city of Omaha. But in Douglas County, first-generation Czechs and Swedes made up less than 7 percent of the population.

Saunders County is situated in eastern Nebraska directly north of Lancaster County, where the city of Lincoln, the state capitol, is located. The Platte River borders Saunders County on the north and east. On the east side of the county, across the Platte, lies Douglas County. Saunders County began to be heavily settled during the 1860s and 1870s. However, during the 1840s, Euro-American migrants traveled across the county on the Ox-Bow Trail. A small community developed in what became southeast Saunders County, and it eventually was called Ashland. Ashland became the county seat, a distinction it held until 1873, when the seat was moved to the town of Wahoo, located in central Saunders County. Besides Czechs and Swedes, old-stock Americans as well as Germans found Saunders County to their liking. As a rule, Germans did not settle among the Czechs and Swedes.

Although Czechs and Swedes in Saunders County lived in close proximity to each other in some cases, for the most part, they both carved out their own clustered areas. In fact, the clustered areas were basically

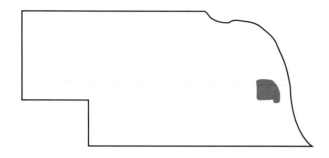

Figure 1   State of Nebraska, Saunders County Highlighted

rural and homogenous. The Czech area developed in the western section of Saunders County and extended west into Butler County. In 1880, almost 80 percent of the people living in four western Saunders County precincts were Czechs. Slightly more than 69 percent of all Czechs in the county in 1880 lived in this clustered area. Only eight Swedes called this section of the county home and all lived in one precinct.

Three decades later, in 1910, the Czech-clustered area expanded to five precincts and included the small Czech town of Prague. Of the 3,896 people living in this section of the county, 3,453 were Czechs, which means first-generation immigrants and their descendents. This constituted more than 88 percent of the population. Close to 65 percent of all Czechs in Saunders County lived in this clustered area. In Elk precinct, which supported no towns or villages, 99.9 percent of the population was Czechs. The only non-Czech was a hired hand from Slovakia. Bohemia precinct in 1910 had a Czech population of 97 percent and the village of Prague supported a Czech population of more than 97 percent. As in 1880, few Swedes resided in the Czech clustered section of Saunders County.

In 1880, the Swedish clustered area of the county was still developing, and during the next decade, it became defined. The Swedish section was the central area of the county and extended south to the border of Lancaster County. About 39 percent of the population in these precincts (excluding the town of Wahoo) was Swedes. However, unlike the Czech area, the line of the Swedish clustered area did not extend to the borders of the main Swedish precincts. Consequently, the percentage of Swedes in the area seems low. But more

than 77 percent of all Swedes in the county lived in the Swedish area in 1880. A few Czechs did live in the precincts of the Swedish section of Saunders County, but more than half lived in Stocking precinct where the town of Wahoo sits.

In 1910, there were several villages in the Swedish clustered area, including the towns of Malmo, Swedeburg, and Mead. Close to 55 percent of area's population were from Sweden or were second- and third-generation Swedes. About 65 percent of all Swedes in Saunders County resided in the Swedish clustered area. However, if the town of Wahoo is included, almost 80 percent of Swedes in the county were in the Swedish section. Czechs made up more than 10 percent of the population in the Swedish precincts, but the Swedes were just as clustered in their area as the Czechs were in their section. For example, in Wahoo precinct (not the town), Swedes were heavily settled in one area, but were virtually nonexistent on one edge.

The town of Wahoo was an island in the middle of the Swedish cluster of Saunders County. As the county seat, Wahoo harbored Czechs, Swedes, Germans, and many older-stock Americans. In Wahoo, Czech and Swede churches and organizations were to be found, and the Swedish school, Luther Academy, was established there. In 1880, not many Czechs and Swedes called the town of Wahoo home, but this changed by 1910. Swedes constituted more than 28 percent of the town's population and the Czechs made up more than 18 percent in 1910.

Because Saunders County was rural, the majority of both Czechs and Swedes were involved in agriculture. Saunders County offered fertile farmland for immigrants, and the Czechs and Swedes took advantage. In 1910, more than 6 out of 10 Swedish men in the county were farmers, and close to 7 out of 10 Czechs were engaged in agriculture. Partly because of the rural environment and clustering, many Czechs and Swedes maintained their native languages. However, many learned to speak English, especially the Swedes. Countywide in 1910, about 95 percent of Swedish men and more than 85 percent of Swedish women spoke English. Among the Czechs, about 76 percent of the men and close to 66 percent of the women spoke English. However, in Bohemia precinct, situated in the Czech area, a high majority of adult Czechs were unable to speak English: More than 78 percent of

Czech men in this precinct spoke exclusively the Czech language, and the rate for the women was almost 87 percent.

Besides clustering, the Czechs and Swedes in Saunders County maintained ethnic identity and slowed the assimilative process through churches, education, fraternal organizations, and the practice of endogamy. Of course, with such highly concentrated areas of Czechs and Swedes, there were few opportunities to marry outside one's ethnic group. Homogenous areas and endogamy went hand in hand, and each strengthened the other. Together, these two factors allowed ethnic churches, schools, and organizations to flourish in the Czech and Swedish communities.

For the Czechs and Swedes who immigrated to America and ultimately to Saunders County, clustering made the transition to American society much less arduous. These two ethnic groups were then able to build their churches and educate their children with few pressures and influences from outside the borders of their communities, especially in rural areas. Through 1910, ethnic churches were the most important institutions for both groups in the county.

The Lutheran Church along with the Swedish Covenant Mission Church dominated the Swedish community in the county. The Swedish Lutheran churches, which belonged to the Nebraska Conference of the Augustana Synod, fought hard to preserve Swedish ethnic identity. The Swedish language was used in these Lutheran churches, as it was in the other Swedish denominations. Swedish preachers who could not speak and read the Swedish language found it difficult to find a Swedish church in which to deliver a sermon. Swedish Lutheran Pastor S. G. Larson was sent to Saunders County early on, and by 1871 his influence was felt. Larson strongly encouraged Swedes to cluster so that the churches of the Augustana Synod had substantial-enough populations to serve. Larson was the first Augustana pastor in Nebraska, and he established several Swedish Lutheran communities in Saunders County. Larson was the most important figure in establishing Swedish clusters in the county.

Other Swedish denominations clamored for members as well. The most influential was the Swedish Evangelical Mission Covenant Church. Swedeburg, a small village situated south of the town

of Wahoo, was a key Mission Covenant community. Many members of the Mission Covenant Churches had left the Swedish Lutheran denominations. Most of the founders of the Evangelical Covenant Church in the village of Mead had left the Lutheran Church. Like the Swedish Lutheran Churches of the Augustana Synod, the Swedish Covenant churches in Saunders County promoted Swedish identity. They believed in maintaining a strong Swedish community and the continued use of the Swedish language in church. Covenant churches in the county, such as the Mead church, joined the Swedish Evangelical Mission Covenant of America, which like the Lutheran's Augustana Synod was an association that promoted Swedish identity.

As with the Swedish churches, Czech churches in Saunders County promoted the retention of ethnic identity. During the late 19th and early 20th centuries, many Catholic priests at Czech congregations were themselves Czech. In 1871, the first Mass for Nebraska's Catholic Czechs was delivered by a Czech priest in the home of a Czech farmer in Saunders County. Not long after this, the first Czech Catholic parish in the state was founded in western Saunders County. Other Czech Catholic churches followed. In the early days, the town of Wahoo did not have a Czech Catholic church, and people were forced to travel more than 15 miles to the Czech clustered area in western Saunders County to attend Mass. However, during the mid-1870s, Czechs from Moravia began a Catholic parish in the county seat, and by 1878 St. Wenceslaus Catholic Church was built.

Although there were fewer Czech Protestants than Catholics, they still established several congregations in the county. Many of Nebraska's Protestant Czechs resided in Saunders County during the late 19th century and after the turn of the 20th century. Protestant Czech churches, like the Catholic ones, fostered Czech identity and used the native tongue in their services and church affairs. But, for the most part, Czech Catholics and Protestants did not interact although they lived in the same clustered area. Protestant Czechs mistrusted Catholics, a sentiment that had been carried over from Europe.

Although not as numerous as the Catholics, Czech freethinkers had an influence in Saunders County. Non-Catholic and Protestant Czechs, or freethinkers, established several cemeteries in the county. During the 1870s, a Catholic Czech monastery was planned for western Saunders County, but it was never established, in part because Czech freethinkers in the county fought against it. By the late 1880s, the original Czech Catholic church's organization was run by freethinkers who had rejected Catholicism. This caused a multitude of internal problems for the parish. Despite the fight between Czech Catholics and freethinkers, both groups maintained a goal of promoting Czech identity.

Because Saunders County's Swedish and Czech children were often isolated geographically, schools usually decelerated the assimilation process. Most or all the students were members of one ethnic group, as was the teacher, so ethnic identity was reinforced. This even held true in public schools located in ethnically homogenous areas. Both the Czechs and Swedes in the county mistrusted public schools to a certain degree, but both groups utilized them. However, the Swedes in the county built a Swedish Lutheran school in Wahoo in 1883 that was established to serve not just Saunders County, but also the entire Swedish Lutheran population in Nebraska. Luther Academy was constructed on the northwest corner of Wahoo. Luther Academy continued educating Swedish Lutherans long after 1900. In 1903, the school added a two-year post–high school program and became Luther College and Academy.

There were many Swedish children living in Saunders County who did not attend Luther Academy, but rather went to public schools. Many Swedish children were not Lutherans. But whether they were Lutheran or belonged to the Covenant Church, many Swedish children who attended public schools had their education supplemented with the Swedish summer school. The Swede school taught religion and the Swedish language, which public schools could not. Also, many Swedes in the county sent their children to Sunday schools, which gave them a religious education and helped perpetuate Swedish ethnic identity. In fact, the Swedish summer schools and Luther Academy were major factors in the maintenance of Swedish ethnic identity in Saunders County.

Education was also important to the Czechs. However, through 1910, many Czech children in Saunders County did not attend high school. Most Czechs did go to elementary school, but although the

English language was usually used in the small rural schools for instruction, the children in the clustered area still communicated in the Czech language. Catholic Czechs also favored parochial schools. Eventually, Czechs sent their children to both parochial and public schools. Of course, Protestants and freethinkers sent their children to public schools. Early on, most teachers in the Czech area were not Czechs, but that changed by 1900 as more and more Czechs became educated and entered the teaching profession.

Most Swedes in Saunders County did not belong to fraternal organizations, but they were utilized by Czechs. Both Catholic and freethinker organizations were important in the Czech community. These clubs and organizations were instruments of Czech ethnic identity. Several Czech organizations existed in the county, including *sokols* (athletic societies) and a hand full of lodges. Two of these lodges were the Czech Slavonic Benevolent Society and the Western Bohemian Fraternal Association (ZCBJ). Catholic Czechs also formed their own fraternal organizations in the county.

In the early 21st century, many signs of Czech and Swedish identity still exist in Saunders County, Nebraska. For the most part, both clustered areas are still intact. Although their native languages are mostly lost, a few Czechs, especially some older ones, can still speak the language. Czech and Swedish descendants are proud of their heritage, and most of their ethnic churches still exist, although the English language is now used in the services and non-Czechs and non-Swedes are members of the congregations. Luther Academy discontinued their high school during the 1950s, and the college closed during the early 1960s, merging with Midland College in Fremont, Nebraska, to become Midland Lutheran College, ending the last vestige of ethnic education in the county. Still, ethnic identity is important to the Czechs and Swedes in Saunders County several generations after their ancestors arrived from Europe.

—*Raymond Douglas Screws*

Suggested Reading

Dowie, James Iverne. *Prairie Grass Dividing.* Rock Island, IL: Augustana Historical Society, 1959.

Kastrup, Allan. *The Swedish Heritage in America: The Swedish Element in America and American-Swedish*

Relations in Their Historical Perspective. Minneapolis, MN: Swedish Council of America, 1975.

Lindell, Terrance Jon. "Acculturation Among Swedish Immigrants in Kansas and Nebraska, 1870–1900." Ph.D. Dissertation, University of Nebraska–Lincoln, 1987.

Miller, Kenneth. *The Czecho-Slovaks in America.* New York: George H. Doran, 1922.

Rosicky, Rose. *A History of Czechs (Bohemians) in Nebraska.* Omaha: Czech Historical Society of Nebraska, 1929.

Saunders County History. Dallas, TX: Taylor, 1983.

Screws, Raymond D. "Not a Melting Pot: A Comparative Study of Swedes and Czechs in Saunders County, Nebraska, 1880–1910." *Heritage of the Great Plains* 35, no. 1 (2002): 4–22.

Screws, Raymond Douglas. "Retaining Their Culture and Ethnic Identity: Assimilation Among Czechs and Swedes in Saunders County, Nebraska, 1880–1910." Ph.D. Dissertation, University of Nebraska–Lincoln, 2003.

D

✠ DAWES ALLOTMENT ACT OF 1887

See BLACKFOOT NATION, BUREAU OF
INDIAN AFFAIRS, CHEMEHUEVI

✠ DEARFIELD, COLORADO

In the post–Civil War era, it became clear to African
Americans in the South that emancipation did not mean
equality. Beginning in the 1890s, tens of thousands of
southern blacks facing racism, Jim Crow laws, lynching, and economic and social inferiority decided to
migrate to other regions within the United States. This
so-called Great Migration of southern blacks to northern and western lands took place starting in the 1890s
and lasted well into the 1970s. The majority of African
Americans relocated to urban areas in the north. It is
estimated that perhaps more than 1 million blacks
migrated to northern cities between 1890 and 1920 in
order to occupy unskilled positions in factories.
However, other African Americans felt that, in order to
improve their status, they ought to move west.

The story of African American migration to the
West and their role on the frontier has often been
overlooked in U.S. history. For these black pioneers,
the West offered the possibility to take on new roles
as explorers, fur trappers, gold miners, cowboys, and
homesteaders. Often, these African Americans embodied the American frontier experience as they carved
out new farming communities where they could exercise
autonomy and independence. One such community
was in Dearfield, Colorado.

Some African Americans felt that city life in the
north left little room for advancement due to the constant competition with whites. These individuals sought
new opportunities by moving westward. Between 1890
and 1910, nearly 35,000 blacks decided to move to the
frontier. Many African Americans argued that blacks
should depart from the factories and return to the land
where they can "work out their salvation from the land
up." Black entrepreneurs pooled their meager resources
and formed black farming communities in order to
collectively better their lives. Colorado was seen as a
region where African Americans could work hard and
enjoy the fruits of their labor. By 1890, the vast majority of the black population that settled in Colorado
owned land. According to the U.S. census, about 6,000
African Americans were living in Colorado, and 5,000
of them had purchased their own land.

African American entrepreneurs such as Oliver
Toussaint Jackson sought to create a black farming
community in Colorado after being inspired by the
writings of Booker T. Washington. Washington urged
African Americans to return to the land and earn
their own way with their own hands. Influenced by
Washington's writings, Oliver Toussaint Jackson
arrived in Colorado in 1887 where he envisioned the
establishment of an African American farming colony.
His idea inspired a settlement in Weld County, where
Jackson and his wife, Minerva, helped found the city
of Dearfield, located about 85 miles northeast of
Denver. Oliver and Minerva Jackson filed for the original

160 acres of land in 1910, and by the end of 1911 there were seven families and three teams of horses, making Jackson's dream a reality. Efforts to recruit homesteaders to the new African American colony, where settlers could live off the land and become self-sufficient, were successful and the original residents were soon joined by 60 newcomers. Within five years, Dearfield, Colorado, had more than 40 wooden homes, two churches, a schoolhouse, a doctor's office, a cement factory, and a filling station. Over the next decade, the population increased to nearly 700 residents, as black men and women flocked to the colony to start a new life.

The African American farming colony had its share of struggles. Most of the would-be farmers had little agricultural experience. The settlers who came to Dearfield were drawn from the working classes and included coal miners, janitors, teamsters, barbers, maids, and waiters. Jackson stated that many of these initial colonists were penniless upon their arrival to their homesteads in Colorado and were forced to forge an existence out of nothing. In the initial phases of settlement, some colonists lived in tents or homes dug out of hillsides, relying on buffalo chips as their primary source of fuel through the winters.

Despite the obstacles facing the men and women who came to Dearfield, they soon settled on their homesteads and learned to raise livestock and mastered the techniques of dry land farming. By 1914, Dearfield had nearly a thousand acres of land under cultivation and colonists, besides raising livestock, planted an array of crops including corn, potatoes, watermelon, and sugar. After a few successful harvests, the circumstances and lives of these homesteaders improved, and by the fall of 1915 Dearfield could boast that their new community was self-sufficient. Dearfield had the added benefit of being situated on the Union Pacific railway line, so that once crops were harvested, they could easily be transported to local markets in Colorado. The colony continued to prosper through World War I, and Dearfield reached its economic peak in 1921, when the value of the community's land and livestock were estimated to be worth $950,000 and the annual production of the settlement grossed nearly $125,000.

The Great Depression and the Dust Bowl in the 1920s and 1930s ushered in a period of steep decline seen in many small farming communities on the American frontier. Ultimately, these events brought about the demise of the African American agricultural community in Dearfield. Many colonists were forced to leave Dearfield to look for work in Denver. By 1940, only 12 people, including Oliver and Minerva Jackson, continued to live in the Dearfield settlement. Jackson attempted to offer the colony to the governor of Colorado in World War II to be used as a camp for Japanese prisoners of war. When this failed, he tried to sell the abandoned town, but no buyers were interested. Jackson died in 1948, and after his death his niece, Jenny Jackson, remained the last resident of Dearfield until her death in 1973. Since then, Jackson's house has been rebuilt and efforts to preserve what remains of the settlement are being undertaken by the Black American West Museum in Denver.

Not only is Dearfield a testament to how African Americans were participants in the American frontier experience, but the settlement also provides an example of how black Americans formed and populated their own communities, where they could be self-sufficient, free from the restrictions of racism, and follow the philosophy of Booker T. Washington in an attempt to advance their circumstances through hard work.

—*Mary Marki*

Suggested Reading

Betts, Donnie. *Dearfield: The Road Less Traveled,* VHS. No Credits Production, 1996.

Katz, William Loren. *The Black West.* New York: Touchstone, 1996.

Milner, Clyde A., II. *A New Significance: Re-Envisioning the History of the American West.* New York: Oxford University Press, 1996.

Porter, W. Kenneth. *The Negro on the American Frontier.* New York: Arno, 1971.

Savage, Sherman. *Blacks in the West.* Westport, CT: Greenwood, 1976.

Taylor, Quintard. *In Search of the Racial Frontier: African Americans in the American West 1528–1990.* New York: Norton, 1998.

⊞ DEFENSE INDUSTRY

The defense industry in California during the last century has several distinct periods that have provided the tempo for California's overall growth: World War I through the interwar years, leading up to mobilization in 1940; World War II from 1940 to 1945; the Cold War; and the defense consolidation period from 1988 through the early 1990s. The population of the state, its economy, its social and cultural fabric, and its overall success and failure is mirrored in the developments linked with the growth and decline of the defense industry.

The growth of the U.S. Navy in the Pacific after World War I was but one of the first steps in the dramatic growth of the state of California that was heavily linked to the military and the defense industry. With the mothballing of the excess destroyer fleet in San Diego in 1919 and establishment of San Diego as an operating base, and subsequently as the headquarters for the Eleventh Naval District, the fortunes of that city came to rely upon military and defense industry dollars to ensure its survival.

While the naval presence on the West Coast grew larger in the years immediately following the Versailles Treaty, the aircraft industries began to grow dramatically in the latter part of the period leading up to World War II. Due to a coordinated effort by boosters in southern California, a high concentration of pre-war military aviation existed there. This drew Consolidated Aircraft Corporation and North American Aviation Corporation to locate factories there in 1935. The Douglas Aircraft Corporation and Northrop Aircraft were already in southern California by this time. Roger Lotchin that, by 1939, more than a third of the nation's aircraft and parts workers and half of those who built airframes were hard at work in southern California's airplane production facilities. As the 1930s drew to a close and tensions boiled in Europe, orders for military planes grew dramatically. Southern California aircraft companies had back orders for $240 million worth of planes at the beginning of 1940, more than twice the total manufactured in 1939. The year 1940 drew to a close with $1.5 billion in unfulfilled orders, as the war in Europe moved beyond tensions to become a bitter reality.

In *The Second Gold Rush,* Marilynn S. Johnson describes the booming growth of Oakland and the Bay Area during World War II. The book's apropos title also fittingly describes the growth spurt in southern California brought on by the war. During the war, nearly 500,000 people a year migrated to California, bringing the total to 1,987,000 people. Yet not every part of the state grew at such a rapid rate, if at all. Just fewer than half of California's counties actually decreased in population, while dramatic increases occurred in the coastal cities—San Diego's population, for example, more than doubled during the war.

The Bay Area grew at a pace second only to that of San Diego during World War II. Its overall population grew by 39.9 percent; in comparison, Los Angeles grew by 17.8 percent, Seattle by 30.5 percent, and Portland by 33.6 percent (though in real numbers, Los Angeles gained the most new residents). This massive urban growth on the West Coast came at a cost. It is apparent that people were migrating not only from other states, but also from the hinterlands to the cities in droves. Rural areas lost one eighth of their residents during the war boom to urban centers like the Bay Area. Nearly one third of the migrants who settled in California did so in the San Francisco–Oakland area.

Aircraft and ship manufacturing in California drove the growth of overall manufacturing jobs. They increased by nearly 150 percent while the federal government directed nearly $20 billion to the war effort in the state. That California's labor force grew by 26 percent between 1940 and 1944, while the national average was only 2 percent, indicated that there was indeed a steady stream of California-bound caravans on U.S. Routes 40 and 66 during the war. The state's aircraft and ship manufacturers grew from a combined total of 21,000 in 1939 to more than 530,000 by the end of 1944. Even though airplane manufacturing plants were built elsewhere in the country at a rapid pace, production in southern California still accounted for nearly half of the national total during the war.

Manufacturing in California brought a disproportionate rise in the employment of women during the war. Nearly 50 percent of women employed in shipyards throughout the country were in California, and women accounted for between 16 and 18 percent of the labor force there. According to Rhode, other factors responsible for the rapid expansion of job opportunities included soaring labor force participation rates among housewives, students, and retirees who had been discouraged from work by the calamitous decade-long depression prior to the war.

Migration to California during the war changed the cultural and social makeup in significant ways. Johnson states that war migration made the Bay Area "more black" and more Southern than it had ever been. Racial barriers were significantly lowered, even if equality was still a long way off. Later in the war, shipbuilders such as Kaiser actively recruited black workers. It is estimated that more than 5,000 Chinese Americans joined the workforce, including as many as 500 women who daily joined a nonsegregated workforce and commingled in ways that were uncommon prior to the war. By the end of World War II, Bay Area defense contractors were advertising for workers within the Chinese community. For the first time in its history, the majority of migrants to the Bay Area came mostly from the Southern states of Oklahoma, Texas, Arkansas, and Missouri. At over 620,000, these Okies of the second gold rush were more than double the number of their more infamous brethren, who came to California during the Great Depression.

In Los Angeles late in 1944, 14.7 percent of the workforce at the California Shipbuilding Corporation were black, while the black population in the area was less than 7 percent. Meanwhile, Lockheed Aircraft Corporation went out of its way to employ minorities by arranging busing for many of its black employees who worked the swing shifts, when transportation to and fro was most difficult to arrange. By the end of the war, blacks held nearly 30,000 assembly line (not custodial) jobs in the aviation industry.

Not quite 15 years after the end of World War II, southern California directly employed more than 320,000 people in defense-related industries. The Southern California Associates of the Committee for Economic Development reported in 1961 that nearly 1 million jobs were directly and indirectly accountable to the military and defense industries in the region. This 1-million-jobs figure equated to one third of the available work in the region at the time. The report projected that the correlating $9 billion in defense related expenditures was nearly a third of the $30 billion regional domestic product. During approximately the same time frame, California's percentage of the nation's total procurement grew from 11.99 percent in 1952 to 18.68 percent in 1956 and was further enlarged in 1962 to 21.27 percent. Meanwhile, the state's overall population grew by its second largest amount of the 20th century, from 10.6 million in 1950 to 15.7 million in the 1960 census, while adding nearly a million more to its rolls between 1960 and 1962.

In the last half of the Cold War, California's reliance upon defense spending and defense-related jobs appeared to be the state's Achilles heel. In 1962, both directly and indirectly, 43 percent of manufacturing in Los Angeles and Orange Counties depended upon military expenditures. As late as 1960, San Diego counted on aerospace jobs for 75 percent of its manufacturing output. In 1982, California was home to almost 30 percent of the nation's aerospace plants and employment, with employment slipping slightly to 25 percent by 1987. Also in 1982, California-based companies controlled almost 30 percent of the aerospace electronics and computer industries. In 1988, before the beginning of the end, California's aerospace industry was valued at $30 billion and employed more than 250,000 people.

In the era of defense industry consolidations during the late 1980s and early 1990s, California lost significant numbers of white- and blue-collar jobs. Lockheed, while merging with Martin Marietta, General Electric Aerospace, and General Dynamics' space division, eliminated its California headquarters. Thousands of ex–General Dynamics workers left the state for work at the Hughes Missile Systems' plant in Tucson, Arizona. Immediately following the boom created by increased military budgets (brought about by the state's former governor-turned-president), the fortunes of California's defense industries collectively fell. Aerospace companies based in southern California laid off thousands of workers. Consolidation caused many of these jobs to be moved to other regions of the country that had lower costs of living and by the end of 1991, more than 60,000 aerospace jobs had disappeared. By 1994, this number more than tripled to just shy of 200,000 jobs lost, with Los Angeles suffering a decline of nearly 11 percent of its job base. During the same period, San Diego, which received more than one fifth of its annual gross product from the military and defense industries, had to cope with losing several large—and hundreds of small—defense contractors. Almost 40 percent of those that lost their jobs during this downturn completely dropped out of the workforce.

The federal expenditures via the military and defense industries clearly played a large role in the economic and population growth of California. Metropolitan areas such as southern California and the San Francisco Bay area grew in direct relation to the job opportunities created. Up and down its coast, California's burgeoning metropolises came to rely upon a mix of military and defense industry money to achieve phenomenal growth throughout the majority of the 20th century. Though the growth of defense-related industries in the state would not see a decline until the late 1980s, the explosion of the military and defense industries and the overall population increase linked directly to the second California gold rush and World War II were most remarkable. Even though the permanence of long-term changes in the economy of the West Coast cities is disputed, the reality that those who migrated to the West during World War II generally stayed is fixed with the clear cultural and social changes that resulted from this rapid expansion. The growth spurred on by World War II, and later by the Cold War that followed, made it possible for California, at nearly 34 million people in the year 2000, to become the most populous state and one of the largest economies in the world.

—*Scott M. Behen*

See also World War II Defense Industries

Suggested Reading

Bolton, Roger E. *Defense Purchases and Regional Growth.* Washington, DC: The Brookings Institution, 1966.

Breese, Gerald, et al. *The Impact of Large Installations on Nearby Areas: Accelerated Urban Growth.* Beverly Hills, CA: Sage, 1965.

California Agriculture and Industry State Chamber of Commerce. *Summary of Stanford Research Institute Report on California's Economy, 1947–1980.* San Francisco: California State Chamber of Commerce, 1961.

California Department of Commerce, Department of Finance, Budget Division, Financial and Population Research Section. *California Migration 1955–1960: Age Distribution of 1955–1960 California Migrant Population.* Sacramento, 1964.

California Department of Commerce, Office of Economic Research. *The Aerospace Industry in California.* By Chris Cochran. Sacramento, 1988.

California Department of Economic and Business Development, Office of Economic Policy, Planning, and Research. *The Aerospace Industry in California.* Sacramento, 1981.

California Department of Economic and Business Development, Office of Economic Policy, Planning, and Research. *The Effect of Increase Military Spending in California.* Sacramento, 1982.

Ellsworth, Ted. *Employment Problems in the Defense Industry: Proceedings of a Conference on Economic Security in the Aerospace and Defense Related Industry in California.* Los Angeles: University of California–Los Angeles, Institute of Industrial Relations, 1970.

Gottlieb, Sanford. *Defense Addiction: Can America Kick the Habit?* Boulder, CO: Westview, 1997.

Greider, William. *Fortress America: The American Military and the Consequences of Peace.* New York: Public Affairs, 1998.

Johnson, Hans. "Immigrants in California: Findings From the 1990 Census." *California Research Bureau Issue Summary* (CRB-93-009). Sacramento: California Research Bureau, 1993. Available from http://www.library.ca.gov/html/statseg2a.cfm

Lotchin, Roger W. *The Bad City in the Good War: San Francisco, Los Angeles, Oakland, and San Diego.* Bloomington: Indiana University Press, 2003.

Lotchin, Roger W. *Fortress California 1910–1961: From Warfare to Welfare.* New York: Oxford University Press, 1992.

Nation, Joseph E. *Defense Industry Transition in California.* Under Direction of the Senate Office of Research Pursuant to Rules Committee Contract Number LCB 17384. Sacramento, 1994.

Rhode, Paul. "The Impact of World War Two Spending on the California Economy," in Roger Lotchin, ed., *The Way We Really Were: The Golden State in the Second Great War.* Urbana: University of Illinois Press, 2000.

Southern California Associates Committee for Economic Development. *National Defense and Southern California 1961–1970: A Statement of Policy by the Southern California CED Associates Together With a Research Report by George A. Steiner.* Los Angeles: Southern California CED Associates, 1961.

⌗ DELLUMS, COTTRELL LAWRENCE (1900–1989)

Cottrell Lawrence (C. L.) Dellums was born in 1900 in Corsicana, Texas. His father was born in slavery, just two and a half months before "Juneteenth" (June 19, 1865), the date emancipation belatedly came to Texas.

As a self-taught young man, Dellums was determined to become a lawyer, stating, "I don't plan to wear these overalls for the rest of my life." He was articulate, eloquent, and knowledgeable. However, in the 1920s, African Americans had few options for a decent job. In January of 1924, Dellums began work as a porter with the Pullman Company's sleeping cars for $2.00 a day, plus tips. The company provided sleeping cars for all long-distance trains and was the country's first large hotel chain.

In some ways, Pullman porters represented higher status. Porters were admired by family and friends for taking on the work, for the travel the work afforded them (instead of being rooted in one place), and for the money they earned, which provided families a chance to be self-sufficient. They were respected even in terms of their attire: Porters donned professional uniforms as opposed to laborers' denims. During this time, all of the porters were black, and the bosses were white. The hours were long, there was no overtime, and the Pullman Company reminded the porters of their social class with the enforcement of arbitrary rules.

C. L. Dellums did not have a long career with the company, though the union was the focus of much of his life. He became one of the founding officers of the Brotherhood of Sleeping Car Porters (BSCP), along with A. Phillip Randolph, BSCP's first president. Dellums helped create and organize the Pullman porters' labor union in August of 1925. The BSCP did not have a very auspicious beginning; no more than half the porters joined the movement at its inception. In October of 1927, the company fired Dellums for his union-raising activities, and in order to make a living after losing his job, he ran a billiard parlor that became one of the centers of west Oakland social life.

The BSCP was created as a union for Pullman porters and maids, and was the first African American labor organization to receive a charter from the American Federation of Labor. Dellums helped organize the union at a time when railroad workers constituted approximately one third of all documented African American wage earners. As such, the BSCP became a powerful, if not lone, advocate for the black workers it represented.

As part of the first campaign, the BSCP demanded improved wages and better working conditions. On September 7, 1927, the brotherhood filed a case with the Interstate Commerce Commission, hoping to get an investigation of the Pullman Company in order to shed light upon the plight of its union members. The BSCP finally gained official recognition a decade later, in 1937, when the union finally forced the Pullman Company to negotiate a labor contract for its representative members. Through the union's efforts in those first years, African Americans acquired control of Pullman porters' and dining car workers' positions throughout the railroad system. These positions were some of the best available and most sought after jobs for black working men. Dellums was elected vice president of the union in 1929 and became its president in 1966, when he succeeded Randolph—though by then the heyday of the Pullman cars was already past.

The BSCP also served as a springboard for Dellums' growing role in future civil rights advocacy. Throughout the 1930s and 1940s, Dellums lent his support to many local black ministers and civil rights workers. In 1941, pressured by Randolph and the BSCP and in fear of a black march on the nation's capital, President Franklin D. Roosevelt signed an executive order that mandated nondiscriminatory employment practices in many of the wartime industries. In 1948, Dellums became the first West Coast Regional Director of the National Association for the Advancement of Colored People (NAACP). In 1959, California Governor Edmund (Pat) Brown appointed Dellums to the state's first Fair Employment Practices Commission, which later transformed into the modern Fair Employment and Housing Commission. Reappointed by Governor Ronald Reagan in 1966, Dellums served on the commission until the mid-1980s. During this time, he also led the first black voter registration drive in Oakland. Dellums was also the uncle of Representative Ronald V. Dellums of California, one of the first African Americans voted into Congress.

Mostly forgotten, C. L. Dellums died in his home of a heart attack December 7, 1989. Though not mentioned in school textbooks, Dellums played an integral part in the origins of the labor and civil rights movements. To commemorate the 10th anniversary of Dellums' passing, the city of Oakland erected a statue of him in front of the train station at Jack London Square.

—*Scott M. Behen*

Suggested Reading

Bates, Beth Tompkins. *Pullman Porters and the Rise of Protest Politics in Black America, 1925–1945*. Chapel Hill: University of North Carolina Press, 2001.

Brazeal, Brailsford Reese. *The Brotherhood of Sleeping Car Porters: Its Origin and Development.* New York: Harper, 1946.

Chateauvert, Melinda. *Marching Together: Women of the Brotherhood of Sleeping Car Porters.* Urbana: University of Illinois Press, 1998.

Dellums, Ronald V., and H. Lee Halterman. *Lying Down With the Lions: A Public Life From the Streets of Oakland to the Halls of Power.* Boston: Beacon, 2000.

Flemming, Thomas C. *C. L. Dellums and Mr. Bojangles, Reflections on Black History, Part 47.* New York: Free Press, 1998. Available from http://www.freepress.org/fleming/flemng47.html

Harris, William H. *Keeping the Faith: A. Philip Randolph, Milton P. Webster, and the Brotherhood of Sleeping Car Porters, 1925–37.* Urbana: University of Illinois Press, 1977.

Lannon, Albert. "Fight or Be Slaves!" *BRC-NEWS.* Black Radical Congress Web Site. Available from http://www.hartford-hwp.com/archives/45a/314.html

Santino, Jack. *Miles of Smiles: Stories of Black Pullman Porters.* Urbana: University of Illinois Press, 1989.

Tye, Larry. *Rising from the Rails: Pullman Porters and the Making of the Black Middle Class.* New York: Henry Holt, 2004.

Wilson, Joseph F. *Tearing Down the Color Bar: A Documentary History and Analysis of the Brotherhood of Sleeping Car Porters.* New York: Columbia University Press, 1989.

⊞ DENVER, PUEBLO, BOULDER, FORT COLLINS, AND COLORADO SPRINGS, COLORADO

Contemplating the 19th-century origins of the five cities that dominate the Front Range of Colorado's Rocky Mountains, thoughts turn to the gold discoveries that launched a new socioeconomic system in the region. Founded within 13 years of the first strikes in 1858, the communities of Denver, Pueblo, Colorado Springs, Boulder, and Fort Collins were tied to the environments from which they emerged. These were cities of nature. Their origins, growth, and survival in the 19th century depended upon the extraction, processing, shipment, or marketing of the region's natural capital—its gold, silver, coal, timber, iron, cattle, sheep, grain, sugar beets, and, in the case of Colorado Springs, scenery and climate.

The so-called fifty-niners who made the dash to Colorado were not the first people to imagine life along the Front Range. For centuries, Native Americans traveled in the shadows of the mountains and along the Platte and Arkansas Rivers flowing eastward. At the time of the gold rush, two tribes—the Arapaho and Cheyenne—occupied the eastern slope plains and lived as one. Originally of Algonquian stock, the Arapaho Indians fled the Great Lakes in the 18th century under pressure from the warlike Sioux and slowly advancing Euro-Americans. Escaping the Sioux's growing power, Cheyenne Indians became nomadic hunters dependent on the bison of the plains. They encountered the Arapaho in the Black Hills. Sharing similar traditions, the Southern Cheyenne Indians moved southward along the base of the Rockies with the Arapaho. The Northern Cheyenne remained in Wyoming. By 1815, these two tribes pushed the Kiowa Indians south of the Arkansas River and into an alliance with the Comanches. Spain claimed title to this land, but remained an ineffective, if not invisible, force.

The Arapaho and Southern Cheyenne Indians hunted and camped along the Front Range where these cities appeared 40 years later. An early American visitor foresaw little chance for significant occupation by his compatriots. Major Stephen Long's 1820 expedition explored the present sites of Fort Collins, Denver, and Colorado Springs. He labeled the plains "the Great American Desert" and concluded the area was best left to Native hunters rather than people dependent upon cultivation.

A burgeoning fur trade soon doubled the small human population of the plains. Sparked by Mexican independence in 1821 and the new nation's reversal of Spain's restrictive policies, this commerce attracted American and European trappers and traders. These migrants were universally male. Because the tribes were matrilineal, the white men captured personal and economic advantages by marrying into Indian families. They were expected to provide trade goods and represent their in-laws' interests.

By 1830, bison hides replaced beaver pelts as the primary medium of exchange. Hides required greater processing, and trading posts appeared along the Front Range. Indian women provided the labor. The bison economy proved short lived. By the early 1850s, markets declined while hunting had left the herds in disarray. The Indians contributed to the bison's plight.

Participating in the market economy, they selected cows whose hides were easier to process and whose meat was more tender, and in so doing undermined bison reproduction. Other factors were also significant: The introduction of cattle to the southern plains brought bovine diseases for which the bison had no immunities, and cattle and horses competed with the bison for water and grass limited by a two-decade drought.

In 1851, the Cheyenne and Arapaho joined other western Indians at the Fort Laramie Council, and under the treaty with the United States, they "received" the land from the Continental Divide to western Kansas and Nebraska, and from the North Platte to the Arkansas Rivers, where they already lived. Emigrants to California, Oregon, and Utah could cross the land, but in return, the treaty required the government to distribute goods. Congress reduced these reparations and rarely provided any goods. Because they were dependent on a shrinking bison population and a floundering fur trade, Indians faced near starvation in the 1850s, a relatively peaceful period.

The gold rush and the cities it spawned challenged this peace. The Plains Indians had dealt with Europeans and Americans for decades, but gold brought larger numbers of people with no interest in the social ties that facilitated the fur trade. Some traders helped found new towns, but boosters quickly squeezed them out. New communities had no place for the traders, their unions, or their children. With travelers to Denver and the mines exceeding 60,000 in 1859, the Indians found themselves isolated, denied access to hunting grounds and campsites, and destitute of food. After 1864 and the Sand Creek Massacre, three years of escalating violence effectively removed all Cheyenne and Arapaho from Colorado.

Gold was the impetus for change. In summer of 1858, prospectors from Georgia, with experience there and in California, discovered gold at the base of the Rockies near the confluence of Cherry Creek and the South Platte River. News of the strikes reached Mississippi and Missouri river towns devastated by the 1857 panic. The nation remained mired in an economic depression, but many potential prospectors believed it too late to begin the journey and launch their diggings. In the spring, their westward trek earned them the sobriquet "the fifty-niners."

DENVER

While prospectors waited, urban entrepreneurs did not. The market center that controlled the mineral trade would, many predicted, become an important city. A decade earlier, Sierra Nevada ores enhanced the nation's international role, expanded its credit, and created a trade surplus. New Front Range towns aspired to regional leadership, but one emerged to dominate the new urban hierarchy. Denver's leadership was not preordained. Its physical location offered no advantages. Nearby placer mines played out quickly. Other towns were closer to mining districts and migration routes along the Platte and the Santa Fe Trail. Americans historically built metropolises on major waterways. In springtime, the nonnavigable South Platte River and Cherry Creek became torrents, but their frequently dry beds provided inadequate drinking water.

Denver, however, enjoyed a few advantages. Entrepreneurs established two towns there in autumn of 1858, merging them within 16 months. Their founders recognized that cities offered greater, more consistent wealth than gold camps. Diggings had shifted to the adjacent mountains, but Denver anchored the nascent economy when the fifty-niners arrived. In a form of "urban primogeniture" earned as the first city and as the locus of the first finds, Denver was the name the prospectors associated with the fortunes that awaited them. This migration to Denver and the camps was overwhelmingly male. Most emigrants were white and between the ages of 18 and 40. Hard times had devastated many. Some charlatans and criminals filled their ranks. Unprepared and inexperienced, many moved west without the necessary equipment for the journey or for mining. In Denver, these sojourners found merchants and tradesmen ready to exploit their needs. While half of the prospectors "saw the elephant," others replaced them when new digs opened. ("Seeing the elephant," a common gold rush phrase, meant doing something that surpassed anything you had done before or experiencing something on the trail that was so big, so terrifying, so huge that it was unheard of, beyond belief.)

Boosters who settled in Denver brought experience from other communities in Missouri, Kansas, Nebraska, and the Midwest. They captured key financial, transportation, and communication systems that allowed the ascendant city to hold sway over the movement of people, goods, information, and money. Denverites grabbed the first cross-country and intraregional overland freight lines. As the primary transshipment point, Denver's merchants determined prices and built warehouses to store goods. Teamsters worked regularly. In April of 1859, William Byers published the region's first newspaper while maintaining his ties to the Omaha business community. Lobbying led the Western Union railroad to identify Denver as its terminus four years later. Given its urban primogeniture and its boosters' connections, the city attracted more and more capable bankers from the start. Within five years of Denver's founding, these bankers successfully petitioned Congress to establish a branch mint and the region's first national bank. Jerome Chaffee and David Moffat, Denverites with prior banking experience, used their positions with the First National Bank of Denver to access information on viable mines, attract and manage outside investments in those ventures, and dominate the mining frontier.

Throughout its first decade, Denver remained a predominantly white community. In those early years, its permanent population only grew by 10 to 4,759, but hundreds of thousands traveled through its doors. And the town's makeup changed. A mining frontier required more people to support it than actually worked the mines. As the entrepot, Denver attracted the tradesmen and services that defined 19th-century urban living—bakers, barbers, butchers, and brewers along with bankers, lawyers, doctors, and others. The city became more domesticated as wives and families accompanied them. When the transcontinental railroad's decision to bypass Denver threatened its future, entrenched elites raised capital within the city and from outside investors to guarantee that homegrown railroads reached the main line by 1870. Within a decade of joining the main rail line, Denver's population soared to 35,629. Dominating the cityscape, pioneers came from such states as New York, Ohio, and Illinois and other midwestern places with sizable German, Irish, and English contingents.

PUEBLO AND BOULDER

Two Front Range communities—Pueblo to the south and Boulder to the north—emerged shortly after Denver. Before 1859, various settlements existed near the confluence of Fountain Creek and the Arkansas River, where Pueblo now stands. Trader John Gantt raised Fort Cass in 1833, but abandoned it two years later after unsuccessful competition with Bent's Fort. Nine years later, George Simpson and Robert Fisher constructed a building called "the Pueblo." Independent traders soon took possession with their families, tending livestock, cultivating bottomland, and bartering with Indians. The nearest U.S. location to Taos, New Mexico, it offered easy access to the Santa Fe Trail, routes south to Mexico, and others north to the South Platte posts. Overgrazing, the declining fur trade, and the temptations of Oregon and California soon undermined the Pueblo. In 1853, new settlers, primarily from New Mexico, arrived at an almost derelict Pueblo following news of congressional approval of a transcontinental railroad through the Arkansas Valley. After sectional tensions halted its construction and violent confrontations with the Utes occurred, white settlers again deserted the Pueblo.

Gold renewed interest in the confluence of the Arkansas River and Fountain Creek. Two hundred Kansans claimed the east side of the creek in February of 1859. Ten months later, a new camp across the creek adopted the name Pueblo. The settlements merged under this name. Some emigrants established mercantile outlets to supply prospectors moving up the Arkansas River to the California Gulch diggings and miners who had opted for farming.

Pueblo's founders could not overcome Denver's advantages and entrepreneurial leadership, and an initial advantage, its proximity to the Santa Fe Trail, soon hurt Pueblo. Northerly trails to Denver allowed it to trade consistently during the Civil War. Pueblo built early linkages with Kansas and Missouri, where connections to the Confederacy hindered business and outward migrations. With Colorado Territory pledged to the Union, travelers generally chose the Platte River trail or the new Republic River route to Denver. From there, they took a shorter, albeit more difficult, path to California Gulch across the 11,200-foot Weston Pass, bypassing Pueblo. Additionally, for almost two decades, Arkansas Valley mines offered an insubstantial hinterland. Nearly 10,000 people prospected there in the early 1860s, but within five years, placers played out and Oro City, the primary camp, stagnated. Lacking technological knowledge, the prospectors failed to appreciate the value of silver-bearing lead carbonate ores that later made Leadville, Colorado, the center of the mining world. By 1870, only 500 souls resided in Lake County, home to California Gulch and Pueblo's backyard. Pueblo fell into dormancy until the mid-1870s, acting as the local wholesaler to nearby Fort Lyon, the remaining miners, and 80 or so Anglo and Hispanic stockmen who filled its tributary sphere. Its proximity to New Mexico added a few citizens of Mexican heritage.

Also founded in February 1859, Boulder offered Denver limited competition. Leading gold seekers to the Cherry Creek diggings, Thomas Aikins encountered the confluence of the St. Vrain River and what he named Boulder Creek. After some prospecting, Aikins decided to settle there. His base camp at the mouth of Boulder Canyon became a supply hub for nearby mines. The Arapaho had hunted in the area for decades and, led by Chief Niwot, welcomed the white men. (Aikins and a company from Boulder later participated at Sand Creek where Niwot died.) Aikins platted a two-mile-long town and offered 4,000 home sites at $1,000 each. Larger and more expensive than lots in Denver, they suggested an early precedent for restrictive land management policies. With flour, gold, and lumber mills, Boulder became a supply center for farmers and miners. The town survived through ties to hinterlands rich in coal, copper, gold, lead, nickel, silver, and tungsten. Most of Boulder's coal fed Denver's railroads and manufactories. When other minerals played out by 1900, its tungsten mines helped the World War I effort, producing 80 percent of the nation's supply. The city's population mirrored Denver's limited racial diversity and the limited economic diversity of small American towns.

In the early scramble for territorial institutions, Boulder lost the most valued prizes. Denver became the capital. Canon City acquired the penitentiary. Boulder received the state university, but the legislature delayed its financing until 1875 and underfunded it for decades. The university opened with 44 students in 1877, and still had only 433 students by 1900. The University of Colorado survived its first few decades due to local donations of money, labor, and land, including a 45-acre hilltop site. By 1914, the university claimed more colleges but only dramatically changed Boulder's fortunes and drew more immigrants after World War II.

FORT COLLINS

Similar to the Boulder and Pueblo merchants who serviced local farmers, Denver entrepreneurs recognized from their city's earliest days that minerals alone did not ensure their prosperity nor their posterity. A diversified, and thus more competitive and autonomous, regional economy required a viable agricultural sector. Moreover, urbanites believed farm families provided a stability badly needed on the predominantly male frontier. Working with regional railroads, boosters established land companies to recruit farmers who believed that the "Great American Desert" could be defeated through cooperative irrigation. Irrigation was too expensive, too time-consuming, and too backbreaking for an individual farmer. These agriculturalists applied the same cooperative community values in the towns that centered their colonies. Often organized in the East or Midwest, colonies purchased land from railroads or their subsidiary companies and set terms for admission.

Occupying a desolate military reservation of the same name, the Fort Collins Agricultural Colony settled north of Denver and offered persons of "good moral character" membership for $50, $150, or $250. Membership purchased city lots, farms, or both. The colony completed most homes and commercial buildings by 1873. As an inducement to migration, the company built the canals for the entire settlement. Fort Collins attracted white people from middle-class families in the Midwest. Poor people could not afford membership. Located on one of two lines that connected Denver to the transcontinental railroad, Fort Collins remained a small, but stable and relatively prosperous supply and processing center for local farmers. Fort Collins lobbied the legislature for the establishment of the College of Agriculture (now Colorado State University), a land-grant institution. It opened in 1879 with 19 students, but did not affect migration patterns until the 20th century. The 1880 census identified 1,356 residents; a decade later, the population only reached 3,053.

COLORADO SPRINGS

Colorado Springs began as a distinctly different venture that sometimes earned the scorn of farmers from Fort Collins and similar communities. As a scout for the Union Pacific Railroad and chief engineer for the Kansas Pacific, William Palmer became convinced of Colorado's and the Southwest's economic potential. In 1870, he formed the Denver and Rio Grande Railway (D&RG) to exploit the 1,000-mile distance from St. Louis that served as a natural tariff protection for the region's native production. He and his partners planned a new city. Although heavily invested in mining and transportation, they started Colorado Springs as a resort that packaged amorphous resources such as scenery, climate, sunshine, altitude, and waters to those who could afford traveling. Founded in 1871 in the shadow of Pike's Peak, the town had 800 residents within six months, entertained 1,500 visitors at its new and elegant hostelry the following summer, and by 1874 was home to 3,000. Recruiting among the better classes of Europe, the town company enjoyed great success in Great Britain. Two thousand English immigrants elevated Colorado Springs's social tone in an Anglophile age. Many elites, both British and American, believed nearby mountains offered a "pristine wilderness" long gone from their industrialized homes, but returned each evening to the comforts of their luxury hotels.

Others, including author Helen Hunt Jackson, sought respite from respiratory ailments in Colorado Springs. Since 1858, emigrants wrote of gentle Front Range winters, the absence of extreme temperatures, and the dry air's healing qualities. The Territorial Board of Immigration and boosters echoed Colorado's role as a sanatorium. Enterprising physicians moved to Colorado Springs to exploit this health market. The migration to Colorado Springs and other southwestern spas represented one of the last expressions of medical geography that began in antiquity: the belief that the environment improved individuals' chemistry. Tuberculosis, a disease with different meanings based on class and race, centered these medical migrations. Before the Civil War, the rich perceived the deaths of their tubercular relatives and friends as transcendent moments between this world and eternal peace. With new understandings of disease, such romantic notions changed. Tuberculosis became a degrading but treatable illness instead of a spiritual burden. A commensurate shift from the construct of invalidism with home care to one of health seeking followed. A new residence became the preferred treatment.

Colorado Springs became a restorative sanctuary and idyllic retreat. Wealthy eastern urbanites led this migration. Poor and working-class consumptives could afford neither the journey nor leisurely residence in Colorado Springs. By 1880, the town held a population of 4,226, trailing only Denver and the new, but temporarily successful, boomtown of Leadville. Large, expensive residential lots preserved the most attractive districts for the wealthy. At the same time, workers who serviced the tourist industry and other local businesses filled surrounding neighborhoods. Colorado Springs remained a predominantly white town in its first few decades.

The discovery of gold at Cripple Creek beneath Pike's Peak in the 1890s gave entrepreneurs and wealthy residents from Colorado Springs new investment opportunities. They developed new camps and created an exchange to trade mining stocks. The city's role as a supply center expanded. The nation remained mired in economic depression, but Cripple Creek allowed Colorado Springs's population to double to more than 20,000 by the turn of the century.

William Palmer and his associates also changed Pueblo's fortunes. His D&RG bypassed Pueblo in 1872 in favor of its newly constructed town of South Pueblo, just across the Arkansas River. After initial animosity, Pueblo's boosters anticipated the eventual merger with South Pueblo in 1886 and recognized that a railroad, even on the wrong side of the river, meant more business. Pueblo emerged in the 1870s as a manufacturing center when Palmer's subsidiary companies developed nearby coal and iron resources. Coal attracted factories and other railroads. Like Denver, Pueblo became a smelting center with the rejuvenation of California Gulch. New technologies allowed for the reduction of lead carbonate ores and sparked a migration of more than 25,000, with most settling in Leadville. With its rail connections, Pueblo now provided easier access to California Gulch than Denver. Smelter owners realized that the Front Range offered greater economies of scale. It cost less to bring the ores down the mountains than to ship the fuel up. The first Pueblo smelter went into operation in 1878. Others, including one controlled by Meyer Guggenheim, followed.

The smelters provided jobs for hundreds, but the biggest boom came in 1879 with the formation of the Colorado Coal and Iron Company from three D&RG affiliates. It later merged with another corporation as the Colorado Fuel and Iron Company (CF&I) and by 1910 employed one out of 10 Coloradans. Pueblo attracted more manufacturers whose capital needs might be met by the steel works that opened in 1882. Pueblo grew eightfold, reaching a population of 24,558 in 1890, to become Colorado's second largest city.

In the late 19th and early 20th centuries, smelters in Denver and Pueblo and the CF&I works required vast numbers of workers. In 1880, fewer than 900 immigrants from southeastern Europe resided in Denver. Over the next three decades, Italians, Austrians, Croats, Serbs, Slovenes, and others provided much of the unskilled labor for both towns' industries and the mines. Some 16,000 called Denver home by 1910. Denver's early suburbs deepened social divisions because their houses were inaccessible to these southeastern European immigrants. Needing homes near the factories, they created ethnic enclaves isolated from the rest of the city. Pueblo also drew small numbers from New Mexico and Mexico who lived in segregated neighborhoods.

Most workers, whether native- or foreign-born, achieved little upward mobility in the late 19th century. Class warfare erupted across Colorado between 1894 and 1914. In southern Colorado, for example, the Pueblo-based CF&I controlled housing, stores, schools, saloons, newspapers, and officials in many small towns. Owned by the Rockefellers after 1903, CF&I's nonunionized and often non-English-speaking workers offered weak challenges to the company's power structure. Only the deaths of 11 women and children in the 1914 Ludlow Massacre finally prompted calls for reform and investigations into unsafe conditions.

African Americans in Denver also found themselves isolated. Numbering less than 1,000 in 1880, the community grew sixfold over the next 30 years. Its members filled menial, dead-end jobs, and found few opportunities for advancement. Most found themselves restricted to the Five Points neighborhood until the 1960s and 1970s. Chinese immigrants, whose numbers in Denver peaked at 1,002 in 1890, faced harsher treatment. Riots in 1880 destroyed the laundries where many worked. With the 1882 Chinese Exclusion Act, their numbers dwindled to only 200 within the next 30 years.

20TH-CENTURY COLORADO

Still tied to volatile mining and agricultural industries, these five front-range cities and their economy stagnated between 1919 and 1939. Population growth stalled, but the trend toward fewer, larger urban areas began. Approximately 50 percent of the residents lived in cities and most were in these communities. During this same period, the region grew more homogeneous. Smaller numbers of foreign-born people found their way west due to federal immigration quotas and declines in mining and smelting. In 1910, foreign-born residents constituted almost 16 percent of the total population; 20 years later, the percentage was cut in half. The sugar beet industry provided one exception. It initially relied on Russian and German labor, but replaced them with Mexican migrant workers in the early 1900s. Several thousand spent winters in the piedmont cities and worked crops in the summer. American-born residents dominated the Front Range population by the 1920s, constituting more than 85 percent of Denver, although half were the children of European immigrants. Although there was little violence, persistent discrimination against racial and religious minorities crystallized in the Ku Klux Klan's rapid rise in Denver in 1924. It soon controlled the state Republican Assembly, the governor, and the new House of Representatives. Led by businessmen and professionals, it gained respectability until its leader became mired in a financial scandal in 1925.

With the Great Depression and hostile state border policies, overall immigration from Mexico faltered, but after their rural jobs as railroad hands and farm laborers disappeared, Mexican Americans flooded Denver and other cities where they competed with African Americans for low-paying jobs. More established African Americans were more likely to own their own homes and experienced better health. The newest arrivals faced an infant mortality rate of 20 percent.

World War II gave new life to the Front Range economy and drew more than 100,000 new residents, who encountered overpriced and insufficient housing. The federal government pumped almost $400 million into the region, and most of it found its way to these communities. Built by the federal government in 1941 and operated by Remington Company and then Henry Kaiser, the arsenal and ammunitions works employed almost 20,000 people at the height of its operation. The Rocky Mountain Arsenal in Denver occupied another 15,000 people in chemical weapons production. When Mare Island shipyards reached their capacity, a Denver plant manufactured ship hulls that were transported across the Rockies by train. Pueblo housed a large new ordinance depot and its manufactories retooled for wartime production. Men and women who migrated to the Front Range for employment or military service stayed because they loved its beauty and climate.

After the war, Colorado became home to a complex of scientific, research, and military installations in the corridor from Pueblo to Fort Collins. Located far from both coasts, these cities made ideal hosts for military bases. Lowry Air Force Base and Buckley Field near Denver, Peterson Air Field near Colorado Springs, and the Pueblo Army Air Base provided civilian jobs and boosted local economies. With Cold War tensions, Colorado Springs welcomed the Air Force Academy and the North American Air Defense Command (NORAD).

Between 1948 and 1964, manufacturing became more diversified, particularly with the aerospace industry and the movement of eastern-based companies to these centers, although with the conservatism of Denver's bankers, these changes resulted from outside investments. Martin Marietta, IBM, and Ball Brothers arrived from distant states, while Storage Technology Corporation was a homegrown Boulder entity. Hewlett Packard employed more than 8,000 people in Colorado Springs and Fort Collins. Yet older industries declined. The 1960s saw the closure of CF&I in Pueblo. The city never found a substitute and suffered in comparison to the other Front Range cities.

Federal agencies found homes in the region after World War II, leading some to call Denver the nation's second capital. President Ronald Reagan's efforts to retrench the federal government meant that the Front Range could not rely as thoroughly on federal dollars to stimulate its communities. Nonetheless, by 1988, the Department of Defense still spent 8 percent of its research budget in the Denver-Boulder area. Despite cutbacks, dozens of other federal agencies, from the Veterans Administration to the Environmental Protection Agency, called Denver home and pushed Colorado to eleventh nationally in per capita federal expenditures. Denver's share exceeded $2.3 billion annually. Federal spending provided 11,620 jobs in Denver alone. Agencies in Boulder, such as the National Center for Atmospheric Research and the National Bureau of Standards, created another 3,262. The University of Colorado, which benefited like other educational institutions from the G.I. Bill and the baby boom, estimated in 1982 that it received 23 percent of its research funds from defense, space, and government-based energy contracts. Government employment and the military-research enterprises attracted one of the nation's most white-collar, highly educated workforces, but blue-collar jobs declined as Denver, Colorado Springs, Boulder, and Fort Collins converted to a service-based, information-based economy. Disenchanted Californians migrated in droves. By 1990, more than 80 percent of Colorado's residents lived in the Pueblo–Fort Collins corridor.

By controlling the explosive growth that overwhelmed other cities in the corridor, Boulder became one of the most desirable areas along the Front Range. In addition to capitalizing on its role as an educational center, Boulder developed cultural and recreational amenities that drew a well-educated, health-seeking, and increasingly upper-middle-class populace. Strongly supported by the university community, slow-growth regulations protected the natural setting and older neighborhoods, and despite concerns did not scare away high tech businesses. It became a small-business haven, particularly in the communications and information technology sectors. Boulder's population grew from 19,000 to 83,000 between 1950 and 1990, while other areas experienced much greater expansion.

A prosperous agricultural center through most of its first seven decades, Fort Collins found new opportunities for economic expansion. With the exception of Hewlett Packard and a few others, Fort Collins did not attract as much business as Boulder and Denver did. Nonetheless, Fort Collins enjoyed the prosperity of the postwar boom and saw its population climb from 12,000 in 1940 to almost 90,000 five decades later. Like Boulder, Fort Collins benefited from the presence of Colorado State University and its rapid postwar expansion.

Minorities followed the migration paths to the Front Range cities during and after the war in search of new employment opportunities. The number of African Americans and Spanish-speaking Americans in Denver grew substantially, but segregation and discrimination persisted. African Americans initially did better than Hispanic Americans, finding employment at government offices and military facilities at a rate higher than the general population. Economic gains allowed blacks to leave Five Points for newer, better housing on the city's eastern edge, but did not lead to social integration. Having become the city's largest minority in the 1940s, Hispanic Americans remained in the city center, with at least 88 percent in substandard housing.

The Rocky Mountain minority representative of the War Manpower Commission reported in 1944 about Denver employers who refuse to hire "Mexicans," the segregation of Spanish-speaking laborers on construction projects, and differential wage scales. Nonetheless, labor shortages and efforts of the War Manpower Commission and the Fair Employment Practices Committee broke through more discrimination than efforts in the previous 80 years. After the 1960s, Mexican Americans assimilated more easily into Anglo-American society than did African Americans, even gaining the mayor's office.

More Native Americans now lived in Denver than the state's two reservations. Most migrated from other states. Despite a comparatively high education rate, Indians trailed other ethnic groups in median family income. At the same time, white Denverites continued their long-standing flight to suburbia. Despite a booming regional economy, the city's tax base declined. Poor people and minorities stayed behind, while white, middle-class families filled the suburbs, although the last decade witnessed gentrification of downtown and some older neighborhoods.

—*Kathleen A. Brosnan*

See also Cripple Creek, Colorado; Leadville, Colorado

Suggested Reading

Abbott, Carl. *Colorado: A History of the Centennial State.* Boulder: Colorado Associated University Press, 1976.

Barth, Gunther. *Instant Cities: Urbanization and the Rise of San Francisco and Denver.* New York: Oxford University Press, 1965.

Brosnan, Kathleen A. *Uniting Mountain and Plain: Cities, Law, and Environmental Change Along the Front Range.* Albuquerque: University of New Mexico Press, 2002.

Fell, James E., Jr. *Ores to Metals: The Rocky Mountain Smelting Industry.* Lincoln: University of Nebraska Press, 1979.

Hogan, Richard. *Class and Community in Frontier Colorado.* Lawrence: University Press of Kansas, 1990.

Lecompte, Janet. *Pueblo, Hardscrabble, Greenhorn: The Upper Arkansas, 1832–1856.* Norman: University of Oklahoma Press, 1978.

Leonard, Stephen J., and Thomas J. Noel. *Denver: Mining Camp to Metropolis.* Niwot: University Press of Colorado, 1990.

Noel, Thomas J., Paul F. Mahoney, and Richard E. Stevens. *Historical Atlas of Colorado.* Norman: University of Oklahoma Press, 1993.

Smith, Duane A. *Rocky Mountain West: Colorado, Wyoming, and Montana, 1859–1915.* Albuquerque: University of New Mexico Press, 1992.

Sprague, Marshall. *Newport in the Rockies: The Life and Good Times of Colorado Springs.* Rev. ed. Chicago: Sage Books, 1971.

Ubbelohde, Carl, Maxine Benson, and Duane A. Smith. *A Colorado History.* 8th ed. Boulder: Pruett, 2001.

West, Elliott. *The Contested Plains: Indians, Goldseekers, and the Rush to Colorado.* Lawrence: University Press of Kansas, 1998.

Wyckoff, William. *Creating Colorado: The Making of a Western Landscape, 1860–1940.* New Haven, CT: Yale University Press, 1999.

⊞ DILLINGHAM COMMISSION

See Immigration and Naturalization Service (INS)

⊞ DONNER, GEORGE AND JACOB

See Donner Party

⊞ DONNER PARTY

During the winter of 1846–1847, the Donner party of 79 overland trail emigrants were trapped in the snows of the Sierra Mountain Range and resorted to cannibalism for survival. One might feel pity and sympathy for their sufferings, but one might wonder if their fate was unavoidable. Thousands made the same journey at about the same period, meeting similar dangers yet arriving in Oregon or California safely. What made the Donner party different?

George and Jacob Donner and James Reed organized families from Illinois, Iowa, Tennessee, Missouri, and Ohio into a wagon train in April of 1846 and set out from Springfield, Illinois. After crossing the crest of the Rocky Mountains, the party split up, some wagons joining other trains. George Donner, a 62-year-old farmer, led his party and made a fateful decision.

At Fort Bridger, Lansford Warren Hastings' *Emigrants Guide to Oregon and California* (1845) gave the emigrants an option. It told of a good road, 300 miles shorter than the route usually followed by wagon trains to California, which led southwest of Fort Bridger, then through Utah's Wasatch Mountains, along the fringe of the Salt Lake Desert, and rejoined the main California trail. George and Jacob Donner and James Reed thought this the best route to follow, and thus led their party away from the main trail into the miseries of the desert and trackless mountains.

Opinions of historians regarding Lansford Hastings differ. Julia Altrocchi (1945) calls him "well intentioned but utterly unwise" and tells that "he had made all his Western investigations on horseback and knew nothing of the 15 miles a day travel by oxen, with long intervals between watering places." Joseph Pigney states that "Hastings and James Clyman had crossed the Sierra Nevadas on horseback a few weeks before the Donners reached Little Sandy (the beginning of the cut-off) and had barely made it through." He went on to say that, at the time, Hastings knew nothing of his "cut-off," and Pigney (1961) called Hastings "an ambitious young man seeking colonists for a new empire that he, himself, hoped to rule." Pigney's statement was supported by a contemporary, John Bidwell. According to Morgan (1963), Bidwell asserted that Hastings wanted to instigate a revolution that would wrest California from Mexico and establish an independent republic, of which Hastings might be president:

> And to accomplish that purpose, . . . the bringing of a large immigration from the United States, Hastings determined to return and write a book giving a glowing

account of Cal. & its resources and have it published as soon as possible. . . . It did much to attract settlers to Cal.

There was another motive attributed to Hastings. He was employed as an agent for Jim Bridger and Louis Vasquez, who operated the trading post that was virtually the whole town of Fort Bridger, which lay on the route of the cut-off Hastings was to describe in his guide. In this capacity, Hastings would have every reason to lead all prospective customers possible through Fort Bridger, which lay on the route of the cut-off. In fact, C. F. McGlashan (1962), publisher of the *Santa Barbara Press* and the *Truckee Republican* in the 1870s, who interviewed many of the survivors of the Donner party, stated that

> but for the earnest advice and solicitation of Bridger and Vasquez, who had charge of the fort, the entire party would have continued by the accustomed route. These men had a direct interest in the Hastings Cut-off as they furnished the emigrants with supplies and had employed Hastings to pilot the first company over the road to Salt Lake.

The Donner party probably decided to take the cut-off because of the savings in time and mileage they supposed it would make, because when they left Fort Bridger on July 31 they were one of the last trains on the move and hundreds of miles still remained between them and California. The party averaged approximately 15 miles a day. Hastings was, even then, only a few days ahead of them on the trail, guiding a large party of 66 wagons through the mountains. The Donner party was assured that he would leave markers for them so there would be no possibility of their getting lost.

At least one member of the Donner party, however, had been warned against the cut-off. James Reed was acquainted with Jim Clyman, who had been in the Hastings party when they rode horseback on the trail that he later called the Hastings Cut-off. Clyman, therefore, was in a good position to speak from first-hand experience. In his diary, Clyman related that his party (another group, not the same one that had included Hastings) camped with the Donners one night at Laramie. Clyman knew John Reed from "the Sauk war" (also known as the Black Hawk War of 1832, a war between the U.S. Army and Sauk and Fox Indians). Reed inquired about the Hastings Cut-off, and Clyman told him to "take the regular wagon track and never leave it—it is barely possible to get through if you follow it—and it may be impossible if you don't." Reed replied, "There is another route and it is of no use to take so much of a roundabout course. Clyman admitted the fact but told him about the great desert and the roughness of the Sierras, and that a straight route might turn out to be impracticable."

Reed was one of the wealthiest members of the Donner party, and a man of good reputation and much influence. If he had taken this advice from Clyman, he would surely have been able to persuade the rest of the party to take the main California route. Yet Reed chose not to heed Clyman's advice.

Unknown to the Donner party, Edwin Bryant, another emigrant and friend of Reed who was traveling on horseback ahead of the Donner party, left a letter with Vasquez to be given to Reed when he reached Fort Bridger. Vasquez never gave the letter to Reed. He probably knew it contained a warning against traveling via the Hastings Cut-off. It is also known that Vasquez and Bridger deliberately misrepresented the conditions of the road beyond Fort Bridger. Reed wrote to his brothers-in-law from Fort Bridger (Morgan 1963):

> The new road, or the Hastings Cut-off, leaves the Fort Hall road here, and it is said to be a saving of 350 or 400 miles in going to California, and a better route. Mr. Bridger, and other gentlemen here who have trapped in that country, say that the Lake has receded from the tract of country in question. There is plenty of grass which we can cut and put into the wagons, for our cattle while crossing it. Mr. Bridger informs me that the route we design to take is a fine level road, with plenty of water and grass.

When the Donner party reached the Weber River crossing, they found a note left for the followers of Hastings, telling them that Weber Canyon was very bad and advising them to camp at the crossing and send a messenger into the canyon to fetch Hastings. He would return to see them safely off on a detour. Reed and two other men rode off to bring Hastings back. Reed returned five days later, saying the canyon was impassable. In spite of his promise, Hastings had

not returned to guide the Donner party, but merely rode with Reed back as far as the summit of the Wasatch Mountains, because the train he was guiding might not make it on their present course. The Donner party decided to travel across the mountains in a more direct line toward Salt Lake. They found, however, the way they had chosen was impassable. Almost all the oxen in the train had to be to used to draw each wagon out of the canyon and up the steep, overhanging mountains. Instead of reaching Salt Lake in a week, as Hastings had promised, they were more than 30 days making the trip. Now, summer was past, the men and oxen were exhausted, and the provisions nearly gone.

The Salt Desert proved a torture to cross. It was much larger than Hastings, Bridger, or Vasquez had let them know. The distances between the water holes were unbearably long, so that some of the livestock perished from thirst and some of the wagons had to be abandoned.

The character of this company had a critical bearing on their tragic fate. At about this point in the journey, an old Belgian, traveling alone in one of the wagons with a German family, was put out and told to walk or die. When the rest of the party learned of this abandonment, not one person offered to go back and look for him. William Pike, a member of the party, was killed when a "pepper box" gun accidentally discharged. Although his brother-in-law was with him at the time, there were no other witnesses to verify that it was indeed an accident. Further, a wealthy man mysteriously disappeared. Finally, Reed stabbed one of the party during a quarrel, killing him. Callous disinterest, violence, evil, and greed seemed to personify this wagon train.

Bad luck also played a part in the Donner tragedy. Most years, the first snow fell during the last part of November, but in 1846 it began to snow near present-day Donner Pass on October 23, 1846. By October 28, snow lay two to five feet deep on the summit.

The party straggled in segments as far as what is now known as Donner Lake and were forced to camp there. In the following days, several small groups, acting independently, made efforts to cross the mountain barrier. These efforts were irregular, the party lacking good leadership and a spirit of unity that might have saved them. Even though these people were exhausted and discouraged and their supplies were low, if they had abandoned their possessions at this point and forgotten the hostilities that were felt among them, their journey might have had a different ending. They refused, however, to discard the hindering wagons and were reluctant to pool their oxen and manpower to make a great, single push to take a few wagons over the cliffs to safety.

There was little generosity or community spirit exhibited in the settlement now established at Donner Lake. One of the men, who had previously shot some game and distributed the meat, tried to beg an ox from another member of the party. This other member demanded $25 for the ox and at last parted with it on the promise of receiving the money when they were safely in California. Mrs. Reed, now without her husband (who had been banished from the party when he killed Snyder and rode ahead to California, returning later as one of the rescuers), had to promise to later pay two oxen for each one she received as food. Another member had to pay his gold watch and other goods for food.

Some people, however, still had ample food in the cattle and mules they brought with them. If these animals had been penned, or carefully watched, there could have been meat enough to last them through the winter. No care was taken of these animals, so they wandered off and died and then were covered with snow so no one could find them.

Although most of the bears were in hibernation, the trout in Donner Lake were semihibernating, and the deer had moved to less snowy altitudes, there is evidence that there was animal life that could have supplied the starving people with food. There were rabbits, grouse, and other animals still active, living under the protective fir branches, eating spruce buds, and staying out of the snow. William Eddy seems to be the only person who made any attempt to hunt. On November 4, 1846, he succeeded in killing a prairie wolf. On November 5, he killed an owl, and on other occasions he killed several ducks, a squirrel, and once even a bear weighing more than 800 pounds, which provided food for many days. Morgan (1963) recounts that Patrick Breen, who kept a diary while the party remained snowbound that winter, made an entry on Thursday, February 25, 1847: "Mrs Murphy says the wolves are about to dig up the dead bodies at her shanty, the nights too cold to watch them, we hear them howling." The wolves certainly must have had

smaller animals to live on, so it is likely that if traps had been improvised, or any serious effort made to catch game, this could have been done.

In his entry of February 26, 1847, Breen wrote, "Hungry times in camp, plenty hides but the folks will not eat them, we eat them with a tolerable good appetite, Thanks be to Almighty God, Amen." In the same entry, he goes on to mention that the Donners were trying to locate the bodies of their lost cattle: "Donners told the California folks that they [would] commence to eat dead people 4 days ago, if they did not succeed that day or the next in finding the cattle under ten to twelve feet of snow & did not know the spot or near it I suppose They have done so ere this time." On February 27, Breen's diary records the fact that he heard some geese flying overhead, so there were birds to be hunted, had anyone tried. However, the members of the Donner party, when the domestic animals were gone and they faced starvation, allegedly fed on human flesh. Members of several relief parties sent to find them found them lying weakly in filth, crawling with lice, looking like ghosts rather than people and supposedly surrounded by the dismembered bodies of their relatives and friends. But recently, scientists say this cannibalism has not been proven during the course of a three-year archaeological dig. In any case, only 47 reached California alive, and they bore physical and mental scars for the rest of their lives.

Interestingly, in 1844, a 17-year-old boy named Moses Schallenberger had stayed at Donner Lake by himself from mid-October until February. He had gone with the Stevens party en route to California via Donner Lake. In order to get through, some of the wagons had to be left at the lake, so Schallenberger and two others volunteered to stay and guard the goods they contained, while the rest of the party went on. The three of them built a cabin (which was later used by the Donner party). According to Schallenberger, game seemed to be abundant, as deer and bear had been seen, and there were Indians living in the vicinity. As winter progressed and the game got scarcer, all they could find were coyote and fox tracks. The two other men improvised snowshoes and hiked out, but Schallenberger could not make it, so he agreed to stay with the cabin. Among the stores he guarded, he found some traps and used them to catch coyotes and foxes, feeding himself on these until his party returned. It would seem that a 17-year-old boy could do by himself what scores of grown men could not do.

Also, on record is the fact that Lansford Warren Hastings crossed the Sierra Nevadas on horseback with a party of 10 men in mid-December of 1845. While they were near Donner Lake, they shot a deer.

Another fact must be mentioned. According to Morgan (1963), there were Indians living in the vicinity who knew of the Donner party's plight. "We could have saved them," wrote Sarah Winnemucca Hopkins, granddaughter of Chief Truckee, in her book *Life Among the Piutes,* "only my people were afraid of them."

In the penultimate entry made in his diary on February 28, 1847, Patrick Breen wrote that one "solitary Indian passed by yesterday come from the lake had a heavy pack on his back gave 5 or 6 roots resembling Onions in shape taste some like sweet potatoe, all full of little tough fibres." He expresses no surprise at the sudden appearance of this Indian, and one wonders if the Donner party members were aware of the Indians' proximity. If they were, then they must have known the Indians could help them survive the winter and could have asked for their help.

The fate of the Donner party was, to a great extent, in their own hands. This fact was apparently recognized by James Reed when he wrote a letter to his brother-in-law on July 2, 1847 (Morgan 1963), after safely arriving with his family in Napa Valley, California:

> The disasters of the company to which I belonged, should not deter any person from coming who wishes to try his fortune. Our misfortunes were the result of bad management. Had I remained with the company, I would have had the whole of them over the mountains before the snow would have caught them; and those who have got through have admitted this to be true.

> —Kellin Francis

See also Sutter, Johann August

Suggested Reading

Altrocchi, Julia C. *The Old California Trail.* Caldwell, ID: The Caxton Printers, 1945.

Croy, Homer. *Wheels West.* New York: Hastings House, 1955.

King, Joseph A. "The Breens Versus Persistent Donner Party Mythology: Critiquing the Chroniclers." *The Californians* 10 (July–August 1992): 8–21.

King, Joseph A. *Winter of Entrapment: A New Look at the Donner Party.* Toronto: P. D. Meany, 1992.

McGlashan, C. F. *History of the Donner Party.* Stanford, CA: Stanford University Press, 1962.

Morgan, Dale, ed. *Overland in 1846: Diaries and Letters of the California-Oregon Trail.* Georgetown, CA: Talisman, 1963.

Pigney, Joseph. *For Fear We Shall Perish.* New York: Dutton, 1961.

Schallenberger, Moses. *The Opening of the California Trail.* Berkeley: University of California Press, 1953.

Sonner, Scott. "Research: Donners Didn't Resort to Cannibalism." Available from http://www.cnn.com/2006/US/01/12/donner.party.ap/index.html

Stewart, George R. *Donner Pass.* San Francisco: California Historical Society, 1960.

Thornton, Jesse Quinn. *The California Tragedy.* Oakland: California Biobooks, 1945.

DOUGLAS, ARIZONA

See Bisbee and Douglas, Arizona

DRY FARMING

Hardy Webster Campbell's contributions regarding dry farming are best understood within the context of the intensive boosterism accompanying the rapid agricultural settlement of the northern plains. The region had already demonstrated that new approaches to farming were needed prior to the widespread publication of his techniques and the belief that they represented a remedy for the region's agricultural challenges. As early as the 1870s, farming settlements had already emerged on the Great Plains. Although many of these farmers experienced success during ample rain, the inevitable return of dry conditions often resulted in financial ruin. Despite such precedents, dry farming's promoters enthusiastically embraced the notion that Campbell's approach possessed the necessary tools for prosperity.

During the initial phase of agricultural settlement, many Americans had also embraced grandiose notions; they had abandoned the notion that the plains represented nothing more than an unpromising, infertile desert. Settlers replaced this negative view with the naive notion that settlement itself might produce increased precipitation and agricultural prosperity. In 1873, the federal policymakers also miscalculated the stubbornness of the region's aridity by enacting the Timber Culture Act, which entitled settlers with 160 acres if they planted 40 acres of trees. This provision proved to be unrealistic, and the planting requirements had to be reduced to 10 acres five years later. In the late 1880s, settlers' optimism was severely tested with the onset of a sustained period of low rainfall, resulting in large numbers of abandoned farms. Such conditions necessitated the development of new agricultural approaches, improved farming techniques, and hardier crops capable of withstanding the plains environment.

Although Campbell's important role in Western settlement distinguishes him from the typical plains resident, his early experience is not atypical. Campbell spent his childhood on a Vermont farm and shortly after leaving New England had established himself as a Dakota farmer. Although initially experiencing success, he soon faced considerable difficulties with the onset of drought. This experience encouraged his search for farming methods that would be more suitable for dry conditions. By the 1890s, his initial experiments had been promising and had gained the interest of a number of railroad companies. A number of railroads appointed him as a director of their model farms. Campbell became involved in the activities of over 40 such institutions throughout the West. These positions provided Campbell with opportunities to further explore his dry farming techniques, enabling him to develop a system aimed at conserving soil moisture. His approach included such methods as plowing fields deeply and extensively packing the soil. His close involvement with the railroads reveals how his ideas became intertwined in the efforts to encourage settlement on the plains.

Soon, Campbell's ideas were being published in *The Western Soil Culture Journal* and a variety of national publications. He also fully articulated his ideas in multiple editions of his *Soil Culture Manual,* which appeared in the early years of the 20th century. His soil manuals soon enjoyed national popularity. Campbell's writings not only outlined his dry farming methods, but also expressed his view that their proper implementation would produce agricultural abundance. In the opening pages of a 1907 edition of his *Soil Culture Manual,* he

stated the region was "destined to be covered with countless homes of happy American families, with cities and towns prosperous and growing." Soon, other dry farming enthusiasts were authoring their own handbooks and echoing Campbell's confident sentiments. In 1912, John Widtsoe, an official at Utah's experiment station, published *Dry Farming: A System of Agriculture for Counties Under Low Rainfall* and also received wide readership. Widtsoe agreed with most of Campbell's methods, and his sentiments were equally boosteristic. He expressed that dry farming could unleash the region's agricultural potential and bring prosperity to both current and future immigrants. He stated that, when dry farming principles were applied correctly, "the practice is almost always successful."

Groups, such as land developers, town boosters, and a large number of railroad officials, praised dry farming as a way to overcome the northern plains' limitations regarding irrigation possibilities. The approach was particularly alluring for regions in which irrigation projects were not viable. In 1902, the passage of the Newlands Reclamation Act represented significant federal effort to develop western irrigation projects. Unfortunately, for the developers, many aspects of the region's geography presented serious irrigation obstacles. For instance, many of the area's rivers were very inconsistent in their water flows. Many residents, therefore, discovered that irrigating was both impractical or cost prohibitive. Thus, in 1900, large sections of Montana, South Dakota, and North Dakota remained devoid of intensive agricultural settlement.

However, during the first two decades of the 20th century, this lack of development did not last as immigration expanded rapidly into some of the northern plains' most dry and sparsely settled regions. This hasty influx of settlers was encouraged by the sustained boosterism of town newspapers and the pamphlets published by both land developers and railroad companies. Some ranchers even praised dry farming's potential, recognizing its possibilities for profit from land sales. Federal policymakers also assisted with the development of the plains by crafting legislation better suited to the region's larger land requirements. In 1904, Congress voted for the Kincaid Act, which offered settlers a 640-acre tract of land, but exclusively in the state of Nebraska. In 1909, Congress passed a more regionally inclusive legislation in the enlarged Homestead Act. This legislation offered settlers 320 acres after farming it for five years. Such acts symbolized efforts to craft land policy better suited to the region's characteristics.

Dry farming's role in encouraging this rapid migration onto the plains is particularly apparent in the creation of the Trans-Missouri Dry Farming Congress. In 1907, the organization was established and, despite twice renaming itself (first to the Dry-Farming Congress and then to the International Dry-Farming Congress), its mission remained the same: to promote settlement on the Great Plains by advocating dry farming's potential. The organization garnered support from land speculators, state promotional organizations, railroad companies, and investors. The annual meetings often attracted large numbers of people. In 1912, a meeting held in Lethbridge, Canada, hosted 10,000 people, and other meetings of the congress attracted similarly substantial participants. The meetings' attendees were showered with verbose speeches celebrating dry farming's potential. In 1909, the congress was held at Billings, Montana. One local town leader stated that "we believe the dry lands of Montana offer the home seeker the best returns, the best living and the easiest way to make a living of any place in the United States today." Meetings included many such examples of overstated enthusiasm regarding the actual effort required to wrestle a living from the Great Plains.

Some writers, observers, and researchers provided more cautionary remarks than the enthusiastic proclamations by speakers at the annual congress meetings. Some stressed that although some portions of the plains produced ample rainfall in good years, droughts were inevitable. Other writers also suggested that farms should be as large as 1,000 acres and ideally accompanied by substantial investment in expensive machinery. In addition, some agricultural researchers believed that further study of appropriate farming methods needed to be undertaken before optimistic appraisals were accepted. For instance, in 1906, Ellery Channing Chilcott, an agricultural scientist for South Dakota's experiment station, acknowledged that understanding what adaptations were required for the region's extreme environment still required further research. Thus, many researchers believed that further investigation of drought-resistant plant varieties needed to be undertaken prior to an accurate understanding of the dry farming approach. Nevertheless, both the amount of scientific knowledge and the detractors' organizational strength proved insufficient caution in averting hasty settlement.

During the first two decades of the 20th century, settlers flooded into regions such as the Dakotas and eastern Montana. They initially enjoyed the combined benefits of high wheat prices and favorable weather conditions, which led to the rapid development of a number of thriving communities on the plains. During the prosperous years, town businesses expanded and prospered while serving the needs of surrounding farmers. Nevertheless, pioneers also quickly became acquainted with the region's challenging climate, isolation, and rough living conditions. These difficulties were severely intensified upon the onset of drought conditions. The farmers of western South Dakota experienced a particularly rough period between 1910 and 1913 that forced the abandonment of large stretches of recently settled land. In the late 1910s, eastern Montana farmers faced a devastating combination of widespread drought and the onset of low farm prices. Such conditions were sometimes complicated by other challenges, including widespread grasshopper infestations. These prolific pests wreaked further havoc on the crops that were already weakened by dry conditions. Although experiment station researchers did discover methods to combat the insect threat, such developments required time and thus many settlers left the plains before benefiting from them. Farmers also experienced failure for a variety of other reasons: They often lacked adequate farming knowledge, had settled on poor lands, or were financially overextended and thus unable to survive periods of crisis.

Regardless of the specific reason for failure, suffering during times of drought was severe. Western South Dakota was so decimated by the drought that outright hunger was evidenced throughout the region. The farm populations suffered further because relief efforts were often insufficient in addressing the problem's scope. In addition, widespread bank closings, business failures, and other components of the rural economy contracted as a result of flight from the plains. Thus, the small towns that had arisen to provide services to the surrounding farm regions declined as larger numbers of settlers made a hasty retreat from the plains. The landscape of the northern plains quickly became dotted with declining communities following such periods. Although some newspaper writers continued to maintain that applying dry farming techniques could avert financial ruin, such advice was of little help to the vast throngs of overwhelmed settlers. Nevertheless, the region continued to possess a contingent of promoters who praised its agricultural potential.

In summary, Hardy Webster Campbell's role in the development of a dry farming approach represents a part of the continuing story of plains farmers' continual adjustment to their situation. The region's farmers have recurrently had to adjust to unreliable weather, changing government policies, and fluctuating commodity prices. Although an observer could justifiably place much culpability for the widespread farm failure during the early part of the 20th century on the region's boosters, it is also important to acknowledge other factors as well. Such contextual considerations include many settlers' relative agricultural inexperience prior to their migration onto the plains. Historian W. M. Hargreaves has pointed to settlers' and farmers' lack of experience as greatly contributing to their demise. She has indicated that large numbers of settlers on the northern plains during the period had previously worked in nonagricultural occupations. Thus, many were either unable or unwilling to practice Campbell's dry farming methods as well as other practitioners of the approach. In addition, settlers were also often shocked by the harsh conditions, which included the very basics of life. Settlers struggled to procure adequate wood and water sources, even for home use. Such difficult conditions persisted on the Great Plains well into the 20th century.

Despite such hardship, those that remained often maintained an optimistic attitude upon the conclusion of the region's many crises. Farmers who survived were often those that best demonstrated their ability to adapt to the region's harsh climatic and economic realities. Such farmers employed improved farming techniques developed by various federal and state agencies, purchased suitable equipment, and sometimes returned the most marginal lands to livestock. Thus, the northern plains continued to be an agricultural region throughout the 20th century. States such as Montana and North Dakota continued to be among the leaders in total wheat production. In addition, farming without the aid of irrigation remained a crucial component to the region's agricultural vitality. The fact that a majority of the region's crop acreage continued to be produced without the assistance of irrigation testifies to the importance of Campbell and other dry farming innovators. Thus, although farmers continually utilized new machinery and refined farming methods, early 20th-century farming discoveries in precipitation-scarce regions represent an important stage in this continued development. Undoubtedly, farmers will be forced to make continued adjustments to the plains, just as their early 20th-century predecessors adapted.

—*Derek Oden*

See also Gallatin Valley, Montana; Hopi

Suggested Reading

Campbell, Hardy Webster. *Campbell's 1907 Soil Culture Manual,* Lincoln, NE: H. W. Campbell, 1907.

Hargreaves, Mary. *Dry Farming in the Northern Great Plains, 1900–1925.* Cambridge, MA: Harvard University Press, 1957.

Hargreaves, Mary. *Dry Farming in the Northern Great Plains: Years of Readjustment, 1920–1990.* Lawrence: University Press of Kansas, 1993.

Hurt, R. Douglas. *American Agriculture: A Brief History.* Ames: Iowa State University Press, 1994.

Nelson, Paula M. *After the West Was Won: Homesteaders and Town-Builders in Western South Dakota, 1900–1917.* Iowa City: University of Iowa Press, 1986.

Proceedings of the Fourth Annual Session of the Dry Farming Congress. Billings, MT: Billings Chamber of Commerce, 1909.

Proceedings of the Trans-Missouri Dry Farming Congress. Denver, CO: Denver Chamber of Commerce, 1907.

Widtsoe, John A. *Dry-Farming: A System of Agriculture for Countries Under a Low Rainfall.* New York: Macmillan, 1911.

⊞ DUNIWAY, ABIGAIL SCOTT (1834–1915)

Abigail Scott Duniway was a prominent editor, writer, and champion for women's rights. She was born Abigail Jane Scott on October 22, 1834, in a log cabin in Tazewell County, Illinois. Jenny Scott, as her family knew her, grew up on a hardscrabble farm on the Illinois frontier, surrounded by numerous siblings and by kin who had migrated to Illinois from Kentucky during the 1820s.

In 1852, the Scott family and thousands of others traveled west by covered wagon on the Oregon Trail. For the duration of the six-month journey, John Tucker Scott assigned specific tasks to each of his children. His eldest daughter was responsible for traditional women's work, such as cooking. Seventeen-year-old Jenny also kept the detailed family journal each day, which her father intended for later publication. This was an ideal assignment for Jenny, who was outspoken and intelligent, but who chafed at domestic work. Jenny soon discovered, however, that it was challenging to write at the end of long days on the trail. Keeping the Scott family journal was Jenny's first step toward her future career as a feminist writer and publisher.

Upon reaching the Oregon Territory, Jenny Scott played the role of a respectable mid-19th-century young woman, teaching school for several months before marrying Benjamin C. Duniway on August 2, 1853. The Duniways settled on Ben's 320-acre donation land claim near Oregon City, in the northern Willamette Valley. Abigail Duniway soon grew discontented with the unceasing labor of a frontier farmer's wife.

Duniway gradually moved from churning butter to writing features for local newspapers. In 1859, she published *Captain Gray's Company,* the first of several novels that she drew from her experiences on the Illinois and Oregon frontiers. When her husband lost their farm after unwisely cosigning interest-bearing notes for a friend, Duniway returned to teaching. After Ben Duniway suffered a debilitating accident, she used her earnings as a teacher to establish a successful millinery business—one of the few acceptable business enterprises for 19th-century women—in Albany, Oregon.

Duniway's financial struggles and those of her millinery customers inspired her to dedicate her life to women's empowerment. The more suffering she observed on the part of rural women, the more devoted she became to the cause of woman suffrage. In 1871, the Duniway family moved to Portland, and Abigail began publishing a weekly equal rights newspaper, the *New Northwest.* For 16 years, Duniway published articles advocating women's rights, fashion tips, domestic advice, and her own serial fiction. She sought to debunk men's arguments against women's suffrage without challenging their belief in separate social roles for men and women, contending that women's moral superiority justified granting them political rights.

Duniway developed into a skilled public speaker through her participation in women's clubs and the temperance movement. Beginning in 1876, she went on lecture tours throughout the Pacific Northwest to promote women's suffrage, lecturing on such topics as "The Future of Woman, as Foreshadowed by her Past" and "The Moral Responsibility of Womanhood." Throughout her campaign for women's suffrage, Duniway's biggest opponent was her own brother: Harvey Scott, who published the influential newspaper *The Oregonian* for more than 30 years, outspokenly opposed the suffrage cause.

Abigail Scott Duniway became a prominent member of the nationwide suffrage movement. She was elected one of five vice presidents at-large of the National American Woman Suffrage Association (NAWSA), and in 1887 was invited to speak before the U.S. House of Representatives. By the turn of the century, however, Duniway found herself at odds with many suffrage leaders because she disagreed with their methods. Duniway believed that outside organizers should stay out of the Pacific Northwest because they did not understand local conditions. Despite numerous setbacks, Duniway persevered until all of the northwestern states granted suffrage to women: Idaho in 1896, Washington State in 1910, and finally Oregon in 1912. After 28 years of effort and five defeats at the polls, Duniway wrote and signed Oregon's Equal Suffrage Proclamation in 1912 and became the first Oregon woman to register to vote. She died in Portland in 1915 at the age of 80.

—Cynthia Culver

Suggested Reading

Duniway, Abigail Scott. *Path Breaking: An Autobiographical History of the Equal Suffrage Movement in Pacific Coast States.* 2nd ed. Portland, OR: James, Kerns & Abbott, 1914.

Moynihan, Ruth Barnes. *Rebel for Rights: Abigail Scott Duniway.* New Haven, CT: Yale University Press, 1983.

E

☷ EMERGENCY IMMIGRATION ACT OF 1921

See IMMIGRATION AND NATURALIZATION SERVICE (INS)

☷ ENLARGED HOMESTEAD ACT OF 1909

In 1862, the U.S. Congress passed one of the most influential pieces of legislation ever written. The Homestead Act of 1862 was a result of vigorous agitation by many western settlers. The act allotted settlers the opportunity to homestead 160 acres of land if, in return, they would cultivate the land for five years. The 1862 act, however, failed in many ways to bring the number of expected homesteaders to the West. The primary reason for this shortcoming was Congress. In 1873, Congress passed the Timber Culture Act, enabling settlers to acquire additional land. Yet Congress granted millions of acres to Native Americans, states of the union, and railroad companies rather than individual settlers. As a result, the Homestead Act of 1862 failed to accomplish the migratory goals of many legislators and became part of an incongruous land system.

In 1909, many state governments, legislatures, railroad companies, real estate, agents, and immigration bureaus looked to the semiarid West with hopes for further development. Much of the land was fit for livestock industry, but many felt that different methods of farming would hasten immigration. Such an alternative was dry farming, endorsed by railroad companies, real estate agents, and land locators. Another was a mixed farming-grazing approach, supported by the U.S. Department of Agriculture. The problem with the second choice, however, was to decide if farmers should grow feed for livestock or raise livestock while also growing food for resale. Consequently, the congressional majority decided that the mixed farming-grazing approach created much uncertainty, and dry farming eventually took hold with the 1909 amendment.

The Enlarged Homestead Act of 1909 increased the acreage available for homesteading from 160 to 320 acres. Furthermore, it stated that the land must be nonmineral, nonirrigable, and without merchantable timber. In addition, the act required that one eighth of the land be continuously cultivated for crops other than native grasses. Finally, homesteaders had to remain on the land for five years, during which time there could be no commutation, an exchange or interchange of lands. Classification of the new lands was to be done by the Department of the Interior through a geological survey. The Enlarged Homestead Act affected nine states: Oregon, Washington, Arizona, New Mexico, Colorado, Utah, Montana, Wyoming, and Nevada. The remaining western states—California, Idaho, Kansas, and North and South Dakota—did not want to be regarded as semiarid and did not participate under the amended act. In 1912, the act was further amended, lowering the required period of residence from five to three years.

In 1916, Congress passed the Stock Raising Homestead Act, raising the amount of acreage from

320 to 640. One exception to the act was for the state of Utah. Because Utah had no known areas with a good source of domestic water, the act stated that residency for up to 2 million acres of land would not be required. Just like its predecessor, the Enlarged Homestead Act failed to accomplish its goals. In actuality, the 1909 act did almost the opposite of what Congress had hoped.

Prior to the Enlarged Homestead Act, the number of settlers putting in entries rose and fell. In fact, in 1910, the first year of the new act, the number of entries had reached its second highest peak at 98,598 entries. Many, however, placed a great deal of faith in the new act, confidently awaiting the arrival of many homesteaders. Confidence was so high that the state of Wyoming claimed that their soil was very rich and fertile. This, however, proved not to be the case. In 1910, before much change could take place, Wyoming had 10,987 entries. In the next 24 years, this number rose to 88,687, yet half of the entrants never homesteaded. Also, those who migrated to Wyoming would find the years that followed plagued by drought. The number of homestead entries drastically declined in 1911 and 1912. Furthermore, the 1909 act came during a wet period in Montana; thus prospects for farming looked good, bringing more than 80,000 settlers to the state. As a result, by 1920 it became evident that farmers had overgrazed and the land was unproductive. In addition, Colorado faced a similar experience with the amended act. Like Wyoming, Colorado claimed that its land was very good and that settlers could become wealthy off their land. Colorado booster literature brought more than 77,000 homesteaders to Colorado. Despite such large numbers of migrants, those who filed entries from 1910 to 1919 increased by only 24 percent.

The hopes that the Enlarged Homestead Act would ignite migration soon faded as many settlers found themselves farming inadequate land. Attempts at amending the 1909 act, such as the 1912 and 1916 acts, also proved unsuccessful. A final attempt at populating the West and homesteading occurred when many settlers attempted to farm the Great Plains. Consequently, such actions resulted in the great Dust Bowl of the 1930s.

—Scott Keys

Suggested Reading

Gates, Paul W. *History of Public Land Law Development.* New York: Arno, 1979.

George Mason University. "The Sale of Federal Land: Free Homesteads." *A History of United States Public Land Law and the Evolution of the National Forest System.* [Online course PRLS 542]. Available from http://classweb.gmu.edu/erodger1/prls542/one/dispos7.htm

Montanakids.com. "They Settled in Montana: The Act." Available from http://montanakids.com/db_engine/presentations/presentation.asp?pid=329&sub=The+Act

⊞ ESPIONAGE ACT OF 1917

See Forced Migration of Anarchists

⊞ EURO-AMERICAN MIGRATION ON THE OVERLAND TRAILS

The possibility of a better life, the lure of the unknown trans-Mississippi West, and the idea of manifest destiny appealed to American expansionist sentiments during the mid-19th century. A shortage of land in the East, untapped sources of wealth in the West, and a desire for adventure encouraged more than a quarter of a million people to emigrate to the American West between 1840 and 1860. Fur traders blazed the first paths to the West, and the American Board of Commissioners for Foreign Missions followed in their footsteps. In 1836, pioneering missionaries, such as Marcus and Narcissa Whitman and Henry and Eliza Spalding, traveled to the West to convert Native Americans to Christianity. Once it had been proven that wagons could survive the trip, overland travel increased with a rising number of farming families seeking fertile land, good health, and a richer life.

The character of westward emigration changed with the discovery of gold in California, and beginning in 1849 men flocked to seek instant riches before returning home. This mass migration disrupted wide swaths of western landscape by displacing Native Americans, by littering the trails with carcasses of dead animals and mounds of unwanted goods, and by slaughtering great numbers of buffalo. But the argonauts also established support systems along the trails and made it easier for families to travel by covered wagon. Emigrants thus headed west on the trails and settled in Oregon, Washington, California, and Colorado, turning the trails into a national highway. The country celebrated the completion of the transcontinental railroad in 1869, but three decades of trail travel represented a migration never to be repeated in American history.

The overland trails were unfamiliar and dangerous, yet thousands of men risked their lives, and the lives of their wives and children, to reach their destinations. The Northern Route crossed Kansas, Nebraska, and Utah. Emigrants on this route generally followed the Oregon-California Trail along the Platte River northwest from Independence, St. Joseph, or Kanesville (now Council Bluffs) in Missouri and Iowa, respectively. The route crossed over the prairies, passing military stations like Fort Kearney and Fort Laramie and notable landmarks such as Courthouse Rock, Chimney Rock, and Independence Rock. Emigrants proceeded through the south pass of the Rocky Mountains, which offered some relief from the freezing weather and steep inclines that challenged the strength of the animals and the determination of the emigrants. Once east of the Rockies, the Northern Route split, leading emigrants either to Oregon or to California. Future Oregonians passed Soda Springs, Idaho, and followed the Snake, Columbia, and The Dalles rivers, which led emigrants to their destination: the Willamette River Valley. The overlanders who took the route to California passed the Great Salt Lake and struggled through the Great Basin, where they encountered a three- to four-day trek through a desert marked by 120-degree heat, dusty paths volcanic in appearance, and, worst of all, no water. Emigrants made the final crossing over the steep ridges of the snow-covered Sierra Nevada mountains on foot, as animals could not pull wagons over nearly impassable and often nonexistent tracks. Once across the mountains, emigrants sought the gold fields and fertile land along the Sacramento River.

Lesser known, but also of importance, were a number of trails on the Southern Route. These crossed the present-day states of Kansas, Oklahoma, Texas, New Mexico, and Arizona and even portions of Mexican territory before reaching California. Like the Northern Route, the Southern Route consisted of a number of trails, the most famous of which were the Gila Trail, the Santa Fe Trail, and the Apache Pass Trail. The starting points for the Southern Route included Independence, Missouri; Fort Smith, Arkansas; and several towns in Texas and Louisiana. The routes to the south crossed Oklahoma, spread throughout Texas, and followed either the Pecos River or the Rio Grande. From New Mexico, emigrants traveled along either the Santa Cruz River or the Gila River, then across the Colorado River where the Gila Trail led emigrants through Devil's Turnpike and the deserts of Gila Bend and Yuma. The 2,500-mile trek ended in southern California.

The year in which emigrants traveled determined the goods that they would bring. In the years before the California gold rush, government forts and the Latter-day Saints (Mormon) community of Salt Lake City offered the only respites for weary travelers, and many emigrants brought goods necessary to sustain them for more than five months. Lansford W. Hastings, whose guidebook promoted American settlement of the West, recommended "a good gun; at least five pounds of powder, and twenty pounds of lead; . . . two hundred pounds of flour, or meal; one hundred and fifty pounds of bacon; ten pounds of coffee; twenty pounds of sugar; . . . and ten pounds of salt." He further suggested emigrants bring cooking utensils, blankets, coffeepots, spare wagon parts, and goods for trade with Indians. "Medicines such as quinine, bluemass opium, whiskey and hartshorn for snake bites and citric acid- an antidote for scurvy" could mean the difference between life and death on the trails, and emigrants prepared for the worst. Other necessities included mattresses, pillows, cook stoves, and buckets or rubber containers for water. Emigrants also packed mementos from home, including bibles, knickknacks, dolls, and even grandfather clocks. As a whole, emigrants on both the Northern and Southern Routes packed according to general guidebook suggestions and speculation.

At the same time, emigrants consistently brought with them several aspects of American culture, emphasizing the importance of democracy, independence, women's domesticity, and white superiority. It was with these notions that many emigrants crossed the continent, bringing with them ideals from the eastern

United States—notions that dominated their experiences and made the trip truly American in character. Emigrants transported the concepts of democracy and self-reliance while looking to the federal government for assistance with supplies and Native Americans. Overlanders carried with them many of the Victorian ideals of domesticity but found that these served as prescription rather than the rule of practice. But emigrants did manage to practice the eastern notions of Anglo-American superiority and condescension.

True to American ideology of the era, democracy and Christian morality characterized the trip from the start. Travelers consisted of a motley assortment of men and no official government to rule them. To keep order along the trail, the emigrants followed the models of democracy that they learned in the United States. Emigrants on both the Northern and Southern Routes organized their traveling parties based on male voting rights, giving each man a say in the decisions of the company; they also allowed each man the opportunity to lead the band of travelers. Large groups were broken into smaller ones, as parties of men formed militia companies of 100. These companies, in turn, were divided into smaller units of 50 and 10. Captains, elected through a democratic vote to take charge of individual wagon trains, could also be removed in the same way. The general vote of men decided important choices, such as which route to take. Even after leaving the jurisdiction of the United States, the emigrants continued to apply the forms and procedures of Anglo-American legal culture. Although companies occasionally took the law into their own hands, they often held trials by jury and usually did not choose random ways to deal with crime and punishment. In doing so, emigrants followed the traditions established by the Constitution of the United States of America and the rule of law across the nation.

Furthermore, emigrants' views of the federal government along the trails followed the notions of republican virtue. Since emigrants practiced self-rule and hoped to become self-made men with property and riches, they had ambivalent feelings about the proper role of the federal government. The assistance of the federal government contradicted the myth of the self-made man in the West, yet it often resulted in the survival of emigrant parties during times of hardships.

Military forts allowed emigrants a chance to restock supplies and to find safe places for rest and recuperation. By 1860, 90 percent of the U.S. Army was deployed in 79 posts throughout the trans-Mississippi west. Emigrants on the Northern Route expected assistance from the federal government and even anticipated their arrival at the forts so that they could take advantage of the goods and services there. Emigrants also saw the federal government offering as protection when dealing with Native Americans. The government responded by negotiating treaties, distributing presents, establishing reservations, dispatching military expeditions, and providing military escorts and Indian agents along the trail. Military companies also allowed emigrants to camp near them at night, offering further protection from Indian attacks. Thus, many men left the East to realize the American dream of the self-made man, but they soon realized that they could not survive the trails without the help of the federal government.

One of the most telling signs of American culture that emigrants transported to the West was the notion of separate spheres and women's domesticity. The emigrant experiences emphasized the prescribed gender norms, including women's duties of cleaning, cooking, and mending. Women struggled to adjust to trail life, learning to wash clothes in scalding hot springs and to cook over buffalo chips when lacking other fuel. The men concerned themselves with driving the wagons, hunting, guarding against Native Americans, and surviving on the trail. Working in the domestic space of women, by contrast, called masculine identity into question. Men even joked about their companions who had to do "women's work," and some refused to do laundry, wearing the same dirty clothes for the entire trip. But both the men and the women found that the circumstances of travel—having no home, having no physically separate spheres, having no spouses, and having no established society—required them to relax their gender ideals.

As men and women transported the customs of Anglo-American society with them on the trails, they also applied these values to peoples from different cultures. Anglo Americans demonstrated their religious biases in their dealings with the Mormon community of Salt Lake City, which was established in

1847. The city's location near the south end of the Great Salt Lake made it a popular rest stop for many Northern Route emigrants, and they used the opportunity to buy vegetables, milk, and cheese. Those who had no cash traded cooking utensils, tools, and extra flour, bacon, and clothing. However, the religious prejudices of the emigrants pushed Mormons and overlanders into conflict. Although not hesitating to take advantage of the goods and services provided by Mormons, emigrants insulted Mormons, complaining about the religious services, the lodging, and the high prices. Mormons and Gentiles (as the Mormons referred to nonmembers) oftentimes clashed, and the lifestyle of the Mormons caused a variety of comments from emigrants. Yet, despite their hostility and condescension, emigrants found Salt Lake City to be a welcomed respite from the trails.

On the Southern Route, the unfamiliar culture of Mexicans caused much comment among emigrants. The Southern Route crossed through Mexican territory, and overlanders interacted with the natives. Mexicans often provided warnings of trail conditions and of Indians and offered to serve as guides for the emigrants. Travelers often noted cultural differences between emigrants and Mexicans. They commented on unfamiliar furniture and housing, disparaged the hygiene and housekeeping, and yet took advantage of opportunities to trade for fresh eggs and produce. Emigrants who visited Mexican towns learned to indulge in Mexican treats, such as tortillas, chilis, cacti, and mescal. Furthermore, Mexican fandangos brought great joy to the emigrants by offering a break from the monotony of overland travel, a chance for socialization, an opportunity for women's companionship (including dancing), and an occasion to drink and gamble.

Emigrants on both the Northern and Southern Routes crossed the paths of Native Americans. Most Anglos never differentiated between the various tribes, but emigrants encountered Natives ranging from Apache to Yakama, Sioux to Shoshone. Federal Indian policy continually supported the invasion of Native American land by Anglo Americans, and many emigrants carried this view with them to the West. Natives offered emigrants advice and guidance, as well as resources such as food and animals. But the heavy traffic on the trails taxed the resources and

patience of Native Americans, and the relations between Native Americans and Anglo Americans worsened over time. Many emigrants practiced "Indian drills," responding as they would in actual attacks: Men grabbed their guns and women sought shelter, screamed, and even fainted. The majority of the attacks in the 1840s and 1850s were isolated incidents, occurring when emigrants left the wagon train, when on guard duty, or when emigrants refused to pay tribute for crossing over what Indians believed to be their land. Throughout, rumors and bigotry colored emigrants' reactions to Native Americans. They faced Native Americans with their prejudices in mind, and by the end of the overland trails era, more Indians had been killed by Anglo Americans than vice versa.

At the height of the westward movement during the 1840s and 1850s, the overland experience proved perilous, exciting, and unsettling. Those cultural values that emigrants brought with them on the trails both helped and hindered their efforts. Man, woman, child, and beast forged trails, crossing over mountains and rivers, through deserts and plains, turning them into national highways that stretched from the Missouri River to the Pacific Ocean. While many of the emigrants left their homes for good, they could not leave behind the culture that influenced their lives. Studies of frontier justice, social structures, and human interactions on the overland trails prove that the West did indeed imitate the patterns of the East. Many Americans saw the West as uncharted, virgin land open to settlement—a place where men and women could make a new start. Yet the emigrants who undertook the adventure of the trails could not shed the values that were integral parts of their lives as Anglo Americans.

The mass migration of nearly 300,000 people changed the face of the country. The westward movement not only expanded U.S. territory, but it also fueled the American dream of abundant land, riches, opportunity, independence, and autonomy. Emigrants who braved the overland trails during the mid-19th century had an adventure that they would never forget. Every step along the way of both the Northern and Southern Routes offered emigrants glimpses of "the elephant" (a popular phrase signifying something so big, so terrifying as to be unheard of or beyond belief), ranging from natural catastrophes and threats to life and limb to encounters with exotic and the unfamiliar that upset their established views of the world. Regardless of the route, it was truly the trip of a lifetime, and emigrants carved their niche in American history.

—Melody Miyamoto

Suggested Reading

1820–1870 Western Emigrant Trails: Historic Trails, Cutoffs, and Alternates. [Map]. Omaha, NE: Western Emigrant Trails Research Center, 1999.

Hastings, Lansford W. *The 1845 Pioneer's Guide for the Westward Traveler: The Emigrants' Guide to Oregon and California.* Cincinnati, OH: G. Conclin, 1845. Reprint, Bedford, MA: Appleworks Books, 1994.

Holmes, Kenneth L., ed. *Covered Wagon Women: Diaries & Letters from the Western Trails, 1840–1890.* 11 vols. Glendale, CA: Arthur H. Clark, 1983.

Mattes, Merrill J. *Platte River Road Narratives: A Descriptive Bibliography of Travel Over the Great Central Overland Route to Oregon, California, Utah, Colorado, Montana, and Other Western States and Territories, 1812–1866.* Urbana: University of Illinois Press, 1988.

Mintz, Lannon W. *The Trail: A Bibliography of the Travelers on the Overland Trail to California, Oregon, Salt Lake City, and Montana During the Years 1841–1864.* Albuquerque: University of New Mexico Press, 1987.

Reid, John Philip. *Policing the Elephant: Crime, Punishment, and Social Behavior on the Overland Trail.* San Marino, CA: The Huntington Library, 1997.

Stegner, Wallace. *The Gathering of Zion: The Story of the Mormon Trail.* New York: McGraw-Hill, 1974.

Unruh, John D. *The Plains Across: The Overland Emigrants and the Trans-Mississippi West, 1840–1860.* Urbana: University of Illinois Press, 1993.

Utley, Robert M. *The Indian Frontier of the American West, 1846–1890.* Albuquerque: University of New Mexico Press, 1984.

EXECUTIVE ORDER 9066

See FORCED MIGRATION OF ITALIANS DURING WORLD WAR II, GERMAN AND ITALIAN INTERNMENT, JAPANESE INTERNMENT

EXODUSTERS

See TOPEKA, KANSAS; WICHITA, KANSAS

F

⊞ FARMING FAMILIES ON THE OREGON FRONTIER

Tens of thousands of Anglo Americans toiling on farms on the Ohio Valley frontier caught "Oregon fever" during the 1840s and 1850s. They dreamed of settling in western Oregon's vast Willamette Valley, which was lauded for its mild, humid climate and fertile soil. Thanks to annual burning by local American Indians, tall grasses covered much of the valley floor, which stretched 100 miles south from the Columbia River and measured 20 to 30 miles wide. To farmers who had struggled to clear midwestern woodlands, the Willamette Valley sounded like a veritable paradise. It was the promise of large quantities of free land, however, that convinced many to uproot their families and migrate 2,000 miles overland to the Willamette Valley.

To attract farming families to Oregon country (which included the present-day states of Oregon, Washington, and part of Idaho, Montana, and Wyoming), the Oregon provisional government, and later the U.S. Congress, offered generous quantities of free land to families who would settle on and work the land. The September 27, 1850, Donation Land Law (better known as the Donation Land Claim Act) granted 320 acres to single, white men and 640 acres to married couples who established residency prior to December 1, 1851. Those arriving in Oregon after December of 1851 could claim up to half that amount. Because most frontier farmers would use fewer than 100 acres to grow crops and graze livestock, 640 acres offered the promise of a substantial

patrimony. So many took advantage of these land grants that by 1857 the territorial surveyor general declared that the Oregon frontier was closed.

Oregon's Willamette Valley was primarily settled by Anglo-American farming families whose ancestors had been gradually pushing westward from the eastern seaboard for three or more generations. Nearly one third of Oregon's population in 1850 was born in the midwestern states of Ohio, Indiana, Illinois, and Iowa. An additional 30 percent hailed from neighboring Missouri and Kentucky. Many Oregon settlers had been born in the older states of Kentucky, Tennessee, or Ohio, but had later migrated to newer frontier regions. They frequently had children who were born in Iowa or Missouri, or both. Only 6 percent of Oregon's 1850 population was foreign born, and of those, one third were Canadian. Greater than 99 percent of the Willamette Valley's population was white throughout the 1850s. As late as 1890, only 4 percent of Oregonians were persons of color.

Nineteenth-century Americans believed that women and men should have distinct social roles. They expected men to go out to work each day in a business or trade, while their wives stayed home to supervise domestic servants and nurture their children. While these disparate gender roles were increasingly possible for the middle class developing in Boston and New York, they remained a distant dream for urban laboring classes and rural families. Although rural women could not afford to be merely decorative members of their household, they nonetheless sought to limit themselves to domestic labor. Their husbands' masculinity depended on their ability to provide for their families and free their wives from fieldwork. However, people on the midwestern and far western frontiers struggled to achieve even this more attainable goal of separate work roles for men and women.

Anglo-American settlers brought with them to Oregon their dream of distinct gender roles. According to this gender code, men and women separated their labor spacially. Women were responsible for child rearing and productive work in and around the home. They grew produce in large gardens, raised poultry, and churned butter in the barnyard. They prepared meals for their families from the food that they produced and preserved foodstuffs for future use. Women also sewed, laundered, and repaired clothing for their families. Throughout these many tasks, women also cared for young children and taught their daughters domestic skills to prepare them for their future role as farmers' wives. Meanwhile, men maintained the farm beyond the barn. They cleared and fenced land, and then plowed, planted, and harvested wheat and other crops. In addition, men tended large livestock, such as horses and cattle, and slaughtered cattle and hogs annually. By the age of 10, boys were apprenticed to their fathers to learn these masculine tasks.

While it had been difficult for rural families to abide by these labor divisions in the Midwest, it was nearly impossible during their first few years on the Oregon frontier. Establishing viable farms on previously untilled soil made labor demands particularly intense. Everyone assisted one another with the most pressing needs. Wives and daughters joined men in the fields, particularly during planting and harvest. Men performed the heaviest labor, such as cutting the wheat, but women and children could help by threshing and winnowing the grain. Men, in turn, assisted with the more physically challenging women's tasks, such as hauling water and firewood or churning butter. Younger boys assisted with simple domestic tasks, such as milking and gathering eggs.

Boys and girls crossed gender boundaries more easily than did their parents, whose gender identities were more firmly established. Because adult men's and women's gender identities were more threatened by crossing gender boundaries, they typically referred to men's domestic work and women's field labor as "helping"

their spouses. Men's masculinity and women's femininity were not questioned so long as they merely helped their spouses with tasks that were clearly not their own.

Female and male workspaces overlapped in the barnyard. Within this border region, men and women cooperated to complete tasks such as milking and gardening. Over time, however, favorable farming conditions in the Willamette Valley enabled many families to distinguish more clearly between men's and women's work. The barnyard developed into a clear and rarely crossed boundary between male and female workspace. While their workspaces continued to intersect in the barnyard, men and women increasingly divided their work within that region into gender-specific tasks. For example, men typically plowed the soil for a garden, which their wives planted and tended. Women raised hogs, but their husbands slaughtered them. Men and women increasingly pursued separate work roles, until old age forced them to once again cross the boundary they had erected between men's and women's roles.

The region's labor shortage began to ease as the children of Oregon settlers reached adolescence. The increased availability of male field hands permitted men and women to separate their work roles to an extent that had previously been impossible. Oregonians expected men to support their families with their field labor, thereby enabling their wives to withdraw into the confines of their domestic space. Freed from field labor, these women's daily lives began to approximate their feminine ideal. Although rural women could not afford to be merely ornamental, they sought to be homemakers, providing a pleasant and nurturing environment for their husbands and children.

Oregon settlers looked forward to enjoying the fruits of their labors in their twilight years. However, a number of these settlers struggled to maintain their separate gender roles as advanced age reduced their ability to perform heavy labor. Older men relied increasingly on their sons and hired hands to perform field labor, gradually moving into managerial positions on their farms. While their supervisory role reinforced their masculine identity, however, many men also found themselves once again assisting their wives with physically demanding domestic labor. Yet men's return to domestic labor actually helped increase their spouses' status as proper women, allowing them to turn from churning and laundry to fine needlework and caring for the emotional and spiritual needs of their community. Unable to materially provide for their families, and once more required to perform domestic work, elderly men clung to their power as household heads, directing the labor of their more physically able sons and employees.

The sons of Oregon settlers learned farming skills and contributed to family labor needs through informal apprenticeships to their fathers or neighboring men. As the first generation aged and land became scarcer, second-generation men tended to extend their period of semidependency on their fathers. During the 1840s and early1850s, there had been intense pressure on young men and women to marry quickly in order to claim land. In contrast, by the time the second generation reached adulthood, most of the tillable land in the Willamette Valley had been claimed. Large portions of most farms nonetheless remained unbroken, awaiting the labor of future generations. Second-generation men who came of age in the 1860s and 1870s were therefore forced to choose between remaining as a laborer on their fathers' land until they inherited a portion of that land, or striking out in search of work in Oregon's growing cities or land of their own in distant frontier regions.

Most first-generation men were unwilling to give up control over their farms, even if they held far more acreage than they were able to work in their lifetime. A majority of young men living in the Willamette Valley in 1880 therefore remained dependents within another man's household past the age of 25. While fathers might assist their elder sons to attain land of their own, younger sons typically remained at home until infirmity forced their fathers to gradually yield control of the farm. Many younger sons would not gain title to the land that they worked until their fathers died.

When they finally did acquire land of their own, second-generation farmers plowed the soil, planted and harvested crops, cut wood, and hauled goods to and from town, as their fathers had done. However, the nature of their specific tasks changed as the second generation responded to economic changes brought by the railroad and growing urbanization. Where their fathers had grown wheat and a variety of other crops for home consumption, many second-generation farmers emphasized fruits, vegetables, or cash crops such as hops. Willamette Valley farmland gradually became

consolidated as a growing pool of paid labor and new technology, such as horse-driven harvesters, enabled some men to manage much larger farms than had been possible for settlers at midcentury. Those who could not afford to embrace farming on this larger scale worked as field hands or moved to burgeoning towns such as Portland, where they opened small businesses or worked as teachers or store clerks.

Many men who could not afford increasingly valuable farmland in the Willamette Valley chose to cross the Cascade Mountains and settle in more arid eastern Oregon. Under the terms of the federal Homestead Act of 1862, citizens could claim 160 acres of land if they settled on it for five years and paid a small fee. Homesteading on land too arid to farm, most settlers of eastern Oregon turned to cattle or sheep ranching.

Changing economic conditions combined with shifting cultural norms to delay marriage among second-generation Oregonians. Second-generation men's prolonged semidependency on their fathers encouraged them to postpone marriage until their late 20s or early 30s. At the same time, second-generation women and men were influenced by a new nationwide emphasis on marrying for romantic love, rather than seeking primarily a financial partnership with their spouse. Although their ability to share labor remained important, second-generation women increasingly were willing to wait for the "right man." While first-generation women had generally married by age 19, their daughters typically did not marry until their early 20s. When they finally did marry, second-generation men and women expected to be partners in life as well as labor.

While the first generation strove after middle-class status by separating men's and women's work spheres, the second generation sought to meet new middle-class standards for consumption that developed in eastern cities during the late 19th century. Although women's domestic tasks did not change significantly from the first to the second generation, increased availability of sewing machines, mechanical washing machines, cheap fabrics, and ready-made clothing reduced the burden of women's work. Freed from field labor and relieved of the most burdensome aspects of domestic labor, second-generation women were able to participate in the women's club movement, or even to join women such as Abigail Scott Duniway in pursuing greater political rights.

Oregon's pioneer heritage remains influential to this day. Throughout the 20th century, pioneer iconography emphasized the distinct gender roles of Oregon settlers. During the 1920s and 1930s, statues honoring brave male pioneers and nurturing "pioneer mothers" were placed atop and at the entrance of the Oregon Statehouse, on the campus of the University of Oregon, and elsewhere throughout the state. As recently as 1987, the state legislature honored 1846 settler and educator Tabitha Moffat Brown by naming her the "Mother of Oregon."

By 2000, less than 2 percent of the state's employed population were farmers, although agriculture remains an important part of the Willamette Valley economy. Family farms persist amid the vast agribusiness structure whose roots date to the late 19th century. More than 1,000 farms and ranches have been continuously operated by the same family for more than 100 years and are registered through the statewide Century Farm and Ranch Program since it began in 1958. Throughout 150 years of social and economic transformations, the legacy of Oregon pioneer men and women remains alive in the state's rich Willamette Valley.

—*Cynthia Culver*

See also DUNIWAY, ABIGAIL SCOTT

Suggested Reading

Boag, Peter G. *Environment and Experience: Settlement Culture in Nineteenth-Century Oregon.* Berkeley: University of California Press, 1992.

Bowen, William A. *The Willamette Valley: Migration and Settlement on the Oregon Frontier.* Seattle: University of Washington Press, 1978.

⊞ FARNHAM, THOMAS J.

See BARTLESON, JOHN; BIDWELL, JOHN

⊞ FELDENHEIMER, EDITH
(1900–1984)

Edith Levy Feldenheimer was born on August 29, 1900, to Estell and Samuel Henry Levy, part of a wealthy and privileged family. She was sent to a private all-girls school, Miss Calhoun's School, in New York. The family spent summers in Europe, and the children were enrolled in French boarding schools. The outbreak of World War I nearly stranded Edith and her family in Europe, though they eventually managed to return safely home to New York.

Edith Levy attended Smith College from 1916 to 1920, a time she enjoyed immensely. Her academic focus there was writing, and she wrote for the college paper. Her personal interest, however, was piqued by Smith's Theater Department, where she worked with Sam Elliott, then head of the department, who encouraged her upon graduation to pursue a career on stage.

In 1922, after graduating from college, Edith and several Smith College students joined an archaeological expedition led by Professor Charles Peabody, curator of European Archeology at Harvard's Peabody Museum. He usually took male students interested in French archaeology on these expeditions; Edith was an exception to the norm. Through this expedition, she was able to make a small collection, which she subsequently donated to Smith College.

Much to Edith's sadness, her parents disapproved of their daughter's pursuit of a career in theater, which they felt did not suit their child's upbringing. She abandoned the theater and pursued her other talent, writing. For a few years, she wrote reviews for the *Bookman,* the *New York Times,* and the *New York Herald.*

On January 15, 1925, Edith Levy married Paul Feldenheimer, moved out West with him, and began a new chapter of her life in Portland, Oregon. Once arrived, she also revived her interest in the theater and actually played the lead in a play, *The Thirteenth Chair,* in 1926.

She became involved with the newly established Portland Art Museum. Before long, Feldenheimer was invited to become a member of the board in 1930. The early board of directors was committed to expanding and improving the museum and desired that Portland have something that compared with that they saw in similar sized cities back East.

Another passion that Feldenheimer brought with her to Portland was for the symphony. However, unlike the museum with its dedicated board, it was difficult to find support for the symphony project.

Symptomatic of its level of support, the symphony's first home was cold and uncomfortable. After its opening night, the small and underfunded orchestra regularly failed to play to a full house. It took a major investment in time and effort to establish the symphony. Feldenheimer eventually served two terms as president of the symphony.

After her first term as president of the symphony, Edith Feldenheimer received an invitation to join the board at Reed College, a position she accepted with some reluctance, because most of her experience was in music and the arts. In 1961, in cooperation with Hubert Crehan, director of the art department at the time, Feldenheimer established the Reed College Art Associates program, which funded and sponsored various art shows. She was also a trustee for several years and eventually received an honorary degree from Reed College.

Edith Feldenheimer participated in numerous boards and was an adroit and active patron of the arts within the Portland community during the 48 years she resided there. Paul, her husband of nearly 60 years, passed away at the end of 1983. Just over two months later, on January 19, 1984, Edith Feldenheimer succumbed to cancer. Her legacy was a vibrant arts landscape in one of the most underrated cities in the entire nation.

—*Scott M. Behen*

Suggested Reading

Feldenheimer, Edith. Interview by Marian W. Kolisch, November 23 and December 1, 1982. Smithsonian Archives of American Art. Available from http://archivesofamericanart.si.edu/oralhist/oralhist.htm

FIFTY-NINERS

See DENVER, PUEBLO, BOULDER, FORT COLLINS, AND COLORADO SPRINGS, COLORADO

FITZPATRICK, THOMAS

See BARTLESON, JOHN; BIDWELL, JOHN

FLATHEAD VALLEY

See KALISPELL, MONTANA

FOLTZ, CLARA SHORTRIDGE (1849–1934)

In 1878, Clara Shortridge Foltz was the first woman admitted to the California bar. She was the first woman to attend the Hastings Law School in San Francisco; the first woman to practice law in San Jose, San Francisco, and San Diego; the first woman to serve on the Board of Charities and Corrections; the first person to argue for a public defender's office; and the first woman to be a deputy district attorney in Los Angeles.

Foltz was an astute politician in the cause of women's rights and women's access to employment. Finding that women could not practice law in California because of a statutory limitation, she conducted a personal lobbying campaign to amend California Civil Code, section 275, by deleting the word "male." With the legislation in hand, she made a personal visit to Governor William Irwin's office to make sure that he signed the bill. The bill became known as the Foltz Woman Lawyer's Act, and she took advantage of it by passing the California bar examination. She then applied to law school, and Hastings Law School promptly informed her that women were not admitted to study. She immediately sued the law school and won a California Supreme Court decision allowing women into law school.

In addition to private practice, Foltz continued her reform efforts. She was one of the creators of the California parole system in 1893 and the author of the Foltz Defender Bill, which created a state system of public defenders for the criminally accused. This latter reform gained great national notoriety because Foltz presented the concept at the Congress of Jurisprudence and Legal Reform at the 1893 World's Columbian Exhibition. Her formal concept for the office of public defender was her greatest accomplishment. Women soon found the defender's role an important part of their legal career path.

On February 8, 2002, the Clara Shortridge Foltz Criminal Justice Center at the corner of Temple and

Broadway streets in Los Angeles was rededicated in her name. The 19-story building housing 60 courtrooms, the offices of the Public Defender and the District Attorney, and numerous other departments sits on the site of the old Red Sandstone Courthouse, the early home of the Los Angeles Superior Court. Foltz practiced at the old Red Sandstone Courthouse, both as a defense attorney and a deputy district attorney for Los Angeles.

—Gordon Morris Bakken

Suggested Reading

Babcock, Barbara Allen. "Clara Shortridge Foltz: 'First Woman.'" *Arizona Law Review* 30 (1988): 673–717.

Babcock, Barbara Allen. "Women Defenders in the West." *Nevada Law Journal* 1 (Spring 2001): 1–18.

Bakken, Gordon Morris, ed. *Law in the Western United States* Norman: University of Oklahoma Press, 2000.

Bakken, Gordon Morris. "Lawyers in the American West, 1820–1920: A Comment." *Nevada Law Journal* 1 (Spring 2001): 88–111.

Bakken, Gordon Morris. *Practicing Law in Frontier California.* Lincoln: University of Nebraska Press, 1991.

Women's Legal History Biography Project. "Clara Shortridge Foltz." Available from http://www.stanford.edu/group/ WLHP.

⊞ FOOTE, MARY HALLOCK
(1847–1938)

Mary Hallock Foote was America's leading literary and artistic figure from the 1880s until the 1920s. Combining a gift for pen-and-ink illustration with a dedicated and disciplined literary pen, she authored 16 books, 20 short stories, 7 sketches, 16 children's stories, and numerous published illustrations. Much of her work depicts life in the American West.

Raised in a Quaker home in the East, she married Arthur Foote, a mining engineer, on February 9, 1876, and moved to the West. Already an accomplished artist, Molly (as she was known) boarded the Overland Limited with her husband and set out for San Francisco and then the New Almaden Mine in California. New Almaden was a well-ordered company town with an ethnically diverse population. This setting provided her with material for "A California Mining Camp," which appeared in the February 1878 issue of *Scribner's.* The story depicted passing seasons in a mining camp with its "curious mixture of races." The Foote home at New Almaden was a social center in the town where people gathered to discuss numerous subjects.

The reading public in the East now had a realistic view of part of the West. A visit to Santa Cruz, California, resulted in "A Sea-Port on the Pacific" in the August issue of *Scribner's,* telling readers of the "heterogeneous mass of transplanted life growing and blooming together."

In 1881, her first work of mature fiction appeared as "In Exile." This work placed her squarely within the local-color movement that dominated the literature of her times. *The Led-Horse Claim* (1883) was the first of three Leadville, Colorado, novels that established her as a western writer. Just as her home in New Almaden had been a center of social intercourse, the Foote log cabin above Leadville served as a place for educated guests to discuss literature, philosophy, art, and science. She mixed the western mining life with the letters emerging from this discourse.

Other short stories and novels of the mining West followed. *John Bodewin's Testimony* was published as a serial in *Century* starting in November 1885 and appeared later in book form in 1886. It focused on a boundary claim dispute between mining companies. Molly's descriptions and characterizations were realistic and artistically constructed, further establishing her reputation as a leading western writer. "The Fate of a Voice" appeared in *Century* in 1886 and accurately described the Boise Canyon of Idaho and the work of mining engineers. These men were bright, attractive, and loving men given personality with her well-crafted prose. *The Last Assembly Ball,* another Leadville novel, appeared in *Century* in 1889 and as a book from Houghton Mifflin and Company the same year. In this work, Molly described the rigid class structure of western mining communities. *The Chosen Valley* saw print in *Century* in 1892 and came out in book form from Houghton Mifflin the same year. The stark realism of Idaho landscapes, the human costs of exploitation, and the degradation of the environment resonate throughout the novel.

Molly and Arthur moved to Grass Valley, California, in 1895 and took up residence at North Star Cottage for more than three decades. Her short stories and a further novel drew upon her experiences in Grass Valley. Her emphasis was on real families and ordinary events, like the failure of a mine pump bringing personal and economic disaster to a community. Molly described local color with great detail and realism—a day-to-day realism unavailable in many of the contemporary novels about the West in her day.

Mary Hallock Foote, throughout her artistic and literary career, put family first, voiced compassion for the working class while criticizing labor unionism, and allowed reading Americans to visualize the West from the kitchen window, within a household, and with a verbal acuity seldom matched. She also left vivid descriptions of mining town life and mining litigation that enabled historians to understand various aspects of mining towns in the American West.

—*Gordon Morris Bakken*

See also Leadville, Colorado

Suggested Reading

Miller, Darlis A. *Mary Hallock Foote, Author-Illustrator of the American West.* Norman: University of Oklahoma Press, 2002.

Spence, Clark C. *Mining Engineers and the American West: The Lace-Boot Brigade, 1849–1933.* New Haven, CT: Yale University Press, 1970.

⊞ FORCED MIGRATION OF ANARCHISTS

In contemporary, popular culture, anarchism is commonly associated with anarchy or chaos and is often symbolized by a black flag or a "circle A." Anarchists themselves are perceived as members of a counterculture rebeling against a higher authority. However, these perceptions of anarchists do not provide a defined representation of their movement. Outside of scholarly work, anarchists and their role in history rarely receive much attention. There is relatively little focus on the past activities of anarchists, and events that took place in the western United States are often overshadowed by the more well-known events that occurred in the eastern region of the country. Nevertheless, the U.S. government has consistently responded to anarchism with laws meant to eradicate the philosophy, as well as its proponents.

As with other political theories, the anarchist doctrine consists of variations of its primary tenets and at times contrasting arguments. However, the philosophy distinguishes itself from other radical beliefs in that anarchism advocates the complete elimination of the state. Anarchists promote the abolition of organized authority of any kind based on their belief that all government is fundamentally unjust and evil. According to Emma Goldman (1869–1940), a prominent American anarchist, the oppressive restraint of any external authority causes humans to commit crime and perpetuate war. Anarchists assert that when mankind is free from the coercion of government, society will act rationally toward its own best interest, thereby eliminating the need for manmade laws. According to anarchists, in the absence of authoritarian restraints, people would assemble in voluntary associations in which they would seek to contribute to the common good, taking only what they need and rightfully deserve.

Most of what history records as significant in the anarchist movement has transpired in the eastern United States. During the 19th century, anarchists publicly spoke against the government, advocated reforms, and participated in labor strikes in New York, Pennsylvania, and throughout the East Coast. The Haymarket Square Riot, which occurred on May 4, 1886, in Chicago, started as a protest demonstration held by a group mainly composed of German-born anarchists. It quickly turned into a riot when the police attempted to disperse the armed protesters. A bomb was thrown during the course of the riot, which killed several people and injured more than 60 in the crowd. Government officials reacted swiftly, and without evidence that linked the prosecuted to the bomb, four anarchists were hanged, one committed suicide, and three others were pardoned seven years later by the governor of Illinois for insufficient evidence. Nevertheless, in the minds of the public, the Haymarket Square incident served to link foreigners with anarchism and anarchism with violence and terror.

Through the years, popular culture has misrepresented the authentic principles of the anarchist doctrine by simply equating it with an absolute lack of control. Likewise, popular culture has created a mythological perception of the American West. The early history of the western territories in the United States is often portrayed as "wild," lawless, or lacking any true governmental authority. Yet the legend of the individual, or even the town banding together in communal brotherhood for the sake of survival, is analogous to the individualism and communal spirit promoted by anarchism.

However, the western territories did not produce an anarchist haven. In the decades following the American Civil War, the West began a slow shift to an urban and industrial economy. In the last half of the 19th century, gold, silver, copper, and lead mines started to appear. By the end of the 19th century, the western United States experienced industrial progress. As the western territory developed, nine new states were admitted to the nation. These states began as mining towns governed by little more than vigilante committees. But before long, the frontier settlers established provisional local governments. This temporary form of government existed in California, Nevada, Colorado, and Oregon until the federal government extended its formal authority to the western states.

During the first half of the 1800s, a substantial group of northern Europeans entered the United States. Consequently, the immigrant population in the East continued to grow. However, while some of the English, Irish, and Germans that came to the United States settled in the East, many eventually migrated to what is now the Midwest. Nevertheless, as the immigrants continued to settle, the frontier continued to expand. For example, the number of foreign-born persons living in the Wyoming and Montana territories in 1870 increased to as high as 39 percent of the population. In total, the foreign-born population in the American West nearly doubled between the years of 1890 and 1910. As a result, the western settlements rapidly increased during this time as they filled with European immigrants. Although members of almost every ethnic group inhabited this new region, southern and eastern European immigrants were the major sources of the new labor. And mining camps provided a source of income for these new settlers.

Work in the mines had few benefits for the miners. They worked long hours in poor conditions and received low wages. However, as early as 1825, a union of carpenters in Boston held a strike for the 10-hour workday. This marked the beginning of a new struggle

between those who owned the businesses and those who labored for the businesses. In the last quarter of the 19th century, union members in the East began to agitate for a shorter workday and to raise awareness about the plight of the working class. On September 5, 1882, 30,000 workers marched in the first Labor Day parade in New York City. But it was in the West in 1887 that Colorado's state legislature passed the first law in the nation that declared Labor Day a legal holiday. By the 1880s, the eight-hour workday became the central goal of the American labor movement, which had by this time spread to the American West.

In addition to the length of the workday, the labor movement also focused on working conditions in the West. Death rates for miners in the West outnumbered the death rates of miners in the eastern United States. Between the 1880s and early 1910s, the state of Utah averaged 10 deaths for every 1,000 workers per year. In states such as Colorado, New Mexico, and Wyoming, during the same period of time, the rate averaged approximately six deaths per 1,000 workers. However, the nation as a whole averaged less than four deaths for every 1,000 workers per year. In addition to a higher death rate in the western mines, "nonfatal" accidents were also high. Because there was a greater percentage of citizens that worked in dangerous occupations in the western states, issues of safety affected the new settlers' decision to join the labor unions.

Labor unions did not appear in the West with the first mining camps. And while smaller unions made a few insignificant attempts at improving miners' conditions, two labor unions actively fought battles for real change in the American West. The Western Federation of Miners (WFM) and the Industrial Workers of the World (IWW) sponsored radical acts in their efforts to bring about reform in labor conditions. Both unions evolved from smaller unions, and both ultimately emphasized the same objective. The leadership of the WFM and the IWW sought to defeat the business owners ("capital") through the organized efforts of their membership. Both unions asserted many of the beliefs articulated in the anarchist doctrine, the foundation of which is *direct action*. Direct action refers to activities such as general strikes, boycotts, use of propaganda, and sabotage; anarchist also refer to this as "propaganda of the deed." Based in some cases on membership alone, miners who joined these unions would suffer the consequences imposed by the U.S. government, as well as the American public, regardless of whether they embraced anarchism or not.

In 1893, several unions merged to form the WFM. This radical labor union, which included miners and smelters, employed direct action and used terrorist tactics, such as the use of dynamite to destroy a $250,000 mill in Wardner, Idaho, in April of 1899. However, the WFM later staged two strikes in the district of Cripple Creek, Colorado, that far exceeded the destruction of past strikes and that would ultimately spell the demise of the union in that state.

Late in the year 1893, a WFM local union organized a strike that included two thirds of its members (approximately 800 men) in the town of Altman, Colorado. The union demanded a shortened workday and a just wage. In response to the strike, some of the mines in the district began hiring nonunion workers. The strike lasted into the early months of 1894. During that time, union men damaged buildings in the city and attacked the homes of nonunion workers. After the use of more explosives, which resulted in the death of two cows, deputies from Denver captured five of the strikers. The strike finally ended when the governor helped the union reach their desired outcome of $3.00 pay for an eight-hour workday.

Following the Cripple Creek strike of 1893–1894, mining company officials hired outsiders to provide security and funded much of the county's law enforcement activities. Approximately 10 years after the first strike, the Cripple Creek district experienced a second strike, which proved to be far more destructive and deadlier than the first. Even though the three ore-reducing mills in Colorado City, which employed mostly nonunion workers, were the union's chief grievance, the WFM once again made demands for higher wages and shorter workdays in 1903. After several assaults, the governor called in extra "troops." The union realized their efforts did not have the desired effects, at which time the WFM decided to expand the strike to several of the mines in Cripple Creek. When that measure did not work, the union extended the strike to all of the mines and mills in Cripple Creek, effectively paralyzing the industry with a walkout. During the course of the strike, the WFM practiced intimidation and committed minor acts of terror to persuade the state government to give in to its demands.

In late 1903, the governor of Colorado called in the state militia and declared martial law after the union began using bombs and several people were murdered. In response to the strike, the mine owners formed the Mine Owners Association and brought in strikebreakers. One hundred out of the 250 strikebreakers were intercepted by union members, who used violence to force the men out of town. Soon it became apparent that this strike would not be successful, as more than 2,000 union men went back to work in the mines and more of the mines began to run without union labor. By July of 1904, the strike ended with the questioning of more than 1,000 men and the military enforced deportation of 238 "troublemakers" to Denver, as well as to other cities close to the state's border. At the end of the yearlong strike, the death toll amounted to 33, and all of the mines were back in operation with nonunion employees. The WFM never recovered from the Cripple Creek strike of 1903–1904.

At the same time that the WFM organized to reform the working conditions of miners in the West, anarchists across the nation organized against perceived authority figures, which they believed perpetuated conditions that oppressed the lower classes. As immigrants came to the United States, it was not unusual for them to retain elements of the values and culture native to their homeland. Many of the emigrants from southern or eastern Europe and Russia had been exposed to anarchism in their own countries. As these new Americans settled in more populated areas, some established formal and informal associations with native and foreign-born anarchists.

While the fundamental aspect of anarchism is the elimination of a repressive power structure, not all anarchists subscribe to the same tenets of the theory. Opinions differ on how the power structure should be eradicated, whether by violent force and assassination, or through a natural process in which society will evolve into a perfect voluntary association. In September of 1901, Leon Czolgosz, a self-professed anarchist, assassinated President William McKinley. As a result of this act, anarchists throughout the United States were vilified, many were threatened and, in some instances, became the target of violence themselves. Anarchists became the object of unwanted government attention and the public's outrage. However, anarchists were not the only ones to suffer as a result of this act. Socialists, communists, and foreigners in general suddenly faced the wrath of the American people, as well as intensified pressures from the U.S. government. The government found it difficult to establish laws against those who practiced anarchism due to the challenge of identifying individuals who believe in a political theory. However, Congress enacted legislation in 1903 that excluded anarchists, or any person who believed in or advocated the removal of government, from immigrating into the United States. Despite the government's effort, and in spite of the public fury, the anarchist movement survived in part through trade unions.

While still in its early years, the WFM underwent several transformations, and in 1905 helped form the IWW. Although originally founded in Chicago, the IWW had a dramatic impact on labor relations in the American West. The IWW asserted the values of anarcho-syndicalism, which is one of many mutations based on the original anarchist doctrine. Adherents to this principle believe that the profit system should be abolished, yet also promote the ideal that control of both industry and government should be in the hands of labor unions. Although the IWW acted in accordance with many of the anarchist beliefs, membership was not dependent on being a practicing anarchist. Many laborers joined the IWW because of the union's efforts to promote better working conditions. The IWW militantly fought in the struggle against forces that bred the frustrations of the laboring class.

For each success boasted by the IWW, there were two or three failures that detract from the union's overall grandeur. The IWW succeeded in the Seattle shipyard strike in 1917, which in turn improved working conditions for the shipyard workers throughout the Pacific Northwest. And in 1934 with San Francisco's Longshoreman Association, there were improved conditions. However, the IWW's policy of direct action and its unwillingness to compromise cost the lives of many union members. In 1909, more than 500 people went to jail and four people died in Spokane, Washington, as the IWW took a stand on free speech after a member was arrested.

The tactics employed by the IWW won them more critics than fans. During World War I, the opposition to the IWW intensified. However, it was not only the policy of direct action that created such animosity toward the union. Due to its socialist and anarchist foundation, the radical union was accused of being pro-German. In May of 1917, when each of the copper mines in Jerome, Arizona, went on strike, a union power struggle took place between the IWW and two other unions. By June, the IWW had increased its demands until a statewide copper mine strike arose. The situation became critical for the IWW when an opposing union joined the citizens of Jerome in July of 1917. As a result, the small town returned for a time to the vigilante justice of the old West, as the group sought out members of the IWW. When the roundup ended, 75 men were loaded into cattle cars and deported to another city with a directive that they not return to Jerome.

The Jerome deportation was an act against an organization that perpetuated direct action by anarchists. However, the deportation that took place on July 12, 1917, in Bisbee, Arizona, dwarfed the events that had taken place in Jerome just two days earlier. In the last week of June, the IWW presented a list of demands to the Bisbee copper mines. When the mines refused the demands, the union called a strike. Once again, in the patriotic fervor of World War I, the IWW was accused of being pro-German, and the town's citizen protection league prompted a meeting of vigilante groups to devise a plan to halt the union in their town. The city assembled 2,000 deputies from across the state, which in turn rounded up 1,186 men who were put into boxcars with armed guards and deported to New Mexico. The town of Bisbee assigned guards to each of the roads to the town to guarantee none of the deportees returned.

The deportations from Jerome and Bisbee symbolized the extent to which the American public and U.S. government acted against the labor unions and anarchists alike. Nevertheless, the federal government established further laws that sought to limit the activities and rid the nation of anarchists. The Immigrant Act of 1917 expanded the class of foreigners excluded from the United States. In 1921, Congress also established a quota system that regulated the number of immigrants allowed in the United States. The quota system was reaffirmed with the 1924 National Origins

Act. This law reduced the number of entries allowed, and was in part the legislature's attempt, based on the assumption that the southern and eastern Europeans imported the practice of anarchism, to limit the anarchist activity in the United States.

The anarchist movement in the United States suffered its most serious attack as a result of America's entry into World War I, and the events that occurred in the years following that war. The labor unions and anarchists alike outwardly opposed the war effort. Emma Goldman formed an anticonscription league and asserted that the state did not have the right to make war. In the midst of wartime patriotism, Congress passed the Sedition Act in 1918. This law made it a crime to criticize the American government or the Constitution either by speech or in writing. Through the application of the Sedition Act and the Espionage Act of 1917, Attorney General A. Mitchell Palmer arrested radicals associated with objectionable organizations. Though many were eventually released, 248 people were deported to the Soviet Union. Those who were deported included socialists, communists, labor agitators, and anarchists. Following these events, the attention of the American government and the fear of the American people turned toward communism as a source of the subversive influence in the United States.

Today, anarchism still exists, though by far it is not considered the menace that it once was. The 1960s saw a brief connection to the theories of anarchists with the radicalism that became associated with the movement against the Vietnam War and resistance to authority. The 1970s punk rock bands seized upon some of the attitudes, but tended more toward anarchy than anarchism. Moreover, the political philosophy has to some extent been renewed with the advents of technology. Through new ways of communicating, the anarchist movement has perhaps reached its largest audience. The Internet provides a safe meeting place to discuss and debate and allows anarchists an outlet to express their ideas. Despite any strengthening of the anarchist movement, there does not seem to be a prominent leader of the anarchist community. However, some of today's intellectuals advocate differing versions of anarchism, yet none can compare to the early figures such as Emma Goldman, Johann Most, or Voltairine de Cleyre. And while several groups still exist, including the IWW, there is not one dominant group that espouses the ideals of the doctrine.

Yet another source of renewal for the anarchist movement is the protest against globalization, as with the protest against the World Trade Organization that took place in Seattle in 1999. Such actions demonstrate that various anarchist groups still speak publicly against the government, advocate reforms, and participate in various strikes. Nevertheless, the government of the United States attempted to use its laws to forcibly remove anarchists from troubled areas and to exclude anarchists from the country through immigration laws, which in turn affected the landscape of the American West.

—*Karen Rosa*

See also BISBEE AND DOUGLAS, ARIZONA; CRIPPLE CREEK, COLORADO

Suggested Reading

Clark, Jane Perry. *Deportation of Aliens from the United States to Europe.* New York: AMS Press, 1968. First published 1931 by Columbia University Press.

Lingenfelter, Richard E. *The Hardrock Miners: A History of the Mining Labor Movement in the American West, 1863–1893.* Berkeley: University of California Press, 1974.

Preston, William, Jr. *Aliens and Dissenters: Federal Suppression of Radicals, 1903–1933.* Cambridge, MA: Harvard University Press, 1963.

⊞ FORCED MIGRATION OF ITALIANS DURING WORLD WAR II

Forced migration of Italians during World War II falls into two categories. The first includes nonnaturalized Italians in the United States who, because of their noncitizenship status, were declared enemy aliens. Hundreds of Italian Americans were sent to internment facilities; thousands more were "excluded," that is, forced to move away from their homes and/or businesses in areas considered vital for national security. The second category of forced migration comprises Italian soldiers transported from European and African battlefields to prisoner-of-war camps in America, many of which were located in the West.

The forced migration of noncitizen Italians is best understood in the context of U.S.–Italian relations in the years following World War I. The deteriorating political and economic conditions in Italy led to mass emigration, and, as Stephen Fox writes, Italians became "the last great immigration group to arrive in the United States before the Second World War." In 1922, Benito Mussolini and his fascist regime took political control of Italy. Hoping to cultivate political support for his new regime, Mussolini developed a favorable relationship with U.S. presidents that continued into the New Deal era with President Franklin D. Roosevelt. Indeed, Roosevelt looked to the social welfare programs instituted by Mussolini to help with Depression needs in the United States. Mussolini's popularity throughout the United States helped elevate the status of Italians in America, a welcome change for an ethnic group that had historically suffered from discrimination.

Mussolini also worked to develop political support abroad from Italian expatriates for his policies. Capitalizing on emotional ties to Italy, he encouraged Italians living in the United States to maintain their cultural bond with their mother country, to cultivate their *italianita,* reminding them that once an Italian, always an Italian. Language classes were subsidized by the Italian government; fraternal organizations, such as the Sons of Italy and Italian War Veterans Society and its women's auxiliary, increased their membership; and youth groups such as the Gruppo Giovaniti appealed to the patriotism of the Italians and their hopes for Mussolini to rejuvenate Italy into a world power.

When Mussolini invaded Ethiopia in 1935, feelings between the United States and Italy changed abruptly. Almost overnight, Italians who had publicly and proudly supported Mussolini found themselves in the spotlight, suspected of supporting the dictator's fascist ideology. During the early part of 1936, the U.S. government began collecting information on prominent Italians whom it considered potentially dangerous— Italian language teachers, newspaper editors and writers, community leaders, and especially members of the Italian War Veterans Society. The information was used to create a Custodial Detention List, which would enable the government to quickly detain individuals in the event of a national emergency. Government scrutiny of nonnaturalized Italians increased when Mussolini and Hitler joined together with the Pact of Steel on May 22, 1939.

The first acts of forced migration began months before the United States' entry into war. Using precedent set during World War I, Roosevelt forced two groups of Italian citizens who were in the United States into detention camps. On March 31, 1941, the United States seized Italian merchant marine ships in American ports and sent the officers and crew to temporary detainment facilities. In May, the sailors found themselves on a train for the Immigration and Naturalization Service internment facility at Fort Missoula, Montana. Also in May, government officials detained a group of Italian men who had traveled to New York City to work in restaurants on the grounds of the 1939–1940 World's Fair. Both the sailors and restaurant workers spent the duration of the war at Fort Missoula.

Growing fear among Americans that nonnaturalized citizens from belligerent countries would put loyalty to their homeland ahead of loyalty to the United States— and perhaps engage in subversive activities—played a significant role in driving federal policy. In June of 1940, the U.S. government passed the Alien Registration Act of 1940. Also known as the Smith Act, its purpose was to "prohibit certain subversive activities; to amend certain provisions of law with respect to the admission and deportation of aliens; to require the fingerprinting and registration of aliens; and for other purposes." In addition to describing subversive activities, the law required all alien residents over the age of 14 years to register with Immigration and Naturalization officials and to report any changes in their residency or employment. As the largest immigrant group in the country at the time, and with perhaps only 30 percent of Italian immigrants from the last wave having undergone naturalization, this act had an enormous impact on the Italian community: Six hundred thousand nonnaturalized Italian Americans were required to register as enemy aliens—twice as many as German Americans, and six times as many as Japanese Americans. The majority of these enemy aliens were elderly people who had been in the United States for more than 20 years, who had married Americans, and who had children in the American armed services fighting Axis forces.

The situation for resident, nonnaturalized Italians worsened after the attack on Pearl Harbor and when, on December 11, 1941, the United States declared war on Italy. Italian Americans who lived on the West Coast remembered December of 1941 as the month of hysteria. Within hours after the Pearl Harbor attack, more than 1,500 citizens on the Custodial Detention List were secreted away to Immigration and Naturalization Service detention centers; their families received no information as to the reason for the arrest, holding site, or length of detention (which varied from a few hours to years). Information the government had collected against suspects was used as evidence in oftentimes hasty official hearings.

Detainees, considered guilty unless they could prove their innocence and denied access to legal advice, had little chance to defend themselves. If the government determined the suspect a danger to national security, the detainee found himself or herself subject to a common pattern—moved from one temporary internment facility to another, until final location at a permanent facility, which, in the West, could be either Fort Missoula in Montana, Camp McAlester in Oklahoma, or Fort Sam Houston in Texas. Filippo Milinari recalled,

> I was the first one arrested in San Jose the night of the attack on Pearl Harbor. At 11 P.M. three policemen came to the front door and two at the back. They told me that, by order of President Roosevelt, I must go with them. They didn't even give me time to go to my room and put on my shoes. I was wearing slippers. They took me to prison . . . and finally to Missoula, Montana, on the train, over snow, still with slippers on my feet, the temperature at seventeen below and no coat or heavy clothes!

Even though Italy joined the Allies in 1943, the detainees were not allowed to return home until the end of the war.

Beginning with the bombing of Pearl Harbor, Italian Americans faced increased restrictions on their civil liberties. Enemy aliens were ordered to surrender items that could be used for sabotage—cameras, radios, flashlights, binoculars—or face internment. Italian Americans on the West Coast were the most severely impacted. By the end of January of 1942, Attorney General Francis Biddle announced strategic zones along the Pacific coast; prohibited zones in California

forced the evacuation of 10,000 Italians from their homes, and 52,000 were subject to dusk-to-dawn curfew. In January, travel restrictions also began.

On February 19, 1942, President Franklin D. Roosevelt signed Executive Order 9066, which stipulated that "every possible protection against espionage and against sabotage to national-defense material, national-defense premises, and national-defense utilities." The secretary of war and his chosen military commanders were given virtually unlimited power to protect the United States against internal enemies. They did this by proscribing military zones, "from which any or all persons may be excluded, and with respect to which, the right of any person to enter, remain in, or leave shall be subject to whatever restrictions the Secretary of War for the appropriate Military Commander may impose at his discretion." The impact of this brief document meant the immediate detention of alien enemies, imposition of restrictions, and exclusion of enemy aliens from designated zones, which led to the internment of Japanese, Italian, and German Americans.

Although commonly known as the Japanese Relocation Order, Executive Order 9066 did not single out any particular ethnic group. However, the vague language and the lack of executive oversight left open the possibility of removing any ethnic group from a military zone if they were deemed a threat to national security. Lieutenant General John Dewitt, commander of the Western Defense Command, requested an expansion of the prohibited zone to include the entire western half of the United States; in April of 1942, the commander of the Eastern Defense Command announced his intention to institute restricted and prohibited zones over 16 states, including the entire Atlantic seaboard. DeWitt, with an overzealous interpretation of Executive Order 9066, also envisioned interning all enemy aliens in the United States, "as soon as he [finished] with the Japanese." Fortunately, calmer heads prevailed. A series of policy papers suggest President Roosevelt became increasingly concerned with the logistics and costs of interning over a million Italians, nationwide. Exclusion restrictions on Italians gradually eased until, on Columbus Day, October 1942, they were fully lifted.

For many families, their return to homes, schools, and businesses signaled the end of a nightmare ordeal. For others, exclusion from their livelihood left families financially ruined—the fishermen along the California coast suffered particularly severe economic losses—and the psychological consequences were equally devastating. When told to evacuate their homes in mid-February of 1942, four elderly Italian men committed suicide, unable to understand why the U.S. government had turned against residents loyal to their adopted homeland.

For the majority of other Italians, their reaction was less overtly destructive, yet overall the effects of the experience lingered for years; whether forced from their homes in the military zones, detained in internment facilities, or living with the stigma of being an "enemy alien," many felt shame and embarrassment over their ordeal. The exclusion policy reflected a combination of wartime hysteria on the part of the American public and lack of responsible oversight on the part of the president and his advisors. As Lawrence DiStasi writes, "During the war, no person of Italian extraction was ever charged with, much less convicted of, espionage, or sabotage or any other hostile action. Virtually all were interned for what authorities thought they *might* do, based on their past sentiments or writings or associations."

In addition to the resident Italians forced to endure exclusion or internment, another group experienced forced migration in the West: Italian soldiers transported to the United States as prisoners of war (POWs). Government records indicate Italian soldiers constituted 51,071 of the total 425,000 POWs held in American camps. The Italian soldiers, most of whom were captured during the campaigns in Sicily and Africa, began to arrive in the United States in 1942.

As soon as the United States entered the war, the military began an aggressive plan to increase POW facilities, which, in 1941, could only accommodate approximately 8,000 prisoners. With rare exceptions POW camps held either Italian, German, or Japanese prisoners. In September of 1943, shortly after Italy surrendered to the Allies, six POW camps in the West held 19,093 Italian prisoners: Douglas, Wyoming (912); Ogden, Utah (1,729); Scottsbluff, Nebraska (2,720); Hereford, Texas (3,607); Lordsburg, New Mexico (3,903); and Florence, Arizona (6,222). Numbers continued to grow as new POWs were sent to camps in the United States, ultimately reaching a total of 3,755 officers and 47,282 enlisted men, nationwide, with a little more than half of the total number—669 officers and 27,644 enlisted men—held in western camps.

Changing dynamics of the war in Europe affected the status of Italian POWs in the United States. When Italy abandoned its alliance with Hitler's regime, captive soldiers faced a decision: remain loyal to the fascists or support the Allies by joining Italian Service Units. The new Italian government urged POWs to join the service units, where, "though still restricted and kept under guard . . . [the men] worked in 26 states under the direction of American soldiers and were permitted both to receive visitors and to visit the homes of U.S. citizens on weekends." Beginning in April of 1944, the number of POWs who joined the service units grew slowly, from 115 officers and 823 enlisted men, to 1,114 officers and 44,650 enlisted men by war's end. Tracking the movement of Italian soldiers becomes more difficult once the service units began, because the men who joined disappeared from the POW camp rosters. As the war drew to an end, 30 percent of Italians in the service units had been assigned to the western, agricultural regions. The officers and enlisted men who refused to join the service units remained in POW camps, under the same restriction as German prisoners. By war's end, facilities for these recalcitrant officers and soldiers had been consolidated into nine main camps and six branch camps, the largest in Hereford, Texas. If the Territory of Hawaii is included in the definition of the West, it held the largest number of Italian POWs (4,931).

The 1929 Geneva Convention allowed captive soldiers to perform necessary maintenance and cooking work in the camps and also to perform military and civilian duties (with the exception of engaging in actual combat duty). The need for laborers determined the locations of new campsites; western, rural areas in particular clamored for workers to replace American men fighting overseas. Yet the decision of where to send prisoners varied according to the local demographics. In Greeley, Colorado, an area with a large German population, both Germans and Italians were welcomed as laborers. However, in Albuquerque, New Mexico, a town with a large Italian population, citizens threatened a riot at the prospect of having German POWs come into the area, but welcomed the Italian prisoners.

Either as POWs or, later, as members of the Italian Service Units, the soldiers performed a wide variety of agricultural chores as they planted, weeded, hoed, shelled, shucked, harvested, and bagged agricultural produce throughout the West. They chopped cotton in south Texas, worked beet fields in Colorado, hoed corn fields in Nebraska, and cleared hundreds of miles of irrigation ditches in New Mexico. Although war in the European theater ended in May, Italians stayed and worked through the 1945 harvest. By December 15, 1945, only 13 units remained in the West: three units in Sidney, Nebraska, nine units scattered throughout California, and one unit in Washington State. By June of 1946, all but 25 POWs had been repatriated.

The story of forced Italian migration in the West has a strange place in the American historical memory. Young soldiers brought to the United States as POWs interacted with farm families and townspeople across the West, and had a generally positive experience. Farm employers were impressed with their hard work and cheerful attitude, and oral histories reveal that Italian soldiers, town residents, and farm families who made friendships during the war continued to correspond, and even traveled to visit one another. In a number of cases, romances between POWs and American women during the war lead to marriages as soon as the war ended. Over time, however, the recollection of Italian POWs has nearly disintegrated from western memory. On the other hand, the story of Italian internment or exclusion from homes and businesses remained outside historical discourse for nearly 50 years. Only within the past decade has this chapter in American wartime experience been brought to the public's attention through the work of Italian American scholars.

—*Renee M. Laegreid*

See also German and Italian Internment, World War II– Postwar Effects on Western Migration, World War II Relocation Program

Suggested Reading

Benedetti, Umberto. *The Lifestyles of Italian Internees at Fort Missoula, Montana, 1941–1943.* Missoula: University of Montana Press, 1986.

DiStasi, Lawrence, ed. *Una Storia Segreta: The Secret History of Italian American Evacuation and Internment during World War II.* Berkeley, CA: Heyday Books, 2001.

Fox, Stephen R. *The Unknown Internment: An Oral History of the Relocation of Italian Americans during World War II.* Boston: Twayne, 1990.

Keefer, Louis E. *Italian Prisoners of War in America, 1942–1946: Captives or Allies?* New York: Praeger, 1992.

Weglyn, Michi. *Years of Infamy: The Untold Story of America's Concentration Camps.* New York: William Morrow, 1976.

⊞ FORT LARAMIE TREATY

See Black Hills Gold Rush of 1874

⊞ FORT WORTH, TEXAS

In Fort Worth, a very laid-back western city that residents proudly call a "cowtown" and in which they continually look for ways to be different from its big-city rival Dallas 30 miles to the east, most folks consider themselves just "Texans." They do not know of immigration in the past nor the impact that it has made on their community. In its 150-year history, the city has seen three waves of immigration, each in its own successive half century. First came newcomers from the eastern United States shortly after the Lone Star State emerged in 1845. Then the so-called "new immigration" to America from southern and eastern Europe, beginning in the 1890s, dominated the next 50 years. Third, from the 1950s to the present, Hispanic immigration changed the demographics of the original blue-collar stockyards area of the north side of Fort Worth.

Earliest settlers came from east Texas and the southern states to the little frontier fort in north central Texas that U.S. troops established in 1849 on a bluff overlooking two forks of the Trinity River. In that year, the four-year-old state of Texas enjoyed a population boom that moved the 1850 census figures of 212,592 to 604,215 in 1860. However, farm families moved slowly into the new Tarrant County, in which the fort was located at the edge of settlement. The fort city only grew to 20 log cabins and a couple of general stores by the 1870s, but residents aggressively sought railroads and expansion. Cattle drives and agricultural pursuits continued to draw settlers, especially when slaughtering plants began operations north of the bluff. Some of the workers were African Americans, their ancestors having been brought to Texas by slaveholders before the Civil War.

Meat-packing plants attracted millions of immigrants from southern and eastern Europe to major livestock markets such as Chicago, Kansas City, St. Paul, St. Louis, Omaha, and Fort Worth. European poverty or oppression, as well as cheaper steamship passenger tickets and those jobs, brought nearly twenty million immigrants to America in the three decades after 1890. This "new immigration" meant that by 1900 Fort Worth swelled to 25,000. When the two largest of the "Big Four" meatpacking giants, Armour and Swift, built large, modern slaughtering plants in 1902, Fort Worth's growth was assured. The city became a railroad hub, as 10 different lines connected there. Because of the growth of its livestock market—with its meatpacking plants and the immigrants having arrived to work in them—Fort Worth's population tripled to 75,000 in 1910.

A new community called North Fort Worth, north of the bluff and its fort, developed between the Trinity River and the stockyards area. The larger city of Fort Worth annexed it in 1909. In 1923, Fort Worth annexed the stockyards area, which had operated for over a decade as Niles City, called the "richest little city in the U.S." because of the population ratio of its small numbers in the company town in relation to the $30 million property value wealth of the stockyards industrial district.

The first generation of these southern and eastern European immigrants continued to speak their languages at home and among friends of the same nationality. They usually married only within their group and continued to practice customs and to prepare foods in European ways. Their children, however, spoke mostly English and chose girlfriends or boyfriends from any race.

Unfortunately, many Anglo neighbors of the newcomers referred to any and all of them as "Bohunks" and looked down on their frugal living conditions in crowded rooming houses. Bohemia was the motherland of some of the Fort Worth immigrants, but others came from Slovakia, Austria, Serbia, Romania, Italy, Poland, Greece, Yugoslavia, Croatia, and Russia. A large German contingent came to Fort Worth as well.

Certainly, the newcomers disliked discrimination, but even with it and their early crowded conditions, they were happy, for they earned more in a month or two than they could make in a year in the old country.

Old World customs that the newcomers fostered during the first two decades of the 20th century included a *biergarten* located on the north side of the Trinity River just east of the junction of the West Fork and Clear Fork. In 1900, the German Society, *Deutscher Verein* or Sons of Hermann, constructed an open-air pavilion among some large trees in a larger area they called Hermann Park, located in the 300 block of North Main Street. People from several of the ethnic groups gathered on Saturday or Sunday evenings for dancing and socializing. Strauss waltzes and Viennese music emanated from the pavilion to surrounding neighborhoods. In the spring of that year, the Sons of Hermann sponsored a three-day May festival and crowned a queen. While young people from differing ethnic groups met in this setting, some of the older Fort Worth Protestant residents tried to keep their youngsters away from the dancing and serving of alcohol. Many of the new immigrants were Catholic or Jewish and did not feel the same aversion to dancing or alcohol as some Protestants did. Unfortunately, by the mid-1920s, a large Ku Klux Klan organization developed among Anglos in North Fort Worth and elsewhere in the city because of these differences.

Prohibition affected the immigrants perhaps more than the white Anglo-Saxon Protestants in Fort Worth during the 1920s. Karel Haba, a Czech, lost his job operating a saloon, so he took his wife and small children back to Europe while two grown children stayed in Fort Worth. Then, years later, when Haba died in a farm accident, his widow with small children came back to America to live with her established children here, again leaving two children to reach maturity in Czechoslovakia. The family remained separated.

New immigrants in Fort Worth and elsewhere often felt mistrustful of smooth-talking English insurance salesmen, making promises in a language the new immigrants did not yet fully comprehend. Consequently, the North Fort Worth immigrants formed their own protection societies. A Czech fraternal insurance organization called the Slavonic Benevolent Order of the State of Texas filled this need. It had been created in LaGrange, Texas, in 1896. The organization constructed a lodge at 2400 North Houston Street and provided reliable and inexpensive death benefits to those immigrants who signed up.

In addition, Czech immigrants brought with them to America an organization called *Sokol,* meaning "falcon," that had been created in the Old Country in 1862 to encourage their citizens to keep themselves physically and morally strong to fight for their freedom from Austrian oppression. Sokol sponsored gymnastic activities to teach healthy living and discipline to their young people. In the gymnasium, which in Fort Worth in the early days was in a building shared with the Slavic insurance order, families gathered on Friday nights for food and socializing. Local promoters of gymnastics, which has lasted in popularity into the 21st century, are descended from these earlier Czech immigrants. They continue to provide facilities for training in a well-equipped, modern gym.

Various ethnic groups created their own churches if enough members existed to do so. By 1911, about 200 young Greek men, mostly single, had arrived in Fort Worth, fleeing Turkish oppression. Most of them initially found jobs in the stockyards, lacking any but agricultural skills. Although originally intending to return home to Greece, most of the young men stayed and eventually married local girls. By the 1930s, approximately 75 percent of them had saved their packing-house wages, purchased or leased fertile land along the Trinity River, and become truck farmers. Many of the other 25 percent operated other businesses. The Greek immigrants worked decades to afford to build their beautiful Greek Orthodox Church on Jacksboro Highway. Another lasting result of their efforts to raise money for the church is an annual three-day Greek Festival that attracts many Fort Worthians who enjoy the ethnic food. Early Greek families in Fort Worth were Sparto, Pappajohn, Salicos, and Anagnostakis.

Twenty-three Russian students from a Philadelphia Baptist seminary that closed in 1921 came to a seminary in Fort Worth to complete their studies. They established a Baptist church in the North Side, the Clinton Avenue Baptist Church for Slavic People. Services were held in three languages, Russian, Polish, and English, and attendance grew to 150 by the 1930s. Only in 1961 after second- and third-generation children had moved away from the north side of the city did the three-language services cease and the church close its doors. More than 40 years later, as a new century began, some of those former youngsters who grew up in the Russian-Polish community still held twice-yearly reunions.

Jewish immigrants succeeded in numerous downtown Fort Worth and North Side businesses. Meyer Greines operated a furniture store on North Main Street and encouraged his children to get a good education. A daughter became a teacher, and sons became a doctor, a lawyer, and a storekeeper. Harry Jacobson, from Romania, and his wife, Sarah, from Russia, operated a dry-goods store on North Main for more than 40 years. Their son later began selling Western clothes exclusively in the same location.

Polish immigrant Joe Riscky began a barbecue business in 1927. His grandson now operates several restaurants derivative of Riscky's first place.

Some eastern European immigrants shortened or Anglicized their names so their children would be more readily accepted in school. Bunkervich became Bunker; Milankovich became Milan; Kablukov became Cabluck, and Rosen was a shortened form of either Rosenberg or Rosenbaum. Others kept their Old World names, such as Pokluda, Shepelwich, Lozuk, and Makariwich.

Children of these first-generation immigrants attended North Side schools, eventually spoke English well, and made friends with youngsters of other ethnic backgrounds. Upon graduation from high school, they found good blue-collar jobs, joined the army, or worked in defense plants in west Fort Worth. They established homes in the North Side. By the third generation, most of them attended one of the many colleges or universities in the area and became schoolteachers or principals, acquired other well-paying jobs, established businesses, and moved into upscale homes in more affluent neighborhoods than the North Side.

Hispanics, mostly Mexicans, dominated the third wave of immigration into Fort Worth. The North Side became their destination as well. Only a few had arrived in the first decade or so of the 20th century, sparked to emigrate by the 1910 Mexican Revolution. They continued to trickle in, acquiring jobs in the meat-packing plants until the 1930s, when job opportunities diminished. Assimilation of these early Mexican immigrants into the mainstream culture followed closely the same pattern as that of the second- and third-generation immigrants from southern and eastern Europe. Second- and third-generation Mexicans became postal workers, defense workers, schoolteachers, soldiers and sailors, and entrepreneurs. One of the better-known Mexican restaurants, Joe T. Garcia's, began in 1935 when Garcia took orders for plate lunches of his wife's cooking while he still worked at Armour and Company meat-packing plant. Garcia's grandchildren still operated the greatly expanded, successful, and popular restaurant as the 21st century began.

J. Pete Zepeda's family came to Fort Worth in 1915 in a covered wagon from Nacogdoches, the Zepeda family having settled in east Texas two centuries earlier. Zepeda became a printer and later worked at General Dynamics (later Lockheed-Martin). He became the first Hispanic on the Tarrant County College District Board.

Most of both waves of immigrant cultures, European and Hispanic, originally lived east of North Main Street and south of the stockyards. The Europeans began moving west of North Main Street first, obtaining lots or homes in Rosen Heights, an addition created by successful immigrant Sam Rosen. Mexicans faced more discrimination and were expected to "keep their place" and stay east of North Main Street, not even crossing over to view the free summertime movies at Marine Park during the Depression years. Angry gangs on either side often threw bottles or rocks at each other.

A crime rate during the 1930s in the blue-collar North Side that was much higher than that in the larger Fort Worth community inspired some wealthy society ladies to beg the help of a men's Kiwanis group, and together they began a boys' club. The Fort Worth Boys' Club operated on the North Side after school and on Saturdays, the ladies providing snacks and helping the youngsters with their homework and the men organizing sports and shop activities. In the 1990s, the club merged into the nationwide Boys' and Girls' Club movement.

The crisis of World War II created tremendous changes in the immigrant community on the North Side. Mexican migration arrived to fill the demand for labor at a time when the U.S. government placed no quotas on their group. Good jobs also meant that many of the Europeans on the North Side could purchase homes in new suburban additions in the larger city, leaving small frame houses that the Mexicans either rented or purchased. Returning veterans of both groups acquired educations and good jobs. Hispanic soldiers returning from World War II found homes in the broader North Side, even though neighborhood associations tried to keep them out for a time.

All Saints Catholic Church, located just west of North Main Street, merged in 1955 with a smaller San Jose Church and school to the east and continues to serve its mostly Hispanic congregation in the 21st century.

Fort Worth's North Side continued to attract large numbers of Hispanics during the last half of the 20th century until they dominated in the area. Many Hispanic businesses proliferated. In 1973, the business people created a Fort Worth Hispanic Chamber of Commerce, only the fourth such Hispanic chamber in Texas.

The larger and more rapid Hispanic migration in recent decades has not assimilated as rapidly into the broader Fort Worth society as the southern and eastern European immigrants did. Too many people arrived too fast, some of them illegally. As a consequence, poverty and unemployment, language differences, crime, drug use, and juvenile gangs created problems. Keeping neighborhood youngsters from congregating every night in the stockyards area and cruising along Exchange Avenue and North Main Street in their revved up hot rods forced the city to adopt some creative solutions, including one-way streets and additional police patrols throughout the tourist area.

Ironically, the historic district that made Fort Worth a "cowtown" and attracts millions of tourists to the stockyards-area shops, museums, and restaurants sits in the middle of a large barrio that includes many run-down or boarded up homes and bars—the leftover blue-collar industrial district where all those immigrants first came. Certainly, efforts are underway to encourage redevelopment, particularly on North Main Street. Not all Hispanics live in the historic district, however. Scattered throughout the city, they represent 30 percent of the Fort Worth population. Hispanics made up 47 percent of the enrollment in the Fort

Worth Independent School District at the beginning of the 21st century, according to the Hispanic Chamber of Commerce.

Certainly, Hispanic culture reigns, as *Cinco de Mayo* and *Diez y Seis de Septembre* celebrations highlight the streets in honor of festivals honoring revered holidays in Mexico. All Saints Catholic Church is a center for this activity.

The immigrants' work—all three migrations over 150 years—contributed greatly in making Fort Worth the beautiful and prosperous city it is today. Their arrival especially allowed the stockyards and meat-packing plants to become the biggest business in Fort Worth during the first half of the 20th century.

—J'Nell L. Pate

Suggested Reading

Cuellar, Carlos E. *Stories From the Barrio: A History of Mexican Fort Worth.* Fort Worth: Texas Christian University Press, 2003.

Pate, J'Nell L. *Livestock Legacy: The Fort Worth Stockyards, 1887–1987.* Fort Worth: Texas A & M University Press, 1988.

Pate, J'Nell L. *North of the River: A Brief History of North Fort Worth.* Fort Worth: Texas Christian University Press, 1994.

⊞ FRANK, RAY (1861–1948)

Rachel "Ray" Frank was known as the "Girl Rabbi of the Golden West," although she was not a rabbi at all. She was, however, the first Jewish woman to give a formal sermon in the United States. In doing so, she became an American Jewish icon during the 1890s and early 1900s. Through her actions, she helped foster thought on the roles of women among American Jews, and she provided an impetus for change in the traditional function of women in the synagogue.

Ray Frank was born on April 10, 1861, in San Francisco to Polish immigrant parents. Her parents were Orthodox Jews, but they had liberal spirits that would later influence Ray. The western frontier was not a place teaming with a Jewish presence, and Ray was quick to notice the differences between the Gentile majority culture as opposed to the Jewish home in which she was raised. After graduating from high school in 1879, Ray moved to Ruby Hill, Nevada, which was a silver mining town. There, she taught school for six years. The lack of a Jewish presence in Ruby Hill gave Ray further insight into and curiosity about the mainstream population and its prejudice against Jews.

In 1885, Ray moved to Oakland, California, where she took courses in philosophy at the University of California at Berkeley and began teaching at a Sabbath school in the Oakland area. Her skills as an orator became apparent, and she developed a following within the Jewish community in California. She also worked as a correspondent for various newspapers in the San Francisco metropolitan area, which further boosted her reputation as a spokesperson on Jewish issues.

It was her newspaper work that took her to Spokane, Washington, in late 1890. She was upset at the hostility among the Reform and Orthodox Jews of the area. Knowing her reputation, a member of the community arranged for her to give a sermon for Rosh Hashanah. Jews and Gentiles alike flocked to the Opera House to listen to Ray speak. Ray's speech discussed "The Obligations of a Jew as a Jew and Citizen," and it was so well received that a Christian man donated land for the building of a synagogue in the Spokane area.

When Ray enrolled at Hebrew Union College, a leading Reform seminary, word began to spread that she was to become the first woman rabbi. It was said that she was offered several pulpits; however, Ray's views about women as rabbis were somewhat ambiguous. She definitely wanted an increased presence of women in the synagogues, yet she made it clear that she had no interest in becoming a rabbi herself. Whether she wanted to be a rabbi or not, Jews in America at that time were unwilling to take such a progressive step. Not until 1972 did a Jewish woman become a rabbi.

Regardless of Ray's feelings about women rabbis, she continued to advocate increased roles for Jewish women in America. Ray was a prominent drawing point for the Jewish Women's Congress, held in conjunction with the Chicago World's Fair in 1893. This was the first mass gathering of Jewish women in America, and Ray delivered the opening and closing prayers. She also gave a speech entitled "Women in the Synagogue," in which she argued in favor of freeing

Jewish women to be more active in society while still appreciating their important traditional roles as wives and mothers.

In the late 1890s, Ray became tired of the endless speaking tours. While taking vacation in Europe, she met and fell in love with Simon Litman, the man who became her husband. Keeping her belief that married women should not be employed outside of the home, Ray Frank removed herself from her prominent public life. She moved to Illinois, and though she and her husband remained active in their Jewish community, the "Girl Rabbi of the Golden West" was no more. Nevertheless, the legend lives on as the first inspiration for an increased role for Jewish women in America. Ray Frank's experiences showed that women could contribute to religious life just as they did in other aspects.

—Douglas Gibb

Suggested Reading

Jewish Women's Archive. "Ray Frank—Breaking Down Barriers." Available from http:/www.jwa.org/exhibits/wov/break.html

Jewish Women's Archive. "Ray Frank—Jewish Women's Congress." Available from http://www.jwa.org/exhibits/wov/frank/jwc.html

Jewish Women's Archive. "Ray Frank—The Maiden in the Temple." Available from http://www.jwa.org/exhibits/wov/frank/maiden.html

Jewish Women's Archive. "Ray Frank—Marriage and New Directions." Available from http://www.jwa.org/exhibits/wov/frank/marriage.html

Kuzmack, Linda Gordon. *Woman's Cause: The Jewish Woman's Movement in England and the United States, 1881–1933.* Columbus: Ohio State University Press, 1990.

Rischin, Moses, and John Livingston. *Jews of the American West.* Detroit, MI: Wayne State University Press, 1991.

⊞ FRASER RIVER GOLD RUSH OF 1858

Gold fever brought the forty-niners to California in search of fortune. By 1858, most of the gold had been mined and thousands of miners stood idle or worked subsistence claims. News came that gold had been found on the Fraser River in New Caledonia, present-day British Columbia, and another gold rush had begun.

The Hudson's Bay Company (HBC) received a charter from the English government in the 17th century to carry on the fur trade and other commerce in New Caledonia. In the early 1850s, Indians from the First Nations realized that the English placed a value on gold, a mineral the Indians had previously ignored. They began to mine gold, trading it to trappers and miners for other supplies. In 1857, James Houston, originally from Scotland, hearing that there might be gold on the Columbia River, deserted ship in Vancouver and traveled overland, eventually making his way to Fort Kamloops on the Thompson River. He found gold on the river and traded it, in exchange for his room and board, to Donald McLean, Chief Trader in charge of the fort for HBC, and stories of gold in the Fraser River and Thompson River valleys started to make their way out of the valleys. The Indians continued to mine gold through this period, but McLean had convinced them to now trade directly with the fort.

McLean sent the gold he collected to the HBC headquarters at Fort Victoria, where it was forwarded to the San Francisco mint. HBC sent more than 800 ounces to the mint. Miners in San Francisco heard the news, and a new gold fever started to rise. By the spring of 1858, more than 30,000 miners came to the Fraser River Valley, with new towns springing from nowhere.

Much of the news of the gold strike came from letters sent by miners to their families and homes. One such letter, by an unknown Norwegian, was published in his hometown newspaper in Stavenger, Norway. He told of arriving in Victoria and walking to a new town, Whatkom, at the trail's head. Two months old, the town repeated the story of many towns in gold strike country. The letter writer relates how his friend, a gunsmith named Gullickson, had purchased a lot for $50. Six weeks later, with a new house on the lot, Gullickson was offered $3,000, which he declined. As the only gunsmith in town, Gullickson said that he had earned more money in six weeks of mining than an entire year's work in San Francisco could command.

Letters published in the San Francisco newspapers told of miners, who had been making $5 per week on their California claims or $5 per day working for a large mining company, now making from $8 to $100 per day and more. The newspaper *Alta California* sent correspondents into the gold strike country to provide an accurate picture to its readers. One man reported taking $2,600 of gold dust in two months. Stories told of miners finding 50 to 60 ounces in a day, when gold was selling for $18 an ounce. It was reported that "almost every Indian on Fraser's river has within his buckskin purse, from one to six inches of dust."

Miners traveling to the gold strike usually started from Fort Victoria, going up river to Fort Langley (30 miles from Victoria) and on to Fort Hope (100 miles from Victoria), then another 15 miles on to Fort Yale on the Fraser and on to Fort Thompson on the Thompson River. The Fraser River Valley runs 600 miles north and south, and is several hundred miles wide, bordered on the east by the Rocky Mountains and on the west by the Coastal Range. The Fraser River runs 500 miles through the valley on the coastal side before turning west to its mouth. About 190 miles above this mouth, the Thompson River, running down the eastern half of the valley, joins the Fraser. Large ships navigated the first 20 miles from the mouth, with smaller vessels easily reaching Fort Langley. To go farther north, to the area of the gold strikes, required transportation by canoe or overland. The Fraser River ran with a very strong current and many rapids, making travel treacherous. Above Fort Yale, the Fraser ran through steep and narrow canyons, requiring that goods and mining supplies be portaged to the next navigable portion of the river. North of the canyons, to the fork with the Thompson, were sandbars that yielded significant amounts of gold.

During the latter part of 1857, the British government, realizing the economic benefit of a gold boom, declined to renew HBC's charter and installed a provincial governor who instituted a scheme of licensing the miners and regulating the working of claims. The fee was 21 shillings per claim per month and had to be paid in Victoria prior to entering the gold fields. Much like the gold rush of California, miners abided by the regulations for the most part, knowing that their claims and work would be protected by enforcement of the regulations.

It is estimated that the gold taken from the Fraser River gold rush, lasting from February to September of 1858, was in excess of $50 million. It is interesting to note that during the same period in the depleted California fields, most of the large mining companies were still taking about $1 million per month. By late September of 1858, the Fraser River had dropped, leaving many of the banks dry and unyielding of gold. More people were leaving for California than were arriving to enter the fields. A special correspondent for the *San Francisco Bulletin,* in a letter dated September 21, 1858, wrote, "I have just returned from a trip up the river, and I am able to speak from personal observation as to the prospects of the miners there. In a word they are not doing well." One miner, having taken $15,000 from his claim at Hill's Bar, sold the claim for $200, believing it to be nearly exhausted. By the end of October of 1958, the run had effectively ended. Many of these miners drifted back to the American West and other mineral strikes.

Over the next few years, there were other, substantially smaller gold strikes farther up the Thompson and Fraser Rivers. One, the Cariboo gold rush, brought thousands of Chinese to the upper Thompson River, establishing the first Chinese community in Canada.

—*Patrick K. Brown*

Suggested Reading

Swindle, Lewis J. *The Fraser River Gold Rush of 1858, As Reported by the California Newspapers of 1858.* Victoria, British Columbia: Trafford, 2001.

Waite, Donald E. *The Langley Story Illustrated: An Early History of the Municipality of Langley.* Altona, Manitoba: D. W. Friesen, 1977.

⊞ FRÉMONT, JOHN CHARLES (1813–1890)

John Charles Frémont was born in Savannah, Georgia, on January 31, 1813, and died in New York, New York, on July 13, 1890. Frémont was the son of Jean Charles Frémont and Anne Whiting Pryor. He was educated at various schools in Virginia and South Carolina, attended Charleston College, and taught mathematics prior to becoming a surveyor. In 1838, Frémont was appointed a second lieutenant in the United States Topographical Corps. In 1841, he married Jessie Benton, the daughter of Missouri Senator Thomas Hart Benton.

The next year, Frémont was named head of an expedition that mapped South Pass, the critical passage to the West for Overland Trail emigrants. His account of the expedition, published in 1843, further encouraged migration to Oregon and California. Frémont led a second expedition to Oregon in 1843 and returned to St. Louis via Sutter's Fort and the Old Spanish Trail. Frémont's exploratory exploits earned him the popular title, "the Pathfinder." His third expedition to California in 1845 concluded with Frémont's participation in the Bear Flag Revolt, his formation of the California Battalion, and the surrender of Mexican forces at Cahuenga on January 13, 1847. Frémont's conduct during the military occupation of California involved a dispute of authority between Commodore Robert F. Stockton and General Stephen W. Kearney, resulting in a court-martial and Frémont's dismissal from the service.

He led a fourth expedition in 1848 that lost 11 men to winter's harsh realities in the San Juan Mountains, but reconstituted the party and continued on to California. There, Frémont was elected one of the state's first two senators and served from September 9, 1850, until March 4, 1851. In 1856, Frémont was the new Republican Party's first candidate for the presidency of the United States. After he lost the election to James Buchanan, Frémont moved to Mariposa, California, to pursue mining ventures.

With the outbreak of the Civil War, Frémont returned to St. Louis as one of the first four major generals appointed by President Lincoln. He arrived in St. Louis as commander of the Department of the West on July 25, 1861. His theater included Tennessee, Missouri, and Kentucky. He had 30,000 raw troops. The specter of Confederates in St. Louis caused him to declare martial law on August 4, 1861, and to march troops regularly through the city streets. Frémont also sent a flurry of letters to Washington seeking supplies, worked with private parties to obtain equipment, and recruited foreign soldiers whom he formed into units bearing either the Benton or Frémont name.

Frémont's attempts at creating a military organization were haphazard. He formed Benton Cadets, a school for infantry officers, and regiments of Benton Hussars and Frémont Hussars, but did little to bring West Point–trained military officers into any training regimen. Rather, he brought Hungarian, German, and Austrian officers into an inner circle of 18 personal aides. These officers hovered around Frémont's headquarters like peacocks and gave regular army officers increased cause for complaint. Further, his chief of

staff was Brigadier General Alexander Asboth, a veteran of Louis (Lajos) Kossuth's Hungarian revolt. Also part of the staff was a postal chief and musical director, all foreign-born. Part of Frémont's personnel strategy was to recruit foreign-born soldiers to obtain experience and military decorum without extensive training. He forgot, however, that all military units require the discipline of the training field.

Frémont's military problems were immediately upon him when he assumed command. Confederate leader Sterling "Old Pap" Price had worked to form his mob of civilians into military units and had used improvisation to create ammunition for artillery and infantry weapons. Price ordered Major General Gideon Pillow to invade southeastern Missouri and join Brigadier General M. Jeff Thompson for an attack upon St. Louis. Pillow only got as far as New Madrid, but the maneuver caused Frémont to act. Further, on July 25, 1861, Sterling left Cowskin Prairie, south of Carthage, Missouri, and made a three-day march eastward across the Ozarks; by August 2, his southern column and federal artillery found one another at Crane Creek, Missouri. On August 6, Price had encamped along the Telegraph Road at Wilson's Creek, 10 miles southwest of Springfield. At the same time, Brigadier General Ben McCulloch's Confederate troops were scouring the country for intelligence on Union forces under the command of Brigadier General Nathaniel Lyon's army.

The armies joined in mortal combat at dawn on August 10, 1861, with Brigadier General Franz Sigel striking Price's Confederate forces from the south and Lyon smashing into the camp from the north. Sigel's 1,200-man flanking column achieved initial success until a murderous volley from Colonel Louis Hebert's Third Louisiana regiment decimated the column. Sigel retreated to Springfield, leaving Lyon to face a Confederate force triple his. Lyon died, the first Union general to perish in combat. Frémont's failure to reinforce Lyon and Lyon's tactical impetuosity combined to give the Confederates a major strategic victory in Missouri. The accomplishments of Price, contrasted with the dilatory practices of Frémont, made clear Frémont's shortcomings in the military arts.

The Battle of Wilson's Creek, as this engagement came to be known, created a storm of criticism, but on August 30, 1861, Frémont would increase the intensity of the tempest with an emancipation proclamation.

With a stroke of the pen, Frémont declared martial law, took over the administrative powers of the state, pronounced the death penalty for guerrillas caught behind Union lines, ordered the confiscation of property owned by Confederate sympathizers, and freed all the slaves in Missouri. President Abraham Lincoln wrote privately to the defiant Frémont, warning him not to shoot guerrillas without presidential consent because the Confederates were likely to shoot Union captives in return. Further, the president cautioned that freeing the slaves would alarm Unionists in the South, particularly Kentucky, and dash efforts there. Lincoln told Frémont to modify his proclamation to bring it into conformance with an act of Congress that authorized the confiscation of property, including slaves, if used directly in the Confederate war effort. Frémont refused to do so without a public order.

Rather than modify the proclamation, Frémont sent his wife, Jessie, to the nation's capital to convince Lincoln of his folly. Jessie failed to do so and, in fact, antagonized the president. Lincoln then publicly ordered Frémont to modify his proclamation. On November 2, 1861, the commander-in-chief relieved the Pathfinder of command.

Frémont's abolitionist friends in and out of Congress quickly took up his cause, and on March 11, 1862, Lincoln created the new military department of West Virginia and appointed Frémont to the post. His Mountain Department included western Virginia and parts of Kentucky and Tennessee. Ordered to break the Virginia and Tennessee Railroad and close the Shenandoah Valley to Confederate forces, Frémont slogged into the valley only to be bogged down by torrential rains and his inability to lighten his baggage train of excess gear, including useless river-crossing equipment.

Meanwhile, Frémont's Confederate nemesis, Major General Thomas "Stonewall" Jackson, was creating textbook examples of maneuver, reconnaissance, concentration, and terrain utilization in his valley campaign. In an effort to stop Jackson, President Lincoln ordered Frémont to Harrisonburg, Virginia. Finding the mountain passes blocked by small Confederate forces, Frémont opted to march 40 miles northward to cross northwest of Strasburg, Virginia. At Strasburg, contact with skirmishers induced Frémont to halt long enough for the Stonewall brigade to pass. Frémont wired Lincoln that pursuit was hampered by terrible thunderstorms and egg-sized hail. Jackson kept marching. In all, Jackson was able to escape with 16,000 men, despite being pursued by three federal armies. Once past the Union forces, including Frémont's, Jackson won the race to Port Republic and across the Shenandoah River.

Frémont did catch up with Major General Richard "Old Bald Head" Ewell's Confederate division at Cross Keys, Virginia. On June 8, 1862, Frémont attacked with a numerical advantage of 11,000 to 6,000, but the attack was piecemeal. Opening with an assault by a New York regiment, the attack faltered and then failed. Rather than attacking in force, Frémont reverted to cannonade. He lost 6,084 men, with the South suffering only 288 casualties. Frémont's inaction despite obvious superiority enabled Jackson to move most of Ewell's troops that night for an attack on another Union army commanded by Brigadier General James Shields at Port Republic. Shields' defense, although outnumbered two to one, held and foiled Jackson's plan to then turn on Frémont and destroy both armies in detail. While Shields fought, Frémont rested and Jackson escaped. The Valley Campaign was history. On June 26, 1862, President Lincoln again relieved Frémont of command. Dalliance on the battlefield could not be tolerated. On August 12, 1863, Frémont resigned from the army.

Throughout the Civil War, Frémont exhibited few military skills. In St. Louis in July of 1861, he marched troops rather than training them for combat. He recruited special forces with Frémont family names rather than national, regional, or state labels, focusing his military image and reputation inward rather than outward and against the enemy. Frémont's lack of military preparedness resulted in poorly planned and poorly executed operations against Sterling Price, a man beloved by his men but hardly a skilled military tactician. General Nathaniel Lyon's death was as much a consequence of his tactical bravado as it was Frémont's timid reactions. Frémont's failure to condition, discipline, and prepare troops for maneuver and fire control were part of his personal failure in command.

When Frémont decided to shoot guerrillas caught behind Union lines, he further demonstrated a lack of command judgment. Rather than obey Lincoln on his emancipation proclamation, Frémont resigned. In this act, Frémont displayed the moral courage necessary in command.

Frémont's Valley Campaign further evinced his failure of generalship. He could not bear the specter of travel under the most adverse circumstances, with his personal creature comforts compromised. He could not visualize the need for highly maneuverable units cut free from lumbering supply wagons. He failed to take advantage of terrain and reconnaissance. He allowed the slightest contact with the enemy to deter decisive offensive assault. The fact that Frémont had experienced field commanders with him at this time further condemns his inaction. Brigadier General Carl Schurz was a division commander for Frémont. Major General Franz Sigel, already distinguished on the offensive for his daring and decisive charge at Pea Ridge, was under Frémont's command. Colonel Charles Zagonyi, the Hungarian commander of Frémont's Missouri cavalry, which routed Confederate forces with sabers at Springfield, was at the ready. But Frémont wallowed while Jackson marched, regardless of terrain or weather. Frémont was one of the war's failed generals.

In 1864, Frémont briefly returned to the political limelight when a Cleveland, Ohio, rump convention controlled by 350 radical Republicans, including Wendell Phillips, Schuyler Colfax, Frederick Douglas, Horace Greeley, and Elizabeth Cady Stanton, nominated him for president of the United States. Frémont's candidacy concerned many, because they feared that Frémont and Lincoln would split the vote, resulting in the election of General George McClellan. But Frémont's candidacy was short lived. Massachusetts Senator Charles Sumner, a supporter of Frémont's in 1856, was not a supporter in 1864. Sumner thought Frémont's return to politics would be divisive and hurt the Republican Party. Francis Lieber refused to head up a Frémont Campaign Club because he saw Frémont's candidacy splitting the Republican Party. Flagging support and increased opposition brought Frémont to the point of withdrawal, but his supporters wanted a price for his retirement. A September 1864 bargain struck at New York's Astor House resulted in Frémont's withdrawal and Lincoln's sacking of Montgomery Blair, a Frémont critic, from the cabinet. For Frémont, it was a time to stand aside for a Lincoln second term.

After the war, the Frémonts settled in New York and into a life of high society. Frémont's social prominence did not keep him from bad financial decisions and a decline of fortune. So bad was this decline, in fact, that Frémont accepted the post of territorial governor of Arizona in 1878 with the salary of $2,600. Frémont journeyed to Arizona via Chicago, Omaha, and San Francisco, with numerous receptions at railroad stops. Arriving in Yuma, Arizona, the Frémont family traveled to Prescott in the town's only barouche and with three ambulances. The Frémonts settled first in the home of Thomas Fitch, former editor of the *Milwaukee* (Wisconsin) *Free Democrat,* the Placerville (California) *Republican,* and the *Virginia City* (Nevada) *Union,* as well as member of the 1864 Nevada Constitutional Convention and Prescott attorney, but the family soon moved to a hilltop home. Jessie quickly entered Prescott's social life, but exited Arizona within the year, citing altitude sickness.

Governor Frémont addressed the Tenth Legislative Assembly in January of 1879, outlining his vision of the future. He recommended spending $500,000 on good roads, establishing an assay office and refinery at Prescott to eliminate ore transportation costs, and diverting of the Gulf of California into the Imperial Valley to provide irrigation waters for Arizona. This latter scheme could be accomplished with the Frémont Canal. The editor of the *Arizona Citizen* wrote that Frémont was "as ignorant as the Ameer of Afghanistan of Arizona Affairs."

After the legislature adjourned, Frémont left for the East on a special mission for the territory and to raise money for mining schemes. He achieved the goal of the special mission by convincing President Rutherford B. Hayes and Secretary of the Interior Carl Schurz to withdraw an order extending the Gila River Indian Reservation into the Salt River Valley. He returned only two months before he had to address the Eleventh Legislative Assembly in January of 1881.

In the summer of 1881, the acting governor, John J. Gosper, submitted a report to the secretary of the interior. He recommended that Frémont be required to return to Arizona and perform his official duties or resign. This was only one of many requests mailed to Washington criticizing the carpetbag governor. The storm of protest resulted in Frémont's resignation on October 11, 1881. A close student of Arizona history has written that he perhaps did less for the territory than any other governor.

Frémont returned to the East and spent the last years of his life working on his memoirs. He died of peritonitis in a cheap rooming house at 49 West 25th Street in Manhattan on July 13, 1890.

—*Gordon Morris Bakken*

See also HARTNELL, WILLIAM; INYO COUNTY, CALIFORNIA; LAS VEGAS, NEVADA

Suggested Reading

Castel, Albert. *General Sterling Price and the Civil War in the West.* Baton Rouge: Louisiana State University Press, 1968.

Cozzens, Peter. *General John Pope: A Life for the Nation.* Urbana: University of Illinois Press, 2000.

Goodwin, Cardinal. *John Charles Frémont: An Explanation of His Career.* Stanford, CA: Stanford University Press, 1930.

McPherson, James M. *Battle Cry of Freedom: The Civil War Era.* New York: Oxford University Press, 1988.

Monaghan, Jay. *Civil War on the Western Border, 1854–1865.* Boston: Little, Brown, 1955.

Rolle, Andrew. *John Charles Frémont: Character as Destiny.* Norman: University of Oklahoma Press, 1991.

Wagoner, Jay J. *Arizona Territory, 1863–1912: A Political History.* Tucson: University of Arizona Press, 1970.

⊞ FRENCH BASQUES OF BAKERSFIELD, CALIFORNIA

The itinerant Basque sheepherder moving his flock from central California's San Joaquin Valley across remote desert wastes into alpine meadows of the Sierra Nevada mountain range and the Basque matron working tireless hours in hotels, boardinghouses, and ranches to create enclaves of familiarity and domestic comfort remain as much a part of the collective imagery of expanding European settlement in the American West as do the cowboy, farmer, and miner. Yet immigration to America for many French Basques in the West was only a way to escape the various hardships experienced in their home country. For most, immigration and subsequent shepherding in the western United States was a means toward later acquiring their own flocks or establishing a small business. The vast majority were single males, whose purpose and drive was for financial independence—acquiring enough money to return home or to marry. Bakersfield, in California's San Joaquin Valley, became one focal point of French Basque culture. Today, French Basques have assimilated into the multitiered social fabric of Bakersfield as doctors, lawyers, judges, businesspeople, farmers, ranchers, and, of course, sheepmen.

Kern County's more than 8,000 square miles lie at the southern end of California's Central Valley and includes the San Joaquin Valley. Geographically, it covers areas that include the Mojave Desert and its desert-dwelling Joshua tree, to the Sequoias high in the Sierra Nevada. It straddles the San Andreas Fault and is used today primarily for livestock grazing, and petroleum. Bakersfield, California, lies in the heart of Kern County. Established in 1853 by a group of small farmers whose interest was settlement rather than the search for gold, it was named after one of these early settlers, Colonel Thomas Baker. Baker's Field was primarily a resting place for travelers before they began moving into the dry reaches of the Owens Valley. Surveyed and planned by Colonel Baker in 1863, the town of Bakersfield was part of the 87,120 acres he received for having reclaimed 400,000 acres of swamp and overflow land. Baker's title would make up a large portion of what is today Kern County, which was then part of both Tulare and Los Angeles Counties. The town of Bakersfield was incorporated in 1873, and a year later it replaced the town of Havilah as the county seat.

The French Basque colony that established itself in 1874 in east Bakersfield coincided with the coming of the Southern Pacific Railroad and would lie across the Kern River from Bakersfield in what was once the town of Sumner in 1874. From the 1870s through to the 1880s, there remained a competition for rail service throughout California. This competition, coupled with land speculation, created "not a cattle boom, but a farm boom." In less than one year, land prices had jumped 200 percent. In 1893, Sumner was incorporated as Kern City. With the rapid growth and expansion of Bakersfield, Kern City would be absorbed into its larger neighbor in 1910, and subsequently designated east Bakersfield.

French Basques are identified as those coming from the three French regions of Lapurdi, Behe-Nafarro ("Lower Navarre"), and Zuberoa. These same regions today are known in France as Labourd, Basse-Navarre, and La Soule, and are part of the *Pyrénées Atlantiques département*, or Bayonne. Basques refer to their home territory as *Euskal Herria*. Their language, *Euskera*, is shared with the four Spanish Basque regions of Vizcaya, Guipuzcoa, Alava, and Navarra.

Euskera has no word for "Basque." Basques use the only word in their language, *Euskaldun* (*Euskera* speaker), to identify themselves and other members of their group. Evidence indicates that Euskera predates Indo-European, and it has been speculated that it may be an early Bronze Age tongue, making it the oldest of European languages.

The early Basques left no early written records, but are mentioned by Roman chroniclers as being an established and ancient people. In the past, when the French were typically physically small, the Basques were characteristically broad shouldered, barrel-chested, and burly. These comparisons have led to the theory that Basques may be the descendants of Cro-Magnon, of nearly 40,000 years ago.

Basque culture is known as enigmatic, clannish, and nationalistic. Individual characteristics show a people that are fiercely independent, hard working, and practical. Basques are Roman Catholic and have maintained their faith and religious holidays throughout their history, even during the French Revolution, when anti-Catholic sentiment attempted to force the closing of many churches.

In the French Basque provinces, separate Basque rural land plots were unified through patrimony with only a single heir inheriting the family estates, in strict Basque primogeniture. This arrangement in multisibling families invariably forced noninheriting family members to migrate away from home until they had acquired the wealth to return. Therefore, immigration was nothing new within the Basque view and was certainly the pattern of those French Basques who were to emigrate to California's Kern County and the town of Bakersfield.

Early immigration of French Basques can be traced as a reaction to the Spanish Carlist Wars (1833–1840, 1846, and 1872–1876), and a desire to avoid the mandatory military service imposed by Napoleon III of France. Another factor that increased Basque immigration in the late 19th and early 20th centuries was the Industrial Revolution. Its manufacturing and distribution of cheap goods disrupted the traditional agricultural economies and affected the markets for crafted Basque goods. Urban employment in France or Spain was not seen as a valued avenue by young rural Basques. The majority of French Basque immigration was composed of single males between the ages of 18 and 25. Statistics show that 84 percent of all French Basques born between 1876 and 1879 left to seek a better life and of these only half ever returned to their homeland. Migration of French Basques supported this demographic well into the 20th century.

Single women immigrated too, but in much smaller numbers. Relatives who had emigrated earlier, and who had established themselves in some sort of business, would recruit single female family members from their home districts to work as cooks in Basque restaurants and hotels or to care and work for those family members that had sponsored their emigration. Brothers would often arrange for the immigration of their younger sisters and female relatives. With the vast majority of pioneer Basque women working briefly in the various hotels as maids and cooks, they invariably found prospective husbands.

The young men immigrating to Kern County were not artisans, but agriculturalists and herders of sheep from small rural villages. They would be either contracted or hired by large sheep-raising cartels that found the Basque aptitude for life in the mountains and deserts of California a beneficial extension of their business. Many of the young men that came to herd sheep were familiar with the seasonal movement of small family-owned flocks in their mountainous homeland. But few could have imagined the vastness of the country or the range and diversity of ecosystems. And where they may have had experience moving a few hundred head of sheep, the flocks they now tended were counted in the thousands. Perhaps of most impact were the protracted periods of loneliness, with only a mule and a dog for company.

Conflicts that arose between American Anglos and Basques were based outside of the town of Bakersfield and played themselves out on the open grazing lands. Here, there was competition for grazing resources and space. Anglos saw the Basque as interlopers in the shared vested interest of preservation of the common grazing and tax support systems. There was also the fact that the Basques were able to succeed because they moved their flocks farther away than would Anglo ranchers who were more affixed to conditions. Tensions were eased by the 1880s, when many Anglos withdrew from the sheep business after the extended drought of the 1870s. Again, it was because the Basques were willing to move their flocks away from the common pastures and into the higher mountain ranges during drought that allowed them to further establish themselves as the dominant sheepherders of the region.

Like many other emigrant groups, Basques used a system of informational and assistance networks of those already established to inform others of economic opportunities. Though it is known that Basques were already ranging herds of sheep and cattle in the area of Bakersfield during both the Spanish and Mexican periods, it was not until the start of the American period that Bakersfield began to draw these people in increasing numbers.

The majority of French Basques that came to Bakersfield and its surrounding areas were from Altuldes and Urepel in the Basse-Navarre, and they are noted for having one the highest emigration rates in Europe in the latter half of the 19th century. However, there was a smaller group of Frenchmen from Béarnais in southwestern France that may have been the focus for Basque immigration to Kern County and Bakersfield. French Basques felt a kind of kinship with these French, who were also from the Pyrenees, and so the two groups often married. This marrying of familiar French Béarnaise reflects a trust in marrying other Basques and fits within the Basque view of family and the Old World Basque view that saw non-Basques as a threat to liberty and privacy.

The forming of a French Basque colony in east Bakersfield had its start in 1873 with the building of the French Basque–owned French Hotel and the coming of the railroad. Soon, there would be other hotels with names like the Pyrenees, Metropole, and the Noriega Hotel and Restaurant. As the hotels sprang up, so did other French Basque businesses, all in a one-block area between Baker and Humboldt streets, and between 19th Street and what is now Highway 78. These hotels and businesses ran diagonally to the railroad station. The purpose was to avail the latest Basque arrivals that did not speak English with a place to stay and be surrounded by

a familiar language and culture. Basque hotels were also places where Basques gathered and mingled with those from the same culture.

Though French Basque males had established a hard-earned reputation as lone traveling sheepmen and small business entrepreneurs, it was the wives, mothers, sisters, and those young women recruited from the Basse-Navarre that truly made the reputation of the "French hotels" in east Bakersfield and that created a Basque cultural center. These women were oftentimes the first Basque speakers many new immigrants met after they had come from the old country. It was these same women who were responsible for helping them get their first jobs and seeing that letters were posted and that savings accounts were established. While the men were on the sheep ranges, managing another family business, or on a long-term business trip, the women who managed the French Basque hotels routinely worked 16 hours a day, seven days a week, in the daily maintenance of the hotel, as well as taking care of their own children. It is no wonder that Basques who later wrote about them referred to their lodgings as *osatuak,* or "home away from home." At the same time, these long hours of endless work left some women feeling alone, embittered, and occasionally depressed. Yet it was they who could truly be called the creators of a Basque cultural enclave in east Bakersfield.

The hotels in east Bakersfield were also places where Basques could come and play *pelote,* or handball, against a front and left-handed wall. It was the Basques that brought *jai alai* to America, which when translated from *Euskera* means "happy game." The handball court next to the old Hotel Noriega had been in constant use from 1893 until a new court was built by the Kern County Basque Club in 1975. Today, the North American Basque Organization and the Kern County Basque Club sponsor Basque handball tournaments in Bakersfield.

In 1898, an arsonist was responsible for the fire that destroyed the entire business district of east Bakersfield. The businesses were rebuilt, mostly by Frenchmen, but were later acquired by Basques. These Basque hotels became centers for a growing Basque community in Bakersfield. At the same time, Basques were expanding into other commercial ventures such as butchers, bakers, blacksmiths, and restaurateurs. This established Basque community, seen as being predominately rural, soon dispersed into divergent occupations while remaining in varied agricultural specializations, such as dairy, citrus cultivation, and wheat cultivation.

The years between 1872 and 1914 saw the largest influx of French Basques into Bakersfield. They established themselves permanently as sheepmen, agriculturalists, hotel proprietors, and small business owners. Once established, Basque men sought out other French or Spanish Basques to marry. The end of World War I brought subsequent immigration quotas and land use reforms in California, which restricted both the use of government lands for grazing and the immigration of French Basques as the demand for shepherds declined. French Basque immigration continued until the 1924 Quota Law restricted Basque immigration to America. This event hastened the acculturation of Basques into the American mainstream. In 1960, the California Range Association established the national Western Range Association, whose function it was to recruit Basques as sheepherders. Most of the respondents were Spanish Basques, with few French Basques immigrating due to improved economies and circumstances in France.

In 1944, five men met at a Basque restaurant in Bakersfield and drew up articles and bylaws for the formation of the Kern County Basque Club. Organized to perpetuate Basque culture, the club sponsors ongoing cultural events and a spring picnic that begins with a Mass given by a Basque priest. During the picnic, there are demonstrations of Basque arts, handball, folk dancing, and traditional music.

The 2000 U.S. census gives Bakersfield a population of more than 247,000. Its once ethnocentric French Basque community has dispersed into the broader general community. Basque business interests have diversified, and few of the children or grandchildren of the early French Basque immigrants to Bakersfield are engaged in the sheep business. Yet it was the early French Basque men and women who came to Bakersfield that were willing to pay the price in personal privation in order to reach the long-range goal of economic success that has woven them into the local and national iconography.

—*George M. Stantis*

See also BASQUE AMERICANS

Suggested Reading

Burmeister, Eugene. *City along the Kern: Bakersfield, California, 1869–1969.* Bakersfield, CA: Kern Publishing, 1969.

Douglass, William A., and Jon Bilbao. *Amerikanuak: Basques in the New World.* Reno: University of Nevada Press, 1975.

Eagle, Sonia Jacqueline. *Work and Play Among the Basques of Southern California.* Ph.D. Dissertation, Purdue University, 1979.

Etulain, Richard W., and Jeronima Echeverria. *Portraits of Basques in the New World.* Reno: University of Nevada Press, 1999.

Kurlansky, Mark. *The Basque History of the World.* New York: Walker, 1999.

Paquette, Mary Grace. *Basques to Bakersfield.* Bakersfield, CA: Kern County Historical Society, 1982.

Paquette, Mary Grace. *Lest We Forget: The History of the French in Kern County.* Fresno, CA: Valley Publishers, 1978.

Stafford, John Allen. *Basque Ethnohistory in Kern County, California: 1872–1934 A.D.* M.A. Thesis, Sacramento State College, 1971.

U.S. Census Bureau. "Table DP-1. Profile of General Demographic Characteristics: 2000." Available from http://wwwstatic.kern.org/gems/KernCOG/Bakersfield.pdf

FRESNO, CALIFORNIA

As the mad auriferous rush wound down in the Sierras, and many miners continued along the craggy Rockies, there were those who sought their fortune in other forms of gold. They climbed down to the Central Valley in California, returning to the occupations of the majority of mankind over the last few millennia, agriculture. Though not at first obvious, the riches of the valley were there for the taking, given a little ingenuity and a lot of work. Fresno was a product of all this.

In 1813, Lieutenant Gabriel Moraga of the Spanish army had named the area Fresno after all the large ash trees growing along the banks of the San Joaquin and the slough where the old pueblo of Las Juntas existed. Eighteen miles south, at the head of the slough, the city of the ash trees came into being.

A handful of shacks along a railroad came to be known as Fresno Station in 1872. It served Millerton, the county seat at the time. However, Millerton, a town serving miners, fell into decline when, in 1874, the county seat was moved to Fresno, in the heart of an agricultural area. The town was incorporated in 1885.

The Yokut Indians had lived around Las Juntas at one time but were taken to the Mission San Juan Bautista at the turn of the 19th century. Spaniards inhabited the old pueblo Las Juntas after that, and later Mexicans after independence. It was an out-of-the-way place where criminals, such as the Murrieta and Vasquez gangs, later found refuge. By the 1880s, the land had been bought up by Henry Miller and the residents forced to leave, relocating to Firebaugh and deserting Las Juntas.

Fresno County came into being in 1856. There already were some Basque sheepherders in the county. Over the course of the next decade, Moses Church settled in the area and irrigated to grow wheat and grain. Others were attracted to the site, such as Frances Eisen. Eisen grew grapes and produced wine, but also inadvertently came across what became Fresno's famous crop, raisins, after his grapes dried on the vine. By the later 1870s, raisins became a great success, because the preservation of food was still rather primitive and the dried grapes lasted a considerable time and continued to be delicious. Martin Kearney, another famed grower, founded the California Raisin Growers' Association by 1899. The ranch and fields of Clovis Cole, "the Wheat King of the Nation," raised crops on large acreage as well.

The agricultural success of the 1870s meant that a lot of labor was needed to maintain production. As it was, the local population, dating to the annexation of California from Mexico, was insufficient. Chinese labor was brought in, but the Chinese Exclusion Act of 1882 forbade further importation, and competition with the railroads for workers led to even greater demand. Fresno's ranchers found a new source of cheap labor in Japan.

Despite the devastation of the city itself by fires in 1882 and 1883, growth in the area continued in the 1890s, with the construction of a flume from the mountains into the city. Primarily conceived to carry lumber, it led to the evolution of that industry, but it also carried water for further irrigation. Across the world in Russia, at about the same time, the Volga Germans, encouraged and welcomed by Catherine the Great more than a century before, suffered the consequences of a poorly run nation and a series of revolutions. Many immigrated to the United States, and from 1890 to 1920 more than 7,000 settled in the Fresno area. About a quarter of them lived in the city proper, as the 1920 census illustrates. The majority left in the 1910s.

In the city itself, in 1893, there were 25 Danes, 17 German Russians, 34 Japanese, and some Basques, Portuguese, Serbs, Croats, and Swedes. Ethnic pressures in the Anatolian peninsula also caused another ethnic group, the Armenians, to begin a diaspora. Those who did not leave died in the ensuing genocide. Many of them made the Fresno area their destination and worked as field hands until they had the money to move into town and start commercial enterprises.

These ethnic minorities, along with the Chinese, lived on the west side of Fresno. The area was to the southwest of the railroad tracks and known as Chinatown. The objective for each ethnic group was to move north and become more respectable. Today, Armenian Town is just north of the tracks and has been a prosperous community since the 1920s, despite the fact that a large number of Armenians relocated to Los Angeles in the 1930s.

To get an idea of the city's growth in the early 20th century, one can look at the census numbers: In 1900, there were 13,000 people; 1910 saw nearly a doubling of them to 24,892; and by 1920, there were 45,000 inhabitants. The population more than trebled over the period due to a number of factors. As the technology for refrigeration and food preservation evolved, more agricultural goods could be produced, transported, and sold. Labor-saving machinery led to the cultivation of more land, and the city became a larger center for commerce. Immigration allowed for a constant influx of laborers from the fields, and there was prosperity.

Two events in the latter part of the 1910s led to an even faster growth in population and ethnic diversity. The first was the Mexican Revolution (1910–1917). The consequences for many people in that country were dire, and there were many displaced by the ongoing war. Mexicans began coming to the United States in large numbers as a result. The exodus's labor was needed, not only in the industrial centers of the north, such as Chicago, which continues to enjoy a large Mexican American community as a result, but also in the fields of the San Joaquin River Valley. As American farmers supplied European powers during World War I, farmers expanded production, increasing their incomes and U.S. connections to belligerents. This proved to be a double-edged sword, because it is one of the reasons the United States later entered the war. However, the need for supplies in time of war led to increased production, and the ensuing need for labor was filled by the Mexican immigrants to Fresno.

The prosperity of the Roaring Twenties further fueled the shortage of labor. Fresno's farmers again looked east, as immigration from the south petered out, and the Emergency Quota Act of the early 1920s limited new-comers from southern and eastern Europe. Filipinos, from our then recently acquired and pacified protectorate, were imported to toil as field hands. Today, they consti-tute the largest Asian minority in the San Joaquin Valley. The city's ethnic mix continued to grow, but its economy, as well as the nation's, came to a grinding halt by the end of the decade and onset of the Great Depression.

As though economic depression were not enough, nature took its toll as well. Drought, among other prob-lems, in the Central Plains led to terrible dust storms. Because of the Dust Bowl, tens of thousands of farmers left the plains in the 1930s. The majority moved south to Texas and west to California, where they found both grapes and wrath in the latter. Yet many found employ-ment in the Fresno area. The Arkies and the Okies dis-placed some of the extant minority field hands, such as Filipinos and Mexicans, as now the competition for labor was great and the demand had dwindled in spite of President Franklin Roosevelt's New Deal program and economic manipulation.

While New Deal programs provided much-needed relief during the Depression, Roosevelt and other New Dealers were unable to fix the economy. World War II proved to be a boon to the economy, however. With the infamous internment of the Japanese (a little more than 3,000 of them from the Fresno area) and the drafting of able-bodied men, new sources of field labor were again sought. Many African American sharecroppers from the South moved to factories in the West, and some ended up in Fresno, along with migrant workers from Mexico.

After World War II, improved technology in agri-culture, medicine, genetics, machinery, and the build-ing of the freeway system, expansion of irrigation systems, and other transportation improvements have paved the way for greater production and even greater need for workers. Mexican laborers have ended up working those fields to the present day, be it through the Bracero Program of the 1940s and 1950s or as

illegal immigrants. It was not far from the city of Fresno that César Chávez and the United Farm Workers protested in the 1970s. More recently, 15,000 Hmong tribe members have been allowed to resettle in the United States. California expected more than 5,000 of them, and Fresno was estimated to take in close to 2,000.

The 2000 census shows a sprinkling of Cubans, Puerto Ricans, Vietnamese, Koreans, Pacific Islanders, Indians from the subcontinent, and Native Americans. None of these groups constitute more than 1 percent of the total Fresno population. "Other Asian" is described as "other Asian alone, or two or more Asians." Because the major Asian groups are speci-fied in the census, most of the people in this category appear to be of mixed background. They constitute 7.3 percent of the population. It may be surmised that most immigrated in the last decade, because there were 32,821 immigrants from Asia from 1990 to 2000, out of a total of 34,244 total immigrants in the same period. The majority are Caucasian and Hispanics. The city grew by 73,000 since 1990, an increase of a little more than 20 percent.

Fresno city is a bustling metropolis of 445,000 people, according to the 2002 census, in a county that is the greatest agricultural producer in the nation. The descendents of many cultures live there and are con-stantly supplanted by new ethnocultural groups. There is still a Chinatown and an Armenian Town, the Russo-Germans still have Orthodox churches, and the Hispanic community has grown to be the predominant minority group. With the exception of some Armenian Americans going to Los Angeles, it seems that most of those who go to Fresno seeking their fortune stay and prosper, finding much opportunity in the heart-land of the Central Valley.

—Ion Puschila

Suggested Reading

Austin, Mary. *The Lands of the Sun*. 2nd ed. Boston: Houghton Mifflin, 1927.

Bulbulian, Berge. *History of a Diaspora Community*. Fresno: The Press at the California State University, 2000.

Matthiessen, Peter. *Sal Si Puedes (Escape If You Can): Cesar Chavez and the New American Revolution*. Berkeley: University of California Press, 2000.

⊞ FRISCO MINE, BEAVER COUNTY, UTAH

Settlement of Utah began as early as the summer of 1847, with a population of 155 men, women, and children. Within three years, the population, mostly Mormon families, had risen to 11,000. This led to the formation of the Utah Territory. Statehood would not be granted until 1896, however. Prior to the 1850s, settlement in the area included those interested in pursuing farming activities.

Beaver County, in southwestern Utah, soon became the first in the Utah Territory to focus its economy on mining. Beaver County was formed in 1856 from lands in the former Iron and Millard Counties. Iron County was established in 1852, while Millard had formed in 1851 from Juab County. Among the earliest towns in Beaver County were the county seat at Beaver and the towns of Minersville and Milford. The 1860 census indicates that there were immigrants from Australia, England, Scotland, Wales, Ireland, Denmark, Spain, and Canada, and emigrants from 21 different states in the area; occupations noted in the census included farmers, farm laborers, carpenters, blacksmiths, teamsters, shoemakers, servants, and school teachers, and virtually all of the landowners were recorded as men.

As noted in A. H. Ricketts' 1931 publication, *American Mining Law With Forms and Precedents,* by July of 1866, Congress had passed several acts declaring public lands open to mineral exploration. At the same time, a number of mining districts had formed in the surrounding mountains, including claims in both the Mineral and San Francisco Mountains, indicating that some of these residents sought to supplement their incomes. Following the completion of the transcontinental railroad in 1869, prospecting and exploitation activities increased throughout Utah. In 1872, Congress revised this legislation under the Act of Congress of 1872 (Title XXII Revised Statutes of the U.S. Section 2319–2346), also known as the General Law of Mining, to promote the development of the mining resources of the United States.

Approximately 50 miles northwest of the town of Beaver and 17 miles west of Milford, miners had by the 1870s discovered silver, copper, lead, zinc, and gold in the San Francisco Mountains. The San Francisco Mining District formed in August of 1871, and by February of 1879, the Horn Silver Mining Company organized, encompassing the claims for the Silver Horn, Blackbird, King David, Cactus, Carbonate, Rattler, Comet, Yellow Jacket, and Imperial mines. By 1920, more than 74 claims had been filed within the San Francisco Mining District.

One of the earliest and most lucrative of these discoveries was made near a stage stop at Squaw Springs by James Ryan and Samuel Hawkes. These men located a high-grade silver vein, which they sold to Matt Cullen, Dennis Ryan, and A. G. Campbell. Investors, including Jay Cooke, J. P. Morgan, and several financiers from Salt Lake City, purchased the Horn Silver Mine in 1879 for $5 million. The Horn Silver stake has been likened to the ore body found at the Comstock Lode in Virginia City, Nevada. In 1879, the United States Annual Mining Review and Stock Ledger recorded the Horn Silver Mine as "the richest silver mine in the world now being worked." The Frisco Mining and Smelting Company employed 18 men on 8- to 12-hour shifts to work the Horn Silver Mine, paying them wages of $3.00 to $4.00 per day. Minerals and ores recovered from the Horn Silver Mine included lead, copper, silver, gold, zinc, antimony, and arsenic.

During the 1870s, two smelters, the Frisco Smelter and the Horn Silver Smelter, had been constructed at the base of the mine; also constructed were a 40-mile telegraph line to Beaver and two company stores. Although several improvements had been made to the surrounding area, problems stemmed from a lack of water in the area and little wood for fuel until the construction of a railroad line had been completed. The Frisco Mining and Smelting Company constructed a series of charcoal kilns to the northeast of the mine for the smelting process; prior to the construction of the kilns, charcoal was made in pits west of the mine in the Wahwah Mountains. The company hired one man per kiln, and each kiln was operated for a 24-hour period.

Directories from 1879 and 1880 indicate at least 33 active businesses, including eight saloons, operating in what was to become Frisco. By June of 1880, Jay Cooke, Sidney Dillon, John Sharp, and Silas H. Clark orchestrated the construction of a railroad line extending from Milford to Frisco to help transport the ore and bring supplies to the growing mining community. The San Pedro, Los Angeles and Salt Lake Railroad, later to become the Union Pacific, extended through Milford at that time. Within the next six years, according to Leonard J. Arrington and Wayne K. Hinton, the Horn Silver Mine became one of the territory's and nation's leading producers of both silver and lead. According to Charlice J. Brown, between 1875 and 1879, more than 22,712 tons of ore had been removed from the Horn Silver Mine, with 90 tons being extracted daily during February of 1879 alone. Shipments of ore in March of 1879 included 10,352 tons of lead and 1,293,250 ounces of silver.

In 1880, the mining community centered on the Horn Silver Mine boasted of a population of 800 people. According to the June 1880 census, the residents included four coal contractors, 21 coal burners, seven stonemasons, one brick mason, four wood contractors, and five wood choppers. Most of the residents were aged between 27 and 42 years; several of these men were immigrants from Germany and England. By 1885, activities at the mine helped prompt the establishment of Frisco, a mining community located along the southeastern slope of the San Francisco Mountains near the Squaw Springs stage stop. Frisco also served as the post office and commercial center for the area's mining operations. During the late 1880s, more than 6,000 residents lived at Frisco and readily constructed several brick and wood frame buildings, including housing, 23 saloons, restaurants, churches, a school house, stores, a hotel with a dance hall, a hospital, and brothels. At least 4,000 of these individuals also worked in the mines. A letter dated February 11, 1880, from Fred Hewitt, a California mining engineer at Frisco, noted several shanties surrounding the mine, as well as a company-operated boarding house and two Chinese washhouses in Frisco. Also operating in the town was a newspaper, the *Frisco Times*. Frisco continued to serve as an active mining camp from 1879 until 1929. The population included both Mormon and non-Mormon residents.

By 1881, an additional smelter, the Francklyn Smelter, was constructed, but was located closer to Salt Lake City, at Murray; the smelter employed 180 men. The following year, smelting activities at Frisco were discontinued when costs became too prohibitive to continue smelting at the mine itself. Around this time, the Horn Silver Mining Company also operated refining works in Chicago, Illinois, and a number of iron flux mines near Frisco.

Like most mining towns, Frisco was faced with a high crime rate. Gambling, gun fighting, and prostitution were well documented as far away as Salt Lake City, as noted by an article from the December 28, 1880, edition of the *Salt Lake Tribune* and by the *Southern Utah Times*. A lawman known only as Marshal Pearson was hired from Pioche, Nevada, to enforce the law. Charlice J. Brown states that the marshal shot criminals rather than bringing them before a judge or to jail. It should be noted, however, that a cemetery is located at Frisco. It is unclear whether the criminals were buried at this location, as the only remaining tombstones primarily display the names and ages of children. Many of these deaths are attributed to an 1885 influenza epidemic that struck the town.

In late 1885, the primary mine shaft of the Horn Silver Mine collapsed, a disaster that halted most of the production until the 1900s, when a short revival of silver ore revitalized Frisco. In 1891, according to Philip F. Notarianni, a historian with the Utah State Historical Society, the Horn Silver Mine continued to be one of the leading silver mines in the United States; the mine itself produced more than half of the total silver production value in the nation at that time.

In April of 1894, a fire destroyed most of the mine workings, creating a financial hardship on Beaver County. Only a few of the buildings were rebuilt. One store, S. N. Slaughter General Merchandise, continued to operate in Frisco. Six years later, in 1900, only 14 establishments were operating at Frisco, and the population had declined to 500 people; the decline continued, and by 1903, only 20 businesses remained in operation in the formerly bustling mining town.

In 1907, Caldo Leasing Company built a concentrating mill at Frisco in order to work the old tailings. Despite the addition of the mill, only 12 businesses were operating, and the population had declined to 150 people. The mill utilized flotation methods in 1915. In 1917, the Quad Metal Mill was constructed at the Carbonate-Rattler Mines, approximately two miles north of Frisco; however, these operations ended in 1925. In 1918, the Frisco community had a small surge in the population, which rose to 300 people; 16 businesses were operating at that time. In 1920, it was believed that most of the ore had run out, and many residents abandoned the town. Between 1922 and 1923, 10 of these 16 businesses open in 1918 had closed and the population dropped to 100 people. Between 1928 and 1931, Tintic Lead Company acquired the Horn Silver Mine. Only two businesses remained open, although the population remained at 100.

In October of 1940, the War Production Board passed Limitation Order L-208, which required nonessential mines to close; this legislation mostly affected gold mines throughout the United States. During World War II, however, metal was mined at the Horn Silver Mine in support of the war. In 1943, the King David shaft was retimbered and connected to the Horn Silver Mine. As a result, added production was noted in 1945 and 1946. At that time, the mine was leased by Metal Producers Incorporated of Los Angeles; they continued to lease the mine until 1952. In 1957, P. S. Martin operated the Horn Silver Mine. The following year, Herman and George Heinecke leased the property until 1960. In 1960, the lease was acquired by the Anaconda Company.

The total output of the Horn Silver Mine for its more than 46 years of production massed $70 million–plus. Today, only the remnants of a few dozen buildings are extant. The charcoal kilns have been listed on the National Park Services' National Register of Historic Places, and the Daughters of Utah Pioneers have erected a plaque (number 268) commemorating the Frisco mining community.

—*Heather Puckett*

See also COMSTOCK LODE, 1859

Suggested Reading

Arrington, Leonard J., and Wayne K. Hinton. "The Horn Silver Bonanza." In *The American West: A Reorientation*, edited by Gene M. Gressley. Laramie: University of Wyoming Publications, 1996.

Bradley, Martha Sonntag. *A History of Beaver County.* Salt Lake City: Utah State Historical Society, 1999.

Brown, Charlice J. *Someone Should Remember: Frisco, Utah, Horn Silver Mine.* Cedar City, UT: The Print Shoppe, 1996.

Carr, Stephen L. *The Historical Guide to Utah Ghost Towns.* Salt Lake City, UT: Western Epics, 1972.

Christiansen, Wayne S. "Frisco: Wildest Camp in Utah." *Old West Magazine* 21, no. 1 (1984): 45–47.

Miller, Donald C. *Ghost Towns of the Southwest: Arizona, Utah, New Mexico.* Boulder, CO: Pruett, 1980.

Notarianni, Philip F. "The Frisco Charcoal Kilns." National Register of Historic Places Nomination Form, 1981.

Notarianni, Philip F. "The Frisco Charcoal Kilns." *Utah Historical Quarterly* 50 (1982): 40–46.

Robertson, Frank C., and Beth Kay Harris. *Boom Towns of the Great Basin.* Denver, CO: Sage Books, 1962.

U.S. Bureau of the Census. June 1880 Federal Census. Washington, DC.

⊞ FRISIANS

Early Frisians were a Teutonic tribe that lived on the northern coast of the Netherlands. Fryslân was a sovereign nation until the early Middle Ages. It became a province of the Netherlands in 1814, when the Netherlands became a monarchy. Frisians are a distinct ethnic group often mistaken by Americans as being German, Dutch, or Danish.

Frisian migration to the United States divides into three distinct periods. During the 17th century, the most notable immigration was that of the Anabaptists, later known as the Mennonites, who were escaping religious persecution. The second and third migrations occurred during the 19th century and after World War II. These later migrations were due to economic factors. The largest migration of Frisians occurred during the 19th century.

The motivation for the out-migration from Fryslân during the 19th century was economic, although the religious pillorization of the Netherlands also motivated movement out of rural agricultural districts. The main problem facing Frisians was the mechanization of agriculture. Economics differed regionally, according to soil type, but throughout the province, mechanized farming displaced huge numbers of dairy farmers.

Frisian immigration to the United States peaked in the late 1800s. These immigrants were married, with children. They were a rural immigrant group who moved to ethnic enclaves in the Midwest. During the 1880s and 1890s, record numbers of Frisians arrived in the United States in hopes of renewing their agrarian way of life. Many joined family members already established in Frisian communities. The fact that Netherlanders, particularly from Fryslân, had arrived during the 17th and 18th centuries made the 19th-century immigration easier.

Frisians first settled in the midwestern states of Wisconsin and Michigan. Soon, they began to migrate west to Iowa, then to the Dakotas and Minnesota. Finally, the lure of the frontier called Frisians farther west. There were good reasons to make the journey westward. In the Midwest, farmers faced freezing winters and boiling, humid summers combined with crop failures and rising land prices. The western frontier promised cheap land, a more temperate climate, and healthy crops.

Frisians migrated to Montana, to Crow Indian Country during the 1880s and 1890s. These Frisian pioneers had little or no family to connect with in the West. For that reason, they settled into farms in Dutch communities such as Manhattan and Amsterdam. In Montana, Frisians attended the Christian Reformed Church and raised dairy cattle or worked on farms. These Frisians made more contacts outside of their ethnic circle because there were fewer Frisians to interact with in Montana than in the Midwest. Minority status in the West was not a new challenge for Frisians, who were used to being a minority in the Netherlands.

Another western migration destination for Frisians was Washington State. Their movement to Washington differed from their migration to Montana. Almost all of the Frisians who moved to Montana had moved from the Midwest; the migration to Washington State included many more people who came directly from the Netherlands. The largest migration of Frisians to Washington took place between 1894 and 1895. The railroads conducted a massive advertising campaign aimed at attracting immigrants to Washington via the newly completed rails. Mortgage companies also campaigned to attract Frisians and other Netherlanders. The Northwestern and Pacific Mortgage Company opened a large office in Olympia, Washington, and later opened a branch in the Netherlands. In Leeuwarden, Fryslân, *Noord-Amerikaansch Hypotheek Bank,* along with some real estate agents in Washington, advertised inexpensive, fertile land and low-interest mortgages. The greatest concentration of Frisians settled in Whatcom County,

specifically in Lynden, Washington, a Dutch community established in the 1850s. Because a large number of Frisians emigrated directly from the Netherlands to Washington, they could afford to indulge in more clannish behavior. In Washington, the Frisians became hugely successful dairy farmers and producers of high-quality cheeses that remain in demand today.

During the late 19th century, brochures and newspapers in Fryslân broadcast the advantage of life in the American West. This literature depicted frontier families traveling across open fields with large teams of horses. Pamphlets and advertisements from companies such as the Royal Dutch Steamship Company, the Northern Pacific Railroad, and the North American Mortgage Company portrayed promising venues such as apple farms in Washington State and the wide-open spaces of the frontier.

Newspapers in the Netherlands played a material role in immigration by keeping readers informed about available opportunities in the United States. These newspapers published letters from Frisians that praised the accomplishments of fellow Netherlanders in America. One of the main topics in letters to Fryslân was the good, inexpensive food available in America. Letters from Frisians in America contained so many reports about food, especially pork, that Netherlanders dubbed the letters *spekbrieven,* "bacon letters."

After the completion of the transcontinental railroad, immigrants from the East Coast inundated California, Frisians among them. Frisian immigrants to California settled in urban areas that offered them the opportunity to mix seasonal work in agriculture with other activities. They joined other immigrant groups who worked in factories during the summer and attended school to learn English during the off-season. California was different from the Midwest; it was hot and dusty, there were fewer churches, and fewer Netherlanders in general. In the late 1800s, California was still the Wild West, and it appealed to the hard-working pioneer spirit of the Frisians. The warm California weather was a concern to some Frisians, because they were used to the seasons of the Netherlands, and later of Wisconsin and Michigan. Netherlanders traditionally related climate to health, and one person's illness jeopardized the entire family.

The Church was important to Frisians, and the lack of religious observance among Californians was a concern. The majority of Frisians in the Netherlands were associated with the *Nederlandse Hervormde Kerk,* the Netherlands Reformed Church. The Frisian population in the United States was smaller than the Dutch, so after migration they usually attended the Dutch Reformed Church. Netherlanders brought religious controversies with them to the American frontier. The difference in ethnicity and language between Frisians and Dutch was a constant source of argument. The main controversy regarded which language should be used in church services.

Out of necessity, Frisians in the West were fairly open-minded about marrying across ethnic and religious lines. In California, it was not possible to live in strict ethnic enclaves because the distance between communities was so great and the number of Frisians was relatively small. Intermarriage was not a new idea to Frisians; they were an ethnic minority in the Netherlands, and they considered marriage between people of different provinces intermarriage. One example of a successful western intermarriage that crossed both ethnic and religious lines was between Captain Cornelius Boy Jensen and Mercedes Alvarado. Jensen was born on the island of Sylt, North Fryslân, Germany, in 1814. He was a trader who sailed into San Francisco Bay in 1848. Legend has it that his crew heard shouts of "Gold! Gold! Gold!" and deserted ship. Jensen opened a shop in Sacramento and traded cattle. In 1854, he married Alvarado, the daughter of a wealthy Californio family. They acquired a large ranch in what is today Riverside, California. By 1873, Jensen was ranked the fifteenth richest man in San Bernardino County. Their home is now the Jensen Alvarado Historic Ranch and Museum.

California afforded Frisian women nontraditional careers and new perspectives on traditional gender roles. Men and women in the American West divided labor differently than they did in the Netherlands. In the United States, men did the milking and shoveled manure, jobs that had typically fallen to women in Fryslân. On the frontier, Frisian women had to work especially hard to maintain the housekeeping standards of the Netherlands. The dirt of the frontier was a constant challenge to the devoted housekeeper. Both

Cornelius Boy Jensen and Mercedes Alvarado Jensen. Photo c. 1866 by Steve A. Rendall, Los Angeles.

Source: Photo courtesy of Jensen Alvarado Historic Ranch and Museum.

Frisian men and women often viewed American women as "lazy" and considered them lacking in housekeeping skills. Frisians sent many letters to their homeland that contained unfavorable descriptions of American women and their poor housekeeping ethic. Frisian men criticized American men for marrying good-looking women rather than women who were smart and hard working. Consequently, Frisian men in the United States wrote letters to the Netherlands asking for help in obtaining good Frisian brides.

Not all Frisian women rejected the American women's notion that a career was more important than housework. Korneliske de Groot (later known as Cornelia De Groot) was born in Dearsum, Fryslân, Netherlands, in 1878. After migration, de Groot moved to San Francisco and became a journalist for the *San Francisco Chronicle.* She published an autobiography and worked for women's suffrage. In her writings, de Groot defended American women, contending that they were not lazy, but rather that American women focused their energies on their careers.

Traditional Frisian dress lasted only a few decades in the United States, and less in urban areas like California.

Traditional Frisian women's headgear: oorijzer. *E. Sander Jr. Groningen photo.*

Source: Veenkoloniaal Museum Veendam.

In cities, men and women rapidly adopted modern American styles. Many Frisian women were reluctant to give up their traditional headgear, the *oorijzer,* a tightly fitted cap decorated with ornaments. In rural areas, women and their daughters continued to wear the oorijzer for decades. In the city, Frisian styles gave way to ready-made clothing almost immediately. Ethnic clothing marked one as an immigrant, and the oorijzer indicated a woman's province of origin and social status.

Frisian immigrants in the West had advantages over other immigrants because they were literate and came from a multilingual homeland. Their native language was Frysk (*Frisian, Frasch, Fresk, Friisk*), an Indo-European/Germanic language with many dialect divisions that phonetically resembled English. Americans often confused Frysk with Dutch or German, which Frisian immigrants may or may not have been able to understand. Once in America, Frisians were again in a multilingual environment. In their American homes, they spoke Frysk; in the workplace and the greater community, they used English; and at church services and school, they used Dutch.

Before leaving Fryslân, most children completed at least an elementary education, and therefore those immigrating to the United States were literate. At the turn of the 19th century, the three provinces in the Netherlands with the highest rates of literacy also had the highest rate of out-migration. Literacy among school-age children was approximately 98 percent in Fryslân. Once in America, Frisian children attended one-room schoolhouses on the prairie and on the western frontier that were much like their schools back home. The lessons were in Dutch, and the preference of Dutch American Protestants was for Christian schools. This attitude in favor of Protestant schools accounts for an increase in Christian schools on the prairie and the frontier.

The majority of Frisian immigrants who settled in the American West originally came from the agrarian provinces of Groningen, Zeeland, and Fryslân. Thousands of Frisians left their homeland during the late 1800s, when industrialization and a worldwide depression affected the local economy. The immigration process lasted several decades. Frisians joined people from the same families, towns, and congregations, settling in ethnic communities in the United States. As with many other European immigrants, the Frisians arrived in the East and then continued to the Midwest. After the 1880s, Frisians who had originally settled in Michigan and Wisconsin moved to the western frontier. By 1900, significant numbers of Frisians had settled in Montana, Washington, and California. Most of these Frisians worked on farms and soon became farm owners; however, others moved to urban areas.

In many regions across the United States, the supposedly Dutch and German immigrants were actually Frisians. Most Frisian immigrants were multilingual and literate. Education, worship, and the home remained a focal point of life for Frisians in America. When they began to purchase land and conduct business with Americans, Frisians were quick to learn English. By 1900, 40 percent of Frisian males in the United States were naturalized citizens.

The number of Frisians who settled in the American West was smaller than the number who settled in the Midwest. Minority status was not a new challenge to Frisians in the West. They had experienced discrimination in their homeland due to their minority status. The Frisians of the American West did not live in strict ethnic enclaves as did the Frisians in the Midwest. The

Frisians who migrated to the West were more likely to marry across ethnic lines, choose nontraditional careers, and explore alternatives in religious worship.

—Rhonda Tintle

Suggested Reading

Galema, Annemieke. *Frisians to America 1880–1914: With the Baggage of the Fatherland.* Groningen, The Netherlands: REGIO-Projekt Utigevers, 1996.

Lucas, Henry Stephen, ed. *Dutch Immigrant Memoirs and Related Writings.* Grand Rapids, MI: W. B. Eerdmans, 1997.

Mahmood, Cynthia Keppley. *Frisian and Free: Study of an Ethnic Minority of the Netherlands.* Prospect Heights, IL: Waveland, 1989.

Onsman, Andrys. *Defining Indigeneity in the Twenty-First Century: A Case Study of the Frisians.* Lewiston, NY: E. Mellen, 2004.

Sinke, Suzanne M. *Dutch Immigrant Women in the United States, 1880–1920.* Urbana: University of Illinois Press, 2002.

Swierenga, Robert P., ed. *The Dutch in America: Immigration, Settlement, and Cultural Change.* New Brunswick, NJ: Rutgers University Press, 1985.

van Hinte, Jacob. *Netherlanders in America: A Study of Emigration and Settlement in the Nineteenth and Twentieth Centuries in the United States of America.* Robert P. Swierenga, gen. ed.; Adriaan de Wit, chief trans. Grand Rapids, MI: Historical Committee of the Christian Reformed Church, 2003.

G

⊞ GABRIELINO

The first Spanish explorations into Alta California in the 16th century by Juan Rodríguez Cabrillo described a native population that included the Gabrielino (sometimes also Gabrieleno or Gabrileno). Two centuries passed, however, before Gaspar de Portolá and Franciscan Father Junípero Serra arrived in 1769 to establish a Spanish settlement in Alta California through the creation of the mission system. Spaniards encountered a Gabrielino population, numbering as many as five thousand, in the region of present-day Los Angeles and Orange Counties and confirmed earlier reports of natives in the region with descriptions varying from primitive stone-age survivors to sophisticated civilizations. Gabrielino resource wealth, sophisticated culture, and economy impressed these visitors, who ranked them second only to the Chumash in their level of civilization. Mission San Gabriel Arcángel, established in 1771 as the fourth of twenty-one missions, not only controlled the lives and destiny of this indigenous population; their attachment to this mission conferred on them the name Gabrielino.

As with countless other Native American tribes in the Southwest, the lives of the Gabrielino irrevocably changed with the arrival of Spanish explorers and Franciscan padres, armed with muskets, Bibles, and a plan to turn California's first peoples into *gente de razon,* people of quality. California, the site of numerous myths, lay thousands of miles and many months of difficult travel from Mexico City, capital of New Spain, and even further from Spain itself. Finding settlers for this remote possession eluded Spanish authorities, who eventually devised a plan to convert, Christianize, and civilize Indians to become the settlers so desperately needed.

Contrary to the commonly held perception, Gabrielino Indians were not the original human inhabitants of present-day Los Angeles and Orange Counties. William McCawley's *The First Angelinos* suggests by its title they were the first; however, he and others explicitly acknowledge the "shadowy existence" of an earlier Hokan population in the region. Neither of these populations possessed a written language, and the subsequent lack of written records creates the necessity for archaeological and anthropological evidence verifying that the Gabrielino replaced a Hokan-speaking Chumash civilization on the southern Channel Islands. Techniques such as radiocarbon dating provide scientific evidence of the existence of human cultures in the southern Channel Islands off the coast of southern California. Recent testing confirms sites on San Clemente Island as early as 7785 BCE and on San Nicolas Island by 6210 BCE.

The Gabrielino belong to the Uto-Aztecan linguistic group, which once extended from the Great Basin area of Oregon, Utah, Nevada, and California into Mexico. (Earlier literature referred to this group as a Shoshonean culture.) There is solid evidence dating their migration from the Great Basin region into southern California around 6000 BCE. Gabrielino legend identifies a settlement of "first people" in the Cajon Pass during a time when "the earth was still soft," a people who were "naked, cold and lonely . . . led by a wise captain southward into an ever-expanding land" (Johnston 1962). The fertile environment of southern California, compared to the less hospitable deserts of Nevada, affords the most likely reason for migration, although warfare cannot be entirely ruled out. The land chosen by this migratory people was rich in resources, virtually eliminating the danger of famine, and by the time of contact with the Spaniards, the Gabrielino developed a society marked by material wealth and cultural sophistication. Ethnographic and ethnohistoric accounts suggest the area supported a peaceful population of approximately five thousand living in fifty to a hundred settlements on both the mainland and coastal islands.

Juan Rodríguez Cabrillo in 1542 provided the first European description of the Gabrielino. Searching for Río de la Señora, or the Northwest Passage, Cabrillo's crew encountered the Gabrielino first at Avalon Harbor on Santa Catalina Island (Wagner 1966):

> As the boat was nearing land a great number of Indians came out of the bushes and grass, shouting, dancing, and making signs to come ashore.... Launching into the water a fine canoe containing eight or ten Indians, they came out to the ships. These were given some beads and presents with which they were well pleased, and shortly went back. The Spaniards afterwards went ashore and both the Indian men and women and everybody felt very secure.

The next day the Spaniards crossed to the mainland and, seeing great clouds of smoke, named San Pedro Bay the "Bay of Smokes." It is unknown whether fires creating the smoke came from Gabrielino signal fires intended to attract the explorers or were the result of seasonal burning of grasslands, a technique used to promote growth and enhance the hunting of small animals.

Fifty years later, Sebastian Vizcaino recorded the next European contact with the Gabrielino, describing their hospitable reception and the favorable impression they left with the Spaniards. Records kept by Vizcaino shed light on Indian trade networks, religious practices, and navigational ability. Another one hundred fifty years passed before Spaniards returned to establish settlements. In 1769, Gaspar de Portolá and Father Junípero Serra traveled north from Mexico, stopping in San Diego, where Serra remained to establish the first

of twenty-one missions. Father Juan Crespí continued north to Monterey with Portola, recording in journals the generosity and kindly nature of the Gabrielino Indians near present-day La Puente. Writing in the late summer, he described ritual activity and festivals associated with harvesting acorns, the staple food product of the Gabrielino diet, and telling of an abundance of food in every settlement.

Crespi, in his journals, notes the frequent occurrence of earthquakes in the area and refers to the San Gabriel River as Rio de las Temblores, or earthquake river, and the mission as "Mission de las Temblores." According to Hugo Reid (1968), the "names [were] given from the frequency of terrestrial convulsions at that time and for many years after. They were not only monthly and weekly, but oftentimes daily." Crespí suggests the Gabrielino held Spaniards in high regard, not surprising considering his ecclesiastical goals in Alta California, and commensurate with attitudes of early historians that imply Indians welcomed Spaniards and their mission system unconditionally.

On September 8, 1771, with the building of Mission San Gabriel Arcángel near Whittier Narrows, the first extended European contact with the Gabrielino began. This mission was moved to its present location in the city of San Gabriel in 1774. Mission San Fernando Rey, built in 1797, lay within Gabrielino territory, and although the Spaniards referred to the native population at this mission as Fernandeño, they demonstrate no significant difference from the Gabrielino. Some Gabrielino also lived at Mission San Juan Capistrano. The boundaries of Gabrielino territory, according to both historical and anthropological sources, stretched north from Aliso Creek near present-day El Toro Road to the base of Mount Wilson in the San Gabriel Mountains and Topanga Canyon in the northwest. The boundaries reached inland to the vicinity of San Bernardino and into the Pacific Ocean to include several of the southern Channel Islands, notably Santa Catalina, San Nicholas, and San Clemente Islands.

Americans traveling to California in the Mexican era included mountain men and seamen following the fur trade. In 1805, William Shaler (1935), a Yankee sea captain, observed Gabrielinos living in the Channel Islands. Impressed by the navigational skills of these people, he described their boats as small pine boards, sewed together in a very curious manner; these are generally capable of carrying from six to fourteen people, and are in form not unlike a whale boat; they are managed with paddles, and go with surprising velocity.

The Gabrielino learned navigational skills from their northerly neighbors, the Chumash, and appropriated their canoe-making skills. Life on a seacoast and island settlements demanded contact with the ocean as a means of travel and source of food and trade products.

California Indians maintained widespread trade networks, and Gabrielinos enjoyed the benefit of their central location between the Chumash, Luiseño, Serrano, Cahuilla, and Mojave. The extensive area occupied by the Gabrielino presented a wealth of natural resources in three categories—fauna, flora, and mineral—and archaeological sites provide evidence that trade between coastal and inland tribes existed by 900 CE. Popular items of trade included soapstone, asphaltum, shell beads, and marine-life products that the Gabrielino exchanged for furs and hides, food products, and obsidian. Rituals and social gatherings closely associated with the trade process were friendly gatherings that played an integral role in stabilizing native society and ensuring minimal incidents of violence and warfare. Trade continued during mission days but in increasingly smaller proportions due to disruptions in Indian lifestyle, decline in population, and diminished resources.

Forty years of colonization did not confer on the Spanish a meaningful understanding of the indigenous population's cultural lifestyles, and consequently a series of questions about the Indians were sent to each mission. The *Interrogatorios of 1812–1813* were the first attempt by Spain to document Indian culture, and though they were intended to improve colonial administration, they also provided an invaluable source for academic study. Father Gerónimo Boscano (1978), one of the priests involved in this study at Mission San Juan Capistrano, in 1822 used firsthand observations and information gained from "three aged Indians" to write the first comprehensive study of California Indian culture. To learn "their secrets with their explanations" and to observe ritual ceremonies, the priest used "gifts, endearments, and kindness." Some

Gabrielino lived at San Juan Capistrano, and anthropologists, such as Alfred Kroeber, claim that much of the information in Boscano's study is of Gabrielino origin. Boscano's book *Chinigchinich,* originally titled *Historical Account of the Belief, Usages, Customs and Extravagancies of the Indians of this Mission of San Juan Capistrano Called the Acagchemem Tribe,* describes the ritual belief system attached to the supernatural being *Chinigchinich.* Kroeber (1976) called it "the most intensive and best written account of the customs and religion of any group of California Indians in the mission days." Comprehensive descriptions of everyday life, written when Gabrielino culture remained intact, are among the strengths of this book.

Thirty years passed before another landmark study of the Gabrielino was written, this time by an immigrant from Scotland. Hugo Reid arrived in 1832 and by 1837 had married Bartolomea Comicrabit, whom he renamed Victoria, daughter of the Gabrielino chief of the Comicrabit ranchería. His life on a rancho near the San Gabriel Mission and his marriage offered Reid a rare opportunity to discover Gabrielino culture firsthand, at a time when its decline was palpable. The Spanish colonization, the mission system, and European diseases exacted an enormous toll on Gabrielino culture. *The Indians of Los Angeles County: Hugo Reid's Letters of 1852* first appeared in the *Los Angeles Star* in weekly installments beginning February 21, 1852. Reid's motivation for writing these letters is unknown; however, this once prosperous rancher and owner of Rancho Santa Anita had fallen on bad times and perhaps hoped his knowledge of the Gabrielino would bring him an appointment as an Indian agent with the new American government in California. His sensitivity to the Gabrielino promised help for them; however, his death shortly after the letters were published precluded any such appointment. Don Benito Wilson, who received the appointment, did not possess Reid's sentiments.

The most likely source for Reid was his wife's family; however, there are several other possibilities, including Canoa, a chief at San Fernando, whom Reid describes as "a great wizard [shaman]," and Bona, an old woman living in San Gabriel. Both Canoa and Bona held respectable positions in Gabrielino society and spoke the "court language," giving them access to Gabrielino religious, economic, and cultural history.

The deterioration of the language troubled Reid and provided yet another indicator of a culture in decline; the younger generation could barely understand the court language of their elders. Understanding language can be problematic for researchers, as several languages and dialects were spoken within Gabrielino territory. Differences compounded with tribes living close to the boundaries, and evidence found in the registers of Mission San Fernando shows three languages spoken. The three languages at San Fernando most likely were Gabrielino, Chumash, and Serrano.

Reid recounted the earliest days of the Gabrielino through creation myths.

> The world was at one time in a state of chaos, until God gave it its present formation; fixing it on the shoulders of *Seven Giants,* made expressly for this end. . . . when they move themselves, an earthquake is the consequence. Animals were then formed; and lastly man and woman. . . . man's name was TOBO-HAR, the woman's PABAVIT. God ascended to Heaven immediately afterwards, where he receives the souls of all who die. They had no bad spirit connected with their creed; and never heard of a "Devil" or a "Hell" until the coming of the Spanish.

The Gabrielino believed in one god, Qua-o-ar, the creator of all things, holding him in such high esteem his name was seldom spoken, and then only in hushed tones. Animals vital to the diet of hunter-gatherers were venerated, and the respect shown to wildlife, such as the eagle, led some whites to believe the Gabrielino thought them to be gods. The eagle, according to Reid, was actually the reincarnation of "a remarkably clever, industrious man, chief of a large tribe . . . who, when dying, told his people that he intended becoming an eagle, and that he bequeathed them his feathers, from henceforth to be employed at their feasts and ceremonies." Gabrielino understood porpoises to be intelligent, viewing them as guardians and protectors of the world. The owl was "held in deep reverence, and supposed to predict death, by screeching near the residence of the doomed one. It was never killed." Crows "advised when a stranger was coming on a visit." Although the Gabrielino did not believe in resurrection, they did believe in "the transmigration of the souls of wizards for a time into the bodies of animals, particularly of the Bear."

Each Gabrielino community, or ranchería as the Spaniards called them, was led by a chief, or *tomyaar.* Although this was a hereditary position generally passed from father to son, reports exist of female *tomyaars* when no male heir survived. They held both religious and secular responsibility, the most important being the management of economic affairs and maintenance of food stores. Because women played a vital role in the collection and processing of food sources, the *tomyaar* often had two or more wives. Multiple wives also allowed the *tomyaar* to mediate conflict and form alliances with other families and communities. Polygamy for other members of the tribe was not generally accepted and ended with the mission system. Some *tomyaars,* such as Canoa, were considered shamans.

One of the most highly venerated and feared positions within Gabrielino society was the shaman, or medicine man. His power to mediate with the supernatural world placed him in a crucial position to influence not only religious and medical affairs but also political, economic, and legal affairs of Gabrielino society. Called *A-hyb-su-voi-rot,* shamans, points out Reid, "not only cured diseases, but created them; they poisoned people with herbs and ceremonies, made it rain when required, consulted the good spirit and received answers, changed themselves into the form of diverse animals, and foretold coming events."

Gabrielino lived in dome-shaped huts called wikkiups, the largest of which held up to fifty people. Constructed of plant materials abundant in the area, these huts were often burned to the ground to remove infestations of fleas or other vermin and quickly replaced. The Gabrielino enjoyed a diet high in protein and calories, superior to that of most Europeans at the time, which included plants and seeds, small game animals, and, in coastal areas, fish and marine mammals. An abundance of oak trees throughout the region gave the Gabrielino unlimited access to acorns, the staple of their diet. Women of the tribe leeched tannic acids from the acorn and ground it into meal, which was used to make a porridgelike food they often supplemented with berries or chunks of meat. They also enjoyed the kernel of a species of plum sometimes called the mountain cherry. Although they used fire, they ate most of their foods cold, which helped preserve their teeth. Little salt was used because they believed it turned hair gray.

Women's roles in food preparation increased their value within society, as did their basket-making expertise. Decorative baskets were made for trade and gifts and utilitarian baskets were used to store food and cooking. Tightly woven coiled baskets were used for cooking and to hold water.

Within this society, most males had only one wife, and when a Gabrielino male decided who he wanted to marry, his male relatives visited the bride's female relatives bearing gifts of beads (money) to be distributed equally among the women as if to purchase the bride. According to Reid, "After a few days the bride's female relations would return the compliment by taking to the bridegroom's dwelling baskets of meal made of Chia, which was distributed among his male relations." The formalities taken care of, the day for the ceremony was set. After the ceremony, the wife never again visited her relations, although they could visit her. If they found abusive behavior, they gathered all the money originally paid them, took it back to the husband, walked away with the wife, and married her off to another immediately.

Extensive laws and codes of behavior ensured social control among the Gabrielino. The *tomyaar* mediated disputes with the assistance of a council of elders. Legends and stories, passed down through oral tradition, served to reinforce tribal laws and provide moral guidance. Reid indicated that robbery was unknown within communities and members of the same lineage and that trespassing on the lands of another lineage, especially in areas set aside for hunting and gathering, was considered a very serious offense threatening valuable food resources. This type of offense might lead to warfare between communities and was therefore punishable by death. Murder was rare and carried a death penalty, as did incest. "Incest . . . being held in such abhorrence, that marriages between kinsfolk were not allowed." The death penalty was administered by shooting a person with arrows; fines were paid with food, animal skins, or money; and whipping was never used as punishment. A husband had the right to kill his wife if he caught her in the act of adultery, but he could also choose to give her to her paramour and take her lover's wife as his own. In all matters regarding laws, the *tomyaar* was the mediator and final authority.

Although some Indians assumed the Spaniards to be gods, Reid described the arrival of Spaniards in 1769 generally as a curiosity to tribal members. The Portolá party did not remain long that first year, and there was no violence. Portolá passed by Gabrielino territory twice on his 1769 expedition, camping near present-day La Puente and El Monte, and two years later, Fathers Pedro Benito Cambón and Josef Angel Fernández de la Somera arrived to establish Mission San Gabriel. In 1774 it was relocated in San Gabriel, on land more suitable for agriculture. The establishment of Mission San Gabriel signaled the first extended contact, and conflict, between the Gabrielino and the Spanish. Gifts, often used to entice the Indians into the missions and convince them of conversion, were accepted; however, food items were rejected and buried in the woods.

The labor of the California Indians built the missions, plowed the fields for European-style agriculture, dug ditches for irrigation, and tended herds of cattle, as the Franciscan padres literally enjoyed the fruits of the land. The missions grew wealthy, controlling some of the finest land in the state; missionaries at the Mission San Gabriel oversaw territory between the Pacific Ocean and San Bernardino. Although life changed drastically for the Gabrielino under the Spanish mission system, it did not improve with that system's closure. Secularization during the Mexican period at first included a proposal that valuable mission lands be distributed to Indian neophytes and Mexican settlers; however, lands intended for mission Indians rarely remained in their control and soon became part of the large rancho land grants or were owned by American settlers. Options available to the Gabrielino with secularization included joining the labor force in the growing pueblo of Los Angeles or laboring on one of the nearby ranchos. A core group remained near the mission, holding on to traditional Gabrielino culture and petitioning Governor Pío Pico in 1846 to declare the mission a pueblo and end ecclesiastical control. According to Reid,

[T]heir chiefs still exist [but] . . . have no jurisdiction more than to appoint times for holding of Feasts and regulating affairs connected with the church. . . . Their food continues the same, with the addition . . . of what the Spaniards introduced. Their clothing is of course distinct, and a cloak made of rabbit skins, has within this year or two become a novelty.

Some chose to remain, but the oppressive treatment by Mexican officials and further disruptions in their lives led many of the remaining Gabrielino to set out on a second migration, leaving the homeland they had known for thousands of years and heading north to Monterey County. The letters of Hugo Reid hold little praise for the missions and padres in their treatment of the Gabrielino. The closing of the missions and subsequent American settlement and American statehood did not promise improvement in the lives of the Indians of California. It was in fact the arrival of American settlers that led to the downfall of Hugo Reid and resulted in the publication of his letters in 1852.

Disease, migration away from San Gabriel, and to some degree assimilation into the Mexican population contributed to a further decline of the Gabrielino after 1852. For the remainder of the 19th century, the only studies on the Gabrielino were by American and European linguists compiling data on language. The turn of the century and the establishment of the Department and Museum of Anthropology at the University of California, Berkeley marked a new era in studies of the California Indian, a turning point in both research and understanding. The most productive of the 20th-century researchers was John P. Harrington. His extensive field research resulted in more than one thousand boxes of field notes, deposited in the National Anthropological Archives at the Smithsonian Institution. In addition to field research, Harrington annotated Boscano's *Chinigchinich* in 1933.

Alfred L. Kroeber led the field of anthropology in its formative years and offered distinguished support for the study of California Indian cultures. Kroeber conducted the first complete survey of Indian cultures in California, published in 1925 in his *Handbook of the Indians of California.* He analyzed earlier manuscripts and worked with two Gabrielino consultants to document the Gabrielino's cultural wealth and considerate nature, placing them, as did the early Spaniards, at the pinnacle of civilization in the state. C. Hart Merriam, a field researcher in the early 1900s, is notable for his work with the mission registers. Like Kroeber,

Merriam worked with Gabrielino consultants to compile a list of village names and additional information gathered from the registers. Each of these men contributed significantly to the study of the Gabrielino.

The Works Progress Administration and the State Emergency Relief Administration supported the archaeological excavation of twenty-four sites in Orange County between 1935 and 1940. In 1926, the Natural History Museum of Los Angeles County undertook excavations and fieldwork on San Nicolas Island and, in 1939, on San Clemente Island. The University of Southern California excavated the Malaga Cove site on Santa Monica Bay in the late 1930s. Although each of these projects yielded valuable information, there has been some criticism of the WPA excavation techniques.

The second half of the 20th century witnessed an increase in public awareness of the state's indigenous population, in part due to the publication of academic and fictional accounts of the Gabrielino that appealed to a popular audience. Bernice Eastman Johnston's 1962 *California's Gabrielino Indians* represents a synthesis of previously reported findings and is based on field notes, especially those of John P. Harrrington. Johnston's work, supported and published by the Southwest Museum in Los Angeles, received acclaim. Harrington himself offered praise in his foreword to the book.

> Archeologists, ethnologists and historians will alike find the book intensely interesting and filling a long-felt want, for it tells not only what is known of the native culture but also gives all the Indian names of places and connects many of these with known archeological sites. The book deals oftentimes with the very outposts of human knowledge and presents throughout in well-written form what can be snatched, even at this late date, from the fading memories of survivors.

In 1960, Scott O'Dell published a fictionalized account of the lost woman of San Nicolas Island, the tale of Juana María, a Gabrielino woman marooned for eighteen years on the island and rescued in 1853. This poignant tale is of particular interest to young readers and those working with them, as it presents a historical event in an appealing format. Both Johnston and O'Dell provided interesting accounts for readers and in so doing helped promote awareness of the Gabrielino history and culture. Most recently, the publication of William McCawley's *The First Angelinos: The Gabrielino Indians of Los Angeles* (1996) offers both academics and the lay public a comprehensive study of the Gabrielino. McCawley's extensive use of sources and accessible writing style make this book a must for any student of aboriginal history in Los Angeles.

Much has been written on the Spanish mission system and its oppressive treatment of indigenous Californians. The experience of the Gabrielino mirrors those of other California Indians in areas of religious conversion, cultural conflict, disease, and rebellion. Immediately after the founding of Mission San Gabriel, a violent rebellion erupted over the rape of a *tomyaar's* wife by a Spanish soldier. Priests found quickly that their goals could be easily subverted by the behavior of the very soldiers they looked to for protection and assistance. Incidents like this ensured that the conversion and acculturation of the Gabrielino progressed at a slow pace. Decline of the Gabrielino, on the other hand, proceeded quickly. Overcrowded conditions at the mission amplified the spread of diseases, and the lack of tolerance for Indian customs and ceremonies led many Gabrielino to become fugitives, fleeing their homeland and migrating to other parts of the state. American territorial expansion, along with repressive laws and discrimination, had damaging consequences for the Gabrielino, and their migrations continued after 1850.

The population boom of the 1880s in Los Angeles exacted a heavy toll on the remaining Gabrielino, not the least of which was eviction from lands they had occupied for generations. American settlers took advantage of the Gabrielino through the court system, as most did not hold legal titles for their lands. Public outcry and the "well-meaning" efforts of reformers, instead of assisting the Indians, resulted in the establishment of reservations and eventually a plan to assimilate Gabrielino children by enrolling them in the Sherman Indian School in Riverside. School records list an average of fifty Gabrielino children per year between 1890 and 1920. As conditions worsened for California Indians, activism emerged with the formation of the Mission Indian Federation after 1910. The federation was instrumental in the 1928 California Indians Jurisdictional Act, which authorized the creation of a roll of California Indians eligible for payments from a judgment fund. To be placed on this roll required proof of ancestry from an Indian living in California in 1852, and more than one hundred and fifty Indians identified themselves as Gabrielino. Decades of migration and absorption into the Hispanic population of California, however, makes it difficult, if not impossible, to ascertain the present-day Gabrielino population. In recent decades, the Gabrielino have emerged on the political scene, fighting to save cultural landmarks, to accomplish the reinterment of ancestral remains, to receive compensation for lands lost, and to educate the public about their history and struggles for federal recognition.

—*Linda Molno*

See also Cahuilla Nation; Chemehuevi; Los Angeles, California

Suggested Reading

Bolton, Herbert Eugene. *Fray Juan Crespi: Missionary Explorer on the Pacific Coast, 1769–1771*. Berkeley: University of California Press, 1927.

Boscana, Father Gerónimo. *A Revised and Annotated Version of Alfred Robinson's Translation of Father Gerónimo Boscano's Historical Account of the Belief, Usages, Customs and Extravagancies of the Indians of This Mission if San Juan Capistrano Called the Acagchemem Tribe*. Reprinted ed. Banning, CA: Malki Museum Press, 1978.

Boulé, May Null. *Gabrielino Tribe*. Vashon, WA: Merryant, 1992.

Castillo, Edward D. "Blood Came from Their Mouths: Tongva and Chumash Responses to the Pandemic of 1801." *American Indian Culture and Research Journal* 23, no. 3 (1999).

Castillo, Edward D. "Gender Status Decline, Resistance, and Accommodation among Female Neophytes in the Missions of California: A San Gabriel Case Study." *American Indian Culture and Research Journal* 18, no. 1 (1994).

Cleland, Robert. *The Cattle on a Thousand Hills*. San Marino, CA: Huntington Library and Art Gallery, 1951.

Dakin, Susanna Bryant. *A Scotch Paisano in Old Los Angeles: Hugo Reid's Life in California, 1832–1852, Derived from His Correspondence*. Berkeley: University of California Press, 1939.

Dana, Richard Henry. *Two Years Before the Mast: A Personal Narrative*. New York: Harper and Brothers, 1840.

Engelhardt, Fr. Zephyrin, O.F.M. *San Fernando Rey: The Mission of the Valley*. Chicago: Franciscan Herald Press, 1927.

Engelhardt, Fr. Zephyrin, O.F.M. *San Gabriel Mission and the Beginning of Los Angeles*. Chicago: Franciscan Herald Press, 1927.

Guest, Francis, O.F.M. "Mission Colonization and Political Control in Spanish California." *Journal of San Diego History* 24, no. 1 (1978). Available from http://www.sandiegohistory.org/journal/78winter/mission.htm

Hackel, Steven W. "Sources of Rebellion: Indian Testimony and the Mission San Gabriel Uprising of 1785." *Ethnohistory* 50, no. 4 (2003).

Harrington, John P. Annotations. In *Chinigchinich: A Revised and Annotated Version of Alfred Robinson's Translation of Father Gerónimo Boscano's Historical Account of the Belief, Usages, Customs and Extravagancies of the Indians of This Mission of San Juan Capistrano Called the Acagchemem Tribe.* 2nd ed. Banning, CA: Malki Museum Press, 1978.

Harrington, John P. "A Rare Account of Gabrielino Shamanism from the Notes of John P. Harrington." *Journal of California and Great Basin Anthropology* 1, no. 2 (1979).

Heizer, R. F., and M. A. Whipple. *The California Indians: A Source Book.* Berkeley: University of California Press, 1971.

Johnston, Bernice E. *California's Gabrielino Indians.* Los Angeles: Southwest Museum, 1962.

Kroeber, Alfred. *Handbook of the Indians of California.* 2nd ed. New York: Dover Publications, 1976.

McCawley, William. *The First Angelinos: The Gabrielino Indians of Los Angeles.* Novato, CA: Ballena Press Publishers' Services, 1996.

Miller, Bruce. *The Gabrielinos.* Los Osos, CA: Sand River Press, 1991.

O'Dell, Scott. *Island of the Blue Dolphins.* Boston: Houghton Mifflin and Riverside Press, 1960.

Reid, Hugo. *Indians of Los Angeles County.* Edited and annotated by Robert F. Heizer. Los Angeles: Southwest Museum, 1968.

San Gabriel Mission Registers. San Fernando, CA: Chancery Archives of the Archdiocese of Los Angeles at Mission San Fernando, various years.

Shaler, William. *Journal of a Voyage Between China and the North Western Coast of America, Made in 1804 by William Shaler.* Claremont, CA: Saunders Studio Press, 1935.

Singleton, Heather Valdez. "Surviving Urbanization: The Gabrielino, 1850–1928." *Wicazo SA Review* 19 (Fall 2004).

Vizcaino, Fr. Juan. *The Sea Diary of Fr. Juan Vizcaino to Alta California 1769.* Los Angeles: Glen Dawson, 1959.

Wagner, Henry R. *Spanish Voyages to the Northwest Coast of America in the Sixteenth Century.* 2nd ed. San Francisco: California Historical Society, 1966.

⊞ GALE, WILLIAM ALDEN (? –1841)

William Alden Gale was born to William Gale and Hannah Pim Bean Gale in Boston, Massachusetts.

W. A. Gale had two sisters named Elizabeth and Lydia Symmes, but little else is known about his family life. Gale was the first American to pioneer the hide and tallow trade between California and New England in the early 19th century, which subsequently opened the commercial gates of the previously isolated Spanish province.

American interest in California began during the late-18th-century sea otter trade with China. In 1810, Gale sailed to California as a clerk on the *Albatross* to the Farallon Islands. As the Russians sailed down to California from the north, British and American companies from New England ventured toward California via the Horn. Whalers began to visit California more frequently, but the predominant American trading interest in the long-isolated region shifted to cowhides and tallow.

Gale and other traders continued to barter their cargo for California's natural products, which provided the essential materials for New England factories. Because money was not used as an exchange medium, the Californians exchanged hides, or "California bank notes," which ranged in value from one to three pesos. The Spanish padres (priests) were the chief customers, acquiring clothing, farming implements, and other necessities. Despite this mutually beneficial relationship, the Mexican authorities passed stringent regulations prohibiting trade with merchants. However, Governor José Darío Argüello's statement, "Necessity makes licit what is not licit by law," explains the emergence of an extremely successful contraband business.

The hide and tallow business gained momentum with Mexico's independence in 1822, when the ports of Monterey and San Diego opened to foreign trade. That year, the frigate *John Begg* arrived. Agents aboard the ship from the British trading firm John Begg and Company included Hugh McCulloch and William E. P. Hartnell, who became known as "Macala and Arnel." They secured an exclusive three-year contract with Governor Pablo Vicente Solá and prefect Payéras to pay one peso per hide and buy at least 25,000 arrobas of tallow at two pesos an arroba (25 pounds).

Because of Gale's reports of the region's vast resources, the Boston mercantile house of Bryant, Sturgis & Co. outfitted a vessel to trade with California. Less than a month after the British arrival, shipmaster Henry Gyzelaar and supercargo W. A. Gale arrived in the *Sachem*. Their arrival initiated trade between the two coasts, as well as a long and prosperous exportation of hides and tallow that became the primary economic business of the region. Because of the British contract, Gale only exported two cargoes until its expiration in 1826. However, his counteroffer of double the British rate caused discontent among the padres and helped the Boston firm weaken the British hold on California trade. With Bryant, Sturgis & Co. and other New England firms' subsequent successes, the United States was commonly known in California as "Boston."

Despite a thriving market, restricted access to ports and high duties obstructed business. Merchants were only permitted to discharge cargoes at the ports of Monterey and San Diego. In 1829, Gale wrote to Governor Echeandía in San Diego, threatening to abandon trade unless the government offered more favorable terms. Dissatisfied with the response, he sailed to San Diego to negotiate in person. As a result, Governor Echeandía reinstated Gale's access to all ports, including San Francisco, Monterey, Santa Barbara, San Pedro, and San Diego. Along with this success, Gale also established the first American mercantile house in California.

Gale's daughter, Anita, was born on the Hawaiian Sandwich Islands in 1817. In 1822, he brought her to live with Pio Pico's widowed mother. The influx of American merchants also had significant social impacts, as many traders became naturalized, married the daughters of leading Mexican families, and obtained large grants of land. For example, in 1836, Anita married Jonathan Trumbull (Don Juan José) Warner, an American overland trader who became naturalized and obtained a land grant. Anita bore two daughters before her death in 1857. Her father followed this pattern when he married Marcelina of the prominent Estudillo family. In 1827, Marcelina sailed to Boston with Gale on the *Sachem,* becoming the first California woman to visit the "hub." She reportedly never returned to California.

Besides engaging in trade on land, Gale and other merchants bartered on board the ships. A trade room in a merchant vessel was configured like a country store, where the goods could be displayed in an appealing manner. According to Richard Henry Dana's account regarding his participation as an agent of Bryant, Sturgis & Co., the vessels were "floating department stores" that contained myriad items such as liquor, sugar, spices, fine and coarse linens, furniture, guns and powder, coffee, tea, crockery and tinware, agricultural implements, clothing, jewelry, toothbrushes, millstones, and an occasional billiard table or piano, as well as "everything that can be imagined, from Chinese fire-works to English cart-wheels."

From his experience on land, Gale was known as "Cambalache" (barter), as well as Don Guillermo "Cuatros Ojos" (four eyes), because of his glasses. According to William Heath Davis, "Cuatros Ojos" and Alfred Robinson, another agent of the Boston house, concocted a plan to boost sales. They would pretend to be rivals, and Gale would descend alone on horseback to a mission and secure a sale. After completion, Robinson, who was well liked by the padres, would also obtain an order. Repeating this ploy, Gale and Robinson collectively sold an extensive quantity of merchandise.

Gale's participation in the hide and tallow trade continued until Bryant, Sturgis & Co. dissolved due to a plummeting market, California politics, and the onset of the gold rush. With the dissolution of the company, Gale returned to Massachusetts, where he lived until his death in 1841. Besides facilitating the establishment of California's commercial market, which provided much of the raw material for New England's extensive manufacturing industries, the hide and tallow trade became a powerful factor that laid the foundation for the American movement to annex the province into the United States.

—*Catherine M. Bilanchone*

Suggested Reading

Bancroft, Hubert Howe. *History of California.* Vols. I–VII. Reprinted ed. Santa Barbara, CA: Wallace Hebberd, 1963–1970.

Bancroft, Hubert Howe. *History of the Pacific States of North America.* Vols. I–V. San Francisco: H. H. Bancroft, 1883–1891.

Castro, Doris Shaw. *California Colony: Genealogy, Land Grants, & Notes of Spanish Colonial California.* Bloomington, IN: AuthorHouse, 2004.

Cleland, Robert Glass. *From Wilderness to Empire: A History of California, 1542–1900.* New York: Alfred A. Knopf, 1944.

Dana, Richard Henry. *Two Years Before the Mast: A Personal Narrative.* New York: Harper and Brothers, 1840.

Davis, William Heath. *Seventy-Five Years in California.* San Francisco: John Howell, 1929.

Eldrege, Zoeth Skinner. *The Beginnings of San Francisco from the Expedition of Anza, 1774 to the City Charter of April 15, 1850.* Vol. I. New York: John C. Rankin, 1912.

Hunt, Rockwell D., ed. *California and Californians: The Spanish Period, the American Period, and a California Bibliography.* Vol. I. Cherry Hill, NJ: Lewis, 1932.

Ogden, Adele. "Boston Hide Droghers Along California Shores." *California Historical Society Quarterly* 8 (1929).

Ogden, Adele. "Hides and Tallow: McCulloch, Hartnell and Company 1822–1828." *California Historical Society Quarterly* 6 (1927).

⊞ GALLATIN VALLEY, MONTANA

Gallatin Valley is often referred to as the "Valley of the Flowers" or "The Egypt of America." Both are idyllic descriptions. Legend is the basis for the first description and boosters imagination for the second. Overlooking the valley from the mouth of a canyon in the Bridger Mountains (named for Jim Bridger) stood the mythical Maiden of the Rock. When the Blackfoot roamed most of the valley, they fiercely tried to protect the valley from intruders trying to enter their prime hunting ground. It did not seem to matter whether it was another tribe, explorer, trapper, or settler. The Blackfoot fought bloody battles but found it difficult to keep intruders at bay. It was the maiden who declared that flowers would grow where blood had been shed and the valley would remain peaceful. So it was that no warfare raged in the valley. Actually, the Indian tribes in the area used the valley to hunt or as a transition from one place to another.

A 1908 pamphlet named some of the superior points of the "Egypt of America": "Gallatin Valley has the blackest, richest deepest soil in Montana. It has the most beautiful climate in the northwest. It is the greatest grain and barley district in the northwest. It has worlds of undeveloped timber and mineral resources." This was published by the Sugar Beet Committee of Bozeman, Montana, advertising the many benefits of coming to the Gallatin Valley. Other benefits were businesses, the railroad, and the agricultural college, but mainly it was the lure of the land.

Gold was the primary temptation for emigration through Gallatin County as miners traveled to gold fields of Bannack (Beaverhead County) and Virginia City and Alder Gulch (Madison County) in 1863. The following year, the Montana Territory was created, and Gallatin was one of the nine original counties in the territory. Get-rich-quick schemes brought men from the East Coast, West Coast, and Europe to scrabble for gold. In 1865, Gallatin County was established by the first territorial legislature of Idaho and reestablished by the first territorial assembly of Montana in February, 1865. The county included a vast area extending beyond the present site of Columbus, Montana. In addition, the unorganized county of Big Horn, which included the entire southeastern section of Montana Territory, was attached to it. The legislature created several more counties after statehood was won in 1889.

Since 1867, there has been little change to the western boundary, but in 1877, Park County was carved out of the eastern part of Gallatin County. Today, Gallatin is one of 56 counties.

Gallatin Valley statistics reveal that it is 2,540 square miles, 116 miles long and from 12 to 49 miles wide. Most of it is less than 28 miles wide. The altitude ranges from the 4,000-foot valley floor to a height of 11,000 feet above sea level. All surveying for Montana begins with the Principal Parallel, which is in Willow Creek, Gallatin County, Montana.

The Gallatin River begins in Yellowstone National Park and is the main tributary of the county. This was one of the rivers named by the Lewis and Clark expedition when they reached the headwaters of the Missouri in 1805. This is also the area from which Sacajawea, the intrepid Indian guide, was originally kidnapped. After Lewis and Clark followed traders and trappers, using the routes of the original inhabitants, the Blackfoot and Crow nations. White men, under the auspices of the Idaho Territory, began to traverse Gallatin County regularly. As early as 1810, a trading post was established at the three forks of the Missouri River. It became a crossroads for traders, trappers, and explorers, who found the county to have rich resources of fur. This post was abandoned one year later due to skirmishes and some attacks by Indians, although the region remained a crossroads for trading.

In 1840, Father Peter deSmet camped here on his mission in the territory. The first permanent settlement in Gallatin County was several miles north of present-day Three Forks, Montana. When it lost the bid to become the county seat in 1867 to Bozeman, the settlement slowly disappeared.

Three Forks, Montana, is descriptive of the three rivers that form the headwaters of the Missouri River: the Gallatin, Jefferson, and Madison Rivers, all named by the Lewis and Clark expedition. A Swiss immigrant, Albert Gallatin, is the namesake for all things Gallatin. He was the secretary of the treasury under President Thomas Jefferson. Gallatin was responsible for gathering the money to make the Louisiana Purchase from France. Spurred to find a passageway to the Pacific and also to learn more about the people, land, flora, and fauna of the large land purchase, Lewis and Clark were sent west with 38 men.

Settlement in Gallatin County began in earnest in 1863, but navigating the Missouri River to this point was fruitless, due to the great falls of the Missouri. Some settlers to the valley boated to Fort Benton, Montana, and continued the trip to the Gallatin Valley by wagon train. When the Bozeman Trail brought settlers through the Bozeman Pass at the east of the county, it became an entrance into the valley from 1863 to early 1867.

Residents and nonresidents also made the land the source of their financial interests. Coal mining was the most important industry and was exploited in the eastern part of the valley, in areas called Chesnut, Storrs, and Cokedale. As soon as the Northern Pacific Railroad went through Rocky Canyon (1883), coal was more easily transported out of the valley.

Other mineral deposits were discovered and attracted economic exploitation. However, none was successfully mined because the deposits were situated in narrow and shallow seams. This made mining a costly endeavor. In the late 20th century, other minerals were in the forefront, such as coal bed methane, much to the consternation of many Gallatin County residents, who fear it will ruin the beauty and fertility of the land.

The lure of gold and mining was followed by agricultural endeavors. Adjusting to the geographic conditions enabled farmers to discover which short-season crops did best, ranchers to discover that the grass cover benefited their Angus cattle, and lumbermen to discover that forest products were plentiful in the high reaches of the valley's mountains.

The county was serviced by three railroads: the Northern Pacific reached the county in March 1883;

the Oregon Short Line of the Union Pacific was built to West Yellowstone in 1907; and the Chicago, Milwaukee, St. Paul and Pacific was built through to Three Forks in 1907.

The original tide of emigration came from all nationalities and continued through the homestead era. The Chinese came to work the mines, the English to raise horses, and the Germans to farm. After gold, the richness of the soil enabled farmers and ranchers to thrive, especially after the dry-farming technique was used along with irrigated fields. Wheat became the gold for farmers.

At the southern end of the county is West Yellowstone and the western gateway to Yellowstone National Park. West Yellowstone began as a small development around 1907. The Union Pacific line brought tourists to the western entrance to Yellowstone Park. At this time, stores, livery stables, and hotels were established to cater to the needs of the tourists who flocked to the area. Improvements to roads from West Yellowstone to the north enabled travelers to reach the park, but mainly in the summer. By the 1950s, winter sports, mainly snowmobiling and dog sledding, led to the area becoming more permanently settled.

Sports and recreation have always been part of the growth of the valley. Hunting and fishing at first brought easterners to the area for vacations. In early 1970, Big Sky became a destination for recreational skiing, one that would rival Aspen and Vail in Colorado. At first this development was contested on environmental grounds, but this area continues to grow and flourish, especially for the rich and famous, who like expansive views along with privacy.

Local residents of Bozeman also established in 1954 another recreational ski area. This area, in Bridger Canyon, 13 miles from Bozeman, is a local favorite for its steep, challenging runs. All forms of skiing—cross-country, skate, downhill, telemark, and backcountry—are enjoyed across the Gallatin Valley. Recreational skiing is a main source of the tourism industry's support of the county coffers.

The southern and eastern parts of the county provided recreational opportunities, but the Gallatin Canyon area also had many mining claims, and later much of the land was encompassed in Charles

Anceney, Jr.'s large ranching operation. This part of the valley was very rugged and was mostly used for hunting, camping, and fishing. However, the Anceney family persevered and acquired a ranch that was 24 miles wide and 26 miles long. This ranch was so large that some men were born, worked the ranching operation, and later died on the same land. Today, Ted Turner Enterprises owns and manages the land as a large bison refuge and conservation area, off-limits to any public participation.

Very early in the 20th century, men from Bozeman set up logging and mill operations to provide building materials for the growing town of Bozeman. The logging activities made a road into the canyon possible. It was opened in 1910, but this too was seasonal and difficult to travel in bad weather. By 1927, a passable road was completed, and improvements continue to be made.

The improved road situation made it possible to open dude ranching enterprises in the canyon. As vacationers came from the east, the dude ranches flourished, mainly the Karst Ranch, the 320 Ranch, and the Nine Quarter Circle. Several of the ranches begun in the early 1920s are still tourist destinations. The mouth of the canyon is close to Gallatin Gateway, so named because it was considered the "gateway" to Yellowstone. At the gateway, the Milwaukee Road terminated, and tourists spent the night before being driven to West Yellowstone to begin their vacations in the park.

A short way straight north of the Gallatin Canyon is Belgrade, Montana, sometimes called "The Hub of the Gallatin." Belgrade was incorporated in 1906 but began in a speculative manner, betting on a railroad terminal and ample grain to ship to market. If the railroad came, transporting the grain would be much easier than by wagon. The Northern Pacific reached Belgrade, and the area began to prosper and grow, with livery stables, mercantiles, saloons, and gambling, as well as horse trading. In 1913, the Northern Pacific Railroad sent out branch lines to the north to pick up grain from Accola, Springhill, and other farms north of Menard. Belgrade was in close competition with Bozeman in the early years of the 20th century. Bozeman won, but Belgrade continued to hang on and in 1910 was the leading hub of grain export from the valley as farmers came from the north of the valley with the famous turkey red wheat. The name Belgrade was chosen by Thomas B. Quaw, who was trying to impress a group of Serbian investors in town to survey the land they had purchased. They were also on their way to see the Northern Pacific's driving of the gold spike.

The northern part of the valley remains rich agricultural land and ranching. This part of the valley was settled early. Many Mormons entered into Montana at Virginia City, accumulated some money, and began homesteading just north of Bozeman. These Mormon contingents were leaving the Salt Lake City area of Utah to escape the current teachings of the church and were known as Josephites. Hardy and inventive farmers, the Mormons managed to cultivate, with dry-land techniques and irrigation, large acreages and produce volumes of wheat, barley, and hay.

Manhattan, Montana, began as Moreland, but was soon renamed by a group of New Yorkers in 1891. These men had large landholdings, along with some from England. Manhattan residents were fairly prosperous, supporting a store, a blacksmith's shop, a school, and several dwellings, but unlike Belgrade, it had no saloon. When the railroad came through, the lines bypassed the town of Hamilton, which until that time had been one of the three largest towns in the valley (the others were Bozeman and Gallatin City). Hamilton residents slowly migrated into Manhattan. The easterners from New York were interested in growing a superior quality malting barley and established the Manhattan Malting Company. The seasons and soil were favorable, and the venture began. Prohibition brought to a close the prosperity of the Manhattan Malting Company, which had provided malt to Montana's breweries as well as to those of other states. One of the succeeding ventures was to use straw to make paper, but the paper mill was not a success. However, the town of Manhattan remained and became an important agricultural center.

As the area north of Bozeman was homesteaded by Germans and French Canadians, the area to the south of Belgrade was settled by the Dutch in a place called Amsterdam.

To promote cultivation and get farmers to work the land for the malting company, fliers were sent to Holland to secure farmers to provide the crops. The first influx of Dutch immigrants to the Gallatin Valley came in 1893. With a strong religious foundation and work ethic, the Dutch became successful and prosperous. Their farming practices and yields were high.

Word spread to other Dutch settlements in the United States and back to Holland. By 1904, there were 40 families in the area prospering in agricultural endeavors. This brought the resulting businesses: garages, implement stores, grain elevators, and mercantiles. The neighboring settlement of Church Hill was slower in growing, but since 1950 the area has seen steady growth. The descendents of the original families till the land; raise wheat, barley, and oats; and maintain the Dutch culture. The Dutch farmers also joined Bozeman in the production of sweet peas and now are known for their potato-growing ability. Big Dutch barns dot the rolling countryside and hills. This is one of the few places in the Gallatin Valley that diary cattle and hogs are raised. The foods and traditions of the Dutch remain strong and vibrant.

Emigration into the Gallatin Valley began in the 19th century and continues into the 21st century. The population of the area continues to grow. The Bozeman *Avant Courier* declared, "The county has a population of about 3,500 and over 1,000,000 bushels of grain have been produced in a single season. There are eight steam threshing machines in the Gallatin Valley and . . . six flour mills." The year 1975 showed 44,748 inhabitants, and at that time it was estimated that the county would grow to 59,787 by 1990. County growth indeed continued to spiral, with a 10 percent increase from 2000 to 2004, and the population at that time was 73,000.

This marked increase is no longer attributed to finding the richness of gold. It is the richness of the landscape, the provision of an escape from the cities, room to grow, the richness of natural resources, and the quality of the wilderness.

—Ann Butterfield

Suggested Reading

Avant Courier. "Gallatin County in 1878" [Pamphlet]. Bozeman, MT: Gallatin Historical Society Pioneer Museum vertical files (January 30, 1879).

Bates, Grace. *Gallatin County (Montana) Places and Things Present and Past.* Self-published, 1995.

Belgrade Centennial Committee. *Belgrade, Montana: The First 100 Years.* Dallas, TX: Taylor, 1986.

Burlingame, Merrill. *Gallatin Century of Progress.* Bozeman, MT: Gallatin County Centennial Publications, 1964.

Burlingame, Merrill G. *Gallatin County's Heritage: A Report of Progress, 1805–1976.* Bozeman, MT: Gallatin County Centennial Publications, 1977.

Cheney, Roberta Carkeek. *Names on the Face of Montana.* Missoula, MT: Mountain Press Publishing, 1983.

Cronin, Janet, and Dorothy Vick. *Montana's Gallatin Canyon.* Missoula, MT: Matain Press, 1988.

Gallatin Pioneers: The First 50 Years, 1868–1918. Privately published, 1984.

A Goodly Heritage: A History of the Churchill and Amsterdam Area of Montana. Billings, MT: Churchill-Amsterdam Historical Society, 1989.

Graves, F. Lee. *Montana's Fur Trade Era.* Helena, MT: Unicron, 1994.

Iverson, Ronald. J. *The Princess of the Prairie: A History of Belgrade, Montana.* Self-published, 1965.

Jones, Landon Y. *The Essential Lewis and Clark.* New York: HarperCollins, 2000.

Maher, Sandy, and Ann Butterfield. *This History of Reese Creek.* Self-published, 2003.

Malone, Michael P., Richard Roeder, and William L. Lang. *Montana: A History of Two Centuries.* Rev. ed. Seattle: University of Washington Press, 1991.

Michener, Thomas. "The South End of the Gallatin County." *The Coast* 15 (June 1908).

Niven, Francis. *Manhattan Omnibus.* Bozeman, MT: Self-published, 1984.

Smith, Phyllis. *Bozeman and the Gallatin Valley: A History.* Helena, MT: Falcon, 1996.

Spring, Wilbur. Interviews by Ann Butterfield, Bozeman, MT, October 2003–January 2005.

Vichorek, Daniel N. *Montana's Homestead Era.* Helena: Montana Magazine, 1987.

Whithorn, Doris. *Photo History of Livingston-Bozeman Coal Country.* Livingston, MT: Park County News, n.d.

⊞ GARRA, ANTONIO

See CAHUILLA NATION, CUPEÑOS

⊞ GEARY ACT

See CHINESE EXCLUSION ACT

⊞ GENTLEMAN'S AGREEMENT

The Gentleman's Agreement was an agreement by the Japanese government to curtail the number of immigrants to the United States in 1907. The agreement came about in light of growing anti-Japanese sentiment on the West Coast, particularly California, and concerns about Japan's growing power in East Asia by policy makers in Washington.

Diplomatic relations between the United States and Japan commenced in 1854 when Commodore Matthew Perry opened Japan to trade with the West after more than two hundred years of isolation. U.S–Japan relations throughout the middle of the 19th century were indifferent. During the 1860s, Japan had been undergoing internal change, culminating in the Meiji Restoration, as the United States was embroiled in its civil war. Neither country was in a position to compete with the other. The United States, though a growing industrial power, maintained its traditional distaste for European power politics, and Japan was at the mercy of European extraterritorial privileges.

By the 1890s, however, the international balance of power had changed. Having won a decisive victory over Spain in 1898, the United States acquired a small colonial empire, consisting of islands in the Caribbean and in the Pacific, most notably, the Philippines. In the same year, the United States annexed Hawaii, a strategic location from which to fuel its navy. At the same time, Japan's rise from an isolated country to an emerging power in Asia astounded the West. In 1895, Japan defeated China in the Sino-Japanese War, resulting in the annexation of Taiwan and growing influence in Korea. In 1905, the Japanese navy resoundingly destroyed the Russian navy in the Russo-Japanese War. Such developments prompted the U.S. Navy to add Japan to its list of potential enemies in 1907 and to draft a war plan titled *War Plan Orange*. The view of each other as rivals in the Pacific set the tone in future dealings between both countries, particularly in immigration.

The first Japanese immigrants were student laborers, who arrived in the United States during the Meiji Restoration. Their original intention was to learn English, acquire a skill, and return to Japan to apply the skills they had learned in the United States. When they arrived in the United States, they found work as domestic servants. According to the 1890 U.S. census, there were 2,039 Japanese residents, of whom 1,147 were in California, particularly in San Francisco. Between 1882 and 1890, 3,475 passports were issued by the Japanese government, of which 1,519 were issued to private students. Many of the students who left Japan

came to the United States for a variety of reasons, ranging from the lack of opportunities at home to escaping conscription. By 1900, 24,000 Japanese were residing in the United States, with the number of arrivals increasing yearly.

Between 1900 and 1908, 140,000 Japanese entered the United States, about an average of 15,000 per year. The white population of the West Coast, particularly California, was alarmed at such numbers and perceived this large influx as a prelude to an invasion. Like the Chinese laborers before them, the white population of California resented the Japanese for working for far less money. On March 1, 1905, the California legislature passed a resolution urging the limitation of Japanese immigrants, characterizing them as "immoral, intemperate, quarrelsome men bound to labor for a pittance." In California, groups such as the Japanese and Korean Exclusion League, formed in May of that year, advocated the exclusion of Japanese immigrants to California, based on the model of the Chinese Exclusion Act that was passed in 1882. President Theodore Roosevelt, who had been mediating a resolution to the Russo-Japanese War, was exasperated at the tactless language of the California legislature. However, further outrages against Japanese immigrants continued.

In 1906, in the aftermath of its great earthquake, incidents of anti-Japanese attacks arose in San Francisco. Additionally, the Japanese and Korean Exclusion League called for the boycott of Japanese-owned businesses. To add further insult to injury, the San Francisco Board of Education ordered that Asian children attend segregated elementary schools, citing the lack of space as an excuse. The Japanese government was incensed at such treatment of its citizens, especially considering that it had provided significant aid to the earthquake victims. The decision to segregate Japanese students stung at the core of Japan's efforts to attain great power status and to be treated as an equal by the West, especially the United States. A Japanese exclusion act would have been a mark of dishonor for Japan.

On December 4, 1906, Roosevelt's message to Congress included an excoriation of the San Francisco Board of Education's actions against its Japanese residents and praised Japan's rise as a great power. Although his address mollified the Japanese, it aroused the anger of many in the West Coast. Roosevelt, however, was not blind to the consequences of Japanese immigration to California and other Pacific states. He was in the delicate position of needing to put an end to diplomatic crises with Japan without alienating voters in the West.

Between December 1906 and February 1907, Secretary of State Elihu Root from the United States and Japanese Ambassador Aoki negotiated over Japanese immigration. The settlement that arose from those negotiations became the Gentlemen's Agreement. The Gentleman's Agreement had three components: (1) the San Francisco Board of Education would withdraw its segregation order; (2) with the exception of students and businessmen, the Japanese government would withhold passports to the mainland United States; and (3) Hawaii, Canada, and Mexico would be closed off as channels of immigration through federal legislation. After the implementation of the Gentlemen's Agreement, Japanese immigration to the United States slowed considerably, from 2,208 in June 1907 to 702 in June 1908. In fact, the number of departures from the United States exceeded the number of arrivals.

The Gentlemen's Agreement did not fully satisfy Californians, who wanted tighter restrictions on Japanese immigration and on the rights of Japanese residents. As soon as the San Francisco school board began complying with the repeal of segregation, riots erupted throughout the city, prompting a war scare between Japan and the United States in 1907. However, Roosevelt's diplomacy diffused tensions and began the process of a *rapprochement* with Japan, culminating in the Root-Takahira notes, by which Japan and the United States recognized each other's claims in the Pacific.

—*Dino E. Buenviaje*

See also Alien Land Law of 1913

Suggested Reading

Esthus, Raymond A. *Theodore Roosevelt and Japan.* Seattle: University of Washington Press, 1966.

Hirobe, Izumi. *Japanese Pride, American Prejudice: Modifying the Exclusion Clause of the 1924 Immigration Act.* Stanford, CA: Stanford University Press, 2001.

Ichioka, Yuji. *The Issei: The World of the First Generation Japanese Immigrants, 1885–1924.* New York: Free Press, 1988.

Iriye, Akira. *Pacific Estrangement: Japanese and American Expansion 1897–1911.* Cambridge, MA: Harvard University Press, 1972.

La Feber, Walter. *The Clash: A History of U.S.–Japan Relations.* New York: W. W. Norton, 1997.

Nimmo, William F. *Stars and Stripes Across the Pacific: The United States, Japan, and the Asia/Pacific Region, 1895–1945.* Westport, CT: Praeger, 2001.

GERMAN IMMIGRATION PATTERNS

See German and Italian Internment; Helena, Montana

GERMAN AND ITALIAN INTERNMENT

The Japanese relocation during World War II has become widely publicized in the media and securely embedded in secondary school curriculums across the country. Its notoriety has greatly overshadowed the relocation and selective internment of Italians and Germans, to the point that many people who write and teach about the subject of internment remain unaware of the fate of thousands of other enemy aliens during and after World War II. It is a common misconception that Executive Order 9066, issued by President Franklin Delano Roosevelt on February 19, 1942, applied only to Japanese (and Japanese Americans) living in the western states. Presently, even quality newspapers such as the *San Francisco Examiner* have unequivocally stated that no Germans or Italians were held in concentration camps.

The roots of the internment lay in 1939 and 1940, when the United States government compiled lists of dangerous enemy aliens and citizens in departments such as the FBI, intelligence divisions of the Justice Department, and various military intelligence agencies. The 1940 national census included information that was later used to locate persons based on their ethnicity. Also in 1940, the Alien Registration Act was passed, which required all aliens 14 years of age and older to register with the federal government. In all, 4.9 million aliens were registered, including 695,000 Italians, 315,000

Germans, and only 91,000 Japanese; one of every 26 people in the country in 1940 was foreign born.

On the day Pearl Harbor was attacked, based on the intelligence gathered in 1939 and 1940, Roosevelt authorized Attorney General Biddle to issue a blanket warrant to have large numbers of predesignated "dangerous enemy aliens" arrested. Raids by the FBI netted 737 Japanese Americans and hundreds of German and Italian aliens by the end of the day. War was not declared on Germany until four days later, on December 11, 1941. The next day, Roosevelt issued Presidential Proclamations 2525, 2526, and 2527, branding German, Italian, and Japanese nationals as enemy aliens. In accordance with the enemy alien act of 1798, these nearly identical proclamations authorized internment as well as travel and property ownership restrictions.

In the weeks following America's entrance into World War II, many additional restrictions were placed upon enemy aliens. On December 27, 1941, the California Division of Fish and Game announced that no hunting or fishing licenses would be sold to enemy aliens. This restriction took away the livelihood of many of the Italians on the West Coast, who were commercial fishermen. To further compound this, enemy aliens were prohibited from entering coastal waters. A day later, it was announced that cameras and shortwave radios were contraband items and that all enemy aliens must immediately turn these items in to the authorities, usually the local police departments or sheriffs.

Pursuant to Presidential Proclamation 2525, 2526, 2527, and 2537, issued January 14, 1942, Attorney General Biddle ordered additional regulations requiring application for certificates of identification of all enemy aliens aged 14 and older and outlining restrictions on their movement and property rights. Approximately one million enemy aliens had to reregister, including hundreds of thousands of German and Italian aliens. Registrants submitted their applications to both the Department of Justice's Alien Registration Division and the FBI. Furthermore, it was necessary for enemy aliens to report any changes of address, employment, or name to the FBI. The Department of Justice worked with the military to create numerous, prohibited zones strictly off-limits to any enemy aliens. At this time, they also established large restricted areas in which enemy aliens were subject to stringent curfew and travel restrictions, particularly on

the West Coast. Later, on February 19, 1942, Roosevelt signed Executive Order 9066, authorizing the secretary of war to define military areas in which "the right of any person to enter, remain in or leave shall be subject to whatever restrictions" were deemed necessary or desirable by the appropriate authorities. This order applied to all axis aliens, and if they violated these or other applicable regulations, they became subject to internment for the remainder of the war. Two days after the signing of Executive Order 9066, 119 Japanese, 54 Italians, and 9 Germans were arrested in California. Over the first several weeks of the war, 1,540 Japanese Americans, 1,260 German Americans, and 231 Italian Americans were detained by the FBI.

Racial and political factors were behind the differentiation of German and Italian aliens from their axis counterparts. California Attorney General Earl Warren, eventual governor and Supreme Court chief justice, was an ardent proponent of Japanese relocation. Warren demonstrated his own racist attitudes when he stated that "When we are dealing with the Caucasian race we have methods that will test the loyalty of them," further stating that the Japanese "race" was an altogether different matter. In addition to obvious racist sentiments, there were political factors that led to a perhaps less harsh treatment of Italian and Germans aliens. The influence of politicians from major East Coast cities with large immigrant populations, such as Boston and New York, helped sway the administration against large-scale Italian and German internment on the West Coast.

The sheer number of German and Italian aliens and their descendants made complete relocation and internment unfeasible. Several hundred thousand Germans and Italians and upwards of 11 million of their children and grandchildren—not to mention the president of Bank of America, the mayors of New York and San Francisco, and the parents of Joe DiMaggio—would have had to be interned. According to Stephen Fox, "The withdrawal of perhaps millions of Italians and Germans from civilian production jobs, many in heavy industry—or even the shutdown of commercial fishing in California—was ultimately judged too high a price to pay to thwart potential sabotage," implying that race was only a factor in the ultimate decision to only intern selected German and Italian aliens.

By late March, the idea of evacuating Italian and German residents out of the state was losing support, but the movement to relocate all Japanese residents was gaining momentum. By mid-1942, it seemed clear that General DeWitt's threat to follow up the Japanese evacuation with those of the more than 200,000 Italian and German aliens in the western states would never became a reality. On Columbus Day, October 12, 1942, in a move designed solely to generate political support among Italian Americans, Roosevelt had Attorney General Biddle announce that Italian nationals in the United States would no longer be classified as enemy aliens. In California, General DeWitt reluctantly lifted all military restrictions on Italians. A few months later, in January 1943, the restrictions were also removed on German aliens who had not been selectively interned. Life gradually returned to normal, although certain work, residency, travel, and other restrictions in the coastal zones continued throughout the rest of the war.

Internment camps administered by the military and the Department of Justice were established throughout the country. The largest were located at Crystal City and Seagoville, Texas, and Ft. Lincoln, North Dakota. There were at least 50 temporary detention and long-term internment facilities. Internees were transferred from camp to camp under armed guard and were observed from guard towers. Armed men, often with guard dogs, watched over the internees, who lived surrounded by barbed wire in huts or dormitories that were usually located in desolate settings. What further disrupted their lives and made it even more difficult for their families to find them was the censoring of their mail and their severely limited contact with the world outside. Many internees incessantly appealed their internment orders, although their pleas were generally ignored. The Department of Justice fabricated impossible standards of obtaining evidence to get another hearing; few internees were granted rehearings, and an even smaller number was released. Internees who were released did not know why, and they never learned the original reason for their internment either. FBI records indicate there were three general categories of enemy aliens that were selectively interned. First were members who served their native country in World War I; next were the editors, writers, and radio announcers of native language media; and last were the language instructors at foreign language schools supported by foreign consulates. Those finally released were generally subject to parole restrictions until the end of the war.

An even lesser known aspect of the German and Italian internment was the way many of the internees were pressured to repatriate in exchange for American nationals, specifically those who were interned by Germany. The U.S. government exchanged approximately 2,000 internees for Americans held in Germany. This included many families, consisting of American-born children and American citizen spouses. Sadly, these exchangees were often treated even worse in Germany than they had been in America and upon arrival in war-torn Germany found themselves both unexpected and undesired by their German families. A dark twist to this was a cooperative program initiated with Latin American countries at the U.S. government's direction. German Latin Americans, including German and Austrian Jews who had fled Europe, were captured by their host countries and shipped under U.S. military supervision to internment camps in the United States. They were interned without being told what was happening to them until they found themselves aboard another ship bound for Germany. By the end of the war, more than 4,000 German Latin Americans were brought to American internment camps and subsequently used in exchange for American nationals held abroad.

After the German surrender, Truman issued Presidential Proclamation 2655 in July 1945 authorizing the deportation of all enemy aliens still deemed dangerous to national security. This affected the hundreds of internees who remained imprisoned. Finally, in November 1945, most internees gained their release from the internment camps. Parole limitations for most persons previously considered enemy aliens were terminated. The internment camps were successively closed and the remainder of the internees was eventually secured at Crystal City and Ellis Island. When the Crystal City family camp was closed in 1947, the remaining internees, almost exclusively of German descent, were crammed into Ellis Island. Over the next year, many additional persons were returned to Germany; others finally received parole or were simply released to return to their homes. The last person, a German American, was finally released from Ellis Island three years after the end of the war with Germany. In all, 10,905 Germans and 3,278 Italians were rounded up and placed in camps for the duration of the war, and in many cases beyond.

A direct comparison between the German and Italian relocation and internment and what was suffered by the West Coast Japanese aliens and their American-born offspring can only be made in principle. Ultimately, different standards were used for different groups and individuals. The disparity between how the Japanese Americans in Hawaii were predominantly treated versus the more than 110,000 Japanese and Japanese Americans on the West Coast who were relocated and interned is evidence of this reality. Politics, economics, and the fact that Germans and Italians were two of the largest immigrant groups in the country at the time were the most significant factors in reducing the overall effects of the relocation and internment programs on their communities. Although the Italian and German internees have never sought, or gained, the redress that has been received by their Japanese counterparts, theirs is a vital component to understanding the history of America in World War II and as such should not remain forgotten.

—Scott M. Behen

See also Forced Migration of Italians During World War II

Suggested Reading

DiStasi, Lawrence, ed. *Una Storia Segreta: The Secret History of Italian American Evacuation and Internment during World War II.* Berkeley, CA: Heyday Books, 2001.

Fox, Stephen. *The Unknown Internment: An Oral History of the Relocation of Italian Americans during World War II.* Boston: Twayne, 1990.

Friedman, Max Paul. *Nazis and Good Neighbors: The United States Campaign Against the Germans of Latin America in World War II.* Cambridge, UK: Cambridge University Press, 2003.

Iacovetta, Franca, Roberto Perin, and Angelo Principe, eds. *Enemies Within: Italian and Other Internees in Canada and Abroad.* Toronto, ON: University of Toronto Press, 2000.

⊞ GIANFORTE, GREG (1961–)

When Thomas Jefferson bought a large section of the land west of the Mississippi, immigration and migration was inevitable. However, it was new technology that helped mitigate the challenges of migration. In western expansion, the steam engine and railroad had profound effects on immigration. The railroad compressed time and space immediately, and allowed settlers and tourists alike to travel from coast to coast in days or weeks instead of months. In addition, new markets became available everywhere.

Just as the railroad transformed time and space, the Internet is now having the same effect on immigration to the West. Being able to communicate and work on the Internet completely eliminates geographical constraints. Mountain ranges and remote locations do not carry the same effects they once did on immigration patterns. Global markets can easily be reached with a computer. One such example of this new trend is Greg Gianforte and his company RightNow Technologies. Based in Bozeman, Montana, RightNow Technologies is an Internet-driven company that is able to do business with clients all over the world without ever setting foot outside Bozeman. Not only has Gianforte started a very successful company, but also by locating its headquarters in Bozeman, he has started a migration trend that is similar to trends of past migrations.

Greg Gianforte was born April 17, 1961, in San Diego, California. His family then moved to Daytona Beach, Florida. Gianforte's father worked in the aerospace industry, so the family spent time in multiple locations but finally settled in Valley Forge, Pennsylvania. He describes the area as a normal, big-city suburb and says that his activities were similarly normal: He played football, basketball, and wrestling. He also enjoyed any chance to be outdoors fishing or catching snakes.

It was in junior high school that Gianforte had his most profound experience with the Big Sky and open spaces of Montana. A teacher at his junior high loved Montana, but the limitations of a teacher's salary made the trip very difficult to make. However, if one brought 18 eighth graders along with him, then it was possible. Thus in 1976, Gianforte made his first trip to Montana. He spent his summer in the Absorkee-Beartooth wilderness, hiking and fishing, and fell in love with everything western—towering peaks, alpine lakes, and a sheer abundance of wildlife. It was also at this time that his natural talent for business became apparent.

Gianforte is a self-titled "serial entrepreneur," and his talent for business showed at an early age. His first entrepreneurial effort was a lawn-cutting business. Prior to the beginning of the lawn season, he went around the neighborhood and collected contracts for his services. He quickly discovered two things: First, he had collected far too many contracts was unable to fulfill his obligations; second, mowing lawns in the summer was hot, sweaty work. Gianforte found some other kids in the area that he could hire to mow the lawns and still come out ahead. At a very early age, he demonstrated a firm grasp on basic business practices, such as creating contractual relationships and labor relations. Over time, the lawn business became repetitious, and soon he turned to computers and software for his next endeavor.

In high school, Gianforte got his first computer, a Radio Shack TRS 80. His first programs were simple business programs that performed calculations. For example, one of Gianforte's commercial programs was used in a trauma ward at a Philadelphia hospital. The user of the program input the patient's vitals and other information and the program calculated the amount of electrical shock that would be administered to the patient. In hindsight, Gianforte finds it very amusing; today he would never attempt something of the sort, due to the liability issue that could arise from such a program.

Gianforte received his advanced education at Stevens Institute of Technology, Hoboken, New Jersey, where he earned a bachelor's degree in engineering and an MS in computer science. His experience there was wonderful. The combination of the curriculum and the background of the student body created an atmosphere that was very challenging. Furthermore, Stevens Institute excelled in engaging people to solve problems, which is the primary job of an engineer.

Upon graduation from Stevens Institute, Gianforte went to work for Bell Laboratories. It was there that he met his wife, Susan. The two shared many interests but, most important, a love for the outdoors. In addition to their enthusiasm for outdoor activities, they worked well together. In the early phases of RightNow, Susan handled the accounting. Gianforte described her as his "safety net," because he needed to have someone he felt he could trust. He and Susan have four children: Richard, David, Adam, and Rachael. Family is his proudest achievement.

Although Gianforte enjoyed his work at Bell Laboratories, he had a strong desire to build his own creation. Gianforte's first company to really grow to a large

size was Brightwork Development. Brightwork developed network management applications. These applications are the brooms and mops of a computer network. A network is the wire connecting various computers. Over time, the wires start to operate in a less efficient manner, and a tool is needed to clean up the problem. Brightwork is (metaphorically) a toolbox for the network manager to use to fix any problems that may arise. The software was used on more than 150,000 systems nationwide. Gianforte grew the Brightworks operation from $25 million in sales to $60 million in less than a year before selling the company in 1994.

After leaving Brightwork, Gianforte moved to Bozeman, where he purchased a house along a nice trout stream so that he could fish whenever he had the desire. Gianforte soon grew restless and started to work in investment banking but knew that he was destined to start another company of his own. It was obvious that the company would involve some type of a software application. Back in 1996 and 1997, the only software opportunities existed in the Internet. Gianforte's work in network management gave him the feeling of only putting on the finished touches. "It was like pin striping a car and I wanted to build the engine or transmission." Gianforte sought a business function that could really be affected by Internet software. He decided that the Internet had the most promise and that software for customer service was a virtually nonexistent product.

In a spare room of his house, RightNow Technologies was founded in 1997. Since that time, the company has moved from Gianforte's house to a real estate office, then to an old elementary school, and finally to a new office complex located in close proximity to Montana State University at Bozeman. RightNow Technologies provides customer relationship management software. "The RightNow mission is to be the leading global provider of customer relationship management solutions to mid-market and departments of large businesses through uncompromised focus on our customers' success." Worldwide, 1,200 organizations use RightNow solutions. In fact, Greg has been so successful in this endeavor that he was awarded the 2003 Pacific Northwest Entrepreneur of the Year by Ernst and Young in the software category. "Ernst and Young use a panel of independent judges who evaluate the excellence and extraordinary success in areas of innovation, financial performance, and personal commitment to business and community."

Gianforte credits the success of RightNow to his business philosophy of "Bootstrap it." The typical western image of this metaphor—pinching pennies—is not actually what bootstrapping is; rather, it is an idea that it is possible to start a business with very few resources. Lack of resources has traditionally been seen as a disadvantage, but Gianforte sees it rather as a huge advantage. In a February 2002 article in *Inc. Magazine,* he explained that "in war you're either making bullets or shooting bullets. . . . Bootstrapping clears away the clutter and makes you focus single-mindedly on the customer, which is what any smart entrepreneur needs to do anyway." Furthermore, bootstrapping is a protective measure because "if you wind up with no sales, no customers, and no business, well at least all you've lost is time." This philosophy is almost reminiscent of early miners, who set off with only a pan and some supplies. If a prospector did not find anything, all he had spent was the money for that pan, and his time.

Due to the nature of RightNow's customer relationship management solutions, the company could be headquartered anywhere in the world, as long as there were electricity and an Internet connection. With the globe at his fingertips, why did Gianforte choose a small town in Montana?

The most appreciated feature of Montana and the West is its open space. Gianforte believes that there is a certain dividend that is paid to the employees of his company. By locating themselves in a small western mountain town, the employees enjoy the benefits that come with that location. The average commuting time is 15 minutes, and a traffic jam is five cars at a stop sign. There is a plethora of outdoor activities for every season. World-class skiing is only 45 miles away, and they can raft, kayak, or fish in the summer on the same river they drive by on the way to the ski lifts. The close proximity to nature means employees enjoy many after-work opportunities. The effects of open space and close proximity to outdoor recreation have an obvious effect on employees. These conditions contribute to a much more balanced lifestyle, which increases productivity in the mind of Gianforte.

Furthermore, the effects of small town living and the rugged outdoors have a very positive outcome for the work ethic. It has been Gianforte's feeling that in the West, "what you see is what you get." Small towns, through their lack of anonymity, create a certain type of accountability. In a big city, you can perform very poorly at your job and go home and remain completely anonymous. However, in a small community, you are very likely to know your coworker through other activities within that community, possibly making for uncomfortable situations. These factors foster a very deep work ethic.

In addition to the collective effects of open spaces, Gianforte felt that it was important to locate his company in close proximity to a university, for several reasons. Bozeman, being the home to Montana State University, became an ideal choice. The university could supply his company with a large pool of interns. Many of those interns fall in love with the town of Bozeman and jump at the chance to make it their home. In addition to the wonderful employment resource the university provides, it also ensures that there is quite a bit of culture in the town. This can make the transition from city to country much easier.

By locating RightNow Technologies in Montana, Gianforte has created a new pattern of migration. Yet this pattern is very similar to immigration to the area in the late 1800s. Emily Barker, in an article in *Inc. Magazine* in February 2002, writes that

> Mountain ringed Bozeman, population 27,000, home of Montana State University, was half college town, half cow town, a place that offered gorgeous scenery, an active outdoor lifestyle and not much in the way of employment. Gianforte decided that his personal mission was to create 2,000 high paying high tech jobs in town.

In fact, RightNow's main recruiting Web address is http://www.iloveithere.com. The site reads, "Great careers right here right now." This slogan is imposed over two people skiing down a slope with huge grins on their faces. Below the image a paragraph reads,

> Bozeman, Montana is a long way from Silicon Valley, and hundreds of bright people who work at RightNow Technologies think that's a very good thing. Maybe

you can have it all. Big Sky vistas, Rocky Mountain recreation, a historic main street, a vibrant family town, short commutes, and a career in a pioneering customer service software firm. Take a fly fishing break at our trout ponds on campus, or use the time to call for theater tickets at night. On winter weekends, head for the ski slopes; there's celebrated vertical, deep powder snow. I love it here, you will too.

This Internet advertisement is very similar to posters printed by railroad companies in the 1800s urging people to go west so that they too could "maybe have it all."

Personally, deciding to live in the west was for Gianforte a simple decision. "God seems to be a lot closer when you're in the outdoors and the outdoors is just so much more accessible in Montana." In addition, there are many very valuable lessons that can be learned from the outdoors. Hiking up 2,000 vertical feet to fish a high alpine lake gives the participant many lessons about life. Not only does it teach people to be self-reliant, but it also demonstrates that one is capable of anything one puts one's mind to.

A recurring theme in Gianforte's personal and business life is a deeper sense of accountability. "God gives every individual certain skills and it's not our responsibility or our right to take responsibility for the accomplishments. All we can do is take our skills and apply them with diligence and that's all we are asked to do." Not only does Gianforte take accountability in his personal life, he also applies it to business relationships. "RightNow pledges to abide [by] the following promise when engaging with its customers. RightNow will prove the value of our solutions, will fairly and accurately represent the capabilities of our software and will continually invest in your success." In a culture of corporate scandal, as with Enron and other companies, Greg Gianforte is a breath of fresh air. Not only is he concerned with his responsibilities and being accountable for his actions, he carries that to his company. RightNow encourages its employees to volunteer in the community, and it has a matching donation program. Greg Gianforte is a pioneer and leader, not only in the Internet software business but also in his personal life. He is an excellent example of a modern, western person.

—*Elwood Bakken*

Suggested Reading

Barker, Emily. "Start With Nothing." *Inc. Magazine* (February 2002).
Gianforte, Greg. Interview by Elwood Bakken, November 24, 2004.
RightNow Technologies [Home page]. Available from http://www.rightnow.com

⊞ GILA TRAIL

See Euro-American Migration on the Overland Trails

⊞ GILEAD, KANSAS

One of seven Jewish farming communities founded in the 1880s in Kansas, Gilead is in the Gyp Hills on the banks of the Salt Fork River, three miles south of Evansville. A dozen Romanian Jewish families settled the town in March 1886. A few years later, Gilead was no longer in operation. Although the residents of Gilead did receive initial support, Gilead was not, unlike other Jewish settlements in Kansas, a utopian society in which the land and equipment were owned by sponsoring organizations; the residents owned the land. Nearly every resident of Gilead belonged to the orthodox Jewish faith. By 1895 there were no Jewish residents still in the area.

Hebron was a neighboring Jewish settlement that had been settled prior to the founding of Gilead. The town of Hebron grew into a community of 300, among which were Russian, Romanian, Polish, and Hungarian Jews. In 1884, the Montefiore Agricultural Aid Society sent six Russians to inspect the farmland near Medicine Lodge, Kansas. After inspecting the region entirely on foot and finding land that was considered suitable, about 30 families made up the colony of Hebron, Kansas. The colony did so well when it was first founded that the society decided to start a second farming community. Thus Gilead was established.

During the 1880s, there was a mass migration to the United States of Jews from eastern Europe and Russia, in part to flee from religious persecution. Aid societies were established to help the new immigrants adjust to life in the United States. Am Olam, the Hebrew Emmigrant Aid Society, and the Montefiore Agricultural

Aid Society were a few of the groups that aided the new immigrants. Most of the Jewish immigrants had not been farmers in their homelands; rather, they tended to have lived in villages and towns and worked as merchants. These Jewish migrants tended to include a high proportion of intellectuals. There were only a few Jews who had been farmers in their native countries.

The expectation in the 1880s was that the best way these Jewish immigrants could fit within the United States was to take up agriculture as a profession. Most had no idea what was involved in farming. As late as the early 20th century, many viewed farming as the most important industry in the United States. The recent arrivals hoped not to replicate their experiences in being treated harshly and persecuted; rather, they wanted to fit in. By taking up farming, the Jewish migrants believed they would be assimilated and face little persecution.

Despite their best efforts, the town was not a success. There were several reasons for the failure of Gilead. Prior to the establishment of the town, Kansas had had a relatively rainy season, making the land more fertile. The following year, a 10-year drought began. A second reason for the demise of Gilead was that the soil was low in nitrogen and high in evaporation. The poor soil added to drought conditions that made for bad farming. Wheat and sorghum could be grown in times of good rainfall, but farmers found it difficult to continue in drought years, when the hard soil made plowing a challenge.

Two other reasons for the failure of Gilead were the location of the town and falling prices. The town was located on former ranch land. It was far from any market or railroad, and thus selling crops profitably was a problem. Deep wells had to be dug, and getting enough water was often very difficult; the cost of digging deep wells was also high. There was little wood in the region, so people had to live in sod houses. Previous settlers who settled in Kansas following the Civil War took the last of the good farming lands, leaving lands that were better suited for raising cattle than raising crops. Perhaps the greatest impediment to success was the inexperience of the Jewish settlers at farming. For many of the new farmers, life in Gilead was their first taste of the agriculture.

—*Timothy A. Strand*

Suggested Reading

Douglas, Donald M. "Forgotton Zions: Jewish Agricultural Colonies in Kansas in the 1880s." *Kansas History: A Journal of the Central Plains* 16 (Summer 1993).

Goodwin, Edward A. *Our Jewish Farmers and the Story of the Jewish Agricultural Society.* New York: Fischer, 1943.

Harris, L. David. "Sod Jerusalems: Jewish Agricultural Communities in Frontier Kansas." Unpublished manuscript, Library and Archives Division, Kansas State Historical Society, 1984.

Herscher, Uri D. *Jewish Agricultural Utopias in America 1880–1910.* Detroit, MI: Wayne State University Press, 1981.

Miner, H. Craig. *Kansas: The History of the Sunflower State, 1854–2000.* Lawrence: University of Kansas Press, 2002.

Sachar, Howard Morley. *The Course of Modern Jewish History.* New York: Dell, 1977.

GOLD

See BLACK HILLS GOLD RUSH OF 1874; CHILEANS AND THE CALIFORNIA GOLD RUSH; GALLATIN VALLEY, MONTANA; GOLDFIELD, NEVADA; GRASS VALLEY, CALIFORNIA; HELENA, MONTANA; KALISPELL, MONTANA; SUTTER, JOHANN AUGUST; TONOPAH, NEVADA; VIRGINIA CITY, MONTANA

GOLDFIELD, NEVADA

Goldfield, Nevada, is located in Esmeralda County, twenty-four miles due south of Tonopah. Goldfield was the second most important of the new wave of mining fields that included Tonopah and Bullfrog-Rhyolite. The town was founded in 1902, after gold was discovered. As mining developed in 1903, the district soon became one of the top gold producers.

A typical boomtown, Goldfield had a population of eighteen thousand in 1907, but this dropped to 5,435 in 1910 when the gold rush atmosphere evaporated. No definitive figures on the size and characteristics of Goldfield's population exist because the mining booms occurred between census dates. Indirect evidence shows that like other boomtowns, Goldfield had a large number of young, single men. Most of Goldfield's residents were foreign born, especially Welsh and Irish miners. There was also a small community of African

Americans and some Indians. Asians were driven from the city in 1904, and none was permitted to return during the boom year. A newspaper report from 1907 declared that Goldfield had every manner of humanity: forty-eight exconvicts; twelve college graduates; card sharks; and men from the Yukon, Australia, and Argentina.

The Goldfield mines had a series of labor disputes from 1906 to 1908, which arose as a result of the Western Federation of Miners (WFM) and the Industrial Workers of the World (IWW) trying to supplant the traditional craft union in Goldfield with their "new unionism." The strikes resulted in shutdowns in the mines and ended with the call-in of federal troops in 1904. The Goldfield mine operators also had labor disputes arising from the practice of "high grading"; that is, the theft of rich ore, usually by a miner working for the company that owned the mine.

The town was replete with saloons, bordellos, opium dens, and "hop joints." One of the saloons, George Lewis "Tex" Rickard's Northern, had the longest bar in the history of mining towns, boasting eighty tenders to serve customers. Rickard was one of the most noted speculators and, along with con artist George Graham Rice, promoted Goldfield through a championship boxing match. They staged a prize fight on Labor Day 1906, when Joe Gans and Battling Nelson fought for the Lightweight Championship of the World. In the forty-second round, Nelson was disqualified, and Joe Gans was declared the winner of the $30,000 purse. The men also promoted the town through the use of excursion trains from Los Angeles, Salt Lake City, and Denver. These trains brought would-be speculators to Goldfield, and their success led to the establishment of the Goldfield stock exchange on October 2, 1905.

Although Goldfield had a completely organized fire department, the town suffered many disasters in its short lifetime. Goldfield was the victim of a major fire on July 8, 1905, when two blocks of buildings were burned to the ground. A massive flash flood in September 1913 swept hundreds of buildings and their contents off into a large flat outside of town. In 1923, another fire ravaged fifty-three square blocks of Goldfield, leaving only burned foundations.

The area initially relied on freight-wagon trade, but transportation improvement was soon realized when a narrow gauge railroad reached Tonopah in July 1904. By September 1905, it had been increased to standard gauge and rechristened the Tonopah & Goldfield Railroad. The first railroad into the boom area of southern Nevada, the Tonopah and Goldfield, was the last to leave in 1946. Automobiles were a common means of travel for the prospectors.

Since 1907, Goldfield has been the county seat for Esmeralda County. The government in Goldfield was simple, with a sheriff, district attorney, and justice of the peace in town. Western lawman Wyatt Earp once worked as pit boss in the Northern. His brother, Virgil Earp, arrived in the spring of 1904. Virgil Earp was Goldfield's deputy sheriff, where he lived until he died of pneumonia in September 1905. Wyatt Earp left Goldfield shortly after his brother's death. Other important residents included George Wingfield, Death Valley Scotty, Jack Dempsey, and Governor and Senator Tasher Oddie. After the boom came to a close, the hotel shut its doors in 1936, and the mines finally closed in 1942.

Although it was the largest city in Nevada from 1903 to 1910, today Goldfield is a shadow of its former self, with a population of about nine hundred people. Eighty-two percent of Goldfield's residents are white and non-Hispanic. The community advertises its mild climate, excellent school system, and favorable, probusiness tax structure.

—*Caroline Owen*

See also Nevada Mining Discoveries of the 20th Century; Rawhide, Nevada; Rhyolite, Nevada; Tonopah, Nevada

Suggested Reading

Elliott, Russell R. *Nevada's Twentieth-Century Mining Boom: Tonopah, Goldfield, Ely.* Reno: University of Nevada Press, 1966.

Esmeralda County, NV, Web Site. Available from http://www.accessesmeralda.com

Ransome, F. L. *Mines of Goldfield, Bullfrog and Other Southern Nevada Districts.* Las Vegas: Nevada Publications, 1907.

Zanjani, Sally S. "To Die in Goldfield: Mortality in the Last Boomtown on the Mining Frontier." *Western Historical Quarterly* 21 (February 1990).

GOLDMAN, EMMA

See FORCED MIGRATION OF ANARCHISTS

GRASS VALLEY, CALIFORNIA

In Grass Valley, the richest and most famous gold-mining district in California, the shift from placer mining to hard-rock quartz mining took place. One of the original boomtowns of the 1849–1850 California Gold Rush, Grass Valley is situated in the Sierra Nevada foothills in California's mother lode, approximately 52 miles northeast of Sacramento. It is between Nevada City and Rough and Ready, 33 miles north of Coloma, at an elevation of 2,100 feet. By the mid-19th century, Grass Valley was the eighth largest town in California, and unlike many mining towns, it never really experienced a decline and fall. Its mining activity continued for more than 100 years.

Previously named Boston Ravine, Hangtown, Centreville, and Gold Flat, the "grassy valley" by the banks of Wolf Creek was settled in 1849 by two small bands of emigrants from Boston. A party of French emigrants passed by in 1846 but did not stay. A thriving camp soon formed, and placer gold was panned along the sides of the creeks. The rapid growth of the camp created a need for lumber, and several saw mills were also erected. After Marshall's 1850 American River gold strike, George McKnight discovered gold locked in quartz deposits at Gold Hill, introduced the area to hard-rock mining, and turned Grass Valley into an overnight boomtown. By March 1851, more than 150 wooden structures had been built, including hotels, saloons, and many stores.

Most of Grass Valley's gold was locked in quartz deposits, where the potential payoff was enormous, but the business of reaching and processing this ore was risky, complicated, and costly. Hard-rock mining demanded large-scale corporate investment and heavy complicated machinery to crush the quartz so the gold could be extracted. However, hard-rock quartz mining was more stable, and it better supported a balanced, long-term economic development than did placer mining. The first machinery was installed in Boston Ravine, and as early as the summer of 1851, large mining companies were being established. The Gold Hill Company was the first, and other companies followed, including Empire, North Star, Pennsylvania, Idaho-Maryland, and Brunswick. Mining shafts were sunk deeper, and improved equipment, including rock breakers and automatic ore feeders, replaced manual labor. Hard-rock mining proved profitable; more than $25,000,000 worth of gold was taken from Deer, Bear, and Wolf Creeks in less than eight years.

The changes brought about by corporate mining also affected Grass Valley's labor force. Initially, Mexican miners had built *arrastres* (millstones that ground rock by single mule power) and stamp mills. Later, however, hard-rock quartz mining required a stable and experienced labor force, and this was found in immigrant miners from Cornwall, England. One seventh of the population of Grass Valley in 1870 was Cornish, with most miners being Cornish or Irish. The Cornish, or "Cousin Jacks," as they were called, understood the machinery and techniques needed for quartz load mining. The 1860 census of Grass Valley reported 3,940 residents, including 530 "English" and 470 miners. Ten years later, the population was nearly 7,000, including 1,245 born in England. Three fourths of these people had come directly from the Old Country, but one fourth had lived in Wisconsin or the East before emigrating to Grass Valley. The 1860 census also enumerated 200 women and children, whose presence helped Grass Valley take on a more stable atmosphere. Adding to Grass Valley's local color, Cornish miners had many superstitions. For instance, they thought it was bad luck for a woman to go underground or to start a new operation on Friday. Whistling was also frowned upon.

Miners unions formed at Grass Valley, and strikes broke out in 1869 and 1872. In 1869, the first strike centered on the mine employers' attempt to introduce dynamite in place of black powder and the related economy of "single-handed" drilling (one man working alone) instead of "double handed" (two men working as a team, one to hold and turn the drill and one to strike it). Because dynamite did not require the large holes that black powder did, one man could do the work of two. Grass Valley had become a Cornish town, and the Cornish were against single-handed drilling because it might reduce the underground labor force. The mine operators tried to reopen the mines with non-Cornish scabs, and the strikebreakers were beaten. Victory lay with the employers, however, because the union, not strong enough, resorted to violence, which upset the public.

One of Grass Valley's most famous residents was Lola Montez, the fiery and exotic dancer, renowned for her erotic "Spider Dance." Montez made her home in Grass Valley for several years, and legend has it that in 1853, miners paid $100 for admission to her show. Lola Montez made an impression on another resident dancer, Lotta Crabtree, who became a famous actress and the first female millionaire in the country.

Grass Valley became a charter city in 1893. By 1880, the seven camps around Grass Valley and Nevada City had disappeared, leaving only the two and the farm-supplying town of Rough and Ready. Today, Grass Valley is the commercial center of western Nevada County. The area is called "Little Silicon Valley," and many residents are involved in the high-tech industry, including electrical, mechanical, and software engineering; development of broadcasting equipment; circuit design laboratories; and computer and medical product design firms. Downtown Grass Valley is considered by many to be one of the best preserved historic towns in the United States. Grass Valley's population in 2000 was 10,992, approximately 88 percent of which was white and non-Hispanic. *Time* magazine has tooted Grass Valley's horn, calling it "one of the top ten best small towns to live in."

—*Caroline Owen*

Suggested Reading

Dilsaver, Larry M. "After the Gold Rush." *Geographical Review* 75 (January 1985).

Mann, Ralph. *After the Gold Rush: Society in Grass Valley and Nevada City, California, 1849–1870.* Stanford, CA: Stanford University Press, 1982.

Rowe, John. *The Hard-Rock Men: Cornish Immigrants and the North American Mining Frontier.* Liverpool, England: Liverpool University Press, 1974.

⊞ GREAT EXODUS, THE

See TOPEKA, KANSAS; WICHITA, KANSAS

⊞ GREAT FALLS, MONTANA

Great Falls is known as the "Electric City" because of its numerous dams and power plants. Montana's third largest city is located on the Missouri River among the five falls that were both a magnificent spectacle and formidable barrier to early river travel.

This area held great significance for the Lewis and Clark expedition. The explorers were forced to spend nearly a month portaging around the falls in June 1805. Much of the Missouri River in this area remains as it was when Lewis and Clark first viewed it more than 190 years ago.

Until the 1880s, a majority of settlers bypassed the Great Falls area, heading to Helena or southwestern Montana from Fort Benton. Fort Benton was the stopping place for steamships heading up the Missouri River. It was not until an entrepreneur named Paris Gibson visited the area of the "Great Falls" that the realization existed that a town in that location might have possibilities.

Gibson came into the Great Falls area for the first time in 1880. He took one look at the Missouri and appreciated the potential power the river might supply. With financial help from a friend, James J. Hill (who later built the Great Northern Railroad), Gibson set about the task of building a city where the falls existed. With enthusiasm and never-ending optimism, Gibson planned every detail of his city. Six years after its beginning, Great Falls grew into a sizable transportation, commercial, and manufacturing center.

By 1887, there were rail connections, hotels, stores, lumberyards, flour mills, churches, newspapers, and a school. In 1888, Gibson broke ground for the silver smelter, which was located on the south bank of the Missouri River.

Great Falls continued its rapid growth. The first dam was built at Black Eagle Falls; a new iron works was started, and a copper smelter was built. The city quickly became a thriving industrial center, boasting a rich ethnic mix of workers. The community continued to thrive and prosper, and the population grew with every passing year. The city's prosperity tied in with national trends in railroading, manufacturing, agriculture, and the price of silver. After two decades of frantic building and expansion, the bottom fell out of the economy, and the nation was in for several years of high unemployment, declining prices, and a shrinking market for the products of farms and factories. During the 1890s, Great Falls found itself ideally situated to take advantage of opportunities offered by new technological developments.

Today, Great Falls is Montana's second largest city and the gateway to the lower Missouri River. Great Falls is also home to Malmstrom Air Force Base and the Lewis and Clark National Historic Trail Interpretive Center.

—Brandon Davis

Suggested Reading

Furdell, William J. "The Great Falls Home Front during World War II." In *Montana Legacy*, edited by Harry Fritz, Mary Murphy, and Robert Swartout, Jr. Helena: Montana Historical Society Press, 2002.

⊞ GREAT NORTHERN RAILROAD

See KALISPELL, MONTANA

⊞ GROS VENTRE

The name Gros Ventre historically referred to two different Indian groups. The first was a band of the Arapaho called the Atsina, whose language came from the Algonquian family. The second was the Hidatsa, who spoke a Siouan language. There are a couple of theories as to the origin of the name Gros Ventre, which is French for "big belly." French fur traders who encountered them in Canada may have used the name for both groups due to confusion about the similarity of signs in the Indian sign language, one of which described the Atsina by communicating hunger and the other of which described the chest-tattooed Hidatsa. Another possibility is that other tribes referred to the Gros Ventre as "The Water Fall People." Passing the hand over the stomach was the sign for waterfall, which could have been interpreted as "big belly."

The Atsina originated in the northeastern United States; the Hidatsa were among the tribes that came from the southeast. Both groups arrived on the Great Plains in the 1600s and 1700s as European settlement pushed west. Guns obtained through trade with English and French settlers and horses obtained from the Spanish helped to create the nomadic and warlike way of life of the Plains Indians. The Atsina, who call themselves the A'ani, which means "White Clay People," were once joined with the Arapaho and living on the plains of Canada. Around 1700, they separated from the Arapaho and by midcentury were located between the north and south branches of the Saskatchewan River. An outbreak of smallpox in 1780 dramatically reduced their population, and the tribe drifted south due to pressure from Crees and Assiniboines, who possessed firearms. Half of the A'ani rejoined the Arapaho in 1826 to move further south and trade with the Mexicans. Eventually they returned to Montana and their fellow tribe members. In 1855, the A'ani and the Blackfoot signed a treaty with the federal government to ensure hunting grounds and provisions. After splitting from the Blackfoot, the A'ani began living at Fort Belknap in Montana in 1888. They have shared the reservation with the Assiniboine ever since. The A'ani are sometimes referred to as the Gros Ventre of the Prairie. The Hidatsa, who live in North Dakota's Missouri River area, are occasionally known as the Gros Ventre of the Missouri. In 1930, the U.S. census began to distinguish between the two groups. Today the name Gros Ventre is usually only applied to the A'ani.

Catholic missionaries arrived in 1862 and were very successful in converting the A'ani on the reservation. St. Paul's Mission was built in 1887, and Catholicism at Fort Belknap proceeded to erode traditional religious practice. In 1895, the A'ani, or Gros Ventre of Fort Belknap, numbered only 596, the lowest total in their history. Although they had acquired a certain degree of immunity from smallpox, declining buffalo herds, on which all Plains Indian tribes depended, made survival much more difficult. The Gros Ventre were also forced to give up the sacred Little Rockies on the southern part of the Fort Belknap Reservation to gold miners. Members of the Gros Ventre have continued to make pilgrimages to the Little Rockies up to the present.

In 1908, the Fort Belknap Reservation was involved in *Winters v. United States,* a U.S. Supreme Court decision that altered water rights in the American West. Previously, the common law of water in the East, or riparian doctrine, protected all users with property located along the side of a river or stream. This was practical east of the Mississippi and in England, where water was abundant. In 1855, the

California Supreme Court ruled in *Irwin v. Phillips* that the water law of the East did not apply in the arid West, where prior appropriation, or "first come, first served," would be the rule. If a user diverted a stream for a mining operation and later another user found there was not enough water as a result, the first user was protected. Otherwise there would not be enough water to meet most farming or mining needs. The *Winters* doctrine was a combination of the law of the East and West. One of the court's rulings was that the Fort Belknap tribes had "reserved rights" to water in the Milk River, which formed one of the reservation's boundaries when it was created in 1888. The court agreed with the U.S. government's position that if upstream users were allowed to use as much water as they wished, as the right of prior appropriation would dictate, then the reservation would be unlivable for the Gros Ventre and Assiniboine who called it home. As the reservation had been created specifically for the purpose of providing a home to the tribes, the government said there were reserved rights to the water that adjoined reservation land. Therefore, upstream settlers were not entitled to unlimited use of water. The *Winters* decision helped the federal government support its interests in reclamation from 1905 until 1930 and subsequently helped tribes with water rights and sovereignty claims.

In later years, the tribes accepted the Indian Reorganization Act of 1934, which made the Fort Belknap Indian Community Council the recognized governing body on the reservation. The tribal members also adopted a constitution in 1935 and a corporate charter in 1937. The constitution was revised in 1974 and replaced in 1994. The current constitution of the Fort Belknap Indian Community vests leadership in a governing council, which is composed of six Gros Ventre and six Assiniboine members who are popularly elected every two years by the community. Officers include a president, a vice president, and a secretary treasurer, who are selected by the council. One member of each tribe must be represented on the presidential–vice presidential ticket. The constitution defines members of the community as those having a least one-fourth Indian blood who were born of Indians residing on the reservation. However, any person with as little as one-eighth Indian blood may be adopted if he or she is a descendant of a member of the Fort Belknap Tribes or community and has resided on the reservation for at least three years. Membership cannot be lost unless the member makes a written request or establishes residence in a foreign country. All members of the community 21 years old and older are eligible to vote in the elections, which are held every two years.

The Little Rockies, or "Island Mountains," as the Gros Ventre call them, became the site of heap leach gold mining after the federal government approved the operations in 1979 of the Zortman Mining Company, a subsidiary of Pegasus Gold, Inc. Despite cyanide spills and illegal dumping of toxic waste, the government continued to grant expansion of the operation. The company had used cyanide to leach gold from the ore. Later studies revealed that acid mine drainage, water pollution, and declining water quality were even worse than anticipated. The tribes of Fort Belknap sued Pegasus in 1993 for violations of the Federal Clean Water Act. The two parties settled the suit after Pegasus agreed to clean up the mines. Five years later, Pegasus went bankrupt, and the mines subsequently became inactive. In April 1999, the Western Environmental Law Center filed a lawsuit against the U.S. government, seeking full reclamation of the mine sites. The suit claimed that the federal and state governments were responsible for the cleanup due to the Pegasus bankruptcy. The suit further alleged that the federal government violated its trust obligations with the Fort Belknap Indian Community because the tribes were told when they ceded the land in 1895 that their water supplies would not be affected. The Grinnell Agreement was a document that took the Island Mountains out of the reservation for this purpose. The tribes filed a new complaint in federal district court in January 2004 against the U.S. Bureau of Land Management and the Montana Department of Environmental Quality for pollution in the 1990s and against the mine's new owner for pollution since. They claimed that not enough was being done to clean up the two mines. In July 2004, a federal judge refused to issue a ruling in the suit because reclamation was already taking place.

The community of Fort Belknap has undertaken several measures intended to improve health care and education. The council created the Fort Belknap Tribal

Health Department in 1976, which addresses needs such as chemical dependency, family planning, and diabetes. However, the Center for Disease Control reported five cases of tuberculosis at Fort Belknap between May 2000 and January 2001, after only one reported case since 1992. The rate of tuberculosis among American Indians is about twice the national average, and an investigation by the Tribal Health Department and the Indian Health Service, with the assistance of the Montana State Department of Public Health and Human Services and the Centers for Disease Control and Prevention, revealed that the initial victim drank large amounts of alcohol with others in confined spaces. The investigation's report stressed the importance of "rapid expansion of local capacity for TB control . . . to eliminate TB in the United States."

Public schools for children on the reservation are run at Harlem, Lodge Pole, and Dodson. There is also a public junior high and senior high school and elementary mission school at Hays and public high schools at Harlem and Dodson. Head Start has been on the reservation since 1965. In an effort to preserve traditional languages, the tribes started a child and family bilingual program in 2000 to teach the Gros Ventre and Assiniboine languages. Two-year degrees in arts and sciences are offered at the Fort Belknap Community College near Harlem, Montana. The college also has a Small Business Development Center that assists small business owners or those wishing to start a small business. In 2002, the college expanded by adding a Gros Ventre and Assiniboine cultural learning center. Two science laboratories for teaching microbiology and conducting microbial research were also a part of the expansion. Two years later, Fort Belknap College received a $1,287,000 grant from the U.S. Department of Education's Tribally Controlled Colleges and Universities Program to construct a technological center. The center will feature vocational and technical courses and include computer laboratories, classrooms, a management information systems center, and faculty and staff offices.

In recent years, the council has attempted to increase American Indian self-determination and self-sufficiency. In 2001, the Fort Belknap leadership entered into a compact with the State of Montana concerning water rights. According to the agreement, the reservation would receive federal and state funds for irrigation and other projects. New reservoirs and other "mitigation measures" protected nontribe members further downstream from a loss of water. The following year, the Fort Belknap tribes took control of fire management, road maintenance, probate, enrollment, and sewer and water systems, programs that the Bureau of Indian Affairs and the Indian Health Service had handled for years. This continued a trend that began when Congress passed the Indian Self-Determination and Education Assistance Act of 1975. The tribes had already taken over water resources, tribal courts, credit, law enforcement, transportation, criminal investigation, planning, and various health programs. The tribal council opened the Fort Belknap Little Rockies Meat Packing plant in August 2003. The plant has brought jobs cutting, processing, wrapping, selling, and delivering buffalo, beef, hogs, and lamb products to the reservation. It has five acres and can process up to 125 head of livestock daily. Seventy to 80 percent unemployment on the reservation helped prompt the $50,000 purchase of the former Big Sky Beef building 53 miles northeast of Fort Belknap. Malmstrom Air Force Base, the Montana Air National Guard, USDA commodities, and state and federal prisons are all potential markets for the plant. The tribal government also hopes to open a $65 million plant that will make ethanol, feed cattle with the byproducts, and then process manure to power the plant. The plant would be powered by 60,000 head of cattle and 10 million bushels of grain and would annually produce 20 million gallons of ethanol, an alcohol derived from grain and added to gasoline to reduce pollution. The proposal could create 60 jobs at the plant and 240 more by stimulating the local economy. The Federal Department of Agriculture Rural Development awarded $50,000 toward a feasibility study estimated to cost $150,000.

The issue of taxation on Indian reservations frequently brings up questions of state versus tribal sovereignty. The State of Montana and the Fort Belknap Indian Community Council reached an agreement on tobacco taxation in September 2003 to avoid controversy and litigation as much as possible. The state and tribes agreed to charge the same amount on all cigarettes and tobacco products sold on the reservation.

Tobacco will be taxed only once. Montana will pre-collect all taxes from tobacco wholesalers for tobacco products sold on the Fort Belknap Reservation and then share the revenue with the tribes. The tribes' share will nearly triple, from about $50,000 in 2003–2004 to $150,000 in 2004–2005. The agreement was for one year and automatically renews. Either side may cancel the agreement provided they give the other party 30 days' notice.

One of the most important industries on the Fort Belknap Reservation is cattle ranching. As a result of increased fees that began in July 2004, ranchers pay grazing fees that are the highest on any reservation in Montana and higher than the average for state, federal, and privately owned land there. The federal Bureau of Indian Affairs manages and sets grazing fees for reservation trust land, called allotments, that are owned by individual tribe members, and the tribes collectively own the rest of the reservation land and set those grazing prices. The system is a source of controversy, as Indian ranchers claim that non-Indians are driving them out of business. Reservation ranchers stress the importance of preserving the ranching industry and tradition, but the BIA is concerned with getting the best deal for the individual allotment owners.

Fort Belknap Indian Community Council president Ben Speakthunder resigned in May 2004 after seven years in office when the council voted down a plan with the Montana Air National Guard to build a practice bombing range near the reservation. Speakthunder had hoped the target range would bring jobs to the reservation, where unemployment is a chronic problem. Vice-President Darrell Martin succeeded Speakthunder. Current council members are Martin, who is a member of the Gros Ventre; Vice-President Julia Donney, an Assiniboine; Secretary-Treasurer Julie King Kulbeck; and council members Raymond Chandler, Ken Lewis, Harold "Jiggs" Main, Doreen Bell, Selena Ditmar, Tracy "Ching" King, Craig Chandler, and Velva Doore.

On September 21, 2004, the National Museum of the American Indian reopened in its new home on the mall in Washington, DC. Gros Ventre historian George Horse Capture has worked at the Plains Indian Museum of the Buffalo Bill Historical Center in Cody, Montana, and the National Museum of the American Indian in New York. The opening is in large part due to Horse Capture, who has spent his life chronicling Indian history. He is the senior counselor to the director of the museum and has worked with tribes across America to present their origins, history, and current lifestyles as accurately as possible. Over the next few years, approximately 850,000 pieces will be transported from the Bronx to the museum's new building near the capitol.

—*Daniel S. Stackhouse, Jr.*

See also ARAPAHO, ASSINIBOINE

Suggested Reading

Constitution of the Fort Belknap Indian Community of the Fort Belknap Reservation, Montana. Available from http://www.tribalresourcecenter.org/ccfolder/fort_belknap_const.htm

Fort Belknap Indian Community Council–State of Montana Tobacco Tax Agreement. Available from http://www.state.mt.us

Fort Belknap Indian Community Official Web Site. Available from http://www.fortbelknapnations-nsn.gov/

"Fort Belknap Indian Tribe Sues Over Gold Mine Pollution." *Billings Gazette,* January 30, 2004. Available from http://www.billingsgazette.com/index.php?id=1&display=red news/2004/01/30/build/state/40-tribeminelaw suit.inc

"Gros Ventre." *Columbia Encyclopedia.* 6th ed. New York: Columbia University Press, 2004.

Hall, Kermit L., William M. Wiecek, and Paul Finkelman. *American Legal History.* New York: Oxford University Press, 1991.

Hoxie, Frederick, ed. *Encyclopedia of North American Indians.* New York: Houghton Mifflin, 1996.

"Judge Finds No Action to Take in Belknap Mining Dispute." *Billings Gazette,* July 3, 2004. Available from http://www.billingsgazette.com/index.php?id=1&display=rednews/2004/07/03/build/state/70-belknap-mining.inc

Kerstetter, Todd M. Review of *Indian Reserved Water Rights: The Winters Doctrine in Its Social and Legal Context, 1800s-1930s.* By John Shurts [Book review]. *Western Historical Quarterly* 32, no. 2 (Summer 2001). Available from http://www.historycooperative.org/cgi-bin/justtop.cgi?act=justtop&url=http://www.historycooperative.org/journals/whq/32.2/br_14.html

"Leader of Indian Tribes Resigns Suddenly; Decision Followed Canceling of Bombing Range Plans." *Billings Gazette,* May 13, 2004. Available from http://www.billingsgazette.com/index.php?id=1&display=rednews/2004/05/13/build/state/65-speakthunder-resigns.inc

Leeds, Tim. "Fort Belknap Pursues Development of Ethanol Plant." *Havre Daily News,* December 2, 2003. Available from http://www.havredailynews.com/articles/2003/12/02/local_headlines/ethanol.txt

Miller, Jared. "Fort Belknap Grazing Rates Soar." *Great Falls Tribune,* July 4, 2004. Available from http://www.greatfalls tribune.com

Montana Indians: Their History and Location. Helena: Montana Office of Public Instruction, 2004.

Montana Office of Public Instruction. Fort Belknap-Montana Compact Ratified, Montana Code Annotated. Helena: Montana Office of Public Instruction, 2003. Available from http://www.opi.mt.gov/

O'Connor, Bryan. "Indian Historian to Realize Dream." *Billings Gazette,* September 27, 2003. Available from http://www.billingsgazette.com/index.php?id=1&display= rednews/2003/09/27/build/local/28-capture.inc

"Rehberg Announces $5.7 Million in Grants to Montana Tribal Colleges." Press release, August 4, 2004. Available from http://www.house.gov

Taylor, Colin F. *The American Indian.* London: Salamander Books, 2004.

Thackeray, Lorna. "Fort Belknap Tribal College to Grow." *Billings Gazette,* November 27, 2001. Available from http://www.billingsgazette.com/index.php?section=local& display=rednews/2001/11/27/build/local/ftbelknap.inc

"Tribal Packing Plant Opens Aug. 4." *Billings Gazette,* July 25, 2003. Available from http://www.billingsgazette.com/ index.php?id=1&display=rednews/2003/07/25/build/local/ 46-packing.inc

"Tribe Signs Water Compact with State." *Billings Gazette,* February 26, 2001. Available from http://www.billings gazette.com/index.php?section=local&display=rednews/ 2001/02/26/build/local/tribe.inc

"Tribes Take Control of More Programs." *Billings Gazette,* October 4, 2002. Available from http://www.billings gazette.com/index.php?id=1&display=rednews/2002/10/ 04/build/local/88-tribes.inc

"Tuberculosis Outbreak on an American Indian Reservation— Montana, 2000–2001." *Montana Mortality Weekly Report* 51, no. 11.

Western Environmental Law Center Web Site. Available from http://www.westernlaw.org

H

HART–CELLAR ACT

See IMMIGRATION ACT OF 1965

HARTNELL, WILLIAM (1798–1854)

William Hartnell was born in Backbarrow, England. At the age of 16, he was sent to the College of Commerce in Bremmen, but young William's study only lasted a year, due to the unexpected death of his father. To support his family, Hartnell took a job as a bookkeeper and accountant. In 1819, he arrived in Santiago, Peru, but soon left for Lima to open an office for his employer. While working in Lima, Hartnell met Hugh McColloch. The two became partners and headed for California to enter the hide business.

In 1822, the two men arrived at Monterey, which was the capital at the time. The men had agreed to a five-year contract for their business, with at least three of the years guaranteed that they be partners. Hartnell set out from Monterey attempting to get all the northern California missions to agree to three-year contracts. All but two of the missions agreed to sell their hides to Hartnell and McColloch. At the time, only a handful of foreigners resided in California. The two partners were able to secure the right to trade in any port in California; all other traders were only allowed to use the ports of Monterey and San Diego. In addition to the trading rights, California Governor Pablo Vicente Sola also gave the two partners land for their business venture. McColloch did not stay long, as he was called back to South America, leaving Hartnell alone to run the business.

In April 1825, Hartnell married Maria Teresa de la Guerra. Teresa was sixteen at the time of the marriage. Teresa's father was Don Jose de la Guerra y Noriega, who was considered the richest and most influential man in the Santa Barbara district. Through 25 years of marriage, the Hartnells had nineteen children and adopted five additional children.

The business started by Hartnell and McColloch became involved in tallow as well as hides. The hide and tallow business came to be a significant economic success in California; however, this did not prevent the partnership from failing. Hartnell was left with a total debt amounting to about $18,000. The entrepreneur did eventually pay off his debts. Even after the collapse of his partnership, Hartnell continued to work in the hide and tallow business.

Hartnell was able to secure 2,900 acres from the Spanish government for the purpose of ranching. Hartnell proved to be a good rancher, but the income from the ranch proved to be insufficient by itself. An adobe house was built on the property and is reported to be the first home in California to have glass windows. The ranch, called El Patrocinio de San Jose, was near the present-day city of Salinas, about 20 miles east of Monterey. The Hartnell family gained a reputation as gracious hosts who welcomed visitors to their home.

In late 1833, the educated Hartnell announced that he was going to open a post–secondary school on his ranch. In early 1834, the school began, with only fifteen students. Among the subjects taught were

French, Spanish, German, Latin, reading, writing, mathematics, and philosophy. The school was located on the Hartnell ranch. Two buildings were erected that held a classroom, chapel, kitchen, and dormitory. The purpose of the school was to prepare students for study at a university. Due to low enrollment, the school lasted only two years. The Hartnell School was the first post–secondary school in California.

Following the closing of his school, Hartnell was appointed customs administrator of Monterey. The appointment came from Governor Alvarado, his wife's cousin. During the period from 1839 to 1840, Hartnell was visitador-general of the missions. His responsibility included the administrative functions of the missions, from San Diego to San Fernando. Although the Mexican government had promised Hartnell an annual salary of $2,000, it never paid him. Hartnell resigned from his post after receiving several threats.

Captain John C. Frémont visited California for the second time in 1846. Hartnell allowed Frémont and his 60 soldiers to stay on his property for three days. Officially, Frémont and his men were on a scientific exploration. Over the three days, Frémont and his men raised a U.S. flag, after which they left Hartnell's property and headed toward Oregon. William Hartnell did not want California to become part of the United States; he hoped that the land would become part of the British Empire. Thanks to a large migration of U.S. citizens to California, however, Hartnell eventually gave up the dream of California becoming a jewel in the crown of the British Empire.

Four months after Frémont and his men left the Hartnell properties, Commodore John Sloat of the U.S. Navy took control of Monterey and raised the U.S. flag. Hartnell was asked to translate a proclamation and later became a land auctioneer, surveyor, and an appraiser in the customs house of the U.S. government. Hartnell quickly became known as the man who could translate for the new government.

In Monterey's first election under the U.S. flag, Hartnell was elected to the position of alcalde counselor. Additionally, Hartnell was paid $2,000 by John C. Frémont to translate Mexican laws into English. It took Hartnell a year to finish the job. William Hartnell's work as an interpreter became the main source of income for him and his family.

During California's first constitutional convention, William Hartnell worked to translate the new constitution into Spanish. Due in part to Hartnell's efforts, California became the only state to recognize Spanish as an official language along with English. In addition to his work in translating the constitution into Spanish, the English-born Hartnell translated many of the new laws into Spanish.

On February 2, 1854, William Hartnell died at the age of 56. He left behind his wife, Teresa, and 13 children.

—*Timothy A. Strand*

Suggested Reading

Beebe, Rose Marie, and Robert M. Senkewicz, eds. *Lands of Promise and Despair: Chronicles of Early California, 1535–1846.* Berkeley, CA: Heyday Books, 2001.

Chapman, Charles. *A History of California: The Spanish Period.* New York: Macmillan, 1921.

Dakin, Susanna Bryant. *The Lives of William Hartnell.* Stanford, CA: Stanford University Press, 1949.

Gutierrez, Ramon, and Richard J. Orsi, eds. *Contested Eden: California Before the Gold Rush.* Berkeley: University of California Press, 1998.

Hurtado, Albert L. *Intimate Frontiers: Sex, Gender, and Culture in Old California.* Albuquerque: University of New Mexico Press, 1999.

Lewis, Donovan. *Pioneers of California: True Stories of Early Settlers in the Golden State.* San Francisco: Scottwall, 1993.

Rolle, Andrew. *California: A History.* 4th ed. Arlington Heights, IL: Harlan Davidson, 1987.

HARVEY, FREDERICK HENRY (1835–1901)

As a successful entrepreneur of the late 1800s, Frederick Henry Harvey developed a legacy of elegant dining and hotel services that has lasted more than a century. Building up his business and reputation along the rails of the Atchison, Topeka and Santa Fe Railway, Fred Harvey rose from immigrant dishwasher to consummate creator of a restaurant and hotel empire. Armed only with alpaca jackets and fine silver, Harvey earned the reputation of "civilizer of the West." According to Harvey House Web master John

Howell, "Where the grunt and growl of frontier barbarism had held sway, Fred Harvey endorsed a law of 'please' and 'thank you.' Where the inhabitants had rooted about in a beans and bacon wilderness, he made the desert bloom with vintage claret and quail in aspic." Like the enterprising businessmen described in historian David Dary's *Entrepreneurs of the Old West*, Harvey sought not the "wild and free outdoor life as many early pioneers appear to be doing in romantic historical myths." Vanguard of elegant dining no matter the location, Harvey was "seeking profit, and in so doing [linked] the East with the West." Western tourism fortified this bond between the coasts, as Harvey and the railroad advertisers merged their expertise to entice travelers to the Southwest.

Dary named these entrepreneurs the "silent army," composed not of disciplined soldiers but "highly mobilized individuals, each seeking opportunity and profit in the American West." Harvey saw his opportunity for prosperity in the restaurant field in replacing deplorable eating conditions with palatable options, and he demanded civilized behavior from those who wished to partake. The fundamental need for food gave Harvey the power to tame; the result was a chain of restaurants and a change of lifestyle that followed the Santa Fe Railway from the Missouri River deep into the West.

Three features contributed to Harvey's early success: exclusive contracts with the Atchison, Topeka and Santa Fe Railway; exquisite cuisine; and the handsome Harvey Girls. The combination created an unbeatable formula for fame, and the history of Harvey's restaurants and hotels stands as testament to the effect one man had on a region rampant with bad manners and worse food.

At the age of fifteen, London-born Harvey found work in New York City as a "pot wollaper" (dishwasher), his first experience in the restaurant field. From then on, the desire to own and manage his own restaurants drove him, and although several years passed and many failed attempts occurred before the Harvey Houses flourished, he never lost his desire for the fulfillment of his dream. From dishwasher to failed restaurant partnerships to being one of two of the first clerks to sort, pick up, and deliver mail through the Railway Post Office, Harvey made his way to New Orleans, St. Louis, and then Kansas. In 1865, Harvey made Leavenworth his home base as freight agent and General Western agent.

As a traveling railroad employee, Harvey observed and tasted the food fare offered in the West. Trains pulled into depots; their passengers departed in a rush and tried to down a meal in the twenty allotted minutes. Elbows jabbed and behinds jockeyed for too few seats. Beaneries (common names for eating houses) often served rancid bacon, unidentified meat stews, eggs preserved in lime, and coffee that had perhaps been made in the same week, perhaps not. If passengers did not have time to eat all the food, some proprietors scraped the plates into a stewpot for the next crowd. Wise passengers avoided these offerings altogether; brave ones chugged a bit of Irish whiskey before and after the meal to diminish gastronomic effects. Carrying picnics aboard the train was an option, but the cloying smell of days-old chicken tempted only mice and flies. Something had to be done, and Harvey was just the man for the job.

In 1876, Harvey met with Charles F. Morse, superintendent of the Atchison, Topeka and Santa Fe Railway. Morse had recently returned from an inspection trip of all the railroad facilities. His own upset stomach was proof enough that Harvey's plan could work. With the two gentlemen in agreement, Morse and Harvey shook hands and thus established the first Harvey House.

Using a former lunchroom in Topeka, Harvey went to work in the spring of 1876. In this first location he set the standard for his restaurants to come, and he spared no expense or amenity. English silver, Irish linens, the best condiments, and moderately priced menu items graced the tables. Following this first successful venture, Morse encouraged Harvey to build a second eating house at the Clifton Hotel, one hundred miles down the rails in Florence, Kansas. As in the first agreement, the Santa Fe picked up the tab, and Harvey contributed his expertise. In 1878, Harvey signed his "first formal contract" with the Santa Fe, but the Morse and Harvey relationship began and continued based on "Whatever is fair and right," and all deals were sealed with a handshake.

In the decades to come, buying old buildings adjacent to Santa Fe depots, fixing them up, and then moving in became Harvey's mode of operation.

Despite many closings during the Great Depression, by 1951, the Harvey and Santa Fe partnership had fifteen hotels, forty-seven restaurants, and thirty dining cars in service. In 1943, Harvey Houses served thirty million meals. Before the Harvey System closed its doors (most locations by the mid-1950s), more than one hundred locations along the Atchison, Topeka and Santa Fe Railway lines served travelers to and from the West.

Exclusivity was the genius of Harvey's arrangement with the Santa Fe. In a formal contract, May 1, 1899, Harvey received the "exclusive right . . . to manage and operate the eating houses, lunch stands, and hotel facilities which the Harvey company then owned, leased, or was to lease at any time in the future upon any of the Santa Fe's railroads west of the Missouri River." The growth of the Atchison, Topeka and Santa Fe provided Harvey with the opportunity to exploit the contract, which allowed for no competition. A symbiotic relationship developed in that the railroad service became more attractive to travelers because of the meals provided by Fred Harvey. Based on the reputation of service and good food, travelers were choosing train service by whether or not it stopped at a Harvey House along the way. The Santa Fe was happy to oblige. Therefore, with a gentleman's handshake, steps toward molding a domesticated West took place.

The second component for Harvey's success derived from the aromas and tastes of a cuisine unprecedented in western travel. Only ingredients of the highest quality steamed in pots throughout the Harvey kitchens. Only the best chefs were brought in to cook. The results astonished the dignified traveler and ruffian alike: Exotic menu items such as turtle steak with giant sea celery salad formed standard fare from one end of the Santa Fe to the other. Harvey took pride in the fact that even in the winter months, no food came from a can. According to the Santa Fe's agreement to provide carrier service for supplies, Harvey had at his disposal the freshest produce at all times. Where the procurement of fresh milk products became a problem, Harvey opened his own dairies. Las Vegas, New Mexico; Newton, Kansas; and Temple, Texas, supplied regional areas. Harvey Houses always served the freshest milk, butter, and even ice cream, no matter the location of the restaurant.

Travelers did not see the same choices repeated during any trip; menus were based on foods that were in season and "coordinated with the eastbound and westbound manifests for the . . . refrigerator cars." Servings were generous: Pies were cut into fourths; managers were chastised and even fired if cuts of meat were trimmed too much. Reportedly, Harvey's dying words to his sons were, "Don't cut the ham too thin, boys."

In addition to fresh milk, all tables were set with silver pitchers of ice water to refresh thirsty passengers. A special blend of coffee was prepared so that the taste was the same no matter what Harvey House was visited. Water was analyzed and, if found unsatisfactory, replaced with fresh water brought in by rail. Employees followed a meticulous procedure for preparing the coffee, and fresh batches were brewed in the huge urns every two hours. Silver coffee pots sat at each table so customers could refill their cups whenever they were ready.

Harvey's sophisticating effects reached further than the dinner table. His introduction of attractive young women, smart, well mannered, and of good character, permeated the West with ripples of effect. These "gentle tamers" (the descriptor historian Dee Brown uses in his book of the same name) were a "force against which the males' brute force could not contend, and which ultimately brought the Wild West under complete domination." Thousands of these gentle tamers, or Harvey Girls, as they were popularly known, married, generally pairing up with well-to-do westerners, railroad engineers, and conductors. The former waitresses became a driving force behind the formation of clubs and the construction of churches, stores, and schools. Red-light districts diminished and in some cases disappeared; saloons lost business. The men and women of the resultant marriages went on to become community founding fathers and mothers.

Harvey's first restaurants employed male waiters, but brawls, knifings, and drunken stupors convinced him to make a change. He opted for sober women, but Harvey had social hurdles to jump before his idea could be implemented. Although schoolteachers and nurses were tolerated, other employed women were thought to be of questionable character; good women "worked" in the home. Waitresses were especially low on the ladder of respectability, slightly above "soiled doves." To overcome negative connotations, the women were seldom referred to as waitresses; instead, they actually were called Harvey Girls.

To overcome the question of character, each applicant was carefully screened and scrutinized for acceptability. Harvey ran newspaper advertisements calling for "Young women, 18 to 30 years of age, of good character, attractive and intelligent." During three quarters of a century, from 1883 until the late 1950s, approximately one hundred thousand women answered the call for a variety of reasons, including matrimonial prospects, financial success, and the lure of adventure. About half probably remained in the Southwest, marrying or settling into ranch, farm, mining, and railroad communities, changing forever and given much credit for cultivating the West.

If a prospective candidate met the qualifications, she was hired immediately and sent to her first assignment within twenty-four hours. She had to sign a six-, nine-, or twelve-month contract, agreeing not to marry during the contract term. Provisions of the contract included $17.50 plus tips each month, free uniform laundering and room cleaning, and room and board. Carrying a first-class ticket for the Pullman car and free food and lodging at the Harvey House stops along the way, she began her westward journey. Harvey Girls lived in mandatory dormitory settings that either adjoined or were located above the Harvey House restaurants. Strict rules applied. Hired matrons rigidly enforced curfews. The Harvey system improved on the good fortune of women, who in large numbers earned above-average wages with excellent working conditions. The image of fine, moral young women made its way into the public's domain through poetry, song, novels, and even film. Harvey Girls remained loyal to the Harvey House system, still speaking highly at a reunion held in the early 1980s of the opportunities they had as members of the Harvey House family.

The girls were admired for their demeanor, their looks, and their intelligence, but also for the service they provided. Each waitress, in rushed thirty-minute periods, served full-course meals to twenty customers. When the train whistle blew from a mile down the track, the Harvey Girls prepared for arriving passengers. While en route, passengers told conductors their meal preferences; the information was wired forward to the Harvey House, where chefs had the food prepared and steaming when the passengers disembarked. The Harvey Girls employed a unique cup code for efficient service of the drinks. The drink girl would make her way around the room, asking patrons their drink preference. She then arranged the cups as follows: cup upright in the saucer, coffee; cup upside down in the saucer, hot tea; cup upside down, tilted against the saucer, iced tea; and cup upside down, away from the saucer, milk. Other girls followed the drink girl, swiftly serving up the preferred beverage.

Desire to be fed so well and to be in the company of the lovely Harvey Girls had cowboys washing up before supper, miners visiting the barber, and moneyed travelers dusting off their cuffs. Similar to 21st century etiquette of "no shirt, no shoes, no service," men entering a Harvey House were required to don a jacket. If a fellow did not own one, the Harvey House establishment was happy to provide an alpaca jacket for him. Without proper attire and attitude, service was refused. On occasion, rowdies protested the dress restrictions they thought to be "sissified." However, Harvey insisted on compliance and courteous behavior.

Fred Harvey died on February 9, 1901, but the institution he developed would last into the next century. Harvey's sons, Ford Ferguson and Byron W. Harvey, implemented company leadership immediately. Ford stayed at his Kansas City office, "overseeing hotels, restaurants, and shops," while Byron, in Chicago, managed the railroad dining cars. In 1906, the Fred Harvey Company incorporated.

The Fred Harvey Company and the Santa Fe were not the only entities and entrepreneurs to prosper from the Harvey House system. Women in general, as well as one in particular, gained prosperity and recognition. Architect Mary Colter designed and decorated many of the structures used by Harvey and the Santa Fe, incorporating southwestern themes in each building. Some locations are still in use, perhaps the most famous being the Phantom Ranch on the banks of the Colorado, the Desert View Watchtower, the Hopi House, and the Bright Angel Lodge, all located in Grand Canyon National Park. Other architects employed by Harvey and the Santa Fe include Frederick L. Roehrig (Castañeda Hotel, Las Vegas, New Mexico, 1899), Charles F. Whittlesey (Alvarado Hotel, Albuquerque, New Mexico, 1902; El Tovar Hotel, Grand Canyon, 1905), and Isaac Hamilton Rapp (La Fonda, Santa Fe, New Mexico, 1920).

Also benefiting financially were the Pimas and Papagos, Zunis and Navajos, Hopi and Mimbreño. The Fred Harvey Indian Department provided an outlet for museum-quality baskets, turquoise and silver jewelry, and collector quality art, thus forging the field of southwestern art appreciation. Native craftsmen exhibited their skills near the hotels, providing tourists with weaving and pottery-making demonstrations and adding to the tourist lure of seeing Indians of the West. Several Native Americans employed by the Fred Harvey Company earned fame as a result of the exposure of their artistic talents to the leisure crowd who toured the Southwest.

Elle of Ganado, an employee of the Fred Harvey Company for more than twenty years, is one of the Harvey Indian Department's best-known artists. According to authors Kathleen L. Howard and Diana F. Pardue, Elle "demonstrated Navajo weaving and represented the Fred Harvey Company and the Santa Fe Railway" in locations including "The Alvarado Hotel in Albuquerque, Hopi House at the Grand Canyon, the Panama-Pacific International Exposition in San Francisco, and Land Shows in Chicago." Howard and Pardue also note, "Elle's image appears in more Harvey publications than any other individual associated with the Harvey Company." Other artists include William and Mary Benson (Pomo, basketweavers), Maria and Julian Martinez (San Ildefonso Pueblo, renowned pottery makers), and Miguelito (Navajo, chanter and sandpainting artist).

Historian Marta Weigle observes a further promotion of Native American history and culture perpetuated by the Harvey House Company. Beginning in 1926, "Indian Detours" provided "authentic encounters" with the "natives in the exotic setting of Santa Fe and environs." Tourists rode in plush "Harveycars" driven by "dudes" and escorted by attractive and intelligent "couriers"—young women adorned in concho belts and turquoise jewelry who provided informed narratives about the "region rich in history and mystery—the Enchanted Empire."

Although Harvey Girls, Native American artisans, and Indian Detours couriers helped draw tourists into the Southwest, the promotional publications produced by the Fred Harvey Company and the Santa Fe are among the most attractive promotional lures. Illustrations of the southwestern vistas, canyons, and sunsets adorned booklets, calendars, and posters published by the Passenger Department of the Santa Fe Route. Artists, among them Thomas Moran, received free fare to points west in return for original paintings that were hung in the halls of the Fred Harvey hotels or were reproduced on the covers of publications.

Prior to the establishment of the Harvey Houses, train-stop lunches were only for the stout of stomach; both servers and customers alike were of the roughest character, often ill-mannered, unclean, and certainly blasé about repeat business or reputation. Gun fighting, fist fighting, and food poisoning were real threats to those travelers who sought destinations west of the Missouri. After the founding of the Harvey Houses, there was at least one building at every Santa Fe stop where decorous behavior was expected. As a member of the "silent army," and with the enlistment of "gentle tamers," Fred Harvey realized his dreams of becoming a successful restaurateur and simultaneously refined and reformed wild ways of the West.

—*Suzzanne Kelley*

Suggested Reading

Adams, Samuel Hopkins. *The Harvey Girls.* Cleveland, OH: Random House, 1944.

Bryant, Keith L., Jr. *History of the Atchison, Topeka and Santa Fe Railway.* Lincoln: University of Nebraska Press, 1982.

Dary, David. *Entrepreneurs of the Old West.* Al M. Napoletano, illus. New York: Knopf, 1986.

Foster, George H., and Peter C. Weiglin. *The Harvey House Cookbook: Memories of Dining Along the Santa Fe Railroad.* Athens, GA: Longstreet Press, 1999.

Howard, Kathleen L., and Diana F. Pardue. *Inventing the Southwest: The Fred Harvey Company and Native American Art.* Flagstaff, AZ: Northland, 1996.

Morris, Juddi. *The Harvey Girls: The Women Who Civilized the West.* New York: Walker, 1994.

Poling-Kempes, Lesley. *The Harvey Girls: Women Who Opened the West.* New York: Marlow, 1991.

Weigle, Marta, and Barbara A. Babcock. *The Great Southwest of the Fred Harvey Company and the Santa Fe Railway.* Phoenix, AZ: Heard Museum, 1996.

⊞ HASTINGS, LANSFORD WARREN

See Donner Party, Euro-American Migration on the Overland Trails

⌗ HAVASUPAIS

See UPLAND YUMANS

⌗ HEART MOUNTAIN

See CODY, WYOMING

⌗ HELENA, MONTANA

The three great gold discoveries in Montana—at Grasshopper Creek in 1862, Alder Gulch in 1863, and Last Chance Gulch in 1864—caused the population to leapfrog from one place to the next. Miners had no sooner settled at one area when another discovery promised new opportunity. In this way, gold attracted a fickle population. On July 14, 1864, four miners— Reginald (Bob) Stanley of Nuneaton, England; John S. Cowan of Georgia; D. J. Miller of Alabama; and John Crabb of Iowa—were headed back to Virginia City for provisions. Hungry, tired, and down on their luck, the men took one more swing through a gulch they had prospected previously. This time, they made a lucky strike.

The four men, known to posterity erroneously as the "Four Georgians" (probably so named for their mining techniques), found the site so remote that they took their time testing up and down the gulch before two of them went on to Virginia City for supplies. It was a most unusual bonanza because there was no stampede. Rather, these men were so discreet that others only trickled in, in small groups. By fall, there were two hundred residents, and the camp had been formally christened Helena. By January 1865 there were many stores and businesses. The population swelled from one thousand in the spring to three thousand—most of them from Alder Gulch—by midsummer. As in Virginia City, Masons were a prominent group. The first death in the camp was that of Dr. L. Rodney Pococke, who succumbed to tuberculosis in March 1865. Pococke was a Mason, and his funeral brought Masons together for the first time in the new settlement. The lodge had thirty-two members at the start of 1866, and from this time forward, Masons were a significant presence in Helena, as they had been in Virginia City.

Helena's first population mirrored that of Virginia City's, with miners, merchants, service providers, saloonkeepers, freighters, gamblers, and prostitutes forming a noisy, boisterous community. Within its first two years, Helena had formally established Protestant, Catholic, and Jewish cemeteries. Andrew J. Fisk visited Helena in October 1866 and noted, "There are a good many Chinese there and all of them (I guess) wash clothes for a living." There were 188 retail and wholesale business houses; forty-five of them were food stores. Helena boasted both Democratic and Republican newspapers and a public school with one hundred students. Daily coaches traveled from Helena to Salt Lake City or Fort Benton. A ticket from Helena to Corinne, Utah, on the Wells Fargo stage cost $145, and the trip took at least four and a half days, traveling twenty-four hours a day, to cover the 550 miles. Arrival of the telegraph in 1866 provided a critical link with eastern states.

With the end of the Civil War, more newcomers flooded into the Montana Territory, and Helena's population continued to grow. A. K. McClure wrote in 1867:

> Helena has all the vim, recklessness, extravagance, and jolly progress of a new camp. It is but little over two years old, but it boasts a population of 7,500 and more solid men, more capital, more handsome and well-filled stores, more fast boys and frail women, more substance and pretense, more virtue and vice, more preachers and groggeries, and more go-ahead activeness generally than any other city in the mountain mining region.

The Montana Territorial Legislature met in Virginia City in 1868 and passed a bill allowing a vote to relocate the territorial capital to Helena. Although Governor Green Clay Smith vetoed the bill, it illustrates the decline of the one gold camp and rise of the other. In 1874, Congress passed a bill that established a federal assay office in Helena, built in 1875 at government expense. There were only five others—in New York, St. Louis, Charlotte (North Carolina), Deadwood, and Boise—and this illustrated Helena's strategic location at the headwaters of the Missouri, its importance as a regional center, and its wealth of gold. The capital moved to Helena in 1875, and along with it came the attendant territorial offices and officials, boosting the town's prestige and population. Helena

Helena's Main Street, from Harper's Weekly, *February 2, 1878. Drawn by W. M. Cary.*

Source: Montana Historical Society Photograph Archives.

by this time had diverse industries, including a foundry, several breweries and brickworks, lime kilns for the manufacture of mortar, and stone quarries.

When the first federal census was taken in 1870, Helena's population was approximately three thousand. Although it lost significant numbers when placer mining was finished toward the end of the 1860s, even so, Helena was the largest urban area in the territory. Men outnumbered women three to one, and residents came from all over the world and every state. The most significant ethnic groups in the earliest community were Jews, Chinese, and Irish. Blacks, Germans, and Japanese were also important to Helena's later cultural landscape.

As Helena endured a series of nine devastating fires between 1869 and 1874, it was the Jewish community that helped keep the fledgling mining camp solvent. Jewish merchants and businessmen had ties to a financial network reaching well beyond the Montana frontier that provided them with the financial resources to rebuild, sometimes again and again. Marcus Lissner, who ran Helena's acclaimed

International Hotel (for example), lost his uninsured business so many times during the 1860s and 1870s that it became known as "the Phoenix." In 1867, among Helena's twenty dry goods merchants, seventeen of them were Jews. By 1877, 20 percent of Helena's Board of Trade was Jewish.

Jews served in public offices (Marcus Lissner was elected to the city council six times), maintained some of Helena's most beautiful homes, and were well respected by the gentile community. Jews participated widely in the economic community and were lawyers, judges, bankers, merchants, and service providers. The prestigious Montana Club, founded in 1885, counted Jews among its elite members. The Jewish congregation built the first Jewish temple between St. Paul, Minnesota, and Portland, Oregon, in 1891. The Jewish population peaked in 1900 at 138 adults, then rapidly declined, due largely to lack of job opportunities. By 1930, members were so few that the temple closed.

As in Alder Gulch, Chinese were the largest ethnic group in Helena (Lewis and Clark County) numbering 633 in 1870, more than 10 percent of the city's

Temple Emanu-El, Helena, circa 1891.

Source: Montana Historical Society Photograph Archives.

population. The almost exclusively male community was confined to the south end of town. The Chinese worked abandoned placer claims, owned businesses, and cultivated market gardens. There were doctors, tailors, herbalists, grocers, restaurateurs, and laborers, as well as Chinese-run laundries and gambling houses and a Chinese Masonic temple.

The Chinese community diminished, with 359 in Lewis and Clark County (Helena) in 1880. With the advent of the Northern Pacific Railroad in 1883, the number increased and nearly doubled in 1890. Chinese workers helped lay the tracks across Montana, did the dangerous blasting that built early roads, and blasted the mountainside to build the Mullan Tunnel, making rail travel possible across the Great Divide. In Helena, in the 1890s, a substantial Chinese community operated a variety of businesses, provided services, and paid local taxes.

Despite their contributions, there was always blatant discrimination against the Chinese. In 1892,

for example, a public meeting was held in Helena to encourage employers to dismiss Chinese help. At the time, there were eighteen Chinese employed in Helena's seven hotels, nine worked for private families, and ninety-six had jobs in the town's fourteen laundries. A. F. Smith, an African American, declared that cooks and waiters should "form a union that they might stand solidly against the Chinese." By the turn of the 20th century, the Chinese community lessened in number again. Helena's Chinese population followed the state trend, dwindling partly because it was almost exclusively male and partly because of discriminatory legislation. Many Chinese, following their original intent, eventually returned to their families in China. In 1910, there were still five laundries run by Chinese proprietors, but by 1930, few Chinese remained in Helena. The only physical remnant of Helena's Chinese community lies in a barren field known as China Row, outside the boundaries of Forestvale Cemetery. The two hundred unmarked graves of Helena's Chinese residents date from 1892 to 1941. During the 1940s, relatives removed perhaps a dozen graves and returned the bones to ancestral soil in China.

Irish Catholics came with the first groups of miners and were among the most prevalent mining camp groups. Usually Union Democrats, men like Martin Maginnis and Peter Ronan—both involved in the publication of the Democratic *Rocky Mountain Gazette*—became prominent, well-respected men in Montana, involved in territorial politics and supporters of their compatriot, the controversial acting territorial governor Thomas Francis Meagher. Meagher's presence lingers in the statue that dominates the lawn around the state capitol. Thomas Cruse was another Irishman who rose from poverty to riches with his Drum Lummon mine at nearby Marysville and later contributed much of his wealth to build the awe-inspiring St. Helena Cathedral. Helena's modern population reflects this large group, with 21 percent claiming Irish ancestry.

German immigrants are another group that came in significant numbers to Helena, particularly after the advent of the railroad in 1883. There were German Lutheran and German Methodist churches in the 1890s, and when there was a German-speaking priest in the mid-1890s, St. Helena's Catholic Church offered Mass in German. The Helena Turnverein built an athletic club in 1890, a German school opened in 1893, and the state's German-language newspaper, the *Montana Staats Zeitung,* was published in Helena. This community flourished until World War I, when anti-German legislation outlawed use of the German language. Today, Helena's German-American population is the largest ancestral group in the city, with more than 26 percent of Helena residents claiming German ancestry.

Blacks on the Montana frontier are little documented, and the history of this minority group has been largely overlooked. For example, when the local newspaper published a descriptive pamphlet in 1908 boosting the capital city, its sizable black population received no mention. The publication praised Helena's churches, fraternal organizations, benevolent societies, civic improvement groups, and social clubs, but it failed to mention that Helena's progressive African American population boasted similar institutions as well as its own politically active newspaper, the *Montana Plaindealer.*

Helena's first mayor, before the town incorporated in the 1870s, was an African American barber by the name of E. W. Johnson. By 1870, there were seventy-one African Americans residing in Helena. Two decades later, in 1890, the African American community numbered 279 in a total population of 13,834. In 1888, the St. James African Methodist Episcopal Church organized, and by 1894, it had sufficient national prestige to host an annual convention in Helena. From the beginning, churches and social organizations were segregated, and territorial legislation in 1872 segregated schools as well. However, financial considerations stemming from the small black population ended school segregation by electorate vote in 1882. Helena never experienced residential segregation; whites and blacks lived together in all neighborhoods except the wealthy West Side. Despite the prejudice that was obvious in social segregation, Helena offered its African American citizens opportunity, and a few businessmen were quite successful.

Joseph Bass, publisher of the *Montana Plaindealer,* proudly claimed in 1907 that Helena's blacks could compete with anyone. When Charles Mason and his professional crew of African American waiters from Hot Springs, Arkansas, came to Helena's famed Broadwater Hotel, Bass could not resist comparing their skill and expertise to the "bum" service previously provided by "the young white men who were imported as waiters."

Helena's African American community was at its height in 1910, numbering 420 persons out of a total population of 12,515. Its active, civic-minded residents were articulate and outspoken through the voice of the *Plaindealer,* protesting acts of prejudice and discrimination. One political organization, the Colored Progressive League, had sixty active members who pledged to expel black pimps, prostitutes, gamblers, and hustlers from their midst and to defend unjustly harassed local African Americans. Helena's vibrant black community also enjoyed recitals, plays, socials, and formal debates staged by an active literary society. The AME church hosted an annual Thanksgiving opossum dinner, held in a downtown hall, and invited the public.

With the onset of World War I, Montana experienced heavier draft calls than other states, and many Helena African Americans were called into service. War-related jobs out of state probably drew others away from Montana. As a result, Helena's African American population declined. In 1920, there were 220 African Americans in the community; by 1930, 131. In 1970, there were only forty-five.

In 1910, when the Northern Pacific Railroad revamped its line across Montana, some forty Japanese laborers, all male, came to work on this project in Helena. They lived in railroad "warehouses," according to the U.S. Census, along the Northern Pacific tracks. Local residents maintain that some of these workers continued to live at the extreme east end of the railyards until the onset of World War II. They cultivated gardens, hauled water from a nearby spring by wagon, and sold their produce locally.

Helena has been called the "City of Churches" for its many houses of religion representing its diverse group of immigrants. Besides the German churches and the Jewish temple, there were Scandinavian Evangelical and Norwegian Lutheran churches, as well as Unitarian, Episcopal, Methodist, Congregational, Christian, Presbyterian, Methodist Episcopal, Baptist, and other denominations. The most visible religious presence in the community, however, was and is Roman Catholic. Foreign-born Jesuit priests very early began a boys' school, and in 1869, five Sisters of Charity from Leavenworth, Kansas, arrived to establish the first Catholic institutions in Montana, including St. John's Hospital, St. Vincent's Academy for Girls, and St. Joseph's Children's Home. This religious group, although small, had a profound effect on social services in Montana. These and other Catholic sisters were a familiar presence on the streets of Helena until the mid-20th century. Crowning achievements of the Catholic Church in Helena include the establishment of the Diocese of Helena in 1884, construction of Mount St. Charles College (the present Carroll College, a private Catholic liberal arts college) in 1910, and St. Helena Cathedral, constructed between 1908 and 1924.

Of the three territorial capitals born of the gold rush, only Helena evolved into an urban center. Men who made fortunes in freighting, real estate, mining, cattle, banking, and other ventures settled there, built handsome business blocks, and left their mansions on the west side of town. With their financial and political backing, statehood came in 1889, and the capital permanently located at Helena in 1894. Since that time, Helena's future has been secure.

From its gold rush roots to its historic downtown, Helena remains an eclectic community, but the remnants of its once distinct ethnic groups have been assimilated into the mainstream. Today, most of its residents are employees of the State of Montana. The capital city has few other industries and a population that fluctuates according to the economy and the political climate; it remains fewer than thirty thousand, the state's smallest urban center. Nestled in its narrow gulch and built upon its golden mining history, Helena has earned its nickname, "Queen City of the Rockies."

—Ellen Baumler

See also HELENA'S EXPLOITED RESOURCES; LAST CHANCE GULCH, MONTANA; VIRGINIA CITY, MONTANA

Suggested Reading

Baumler, Ellen, ed. *Girl from the Gulches: The Story of Mary Ronan.* Helena: Montana Historical Society Press, 2003.

Baumler, Ellen. "Temple Emanu-El: First Temple Amidst the Rockies." *More from the Quarries of Last Chance Gulch Volume I.* Helena, MT: American and World Geographic, 1995.

Lang, William L. "The Nearly Forgotten Blacks on Last Chance Gulch, 1900–1912." *Pacific Northwest Quarterly* 70 (1979).

Paladin, Vivian, and Jean Baucus. *Helena: An Illustrated History.* Helena: Montana Historical Society, 1996.

Swarthout, Robert R., Jr. "From Kwangtung to Big Sky: The Chinese Experience in Frontier Montana." *Montana: The Magazine of Western History* 38 (1988).

⊞ HELENA'S EXPLOITED RESOURCES

In the summer of 1864, Helena's pristine wilderness teemed with wildlife—pronghorn antelope, grizzly bears, coyotes, wolves, and rattlesnakes. The area was rich in other natural resources as well: water, timber, and especially gold. As the men worked, Indians of various tribes watched in silence as the men began to destroy ancestral hunting grounds. Miners trickled in

Helena's impressive St. Peter's Hospital, constructed in 1890, reveals a bleak landscape littered with tailing piles.

Source: Used with permission of the Montana Historical Society.

that summer, and those who decided to stay began to harvest the hillsides, which were overgrown with large trees. Before winter set in, two hundred men swarmed the gulch, building sluice boxes and log shelters along the stream that ran through it and provided miners with the necessary water to placer their claims.

As placer operations along the gulch expanded and men and their animals trampled through the gulch, it was not long before the water source—sufficient for the small party of discoverers—became polluted. By 1865, the water that was so fortuitously located was unfit to drink. Miners relied on teams to bring in a daily supply of potable water. Although once plentiful, there was not enough water to serve so many, and newcomers sometimes left in disgust over its scarcity. Construction of the Yaw Yaw Ditch (also known as the Chessman and Cowan Ditch) remedied the water situation. A wooden flume, built around the base of Mount Helena, harnessed water from a reservoir supplied by Ten Mile Creek. This made sluicing, and further upheaval of the land, much more efficient. In 1869, the Park Ditch Company brought a second water source into Helena from Park Lake twenty miles away. Other water systems followed, and numerous small companies supplied water from various sources.

By the middle of summer in 1865, three thousand people choked Last Chance Gulch. The countryside was barren; stumps remained on the once-forested

slopes. The gulch was a jumble of claims where prospect holes and mine shafts made the area treacherous. Tunnels undermined buildings, and stilts held them up. Streets ended abruptly in tailing piles, and prospect holes filled with water put residents and especially children at grave risk. By 1868, sluicing on the gulch had ended and a city covered the old placer diggings.

Some men worked to recover the more easily obtained gold along the gulch near the discovery site; others discovered gold veins south of Last Chance where the main gulch divides into Grizzly and Oro Fino gulches. James Whitlach made the first lode discovery in the fall of 1864. Discovery of the Whitlach-Union Mine inspired others to comb the surrounding hillsides and explore the gulches. Discoveries followed, and small mining camps dotted the area, with Helena at the hub of these smaller operations. The main lode-mining settlement was Unionville, where the Whitlach-Union Mine produced $3.5 million worth of gold between 1864 and 1872. The Spring Hill was discovered in 1870 in Grizzly Gulch. The Spring Hill's major contribution lay in the twenty-three thousand tons of flux it provided between 1885 and 1890 for the territory's first silver-lead smelter at Wickes, eighteen miles south of Helena. Mining at the Whitlach-Union and the Spring Hill mines continued into the mid-20th century.

Placer mining in the area was essentially over by 1875, although Chinese miners, as in Alder Gulch, continued to mine small claims. Hydraulic mining (power washing of the hillsides) in the 1870s further changed the surrounding landscape. Early maps show reservoirs in some neighborhoods to accommodate this type of mining. When mining operations, either hydraulic or placer or both, were finished in an area, it was then developed for residential use, and many of Helena's wealthiest citizens made their fortunes in these lucrative, secondary real estate ventures. Sanborn Perris fire insurance maps of 1888 reveal placer diggings still bordering some neighborhoods, and photographs of fine new buildings often have tailing piles instead of landscaping.

Stone was another essential resource. Fires that plagued the mining camp destroyed first-generation buildings. With no wood left to harvest and a need for fireproof materials, citizens looked to stone for building needs. Quarries in the vicinity of Mount Helena

Destructive hydraulic mining operations like the one shown here in Nelson Gulch near Helena drastically altered natural topography.

Source: Used with permission of the Montana Historical Society.

provided essential building material before the end of the 1860s. Limestone quarried in great quantities at the south end of Last Chance Gulch provided lime used to manufacture mortar. Limestone quarrying continued on a significant scale until the 1890s, when lack of railroad accessibility made it unprofitable.

Although most placers had played out, Last Chance Gulch was still producing gold in the 1890s. Dirt excavated for new buildings on Main Street was carefully washed for gold with good results, and even in the 1940s, as workers dug the foundation for a new business block, sidewalk miners waited to sluice the dirt, with fair returns.

In 1938, placer mining revived in the form of dredging. The Porter Brothers Corporation began operating

an electric dredge in the flats north of Helena. The company recovered forty-five thousand ounces of gold from the gravel. A second dredge began operating between 1940 and 1941. The Gold Mine Closing Order in 1943 shut down dredging activities. Porter Brothers resumed in 1945 for one final season. Gold from dredging this area reportedly exceeded $2.5 million.

The Helena mining district boundaries extend south for six to ten miles and include Helena and Last Chance, Grizzly, Oro Fino, Dry, and Nelson gulches. Second only to Alder Gulch, in the first four years the area produced an estimated $19 million in gold. The Last Chance placers alone produced $6,724,000, most of it before 1868. The tunnels that run everywhere beneath Helena sometimes pose difficulties when foundations for new buildings are being sunk. They are also the source of legends and misconceptions and most often are mistakenly called "Chinese tunnels."

Time and human effort have softened the scars. Most tailing piles have disappeared, and vegetation frames the stone-quarried slopes to the south. In the late 1890s, a lightning-sparked fire blackened Mount Helena's barren hillside. On Arbor Day in 1899, children armed with seedling trees began replanting the slopes that now make up a city park. Little remains visually to document the frenzied activity on which Montana's capital city rests.

—Ellen Baumler

See also Helena, Montana

Suggested Reading

Montana Department of Environmental Quality. "Helena Mining District." Available from http://www.deq.state .mt.us/AbandonedMines/linkdocs/techdocs/98tech.asp
Wolle, Muriel Sibell. *Montana Pay Dirt: A Guide to the Mining Camps of the Treasure State.* Athens: Ohio University Press, 1983.

⊞ HOMESTEAD ACT

In 1862, Congress passed the Homestead Act to open government lands to settlement, primarily those west of the Mississippi River. Most of the available land lay in the arid territory west of the ninety-eighth meridian. Small farms of 160 acres could be purchased for $1.25 per acre, with an initial filing fee due at the time of initial selection. The remainder of the money was due after five years of mandatory residence and improvement on the land.

Although the terms of purchase seemed generous, the actualities of life on a homestead claim required an initial investment for animals, equipment, and seed. For immigrants, the challenge often required financing with high interest rates. By 1880, much of the land located near water and wood sources had already been claimed by Civil War veterans and emigrants from eastern states. Immigrants often purchased their land from speculators or railroad companies for slightly higher prices. Enterprising town developers also recruited in Europe through pamphlets, brochures, and newspaper advertisements. Through the 1880s, homestead claims rose correspondingly with increasing numbers of immigrants. The act did not require U.S. citizenship for purchase as long as the homesteader declared his or her intent to become a citizen in the future. It also allowed women to claim 160 acres as heads of their household. Many families acquired larger farms by using older daughters and sons to homestead claims adjacent to their parents' claims.

Homesteading immigrants played an important role in the development of crops on the semiarid plains. German Russians brought hard red wheat that developed into the staple grain crop of homesteaders in the arid West. Government regulations attempted to prevent blocs of immigrants from settling together and forming isolated communities, but many managed to preserve their native language, customs, and religion until World War I. Residents of the Dakota Territories and Nebraska filed the most claims under the Homestead Act and corresponding legislation such as the Timber Culture Act. Between 1868 and 1904, more than 700,000 claims were filed by farmers on almost 97 million acres of government land. Railroad companies and speculators were granted or purchased the bulk of available land, which totaled around 400 million acres.

—*Megan Birk*

See also ENLARGED HOMESTEAD ACT OF 1909, NINETEENTH CENTURY LAND POLICY

Suggested Reading

Gates, Paul Wallace. *History of Public Land Law Development.* Washington, DC: Government Printing Office, 1968.

Hurt, R. Douglas. *American Agriculture: A Brief History.* Ames: Iowa State University Press, 1994.

Nelson, Paula M. *After the West Was Won: Homesteaders and Town-Builders in Western South Dakota, 1900–1917.* Iowa City: University of Iowa Press, 1986.

HOPI

The Hopi Reservation is located on approximately 1.6 million acres in northeastern Arizona, a relatively small Indian reservation compared to its surrounding neighbor, the Navajo Nation. Described by historians and anthropologists as the "westernmost of the Pueblo Indians," the Hopi people are direct descendents of the *hisatyesqam,* or "ancient people," and have continuously inhabited present-day northeastern Arizona since 500 CE. Although the term "Hopi" is generally used and accepted by Hopis and non-Hopis, the Hopis have historically referred to themselves as *Hopitu-Shinumu,* meaning "all people peaceful."

Currently, the Hopi Reservation consists of twelve autonomous villages situated almost entirely on three mesas named "First," "Second," and "Third Mesa." On First Mesa, the Hopi villages include Hanoki (Tewa), Sichomovi, Walpi, and Polacca. Ten miles west of First Mesa are the Second Mesa villages of Mishongnovi, Sipaulovi, and Shungopavi. On the western edge of the Hopi Reservation, the villages of Third Mesa include Hotevilla, Bacavi, Oraibi, and Kykotsmovi at the foot of the mesa. The ancient village of Oraibi has long been considered "by outsiders" as the most important and largest Hopi village on the reservation. Although the present-day population of Oraibi is only a fraction of 18th- and 19th-century estimates, Oraibi remains the "oldest continuously inhabited village [in] all of North America," and throughout history it has played an important role in Hopi society.

In September 1906, Oraibi experienced a severe internal division between two opposing Hopi factions. Referred to as the Oraibi Split, the division developed over whether or not Hopis at Oraibi should adopt some aspects of western life and values. Those who favored western progression were given the imposed name "Friendlies" by the government, and those who opposed were called the "Hostiles." The two factions settled their long dispute by a pushing battle near Oraibi. The "Hostiles" lost the battle, and Tawaquaptewa, *kikmongwi* (village chief) of Oraibi, forced the opposing faction out of the village. Shortly thereafter, the government forced Tawaquaptewa, along with seventy Hopi pupils, to attend Sherman Institute, an Indian boarding school in Riverside, California. The government sent the children of the "Hostile" families to Phoenix Indian School, in Phoenix, Arizona. In the early 20th century, the government created Indian boarding schools to assimilate Native people and to destroy Indian culture. However, the Hopis, as did many other Indian tribes, used their boarding school education as a tool to ultimately preserve the Hopi culture.

Although each is distinctly Hopi, the villages function independently from one another, with traditions, clans, and religious ceremonies that reflect the unique characteristics of each village. In addition to the twelve villages, Hopi and Hopi-Tewa families founded the Hopi community of Yu Weh Loo Pah Ki (Spider Mound), at the Jeddito Wash area near Keams Canyon, Arizona. Within the boundaries of the Hopi Reservation, Yu Weh Loo Pah Ki is a growing community with nearly one hundred occupants.

Of the original seventy-five clans, thirty-four clans exist in Hopi culture today, including the Rabbit Clan, Bear Clan, Eagle Clan, and Sand Clan. Clan membership is traced through the maternal lineage, and it is absolutely forbidden for a Hopi to marry within his or her own clan. Associated with each clan is a creation story that tells how the clan came to be. To understand the Hopi as a whole, one must understand the Hopi creation story. As with many other Indian tribes, the Hopi creation story varies in detail among Hopi villages and clans. Although complex, the Hopi emergence story continues to be held and taught among the Hopi people and serves as the foundation of Hopi culture.

According to Hopi belief, before matter, *Tokpella,* or endless space, existed with the Sun Spirit, *Dawa,* and other lower gods. By taking the elements from Tokpella, Dawa created the First World, which consisted of insectlike creatures. These creatures eventually disappointed Dawa, for they did not understand the meaning or significance of life. Saddened by what he saw in the insectlike creatures, Dawa sent his messenger, Spider Grandmother (*Gogyeng Sowuhuti*), to the creatures and told them they would soon migrate to the Second World. After a long journey to the Second World, Spider Grandmother took the creatures to a cave, where they discovered that Dawa had changed them into animals. Although they were initially glad to be animals, internal division eventually developed, and Dawa, again saddened by what he saw, had Spider Grandmother take them to the Third World, a world prepared and created by Dawa.

When they arrived in the Third World, Dawa changed their animal bodies into people, and shortly thereafter, the people established villages and planted corn. Due to the cold and lack of adequate light, however, the corn did not grow. On one occasion, a hummingbird spoke to a group of people in the fields and told them that his ruler, *Maa'saw,* Ruler of the Upper World, had observed their desperate condition and sent the hummingbird to teach the people how to make warmth by fire. However, even with the introduction of fire, which eliminated many problems, the people did not all live harmoniously with each other. Some, such as the *powakas,* or sorcerers, caused trouble among the people and proclaimed that they had created themselves. When Dawa heard about the trouble developing in the Third World, he sent Spider Grandmother to the people with a message that all people of good hearts must leave the powakas behind. The people understood that they had to leave, but they did not know where they would go.

At this time, the people heard footsteps above the sky, and some suggested that they set out to discover the world above them. As the chiefs and medicine men met in the kiva to discuss the issue, they made a live swallow out of clay. The swallow attempted to fly through the opening to the Fourth World, but he became tired and returned, unable to continue on. Convinced that there was a world above their own, the chiefs and medicine men fashioned a white dove, and they told the dove to fly high in the sky. Although the dove passed through the opening in the sky and saw that land existed in the Upper World, he did not see any living things. After the chiefs and medicine men attempted a third time with a hawk, they created a catbird out of clay and sent him to explore the Upper World. The catbird flew much farther than the others, and he came to a location of mesas surrounded by sand, with gardens full of melons and squash. As the catbird flew overhead, he noticed a man with his head down, sleeping near a house made of stone. The catbird quickly realized it was *Maa'saw,* and he spoke with the Ruler of the Upper World. The catbird asked *Maa'saw's* permission for people of the good hearts to enter his land, and *Maa'saw* granted his permission.

After the catbird returned to the Third World and told the chiefs and medicine men of his journey, the people eagerly wanted to go to the Fourth World. Because the people did not have wings like the swallow, dove, hawk, or catbird, however, they questioned how they would ever reach the opening in the sky. To solve this problem, Spider Grandmother sent her two grandsons, the warrior gods *Pokanghoya* and *Polongahoya,* to find chipmunk, the great planter. Chipmunk planted sunflower seeds in the middle of the plaza, and the people made the sunflower grow by praying and singing songs. Although the sunflower reached the opening in the sky, it did not pass through the opening due to the weight of its blossom. Finally, after chipmunk attempted with a spruce seed and pine seed, he planted a bamboo seed, which grew very tall and passed through the opening in the sky. Thus the bamboo became the road of migration the people took to the Upper World, also known as the Fourth World. After the people emerged from the Under World, groups of Hopi wandered the land in all four directions. These groups were made up of the many Hopi clans who migrated to the mesas. Although each clan has its own story of migration, it is commonly believed that those of the Bear Clan arrived first on Hopi land, or Hopi *Tusqua* (Hopi aboriginal lands).

For more than a thousand years, the Hopi lived and flourished on their mesa tops without any European contact. The first Hopi contact with Spanish explorers came in the summer of 1540. In search of the legendary Seven Cities of Gold, Spanish explorer Don Pedro de Tovar, along with seventeen armed men and at least one Zuni guide, arrived from the pueblo villages of present-day New Mexico. As part of General Francisco Vazquez de Coronado's expedition, de Tovar

and his men came to the Hopi people with little respect or regard for Hopi ways. The Spaniards were spotted first by the Hopis near the village of Awat'ovi, and the Hopis cautiously allowed them to enter their land. Seeing that Hopi Country, or "Tusayan," as the Spaniards called it, had no permanent streams, in 1610 the Spaniards established their colonial capital six hundred miles east in Santa Fe, New Mexico.

Between 1628 and 1633, Spanish missionaries persuaded some of the Hopis to build three large churches made of stone at the villages of Oraibi, Awat'ovi, and Shungopovi. After a number of priestly abuses and fierce persecution experienced by the Hopis when they attempted to practice their traditional religion, Hopi resentment toward the Spanish intruders eventually came to a deadly climax, known as the Pueblo Revolt. In 1680, the Puebloans of the Rio Grande proposed an anti-Spanish rebellion, and the Hopis gladly participated and killed the priests at Awat'ovi. After 1680, the Spanish never regained a strong presence on Hopi land. In addition to the Spaniards, others attempted to Christianize the Hopi, most notably the Mormons, Mennonites, and Baptists.

In spite of the dry and arid climate of the Hopi Reservation, the Hopi continue to successfully use ancient farming techniques that have been passed on from one generation to the next. Primarily an agricultural-based society, Hopi culture is closely connected with planting and harvesting crops. Apart from squash, beans, melons, grapes, peaches, apricots, and wheat, the Hopi are perhaps best known for their corn. Corn plays an extremely important role in Hopi society, for the "Hopi way of life is the corn—humility, cooperation, respect, and universal earth stewardship." In mid-April of each year, the Hopi begin the first corn planting on numerous cornfields scattered throughout the mesas. A second corn planting begins in May or early June, which is considered the main corn crop. Varying in size from half an acre to more than eleven acres, Hopi corn fields typically belong to individual Hopi clans and have been passed down through the female lineage.

Hopi agricultural success can be attributed to tried and tested methods, the ability to adapt to the environment, and Hopi religion. Considered the master dry farmers of the world, the Hopi have long used the dry farm technique with the seasonal planting of corn. Although some fields exist in close proximity to springs and washes, the Hopi have traditionally relied on seasonal rains to water their crops. By using a sharpened digging stick, Hopi men dig holes of eight inches or more and place ten or so kernels of corn into the moist sandy dirt. Once the corn plant emerges from the ground, the farmer tenderly protects the young plant, much as a Hopi mother would take care of her infant child. Forty miles west of Oraibi, the village of Moencopi near present-day Tuba City, Arizona, has been used by Hopis throughout history as an important farming community. A strategic satellite village of Oraibi, Moencopi is the only Hopi village that is not located on or near the Three Mesas of the Hopi Reservation. Likely attracted by the running springs and wash, the Hopi developed a seasonal community in Moencopi for agricultural purposes. Today, Moencopi is divided into two sections, named Upper Moencopi and Lower Moencopi.

In addition to agriculture, Hopi have excelled in various forms of native arts and crafts and are especially known for their ability to make baskets, silver jewelry, pottery, rugs, and *tihu,* or kachina dolls. In traditional Hopi culture, basket making is performed by the women and is a skill learned by Hopi girls at a young age. Since the 1890s, the Hopi have worked with silver to make beautiful and intricate bracelets, necklaces, earrings, watches, and rings. By adapting the overlay technique from other Indians of the Southwest, the Hopis have been able to produce distinctly Hopi jewelry that reflects the values and symbolism of Hopi society.

In 1882, President Chester Arthur established a 2.5 million-acre reservation for the Hopi people. Prior to this, an official "Hopi Tribe" did not exist. Following the Reorganization Act in 1934, the Hopi people created the Hopi Tribal Council in 1936. As the first government body intended to represent the entire Hopi community, the Hopi Tribal Council devoted itself to carrying out the "goals and objectives of the Hopi Tribal Government in the best interest of the Hopi people; and to institute a collaborative and cooperative relationship between and among all levels of tribal and village governments, and the Hopi people."

An important responsibility of the tribal government is to provide educational opportunities for the Hopi people. The Hopi Tribe actively promotes and encourages education among its eleven thousand–plus members. In 2000, under the leadership of tribal Chairman Wayne Taylor, Jr., the Hopi Tribal Council agreed to allocate $10 million for Hopi educational purposes and established the Hopi Education Endowment Fund (HEEF) to oversee and secure funds intended for Hopi students and programs. With a philosophy geared toward the survival and furtherance of Hopi culture, HEEF administrators firmly believe that "Only through the education of the Hopi people can the continuance of Hopi culture and the Hopi homeland be ensured." Working alongside HEEF, the Hopi Tribe Grants and Scholarship Program has provided hundreds of Hopi students with financial assistance for college and graduate school, with the hope that students would later return and contribute to the tribe and community. Hopi education is closely associated with the preservation of Hopi culture, and the Hopi Tribe established the Hopi Cultural Preservation Office to preserve and protect Hopi culture. This office essentially acts as the "central tribal clearinghouse for culturally related issues coming to the attention of the Hopi Tribe."

In connection with the migration of Hopi students who sought educational opportunities off the reservation, Hopis have secured teaching and staff positions at numerous institutions, including the University of California, Los Angeles; Cornell University; Northern Arizona University; and the University of Arizona. In 1998, Emory Sekaquaptewa from the University of Arizona, along with others, published the first comprehensive Hopi dictionary. The *Hopi Dictionary* is by far the most complete and esteemed Hopi language tool and is used by Hopis and non-Hopis alike.

Although visitors are welcomed and encouraged at the Hopi Reservation, the Hopi people do ask that all visitors adhere to the regulations posted at the entrance of each village. Visitors are also encouraged to view and purchase traditional Hopi arts and crafts sold throughout the reservation by authentic Hopi and Hopi-Tewa artists. For additional information regarding visitor etiquette, contact the Hopi Office of Public Information.

—Matt Sakiestewa Gilbert

Suggested Reading

Clemmer, Richard O. *Roads in the Sky: The Hopi Indians in a Century of Change.* Boulder, CO: Westview Press, 1995.

Hopi Dictionary Project, Bureau of Applied Research in Anthropology, University of Arizona. *Hopi Dictionary = Hopìikwa Lavàyatutveni: A Hopi-English Dictionary of the Third Mesa Dialect with an English-Hopi Finder List and a Sketch of Hopi Grammar.* Tucson: University of Arizona Press, 1998.

The Hopi Tribe Web Site. Available from http://www.hopi .nsn.us

James, Harry C. *Pages from Hopi History.* 8th ed. Tucson: University of Arizona Press, 1994.

Qoyawayma, Polingaysi. *No Turning Back: A Hopi Indian Woman's Struggle to Live in Two Worlds.* Albuquerque: University of New Mexico Press, 1964.

Simmons, Leo W., ed. *Sun Chief: The Autobiography of a Hopi Indian.* Fredericksburg, VA: BookCrafters, 1970.

Spicer, Edward H. *Cycles of Conquest: The Impact of Spain, Mexico, and the United States on the Indians of the Southwest, 1533–1960.* 6th ed. Tucson: University of Arizona Press, 1976.

Udall, Louise. *Me and Mine: The Life Story of Helen Sekaquaptewa.* Tucson: University of Arizona Press, 1969.

Whiteley, Peter M. *Deliberate Acts: Changing Hopi Culture Through the Oraibi Split.* Tucson: University of Arizona Press, 1988.

⊞ HOUSTON, SAMUEL

See AUSTIN, STEPHEN FULLER

⊞ HUALAPAIS

See UPLAND YUMANS

⊞ HUNTINGTON BEACH, CALIFORNIA

The city of Huntington Beach sits on the shores of the Pacific some 40 miles south of Los Angeles in neighboring Orange County. With a current population of nearly 200,000, it benefits from its now famous beach-oriented recreational activities and plays host to such events as the U.S. Open of Surfing, Association of Volleyball Professionals Pro Beach Volleyball, and Van's World Championship of Skateboarding. However,

Huntington Beach's initial notoriety sprung not from its sandy shores but from resources beneath the ground. In 1920, a Standard Oil Company oil well tapped into one of the largest pools of crude oil ever discovered at the time, thus launching a bona fide southern California oil rush. Huntington Beach became the forerunner to a series of regional oil towns that not only changed the landscape of southern California through the sudden construction of thousands of derricks and rapidly built housing but also altered the regional composition of the population. In the decade that followed the Huntington Beach gusher, Long Beach (Signal Hill), Torrance, Dominguez, Inglewood, and Seal Beach all found oil beneath their city limits. One consequence of these discoveries was the massive influx of working-class migrants distinct from the middle-class midwesterners that had previously flowed into southern California. Hence, the migration to Huntington Beach in many ways works as a model for the development of working-class suburbs of Los Angeles and Orange Counties.

Before the boom, Huntington Beach served greater Los Angeles as a potential recreational hub. Linked to the metropolis by Henry E. Huntington's Pacific Electric Railroad in 1904, the founders of Huntington Beach planned the city as a western version of Atlantic City—a playground for urbanites. Hoping for weary but affluent Angelenos, Huntington Beach officially opened for recreational business in 1909 with a population of 915. That year, a writer for *Outwest Magazine* attempted to boost the city's fortunes by claiming the beach town had a "dignified appearance." According to the author, Charles Lawrence Edholm, Huntington Beach "is not only a watering-place but a permanent and settled community whose existence is justified by the highly developed region round it" (p. 440). Unfortunately for developers and hopeful residents, few Angelenos ventured to the city's shores (partially due to Huntington Beach's location in a dry county), and commerce stagnated. The city then diversified economically with the opening of the Holly Sugar Company, which became the largest municipal employer and caused local farmers to grow more sugar beets. Even with the new industry (which brought in an additional 250 families), by 1920 Huntington Beach only held a mere 1,700 residents.

The sleepy agricultural existence of the city's residents, however, was forever altered by the discovery of oil in 1920. Once Standard Oil's well—Bolsa Chica no. 1—began producing crude oil, Huntington Beach was quickly transformed into a crowded petroleum boomtown of some 12,000 people. At first, local residents resoundingly welcomed the coming of the oil age into the city limits. Soon after the city's big gusher arose, the editor of the *Huntington Beach News* declared that the "effect of oil development work to date has been as though Aladdin had given his big brass lamp a rub for our benefit" (*Huntington Beach News*, August 13, 1920). One *Los Angeles Times* writer did little to temper local residents' hopes, declaring that in Huntington Beach "under the fertile acres and city lots there lay hidden from man's eye the black gold called oil." Thus, as the residents of Huntington Beach dreamed of untold riches, the city itself rapidly acquiesced to the demands of the oil industry. Initially cautious, the local government attempted to place limited restrictions on the drilling, but by mid-decade, as residents clamored for drilling in their own backyards, most of those limitations had been lifted. Starting with a handful of wells in 1920, various oil operators erected nearly 300 by 1924. As the oil boom continued and new areas of the city opened for drilling, that number continued to climb. In a two-month period in 1927, an estimated 250 wells were built in the western section of the city alone.

Equal to the transformation of the landscape were the vast changes brought about by scores of migrant oil workers searching for employment. "People came pouring in here like there was a gold rush," remembered one Huntington Beach resident. "They flocked here by the hundreds from Texas, Oklahoma and Wyoming and all the various oil producing states." By 1921, hundreds, if not thousands, of oil workers, or "roughnecks," pitched army tents on city beaches, often renting cots for eight-hour shifts before relinquishing them to the next worker. The problem of beach tents became so acute that in 1922 and 1923, responding to local complaints of blight and rowdy behavior, the police swept through the beach's "tent cities" and "tent hotels" in an attempt to dislodge troublesome oil workers. City boosters with connections to the oil industry, however, lobbied to suspend the sweeps, claiming that many of the tents belonged to adventurous vacationers who chose to camp on the city's pleasant shoreline.

The slew of oil workers created other challenges as well. As happened in other boomtowns from San Francisco to Desdemona, Texas, vice followed the young male workers. One of the first police officers on Huntington Beach's police force, Delbert "Bud" Higgins, described the chaos of the era:

> The town was full of bootleggers selling whiskey during those days. Many of the downtown hotels were loaded with prostitutes. There were a number of gambling places running. I think it's like any boomtown. When you get a boomtown, anything goes. . . . They had the same thing at Signal Hill after they left Huntington Beach. (p. 66)

Pool halls, boxing matches, and dance halls crowded into a city that had previously prided itself on its rather puritanical nature. Pool halls, especially, were central to roughnecks' recreation. The city's pool halls "were open twenty-four hours a day and the tables were full all the time" with oil workers. Pool halls were also notoriously dangerous. As one observer reported, the young men that flooded into Huntington Beach "didn't have any responsibility; they'd work, eat, sleep, and just raise cane on Saturday night. They'd have a pool hall here and the workers would gather every night and play pool, drink, fight, stab and shoot each other."

The wild young men of Huntington Beach were a far cry from the first wave of interregional migrants that relocated to southern California from the turn of the century to the 1920s. Prior to the discovery of oil and the subsequent rise of heavy industry, the peopling of southern California depended on the abundance of white middle-class midwesterners. This new group, although still white, differed in class and regional origins from its predecessors. First of all, the majority of employed men in Huntington Beach in the 1920s worked as roughnecks in the oil fields. This demanding and often dangerous labor paid relatively well but fell squarely into the category of wage labor. Distinct from the white-collar workers, small farmers, retirees, and small shopkeepers that defined southern California's population before World War I, these blue-collar workers not only dominated the neighborhoods of Huntington Beach but spread out into the working-class suburbs that surround Los Angeles, such as Signal Hill, South Gate, and Compton. So dependent were they on the extractive industry that these cities were later dubbed the "black gold suburbs."

Studies have found that the working-class residents of the black gold suburbs preferred to move outside of large cities and purchase homes in the search for independence. Younger, poorer, and less educated than their predecessors, these migrants often found the city chaotic and benefited from the industrial opportunities located beyond the metropolis. Furthermore, they decidedly rejected the residential mixing of the races found within some city areas. In working-class suburbs, some minorities, such as Mexican laborers, were relegated to labor camps on the edges of town. African Americans, however, found little if any refuge in the working-class suburbs. By 1930, the oil towns of Brea, Signal Hill, and Torrance reported no black residents whatsoever; Huntington Beach claimed only three.

At least part of this aversion to interracial mingling was due to the second distinction between the old wave of interregional migrants and the new. Those that ventured to southern California after World War I often came from the American South and southern border states. This was particularly true of oil workers. By 1930, nearly 30 percent of all southern California oil workers were born in the South. Although southerners accounted for only 7 percent of California's aggregate population, they amounted to around 15 percent of southern California's oil-town residents. The reason for these elevated numbers is related to the nature of the oil industry itself, as well as the timing and location of oil discoveries. From the turn of the century to the 1920s (and beyond), oil discoveries in Texas and Oklahoma drew countless young men from the farms of not only those two states but from Louisiana, Arkansas, Missouri, and Tennessee. With each discovery came another boomtown. Cities appeared seemingly overnight, and, once the wells were too tapped to produce, often disappeared at the same rate. Wages in the large fields, such as the Mid-continent Oil Field in Oklahoma, offered decent wages to anxious young men in a time of agricultural decline. The result was a large and highly mobile workforce of former southern farmers accustomed to the harshest of conditions. Unsanitary and unsafe conditions were a fact of life for the residents in these boom-to-bust communities. In

such cities, "garbage and decaying vegetable matter, tin cans, old rags and scrap paper lie in heaps around temporary structures, or are strewn over vacant lots" ("Cleaning Up the Oil Camps," p. 20). In 1921, the U.S. Bureau of Mines decried the squalor of Texas boomtowns that brought "unnecessary hardship to a class of migratory workers":

> So it is that a stretch of trackless prairie sometimes becomes, almost overnight, a community numbering thousands of people who establish themselves in temporary buildings, tents, dugouts, lean-to shelters, or even within four topless walls of burlap, or in the open. ("Cleaning Up the Oil Camps," p. 20)

These mushroom communities were rather sadly termed "rag towns." Ranger, Desdemona, and Burk-Burnett, Texas, were towns of this type in 1919.

One oil worker from Seminole, Oklahoma, complained that the oil patch environment was not only unhealthy but truly dire. "Here in the Mid-Continent oil fields," he lamented, "there are hundreds of little innocent children, mothers and fathers, all sinking gradually but surely to a death more horrid than drowning."

Hence, with the advent of oil production in southern California, southerners and southwesterners attempting to escape the grim conditions of other boomtowns arrived in droves. On the shores of the Pacific, they found both higher wages and better hours. In southern California, they earned $160 per month, compared to the $145 per month paid in Oklahoma and Texas. Additionally, the oil companies in southern California recognized—but did not always respect—the policy of eight-hour days. Immigrants to the Pacific oilfields also found considerably better living conditions. Unlike the boomtowns of Oklahoma and Texas, Huntington Beach and Los Angeles' black gold suburbs were relatively close to a highly modern metropolis and offered amenities unheard of in isolated oil camps. Oil workers concerned with sanitation, single-unit housing, and public schools were pleased with what they found in southern California. One roughneck from Arkansas (by way of Oklahoma) who worked in Orange County claimed that southern California was "paradise from where I lived."

By 1930, however, the boom had receded, and many of the single young men that had flooded the boarding houses and camped on the sands of Huntington Beach left for other oil fields. Some found work in the Signal Hills fields outside of Long Beach; others drifted to the derricks near Bakersfield. Census data strongly suggest that most of the oil workers who migrated from the oil fields of Texas and Oklahoma to California ultimately planted roots in the West, but in the case of Huntington Beach—a true one-industry town in the 1920s—most workers had no choice but to leave. As the industry declined, not only did workers find little opportunity, they had little interest in any other type of labor. From its peak population of 12,000 in the early 1920s, only 3,700 remained in Huntington Beach by 1930.

Although still quite typical of the second wave of interregional migrants, those who stayed behind in Huntington Beach differed from the throngs of young, single oil workers. Most noticeably, the group that remained had sought—and found—a measure of stability. Even in the case of the most mobile group, southern oil workers, this pattern is apparent. An analysis of all southern-born heads of households in the city of Huntington Beach reveals the disparity between the boomtowns of Oklahoma and Texas and this particular black gold suburb. In the Texas and Oklahoma oil camps, there was a dearth of women and few permanent structures. Huntington Beach, on the other hand, differed little from any other city on Los Angeles's periphery. Of the southern-born heads of households (62 percent of whom were oil workers), 93 percent were married, and of that group more than 80 percent had children. Additionally, nearly all lived in single-family dwellings, and few housed nonfamily members. Although many of these men and women undoubtedly began families after migrating to California, others moved with their families in tow. Delbert Higgins recalled, "in the oil boom days, a lot of these fellas that came here had boys going to school" (p. 70). Even the local union representative recognized the presence of stable families in Huntington Beach, claiming in 1921 that the "future of the [Huntington Beach] oil field has good promise and it's up to you married folks . . . to look to the economic point regarding your future home and work in harmony with the OFG&W Refinery Union" (*Huntington Beach News*, August 26, 1921).

The presence of working-class families in Huntington Beach—the majority of which were headed by oil workers—illustrates that by 1930 the city had a resoundingly blue-collar population. On the whole, these workers paid half the monthly rent of the average Angeleno and were far more likely to work wage labor. These families, however, enjoyed a quality of life undreamed of in the dusty boomtowns of Oklahoma and Texas. Not only could these families find superior work conditions and modern amenities, but workers and their families could enjoy a variety of recreational benefits, such as a large, heated salt water plunge at Huntington Beach pier and the ability to lunch on the sand within yards of towering oil derricks.

Patterns of migration to Huntington Beach also presage the conservatism of Orange County after World War I. Like the men and women that flooded into Orange County 30 years later, the families of the 1920s sought stability through conservatism. They feared the perceived social chaos of large cities, joined evangelical churches, fought the teaching of evolution in public schools, rejected integration in the workforce and neighborhoods, and distanced themselves from radicalism (particularly in the form of the Industrial Workers of the World). On Sunday afternoons, the residents of Huntington Beach could attend the Pentecostal Mission's song services at the open air dance pavilion on the pier or walk anytime into the Reverend W. H. Bradley's massive beach tent (which supplanted the workers' tents) where he held his "Bible Chautauqua." The people of Huntington Beach refused to allow Eugene Debs to speak publicly but crowded the bleachers when Los Angeles's Ku Klux Klan no. 1 played its Ku Klux Klan no. 2 in an exhibition baseball game within the city limits. When black Angelenos built a beach club on a local strip of sand, Huntington Beach residents first fought through legal channels, then—after having failed—burned the club to the ground.

—*Daniel Cady*

See also AFRICAN AMERICAN COMMUNITIES IN CALIFORNIA

Suggested Reading

"Cleaning Up the Oil Camps," *Literary Digest* 71 (October 22, 1921): 20.

Edholm, Charles Lawrence. "The Seaward Suburbs of Los Angeles." *Outwest Magazine* (May 1909): 440.

Franks, Kenny A., and Paul F. Lambert. *Early California Oil: A Photographic History, 1865–1940.* College Station: Texas A&M Press, 1985.

Higgins, Delbert "Bud," interviewed by Harry Henslick, May 9, 1968, Huntington Beach, California, for the Huntington Beach Community History Project. Unpublished collection of oral histories, California State University at Fullerton, Special Collections, 66, 70.

Huntington Beach News, August 13, 1920.

Huntington Beach News, August 26, 1921.

Nicolaides, Becky M. *My Blue Heaven: Life and Politics in the Working-Class Suburb of Los Angeles, 1920–1965.* Chicago: University of Chicago Press, 2002.

Quam-Wickham, Nancy. "'Another World': Home, Work, and Autonomy in Blue Collar Suburbs." In *Metropolis in the Making: Los Angeles in the 1920s,* edited by William Deverell and Tom Sitton. Berkeley: University of California Press, 2001.

Tolnay, Stewart E., Kyle D. Crowder, and Robert M. Adelman. "Race, Regional Origin, and Residence in Northern Cities at the Beginning of the Great Migration." *American Sociological Review* 67 (June 2002): 456–475.

Viehe, Fred W. "Black Gold Suburbs: The Influence of the Extractive Industry on the Suburbanization of Los Angeles, 1890–1930." *Journal of Urban History* 8 (November 1981): 3–26.

I

⎄ IDAHO SILVER STRIKES

Although the Wood River area first attracted attention during the gold rush in Boise Basin in 1862, miners largely disregarded the area. Indians discouraged development until the end of the Bannock War in 1878. This interval saw the creation of more effective means of smelting lead and silver in Nevada and Colorado. Furthermore, the railroads now almost reached Wood River, making the development of the area's lead deposits profitable. Prospectors returned to the area by 1879, and thousands rushed to Wood River the following year. Miners organized new towns such as Galena, and Bellevue showed great potential due to the discovery of the Minnie Moore Mine in the vicinity. Galena reached a peak of about 800 residents, but by 1890, it had become a ghost town.

Capital from Philadelphia placed a smelter in Ketchum for the 1882 mining season. However, companies still shipped their ore to Denver, Kansas City, Omaha, or Salt Lake City, prompting the Philadelphia Company to lower prices and double the size of the plant. In 1883, the Oregon Short Line reached Hailey, and the following year, it reached Ketchum, enabling mines to reach their maximum production. Until the arrival of the railroads, the mines deliberately held back production due to the higher transportation costs of shipping ore by wagon. Ketchum would contain two thousand residents by 1889. However, some of the mines, such as the Minnie Moore, eventually shut down after the drop in the price of silver pushed production

costs higher than potential profits. Unlike other boomtowns, Ketchum survived due to the sheep industry.

By 1867, more than a thousand Chinese worked in the mines of the Boise Basin. The Chinese started coming to Idaho in large numbers after the completion of the transcontinental railroad released thousands of Chinese workers into the West in search of employment. The additional competition from the Chinese contributed to driving prospectors to either Montana or British Columbia, but some made their way to the Owyhee Basin.

Prospectors found gold on Jordan Creek in 1863, but the deposits did not last long. The silver-bearing quartz ledges found in fall 1863 did create excitement, as assays hinted at wealth to dwarf the Comstock. Investors created several mines by the end of the following year, with the Orofino and Morningstar mines being the most prominent. The mines launched the cities of Silver City and Ruby City. Promoters encouraged the further growth of these cities with the construction of the Silver-Ruby wagon road. Silver City eventually eclipsed Ruby City and attracted most of its inhabitants due to its proximity to important mines. For similar reasons, Silver City had the largest Chinese population in the Owyhees, although Irish, Australian, and Cornish immigrants could also be found in the region. In 1870, 118 of Silver City's 599 residents were Chinese. The Irish made up about 25 percent of southern Idaho's miners in the 1870s. During the 1860s, a depression in Cornish mines drove many workers to the United States, where they expected to earn more money. From 1860 to 1880, approximately one third of Cornish mine workers left their country. Although the Silver City mines continued their operations after the failure of the Bank of California in 1875, the operations started to fade as companies depleted the mines. Silver City itself remained the county seat of Owyhee County until 1935, when Murphy took this distinction for itself. Silver City continued its decline until it became a ghost town.

Prospectors made other discoveries at Sheep Mountain, Greyhound Ridge, and Seaform. Although these areas experienced a high level of investment prior to 1888 because of the severe drop in lead and silver prices after 1892, they did not take off. However, heavy investment from Salt Lake City did bring development to the area by the end of the 19th century. Seaform's relative isolation from the railroads hindered its development. Even though Hecla, a mining corporation from Coeur d'Alene, made major investments in the area in 1926, these did not include improved transportation, and Seaform continued to be cut off.

Andrew Prichard discovered gold in the Coeur d'Alene region in the early 1880s and tried to keep the find secret. After 1883, this became impossible, as the Northern Pacific Railroad advertised the presence of gold to encourage traffic on its new track crossing northern Idaho. The company claimed that gold seekers could take the train almost to Coeur d'Alene itself. The town grew to one thousand by 1888 and eight thousand by 1910. However, this initial emphasis on gold ignored the real wealth of Coeur d'Alene. Mineral seekers noted that the true wealth of the region was its lead-silver ore. Investments from Montana, Portland, and San Francisco covered the area with mills, mines, and smelters. In 1885, Noah Kellogg's discovery of the Bunker Hill mine set off a legal battle that delayed the mine's development. The dispute centered on Kellogg's refusal to inform his backers, Dr. John Cooper and Origin Peck, of his findings. The courts eventually decided in favor of Cooper and Peck. Once operations began, work continued at the mine until the 1980s.

Coeur d'Alene's lead-silver extraction soon made up more than 80 percent of the total mineral production in the state, easily surpassing gold mining. The operations required large-scale corporate investments, pushing out the small and medium-sized placer and lode producers. This also created labor problems due to disputes between workers and management. The Twenty-fifth Infantry Regiment from Missoula, a unit of black soldiers, came to the region in July 1892 to restore order. During the labor strike, the mine owners brought in strikebreakers that included Eastern Europeans. Within the region, one could also find Finnish, Swedish, Irish, and Italian workers. However, the miners prevented Chinese from entering the Coeur d'Alene mining district.

In 1880, John A. James and Jim Peck prospected south of Heath below Sturgil Park and discovered several fine lodes of silver. Initially, they named the discovery for presidential candidate Winfield Scott Hancock, but they soon changed the name to Mineral City. The area's development had to wait until a smelter arrived in 1890, as earlier equipment failed. Mineral City experienced prosperity until silver prices dropped in 1893. Despite these difficulties, Mineral City did have a distinct advantage, as it lay only four miles from a branch line. Furthermore, winter snows did not cut off Mineral City, distinguishing it from other mining camps. Investors tried unsuccessfully to revive Mineral City in 1900 and 1902, but the area did experience a revival when silver prices rose in 1918–1922 and the early 1940s. Mineral City is now a ghost town.

The Lemhi Range near Birch Creek also attracted mining interest over a period of several decades. Initial interest in the area went back to 1867, but prospectors did not organize it until 1880. However, additional discoveries found additional lead-silver deposits 10 miles to the south at Spring Mountain. Once prospectors found the Viola mine, this expanded the scope of the minerals almost to the continental divide. Although problems shut the mines down, the Gilmore mine reopened in the 20th century, and its production expanded after railroads improved transportation in the area. Extensive mining continued until a power plant explosion in 1929.

Southern Idaho's major lead-silver-zinc discoveries continued into the 20th century. The 1925 discoveries at Livingston proved to be the most significant in 30 years. New investments created a new plant and bought the latest equipment for 1926. These improvements made the area southern Idaho's largest mining employer within a year. At the time, Livingston became the second largest metal-producing area in the state, but it was not alone in its 20th-century success. The Triumph mine reached its peak from 1936 to 1957, and rising silver prices enabled some mines around Bellevue to reopen in 1967, although they shut down again in 1970. Wood River also saw the digging of a 500-foot tunnel in 1977 to access a vein found near Ketchum.

—Robert Miller

Suggested Reading

Hanley, Mike. *Owyhee Trails: The West's Forgotten Corner.* Caldwell, ID: Caxton, 1988.

Magnuson, Richard G. *Coeur d'Alene Diary: The First Ten Years of Hardrock Mining in North Idaho.* Portland, OR: Metropolitan Press, 1968.

Mercier, Laurie, and Carole Simon-Smolinski, eds. *Idaho's Ethnic Heritage: Historical Overviews.* Boise: Idaho Ethnic Heritage Project, 1990.

Paul, Rodman Wilson. *Mining Frontiers of the Far West, 1848–1880.* Revised edition edited by Elliot West. Albuquerque: University of New Mexico Press, 2001.

Wells, Merle W. *Gold Camps & Silver Cities: Nineteenth Century Mining in Central and Southern Idaho.* Moscow: University of Idaho Press, 2002.

⊞ ILLEGAL IMMIGRATION REFORM AND IMMIGRANT RESPONSIBILITY ACT

See IMMIGRATION AND NATURALIZATION SERVICE (INS), IMMIGRATION REFORM AND CONTROL ACT OF 1986

⊞ IMMIGRANT ACT OF 1917

See FORCED MIGRATION OF ANARCHISTS

⊞ IMMIGRATION ACT OF 1924

See IMMIGRATION ACT OF 1965, IMMIGRATION AND NATURALIZATION SERVICE (INS), IMMIGRATION REFORM AND CONTROL ACT OF 1986, OPERATION WETBACK

⊞ IMMIGRATION ACT OF 1965

The Immigration Act of 1965 (the Hart-Cellar Act), signed by President Lyndon Johnson, changed the structure and application of U.S. immigration policies. The act altered the requirements for admission into the United States by abolishing the quota system created 41 years earlier. The prior statute, known as the Immigration Act of 1924, grew out of fear that immigrants would occupy American jobs and corrupt American Christian values. It established a system of immigration that severely limited the number of immigrants admitted to the United States annually and excluded immigrants who were unable to obtain U.S. citizenship. The Naturalization Law of 1790 stipulated that only whites could obtain citizenship, thus excluding all those of Asian background, including Japanese. As a result, the Immigration Act of 1924 barred all Asian immigrants from entering the United States. Immigration reform emerged in 1952 when Congress passed the Immigration and Nationality Act (the McCarran-Walter Act), which President Harry Truman vetoed. Truman believed the quota system contradicted the goals of the United States, and in September 1952 he ordered a commission to make recommendations. Those recommendations included the abolition of the quota system and an increase in the maximum annual quota. Congress overturned the veto. The McCarran-Walter Act granted the president power to exclude any immigrant believed to be a threat to national security and increased the number of immigrants from Asian countries. This increase was minimal, raising the number from zero to 100 people per year. Additionally, fears over the threat of communism limited significantly the number of immigrants allowed in the country from nations under communist rule. The breakdown of the law was that those with family residing and holding citizenship in the United States made up 50 percent of immigrants allowed to enter the country. The other 50 percent, however, were those highly skilled in some trade that would aid America in some way. Still, despite minor modifications, the McCarran-Walter Act did little in the way of reforming the quota system. In many ways, the Immigration and Nationality Act resembled the Immigration Act of 1924, maintaining the quota system and low Asian numbers.

As tensions arose over civil liberties, it became apparent that past immigration policies proved racially and ethnically discriminatory. Such legislation as the Civil Rights Act of 1964 demonstrated the Johnson administration's desire to eradicate such discrimination. It was in response to this issue that the Immigration Act of 1965 was adopted. Other factors, such as calls for immigration reform, also played a role in its passage. Prior to its adoption, President John F. Kennedy had intended to reduce the quotas by 20 percent every year, as well as making a number of other changes. Due to internal conflict in Congress, however, the proposed legislation died along with President Kennedy in 1963. Despite such setbacks, the Johnson administration was able to promote and pass the Immigration Act of 1965.

Effective December 1, 1965, the Immigration Act abolished immigration quotas and placed a cap on overall hemispheric immigration. The cap on visas for immigrants coming from the Eastern Hemisphere was 170,000, and from the Western Hemisphere, 120,000. The act further required that the number of visas granted each year not exceed 20,000 for any country in the Eastern Hemisphere. The hemispheric caps, however, would be abolished in 1976 and replaced by a global ceiling. The 1976 statute granted 290,000 visas per year, with a 20,000-visa cap per country. In addition, on the same day he signed the Immigration Act of 1965, President Johnson granted an open invitation to Cubans trying to flee from the communist rule of Fidel Castro. This invitation has caused approximately 17,400 Cubans to enter the United States annually since that time. Furthermore, Cold War tensions played a significant role in the shaping of immigration policy. By admitting immigrants previously ignored or seen as a national threat, the United States was demonstrating the kindness of America and democracy. In a time when communism seemed an international threat, this positive aspect of American democracy, Johnson hoped, would shift sympathies in America's favor.

Unlike the Immigration Act of 1924 and the McCarran-Walter Act of 1952, the 1965 statute was not restricted to admitting immigrants from specified regions. Prior immigration acts had required that immigrants come from a specific region, mostly Europe. The Immigration Act of 1965, however, abolished this, and as a result, many immigrants, such as Asians, were permitted to enter the country. As a result, more than 2 million Asian people have immigrated to the United States since 1965. Immigrants were to be welcomed not for their place of origin but rather for their skills and profession. Family reunification also played a significant role in the admittance process. One major difference between the 1965 act and the Immigration and Nationality Act of 1952 was the preference provisions. The Immigration Act of 1965 issued 20 percent of its visas to unmarried adult children of United States citizens and another 20 to spouses and unmarried adult children of permanent resident aliens. Additionally, 10 percent were given to scientists and artists who possessed great talents for their trade and to brothers and sisters of United States citizens older than 21. Finally, 24 percent was given to skilled and unskilled workers of occupations where labor was in short demand, and 10 percent was given to refugees from communist nations and the Middle East.

As a result of the Immigration Act of 1965, more than 22,000 Asian immigrants have migrated to the United States. In the year 2000, 10,243 Asians migrated to the United States, including Chinese, accounting for 2,433 immigrants, and Vietnamese accounting for 1,123. Other nations, such as Mexico, from which in 1985 48,000 people emigrated legally to the United States, have been greatly affected by the Immigration Act of 1965, making it a cornerstone statute in immigration policy.

—*Scott Keys*

See also CHINATOWNS, CHINESE EXCLUSION ACT, IMMIGRATION AND NATURALIZATION SERVICE (INS), IMMIGRATION REFORM AND CONTROL ACT OF 1986

Suggested Reading

Braziel, Jana Evans. "History of Migration and Immigration Laws in the United States." Available from http://www.umass.edu/complit/aclanet/USMigrat.html

Carroll, Peter N., and David A. Horowitz. *On the Edge: The U.S. in the 20th Century.* New York: West/Wadsworth, 1998.

Daniels, Roger. *Guarding the Golden Door.* New York: Hill and Wang, 2004.

Handlin, Oscar, ed. *Immigration as a Factor in American History.* Englewood Cliffs, NJ: Prentice-Hall, 1959.

Love-Andrews, Devin. "Immigration Act of 1965." Available from http://campus.northpark.edu/history/WebChron/USA/ImmigrationAct.CP.html

IMMIGRATION COMMISSION, U.S.

See IMMIGRATION AND NATURALIZATION SERVICE (INS)

IMMIGRATION AND NATURALIZATION SERVICE (INS)

In 1891, Congress created the Bureau of Immigration, with the sole responsibility of enforcing United States immigration laws. Unfortunately, it only had 28 employees, tasked not only with keeping out the thousands of Chinese attempting to immigrate by many subterfuges but also with screening the millions of European immigrants to weed out legally excludable social undesirables such as lunatics and criminals. The 1891 amendment even expanded the list to include immigrants likely to become public charges and polygamists. The 1891 amendment expanded the reach of the law so that aliens could not only be excluded for actions prior to entry; they could henceforth be deported for actions occurring after entry that fell within the excludable charges. In addition to those laws, immigration officials had to screen immigrants for violation of the 1885 Alien Contract Labor Law, passed during the economic depression of 1883–1886. This law forbade an immigrant from contracting with an employer prior to immigrating to the United States. Avoiding this law only required that aliens wait until they cleared immigration to contract for labor, and labor contractors waited like jackals for the fresh immigrants to emerge from the ports of entry.

The new bureau did begin to make itself felt with Chinese immigration, and it proved successful in court. During the period from 1893 to 1894, the Bureau of Immigration managed to have 75 percent of its Chinese deportation and exclusion cases upheld. However, criminal convictions within the "crimes involving moral turpitude" provisions of the law and not the Chinese Exclusion Act provided the basis of removal from the United States.

The Bureau of Immigration would receive added resources and impetus with the passage of the 1924 Immigration Act. The passage of that legislation was the culmination of a movement that had begun in the previous century. In the 1890s, there was a growing conviction that fewer opportunities existed. The economic downturn of that decade, and the prevailing economic theories of the era, including the inability of the economy to grow sufficiently to produce enough jobs to match population growth, reinforced that sentiment. The Immigration Restriction League was founded in 1894 in Boston, Massachusetts. Harvard graduate Prescott F. Hall functioned as chief political officer, and membership included Henry Cabot Lodge, who functioned as spokesman. In addition to increased enforcement of existing immigration laws, the league pushed hard to increase the strength of the Bureau of Immigration, which by 1906 employed 1,200 people. The league also advocated general restrictions for immigration, principally involving a literacy test. Advocates felt that the literacy test would prevent the immigration of supposedly illiterate peasants from eastern and southern Europe and from Asia who brought with them unacceptable cultural baggage. The league gained strength as immigration rates increased. By 1910, the league reached its peak strength, shortly after immigration levels peaked in 1907.

In 1900, immigrants constituted 10 percent of the population of the United States. This was the first time immigration had accounted for the majority of the increase in population from a previous census. Within cities, the proportion of immigrants ran even higher. In the 12 largest cities, immigrants made up 40 percent of the urban dwellers, with second-generation Americans adding up to another 20 percent. The rate of immigration increased after 1900 to almost double the levels sustained through most of the second half of the 19th century.

Not only the cities felt the seismic shift in demographics; regional changes in proportions of immigrants also changed opinions about restrictions on immigration. In the southern United States, immigrants had been initially welcomed as cheap replacements for black slaves. The immigrants fit in well until they became so numerous that their alien culture began to clash with southern white culture. When this conflict occurred, southern whites no longer cared for the cheap labor.

The immense numbers of immigrants concentrated in urban centers constituted the largest proportion of urban poor. Consequently, social workers also began to argue for restrictions on immigration. As they saw it, the restrictions would be for the immigrants' own good.

However, the most significant urban-based source of restrictionist sentiment came from organized labor. Many of the members of organized labor came to the United States as immigrants themselves. Samuel Gompers, head of the American Federation of Labor (AFL), immigrated to the United States. However, the massive numbers of new immigrants, many of them now skilled workers, depressed wages, undermining one of the principle goals of organized labor: better wages. In addition, many of the immigrants coming to America after 1900 scared organized labor with their socialist ideas and talk. Labor leaders feared the radicalism would gain broad appeal. Radicalism was what business leaders had used previously to claim that organized labor constituted a threat to civil order, so that the use of force to quell the threat was justified. Organized labor did not want the newcomers giving business and government reason to fear radicalism within organized labor.

The fear of radicalism gained reinforcement with the assassination of President William McKinley in 1901. The assassin, an immigrant anarchist, gave restrictionists literally a "smoking gun." This act resulted in legislation passed in 1903 strengthening laws regarding anarchists, but it did not result in significant changes in immigration law.

With all the pressure building from the disparate coalition that constituted the restrictionist movement, in 1907 the Congress formed the U.S. Immigration Commission, alternatively known as the Dillingham Commission for its chair, Senator William P. Dillingham. Congress mandated the commission to study immigration and recommend actions that Congress should take. The commission's results appeared in a 41-volume report. The report provided, among other things, the origin of the terms "old" and "new" immigration in discussing immigration to the United States. The exact cut-off date between the two was left undefined; the real meaning was more closely associated with the source country than the date of arrival. Immigrants from northern and western Europe constituted the bulk of the earlier immigrants to the United States, and so became part of the "old"

immigration. Most immigrants from eastern and southern Europe, having arrived more recently, fell within the meaning of "new" immigration. Asian immigrants failed to meet either definition. They were unwanted in either case. The commission recommended a literacy test as the best means to control immigration. However, by 1911, even Senator Dillingham began to call for quotas.

The opposition to restrictionism now came from political machines and business. Political machines welcomed new immigrants, especially as ethnic blocks began to create their own political power. Immigrant groups formed their own political action organizations, primarily supporting Republican candidates and issues.

President Theodore Roosevelt, for instance, generally took a neutral stance on immigration. However, he appointed Oscar Straus, a Jewish American, as secretary of commerce and labor and, therefore, head of the Bureau of Immigration. Straus, an antirestrictionist, retarded anti-immigrant legislation. On the other hand, in 1905, a crisis occurred between Japan and California over immigration. Roosevelt, taking advantage of the international situation between Japan and Russia, negotiated a "Gentleman's Agreement." Japan had to "voluntarily" stop its citizens from immigrating to the United States, and in return, Roosevelt would convince the Russians to surrender control of Korea, Manchuria, and northern China to Japan.

Manufacturers strongly opposed the literacy test and other forms of immigration restriction. Business saw immigration and immigrants as a ready supply of cheap labor. This attitude changed as the demand for cheap labor declined and fear of radicals increased.

As a bill, the literacy test passed only the House in 1895, but it gained full passage in 1897, 1913, 1915, and 1917. Every time it passed Congress, the president in office at the time vetoed the bill. However, in 1917, the Congress overrode President Woodrow Wilson's veto, and the literacy test became law. It had little or no effect on immigration, as by the time it passed, World War I had halted almost all immigration. Moreover, education levels had improved in eastern and southern Europe to the point that almost all prospective immigrants could read and write. Enforcement of the test fell on the Bureau of Immigration inspectors at the designated ports of entry as part of the overall screening of immigrants.

Within weeks of passage of the law, agriculturists in the southwestern United States pressed for an exemption for Mexican laborers. Mexicans did not constitute a perceived threat, as they were close to the United States anyway, worked cheap, and went home. Secretary of Labor William Wilson, whose department included the Bureau of Immigration, subsequently exempted Mexicans from the existing immigration laws.

World War I brought fear and hatred into the political mainstream of America. The wartime propaganda fueled nascent fears of immigrants to a fever pitch. As intended by the propagandists, Americans directed their fear and hatred toward Germans, but all "hyphenated Americans" came under suspicion.

Anti-German propaganda contributed directly to nativism after World War I. The fear continued unabated; first of all, of refugees from the destruction and political turmoil the war had caused. The Russian Revolution in 1917, followed by labor disputes, unrest, and strikes at home and abroad poured fuel on the fires of fear in America. The strikes convinced business leaders that the value of the supply of cheap labor from immigration need not outweigh their fear of subversives.

All of this fear led to a postwar "Red Scare," the first of many in American history, and the Palmer Raids, led by that irascible defender of justice, J. Edgar Hoover. A terrorist bombing attack on Attorney General A. Mitchell Palmer's house in Washington, DC, touched off the wave of anticommunist hysteria. Palmer had presidential ambitions and hoped to use the notoriety to promote himself. Relying on Hoover, his eager subordinate, he undertook the "Palmer Raids," which consisted of Federal Bureau of Investigation (FBI) operations rounding up hundreds of aliens on questionable charges of subversive activity. Hoover, unable to prove criminal cases against the aliens, attempted to have them deported, although he had no legal authority to remove aliens from the United States (that authority resided with the Bureau of Immigration). President Woodrow Wilson, Secretary of Labor William Wilson, and Commissioner of Immigration Louis F. Post blocked Hoover's efforts to deport most of the aliens arrested.

In addition to the Red Scare, the effect of the nativistic fear from the war increased the popularity of a reborn Ku Klux Klan. The Klan gained in popularity at the same time new efforts to severely restrict immigration began to emerge from Congress. The KKK eventually grew to become, briefly, one of the most popular social organizations in the United States.

During the war, Congress had passed the Alien Act of 1918, allowing for the deportation of aliens suspected of hostile actions or beliefs, such as anarchists, communists, or other violent revolutionaries. The act, however, did not constitute a restriction on new immigration. After the war, in 1920, Congress passed the first immigration quota bill. However, Woodrow Wilson used his "pocket veto" authority to kill the bill as he left office.

President Warren G. Harding, who took office in 1921, did not oppose immigration restriction. Consequently, the Emergency Immigration Act of 1921 became law, and in 1922 Congress extended the law without difficulty. This act fixed the amount of aliens allowed to come into the United States and divided that fixed number into quotas based on national origin. The quota for Europeans established by this law stood at 3 percent of all foreign born in the United States at the time of the 1910 census. The act did not apply to immigration from the Western Hemisphere and expired in 1924.

Consequently, Congress set out to establish permanently the national origins quota system of immigration in 1924 with the Johnson-Reed Act. Representative Albert Johnson, one of the cosponsors, had a reputation as a radical and an anti-Semite, in contrast to Senator William Dillingham, the proponent of the literacy test and a relative moderate regarding restriction. The nature of the bill's sponsor indicates the level of emotionalism associated with the background of the bill.

There is very little doubt that the impetus for the bill still came from World War I. During the debate on the bill, Representative Grant M. Hudson of Michigan stated in justification for the restrictions, "Then came the World War and the conditions rising from it." Hudson then explained the necessity of the bill to stop the "hordes" from eastern and southern Europe and Asia. Further justifications included descriptions of the "cruelties" and "insufficiencies" of many would-be immigrants. Much of the argument relied on Darwinian anthropological reasoning, theorizing the superiority of some ethnic origins over others.

The 1924 Immigration Act passed, creating substantial quotas and containing several other provisions. The act exempted the Western Hemisphere. Legislators from the Southwest and West insisted that their agricultural constituents needed Mexican workers. The Gentleman's Agreement with Japan remained intact. The law created the Border Patrol and expanded the Bureau of Immigration, giving it both the power and the personnel to enforce the law. The 1929 Immigration Act made the 1924 act permanent.

The creation of the Border Patrol relieved the United States Army from responsibility for patrolling the land borders of the United States. Illegal immigrants from China through Mexico constituted the primary target of the Border Patrol initially. This is hardly surprising, because the new law did not restrict immigration from the western hemisphere, and illegal immigration from China through Mexico had been occurring since the passage of the Chinese Exclusion Act in 1882. For 42 years there had been no agency specifically responsible for enforcing the Exclusion Act. It is interesting (and not surprising) that many of the early recruits for the Border Patrol came from the Ku Klux Klan. The Klan had grown to be the largest social organization in the United States by the time of the creation of the Border Patrol, and the ideas advocated by the Klan did not conflict with the intended mission of the Border Patrol.

Enforcement of the new quotas of the 1924 Immigration Act fell on two departments that had to coordinate their activities. The Bureau of Immigration ensured that applicants qualified for admission as immigrants, and the State Department ensured adherence to the visa quotas. European refugees from eastern and southern Europe did not constitute a major source of illegal immigration, as they did not have the resources, or the support networks, to travel to a third country such as Mexico or Canada and attempt entry by crossing a land border. Therefore, most enforcement of the 1924 Act, as well as all of the other exclusionary laws, occurred at ports of entry by Bureau of Immigration inspectors.

The new laws set quotas of immigrants, and the limits appeared harsh. Nevertheless, in the years following enactment, the quotas, however harsh, were not filled. In some years, more aliens departed the United States than arrived. By the time of the Great Depression, the "immigrant wave" that began in the 19th century had ended.

The exemption granted to the Western Hemisphere had the effect of shifting the source of new immigrants to Mexico and Canada instead of northern and western Europe, as intended. The resources committed to enforcing the act did not result in any significant impact. Deportations never constituted a significant percentage of immigrants. In 1926, the Bureau of Immigration managed to deport 16,000 persons, an unusually high number. Immigration officials did not exceed 20,000 deportations in one year until 1948. The 1924 act did succeed in reducing the recruitment levels of the Ku Klux Klan, whose membership dropped significantly after 1924. However, during the Great Depression, Herbert Hoover issued an executive order to use the "public charge" exclusion grounds to bar Mexicans from entry into the United States.

During World War II, attitudes in the United States toward immigration changed dramatically. The incongruity of being China's ally and barring immigration with them at the same time ended in 1943 with the repeal of the Chinese Exclusion Act. The wartime economy boomed, and the military demands for manpower and industrial output created a tremendous demand for fresh sources of labor. The business community and the government of the United States turned to the closest source of manpower: Mexico.

Until 1924 and the creation of the U.S. Border Patrol, no law enforcement presence existed on the Mexican border with the United States, and Mexicans came and went legally and illegally without much concern. As stated earlier, the U.S. government provided specific exemptions for Mexican workers to the literacy requirements of 1917, and the 1924 act did not restrict immigration from the Western Hemisphere. The Mexican Revolution in the early decades of the 20th century accelerated immigration from Mexico with an increase in refugees from the war.

However, after 1920, American business, including agriculture, began to rely more heavily on native-born

American labor. African Americans in particular found employment in agriculture in the Southwest, filling the demand that had been supplied by Mexican labor. Demand for Mexican labor waned until World War II.

World War II massively increased the demand for labor at home, with the mobilization of men for military service and the rapid expansion of industrial capacity to produce war goods combined with the need to maintain the production of most domestic consumer products. Working women accounted for some increases in the labor pool, but outside sources became necessary, especially in the Southwest United States, where many of the new shipbuilding and aerospace manufacturing facilities were. The primary foreign source became Mexico, with the creation of two war programs, a railroad worker program, and, more important, the Bracero Program to import agricultural workers.

The creation of the Bracero Program in 1942 led to a migratory pattern that has changed only in legality since that time. In the same year, Congress passed legislation transferring the Bureau of Immigration from the Department of Labor to the Department of Justice and changed its name to the Immigration and Naturalization Service. Much of the impetus for the change had come from J. Edgar Hoover and the FBI. Hoover wanted authority to enforce immigration law as a weapon to use against communists and other subversives. However, early FBI frustrations in the handling of immigration cases, as well as the other responsibilities heaped on the FBI during World War II, resulted in the waning of Hoover's interest in specific authority for enforcement of immigration law being accorded to the FBI. Consequently, administration of the Bracero Program, and enforcement, fell on the new Immigration and Naturalization Service.

The Bracero Program addressed the labor shortage claim by agricultural employers in the Southwest United States. On the basis of this claim, the United States entered into an agreement with Mexico to allow Mexican nationals to temporarily work in the United States. The agreement provided safeguards for the workers, called *braceros*, intended to ensure that they were not exploited and were properly treated. This agreement became Public Law 45. The program officially terminated in 1947, but under pressure from

agricultural business interests and the Mexican government, the program started officially again in 1951 as Public Law 78. However, in the interim, the program had continued "unofficially." One characteristic of the program arose from the avoidance or circumvention of many of the protections in the Bracero Program by employers. Another aspect was that thousands of braceros overstayed their permits, becoming illegal aliens.

In response to the growth of illegal immigration, the first congressional effort at passage of employer sanctions came on February 5, 1952. Senator Paul Douglas of Illinois submitted an employer sanctions amendment to the 1952 Immigration and Naturalization Act on the floor of the Senate. The 1951 Truman Commission on Migratory Labor had suggested that employer sanctions might be a useful tool in combating illegal immigration. Instead, Congress passed what became known as the "Texas Proviso" as part of the 1952 McCarran-Walter Act. This provision of the act specifically prohibited criminal penalties for employers who "harbored" illegal aliens. Although any other type of assistance to an illegal alien, such as providing room and board, constituted felony harboring, the most significant assistance one could provide, a job, did not meet the statutory definition of harboring. Truman vetoed the act, but Congress voted to override his veto and the act became law.

Efforts to stem illegal immigration after passage of the Texas Proviso concentrated on apprehending illegal immigrants. As part of the effort to combat illegal immigration, the U.S. Border Patrol conducted "Operation Wetback" in 1954. The operation, led by the commissioner of the Immigration and Naturalization Service, General Joseph Swing (ret.), had a military flavor and involved approximately 800 border patrol agents. The sweep began in Los Angeles, then moved east across the Southwest. In all it netted approximately 1.3 million illegal aliens. Though acclaimed by the Border Patrol as a success, no means of measuring what effect the program had on illegal immigration existed.

The numbers apprehended in Operation Wetback were deceptive. The Border Patrol "dried out" many of the illegal aliens by making them braceros, in contravention of the agreements with Mexico. This process helped to encourage illegal immigration rather than deter it. In addition, the dramatic increases in the number of braceros allowed into the United States reduced the demand for illegal workers and increased the opportunities to be "dried out." In any case, Operation Wetback predated the beginning of the upsurge in illegal immigration that began in 1964.

The event that triggered the increase in illegal immigration in 1964 was the repeal of the Bracero Program. Despite the program's popularity with employers, by 1964, public opposition to the Bracero Program had grown due to the exposure by the media and the growing civil rights movement of the living conditions of migrant participants. In addition, labor, church, and ethnic organizations had voiced opposition to the continuation of the Bracero Program. After the termination of the program, illegal immigration increased immediately.

The end of the Bracero Program did not stop Mexican migrants from coming to the United States, but it did change the nature of the migration. According to a RAND Corporation study, "Perhaps the most significant legacy of the Bracero Program for the country was that what was thought to be mostly temporary migration often turned into permanent immigration." This should not have come as a surprise, as the Department of State had warned that if the program ended, the Mexican workers would come anyway, as illegal aliens. The upsurge in illegal immigration clearly dates from the termination of the Bracero Program. Unfortunately, no effort to increase the resources of the Immigration and Naturalization Service followed the legislative acts that dramatically increased the enforcement problem that the INS now faced.

The rise in immigration, both legal and illegal, during the 1970s and 1980s inspired a movement to reform immigration law and policy. The majority of the public was convinced that illegal immigration was a problem. Popular consensus held that illegal aliens took jobs from American citizens and legal immigrants. The American public also blamed the erosion of wages and working conditions on the employment of undocumented workers.

During the 1970s, successive administrations proposed some form of employer sanctions to address the problem of illegal immigration. In 1973, the Nixon administration issued the Crampton Report, which recommended sanctions against employers as a means of restricting illegal immigration. The Ford administration's Domestic Council Committee Report on Illegal Aliens also recommended employer sanctions as a system for controlling the problem. The Alien Employment Act of 1977 suggested employer sanctions as a possible policy choice for combating illegal immigration.

During the same time period, some states assumed the mantle of leadership in addressing illegal immigration. Again, California came to the forefront of legislation. The dozen states that attempted to address illegal immigration all used some form of employer sanctions, banning the employment of illegal aliens and providing for penalties against employers who did so. However, the states passing these laws, including California, failed to enforce them. It was a surprise when the U.S. Supreme Court upheld the California law in *DeCanas v. Bica.* Even though the law was upheld, it remained unenforced. State officials responsible for enforcing the law proved ignorant of the Supreme Court decision and allowed the law to lapse through neglect.

In 1978, Congress formed the Select Commission on Immigration and Refugee Policy. The commission concluded that controlling illegal immigration constituted the most crucial challenge facing the United States in the realm of immigration policy. The commission recommended employer sanctions as a means of addressing the challenge.

The existence of a problem with illegal immigration was supported by the 1980 census. According to this census, there were 2.1 million illegal aliens in the United States. The results also indicated that certain states were more significantly affected than others. The states of California, New York, Texas, Illinois, and Florida contained 81 percent of the illegal aliens counted by the Census Bureau. The same states also received a disproportionate share of legal immigration. Although they contained only 34 percent of the total population, these five states absorbed 67 percent of legal immigrants. These demographic changes certainly added to the public perception of an immigration problem in these states.

The debate over immigration, when reduced to its basic form, consists of two viewpoints: those favoring immigration and those supporting restriction. These two basic viewpoints cut across "liberal" and "conservative" lines, political parties, ethnicities, and social classes. Beyond this basic division, there are a myriad of reasons for either position. The heterogeneous nature of the opposing viewpoints makes it difficult for a consensus to be formed in either camp. This was the environment that produced the Immigration Reform and Control Act (IRC) of 1986.

The IRC compromised the opposing positions on immigration by providing employer sanctions, which were expected to reduce illegal immigration, and an "amnesty" program for illegal immigrants who had resided continuously in the United States since January 1, 1982.

This act made neither side happy. Opponents of employer sanctions attacked the sanctions provisions on the basis that they would lead to discrimination. Amnesty was attacked for possibly encouraging further illegal immigration and exacerbating the number of immigrants through chain migration. In the end, both sides agreed that the act failed to accomplish any of its goals. We will see how the political process that shaped IRC, resulting in its inherent contradictions, contributed to the nature of the impact the law made after its implementation. Compromises made to gain passage for the law resulted in a compromised effectiveness. The process of political compromise doomed the act to failure in achieving its intended goals.

Those opposed to employer sanctions claimed that the change in public mood and perceptions was the result of suspicions being engendered by the media. Immigration advocates provided alternative solutions to controlling illegal immigration. One argument centered on the demographics of illegal immigration. Because most illegal aliens came from Mexico, more effort to seal the Mexican border was advocated. The opposition to sanctions also suggested that more resources be committed to keeping control of the interior of the United States and removing illegal aliens if they were located. Both positions found a place in the compromise legislation.

Proponents of sanctions maintained that for the program to be successful, several necessary prerequisites must be met. One prerequisite was that the Immigration and Naturalization Service "would have to be funded adequately and modernized in order to make the law work." Furthermore, the Border Patrol needed to be expanded to stop illegal immigration across the border with Mexico. As long as it remained relatively easy to cross the border illegally, employers would have a ready supply of cheap, illegal labor and would therefore have a cost-beneficial alternative to complying with the law. Some advocated the creation of a national identification system as a necessary prerequisite. Consequently, the IRC provided for increases in the numbers of Border Patrol agents and special agents of the investigative branch of the Immigration and Naturalization Service.

The investigations branch of INS was charged with enforcement of immigration law in the interior of the United States. It had originally been composed of inspectors assigned to working cases away from the ports of entry. In the 1960s, the title of these inspectors was changed to "investigator," and many Border Patrol agents began to transfer into the branch. By the 1970s, new investigators were being hired directly into the job, and the title changed again to "criminal investigator." In 1987, as a result of IRC, the position was upgraded to "special agent," classifying immigration investigators together with other federal law enforcement investigators.

President Ronald Reagan signed the Immigration Reform and Control Act into law on November 6, 1986. Its passage into law did not end the debating. Immediately after its signing, complaints of discrimination arose. In congressional hearings, some alleged that the administration had no intention of enforcing the antidiscrimination provisions of the law. Other questioning attacked the administration for insufficient budgeting to make the law work. The commissioner of the INS, Alan Nelson, testified to Congress that INS intended to rely on voluntary compliance rather than aggressive enforcement.

The administration's plan to rely on voluntary cooperation did not reassure the advocates of employer sanctions. Representative Dan Lungren of California denied accusations that the law would not work or that the government did not want it to work. John R. Schroeder, assistant commissioner of the INS, argued that IRC should control the borders by removing the work incentive for illegal immigration. He also argued that the sanctions provisions should not be punitive.

As a program to combat illegal immigration, IRC failed miserably. Inadequate enforcement by INS undermined its credibility and exacerbated hostility toward it as an organization. The legalization programs, amnesty, and the special agricultural workers provided the biggest opportunity for fraudulent immigration since the San Francisco earthquake and fire enabled Chinese to claim they were born in the United States. The resulting explosion in now-legal immigrant applications overwhelmed INS and led to numerous adjudication scandals in the 1990s stemming from inadequate background checks on applicants. Throughout the 1990s, opponents of employer sanctions succeeded in removing almost all possibility of penalties being levied against employers and shifted the focus of enforcement back on arresting the aliens instead of punishing the employer.

The Border Patrol did not escape criticism either. IRC authorized increases in the number of Border Patrol agents to increase vigilance along the U.S.–Mexican border. However, the Border Patrol increased its personnel at a slow rate. This came in part from intransigence in the Border Patrol to change its recruiting and training scale and methods and in part due to the laggardly manner in which Congress funded the positions authorized by IRC.

In addition, the Border Patrol dispersed its limited resources by unilaterally expanding the scope of its duties. In addition to interdicting illegal aliens, the Border Patrol also assumed primary responsibility for interdicting drugs. Numerous other agencies had drug enforcement authority, but only the Border Patrol (and INS) had authority to enforce immigration law.

As if that were not enough, the Border Patrol also took it upon itself to enforce employer sanctions. It had no mandate to do so, and Congress had no intent when it passed IRC that the Border Patrol would be the agency that would conduct sanctions investigations. Besides contributing to the dissipation of Border Patrol effort, the enforcement of sanctions by Border Patrol contributed to the unevenness and inconsistency in the manner that employer sanctions were enforced. The Border Patrol conducted its inspections radically differently than the manner in which INS conducted its

investigations. Consequently, some employers investigated by both the Border Patrol and the INS received radically different experiences and results.

As a result of the dissipation of Border Patrol resources, the amount of "line watch" hours conducted by the Border Patrol actually declined after the passage of IRC. Congress had intended that interdiction of illegal crossings of the border would be an inherent component of the success of employer sanctions. The failure to restrict illegal immigration at the border contributed instead to the failure of employer sanctions, and INS in general, to accomplish its goals.

The INS plan of enforcement ensured that any hope of success for employer sanctions vanished. INS intended to rely primarily on voluntary compliance by employers who did not like the law in the first place. The law provided no carrot for employers, and the INS never picked up a stick to provide a negative incentive. INS failed to control its enforcement effort, which deprived the government of the only incentive for employers who were dependent on illegal workers to change their employment patterns. The only thing INS seems to have done correctly was to concentrate on small employers. However, even this was done for all the wrong reasons. As a consequence, INS could not claim justification for its actions and was duly criticized by supporters of the law for not going after larger employers.

After the failure of IRC, attempts to combat illegal immigration continued, resulting in some legislation but no serious impact. Economic factors typically motivate immigration. The booming 1990s provided plenty of motivation. INS downgraded emphasis on employer sanctions and shifted its focus to rapid approval of applications, deportation of criminal aliens, and an increased emphasis by the Border Patrol on the border with Mexico.

No significant changes to immigration law occurred until 1996. However, in California, the restrictionist movement that had started in the 1970s continued. Governor Pete Wilson led efforts to bar citizenship to children of illegal aliens, require illegal aliens to pay for emergency medical assistance, deny illegal aliens admission to public school, and require the issuance of a national identity card. Much of this angst in California derived from the massive economic blow the state felt with the end of the Cold War. Numerous military bases closed, such as the Presidio in San

Francisco, Fort Ord near Monterey, and El Toro Marine Air Base in Orange County. The defense industry, and in particular the aerospace industry, had to downsize significantly. Companies such as McDonnell-Douglas had difficulty operating without Cold War military orders. Boeing eventually bought McDonnell-Douglas, and most of its operations have moved out of California. The economic readjustments in California caused a great deal of pain, and those feeling the pain had little sympathy for illegal aliens.

Popular feeling ran decidedly against immigration. The public had no support for continued illegal immigration. Polls also indicated that the public overall supported general reductions in immigration. As indicated earlier, restriction began in the 1970s and continued through the 1980s into the last decade of the 20th century. Just as restrictionism grew at the beginning of the 20th century as a result of social friction generated by uncontrolled immigration, at the end of the century, uncontrolled illegal immigration created the same popular sentiment to restrict immigration. Immigration in the 1980s reached massive levels, although no conscious decision to allow such high levels of immigration had occurred.

However, instead of taking steps to control illegal immigration, the government of the United States expended most of its energy and effort in speeding up processing and reducing the time necessary to immigrate, to naturalize, and to pass through immigration inspection at airports. In 1996, a major scandal broke involving naturalization in the Los Angeles District Office in California. The INS, in the interest of speeding up the process, and at the insistence of officials of the administration of President Bill Clinton, had failed to do criminal background checks on naturalization applicants. Consequently, thousands of aliens with criminal records, who should have had their applications denied, instead became United States citizens. Although INS claimed that most of the applicants had concealed minor criminal convictions, some of the new citizens were also registered sex offenders with felony convictions for child molestation and rape.

The only program to come out of INS during the 1990s to combat illegal immigration besides the failed IRC came from the initiative of an employee, in the face of official opposition. Operation Hold the Line began in El Paso, Texas, in 1994. Border Patrol Sector Chief Silvestre Reyes felt that the Border Patrol's tactics of hiding and lying in wait for the illegal aliens to cross the border failed to deter illegal immigration. In an effort to increase officer presence on the border, the sector chief ordered his agents to make a visible presence along the border to deter aliens from crossing illegally in the first place. The operation succeeded, and the program expanded under the name Operation Gatekeeper to include most areas of high illegal crossing traffic. The only problem with the program came from the smugglers' response. To avoid the visible patrols, the smugglers, or "coyotes," took their contraband, or "pollos," into more remote areas, often at great risk to the lives of the aliens.

In addition to welfare reform, in 1996 Congress passed a major reorganization of immigration deportation and exclusion provisions in the 1996 Illegal Immigration Reform and Immigrant Responsibility Act (IIRAIRA, pronounced "irah irah"). This law expanded the "aggravated felony" definition to many more crimes, denied relief from deportation to "aggravated felons," applied the law to any conviction for an aggravated felony regardless of when it occurred, denied bond to aggravated felons, and limited appeals to only the administrative Board of Immigration Appeals. All of these provisions faced challenges in court, and all have been upheld. The law also increased the sentence for a conviction of a deported alien returning to the United States with an aggravated felony for a prior conviction. This provision spurred serious attempts by INS to attack recidivism among serious criminal aliens who routinely returned to the United States illegally after deportation. The law also created a few new "removal" charges, such as for domestic violence convictions and terrorism. In reality, although this law catered to restrictionists, it did little to stop illegal immigrants, most of whom do not spend time in local jails, enabling INS agents to interview them. It also did nothing about the asylum program.

The most interesting aspect of IIRAIRA is that it passed in a period when the American economy was growing by leaps and bounds and unemployment was low. This evidence alone shows the level that restrictionism had reached by the mid-1990s. On the other hand, aside from Operation Gatekeeper, little enforcement effort occurred that was directed at stopping new illegal immigration.

By the mid-1990s, half of the aliens coming to the United States did so with visas, making lawful entries. At the same time Congress strengthened laws to remove criminal aliens, it massively increased the numbers of worker visas (H-1B visas) for nurses and computer engineers. Many of these nonimmigrants become illegal aliens when their admissions expire, their company goes out of business, or they simply change jobs. Many more aliens come as tourists, many without visas under new agreements reached with "friendly" countries, and settle in the United States illegally.

The catastrophic event that led to the destruction of INS came on September 11, 2001. Nineteen aliens succeed in hijacking four airliners. Two crashed into the twin towers of the World Trade Center of New York, one crashed into the Pentagon in Washington, DC, and one crashed into an empty field in Pennsylvania. The fear and alarm caused by this terrorist attack led to the creation of the Department of Homeland Security. President George W. Bush signed the bill reorganizing most of law enforcement in the federal government on November 25, 2002. On March 1, 2003, three new agencies rose from the ashes of what had been the Immigration and Naturalization Service. The Bureau of Customs and Border Protection combined the U.S. Border Patrol, U.S. Coast Guard, Immigration Inspections, Customs Inspections, and Department of Agriculture inspections into a single agency. The Bureau of Immigration and Customs Enforcement (ICE) combined Customs Investigations, INS Investigations, the INS Detention and Removal Branch, the Air Marshals Service, and the Federal Protective Police into a single interior enforcement. The remainder of INS, the services that handled applications and their adjudications, became its own agency, the Bureau of Immigration and Citizenship Services. The stated primary objective of the Department of Homeland Security and its constituent agencies is combating terrorism.

Although INS has been broken into several parts, immigration law has not really changed much. Plans to break INS up into enforcement and service halves predated September 11, 2001. The terrorist attacks served to facilitate and expedite the breakup. The breakup into Homeland Security became more extensive

than the plans that predated September 11, 2001. The surprising development is that Customs and several other agencies also became part of the reorganization.

Certainly, terrorist attacks by aliens had occurred before in the 1990s. Mir Aimal Kansi gunned down several people outside CIA headquarters. The most serious occurred in 1993, when a group of extremist Muslims, led by Sheik Omar Abdel Rahman, attacked the World Trade Center in New York with the intent of toppling one of the towers. Sheik Rahman had originally obtained legal permanent resident alien status through fraud. When this was discovered, INS revoked Rahman's status. However, he requested asylum, and his application was pending at the time of the bombing.

After the September 11 terrorist attack, several immigration initiatives began to address past failures in enforcement. A registration program (the National Security Entry-Exit Registration System) began for nonimmigrants from target countries, but this simply constituted the application of preexisting law that had been allowed to lapse. The Alien Absconder Initiative was aimed at clearing the immense backlog of cases in which aliens ordered deported had not been arrested and removed, but this was no more than remedial action in cases that should have been investigated years earlier but in which inadequate resources had prevented INS from doing so. Finally, Congress funded a new computer tracking system for alien students. INS had requested and Congress had denied funds for the system prior to September 11, 2001. After the attacks, several members of Congress, some of whom had voted against the computer system when INS requested it, criticized INS for not having a system to track alien students. Such are the politics of immigration.

The federal government no longer has any agency specifically responsible for enforcing immigration law. The Border Patrol, as its name implies, patrols the border and has no interior enforcement authority. Because its emphasis is now specifically stopping terrorists, nonterrorist illegal aliens are not a top priority. ICE, the agency with interior enforcement authority, has a diverse set of missions. As with any agency with multiple missions, it must prioritize its resources. Under INS, investigations had to be prioritized between criminal aliens, fraud, smuggling, and employer sanctions. Now, under ICE, immigration is a low priority, and the enforcement of its administrative provisions is perceived as being nonprestigious to a management team that has little or no background in immigration. Consequently, enforcement of immigration law in the interior of the United States is waning rapidly. Most enforcement of immigration is again now, as it was at the beginning of the 20th century, focused on the ports of entry and the inspection process. Instead of a more efficient immigration enforcement agency, September 11, 2001, has produced a disjointed, uncoordinated, and minimized immigration law enforcement effort. It remains to be seen if improvements will be made to ensure adequate enforcement. What is certain is that there is no longer a single immigration agency.

—Lonnie Wilson

See also Asian Immigration Law, Chinese Exclusion Act, Gentlemen's Agreement, Immigration Act of 1965, Immigration Reform and Control Act of 1986

Suggested Reading

Bodnar, John. *The Transplanted: A History of Immigrants in Urban America.* Bloomington: Indiana University Press, 1985.

Daniels, Roger. *Not Like Us: Immigrants and Minorities in America 1890–1924.* Chicago: Ivan R. Dee, 1997.

Gyory, Andrew. *Closing the Gate: Race, Politics, and the Chinese Exclusion Act.* Chapel Hill: University of North Carolina Press, 1998.

Handlin, Oscar. *The Uprooted: The Epic Story of the Great Migration That Made the American People.* 2nd ed. New York: Little, Brown, 1979.

Hays, Samuel P. *The Response to Industrialism 1885–1914.* Chicago: University of Chicago Press, 1957.

Lee, Erika. *At America's Gates: Chinese Immigration During the Exclusion Era, 1882–1943.* Chapel Hill: University of North Carolina Press, 2003.

Reimers, David M. *Still the Golden Door: The Third World Comes to America.* New York: Columbia University Press, 1985.

Reimers, David M. *Unwelcome Strangers: American Identity and the Turn Against Immigration.* New York: Columbia University Press, 1998.

Salyer, Lucy E. *Laws Harsh as Tigers: Chinese Immigrants and the Shaping of Modern Immigration Law.* Chapel Hill: University of North Carolina Press, 1995.

Ueda, Reed. *Postwar Immigrant America: A Social History.* New York: Bedford Books, 1994.

Yans-McLaughlin, Virginia, ed. *Immigration Reconsidered: History, Sociology, and Politics.* New York: Oxford University Press, 1990.

⊞ IMMIGRATION REFORM AND CONTROL ACT OF 1986

The Immigration Reform and Control Act restricted not so much the number of immigrants allowed in the nation but who could be employed. Prior immigration policies had focused primarily on restricting, amending, or maintaining the number and nationality of immigrants allowed in America. The Immigration and Naturalization Act differed slightly from this trend.

In 1924, the U.S. government established the quota system, a policy that allotted a specific number of immigrant visas by country. As a result of racial perceptions, no immigrants from Asian countries would be admitted. The Immigration Act of 1924 guided immigration policy until 1952, when it was amended. The Immigration and Naturalization Service, created in 1940, was an agency in the Department of Justice from 1940 to 2002. It originally oversaw the admittance, exclusion, and deportation of all aliens. Furthermore, it investigated candidates for citizenship and provided the textbooks required for teaching the information necessary to gain citizenship. In 2002, the functions of the Immigration and Naturalization Service were transferred to the Department of Homeland Security.

In 1952, the U.S. Congress passed the Immigration and Nationality Act, also known as the McCarran-Walter Act. The Immigration and Nationality Act gave the president power to exclude immigrants thought to be a threat to national security and increased the number of immigrants from Asian countries. The act raised the Asian immigration number to only 100 people a year despite opposition from the executive branch. Major immigration reform would not occur for almost another decade and a half. Still, in 1965, the Johnson administration was successful in passing the Immigration Act of 1965. As a result of the Civil Rights movement, Lyndon Johnson passed multiple bills granting African Americans relief from political oppression. Johnson believed that past immigration policies also were racist and biased. The Johnson administration successfully abolished the oppressive quota system and granted visas on the basis of family reunification, not by place of origin. The 1965 act opened the doors of America to immigrants. Twenty-one years passed before major reform took place in 1986. This time; however, the focus was on employment restriction.

Although the Immigration Reform and Control Act supplemented the Immigration Naturalization Act, it can be seen as an original piece of legislation. As a result of the Immigration Act of 1965, immigrants from Asia and Latin America poured into the United States in alarming numbers. Large numbers of people from Latin American countries, primarily Mexico, immigrated to the United States illegally and obtained numerous jobs. Many in the United States felt that America had no control over its borders. Others, however, felt that Latin Americans would cause social, political, and economic problems similar to those in their native countries. Consequently, fear of American unemployment started to grow, as many illegal immigrants began holding jobs previously held by U.S. citizens. Therefore, after much deliberation in Congress, the U.S. government passed the Immigration Reform and Control Act of 1986.

The Immigration Reform and Control Act (IRC) was revolutionary in that it, for the first time, regulated undocumented employment. The IRC required all employers to make a background check of future employees as well as any employed after November 1966. Employers had to verify the legal status of immigrants and eligibility to work in the United States. After this process was completed, employers had to complete an INS I-9 form that stated the status of each employee and listed the documents used to verify an immigrant's legal status to work. Acceptable forms of identification to prove an alien's identity and eligibility for work include a U.S. passport or an Alien Registration Receipt card. The IRC further established sanctions prohibiting employers from knowingly hiring or recruiting illegal immigrants. In 1998, the Immigration and Naturalization Service (INS) reported that it had apprehended and expelled 1,008,145 immigrants. Of those, 985,479 (97.8 percent) were found to have entered the United States

illegally or, as the INS states, "entered without inspection." If an employer was found guilty of knowingly hiring illegal aliens, that employer could be fined anywhere from $250 to $10,000. If the offense was repeated, the employer could serve up to six months in jail.

The act further authorized legalization. Legalization created a situation where immigrants who had entered the United States illegally since 1982 could obtain temporary and then permanent status as citizens of the United States. In addition, a new classification of workers, known as seasonal agricultural workers (SAW), was created with the intention of providing these immigrants the chance at applying for legalization. As a result of the SAW provision, more than 1.3 million applicants were accepted in the United States. Furthermore, the act allocated five thousand special preference visas during 1987 and 1988 to nations affected by the Immigration Act of 1965. Outside the INS, many referred to this provision as "the lottery." Finally, the act established "get tough" provisions, hoping that these would reduce the number of illegal immigrants pouring into the United States; one such provision strengthened the boarder patrol.

By 1998, about 2.68 million illegal immigrants, 88 percent of those legalized aliens, had obtained legal status through the legalization process. Still, despite these numbers, the Immigration Reform and Control Act failed to keep illegal immigrants from crossing the boarder. Illegal immigration continued to grow through the 1980s and 1990s, encouraging many to call for stricter immigration laws.

—Scott Keys

See also Asian Immigration Law, Immigration Act of 1965, Immigration and Naturalization Service (INS)

Suggested Reading

Daniels, Roger. *Guarding the Golden Door.* New York: Hill and Wang, 2004.

⊞ INDIAN PEACE POLICY

See Bureau of Indian Affairs

⌗ INDIAN REMOVAL ACT OF 1830

As the United States steadily grew in population during its infancy, the need for more land became an unavoidable topic. The most feasible and easiest route to solving the problem, as far as Congress could see, was simply to remove the American Indians from their land. Although numerous treaties had been signed with the Indians throughout the first years of America's existence designating some lands as off-limits, the white man, Congress, and a large part of the nation felt the need to terminate such contracts and send the Indians west. The premiere example of this sort of diplomacy is the Indian Removal Act of 1830.

On May 26, 1830, the Indian Removal Act legally allowed state and federal agencies to facilitate the removal of all Indian tribes east of the Mississippi River to various locations situated in the West. During the years preceding 1830, tribes were moved to various lands in Arkansas and Tennessee, but by 1830 this land was also coveted by white settlers pushing west. Instead, the territory of Oklahoma was designated for the Indians, without concern for their lifestyles, background, or livelihood. The act, which was signed by President Andrew Jackson almost immediately after being passed, was lobbied for heavily on behalf of the Southern states. Georgia, the state that stood to gain the most if Indian tribes vacated its land, led the charge for the removal act. The Senate passed the bill with 28 votes in favor of and 19 opposed, and the House of Representatives split even more closely, with 102 voting in favor of the bill and 97 against. Although it was named the Indian Removal Act, the actual bill did not immediately demand the vacation of tribes from the east. Instead, the president of the United States was given the power (meaning the financial means and ability) to directly negotiate with Indian tribes to obtain all lands that lay within the boundaries of an existing state. In return, lands lying to the west and not part of an existing state would be given back to the Indians.

President Jackson was a heavy proponent of this bill from its inception into Congress and did not try to hide his thoughts. He did, indeed, favor a plan to move the Indians west, but for reasons concerning both national security and for the security of the Indians themselves. According to Jackson's own personal writings, he felt that Indians would be targets of jealousy if they were to remain on lands lying within state borders. He also felt that as a result, there would be too many opportunities for violence and destruction, either of land or life.

The Reservation Policy, as we understand it today, did not exist at the time of the Indian Removal Act. Instead, it was developed primarily during the presidency of Ulysses S. Grant, nearly 40 years later. During the late 1860s and 1870s, the Indian Wars began to cause a large problem in domestic defense for the military. The "Indian Problem," as it was dubbed, consisted of constant fighting between settlers and Indians as the perpetual idea of Manifest Destiny moved people westward. This caused the trespassing of white settlers on Indian territory and hunting grounds, much of which had been guaranteed to the Indians through federal charters and treaties.

The policy that emerged from Grant's presidency centered on the assimilation of Indians into American culture, along with the granting of citizenship to them. Certain tracts of land were to be set aside strictly for use as Indian land, and the reservation systems were to be run not by government officials but rather by Christian leaders, a role that the Quakers aptly filled. The Indians were to become good Christians, which would in turn lead to their qualification as citizens of the United States. In addition to the Christianization of the Indians, they were also to be taught the art of agriculture as they were assimilated into the white lifestyle. This made sense because most reservations were not given enough land to hunt on, and those that did saw little to no game; certainly not enough to sustain an entire tribe. However, in many instances, the land was not adequate for farming. Although many reservations received federal stipends for food and supplies, in many cases the delivery of such stipends was undependable and erratic.

The reservation policy under President Grant nearly ended up a complete failure. In many cases, the land tracts did not sufficiently suit the needs of the tribes placed on them. In addition, corruption spread among various Indian agencies, and the overall standard of living for the Indians was considered poor at best. After seeing the failure of the reservation system, many tribes tried to revert back to their previous lifestyles and left the reservation system. Other tribes, such as the Lakota and Nez Perce, saw the conditions of Indians on the reservation and opted to either fight the U.S. Army or flee. Under President Rutherford B. Hayes, Grant's policy was completely disposed of and all religious groups that had been placed in charge of various reservations were removed.

What replaced the Grant policy was a policy that awarded land individually to Indians instead of awarding large tracts to tribes. The Dawes Act, which was passed in 1887, was the bill that enacted this policy. Although the policy was better for the federal government, the plight of the Indians was hardly improved. This policy of individual appropriations lasted until the Indian Reorganization Act of 1934.

—*Matthew Adam Henderson*

See also BUREAU OF INDIAN AFFAIRS, CAHUILLA NATION, CREEK NATION, TRAIL OF TEARS

Suggested Reading

Ehle, John. *Trail of Tears: The Rise and Fall of the Cherokee Nation.* New York: Doubleday Press, 1988.

Foreman, Grant. *Indian Removal: The Emigration of the Five Civilized Tribes of Indians.* Norman: University of Oklahoma Press, 1993.

Gates, Paul Wallace, ed. *The Rape of Indian Lands.* New York: Arno Press, 1979.

Perdue, Theda, and Michael D. Green, eds. *The Cherokee Removal: A Brief History with Documents.* Boston: Bedford St. Martin's Press, 1995.

Prucha, Francis Paul. *The Indian in American History.* New York: Holt, Rinehart and Winston, 1971.

⊞ INDIAN REORGANIZATION ACT

See BLACKFOOT NATION, BUREAU OF INDIAN AFFAIRS

⊞ INYO COUNTY, CALIFORNIA

The gold rush created enormous population growth in California during the 1850s. However, as the population grew, success in small-scale mining diminished over time. The diminishing returns led to skepticism over reports of new gold strikes by the later 1850s.

The discovery of the Comstock Lode in 1859 reignited interest in a way gold could not. It generated a new enthusiasm among a population suffering from high unemployment and created a rush of miners and prospectors across the Sierra Nevada to work in the Comstock and also to explore other eastern Sierra regions.

The Owens Valley, in the future Inyo County, California, was one of these other areas where silver was found. The pioneers and entrepreneurs who opened and operated this region were representative of those who moved east and north to the new areas. Inyo was unique in that the supply and administrative centers were separate from the actual mining towns geographically but very similar to them in culture.

The earliest Anglo American to visit the Owens Valley was the explorer and mountain man Joseph Walker. Walker had entered California in 1833, crossing the Sierra well to the north of the Owens Valley and viewing Yosemite Valley in the process. He then traveled down the San Joaquin River, turned east, recrossed the Sierra through Walker's Pass, and turned north through the Owens Valley. Returning in 1843 with the Chiles-Walker parties, Walker again passed through the Owens Valley from north to south and crossed the Sierra via Walker's Pass with some fifty immigrants. In 1845, Walker was with John C. Frémont on the expedition that would play a critical role in the Bear Flag Revolt and Mexican War in California. Frémont and a small group crossed the Sierra via Truckee's Pass as Walker took the main party south through Owens Valley and crossed again into the San Joaquin Valley through Walker's Pass. It was this last passage through the valley that led to its name.

Two men who would lend their names to regions of California accompanied Walker on this trip. These were Richard Owens and Edward Meyer Kern. With Walker and the Frémont Party, they passed down the western side of the river to the lake, both of which now bear Owens' name. The party continued south and crossed the Sierra at Walker's Pass.

The expeditions led by Joseph Walker did not, however, lead to the settlement of the valley. This would come from two other events during the 1860s and bring people from both the north and south of the region.

The first and most important of these was the discovery of gold and then silver in the Comstock. The rush to this area, some two hundred miles north of the Owens Valley, began with the discovery of the Comstock Lode in 1859 by Peter O'Reilly and Patrick McLaughlin and the subsequent wide-ranging hunt for silver. Early Comstock ore samples assayed by Meville Atwood in Grass Valley showed gold at $1,000 per ton and silver at more than $3,000 per ton. Nowhere else in the region would silver ore be this pure, but its richness and vast quantity would spur exploration throughout the area. Historian Remi Nadeau, great-grandson and namesake of Inyo's major freight company operator during the 1870s, contends that only silver could excite California in 1859. There had been too many disappointments chasing rumored gold strikes. Also, unemployment was high in California in 1859, and many were eager for work or a new chance to strike it rich. By April 1860, one hundred fifty men a day were arriving at the Comstock. The population of the area had reached ten thousand, with more on the way. Only an Indian uprising in May stopped the first rush, but it resumed later in the summer and continued into 1863. This large influx naturally led to the search for other Comstocks. Although nothing found later would rival its wealth, it spurred numerous searches, discoveries, booms, and busts. By 1880, $310 million in gold and silver had been mined in the Comstock, and the logical assumption was that other, similar veins were likely to exist in the hills and mountains to the south.

In 1861, discoveries at Monoville, approximately ninety miles south of Virginia City, began the rush to the Esmeralda-Aurora area. Many came from the Virginia City area; some also came from the south via Walker's Pass or up from the Los Angeles area across the Mojave Desert, establishing the routes that would later serve the shipment of Owens Valley silver-lead bullion. This led to the discovery of sites in the Coso District of Inyo at San Carlos, Bend City, and Cerro Gordo.

The second factor that brought prospectors to the region was the mythical Lost Gunsight Mine. While the Gunsight Lode would never be found, the story

became widely known, leading to increased prospecting in the area. This led to the discovery of silver in various regions between Owens Valley and Death Valley, particularly in the Coso Range and Panamints.

The most notable of those searching for the Gunsight in terms of Inyo was Darwin French. The discovery of the Comstock in 1859 had renewed interest in prospecting, and French was no exception. Leaving his ranch at Tejon, French and about a dozen others from Oroville and Sacramento headed to Death Valley. Returning to the Coso Range, they found the others had discovered some rich silver-lead deposits. They named the spot Silver Mountain, and on May 28 they named the district Coso, Paiute for fire.

Another party searching for the Gunsight opened the first mine in the Panamints. Led by Dr. Samuel G. George, it organized the Telescope Mining District and formed the Combination Gold and Silver Mining Company.

With the return of the military and the end of the Indian trouble in the late 1860s, the stage was set for a renewed exploration and settlement of the valley. This new migration came from both the north and the south. From the north came veterans of the Comstock and Aurora, moving out to find their own strikes or looking for employment in the new mines and mills. From the south, people came from the Los Angeles area via trails across the Mojave or from the central valley through Walker's Pass. Many of the people in this southern group were Hispanics, with experience in the southern Sierra gold fields or in the Sinaloa, Mexico, silver mines. They would be the discoverers of many of the mines in the region, and early processing of ores would use long-existing Spanish-Mexican systems. Members of this group would discover Inyo's first and longest lasting silver lode at Cerro Gordo and become the majority of the town of Lone Pine's population.

Lone Pine and Independence, which became the county seat with the formation of Inyo County in 1866, were the major supply and administrative centers of this region. Lone Pine was at the intersection of the major north-south trail and the road to Cerro Gordo and later to Panamint and Darwin, the other two major mining towns of the era in Inyo. The location of Independence, sixteen miles north, was due to the site of the military camp. It was a community of ranchers, farmers, shopkeepers, saloon owners, lawyers, county officials, and the military. There were churches, schools, social organizations, and a much higher number of women and children than in the mining camps. The towns did a brisk business supplying the miners, as well as the soldiers stationed at Camp Independence.

Silver ore was discovered at Cerro Gordo in 1864 or 1865, but the discovery remained virtually unknown until 1867, when one of the pioneers appeared in Virginia City with samples of ore. Traditionally the first strike was credited to Pablo Flores and two other Mexicans. He was also credited with naming the area Cerro Gordo, Spanish for fat mountain or hill. With the increased number of miners arriving in the area, the mining district was officially organized at Lone Pine on April 5, 1866. Early arrivals included Mortimer William Belshaw, Victor Beaudry, and A. B. Elder, who would later be elected county sheriff.

M. W. Belshaw was a practical engineer by training. His great-grandparents had immigrated to America from County Antrim, Ireland, in 1770, settling in central New York as farmers. This is where Belshaw was born in 1830. He graduated from Geneva College and went to work as a toll collector on the Erie Canal. Gold fever struck, and he traveled by steamer to San Francisco in 1852. He opened a watch and jewelry store in Fiddletown and also became the local Wells Fargo agent. In 1858, he returned to New York to marry Jenny Oxmer and returned with her to California. In 1862, he left for the silver mines of Sinaola, Mexico, where he spent two years learning the techniques of silver mining. There Belshaw met A. B. Elder, who became his partner. Elder was a Civil War veteran and a native of western Ohio. Belshaw and Elder arrived in Cerro Gordo in April 1868.

Victor Beaudry was a French Canadian from Montreal who had joined the gold rush in 1849. At the outbreak of the Civil War, he became a sutler for the garrison of U.S. Army troops in Los Angeles and expanded the enterprise to San Bernardino and, with the arrival of troops in Inyo in 1862, to Camp Independence.

Here he provided generous credit to the mostly Mexican miners. Unpaid debts led to mortgaged mining claims. Foreclosure led to ownership, and Beaudry was in the mining business. He used this technique to acquire interests in the Union and San Felipe mines, Cerro Gordo's most profitable.

Beaudry and Belshaw would form the dominant company in the area, under their names. The company's dominance resulted not only from claim ownership but also from developing and monopolizing the water resources and delivery to the area, which was essential to the processing of the ore.

The silver-lead bullion from Cerro Gordo was shipped south around the end of the Sierras and across the Mojave Desert to Los Angeles. These bullion shipments coincided with the influx of farmers into the Los Angeles area. Cerro Gordo provided a ready market for their produce, as well as for manufactured goods. This trade was a major economic benefit to Los Angeles in the early 1870s.

Panamint was the next Inyo boomtown, with its mining district organized in the spring of 1873. Jacobs, R. B. Stewart, and W. L. Kennedy held early claims. By June, eighty more sites had been registered. The first business in town was the *Hotel de Bum,* which offered free entertainment and served food, as it had the only cook in town. It was rumored that a U.S. senator owned it. Saloons were quick to follow, and the two most prominent were Dave Neagle's *Oriental* and Ned Reddy's *Independent,* which opened shortly after the *Oriental.* Dave Neagle later achieved further notoriety by shooting former California Supreme Court Chief Justice David Terry. In March 1874, Panamint's population was about one hundred. By November, it had reached one thousand. Throughout the spring of 1875, workers rushed to complete a mill and furnaces. William C. Smith had been made justice of the peace in July 1874, and T. S. Harris, a printer from Sacramento, had started the *Panamint News.* Martha Camp arrived in the fall of 1874 to begin the "Maiden Lane" section of town.

Two U.S. senators from Nevada were Panamint's major mine owners. William Stewart had been elected senator in 1865 and 1869, J. P. Jones in 1873 and 1879. Together they organized the Panamint Mining Company and issued $2 million worth of stock. They paid $350,000 for a number of prominent claims. An additional part of the purchase price on some occasions

Table 1   Population Statistics for Inyo County, 1870 and 1880

	Census Year	
	1870	*1880*
Total Population	1,956	2,928
Sex		
Male	n.a.	1,853
Female	n.a.	1,065
Race		
White	1,608	2,197
American Indian	311	637
Chinese	29	90
African American	8	4

n.a. = not applicable.

was amnesty for the criminals selling the claim. The most interesting incident of "amnesty" involved Panamint's favorite outlaws, John Small and John MacDonald. These bandits were accepted in Panamint and lived in nearby Wildrose Canyon.

An indication of their acceptance was their leadership in an attack on Panamint's Chinese community on New Year's 1875. Attacking and denouncing Chinese was a popular pastime in 1870s California. Denis Kearny was building the Workingmen's Party in San Francisco at this time, for example, which denounced the Chinese for their real or perceived economic problems. Panamint followed the statewide political climate by passing its own exclusion resolution on July 4, 1876. Panamint's Chinese community consisted of the two hundred men employed to chip the trails from the cliffs and build the road to the valley.

Darwin, south of Owens Lake in the Coso range, began with the discovery of rich silver-lead deposits in late October 1874. It was named for the early explorer Dr. Darwin French. Victor Beaudry was one of the first arrivals. He bought a nearby spring and laid pipes to town, ensuring his dominance by controlling the water supply, as he had in Cerro Gordo. In 1875, Darwin saw explosive growth. By the end of 1875, there were two smelters, two hundred frame houses, and more than seven hundred citizens. Lola Travis moved her girls from Cerro Gordo and opened a dance hall. The influx of people came from Cerro Gordo and Panamint, plus the tough Nevada towns of Pioche,

Columbus, and Eureka. In February, George Hearst of Comstock fame, U.S. senator and father of newspaper baron George Randolph Hearst, arrived and formed the New Coso Mining Company by purchasing the Christmas Gift and Lucky Jim mines for $50,000. Darwin reached its peak in 1876 with fifteen saloons and more than a thousand residents. In August 1876, the largest smelter temporarily closed. The problem was a drop in silver-lead prices, combined with an increased difficulty in extracting ore. This resulted in wage reductions and an exodus to new areas such as Bodie, Mammoth, and the state of Idaho.

The populace was mostly young, male, transient, and prone to violence. The administrative and supply centers were more settled. Wives and children were common. There were schools, churches, a drama club, social and fraternal organizations, sporting events, and other events that were attended together by members of the various ethnic groups that made up Inyo's population. The crime and violence that is assumed to be part of mining camp life, but not of other types of communities, was in fact part of day-to-day life in both types of communities. It affected miners, merchants, ranchers, lawyers, and other members of the community. These towns were simultaneously mining towns, frontier towns, and industrialized towns. They had sprung to life essentially intact. Businesses and civic institutions had been established by statute or were imported from earlier communities, as were the materials from which the towns were built.

The judicial and law enforcement community in Inyo reflected in many ways the culture and attitudes of all sectors of the county population. Members of this community were transients like most members of the greater community. They came with the news of silver strikes and left when it played out or their own expectations were not met. They also were directly or indirectly involved in mining. From the justices of the peace to the circuit judge, they owned mining stock, prospected, or engaged in related businesses. They owned water companies, built furnaces, and served as mining district officers. A lawyer's primary income flowed from litigation concerning mining suits, and often clients paid in mining company stock. They were "mining the miners" as directly as those who sold the forty-niners clothing, pans, and shovels. The entire judicial system was tied to the mining economy, as was the county as a whole. It was the reason for the county's existence.

The most prominent law enforcement officials were A. B Elder, C. Mulkey, Thomas Passmore, and the Moore brothers, W. L. "Dad" Moore and J. J. "Jack" Moore. All of these men were early county residents and had other financial interests within the area, particularly in mining.

A. B. Elder was the sheriff at the beginning of the period of this study. He had been one of the early pioneers of Inyo and was instrumental in the development of the Coso Mining District, with interest in supplying water and as the operator of a furnace in Cerro Gordo with Belshaw.

In July 1871, Elder withdrew as a candidate for reelection so he could move his furnace operation to the Clarke District along the Colorado River in Arizona. This required the shipment of 60,000 pounds of machinery to the new site. In 1874 he returned to Inyo, following the failure of the Clarke District.

On his return, he became reinvolved in Cerro Gordo, this time with Beaudry's furnace, which on October 1, 1874, produced a record twenty-four-hour run of 305 bars of silver-lead bullion. In December of that year, the *Independent* indicated that Elder held the office of recorder for the Coso Mining District. In May 1875, he traveled to San Francisco to purchase furnace machinery for Pine Mountain and set up the furnace in that location.

After being a successful furnace man, a sheriff, and an unsuccessful furnace man, Elder turned to ranching. In the spring of 1877, he went to Los Angeles to buy four thousand head of sheep, with three thousand to be supplied later. He also planned "to irrigate and turn a section of sage brush into alfalfa for the purpose of maintaining his herds."

Jack Moore, known locally as J. J., and his brother W. L. "Dad" Moore, both served Inyo County as sheriff. One died violently in office. The brothers were originally from the Carolinas and arrived in Inyo in the 1860s. They were true county pioneers and leaders during the Indian troubles, particularly during the period in which the U.S. Army was absent from the county.

Passmore was, like the Moore brothers, a county pioneer. Born in Ohio, Passmore came west in 1852 and settled in the Sierra County gold country, in the western Sierra. Following the silver strikes of the late 1850s, he moved to the Aurora area, and in February 1862, he moved south to Inyo, establishing a farm at Georges Creek. He was renowned for his bravery during the Indian troubles of the 1860s. He was described as "self confident to the last degree" and "quick to act."

With the incorporation of the county in 1866, Passmore, a Republican now living in Olancha, was elected the first county clerk. In business, he was directly involved in the support of the mining development of the area. In 1874, he and his partner Walker were awarded a contract by the county supervisors to build a toll road to the new mining strikes at Panamint. Later, along with another partner, a Mr. Dodge, he drilled wells in Lone Pine. Water was a key ingredient, along with combustible material, for the operation of the ore furnaces located throughout the area.

During his time as sheriff, Passmore was best known for cracking down on the selling of whiskey to Indians, arresting the sellers as well as the Indians. He was married to Miss M. Walker at Olancha by Judge Hannah on May 13, 1875. He also was a member of the Episcopal Church and Masonic Lodge.

Several common themes characterize the men in law enforcement. They tended to be county pioneers and held in high esteem by the business community, a necessity if one wanted to be able to post the required bond to hold office. They also were all involved in mining or in businesses directly related to it. In addition, they had followed the mining strikes, often after several stops, to Inyo and beyond. They were, although more settled (with their families and businesses) than the itinerant miners, in reality just as transient.

The judges of Inyo during this period were also directly involved or tied to the mining industry by business interests. They were less transient, although they had clearly been initially attracted to Inyo because of its mining possibilities. The exception was Theron Reed, the Circuit Court judge, to whose circuit Independence was added on its incorporation in 1866. His occasional residence, however, did not preclude an interest in mining.

A. C. Hanson, originally from Vermont, served as Inyo's first county judge. Later he would serve as Cerro Gordo's justice of the peace. His term of office as county judge expired in December 1871, and he did not seek reelection, preferring to return to his business interests.

He maintained his interest in mining, and in 1874, Hanson prospected the areas around Panamint and also in the Mineral King area of the western Sierra. He also became secretary of the Coso Mining District that year, with former sheriff A. B. Elder as mining district recorder.

Like many in the county, Hanson's interests had moved from Panamint, which failed to live up to its hype, back to Coso and the new mining town of Darwin in 1875. He and a partner, Mr. Thompson, established the Darwin House hotel, which became the county's largest. A March 1875 advertisement in the *Independent* claimed that it was a "new and commodious hotel . . . furnished in a style unprecedented in the district." Hanson's interests that year also included a partnership in the "Promontorio" Mine in the Coso District.

In 1876, Hanson was mentioned in print as being in Darwin. He had previously, in 1874, talked of returning to Vermont, and he did return for a visit. Because no further mention of this prominent Inyo citizen appears in any of the county papers, it is likely that he finally did return to Vermont or followed new mining strikes as he had done during his time in Inyo.

When Hanson chose not to run for reelection, the judicial election in the fall of 1871 brought John A. Hannah to office as the Democratic candidate for county judge. A reluctant candidate at the time, expressing doubts whether he would accept the office, Hannah went on to serve throughout the decade.

Prior to becoming county judge, Hannah served as recorder of the Cerro Gordo mining district. At the beginning of his term as judge, he was still the official notary for Cerro Gordo, but his term expired in October 1872.

With the incorporation of the county, Independence became a stop on the Sixteenth District Circuit Court. The judge for this circuit during the entire period was Theron B. Reed. He was married and politically a Republican. The district encompassed both sides of the southern Sierra. Reed traveled by stage lines and held court in Inyo every six months, in May and November.

Judge John A. Hannah.

Source: Published with permission of the Country of Inyo, Eastern California Museum.

As was the case in the county court, the vast majority of each term was taken up by civil litigation, the preponderance of which involved mining litigation.

Reed, despite not having migrated to Inyo following the silver strikes, as had most of those involved in the criminal and civil judicial system, nevertheless was involved in the mining industry. He was part owner, along with attorney V. A. Gregg and William D. and Robert D. Brown, of the Grand Mine in Darwin. He was also a close friend of long-time Inyo district attorney Paul W. Bennett, along with Judge Fox of Cerro Gordo, Colonel Putney, and ex-sheriff and mining furnace and water supplier A. B. Elder.

The attorneys of Inyo follow the same patterns of transience and interests in mining. They came with the silver strikes, not long after the miners and saloon proprietors, and stayed for varying lengths of time based on their success, financially and professionally. These areas obviously were intimately connected, as it was common for legal fees to be paid in mining stock. Participation in criminal cases was a duty to the court, much like that of a public defender, and was performed

Attorney Patrick Reddy.

Source: Published with permission of the County of Inyo, Eastern California Museum.

by these men as an adjunct to their civil practices or, in the case of the district attorney, as part of his duties of office. A number of attorneys appear and leave, undistinguished, throughout the decade, but two stand out. Paul W. Bennett, long-time district attorney, and Patrick Reddy, arguably the most successful criminal defense attorney in 19th-century California, distinguished themselves with long and successful careers including their time in Inyo during the 1870s.

Bennett had moved south to Inyo from the Aurora area in the mid-1860s. The limited criminal court calendar left plenty of time after his duties as district attorney were fulfilled for him to pursue his private law practice and mining interests. In late 1870, the *Independent* reports his chairing a meeting forming the Granite Mountain Mining District. In late 1871, a district court judgment against a Mr. Dorr awarded Bennett $97,000. With this money, he bought the Santa Maria mine at a sheriff's sale for $100,041.50, with the expectation of the prior owners redeeming the sale. Patrick Reddy was also a partner in this venture, and in July 1872, Bennett sold shares to William Watt for $30,000. In January 1874, he and Reddy filed suit

against Watt and others for recovery of the $30,000 due on the mine. These proceedings were typical of the methods employed to leverage a debt into mine ownership. Often the plaintiff was awarded a judgment redeemed by the owners to clear title or kept ownership in a particularly promising mine with hope of future profits. Bennett and Reddy were the most successful of the Inyo attorneys in this enterprise.

In January 1874, Bennett was appointed chairman of a committee to organize the Society of Pioneers of Owens River Valley. Others on the committee included future sheriff Passmore and V. A. Gregg, Bennett's law partner since mid-1873. Membership required residence in the valley prior to June 6, 1865. This labeled Bennett, together with many of the principals in the legal system, as early residents who had established their influence during the difficulties of the 1860s.

Bennett's partner Gregg, originally from Iowa, also had mining interests in both the Panamint and Darwin regions. In 1874, he was appointed deputy internal revenue collector for the Eighth District, having previously served as deputy in Mono and Inyo Counties. In 1878, he was nominated by the governor to the Constitutional Convention of 1878 as a representative of Kern County, where he had moved some time after 1875.

In March 1877, Bennett had been having health problems and resigned as district attorney in midtrial. It was during this time that Bennett planned a move to Aurora or Bodie to the north, as the mining activity in Inyo had tapered off. Reddy would also move to Bodie when the news broke of significant ore discoveries in that region.

Patrick Reddy and his brother Ned were born in Woonsocket, Rhode Island, Patrick in 1839 and Ned in 1844. Pat came to California in 1861 and worked as a miner in Placer County and as a laborer in Contra Costa. In 1863, Pat traveled to the new mining camp of Aurora, which was then the county seat of Mono County, California, and Esmeralda County, Nevada. Pat Reddy rose from obscurity as a bouncer to prosperity by application of the litigious techniques previously discussed. Ned would check out the mining camps for opportunities, and if the situation was favorable, he would move to the new town to protect the brothers' interests. They used this technique in Virginia

City, Cerro Gordo, Columbus, Panamint, Darwin, and Bodie. Pat Reddy moved to Independence, the future county seat of Inyo, in 1865, worked as a notary, and on November 11, 1867, he was enrolled as a member of the California Bar.

Pat Reddy also became the most successful criminal attorney in the region, purportedly defending one hundred accused murderers without losing a case. He served as a delegate to the California 1879 constitutional convention and as state senator after moving to Sacramento.

These men, the miners, lawmen, and lawyers, typified the mining rushes of the post–California gold rush era. They traveled from rush to rush, from Virginia City to Aurora to Inyo, to Bodie or Tombstone, Montana, and the Dakotas. They brought enterprise, jobs, and expertise. Eventually they returned home or to more settled areas, resuming previous careers or starting new ones. The areas they opened evolved and remain in some cases or became ghost towns, some of which survive today as tourist destinations.

—*Hank Thayer*

Suggested Reading

Barth, Gunther. *Instant Cities: Urbanization and the Rise of San Francisco and Denver.* New York: Oxford University Press, 1975.

Chalfant, W. A. *Gold, Guns & Ghost Towns.* Stanford, CA: Stanford University Press, 1947.

Chalfant, W. A. *The Story of Inyo.* Chicago: Author, 1922.

Chalfant, W. A. *Tales of the Pioneers.* Stanford, CA: Stanford University Press, 1942.

Elliot, Russel R. *Servant of Power: A Political Biography of Senator William M. Stewart.* Reno: University of Nevada Press, 1983.

Holliday, J. S. *The World Rushed In.* New York: Simon & Schuster, 1981.

Lingenfelter, Richard E. *Death Valley and the Amargosa.* Berkeley: University of California Press, 1986.

Mann, Ralph. *After the Gold Rush.* Stanford, CA: Stanford University Press, 1982.

McGrath, Roger. *Gunfighters, Highwaymen, and Vigilantes.* Berkeley: University of California Press, 1984.

Murphy, Mary. *Mining Cultures: Men, Women, and Leisure in Butte: 1914–41.* Urbana: University of Illinois Press, 1997.

Nadeau, Remi A. *City Makers.* New York: Doubleday, 1948.

Nadeau, Remi A. *The Silver Seekers.* Santa Barbara, CA: Crest, 1999.

Paul, Rodman Wilson. *Mining Frontiers of the Far West 1848–1880.* New York: Holt, Rinehart and Winston, 1963.

IRAN-IRAQ WAR AND THE MIGRATION OF IRANIAN YOUTH TO CALIFORNIA

America's West in the 1980s experienced a new wave of immigrants as never before. The Golden State had always been wealthy Iranians' highly sought-after vacation and investment destination, starting in the late 1940s, but 40 years later, the exciting shorelines of California were sought by other Iranians, those for whom wealth and social class were not necessarily a fundamental part of the background. By 1966, more than 1,000 Iranians lived in the United States. The years between 1960 and 1969 saw the biggest surge of Iranian immigrants to the states: a total of 8,895. The steady climb in the number of immigrants totaled 37,567 by the 1970s. The 1979 Islamic Revolution in Iran, led by Ayatollah Ruhollah Khomeini, which consequently ended the 65-year-old Pahlavi Dynasty and toppled the regime of American-supported Shah Muhammad Reza Pahlavi, opened a new chapter of Middle Eastern history that was to have an affect on the 21st century's global sociopolitical and economic future. The Iraqi government in the hands of strongman Saddam Hussein initiated a war against Iran in 1980, which lasted more than eight years, causing an unprecedented outflow of male Iranian teenagers and young adults. Their ages ranged between 13 and 20, with the majority of them ultimately heading for the United States in general and California specifically. The number of nonimmigrant Iranians coming to America between 1980 and 1989 broke all previous records, and more than 60 percent of the total 136,202 changed their status to immigrants. Among these émigrés, youths of different faiths and ethnicities, such as Armenians, Assyrians, Bahá'ís, Christians, Jews, Muslims, and Zoroastrians, made the historic journey.

Running away from a violent atmosphere, the base population of Iranian youth found itself between the difficulty of dodging military conscription and the difficulty of attaining an American or European entry visa. One without the other was usually the norm. That is, by paying a high ransom, one could obtain a passport to leave the country, but the destination was still unknown, because no European country or any nation on the American continent would grant a visa for entry to this group of runaways.

Although the Western European nations, such as Great Britain, Germany, and France, received a large population of Iranian youths, the majority of these immigrants preferred the United States as their permanent home outside of Iran. The peak time of immigration for Iranians, 1975, is the time in history that 90% of the total 224,456 immigrated to the United States, according to the Immigration and Naturalization Service, until 1993. Based on the same source, California received more than half the total number of immigrants (108,572) between 1975 and 1993.

Immigration attorneys and brokers with high-level connections in the Consular Section of the American State Department and local embassies and consulates were the key to obtaining entry permits into the United States for this desperate group of Iranian youth. These miracle workers charged a fee anywhere between $3,000 and $25,000 for securing a student, worker, or tourist visa, and the Iranian youth made their way into the United States, with a majority settling in and around Los Angeles.

A free society, along with a world-class educational system, the multiethnic and multinational makeup of California's population, a mild and pleasant climate, a relatively liberal society, and a free market economy, accompanied by a persevering character, decided the Iranian youth to settle in the West. These notable characteristics eventually assisted the young immigrants in their successes, which ultimately led to their unsurpassed contributions to their adopted country through entrepreneurship and scholarship.

The challenge of staying in the West legally and honorably was the next step that these Iranian youths had to take. On settling in their newfound home in California, the Iranian youth had to overcome numerous challenges. These challenges, however, were met with a certain resilience that can be attributed to the youths' growing up in the time of a bloody revolution and war back in their native land. It can be argued that if one is threatened with the loss of life or the possibility of becoming physically disabled, one does not consider the challenges of learning a new language or adopting new customs and cultures of a new society

to be very difficult. The Iranian teenagers and young adults' first priority was attaining the best education possible in the American academic system to grow distinctively in their new home. Aiming for the highest degrees and professions by attaining bachelors, masters, Ph.D.s, M.D.s, and J.D.s, after 25 years of hard work, the Iranian exiles rank among the highest in the minority groups currently living in the United States, especially in California. According to a University of Arizona doctoral dissertation, the majority of the California-based population of Iranians is concentrated in 15 zip codes within Los Angeles County. In 1993, their average per capita income was twice that of the national average and two times that of the county average.

On graduating from universities, professional schools, and institutions, these Iranian youth persevered to reach the highest professional ladders that the state of California would allow. The young Iranian immigrants of the 1980s currently hold the highest posts in the California state government. The success of the Iranian émigré has been noticeable on the technological frontier as well; they have taken part in the great technological revolution of the 1980s and 1990s and have benefited handsomely from its financial rewards. Silicon Valley, which by all measures and standards has been held as one of the top technological centers in the world, has seen the growth of many Iranian engineers who made their journey to the West because of the Iran-Iraq War (1980–1988).

West Los Angeles specifically has become the nucleus of the Iranian community as far as businesses and community activities are concerned. Although most of the Iranians live in and around Los Angeles County, Westwood Village has unofficially been called TehrAngeles, which is a combination of the name of the Iranian capital Tehran and Los Angeles. An estimated 70 percent of businesses in Westwood are Iranian owned. Persian was the most widely spoken language in Beverly Hills High School during the 1990s, even before the official language of English.

Believing in family as the most important part of society and also esteeming it as the most necessary part of a healthy and stable community, the Iranian youth strove to create a social setting that family, friends, and associates would enjoy and benefit from.

Hence a large number of these Iranian youths who had begun to put down roots in California started the long process of petitioning for immigrant visas from the Department of State for their immediate families and relatives, which subsequently raised the number of Iranians living in California by tens of thousands. This specific characteristic of Iranian émigrés, it can be argued, allowed them to live and work side by side with the Mexican and Latin American population of California. The similarity of Mexican American and Iranian family and social values has created a symbiotic relationship to which the success of the Iranian immigrants in the greater Los Angeles area can be attributed. The inclusion of family elders, such as grandparents and great-grandparents, as part of the family and the utter and unconditional respect for them by all family members is another point of similarity between the Spanish-speaking population of California and Iranians, causing a more stable and successful existence in the West. In a more detailed analysis, one can take into account the role of food, music, and a festive lifestyle that has allowed Iranian immigrants to succeed in having a healthy relationship with all California residents in the 1980s, 1990s, and the opening years of the new millennium.

The Iranian youth in exile have not participated much in the political fight against the Islamic government of Iran for the past 25 years. This can be attributed to their dedication of time and energy to education, business, and commerce. Among the different businesses that these youths have been involved in was the burgeoning business of Persian music and entertainment. Although many believe that the effect of Persian music and its products has been nothing but a total disappointment musically and professionally, nevertheless this highly lucrative business has given birth to a new wave of Iranian youth, the children of the escapees of the Iranian war. Still, it is no match for the traditional and mainstream Hollywood entertainment machine.

The young immigrants of 20 years ago and their families have and are growing every year and are becoming a part of the vast western fabric of America that has made California a special place for those who seek opportunity, safety, and freedom.

—*Mateo Mohammad Farzaneh*

Suggested Reading

Ansari, Abdoulmaboud. "A Community in Progress: The First Generation of the Iranian Professional Middle-Class Immigrants in the United States." *International Review of Modern Sociology* 7 (1977).

Ansari, Abdoulmaboud. *Iranian Immigrants in the United States: A Case Study of Dual Marginality.* Millwood, NY: Associated Faculty Press, 1992.

Askari, Hossein, John T. Cummings, and Mehmet Isbudak. "Iran's Migration of Skilled Labor to the United States." *Iranian Studies* 10 (1977).

Bozorgmehr, Mehdi. "Internal Ethnicity: Iranians in Los Angeles." *Sociological Perspectives* 40 (1997).

Bozorgmehr, Mehdi. "Iranians." In *Refugees in America in the 1990s*, edited by David Haines. Westport, CT: Greenwood Press, 1996.

Bozorgmehr, Mehdi, and Georges Sabagh. "Iranian Exiles and Immigrants in Los Angeles." In *Iranian Exiles and Refugees Since Khomeini*, edited by Asghar Fathi. Costa Mesa, CA: Mazda, 1991.

Brown, Ian. *Khomeini's Forgotten Sons: The Story of Iran's Boy Soldiers.* London: Grey Seal, 1990.

Dallalfar, Arlene. "The Iranian Ethnic Economy in Los Angeles: Gender and Entrepreneurship." In *Family and Gender Among American Muslims*, edited by Barbara Aswad and Barbara Bilge. Philadelphia: Temple University Press, 1996.

Der-Martirosian, Claudia. "Economic Embeddedness and Social Capital of Immigrants: Iranians in Los Angeles." Ph.D. Dissertation, University of California, Los Angeles, 1996.

Feher, Shoshanah. "From the Rivers of Babylon to the Valleys of Los Angeles: The Exodus and Adaptation of Iranian Jews." In *Gatherings in Diaspora*, edited by R. Stephen Warner and Judith G. Wittner. Philadelphia: Temple University Press, 1998.

Ghaffarian, Shireen. "The Acculturation of Iranians in the United States." *Journal of Psychology* 127 (1987).

Jones, Allen. "Iranian Refugees: The Many Faces of Persecution." Washington, DC: U.S. Committee for Refugees, 1984.

Karim, Persis, and Mohammad Mehdi Khorrami, eds. *A World Between: Poems, Stories, and Essays by Iranian-Americans. An Anthology.* New York: George Braziller, 1998.

Kelly, Ron, and Jonathan Friedlander, eds. *Irangeles: Iranians in Los Angeles.* Berkeley: University of California Press, 1993.

Lorentz, John, and John Wertime. "Iranians." In *Harvard Encyclopedia of American Ethnic Groups*, edited by Stephen Thernstrom. Cambridge, MA: Harvard University Press, 1980.

Modarres, Ali. "Settlement Patterns of Iranians in the United States." *Journal of the Society for Iranian Studies* 3, no. 1 (Winter 1998).

Rajaee, Farhang. *Iranian Perspectives on the Iran-Iraq War.* Gainesville, FL: University Press of Florida, 1997.

Sabagh, Georges, and Mehdi Bozorgmehr. "Are the Characteristics of Exiles Different from Immigrants? The Case of Iranians in Los Angeles." *Sociology and Social Research* 71 (1987).

Willett, Edward. *Iran-Iraq War.* New York: Rosen, 2004.

⊞ IRISH IN THE WEST

For the Irish, the first western frontier they confronted was the West of trapping and the fur trade. Like other trappers, Irish trappers were in search of beaver. Irish trappers traveled in parts of the Far West that few other white men had trod. They were among the first Americans to see the Rocky and Sierra Nevada mountains. There were other Irishmen who settled early in the Far West who did not make a living in the fur trade. A few married into wealthy Mexican families and lived as ranch owners; others made their fortunes by trading.

The first great Irish migration west came as a result of the California Gold Rush in 1849. Initially, it was gold that was the lure, but other metals proved to be far more valuable to the growth of the United States. Irish miners would eventually make up one third of those digging for gold, silver, copper, lead, and other resources. Mining camps often had an Irish feel to them. Conditions in the camps could often be harsh; miners had to live off low wages and worked long hours. Due to these harsh conditions, groups such as the Knights of Labor and the Industrial Workers of the World were often successful in getting Irish miners to join their organizations. Not all Irish came with the intention of staying. Many Irishmen came west looking to earn money that they could take back with them to Ireland.

One of the first western cities to feel the impact of the Irish-American migration was San Francisco. Many of the Irish came as a result of serving in the U.S. Army during the Mexican War, but it was the gold rush of 1849 that really attracted them. In 1850, there were four thousand Irish in the Bay Area in search of a better life. By 1890, half of San Francisco's population of 150,000 was of Irish descent. The number of Irish that settled in San Francisco waxed and waned from the time of the gold rush in 1849 to the 1920s. During the Great Depression there was very little Irish immigration, but that changed in the 1950s and 1960s. Today, about 10 percent of San Francisco's population is of Irish origin. For early settlers of the Bay Area, there was opportunity, particularly if one could speak English.

Politics was an area in which many Irishmen got involved. In 1867, Frank McCoppin was elected San Francisco's first mayor, two decades before Boston elected its first Irish mayor. David Broderick was the first Irish Catholic elected to the U.S. Senate. He had originally got his political start in San Francisco. The Irish did face their share of prejudice in the Bay Area. Graves can be found of those who died at the hands of vigilantes, but conditions were not so bad that the Irish had to live in separate areas of the city, as in Boston.

A second city that drew a large Irish population in the Far West was Butte, Montana. In 1900, there were 12,000 people of Irish descent residing in the mining town of Butte. The majority of the Irish living in Butte originally came from Cork in Ireland. Many of those who came from Cork had worked in copper mines, which came to be an advantage in Butte. The Anaconda Copper Company, owned by Irishman Marcus Daly, was by the 1890s supplying the United States with a third of its copper. Anaconda miners were paid twice the normal rate of $3.50 for an eight-hour workday and led the nation in per capita income and union membership. Daly, a former miner, did much to endear himself to the miners and the people of Butte, such as constructing banks and irrigation systems. Following Daly's tenure as chief executive officer of the corporation, three other Irish Catholics would serve as chief executive officer of the Anaconda Copper Company. Irish mutual aid societies were created, including the Ancient Order of Hibernians, the Robert Emmet Literary Society, and the Clan-na-Gael.

Butte developed a reputation as a tough town. The sheriff had difficulty keeping some of the miners from breaking the law. On a few occasions at the local theater house, when some of the residents did not like the presentation, they beat up the actors. When Carrie Nation came to town with a hatchet in an attempt to shut down the local saloons, a female saloon owner chased her out of town.

Perhaps one of the most famous cases of Irish Americans making it big in the American West was J. J. Brown and his wife Molly Tobin Brown. J. J. Brown made a fortune as a mine manager, and the two built a mansion in Denver, where Molly Brown developed a reputation as a nouveau riche social climber. She was often excluded from upper society events due to her Irish heritage. She was on board the Titanic and was able to get into a rescue boat, where she calmed the fears of others by telling stories, leading the survivors in song, and proclaiming that they were safe, as she was the "unsinkable Molly Brown." She later collected $10,000 from other wealthy survivors to give to the less fortunate, and her story was turned into a musical comedy.

One of the occupations of Irishmen in the West was that of soldier. It is estimated that following the Civil War, through the 1870s, about 20 percent of the army was made up of Irish Americans. Many Irishmen served as noncommissioned officers, which made up the backbone of the army. The western army units were often charged with keeping the peace between white settlers and American Indians. In fulfilling their duties, Irish-Americans did become involved in combat. At the Battle of Little Big Horn, 31 Irish-Americans were killed.

—Timothy A. Strand

See also HELENA, MONTANA; IDAHO SILVER STRIKES; LEADVILLE, COLORADO

Suggested Reading

Clark, Dennis. *Hibernia America: the Irish and Regional Cultures.* Westport, CT: Greenwood Press, 1986.

Dezell, Maureen. *Irish America: Coming Into Clover: The Evolution of a People and a Culture.* New York: Doubleday, 2000.

Erie, Steven P. *Rainbow's End: Irish-Americans and the Dilemmas of Urban Machine Politics, 1840–1985.* Berkeley: University of California Press, 1988.

Fitzgerald, Margaret E., and Joseph A. King. *The Uncounted Irish in Canada and the United States.* Toronto: Meany, 1990.

Griffin, William D. *A Portrait of the Irish in America.* New York: Scribner, 1981.

Maguire, John Francis. *The Irish in America.* New York: Arno Press, 1969.

Malone, Michael P., Richard B. Roeder, and William L. Lang. *Montana: A History of Two Centuries.* Seattle: University of Washington Press, 1991.

Murphy, Mary. *Mining Cultures: Men, Women, and Leisure in Butte, 1914–41.* Urbana: University of Illinois Press, 1997.

Rolle, Andrew. *California: A History.* 4th ed. Arlington Heights, IL: Harlan Davidson, 1987.

⊞ IRVINE, JAMES HARVEY (1827–1886)

James Irvine was born in Anabilt, County Down, Ireland, on December 27, 1827, and immigrated to New York in 1846. Penniless but determined, Irvine sailed to San Francisco as a merchant and miner during the California Gold Rush. In 1854, Irvine's subsequent success enabled him to purchase interest in a business that was renamed Irvine & Co., Wholesale Produce and Grocery Merchants. Wanting to expand his mercantile enterprise into sheep ranching and real estate investments, Irvine purchased property in northern California. Partnering with Flint Bixby & Co., Irvine purchased three major Spanish ranchos south of Los Angeles during the Great Drought of 1864. The land, covering about 110,000 acres, included the 47,000-acre Rancho Lomas de Santiago, which was purchased for $7,000. Although the rancho's terrain was unsuitable for cultivation, the fact that the property bordered the northern bend of the Santa Ana River secured valuable water rights. The second property included 13,000 acres of the Rancho Santiago de Santa Ana. The last parcel, the Rancho San Joaquín, was purchased for $18,000 and covered 50,000 acres.

A few years later, Irvine married Nettie Rice, who bore him a son, James Harvey, in 1867. In 1868, Irvine began construction on San Joaquín Ranch house, the first wooden house erected in southern California. A prolonged drought destroyed grazing lands and thwarted attempts to make the land profitable. Catering to the semiarid environment, Irvine planted wheat and barley, crops that did not require irrigation and were moderately drought resistant. Other produce grown on the ranch included corn, potatoes, and fruit. Despite Irvine's successful harvests, the area lacked an adequate transportation infrastructure that could transport the crops to distant markets. In addition to the ranch's problems, Irvine lost his infant son Harvey in 1873, along with his wife, Nettie, who died of tuberculosis in 1874. Six years later, James Irvine married Margaret Byrne.

Adding tenant farms to an extensive sheep-grazing enterprise in 1876, Irvine bought the interests of his partner, Flint Bixby & Co., for $150,000, and renamed the property the "Irvine Rancho San Joaquín." Irvine attempted to defend his extensive lands from squatters, whom courts and journalists supported as the rightful owners if they "improved" property according to usufruct ideals.

Although the Southern Pacific Railroad laid track in 1876 along the ranch's northern border, Irvine refused to allow the company to build on his property due to a personal feud with the company's owner, Mr. Collis Huntington. Despite the negative press attention Irvine received from blocking the railroad's access to San Diego, transportation of the crops via the railroad was ultimately realized by Southern Pacific's competitor, the Santa Fe Railroad, in 1887. Before his death from Bright's disease in 1886, James Harvey Irvine's extensive real estate holdings, sheep ranching, and agricultural empire made him one of the wealthiest men in California, with an estimated worth of $1,283,000.

Following in his father's footsteps, James Irvine II began to replace dominant sheep herds with cattle, transformed a large portion of the rancho's chaparral environment suitable for grazing into diversified farming, and was one of the first to engage in large-scale agribusiness. Groves of olive and walnut trees were introduced, along with massive stands of eucalyptus trees, which shielded the property from the Santa Ana inland winds. By 1888, Irvine had leased more than 5,000 acres to tenants or sharecroppers. Beginning in 1890 and continuing for the next 44 years, Irvine built homes and barns for the tenant farmers, paid for their maintenance and repairs, and charged $6.00 a month for rent. The Irvine family's generosity toward their tenants was not shown to other families who illegally lived on the Irvine Ranch. After years of battling squatters in and out of court, their opportunistic attempts to settle on the Irvine Ranch dissipated by 1890. Around the turn of the century, coal and gypsum deposits were discovered near the property's eastern border, and these yielded more than 20,000 tons of coal.

One year after James Irvine II's wife Frances Anita Plum gave birth to their son, James Harvey, Jr., in 1893, Irvine Sr. incorporated the ranch's holdings into the Irvine Company. In the following years, Irvine Sr.'s daughter Kathryn Helena and son Myford Plum were born, and the family lived in the Irvine mansion after 1906. Close to the residence, the ranch's agricultural station housed maintenance shops, a walnut dehydrator, warehouses, barns, administrative offices, garages, and a service station. Myriad pests, diseases, and other catastrophic events plagued the family in 1907. However, the Irvine Company's ingenuity and prosperity in the face of adversity created a legacy that continues to the present day.

Thanks to its bean and barley production, the Irvine Ranch became California's most productive farm in 1910. Irvine's access to and distribution of water in this semiarid region allowed him to expand the agribusiness. Irvine diversified further and planted groves of avocado, lemon, papaya, and orange trees, as well as asparagus, black-eyed peas, alfalfa, rhubarb, artichokes, peanuts, persimmons, grapes, strawberries, celery, and cauliflower. The ranch's successful harvest of 100,000 tons of delicate sugar beets resulted in the establishment of the Santa Ana Cooperative Sugar Company in 1911. This plant and five others supplied one quarter of the nation's sugar during World War I. Despite these improvements, Irvine realized that the wells were depleting the groundwater basin in the 1920s. Irvine subsequently built 2,500 miles of irrigation pipeline and constructed canals and dams that collected natural runoff into reservoirs.

After James Irvine, Sr.'s death in 1947, his son Myford promoted urban development on small portions of land. Exponential urban growth hallmarked increasing agrarian and domestic demands. These demands were met by the accomplishments and ingenuity of James Irvine I, his family, and the Irvine Company, which had pioneered large-scale agribusiness, developed access to and distribution methods for water for agricultural and domestic purposes, and subsequently founded the 21st-century award-winning, master-planned community of Irvine.

—Catherine M. Bilanchone

Suggested Reading

American National Biography. New York: Oxford University Press, 1999.

Baxter, Gavin H. *James Irvine II and the Irvine Ranch: As Remembered by Gavin H. Baxter, F.F. "Fay" Irwin, Thomas McBride.* Interviews by Jim Sleeper. Fullerton: California State University Fullerton Oral History Program, 1992.

City of Irvine. "History of the City." Available from http://www.cityofirvine.org/about/history.asp

Cleland, Robert Glass. *The Irvine Ranch.* 3rd ed. Pasadena, CA: Huntington Library Press, 2003.

Forsyth, Ann. *Reforming Suburbia: The Planned Communities of Irvine, Columbia, and the Woodlands.* Pasadena: University of California Press and the Huntington Library, 2005.

Irvine, James. *Last Will and Testament.* San Francisco, circa 1886.

Irvine Ranch Water District. "About IRWD: History." Available from http://www.irwd.com/AboutIRWD/history.php

Liebeck, Judy. *Irvine: A History of Innovation and Growth,* edited by Myrtle Malone. Houston, TX: Pioneer, 1990.

Stern, Jean, Janet Blake Dominik, and Harvey L. Jones. *Selections from the Irvine Museum.* Irvine, CA: Irvine Museum, 1992.

⊞ IRVINE RANCH

See IRVINE, JAMES HARVEY

⊞ ITALIAN IMMIGRANTS

See GERMAN AND ITALIAN INTERNMENT

J

⧉ JACKS, DAVID BAIRD
(1822–1909)

"It's the Cheese!" This motto graces television advertisements across the country extolling the quality of California cheeses and their positive impact on life in California. The implication is that you too can have a California life by eating lots and lots of California cheese. The most famous of these cheeses is Monterey Jack, a soft white cheese native to California. Its name combines the city of its origin, Monterey and the name of the man credited with its creation, David Jacks.

David Jacks was born David Jack in Crief, Perthshire, Scotland, on April 18, 1822. Two of his brothers immigrated to New York, becoming successful storekeepers. In 1841 or 1842, he joined his brothers in Long Island, finding work at Fort Hamilton, in Brooklyn. He tells of meeting Robert E. Lee, then a captain in the army, who came to inspect caisson wheels. In 1848, Jack heard of California gold and decided to seek his fortune. He spent his savings of $1,400 on revolvers and booked passage around the Horn, landing in San Francisco in April 1849 and selling the guns for $4,000, which he then lent out at the rate of 2 percent per month. He found employment in the Custom House and was legally naturalized on December 3, 1849.

In 1850, he moved to Monterey and lived there the rest of his life. At some point in his residence in California, probably during his time in Monterey, the surname "Jack" became "Jacks." He went to work for Joseph Boston as a clerk in Boston's store, the Casa del Oro. By 1855, he had purchased the building. In 1851, Jacks worked as a clerk for a fellow Scot, James McKinley, who owned a dry goods store in the Pacific Building. Jacks bought that building in 1869. The first record of his real estate purchases shows that within a year of arriving in Monterey, he was lending money secured by land. The next year he was chosen treasurer of Monterey County, and he purchased his first piece of land. It was at this time that he acquired some property through foreclosing on his loans or buying at tax sales. In 1856, he returned to Scotland for a year following the death of his father. His holdings in Monterey were left in the care of an agent, and he returned in 1857.

The acquisition that set him on the path to becoming the largest landowner in Monterey County started with the Treaty of Guadalupe Hidalgo in 1848 and litigation to legitimize Monterey's title to an 1830 Mexican pueblo land grant of 29,698 acres. The city hired an attorney, Delos Rodeyn Ashley, to press its claim to the land grant before the U.S. Land Claims Commission. Ashley was successful and presented the city with a bill for $991.50. The city had no funds to pay the fee, and the state legislature authorized the Monterey city government to auction off the lands to pay off the Ashley debt. On February 5, 1859, Jacks, in partnership with attorney Delos, made the only bid on the property, for $1,002.50, the amount of the debt and costs of sale. All of the money went to Delos, who later sold his interest to Jacks for $500.00. The sale of the land at auction came to be known as "The Rape of Monterey."

The city tried to regain ownership of the land, suing Jacks in court. The case went all the way to the U.S. Supreme Court, which ruled in Jacks' favor on July 11, 1903. By this time, Jacks had acquired another 30,000 acres of land. He had begun paying overdue taxes on local land, claiming the lands when the owners could not pay the back taxes with interest. He continued his practice of foreclosing on loans that went into default. It was his choice of tactics that drew condemnation from the locals. He would, allegedly, post foreclosure notices on the outlying reaches of the property. If the owner was Spanish speaking, he would post the notice in English; if the owner was English speaking, he would post the notice in Spanish. Those who lost their land considered him a land shark, and he considered them to be squatters on his land. At the height of his land ownership, the total acreage in his possession exceeded 100,000 acres.

The enmity led to formation of "The Squatters League of Monterey County." In 1872, the league wrote to Jacks, threatening his life. Robert Louis Stevenson was visiting California, and in his book *Across the Plains,* he wrote that the lands in Monterey were all in the hands of a single man, "who is hated with a great hatred." Denis Kearny, the radical Irishman who would later lead the Workingmen's Party of California, visited Monterey and counseled the league to "hang David Jacks." Jacks started to travel with bodyguards.

Within the acres amassed by Jacks are the present-day cities of Pacific Grove, Del Rey Oaks, Seaside, Fort Ord, and the Del Monte Forest, including the 17 Mile Drive coastline. His holdings extended inland, with the highest point known as Jacks Peak.

Jacks also owned a dairy on the Salinas River, where he produced a cheese from a recipe brought to the area by the Franciscan friars. An oversupply of milk led the brothers to devise a way of preserving the milk by turning it into cheese. It was known as "queso blanco pais," white country cheese, or simply "queso blanco," white cheese. It had become a staple in the diet of the Spanish-speaking settlers. Jacks eventually became a partner in 14 dairies, with Spanish and Portuguese dairymen, dominating the market. Like the Franciscans, Jacks solved the problem of excess milk by making the cheese and marketing it as "Jacks Cheese." It was stamped as originating from Monterey, and people started to ask for the Monterey Jack cheese.

There is a debate as to who first made and marketed the cheese. A local dairyman, Domingo Pedrazzi of Carmel Valley, manufactured a similar cheese that required the application of pressure by means of a "house jack." As a result, the cheese was called "jack cheese." Another credited with the cheese was Juana Cota de Boronda, who sold her cheese door to door to support her family and called the cheese by its traditional name. What is certain is that Jacks was the first to commercially market the cheese.

Jacks was a devout Presbyterian who taught Sunday school for more than 50 years. He supported many local churches, donating the land and financially supporting the Pacific Grove Methodist Retreat. He sold the retreat 100 acres of oceanfront land for $1 and donated $30,000 for its support. He served on the University of the Pacific Board of Trustees, contributing to the institution many times over the years. He was a major investor in the Monterey & Salinas Valley Railroad, which had been established to force the Southern Pacific to lower its freight rates for local ranchers. He continually contributed to his family in Scotland when they were in need.

Jacks and his wife had nine children, seven of whom survived, and he encouraged and supported them in attaining an education. In 1907, at the age of 85, he turned control of the family business over to his wife. She deeded all the property to the David Jacks Corporation, run by his children. He died on January 11, 1909, a multimillionaire and the richest landowner in Monterey County.

—Patrick K. Brown

Suggested Reading

Bestor, A. E., Jr. *David Jacks of Monterey, and Lee L. Jacks, His Daughter.* Stanford, CA: Stanford University Press, 1945.

Freeman, Cathleen A. *David Jacks (1822–1909)* [Local history pages]. Monterey, CA: Monterey Historical Society, 1996.

Jack, Kenneth C. *Land King: The Story of David Jack* [Local history pages]. Monterey, CA: Monterey Historical Society, 1999.

Land King: The Story of David Jack. Available from http://www.electricscotland.com/history/jack/chap3.htm

⊞ JACKSON, OLIVER TOUISSANT

See DEARFIELD, COLORADO

⊞ JACKSON, WYOMING

The stretch of land now occupied by the town of Jackson, Wyoming, lies at the southern end of a valley known as Jackson Hole, in the northeastern section of the state. The valley was named for David E. Jackson, a 19th-century American fur trapper. His trapping partner referred to the broad, flat valley as "Jackson's Hole" after they wintered there in 1829 (Betts, p. 3). The valley is 48 miles long and 8 to 15 miles wide, with an elevation from 6,779 feet above sea level in the north to about 6,069 feet at the southern end. Its seemingly flat bottom is encircled by the spectacular mountains, giving it the appearance of a "hole" to early trappers. Along the western slope of the valley, the Tetons soar above the basin without any sign of foothills. The Grand Teton, the tallest mountain in the range, is 13,772 feet above sea level. The range itself, 40 miles long and 10 miles wide, is still rising as the valley floor sinks. The Snake River, originating in the high Yellowstone area above Jackson Hole, is the valley's main drainage.

EARLY HABITATION

The earliest evidence of human presence in the Jackson Hole area is from at least 11,000 years ago. As the glaciers that had formed in the preceding 200 years began to recede, renewed vegetation brought more game and more animal and plant life to the region. Hunters followed, presumably over Teton pass at the south end of the basin. Throughout this early period, only small bands of hunters and gatherers came, periodically, to look for food and materials for tools. More roasting pits and teepee rings among archaeological ruins from 5,000 to 3,000 years ago indicate an increased presence of travelers in and out of the valley. During winter, it is thought, native hunters and gathers took various routes out of the valley to what became Idaho, the Green River, or the Bighorns in eastern Wyoming. Just before contact with Europeans, Bannock, Eastern Shoshone, Blackfoot, and Gros Ventres Indians had developed many routes through the valley and had even frequented the high stone masses above the valley floor. As Indian-built stone enclosures in the mountains testify, the peaks probably served as places of spiritual refuge before contact.

AMERICAN EXPLORATION

Whites came in waves to the Jackson Hole valley. John Colter may have visited Jackson Hole following his departure from the Lewis and Clark expedition. With his partner, Manuel Lisa, who had established a trading fort in the Bighorn Basin to the east of Jackson Hole, Colter took a winter trip from the Bighorn Basin, up the Shoshone river and possibly into the Tetons, to encourage Indian trade.

Evidence more firmly supports later commercial ventures into the valley, beginning with representatives of John Jacob Aster's American Fur Trade Company in 1811 and 1812. By the 1830s, the Tetons became important landmarks for trapping expeditions. One such early team included an Irish trapper by the name of Robert Campbell. After migrating to the United States, Campbell accompanied Jed Smith west to improve his health. He later joined Bill Sublette in supplying goods to the Rocky Mountain Fur Company and moved to Saint Louis to become a wealthy merchant and banker. French Canadian trappers gave the Tetons their name when they traveled with the Northwest Company to Jackson Hole in 1819. Proof of ethnic diversity in the area's roots, these trapping expeditions tapered out by 1840 when the last trappers' rendezvous was held. The country went back to being primarily Indian hunting grounds between 1840 and 1871, when there were only six recorded white visits to Jackson Hole.

As the U.S. Army determined to "ascertain the numbers, habits and disposition of the American Indians inhabiting the country" in the "far west" following acquisition of land from Britain and Mexico, government surveyors and explorers moved through the Jackson region and throughout the West with greater frequency starting in the 1860s. The most famous of those explorations, led by geologist Ferdinand Hayden, sent a spur expedition into the Snake River region in 1871. Together, Hayden, famous photographer William Henry Jackson, and the other scientists and artists on the route publicized and popularized the areas surrounding what became, in 1872, Yellowstone National Park.

It was more than ten years later, however, that the first white settlers began to populate the Jackson area with any level of permanence. Many of the earliest settlers came from surrounding western areas, such as Montana, Idaho, and Utah. Settlement began with a slow progression of individual homesteaders, many of them Civil War veterans who had migrated west after the war. By 1880, the established population of the valley included 20 men, 2 women, and 1 child. In 1889, 20 Mormon settlers boosted the town's population, building a series of homes on what became known as "Mormon row." By 1890, the town had more than 60 people. In response, a post office was opened in 1892, and between 1892 and 1893, William Owen surveyed township lines for the town of Jackson. With mail and most supplies entering the valley over the Teton pass to the south of Jackson, by 1899 the settlement was ready for its first general mercantile store.

Included in the original settlers were a host of foreign-born immigrants. Emile Wolff came to Jackson from Luxembourg. He returned there in 1887 to find a wife. In 1892, Marie Wolff, his new wife, moved to Jackson, contributing to the immigrant population. An Englishman known as Richard "Beaver Dick" Leigh was another of Jackson's foreign-born settlers. The son of a British navy man, Leigh was born in 1831 in Manchester, England. After moving to the United States, he made it to the Rockies and built a cabin in the Jackson Hole valley well before it became settled. He guided well-to-do easterners, including members of the Hayden survey, during the 1870s. Leigh married a Shoshone woman named Jenny who, along with all of the couple's children, died of smallpox in December 1876. Jenny's death symbolized American Indian displacement from the valley that had formerly provided their sustenance.

Early settlers in Jackson, like the rest of American settlers who moved into the West, took part in often violent confrontations between themselves and American Indians during this period. By 1900, there were 638 settled white people in the Jackson Hole. As the white population grew and Wyoming shifted from a federal territory to a state in 1890, Indian hunting rights, protected in earlier federal treaties of the 1860s, became a hotly contested matter in Jackson Hole. The State of Wyoming created big game laws to limit hunting just as many settlers began to see the huge elk herd in the area as more commercially valuable than cattle. Twenty-five of the 75 families in the town of Jackson made more money by guiding hunters than by raising cattle in the 1890s.

In this context, by June 1895, Jackson authorities arrested a lone Bannock man for shooting an elk. In July, directly stating that they hoped to "keep the Indians out" of the valley from then on, authorities arrested 28 more Bannocks, including women and children (Betts, p. 155). When the Indians ran away on their march to confinement, the arrestors shot at them, killing two men, one of them blind. Although the rest of the Bannocks escaped that incident, by the late 1800s, Indian wars throughout the West peaked. The Bannocks and Eastern Shoshones, depleted in numbers and strength, were forced onto reservations and denied access rights to their former hunting lands in Jackson Hole.

It was not until the early years of the 20th century that Anglo Americans overcame the isolation inherent in sporadic and unreliable transportation networks to the valley. Severe winters with temperatures below zero and devastating snow slides could cut off transportation routes for many days at a time, even into the 1930s. The main route came from Rexburg, Idaho, to the southwest, over the Teton pass. By 1901, that course was surveyed, and it was improved in 1918. The road was not surfaced, however, until 1925. It linked Jackson to the railroad in Idaho, which by 1912 had reached Driggs, about 40 miles to the west of Jackson.

Improved transportation and containment of a perceived Indian threat brought another round of homesteaders to Jackson that peaked between 1908 and 1919. In this era, immigrants such as Albert Nelson diversified the town. Born in Sweden in 1861, Nelson moved to Nebraska in 1883 and shortly thereafter found work in the coal mines of Rock Springs,

Wyoming. Later migrating nearly 200 miles north, to Jackson, he became the town's most prominent taxidermist and a very successful businessman. Nelson was among the 10 percent of Jackson's residents who, in 1900, were foreign born. Also included in that group were Gottfried Freuz, one of three homesteaders from Switzerland, and John P. Nelson, who was among four residents from Denmark in 1900. The majority of Jackson's foreign born that year, 15, were from Sweden.

Together, the diverse citizens of Jackson entered the 20th century when, by 1905, the first telephones began to operate and residents became a bit less isolated. Three years later, in 1908, the first automobile drove into Jackson after being hauled through Yellowstone Park on a freight wagon because the National Park Service did not allow cars there until 1915. Actually, most early cars required assistance to go over the Teton pass. In any case, the days of severe isolation in the valley were over, as spatial and temporal boundaries shrank with new national technologies. Its first airstrip served Jackson Hole from 1934 until, by 1946, commercial service operated out of a new airport on land leased from Grand Teton National Park. By 1930, the town had 533 residents, and by 1940, the population had nearly doubled to 1,046. Ongoing settlement of the town, however, became a hot political issue by the late 1920s, when, as the conservation movement gained followers and tourism increased in the area, one of the nation's most powerful men took an interest in the Jackson area. His attention forever changed the future of migration in and to the region.

CONSERVATION

Perhaps the earliest recreational (at least in the modern sense of the term) interest in Jackson came in 1883 when then President Chester Arthur visited the area for a fishing and camping trip with his pals and political allies. Just more than 40 years later, another very powerful man, John D. Rockefeller, formed the Snake River Land Company, with the purpose of purchasing Jackson Hole ranches to set aside for conservation. In 1927, before the process even began, the company convinced President Coolidge to set 23,000

acres of the valley's land apart from private settlement. By 1929, Congress had established Grand Teton National Park in the Teton Mountains. It did not include large sections of the valley floor until, in 1942, after a heated and tumultuous process, Rockefeller persuaded Franklin Delano Roosevelt to create a national monument out of remaining Snake River lands in the valley. By 1950, Congress had merged those lands into the Grand Teton National Park holdings, creating the present borders of the park. In addition, the National Elk Refuge, established in 1948, right outside the town of Jackson, is the winter home of the largest elk herd in North America. Now, with only 3 percent of Teton County in private hands, the complicated history of conservation in a community sustained by tourists and ranchers helped form the migration and immigration the town would see during the last half of the 20th century and into today.

20TH-CENTURY TOURISM

Since the beginnings of Jackson, and even before its official settlement, residents have guided wealthy easterners and Europeans around the surrounding landscape on tours and hunts. By the 1910s, dude ranches had been established in large numbers. Tourists also began frequenting the national park outside Jackson as soon as it was established. Now Jackson Hole sees around 2.5 million visitors a year.

The town's proximity to some of the world's most prestigious mountains contributes to the advent of large numbers of outdoor enthusiasts in the area. Nathaniel Langford and James Stevenson, members of the 1871 Hayden expedition, were the first to claim an ascent of Grand Teton. There is also a possibility that a French trapper and explorer may have ascended the Matterhorn-like peak as early as 1843. In 1898, William O. Owen reached the summit and claimed his trip as the first. In 1929, the Wyoming legislature officially recognized his claim. Since then, thousands of climbers have traveled worldwide to attempt some of the 800 climbs on the 200 or more Teton peaks. Today, the range sees tens of thousands of climbers all year-round. Skiing has also brought in rounds of visitors to the region in the 20th century.

Wyoming's first ski area was Snow King, which opened near Jackson in 1939. The region also includes the Jackson Hole ski area and, not far from town, Grand Targhee resort. Skiers and climbers are part of an overall trend in Jackson represented by generally increased backcountry use in Grand Teton National Park during the last 10 years. In 1997, for example, the park underwent an 884.5 percent increase of backcountry use. Just under three thousand people used the Teton backcountry in 1996, and nearly 28,000 used it in 1997.

Jackson's population base has been significantly affected, especially in the last 10 years, by this rampant tourism and recreational use. The number of temporary residents from all over the globe swells each summer by up to 50,000. In the 1980s, about 54 percent of the county's residential building permits were for second homes. Between 1990 and 2000, the town's population grew generally by 63.3 percent. Most of that growth is from well-educated, wealthy whites. In Jackson, 45.8 percent of residents hold a college degree, compared to 21.9 percent of the state as a whole. With the median value of owner-occupied housing units at $365,400 in 1990, the valley's wealth is evident.

Along with recent economic trends, Jackson has simultaneously seen a sharp rise in its minority population, which increased an incredible 603 percent between 1990 and 2000, compared to a 34.5 percent rise in the rest of Wyoming during the same period. The growth came particularly in the number of Hispanics. Remarkably, during the 1990s, the Hispanic population in Jackson rose 1,164.2 percent (from 81 residents to 1,024). By 2000, the town was 14.4 percent Hispanic.

The character of Jackson has responded to its increasing prosperity. The New York Philharmonic held its first summer residency in 147 years in Jackson in 1989. Vice President Dick Cheney, World Bank president James Wolfensohn, and many Fortune 500 CEOs have vacation property there. At the newly opened Four Seasons Hotel, at the base of the Jackson ski resort, visitors pay $475 a night during the winter. Jackson has its roots as an American Indian seasonal hunting ground, a fur-trapping crossroads, and a hotbed of the conservation wars, and it is changing into a wealthy vacation town and undergoing rampant growth. Its history has included waves of diverse people migrating, sometimes staying, and always transforming Jackson Hole.

—*Laurie Hinck*

Suggested Reading

Betts, Robert. *Along the Ramparts of the Tetons: the Saga of Jackson Hole.* Boulder: Colorado Associated University Press, 1978.

Bonney, Orrin H., and Lorraine G. Bonney. *Guide to the Wyoming Mountains and Wilderness Areas.* 3rd rev. ed. Chicago: Swallow Press, 1977.

Burt, Nathaniel. *Jackson Hole Journal.* Norman: University of Oklahoma Press, 1983.

Calkins, Frank. *Jackson Hole.* New York: Knopf, 1973.

Daugherty, John A. *Jackson Hole: The Historic Resource Study of Grand Teton National Park.* Moose, WY: National Park Service, 1999.

Jackson Hole Chamber of Commerce. "Grand Teton National Park." Available from http://www.jacksonholechamber.com/chamber/index.php?option=content&task=view&id=22

"Jackson Hole Gang," *The Progressive*, 57, no. 5 (May 1993).

Larson, T. A. *History of Wyoming.* 2nd ed., rev. Lincoln: University of Wyoming Press, 1978.

Nelson, Fern K. *This Was Jackson's Hole: Incidents and Profiles from the Settlement of Jackson Hole.* Glendo, WY: High Plains Press, 1994.

Righter, Robert. *Crucible for Conservation: The Creation of Grand Teton National Park.* Boulder: Colorado Associated University Press, 1982.

Saylor, David J. *Jackson Hole, Wyoming: In the Shadow of the Tetons.* Norman: University of Oklahoma Press, 1970.

"Showdown at Jackson Hole." *USA Today,* February 6, 2004.

⊞ JAPANESE IMMIGRATION

See GENTLEMEN'S AGREEMENT; HELENA, MONTANA

⊞ JAPANESE INTERNMENT

As early as September 1936, the federal government took the first direct step toward wartime internment. With the approval of President Franklin D. Roosevelt, J. Edgar Hoover's FBI began a five-year plan of clandestine surveillance of people it considered to be a risk to American security. In September 1939, Roosevelt authorized the creation of the Emergency Detention Program. He also instructed the Justice Department to be prepared to arrest and detain those who might prove dangerous in the event of war. This came only months after the passage of the Hobbs Bill in May, which allowed for the detainment of suspicious foreigners. Even though the FBI had been working on its lists for years, Hoover made the compilation of the list of dangerous aliens and citizens the top priority. For the next two years, the U.S. government compiled lists of dangerous enemy aliens and citizens in departments such as the FBI, the intelligence divisions of the Justice Department, and various military intelligence agencies into the Custodial Detention Index. The 1940 census also included information that was used to locate persons based on their ethnicity. Also in 1940, the Alien Registration Act was passed and required all aliens 14 years of age and older to register with the federal government. In all, the Justice Department registered 4,900,000 aliens, including 695,000 Italians, 315,000 Germans, and 91,000 Japanese; one of every 26 people in the country in 1940 was foreign born.

On the day of the attack on Pearl Harbor, based on the intelligence gathered in the previous years, Roosevelt authorized Attorney General Biddle to issue a blanket warrant to have large numbers of predetermined "dangerous enemy aliens" arrested. Raids by the FBI netted 737 Japanese Americans and hundreds of German and Italian aliens by the end of the day. The next day, Roosevelt issued Presidential Proclamation 2527, branding Japanese nationals as enemy aliens. In the weeks following America's entrance into World War II, many additional restrictions fell upon the so-called enemy aliens. According to War Relocation Statistics, the FBI detained five thousand people of Japanese descent for questioning in the first few weeks of the war.

Life changed dramatically for all people of Japanese descent on the West Coast with the issuance of the blanket warrants. The federal government closed the borders to all Japanese, and those who were not citizens could no longer transfer ownership of, or register, their cars. Issei (Japanese who had emigrated to America from Japan) also had all of their assets frozen, their banks closed, and all business licenses revoked; they had only the cash they had on hand on the morning of the attack on Pearl Harbor. Because of a dramatic fall-off in the volume of produce available at the markets, on December 11 the government—specifically the Treasury secretary—issued General License 77 along with a press release. The General License "permitted" foreign nationals to engage in making and selling food products; the press release urged the Japanese nationals to bring their products to market as "evidence of their loyalty to the United States." This arm twisting restored the availability of produce to 75 percent of prewar levels. Other general licenses allowed Issei to resume control of their produce houses and, by New Year's Day, to withdraw $100 a month from their frozen bank accounts. On December 27, 1941, the California Division of Fish and Game curtailed the issuance of hunting and fishing licenses to enemy aliens. A day later, it was announced that cameras, shortwave radios, guns, swords, and even record players were contraband items and that all enemy aliens must immediately turn these items in to the authorities, who usually consisted of the local police or sheriff's departments.

Japanese Americans in Hawaii were not subject to the same problems as those on the mainland. About one third of the population of Hawaii was Japanese American, and thus economic factors forestalled the mass evacuation and internment of people of Japanese descent. Although some Japanese Americans from Hawaii found themselves selectively interned in camps on the mainland, the imprisonment of Japanese Americans in Hawaii was not as severe as the treatment of the prisoners on the mainland. The conditions, however, were much more favorable in Hawaii, as the interned received more time and warning and could more easily give or sell their property to friends and relatives. This differentiation in treatment showed that politics, race, and economics, in varying degrees, were significant factors in the decision to relocate and intern those of Japanese descent as well as those of German and Italian descent.

The state of California and its local and federal representatives in government began in earnest to call for the removal of all Japanese and Japanese Americans from the coastal region. Los Angeles Congressman

Leland Ford telegrammed Secretary of State Cordell Hull to say he did not believe the government could be too strict in its "consideration of the Japanese in the face of the treacherous way in which they do things" when he asked for their removal from the West Coast. On January 21, Congressman Ford urged officials in Washington to remove all Japanese, whether they were alien or native born, to "concentration camps." On January 28, the California State Personnel Board voted to bar all Japanese descendants from its civil service positions. As cries from the state of California arose demanding the removal of the Japanese and their descendants, Senator Hiram Johnson called for a meeting of the Pacific Coast delegates to discuss the situation. By the end of January, the call for the removal of Japanese from the West Coast had gained unstoppable momentum. Racial and political factors were behind the differentiation of Japanese aliens from their axis counterparts. California Attorney General Earl Warren, eventual governor and Supreme Court chief justice, was an ardent proponent of Japanese relocation. Warren demonstrated his own racist attitudes, stating that "When we are dealing with the Caucasian race we have methods that will test the loyalty of them," further stating that the Japanese "race" was an altogether different matter.

Newspapers and other media accelerated this momentum with a growing dissemination of anti-Japanese rhetoric and propaganda. A *Los Angeles Times* headline dated February 2, 1942, said, "A Viper is Nonetheless a Viper Wherever the Egg is Hatched. So a Japanese-American . . . Grows up to be a Japanese, not an American," reflecting the growing racist sentiment. The following day, the *Orange County News* printed the misleading headline "Grand Jury Asks Removal of Jap Aliens," when, in fact, the jury in question had suggested the removal of all enemy aliens from coastal areas. At the same time, prominent radio newsman John Hughes was insistently pointing out the dangers of sabotage from Japanese aliens, as well as the need to remove them from the coast. Well-known columnist Walter Lippman railed about the inevitability of sabotage, claiming it was a fact that "communication takes place between the enemy at sea and enemy aliens on land." Newspapers up and down the West Coast increasingly reported many such "facts."

The Justice Department worked with the military to create numerous, prohibited zones that were strictly off-limits to enemy aliens. On January 29, 1942, the Department of Justice created 99 "spot" zones, on the recommendation of the military, in areas near dams, electric plants, and other vital installations such as military bases. The largest of these "spot" zones were in San Francisco, San Diego, and the Los Angeles Harbor at Terminal Island in Wilmington. At this time, the Justice Department also established large restricted areas in which enemy aliens were subject to stringent curfew and travel restrictions, particularly on the West Coast. Despite pleas for fairness on the part of Attorney General Biddle and the stated position of the Justice Department that the mass evacuation was both unnecessary and unconstitutional, it ultimately went along with the military in recommending Executive Order 9066. Later, on February 19, 1942, Roosevelt signed Executive Order 9066, authorizing the secretary of war to define military areas in which "the right of any person to enter, remain in or leave shall be subject to whatever restrictions" were deemed necessary or desirable by the given military and civil authorities. This order applied to all axis aliens, and if they violated these or other applicable regulations, they were subject to internment for the remainder of the war. Two days after the signing of Executive Order 9066, the FBI detained an additional 119 Japanese, 54 Italians, and 9 Germans in the state of California alone. Over the first several weeks of the war, the FBI detained a total of 1,540 Japanese, 1,260 Germans, and 231 Italians. On March 18, Executive Order 9102 created the War Relocation Authority (WRA) and named Milton S. Eisenhower its first director.

In contrast, the sheer number of German and Italian aliens and their descendants made their complete relocation and internment unfeasible. Several hundred thousand Germans and Italians and upwards of 11 million of their children and grandchildren, not to mention some prominent politicians, business leaders, and athletes, would have required internment. By late March, the idea of evacuating Italian and German residents from the state was losing support, but the movement to relocate all Japanese residents was gaining momentum. Juxtaposed to this, on March 27, 1942,

General DeWitt's Proclamation No. 4 prohibited all those of Japanese ancestry from leaving Military Area 1 for any reason, thus ending the voluntary evacuation. By mid-1942, it seemed clear that General DeWitt's threat to follow up the Japanese evacuation with those of the more than 200,000 Italian and German aliens in the western states would never become a reality. On Columbus Day, October 12, 1942, in a move designed solely to generate political support among Italian Americans, Roosevelt had Attorney General Biddle announce the end of the enemy alien classification for Italian nationals in the United States. In California, General DeWitt reluctantly lifted all military restrictions on Italians. A few months later, in January 1943, the government also removed the restrictions on German aliens not already selectively interned.

The initial WRA plans to disperse Japanese internees to the interior states met with vehement opposition from the politicians and residents of those states. This was in response to the ongoing voluntary evacuation of the Japanese out of Military Area 1, as designated by General DeWitt. Many of the states immediately to the east of California felt that California was dumping its undesirables on them. The Salt Lake Conference, held on April 7, 1942, attempted to explain the tentative goals of the WRA to the representatives of the 10 western states who attended. It met with so much resistance from the political representatives of these 10 states that it was clear that anything less than concentration camps with slave labor under armed guards would be generally unacceptable. According to a WRA report, this conference was "fundamental in setting the character of relocation centers" as they finally came into being.

On May 3, 1942, General DeWitt issued Civilian Exclusion Order No. 346, ordering all citizens and noncitizens of Japanese ancestry to report to the Assembly Centers, where they would live until they were moved to permanent Relocation Centers. This order began the forced relocation to the 16 army-controlled Assembly Centers, operated by the Wartime Civil Control Administration, that were located up and down the West Coast. Between 112,000 and 120,000 people of Japanese ancestry were subject to this mass exclusion and internment program. The temporary

centers were usually located in race tracks and converted fairgrounds: Santa Anita Race Track, in the environs of Los Angeles, held as many as 18,000 evacuees. Almost no privacy existed; families were jammed together into horse stalls and 20- by 20-foot living areas; meanwhile, all eating, bathing, and toilet facilities were communal. The presence of barbed wire, military police, and guard dogs made it clear that these assembly centers were *de facto* prisons. Only 30 to 40 percent of the internees were aliens the government could legally intern during wartime. By October, barely nine months after the beginning of the war, the first component of internment was finished. In all, almost 4,900 people voluntarily left for nonrestricted areas, predominantly Colorado, Utah, Idaho, and the eastern parts of Oregon and Washington, although roughly 800 of these evacuees found refuge in states farther east. Another four thousand moved to Military Area 2, hoping that if they voluntarily moved out of Military Area 1, General DeWitt would allow them to stay in their new residences. Unfortunately, these people probably suffered the most because of the loss of property and material goods when they moved the first time, compounded by the harsh, unexpected, and abrupt relocation that occurred with the forcible evacuation of Military Area 2.

The WRA gradually transferred the internees to their permanent homes as construction progressed and the Relocation Centers were completed. At any one time, the camps held as many Japanese as the total number of Germans and Italians interned during the scope of the entire war. For instance, there were 16,665 Japanese and their descendants interned at Gila River, Arizona; 19,534 at Poston, Arizona; 10,241 in Jerome, Arkansas; and 11,928 in Rohwer, Arkansas. Other camps, such as Manzanar, California, held 11,062; Tule Lake, California, 29,490; and there were an additional 10,295 at Granada, Colorado; 13,078 at Minidoka, Idaho; 11,212 at Topaz, Utah; and 14,025 at Heart Mountain, Wyoming. Although these figures include those transferred between camps, they make clear the significantly large scale of the Japanese internment. Upon completion of the camps by the end of 1942, there were 10 permanent detention facilities in operation holding more than 110,000 Japanese and Japanese Americans. The majority of these centers were located on Indian land, but the tribes never received remuneration, nor did they gain from the upgrades to the land, because the federal government sold or demolished most of the facilities on closure.

Unique communities evolved inside the camps over the course of the internment. The Relocation Centers were often unfinished when the first shipments of internees arrived. An internee at Heart Mountain described how the first group that arrived had to put tarpaper on the outside and finish the inside of their new homes. This same internee felt fortunate about only having to finish the inside on arrival. Newly arrived internees waited on the stoops of their barracks for their luggage to be distributed. In fact, internees often found themselves waiting for food, water, latrines, and showers. Barracks were broken up into fixed spaces and given out on a per-family basis regardless of the size of the family. These could be described as slightly larger versions of the Assembly Center set-up. The utter barrenness of the land surrounding the Relocation Centers shocked many of the internees. Often neither trees nor anything green existed for miles around, and barbed wire and machine gun towers surrounded the camps. In the fall, schools started that were woefully short on space, teachers, and supplies. Many people took on jobs based on their various skills, some as nurses, some as cooks, and others as musicians. As with the Assembly Centers, the presence of barbed wire, military police, and guard dogs made it clear that these people were there against their will.

The Department of Justice and the military established other internment camps throughout the country. The largest were located at Crystal City and Seagoville, Texas, and Ft. Lincoln, North Dakota. There were at least 50 temporary detention and long-term internment facilities. FBI records indicate that there were certain categories of enemy aliens that became selectively interred in Justice Department internment camps instead of one of the 10 permanent detention centers. Often these internees were the editors, writers, and radio announcers of native language media or language instructors at foreign language schools sometimes supported by foreign consulates. Internees transferred from camp to camp under armed guard, under observation from machine gun towers

and armed men, often with guard dogs, and lived surrounded by barbed wire in huts or dormitories often located in desolate settings. One Los Angeles evacuee spent time at three different local jails before entrainment to Fort Sill in Missoula, Montana. After one month, the internee was off to Livingston, Louisiana, and a month after that, finally, to Santa Fe, New Mexico, until February 1946. Along the way, internees joined Japanese from Costa Rica, Hawaii, and Peru and even some Japanese prisoners of war from the battle of Midway. What further disrupted their lives and made it even more difficult for their families to find them was the censoring of their mail and their severely limited contact with the world outside. Many internees incessantly appealed their internment orders, although their pleas often went unheard. The Department of Justice fabricated impossible standards for obtaining evidence to receive another hearing; few internees obtained rehearings and an even smaller number eventual release. Those who did obtain release simply exchanged prisons of a sort; they often traded one kind of internship for another.

The WRA regulations initially provided for four types of leave. The first successful leave program involved 250 students, none of whom could ever have studied in Japan, who in the summer and fall of 1942 were granted permission to attend colleges such as Gonzaga, Swarthmore, Smith, Radcliffe, and larger institutions such as Texas State and Nebraska State universities. The student leave program involved 2,263 students by the end of 1943. There were generally three other types of leave programs. The first, short-term leave, offered defined periods of leave of short duration. Work-group, or seasonal, leave allowed for longer periods revolving around the needs of agricultural interests. Finally, indefinite leave, which initially only the national director could grant, included stringent requirements, such as definite means of outside support (usually a verifiable job offer), a clean background check, evidence that the community would accept the internee's presence, and agreement to notify the WRA of any changes of address. By the end of 1942, the authorities had only granted 273 applications for indefinite leave, including those for the students who left for college. According to WRA reports, the 10,000 seasonal workers, which included more than

700 who never returned to the camps, evidenced the possible success of larger-scale relocation.

Disturbances at several camps in late 1942 and early 1943 demonstrated a rising tide of resentment among many of the internees. In Manzanar, during August 1943, a meeting of more than 600 residents grew fractious due to the restriction of leave permits for kibei (Japanese Americans educated in Japan). In November 1942, a disturbance in Poston hinged on the arrest and detention of two internees, on little evidence, for the beating of a third who was extremely unpopular in the camp. One thousand internees posted themselves outside the camp jail to interfere with possible transfer of the two prisoners, and a general strike was called for throughout the camp. The disturbance was resolved by eventually releasing both men, one into the custody of a council of internees. Two weeks after the Poston strike, a similar disturbance led to the death of two internees after a standoff between thousands of internees and soldiers. The deaths of the two young Nisei (second-generation Japanese Americans) led to a strike that did not end until just before Christmas. Ultimately, many of the agitators of these various disturbances ended up in segregation at Tule Lake.

In February 1943, a massive registration program began to gather information, in collusion with the draft-minded military, to speed up the leave clearance process. The mass registration led to crises within the internment centers. The controversial "loyalty oath" questions led to large-scale outcry and the eventual segregation at Tule Lake of more than 5,000 internees whose answers to two specific questions regarding their willingness to serve in the military and loyalty to the United States were ostensibly incorrect. Distributed by the WRA and the army, questions 27 and 28 of the "Statement of U.S. Citizenship of Japanese American Ancestry" were particularly disturbing to Issei and their Nisei children. The first question asked the internees if they were willing serve in the military "on combat duty" wherever ordered. This was a ridiculous question for many of the older Issei, for whom combat duty was entirely unrealistic. Question 28, the "loyalty oath" question, demanded a pledge be sworn to defend the United States and to "forswear any oaths of allegiance to the Japanese emperor" or any other foreign power. This forced

many of the people, disallowed American citizenship by law, into an untenable position. Often, Nisei children older than 17 answered as their parents did to avoid the likeliness of being separated, and those under 17 had no choice but to follow their parents. Those who answered no to both questions were labeled as disloyal and, along with their children, segregated from the other internees and sent to Tule Lake. At Tule Lake, many of the internees would not even fill out the registration forms, and camp authorities arrested and segregated about 40 of them.

Improvements to the relocation program in 1943 helped speed up the overall process of resettling internees. Field offices opened in cities such as Chicago, Minneapolis, and Madison, usually where resettlement committees had previously existed, to help voluntary evacuees settle into their communities. A policy to give limited cash grants to internees who were relocating included $50 for individuals, $75 for those leaving with a dependant, and a maximum of $100 for all others. Further changes to this program eventually included families of those serving in the military and those leaving to seek employment without previously securing its guarantee. The decentralization of the leave clearance bureaucracy also empowered project directors to give permission for indefinite leave without requiring the national director's approval. The WRA had only 8,000 seasonal leaves in 1943. The lower numbers were due in large part to indefinite leaves and those who enlisted in the military; a large portion of those on seasonal leave converted to indefinite leave status and did not return to the camps. In all, 9,000 internees had relocated by mid-year, and more than 17,000 were out by the end of the year. Though slightly diminished, the levels of relocation stayed relatively the same in 1944. Enough internees had received indefinite leave for the WRA to begin planning the closure of some of its facilities. Jerome, Arkansas, was the first to close, on June 30, with the 5,700 remaining internees transferred primarily to Rohwer and Gila River. On December 17, 1944, the War Department announced the forthcoming end to the mass exclusion orders. At this point, approximately 35,000 internees relocated out of the camps; more than 2,300 of these had joined the military.

On December 18, 1944, the WRA announced that it would seek closure of all of its remaining centers, with the exception of Tule Lake, between June 1944 and January 1945. At the time, there were still roughly eighty thousand internees located within the remaining camps. Except for Gila River and Colorado River, where internees still had winter crops to harvest, the WRA immediately terminated the seasonal leave program. The actual timing of the closing was flexible due to the difficulties of relocating tens of thousands of internees within a relatively short period. Even excluding internees and their families who had renounced their citizenship (an estimated 20,000 people), the WRA had to relocate twice as many people in the next year as it had in total during the previous two. Although violence and other forms of resistance toward the returning internees occurred within the former exclusion zones, the WRA closed all centers, except Tule Lake, by December 1945.

The end of the internment witnessed a vastly different geographic settlement of people of Japanese descent than had existed previously in 1940. Only 40 percent of the evacuees returned to the excluded portion of Oregon, and both Washington and California reclaimed only 51 percent of those forced to leave in the first months of the war. Although the number of evacuees that moved to states such as New Hampshire (9), Maine (7), North Carolina (8), and Georgia (10) was extremely limited, significant numbers of internees ended up all across the country. Thousands of former internees ended up in Illinois, Ohio, Missouri, New York, Colorado, Utah, Pennsylvania, New Jersey, and Minnesota. Large cities such as Chicago (11,309), Denver (3,124), New York (2,036), Detroit (1,649), and Minneapolis (1,354) almost overnight became home to enclaves of these former "enemy aliens."

A movement to obtain redress from the federal government began in the late 1960s and took 20 years to come to fruition. The first step toward redress came with the repeal of the Emergency Detention Action in 1971. It was followed in 1976 when President Ford officially rescinded Executive Order 9066. In 1979, the National Council for Japanese American Redress formed, with the sole purpose of obtaining monetary compensation for Japanese American victims of internment. President Carter authorized the Commission on Wartime Relocation and Internment of Civilians in 1980, and its report was published in 1983. The Civil Liberties Act of 1988 authorized $20,000 and an official apology. Finally, in 1990, the federal government gave the first redress payments and apologies to the oldest of the survivors.

—*Scott M. Behen*

See also Cody, Wyoming; German and Italian Internment

Suggested Reading

Akiyama, Kiyoma Henry. Interview by Arthur A. Hansen and Yasko Gamo [Interview no. 1751, transcript], June 10, 1982. Fullerton: California State University Fullerton Oral History Collection.

Broom, Leonard, and Ruth Rienera. *Removal and Return: The Socio-economic Impact of the War on Japanese Americans.* Berkeley: University of California Press, 1974.

Bosworth, Allan R. *America's Concentration Camps.* New York: Norton, 1967.

Bureau of Sociological Research, Colorado River War Relocation Center. "The Japanese Family in America." *Annals of the American Academy of Political and Social Science* 229 (September 1943).

"Center Gets 1246 Japs from South," *Los Angeles Times,* April 9, 1942.

Chamness, Lee, Jr. Interview with John Sprout [Interview no. 78, transcript], November 25, 1968. Fullerton: California State University Fullerton Oral History Collection.

Chin, Frank. *Born in the USA: A Story of Japanese America, 1889–1947.* New York: Rowman & Littlefield, 2002.

Collins, Donald E. *Native American Aliens: Disloyalty and the Renunciation of Citizenship by Japanese Americans during World War II.* Westport, CT: Greenwood Press, 1985.

Congressional Record. 77th Cong., 1st sess, 1941. p. A5554.

Conrat, Maisie, & Richard Conrat. *Executive Order 9066.* Van Nuys: University of California, Los Angeles, Asian American Studies Center, 1992.

Daniels, Roger. *The Politics of Prejudice: The Anti-Japanese Movement in California and the Struggle for Japanese Exclusion.* Berkeley: University of California Press, 1977.

Daniels, Roger, Sandra C. Taylor, and Harry H. L. Kitano. *Japanese Americans: From Relocation to Redress.* Ogden: University of Utah Press, 1986.

De Nevers, Klancy Clark. *The Colonel and the Pacifist: Karl Bendetsen, Perry Saito, and the Incarceration of Japanese Americans during World War II.* Salt Lake City: University of Utah Press, 2004.

DeWitt, J. L. *Final Report: Japanese Evacuation from the West Coast, 1942.* Washington, DC: U.S. Government Printing Office, 1943.

Drinnon, Richard. *Keeper of Concentration Camps: Dillon S. Myer and American Racism.* Berkeley: University of California Press, 1987.

Endo, Aiko Tanimachi. Interview with Marsha Bode [Interview no. 1750, transcript], November 15, 1983. Fullerton: California State University Fullerton Oral History Collection.

Fisher, Galen M. "Japanese Evacuation from the Pacific Coast." *Far Eastern Survey* 11, no. 13 (June 29, 1942).

Gibney, Frank, ed. *Senso: The Japanese Remember the Pacific War.* Armonk, NY: Sharpe, 1995.

Hayasi, Brian Masaru. *Democratizing the Enemy: The Japanese American Internment.* Princeton, NJ: Princeton University Press, 2004.

Herman, Masako, ed. *The Japanese in America 1843–1973: A Chronology and Fact Book.* Dobbs Ferry, NY: Oceana, 1974.

Hohri, William Minoru. *Resistance: Challenging America's Wartime Internment of Japanese-Americans.* Lomita, CA: Espistolarian, 2001.

Ichioka, Yuji. *The Issei.* New York: Free Press, 1988.

Ihara, Craig Kei Sansei. Interview with Betty E. Miton [Interview no.1230, transcript], December 19, 1973. Fullerton: California State University Fullerton Oral History Collection.

Inada, Lawson Fusao. *Only What We Could Carry: The Japanese American Internment Experience.* Berkeley, CA: Heyday Books, 2000.

Iriye, Akira. *Power and Culture: The Japanese-American War, 1941–1945.* Cambridge, MA: Harvard University Press, 1981.

James, Thomas. *Exile Within: The Schooling of Japanese Americans 1942–1945.* Cambridge, MA: Harvard University Press, 1987.

"Japanese on West Coast Face Wholesale Uprooting," *San Francisco News,* 4 March 1942.

Kaihard, Rodney. Interview with Patricia Morgan [Interview no. 1277, transcript], March 25, 1973. Fullerton: California State University Fullerton Oral History Collection.

Kanegae, Henry. Interview with Richard Curtiss [Interview no. 4, transcript], February 16, 1966. Fullerton: California State University Fullerton Oral History Collection.

Kashima, Tetsuden. "Japanese American Internees Return, 1945 to 1955." *Phylon* 41, no. 2 (1980).

"Manipulating of Market by Jap Farmers Related: Vegetable Profits Assertedly Sent Back to Homeland." *Los Angeles Times,* February 5, 1943.

Moore, Brenda Lee. *Serving Our Country: Japanese American Women in the Military during World War II.* Piscataway, NJ: Rutgers University Press, 2003.

Muller, Eric L. *Free to Die for Their Country: The Story of the Japanese American Draft Resisters in World War II.* Chicago: University of Chicago Press, 2001.

Nakano, Mei. *Japanese American Women: Three Generations, 1890–1990.* San Francisco: National Japanese American Historical Society, 1990.

Niiya, Brian. *Encyclopedia of Japanese American History.* New York: Facts on File, 2000.

O'Brien, David J., and Stephen S. Fugita. *The Japanese American Experience.* Bloomington: Indiana University Press, 1991.

Personal Justice Denied: Report of the Commission on Wartime Relocation and Internment of Civilians. Seattle: University of Washington Press, 1997.

Robinson, Greg. *By Order of the President.* Cambridge, MA: Harvard University Press, 2001.

Smith, Elmer R. "Resettlement of Japanese Americans." *Far Eastern Survey* 18, no. 10 (May 18, 1949).

Stanley, Jerry. *I Am an American: A True Story of Japanese Interment.* New York: Crown, 1994.

Takami, David. *Executive Order 9066: Fifty Years Before and Fifty Years After.* Seattle, WA: Wing Luke Asian Museum, 1992.

Takata, Roy Y. Interview with Mary McCarthy [Interview no. 127a, transcript], April 14, 1974. Fullerton: California State University Fullerton Oral History Collection.

Taylor, Sandra C. *Jewel of the Desert: Japanese American Internment at Topaz.* Berkeley: University of California Press, 1993.

TenBroek, Jacobus, Edward N. Barnhart, and Floyd W. Matson. *Prejudice, War and the Constitution, Causes and Consequences of the Evacuation of the Japanese Americans in World War II.* Berkeley: University of California Press, 1968.

Uchida, Yoshiko. *Desert Exile: The Uprooting of a Japanese American Family.* Seattle: University of Washington Press, 1982.

Uno, Roy. Interview with John McFarlane [Interview no. 1070, transcript], April 25, 1971. Fullerton: California State University Fullerton Oral History Collection.

U.S. Congress. House. Tolan Committee. Report no. 2124, 77th Cong., 2nd sess., 1942.

U.S. Department of Interior, War Relocation Authority. *Administrative Highlights of the WRA Program, Volume 1.* New York: AMS Press, 1975.

U.S. Department of Interior, War Relocation Authority. *Community Government in War Relocation Centers, Volume 2.* New York: AMS Press, 1975.

U.S. Department of Interior, War Relocation Authority. *Legal and Constitutional Phases of the WRA Program, Volume 4.* New York: AMS Press, 1975.

U.S. Department of Interior, War Relocation Authority. *People in Motion: The Postwar Adjustment of the Evacuated Japanese Americans.* Washington, DC: U.S. Government Printing Office, 1946.

U.S. Department of Interior, War Relocation Authority. *A Quantitative Data.* Washington, DC: U.S. Government Printing Office, 1946.

U.S. Department of Interior, War Relocation Authority. *Relocation of Japanese Americans.* Washington, DC: U.S. Government Printing Office, May 1943.

U.S. Department of Interior, War Relocation Authority. *The Relocation Program, Volume 7.* New York: AMS Press, 1975.

U.S. Department of Interior, War Relocation Authority. *A Story of Human Conservation.* Washington, DC: U.S. Government Printing Office, 1946.

U.S. Department of Interior, War Relocation Authority. *Token Shipment: The Story of America's War Refugee Shelter, Volume 8.* New York: AMS Press, 1975.

U.S. Department of Interior, War Relocation Authority. *The War Time Handling of Evacuee Property, Volume 11.* New York: AMS Press, 1975.

"A Viper Is Nonetheless a Viper Wherever the Egg Is Hatched. So a Japanese-American . . . Grows up to Be a Japanese, Not an American." *Los Angeles Times,* February 2, 1942.

Weglyn, Michi. *Years of Infamy: The Untold Story of America's Concentration Camps.* San Francisco: National Japanese American Society, 1996.

Yoo, David. *Growing Up Nisei: Race, Generation, and Culture among Japanese Americans of California, 1924– 49.* Champaign: University of Illinois Press, 2000.

▦ JAPANTOWN

See LITTLE TOKYO AND JAPANTOWN

▦ JEWISH MIGRATION PATTERNS

See GILEAD, KANSAS; HELENA, MONTANA

▦ JICARILLA

See APACHE

▦ JOHNSON–REED ACT

See IMMIGRATION AND NATURALIZATION SERVICE (INS)

▦ JUANEÑOS

The Indians of the Acjachemen Nation are the original inhabitants of lands that comprise much of Orange and San Diego Counties in southern California today. They occupied the coastal region from Long Beach to Oceanside, fished off the shores of Santa Catalina and San Clemente Islands, and hunted the inland areas as far east as Lake Elsinore. Originally, they migrated into this region from the Great Basin and later experienced forced migrations within their tribal lands when Spanish, Mexican, and American invaders took their land and homes.

Wedged between two linguistically similar Indian groups, the Gabrielinos to the north and the Luiseños to the south, the Acjachemen became known as the Juaneño Indians. The Spanish discarded the Indian names of these tribes and renamed each of them after the nearby missions, including San Gabriel (Gabrielinos), San Luis Rey (Luiseños), and San Juan Capistrano (Juaneños). The Juaneños flourished before the arrival of the Europeans, living by a productive and reliable substance economy based on the hunting and gathering of naturally occurring foods and materials. The songs and stories of the tribe tell of seasonal migrations to harvest and hunt. Elaborate trade networks and kinship groups formed with other Indians in the region often dictated the migration patterns of the Juaneños. More migrations occurred within the region when the Spanish arrived in California and forced the Juaneños from their land to use it to raise crops and cattle. The Juaneños built the great mission for the invaders as diseases decimated their tribe. The Juaneños maintained their cultural identity and adapted to more changes throughout the Mexican period. The American takeover and occupation of California again forced them to sacrifice their land, relocate, and adapt to yet another new culture and language. After more than two centuries of interaction with these intruders on their land, today the large-scale migrations of the Juaneños have ended, yet their fight to retain control of ancestral lands and sacred burial grounds continues.

In terms of culture, linguistics, and origin theories, the Juaneños share similar characteristics with neighboring native groups. The Juaneño language belongs to the Takic division of the Uto-Aztecan family, and American Indians associated with the San Luis Rey and the San Juan Capistrano missions both spoke the language. These groups share cultural and linguistic traits with their Uto-Aztecan neighbors, the Cupeños, Gabrielinos, and Cahuilla Indians. Early ethnographic literature distinguishes between the Juaneños and the

Luiseños, but modern academics generally agree that they were culturally one tribe. Linguistic distribution studies suggest that these people migrated into southern California from the Great Basin area in a succession of waves rather than in a single migration or drift. There is no evidence to suggest that they crossed the barrier of the Sierra Nevada to penetrate California's Central Valley during their southward migration. Their route into the region may have been via the Cajon Pass, although the San Gorgonio Pass, prominent in many of the travel songs of the Luiseño Indians, is a likely path also. Because pre–contact era ethnographical materials are scarce, no definite migration dates exist. Linguists and authors believe that these Takic-speaking groups arrived between fifteen hundred and three thousand years ago.

The Juaneños established villages along the coast and inland areas of southern California as they gradually became more sedentary. Settlement patterns developed around the seasonal migrations that supported a subsistence economy for the tribe. Some anthropologists suggest that the Juaneños spent equal time during the year in two separate settlements. They occupied one location at a higher altitude during the months of summer and then relocated to a lowland location for the winter months. They migrated to gather acorns, hunt deer, and collect other available foods. A second and more likely theory is that the Juaneños spent most of the year at one settlement, with seasonal trips to specific areas to gather food. The acorn harvest usually took several weeks, eliminating any reason for a four- to six-month occupation of the mountain sites. It was also a standard practice in California to store enough acorns to last for two years, thus eliminating the need to relocate the village every six months. Much of what ethnographers and historians know about these seasonal migration patterns comes from the accounts of Juaneño storytellers, who have passed this information on from one generation to the next.

In addition to providing clues about tribal migration, Juaneño stories also reveal the Juaneños' beliefs about their origins as a people. The creation story of the Juaneños describes a different kind of migration, a journey from the spiritual world to the human world. The story has at least two versions, one told by the

inhabitants of the interior and the other by the people of the coast. In the most commonly told story, the first things in the universe were heaven and the earth, who were brother and sister. Sand, stones, trees, grass, and animals were the products of the union of heaven and earth. This union also created a being called Wiyot, a man-god who th en created men, or rather a first race of beings that preceded humankind. These beings multiplied in number and populated the earth, migrating southward from the north.

The eldest of Wiyot's servants plotted against and poisoned him, and a new deity replaced him. Chinigchinich, a spectral being who appeared after the death of Wiyot, lived in the sky rather than throughout the world. He created a new race, the present human species, and taught them laws, institutions, rites, and ceremonies. This migration from one creation to another produced the Juaneño people of the present day. Chinigchinich foretold his own death and told the people he would ascend to the stars where he would watch over them. He promised to punish with bears, rattlesnakes, famine, and sickness those who disobeyed his commandments, and he promised to reward the faithful. The Indians believe that Chinigchinich is ever-present and can see all things but is invisible to man.

The creation stories of the people of the Capistrano Valley do more than entertain children and tourists. These stories, passed from generation to generation within the tribe, help to preserve their religion, culture, and traditions. To the Juaneños, their history and their identity begin with creation, and many of these stories are the basis for their religious ceremonies. Archeologists trace migration patterns, but Native American storytellers look for their origins in their oral narratives. These stories are the cultural foundation of the people, and they provide moral lessons and guidance in this life. They also form the link between the natural world and the spiritual world. These oral accounts provide clues about past migrations of the Juaneños and help to explain to young tribal members why certain places still have great religious significance to the tribe.

Ceremonial practices developed around the deity Chinigchinich and became the religion of the Juaneños, Gabrielinos, Luiseños, and other native groups in southern California. Chinigchinich lived long before the arrival of the Europeans to the region, but the religion surrounding the man-god developed perhaps in part as a reaction to the decimation of native populations by European diseases. It spread quickly as an indigenous "missionary movement," passed on by one native group to the next.

The Chinigchinich religion provides examples of both the physical and the spiritual migration of the Juaneños. The religion included an extensive number of secret and sacred ceremonies, including rituals for boys' puberty rites, initiation rites for girls, mourning ceremonies, cremation rituals at death, and a dance of thanksgiving during solar eclipses. Often the Juaneños would migrate to specific sites to perform rituals, rites, and ceremonies. To stimulate dreams or revelatory visions during religious rites, shamans often used *toloache,* a powerful hallucinogenic drug prepared from jimsonweed. These dreams and visions symbolize the spiritual migration of the initiate to another realm. The strict laws and rites of the Chinigchinich religion made it possible for the Juaneños to preserve their traditional religious system over time by perpetuating specific practices and beliefs.

The migration of Spaniards into Alta California from Mexico during the 18th century radically altered the religious life and cultural traditions of the Juaneños. The arrival of the Juan Rodriguez Cabrillo expedition in 1542 marked the first interaction between the Europeans and Native Americans in the region. The first recorded contact between the Juaneños and the Europeans did not occur until 1769, when Gaspar de Portolá passed through southern California with an expedition of Spanish soldiers and settlers. The early encounters between the Indians and the newcomers seemed benign enough; the Juaneños welcomed the Spanish with friendship and hospitality. Things changed quickly, however, when the Indians discovered what their role would be in the Spanish plans for colonization.

Father Junípero Serra, the Franciscan priest who arrived in Alta California with Portolá, established a chain of missions along the coast using Indian labor. The founding of the missions at San Juan Capistrano in 1776 and San Luis Rey in 1798 represented the first permanent Spanish settlements on Juaneño land

and the first wave of Spanish migration from Mexico. The Franciscans quickly incorporated the Juaneños and Luiseños into the mission system as converts to Catholicism and as workers in the new Spanish society. Forced migrations soon began as Indians left their villages and settlements to relocate and live as resident laborers inside the walls of the missions. Juaneños also moved to the *asistencias,* the outlying chapels built by the Spanish that served as extensions of the oppressive mission system. Completed by the Indians in 1806 after nine years of labor, the mission at San Juan Capistrano had a 125-foot bell tower, the largest man-made structure west of the Mississippi River. Indians migrating north from Dana Point, six miles away, used cattle-drawn carts to transport the volcanic rock and sandstone used to build the mission.

Once construction of the mission was complete, the Indians then labored as carpenters, tanners, and blacksmiths as the forced relocation of the Juaneños continued. Wheat and corn grown near the mission and sheep and cattle raised by the Indians provided trade goods for visitors and food for the priests and converts. The revenues from the sale of hides and tallow provided the economic foundation for the mission economy. By the end of the Spanish Period, when the missions were one of the few profit-making entities in California, Indian labor was providing the foundation of every aspect of mission production. To keep this system running, the Spanish priests and soldiers forced Juaneños from coastal villages to relocate closer to the mission. As agricultural and grazing acreage increased and the mission economy grew, greater numbers of Indians came from progressively more distant villages to labor at the missions.

The arrival of the Spanish and the imposition of the mission system caused a significant population shift and great disruptions in the daily lives of the Juaneños. The Indians adopted a new language, a different system of religious beliefs, and certain aspects of the new culture. The Franciscans controlled native labor and exercised absolute authority over the converted Indians, ridiculing and repressing native religious practices. In spite of the efforts of the mission fathers to quash native traditions, the Juaneños resisted change and maintained important aspects of their culture by clinging to the rites of the

Chinigchinich religion. Contact with the foreigners and forced servitude led to the increase of diseases, murder, and rape of the Indians. The Juaneño transition to the afterlife (marked by an earthly grave) represents another type of forced migration; the tribe lost more than 60% of its population during the mission period.

In 1821, Mexico achieved its independence from Spain and took possession of California and its native inhabitants. The Juaneños instantly became Mexican citizens and prepared to adapt once again to the new laws of a foreign government. Under Spanish rule, California languished as an economically struggling province on the hinterlands of a once-vast empire. As a Mexican territory, California remained isolated from the new capital in Mexico City and neglected by the new government, so independence initially had little effect upon the Juaneños. Mexican plans to secularize the Franciscan missions changed all that.

After Mexico won its independence, it found that it could no longer afford to keep the missions running as Spain had done. In 1833, the Mexican Congress ordered the process of mission secularization to begin. Over the next fifteen years, the government removed the clergy's authority over the Indians, parish priests replaced the missionaries, and the missions became ordinary churches. The most remarkable part of the plan divided the vast and valuable mission lands and gave them to Indian neophytes, soldiers, colonists, naturalized foreigners, and convicts. The priests dismantled Mission San Juan Capistrano and abandoned the Juaneños completely by 1844, and Governor Pío Pico offered the mission at public auction the following year.

The secularization of the missions affected the Indians profoundly and left their future uncertain. Before secularization, the mission priests held a monopoly on Indian labor, and the closing of the missions caused a scattered migration of the Juaneños over a wide area of southern California. Plans to disperse the mission lands fairly and evenly among the needy never materialized, and the Indians ended up owning very little of the land. Many of the displaced Indians migrated in search of places to live and food to eat. A few Juaneños acquired land grants and attempted to enter into the mainstream of Mexican culture. The Mexican government established several Indian pueblos, but they could not successfully compete in the rancho-dominated economy, and most of these pueblos soon dissolved. Some native people migrated inland and assimilated into groups of nonmission Indians. The mission had been the only home many of the Indians had ever known, so some stayed to look for work at the mission or in the pueblos of the Mexicans. Other Juaneños returned to tribal village sites, where they maintained their traditional subsistence activities with the addition of agriculture and animal husbandry. Many found work on the nearby ranchos, where the landowners continued to exploit their labor; others revolted against the Mexican rancheros, who treated them like slaves. Rancho society in Mexican California became a feudal society, where the Indian workers who tended the fields and herds labored as serfs.

Nothing improved for the Juaneños when the Mexican War and American takeover of California led to more displacement of the Indians from their land. Large numbers of immigrants from the United States and from around the world soon arrived in California, and everyone wanted land. Under the terms of the Treaty of Guadalupe Hidalgo in 1848, the indigenous peoples of California should have received American citizenship and the property ownership protections accorded to all citizens under the U.S. Constitution. Instead, the new government granted no recognition of native rights; Anglos viewed the Indians either as trespassers or as a useful class of migrant laborers, agricultural workers, and domestic servants. The discovery of gold a few days before the signing of the treaty and the subsequent rush of Americans into California exacerbated Anglo-Indian conflicts.

The gold rush that began in the foothills of the Sierra Nevada and in northern California soon affected a far wider area. When the gold panned out, frustrated argonauts became farmers and ranchers, and many set their sights on Juaneño land in southern California. Disputes quickly arose, and Juaneños evicted from their homes had to relocate to nearby towns or ranches. The flood of immigrants into the region from the United States and other countries caused great changes in the traditional lifestyle of the Juaneños. Native grasses decreased, and local game retreated to higher elevations and safer locations. The Indians had to leave their homes and land to pursue the animals or to seek additional grazing lands for their own herds. The sudden influx of American settlers led to an increase in disease, murder, and mayhem, forcing the Juaneños to move to areas far removed from Anglo settlements.

Many of the new California residents believed that Indians were impediments to progress and civilization and saw either extermination or domestication as the solution to the "Indian problem." Other Californians saw ways to use the Indians as an indigenous labor force. In April 1850, the new state government acted quickly to control Indian labor by passing a law titled "An Act for the Government and Protection of the Indians." Under this law, Indians arrested and jailed for crimes such as "strolling about" were then required to work for the person who paid their bail. The law also established a system of Indian "apprenticeship" in which Anglos could legally own Indian children. These child laborers performed many types of work in many different parts of the state, and their story is another example of the forced migration of native peoples. At the same time the U.S. Congress in Washington, DC, was debating whether to admit California to the union as a free state, this new act sanctioned Indian slavery in California.

In addition to the apprenticeship clause, the legislation of 1850 led to an increase in the resettlement and relocation of native peoples for another reason. Indians could do nothing to prevent the taking of their lands and children because the law prohibited Indians from testifying against Anglos in American courts. Because Indians had no legal recourse available, by 1875, whites had expropriated most Juaneño villages and farms and again forced the Indians to migrate to survive. The few Juaneños who escaped the experience of moving from place to place remained in a state of peonage like that which had existed on the Mexican ranchos. The Anglos simply Americanized the Hispanic system of Indian labor exploitation.

Shortly after California's admission to the union in 1850, Congress authorized three federal Indian commissioners to negotiate treaties with the Indians. In January 1852, the commissioners and native leaders signed eighteen treaties with 139 different bands and tribes. The treaties created reservations for Indians and, more significantly, established official relations between the U.S. government and the native people of California. Even though the treaties granted only 7.5% of the state's land to Native Americans, many Californians opposed the pacts because they felt the Indians would receive too much good land. Congress bowed to the pressure and failed to ratify the treaties. This meant that neither the United States nor the State of California recognized Native American land rights, so whites continued to steal Indian land. Migrations increased as more and more Indians became landless and displaced.

In an attempt to find a humane solution to the growing number of Anglo-Indian conflicts in California, the U.S. government tried to establish segregated living areas for the Indians within the state. The first federal Indian reservation opened in California in 1853 and operated for only eleven years, and most subsequent attempts by the government to provide small reservations were only partially successful. The creation of government reservations usually led to the migration of Indians. Large groups of natives had to be organized, transported, and resettled on reservations located far from their original tribal lands. In 1875, the U.S. government created several reservations for the Luiseño Indians, but their plans neglected the needs of the neighboring Juaneños. Federal agents in southern California overlooked the Juaneños and omitted them from their surveys and reports, and consequently the Juaneños never received any reservation lands. Because of Congress' failure to ratify the eighteen treaties and establish reservations, the Juaneños lost much of the land they had retained up to that time. Left to survive as best they might on the fringes of white settlement, many of them did not survive.

The repercussions of the government's failure to provide a reservation for the Juaneños had long-lasting effects on the well-being of the tribe. During the last two decades of the 19th century, in the rare instances when Indian reform advocates succeeded in attaining monetary or material assistance for California natives, federal aid programs excluded the Juaneños because they had no reservation. For example, Congress passed the Act for the Relief of Mission Indians in 1891 to settle land disputes in California and to create ten new reservations. The act also created the Smiley Commission, the purpose of which was to relocate as many Indians as possible onto the new reservation lands. The legislation and the commission ignored the Indians of San Juan Capistrano because the reports of the Indian agents failed to mention them after 1880. The actions of the commission also show that the federal government had no serious interest in ceding coastal land to the Indians for reservations. The decision not to recognize the Juaneños is significant because it compounded the difficulties they would have years later in their efforts to achieve federal recognition.

In acknowledgement of the failure of the U.S. Senate to ratify the eighteen treaties in 1852, Congress passed the California Indians Jurisdictional Act in 1928 to compensate native peoples for lands lost to the United States. To determine who would receive compensation, yet another special government census determined the number of living descendents of California Indians. Litigation over the details of the case dragged on in the legal courts until 1944. In the land seizure settlement, the Indians of California received $5 million, or about $600 per person, after government deductions for goods and services rendered to the Indians. In 1950, the Juaneños finally received payments amounting to about $150 per person, money that many tribal members refused to accept as compensation for their stolen land. The payments authorized by the commissions and legislation represented nothing more than token attempts at reparations. The commissions could not reverse the forced migrations nor fully compensate the displaced Juaneños. The Indians received little land from the government.

The Acjacamen Indian Nation today is a sovereign, organized, democratic body comprising more than twenty-seven hundred members. A five-person elected council guides tribal affairs, and a tribal constitution provides the legal framework for governance. In 1979, the Acjacamen Nation ratified the constitution and organized as the "Juaneño Band of Mission Indians" in an effort to safeguard its sovereignty, improve relations with the federal government, and advance tribal agendas. Part of these agendas included the goal of achieving official recognition by the federal government. The Juaneño Band of Mission Indians still exists today, although there are three different factions within the group who are all seeking a prominent voice in tribal decision making.

Tribal existence does not depend on federal recognition, but approval could affect the future migration of the tribe for several reasons. Recognition creates a trust relationship between the tribe and the federal government and provides protection for the tribe under the Native American Graves Protection and Repatriation Act. Using this act, American Indians can preserve sacred objects and end the type of unwanted migration represented by the desecration of graves and the removal of the skeletal remains of their ancestors. Official government acknowledgment would increase longevity rates among the Juaneños by providing them with access to education and medical programs to address the health problems that afflict urbanized tribal members today, such as diabetes, stress, and obesity. Recognition also makes the tribe eligible for future considerations regarding changes in reservation lands in southern California. Twenty-two years after formally petitioning the U.S. government for recognition, the request of the tribe remains categorized as "ready for active consideration" by the U.S. Bureau of Acknowledgement and Research, one stage away from beginning the ultimate decision-making process.

Today the Juaneños are actively continuing their efforts to end their long history of forced migrations. The most obvious example of this is their ongoing fight to prevent the desecration of native gravesites and the relocation of the sacred remains of their ancestors. The tribe is often embroiled in protracted legal disputes, and they have sought the help of county and state courts to prevent local land developers from turning sacred burial sites into soccer fields and parking lots for convenience stores. The Acjachemen continue to be a strong and active Indian tribe that contributes to American society and fiercely protects its cultural identity.

—*Hal Hoffman*

See also Cahuilla Nation

Suggested Reading

Bean, Lowell J., and Florence C. Shipek. "Luiseño." In *Handbook of North American Indians.* Vol. 8, edited by R. F. Heizer. Washington, DC: Smithsonian Institution, 1978.

Boscana, Geronimo. *Chinigchinich: A Revised and Annotated Version of Alfred Robinson's Translation of Father Geronimo Boscana's Historical Account of the Belief, Usages, Customs, and Extravagances of the Indians of This Mission of San Juan Capistrano Called the Acagchemen Tribe.* Reprinted ed. Banning, CA: Malki Museum Press, 1978.

Henshaw, H. W. "The Luiseño Creation Myth." *Masterkey for Indian Lore and History* 46, no. 3 (1972).

Sparkman, Philip Stedman. "The Culture of the Luiseño Indians." *University of California Publications in American Archaeology and Ethnology* 8, no. 4 (August 7, 1908).

⊞ JULIAN, CALIFORNIA

As one snakes along the serpentine Route 78, meandering through the foothills east of San Diego, one is struck by the beauty of the landscape. Julian is a gem found in that piedmont region. The natives of the area are now mostly gone, many inadvertently killed by diseases spread by the Spaniards who built the tiny Santa Ysabel mission in the early 19th century. There are fewer than 100 Cuyamacas left today, the predominant tribe of the area after whom the local reservation and surrounding countryside were named, and none of the many other smaller tribes remains that used to be indigenous. There was no significant migration to the town after mining died out, and it continues to be a village.

The land once belonged to Don Agustin Olvera, of Los Angeles fame, who sold it in 1869. By that time, there were a handful of East Coast transplants living in the area that was later to become Julian city. They were joined by some ex-Confederates. With the exception of one, the latter went prospecting, something they had been busy doing through Arizona, and found gold. In 1870, there was a gold rush, and the population swelled to 574, according to the census. There were 9 saloons, 2 gunsmiths, 3 teachers, a couple of hotel and restaurant keepers, 1 barber, 38 carpenters, 93 miners, and 80 housekeepers (all of them female), as well as other professionals needed in the affairs of mining.

It was then that the town was born, due to the influx of miners. Julian got its name from one of the former "secesshers" from Georgia. In the heyday of the local gold rush, right after the census, a greater number of miners drifted into the town, generally males, from all over the United States and Western Europe, as well as Chinese who labored and laundered. Among them, a few African American families settled in the boomtown and opened businesses. Coleman Creek is the namesake of a former slave turned prospector. However, as is generally the case in mining, it is a boom and bust business, and by the late 1870s the hills' veins had been bled dry. As the lifeblood of ore trickled out, so did those who had extracted it, and the town's 100 souls returned to farming and ranching.

To that end, James Madison, a New Yorker, arrived in the area of Julian in 1867. His interest lay in horses, and he developed a new breed, the Shilo. Madison's interests were not limited to livestock, however, and from his importation of some central California apples, a new breed of the fruit arose, the Julian apple. Arthur Juch bred them alongside many other popular breeds that took well to the climate. By the 1880s, the surrounding countryside abounded in orchards. In the 20th century, migrant laborers came seasonally to pick the fruit, most of them of Mexican origin, especially after that country's bloody civil war in the 1910s.

Horse ranching and cultivation of apples continue in Julian to this day, although not on as large a scale as a century ago. The population of the town and surrounding area is 3,000. It has become a tourist attraction because it is beautiful, close to hiking trails, lakes, weekend getaway activities, and offers a couple of annual fairs in keeping with the traditional cultivation activities. After the mining boom, Julian became the sleepy hollow it is today.

—Ion Puschila

Suggested Reading

Julian Historical Society. *History of Julian.* Julian, CA: Julian Historical Society, 1969.

LeMenager, Charles R. *Julian City and Cuyamaca Country: A History and Guide to the Past and Present.* Ramona, CA: Eagle Peak, 2001.

K

⊞ KALISPELL, MONTANA

In the winter of 1882–1883, two young men met in Boulder Valley, Montana (30 miles southwest of Helena). Tyscon Duncan and Edgar Brook decided to head to the Bitter Root Valley near present-day Missoula, Montana. At the end of March 1883, they started with a four-horse team and covered wagon, traveling via Helena and crossing the Continental Divide over the Mullen Road. They reached Missoula in the year the Northern Pacific was completed, and it was a very "wide open" town at that time.

In Missoula they met Major Peter Ronan, the Indian agent at the Flathead Indian reservation. The major told them there was no more good land to be taken in the Bitterroot Valley and advised them to go to the Flathead.

Duncan and Brook journeyed along the Northern Pacific up the valley to Flathead Lake. Soon they came to the McGovern ranch, at the gateway of Flathead Valley, which is now the town of Somers. On April 25, 1883, Tyscon Duncan marked out his homestead, which is now Kalispell north, and together he and Brook built a log cabin. Next they built one for Brook three miles to the south. They then returned to Boulder, stopping in Helena to file their claims. In those early years of living in the Flathead Valley, pioneers endured plenty of hardships. Winters were long and severe. The Flathead Valley received generous amounts of snowfall, and temperatures in January and February could fall well below zero. However, these settlers found the soil rich in minerals and good for growing crops. Indian tribes also inhabited the fertile valley, and trade with the Indians became common.

Gold dust was found 60 miles to the west of the valley. News soon spread to all parts of the United States about the new gold strike, and the popularity of the Flathead began to rise.

In the fall of 1890, word was brought that the surveyors of the Great Northern Railroad had crossed the main range of the mountains and were coming down the Middle Fork of the Flathead River. People from beyond the valley heard about this and came by the score. Two men, C. A. Conrad and A. A. White, came with the railroad and, as they had many other cities in Montana, founded the town site of Kalispell. The town site was named after the Kalispel Indians who inhabited the Flathead Valley. Conrad and White began buying land and marking lots for sale. Pioneers and settlers came to Kalispell by the hundreds. In April 1891, Conrad and White began to sell lots faster than they could make out deeds. By 1891, Kalispell had 23 saloons, 12 gambling joints, 2 Chinese restaurants, 2 Chinese laundries, and 4 general stores.

On December 31, 1891, railroad graders and track layers reached the center of Main Street. The next day, New Year's Day 1892, the first locomotive officially arrived. A big celebration was held, at which time a silver spike was driven into the center tie.

The railroad brought in businessmen, tourists, and pioneers looking for a new start. Kalispell soon emerged as an industrial center, as sawmills, flour mills, merchants, and farmers rooted themselves in the area.

Today, Kalispell is a paradise for those wanting to experience the beauty and solitude of Glacier National Park. Flathead Lake offers amazing boating and fishing. Tourism abounds in both the summer and the winter. In recent years, because of Kalispell's success, nearby cities such as Whitefish, Columbia Falls, and Polson have all become popular tourist destinations as well. Kalispell truly has it all.

—*Brandon Davis*

Suggested Reading

Baumler, Ellen. *Girl from the Gulches.* Helena: Montana Historical Society Press, 2003.

McKay, Kathryn. *Montana Mainstreets. Volume 5: A Guide to Historic Kalispell.* Helena: Montana Historical Society Press, 2001.

⊞ KELSEY, BENJAMIN

See BARTLESON, JOHN

⊞ KIOWA-APACHE

See APACHE

⊞ KOREATOWN

The flow of immigrants into America has always been a theme that has woven itself throughout the existence of the United States. Whether European immigrants or Asian immigrants, the continual flow of foreigners to the United States has provided the nation with a plethora of mixed cultures and ethnicities. One of the most predominant of these ethnicities on the West Coast is that of the Koreans.

Outside of Korea, Koreatown in Los Angeles, California, houses the largest population of Koreans anywhere in the world. Koreans first began to migrate to the United States in the early 1900s, and in 1920 and 1940, Los Angeles saw populations of 1,680 and 1,700, respectively. Various immigration laws passed during 1924 helped to close the doors to Asian immigration to the United States, but by the year 1965, new immigration laws had completely overturned the previous statute. Beginning in 1965, and partly resulting from the various civil rights movements of the era, America reopened her borders to twenty thousand persons per Asian country per year. This resulted in a high rate of immigration, not only from Korea but from China, Japan, and various other Asian countries as well.

By the year 1985, 11 percent of all Asians in America were Korean, a big jump from 1960's 1 percent. As a result, Los Angeles served as home for close to 200,000 Koreans by the mid-1980s. As early as 1975, however, *Newsweek* magazine was publishing stories regarding a five-square-mile section of the Olympic district in Los Angeles that was inundated with Korean immigrants, and it dubbed the new community "Koreatown." The publication also reported that by the mid-1970s, there were close to 70 Korean American churches, 12 Korean Buddhist temples, 100 nonprofit organizations (i.e., youth clubs and business associations), and more than 1,400 Korean-owned businesses located in the tiny district located next to South Central Los Angeles.

The Korean Chamber of Commerce, which came into being in Los Angeles during the 1970s, lobbied for Koreans in the Olympic district to share their ethnic identity, print business signs in the native *han'gul* alphabet, and pursue an original Korean culture. Immigrants and Korean businesses flocked to the Olympic district, and by the early 1990s, the Korean population in Koreatown, Los Angeles, had swelled to 350,000.

Although Koreatown is heralded as a community rich in cultural heritage, there are still problems that present themselves to the locals of Koreatown. Few Koreans tend to venture outside of their small, established community in downtown Los Angeles, and therefore there is a high population of Koreans who do not speak enough English to survive outside of Koreatown; some Koreans do not speak any English at all. In most cases, it is the older generations that are affected by this lack of communication between them and the outside world, and thus for these generations there also tends to be a lack of assimilation and acceptance into "American" culture. Younger generations of Koreans, many of whom speak fluent English and, ironically, struggle with their own native tongue, are beginning to venture outside of the Olympic district walls. Korean lawyers, doctors, real estate investors, bankers, and educators are seeing a rise in numbers in their profession outside of Los Angeles, but the majority of businesses inside Koreatown remains dominated by liquor and grocery stores, restaurants, garment vendors, gas stations, and electronics stores.

Because of the inability of many Koreans to properly understand the "American" culture, due in part to the dominance of their own native culture in Koreatown, the Korean community has become the target of many racial incidents, most notably the 1992 L.A. riots. The precursor to this infamous event was the 1991 shooting of Latasha Harlin, a young African American girl who was shot and killed by a Korean merchant over a dispute regarding a bottle of fruit juice. The merchant, who happened to be female, was sentenced to probation and served no jail time. The predominantly African American community of South Central Los Angeles, adjacent to Koreatown, was outraged at the court decision, and tensions between the two groups grew to dangerous levels. The jury decision in the Rodney King case nearly a year later caused Los Angeles, especially the African American population, to explode. Koreatown became a target for looters and thieves, who roamed the streets of Los Angeles for nearly three days creating havoc. Because of racial troubles and stereotypes, Koreatown saw the destruction of nearly 2,000 businesses, only 28 percent of which had been reestablished by 1993.

Koreatown and its inhabitants have since rebuilt businesses and stores, and the community has again become a vibrant center for Korean American culture. Today, Koreatown serves not only local Koreans as a center for commerce but is also heralded as an intriguing tourist destination. Although Korean immigration has been curtailed slightly in the last few years, there is still a movement to help well-educated Koreans exit Koreatown, become successful in a variety of professional occupations, and in turn help older generations to embrace a Korean American culture as opposed to a solely Korean culture.

—*Matthew Adam Henderson*

Suggested Reading

Abelmann, Nancy, and John Lie. *Blue Dreams: Korean Americans and the Los Angeles Riots.* Cambridge, MA: Harvard University Press, 1997.

Knoll, Tricia. *Becoming Americans: Asian Sojourners, Immigrants, and Refugees in the Western United States.* Portland, OR: Coast to Coast Books, 1982.

Takaki, Ronald. *From the Land of Morning Calm: The Koreans in America.* New York: Chelsea House, 1989.

KUMEYAAY (DIEGUEÑO, I'IPAY, AND TIPAI)

In the beginning of time, neither earth nor land existed. A massive salt-water sea enveloped all. Two brothers coexisted beneath the sea. The elder was named Teaipakomat. The brothers always held their eyes closed, for they knew that if their eyes came into contact with salt water it would blind them. One day Teaipakomat decided to surface. He saw nothing but a vast expanse of ocean in every direction. Wanting to rejoin Teaipakomat, the young brother swam toward him. However, while swimming upwards the younger brother opened his eyes, and the salt water instantly blinded him. Lacking the sense of sight, the younger brother could not comprehend the enormity of the sea and therefore submerged back beneath the waves. Teaipakomat remained above the surface and decided that he must endeavor to fill this landless void.

The Kumeyaay creation story begins with movement and upwards migration out of the ocean. The migration of Teaipakomat up to the surface set into motion perpetual migration that resulted in a creative process that continued, bringing into existence the origins of the Kumeyaay world. Teaipakomat first made little red ants, called *miskiluwi* or *ciracir*, whose bodies drifted on the water and clustered to form land. Then he brought black birds with flat bills, named *xanyil*, into existence. The black birds flew aimlessly about, lost in a sea of darkness, for neither the sun nor the moon had been brought into being. To fix this oversight, Teaipakomat gathered three colors of clay—black, yellow, and red—and worked the mass into a flat, circular disk. Taking the tricolor object in his hands, Teaipakomat heaved it at the sky. The clay adhered to the sky and provided a dim light called the moon, or *halya*. Teaipakomat remained unsatisfied, for moonlight did not allow one to see very far, and he desired to create people. Teaipakomat knew that people would require additional light. Again, Teaipakomat gathered more clay. He fashioned the clay into another round, level disk. Then Teaipakomat threw this object against the opposite side of the sky. *Inyau*, or sun, clung to the sky and provided lighting adequate to view the horizon. Using a light-colored piece of clay that he split part way, Teaipakomat made man, or *Avekwame*. After he created man, Teaipakomat removed a rib from him and made *Sinyaxau*, or first woman. The progeny of the man and woman were the people, *Ipai*.

Contemporary Kumeyaay Indians believe they are descendants of Ipai, and they have always inhabited their land. Traditional Kumeyaay territory encompasses San Diego and Imperial Counties in California, continuing sixty miles south of the U.S.–Mexico border. Archaeologists maintain that the Kumeyaay and all other Native peoples living in the San Diego area migrated there after crossing the Bering Strait from Asia to North America. The majority of Native scholars agree that Native peoples first populated the area fifteen to twenty thousand years ago. Scientists claim that specific evidence gives validity to their chronological estimates. Most Kumeyaay elders and additional Native peoples disagree and disregard such hypotheses. Kumeyaay say they are the descendents of the earth. Tribal elders and traditional educators teach that Kumeyaay culture, life, linguistics, belief systems, and history are all site specific.

Near where Rancho Bernardo, California, now stands, in a lush valley, a large village once stood bordering an annual river. By this river, water cascades down an outcropping of rocks, forming a series of miniature waterfalls. Pictographs (paintings or drawings on a rock wall) and petroglyphs (carvings or inscriptions in a rock wall) adorn these rocks, which are sometimes called Piedras Pintadas. A variety of the symbols and characters on the rocks corresponds to the female puberty ceremony, which culturally ushers an adolescent girl into womanhood. Some archeologists and scholars believe Piedras Pintadas was a Kumeyaay site prior to the neighboring Luiseño tribe's usage of the site for the female puberty ceremony. The migration

from girl into woman marked a physical and spiritual transformation that required a symbolic ceremony. Kumeyaay puberty ceremonies for boys and girls differed, but a sand painting marked the conclusion for both. Tribal elders made sand paintings by using a variety of colored sands to create a circular sand sculpture on the ground. The circular nature of sand paintings represents their eternal nature: no beginning and no end. Sand paintings depict images of the celestial bodies, flora, and fauna. When the ceremonial painting was finished, the elder placed white sage (*Salvia apiana*) and salt in a hole in the center of the sand painting. At the conclusion of the ceremony, to protect the power of the sand painting and others, a tribal elder would transfer the sand painting to a secluded location. Kumeyaay and Luiseño learned to revere this area as the birthplace of deities, gods who possess supernatural forces and powers that can adversely or positively affect people. Kumeyaay and Luiseño consider this place sacred, and some natives continue to use it as a place of prayer.

Kumeyaay religion teaches cremation as another important ceremony. Although generally not considered part of migration, cremation is believed by the Kumeyaay to be the occasion when the spirit of a person migrates to the sky world, another plane where life exists but in a different form. It was not until after the 1769 Christian incursion that Kumeyaay and other tribes switched (partially) to inhumation. Before Christianity adversely influenced the cremation ceremony, Kumeyaay cremated their tribal members. However, prehistoric peoples from two thousand years ago or earlier buried their dead. Generally, Kumeyaay incinerated the deceased's home and belongings. Kumeyaay elders claim this practice prevented the departed spirit from returning and provided the dead with possessions to use in the next world. Cremated remains were placed in an *olla*, a medium-to-large-sized earthenware vessel, and interred beneath the ground. After the death of the body, the soul migrated to the next life, and ceremonial practices helped in its journey to the place of the dead. Regardless of the type of burial a Kumeyaay received, the tribe always conducted a respectful ceremony, such as the *Kuruk*.

Kumeyaay believe that relationships and bonds between people are not severed completely by death.

Tribal elders preach that the dead maintain a connection between this world and the next. In honor of this, Kumeyaay conduct Kuruk, or mourning ceremonies. Previously thought by anthropologists to be a forgotten practice, Kuruk ceremonies are still hosted by Kumeyaay today. Kuruks continue throughout the night and sometimes last twenty-four hours. During the Kuruk, Bird Singers share sacred songs, including some Bird Songs. Historically, Bird Songs were cyclical songs sung while others danced. Over the course of a Kuruk, more than one hundred Bird Songs might be recited, to the beat of rattles, not drums. The rhythmic meter of sacred hollowed gourd or tortoiseshell rattles partially filled with indigenous palm seeds keeps the cadence of the singers. The practice of Bird Singing keeps Kumeyaay culture alive and reminds the people of a time prior to European contact.

Before the incursion of Europeans into the southwestern United States, Kumeyaay divided their land into clan, or *Sh'mulq* territories. Sh'mulq lands belonged to one of two clans: I'ipay or Tipai. Topographically speaking, it appears that the two most important factors in the selection of village sites were proximity to a dependable water source and the availability of acorn-bearing trees. Kumeyaay constructed their homes by lashing willow (*Salicaceae)* poles with yucca (*Yucca whipplei*) twine into a domed structure thatched with local grasses or willows. Kumeyaay lived a seasonal migratory lifestyle, maintaining summer and winter villages with smaller temporary villages for specific necessities across the San Diego area. Contrary to the European definition of property as the possession of the landowner, Kumeyaay did not consider themselves superior to Mother Earth. Feeling a reverent connection to the Earth rather than a desire to control it, Kumeyaay held their land in more of a collective. For example, a native trader could cross tribal territories or a hunter could track game through different clans' land without fear of recourse or reproach. However, it required the consent of the local Sh'mulq to settle in another's territory.

Regardless of clan or territory, Kumeyaay were the first to employ environmental management in the San Diego area. Kumeyaay used fire to clear lands overgrown with brush, thus allowing transitional plants time to grow and soil a chance to renew. Placing rocks, limbs, and brush in watershed drainages created wetlands and raised the water table in arid regions. These environmental adaptations increased the abundance and variety of foodstuffs to gather and animals to hunt. Kumeyaay hunted deer, rabbits, bighorn sheep, fowl, and other small animals; caught fish, lobster, and crab; and harvested scallops and other shellfish. Kumeyaay had a six-month lunar calendar that repeated itself once during the year and used the presence of celestial bodies to time their harvests and burns. The Kumeyaay way of life prospered until the middle of the 16th century.

In 1540, the first Spanish explorer, Hernando de Alarcón, reached Alta California via the Colorado River. Alarcón encountered the Quechan, a neighboring socioeconomically related tribe located to the east of the Kumeyaay. By 1542, the Spanish, led by Portuguese explorer Rodriguez de Cabrillo, made first contact with the Kumeyaay, mistakenly called the Diegueño by the Spanish, near Point Loma. Spanish explorer Sebastian Vizcaino briefly stopped in San Diego in 1602 and then proceeded farther up the California coastline. All of these encounters carried with them a momentous importance, for the Spanish, and Europeans, in general believed in the "right of discovery." This idea justifies the intrusion upon, usurpation of, and resettlement of non-Christian lands by Christian countries. Therefore, under European law, the meandering expeditions of Alarcón, Cabrillo, and Vizcaino had rightfully claimed Alta California for Spain.

The Spanish chose to invoke their self-appointed right to resettle the California coastal region on July 2, 1769. On July 16, Franciscan Father Junípero Serra founded Mission San Diego de Alcalá on Kumeyaay land without Sh'mulq approval. A short time later, the Spanish built a presidio or fort, again without Sh'mulq approval, above the Kumeyaay village of Cosoy. The initial actions and ceremonies of the Spaniards did not provoke fear among the Kumeyaay, for the Spanish suffered from scurvy and starvation. However, through continued reinforcements and more sophisticated weaponry, the Spanish slowly grew in strength and number. Whether voluntarily or by pressed service, Kumeyaay ensured the survival of the mission in San Diego. Kumeyaay functioned as masons and carpenters in building the mission, farmers in working the mission's fields, and cowboys and leatherworkers in herding, slaughtering, and skinning the mission's cattle. In 1774, Father Serra granted Father Luis Jayme permission to move Mission San Diego de Alcalá up Mission Valley to the Kumeyaay village of Nipaguay. Latter that year, in November, the suppressed anger of the Kumeyaay erupted in a massive rebellion against Mission San Diego de Alcalá, which ultimately destroyed it. Kumeyaay elders say that more than forty Sh'mulqs provided warriors for the attack, which was led by anti-Christian Kumeyaay religious leaders. Eventually, the Spanish military suppressed the uprising, and by 1776, Kumeyaay labor had rebuilt Mission San Diego de Alcalá where it stands today.

The reasons for the Kumeyaay revolt lie in the contrast between the hardships these people endured and the liberties they were denied. Native peoples possessed little freedom at the mission. Catholic treatment of Kumeyaay and other tribes ranged from outright slavery to childlike supervision. Although some Kumeyaay did choose mission life, others escaped any way they could. Native runaways joined villages farther inland out of Spanish reach, other rancheros, and bands of renegade Natives that ransacked missions and Spanish encampments. If the Spanish military captured a mission escapee, it resulted in the brutal punishment of that individual. Missions throughout Latin and North America punished Natives who were deemed insolent. The president of the California missions, Father Serra, personally authorized the use of whips to administer lashes to men, women, and children for numerous offenses.

Mexico secured its independence from Spain in 1821, but it took another year for San Diego to officially come under Mexican rule. The Catholic missions, loosely unified and in disarray, lost all power when they were secularized by the Mexican government in 1833. Kumeyaay loyal to the missions felt betrayed by the Mexican government for two reasons: first, for granting large tracts of land, called rancheros, to Mexican citizens not Kumeyaay, and second, for the secularization of Catholic missions and the subsequent transfer of their titles to non-Native ownership. Numerous mission priests had promised sections of mission lands to converted Kumeyaay. As the missions dissolved and broke into differing rancheros and land grants, Kumeyaay living at Mission San Diego de Alcalá struggled to find their place in Mexican society. Most moved back to Kumeyaay villages in an effort to reclaim and readjust back to a more Native lifestyle.

Following the conclusion of the United States–Mexican War in 1848, the United States established military control over the economics and politics of the region. With California approved for statehood in 1850, federal Indian policy made all Native peoples wards of the national government. From 1850 to 1851, federal Indian agents quickly crisscrossed California, negotiating and signing treaties with numerous Native tribes. For the greater San Diego area, two treaties, those of Temecula and Santa Ysabel, established the legal relationship between the tribes and the federal government. However, due to the U.S. Senate's rejection of all eighteen California treaties, non-Natives in California refused to acknowledge any Native rights. Prior to the rejection of the California treaties by the Senate, the California state legislature passed Statutes Chapter 133 in 1850. The statutes' title claimed to govern and protect Indians, but they actually became ways to legally discriminate and subjugate Native peoples. Provisions in the statutes legally allowed whites to assume the custody of Native children, prevented Natives from testifying against non-Natives, forced Natives who could not pay court fees or fines into bondage, allowed Natives convicted of vagrancy to be auctioned off, and allowed Natives convicted of stealing to be lashed.

Kumeyaay combated these California statutes until 1870, when after decades of federal negligence the U.S. government established two reservations in San Diego County. Unfortunately, under pressure by local ranchers and businesspersons, the U.S. government rescinded the order less than a year later and abolished the two reservations. Kumeyaay would wait until 1875, when President Ulysses S. Grant signed an executive order founding ten reservations. Only three quarters the size of the two 1870 reservations and scattered across the region, the ten 1875 reservations created a checkerboard pattern across the San Diego landscape. The government forced the Kumeyaay to move onto specific reservation lands and choose which familial ties to sever. The patchwork of reservations proved an insufficient land base and did little to halt the incursion of whites onto Native Kumeyaay lands. Miners dynamited and destroyed the Native landscapes in search of gold, with complete disregard for Kumeyaay reservations. While mining for precious metals, these prospectors intentionally crossed reservation boundaries and further pressed in on Kumeyaay lands. Ranchers and farmers ignored Kumeyaay land boundaries, moving crops and cattle onto Native lands, resulting in the destruction of indigenous plant and animal populations. This additional incursion onto Kumeyaay land pushed the Kumeyaay into portions of their reservations less desirable for continual habitat. These more remote sections of Kumeyaay reservations generally contained less potable water and sustained less vegetation and wildlife. The actions of miners, ranchers, and farmers in disregarding Kumeyaay legal rights to reservation lands compelled Kumeyaay to be subject to forced migration within the boundaries of their reservations. Non-Natives also dismissed Kumeyaay rights to public education by forbidding Natives to attend non-Native schools.

The Bureau of Indian Affairs (BIA) established a limited number of Native day schools in the Kumeyaay's traditional lands. As a direct result of this, agents forced Kumeyaay children to travel more than one hundred miles to the northeast to attend Sherman Institute, among other Native-only schools even farther away. These institutes of learning, which were based on the presupposition of Native mental inferiority to non-Natives, taught mostly vocational skills. Girls were trained to cook, sew, and clean, and boys learned gardening, milking, and metal- and woodworking. These skills provided only a subsistence-level income for most Natives and never granted true economic freedom or movement up the social ladder. In addition, the skills learned by Kumeyaay children in these schools condemned them to a life off the reservation separate from their tribe in a non-Native society. To fully use their new trades, these Natives would have to seek employment in non-Native urban areas, where their heritage would serve as a hindrance to any form of advancement. For unlucky Native children, matriculation in these schools proved deadly. Kumeyaay and other Native children died from exposure to tuberculosis, influenza, and measles. Allowed to return home for visits, infected Native students often unknowingly spread diseases among Kumeyaay villages. Deaths from disease resulted in a declining birth rate and Kumeyaay population during the early 20th century. This demographic shift in the Kumeyaay prompted some non-Natives to predict that the entire Kumeyaay population would transition into the next life before the century's end; however, the Kumeyaay endured and adapted to their ever-changing environment.

The Kumeyaay people diverged into two societal groupings founded on land tenure. The first faction moved into urban non-Native communities in the San Diego area. These Kumeyaay gradually acculturated into white society but never fully divested themselves of their Native culture. Urbanized Kumeyaay found employment as anglers and dockhands and in domestic capacities. The second group of Kumeyaay remained on the executive order reservations. Reservation Kumeyaay worked their land and worked for non-Natives as wranglers, ranchers, and field hands. Because of the Great Depression and the hard economic times that followed, Native Americans from Arizona, Oklahoma, South Dakota, and other states migrated to San Diego seeking new opportunities and employment. This new influx of Natives to San Diego and Kumeyaay lands increased California's Native population to the highest in the United States by 1980.

During the 1960s and 1970s, the federal and California governments increasingly confined and restricted Kumeyaay to reservations. This limited many tribal members' economic options to either wage labor or small agricultural business. However, without sufficient funding, arable land, and water, these agricultural ventures did not thrive. Death, illness, malnutrition, disease, and inadequate education ensured social and economic immobility for the Kumeyaay. Throughout the 1960s and previous decades, the Mission Indian Federation fought to abolish the BIA and win compensation for stolen Native lands. It was not until the 1980s that Kumeyaay bands began to assert their tribal sovereignty to their advantage by starting bingo and other fledgling gaming businesses. Gaming brought with it economic independence and the ability to change the topography of Kumeyaay lands. Kumeyaay purchased businesses, banks, and additional lands with gaming monies. Gaming revenues helped Kumeyaay lift their tribal communities out of squalor by paying for the construction of modern housing, running water, electricity, sewer systems, telephone lines, and paved streets. Casinos provided employment for engineers, designers, consultants, construction workers, and numerous other skilled and unskilled individuals both Native and non-Native. Not all Kumeyaay or San Diego reservations have chosen to pursue gaming. Tribal elders at these reservations argue that gaming could adversely affect the Native environment and culture they are trying to protect. However, numerous other Kumeyaay reservations feel that the benefits gaming brings far outweigh its negative aspects. Nevertheless, Kumeyaay gaming and nongaming reservations still socialize, bond, and champion Native sovereignty together.

Although always politically active, with the advent of gaming, Kumeyaay have substantially increased their political power. Kumeyaay and other Native tribes harnessed this power during the campaign to pass Propositions 5 and 1A, two initiatives that more than 60% of California voters supported, allowing high-stakes gaming at Indian casinos. In 2002, the Kumeyaay reservations of Barona, Viejas, and Sycuan supported a bill establishing a Native commission to enforce the national Native American Graves and Repatriation Act on a California state level. Kumeyaay and other Native tribes sponsor such acts and bills to preserve their Native heritage. Kumeyaay are committed to the conservation of their culture, people, and sovereignty.

Influenced greatly by migration, Kumeyaay have perpetually been a people of movement. Hunting, gathering, fishing, social gatherings, trading, and observation of religious ceremonies all ensured that Kumeyaay never took on a sedentary lifestyle. Throughout the course of U.S. history, Kumeyaay voluntarily chose to migrate off their reservations and bravely participate in U.S. military wars, from World War I to Iraq. Also, Kumeyaay have adapted and endured continual immigration of non-Natives and Natives alike onto traditional Kumeyaay land. Kumeyaay have struggled but survived numerous hardships and misfortunes, many times outside of their control. It is this sense of perseverance that leads the Kumeyaay: knowledge that whatever obstacles may come in the future, Kumeyaay can overcome them together and look to a prosperous future as sovereign First Nations people.

—*Jeffrey Allen Smith*

Suggested Reading

Carrico, Richard L. *Strangers in a Stolen Land: American Indians in San Diego, 1850–1880.* Sacramento, CA: Sierra Oaks, 1987.

Heizer, R. F., ed. *Handbook of North American Indians. Volume 8: California.* Washington, DC: Smithsonian, 1978.

Kroeber, A. L., ed. *Handbook of the Indians of California.* New York: Dover, 1976.

Phillips, George H. *Chiefs and Challengers.* Berkeley: University of California Press, 1975.

Shipek, Florance. *Pushed into the Rocks.* Lincoln: University of Nebraska Press, 1988.

Trafzer, Clifford E. "European Impact on Native California Cultures." In *Early California Reflections,* edited by Nicholas M. Magalousis. San Juan Capistrano, CA: Orange County Public Library, 1987.

L

⌗ LAKE HAVASU CITY, ARIZONA

Robert McCulloch of McCulloch Properties, Inc. convinced state officials to request the transfer of federal land in Mohave County to the State of Arizona. McCulloch purchased all 16,700 acres in an auction. A reporting group known as the Investigative Reporters and Editors scrutinized the transaction. The group claimed that the price McCulloch paid—$1 million—was extremely low, and that the land could have sold for $6.5 million if it had been partitioned. Unfortunately there was no market for this land, because it was undeveloped and in an inhospitable area, and thus not many would have sought it.

The development of the city centered at Lake Havasu—a federal Bureau of Reclamation dam project on the Colorado River. The McCulloch Corporation aimed at creating a community based on recreation and retirement. The severe weather of the region made it very unattractive, but the lake and the advent of air conditioning offset that. The dry arid region can reach temperatures around 120°F and is prone to flash floods.

The development first opened in 1963 and was marketed as a retirement and recreational facility. McCulloch divided the 16,700 acres into 33,514 lots, which sold within a few years. Original predictions stated that Lake Havasu City could sustain 80,000 people. The city experienced rapid development, as developers expected to reach the target population of 80,000 quickly.

By 1970, the region only contained around 5,000 people. In 1968, Robert McCulloch purchased the London Bridge for $2.5 million as a stunt to attract people to the city. McCulloch had it dismantled and shipped to the United States in pieces at the cost of $8 million. The bridge's reconstruction transformed Lake Havasu City into a tourist venue. A "British village," assembled by McCulloch Properties, Inc., emerged near the bridge to further promote tourism.

The village contains a resort complex to accommodate shopping, restaurants, entertainment, and lodging. Golfing, fishing, and camping are great attractors to the region. Gambling in nearby Laughlin to the north draws people to this area as well. Jet skiing, boating, and other water sports have entrenched themselves in Lake Havasu City's economy. Yamaha and Kawasaki installed research plants for personal watercraft, adding to the growing community.

The abundance of cheap land attracted people to Lake Havasu City. As late as the mid-1980s, land lots could be purchased for $5,500. There were catches to buying land: Owners paid assessment fees. Assessment districts created by the developer financed the cost of installing basic services, including a per-acre tax for irrigation and drainage districts. From 1970 to 1974, the population of Lake Havasu doubled, rising to 10,000 people. In the early 1990s, the prices of lots more than tripled in value. A third of the population is currently unwilling to sell their lots, which makes finding land difficult.

Cheap land attracted older people, and many retirees entered the region because fixed incomes created limitations that were offset by moving to the area. The warm weather and dry climate also proved attractive. Today, Lake Havasu City boasts a retired population of about 20 percent out of a total population of 48,000 people. The city was known early on for having an elderly population. Although this community was not necessarily fashioned to accommodate a retired crowd, like Sun City, it did draw many.

Families from northern states have been pulled in because of the warm climate. Havasu also draws on Californians escaping urban centers and their problems. The majority (90 percent) of the people in this region is American born, white, and non-Hispanic. Hispanics have started entering the region, so far representing 8 percent of the population. The second major growth period experienced by Lake Havasu City was from 1980 to 1992; the population gradually increased, doubling to 32,710 people. Lake Havasu City's median age is 37; this low number reflects the growth of younger families. The Sterlite Corporation produces plastic houseware products and employs 400 people at its facility. Other manufacturers produce boats and other watercraft. Cheaper housing and job growth have contributed to the growing younger population. This retirement and recreational community has 4,500 school-aged children, which is a considerable number for a region of this nature. Tourism is a crucial part of the economy, as it brings in more than $100 million annually.

Lake Havasu City is experiencing changes as it continues to develop. This retirement and recreation center has not been as carefully planned as other centers. The uncontrolled growth allowed for poorly laid out housing locations. These locations are endangered when flash floods occur. Other drainage problems leave homes in danger because of their poor placement. The developers have not made optimum use of the land. The region is not growing as fast as anticipated, but its growth is accelerating. This will convert Lake Havasu City into an urban center if it continues its development to the calculated maximum of 80,000 people. It will be just like the areas some were escaping. The region has all the amenities of any major city, such as shopping complexes, a movie theater complex, a city library, and numerous recreational facilities. The only difference is that this center lies in an isolated location.

Although Lake Havasu is not a perfect model for a developed community, it is a successful community. The retirement community is still present, and its tourism is forcing current growth patterns. The influx of younger people staying permanently, rather than visiting, is what is turning Havasu City from a retirement-recreational community to a regular urban area. The rise of industrial manufacturers and school districts is changing the original nature of this community.

—Eduardo Barrios

See also CHEMEHUEVI

Suggested Reading

Sheridan, Thomas. *Arizona: A History.* Tucson: University of Arizona Press, 1996.

Stroud, Hubert. *The Promise of Paradise: Recreational and Retirement Communities in the United States since 1950.* Baltimore, MD: Johns Hopkins University Press, 1995.

Wheeler, Nik. "Bridge Too Far." *Preservation* 53, no. 4 (2001).

LAKOTAS

The history of a great people always begins with a great story. The Lakotas of the northern Plains are no exception. A very long time ago, two Lakota men were searching for buffalo. On reaching the crest of a high hill, they gazed to the north and noticed a woman coming toward them. According to Black Elk, a prominent Lakota spiritual leader, the two scouts saw that the woman "wore a fine white buckskin dress, that her hair was very long and that she was young and very beautiful." One of the men lusted after the young woman and was consequently cursed, quickly turning into a "skeleton covered with worms." The woman informed the other Lakota that she was coming to visit his people and that they should prepare a large teepee for her arrival. When she came, she presented to the people a sacred pipe and taught them seven sacred ceremonies, which serve as the foundation of Lakota culture. As she left the people, she was transformed into a white buffalo cow and disappeared over the horizon.

The story of White Buffalo Calf Woman is the founding story of the Lakotas. Her gift of the sacred pipe, as aptly pointed out by scholar Raymond J. DeMallie, "established kinship between the buffalo and the people; when it was smoked, the spirits would hear the prayer and send buffalo." The seven sacred ceremonies of the Lakotas, including the vision quest, the naming ceremony for children, the Sun Dance, and the purification ceremony of the sweat lodge, have all experienced a renaissance during the last forty or so years. Lakotas today, just as in ancient days, adhere to the culture given to them by their sacred visitor long ago. The account of White Buffalo Calf Woman, along with numerous other stories, defines Lakota culture and identity.

The Lakotas are but one tribe within a larger grouping of Siouan-speaking peoples collectively known as the Sioux. The name "Sioux," a term rarely, if ever, used by Lakotas, is a French corruption of the Ojibwa word *nadoweis-iw*, meaning "enemy" or "little snakes." Instead, the Sioux refer to themselves as *Ocheti Sakowin* or the "Seven Council Fires." More commonly, depending on their dialect, the Sioux call themselves "Dakota" or "Lakota," both of which mean "allies" or "friends." The westernmost Sioux tribe is the Lakota. Furthermore, the Lakotas divide themselves into seven separate bands, the largest of which is the Oglala ("they scatter their own"). The remaining six bands are the Sicangu ("burnt thighs") or Brule, the Hunkpapa ("those who camp at the entrance"), the Miniconjou ("those who plant by the stream"), Sihasapa ("blackfeet"), Itazipco ("without bows"), and Oohenonpa ("two kettles").

The origins of the Lakotas and their Dakota relatives have been a source of controversy, one with significant political implications. In general, anthropologists contend that the ancestors of the Sioux were originally from the lower Ohio and middle Mississippi valleys. By the 16th and 17th centuries, some of these peoples journeyed northward into Wisconsin and Minnesota. About this time, it is believed, these migrants separated into seven tribal groups, constituting the Seven Council Fires. During the 18th century, many of these fanned out into what are now the Dakotas, western Nebraska, and eastern Wyoming. Those who traveled furthest to the west, the Lakotas, eventually made forays into Montana and western Wyoming. In this manner, the Lakotas were expanding their territory at the same time the United States of America was formed.

The Lakotas, on the other hand, believe that they originated in the Black Hills of South Dakota. Long, long ago, before their encounter with White Buffalo Calf Woman, the Lakotas resided underground beneath the Black Hills. At one point, they came to the surface, emerging through Wind Cave in the southern Black Hills. One version of this story recalls that a Lakota leader, knowing the harsh realities the people would soon face, transformed himself into a buffalo to save them from starvation. According to Lakota tribal historian Karen Lone Hill, "it was the buffalo that sustained the people during that early period; it provided food, clothing, shelter, tools—all the necessities of life." For this and other reasons, the Lakotas know the Black Hills as "the heart of everything that is." They are the lands of their origins. The Black Hills are sacred lands, which the Lakotas still visit to perform ceremonies and procure medicines. Besides Wind Cave, other sites in and near the Black Hills continue to hold particular spiritual significance, including Bear Butte, Devil's Tower, and Harney Peak.

For at least two hundred years and perhaps longer, the Lakotas, like many indigenous peoples of the Great Plains, were nomadic. This adaptation to the harsh environment of the plains was both practical and intelligent. As anthropologists have noted, nomadism is an extremely healthy lifestyle, one that requires the least amount of labor. Lakotas and other Native peoples knew approximately where they might locate buffalo herds during a given season of the year and where they could find certain roots and berries. Using their extensive knowledge of the stars, weather patterns, and the environment, Lakotas migrated from place to place, hunting animals and harvesting a wide range of edible plants.

One of the more important events in Lakota history, one that facilitated the ability of Lakotas to move, migrate, and travel, was the acquisition of the horse. As far as can be ascertained, Lakotas first obtained the horse from the Cheyennes around 1750. So impressed were they by this large and swift creature that they called it *sunka wakan*, meaning "sacred-holy dog." Other Native peoples throughout the Great Plains, the Rocky Mountains, and the Pacific

Northwest adopted horses into their cultures as well. This great diaspora of horses commenced during the Pueblo Revolt of 1680, when the Pueblo Indians temporarily expelled the Spanish from northern New Mexico. In their haste to be gone, the Spaniards left behind hundreds of horses, which various indigenous groups gradually secured through theft or trade.

The horse was a transforming influence in the lives of Lakotas for several reasons. First of all, and perhaps most significantly, Lakotas could now travel farther and more quickly than ever before. Consequently, the acquisition of the horse facilitated Lakota migration into western Nebraska, Wyoming, and southeastern Montana. Secondly, Lakotas could hunt buffalo and other animals with greater ease. Their increased ability to procure meat appears to have resulted in an overall population increase. Next, Lakota war parties could approach and attack enemy encampments with tremendous speed. Lakotas were legendary among both Native and non-Native peoples for their skills in battle. Finally, the horse served as an extremely useful beast of burden. Prior to the arrival of horses, Lakotas and other Native Americans often had their belongings hauled by dogs. A horse could transport a large amount of goods, with relative ease, over long distances. Truly, horses were of tremendous value to the Lakotas. It should be, therefore, no surprise that Lakotas and other indigenous peoples in the region viewed horses as a sign of wealth and prestige.

The Lakotas were arguably the most influential and most powerful tribe on the Great Plains during the mid-19th century. Other local Native societies either made alliances with the Lakotas or greatly feared them. American citizens were also generally afraid of the Lakotas yet admired them for their horsemanship and ability to fight and conduct raids. Acknowledging the Lakotas' powerful influence over the northern plains—and determined to ensure safe passage for Anglo immigrants through Nebraska and Wyoming—the United States federal government signed two major treaties with the Lakotas and other Native peoples in the region. The first agreement, the Fort Laramie Treaty of 1851, reflected a highly unrealistic posture by the federal government. In this treaty, the government divided the plains into permanent tribal territories, receiving casual assurances from the various tribes that they would not trespass onto one another's lands. In other words, the government was requesting that Lakotas and others cease raiding one another, a common practice that was highly significant for men in most indigenous societies of the Great Plains.

The second treaty, the Fort Laramie Treaty of 1868, ended more than two years of intense fighting along the Bozeman Trail between the United States Army and a resilient Native alliance composed of Lakotas, Cheyennes, and Arapahos. In this agreement, the federal government recognized most of Nebraska, all lands west of the Missouri River in what became North and South Dakota, and portions of northeastern Wyoming and southeastern Montana as Lakota territory. If the United States had honored this treaty, the nation's history and settlement patterns might have been vastly different. Unfortunately, over the years, the federal government forced the Lakotas to give up vast tracts of their promised lands, including the beautiful and sacred Black Hills, which were stolen in 1877.

The period between 1850 and 1880 was not only a time of negotiations and treaties but of conflict and war. From the Lakota perspective, American citizens traversing the plains were invaders. They traveled through Lakota hunting grounds without permission, shot buffalo and other game, had their livestock graze on the native grasses, and polluted the rivers and streams. During these times of turmoil, several legendary Lakota leaders emerged, most of whom inspired their followers to resist the intruders, although a few sought to negotiate carefully and tenaciously with federal officials in hope of securing maximum benefits from the government. Regardless of the methods and the outcomes, Crazy Horse, Red Cloud, Spotted Tail, Sitting Bull, and others all did what they believed was best for their people. Perhaps one of the most enduring triumphs for the Lakotas, one that is still celebrated today, was the Battle of the Greasy Grass in 1876 (also known as the Battle of the Little Bighorn). Armed conflict between the Lakotas and the U.S. Army concluded with the horrific Wounded Knee Massacre of 1890, which became an unforgettable symbol of the atrocities the federal government, its representatives, and its military had committed against Native peoples for decades.

As was common during the second half of the 19th century, the federal government created Indian reservations on lands deemed undesirable by American citizens. Many of the Oglala Lakotas took up residence at the Red Cloud Agency, created in 1873 in the northwest corner of Nebraska. Although under pressure by government officials to relocate the agency somewhere along the Missouri River, Red Cloud refused to move any farther than the current location of the Pine Ridge Reservation. Pine Ridge was but one of four Lakota reservations created between 1878 and 1889 from the dwindling land base of the former Great Sioux Reservation. The other three reservations include Standing Rock, Cheyenne River, and Rosebud. Each reservation is home to at least one of the seven Lakota bands. At Pine Ridge, for instance, live the Oglalas. On the Standing Rock Reservation there are Hunkpapas and Sihasapas. On Cheyenne River, Sihasapas are also to be found, along with Miniconjous, Itazipcos, and Oohenonpas. Finally, at Rosebud, Brules and Oohenonpas reside.

Quite frequently, Lakota children did not remain on these reservations. In its attempt to divest Native peoples of their cultures and languages, the federal government forced Indian children to leave their families and live in boarding schools, often located hundreds of miles away. Lakota children, along with boys and girls from dozens of other tribes, attended schools in such distant locations as Carlisle, Pennsylvania; Lawrence, Kansas; and Riverside, California. According to scholar Brenda J. Child, this transition to boarding school life was "punctuated by the trauma of separation from family and community, severe bouts of homesickness, and a difficult period of adjustment to a new environment." Rigid discipline, harsh punishments, rampant disease, inadequate food, and even sexual abuse were common in these schools. As a consequence, hundreds of children, including dozens of Lakotas, died far from their parents, loved ones, and homelands. Today many Lakotas maintain that Lakota families are still feeling the disastrous social and emotional effects of the boarding schools.

In addition to the boarding schools, Lakotas lived temporarily in other locations. During the two world wars, hundreds of Lakota men and women left their families, relatives, and reservations to serve in the U.S. Armed Forces. After America's entrance into World War I in 1917, Lakotas volunteered to fight for the U.S. overseas. Down in the trenches with other American troops, they assisted in the defeat of the mighty German army. In World War II, Lakotas fought in Europe and the Pacific, some even assisting the war effort as code talkers. Both conflicts provided Lakotas and other tribes with the opportunity to add new members to their warrior societies.

After World War II, the federal government initiated a relocation program, encouraging Native peoples to migrate to the nation's urban centers. Hoping to improve their lot, some Lakota families moved to Denver, San Francisco, and other metropolitan areas. More often than not, Lakotas found grinding poverty, isolation, discrimination, and other problems in city ghettos. Ironically, one major benefit of the relocation program was that Lakotas frequently interacted with other Native peoples, many of whom lived either down the street or in adjacent neighborhoods. Members of various tribes developed a sense of Native unity, known as *pan-Indianism*. Native political activism emerged at this time as an urban phenomenon. During the 1960s and 1970s, Lakotas and others participated in a variety of protests, including the seizure of Alcatraz, the Trail of Broken Treaties, and, most significantly, the occupation of Wounded Knee.

In recent decades, Lakotas have shared many challenges and opportunities. Most Lakotas continue to live in acute poverty. For years, the Pine Ridge Reservation has had the dubious distinction of being one of the most impoverished areas of the United States. High unemployment and, for some, a sense of hopelessness have resulted in high rates of criminal activity, teen pregnancy, broken families, alcoholism, and drug abuse. When Oglalas from Pine Ridge leave the reservation and move to border communities such as Gordon, Rushville, and Chadron, Nebraska, they oftentimes encounter discrimination from the local white majority. They become, as has been said, "strangers in a stolen land." Similar trends can also be found on the Rosebud, Cheyenne River, and Standing Rock reservations.

Another challenge for Lakotas is the unsettled and unsettling issue of the Black Hills. In the Fort Laramie Treaty of 1868, the federal government openly affirmed Lakota claims to the Black Hills. The agreement also stipulated that three fourths of all Lakota men would have to approve any territorial cessions to the United States. In autumn 1876, just after the Battle of the Little Bighorn—which was a major embarrassment for the United States—federal representatives coaxed approximately one tenth of all Lakota men to relinquish claim to the Black Hills, threatening to withhold rations from their elders, wives, and children if they refused. Recognizing this manipulation as invalid and as a blatant violation of the Fort Laramie Treaty of 1868, Lakotas began to organize monthly meetings as early as 1891. Finally, in 1923, Lakotas sued the United States over the Black Hills. After decades of litigation, the U.S. Supreme Court ruled in 1980 in favor of awarding compensation for the illegal seizure of the Black Hills. The Lakotas have declined the cash award; instead, they simply want their sacred Black Hills back, even though the total award today would be well over $500 million.

Despite these difficulties, there is optimism and resilience among the Lakotas. Since the 1960s, Lakota culture has experienced a renaissance. More than ever, Lakotas participate in the seven sacred ceremonies given to them by White Buffalo Calf Woman. At pow-wows, fathers and mothers present their newborns to the audience in naming ceremonies. Some teenage boys still go on vision quests. Holding a purification ceremony in a sweat lodge is a common occurrence, not only on reservations but also in border communities. Lakotas hold the sacred Sun Dance several times each summer at various locations throughout their reservations. Furthermore, Lakota children learn their language and culture at school in classes taught by Lakota elders and other respected individuals. Without a doubt, the revitalization of their ceremonies and language has given the people strength and courage to endure the economic deprivations of the last century.

Despite economic hardships, Lakotas have had many success stories. For instance, the Lakotas have established tribal colleges, which continue to thrive. On Pine Ridge, Oglala Lakota College opened its doors in 1971. Over the past thirty years, this college has developed an array of degrees, both at the undergraduate and graduate levels. It has satellite campuses in all districts of the reservation. Sinte Gleska University, located on the Rosebud Reservation, also offers an impressive variety of programs designed to meet the educational and intellectual needs of the Sicangu Lakotas and others. On the Cheyenne River Reservation, Si Tanka University prides itself on being a multicultural institution. Students who attend Si Tanka come not only from the United States but from China, Japan, the Bahamas, and Puerto Rico. At these and other colleges, Lakota students are studying to become teachers, school administrators, doctors, librarians, and business owners. Today it is highly common to find Lakotas on reservations and in adjacent communities who own businesses, such as restaurants, flower shops, and gas stations, or who hold professional positions as nurses, social workers, or educators.

According to the 2000 census, there are more than ninety thousand persons who claim to be Sioux, approximately fifty-five thousand of whom are Lakotas. Year after year, their numbers continue to grow. They cling tenaciously to the rich traditions of their past, yet they participate fully in the present. Most Lakota reservations and tribal colleges have Web sites, elementary and secondary schools have computers and Internet access, and well over one hundred Lakota men and women have served in the Armed Forces during the recent and ongoing military campaigns in Afghanistan and Iraq. One of the primary issues for Lakotas today is to find balance between their own culture and the modern forces of the outside world. Certainly, the future is in their hands.

—Joel R. Hyer

See also Bureau of Indian Affairs

Suggested Reading

Biolsi, Thomas. *Organizing the Lakota: The Political Economy of the New Deal on the Pine Ridge and Rosebud Reservations.* Tucson: University of Arizona Press, 1992.

Crow Dog, Mary, and Richard Erdoes. *Lakota Woman.* New York: Grove Weidenfeld, 1995.

DeMallie, Raymond J., and William C. Sturtevant, eds. *Handbook of North American Indians. Volume 13: Plains.* Washington, DC: Smithsonian Institution, 2001.

Gagnon, Gregory, and Karen White Eyes. *Pine Ridge Reservation: Yesterday and Today.* Interior, SD: Badlands Natural History Association, 1992.

Hassrick, Royal B. *The Sioux: Life and Customs of a Warrior Society.* Norman: University of Oklahoma Press, 1964.

Hyde, George E. *Red Cloud's Folk: A History of the Oglala Sioux Indians.* Norman: University of Oklahoma Press, 1957.

Hyde, George E. *A Sioux Chronicle.* Norman: University of Oklahoma Press, 1956.

Hyde, George E. *Spotted Tail's Folk: A History of the Brulé Sioux.* Norman: University of Oklahoma Press, 1961.

Lazarus, Edward. *Black Hills, White Justice: The Sioux Nation versus the United States, 1775 to the Present.* New York: HarperCollins, 1991.

Neihardt, John G. *Black Elk Speaks: Being the Life Story of a Holy Man of the Ogalala Sioux.* New York: William Morrow, 1932.

Olson, James C. *Red Cloud and the Sioux Problem.* Lincoln: University of Nebraska Press, 1965.

Utley, Robert M. *The Lance and the Shield: The Life and Times of Sitting Bull.* New York: Henry Holt, 1993.

⊞ LANKERSHIM, ISAAC
(1818–1882)

Isaac Lankershim, born in West Prussia on April 8, 1818, immigrated with his brother James to San Francisco in 1848. After he built a very successful wheat and wool business in the San Francisco area, Lankershim decided to expand his holdings and traveled south that same year over the Cahuenga Pass into the San Fernando Valley. Lankershim and his partner, Isaac Newton Van Nuys, saw potential in ranching and were impressed by the height of the wild oats. The financial investment of these men eventually led to the greater development of the San Fernando Valley, and Lankershim's story represents many of difficulties Americans found with the Spanish land system as they struggled to buy land after California entered the Union.

As a result, Lankershim hired attorney Major Levi Chase to negotiate the sale of Rancho El Cajon for $36,595 from the Pedrorena family on August 12, 1868. Because the United States did not honor the Pedrorena family's land grant, Lankershim did not immediately receive the deed of the rancho. Despite this setback, in 1869, Lankershim, I. N. Van Nuys, Levi Strauss, the Scholle brothers, and the Sachs family formed a syndicate called the San Fernando Farm Homestead Association. On July 2, the association purchased the 60,000-acre Pico Rancho, which encompassed the southern half of the San Fernando Valley, for $115,000. Problems, however, arose because the Pico family, who sold the southern portion of the rancho to the association, had originally transferred the deed to Eulogio de Celis. This drew the attention of former California governor and railroad baron Leland Stanford, who vowed to extend the Southern Pacific's tracks to the region if Senator Charles Maclay purchased the rancho and established a town. Knowing that boomtowns often accompanied new rail lines, Maclay successfully bribed the de Celis family lawyer and purchased the 56,000-acre property for $117,500. The district court also granted full title of the southern portion of the rancho to the association in 1871. Renaming the area Rancho Ex-Mission San Fernando, the new owners divided the property into southern and northern halves along a 20-mile boundary line that later became Roscoe Boulevard. Lankershim, Van Nuys, Maclay, and Benjamin Porter supervised the subdivision and development of the valley's farmland into agricultural and residential areas.

Lankershim also financed the Patton Ranch, now the site of Tarzana, as well as the Kestor Ranch, which lies nearly two miles southwest of the present town of Van Nuys. The association subsequently established the Old Sheep and Clyman ranches. Seven ranches—owned by various parties—in the San Fernando Valley became the largest farming enterprise in the West at the time. On these ranches, raising sheep and wheat dominated the earliest production.

Between 1872 and 1874, the sheep industry boomed in southern California, and the association temporarily changed its name to the San Fernando Sheep Company, taking advantage of the climate and available markets. The drought of 1874–1875, however, destroyed pasturelands, killed nearly 40,000 head of livestock, and ruined the first wheat crop. After building the first wagon road through Sepulveda Pass to expedite shipping to the port of San Pedro, Lankershim and his partners recovered their losses in 1876 when they exported two cargoes to Liverpool, England, which became California's first international export of grain. To accommodate the bountiful harvests, Lankershim and Van Nuys built a mill and formed the Los Angeles Farming and Milling Company. In 1877, Lankershim also exported 21,000 bushels of wheat from his ranches, at $1.28 a bushel, to San Francisco. The small farming community prospered, grew exponentially, and changed the valley's landscape from pastureland to vast golden fields of wheat.

The region became accessible to local and national markets with the arrival of the railroad in the 1870s and 1880s, as growers used an extensive network of tunnels and track across the valley to transport crops and other goods. By this point, the association had distributed the property to the stockholders, the largest amount belonging to James B. Lankershim, Isaac's son. As the Van Nuys and Lankershim partnership profited economically, it also led to growing family networks in the valley. Van Nuys married Isaac Lankershim's daughter, Susanna H. Lankershim, on February 10, 1880, and lived in the first wood-framed house, called the Home Ranch, which he had built in 1874.

When Isaac Lankershim, the Los Angeles pioneer, farmer, and land baron, died on April 10, 1882, Van Nuys assumed control of the Los Angeles Farm and Milling Company's wheat, ranching, and milling operations. Two years before, James Lankershim and San Francisco investors had formed the Lankershim Ranch, Land and Water Company. James Lankershim's company bought 12,000 acres from Van Nuys' holdings in the Los Angeles Farm and Milling Company to subdivide into small acreages (10–80 acres) for ready sale. An individual settler, then, had the opportunity to purchase one of the farms, which had previously been unavailable for settlement, at $5 to $150 per acre. Subdivision and new rail lines in southern California resulted in a real estate boom in the late 1880s. Economic collapse in the 1890s left families landless, and farmers began squatting on company lands. Approximately 1,200 took possession and drove off company stock. Over the next 10 years, Van Nuys filed and won multiple suits. The litigation and resurveying costs, however, exceeded $50,000. For Van Nuys, the land boom had negative consequences, but it also led to growth in the region, a growth that had been retarded to that point because of extensive wheat production.

Through subdivision of vast acreages, farmers transformed the ranches into small farms, and the town of Toluca grew as new residents needed services. Toluca was eventually renamed Lankershim and

known as the "Home of the Peach." Operators of the Lankershim ranches and local farmers planted vast orchards of peaches, as well as grape vines, smaller groves of pears, and fields of tobacco plants. During the 1880s and 1890s, residents built the infrastructure of the town, including commercial buildings, general stores, and hotels. By 1896, the town had grown sufficiently to have its own post office, school, rail depot, and blacksmith shop. In 1927, the town's name changed to North Hollywood, but the old road connecting the Cahuenga Pass to the valley remained Lankershim Boulevard. As the primary investor, Lankershim's contribution toward the establishment of the farming community and real estate development led to agriculture and, later, the urbanization of the San Fernando Valley.

—*Catherine M. Bilanchone*

Suggested Reading

Durrenberger, Robert, Leonard Pitt, and Richard Preston. *The San Fernando Valley: A Bibliography and Research.* Northridge, CA: San Fernando Valley State College Center for Urban Studies and Bureau of Business, 1967.

Fogelson, Robert M. *The Fragmented Metropolis: Los Angeles, 1850–1930.* Cambridge, MA: Harvard University Press, 1967.

Keffer, Frank. *History of San Fernando Valley.* Glendale, CA: Stillman, 1934.

Los Angeles County Bar Association. "State Bar Symposium Issue: Water Law and the Drought" [Special issue]. *Los Angeles Bar Journal* 53, no. 3 (September 1977).

Robinson, William W. *Land in California.* New York: Arno Press, 1979.

Robinson, William W. *The Spanish and Mexican Ranchos of the San Fernando Valley.* Highland Park, CA: Southwest Museum, 1966.

Robinson, William W. *The Story of the San Fernando Valley.* Los Angeles: Title Insurance and Trust, 1961.

Roderick, Kevin. *The San Fernando Valley: America's Suburb.* Los Angeles: Los Angeles Times Books, 2001.

⊞ LAS VEGAS, NEVADA

The city of Las Vegas, situated almost halfway between Salt Lake City and Los Angeles, was founded on May 5, 1905. The history of the surrounding area, however, dates back to the early 1830s and correlates with the histories of the Old Spanish Trail, the Mormons, and various other mining and railroad communities. As early as 1831, there existed a trade between Los Angeles and Santa Fe dealing with wool blankets and other textiles. The Old Spanish Trail was the quickest means of transporting goods between the two cities, and the Las Vegas area served as a resting stop for convoys. It was the only forgiving region that contained water between the Mojave and Muddy River valleys. The first explorers to travel this path did so in the 1820s and are believed to have been Jedediah Strong Smith and Antonio Armijo. Although it is not known who traveled the area first, it is known that the trail followed Muddy River south to the Virgin River, then west toward the Las Vegas Springs. After this was established as a viable route, traders and explorers made annual journeys to trade and exchange goods, always making sure to stop and rest and water their livestock before making the next leg of the journey. The route was named Las Vegas, or "the meadows," due to its fertile grounds. Because of the Mexican War, however, the trail closed in 1848.

Before the war, American military officer John C. Frémont explored the region in May 1844 and was amazed at the natural springs and the lush vegetation that grew on the banks of the Las Vegas Wash. It was recorded as an important and essential stop for all travelers headed west and held its importance throughout the following decades.

By April 1854, Congress recognized the Las Vegas area and established a postal route that ran from Salt Lake City to San Diego in southern California. Las Vegas was little more than a watering hole for postal officers and travelers, however, until the exploration of the Las Vegas Springs by the Mormons in 1855. During this year, Brigham Young sent a detachment of thirty men from Salt Lake City to Las Vegas to build a fort to protect immigrants and the U.S. mail. It is also likely that Young had ulterior motives in his charity, wishing to convert the locals of the Las Vegas Springs and show them how to raise corn, wheat, squash, and melon. In addition, the Mormons wanted a mission to connect Salt Lake City with San Bernardino and the Pacific Ocean. William Bringhurst, who later became the leading member of the community set up at Las Vegas, led this group.

By April 1856, the Mormon group of men established a small fort and modest agricultural ventures. On April 19 of the same year, lead ore was found in the Potosi Mountain area twenty-seven miles southwest of Las Vegas. The travel back and forth between the fort and Potosi Mountain brought the Mormons into greater contact with the local Paiute Indians, a tribe that retained cordial relations with the Mormons despite the perpetual theft of horses and agricultural goods by these Natives. Due to dissension among the leaders of the Mormon fort, a lack of supplies and food, unsuccessful missionary work, and bad farming because of weather, the mission was forced to close in February 1857.

Four years later in 1861, silver was discovered in the Potosi Mountain area by travelers and laborers still searching for lead ore. Later that year the Union established Fort Baker to defend against any uprisings that might occur in the Confederate-biased Southwest. This fort proved more of a decoy than anything else and allowed the mobilization of Union troops throughout Arizona.

The conclusion of the Civil War saw the return of the Las Vegas establishment to civilian hands. Octavius Decatur Gass, a former miner from northern California, founded a few small lodes in the Potosi mines and rebuilt the Mormon mission turned Union fort. After buying all the land surrounding Las Vegas Springs, Gass opened a small store to sell goods to travelers and miners passing through the Mojave Desert. Gass also grazed cattle on his lands, and by 1866, he found himself in the middle of a newly formed Arizona county, Pah-ute County. Later that year, however, Las Vegas officially became part of the state of Nevada, although it remained under Arizona's control until 1871.

In 1901, the San Pedro, Los Angeles, and Salt Lake City Railroad Company bought Octavius D. Gass's Las Vegas Ranch for a price of $55,000, and by 1904, the railroad was passing through a small tent community located just half a mile west of the ranch. The following year, Las Vegas became a bona fide town because of a population explosion caused by the Bullfrog Mining Company and the freight traffic it created. Although the town's businesses were all run out of canvas buildings, Las Vegas still attracted migrants due to the railroad and labor possibilities. A land auction in

1905 established Las Vegas as an organized town with land tracts and grids. Saloons outnumbered all other businesses in the infant town, and it remained this way for the following few years. In 1906, the former Gass Ranch was converted into a resort with a swimming pool for the Las Vegas residents, and the town itself slowly began seeing more brick and wood edifices.

The next big event to affect Las Vegas was the construction of the Hoover Dam in 1930. Another population boom occurred for the town, and in 1931 gambling was legalized, although the various miners, travelers, and laborers had already been taking part in this pastime for some years. In the 1940s, Las Vegas began to resemble the city as it is known today. Hotels and resorts began being constructed to house the droves of tourists who flocked to visit the Hoover Dam. The Flamingo, promoted by the infamous Bugsy Siegel, was the first major hotel to open its doors in 1946, along with the Golden Nugget. The 1950s followed, with hotels opening such as the Sahara in 1952, the Sands in 1953, and the Riviera in 1954. The latter was the first resort hotel to build up instead of out; it towered nine stories in the air. Following these hotels were the Dunes, Fremont, Hacienda, Tropicana, Stardust, Four Queens, Caesar's Palace, the Aladdin, the Frontier, and the Hilton over the course of the following twelve years.

A series of events helped spur the construction of such hotels, such as the opening of Nellis Air Force Base in 1941 and, in the same year, the building of Basic Magnesium, Inc., a company that produced metallic magnesium to be used in the construction of airplanes, engines, and incendiary bombs. Popular recreation sites, such as Lake Mead and Lake Mojave, also attracted tourists to Las Vegas and necessitated the building of resort hotels. Conversely, the Las Vegas of today houses the resorts as its main areas of interest, with sites such as Hoover Dam being considered afterthoughts. Today's Las Vegas is centered on gambling, entertainment, and shopping for both the individual and the entire family.

—*Matthew Adam Henderson*

Suggested Reading

Cooper, Marc. *The Last Honest Place in America.* New York: Nation Books, 2004.

Moehring, Eugene P. *Resort City in the Sunbelt.* Reno: University of Nevada Press, 1989.

Paher, Stanley W. *Las Vegas: As It Began—As It Grew.* Las Vegas: Nevada Publications, 1971.

LAST CHANCE GULCH, MONTANA

Montana's gold rush began in 1862 on Grasshopper Creek in the southwestern part of the state. This brought the first sizeable population to the remote Montana wilderness east of the Continental Divide. Miners from all over the United States flocked to the sizeable gold fields, and cities such as Bannack and Virginia City sprang up virtually overnight.

On July 21, 1864, a group of men led by John Cowan were returning from the gold fields of Virginia City broke and out of luck. As they moved through the area of present-day Helena, one of the men in their party suggested that they try one more time. To the surprise of everyone, gold was found in abundant quantities near what is now Helena's main street. The claim was staked and named "Last Chance Gulch." The men, known as the "Four Georgians" (consisting of John Cowan, D. J. Miller, John Crab, and Robert Stanley) worked the claim until 1867. They finally had their fill and moved backed to the East Coast. They left behind them an overnight boomtown, with thousands of miners panning for placer gold, quartz gold, and silver, as well as lead. The ensuing gold strike brought thousands of "get-rich-quick" miners to the fabulously rich Last Chance Gulch. These early residents considered the names of Pumpkinville and Squashtown but decided on Helena.

As the gulch began to fill with people, mostly from Virginia City, the miners decided they needed to come up with a name for their town. Its original name was Crabtown, after John Crab, one of the founders. Searching for a name, the miners decided on a town name from Minnesota that was pronounced Saint Hel-E-na. "Saint" was dropped from the name because many thought it was unnecessary. Once the placer gold ran out, Helena could easily have become a ghost town, but the town's key geographical location also made it a vital redistribution center for businesses supplying scores of other gold-mining communities. As the city grew, farms and ranches spread across the fertile Helena valley. The city grew quickly as a supply center for other area mining camps, such as Elkhorn and Marysville, and in 1874 Helena was selected as the capital of the Territory of Montana. The development of the Helena area was slowed by the exhaustion of the early gold mines, but the arrival of the Northern Pacific Railroad in 1883 and the expansion of other mining activities brought renewed prosperity to the area. In the years from 1864 to 1884, Last Chance Gulch produced an estimated $3.6 billion (in today's dollars) in gold. By 1888, an estimated 50 millionaires made Helena their home. Finally, in 1889, Montana became the 41st state, and Helena became the state capital.

Today, Helena is still the seat of Montana's state government and politics. Helena's population has grown moderately throughout the 20th century, despite such disasters as fires and the devastating 1935 earthquake. The city has not experienced the boom-and-bust cycles that have affected many other Montana communities because of its reliance on state government and on a broad-based economy emphasizing goods and services. Tourism abounds in this culturally rich city. There are many lakes and mountains for fishing and hiking, and in the city, the past truly comes alive.

—Brandon Davis

See also HELENA, MONTANA; HELENA'S EXPLOITED RESOURCES

Suggested Reading

Baumler, Ellen. *Girl from the Gulches: The Story of Mary Ronan.* Helena: Montana Historical Society Press, 2003.
Cullen, Ann. *Lilly Cullen: Helena, Montana 1894.* Missoula: Book Montana, 1999.

⊞ LAWYERS AND LEGISLATION

Lawyers were the glue that held much of the American West together. As they moved west, the trappings of regularized business transactions and criminal justice moved with them. The transmission of legal knowledge from one generation to another, the nature of judicial craftsmanship, and the gendered nature of law in the West followed their paths.

For historians, it is easy to understand that Indiana is in the East and Montana and California are in the West. But Indiana at one time was what historians called "the frontier." It was the cutting edge of civilization, where white northern Europeans confronted the savagery of wilderness and American Indians. In this new century, that formulation of "frontier" has passed to some degree, and historians are trying to determine where the West is today in the historical profession.

When University of Wisconsin history professor Frederick Jackson Turner announced his frontier thesis in 1893, most Americans had no doubt where the West was. It was simply across the Mississippi. Turner's frontier thesis, positing that the process of civilizing the West from the colonial period until 1890 produced American democracy and the American character, started historians down the path of proof to find evidence either supporting or debunking it. The process continues. Early supporters of Turner found settlers from the East finding greater democracy in the West. Detractors found evidence that eastern urban factory workers did not migrate to the West in any great numbers, and the West was not a safety value for labor unrest. So it went. Turner argued that the existence of free land, its continuous recession, and the process of settlement from east to west explained American history. Turner cast his net broadly and caught the American character as well as democracy in the seine. Books and articles offered proof on both sides until the New Western historians arrived with publication of Patricia Nelson Limerick's *The Legacy of Conquest: The Unbroken Past of the American West* (1987). Limerick shifted the debate by noting Turner's Eurocentric focus on an east-to-west process of which the viewpoint was strictly that of the pioneers, not those experiencing the process and seeing the pioneers as conquerors, from their perspective looking to the east from the west.

Limerick's call for inclusion in western history was not the first but was clearly the most noticed. Herbert Eugene Bolton already had suggested the utility of borderland studies noting the richness of cultural interaction in New Spain's northern territories. Bolton appreciated the fact that Europeans and Indians had occupied lands together for generations in the American Southwest. Limerick's argument acknowledges the need for such studies but rejects Bolton's emphasis on the opening and closing of Spanish and English empires in favor of the continuity of conquest. Further, Limerick tapped into the scholarly dissatisfaction of the 1960s with the political synthesis in American history. He joined the legions of historians, including women, persons of color, and marginalized classes, in the general fabric of American history. Most important, Limerick called for studies of place. Here the West as a region needed recognition and definition.

It is not difficult to start identifying regions and subregions. The Pacific slope belongs to Earl Pomeroy and was an identified region crying out for analysis. But can the Pacific Northwest stand scrutiny as a region? What ties the states of Oregon, Washington, and Idaho together? They all have extractive industries, and logging clearly characterized Washington and Oregon. Idaho had logging, but mining and potato farming seem clearer markers of identity. Perhaps the salmon would be a better regional icon. The whiteness of the present population of Oregon and Idaho sets these states apart from the multiracial West of the borderlands. The Great Basin Kingdom belongs to Leonard Arrington, but his economic history of the Mormons in Utah gives religion a central part in identity. For Limerick, Mormon history was very much a part of the history of the West, and today Mormon history has multiplied from many scholarly parents.

Beyond the question of "frontier" and the location of the West, these papers raise a closer question of whether urbanization was a central force in legal change. Urbanization in the West also is a question that historians have struggled to analyze in broader terms. Clara Foltz, Laura Gordon, and Lelia Robinson practiced law in cities large enough to produce clients and legal issues. Decius Wade lived in a Montana of instant cities.

Looking at the West in the 21st century, we find the most urbanized region of America. Over 80 percent of the people live in cities, and if we exclude Texas and the Plains states, the West contains almost half the American Indian and Hispanic population and more than one half of the Asian population. The West is urban and diverse. Some of these cities were "instant cities"; that is, they were created by a boom, grew from nothing to city size in months, and took on the trappings of urban America within a few years. San

Francisco, Denver, and Butte fit into this category. Many of the small cities and villages revolved around booms of another sort. The cattle trails out of Texas gave Kansas cities along the railroad instant business and instant economic distress when the herds no longer visited. Many of the cities reached out along routes of transportation for business and population. All sought to prosper and survive—but some did not. The West also is a place for ghost towns, such as Bodie, California, now a tourist destination rather than a place of homes and families. The urban West was many things over time and continues to change with population shifts and telecommuting.

San Francisco was a diverse community from its origins in the gold rush. The flood of humanity that docked there, left there, or stayed there produced a city with clear cultural and ethnic diversity. The Irish and the Chinese were the labor that built the Transcontinental Railroad and populated the city. The Irish moved into politics and the Chinese into Chinatown. Jews, Irish, and Italians moved into the embedded mercantile elite. African Americans formed a small but vibrant community. Chinese and blacks sought legal counsel when threatened within their communities and on the streets. Charlotte Brown's lawsuits would desegregate the San Francisco transit system in the 1860s. A lawsuit would desegregate the school system over a decade later. Anti-Chinese zoning ordinances would be challenged in court and overturned by the United States Supreme Court. Accommodations were not without rough spots, but diversity and accommodation became the mark of the city. Not so in Los Angeles or many other cities of the West. *Brown v. Board of Education* (1954) was a Kansas case. *Sweatt v. Painter* (1950) was a decision attacking segregation in a Texas state law school. *McLaurin v. Oklahoma State Regents* (1950) outlawed the admission of blacks to graduate school and segregated them within classrooms and other facilities. The racial liberalism of San Francisco was not followed throughout the West.

On our southern borders, America has a clear Mexican American West that is both very urban and very sparsely settled. El Paso and San Diego are examples of our binational borderland of intensive interaction with a large cultural region of Hispanic settlement and enterprise. Border cities and borders have a long reach, however. Los Angeles in the 20th century was the designation of many Mexican workers. Beyond the factories in the fields that characterized California's Imperial Valley, urban jobs constituted a substantial lure.

Cities in the West, in turn, have relationships with other western cities. Carl Abbott's *The Metropolitan Frontier: Cities in the Modern American West* (1993) describes a nested hierarchy of smaller cities and towns with strong regional, economic linkages. Most large economic regions are subdivided, with one or more of these cities controlling significant economic interests. Denver's junior economic partner is Salt Lake City. Stockton and Fresno serve the interests of San Francisco. Phoenix and El Paso share economic territory not gobbled up by Dallas in the east or Los Angeles in the west. Much of this territoriality is historical. Dallas, for example, retains a long-term commitment to serving as a comprehensive trading and financial center; its sister city, Fort Worth, concentrated on and continues to serve the west Texas cattle business. Beyond the reach of these trading and financial giants, smaller regional cities serve smaller markets. Lincoln, Nebraska; Bismark, North Dakota; and Billings, Montana are such centers of regional economic activity. It was those railroads that Decius Wade wrote about from the bench that linked these economies. The cities of the West live by these economic relationships that transportation made possible and that the computer sustains with invisible speed.

Other western cities rose with industry and fell with industry. Butte, Montana, is perhaps the most colorful example. Anyone visiting the World Mining Museum or the M & M Bar knows that you are not in Kansas anymore, much less "frontier" Indiana. Mary Murphy's *Mining Cultures: Men, Women, and Leisure in Butte, 1914–41* (1997) is the most insightful book on the subject. Butte was another instant city, growing from three thousand in 1880 to ninety thousand in 1916 on the wealth of its copper deposit, its mining and milling operations, and the diversity of its people. Copper mining was the lifeblood of the city, with three shifts of workers tramping from home to mine every eight hours and back again. Men went to the mines and women to clerical work by 1920. Unions

protected the interests of both. The prosperity of Butte rode on copper wires and the demands of World War I. When the war ended, Butte's economic fortunes turned sour, and one third of its population left by 1921. Prohibition and the crusade to save the world for democracy went hand in hand, but in Butte, the former opened new doors for women. In addition to jobs, the clandestine entertainment industry opened its doors to women. Nightclubs encouraged women to attend. Roadhouses welcomed women, and some women became owner-operators.

Butte was an ethnically diverse city. The Irish dominated the city and its union, but Finntown was the dominant ethnic neighborhood. The East Side of Butte also was home to Lebanese, Serbs, Croatians, Slovenes, Montenegrins, and Slavs. Further east, in Meaderville and McQueen, Austro-Hungarians, Swedes, Norwegians, Germans, and French lived together. These diverse groups organized their social life around the complexities of class and ethnicity. A clear blue-collar normative behavior characterized these neighborhoods, with the challenges of mining and the harsh environment of Montana pasting diverse peoples into a western pastiche.

Another avenue sometimes pursued in explaining change in the American West has been the environment. Clearly, the climate of Indiana was not the arid West of Montana or the desert vistas of southern California or the damp Pacific coast of northern California. For historians, this path of inquiry has led to a variety of tentative conclusions.

Historians of the environment in the American West have adopted a variety of multidisciplinary methods, as well as a variety of topical approaches. What emerges from the literature is a lack of agreement about what should be done to unify this new field—or, rather, the literature lays out a varied landscape, allowing scholars to adopt singular positions yet hold on to a central core of environmental focus.

The variety makes this field exciting. Some historians deal with ideas about the environment. What humans see in the landscape, how they create its image, and how they view its spiritual essence constitute some of their concerns in research. Other scholars look at the institutional and political movements that brought environmental protection and preservation.

Still others look at public policy formation and how it finds its way into law. Legal historians and policy scholars have barely scratched the surface of this field.

The common-law approach to environmental protection was through the law of nuisance. Common-law nuisance was either private nuisance or public nuisance. Private nuisance cases were commonly between a single plaintiff or a small number of plaintiffs and a polluter. These cases usually revolved around land use questions or the interference with another's unimpaired use of private property. Public nuisance related to interference with public access to rivers, ways of necessity, or a breath of air. Polluters had no right to diminish the value of downstream property owners, whether that interest in land had to do with water or air. In the 18th century, *Blackstone's Commentaries* used the example of a smelter too near the land of others, killing crops and damaging cattle as subject to nuisance law. The problem for some plaintiffs was that courts under the common law did have the option of granting damages without putting a halt to the pollution. Landowners had the option, in turn, of accepting contracts in the form of easements for pollution without lawsuit that would compensate them for the continuing pollution. Further, courts could look at the market value created by the polluter and weigh it against the social and economic costs to the community. Courts often determined that the balance was in favor of industry because of employment and deny recovery for the plaintiffs. Common-law remedies did not look beyond market factors and contract issues unless a compelling case regarding public health could be raised.

Common-law liability rules further frustrated the victims of pollution. The theory of negligence is that there is a reasonable standard of conduct for every human situation. Conduct is negligent when there is proof of unreasonable risk of harm to others. Further, plaintiffs must prove that the defendant knew or should have known that the conduct was harmful. As a result, in bringing a lawsuit the plaintiff has four elements to allege and prove: (1) that a legal duty of care was owed the plaintiff, (2) that there was a breach of that duty, (3) that there was a causal relationship between the breach of duty and injury, and (4) that the plaintiff was damaged. Beyond negligence, most jurisdictions provide for strict liability in tort for injury caused by abnormally dangerous activities. In the West, a smelter dumping arsenic into the air and water was sending a known poison onto the property of others. Also, a coal mine in Montana that washed its coal in river water and cleaned its machinery with the same water was putting coal slack downstream to the detriment of irrigators and fish. The substances were different, yet dead fish told the tale in both instances. As the research goes beyond the descriptive to the analytical, we will see that western lawyers were fashioning arguments to keep goldfish alive and return trout to their pristine habitat.

For plaintiffs, strict liability claims did not require proof of negligence, but there were other proof problems. The polluter could defend its poisoning of the air and water by claiming that its value to the community outweighed the dangerous attributes of its operations. Private nuisance law contained these general tort law elements. Plaintiffs had to prove that the polluter's conduct caused the invasion of his or her interest in land, that it was intentional and unreasonable, negligent or reckless, or abnormally dangerous. The polluter could raise the balancing test, asking the court to weigh the gravity of the harm and the utility of the defendant's conduct.

In public nuisance cases, the plaintiff must show that there has been an unreasonable interference with the interests of the community or the rights of the general public. For a citizen rather than a public entity to raise this claim, the citizen must show the injury to be different in kind rather than different in degree.

The final common-law cause of action used in environmental cases was trespass. Trespass usually involved interference with the right of exclusive possession of land. In modern practice, trespass was the basis for *Martin v. Reynolds Metals Co.,* 221 Oregon 86 (1959). We need to remember that this was good law in the East as well as the West. The common-law remedies were continuous yet limited.

Beyond the common law, western legislatures were busy dealing with some of the same problems. In 1852, the California legislature passed an "Act to prevent certain public nuisances." This statute declared it a public nuisance and a misdemeanor to pollute any creek, stream, pond, road, alley, or highway. The same session passed a law to protect salmon runs. In 1862, the solons regulated trout fishing. The next year, their legislative hands moved to protect seals and sea lions. In 1872, they banned the killing of mockingbirds. Six years later, they banned fishing on Lake Bigler. In 1877, the Montana Territorial Legislature outlawed the dumping of coal slack in the waters. As early as *Nelson v. O'Neal,* 1 Montana 284 (1871), the Montana Territorial Supreme Court would declare in a trespass case that there was "no right to fill the channel of a creek with tailings and debris." California's high court would make a similar decision in *California v. Gold Run Ditch and Mining Company,* 66 California 318 (1884). As Robert Bunting points out in his *The Pacific Raincoast: Environment and Culture in an American Eden, 1778–1900* (1997), to protect fish, Washington and Oregon passed laws to forbid the dumping of sawdust in streams. State lawmakers were busy providing piecemeal for environmental protection. Some of this legislation had environmental protection in mind that would increase the profits of farmers. Mark Fiege's *Irrigated Eden: The Making of an Agricultural Landscape in the American West* (1999) surveys water law as well as Idaho seed purity law, finding that the reach of law does not always grasp what it intended.

The federal government got into the pollution control business late in the century. In 1899, Congress passed the Rivers and Harbors Appropriation Act, which came to be known as the Refuse Act of 1899. This act facilitated the Army Corps of Engineers' mission to keep navigation channels free of obstructions. Section 407 forbade the dumping of refuse without a permit in any navigable stream or on the banks where it could be washed into the waters. Section 411 contained criminal penalties and a reward for informants who reported violations. The enforcement of this act federalized pollution control on our nation's waterways and made industry change its ways (in part). The Clean Water Act of 1972 created tougher standards and a bureaucracy to manage permits. The Clean Air Act of 1970 created modern federal regulatory control law, a bureaucracy to administer it, and continuing administrative law and congressional tinkering with emissions standards. The federal bureaucracies in the environmental field must follow the procedures set out in the Administrative Procedures Act of 1946. This statute sets out procedures for agency rule making and adjudication. Implicit in these procedures is public notice and citizen participation in many of the stages of rule making.

The biodiversity of the West was furthered by another federal statute, the Endangered Species Act of 1973. This legislation was in line with the Convention on International Trade in Endangered Species. The federal Fish and Wildlife Service and the Commerce Department's National Marine Fisheries Service administer the program. Under the statute, the services place endangered and threatened species on the federal endangered species list. They also prepare recovery programs. Most important, the law forbids all federal agencies to act in a manner that would jeopardize the existence of a listed species or destroy critical habitats of a listed species. In 1978, Congress created a cabinet-level "God Committee" with the power to issue exemptions after findings of necessity and lack of alternatives. An amendment in 1982 further weakened the statute by allowing petitioners to obtain "incidental take" permits from the secretaries. These petitioners must go through an extensive labyrinth of procedures, including habitat conservation plans that can include strict controls of private projects. The statute does include civil penalties and criminal sanctions for violation. The success of the program can be seen by all Americans in the return of the bald eagle to our skies.

In the federal courts, the U.S. Supreme Court in a 1907 Georgia case involving interstate air pollution recognized that the states have a legally enforceable interest in stopping pollution. Copper heaps and smelting, such as Montana witnessed in Butte, produce acid rain, wiping out forests and crops. This doctrine was dormant until *Texas v. Pankey,* 441 F.2d 236 (1971). This case recognized that states have a right to protect ecological interests from impairment by polluters. Because such pollution is interstate in nature and the federal government has exclusive jurisdiction over commerce under the commerce clause of the Constitution, this judicial recognition of state authority to sue to abate pollution when other governmental entities have not was significant. Questions of federal preemption of state action were raised in *California*

Tahoe Regional Planning Agency v. Jennings, 594 F. 2d 181 (1979). The court found that the Clean Air Act and the Federal Water Pollution Control Act did not preempt state action to protect the environment under the federal nuisance law doctrine.

Although federal and state environmental law draws scholars to the public policy and politics aspects of history, other historians have found biodiversity and its science to be equally illuminating. Mark Fiege's *Irrigated Eden,* Peter Boag's *Environment and Experience: Settlement Culture in Nineteenth-Century Oregon* (1992), and Robert Bunting's *Pacific Rainforest* demonstrate the limits of man's control of the environment through careful discussion of biodiversity and man's impact. Different kinds of grass, insects, rodents, and rabbits inhabit their pages and give readers an understanding of basic ecology to enhance the narrative. Introduced species conflict with native plants and animals, often to the indigenous species' detriment. Science produces insecticides, fungicides, and rodenticides to further alter nature's course. Again, the science that is applied to nature may have unintended consequences, further diminishing nature's economy. The stories vary in time and place, but the consequences frequently converge in human error.

Finally, historians have started the process of promoting the understanding that there is no more a singular "West" than there was "an" American Indian. Region and section in the Turnerian world of yesterday and the regional location of the West in the eyes of "New Western historians" have been further refined by environmental historians who recognize microclimates, watersheds, and arroyos. Again, this is an interdisciplinary enterprise, as Rotberg and Rabb's *Climate and History: Studies in Interdisciplinary History* (1981) demonstrated. Beyond history, these scholars found it necessary to include biology, chemistry, geography, and geology in their quiver of inquiry.

Unfortunately, environmental history has one very arid void: It seldom concerns itself with gender. Simply put, Clara Foltz, Laura Gordon, and a myriad of other women made a substantive difference in the West. Further, the history of women in the American West affords legal historians a growing base on which to build new questions about the gendered nature of law and politics. Clara Foltz was the pioneer for women in gaining access to the bar in the West just as women gained suffrage in the West, giving reformers in the East rhetorical ammunition for their campaigns.

From first contact, American Indians knew that Europeans did not understand the gendered nature of America. Confusion regarding the role of women within tribes and bands continued from first contact well into the late 19th century. European willingness to conflate the 500 tribes and bands into a singular American Indian further confused a growing populace that moved west seeking opportunity in lands long inhabited by Native peoples. In the process of moving to a region that we now call the West, gender played a major role in changing the society that confronted a changing environment and splendidly varied landscape.

The mistaken view of the role of women in American Indian societies opens Sara Evans' *Born for Liberty: A History of Women in America* (1989), making clear the narrow vision of Euro-Americans from the 17th century to the recent past. Many early Euro-Americans overlooked the nuanced cultural complexity of American Indian societies and the dimensions of women's economic, social, and religious roles. Rather, they saw a corrupt, uncivilized people who allowed women to perform men's tasks, such as chopping wood, building dwellings, planting fields, harvesting crops, and leading war parties. Missionaries wanted their neophytes to become "white Indians" in the image of a white Christ. White eyes could not see women at the center of creation myths. God was white and male in white eyes. They could not see American Indian women as Mother Earth, the Keepers of the Game, or the Double Woman Dreamer. God, a white male, created the earth, put men in charge of animal husbandry, and ordained that men alone would be in touch with the Holy Spirit. The divisions between American Indian reality and white perspective were manifest despite the facts that were clearly at hand.

In the recent past, historians have started the process of recovering the gendered past of the American West and recognizing the complexity of western women's history. The stereotypes of western women as civilizers in sunbonnets have yielded to the complexity of western women's history. First, historians have recognized that the West was the most multicultural region of the country. Ethnic and racial backgrounds played a significant part in the roles of women on the West's varied stages. Migration experiences were formative for many but varied widely in time, place, and manner of migration. Women formed bonds with other women of like and dramatically different cultural heritages. The contributions of women to the success of families varied with time, place, and class as well as race. American Indian women were, for example, in charge of economic transactions and the means of production, such as sheep among the Navajo. Women struggled for rights, but in the West we can see variation found in few other regions. White women marched for the vote in California but already had the vote in the Wyoming Territory in 1869. American Indian women found it hard to contemplate the vote without citizenship, and they would wait until 1924 to become citizens. Asian women would wait until World War II to gain rights to citizenship. Black women in Kansas suffered the indignities of racial discrimination in public accommodations long after women of color in the San Francisco Bay Area were riding local streetcars (in the 1860s) and attending desegregated schools (thirty years later). The similarities as well as the differences in female experience because of race further complicate the West.

Race also affected women's outlook on the future and their range of choice in the past. In many ways, these choices had to do with relationships with men. Men obviously wanted women in the West, particularly when gender balances were off center in the 1850s and 1860s. Henry Halleck stood on the floor of the 1849 California Constitutional convention advocating women's legal rights as a lure to bring them west. Wyoming's female franchise found advocates because of another form of lure. When they arrived, women varied by marital status, sexual preference, religion, race, class, and culture. Some came from rural America, others from the factories of the East. Some came west to escape religious persecution in the East and find Zion in Utah or Idaho. All of these factors molded a woman's perception of the West. Although the men of the West looking for women frequently did not recognize these distinctions, historians have done

so, recognizing the diversity of the women of the West. Rather than marginalizing women because of racial or other distinctions, historians have found it necessary to account for differences by critically analyzing the experiences of western women.

Racial and ethnic heritage played a role in female experience, whether the woman was Hispanic, Japanese, or Irish. Women's work was part of western history, but women did not confine themselves to plow handles or brothels. Women were very much a part of most occupations and were certainly part of the process of breaking down barriers of access. They worked in the fields for wages as well as for family welfare and prosperity. Women demanded access to the professions, whether teaching or law, accounting or medicine. The process of eliminating barriers varied in time and space, but the struggle was constant. The story of women in polygamous Utah or Idaho was different yet also an integral part of the fabric of western history. Because of their beliefs and practices, these women suffered at the hands of the federal government and persevered.

One method of illuminating women's lives in a multicultural West is looking from their point of view and analyzing their experiences in their own context before placing their story in the larger West. Rosalina Mendez Gonzalez, Deena J. Gonzalez, and Antonia Castenada have been very successful with this method. In particular, Gonzalez's *Refusing the Favor: The Spanish-Mexican Women of Santa Fe, 1820–1880* (1999) situates women and gender issues within the debate on conquest and colonization as New Mexico politically transforms itself from Mexico to America. More generally, historians Joan Jensen and Darlis Miller have turned to women's documents to look at context through the eyes of 19th-century women. Sarah Deutsch traced Hispanic women within families and communities across the West. These women seasonally migrated north, following the ripening of various crops. They worked fields, maintained families, and created communities. Other Hispanic women remained in traditional villages, seasonally regendered, and took on expanded responsibilities for institutions and social relations. Antonia I. Casteneda found similar struggles without the migrating males in Alta California from 1769 to 1848. Amerindian and mestiza (half Indian, half Spanish or Mexican) women carved out space for themselves and their families, were active agents in their spheres, and resisted Spanish military and clerical power. Laurie K. Mercier's *Anaconda: Labor, Community, and Culture in Montana's Smelter City* (2001) looked at women's documents and preserved women's voices in an oral history that reconstructed the lives of Irish women in Anaconda, Montana. A town created by the Anaconda Copper Mining Company smelting facility, Anaconda was 25 percent Irish. These women constructed a community with economic, social, and political security that persisted until the 1950s. For comparative purposes, readers should consult Murphy's *Mining Cultures*. Murphy, like Mercier, looks at community through the experiences of women in a very multicultural gendered community in the American West.

Perhaps the best book on the multicultural West as seen through women's eyes is Glenda Riley's *A Place to Grow: Women in the American West* (1992), which puts synthesis and documents in the hands of students of western women. Riley's work is foundational in this field of western history. Her *Women and Indians on the Frontier, 1825–1915* (1984) opened the issue of women pioneers and their attitudes concerning the West and American Indians in time and place; *The Female Frontier: A Comparative View of Women and the Prairie and the Plains* (1988) analyzed the lives of women during the 19th century who lived lives in dramatically different places. Their voices play an important role in the analysis. Riley's *Building and Breaking Families in the American West* (1996) took her study of divorce on a national level to the West and included the processes of courting, committing, marrying, intermarrying, separating, and deserting. Open space and opportunity in the American West, as well as divorce law, allowed the creation of a fluid society. Riley's *Prairie Voices: Iowa's Pioneering Women* (1996) brought 19th-century voices to life for 21st-century ears and eyes. In *By Grit & Grace: Eleven Women Who Shaped the American West* (1997), Professor Riley teamed with Professor Richard W. Etulain to provide readers with biographies of significant women. In *By Grit & Grace*, Riley summarized her book *The Life and Legend of Annie Oakley* (1994) as one of the biographies. Riley's attention turned to

the conservation movement in *Women and Nature: Saving the "Wild" West* (1999), which covers botanists, ornithologists, naturalists, authors, photographers, and outdoor enthusiasts who supported the environmental movement. The gendered West owes a great debt to this intrepid historian.

Clearly, the history of gender in the West has a literature basis awaiting new questions and insights. With law as the glue that held western society together and with western lawyers at the center of that political and institutional world, it is incumbent that we understand that gender mattered then as it does now in law and politics.

Western legal history has come of age with the work of John Phillip Reid and others, who have guided a research agenda that recognizes the familiar in civil and criminal law in the West and identifies the uniqueness flowing from water and mining law development. In addition, Professor Reid and others have constructed a research agenda that includes multicultural legal analysis and should illuminate the vitality of western legal history. Reid suggested that there were numerous layers of western legal history, most only partially explored. They included the development of law during the westward expansion, the law of Indian Territory, the law of cattle drives and the open range, the law of the Mormons, mining law, water law, the law of American Indian nations, violence and the law, and transboundary law. His observations in "The Layers of Western Legal History" (1992) clearly delineate a topical and conceptual agenda for research. The work in western legal history is extensive, but as Reid suggests, a great deal of scholarly opportunity awaits researchers.

In addition to Reid's research agenda, the "New Western historians" have offered some insights on law in the American West. Howard Lamar made the following observation in 1992:

> Bureaucracy thrives on rules. Rules suggest laws, and laws lead to litigation. In the past fifty years both citizens and the state and federal governments have hired armies of lawyers to fight their battles in legislative halls or in courts. The current debate[s] over water needs, pollution, the environment, and development has been cast in legal terms. In addition to studying the history of these endless litigations, we should ask

why the debate has taken this form. Are we a legal-minded people, or, as one suspects, have Americans become so accustomed to using the law as a selfish manipulative tool—from the time of the first Indian treaty on through two centuries of abuse of public lands—that it is a fundamental part of our culture? The new bureaucracy itself now seems to be using the law, sometimes callously, to achieve its own ends. The point is not to condemn but to ask how we came to this litigiousness and why we continue it. (pp. 263–264)

Lamar's formulation of the research question is confrontational. Are the American people, particularly those that people the West, law minded, as Reid found on the overland trail, or is the law a tool of capitalistic oppression, as the critical legal studies school would have us believe.

Patricia Nelson Limerick, writing in the same volume, finds the West a place of opportunity for legal history research.

Western history is full of . . . examples of words consulted and puzzled over as if they were Scripture. When mining law awarded ownership of all the "angles, dips, spurs, and variations" of a vein to the person who claimed the "apex" of that vein, lawyers took on the trying task of translating a verbal construction into a geological reality. (p. 181)

Limerick also found lawyers representing "forests and rivers, antelope and coyotes." She offered that

when inarticulate nature found voice in legal proceedings, the world of words had reached its peak of inclusiveness. . . . [L]egal words provide abundant opportunities for cross-cultural comparisons. . . . Written or oral, legal tradition is transmitted in words, by which power and influence flow toward the appointed custodians and interpreters of those words. The study of law and verbal behavior also provides important information on intergroup relations in the West. (p. 182)

The research opportunities, according to Limerick and Reid, are abundant.

Looking at Richard White's *"It's Your Misfortune and None of My Own": A History of the American West* (1991), it is clear that there was plenty of law in the New West, but a good deal of that law remains for analysis and explanation. My conservative count of law references in this text yielded 107 citations. Many of these references should not be surprising to students of legal history or the American West. Numerous federal statutes pertained to the West or had substantial impact in the West, such as the Trade and Intercourse Act of 1834, the Oregon Donation Act of 1850, the Dawes Act of 1887, American land law generally, the Northwest Ordinance of 1787, the Edmunds Acts of 1882 and 1887, the Chinese Exclusion Act of 1882, the California Land Act of 1851, the Sherman Anti-Trust Act, the Alien Land Law of 1887, the Boulder Canyon Act of 1928, the General Mining Law of 1872, the Coal Lands Act of 1873, the Mineral Leasing Act of 1920, the Carey Act of 1894, Newland's National Reclamation Act of 1901, the Forest Management Act of 1897, the Yosemite Act of 1864, the Lacy Act of 1906, the Tydings-McDuffie Act of 1934, the 1917 Immigration Act, the 1917 Literacy Test Act, the 1921 and 1924 Immigration Quota laws, the Emergency Relief and Construction Act of 1934, the Agricultural Marketing Act of 1924, the Silver Purchase Act of 1934, the Lanham Act, the Agricultural Act of 1956, Public Law 283 of 1952, the Sustained Yield Act of 1944, the Multiple Use–Sustained Yield Act of 1960, the U.S. Housing Act of 1949, the Collier-Burns Act of 1948, the Federal Interstate Highway Act of 1956, the Payments in Lieu of Taxes Act of 1976, the Federal Land Policy and Management Act of 1976, the Religious Freedom Act of 1978, the Indian Civil Rights Act of 1968, the Immigration and Naturalization Act of 1952, the Immigration Act of 1965, and the Simpson-Mazzoli Act of 1986. This is quite an impressive list.

State and territorial law are included in the portrait. Women used Spanish law in New Mexico to manage their affairs and gain a great deal of independence, but the law of debt peonage forced Indians to work one year for a creditor. Americans in pre-Revolutionary Texas complained about the Mexican legal system. After the Mexican War, New Mexico had Kearny's Code as a base. In Utah, the Mormons used their probate courts against "Gentile" aggression. California passed a Foreign Miners Tax Act in 1850 to run the Californios off the diggings.

California courts refused to uphold the communal land rights of Hispanics. Mexican and American law was in conflict in California regarding the law of heirship. Western railroad boosters wanted lawmakers to give railroads "breaks." Western miners and smelter workers got the 8-hour day by statute. A California statute of 1850 enabled the peonage of Indians. Western state law and federal statute, in sum, disfranchised western minorities by denying citizenship, imposing poll taxes, and creating white-only primaries. Western states passed prohibition statutes. California enacted a Railroad Commission law, but the Southern Pacific used legal procedures to frustrate or delay the law's impact. Oregon's Compulsory School Act of 1922 was unconstitutional. Texas statutes and court decisions prevented a Standard Oil monopoly in Texas. Western water law was the product of legislatures and courts. Tax law changes in Texas caused a civil war in south Texas from 1915 to 1917. The Japanese often managed to evade California's alien land laws (1913), which were enacted to bar Japanese land use. Later these laws were declared unconstitutional. Texas and Oklahoma used executive orders, statutes, and court actions to regulate the oil industry. State law after World War II made municipal annexation easier, stimulating expansion of city boundaries. Since the 1960s, state law has attacked environmental pollution, taxed extractive industries, regulated land use, and expanded the tax base. The states of the New West were busy using law.

Law at the local level does not escape Professor White's extensive research net. Both elite and peasant women in New Mexico went to court to maintain their rights within marriage. The expansion of the bureaucratic state in the 19th-century West brought with it the growth of administrative law before it was ever noticed in the nation. When it was discovered that trapping beaver violated Mexican law, the Hudson's Bay Company ordered it stopped. Restrictive covenants in deeds proved an effective way of segregating minority communities, particularly Asians. Stockmen often worked out law among themselves without resort to courts. Law at the operational level also is an important part of understanding the New West.

This last issue, like that of the dispossession of the Californios under the California Land Act of 1851, is a volatile one with a great deal of political baggage. From the legal historian's perspective, the analysis usually ends with the issue of due process, that fundamental principle of American constitutional right and liberty. Although American Indians may have both won and lost cases in court, we must remember that the Chinese often used those same courts to win and lose. Perhaps when western historians ask legal history questions, we will learn more about how to play the game than about who won and lost. Perhaps the best players were the winners with the best lawyers sitting at the Mad Hatter's Tea Party trying to make sense of western history.

The best analytic work using questions about law in the New West is Debra L. Donahue's *The Western Range Revisited: Removing Livestock from Public Lands to Conserve Native Biodiversity* (1999). Professor Donahue brings extensive training and experience in rangeland science together with a law professor's analytic quiver of tools to suggest the "unthinkable": the removal of livestock from many western rangelands on the grounds that it makes economic sense, is ecologically wise, and (clearly) is legally justifiable. In the process of arriving at this politically explosive suggestion, Professor Donahue analyzes why the cattle industry has been able to retain such political and bureaucratic clout despite clear evidence that its grazing practices are destroying the region's grasslands. It was most fitting that the publisher released this book in the last month of the millennium, because it brings New Western history into an analytic framework that both informs and convicts public policy.

More broadly, the struggles of female lawyers in the West to access clients is part of a larger inquiry into the nature of women's work in America. What is particularly striking about these studies is the agency of women in achieving access to employment opportunities. These strategies went beyond those of Laura deForce Gordon working in the California Constitutional Convention of 1878–1979 to obtain constitutional access to employment. They were many and varied and are worthy of our consideration in exploring the western experience. Gayle Gullett has done this in part in *Becoming Citizens: The Emergence and Development of the California Women's Movement, 1880–1911* (2000). She places Clara Foltz and Laura

Gordon in a much larger picture of female activism. In 1896, few women were in the workplace, and suffrage lost at the polls. In 1911, more women were in the workforce, were better organized, and were writing copy for newspapers. Women were in the legislature working for a juvenile court system tied to the municipal playground movement. Success in getting their program institutionalized meant jobs for women. Gullett's historical quilt is the work of many hands in and outside the legislature, but all hands were sewing new opportunities for women.

Sally Zanjani's *A Mine of Her Own: Woman Prospectors in the American West, 1850–1950* (1997) focuses on women in the mining business, dividing the periods of 1850–1918 and 1919–1950. The book is mostly biographies of women in the prospecting business and mostly Nevada women. One chapter centers on a Mexican woman in the mines, but the work also ranges from the "famous," such as Josephine "Josie" Marcus Earp, to unknowns now recovered for history.

Her conclusions are important: Few married; few had children, because there was a certain incompatibility in prospecting and raising children; none sought self-worth through what Carl Degler has described as the sense of identification with other women—to be attained by confining one's activities to the domestic sphere—and they relished equaling or exceeding male achievements.

Married women who were also prospectors reverted to a more traditional "feminine" role in mine sales and the promotion phase of prospecting. Forty-seven percent of women in this study began prospecting between 1898 and 1910. They came from a variety of backgrounds and often pursued a variety of occupations and businesses. Jennie Enright, for example, was a cattle rancher, craftswoman, cashier, bakery and boarding house operator, and real estate agent.

Woman prospectors were not domestics and not factory workers. Less than 10 percent of the women in the study ever left prospecting once they started.

Mrs. Helen C. Quigley, a prospector from Utah who ventured into Death Valley alone with a horse and a pack mule in 1907 . . . was found in a cave in the Funeral Mountains . . . barely alive. . . . Her narrow escape deterred Quigley not at all. As soon as her rescuers had nursed her back to health, through weeks of delirium, she set off into the desert to return to the ledge she had discovered. (Zanjani, pp. 309–310)

Some successful prospectors took trophy husbands. Twenty-nine percent of the women who married took men five to thirty years younger than themselves. Mary Grantz "paraded her new husband before her Wisconsin relatives" (Zanjani, pp. 222–223). Social ambition was conspicuously absent, however: No woman prospector built a pretentious seaside mansion with gold doorknobs. Pleasure lay in achievement. In some ways, this sounds like the better lawyers in the western bar.

Those "better" lawyers who achieved positions of influence generally started by reading law in a local lawyer's office. For the women of the bar later in the century, access was the first issue, and Clara Foltz's use of the legislature was significant, yet not uniformly applied. Decius Wade also read law in his uncle's office and used political connections to elevate himself.

When in power, these frontier and western attorneys left important marks. Wade's work on the Montana Supreme Court and as a code commissioner left a substantial heritage. He created a framework for the development of the state's common-law jurisprudence, a jurisprudence so strong that it survived codification. The women defenders of the West, particularly Clara Foltz, created the public defender's office. This supported the justice system and gave women access to important positions and trial practice. Perhaps there was something in frontier soil that allowed lawyers of both genders to grow and make the legal landscape to match the mountains.

—*Gordon Morris Bakken*

See also Brent, Joseph Lancaster; Inyo County, California; Jacks, David Baird; Logging; Rexburg, Idaho, and the Minidoka Project

Suggested Reading

Abbott, Carl. *The Metropolitan Frontier: Cities in the Modern American West.* Tucson: University of Arizona Press, 1993.

Babcock, Barbara Allen. "Women Defenders in the West." *Nevada Law Journal* 1 (Spring 2001): 1–18.

Bakken, Gordon Morris, ed. *Law in the Western United States* Norman: University of Oklahoma Press, 2000.

Bakken, Gordon Morris. "Lawyers in the American West, 1820–1920: A Comment." *Nevada Law Journal* 1 (Spring 2001): 88–111.

Bakken, Gordon Morris. *Practicing Law in Frontier California.* Lincoln: University of Nebraska Press, 1991.

Boag, Peter. *Environment and Experience: Settlement Culture in Nineteenth-Century Oregon.* Berkeley: University of California Press, 1992.

Bunting, Robert. *The Pacific Raincoast: Environment and Culture in an American Eden, 1778–1900.* Lawrence: University of Kansas Press, 1997.

Donahue, Debra L. *The Western Range Revisited: Removing Livestock from Public Lands to Conserve Native Biodiversity.* Norman: University of Oklahoma Press, 1999.

Evans, Sara. *Born for Liberty: A History of Women in America.* New York: Free Press, 1989.

Fiege, Mark. *Irrigated Eden: The Making of an Agricultural Landscape in the American West.* Seattle: University of Washington Press, 1999.

Gonzalez, Deena J. *Refusing the Favor: The Spanish-Mexican Women of Santa Fe, 1820–1880.* New York: Oxford University Press, 1999.

Gullett, Gayle. *Becoming Citizens: The Emergence and Development of the California Women's Movement, 1880–1911.* Urbana: University of Illinois Press, 2000.

Lamar, Howard. "Westering in the Twenty-first Century: Speculations on the Future of the Western Past." In *Under an Open Sky: Rethinking America's Western Past*, edited by William Cronon, George Miles, and Jay Gitlin. New York: Norton, 1992.

Limerick, Patricia Nelson. "Making the Most of Words." In *Under an Open Sky: Rethinking America's Western Past*, edited by William Cronon, George Miles, and Jay Gitlin. New York: Norton, 1992.

Mercier, Laurie K. *Anaconda: Labor, Community, and Culture in Montana's Smelter City.* Normal: University of Illinois Press, 2001.

Morriss, Andrew P. "Legal Arguments in the Opinions of Montana Territorial Chief Justice Decius S. Wade." *Nevada Law Journal* 1 (Spring 2001): 38–87.

Murphy, Mary. *Mining Cultures: Men, Women, and Leisure in Butte, 1914–41.* Urbana: University of Illinois Press, 1997.

Reid, John Phillip. "The Layers of Western Legal History." In *Law for the Elephant, Law for the Beaver: Essays in the Legal History of North America*, edited by John McLaren, Harmar Foster, and Chet Orloff. Pasadena, CA: Ninth Judicial Circuit Historical Society, 1992.

Riley, Glenda. *Building and Breaking Families in the American West.* Albuquerque: University of New Mexico Press, 1996.

Riley, Glenda. *The Female Frontier: A Comparative View of Women and the Prairie and the Plains.* Lawrence: University of Kansas Press, 1988.

Riley, Glenda. *The Life and Legend of Annie Oakley.* Norman: University of Oklahoma Press, 1994.

Riley, Glenda. *A Place to Grow: Women in the American West.* Wheeling, IL: Harlan Davidson, 1992.

Riley, Glenda. *Prairie Voices: Iowa's Pioneering Women.* Ames: Iowa State University Press, 1996.

Riley, Glenda. *Women and Indians on the Frontier, 1825–1915.* Albuquerque: University of New Mexico Press, 1984.

Riley, Glenda. *Women and Nature: Saving the "Wild" West.* Lincoln: University of Nebraska Press, 1999.

Riley, Glenda, and Richard W. Etulain. *By Grit & Grace: Eleven Women Who Shaped the American West.* Golden, CO: Fulcrum Press, 1997.

Rotberg, Robert I., and Rabb, Theodore K. *Climate and History: Studies in Interdisciplinary History.* Princeton: Princeton University Press, 1981.

White, Richard. *"It's Your Misfortune and None of My Own": A History of the American West.* Norman: University of Oklahoma Press, 1991.

Zanjani, Sally. *A Mine of Her Own: Woman Prospectors in the American West, 1850–1950.* Lincoln: University of Nebraska Press, 1997.

⊞ LEADVILLE, COLORADO

Leadville's story, as with all mining towns, begins with geology. Leadville (also called, in various incarnations, Magic City and Silver City) is situated on the western slope of the mountains of the Mosquito Range in the upper Arkansas River Valley, nearly in the middle of Colorado. The mineralization around the city, created by rich hydrothermal solutions seeping into local geologic faults, is diverse—ranging from gold and silver to zinc and iron. At 10,188 feet, making Leadville the highest incorporated city in the United States, Leadville came into being at the intersection of two Ute Indian trails that were later widened to accommodate horses and wagons. One trail came over Frémont Pass, the loftiest in North America, from the east. To the west is a magnificent view of the Sawatch Range, home to the two highest peaks in Colorado. Mount Elbert measures 14,433 feet and Mount Massive, 14,421 feet. Southeast of Leadville, running some seven miles in length, is California Gulch.

It is in California Gulch that initial settlement took place when gold was found in April 1860, sparking a gold rush. A prospector by the name of Abe Lee, along with some companions, had crossed the snowy Mosquito Range, entering into the upper Arkansas

River Valley, and started to prospect in the gulches upstream. On discovering gold in one of the gulches, Lee exclaimed to his companions, "Boys, I have all of Californee right here in my hands!" The area of the gold strike was thus named California Gulch.

Within three months of Lee's discovery, four thousand prospectors were working in California Gulch. This number swelled to ten thousand by the time summer came. During the next five years, California Gulch earned more than $5 million in 1865 prices. By 1866, California Gulch was all played out, as all gold near the surface had been collected. In 1868, the discovery of the Piner Boy Lode in California Gulch brought the opening of the first underground gold mine and another gold rush. Gold miners began to hard-rock mine into the mountainsides between 1868 and 1875 on a small scale.

In 1875, two miners, William Stevens and Alvinus Wood, sent out samples of the heavy black sand that the gold in California Gulch was being found in. They were curious about its mineral content, and to their delight, the test results showed that the sand was made up of 27 percent lead and contained up to fifteen ounces of silver per ton. This discovery sparked a silver rush in 1877, and mining shifted from searching for gold to more widespread hard-rock mining. Miners began to drill and blast into the mountainside to get at the veins of silver.

Active prospecting over the entire region commenced in the spring of 1877, and the development of rich and productive mines from that time on advanced rapidly. At the beginning of this era of prosperity, the settlement consisted of a few log cabins on the edge of California Gulch, with an estimated population of two hundred; its business houses consisted of a "ten by twelve" grocery and two small saloons. The three mines were scarcely started into the mountainsides. Communication with the outside world was by stage or wagon, either across the crests of two high ranges to Denver or by an almost equally difficult road to Colorado Springs. When residents petitioned for a post office, the names Cerusite (the mineralogical name for lead carbonate) and Agassiz were proposed but rejected as being too scientific. Lead City was suggested, but finally a compromise was reached, and the rapidly growing town was named Leadville in 1878. It was incorporated in 1879. By 1879, at the peak of the silver boom, Leadville's population stood above thirty thousand people, just a few thousand shy of Denver's.

It was said that Leadville's streets were "paved with silver" because they were covered with the black, heavy remnants from the silver smelting process. This "slag" cut down on the mud created during each spring runoff. This wealth also helped pay for rapid improvements in communication, transportation, and utilities. In the fall of 1879, gas lighting was installed in the Tabor Opera House and along the city streets. A couple of months later, in December 1879, the Edison lines of Tabor's telephone exchange connected Leadville to Denver. Finally, two railroads, the Denver and Rio Grande and the South Park and Pacific, connected Leadville to the world in 1880. A third rail line, the Colorado Midland, was finished in 1887.

As was typical of mining towns, boom and bust resulted in rapid population increases and decreases. Although Leadville's population in 1879 was thirty thousand, by 1880, the city had fifteen thousand inhabitants; later, the population rose to thirty thousand again. As of 1880, Leadville had twenty-eight miles of streets and more than five miles of water mains. It had eleven hundred pupils in daily attendance at its schools, five churches, three public hospitals, an opera house, six banks, and many business houses constructed of brick and stone. Its assessable property is estimated to have been $30 million, and $1.4 million was expended in 1880 in new buildings and improvements. To support this population, there were more than thirty producing mines and ten large smelting works, and the annual production of gold, silver, and lead amounted to $15 million.

The immense wealth being generated in Leadville made for diverse society. Americans from all over the United States worked alongside Finns, Irish, and Germans in the mines. The Cornish, who lived near the smelters, came to Leadville to apply the smelting talents that they had learned in England.

Opera houses and grand hotels stood just blocks away from cribs, flophouses, and dismal slums; culture and wealth collided face to face with violence, sickness, and poverty. Leadville drew from every level of American and even foreign society; its population of thirty thousand placed honest, hard-working miners, teamsters, and tradesmen shoulder to shoulder with a legion of con men, prostitutes, and criminals.

By 1880, four thousand men were working as miners in the caverns of Leadville, earning roughly $3 for each ten- or twelve-hour shift. Miners often supplemented their wages by high-grading ore (stealing gold nuggets or other valuable pieces).

Meanwhile, the "silver kings," such as Horace Tabor, David May, J. J. Brown and his wife Margaret, the Guggenheims, and the Boettcher family, made their initial millions from the mines and the backbreaking labor of miners. Although Leadville was shaped somewhat by the hardscrabble lot of miners living in and around the city, the wealth amassed was also a magnet for all sorts, famous and infamous, arriving by foot, mule, and, finally, train. The city attracted such notables as Doc Holliday, Susan B. Anthony, Frank and Jesse James, Oscar Wilde, and Buffalo Bill.

Leadville's boom continued until 1893 and the repeal of the Sherman Silver Purchase Act, which stopped the government's mandated support of the silver market and thus allowed the price of silver to drop drastically. With the collapse of silver prices came the economic collapse of Leadville. To counter the effect of falling silver prices, local businessmen financed the building of the Leadville Ice Palace.

It was hoped by the local business men that the four-story Ice Palace, which opened on January 1, 1896, with its ice-skating rink, café, and heated ballroom, would serve as a tourist attraction and bring sorely needed business to Leadville merchants. As a remembrance of better economic times, a frigid statue of "Lady Leadville," holding a scroll embossed with the figure of $207 million, signifying the wealth that Leadville mines had produced, greeted visitors to the palace. Unfortunately, the Ice Palace was not the tourist draw that it had been hoped to be, and it had be closed earlier than originally thought when it started to melt in the unusually warm March of that year.

To add insult to injury, in June 1896, Leadville's ore miners went on strike to gain better wages. The newly formed Cloud City Miners' Union (CCMU) was testing its strength when it decided to ask Leadville mine owners for a $.50 per day wage increase for all mineworkers not already on the $3.00 wage scale. Mine owners

refused, and on June 19 the CCMU voted to strike. To make matters worse, the mine owners locked out all workers a few days later, effectively stopping all mine operations in Leadville. Tensions rose as the miner owners refused to deal with the CCMU and brought in strikebreakers to work the mines.

On the evening of September 21, strikers attacked the Coronado and Emmet mines, where strikebreakers were working. The strikers succeeded in setting the Coronado mine on fire, causing $50,000 worth of damage and killing five people. In response to the violence, Colorado Governor Albert W. McIntire, who had up until that point rebuffed mine owners' request for the state militia to be sent, did so. With the protection of the state militia, the mines reopened, with strikebreakers working them. With support and membership dwindling, the CCMU voted to end the strike on March 9, 1897, and the miners went back to work under the old wage system.

By the 1920s, Leadville's mines shifted away from producing gold and silver to mining molybdenum, a mineral used as an alloy with steel to make it more durable. Production of molybdenum mainly came out of the Climax Mine, which grew with the wartime demand for molybdenum during World War II. Molybdenum was so important to war production that the federal government designated Climax as the nation's highest-priority mine. It was surrounded by three thousand feet of barbed wire–topped chain-link fencing and protected by armed and uniformed guards. In addition, to meet wartime demand, the federal government pushed the limits of men and machines. By the end of the war, the Climax Mine had supplied virtually all the molybdenum that toughened the steel for armor and weaponry that carried the Allies to victory in World War II. In 1957, production remained high, and the mine had grown to be the largest underground mine in the world.

By 1982, the Climax Mine was in trouble. A series of circumstances converged: The price of molybdenum dropped; foreign competition increased; and Phelps Dodge, the company that owned the Climax Mine, had opened Henderson Mine, a new, more efficient operation, near Berthoud Pass. They chose to close the Climax because it was no longer cost effective to operate it.

The closing of the Climax Mine devastated Leadville. Employment in Leadville fell from thirty-four hundred to four hundred. Retail businesses closed, unemployment hit 8 percent, and the county's tax base dropped from $250 million to $44 million. One third of its population left Leadville. Those people remaining took whatever jobs were available, approximately half finding work in the service industry at Copper Mountain and in the Vail Valley. The days when a miner made an annual income of $45,000, with benefits, were gone. The median annual income for men in Leadville as of 2000 was $28,125, and more than 13 percent of the population lived in poverty. The local schools fell into disrepair, forcing Leadville subsequently to become part of a lawsuit against the state of Colorado that sought funds for educational capital construction.

Since the 1980s, Leadville has been shifting its economic base from resource extraction to historical tourism and wilderness recreation. Although Leadville, with its rough and tumble image, cannot compete with the more glamorous neighboring towns of Aspen and Vail in skiing, restaurants, and art galleries, the town has identified abundant opportunities for outdoor activities and is using its exciting, colorful history as the foundation for its revival. This was part of the reason that Leadville became home to the National Mining Hall of Fame and Museum, which was established in 1987. Leadville also has a National Historic Landmark Designation to build on, and the charm of quaint Victorian homes set against the backdrop of the Rocky Mountains holds tremendous appeal. The current population stands at around 2,821.

—G. Wade Franck

See also DENVER, PUEBLO, BOULDER, FORT COLLINS, AND COLORADO SPRINGS, COLORADO; FOOTE, MARY HALLOCK

Suggested Reading

Bamford, Lawrence. "Streets From Silver: Leadville's History Through Its Built Environment." *Colorado Heritage* 4 (1987).

Geist, Christopher D. "The Great Leadville, Colorado, Ice Palace and Winter Festival of 1896." *Journal of American Culture* 7, no. 3 (1985).

Herr, Elizabeth, and Mayes, Jennifer. "Women and Economic Opportunity in Western Mining Towns in the Late 19th Century: The Case of Leadville, Colorado." *Essays in Economic and Business History* 14 (1996).

Philpott, William. *The Lessons of Leadville: Or, Why the Western Federation of Miners Turned Left* [Colorado Historical Society monograph no. 10]. Denver: Colorado Historical Society, 1994.

Voynick, Stephen M. *Climax: The History of Colorado's Climax Molybdenum Mine.* Missoula, MT: Mountain Press, 1996.

Wyman, Mark. *Hard Rock Epic: Western Miners and the Industrial Revolution, 1860–1910.* Berkeley: University of California Press, 1979.

⊞ LEWIS, MERIWETHER

See BLACKFOOT NATION

⊞ LEWISTON AND COEUR D'ALENE, IDAHO

Lewiston's initial growth came from the discovery of gold. However, there were problems, as the land on which the city sat remained under Nez Perce control. An 1861 agreement permitted mining north of the Clearwater, but the south bank of the river was off limits. Although settlers disregarded the agreement, the threat of war with the Nez Perce led to a compromise in which the settlers leased the land. The Nez Perce lost control in 1863, when a new treaty removed Lewiston from their reservation. Although Lewiston boomed, the mines panned out within a few years, and then the town started to shrink as prospectors moved south to the Boise Basin. Consequently, the town had grown to a population of only 849 by 1890. However, it did begin to grow again, and by 1910 it had six thousand residents.

Prior to 1864, laws prevented Asians from working in the mines of northern Idaho, but by February of that year, mining districts experienced a labor shortage. Most miners had left for the gold strikes of the Boise Basin, where the work was not as difficult. For operations to continue, the region needed many workers willing to perform hard work. Consequently, the miners permitted the entrance of Chinese laborers, and by the following year, Chinese began to arrive in the mining districts. They worked as laborers until they amassed enough money to buy claims of their own. The Chinese also set up businesses in the towns, such as laundries and restaurants.

Lewiston's growth also depended on greater self-sufficiency. Until early 1872, the town relied on Walla Walla for its flour, even though farms surrounded Lewiston. However, a shortage of flour from Walla Walla encouraged Lewiston to build a gristmill to make use of the abundant wheat grown in the area. Technological advancements in the 1880s enabled Lewiston's farmers to continue to prosper, although they still desired the farmlands on the Nez Perce reservation. The farmers finally got their way in 1895, when the reservation lands became available for settlement.

However, the Lewiston area required a railroad. Henry Villard, the president of the Northern Pacific, promised to bring a railroad to the town but failed to state just when this would happen. Consequently, Lewiston remained dependent on its rivers to reach other markets. This still proved advantageous, as its location at the confluence of the Snake and Clearwater Rivers made it an important river port. Farmers transported their grain to the Snake River, where they stored their crops at the docks. When the temperature dropped, boatmen needed to deal with ice floes and the freezing of the waterways. Although Lewiston's production of crops remained relatively small, the steamboats could not transport all of it. However, in 1914, a series of improvements in the navigation of the Lower Columbia facilitated a growth in trade.

The railroads made a significant contribution to the development of silver-lead lode mining in the Coeur d'Alene Mountains area of northern Idaho. The railroads brought in heavy equipment and transported ore to smelters in Salt Lake City or Omaha. Just as the railroads required eastern capital, the arrival of the railroads made Idaho's mines more attractive to development by eastern capital. After Pritchard's discovery of gold in the Coeur d'Alenes in 1882, the Northern Pacific started to advertise the area's supposed abundance of gold in late 1883, leading to the emergence of several boomtowns. However, this ignored the true wealth of the region: lead and silver mining.

Investments from Montana, Portland, and San Francisco covered the area with mills, mines, and smelters. Noah Kellogg's 1885 discovery of the Bunker Hill mine set off a legal battle that delayed the mine's development. The dispute centered on Kellogg's refusal to inform his backers, Dr. John Cooper and Origin Peck, of his findings. Although a jury decided for Cooper and Peck, the judge overturned their decision. Once operations began, work continued at the mine until the 1980s. The area soon made up more than 80 percent of the state's mineral production. The work required extensive capital, forcing out smaller companies. The area also experienced labor problems, resulting in the declaration of marshal law and the deployment of federal troops in 1892. Even with the end of production at the Bunker Hill and Sullivan mines, silver mining continues in the Coeur d'Alene area.

Until the 1870s, settlement in the Coeur d'Alenes remained scattered. However, the lumber industry provided important aid for the construction of gold mining camps, railroad construction, and the building of the Mullan Road. When the first commercial sawmill opened in 1880 and the Northern Pacific arrived in 1882, small settlements grew throughout the region, although true growth awaited the recovery from the panic of the mid-1890s.

Colonel Merriam and a detachment of cavalry established Fort Coeur d'Alene in April 1878. A settlement soon appeared at the edge of the fort. After the construction of the first commercial sawmill in 1883, the population started to grow, and a thousand people lived there by 1888. The population neared eight thousand in 1910. Like Lewiston, the town became a supply center for the mines in the area.

Congress intended the 1878 Timber and Stone Act to provide homesteaders with the opportunity to use nearby woodlots as a means of augmenting their income. The act stipulated that each sale could not exceed 160 acres. The land had to be unsuitable for cultivation and the corners and boundaries needed to be plainly indicated. Most important was the act's attempt to eliminate speculation.

However, many of the settlers wanted to sell the land immediately. Although Congress tried to repeal the Timber and Stone Act, it remained in place until

1955. The policy remained shortsighted, as claimants wanted to sell the land to large companies that had the necessary financial resources to fund improvements to both waterways and railroads so that they could transport the timber from remote areas of the Coeur d'Alenes. Despite these difficulties, timber companies purchased timberlands from the Northern Pacific Railroad Company.

The Coeur d'Alenes area reached its peak during the years 1900 through 1925. All of the intermediate and large-scale operations had their roots in this era. This reflected a shift to western sources of lumber as the earlier sources—the lake states and the eastern seaboard—declined. In 1923, the Clearwater Timber Company planned a mill for Lewiston. Construction began in 1926, and the mill began operating in 1927. The completion of railroads to the region during the first decade of the 20th century further convinced eastern lumbermen to invest in the area. Even though the industry faced labor disputes, high insurance costs, and natural disasters, it flourished through 1925.

After 1925, the large sawmills started to close. Of the eleven main sawmills in the area, six closed by 1931. The greatest decline came in 1928 and 1929. By 1933, only twenty-nine mines were still in operation. The real plunge in the number of mills operating began in 1928 and 1929 with the imminence of the Great Depression. Although production increased during and after World War II, it did not reach its pre-Depression levels. The 1960s brought another decline as increased competition focused on a limited supply of timber.

—Robert Miller

See also Boise, Idaho; Palouse Indians

Suggested Reading

Allen, Margaret Day. *Lewiston Country: An Armchair History.* Lewiston, ID: Nez Perce County Historical Society, 1990.

Magnuson, Richard G. *Coeur d'Alene Diary: The First Ten Years of Hardrock Mining in North Idaho.* Portland, OR: Metropolitan Press, 1968.

Nugent, Walter. *Into the West: The Story of Its People.* New York: Knopf, 1999.

Paul, Rodman Wilson. *Mining Frontiers of the Far West, 1848–1880.* Rev. exp. ed., edited by Elliott West. Albuquerque: University of New Mexico Press, 2001.

Strong, Clarence C., and Clyde S. Webb. *White Pine: King of Many Waters.* Missoula, MT: Mountain Press, 1970.

Wells, Merle W. *Gold Camps & Silver Cities: Nineteenth Century Mining in Central and Southern Idaho.* Moscow: University of Idaho Press, 2002.

LIBBY, MONTANA

With the construction of the transcontinental railroads across the United States, it became possible for western timber to reach beyond regional markets and become a part of the national economy. Lumber companies of the Great Lakes region began speculating in western timber as their supply dwindled in Minnesota, Wisconsin, and Michigan. Many recognized that if they were to survive, they would need to find new stands of timber. The Rocky Mountains area and the Pacific Northwest had large tracts of virgin timber and offered logging companies the opportunity to purchase timberlands outright or illegally cut timber from federal land with minimal government interference. The migration of the industry began in the late 1880s and continued on through the first two decades of the 20th century.

This method of logging was continued when the industry arrived in Montana. Initially, the timber industry developed in conjunction with mining. During this embryonic phase of timber production in the West, the fortunes of the logging industry fluctuated with the mining industry. The timber industry peaked during the placer period and underwent adjustment as quartz mining developed, placing different demands on the industry. The industry found its niche within this economy by providing rough-cut lumber to miners and mining companies and later branching out to provide finished lumber for building construction. However, it surfed on an almost continual boom and bust cycle, resulting in an unstable, highly speculative industry that created communities struggling on the margins of economic existence.

The migration west of the nation's lumbermen created a stir of conservative rhetoric. The companies touted new logging policies that moved away from past practices of "cut and run." The lumber companies claimed they had learned their lesson in the forests of

Minnesota, Wisconsin, and Michigan—they predicted their redemption in the West, with careful management and active pursuit of perpetuation, not annihilation, of western forests. Once lumber companies such as Weyerhaeuser, Potlatch, and the J. Neils Lumber Company migrated west, the realization struck in the 1930s that they had no other place to move. These companies needed to manage differently if they expected to survive. Logging companies such as J. Neils began tailoring their logging operations to maintain a sustained yield of merchantable timber. This also meant the employment of company foresters to help them manage their timberlands.

Despite the conservative verbiage adopted by many of the western lumber companies, overall industry habits stayed true to form, resulting in overcutting on privately held timberlands, overproduction, and, ultimately, the abandonment of lumber mills and their supporting communities. Lumbermen still had not grasped the notion of replanting their cutover lands. The practice of harvesting all the merchantable timber and then pulling out still remained the preferred method. Industry recessions during the 1920s and the Depression of the 1930s held in check for two decades the cutting of private timberlands. This changed drastically during World War II and the postwar construction and housing boom. By the 1940s, the nation depended on privately owned timberlands for 90 percent of its timber. Lumbermen continued to practice a "mining" rather than "cropping" philosophy, and timber on private land quickly diminished.

The threat of a "timber famine" was used by industry leaders as a reason for their continuous financial instability throughout the early decades of the 20th century. This threat, they claimed, forced them to purchase vast tracts of timber and then to pay for the land the timber was logged off immediately, without regard for what the market could bear, resulting in overproduction, layoffs, and, in some cases, bankruptcy. In an attempt to check this habitual problem, the U.S. Forest Service began to seriously discuss the topic of sustained yield. The U.S. Forest Service was formally created in 1905 to manage the National Forest System, which had been created eight years earlier with the passage of the Organic Administration Act. The Forest Service's mission was to act as the caretaker of the national forests, which were to provide quality water and timber for the nation's benefit. As a result, by adopting sustained yield as a management principle, the Forest Service hoped to perpetuate the industry, using a combination of private and federal timberlands without denuding both of marketable timber.

During World War II, the Forest Service and the timber industry realized that logging companies were, by necessity, relying more heavily on timber sales from the national forests to help meet growing demands. If there were no access to national forest timberlands, the prospect of an actual timber famine became a distinct possibility. The Forest Service not only wanted to assist in stabilizing the cut on private and federal lands but also sought to stabilize those communities of the West that were dependent on the forest products industry for their economic well-being.

By 1948, 65 percent of the nation's saw timber was in the West, and the U.S. government owned 60 percent of it. Sixty-eight lumber companies owned 30% of western timberlands, and they perceived the national forests as "natural resource reserves conceived to serve the greatest good of the greatest number of people." Due to the alarming rate at which private timberlands were cutover and the realization that timber companies would need to begin cutting in the national forests, the U.S. Congress passed the Sustained Yield Forest Management Act of 1944. This act required that the Forest Service and private industry work together to replant cutover lands and manage the size of subsequent cuts. The Forest Service supported the purposes of the act, and it was clear that formal cooperation between the agency and the timber industry would ensure an adequate supply of timber to stabilize the economic fortunes of the lumber companies, as well as providing enough wood products so that national consumption would not be disrupted.

The Sustained Yield Act permitted the Forest Service and lumber companies to enter into long-term agreements (60 to 100 years) to provide mills with a constant supply of timber, without resorting to competitive bidding. The rationale for the act, according to its supporters, was community stability; it authorized the pooling of federal and private timberlands into cooperative, sustained-yield management units and allowed the creation of similar units from federal land when the stability of a community depended on federal timber. The idea was not to promote competition and more industry but to maintain those operations that currently existed. The act specifically targeted lumber companies that owned large tracts of timber and cutover land. Supporters of the act argued that cooperative, sustained-yield agreements would bring economic stability to timber communities; opponents countered that these proposed agreements neglected small companies and flirted dangerously with the notion of federally supported monopolies.

The J. Neils Lumber Company first arrived in northwest Montana in 1911 and, after a brief hiatus, returned in 1919. Even though 97 percent of Lincoln County was composed of forest, the company did not delude itself into thinking it had an inexhaustible supply of timber. When the company returned to the Libby area in 1919, the J. Neils family understood that opportunities were limited for new stands of timber farther to the west. As a result, the company sought a means to ensure longevity of its operations in Libby and Klickitat, Washington. J. Neils contracted with former University of Washington Professor of Forestry Dr. Walter H. Meyer and, with his professional guidance, formulated a plan for selective cutting on the company's timberlands. The process of selective cutting involved assessing the merchantable timber and cutting dead and decadent (overmature) trees first. The company hired foresters to manage its timberlands for the dual purpose of providing (a) financial security for the company and (b) a continual supply of marketable timber to extend the viability of its Libby operation.

In the 1920s, the J. Neils Lumber Company sawed one third of the timber coming out of Lincoln County, but by 1944 the company was sawing five sixths of the timber, with 90 to 95 percent coming from the Libby-Troy area. Initially the company did not cut any timber on the National Forest, but by the 1940s, 73 percent of J. Neils's annual cut came from the national forests. By 1946, J. Neils's Libby operation employed more than five hundred people, with a monthly payroll of $112,000. An estimated two thirds of the labor force in Lincoln County worked at logging or at the sawmill. Libby came to rely heavily on the company for economic stability, particularly the county school

system, which relied heavily on the taxable timber that J. Neils cut from the national forest.

With the passage of the Sustained Yield Act, the Forest Service and the J. Neils Lumber Company began to actively negotiate a sustained-yield agreement. The proposed unit was composed of approximately two million acres of timberland from the Kootenai National Forest and 325,328 acres of timber and cutover land belonging to the company. According to the Forest Service, J. Neils did not have sufficient stands of merchantable white pine and ponderosa pine on company lands to sustain its operations, at least not without getting the majority of the white pine and ponderosa pine sales from the national forest. The company's large stands of larch, Douglas fir, and lodgepole pine did not have enough market value to support the company's Libby operations. Without a sustained yield agreement, the Forest Service predicted that J. Neils would close the Libby mill in twenty years.

The sustained yield unit selected under the agreement consisted of all the tributaries of the Kootenai River except for the Pleasant Valley Fisher and Tobacco Rivers. This comprised the bulk of the Kootenai National Forest in Lincoln County. The plan gave the J. Neils Lumber Company the right, for a period of 60 years, to purchase all national forest timber in the unit at its appraised price rather than having to bid competitively on each sale. The plan also assured the company of enough timber to maintain its annual cut level of approximately 80 million board feet. The management scheme closely resembled the plan formulated by Professor Meyer for the company in the 1930s. J. Neils would replant the cutover lands with those species most suited to the terrain but keep in mind the value of white and ponderosa pine. Fire and pest control were also essential in the unit to maintain appropriate levels of merchantable timber.

The plan also depended in part on the J. Neils Lumber Company purchasing the Northern Pacific Railroad's timberlands in Lincoln County. Although smaller mills operated in the county, J. Neils had proved, through the recession of the 1920s and the depression of the 1930s, that it had the wherewithal to survive lean times. The plan would affect not only Libby but also Troy, Warland, and Rexford. Two thirds of the approximately fifty-four hundred people living in proximity to the unit depended on the timber industry for their income. The agreement would go a long way to providing economic security for these individuals and their families. The plan further ensured that the Forest Service would manage the road network constructed to access the timber and protect the public's right to recreation on federal lands within the unit.

The push for a sustained yield agreement between the J. Neils Lumber Company and the Forest Service coincided with the implementation of the Montana Study in 1946. Financed by the Rockefeller Foundation and conducted through the University of Montana, the study searched for ways to improve the quality of life in rural areas to halt the urban migration of Montana's young men and women. Rooted firmly in Thomas Jefferson's republican ideology of the yeoman farmer acting as the moral and social underpinning of American society, the Montana Study group in Libby actively supported the proposed sustained yield agreement as a way to buttress these yeoman republican principles.

The Libby study group formed the Greater Libby Association (GLA) to formulate possible solutions for stabilizing Libby's economic fortunes and improving the quality of life. In conjunction with these endeavors, the GLA wrote senators and representatives at both the state and federal levels, throwing its support behind the sustained-yield agreement between the Forest Service and the J. Neils Lumber Company. The GLA began also to actively lobby the local union in an attempt to make the company's workers aware of the benefits of the long-term plan. Without union backing, the GLA believed the agreement would fail, and it urged the company and the labor union to address any concerns.

Opposition quickly arose nationally, against not only the proposed sustained-yield agreement in Lincoln County but also other agreements proposed throughout the timbered regions of the Pacific Northwest. Small operators and the general public alike saw sustained-yield agreements as federally sanctioned monopolies that would strangle smaller lumber companies. The agreements would end the practice of competitive bidding. Timber sales purchased at above the appraised value would cease, cutting the tax base for counties and states. The agreements meant that, in some instances, the large company would pay less than half the bid value for the timberlands, thus effectively freezing out all other competitors.

Even though Troy stood to benefit from the proposed sustained-yield agreement, residents of the small community eighteen miles west of Libby opposed it for a number of reasons. Their main objection stemmed from the fact that the mill in Libby would continue to grow, but any company contemplating a sawmill in Troy would immediately be handicapped by the agreement that offered national forest timber first to J. Neils. The Troy Rod and Gun Club opposed the agreement, saying that it would give the company the power to deny public access to national forest lands for recreational purposes. The club accused the Forest Service and J. Neils of putting a "padlock" on the national forest.

The Western Forest Industries Association of the Pacific Northwest allied itself with the disaffected elements in Lincoln County. The association actively opposed sustained-yield agreements in Washington, Oregon, Idaho, and Montana. They helped organize the Western Montana Lumbermen's Association to combat the proposed agreement in Lincoln County, and this association held a meeting in Kalispell, Montana, in March 1948. The meeting drew almost 80 independent sawmill operators. The association followed this up with a meeting in Eureka, Montana, where 105 loggers and sawmill operators formed a local affiliation with the Western Montana Lumbermen's Association. J. Neils fired back, stating that opposition to the agreement came from mill operators from Kalispell and Flathead County who, due to injudicious cutting practices on their own lands, eyed Lincoln County timber as a logical substitute.

Helena attorney and former Montana State Supreme Court Judge Lief Erickson entered the fray by joining the Western Montana Lumbermen's Association and asking Congress to investigate the cooperative sustained-yield agreement between the Forest Service and J. Neils. The association argued that the agreement gave J. Neils a sixty-year monopoly on 89 percent of the Kootenai National Forest's saw timber. The agreement would not only create a monopoly, Erickson argued, but would also put the communities of Lincoln County at the mercy of the logging company.

J. Neils continued to argue that the agreement would not freeze out small operators in the county.

The plan called for the sale of approximately ten million board-feet of national forest saw timber in the Troy area, six million board-feet for purchase by small operators, and twenty-five million board-feet open for competitive bidding. According to the agreement J. Neils Lumber Company would only receive forty million board-feet of the proposed eighty million board-feet of saw logs cut from the national forest annually. Conservationists and large lumber companies had difficulty countering the argument that the agreements would create monopolies. The communities of Eureka and Troy did not like the idea of being sacrificed because the mill was located in Libby. They further argued that, although they would become ghost towns, Libby would suffer the fate of becoming a company town.

Labor groups squared off in opposition to the agreement as well. Members of the Flathead Valley Loggers Local Union 2446 adopted a resolution opposing the agreement, as did members of the Lumber and Sawmill Workers of the United Brotherhood of Carpenters and Joiners of America in Montana and the Pacific Northwest. Again, the fear of monopoly and the creation of company towns pushed management and labor apart on the issue.

The Montana Study revealed that area residents did not oppose sustained yield as a form of forestry so much as they did the apparent control large lumber companies would have over the social and economic landscape of an area. Of the Libby and Troy residents surveyed by the Montana Study, 84 percent believed that southern Lincoln County would be better off with at least two sawmills. The Montana Study suggested that because they did not have a strong backing by county residents, the Forest Service and J. Neils should delay the agreement until the issues concerning economic and social impact were resolved among all parties.

The cooperative, sustained-yield agreement in Lincoln County had reached an impasse. The Greater Libby Association moved on to less controversial matters, and the Forest Service and J. Neils shelved the proposal. The company admitted that it could continue to operate without the agreement as long as it could successfully get the majority of the Kootenai National Forest's timber sales. J. Neils continued operation in the Libby area until it merged with the St. Regis Paper Company in the 1950s. St. Regis continued the tradition of replanting cutover lands but cut heavily on company-owned timberlands. Champion International purchased the Libby mill in the 1980s and, after stripping the marketable timber from company land, sold the mill to the Stimson Lumber Company and the timberlands to Plum Creek in the 1990s.

Stimson closed the Libby mill in 2003, stating that without their own timberlands the company could not competitively bid on national forest sales. If the Forest Service and J. Neils had signed the Kootenai National Forest Sustained Yield Cooperative Agreement in 1948, the mill would have had four years remaining on the agreement for timber as of 2004. C. C. Crow, editor of *Crow's Pacific Coast Lumber Digest*, stated in a September 1948 editorial, "nothing more un-American was ever proposed, wherein the man of small means is to be deprived of his birthright to harvest a God-given natural resource." These words mock Lincoln County residents as they watch local gyppo loggers transport logs to mills outside the county and the communities of Libby and Troy reel from the loss of an industry that helped sustain them for almost a century.

—*Richard Aarstad*

See also Logging

Suggested Reading

Kaufman, Harold F., and Lois C. Kaufman. *Toward the Stabilization and Enrichment of a Forest Community: The Montana Study*. Missoula: University of Montana, 1946.

Robbins, William G. *Lumberjacks and Legislators: Political Economy of the U.S. Lumber Industry, 1890–1941*. College Station: Texas A&M University Press, 1982.

Robbins, William G. "The Tarnished Dream: The Turbulent World of the Forest Products Industry in the Northwest." *Montana, the Magazine of Western History* 37, no. 1 (Winter 1987).

Robbins, William G. "The Western Lumber Industry: A 20th Century Perspective." In *The 20th Century West: Historical Interpretations*, edited by Gerald Nash and Richard Etulain. Albuquerque: University of New Mexico Press, 1989.

⊞ LIBRARIES AND THE IMMIGRANT

Immigrants in the American West brought with them a vibrant print culture and an abiding appreciation for books and reading. Once settled, they pooled their resources to establish libraries to ease the isolation and tedium of pioneer life. In recreating cultural institutions they had left behind, western community builders considered libraries significant to a town's coming of age and instrumental in promoting growth. Later, as immigration expanded and diversified, local officials augmented their libraries' mission to help with assimilating and "Americanizing" the foreign born. Today public libraries continue to provide books, newspapers, and services to new immigrants, serving as a passage to their fuller participation in civic life.

Soldiers and missionaries who began the westward migration in the 17th century established the first libraries in the West. Territorial administrators were often educated, wealthy men, and they gathered some impressive book collections despite primitive frontier conditions. French explorer René-Robert Cavelier, Sieur de la Salle, built one of the earliest private libraries at Fort St. Louis in Texas. When Spanish soldiers found the fort's ruins in 1689, they discovered more than two thousand books, many with original fine bindings, strewn in the mud. In New Mexico and California, Franciscan padres established small reference and religious libraries in missions built in the late 1700s and early 1800s. Mission Santa Barbara houses the oldest surviving mission library, with about four thousand original books, manuscripts, and musical scores. Protestant missionaries, migrating to the Pacific Northwest in the 1830s, also brought books. By 1870, nearly every county in Oregon had one Protestant library or more serving the local community. In similar fashion, Mormon refugees in Utah created libraries as a cornerstone of their religious mission. In fact, Brigham Young required every Mormon stake to set up a library of "useful and instructive" works to help solidify the Latter-Day Saints' distinctive social order.

In the mid-19th century, the U.S. government added to this steady westward stream by dispatching administrators and soldiers to secure American interests in the West. Recognizing that official emissaries depended on books to inform their work and occupy their leisure, Congress funded legislative libraries in each territory and small regimental reading rooms in every fort and garrison. Additional monies for the latter came from the United States Military Post Library Association, formed by eastern philanthropists in 1861 to ensure that "the soldier on our most remote frontier is . . . regularly supplied with the best reading." Garrison libraries contained four hundred to five hundred books, although a large outpost like Texas's Fort Davis might have more than a thousand books. Territorial libraries could be quite extensive. For example, in 1876, the territorial library in Olympia, Washington, had nearly sixty-five hundred volumes. Its counterpart in Salt Lake City, Utah, had at this time nearly seven thousand volumes.

Despite these early efforts by the church and state to supply books in the West, literate immigrants suffered from a lack of reading matter, triggering what historian Don Walker describes as a "crazy intensification of their interest in anything printed." Walker relates how a Texas cowboy grabbed for a piece of paper caught in a fence, hoping it was something to read. Walker also tells of another range rider who stumbled on an abandoned shack with its ceiling and walls lined with newsprint for insulation. Hungry for print, he read each wall and was reading through the ceiling when he was ordered to move on. Some men working on the range read and reread can labels to the point of memorizing them. Indeed, the expression one "knew his cans" came to signify a seasoned trail rider who spent his leisure time absorbed in a can label.

Westward migrants carried books on the immigrant trail. They depended on sources such as *The Pioneer Traveler* for advice and directions, and their diaries mention reading books ranging from Cooper to Shakespeare to pass the time. Although pioneers often littered the Oregon Trail with their abandoned books, some painstakingly transported their entire personal libraries. Early Los Angeles resident Mary Foy recalled that in the 1860s, Nobel Calhoun traveled from Kentucky to Los Angeles with several mules laden with four thousand books. Calhoun had given her mother one of these treasured volumes, and many years later Foy still remembered its title: *Heroines of History*.

As settlements prospered, newcomers formed library associations to acquire and maintain collections of books and periodicals for themselves and others in the community. In developing these early libraries, pioneers modeled them on cultural organizations they knew in the East. Houston settlers in the 1830s, for instance, organized several voluntary associations emulating Philadelphia examples, including the Franklin Debating Society, the Philosophical Society of Texas, and the Houston Circulating Library. Elsewhere in Texas, pioneers also inaugurated cultural and educational institutions in their towns, most notably reading rooms and libraries. Austin formed its first library association in 1841, Galveston in 1845, Brownsville in 1849, and Nacogdoches and Tyler in 1859. Dallas, a relative latecomer in the Texas library movement, did not organize a viable library association until 1872, and El Paso's first library association appeared in 1884.

Most western states and territories likewise established libraries as part of their communities' formation. Territorial settlers in Kansas, Nebraska, and Washington organized library associations as early as the 1850s. The library movement in Oregon, Wyoming, Colorado, Nevada, and Montana followed in the 1860s. In more sparsely populated areas, such as Arizona, New Mexico, Idaho, and the Dakotas, territorial and post libraries were the only organized book collections until the early 1880s.

Californians were the most active in developing reading rooms during the 19th century. The state's first library association was organized in Monterey in 1849, spearheaded by Connecticut immigrant Reverend Samuel Willey as a "nucleus around which the friends of literary and social refinement, and elevation, may cordially unite." Other towns followed suit, and by the late 1870s, California had eighty-five libraries located in towns such as Alameda (1879), Arcata (1879), Marysville (1858), Oakland (1878), Sacramento (1879), and Ventura (1878). San Francisco was *the* literary mecca for the entire West. Establishing its first library association—the San Francisco Mercantile Library—in 1852, San Franciscans supported twenty-seven libraries in 1876, more than any other state or territory except Texas.

In some communities, a prosperous pioneer donated books and funds to start a town library. In Los Angeles, for instance, Irish immigrant and former California governor John G. Downey gave money, books, and rooms to launch the Los Angeles Library

Table 1   Western Libraries Containing More Than 300 Volumes (1876)

State	No. of Libraries
Arizona	3
California	86
Colorado	8
Dakotas	4
Idaho	1
Kansas	19
Montana	2
Nebraska	14
Nevada	6
New Mexico	4
Oregon	14
Texas	42
Utah	5
Washington	2
Wyoming	3

SOURCE: U.S. Bureau of Education. *Public Libraries in the United States: Their History, Condition, and Management.* Washington, DC: Government Printing Office, 1876, pp. 1012–1142.

Association in 1872. Whereas the Library Association of Portland was the beneficiary of Irish immigrant John Wilson's largesse, San Francisco's Andrew S. Hallidie, a wealthy Scotsman who invented the cable car, sponsored that city's early libraries. In Arizona, Samuel Colt of revolver fame organized the territory's first library in 1862 as a reading room for men working in his Cerro Colorado mine.

Typically, however, the formation of a library association was part of a collective action among local elites to bring culture and stability to their town. The Wyoming Literary and Library Association, for example, was organized in Laramie in 1870 by a formidable group of lawyers, ministers, businessmen, educators, editors, and doctors. Denver's library movement was led by an equally impressive phalanx of local luminaries, including seven members of the territorial legislature, the territorial supreme court chief justice, and the speaker of the House. According to the local press in Billings, Montana, "men of energy and snap" orchestrated that city's library movement, although behind the scenes, women's clubs raised money and oversaw reading room operations. This was also the case in cities such as Dallas, Salt Lake City, Boise,

Phoenix, Flagstaff, and Santa Fe, where women's clubs financed and managed the original libraries. In fact, it has been estimated that women's groups served as the moving force behind more than 75 percent of the nation's public libraries.

Library associations thus played a critical role in the maturation of western towns, providing sure testimony that these nascent communities possessed the same cultural amenities as those in the East. Thus the Omaha Library Association was established in 1856 as confirmation that the Nebraska capital now possessed a "high state of popular culture." Los Angeles developers also considered a library crucial to their city's coming of age. That the city as late as 1872 still did not have a reading room was, in the view of the *Los Angeles Evening Express,* a "public shame which ought to blanch the cheek of every respectable citizen." Denver's newspaper expressed similar dismay that Colorado's capital lagged behind other Western cities in developing a library: "The shame of having 300 saloons and no public library in Denver," editorialized the *Rocky Mountain News* in 1885, "has been borne too long already. Let us all join hands to make the library a splendid success."

Library promoters, as in Denver, often pictured workingmen "drinking fully at the fountain of knowledge" instead of frequenting the saloons to suggest that a reading room could curb the unacceptable behavior of itinerant workingmen dominating the urban West. Prominent San Francisco lawyer and real estate developer Joseph Crockett, for example, argued that a "well conducted" reading room in the city would "do much to counteract the pernicious influence of prevalent vice . . . and in all respects elevate the standard of public morals." Respectable citizens in Butte, Montana, likewise hoped that their library association would offset its reputation as the roughest city on the frontier. With its large population of transient miners, Butte in the late 1800s had more than three hundred saloons and brothels, second only to San Francisco in size and number. Seeking to redress such sordid conditions and refurbish the town's popular image, in 1885 Butte's Women's Christian Temperance Union, backed by local mining companies, opened a reading room. Library organizers expected that interesting books and an inviting place to congregate

would tempt the young men "who now loiter around saloons for want of a better place to go."

As self-created monuments to the new American sociopolitical order, few libraries recognized the diversity of late-19th-century immigrants. Books and periodical collections were largely limited to Anglo-American worthies, and reading rooms were restricted to white residents. Texas cities Dallas and Houston barred African Americans openly, and collections and services catering to Latinos in Arizona would not materialize for another century. Several California library associations had close ties to local nativist organizations. For example, Workingmen's Party leader Denis Kearney, known for his anti-Chinese feelings, was an outspoken advocate for San Francisco's library movement in 1877 and 1878. After gaining control of Los Angeles politics in 1879, Workingmen's Party members installed Patrick Connolly, a party faithful, as city librarian and held meetings in the library association's reading room.

This ethnocentric perspective began to change in the 1890s as librarians discerned that westward migration had dramatically changed. Instead of white Protestants migrating from the East and Midwest, newcomers were increasingly diverse in ethnic and religious backgrounds. The library, which had initially served as a symbol of Anglo-American hegemony, now pursued new immigrant groups to acclimate them to their adopted home and assimilate them into the culture it embodied.

One of the earliest voices in reorienting western libraries was Charles Wesley Smith, an erudite lawyer from New York who in 1895 was appointed director of the Seattle Public Library. In his first annual report, Smith declared that the library could shape "the destinies of free people." Noting that one fourth of Washingtonians were foreign born, Smith argued that the library could help them assimilate into American life. "They must be educated to the status of freemen," Smith maintained, and the library, as "the people's university," was the proper agency to facilitate this laudable objective.

Librarians embraced this new spirit, and over the next several decades—despite a world war and escalating anti-immigrant politics—they sought ways to help foreigners in their communities. Before 1914, librarians focused on purchasing foreign-language books and developing services to acquaint immigrants with the American public library system. "In this way," explained the Los Angeles Public Library director in an 1897 report, "we hope to make the library useful to those of our citizens who were born abroad and desire to partake of knowledge in the language with which they are most familiar." That very year, the Los Angeles Public Library opened a deposit station at Casa de Castelar, a settlement house located in a "neighborhood comprised largely of a foreign and non-reading people." The books proved so popular that a librarian was sent to the settlement house one evening a week. Over the next few years, Los Angeles's library established branches in other immigrant neighborhoods, including Boyle Heights, Hoover Street, East Los Angeles, and Pico Heights. It also operated delivery stations at the YMCA, serving Japanese fishermen in San Pedro and at playgrounds frequented by children in other immigrant enclaves. At the city's main library downtown, librarians placed foreign-language books on open shelves in the central reading room so that non–English-speaking residents would quickly ascertain that materials were available in their native tongues. By 1909, services for the foreign born had a label—"extension work"—and had become a significant component of Los Angeles Public Library's mission.

Western cities apart from Los Angeles were also beginning to respond to their burgeoning immigrant populations. The Seattle Public Library, for example, built a large foreign-language collection so that, to quote from the institution's 1920 annual report, immigrants "might find in the literature of their own language temporary relief from the pangs of homesickness which, unalleviated too long, sap the mental and physical strength which often [are] the immigrant's only assets." As with Los Angeles, Seattle's library operated several deposit stations in immigrant sections of the city: the Yesler Branch for Russians and Jews, the Georgetown Branch for Italians and Germans, and the Ballard Branch for Scandinavians. The Seattle Public Library also experimented with cataloging foreign-language books, especially those not written in Latin characters. Called the "Seattle Plan," the library pioneered in reorienting standard practices to meet the needs of foreign readers who were unable to read English or comprehend the traditional library card-catalog system.

World War I was a turning point for how public libraries worked with immigrants. The war made manifest the West's extensive ties with foreign nations. Residents flocked to the library to find books about U.S. wartime allies and foes and read foreign newspapers to learn more about the war's progress in their respective homelands. At the same time, American public opinion became increasingly hostile to foreigners and anxious over perceived threats to American loyalty and unity. This hypervigilance assumed many forms, ranging from the surveillance and arrest of pacifists and labor organizers to physical violence against German Americans. Many librarians purged their shelves of German-language books and monitored patrons' use of "subversive" books. Other librarians sympathized with immigrants' plight and sought ways to ameliorate the situation. Commiserated Seattle librarian Charles Compton in 1917:

> During the year, the immigrant has had another burden added to that of learning our language and customs— a depressing consciousness that the "foreigner" is not wanted here. . . . More and more frequently have immigrants come to us this year lonely, depressed, and bowed down with the grief of losing relatives and friends in the war-ridden countries of their birth.

As a consequence of these experiences, western librarians embraced the post–World War I Americanization movement. Librarians developed innovative programming to reach foreign residents and partnered with night-school teachers to supply books and reading lists to English-language students. In Aberdeen, South Dakota, librarians worked with Americanization classes by setting up a special collection in the library of simple English-language books on American history and citizenship. The Los Angeles Public Library hosted "naturalization parties" for night-school graduates, using the occasion to bring immigrants into the library and introduce them to its resources and services. Seattle's librarians obtained the names and addresses of recently naturalized citizens so they could send them personalized invitations to visit the library. Denver librarians created a flyer about the library's Americanization materials, which they convinced naturalization officers to include in their citizenship application packets. Rather than rely on such mass, undirected advertisement, Portland librarians first compiled a nationality map to identify different foreign enclaves in their jurisdiction and then hand-delivered specially designed ethnic-specific promotional materials to individual households.

Librarians focused much of their attention on children, appreciating how quickly they absorbed the dominant culture and their usefulness as a conduit to their more reticent parents. Whereas children using the Portland Public Library brought home to their parents specially prepared bibliographies of foreign books, in Los Angeles, children were provided with "hero stories" introducing them to American values and ideals. Los Angeles librarians also featured immigrant children in traditional festivals and pageants, to better incorporate them into the American mainstream. "Have you ever seen an almond-eyed Cinderella or a Japanese Miles Standish in Puritan costume?" inquired librarian Jasmine Britton in 1918. "There is a novelty and piquancy about the sight you will not forget."

Many librarians sought to promote a more general cultural awareness and ethnic tolerance through their work with immigrant groups. Observed a South Dakota librarian in 1920, as an "aftermath of the war spirit . . . it seems as if the people of the state are genuinely interested in promoting a more intelligent, loyal, and harmonious citizenship." Taking advantage of this receptive climate, libraries in Denver and Los Angeles sponsored exhibits and programs to showcase their cities' different ethnic groups. The Seattle Public Library also endeavored to connect immigrants with the dominant community by asking new library card applicants what languages they read. Discovering that collectively their patrons were literate in thirty-two languages, librarians compiled a list of interpreters and translators for distribution to Seattle businesses and civic organizations. As Los Angeles's Jasmine Britton philosophized in a 1918 *Library Journal* article, "The Library's Share in Americanization," librarians were not content with simply "Americanizing the foreigner" but were also committed to "Americanizing the

Americans, until we have a democratic neighborly interest in these strangers whose only fault often is that they speak a language which we do not understand."

Library services to foreigners peaked in the mid-1920s and then evaporated in the wake of restrictive immigration legislation and the Great Depression. As immigration slowed and public funds for library services declined, libraries cut back on programs for immigrants (and all other sectors of the community). In addition, the Red Scare of the 1920s and social unrest of the 1930s resuscitated nativist sentiment and pressured librarians to curtail their internationalist approach to library services. Many libraries closed their foreign literature and extension departments and cut purchases of foreign-language books. In one dramatic 1932 episode, the head of the Seattle Public Library's Foreign Books Division, Natalie Notkin, was fired for purchasing "obscene and Communistic" books for her library's collection.

Thus, by the late 1930s, libraries had turned inward to focus on indigenous rather than foreign migrants. The West, in particular, had to grapple with the influx of Dust Bowl refugees pouring into its agricultural heartland. For example, so-called Okies swelled the population in California's San Joaquin Valley by more than 63 percent, forcing local schools, hospitals, and libraries to scramble to absorb them into already overtaxed services and programs. Responding to popular concern about these newcomers, the Kern County Library System in 1939 purchased sixty copies of John Steinbeck's *Grapes of Wrath,* only to have the county board of supervisors ban the Pulitzer Prize–winning novel. Despite concerted protest from civil libertarians and the library profession, *Grapes of Wrath* was not returned to Kern County library shelves until 1941. This drama was enacted throughout the West.

Myriad economic, legal, and political pressures continued through the 1940s and 1950s to render dormant immigrant library services. Western librarians did respond to exceptional situations, such as assisting European war refugees and sending books to Japanese Americans during their World War II relocation and incarceration. In the late 1940s, the American Library Association investigated the plight of Mexican migrant workers in hopes of developing a nationwide program for them. Although individual libraries experimented with services for migrant workers, the association's more ambitious plans never materialized. During the McCarthy Era, unchecked censorship against controversial and "communistic" books and magazines contributed to the conservatism of public library administrations and their disinterest in non-mainstream clienteles. Indeed, in some western locales, such as Los Angeles County, government employees were required to sign loyalty oaths and forced to submit acquisition lists to a committee of censors.

In the late 1960s, American librarianship entered into a sustained period of social activism, which in many respects still characterizes the profession today. Through organizations such as the American Library Association's Social Responsibilities Round Table (formed in 1967), information professionals reconnected with ethnic and immigrant communities within a wider agenda of social awareness and reform. Library extension work—recast as "multicultural services"—blossomed, reinvigorating programs and methods developed fifty years before. For example, the Tucson Public Library (1969) and the Phoenix Public Library (1972) opened their first branches in Mexican American neighborhoods with services and collections geared specifically to Spanish-speaking residents. These Arizona libraries not only built Spanish-language collections but also hired bilingual staff, showed Spanish-language films, hosted workshops, and sponsored classes. The San Jose Public Library in California followed a similar pattern, opening the Biblioteca Latino Americana Branch in 1976, with 80 percent of its book and periodical collection in Spanish. Over the next decade, this library system continued to respond to the city's increasing diversity, purchasing more than one hundred sixty thousand books in forty different languages, participating in cultural festivals, sponsoring multilingual story hours, and hosting cultural awareness workshops. To further demonstrate the institution's commitment to multiculturalism, the San Jose Public Library purged the word "foreign" from its institutional vocabulary and renamed its Foreign Language Department simply the "Language Department."

Contemporary public libraries remain conscious of their community's changing demographics, and this awareness is evident in library collections,

signage, programming, and staffing. Libraries thus continue to reflect and respond to the history of migration to the American West, ever changing to meet the needs of incoming groups yet faithful to an enduring belief that a literate and informed populace is the foundation on which a democratic society is built and sustained.

—*Debra Gold Hansen*

See also California Libraries in the Post–World War II Era, Mormon Colonization of Utah, Public Libraries in Utah

Suggested Reading

Adams, Eleanor B., and France V. Scholes. "Books in New Mexico, 1598–1680." *New Mexico Historical Review* 17 (1942).

Baker, Hugh S. "Rational Amusement in Our Midst: Public Libraries in California, 1849–1859." *California Historical Society Quarterly* 38 (December 1959).

Bundy, Mary Lee, and Frederick J. Stielow, eds. *Activism in American Librarianship, 1962–1973.* New York: Greenwood Press, 1987.

Clement, Richard W. *Books on the Frontier: Print Culture in the American West, 1763–1875.* Washington, DC: Library of Congress, 2003.

Davis, Donald G., Jr. "The Rise of the Public Library in Texas, 1876–1920." In *Milestones to the Present: Papers from the Library History Seminar V*, edited by Harold Goldstein. Syracuse, NY: Gaylord, 1978.

Fish, James. "Responding to Cultural Diversity: A Library in Transition." *Wilson Library Bulletin* 66 (February 1992).

Freeman, Robert S., and David M. Hovde, eds. *Libraries to the People: Histories of Outreach.* Jefferson, NC: McFarland, 2003.

Gallegos, Bee, and Lisa Kammerlocher. "A History of Library Services to the Mexican American and Native American in Arizona." *Journal of the West* 30 (July 1991).

Geiger, Maynard J. "The Story of California's First Libraries." *Southern California Quarterly* 46 (June 1964).

Gower, Calvin W. "Lectures, Lyceums, and Libraries in Early Kansas, 1854–1864." *Kansas Historical Quarterly* 36 (1970).

Grove, Larry. *Dallas Public Library: The First 75 Years.* Dallas, TX: Dallas Public Library, 1977.

Gunselman, Cheryl. "Illumino for All: Opening the Library Association of Portland to the Public, 1900–1903." *Libraries and Culture* 36 (Summer 2001).

Gunselman, Cheryl. "Pioneering Free Library Service for the City, 1864–1902: The Library Association of Portland and the Portland Public Library." *Oregon Historical Quarterly* 103 (Fall 2002). [Electronic version]

Hatch, Orin Walker. *Lyceum to Library: A Chapter in the Cultural History of Houston.* Houston: Texas Gulf Coast Historical Association, 1965.

Hazel, Michael. *The Dallas Public Library: Celebrating a Century of Service, 1901–2001.* Denton: University of North Texas Press, 2001.

Held, Ray E. *Public Libraries in California, 1849–1878.* Berkeley: University of California Press, 1963.

Held, Ray E. *The Rise of the Public Library in California.* Chicago: American Library Association, 1973.

Jackson, Louise, and Michael Day. "The Wyoming Literary and Library Association, 1870–1978." *Journal of the West* 30 (July 1991).

Jones, Plummer Alston, Jr. *Libraries, Immigrants, and the American Experience.* Westport, CT: Greenwood Press, 1999.

Kalisch, Philip A. "High Culture on the Frontier: The Omaha Library Association." *Nebraska History* 52 (1971).

Lingo, Marci. "Forbidden Fruit: The Banning of *The Grapes of Wrath* in Kern County Free Library." *Libraries and Culture* 38 (Fall 2003).

Luckingham, Bradford. "Agents of Culture in the Urban West: Merchants and Mercantile Libraries in Mid-Nineteenth Century St. Louis and San Francisco." *Journal of the West* 17 (April 1978).

Manning, James W. "Literacy on the Oregon Trail: Books Across the Plans." *Oregon Historical Quarterly* 41 (1940).

Marshall, John Douglas. *Place of Learning, Place of Dreams: A History of the Seattle Public Library.* Seattle: University of Washington Press, 2004.

Mediavilla, Cindy. "The War on Books and Ideas: The California Library Association and Anti-Communist Censorship in the 1940s and 1950s. *Library Trends* 46 (Fall 1997).

Mood, Fulmer. "Andrew S. Hallidie and Libraries in San Francisco, 1868–1879." *Library Quarterly* 16 (July 1946).

Pacific Northwest Libraries: History of Their Early Development in Washington, Oregon, and British Columbia. Seattle: University of Washington Press, 1926.

Passet, Joanne E. "Bringing the Pubic Library Gospel to the American West." *Journal of the West* 30 (July 1991).

Passet, Joanne E. *Cultural Crusaders: Women Librarians in the American West, 1900–1917.* Albuquerque: University of New Mexico Press, 1994.

Reese, Rina. *History of the Denver Public Library, 1860–1928.* Denver, CO: Denver Public Library, 1928.

Ring, Daniel F. "Men of Energy and Snap: The Origins and Early Years of the Billings Public Library." *Libraries and Culture* 36, no. 3 (2001).

Ring, Daniel F. "The Origins of the Butte Public Library: Some Further Thoughts on Public Library Development in the State of Montana." *Libraries and Culture* 28 (Fall 1993).

Rock, Rosalind Z. "A History of Libraries in New Mexico—Spanish Origins to Statehood." *Journal of Library History* 14 (Summer 1979).

Sarber, Mary A. "A Century of Growth: The El Paso Public Library, 1894–1994." *Password* 39 (Spring 1994).

Skinner, A. E. "Books and Libraries in Early Texas." *Texas Libraries* 37 (1975).

Soter, Bernadette Dominique. *The Light of Learning: An Illustrated History of the Los Angeles Public Library.* Los Angeles: Library Foundation of Los Angeles, 1993.

U.S. Bureau of Education. *Public Libraries in the United States: Their History, Condition, and Management.* Washington, DC: U.S. Government Printing Office, 1876.

Walker, Don D. "Reading on the Range: The Literary Habits of the American Cowboy." *Arizona and the West* 2 (Winter 1960).

Wiegand, Wayne A. *"An Active Instrument for Propaganda": The American Public Library During World War I.* Westport, CT: Greenwood Press, 1989.

Wiegand, Wayne A. "Oregon's Public Libraries During the First World War." *Oregon Historical Quarterly* 90 (Spring 1989).

Wiley, Peter Booth. *A Free Library in This City: The Illustrated History of the San Francisco Public Library.* San Francisco: Weldon Owen, 1996.

⊞ LINCOLN, NEBRASKA

Lincoln is the state capital of Nebraska. It formerly was a village known as Lancaster, but with Nebraska entering the Union as the 37th state on March 1, 1867, the village was chosen as the state capital and renamed Lincoln. Lincoln was a very unlikely choice for a city or a capital, as it was not located on a navigable waterway or near a major intersection of trade routes. Lincoln was focused around a small stream with about a dozen other streams nearby, although not even the smallest of boats could use these streams for travel. A portion of the Oregon Trail passed within 10 miles to the south of Lincoln, but a seasonal salt flat was deemed its most advantageous asset.

In reality, it was a problem with other options that led to Lincoln becoming Nebraska's capital city. A commission appointed to locate a capital site wanted it inland from the towns along the Missouri River, such as Omaha. Rivalries among other locales further contributed to the naming of Lancaster—a minute prairie town with few requisite resources such as water, lumber, or other building materials—as Nebraska's state capital. On July 29, 1867, the village of Lancaster was renamed Lincoln, in honor of the slain president.

Progress and development in Lincoln were dependent on the arrival of the westbound railroad lines. The competing rail companies were enticed with bonds and land, and in June 1869, the governor of Nebraska, Nebraska's Capital Commission, and a representative of the Burlington and Missouri River Railroad met to break ground for the terminal in Lincoln. As more railroads began running through the capital, Lincoln attracted the road builders as well. Soon Lincoln was home to a newly formed state university; local, county, and state government offices; a prison; and a hospital. It also became a major point of departure for settlers heading west.

Lincoln sustained explosive growth through its first year as the capital. Population rose from 30 citizens before Nebraska's statehood to more than 2,500 in 1870. However, Lincoln's development was not without difficulties. An economic depression hit the country, lasting through 1876, and this hindered growth. In addition, an infestation of grasshoppers in early 1876 plagued the state's agricultural enterprises. A new growth spurt followed the depression, and Lincoln became a major transportation center, with four railway systems present.

Finding a sufficient supply of water continued to be a problem for the city. The first well was constructed in 1882, and it supplied Lincoln with more than a million usable gallons of water each day. A second well was dug in 1887 to aid the first, as its supply was becoming strained. This second well also supplied the burgeoning city with a million gallons of water per day, and then numerous other wells were created to the south of Lincoln. Lincoln had one last obstacle to overcome in solidifying it as Nebraska's capital city. The original capitol building was falling apart by the late 1880s. The need for construction of a new building led to new cries for moving the state capital. A number of communities called for the change to their cities, but fighting only served to solidify Lincoln's place as Nebraska's capital. When a new capitol building was finished in 1888, all calls for a different capital city were defeated.

Lincoln, Nebraska, has now established itself as a modern Midwest city. The University of Nebraska at Lincoln is a well-known and widely respected research university famous for its football program, among other things. On fall Saturdays, when the football team is playing a home game, the size of Lincoln practically doubles as loyal fans flock from all over the state to see their team play. Known for the friendliness of its people, the prairie capital is now a center for agribusiness, along with its neighbor, Omaha.

—*Douglas Gibb*

Suggested Reading

"City of Lincoln and Lancaster County." Available from http://ci.lincoln.ne.us

"Lincoln—Lancaster County." Available from http://www.casde.unl.edu/history/counties/lancaster/lincoln/index.php

McKee, James L. *Lincoln: The Prairie Capital.* Woodland Hills, CA: Windsor, 1984.

LIPAN

See APACHE

LITTLE BIGHORN

See BLACK HILLS GOLD RUSH OF 1874

LITTLE ITALY

The United States has served as a popular destination for immigrants from around the world since its inception. European immigrants were the dominant group immigrating west during the 19th and 20th centuries, with Italian immigrants composing a substantial portion. As a result, Italian communities dubbed "Little Italy" have popped up in various American cities throughout the last two hundred years. New York, New Haven, Chicago, San Francisco, and Los Angeles have served as home to some of the most popular Italian communities, and the influence of these neighborhoods has proven beneficial to both Italians and Americans alike.

The first Italian communities to surface in the United States were located on the East Coast in cities such as New York and New Haven, Connecticut. The influx of Italian immigrants led to the communal gathering of their dwellings and businesses. Many immigrants, on first arriving in America, often stayed with friends or relatives until enough money had been saved for them to lease a dwelling of their own. When this occurred, it was important for the family and friends to remain near to each other, to promote safety and assurance in their new surroundings. If it was not possible to stay with acquaintances or family, the immigrants looked for neighborhoods in which similar dialects of Italian were spoken. As the communities grew, the patterns of the neighborhoods tended to mirror those of old Italy. The same groceries and foods were sold, the same services were provided, and the same merchandise was peddled. In many cases, Little Italy became almost self-sufficient within the larger city that surrounded it. Everything from ice-houses to coal houses, from hospitals to bakeries was established in the community, and those businesses that were absent from the community were often communally bought and incorporated into the neighborhood.

There were two complications in these new Italian neighborhoods that created conflict: language and attitude among the Italians. The adaptation of English words to Italian, and vice versa, often occurred, creating a hybrid of the two languages. Also, immigrants who had arrived first in America often regarded the new arrivals from Italy with condescending attitudes and made them work to earn respect. Because of language barriers and poor economic status, new immigrants were forced to accept this treatment from their Italian neighbors and work their way up, as opposed to entering the confines of the host city. As a result, social classes formed in Little Italy as they had throughout the United States.

Even with this "earn your way" mentality, Italian neighborhoods remained tight-knit communities that supported each other and aided each other in times of need. The Order of the Sons of Italy was an organization that formed to help supply aid for their countrymen, find jobs for men, schools for children, and provide needed goods for women and their families in the absence of the head of the family. This organization also helped establish hospitals, orphanages, stores, and banks inside Little Italy to ease the transition from Italian life to American life.

The Little Italy communities that formed on the West Coast differed slightly from their Italian predecessors to the east. For instance, the beginning of heavy Italian immigration into San Francisco and Los Angeles did not occur until the 1910s and 1920s. By 1950, San Francisco had an Italian population of fifty thousand, most of which resided in the lower rent districts of North Beach, Mission, and Portola. There was also a large constituency that resided in the countryside and conducted life even more like that of life in Italy.

Italians in the city labored as longshoremen, fishermen, and small business owners, not unlike their Italian counterparts in the East, but Italians that resided outside city limits created their own type of Italian community. Because of the strikingly similar climate, terrain, and fertility of the soil to that of Italy, Italians in the countryside pursued interests in viniculture and viticulture. Where the city dwellers contributed to opera and the arts, the country dwellers created their own wine industry. Vineyards operated by famous families such as the Rossi and Mondavi families flourished outside of San Francisco and throughout the Napa Valley. In addition, the Italian-Swiss Colony was created and produced excellent wines, gaining worldwide acclaim and winning international honors. In addition to viniculture and viticulture, Italians in the countryside also gained prosperity in the dairy and fruit-packing industries.

Back in San Francisco, Little Italy produced numerous traveling opera troupes and founded a fine establishment in the Grand Opera House. This became a necessary stop for all traveling operas, even the great Metropolitan Opera. In addition to the arts, the Italian community also produced figures such as Amadeo Pietro Giannini, the founder of Bank of America, which today is the largest bank in the world. He was acclaimed as the "J. P. Morgan of the West" and became very involved with his customers, especially Italian immigrants who were weary of giving their hard-earned money to someone else for safekeeping. After the 1906 earthquake and fire, Giannini gained even more respect, and his reputation grew as an honest man, as he helped San Francisco, especially the Italian community, to get back on its feet after the tragedy.

Today, the largest remnants of Italian influence on the West Coast have traveled south to Los Angeles, as seen in the plethora of Italian markets and especially St. Peter's Church, all located with the city limits. The contribution of Italian communities throughout the nation cannot be overstated, and the amalgamation and assimilation of Italian culture has become part of American culture and the American way of life.

—*Matthew Adam Henderson*

See also German and Italian Internment; Idaho Silver Strikes

Suggested Reading

Gallo, Patrick J. *Ethnic Alienation: The Italian Americans.* Rutherford, NJ: Farleigh Dickinson University Press, 1974.

Lothrop, Gloria Ricci, ed. *Fulfilling the Promise of California: An Anthology of Essays on the Italian American Experience in California.* Spokane, WA: Arthur H. Clark, 2000.

Luebke, Frederick, ed. *European Immigrants: American West Community Histories.* Albuquerque: University of New Mexico Press, 1998.

Pisani, Lawrence Frank. *The Italian in America.* New York: Exposition Press, 1957.

Rolle, Andrew F. *The Immigrant Upraised: Italian Adventures and Colonists in an Expanding America.* Norman: University of Oklahoma Press, 1968.

⌗ LITTLE TOKYO AND JAPANTOWN

These small enclaves, born out of the need for immigrant Japanese to combine resources to survive in their new country, were once prevalent throughout the West Coast. Due to the passage of time, dispersion after the internment of the Japanese and Japanese Americans during World War II, exodus to the suburbs, and urban renewal, San Jose, San Francisco, and Los Angeles now have the only three remaining thriving Little Tokyos, or Japantowns, on the West Coast.

East of Sixth Street, between Jackson and Taylor, San Jose's Japantown began near what was known as "Heinlenville Chinatown," named after John Heinlen,

who offered his property after the city's second Chinatown burned down. Japantown's early inhabitants were mostly single men who found employment as laborers on surrounding local farms. By 1902, approximately three thousand seasonal workers resided in Japantown during the growing and picking seasons. As a result, a community of Japanese businesses arose that catered to these single men. With the 1907 Gentlemen's Agreement, wives and children were finally allowed to emigrate from Japan. Subsequently, the nature of the town changed as businesses catering to families made their appearance. Japanese merchants often lived with their families in rooms behind their places of business.

In 1921, as anti-immigrant sentiment once again rose in the United States, the government forbade female immigration. At this time, antimiscegenation laws in California and other states strictly forbade marriage between whites and Asians. With 42 percent of the male population still single, this created a serious problem in the Japanese community. An indirect result was the increase in popularity of *kenjinkai,* clubs based on the native prefectures of the Issei (Japanese-born American immigrants), which helped to form tighter bonds within the community as a whole.

The attack on Pearl Harbor on December 7, 1941, and America's entry into World War II nearly made permanent ghost towns out of the Japantowns. The war led to the evacuation and relocation of all the Japanese communities on the West Coast. Most of Santa Clara's three thousand Japanese American residents were eventually interned at the Heart Mountain, Wyoming, Relocation Center after voluntarily relocating or being sent initially to temporary assembly centers run by the U.S. Army. Almost all of Japantown's fifty-three businesses closed during the internment. Little time was given the residents to dispose of personal property and belongings; only what could be carried was allowed to be taken to the relocation centers. The amount of property and personal loss was staggering.

In December 1944, except for those who remained selectively interned, the Japanese internment policy ended, and the camps were emptied during the following twelve months. By 1947, forty businesses and one hundred families had reestablished themselves in the area. Today, although families do not generally still live behind their stores, Japantown in San Jose reflects a cultural blend of history and heritage that is still carefully preserved by nearby residents and shopkeepers.

San Francisco's Japantown first emerged with the original influx of Japanese immigrants in the mid-1800s. It has been at its current location, near Post and Buchanan Streets in the Western Addition, for almost a hundred years. Prior to 1906, Japanese immigrants lived mostly in Chinatown and the alleys south of Market Street between Fifth and Seventh Streets. Unfortunately, both neighborhoods burned in the 1906 earthquake and fire. After their destruction in 1906, the Western Addition was one of the few districts left standing where old Victorian dwellings were turned into apartments and hotels, storefronts were added to front yards, and churches and synagogues doubled as courthouses. As businesses slowly returned to the ravaged downtown, Japanese Americans found this densely built, mixed-use, mixed-race neighborhood ideal and affordable for establishing their community. By 1940, on the eve of World War II, nearly every business within a block of Post and Buchanan was owned by a person of Japanese descent and the district had grown to have one of the largest concentrations of Japanese outside of Japan.

During World War II, approximately five thousand people of Japanese ancestry were interned from San Francisco. Unfortunately, the forced relocation of the Japanese during the war put an end to what had been Japantown's boom era. The Western Addition became home to tens of thousands of African Americans, who had often migrated from the South to work in the wartime industries, such as shipbuilding, that were densely concentrated in San Francisco during the war. After the end of World War II and the earlier revocation of the mass evacuation orders, the former internees were able to reestablish themselves to a limited degree.

Significant changes occurred in Japantown in the decades following the Japanese relocation. In the 1950s, after the Japanese Americans relocated and rebuilt Japantown, the city proposed to redevelop their neighborhood. Scores of old Victorian homes, housing hundreds of residents, were torn down to

widen Geary Boulevard. After more than a decade of delay, urban blight and decay set in, as home-owners were reluctant to invest in repairs. Given all the changes wrought on the Western Addition by redevelopment in the 1960s and 1970s, the district that remained most physically intact was South Park. This area was the center of a small assortment of Japanese hotels from 1906 to 1933: They had moved back to Japantown when the steamships from Japan shifted to piers farther north and immigration restrictions drastically reduced traffic to and from Japan.

San Francisco's Japantown still exists. The area, straddling the few blocks just north of Geary and south of Sutter, between Laguna and Fillmore, has, however, shrunk somewhat from its pre–World War II heights. A two-story mall-like structure filled with shops, restaurants, and galleries is now the focal point of the community. There are about twelve thousand residents of Japanese descent who still call the neighborhood "home," which makes for a small but still-vibrant Japantown.

Los Angeles' Little Tokyo was first inhabited in the early 1880s by Japanese laborers lured by the availability of jobs in the railroad and farm industries. In 1886, Charles Kame, an ex-seaman, established a restaurant on East First Street. The first Japanese-owned business was thus, ironically, an American-style restaurant. By the turn of the century, a small Issei community was firmly established around First and San Pedro Streets. The area became known as Little Tokyo after Issei, recruited from northern California by Henry Huntington for the Pacific Electric Railway in 1903, were later joined by thousands more who fled racial tensions in San Francisco after the 1906 earthquake.

The Japanese-language newspaper *Rafu Shimpo*, which remains a major influence within the city's Japanese community, first christened the town "Little Tokyo" in 1903. As more Japanese migrated to southern California, racially restrictive housing laws necessitated their living either in Little Tokyo or in isolated farming or fishing communities. During its heyday, between 1925 and 1941, Little Tokyo, which spread out to occupy roughly three square miles of downtown Los Angeles, was home to more than half of southern

California's Japanese population and was the center of its community and cultural life.

As it had the communities in San Jose and San Francisco, America's entry into World War II significantly altered Little Tokyo. The mass exclusion orders eventually forced most of Little Tokyo's residents, after temporary stays at assembly centers such as the one located at the Santa Anita Race Track, in which as many as eighteen thousand detainees were housed in horse stalls and twenty- by twenty-foot rooms, into permanent relocation centers. After World War II ended and the majority of those of Japanese ancestry were released from the camps, only a fraction of the preinternment population returned to Little Tokyo. War Relocation Authority records indicate that only 52 percent of evacuees even returned to California, with the remainder largely relocating to the intermountain states and the Midwest. Many of those who chose to return often followed the nationwide exodus to the suburbs.

Little Tokyo's shrinking population was reduced further in the early 1950s, as the city's redevelopment projects destroyed housing and much of the district's commercial space and business frontage. Reacting to these immediate threats, as well as to the problem of long-term decay, the community sponsored a variety of redevelopment proposals of its own. These proposals combined urban renewal with the goal of preserving Little Tokyo as a residential, commercial, and cultural center.

According to a 1991 Japanese American Community League census, approximately 18.8 percent of the 847,562 Japanese Americans in the United States live in Los Angeles County and neighboring Orange County, but Little Tokyo's area proper has dwindled to a scant four square blocks, with only about a thousand residents. Most are elderly, fixed-income Japanese who spent their youths in Little Tokyo. Clearly, for the southern California Japanese community, Little Tokyo has evolved into a sort of cultural touchstone, with its overall survival predicated on the community's tenacity, flexibility, and desire to stay in touch with its roots. Recent changes may have altered the face of the downtown Japanese American community, but after weathering the Great Depression and a three-year-long forced eviction, and with the establishment of cultural centers such as the Japanese American

National Museum, Little Tokyo in one form or another is likely to continue to survive.

—*Scott M. Behen*

Suggested Reading

Laguerre, Michel S. *The Global Ethnopolis: Chinatown, Japantown, and Manilatown in American Society.* New York: St. Martin's Press, 2000.

Lyman, Stanford Morris. *Chinatown and Little Tokyo: Power, Conflict, and Community among Chinese and Japanese Immigrants in America.* Millwood, NY: Associated Faculty Press, 1986.

Murase, Ichiro Mike. *Little Tokyo: One Hundred Years in Pictures.* Los Angeles: Visual Communications/Asian American Studies Central, 1983.

Pease, Ben. "Japantowns." Available from http://www.pease press.com/Japantowns.html

Several, Michael. "Little Tokyo: Historical Background." Available from http://www.publicartinla.com/Downtown/ Little_Tokyo/little_tokyo.html

Shiroishi, Julie. "Return to Little Tokyo." *Asian Week* 17, no. 37 (May 10–16, 1996). Available from http://www.asian week.com/051096/LittleTokyo.html

⌗ LOGGING

American logging companies during the 19th and early 20th centuries habitually practiced a "cut out and get out" policy that required continual fresh stands of timber. Migratory by nature, the timber industry has also relied on a large mobile labor pool. As the logging industry moved west in the 1890s and 1910s, so did its workers; some followed the only industry they had ever worked for, and others melded together a subsistence-level existence over the course of a year logging, mining, and working the harvest. With the development of the western timber industry, the number of workers employed steadily increased between 1899 and 1929. Many carried all their possessions in a bundle on their back as they traveled from job to job. Referred to as "bindlestiffs," they became an unwanted if necessary commodity in the logging regions of the West. This labor pool consisted of recent immigrants to the United States as well as second-generation Americans.

Living conditions in the logging camps of the "short log" country (composed of western Montana, northern Idaho, and eastern Washington and Oregon) in 1909 and 1920 were considered nightmarish in many instances. Cabins with little or no ventilation were crammed with men who slept in muzzle-loader bunks lined with straw or pine boughs. The men endured humid heat in the winter months as they attempted to dry their wet clothing each evening by hanging shirts, pants, and socks from wires around the stovepipe. Denied the basic means of washing their clothes and themselves, they constantly battled lice and bedbugs. Logger Mark Watkins remembered, "when those wires were filled with lumberjacks' sox and underwear the place needed ventilation!" North Idaho logger Joe Halm concurred: "What a scramble for socks in the morning, first come first served."

With these types of working conditions it became common to hear the phrase "three crews, one coming, one going, and one working." When the mood struck them, loggers simply packed their bedrolls and moved on to the next camp. Before World War I, the rate of turnover in the western timber industry exceeded 600 percent annually. The desire of some companies to hire married men came as a direct result of this turnover problem. Bindlestiffs, immigrant and citizen alike, worked in an industry that marginalized their labor and existence.

Communities that relied on the timber companies for economic survival did not often embrace these migratory workers. For example, the Eureka Lumber Company in northwest Montana hired workers every year to bring logs down Grave Creek and the Fortine and Tobacco Rivers to their sawmill. These "river pigs" lived in jungle camps on the outskirts of town. Some Eureka residents were not above flaunting their "native" status as they ridiculed the immigrant workers. During one such discussion, Norwegian tie-hack Hobo Kanute declared hotly, "I is a better citizen of America as you is! I is a citizen by choice but you is a citizen by accident!"

Although the industry transplanted some of its workers when it moved west, the industry itself underwent significant changes as it attempted to adapt to the challenges of logging in this new area. With larger trees and rougher terrain, logging underwent rapid mechanization to deal with these issues. Logging railroads, donkey engines, and yarders replaced oxen and horses. Sawmills adapted to the larger logs by creating bigger and faster band saws. Mechanization also brought an increase in logging accidents. When accidents occurred in the woods, the victim many times had no immediate if any medical aid. If the accident proved fatal and happened early enough in the day, the men finished their shift before returning the body to the camp or town.

The Industrial Workers of the World (IWW), organized in 1905, took it upon themselves to educate the "timber beast" in an attempt to free loggers from the exploitation of the capitalist lumber companies. The first serious attempt at organizing a union resulted in the 1909 strike that affected the Somers Lumber Company, Eureka Lumber Company, and the Anaconda Company's logging operations. Only four years old, the IWW lacked the organizational skills to sustain the strike, and it soon folded without any significant gains for the workers.

By the time the IWW became active in the Montana timber industry, six companies (the two largest were the Northern Pacific Company and the ACM Lumber Company, a subsidiary of the Anaconda Copper Mining Company) owned 80 percent of the private timberlands in the state. As such, they exercised almost feudal control over the industry and its workforce. When the IWW met in March 1917 at Spokane, Washington, their goal was to break the back of these timber giants and restore the timber beast to the status of a man. The IWW preached the radical overthrow of not only the timber industry but also the capitalist system. For the men who worked in the timber industry, the goal was to force the company owners to grant an eight-hour day; clean up the logging camps; and provide clean bedding and steel bunks, better food, and a place to take a shower after a day's work.

Out of the IWW convention, held in Spokane March 4–6, 1917, came the creation of Lumber Workers Industrial Union #500 (LWIU). Strategy for the new union was simple: strike those companies planning on a spring river drive to obtain logs for their mill and follow up with an industrywide strike in June 1917. With the war in Europe, the IWW banked on the lumber companies settling the strikes quickly to maintain increased production. What the union did not count on was the entry of the United States into the war on April 6, 1917.

One of the first targets of opportunity in the spring of 1917 became the Eureka Lumber Company in northwest Montana. As the convention hammered out its agenda, IWW strike delegates James Rowan, John Turner, Louis Miller, and Olin Anderson worked the "jungle camps" along Grave Creek and the Fortine and Tobacco Rivers, recruiting members and passing out literature advocating the eight-hour day, clean camps, and increased pay. Six days after the United States entered the war, the Eureka Lumber Company's river drivers walked off the job.

Eureka Lumber Company manager Charles Weil had already been proactive in his preparation for the coming spring river drive. In February, Weil hired the Thiel Detective Agency in Spokane to infiltrate the logging camps in the Eureka area. As early as March, Weil received reports from the undercover operatives about radical Swedes and Finns who planned to make the company pay by tying up the spring drive—and if it came to violence, then dynamite could settle the issue. Using this information when the strike occurred, Charles Weil appealed to Montana Governor Sam Stewart for assistance. Both men began bombarding Montana's U.S. senators, T. J. Walsh and H. L. Myers, with demands for military protection. Claiming that many of the IWW agitators were foreigners, Weil informed the senators that "patriotic" citizens endorsed the company's appeal for military assistance to break the strike.

When local logger James Gardam learned that Governor Stewart advocated the use of troops in Eureka, he wrote an impassioned plea to President Woodrow Wilson, asking for impartial treatment of the strikers and their demands rather than their vilification because of the IWW's radical reputation. Having firsthand knowledge of the conditions in northwest Montana logging camps, Gardam described the overcrowded, bug-infested, poorly ventilated bunkhouses where loggers sat on eight-inch boards around the bunks discussing the primitive conditions they were forced to endure until lights out at 9 p.m. In Gardam's words, "It finally brews into results not conducive to Peace but revenge."

Although some of the strikers seemingly advocated extreme measures, John Turner assured Charles Weil and the citizens of Eureka that the strike would not become violent. Thiel detectives continued to report that loggers were threatening the use of violence, prompting one loyal company employee to suggest the construction of a bullpen in town to accommodate union organizers—preferably near a fire hydrant to cool off the radicals if need be. The union immediately found itself on the defensive, as it sought to balance its radical rhetoric condoning sabotage and revolution with an ever more wary populace that was being hammered by the propaganda of lumber company owners, state politicians, and newspapers alike, which told workers that the IWW was a "foreign" subversive element intent on tying up the industry to hamper the United States and aid the Kaiser. To further alienate union members, newspapers began referring to the IWW as "I Won't Workers" and "Imperial Wilhelm's Workers." Patriotic fervor overshadowed legitimate grievances.

The Eureka Lumber Company, using its Minnesota connections, hired Chippewa river drivers from the White Earth Reservation and shipped them to Eureka. When these 16 men arrived, they found themselves in the middle of a standoff between the strikers and the company. Federal troops had also arrived on the scene. Captain Gobel arrived from Whitefish, Montana, on the same day and placed 25 of his men at Eureka. He informed Charles Weil that if the IWW caused any trouble, he would place his entire company of soldiers in town, along with a Gatling gun. On April 22, 1917, 150 soldiers from the Vancouver barracks arrived in town under the command of Captain Blanchard. Blanchard promised to place troops at all company camps if need be. The lumber company wanted the military to either immediately force the strikers to return to work or expel them from the area.

Forty of the rank-and-file union members were unwilling to oppose the lumber company and federal troops. They returned to work on April 25, accepting the company's pay increase from $3.50 per day to $4.50. Conditions only improved marginally, as the bulk of the river drivers stayed on strike. Although both sides claimed victory, in reality it was only the opening salvo, as the LWIU—two thousand strong—squared off against the timber industry when it called a general strike on July 1, 1917, that affected Washington,

Oregon, Idaho, and Montana. Law enforcement agencies began arresting union organizers, strike delegates, and IWW members on a number of charges, including vagrancy, in an attempt to break the stranglehold on the timber industry. Western state legislatures began passing criminal syndicalism laws as a way to clamp down on the IWW.

Lumber companies responded by raising wages and, in some cases, granting the eight-hour day. By August, the striking men had reduced the cut for western states by 25 percent. The Libby (Montana) *Western News* advocated a policy whereby "all aliens should be forced by special taxes, to become citizens of this country or return to their native shores." Newspaper editor C. A. Griffen understood the need for alien immigrants but claimed that those who advocated sedition and revolution "should meet speedy and terrible punishment." Griffen claimed that the IWW was filled with foreign subversives who had no allegiance to the United States.

The federal government finally responded to state and local pressure and began raiding IWW union halls, arresting members on charges of treason for striking during a time of war. The federal government raided the LWIU headquarters in Spokane on August 19, 1917. Among those arrested was James Rowan, who had engineered the general strike of the timber industry. Arresting the union's leadership left the rank-and-file union members adrift in an inhospitable landscape. Union membership identified a worker as either an enemy alien or a disloyal American.

With so many of the leadership under arrest and defense attorney fees mounting, the union called for the membership to return to work and strike on the job. In this manner, they could collect their paychecks (and pay their much-needed union dues) and simultaneously cause slowdowns in the already prostate industry. James Rowan encouraged workers to respond to the lumber companies' poor pay, poor food, and poor conditions with poor work.

In an attempt to mend the relationship between workers and the lumber companies in Montana, the Montana Lumber Manufacturers' Association met in Missoula, Montana, in September 1917. Under the direction of Kenneth Ross, general manager of the Anaconda Company's lumber department, the organization took up the demands of the strikers, pushing for clean camps and better food. The association discussed the problem of inedible food with the domestic sciences department of the University of Montana, which provided them with a wholesome menu for the camps. One company manager offered the opinion that if a man got up from the breakfast table with "a grouch on" he was no good the rest of the day.

The Timberman reported the association as saying, "in season and out of season, in the bunkhouses they [the IWW] taught their doctrine of hate. . . . Their pupils accepted the theories and became inoculated with the bacilli of malice and hatred. Their minds were poisoned." As a result, some of the lumber companies suggested that they should provide wholesome literature to their workers. In this way, the companies could help educate their employees about subversive organizations such as the IWW. The implication became clear—the lumber companies only wanted their employees to think for themselves when it did not affect the bottom line.

Although the lumber companies blamed their labor troubles on the IWW and successfully enlisted the aid of local, state, and federal agencies to combat the strike, in reality many organizations recognized the legitimacy of the loggers' strike demands. F. A. Silcox, superintendent of the U.S. Forest Service's Region 1, wrote a lengthy report regarding the strike and conditions in the logging camps, which the federal government ignored. Silcox contended that although the eight-hour day, wages, and sanitary camps were legitimate concerns, the greatest deterrent to the settlement of the labor problems resided with the lack of stable communities to act as support networks for the loggers. He believed the industry needed "some permanency to forest communities to eliminate the migratory worker."

President Woodrow Wilson's own specially appointed mediation commission reported that accusations regarding the disloyalty of striking loggers were a fabrication of the lumber companies to turn public opinion against the union. The commission further reported that the obstinacy of western lumber companies exacerbated the situation by ignoring the demands of the loggers, compelling them to strike in an attempt to seek redress. The investigators revealed in their report that "the operators took advantage of the popular prejudice against the IWW as an unpatriotic organization to break not only the strike but all the unions." The U.S. Labor Department, however, did not entirely give up the theory of foreign subversive elements operating within the IWW; the department claimed that between 60 and 65 percent of the IWW's membership were foreign born.

W. J. Swindlehurst of the Montana Department of Labor and Industry further buttressed this opinion when he conducted an investigation in the areas of the state most affected by the strike. In August 1917, he toured Flathead, Granite, Lincoln, Mineral, Missoula, Powell, and Sanders Counties, observing firsthand the deplorable conditions of the camps. He advocated that the logger should have an opportunity to voice grievances but should not ally himself with an organization as corrupt as the IWW.

Another force for change in the industry occurred with the creation of the Loyal Legion of Loggers and Lumbermen (Four L). Essentially the Four L became a government union under the command of Colonel Brice Disque of the U.S. Army, who organized Spruce Battalions throughout the Pacific Northwest to aid in the harvesting of spruce timber for constructing airplanes and ships. The Four L also acted as a pseudounion, instituting the eight-hour day in camps where its members worked. After the war, the Four L continued to operate as a company union, but it drew little support from wary loggers.

Montana loggers had learned a hard lesson. When the IWW called for a general strike in 1918 to protest the convictions of labor leaders on charges of treason, J. M. Kennedy, chairman of the Lincoln County Council of Defense, happily reported that none of the loggers walked off the job—"men in the Montana woods [were] 100 percent American." Kennedy ignored the fact that any logger expressing support of the union quickly found himself either in jail or invited to leave the area.

The logging communities in Montana coalesced around the population demographic after World War I, and the radical foreigners previously shunned became accepted members of the community. The workers remained unorganized during the timber recession of the 1920s. The opportunity to collectively bargain did not come until President Franklin Roosevelt's New Deal policy in the 1930s.

—Richard Aarstad

See also LIBBY, MONTANA

Suggested Reading

Bowman, A. B. *Management Plan for the Kootenai Sustained Yield Unit: Kootenai National Forest Lincoln County, Montana 1946.* Washington, DC: U.S. Department of Agriculture and U.S. Forest Service, 1946.

Dubofsky, Melvyn. *We Shall Be All: A History of the Industrial Workers of the World.* Chicago: Quadrangle Books, 1969.

Hanson, P. D. *The Proposed Kootenai Sustained Yield Unit: Kootenai National Forest.* U.S. Department of Agricultural and U.S. Forest Service, 1948.

Holter, Anton M. "Pioneer Lumbering in Montana" [Pamphlet]. Portland, OR: *The Timberman*, n.d.

Jensen, Vernon H. *Lumber and Labor.* New York: Farrar and Rinehart, 1945.

Kaufman, Harold, and Lois Kaufman. *Toward the Stabilization and Enrichment of a Forest Community* [Montana Study Research Collection no. MC 270]. Missoula: University of Montana, 1946.

Lukas, Anthony J. *Big Trouble.* New York: Simon and Schuster, 1997.

Morrow, Delores. *Our Sawdust Roots: A History of the Forest Products Industry in Montana.* Helena: Montana Historical Society, n.d.

Neils, Paul. *Julius Neils and the J. Neils Lumber Company.* Seattle: McCaffrey, 1971.

Rader, Benjamin G. "The Montana Lumber Strike of 1917." *Pacific Historical Review* 36 (May 1967).

Robbins, William G. *Lumberjacks and Legislators: Political Economy of the U.S. Lumber Industry, 1890-1941.* College Station: Texas A&M University Press, 1982.

Robbins, William G. "The Tarnished Dream: The Turbulent World of the Forest Products Industry in the Northwest." *Montana: The Magazine of Western History* 37, no. 1 (Winter 1987).

Robbins, William G. "The Western Lumber Industry: A 20th Century Perspective. In *The 20th Century West: Historical Interpretations*, edited by Gerald Nash and Richard Etulain. Albuquerque: University of New Mexico Press, 1989.

Tyler, Robert L. *Rebels of the Woods: The I.W.W. in the Pacific Northwest.* Eugene: University of Oregon, 1967.

⊞ LOS ANGELES, CALIFORNIA

Spanish explorer Gaspar de Portola first explored the area around the present-day city of Los Angeles in the year 1769. Three short years later, Father Junípero Serra established a Franciscan mission at San Gabriel and, in 1797, a mission at San Fernando. In 1781, Felipe de Neve formally founded the city of Los Angeles, or *el Pueblo de Nuestra Señora la Reina de Los Angeles de Porciúncula* (the City of Our Lady the Queen of the Angels of Porciúncula), as it was called by the Spanish, and later the Mexicans. Neve was the Spanish governor of California and helped promote the migration of peoples north from Sonora, Mexico. Juan Bautista de Anza greatly aided this migration with the founding in 1774 of an overland trail that ran between northern Mexico and California.

The first peoples to settle in the Los Angeles Basin throughout the latter part of the 18th century were poor farmers and *rancheros* in search of grazing pastures. By 1784, the first three large ranchos were established in California by Spanish government officials and given to three entrepreneurial families in the business of raising livestock: the Verdugos, Nietos, and Dominguezes. Six years later in 1790, the population of El Pueblo, as it was known throughout the early 19th century, was established at 139.

In 1821, Mexico gained her independence from Spain, but the instability of the infant Mexican government, combined with the distance between Mexico City and California, allowed California to remain quasi-independent, with a distinct identity. As time progressed, more Mexicans began to trickle northward in search of lands, much of which had been confiscated from the Church and dispersed to various ranchero families by the government. Between the years of 1826 and 1831, El Pueblo saw white men for the first time, as men such as Jedediah Strong Smith, James Ohio Pattie, William Wolfskill, and other trappers continued their search for financial gain. In fact, both Smith and Pattie were imprisoned while in El Pueblo, and Pattie was forced by the Mexican mayor, or *alcalde,* to vaccinate the locals against smallpox in 1826. There are several different sources for this fact, and it is believed that Pattie did indeed vaccinate around two thousand local Mexicans in the Los Angeles area.

By 1835, El Pueblo was designated by the Mexican Congress as Alta California's capital, a decision that embittered the former capital of Monterey. It was not until 1845, however, that California's last Mexican governor, Pío Pico, moved the capital to Los Angeles. Throughout the following decade, El Pueblo experienced many factional problems that allowed the influx of numerous white settlers in search of land, financial security, and, by the 1840s and 1850s, gold. Mexico and its northern territories encountered its biggest problem starting on August 13, 1846. On this date, Commodore Robert F. Stockton sailed into the waters just west of El Pueblo and established an American military presence in Alta California. Infuriated by such actions, the locals surrounded a military force under the command of Marine Captain Archibald Gillespie. The American detachment was forced to retreat to what is now San Pedro until reinforcements could arrive. The Battle of the Old Woman's Gun ensued, with the Mexicans emerging victorious. Less than five months later, in January 1847, officers Stockton and Stephen W. Kearney retook El Pueblo, and the end of skirmishes in the Mexican-American War was seen in California. On January 13, 1847, the final band of Mexican forces, led by Andres Pico, surrendered to John C. Frémont, and the Cahuenga Capitulation was signed.

Just prior to California's entrance into the Union in September 1850, Los Angeles, as it slowly became known during the migration of easterners, became the main cattle and beef supplier for the northern part of the state during the great gold rushes of 1849 and the succeeding years. Los Angeles was slowly taken from the Mexican locals, as land speculation redrew boundaries and Americans made new claims in the new state. Shipping also became a viable and prosperous industry, as Phineas Banning, known affectionately as "Father of the Los Angeles Harbor," established a landing at San Pedro in 1854. The white population of Los Angeles continued to climb throughout the following years, but a drop in cattle prices during the 1860s and a series of dry summers forced rancheros and small agricultural farmers off their land. As a result, railroad companies were one of the organizations benefiting during this decade: A transcontinental railroad finally reached Los Angeles in 1869. By 1876, Los Angeles also had a rail that ran to San Francisco, the largest city on the West Coast. The Santa Fe Railroad reached Los Angeles in 1885, providing the city with a second line to the east.

The boom in the railroad industry saw ticket fares from the Midwest to Los Angeles drop to as low as one dollar each way during the 1880s, thus creating a population surge in the young city. By 1890, the population reached 50,395, up from 11,183 ten years prior. The real estate business also boomed; advertisements were sent eastward selling Los Angeles as a series of harmonious neighborhoods and businesses located in a mild, Mediterranean climate. The filial feeling of the new city brought families west, and the harvests of oranges, grapes, various nuts, peaches, figs, vegetables, avocados, and grain brought laborers. Additionally, the cattle industry, which did not completely disappear with the *ranchero,* spawned a thriving dairy industry, and the conversion of locomotives from coal to diesel brought about an oil industry that increased wealth in the Los Angeles Basin. Finally, the allocation of $2.9 million from Congress in 1896 to establish a harbor at San Pedro ushered in a new shipping industry.

By 1900, the population of Los Angeles had reached 170,268, and the arid region proved to have insufficient water for the needs of its population. The city turned northward in a series of protested actions that diverted water from the Owens Valley, San Fernando Valley, and finally during the 1920s, the Colorado River. Culturally, Los Angeles remained an amalgamation of ethnicities from the population boom of the 1920s until today. Landmarks such as the Chinese Theater opened on Hollywood Boulevard in 1929, and the University of California, Los Angeles' Westwood campus opened in the same year. Hollywood and the film industry began to grow during this era, as well as Los Angeles' first municipal airport, the predecessor to Los Angeles International Airport. By 1939, Union Station, located on Alameda Boulevard in the heart of El Pueblo, opened, and the population of the city continued to rise despite the Great Depression.

World War II saw Los Angeles explode as a wartime industry machine, especially in terms of the airplane business. Lockheed and Douglas were just two of many aviation companies that made their home in Los Angeles and the surrounding communities during the 1940s, and they remained there until the end of the Cold War. Since World War II, Los Angeles has continued to grow and remains at the top of the list in terms of the United States' most successful city economies. Los Angeles is a multicultural, multiethnic city that has persevered through two race riots in the last forty years yet remains one of the nation's most populous and most diverse cities.

—*Matthew Adam Henderson*

See also African American Communities in California; Anglo Migration to Southern California Before the Depression; Bass, Charlotta A. Spear(s); Boyle Heights, California; Brent, Joseph Lancaster; Gabrielino; Lankershim, Isaac; Lawyers and Legislation; Libraries and the Immigrant; Little Italy; Little Tokyo and Japantown; Thrall, William H.

Suggested Reading

Berger, Brian. *Los Angeles: Commemorating 200 Years.* Beaverton, OR: Beautiful America, 1980.

Caughey, John, and LaRee Caughey. *Los Angeles: Biography of a City.* Berkeley: University of California Press, 1977.

Flamming, Douglas. *Bound for Freedom: Black Los Angeles in Jim Crow America* Berkeley: University of California Press, 2005.

Nadeau, Remi. *Los Angeles: From Mission to Modern City.* New York: Longmans, Green, 1960.

Poole, John Bruce, and Tevvy Ball. *El Pueblo: The Historic Heart of Los Angeles.* Los Angeles: Getty, 2002.

Rolle, Andrew. *Los Angeles: From Pueblo to City of the Future.* Sacramento, CA: MTL, 1995.

Sides, Josh. *L.A. City Limits: African American Los Angeles from the Great Depression to the Present.* Berkeley: University of California Press, 2003.

Wild, Mark. *Street Meeting: Multiethnic Neighborhoods in Early Twentieth-Century Los Angeles.* Berkeley: University of California Press, 2005.

⊞ LUISEÑO

Luiseño is not an indigenously derived term but, rather, is of Spanish origin, having been used to refer to those native peoples associated with the Mission San Luis Rey de Francia. The mission, founded in 1798, established numerous supporting ranchos throughout what are now southwestern Riverside and northwestern San Diego Counties, and these ranchos encompassed dozens of existing native villages. People living in the villages became the forced labor of the mission, and because they resided within territory claimed by Mission San Luis Rey, they became known as San Luiseños, a term later shortened to Luiseños. Aboriginally, each of the six Luiseño bands identified themselves along village lines but acknowledged tribal identity by language, with distinctions based on the four cardinal directions. Because their tribal territory was located west of the other tribes in the region, the Luiseño, whose language belongs to the Cupan group of the Takic subfamily of the widespread Uto-Aztecan linguistic family, referred to themselves collectively as Payomkawichum (Western People).

The Luiseño, as well as other Takic-speaking people such as the Cupeño, Cahuilla, and Gabrielino, are thought to have migrated into southern California from the Great Basin. Luiseño tradition notes alternately that the people originally came from either the east or north to the places they eventually settled in southern California, but this tradition does not offer a specific place of origin. The belief that the Luiseño migrated from the Great Basin, which is northeast of Luiseño territory, is based on linguistic evidence. Precise estimates of when this migration occurred do not currently exist, although some theorists believe it may have begun as early as 7,000 to 8,000 years ago. Archaeological evidence indicates the presence of aboriginal cultures in the coastal area of San Diego County as early as 7370–7270 BCE, and these peoples are generally considered to be the ancestors of the Luiseño.

The ecologically diverse territory of the Luiseño comprised 1,500 square miles of coastal and inland southern California in what are now northwestern San Diego County and southwestern Riverside County. Their habitat included every ecological zone, ranging from sea level to more than 6,000 feet above sea level, providing an abundant and variable subsistence base. Territorial boundaries of the Luiseño were shared with the Gabrielino and Serrano to the north, the Cahuilla to the east, and the Cupeño and Ipay to the south.

Sedentary and autonomous village groups with strictly delineated land and resource holdings were located in every ecological zone within Luiseño territory. Villages were usually situated near adequate sources of food and water, in defensive locations such as sheltered coves or canyons. Typically, a village was composed of permanent houses, a sweathouse, and a religious edifice. Permanent houses of the Luiseño were earth-covered and built over a two-foot-deep excavation. According to informants' accounts, the dwellings were conical roofs resting on a few logs leaning together, with a smoke hole in the middle of the roof and entrance by a door. Cooking was done outside when possible, on a central hearth when necessary. The sweathouse was similar to the houses except that it was smaller, elliptical, and had its door in one of the long sides. Heat was produced directly by a wood fire. Finally, the religious edifice was usually just a round fence of brush with a main entrance for viewing by the spectators and several narrow openings for entry by the ceremonial dancers.

Each village had specific resource procurement territories, most of which were within one day's travel of the village. However, during the autumn of each year, most of the village population would migrate to the mountain oak groves and camp for several weeks to harvest the acorn crop, hunt, and collect local resources not available near the village. Luiseño subsistence was based on seasonal floral and faunal resource procurement. Game animals, such as deer, could usually be taken throughout the year by individual hunters or small groups. Similarly, small rodents, cottontail, quail, and dove were available during all seasons. Individual hunters typically employed traps, nets, throwing sticks, snares, or clubs for procuring small animals; deer were usually ambushed, then shot with bow and arrow. Antelope and jackrabbits normally were hunted in the autumn by means of communal drives, although individual hunters could often take jackrabbits throughout the year using a bow and arrow. Many other animals were available to the Luiseño during various times of the year but were not eaten. These included dog, coyote, bear, tree squirrel, dove, pigeon, mud hen, eagle, buzzard, raven, lizards, frogs, and turtles. Faunal procurement by inland Luiseño comprised 15 to 20 percent of their total food resources.

Small game was prepared by broiling it on coals. Venison and rabbit were either broiled on coals or cooked in an earthen oven. Whatever meat was not immediately consumed was crushed in a mortar, then dried and stored for future use. Of all the food sources used by the Luiseño, acorns were by far the most important, supplying 25 to 45 percent of the total diet. Six species were collected in great quantities during the autumn of each year, although some were favored more than others. Acorns were prepared for consumption by crushing them in a stone mortar, leaching off the tannic acid, then making them into either a mush or flourlike material.

Herb and grass seeds were used almost as extensively as acorns, comprising 20 to 40 percent of the diet. Many plants produced edible seeds, which were collected between April and November. Important seeds included, but were not limited to, the following: sagebrush, white tidy tips, sunflower, calabazilla, sage, buckwheat, peppergrass, and chamise. Seeds were parched, ground, and cooked as mush or used as flavoring for other foods.

Fruit, berries, corms, tubers, and fresh herbage were collected and often immediately consumed during the spring and summer months. Among those plants commonly used were basketweed, manzanita, miner's lettuce, thimbleberry, California blackberry, holly-leaf cherry, and juniper. Some berries, especially juniper and manzanita berries, were dried and ground into flour to be made into mush at a later time when an occasional large yield occurred.

Tools for food acquisition, preparation, and storage were made from widely available materials. Hunting was done with bow and fire-hardened wood or stone-tipped arrows. Coiled and twined baskets were used in food gathering, preparation, serving, and storage. Seeds were ground with handstones on shallow granitic metates; mortar and pestle were used to pound acorns and other nuts or berries. Food was cooked in clay vessels over fireplaces or in earthen ovens. A wide variety of other utensils was employed in all phases of food acquisition and preparation, and most of these utensils were produced from locally available geological, floral, and faunal resources.

The subsistence system of the Luiseño was constituted of seasonal resource exploitation within their prescribed village-centered procurement territory. In essence, all activities of the Luiseño were based on and centered around this seasonal resource procurement. During the spring, collection of roots, tubers, and greens was emphasized. Seed collection and processing during the summer months shifted this emphasis, although the collection areas and personnel (primarily small groups of women) remained virtually unchanged. However, as autumn and the acorn harvest approached, the entire settlement pattern of the Luiseño was altered. Small groups joined to form the larger groups necessary for the harvest, and village members left the villages for several weeks, migrating to the mountain oak groves. Following the annual acorn harvest, village activities centered on preparation of collected foods for use during the winter. Because few plant food resources were available for collection during the winter, this time was probably spent repairing and manufacturing tools and necessary implements in preparation for the coming resource procurement seasons.

Each Luiseño village was a clan tribelet—a group of people patrilineally related who owned an area in common and who were politically and economically autonomous in regard to neighboring villages. The chief of each village inherited his position and was responsible, with the help of an assistant, for the administration of religious, economic, and warfare powers. A council composed of ritual specialists and a shaman, also hereditary positions, advised the chief on matters concerning the environment, rituals, and supernatural powers.

The social structure of the villages is obscure, since the Luiseño apparently did not practice the organizational system of exogamous moieties used by many of the surrounding Native American groups. At birth, a baby was confirmed into the householding group and the patrilineage. Girls and boys went through numerous puberty initiation rituals, in which they learned about the supernatural beings who governed them and punished any infractions of the rules of behavior and ritual. The boys' ceremonies included the drinking of *toloache* (datura), visions, dancing, ordeals, and the teaching of songs and rituals. Girls' ceremonies included advice and instruction in the knowledge necessary for married life, "roasting" in warm sands, and rock painting. Shortly after the completion of the puberty initiation rituals, girls were married, typically to someone arranged for by the girl's parents.

Although the Luiseño were concerned that marriages not occur between individuals too closely related, cross-cousin marriages may have been the norm prior to Spanish Catholic influences. Luiseño marriages created important economic and social alliances between lineages and were celebrated accordingly with elaborate ceremonies and a bride price. Residence was typically patrilocal, and polygyny, often sororal, was practiced, especially by chiefs and shamans.

One of the most important elements of the Luiseño life cycle was death. At least a dozen successive mourning ceremonies were held following an individual's death, with feasting taking place and gifts being distributed to ceremony guests. Luiseño cosmology was essentially based on a dying-god theme and around Wiyót, a creator-culture hero and teacher who was the son of Earth-mother. The order of the world was established by this entity, and he was one of the first "people," or creations. On the death of Wiyót, the nature of the universe changed, and the world of plants, animals, and men was created. The original creations took on the various life forms they now have and worked out solutions for living. These solutions included a spatial organization of species for living space and a chain of being concept that placed each species into a mutually beneficial relationship with all others.

Although European explorers had observed the Luiseño as early as 1542, it was not until the "Sacred Expedition" of Captain Gaspar de Portola and the Franciscan Father Junípero Serra in 1769 that there was actual contact with them. The purpose of the expedition, which began in San Blas, Baja California, was to establish missions and presidios along the California coast. The first mission and presidio were founded in San Diego in 1769, with missions built at San Juan Capistrano in 1776 and Mission San Luis Rey in 1798. Population figures at the time of contact are estimated to have been as high as 10,000 Luiseño, occupying 50 villages. By 1828, Mission San Luis Rey records show a population of only 3,683, although such figures are somewhat misleading because many individuals and several villages were never incorporated into the mission system and consequently would not have been included in these records.

Spanish missions in California were typically based on the *reducción* model, with Native peoples brought from villages into the mission environs, where they were taught the Spanish language, the Roman Catholic faith, farming, animal husbandry, adobe brick making, and a variety of other European skills. By greatly reducing the area in which native peoples were permitted to live, the missions were able to exert significant control over the Indians and their process of "civilization," as well as maintaining a steady source of laborers for their many commercial endeavors. Due to this closed living environment, nutritional imbalance, stress, and a variety of other factors, European diseases thrived among the Native peoples, accelerating a population decline that had begun at contact.

There is some evidence that the policy of Mission San Luis Rey was to maintain Luiseño settlement patterns instead of bringing them into the mission environs to live. The mission's priest, Father Antonio Peyri, traveled to villages to hold masses, supervised agricultural activities, and performed baptisms and marriages. This policy allowed the Luiseño to maintain their traditional system of leadership and economic subsistence yet still provided labor for the mission, whose holdings were often far distant from the mission itself. Under this policy and the guidance of Fr. Peyri, the mission prospered to such a degree that it was often referred to as the "King of the Missions." At its peak, Mission San Luis Rey controlled six ranches and annually produced 27,000 cattle, 26,000 sheep, 1,300 goats, 500 pigs, 1,900 horses, and 67,000 bushels of grain.

Following the Secularization Act of 1833, the Spanish missions of California were secularized, and the first of the Mexican ranchos were established. The political imbalance that occurred after secularization resulted in Indian revolts and uprising against the Mexican ranchers, many of whom used a system of servitude even more cruel than that of the Spanish. Many Luiseño left the mission and the ranchos at this time, seeking refuge in inland villages, where surviving families regrouped into new organizations called parties. A few individuals, however, acquired land grants and entered into the mainstream of Mexican culture. The Mexican government established several pueblos for some of the Mission San Luis Rey Indians. The pueblos, among which were Los Flores and Santa Margarita, were intended to function as governmental units within the Mexican political system, but few were successful, and most soon succumbed to pressures from Mexican ranchos. Alternatively, many Luiseño villages maintained their traditional orientation, integrated with the agriculture, animal husbandry, and European technological skills learned from the Spanish.

Discovery of gold in 1848 caused California to become a magnet that attracted Anglo-American exploration and colonization. California's population, estimated at 2,000 in 1848, burgeoned to more than 560,000 by 1870, not including Native Americans, whose populations were decimated by this invasion. Although most of the gold-mining activity and population boom occurred in the northern and central portions of California, land included in Luiseño territory was not exempt from impact. This was particularly true in the 1840s and 1850s, when thousands of settlers and prospectors traveled through this part of southern California on the Emigrant Trail, which cut through Luiseño territory, en route to various destinations in the West. With passage of the Homestead Act of 1862, the Luiseños saw the first serious influx of settlers. As Anglo Americans came to this region in increasing numbers, the continued existence of the Luiseños was threatened as their traditional lands were taken from them. By 1875, most Luiseño villages and farmlands had been expropriated by whites. It was at this time that the first reservations of land for Luiseños, at Pala, La Jolla, and Rincon, were set aside by President Ulysses S. Grant's executive order. Passage of the Act for Relief of Mission Indians in 1891 gave legal trust–patent status to these reservations, as well as those established later at Pechanga, Pauma, and Soboba. The act also provided the bureaucratic infrastructure of the Bureau of Indian Affairs for the reservations.

Reservations established for the Luiseño were relatively small and typically established in areas considered undesirable by white settlers. The Luiseños planted crops and orchards, as well as raising livestock and poultry for their own use and occasionally for sale. As they were often faced with insufficient water, extreme topography, and rocky soil that affected their productivity, many turned to wage and subsistence labor on ranches and nearby towns to survive. In many cases, they formed a major portion of the labor pool for local agriculture, ranching, and various forms of wage labor. Despite the fact that most Luiseño could not subsist solely on the products derived from reservation farming, thus necessitating supplemental earnings, few sold their land when given the opportunity. Whereas elsewhere in the United States up to two thirds of Indian land was lost as the result of the Dawes Act of 1887, less than 10 percent of Luiseño acreage was allotted, and some of these fee-patent lands remained in the hands of Indians.

As part of Bureau of Indian Affairs' management, agents, teachers, and medical personnel were placed on the reservations, and a network of Indian captains, judges, policemen, and courts was also established. Children were sent to reservation day schools, to off-reservation BIA boarding schools such as Perris Indian School and Sherman Institute, and to private boarding schools such as St. Boniface, which was run by the Roman Catholic Church. The point of the management and education programs was to develop a self-supporting Indian population that could eventually be assimilated into mainstream American life. The education of Luiseño children, particularly at off-reservation boarding schools, was intended to hasten the assimilation process, as well as to provide a "civilizing" influence on their reservation families.

Beginning with World War I and continuing through World War II, many Luiseños either entered into military service or migrated to urban centers for defense industry jobs. This resulted in substantially decreased reservation populations. After the wars, many Luiseños chose not to return to the reservations, but those who did return often possessed increased job skills that provided opportunities both on and off the reservations. As a result, the personal income level of most Luiseños rose considerably and provided a more stable existence. Discussions regarding the termination of the federal trust responsibility for Indians throughout the country began in earnest with the passage of the Indian Reorganization Act in 1934. These discussions became a reality for many tribes when Public Law (P.L.) 280 was signed into law in 1953. Under the terms of this law, Indians in six states became subject to state civil and criminal jurisdiction, and federal services were reduced to maintenance of the trust status of reservation lands; California was one of the original P.L. 280 states. Due in large part to the fact that P.L. 280 was pushed through both houses of Congress in just two weeks and did not clearly delineate the responsibility of counties and states to Indian tribes, numerous legal problems arose. Still, perhaps because of the confusion engendered by P.L. 280, many tribes chose to focus on the goals of self-government and self-determination instead of the federal benefits that were taken away. The Luiseño chose this track.

Beginning in the late 1960s, the Luiseños began to take advantage of emergent federally funded programs such as low-cost housing and manpower training. These new programs demanded large populations, and to qualify, new organizations were formed that included several reservations, including those of the Luiseño. In organizations such as the Intertribal Council of California, Tribal Chairman's Association, and All-Mission Indian Housing Authority, Luiseños were generally more involved than other southern California tribes, with their participation and leadership becoming more prominent over time.

By the 1970s, most Luiseños were enrolled on one of six reservations located in southwestern Riverside and northwestern San Diego Counties, with approximately one half of enrolled members actually residing on the reservations. Tribal members not residing on reservations generally lived within a 20-mile radius, in nearby towns or on other reservations. The occupations of most Luiseños were in semiskilled or skilled categories, although some professional occupations were represented as well, the result of an increasing focus on higher education in many reservations. Because California is a P.L. 280 state, the Luiseños were able to partake of the same benefits as any other California citizen, including Medicare, unemployment compensation, welfare, and grants for continuing education.

In 1987, the U.S. Supreme Court ruling in *California v. Cabazon Band of Mission Indians* was to have a dramatic and permanent impact on Luiseños, despite the fact that they were not a party to the suit. The court decided that even in P.L. 280 states, state gambling laws do not apply to Indian gaming because they are "regulatory" laws instead of "prohibitory"

laws. This is the key case for the modern proliferation of Indian gaming and one that the Luiseño would take full advantage of. The decision permitted the continued operation of bingo and card rooms on Indian reservations throughout the state.

In 1988, spurred by complaints from state representatives that they had lost control over gaming in their states, Congress passed the Indian Gaming Regulatory Act. This act divided Indian gaming into three classes: Class I would be regulated by tribes alone, Class II would be regulated by tribal and federal government, and Class III would be regulated by tribal, federal, and state governments, with tribes required to enter into a compact with the state. Between 1990 and 1996, attempts were made by California tribes to negotiate gaming compacts with Governor Pete Wilson, but to no avail. During this time, U.S. attorneys in California were ignoring casinos that were springing up on reservations without compacts, except in San Diego County. In 1994, U.S. Attorney Alan Bersin entered into a handshake agreement with leaders of the only tribes in San Diego operating casinos at the time— Barona, Sycuan, and Viejas—thus giving them a tribal gaming monopoly for several years while acceptable compacts were being developed.

In 1997, under continuing pressure to solve the stalemate with California tribes, Governor Wilson finally agreed to negotiate compacts, although he adamantly refused to negotiate with tribes operating illegal casinos. He chose the Pala Band of Mission Indians, a tribe composed of both Luiseño and Cupeño Indians, to negotiate a compact that would serve as the model for all California tribes. Tribes were given the option of signing what became known as the "Pala Compact" or closing their casinos and negotiating compacts of their own, which Wilson assured them would be identical to the model Pala Compact. Despite numerous challenges to the legality of the compacts, ballot measures in 1998 (Proposition A) and 2000 (Proposition 1a) served to legitimize and strengthen California Indian gaming and permit its growth to what has become a multibillion-dollar industry.

Today there are six bands of Luiseño Indians living on independent reservations in southwestern Riverside and northwestern San Diego Counties: the

Pechanga Band in Temecula, Soboba Band near San Jacinto, Pauma Band in Pauma Valley, Rincon Band near Valley Center, La Jolla Band near Palomar, and the Old Pala Band at Pala Reservation. Each reservation currently maintains gaming operations, ranging in size from the large casino, hotel, and conference center at Pechanga to a small slot machine arcade at La Jolla. Estimated to have originally numbered 10,000, enrolled members of the six Luiseño bands currently number approximately 4,000 individuals, slightly more than half of whom reside on the reservations. At present, the six reservations encompass 37,248 acres of tribal land, as well as 3,179 allotted acres and 224 acres in fee lands. Gaming has permitted significant economic growth, allowing the Luiseño to offer tribal members benefits in the form of housing, education, health and social services, and, in many cases, generous monthly stipends. With the stability brought by gaming, each of the six Luiseño bands has sought economic diversity through developments ranging from agribusiness at Pauma to racetracks and a campground at La Jolla.

Each reservation is governed independently by a general council (or general membership), which is composed of all enrolled members over the age of 21. The general council or membership elects a tribal council, whose term is typically two years, and also establishes committees to oversee various tribal activities and projects. Several of the Luiseño bands have made it a priority to create cultural centers on the reservations that will educate tribal members, as well as the general public, about the tribe's cultural history. Although very few Luiseño individuals speak the traditional language, steps are being taken by many reservations to teach its members the language so that oral traditions are not lost. Among the Luiseño today there exists an abiding belief that through the economic foundation wrought by gaming and a return to traditional values, Luiseños will be able to build and plan a better life for their people. In the words of the Pechanga Band of Luiseño Indians, a new day has dawned.

—*Jean A. Keller*

See also CAHUILLA NATION; CUPEÑOS; GABRIELINO; TEMECULA, CALIFORNIA

Suggested Reading

Bean, L. J., and F. G. Shipek. "Luiseno." In *Handbook of North American Indians. Volume 8: California*, edited by Robert F. Heizer. Washington, DC: Smithsonian Institution, 1978.

Bean, W., and J. J. Rawls. *California: An Interpretive History.* New York: McGraw-Hill, 1983.

County of San Diego. *Update of Impacts of Tribal Economic Development Projects in San Diego County.* San Diego, CA: County of San Diego, 2003.

Holmes, E. W. *History of Riverside County.* Los Angeles: Historic Record, 1912.

Moratto, M. J. *California Archaeology.* San Diego, CA: Academic Press, 1984.

Oxendine, J. "The Luiseño Village During the Later Prehistoric Era." Ph.D. Dissertation, University of California, Riverside, 1983.

Sparkman, P. S. "The Culture of the Luiseno Indians." In *University of California Publications in American Archaeology and Ethnology* 8, no. 4 (1908).

Strong, W. D. "Aboriginal Society in Southern California." *University of California Publications in American Archaeology and Ethnology* 26 (1929).

⊞ LUMBER STRIKE OF 1917

See LOGGING

APPENDIX

Master Bibliography

1820–1870 Western Emigrant Trails: Historic Trails, Cutoffs, and Alternates. [Map]. Omaha, NE: Western Emigrant Trails Research Center, 1999.

"A Viper Is Nonetheless a Viper Wherever the Egg Is Hatched. So a Japanese-American . . . Grows Up to Be a Japanese, Not an American." *Los Angeles Times,* February 2, 1942.

Abajian, James. *Blacks and Their Contribution to the American West: A Bibliography and Union List of Library Holdings through 1970.* Boston: G. K. Hall, 1974.

Abbott, Carl. *Colorado: A History of the Centennial State.* Boulder: Colorado Associated University Press, 1976.

Abbott, Carl. *The Metropolitan Frontier: Cities in the Modern American West.* Tucson: University of Arizona Press, 1993.

Abbott, Carl, Stephen J. Leonard, and David McComb. *Colorado: A History of the Centennial State.* Boulder: Colorado Associate University Press, 1982.

Abelmann, Nancy, and John Lie. *Blue Dreams: Korean Americans and the Los Angeles Riots.* Cambridge, MA: Harvard University Press, 1997.

Accordino, John J. *Captives of the Cold War Economy: The Struggle for Defense Conversion in American Communities.* Westport, CT: Praeger, 2000.

Adams, Eleanor B., and France V. Scholes. "Books in New Mexico, 1598–1680." *New Mexico Historical Review* 17 (1942).

Adams, Samuel Hopkins. *The Harvey Girls.* Cleveland, OH: Random House, 1944.

Adler, Patricia. "Watts: From Suburb to Black Ghetto." Ph.D. Dissertation, University of Southern California, 1977.

"The African American Mosaic." Available from http://www.loc.gov/exhibits/african/afam010.html

Aginsky, Burt. "The Socio-Psychological Significance of Death among the Pomo." In *Native Californians: A Theoretical Retrospective,* edited by Lowell J. Bean and T. C. Blackburn. Menlo Park, CA: Ballena Press, 1976.

Agnew, Meaghan. "As the Crow Flies." *USC Trojan Family Magazine* (Summer 2002). Available from http://www.usc.edu

Air University Library Staff. "Base Realignment and Closures: PMCS Financial/Resource Topics." Available from http://www.au.af.mil/au/aul/bibs/brac/brac.htm

Akiyama, Kiyoma Henry. Interview by Arthur A. Hansen and Yasko Gamo [Interview no. 1751, transcript], June 10, 1982. Fullerton: California State University Fullerton Oral History Collection.

Alexander, Thomas G. *Mormons & Gentiles: A History of Salt Lake City.* Boulder, CO: Pruett Press, 1985.

"Alien Land Laws." Available from http://www.santacruzpl.org/history/ww2/9066/land.shtml

"Aliens Must Register First Week in February." *Cody Enterprise,* January 23, 1918.

Allen, Elsie. *Pomo Basketmaking: A Supreme Art for the Weaver.* Happy Camp, CA: Naturegraph, 1972.

Allen, Margaret Day. *Lewiston Country: An Armchair History.* Lewiston, ID: Nez Perce County Historical Society, 1990.

Altrocchi, Julia C. *The Old California Trail.* Caldwell, ID: The Caxton Printers, 1945.

American Enterprise Institute for Public Policy Research. *Military Base Closings: Benefits for Community Adjustment.* Washington, DC: American Enterprise Institute for Public Policy Research, 1977.

"The American Indian in the Great War: Real and Imagined." Available from http://raven.cc.ukans.edu/~ww_one/comment/camurat1.html

American National Biography. New York: Oxford University Press, 1999.

Andrist, Ralph. *The Long Death*. New York: Macmillan, 1974.

Angulo, Jaime de. "Pomo Creation Myth." *Journal of American Folklore* 48 (1935).

Ansari, Abdoulmaboud. "A Community in Progress: The First Generation of the Iranian Professional Middle-Class Immigrants in the United States." *International Review of Modern Sociology* 7 (1977).

Ansari, Abdoulmaboud. *Iranian Immigrants in the United States: A Case Study of Dual Marginality*. Millwood, NY: Associated Faculty Press, 1992.

Apodaca, Paul. "Tradition, Myth, and Performance of Cahuilla Bird Songs." Ph.D. Dissertation, University of California–Los Angeles, 1999.

Apostol, Jane. *Olive Percival, Los Angeles Author and Bibliophile*. Los Angeles: Department of Special Collections, University Research Library, University of California, 1992.

"Arapaho." *Columbia Encyclopedia*. 6th ed. New York: Columbia University Press, 2004.

Armor, Samuel. *History of Orange County, California: With Biographical Sketches of the Leading Men and Women of the County, Who Have Been Identified with the Growth and Development from the Early Days to the Present Time*. Los Angeles: Historic Record, 1911.

Arrington, Leonard J. *Great Basin Kingdom*. Lincoln: University of Nebraska Press, 1958.

Arrington, Leonard J. *History of Idaho*. Moscow: University of Idaho Press, and Boise: Idaho State Historical Society, 1994.

Arrington, Leonard J., and Wayne K. Hinton. "The Horn Silver Bonanza." In *The American West: A Reorientation*, edited by Gene M. Gressley. Laramie: University of Wyoming Publications, 1996.

Askari, Hossein, John T. Cummings, and Mehmet Isbudak. "Iran's Migration of Skilled Labor to the United States." *Iranian Studies* 10 (1977).

Associated Pioneers of the Territorial Days of California. *A Nation's Benefactor: Gen'l John A. Sutter: Memorial of His Life and Public Services, and an Appeal to Congress, to Citizens of California, and the People of the United States, by His Fellow Pioneers of California*. New York: Polydore Barnes, 1880.

Associated Press. "Peace Talks in Little Saigon." *Orange County Register*, May 5, 1989.

Athearn, Robert G. *In Search of Canaan: Black Migration to Kansas, 1879–1880*. Lawrence: The Regents Press of Kansas, 1978.

Austin, Mary. *The Lands of the Sun*. 2nd ed. Boston: Houghton Mifflin, 1927.

Avant Courier. "Gallatin County in 1878" [Pamphlet]. Bozeman, MT: Gallatin Historical Society Pioneer Museum vertical files (January 30, 1879).

Axtell, Horace P., and Margo Aragon. *A Little Bit of Wisdom: Conversations with a Nez Perce Elder*. Lewiston, ID: Confluence Press, 1997.

Ayers, Marion P. "A Study of Stress in Park City, Utah: A Community Impacted by Recreational Development." Ph.D. Dissertation, University of Utah, 1983.

Babcock, Barbara Allen. "Clara Shortridge Foltz: 'First Woman.'" *Arizona Law Review* 30 (1988).

Babcock, Barbara Allen. "Women Defenders in the West." *Nevada Law Journal* 1 (Spring 2001).

Bahr, Diana Meyers. *From Mission to Metropolis: Cupeño Indian Women in Los Angeles*. Norman: University of Oklahoma Press, 1993.

Baker, Hugh S. "Rational Amusement in Our Midst: Public Libraries in California, 1849–1859." *California Historical Society Quarterly* 38 (December 1959).

Bakken, Gordon M. *The Development of Law on the Rocky Mountain Frontier, 1850–1912*. Westport, CT: Greenwood Press, 1983.

Bakken, Gordon Morris, ed. *Law in the Western United States*. Norman: University of Oklahoma Press, 2000.

Bakken, Gordon Morris. "Lawyers in the American West, 1820–1920: A Comment." *Nevada Law Journal* 1 (Spring 2001).

Bakken, Gordon Morris. *Practicing Law in Frontier California*. Lincoln: University of Nebraska Press, 1991.

Bakken, Gordon M. *Surviving the North Dakota Depression*. Pasadena, CA: Wood & Jones, 1992.

Bamford, Lawrence. "Streets from Silver: Leadville's History through Its Built Environment." *Colorado Heritage* 4 (1987).

Bancroft, Hubert Howe. *History of California*. 7 vols. San Francisco: Bancroft Publishing, 1884–1890.

Bancroft, Hubert Howe. *History of California*. Vols. I–VII. Reprinted ed. Santa Barbara, CA: Wallace Hebberd, 1963–1970.

Bancroft, Hubert Howe. *History of the Pacific States of North America*. Vols. I–V. San Francisco: H. H. Bancroft, 1883–1891.

Bancroft, Hubert Howe. *History of Utah*. San Francisco: The History Company, 1889.

Bancroft, Hubert Howe. *The Works of Hubert Howe Bancroft, Vol. 4. History of California.* San Francisco: A. L. Bancroft, 1885.

Bancroft, Hubert Howe. *The Works of Hubert Howe Bancroft, Vol. 19. History of California, 1801–1824.* San Francisco: A. L. Bancroft, 1885.

Bancroft, Hubert Howe. *The Works of Hubert Howe Bancroft, Vol. 20. History of California, 1825–1840.* San Francisco: A. L. Bancroft, 1885.

Barker, Emily. "Start with Nothing." *Inc. Magazine* (February 2002).

Barker, Eugene. *The Life of Stephen F. Austin, Founder of Texas, 1793–1836. A Chapter of the Westward Movement of the Anglo-American People.* New York: Da Capo Press, 1968.

Barnett, Louise. *Touched by Fire.* New York: Henry Holt, 1996.

Barrett, Samuel, and Edward Gifford. "Indian Life of the Yosemite Region: Miwok Material Culture." *Bulletin of Milwaukee Public Museum* 2, no. 4 (March 1933).

Barseness, Larry S. *Gold Camp: Alder Gulch and Virginia City, Montana.* New York: Hastings House, 1962.

Barth, Gunther. *Instant Cities: Urbanization and the Rise of San Francisco and Denver.* New York: Oxford University Press, 1975.

Bartholomew, Becky. "Contemporary Ute Government Reflects Old Ways." Available from http://historytogo .utah.gov/utah_chapters/american_indians

Base Realignment and Closures Commission. *Defense Base Closure and Realignment Commission 1995 Report to the President.* Arlington, VA: Base Realignment and Closures Commission, 1995.

Bass, Charlotta A. *Forty Years: Memoirs from the Pages of a Newspaper.* Los Angeles: Charlotta A. Bass, 1960.

Bassett, Arthur R. "Culture and the American Frontier in Mormon Utah, 1850–1896." Ph.D. Dissertation, Syracuse University, 1975.

Bates, Beth Tompkins. *Pullman Porters and the Rise of Protest Politics in Black America, 1925–1945.* Chapel Hill: University of North Carolina Press, 2001.

Bates, Grace. *Gallatin County (Montana) Places and Things Present and Past.* Self-published, 1995.

Baumler, Ellen. "More than the Glory: Preserving the Gold Rush and Its Outcome at Virginia City." *Montana: The Magazine of Western History* 49 (1999).

Baumler, Ellen. "Temple Emanu-El: First Temple amidst the Rockies." *More from the Quarries of Last Chance Gulch Volume I.* Helena, MT: American and World Geographic, 1995.

Baumler, Ellen, ed. *Girl from the Gulches: The Story of Mary Ronan.* Helena: Montana Historical Society Press, 2003.

Baxter, Gavin H. *James Irvine II and the Irvine Ranch: As Remembered by Gavin H. Baxter, F.F. "Fay" Irwin, Thomas McBride.* Interviews by Jim Sleeper. Fullerton: California State University Fullerton Oral History Program, 1992.

Bean, Lowell. *Mukat's People: The Cahuilla Indians of Southern California.* Los Angeles: University of California Press, 1972.

Bean, Lowell J., and Florence C. Shipek. "Luiseño." In *Handbook of North American Indians, Volume 8: California,* edited by R. F. Heizer. Washington, DC: Smithsonian Institution, 1978.

Bean, Lowell, and Harry Lawton. *The Cahuilla Indians of Southern California.* Banning, CA: Malki Museum Press, 1989.

Bean, W., and J. J. Rawls. *California: An Interpretive History.* New York: McGraw-Hill, 1983.

Beasley, Delilah. *Negro Trail Blazers of California.* Los Angeles, 1919. (Reprinted New York: Negro Universities Press, 1969)

Beattie, G. W., and H. P. Beattie. *Heritage of the Valley: San Bernardino First Century.* Pasadena, CA: San Pasqual Press, 1939.

Bechdolt, Frederick. *Giants of the Old West.* Freeport, NY: Books for Libraries Press, 1930.

Bechdolt, Frederick R. *Giants of the Old West.* Freeport, NY: Century, 1969.

Beebe, Rose Marie, and Robert M. Senkewicz, eds. *Lands of Promise and Despair: Chronicles of Early California, 1535–1846.* Santa Clara, CA: Santa Clara University; Berkeley, CA: Heyday Books, 2001.

"Before Creek and Cherokee: The Colonial Transformation of Prehistoric Georgia." Available from http://members .aol.com/jeworth.gbotxt.htm

Belgrade Centennial Committee. *Belgrade, Montana: The First 100 Years.* Dallas, TX: Taylor, 1986.

Benedek, Emily. *The Wind Won't Know Me: A History of the Navajo-Hopi Land Dispute.* Norman: University of Oklahoma Press, 1992.

Benedetti, Umberto. *The Lifestyles of Italian Internees at Fort Missoula, Montana, 1941–1943.* Missoula: University of Montana Press, 1986.

"Benjamin D. Wilson, Report on California Indians, 1852." Available from http://ancestry.com/search/db.aspx? dbid=3864

"Benjamin 'Pap' Singleton." Available from http://www .pbs.org/weta/thewest/people/s_z/singleton.htm

Benson, Todd. *Race, Health, and Power: The Federal Government and American Indian Health, 1909–1955.* Ph.D. Dissertation, Stanford University, 1993.

Berger, Brian. *Los Angeles: Commemorating 200 Years.* Beaverton, OR: Beautiful America, 1980.

Berthrong, Donald J. *The Cheyenne and Arapaho Ordeal: Reservation and Agency Life in the Indian Territory.* Norman: University of Oklahoma Press, 1976.

Bestor, A. E., Jr. *David Jacks of Monterey, and Lee L. Jacks, His Daughter.* Stanford, CA: Stanford University Press, 1945.

Betts, Donnie. *Dearfield: The Road Less Traveled* [VHS]. No Credits Production, 1996.

Betts, Robert. *Along the Ramparts of the Tetons: The Saga of Jackson Hole.* Boulder: Colorado Associated University Press, 1978.

Bibb, Leland E. "The Location of the Indian Village of Temecula." *Journal of San Diego History* 18, no. 3 (1972).

Bidwell, General John. *Echoes of the Past.* New York: Citadel, 1962.

Biolsi, Thomas. *Organizing the Lakota: The Political Economy of the New Deal on the Pine Ridge and Rosebud Reservations.* Tucson: University of Arizona Press, 1992.

Blackburn, T. C., and Kat Anderson, eds. *Before the Wilderness: Environmental Management by Native Californians.* Menlo Park, CA: Ballena Press, 1993.

Blevins, Bruce H. *Park County, Wyoming: Facts and Maps through Time.* Powell, WY: WIM, 1999.

Block, G. K. "The Russian Colonies in California—A Russian Version." *Quarterly of the California Historical Society* 12 (1933).

"The Bluejacket." Available from http://www.nsamidsouth.navy.mil/publications/bluejacket/2002/bj021128.htm

BlueWater Resort and Casino [Home page]. Available from http://bluewaterfun.com

Boag, Peter G. *Environment and Experience: Settlement Culture in Nineteenth-Century Oregon.* Berkeley: University of California Press, 1992.

Bodnar, John. *The Transplanted: A History of Immigrants in Urban America.* Bloomington: Indiana University Press, 1985.

Bold, Kathryn. "O Little Saigon." *Los Angeles Times,* December 15, 1994.

Bolton, H. E. *Anza's California Expeditions.* Berkeley: University of California Press, 1930.

Bolton, H. E. "The Mission as a Frontier Institution in the Spanish American Colonies." *The American Historical Review* 23, no. 1 (1917–1918).

Bolton, Herbert Eugene. *Fray Juan Crespi: Missionary Explorer on the Pacific Coast, 1769–1771.* Berkeley: University of California Press, 1927.

Bolton, Roger E. *Defense Purchases and Regional Growth.* Washington, DC: The Brookings Institution, 1966.

Bonney, Orrin H., and Lorraine G. Bonney. *Guide to the Wyoming Mountains and Wilderness Areas.* 3rd rev. ed. Chicago: Swallow Press, 1977.

Boscana, Geronimo. *Chinigchinich: A Revised and Annotated Version of Alfred Robinson's Translation of Father Geronimo Boscana's Historical Account of the Belief, Usages, Customs, and Extravagances of the Indians of This Mission of San Juan Capistrano Called the Acagchemen Tribe.* Reprinted ed. Banning, CA: Malki Museum Press, 1978.

Bosworth, Allan R. *America's Concentration Camps.* New York: Norton, 1967.

Boulé, May Null. *Gabrielino Tribe.* Vashon, WA: Merryant, 1992.

Boussy, Henri M., with Edgar Sliney. *First Settlers—Reed and Richardson.* Mill Valley, CA: Mill Valley Historical Society, 1996.

Bowen, William A. *The Willamette Valley: Migration and Settlement on the Oregon Frontier.* Seattle: University of Washington Press, 1978.

Bowman, A. B. *Management Plan for the Kootenai Sustained Yield Unit: Kootenai National Forest Lincoln County, Montana 1946.* Washington, DC: U.S. Department of Agriculture and U.S. Forest Service, 1946.

Boye, Alan. *Holding Stone Hands: On the Trail of the Cheyenne Exodus.* Lincoln and London: University of Nebraska Press, 1999.

Boyne, U.S.A. "Big Sky Resort." Available from http://www.bigskyresort.com

Bozeman Area Chamber of Commerce. *1995 Visitors' Guide.* Bozeman, MT: Bozeman Area Chamber of Commerce, 1995.

Bozeman Area Chamber of Commerce. *2004 Visitors' Guide.* Bozeman, MT: Bozeman Area Chamber of Commerce, 2004.

Bozorgmehr, Mehdi. "Internal Ethnicity: Iranians in Los Angeles." *Sociological Perspectives* 40 (1997).

Bozorgmehr, Mehdi. "Iranians." In *Refugees in America in the 1990s,* edited by David Haines. Westport, CT: Greenwood Press, 1996.

Bozorgmehr, Mehdi, and Georges Sabagh. "Iranian Exiles and Immigrants in Los Angeles." In *Iranian Exiles and Refugees since Khomeini,* edited by Asghar Fathi. Costa Mesa, CA: Mazda, 1991.

Braatz, Timothy. "The Question of Regional Bands and Subtribes among the Preconquest Pai (Hualapai and Havasupai) Indians of Northwestern Arizona." *American Indian Quarterly* 22 (1998).

Braatz, Timothy. *Surviving Conquest: A History of the Yavapai Peoples.* Lincoln: University of Nebraska Press, 2003.

Bradley, Martha S. *A History of Kane County.* Salt Lake City: Utah Historical Society, Kane County Commission, 1996.

Bradley, Martha Sonntag. *A History of Beaver County.* Salt Lake City: Utah State Historical Society, 1999.

Bravo, Leonore M. *Rabbit Skin Blanket: About the Washo of the Eastern Sierra Nevada and Their Neighbors, the Paiute.* Ann Arbor, MI: Braun-Brumfield, 1991.

Brazeal, Brailsford Reese. *The Brotherhood of Sleeping Car Porters: Its Origin and Development.* New York: Harper, 1946.

Braziel, Jana Evans. "History of Migration and Immigration Laws in the United States." Available from http://www.umass.edu/complit/aclanet/USMigrat.html

Breese, Gerald, et al. *The Impact of Large Installations on Nearby Areas: Accelerated Urban Growth.* Beverly Hills, CA: Sage, 1965.

Breschini, Gary S., Trudy Haversat, and R. Paul Hampson. *Cultural Resources Survey: Upper Santa Ana River, California.* Pacific Palisades, CA: Greenwood and Associates, 1988.

Bricken, Gordon. *The Civil War Legacy in Santa Ana.* Tustin, CA: Wilson/Barnett, 2002.

Brigandi, Phil. *Temecula: At the Crossroads of History.* Encinitas, CA: Heritage Media, 1998.

Brimlow, George. "The Life of Sarah Winnemucca: The Formative Years." *Oregon Historical Quarterly* 53 (1952).

Broom, Leonard, and Ruth Rienera. *Removal and Return: The Socio-economic Impact of the War on Japanese Americans.* Berkeley: University of California Press, 1974.

Brosnan, Kathleen A. *Uniting Mountain and Plain: Cities, Law, and Environmental Change along the Front Range.* Albuquerque: University of New Mexico Press, 2002.

Brown, Charlice J. *Someone Should Remember: Frisco, Utah, Horn Silver Mine.* Cedar City, UT: The Print Shoppe, 1996.

Brown, Henry M. *Mineral King Country.* Fresno, CA: Pioneer, 1988.

Brown, Ian. *Khomeini's Forgotten Sons: The Story of Iran's Boy Soldiers.* London: Grey Seal, 1990.

Brown, James T. *Harvest of the Sun: An Illustrated History of Riverside County.* Northridge, CA: Windsor, 1985.

Brown, John H. *Early Days of San Francisco.* Oakland, CA: Biobooks, 1949.

Brown, Robert L. *The Great Pike's Peak Gold Rush.* Caldwell, ID: Caxton Press, 1985.

Brown, S. Kent, Donald Q. Cannon, and Richard H. Jackson, eds. *Historical Atlas of Mormonism.* New York: Simon & Schuster, 1994.

Brown, Vinson, and Douglas Andrews. *The Pomo Indians of California and Their Neighbors.* Happy Camp, CA: Naturegraph, 1969.

Brumgardt, John R., and Larry L. Bowles. *People of the Magic Waters: The Cahuilla of Palm Springs.* Palm Springs, CA: ETC, 1981.

Bryant, Keith L., Jr. *History of the Atchison, Topeka and Santa Fe Railway.* Lincoln: University of Nebraska Press, 1982.

Buchanan, Frederick S. *Culture Clash and Accommodation: Public Schooling in Salt Lake City, 1890–1994.* Salt Lake City, UT: Signature Books, 1996.

Bulbulian, Berge. *History of a Diaspora Community.* Fresno: The Press at the California State University, 2000.

Bullchild, Percy. *The Sun Came Down: The History of the World as My Blackfeet Elders Told It.* San Francisco: Harper & Row, 1985.

Bundy, Mary Lee, and Frederick J. Stielow, eds. *Activism in American Librarianship, 1962–1973.* New York: Greenwood Press, 1987.

Bunting, Robert. *The Pacific Raincoast: Environment and Culture in an American Eden, 1778–1900.* Lawrence: University of Kansas Press, 1997.

Bureau of Sociological Research, Colorado River War Relocation Center. "The Japanese Family in America." *Annals of the American Academy of Political and Social Science* 229 (September 1943).

Burlingame, Merrill. *Gallatin Century of Progress.* Bozeman, MT: Gallatin County Centennial Publications, 1964.

Burlingame, Merrill G. *Gallatin County's Heritage: A Report of Progress, 1805–1976.* Bozeman, MT: Gallatin County Centennial Publications, 1977.

Burmeister, Eugene. *City along the Kern: Bakersfield, California, 1869–1969.* Bakersfield, CA: Kern Publishing, 1969.

Burns, Roger. *Desert Honky-Tonk: The Story of Tombstone's Bird Cage Theatre.* Golden, CO: Fulcrum, 2000.

Burrill, Richard. *River of Sorrows.* Happy Camp, CA: Naturegraph, 1988.

Burrows, Jack. *Black Sun of the Miwok.* Albuquerque: University Press of New Mexico, 2000.

Burt, Nathaniel. *Jackson Hole Journal.* Norman: University of Oklahoma Press, 1983.

Burton, Doris K. *A History of Uintah County.* Salt Lake City: Utah Historical Society, Uintah County Commission, 1996.

Cairns, Kathleen A. *Front-Page Women Journalists, 1920–1950.* Lincoln: University of Nebraska Press, 2003.

Caldwell, George W. *Legends of Southern California.* San Francisco: Phillips and Van Orden, 1919.

California Agriculture and Industry State Chamber of Commerce. *Summary of Stanford Research Institute Report on California's Economy, 1947–1980.* San Francisco: California State Chamber of Commerce, 1961.

California Department of Commerce, Department of Finance, Budget Division, Financial and Population Research Section. *California Migration 1955–1960: Age Distribution of 1955–1960 California Migrant Population.* Sacramento, 1964.

California Department of Commerce, Office of Economic Research. *The Aerospace Industry in California.* Sacramento, 1988.

California Department of Economic and Business Development, Office of Economic Policy, Planning, and Research. *The Aerospace Industry in California.* Sacramento, 1981.

California Department of Economic and Business Development, Office of Economic Policy, Planning, and Research. *The Effect of Increase Military Spending in California.* Sacramento, 1982.

"California Indians." Available from http://allianceofcatribes .org/californiaindians.htm

Calkins, Frank. *Jackson Hole.* New York: Knopf, 1973.

Calloway, Colin G. *The American Revolution in Indian Country.* Cambridge, UK: Cambridge University Press, 1995.

Campbell, Eugene E. *Establishing Zion: The Mormon Church in the American West, 1847–69.* Salt Lake City, UT: Signature Books, 1988.

Campbell, Hardy Webster. *Campbell's 1907 Soil Culture Manual,* Lincoln, NE: H. W. Campbell, 1907.

Canfield, Gae W. *Sarah Winnemucca of the Northern Paiutes.* Norman: University of Oklahoma Press, 1983.

Cano, Debra. "Program Addresses Needs of Amerasians." *Orange County Register,* January 29, 1994.

Cantrell, Greg. *Stephen F. Austin, Empresario of Texas.* New Haven, CT: Yale University Press, 1968.

Cao, Lan, and Himilce Novas. *Everything You Need to Know about Asian American History.* New York: Plume/ Penguin, 1996.

Carlson, Paul H. *The Plains Indians.* College Station: Texas A&M University Press, 1998.

Carpenter, Edmund J. *America in Hawaii: A History of United States Influence in the Hawaiian Islands.* Boston: Small, Maynard, 1899.

Carr, Stephen L. *The Historical Guide to Utah Ghost Towns.* Salt Lake City, UT: Western Epics, 1972.

Carrico, Richard L. *Strangers in a Stolen Land: American Indians in San Diego, 1850–1880.* Sacramento, CA: Sierra Oaks, 1987.

Carroll, Peter N., and David A. Horowitz. *On the Edge: The U.S. in the 20th Century.* New York: West/Wadsworth, 1998.

Carson, Phil. *Across the Northern Frontier.* Boulder, CO: Johnson Books, 1998.

Carvajal, Doreen, "Big Sigh in Little Saigon as New Reality Sinks In." *Orange County Register,* February 4, 1994.

Castel, Albert. *General Sterling Price and the Civil War in the West.* Baton Rouge: Louisiana State University Press, 1968.

Castillo, Edward D. "Blood Came from Their Mouths: Tongva and Chumash Responses to the Pandemic of 1801." *American Indian Culture and Research Journal* 23, no. 3 (1999).

Castillo, Edward D. "Gender Status Decline, Resistance, and Accommodation among Female Neophytes in the Missions of California: A San Gabriel Case Study." *American Indian Culture and Research Journal* 18, no. 1 (1994).

Castro, Doris Shaw. *California Colony: Genealogy, Land Grants, & Notes of Spanish Colonial California.* Bloomington, IN: AuthorHouse, 2004.

Cau, Nguyen. Interview by Trangdai Tranguyen. October 13, 2000. Fremont, California.

Caughey, John Walton. *McGillivray of the Creeks.* Norman: University of Oklahoma Press, 1959.

Caughey, John, and LaRee Caughey. *Los Angeles: Biography of a City.* Berkeley: University of California Press, 1977.

"Census Report." Available from http://www.census.gov/ population/socdemo/race/indian/ailang1.txt

"Center Gets 1246 Japs from South," *Los Angeles Times,* April 9, 1942.

Chalfant, W. A. *Gold, Guns & Ghost Towns.* Stanford, CA: Stanford University Press, 1947.

Chalfant, W. A. *The Story of Inyo.* Chicago: Author, 1922.

Chalfant, W. A. *Tales of the Pioneers.* Stanford, CA: Stanford University Press, 1942.

Chamness, Lee, Jr. Interview with John Sprout [Interview no. 78, transcript], November 25, 1968. Fullerton: California State University Fullerton Oral History Collection.

Chan, Sucheng. *Asian Americans: An Interpretative History.* New York: Twayne, 1991.

Chapman, Charles. *A History of California: The Spanish Period.* New York: Macmillan, 1921.

Charlotta A. Bass Papers. Los Angeles: Southern California Library for Social Studies and Research.

Chateauvert, Melinda. *Marching Together: Women of the Brotherhood of Sleeping Car Porters.* Urbana: University of Illinois Press, 1998.

Chaudhuri, Joyotpaul. *Urban Indians of Arizona: Phoenix, Tucson, and Flagstaff.* Tucson: University of Arizona Press, 1974.

Chen, Yong. *Chinese San Francisco, 1850–1943: A Trans-Pacific Community.* Stanford, CA: Stanford University Press, 2000.

Cheney, Roberta Carkeek. *Names on the Face of Montana.* Missoula, MT: Mountain Press Publishing, 1983.

Cheverton, Richard. "Saigon's' Skin-Deep Sketch." *Orange County Register,* October 28, 1988.

"Cheyenne and Arapaho Tribes of Oklahoma Constitution and By-Laws." Available from http://thorpe.ou.edu/constitution/Chyn_aph.html

Chin, Frank. *Born in the USA: A Story of Japanese America, 1889–1947.* New York: Rowman & Littlefield, 2002.

Christiansen, Wayne S. "Frisco: Wildest Camp in Utah." *Old West Magazine* 21, no. 1 (1984).

Christman, Albert B. *Sailors, Scientists, and Rockets—Origins of the Navy Rocket Program and the Naval Ordnance Test Station, Inyokern.* Vol. 1 of *History of the Naval Weapons Center, China Lake, California.* Washington, DC: U.S. Government Printing Office, Navy History Division, 1971.

Chuman, Frank F. *The Bamboo People: The Law and Japanese-Americans.* Del Mar, CA: Publisher's Inc., 1976.

Churchill, Gail Beryl. *Dams, Ditches and Water.* Cody, WY: Rustler, 1979.

Churchill-Amsterdam Historical Society. *A Goodly Heritage: A History of the Churchill and Amsterdam Area of Montana.* Billings, MT: Churchill-Amsterdam Historical Society, 1989.

City of Irvine. "History of the City." Available from http://www.cityofirvine.org/about/history.asp

"City of Lincoln and Lancaster County." Available from http://ci.lincoln.ne.us

City of San Diego City Clerk's Office. "A History of San Diego Government." Available from http://www.sandiego.gov/city-clerk/history.shtml

Clairmonte, Glenn. *John Sutter of California.* New York: Thomas Nelson & Sons, 1954.

Clark, Blue. "Bury My Heart in Smog: Urban Indians." In *"They Made Us Many Promises": The American Indian Experience 1524 to the Present.* 2nd ed., edited by Philip Weeks. Wheeling, IL: Harlan Davidson, 2002.

Clark, Dennis. *Hibernia America: The Irish and Regional Cultures.* Westport, CT: Greenwood Press, 1986.

Clark, Jane Perry. *Deportation of Aliens from the United States to Europe.* New York: AMS Press, 1968. First published 1931 by Columbia University Press.

Clark, Lynda C. *Nampa, Idaho, 1885–1985: A Journey of Discovery.* Nampa, ID: Pacific Press, 1985.

Clark, Thomas R. *Defending Rights: Law, Labor Politics, and the State in California, 1890–1925.* Detroit, MI: Wayne State University Press, 2002.

Cleland, Robert. *The Cattle on a Thousand Hills.* San Marino, CA: Huntington Library and Art Gallery, 1951.

Cleland, Robert Glass. *From Wilderness to Empire: A History of California, 1542–1900.* New York: Alfred A. Knopf, 1944.

Cleland, Robert Glass. *The Irvine Ranch.* 3rd ed. Pasadena, CA: Huntington Library Press, 2003.

Clement, Richard W. *Books on the Frontier: Print Culture in the American West, 1763–1875.* Washington, DC: Library of Congress, 2003.

Clements, Eric L. *After the Boom in Tombstone and Jerome, Arizona.* Reno: University of Nevada Press, 2003.

Clemmer, Richard O. *Roads in the Sky: The Hopi Indians in a Century of Change.* Boulder, CO: Westview Press, 1995.

Clendenen, Clarence C. "Dan Showalter—California Secessionist." *California Historical Society Quarterly* 40, no. 4 (1961).

Cohen, Warren I. *America's Response to China: A History of Sino-American Relations.* 4th ed. New York: Columbia University Press, 2000.

Cole, Tom. *A Short History of San Francisco.* San Francisco: Lexikos, 1981.

Coleman, Julie. *Golden Opportunities: A Biographical History of Montana's Jewish Communities.* Helena, MT: Skyhouse, 1994.

Collins, Donald E. *Native American Aliens: Disloyalty and the Renunciation of Citizenship by Japanese Americans during World War II.* Westport, CT: Greenwood Press, 1985.

Collins, Jeff, and Katherine Nguyen. "Little Saigon Stores Accused of Illegal Pharmaceutical Sales." *Orange County Register,* July 10, 2002.

Colorado River Indian Tribes Public Library/Archive Web Site. Available from http://critlibrary.com

Comer, Douglas C. *Ritual Ground: Bent's Old Fort, World Formation, and the Annexation of the Southwest.* Berkeley: University of California Press, 1996.

Committee for Economic Development, Research and Policy Committee. *The Economy and National Defense: Adjusting to Military Cutbacks in the Post–Cold War Era.* New York: Committee for Economic Development, 1991.

Congregation Or HaTzafon. "Temple History Or HaTzafon: A Profile." Available from http://www.mosquitonet .com/~orhatzafon/history.htm#temple

Congressional Record. 77th Cong., 1st sess, 1941. p. A5554.

Conrat, Maisie, and Richard Conrat. *Executive Order 9066.* Van Nuys: University of California, Los Angeles, Asian American Studies Center, 1992.

Constitution of the Fort Belknap Indian Community of the Fort Belknap Reservation, Montana. Available from http://www.tribalresourcecenter.org/ccfolder/fort_belk nap_const.htm

Cook, Jeannie, Johnson Lynn Houze, Bob Edgar, and Paul Fees. *Buffalo Bill's Town in the Rockies: A Pictorial History of Cody, Wyoming.* Virginia Beach, VA: Donning, 1996.

Cook, Sherburne F. *The Population of California Indians, 1769–1970.* Berkeley: University of California Press, 1976.

Cooper, Marc. *The Last Honest Place in America.* New York: Nation Books, 2004.

Cordell, Linda S. *Prehistory of the Southwest.* Orlando, FL: Academic Press, 1984.

Corkran, David H. *The Creek Frontier, 1540–1783.* Norman: University of Oklahoma Press, 1967.

Costo, Rupert, and Jeanette H. Costo. *Natives of the Golden State: The California Indians.* San Francisco: The Indian Historian Press, 1995.

Coues, E. *On the Trail of a Spanish Pioneer: The Diary of Francisco Garces.* New York: Harper, 1900.

County of San Diego. *Update of Impacts of Tribal Economic Development Projects in San Diego County.* San Diego, CA: County of San Diego, 2003.

Courlander, Harold. *The Fourth World of the Hopi: The Epic Story of the Hopi Indians as Preserved in Their Legends and Traditions.* Albuquerque: University of New Mexico Press, 1971.

Cowan, Robert. *Ranchos of California: A List of Spanish Concessions 1775–1822 and Mexican Grants 1822– 1846.* Los Angeles: Historical Society of Southern California, 1977.

Cox, Thomas C. *Blacks in Topeka: A Social History, 1865– 1915.* Baton Rouge: Louisiana State University Press, 1982.

Cozzens, Peter. *General John Pope: A Life for the Nation.* Urbana: University of Illinois Press, 2000.

Cramer, Esther, et al., eds. *A Hundred Years of Yesterdays: A Centennial History of the People of Orange County and Their Communities.* Santa Ana, CA: The Orange County Centennial, 1988.

Craver, Rebecca M. C. *The Impact of Intimacy: Mexican-American Intermarriage in New Mexico, 1821–1846.* El Paso: Texas Western Press, 1982.

Cray, Ed. *Levi's.* Boston: Houghton Mifflin, 1978.

"Creek Indians." Available from http://www.rra.dst.txt .us/c_t/indians/CREEK%20INDIANS.cfm

Cronin, Janet, and Dorothy Vick. *Montana's Gallatin Canyon.* Missoula, MT: Matain Press, 1988.

Crouchett, Lawrence, Lonnie Bunch, III, and Martha K. Winnaker, eds. *Visions toward Tomorrow: The History of the East Bay Afro-American Community, 1852– 1977.* Oakland: Northern California Center for Afro-American History and Life, 1989.

"Crow." *Columbia Encyclopedia.* 6th ed. New York: Columbia University Press, 2004.

Crow Dog, Mary, and Richard Erdoes. *Lakota Woman.* New York: Grove Weidenfeld, 1995.

"Crow Seek Investors for Power Plant." *Billings Gazette,* June 22, 2004. Available from http://www.billingsgazette .com

"Crow Tribal Constitution." Available from http://www .tribalresourcecenter.org

"Crow Tribal Government Today." *Library@Little Big Horn College.* Little Big Horn College, 2002. Available from http://lib.lbhc.cc.mt.us

"Crow Tribe of Montana." FEMA Region VIII Tribal Lands Web Page. Available from http://www.fema.gov/ regions/viii/tribal/crowbg.shtm

Crow Tribe Official Web Site. Available from http://tlc .wtp.net/crow.htm

Crowder, David Lester. *Rexburg, Idaho: The First One Hundred Years, 1883–1983.* Rexburg, ID: D. L. Crowder, 1983.

Croy, Homer. *Wheels West.* New York: Hastings House, 1955.

Cuellar, Carlos E. *Stories from the Barrio: A History of Mexican Fort Worth.* Fort Worth: Texas Christian University Press, 2003.

Cullen, Ann. *Lilly Cullen: Helena, Montana 1894.* Missoula: Book Montana, 1999.

D'Azevedo, Warren L. *Straight with the Medicine: Narratives of the Washoe Followers of the Tipi Way.* Reno, NV: Black Rock Press, 1978. (Reprinted Berkeley, CA: Heyday Books, 1985)

D'Azevedo, Warren L. "Washoe." In *The Handbook of North American Indians,* edited by William Sturtevant. Washington, DC: Smithsonian Institution, 1986.

Dakin, Susanna Bryant. *The Lives of William Hartnell.* Stanford, CA: Stanford University Press, 1949.

Dakin, Susanna Bryant. *A Scotch Paisano in Old Los Angeles: Hugo Reid's Life in California, 1832–1852, Derived from His Correspondence.* Berkeley: University of California Press, 1939.

Dallalfar, Arlene. "The Iranian Ethnic Economy in Los Angeles: Gender and Entrepreneurship." In *Family and Gender among American Muslims*, edited by Barbara Aswad and Barbara Bilge. Philadelphia: Temple University Press, 1996.

Dana, Julian. *Sutter of California: A Biography.* New York: The Press of the Pioneers, 1934.

Dana, Richard Henry. *Two Years before the Mast: A Personal Narrative.* New York: Harper and Brothers, 1840.

Daniel, Cletus E. *Bitter Harvest.* Ithaca, NY: Cornell University Press, 1981.

Daniels, Roger. *Asian America: Chinese and Japanese in the United States since 1850.* Seattle: University of Washington Press, 1988.

Daniels, Roger. *Coming to America: A History of Immigration and Ethnicity in American Life.* 2nd ed. New York: Perennial, 2002.

Daniels, Roger. *Guarding the Golden Door.* New York: Hill and Wang, 2004.

Daniels, Roger. *Not Like Us: Immigrants and Minorities in America, 1890–1924.* Chicago: Ivan R. Dee, 1997.

Daniels, Roger. *The Politics of Prejudice: The Anti-Japanese Movement in California and the Struggle for Japanese Exclusion.* Berkeley: University of California Press, 1977.

Daniels, Roger, Sandra C. Taylor, and Harry H. L. Kitano. *Japanese Americans: From Relocation to Redress.* Ogden: University of Utah Press, 1986.

Danky, James P., ed. *The African-American Newspapers and Periodicals: A National Bibliography and Union List.* Cambridge, MA: Harvard University Press, 1999.

Dary, David. *Entrepreneurs of the Old West.* Al M. Napoletano, illus. New York: Knopf, 1986.

Daugherty, John A. *Jackson Hole: The Historic Resource Study of Grand Teton National Park.* Moose, WY: National Park Service, 1999.

Daugherty, Richard D. *The Yakima People.* Series edited by John I. Griffin. Phoenix, AZ: Indian Tribal Series, 1973.

Daughters of Utah Pioneers. *Pioneers Mills and Milling.* Grand County: Daughters of Utah Pioneers, 1983.

Davis, Clark. *Company Men: White Collar Life and Corporate Cultures in Los Angeles, 1892–1941.* Baltimore, MD: Johns Hopkins University Press, 2000.

Davis, Donald G., Jr. "The Rise of the Public Library in Texas, 1876–1920." In *Milestones to the Present: Papers from the Library History Seminar V*, edited by Harold Goldstein. Syracuse, NY: Gaylord, 1978.

Davis, Marianna W., ed. *Contributions of Black Women to America.* 2 vols. Columbia, SC: Kenday Press, 1982.

Davis, Robert Murray. *The Ornamental Hermit: People and Places in the New West.* Lubbock: Texas Tech University Press, 2004.

Davis, William Heath. *Seventy-Five Years in California.* San Francisco: John Howell, 1929.

De Graaf, Lawrence B. "Negro Migration to Los Angeles, 1930–1950." Ph.D. Dissertation, University of California–Los Angeles, 1962.

De La Teja, Jesus F. *San Antonio de Bexar: A Community on New Spain's Northern Frontier.* Albuquerque: University of New Mexico Press, 1995.

De Leon, Arnoldo. *Mexican Americans in Texas: A Brief History.* Arlington Heights, IL: Harlan Davidson, 1993.

De Nevers, Klancy Clark. *The Colonel and the Pacifist: Karl Bendetsen, Perry Saito, and the Incarceration of Japanese Americans during World War II.* Salt Lake City: University of Utah Press, 2004.

Debo, Angie. *The Road to Disappearance.* Norman: University of Oklahoma Press, 1941.

DeClercq, John H. "A History of Rohnert Park." Available from http://libweb.sonoma.edu/regional/subject/rohnert.html

Del Sagrario Ramirez, Maria. "The 1950s Operation Wetback a la 1990s." *Arizona Daily Wildcat*, December 5, 1997. Available from http://wildcat.arizona.edu/papers/91/71/04_3_m.html

Dellums, Ronald V., and H. Lee Halterman. *Lying Down with the Lions: A Public Life from the Streets of Oakland to the Halls of Power.* Boston: Beacon, 2000.

DeMallie, Raymond J., and William C. Sturtevant, eds. *Handbook of North American Indians. Volume 13: Plains.* Washington, DC: Smithsonian Institution, 2001.

"Denton-Rawhide." Available from http://www.pacrim-mining.com/s/Denton-Rawhide.asp

"Denton-Rawhide Mine." Available from http://www.kennecottminerals.com

DeQuille, Dan. *The Big Bonanza.* New York: Knopf, 1947.

Der-Martirosian, Claudia. "Economic Embeddedness and Social Capital of Immigrants: Iranians in Los Angeles." Ph.D. Dissertation, University of California, Los Angeles, 1996.

Deverell, William, and Tom Sitton, eds. *California Progressivism Revisited.* Berkeley: University of California Press, 1994.

DeWitt, J. L. *Final Report: Japanese Evacuation from the West Coast, 1942.* Washington, DC: U.S. Government Printing Office, 1943.

Dezell, Maureen. *Irish America: Coming into Clover: The Evolution of a People and a Culture.* New York: Doubleday, 2000.

Dillon, Richard. *Fool's Gold: The Decline and Fall of Captain John Sutter of California.* New York: Coward-McCann, 1967.

Dillow, Gordon. "Tet in Ho Chi Minh City." *Orange County Register,* January 31, 1995.

Dillow, Gordon, et al. "One Family Two Worlds." *Orange County Register,* January 29, 1995.

Dilsaver, Larry M. "After the Gold Rush." *Geographical Review* 75 (January 1985).

Dinar, Joshua. *Denver Then and Now.* San Francisco: Thunder Bay Press, 2002.

Dirlik, Arlif, ed. *Chinese on the American Frontier.* New York: Rowman & Littlefield, 2001.

DiStasi, Lawrence, ed. *Una Storia Segreta: The Secret History of Italian American Evacuation and Internment during World War II.* Berkeley, CA: Heyday Books, 2001.

Do, Anh. "Anger and Delight Mark Tet in O.C." *Orange County Register,* February 6, 1994.

Do, Anh. "Emerging Markets." *Orange County Register,* October 4, 1999.

Do, Anh. "Little Saigon Is the Big Question." *Orange County Register,* May 13, 2002.

Do, Anh. "Nailing Down a Future Wherever It May Be." *Orange County Register,* October 25, 1999.

Do, Anh. "Register Columnists Will Focus on O.C.'s Vietnamese Society." *Orange County Register,* November 4, 1999.

Do, Anh. "Rock-n-Vote Drums Up Vietnamese Voters." *Orange County Register,* October 18, 1999.

Do, Anh. "Songs for a Troubadour—His Songs in Their Hearts—Pham Duy: Work to Be Done." *Orange County Register,* May 23, 2002.

Do, Anh. "Soy Factory Also a Symbol for the Little Saigon–Factory: Customers Come from All over for Soy Products." *Orange County Register,* September 17, 2002.

Do, Anh. "Vietnamese Have Plenty to Choose from Today." *Orange County Register,* February 5, 1994.

Do, Anh. "Vietnamese Verite." *Orange County Register,* June 7, 1999.

Do, Anh. "We Can All Learn from These Four Students—Vietscape: A Better Life." *Orange County Register,* June 24, 2002.

Do, Quyen. "Keeping the Faith." *Orange County Register,* August 20, 1994.

Dominic, Gloria. *Coyote and the Grasshoppers: A Pomo Legend* (Native American Legends & Lore). Las Vegas, NV: Sagebrush, 1999.

Donahue, Debra L. *The Western Range Revisited: Removing Livestock from Public Lands to Conserve Native Biodiversity.* Norman: University of Oklahoma Press, 1999.

Douglas, Donald M. "Forgotten Zions: Jewish Agricultural Colonies in Kansas in the 1880s." *Kansas History: A Journal of the Central Plains* 16 (Summer 1993).

Douglass, William A., and Jon Bilbao. *Amerikanuak: Basques in the New World.* Reno: University of Nevada Press, 1975.

Douglass, William A., and Richard Etulain. *Basque Americans: A Guide to Information Sources.* Detroit, MI: Gale Research, 1981.

Dowie, James Iverne. *Prairie Grass Dividing.* Rock Island, IL: Augustana Historical Society, 1959.

Downey, Lynn. *501: This Is a Pair of Levi's Jeans: The Official History of the Levi's Brand.* San Francisco: Levi Strauss, 1995.

Downs, James F. *The Two Worlds of the Washo, an Indian Tribe of California and Nevada.* New York: Holt, Rinehart, and Winston, 1966.

Drachman, Roy. *From Cowtown to Desert Metropolis: Ninety Years of Arizona Memories.* San Francisco: Whitewing Press, 1999.

Driggs, Howard R. "The Utah Library-Gymnasium Movement." *Improvement Era* 12 (1909).

Drinnon, Richard. *Keeper of Concentration Camps: Dillon S. Myer and American Racism.* Berkeley: University of California Press, 1987.

Dubofsky, Melvyn. *We Shall Be All: A History of the Industrial Workers of the World.* Chicago: Quadrangle Books, 1969.

Dunbar, Seymour, ed. *The Fort Sutter Papers, Together with Historical Commentaries Accompanying Them, Brought Together in One Volume for Purposes of Reference.* New York: Edward Eberstadt & Sons, 1922.

Duniway, Abigail Scott. *Path Breaking: An Autobiographical History of the Equal Suffrage Movement in Pacific Coast States.* 2nd ed. Portland, OR: James, Kerns & Abbott, 1914.

Durand, Jorge, Douglas S. Massey, and Emilio A. Parrado. "The New Era of Mexican Migration to the United States: Rethinking History and the Nation-State:

Mexico and the United States as a Case Study." *Journal of American History* 86, no. 2 (1999).

Durrenberger, Robert, Leonard Pitt, and Richard Preston. *The San Fernando Valley: A Bibliography and Research*. Northridge, CA: San Fernando Valley State College Center for Urban Studies and Bureau of Business, 1967.

Eagle, Sonia Jacqueline. *Work and Play among the Basques of Southern California*. Ph.D. Dissertation, Purdue University, 1979.

Eargle, Dolan H. *The Earth Is Our Mother: A Guide to the Indians of California, Their Locales and Historic Sites*. San Francisco: Tress, 1986.

Ehle, John. *Trail of Tears: The Rise and Fall of the Cherokee Nation*. New York: Doubleday Press, 1988.

Eldrege, Zoeth Skinner. *The Beginnings of San Francisco from the Expedition of Anza, 1774 to the City Charter of April 15, 1850*. Vol. I. New York: John C. Rankin, 1912.

Elliot, Russel R. *Servant of Power: A Political Biography of Senator William M. Stewart*. Reno: University of Nevada Press, 1983.

Elliot, Wallace B. *History of San Bernardino and San Diego Counties*. San Francisco: W. W. Elliott, 1883. (Reprinted Riverside, CA: Riverside Museum Press, 1965)

Elliott, Russell R. *History of Nevada*. 2nd ed., revised. Lincoln: University of Nebraska Press, 1987.

Elliott, Russell R. *Nevada's Twentieth-Century Mining Boom: Tonopah, Goldfield, Ely*. Reno: University of Nevada Press, 1966.

Elliott, Wallace. *History of San Bernardino County California with Illustrations*. San Francisco: Elliott, 1883. (Reprinted Riverside, CA: Riverside Museum Press, 1965)

Elliott-Scheinberg, Wendy. *Boyle Heights: Jewish Ambiance in a Multi-Cultural Neighborhood*. Ph.D. Dissertation, Claremont Graduate School, 2001.

Ellis, Jerry. *Walking the Trail: One Man's Journey along the Cherokee Trail of Tears*. New York: Delacorte Press, 1991.

Ellsworth, Ted. *Employment Problems in the Defense Industry: Proceedings of a Conference on Economic Security in the Aerospace and Defense Related Industry in California*. Los Angeles: University of California–Los Angeles, Institute of Industrial Relations, 1970.

Emmerich, Lisa. "'Right in the Midst of My Own People': Native American Women and the Field Matron Program." *American Indian Quarterly* 15 (Spring 1991).

Emmons, David. *The Butte Irish: Class and Ethnicity in an American Mining Town, 1875–1925*. Urbana: University of Illinois Press, 1990.

Endo, Aiko Tanimachi. Interview with Marsha Bode [Interview no. 1750, transcript], November 15, 1983. Fullerton: California State University Fullerton Oral History Collection.

Engelhardt, Fr. Zephyrin. *Missions and Missionaries of California, Vol. 8. Upper California*. San Francisco: James H. Barry, 1913.

Engelhardt, Fr. Zephyrin, O.F.M. *San Fernando Rey: The Mission of the Valley*. Chicago: Franciscan Herald Press, 1927.

Engelhardt, Fr. Zephyrin, O.F.M. *San Gabriel Mission and the Beginning of Los Angeles*. Chicago: Franciscan Herald Press, 1927.

Erie, Steven P. *Rainbow's End: Irish-Americans and the Dilemmas of Urban Machine Politics, 1840–1985*. Berkeley: University of California Press, 1988.

Esmeralda County, NV, Web Site. Available from http://www.accessesmeralda.com

Esthus, Raymond A. *Theodore Roosevelt and Japan*. Seattle: University of Washington Press, 1966.

Ethington, Philip J. *The Public City: The Political Construction of Urban Life in San Francisco, 1850–1900*. Cambridge, UK: Cambridge University Press, 1994.

Ethridge, Robbie. *Creek Country: The Creek Indians and Their World*. Chapel Hill: University of North Carolina Press, 2003.

Etter, Patricia. *To California on the Southern Route: A History and Annotated Bibliography*. Spokane, WA: Arthur H. Clark, 1998.

Etulain, Richard W., ed. *Basques of the Pacific Northwest*. Pocatello: Idaho State University Press, 1991.

Etulain, Richard W., and Jeronima Echeverria. *Portraits of Basques in the New World*. Reno: University of Nevada Press, 1999.

Evans, J. R. *Location and Patenting of Mining Claims and Mill Sites in California*. Sacramento, CA: U.S. Department of the Interior, Bureau of Land Management, 2002.

Evans, Martin C. "Catch of Day from Vietnam." *Orange County Register*, December 27, 1994.

Evans, Martin C. "Family Ties." *Orange County Register*, July 28, 1994.

Evans, Martin C. "Trade Issue Splits O.C. Vietnamese." *Orange County Register*, August 21, 1994.

Evans, Max J. "A History of the Public Library Movement in Utah." M.A. Thesis, Utah State University, 1971.

Evans, Sara. *Born for Liberty: A History of Women in America.* New York: Free Press, 1989.

Evans, Terry. *Disarming the Prairie.* Baltimore, MD: Johns Hopkins University Press, 1998.

Everett, Derek. *The Colorado State Capital: History, Politics, and Preservation.* Boulder: University Press of Colorado, 2005.

Ewers, John Canfield. *The Blackfeet Raiders on the Northwest Plains.* Norman: University of Oklahoma Press, 1983.

Faragher, John M. *Women and Men on the Overland Trail.* New Haven, CT: Yale University Press, 1979.

Farrell, Allison. "Tribes Seek Funds; Martz Balks." *Billings Gazette,* October 11, 2003. Available from http://www.billingsgazette.com

Feher, Shoshanah. "From the Rivers of Babylon to the Valleys of Los Angeles: The Exodus and Adaptation of Iranian Jews." In *Gatherings in Diaspora,* edited by R. Stephen Warner and Judith G. Wittner. Philadelphia: Temple University Press, 1998.

Fehrenbach, T. R. *Lone Star: A History of Texas and the Texans.* New York: Macmillan, 1968.

Fehrenbach, T. R. *The San Antonio Story.* Tulsa, OK: Continental Heritage Press, 1978.

Feldenheimer, Edith. Interview by Marian W. Kolisch, November 23 and December 1, 1982. Smithsonian Archives of American Art. Available from http://archivesofamericanart.si.edu/oralhist/oralhist.htm

Fell, James E., Jr. *Ores to Metals: The Rocky Mountain Smelting Industry.* Lincoln: University of Nebraska Press, 1979.

Fellmeth, Robert C., ed. *Politics of Land.* New York: Grossman, 1973.

Ficken, Robert E. *Washington Territory.* Pullman: Washington State University Press, 2002.

Fiege, Mark. *Irrigated Eden: The Making of an Agricultural Landscape in the American West.* Seattle: University of Washington Press, 1999.

Findlay, John. *Magic Lands: Western Cityscapes and American Culture after 1940.* Berkeley: University of California Press, 1992.

"First Stop California: The History of Cruizing Down Route 66." Available from http://calcruising.com/route66.html

Fish, James. "Responding to Cultural Diversity: A Library in Transition." *Wilson Library Bulletin* 66 (February 1992).

Fisher, Galen M. "Japanese Evacuation from the Pacific Coast." *Far Eastern Survey* 11, no. 13 (June 29, 1942).

Fisher, M. F. K. *Spirits of the Valley.* New York: Targ Editions, 1985.

Fitzgerald, Margaret E., and Joseph A. King. *The Uncounted Irish in Canada and the United States.* Toronto: Meany, 1990.

Fitzgibbons, Margaret M. *History of the United Daughters of the Confederacy in California: Centennial Edition, 1896–1996.* Mesa, AZ: Blue Bird, 1997.

Fixico, Donald L. *Termination and Relocation: Federal Indian Policy, 1945–1960.* Albuquerque: University of New Mexico Press, 1986.

Fixico, Donald L. *The Urban Indian Experience in America.* Albuquerque: University of New Mexico Press, 2000.

Flamming, Douglas. *Bound for Freedom: Black Los Angeles in Jim Crow America.* Berkeley: University of California Press, 2005.

Flanner, Hildegarde. *Different Images, Portraits of Remembered People.* Santa Barbara, CA: John Daniel, 1987.

Fleming, Walter L. "'Pap' Singleton, the Moses of the Colored Exodus." *American Journal of Sociology* 15 (1909).

Flemming, Thomas C. *C. L. Dellums and Mr. Bojangles, Reflections on Black History, Part 47.* New York: Free Press, 1998. Available from http://www.freepress.org/fleming/flemng47.html

Flores, Dan. "Zion in Eden: Phases of the Environmental History of Utah." *Environmental Review* 7 (1983).

Fogelson, Robert M. *The Fragmented Metropolis, Los Angeles, 1850–1930.* Cambridge, MA: Harvard University Press, 1967.

Foreman, Grant. *Indian Removal: The Emigration of the Five Civilized Tribes of Indians.* Norman: University of Oklahoma Press, 1993.

Fornander, Abraham. *An Account of the Polynesian Race: Its Origins and Migrations, and Ancient History of the Hawaiian People to the Times of Kamehameha I.* Rutland, VT: C. E. Tuttle, 1969.

Forsgren, Lydia Walker. *History of Box Elder Stake.* Grand County: Daughters of Utah Pioneers, 1937.

Forsyth, Ann. *Reforming Suburbia: The Planned Communities of Irvine, Columbia, and the Woodlands.* Pasadena: University of California Press and the Huntington Library, 2005.

Fort Belknap Curriculum Development Project. *Assiniboine Memories: Legends of the Nakota People.* Hays, MT: Fort Belknap Education Department, 1983.

Fort Belknap Indian Community Council–State of Montana Tobacco Tax Agreement. Available from http://www.state.mt.us

Fort Belknap Indian Community Official Web Site. Available from http://www.fortbelknapnations-nsn.gov/

"Fort Belknap Indian Tribe Sues Over Gold Mine Pollution." *Billings Gazette,* January 30, 2004. Available from http://www.billingsgazette.com/index .php?id=1&display=rednews/2004/01/30/build/ state/40-tribeminelawsuit.inc

Foster, George H., and Peter C. Weiglin. *The Harvey House Cookbook: Memories of Dining along the Santa Fe Railroad.* Athens, GA: Longstreet Press, 1999.

Foster, Mark S. *Henry J. Kaiser: Builder in the Modern American West.* Austin: University of Texas Press, 1989.

Fowler, Catherine S. "Sarah Winnemucca Northern Paiute, ca. 1844–1891." In *American Indian Intellectuals,* edited by Margot Liberty. St. Paul, MN: West Publishing, 1978.

Fowler, Laura. *American Indians of the Great Plains.* New York: Columbia University Press, 2003.

Fox, Stephen R. *The Unknown Internment: An Oral History of the Relocation of Italian Americans during World War II.* Boston: Twayne, 1990.

Francaviglia, Richard V. *Hard Places: Reading the Landscape of America's Historic Mining Districts.* Iowa City: University of Iowa Press, 1991.

Franks, Kenny A., and Paul F. Lambert. *Early California Oil: A Photographic History, 1865–1940.* College Station: Texas A&M Press, 1985.

Frayne, Gabriel, Jr. "Race for Latino California: The Dornan-Sanchez Rematch Will Show the Staying Power of 1996 Coalitions." *Nation* 267, no. 13 (1998).

Frazier, Deborah. "Reservation, Casino in Works Near DIA." *Rocky Mountain News,* December 31, 2003. Available from http://www.rockymountainnews.com

Freeman, Cathleen A. *David Jacks (1822–1909)* [Local history pages]. Monterey, CA: Monterey Historical Society, 1996.

Freeman, Jane, and Glenn Sanberg. *Jubilee: The 25th Anniversary of Sun City, Arizona.* Phoenix, AZ: COL Press, 1984.

Freeman, Robert S., and David M. Hovde, eds. *Libraries to the People: Histories of Outreach.* Jefferson, NC: McFarland, 2003.

Freeth, Nick. *Traveling Route 66.* Norman: University of Oklahoma Press, 2001.

Friedman, Max Paul. *Nazis and Good Neighbors: The United States Campaign against the Germans of Latin America in World War II.* Cambridge, UK: Cambridge University Press, 2003.

Furdell, William J. "The Great Falls Home Front during World War II." In *Montana Legacy,* edited by Harry Fritz, Mary Murphy, and Robert Swartout, Jr. Helena: Montana Historical Society Press, 2002.

Furst, Jill Leslie. *Mojave Pottery, Mojave People: The Dingham Collection of Mojave Ceramics.* Santa Fe, NM: School of American Research Press, 2001.

Gagnon, Gregory, and Karen White Eyes. *Pine Ridge Reservation: Yesterday and Today.* Interior, SD: Badlands Natural History Association, 1992.

Galema, Annemieke. *Frisians to America 1880–1914: With the Baggage of the Fatherland.* Groningen, The Netherlands: REGIO-Projekt Utigevers, 1996.

Gallaci, Caroline D. *The City of Destiny and the South Sound: An Illustrated History of Tacoma and Pierce County.* Carlsbad, CA: Heritage Media Corporation, 2001.

Gallatin Pioneers: The First 50 Years, 1868–1918. Privately published, 1984.

Gallegos, Bee, and Lisa Kammerlocher. "A History of Library Services to the Mexican American and Native American in Arizona." *Journal of the West* 30 (July 1991).

Gallo, Patrick J. *Ethnic Alienation: The Italian Americans.* Rutherford, NJ: Farleigh Dickinson University Press, 1974.

Gamboa, Erasmo. "Braceros in the Pacific Northwest: Laborers on the Domestic Front, 1942–1947." *Pacific Historical Review* 56, no. 3 (1987).

Garcia y Griego, Manuel. "Responses to Migration: The Bracero Program." In *Migration between Mexico and the United States,* Vol. 3. Available from http://www .utexas.edu/lbj/uscir/binpapers/v3c-1garcia.pdf

Gardiner, June Ericson. *Olompali: In the Beginning.* Fort Bragg, CA: Cypress House Press, 1995.

Gaskins, Susanne T. "The Dam that Would Not Stay Put: Henry J. Kaiser and Shipbuilding on the Homefront." M.A. Thesis, California State University, Fullerton, 1987.

Gates, Paul W. *History of Public Land Law Development.* New York: Arno Press, 1979.

Gates, Paul Wallace. *History of Public Land Law Development.* Washington, DC: Government Printing Office, 1968.

Gates, Paul Wallace, ed. *The Rape of Indian Lands.* New York: Arno Press, 1979.

Gatschet, Albert S. *A Migration Legend of the Creek Indians.* Philadelphia: D. G. Brinton, 1884.

Geary, Edward A. *History of Emery County.* Salt Lake City: Utah Historical Society, Emery County Commission, 1996.

Geiger, Maynard J. "The Story of California's First Libraries." *Southern California Quarterly* 46 (June 1964).

Geist, Christopher D. "The Great Leadville, Colorado, Ice Palace and Winter Festival of 1896." *Journal of American Culture* 7, no. 3 (1985).

George Mason University. "The Sale of Federal Land: Free Homesteads." *A History of United States Public Land Law and the Evolution of the National Forest System.* [Online course PRLS 542]. Available from http://class web.gmu.edu/erodger1/prls542/one/dispos7.htm

"German Hide Buyer of Billings Too Much a Friend of Germany, He Criticized U.S. Government, Now Rests in County Jail Awaiting Federal Officers—Undoubtedly Will Be Placed in Detention Camp." *Cody Enterprise,* January 16, 1918.

"German Is Jailed for Seditious Remarks." *Cody Enterprise,* December 26, 1917.

Gerrard-Gough, J. D., and Albert B. Christman. *Grand Experiment at Inyokern: Narrative of the Naval Ordnance Test Station during the Second World War & the Immediate Postwar Years.* Vol. 2 of *History of the Naval Weapons Center, China Lake, California.* Washington, DC: United States Government Printing Office, Navy History Division, 1978.

Ghaffarian, Shireen. "The Acculturation of Iranians in the United States." *Journal of Psychology* 127 (1987).

Gibney, Frank, ed. *Senso: The Japanese Remember the Pacific War.* Armonk, NY: Sharpe, 1995.

Gibson, Arrell Morgan. *The American Indian: Prehistory to the Present.* Lexington, MA: D. C. Heath, 1980.

Gibson, Wayne D. *Tomas Yorba's Santa Ana Viejo: 1769–1847.* Santa Ana, CA: Santa Ana College Foundation Press, 1976.

Gilbert, Benjamin Franklin. "California and the Civil War." *California Historical Society Quarterly* 40, no. 4 (1961).

Gillette, Paul. "The Civil War Legacy of Orange County." Civil War Round Table of Orange County Web Site. Available from http://www.cwrtorangecounty-ca.org/

Gillis, Michael J., and Michael F. Magliari. *John Bidwell and California: The Life and Writings of a Pioneer 1841–1900.* Spokane, WA: Arthur H. Clark, 2003.

Girl Scouts USA. "Farthest North Girl Scout Council, Council History." Available from http://home.gci.net/~fngsc/TLM_Council_History.htm

Gisel, Bonnie Johanna, ed. *Kindred and Related Spirits: The Letters of John Muir and Jeanne C. Carr.* Salt Lake City: University of Utah Press, 2001.

Gittelsohn, John, "Eatery Is Talk of the Town." *Orange County Register,* September 27, 1999.

Gittelsohn, John. "Laotian Refugee a Leader in Hmong Community." *Orange County Register,* July 18, 2002.

Glauthier, Martha. "San Dimas Remembered." Available from http://www.sandimasnews.com/history

GlobalSecurity.org. "Base Realignment and Closure (BRAC)." Available from http://www.globalsecurity.org/military/facility/brac.htm

Godines, Valeria, and Ronald Campbell. "County Sees an Influx of Non-English Speakers—Language: Skills Broadening." *Orange County Register,* May 17, 2002.

Gonzalez, Deena J. *Refusing the Favor: The Spanish-Mexican Women of Santa Fe, 1820–1880.* New York: Oxford University Press, 1999.

Gonzalez, Gilbert. *Labor and Community: Mexican Citrus Worker Villages in a Southern California County, 1900–1950.* Urbana: University of Illinois Press, 1994.

Goodrich, Jennie, Claudia Lawson, and Vana Parrish Lawson. *Kashaya Pomo Plants.* Berkeley, CA: Heyday Books, 1996.

Goodwin, Cardinal. *John Charles Fremont: An Explanation of His Career.* Stanford, CA: Stanford University Press, 1930.

Goodwin, Edward A. *Our Jewish Farmers and the Story of the Jewish Agricultural Society.* New York: Fischer, 1943.

Goodwin, Samuel H. *Freemasonry in Utah: The Masonic Public Library, 1877–1891–1897: With Notes on Movements to Establish Public Libraries in Utah Prior to 1877.* Salt Lake City: Committee on Masonic Education and Instruction, Grand Lodge of Utah, 1929.

Gottlieb, Sanford. *Defense Addiction: Can America Kick the Habit?* Boulder, CO: Westview, 1997.

Gould, Stephen. *The Burning of Santa Ana's Chinatown and the Murder of Anaheim's Mock Lau Fat.* Hollywood, CA: Sun Dance Press, 1995.

Gower, Calvin W. "Lectures, Lyceums, and Libraries in Early Kansas, 1854–1864." *Kansas Historical Quarterly* 36 (1970).

Grand Memories. Grand County: Daughters of Utah Pioneers, 1972.

Grapp, Bonnie. *Footprints: An Early History of Fort Bragg, California and the Pomo.* Happy Camp, CA: Naturegraph, 1985.

Graves, F. Lee. *Montana's Fur Trade Era.* Helena, MT: Unicron, 1994.

Green, Michael D. *The Creeks: A Critical Bibliography.* Bloomington: Indiana University Press, 1979.

Green, Michael D. *The Politics of Indian Removal: Creek Government and Society in Crisis.* Lincoln: University of Nebraska Press, 1982.

Greever, William S. *The Story of the Western Mining Rushes, 1848–1900.* Moscow: University of Idaho Press, 1991.

Gregory, James N. *American Exodus.* New York: Oxford University Press, 1989.

Greider, William. *Fortress America: The American Military and the Consequences of Peace.* New York: Public Affairs, 1998.

Grey, Herman. *Tales from the Mohaves.* Norman: University of Oklahoma Press, 1970.

Griffen, William B. *Apaches at War and Peace: The Janos Presidio, 1750–1858.* Norman: University of Oklahoma Press, 1988.

Griffin, William D. *A Portrait of the Irish in America.* New York: Scribner, 1981.

Grinnell, George Bird. *The Cheyenne Indians*, 2 vols. Lincoln: University of Nebraska Press, 1972.

"Gros Ventre." *Columbia Encyclopedia.* 6th ed. New York: Columbia University Press, 2004.

Grove, Larry. *Dallas Public Library: The First 75 Years.* Dallas, TX: Dallas Public Library, 1977.

Gudde, Erwin G. *Sutter's Own Story: The Life of General John Augustus Sutter and the History of New Helvetia in the Sacramento Valley.* New York: Van Rees Press, 1936.

Guest, Francis. "Mission Colonization and Political Control in Spanish California." *Journal of San Diego History* 24, no. 1 (1978). Available from http://www .sandiegohistory.org/journal/78winter/mission.htm

Guinn, J. M. *Historical and Biographical Record of Los Angeles and Vicinity.* Chicago: Chapman, 1901.

Gullett, Gayle. *Becoming Citizens: The Emergence and Development of the California Women's Movement, 1880–1911.* Urbana: University of Illinois Press, 2000.

Gunnerson, Delores A. *The Jicarilla Apaches: A Study in Survival.* De Kalb: Northern Illinois University Press, 1974.

Gunnerson, James H., and Delores A. Gunnerson. *Ethnohistory of the High Plains.* Denver: Colorado State Office of Bureau of Land Management, 1988.

Gunselman, Cheryl. "Illumino for All: Opening the Library Association of Portland to the Public, 1900–1903." *Libraries and Culture* 36 (Summer 2001).

Gunselman, Cheryl. "Pioneering Free Library Service for the City, 1864–1902: The Library Association of Portland and the Portland Public Library." *Oregon Historical Quarterly* 103 (Fall 2002). [Electronic version]

Gutelius, Scott. *True Secrets of Salt Lake City and the Great Salt Lake Revealed!* Key West, FL: Eden Entertainment, 2002.

Gutierrez, Ramon, and Richard J. Orsi, eds. *Contested Eden: California before the Gold Rush.* Berkeley: University of California Press, 1998.

Gyory, Andrew. *Closing the Gate: Race, Politics, and the Chinese Exclusion Act.* Chapel Hill: University of North Carolina Press, 1998.

Haas, Lisbeth. *Conquests and Historical Identities in California, 1769–1936.* Berkeley: University of California Press, 1995.

Hackel, Steven W. "Sources of Rebellion: Indian Testimony and the Mission San Gabriel Uprising of 1785." *Ethnohistory* 50, no. 4 (2003).

Hafen, Leroy R. *The Mountain Men and the Fur Trade of the Far West: Biographical Sketches of the Participants by Scholars of the Subject and with Introductions by the Editor. Vol. 2, The Far West and the Rockies Historical Series.* Glendale, CA: Arthur H. Clark, 1965.

Hafen, Leroy R., and Ann W. Hafen, eds. *To the Rockies and Oregon 1839–1842: With Diaries and Accounts by Sidney Smith, Amos Cook, Joseph Holman, E. Willard Smith, Francis Fletcher, Joseph Williams, Obadiah Oakley, Robert Shortess, T. J. Farnham. Vol. 3, The Far West and the Rockies Historical Series 1820–1875.* Glendale, CA: Arthur H. Clark, 1955.

Hahn, Steven C. *The Invention of the Creek Nation, 1670–1763.* Lincoln: University of Nebraska Press, 2004.

Haines, Aubrey. *Bannock Indian Trail.* Yellowstone, WY: Library and Museum Association, 1964.

Hall Family Collection: Faracita Hall (Wyatt), Marcus Hall, Tarea Hall (Pittman). Oakland, CA: African American Museum and Library.

Hall, Kermit L., William M. Wiecek, and Paul Finkelman. *American Legal History.* New York: Oxford University Press, 1991.

Hämäläinen, Pekka. "The Rise and Fall of Plains Indian Horse Cultures." *The Journal of American History* 90 (December 2003).

Hamilton, Kenneth Marvin. *Black Towns and Profit: Promotion and Development in the Trans-Appalachian West, 1877–1915.* Urbana: University of Illinois Press, 1991.

Handlin, Oscar, ed. *Immigration as a Factor in American History.* Englewood Cliffs, NJ: Prentice-Hall, 1959.

Handlin, Oscar. *The Uprooted: The Epic Story of the Great Migration That Made the American People.* 2nd ed. Boston: Little, Brown, 1979.

Handy, E. S., et al. *Ancient Hawaiian Civilization: A Series of Lectures Delivered at the Kamehameha Schools.* Rutland, VT: C. E. Tuttle, 1976.

Hanley, Mike. *Owyhee Trails: The West's Forgotten Corner.* Caldwell, ID: Caxton, 1988.

Hanson, Barry, and Bill Jennings. *San Jacinto Valley Railway California Southern–Santa Fe.* Hemet, CA: Save Our Station, 1991.

Hanson, P. D. *The Proposed Kootenai Sustained Yield Unit: Kootenai National Forest.* U.S. Department of Agricultural and U.S. Forest Service, 1948.

Hardesty, Donald L. *The Archaeology of Mining and Miners: A View from the Silver State.* Rockville, MD: Society for Historical Archaeology, 1988.

Hardy, C. Brian. "Education and Mormon Enculturation: The Ogden Public Schools, 1849–1896." Ph.D. Dissertation, University of Utah, 1995.

Hargreaves, Mary. *Dry Farming in the Northern Great Plains, 1900–1925.* Cambridge, MA: Harvard University Press, 1957.

Hargreaves, Mary. *Dry Farming in the Northern Great Plains: Years of Readjustment, 1920–1990.* Lawrence: University Press of Kansas, 1993.

Harrington, John P. Annotations. *Chinigchinich: A Revised and Annotated Version of Alfred Robinson's Translation of Father Gerónimo Boscano's Historical Account of the Belief, Usages, Customs and Extravagancies of the Indians of This Mission of San Juan Capistrano Called the Acagchemem Tribe.* 2nd ed. Banning, CA: Malki Museum Press, 1978.

Harrington, John P. "A Rare Account of Gabrielino Shamanism from the Notes of John P. Harrington." *Journal of California and Great Basin Anthropology* 1, no. 2 (1979).

Harris, L. David. "Sod Jerusalems: Jewish Agricultural Communities in Frontier Kansas." Unpublished manuscript, Library and Archives Division, Kansas State Historical Society, 1984.

Harris, William H. *Keeping the Faith: A. Philip Randolph, Milton P. Webster, and the Brotherhood of Sleeping Car Porters, 1925–37.* Urbana: University of Illinois Press, 1977.

Hart, Arthur A. *The Boiseans: At Home.* Boise, ID: Historic Boise, 1992.

Hart, Arthur A. *Chinatown: Boise, Idaho, 1870–1970.* Boise, ID: Historic Idaho, 2002.

Haskell Indian Nations University Web Site. Available from http://www.haskell.edu/haskell/about.asp

Haslam, Gerald W. *Voices of a Place.* Walnut Creek, CA: Devil Mountain Books, 1987.

Haslam, Gerald W. *Workin' Man Blues.* Berkeley: University of California Press, 1999.

Hassrick, Royal B. *The Sioux: Life and Customs of a Warrior Society.* Norman: University of Oklahoma Press, 1964.

Hastings, Lansford W. *The 1845 Pioneer's Guide for the Westward Traveler: The Emigrants' Guide to Oregon and California.* Cincinnati, OH: G. Conclin, 1845. (Reprinted Bedford, MA: Appleworks Books, 1994)

Hatch, Orin Walker. *Lyceum to Library: A Chapter in the Cultural History of Houston.* Houston: Texas Gulf Coast Historical Association, 1965.

Hayasi, Brian Masaru. *Democratizing the Enemy: The Japanese American Internment.* Princeton, NJ: Princeton University Press, 2004.

Hays, Samuel P. *The Response to Industrialism, 1885–1914.* Chicago: University of Chicago Press, 1957.

Hazel, Michael. *The Dallas Public Library: Celebrating a Century of Service, 1901–2001.* Denton: University of North Texas Press, 2001.

Hedges, James B. *Henry Villard and the Railways of the Northwest.* New Haven, CT: Yale University Press, 1930. (Reprinted New York: Russell and Russell, 1967)

Hedren, Paul L., ed. *The Great Sioux War 1876–77.* Helena: Montana Historical Society Press, 1991.

Heizer, Robert Fleming, ed. *The Destruction of California Indians.* Lincoln: University of Nebraska Press, 1993.

Heizer, Robert Fleming, vol. ed. *Handbook of North American Indians. Volume 8: California.* Washington, DC: Smithsonian, 1978.

Heizer, R. F., and M. A. Whipple. *The California Indians: A Source Book.* 2nd ed. Berkeley: University of California Press, 1971.

Held, Ray E. *Public Libraries in California, 1849–1878.* Berkeley: University of California Press, 1963.

Held, Ray E. *The Rise of the Public Library in California.* Chicago: American Library Association, 1973.

Hemet Land Company. *Hemet Southern California: Its Homes and Scenes.* Hemet, CA: Hemet Land Co., 1902.

Hemet News. *Down Memory Lane: A Historical Record of People and Events in California.* Hemet, CA: The Hemet News, 1960.

Hemet–San Jacinto Genealogical Society. *San Jacinto Valley: Past and Present.* Dallas, TX: Curtis Media, 1989.

Henshaw, H. W. "The Luiseño Creation Myth." *Masterkey for Indian Lore and History* 46, no. 3 (1972).

Henson, Pauline. *Founding of a Wilderness Capital: Prescott.* Flagstaff, AZ: Northland Press, 1965.

Hepworth, Bobbee M. *Utah Libraries: Heritage and Horizons.* Salt Lake City: Utah Library Association, 1976.

Herman, David G. "Neighbors on Golden Mountain: The Americanization of Immigrants in California and

Public Instruction as an Agency of Ethnic Assimilation, 1850–1933." Ph.D. Dissertation, University of California, Berkeley, 1981.

Herman, Masako, ed. *The Japanese in America, 1843–1973: A Chronology and Fact Book.* Dobbs Ferry, NY: Oceana, 1974.

Hernandez, Robert C. *Los Chilenos en San Francisco: Recuerdos historicos de la emigracion por los descubrimientos del oro, iniciada en 1848.* 2 vols. Valparaiso, Chile: Imprenta San Rafael, 1930.

Herr, Elizabeth, and Jennifer Mayes. "Women and Economic Opportunity in Western Mining Towns in the Late 19th Century: The Case of Leadville, Colorado." *Essays in Economic and Business History* 14 (1996).

Herscher, Uri D. *Jewish Agricultural Utopias in America 1880–1910.* Detroit, MI: Wayne State University Press, 1981.

Hickey, Donald R. *Nebraska Moments; Glimpses of Nebraska's Past.* Lincoln: University of Nebraska Press, 1992.

Hicks, Jerry. "Different Paths to a Place of Glory." *Orange County Register,* October 8, 1999.

Higham, John. *Strangers in the Land: Patterns of Nativism, 1860–1925.* New York: Atheneum, 1965.

Hine, Robert V. *California's Utopian Colonies.* New Haven, CT: Yale University Press, 1966.

Hirobe, Izumi. *Japanese Pride, American Prejudice: Modifying the Exclusion Clause of the 1924 Immigration Act.* Stanford, CA: Stanford University Press, 2001.

"Historic Route 66: Facts." Available from http://www.historic66.com/facts

Hoang, Vinh. Interview by Trangdai Tranguyen. January 8, 2000. Fountain Valley, California.

Hobbs, Richard R. *Naval Science 2: Maritime History Science for the NJROTC Student.* Annapolis, MD: Naval Institute Press, 2002.

Hockemeyer, Karen Sue. *The Southern Minority?: The Strength of the Confederate and the Copperhead Sentiment in Santa Clara County, California.* M.A. Thesis, San Jose State University, 1988.

Hogan, Richard. *Class and Community in Frontier Colorado.* Lawrence: University Press of Kansas, 1990.

Hohri, William Minoru. *Resistance: Challenging America's Wartime Internment of Japanese-Americans.* Lomita, CA: Epistolarian, 2001.

Holliday, J. S. *The World Rushed In.* New York: Simon & Schuster, 1981.

Holm, Debra N., Lynda C. Clark, and Norman L. Holm. *Nampa's People, 1886–1986: Discovering Our Heritage.* Nampa, ID: Nampa Centennial Committee, 1986.

Holmes, Alvin C. *Swedish Homesteaders in Idaho on the Minidoka Irrigation Project, Minidoka County, Idaho.* Twin Falls, ID: Ace, 1976.

Holmes, E. W. *History of Riverside County.* Los Angeles: Historic Record, 1912.

Holmes, Kenneth L., ed. *Covered Wagon Women: Diaries & Letters from the Western Trails, 1840–1890.* 11 vols. Glendale, CA: Arthur H. Clark, 1983.

Holter, Anton. M. "Pioneer Lumbering in Montana" [Pamphlet]. Portland, OR: *The Timberman,* n.d.

Holzapfel, Richard N. *History of Utah County.* Salt Lake City: Utah Historical Society, Utah County Commission, 1996.

"Home Defense Club Formed." *Cody Enterprise,* January 23, 1918.

Homer, David. *Moscow at the Turn of the Century.* Moscow, ID: Latah County Historical Society, 1979.

Hoopes, Chad L. *What Makes a Man: The Annie E. Kennedy and John Bidwell Letters 1866–1868.* Fresno, CA: Valley Publishers, 1973.

Hoopes, Lorman. *This Last West: Miles City, Montana Territory, and Environs, 1876–1886: The People, the Geography, the Incredible History.* Missoula, MT: SkyHouse, 1990.

Hoover, J. Howard. *Profile of San Dimas.* San Dimas, CA: San Dimas Press, 1961.

Hop, Thi Nguyen. Interview by Trangdai Tranguyen. March 19, 2000. La Palma, California.

Hopi Dictionary Project, Bureau of Applied Research in Anthropology, University of Arizona. *Hopi Dictionary: Hopìikwa Lavàytutuveni: A Hopi-English Dictionary of the Third Mesa Dialect with an English-Hopi Finder List and a Sketch of Hopi Grammar.* Tucson: University of Arizona Press, 1998.

The Hopi Tribe Web Site. Available from http://www.hopi.nsn.us

"How the Clans Came to Be." Available from http://www.indianlegend.com/cdreek/creek_001.htm

Howard, Kathleen L., and Diana F. Pardue. *Inventing the Southwest: The Fred Harvey Company and Native American Art.* Flagstaff, AZ: Northland, 1996.

Hoxie, Frederick, ed. *Encyclopedia of North American Indians.* New York: Houghton Mifflin, 1996.

Huchel, Frederick M. *A History of Box Elder County.* Salt Lake City: Utah Historical Society, Box Elder County Commission, 1996.

Hudson, Roy F., ed. *Desert Hours with Chief Patencio: As Told to Kate Collins by Chief Francisco Patencio*. Palm Springs, CA: Palm Springs Desert Museum, 1971.

Hughes, Richard B. *Pioneer Years in the Black Hills*. Glendale, CA: Arthur H. Clarke, 1957.

Hungry Wolf, Beverly. *The Ways of My Grandmothers*. New York: Quill, 1982.

Hunt, Rockwell D. *John Bidwell: Prince of California Pioneers*. Caldwell, ID: The Caxton Printers, 1942.

Hunt, Rockwell D., ed. *California and Californians: The Spanish Period, the American Period, and a California Bibliography*. Vol. I. Cherry Hill, NJ: Lewis, 1932.

Hunter, Milton R. *Brigham Young the Colonizer*. Salt Lake City, UT: Deseret News Press, 1940.

Hurt, R. Douglas. *American Agriculture: A Brief History*. Ames: Iowa State University Press, 1994.

Hurtado, Albert L. *Indian Survival on the California Frontier*. New Haven, CT: Yale University Press, 1988.

Hurtado, Albert L. *Intimate Frontiers: Sex, Gender, and Culture in Old California*. Albuquerque: University of New Mexico Press, 1999.

Hyde, Charles. *Copper for America: The United States Copper Industry from Colonial Times to the 1990s*. Tucson: University of Arizona Press, 1998.

Hyde, George E. *Red Cloud's Folk: A History of the Oglala Sioux Indians*. Norman: University of Oklahoma Press, 1957.

Hyde, George E. *A Sioux Chronicle*. Norman: University of Oklahoma Press, 1956.

Hyde, George E. *Spotted Tail's Folk: A History of the Brulé Sioux*. Norman: University of Oklahoma Press, 1961.

Hyer, Joel R. *"We Are Not Savages": Native Americans in Southern California and the Pala Reservation, 1840–1920*. East Lansing: Michigan State University Press, 2001.

Iacovetta, Franca, Roberto Perin, and Angelo Principe, eds. *Enemies Within: Italian and Other Internees in Canada and Abroad*. Toronto: University of Toronto Press, 2000.

Ichioka, Yuji. *The Issei: The World of the First Generation Japanese Immigrants, 1885–1924*. New York: Free Press, 1988.

Ihara, Craig Kei Sansei. Interview with Betty E. Miton [Interview no. 1230, transcript], December 19, 1973. Fullerton: California State University Fullerton Oral History Collection.

Inada, Lawson Fusao. *Only What We Could Carry: The Japanese American Internment Experience*. Berkeley, CA: Heyday Books, 2000.

"The Indian Removal Act of 1830." Available from http://www.thebearbyte.com/NAResource/RemovalAct.htm

"Indian Territory." Available from http://www.nativeamericanrhymes.com/library/territory.htm

Ingersoll, Thomas N. *To Intermix with Our White Brothers: Indian Mixed Bloods in the United States from Earliest Times to the Era of the Removals*. Albuquerque: University of New Mexico Press, 2005.

Inouye, Mamoru. *The Heart Mountain Story*. Park County Archives, Cody, Wyoming, 1997.

Inter Tribal Council of Arizona Web Site. Available from http://itcaonline.com

Inter Tribal Council of Arizona. "Colorado River Indian Tribes." Available from http://itcaonline.com/tribes_colriver.html

Inter Tribal Council of Arizona. "Fort Mojave Indian Tribe." Available from http://itcaonline.com/tribes_mojave.html

Iriye, Akira. *Pacific Estrangement: Japanese and American Expansion 1897–1911*. Cambridge, MA: Harvard University Press, 1972.

Iriye, Akira. *Power and Culture: The Japanese-American War, 1941–1945*. Cambridge, MA: Harvard University Press, 1981.

Irvine, James. *Last Will and Testament*. San Francisco, circa 1886.

Irvine Ranch Water District. "About IRWD: History." Available from http://www.irwd.com/AboutIRWD/history.php

Iverson, Ronald. J. *The Princess of the Prairie: A History of Belgrade, Montana*. Self-published, 1965.

Jack, Kenneth C. *Land King: The Story of David Jack* [Local history pages]. Monterey, CA: Monterey Historical Society, 1999.

Jackson, Donald. *Custer's Gold*. New Haven, CT: Yale University Press, 1966.

Jackson, Louise, and Michael Day. "The Wyoming Literary and Library Association, 1870–1978." *Journal of the West* 30 (July 1991).

Jackson, Robert H., and Edward Castillo. *Indians, Franciscans, and Spanish Colonization: The Impact of the Mission System on California Indians*. Albuquerque: University of New Mexico Press, 1995.

Jackson Hole Chamber of Commerce. "Grand Teton National Park." Available from http://www.jacksonholechamber.com/chamber/index.php?option=content&task=view&id=22

"Jackson Hole Gang." *The Progressive*, 57, no. 5 (May 1993).

Jacob Rader Marcus Center of the American Jewish Archives. "An Inventory to the Robert and Jessie

Bloom Papers, Manuscript Collection No. 93 1897–1980. 5.2 Linear Ft." Available from http://www.huc.edu/aja/Bloom.htm

Jacobson, Max. "Wonderful Vietnamese Food Served amid Mondo Bizarro Décor." *Los Angeles Times,* February 10, 1989.

Jahoda, Gloria. *The Trail of Tears.* New York: Wings Books, 1975.

James, George Wharton. *Old Missions and Mission Indians of California.* Los Angeles: B. R. Baumgardt, 1895.

James, Harry C. *The Cahuilla Indians.* Banning, CA: Malki Museum Press, 1969.

James, Harry C. *Pages from Hopi History.* 8th ed. Tucson: University of Arizona Press, 1994.

James, Thomas. *Exile Within: The Schooling of Japanese Americans, 1942–1945.* Cambridge, MA: Harvard University Press, 1987.

Jameson, Elizabeth. *All That Glitters: Class, Conflict, and Community in Cripple Creek.* Urbana: University of Illinois Press, 1998.

"Japanese on West Coast Face Wholesale Uprooting," *San Francisco News,* March 4, 1942.

Jensen, J. Marinus. *History of Provo, Utah.* Provo, UT: Author, 1924.

Jensen, Joan M., and Gloria R. Lothrop, eds. *California Women: A History.* San Francisco: Boyd & Fraser, 1987.

Jensen, Vernon H. *Lumber and Labor.* New York: Farrar and Rinehart, 1945.

Jeter, James Phillip. "Rough Flying: The *California Eagle* (1879–1965)." Presentation to 12th Annual Conference of the American Journalism Historians Association, Salt Lake City, Utah, 1993.

Jewell, Donald. *Indians of the Feather River: Tales and Legends of the Concow Maidu of California.* Menlo Park, CA: Ballena, 1987.

Jewish Women's Archive. "Personal Information for Jessie S. Bloom." Available from http://www.jwa.org/archive/jsp/perInfo.jsp?personID=338

Jewish Women's Archive. "Ray Frank—Breaking Down Barriers." Available from http:/www.jwa.org/exhibits/wov/break.html

Jewish Women's Archive. "Ray Frank—Jewish Women's Congress." Available from http://www.jwa.org/exhibits/wov/frank/jwc.html

Jewish Women's Archive. "Ray Frank—The Maiden in the Temple." Available from http://www.jwa.org/exhibits/wov/frank/maiden.html

Jewish Women's Archive. "Ray Frank—Marriage and New Directions." Available from http:/www.jwa.org/exhibits/wov/frank/marriage.html

Johnson, Clarence. "Radio Host Tarea Hall Pittman Dies." *San Francisco Chronicle,* August 3, 1991.

Johnson, David Alan. *Founding the Far West.* Berkeley: University of California Press, 1992.

Johnson, Hans. "Immigrants in California: Findings from the 1990 Census." *California Research Bureau Issue Summary* (CRB-93-009). Sacramento: California Research Bureau, 1993. Available from http://www.library.ca.gov/html/statseg2a.cfm

Johnson, Henry S. *Uranium Deposits of the Moab, Monticello, White Canyon, and Monument Valley Districts, Utah and Arizona.* Washington, DC: U.S. Government Printing Office, 1966.

Johnson, Marilynn S. *The Second Gold Rush: Oakland and the East Bay in World War II.* Berkeley: University of California Press, 1993.

Johnson, Troy, Joane Nagel, and Duane Champagne, eds. *American Indian Activism: Alcatraz to the Longest Walk.* Urbana: University of Illinois Press, 1997.

Johnston, Bernice E. *California's Gabrielino Indians.* Los Angeles: Southwest Museum, 1962.

Jolly, Vic. "Refugee Has a Reason to Sing." *Orange County Register,* October 7, 1999.

Jones, Allen. *Iranian Refugees: The Many Faces of Persecution.* Washington, DC: U.S. Committee for Refugees, 1984.

Jones, Cont L. "The Study of a Redevelopment Program: Its Political and Economic Effect on Park City, Utah." M.A. Thesis, Brigham Young University, 1967.

Jones, Donald G., et al. *Ethnohistoric and Ethnographic Information Related to the Fort Carson Military Reservation and Pinon Canyon Maneuver Site in Colorado.* St. Louis, MO: Department of the Army Corps of Engineers, 1998.

Jones, Landon Y. *The Essential Lewis and Clark.* New York: HarpersCollins, 2000.

Jones, Plummer Alston, Jr. *Libraries, Immigrants, and the American Experience.* Westport, CT: Greenwood Press, 1999.

Jorgensen, Lawrence C., ed. *The San Fernando Valley: Past and Present.* Los Angeles: Pacific Rim Research, 1982.

Josephy, Alvin M., Jr. *The Nez Perce Indians and the Opening of the Northwest.* New Haven, CT: Yale University Press, 1965.

"Judge Finds No Action to Take in Belknap Mining Dispute." *Billings Gazette,* July 3, 2004. Available from http://www.billingsgazette.com/index.php?id=1&display=rednews/2004/07/03/build/state/70-belknap- mining.inc

Julian Historical Society. *History of Julian.* Julian, CA: Julian Historical Society, 1969.

Kaihard, Rodney. Interview with Patricia Morgan [Interview no. 1277, transcript], March 25, 1973. Fullerton: California State University Fullerton Oral History Collection.

Kalisch, Philip A. "High Culture on the Frontier: The Omaha Library Association." *Nebraska History* 52 (1971).

Kanegae, Henry. Interview with Richard Curtiss [Interview no. 4, transcript], February 16, 1966. Fullerton: California State University Fullerton Oral History Collection.

"Kansas." Available from http://www.soulofamerica.com/towns/kstowns.html

Karim, Persis, and Mohammad Mehdi Khorrami, eds. *A World Between: Poems, Stories, and Essays by Iranian-Americans. An Anthology.* New York: George Braziller, 1998.

Kashima, Tetsuden. "Japanese American Internees Return, 1945 to 1955." *Phylon* 41, no. 2 (1980).

Kastrup, Allan. *The Swedish Heritage in America: The Swedish Element in America and American-Swedish Relations in Their Historical Perspective.* Minneapolis, MN: Swedish Council of America, 1975.

Kaszynski, William. *Route 66: Images of America's Main Street.* Jefferson, NC: McFarland, 2003.

Katz, Tonnie L. "20 Years after the Fall." *Orange County Register,* January 29, 1985.

Katz, William Loren. *The Black West.* New York: Touchstone, 1996.

Kaufman, Harold F., and Lois C. Kaufman. *Toward the Stabilization and Enrichment of a Forest Community: The Montana Study.* Missoula: University of Montana, 1946.

Kaufmann, William W. *Assessing the Base Force: How Much Is Too Much?* Washington, DC: Brookings Institution, 1992.

Kazin, Michael. *Barons of Labor: The San Francisco Building Trades and Union Power in the Progressive Era.* Urbana: University of Illinois Press, 1987.

Keefer, Louis E. *Italian Prisoners of War in America, 1942–1946: Captives or Allies?* New York: Praeger, 1992.

Keeling, Alma Taylor-Lauder. *The Un-covered Wagon: A Glimpse of Pioneer Days in Moscow, Idaho.* Moscow, ID: Alma Taylor-Lauder Keeling, 1975.

Keffer, Frank. *History of San Fernando Valley.* Glendale, CA: Stillman, 1934.

Keller, Robert. *American Protestantism and United States Indian Policy, 1869–1882.* Lincoln: University of Nebraska Press, 1983.

Kellor, Shelly, and Patty Wong. *Cultivating Change: Redesigning Library Services Using the Partnership for Change Approach.* Available from http://www.library.ca.gov/html/lds.cfm

Kelly, Ron, and Jonathan Friedlander, eds. *Irangeles: Iranians in Los Angeles.* Berkeley: University of California Press, 1993.

Kenner, Charles L. *A History of New Mexican Plains Indian Relations.* Norman: University of Oklahoma Press, 1969.

Kerstetter, Todd M. Review of *Indian Reserved Water Rights: The Winters Doctrine in Its Social and Legal Context, 1800s–1930s.* By John Shurts [Book review]. *Western Historical Quarterly* 32, no. 2 (Summer 2001). Available from http://www.historycooperative.org/cgi-bin/justtop.cgi?act=justtop&url=http://www.historycooperative.org/journals/whq/32.2/br_14.html

Kessel, John L. *Spain in the Southwest: A Narrative History of Colonial New Mexico, Arizona, Texas and California.* Norman: University of Oklahoma Press, 2002.

Kessell, Hudson. *Pahaska Tepee: Buffalo Bill's Old Hunting Lodge and Hotel: A History.* Cody, WY: Buffalo Bill Historical Center, 1987.

Kessell, Velma Berryman. *Behind Barbed Wire: Heart Mountain Relocation Camp.* Billings, MT: Topel, 1992.

Khan, Irfan. "A Tribute to an Alliance." *Los Angeles Times,* September 24, 2002.

King, Joseph A. "The Breens versus Persistent Donner Party Mythology: Critiquing the Chroniclers." *The Californians* 10 (July–August 1992).

King, Joseph A. *Winter of Entrapment: A New Look at the Donner Party.* Toronto: P. D. Meany, 1992.

Kirkland & Ellis. *National Defense Authorization Act for FY 90–FY 91: Legislative History of P.L. 101–189, 103 Stat. 1352* Washington, DC: Kirkland & Ellis, 1989.

Kirkpatrick, Leonard H. "An Introduction to the History of Libraries in Utah, 1957 (?)." *Leonard Henry Kirkpatrick Papers, 1941–1962.* Salt Lake City: Special Collections, Marriott Library, University of Utah.

Kitts, Charles R. *The United States Odyssey in China, 1784–1990.* Lanham, MD: University Press of America, 1991.

Kling, Rob, Spencer Olin, and Mark Poster, eds. *Postsuburban California: The Transformation of Orange County since World War II.* Berkeley: University of California Press, 1991.

Knaut, Andrew L. *The Pueblo Revolt of 1680.* Norman: University of Oklahoma Press, 1995.

Knoll, Tricia. *Becoming Americans: Asian Sojourners, Immigrants, and Refugees in the Western United States.* Portland, OR: Coast to Coast Books, 1982.

Koestler, Fred L. "Operation Wetback." *The Handbook of Texas Online.* Available from http://www.tsha.utexas.edu/handbook.

Kreck, Dick. *Denver in Flames: Forging a New Mile High City.* Golden, CO: Fulcrum, 2000.

Kremer, Rona. "Jewish Involvement in the Early Development of Visalia, California, 1851–1853." *Western States Jewish History* 36 (2003).

Kroeber, A. L. *Handbook of the Indians of California.* Reprinted ed. New York: Dover, 1976.

Kroeber, Alfred Louis. "Report on Aboriginal Territory and Occupancy of the Mohave Tribe." In *American Indian Ethnohistory: California and Basin-Plateau Indians,* edited by David Agee Horr. New York: Garland, 1974.

Kurlansky, Mark. *The Basque History of the World.* New York: Walker, 1999.

Kuzmack, Linda Gordon. *Woman's Cause: The Jewish Woman's Movement in England and the United States, 1881–1933.* Columbus: Ohio State University Press, 1990.

Kvasnicka, Robert M., and Herman J. Viola, eds. *The Commissioners of Indian Affairs, 1824–1977.* Lincoln: University of Nebraska Press, 1979.

La Feber, Walter. *The Clash: A History of U.S.–Japan Relations.* New York: W. W. Norton, 1997.

La Pena, Frank, Craig D. Bates, and Steven P. Medley. *Legends of the Yosemite Miwok.* El Portal, CA: Yosemite Association, 1993.

Laguerre, Michel S. *The Global Ethnopolis: Chinatown, Japantown, and Manilatown in American Society.* New York: St. Martin's Press, 2000.

Lamar, Howard R. *The Far Southwest.* Albuquerque: University of New Mexico Press, 2000.

Lamar, Howard R. "Rites of Passage: Young Men and their Families in the Overland Trails Experience, 1843–69." In *"Soul-Butter and Hog Wash" and Other Essays on the American West,* edited by Thomas G. Alexander. Provo, UT: Brigham Young University Press, 1978.

Lamar, Howard. "Westering in the Twenty-First Century: Speculations on the Future of the Western Past." In *Under an Open Sky: Rethinking America's Western Past,* edited by William Cronon, George Miles, and Jay Gitlin. New York: Norton, 1992.

Land King: The Story of David Jack. Available from http://www.electricscotland.com/history/jack/chap3.htm

Lane, Richard H., and William A. Douglas. *Basque Sheepherders of the American West.* Reno: University of Nevada Press, 1985.

Lang, William L. "The Nearly Forgotten Blacks on Last Chance Gulch, 1900–1912." *Pacific Northwest Quarterly* 70 (1979).

Lange, Dorothea, and Paul S. Taylor. *An American Exodus.* New York: Reynal & Hitchcock, 1939.

Lannon, Albert. "Fight or Be Slaves!" *BRC-NEWS.* Black Radical Congress Web Site. Available from http://www.hartford-hwp.com/archives/45a/314.html

Larsen, Lawrence, and Barbara J. Cottrell. *The Gate City: A History of Omaha.* Lincoln: University of Nebraska Press, 1997.

Larson, A. Karl. *I Was Called to Dixie.* Salt Lake City, UT: Deseret News Press, 1961.

Larson, T. A. *History of Wyoming.* 2nd ed., rev. Lincoln: University of Wyoming Press, 1978.

Latta, Frank. *Handbook of Yokuts Indians.* Bakersfield, CA: Kern County Museum, 1949.

Lavender, David. *Bent's Fort.* New York: Doubleday, 1954.

Lavender, David. *The Southwest.* Albuquerque: University of New Mexico Press, 1980.

Lawson, Michael, and Vine Deloria, Jr. *Damned Indians: The Pick-Sloan Plan and the Missouri River Sioux, 1944–1980.* Norman: University of Oklahoma, 1994.

Lazarus, Edward. *Black Hills White Justice: The Sioux Nation versus the United States, 1775 to the Present.* New York: HarperCollins, 1991.

Le, Du Tu. Interview by Trangdai Tranguyen. February 3, 2002. Garden Grove, California.

Le, Thuan. "Coming Home." *Los Angeles Times,* September 11, 1994.

"Leader of Indian Tribes Resigns Suddenly; Decision Followed Canceling of Bombing Range Plans." *Billings Gazette,* May 13, 2004. Available from http://www.billingsgazette.com/index.php?id=1&display=rednews/2004/05/13/build/state/65-speakthunder-resigns.inc

Lecompte, Janet. *Pueblo, Hardscrabble, Greenhorn: The Upper Arkansas, 1832–1856.* Norman: University of Oklahoma Press, 1978.

Lee, Don. "Power Broker Has New Plan for Little Saigon." *Orange County Register,* August 5, 1997.

Lee, Erika. *At America's Gates: Chinese Immigration during the Exclusion Era, 1882–1943.* Chapel Hill: University of North Carolina Press, 2003.

Lee, Joann. *Asian Americans.* New York: The New Press, 1991.

Lee, Kenneth. "Hasta la Vista: Orange County." *New Republic* 217, no. 17 (1997).

Lee, Lawrence B. *Kansas and the Homestead Act 1862–1905.* New York: Arno Press, 1979.

Lee, Mabel Barbee. *Cripple Creek Days.* Lincoln: University of Nebraska Press, 1958.

Lee, Portia. *Historical and Architectural Evaluation: Prado Basin.* Pacific Palisades, CA: Greenwood and Associates, 1994.

Lee, Rose Hum. *The Growth and Decline of Chinese Communities in the Rocky Mountain Region.* New York: Arno, 1978.

Leeds, Tim. "Fort Belknap Pursues Development of Ethanol Plant." *Havre Daily News,* December 2, 2003. Available from http://www.havredailynews.com/articles/2003/12/02/local_headlines/ethanol.txt

LeMenager, Charles R. *Julian City and Cuyamaca Country: A History and Guide to the Past and Present.* Ramona, CA: Eagle Peak, 2001.

Leonard, Stephen J., and Thomas J. Noel. *Denver: Mining Camp to Metropolis.* Niwot: University Press of Colorado, 1990.

Leong, Russell. *Asian American Sexualities: Dimensions of the Gay & Lesbian Experience.* New York: Routledge, 1996.

Letran, Vivian. "The Other Camps." *Los Angeles Times,* May 1, 2002.

Letran, Vivian. "Rewriting the Books to Teach Vietnamese." *Orange County Register,* July 16, 2002.

Levine, Brian. *Cripple Creek-Victor Mining District.* Colorado Springs: Century One, 1987.

Lewis, David Rich. "Argonauts and the Overland Trail Experience: Method and Theory." *Western Historical Quarterly* 16, no. 3 (July 1985).

Lewis, David, Jr., and Ann T. Jordan. *Creek Indian Medicine Ways: The Enduring Power of Muskoke Religion.* Albuquerque: University of New Mexico Press, 2002.

Lewis, Donovan. *Pioneers of California: True Stories of Early Settlers in the Golden State.* San Francisco: Scottwall, 1993.

Lewis, Oscar. Sutter's *Fort: Gateway to the Gold Fields.* Englewood Cliffs, NJ: Prentice-Hall, 1966.

Liebeck, Judy. *Irvine: A History of Innovation and Growth,* edited by Myrtle Malone. Houston, TX: Pioneer, 1990.

Limerick, Patricia N. "Haunted by Rhyolite: Learning from the Landscape of Failure." *American Art* 6 (1992).

Limerick, Patricia N. *Legacy of Conquest: The Unbroken Past of the American West.* New York: Norton, 1987.

Limerick, Patricia Nelson. "Haunted by Rhyolite: Learning from the Landscape of Failure." In *The Big Empty: Essays on the Land as Narrative,* edited by L. Engel. Albuquerque: University of New Mexico Press, 1994.

Limerick, Patricia Nelson. "Making the Most of Words." In *Under an Open Sky: Rethinking America's Western Past,* edited by William Cronon, George Miles, and Jay Gitlin. New York: Norton, 1992.

"Lincoln—Lancaster County." Available from http://www.casde.unl.edu/history/counties/lancaster/lincoln/lincoln.htm

Lindell, Terrance Jon. "Acculturation among Swedish Immigrants in Kansas and Nebraska, 1870–1900." Ph.D. Dissertation, University of Nebraska–Lincoln, 1987.

Lingenfelter, Richard E. *Death Valley and the Amargosa.* Berkeley: University of California Press, 1986.

Lingenfelter, Richard E. *The Hardrock Miners: A History of the Mining Labor Movement in the American West, 1863–1893.* Berkeley: University of California Press, 1974.

Lingo, Marci. "Forbidden Fruit: The Banning of *The Grapes of Wrath* in Kern County Free Library." *Libraries and Culture* 38 (Fall 2003).

Littlefield, Daniel F., Jr. *Africans and Creeks: From the Colonial Period to the Civil War.* Westport, CT: Greenwood, 1979.

Lobo, Susan, and Kurt Peters, eds. *American Indians and the Urban Experience.* Walnut Creek, CA: AltaMira, 2001.

Logue, Larry. *A Sermon in the Desert: Belief and Behavior in Early St. George.* Urbana: University of Illinois Press, 1988.

Long, James L. *Land of Nakoda: The Story of the Assiniboine Indian.* Helena: Montana Historical Society Press, 2004.

Longacre, William L., ed. *Reconstructing Prehistoric Pueblo Societies.* Albuquerque: University of New Mexico Press, 1970.

Loo, Chalsa. *Chinatown: Most Time, Hard Time.* New York: Praeger, 1991.

Lopez, Carlos U. "Chilenos in California: A study of the 1850, 1852 and 1860 Censuses." Saratoga, CA: R and E Research, 1973.

Lorentz, John, and John Wertime. "Iranians." *Harvard Encyclopedia of American Ethnic Groups,* edited by Stephen Thernstrom. Cambridge, MA: Harvard University Press, 1980.

Los Angeles County Bar Association. "State Bar Symposium Issue: Water Law and the Drought" [Special issue]. *Los Angeles Bar Journal* 53, no. 3 (September 1977).

Lotchin, Roger W. *The Bad City in the Good War: San Francisco, Los Angeles, Oakland, and San Diego.* Bloomington: Indiana University Press, 2003.

Lotchin, Roger W. *Fortress California 1910–1961: From Warfare to Welfare.* New York: Oxford University Press, 1992.

Lotchin, Roger W., ed. "Special Issue: Fortress California at War: San Francisco, Los Angeles, Oakland and San Diego, 1941–1945." *Pacific Historical Review* 63, no. 3 (1994).

Lotchin, Roger W., ed. *The Way We Really Were: The Golden State in the Second Great War.* Urbana: University of Illinois Press, 2000.

Lothrop, Gloria Ricci, ed. *Fulfilling the Promise of California: An Anthology of Essays on the Italian American Experience in California.* Spokane, WA: Arthur H. Clark, 2000.

Love-Andrews, Devin. "Immigration Act of 1965." Available from http://campus.northpark.edu/history/WebChron/USA/ImmigrationAct.CP.html

Lowie, Robert H. *The Assiniboine.* New York: American Museum of Natural History, 1909.

Lucas, Henry Stephen, ed. *Dutch Immigrant Memoirs and Related Writings.* Grand Rapids, MI: W. B. Eerdmans, 1997.

Luckingham, Bradford. "Agents of Culture in the Urban West: Merchants and Mercantile Libraries in Mid-Nineteenth Century St. Louis and San Francisco." *Journal of the West* 17 (April 1978).

Luckingham, Bradford. *Minorities in Phoenix: A Profile of Mexican American, Chinese American, and African American Communities, 1860–1992.* Tucson: University of Arizona Press, 1994.

Luckingham, Bradford. *Phoenix: The History of a Southwestern Metropolis.* Tucson: University of Arizona Press, 1989.

Luebke, Frederick, ed. *European Immigrants: American West Community Histories.* Albuquerque: University of New Mexico Press, 1998.

Lukas, Anthony J. *Big Trouble.* New York: Simon & Schuster, 1997.

Lyman, George D. *John Marsh, Pioneer: The Life Story of a Trail-Blazer on Six Frontiers.* Chautauqua, NY: Chautauqua Press, 1931.

Lyman, George D. *The Saga of the Comstock Lode.* New York: Scribner, 1934.

Lyman, Stanford Morris. *Chinatown and Little Tokyo: Power, Conflict, and Community among Chinese and Japanese Immigrants in America.* Millwood, NY: Associated Faculty Press, 1986.

Lynch, Stephen. "Catching the Spirit of Tet." *Orange County Register,* February 3, 1994.

MacKell, Jan. *Cripple Creek District: Last of Colorado's Gold Booms.* Charleston, SC: Arcadia, 2003.

Madrigal, Anthony. "Ramona and Cahuilla Indian Bird Songs: Contrasting Visions of Southern California." Unpublished paper, University of California–Riverside, 2001.

Magden, Ronald E. *Furusato: Tacoma–Pierce County Japanese, 1888–1977.* Tacoma, WA: Tacoma Longshore Book & Research Committee, 1998.

Magnuson, Richard G. *Coeur d'Alene Diary: The First Ten Years of Hardrock Mining in North Idaho.* Portland, OR: Metropolitan Press, 1968.

Maguire, John Francis. *The Irish in America.* New York: Arno Press, 1969.

Maher, Sandy, and Ann Butterfield. *This History of Reese Creek.* Self-published, 2003.

Mahmood, Cynthia Keppley. *Frisian and Free: Study of an Ethnic Minority of the Netherlands.* Prospect Heights, IL: Waveland, 1989.

Mailman, Stanley. "California's Proposition 187 and Its Lessons." *New York Law Journal,* January 3, 1995. Available from http://ssbb.com/article1.html

Malone, Michael. *The Battle for Butte: Mining and Politics on the Northern Frontier, 1864–1906.* Seattle: University of Washington Press, 1981.

Malone, Michael P., Richard B. Roeder, and William L. Lang. *Montana: A History of Two Centuries.* Seattle: University of Washington Press, 1991.

Malone, Michael P., Richard Roeder, and William L. Lang. *Montana: A History of Two Centuries.* Rev. ed. Seattle: University of Washington Press, 1995.

"Manipulating of Market by Jap Farmers Related: Vegetable Profits Assertedly Sent Back to Homeland." *Los Angeles Times,* February 5, 1943.

Mann, Jim. "Retooling Southeast Asia Geopolitical Map." *Orange County Register,* February 4, 1994.

Mann, Ralph. *After the Gold Rush: Society in Grass Valley and Nevada City, California, 1849–1870.* Stanford, CA: Stanford University Press, 1982.

Manning, James W. "Literacy on the Oregon Trail: Books across the Plans." *Oregon Historical Quarterly* 41 (1940).

"Map of the Old Spanish Trail." Available from http://www.homesteadmuseum.org/family/mapost.htm

Margolin, Malcolm, ed. *The Way We Lived: California Indian Reminiscences, Stories, and Songs.* Berkeley, CA: Heyday Press, 1981.

Margolin, Malcolm, ed. *The Way We Lived: California Indian Stories, Songs, and Reminiscences.* 2nd ed. Berkeley, CA: Heyday Books, 2001.

Marsh, Charles S. *People of the Shining Mountains.* Boulder, CO: Pruett, 1982.

Marsh, Diann. *Santa Ana: An Illustrated History.* Encinitas, CA: Heritage, 1994.

Marshall, John Douglas. *Place of Learning, Place of Dreams: A History of the Seattle Public Library.* Seattle: University of Washington Press, 2004.

Martin, John. "From Judgment to Land Restoration: The Havasupai Land Claims Case." In *Irredeemable*

America: The Indians' Estate and Land Claims, edited by Imre Sutton. Albuquerque: University of New Mexico Press, 1985.

Martin, John. "The Prehistory and Ethnohistory of Havasupai-Hualapai Relations." *Ethnohistory* 32 (1985).

Martin, Philip. "Factors That Influence Migration: Proposition 187 in California." In *Migration between Mexico and the United States,* vol. 3. Available from http://www.utexas.edu/lbj/uscir/binpapers/v3a-4martin.pdf

Martines, Art. *A Brief History of Price.* Price, UT: Price City, 1986.

Mason, Kenneth. "African Americans and Race Relations in San Antonio, Texas, 1867–1937." In *Studies in African American History and Culture,* edited by Graham R. Hodges. New York: Garland, 1998.

Massey, Douglas S., and Audrey Singer. "New Estimates of Undocumented Mexican Migration and the Probability of Apprehension." *Demography* 32, no. 2 (1995).

Mathewson, Donald W. "A Central Public Library for Ogden, Utah, with Facilities for Serving County and Region." B.A. Thesis, University of Utah, 1959.

Matsumoto, Valarie. *Farming the Home Place: A Japanese American Community in California, 1919–1982.* Ithaca, NY: Cornell University Press, 1993.

Mattera, Philip. *World Class Business: A Guide to the 100 Most Powerful Global Corporations.* New York: Henry Holt, 1992.

Mattes, Merrill J. *Platte River Road Narratives: A Descriptive Bibliography of Travel over the Great Central Overland Route to Oregon, California, Utah, Colorado, Montana, and Other Western States and Territories, 1812–1866.* Urbana: University of Illinois Press, 1988.

Matthiessen, Peter. *Sal si Puedes (Escape if You Can): Cesar Chavez and the New American Revolution.* Berkeley: University of California Press, 2000.

Mayers, Jackson. *The San Fernando Valley.* Walnut, CA: John D. McIntyre, 1976.

Mayo, Morrow. *Los Angeles.* New York: Knopf, 1933.

McBroome, Delores N. "African American Boosterism, Agriculture, and Investment in Allensworth and Little Liberia." In *Seeking El Dorado: African Americans in California,* edited by Lawrence B. de Graaf, Kevin Mulroy, and Quintard Taylor. Seattle: University of Washington Press & Autry Museum of Western Heritage, 2001.

McCawley, William. *The First Angelinos: The Gabrielino Indians of Los Angeles.* Novato, CA: Ballena Press Publishers' Services, 1996.

McClean, Norman. *A River Runs through It and Other Stories.* Chicago: University of Chicago Press, 2001.

McClean, Norman. *Young Men and Fire.* Chicago: University of Chicago Press, 1993.

McCleary, Carrie Moran. "Giving Voice to Crow Country—The Crow Place Name Project." *The Tribal College Journal* 12 (Winter 2000). Available from http://www.tribalcollegejournal.org

McClintock, Walter. *Old Indian Trails: An Authentic Look at Native American Life and Culture by the Adopted Son of a Blackfoot Chief.* New York: Houghton Mifflin, 1923.

McCormick, John S. *The Gathering Place: An Illustrated History of Salt Lake City.* Woodland Hills, CA: Windsor, 2000.

McCormick, John S., and John R. Sillito, eds. *World We Thought We Knew: Readings in Utah History.* Salt Lake City: University of Utah Press, 1995.

McCracken, Harold. *The Mummy Cave Project in Northwestern Wyoming.* Cody, WY: Buffalo Bill Historical Center, 1978.

McCullough, Flavia Maria. *The Basques in the Northwest.* San Francisco: R and E Research Associates, 1974.

McDaniel, Wilma E. *The Last Dust Storm.* Brooklyn, NY: Hanging Loose Press, 1995.

McDaniel, Wilma E. *Sleeping in a Truck.* Santa Barbara, CA: Mille Grazie Press, 1998.

McFarren, H. W. *Mining Law for the Prospector, Miner and Engineer.* San Francisco: Mining and Scientific Press, 1911.

McGlashan, C. F. *History of the Donner Party.* Stanford, CA: Stanford University Press, 1962.

McGrath, Roger. *Gunfighters, Highwaymen, and Vigilantes.* Berkeley: University of California Press, 1984.

McKay, Kathryn. *Montana Mainstreets. Volume 5: A Guide to Historic Kalispell.* Helena: Montana Historical Society Press, 2001.

McKee, Delber R. *Chinese Exclusion versus the Open Door Policy 1900–1906: Clashes over China Policy in the Roosevelt Era.* Detroit, MI: Wayne State University Press, 1997.

McKee, James L. *Lincoln: The Prairie Capital.* Woodland Hills, CA: Windsor, 1984.

McLoughlin, William G. *After the Trail of Tears: The Cherokees' Struggle for Sovereignty, 1839–1880.* Chapel Hill: University of North Carolina Press, 1993.

McLynn, Frank. *Wagons West: The Epic Story of America's Overland Trails.* New York: Grove, 2002.

McPherson, James M. *Battle Cry of Freedom: The Civil War Era.* New York: Oxford University Press, 1988.

McWhorter, Lucullus V. *Yellow Wolf: His Own Story.* Rev. and enlarged ed. Caldwell, ID: Caxton Press, 1940–1968.

McWilliams, Carey. *Factories in the Field.* Boston: Little, Brown, 1939. (Reprinted Santa Barbara, CA: Peregrine Smith, 1971)

McWilliams, Carey. *Southern California: An Island on the Land.* Santa Barbara, CA: Peregrine Smith, 1973.

McWilliams, Carey. *Southern California Country: An Island on the Land.* New York: Duell, Sloan, & Pearce, 1946. (Reprinted Santa Barbara, CA: Peregrine Smith, 1973)

Mediavilla, Cindy. "The War on Books and Ideas: The California Library Association and Anti-Communist Censorship in the 1940s and 1950s." *Library Trends* 46 (Fall 1997).

Mediavilla, Cynthia L. *Carma Russell (Zimmerman) Leigh—An Historical Look at a Woman of Vision and Influence.* Ph.D. Dissertation, University of California–Los Angeles, 2000.

Medina, Manuel. Oral history conducted by Leleua Loupe. May 19, 2001. Riverside, California.

Mendez, Sylvia. Interview by Richard Heinemeyer, April 2001. Santa Ana Oral History Collection, City of Santa Ana Library, CA.

Mercer, Martha J. *British Brides, American Wives: The Immigration and Acculturation of War Brides in Mobile, Alabama, 1945–1993.* M.A. Thesis, Florida State University, 1993.

Mercier, Laurie K. *Anaconda: Labor, Community, and Culture in Montana's Smelter City.* Normal: University of Illinois Press, 2001.

Mercier, Laurie, and Carole Simon-Smolinski, eds. *Idaho's Ethnic Heritage: Historical Overviews.* 2 vols. Boise: Idaho Ethnic Heritage Project, 1990.

Merriam, C. Hart. *The Dawn of the World: Myths and Tales of the Miwok Indians of California.* Lincoln, NE: Bison Books, 1993.

Metcalf, R. Warren. *Termination's Legacy: The Discarded Indians of Utah.* Lincoln: University of Nebraska Press, 2002.

Michener, Thomas. "The South End of the Gallatin County." *The Coast* 15 (June 1908).

Miller, Bruce. *The Gabrielinos.* Los Osos, CA: Sand River Press, 1991.

Miller, Darlis A. *Mary Hallock Foote, Author-Illustrator of the American West.* Norman: University of Oklahoma Press, 2002.

Miller, Donald C. *Ghost Towns of the Southwest: Arizona, Utah, New Mexico.* Boulder, CO: Pruett, 1980.

Miller, Jared. "Fort Belknap Grazing Rates Soar." *Great Falls Tribune,* July 4, 2004. Available from http://www.greatfallstribune.com

Miller, John J. "Buffaloed." *National Review* 52 (October 9, 2000).

Miller, John J. "Propped Up: The Unexpected Legacy of Proposition 187." *National Review,* March 3, 2002. Available from http://www.nationalreview.com/miller/miller032802.asp

Miller, Kenneth. *The Czecho-Slovaks in America.* New York: George H. Doran, 1922.

Miller, Ronald Dean, and Peggy Jean Miller. *The Chemehuevi Indians of Southern California.* Banning, CA: Malki Museum Press, 1967.

Milliken, Randall. *A Time of Little Choice: The Disintegration of Tribal Culture in the San Francisco Bay Area, 1769–1810.* Menlo Park, CA: Ballena Press, 1995.

Milner, Clyde A., II. *A New Significance: Re-Envisioning the History of the American West.* New York: Oxford University Press, 1996.

Milner, Clyde A., II, Carol A. O'Connor, and Martha A. Sandweiss, eds. *The Oxford History of the American West.* New York: Oxford University Press, 1994.

Miner, H. Craig. *The Corporation and the Indian: Tribal Sovereignty and Industrial Civilization in Indian Territory, 1865–1907.* Columbia: University of Missouri Press, 1976.

Miner, H. Craig. *Kansas: The History of the Sunflower State, 1854–2000.* Lawrence: University Press of Kansas, 2002.

Miner, H. Craig. *Wichita: The Early Years, 1865–80.* Lincoln: University of Nebraska Press, 1982.

Mintz, Lannon W. *The Trail: A Bibliography of the Travelers on the Overland Trail to California, Oregon, Salt Lake City, and Montana during the Years 1841–1864.* Albuquerque: University of New Mexico Press, 1987.

Mission Tour. "A Virtual Tour of the California Missions, Lavanderia." Available from http://missiontour.org/santaines/tour06.htm

Mitchell, Annie R. *A Modern History of Tulare County.* Visalia, CA: Limited Editions of Visalia, 1974.

Modarres, Ali. "Settlement Patterns of Iranians in the United States." *Journal of the Society for Iranian Studies* 3, no. 1 (Winter 1998).

Moehring, Eugene. "The Comstock Urban Network." *Pacific Historical Review* 66 (August 1997).

Moehring, Eugene P. *Resort City in the Sunbelt.* Reno: University of Nevada Press, 1989.

Monaghan, Jay. *Chile, Peru, and the California Gold Rush of 1849.* Berkeley: University of California Press, 1973.

Monaghan, Jay. *Civil War on the Western Border, 1854–1865.* Boston: Little, Brown, 1955.

Monnett, John H. *Tell Them We Are Going Home: The Odyssey of the Northern Cheyennes.* Norman: University of Oklahoma Press, 2001.

Monroe, Julie R. *Moscow: Living and Learning on the Palouse.* Charleston, SC: Arcadia, 2003.

Monroy, Douglas. *Thrown among Strangers: The Making of Mexican Culture in Frontier California.* Berkeley: University of California Press, 1990.

Montana Ballet Company Web Site. Available from http://www.motanaballet.com

Montana Department of Environmental Quality. "Helena Mining District." Available from http://www.deq.state .mt.us/AbandonedMines/linkdocs/techdocs/98tech.asp

Montana Indians: Their History and Location. Helena: Montana Office of Public Instruction, 2004.

Montana Office of Public Instruction. Fort Belknap-Montana Compact Ratified, Montana Code Annotated. Helena: Montana Office of Public Instruction, 2003. Available from http://www.opi.mt.gov/

Montana State University. "Mountains and Minds." Available from http://www.montana.edu/msu/history

Montana–Wyoming Tribal Leaders Council Web Site. Available from http://tlc.wtp.net

Montanakids.com. "They Settled in Montana: The Act." Available from http://montanakids.com/db_engine/ presentations/presentation.asp?pid=329&sub=The+Act

Montane, Patricia. "Wetback." In *International Dictionary of Racial Language* (2003–2004). Available from http:// kpearson.faculty.tcnj.edu/Dictionary/wetback.htm

Mood, Fulmer. "Andrew S. Hallidie and Libraries in San Francisco, 1868–1879." *Library Quarterly* 16 (July 1946).

Moon, Danelle. "Educational Housekeepers: Female Reformers and the California Americanization Program, 1900–1927." In *California History: A Topical Approach*, edited by Gordon M. Bakken. Wheeling, IL: Harlan Davidson, 2003.

Moore, Brenda Lee. *Serving Our Country: Japanese American Women in the Military during World War II.* Piscataway, NJ: Rutgers University Press, 2003.

Moore, John H. *The Cheyenne.* Cambridge, MA: Blackwell, 1996.

Moore, John H. *The Cheyenne Nation: A Social and Demographic History.* Lincoln: University of Nebraska Press, 1988.

Moratto, M. J. *California Archaeology.* San Diego, CA: Academic Press, 1984.

Morgan, Dale, ed. *Overland in 1846: Diaries and Letters of the California-Oregon Trail.* Georgetown, CA: Talisman, 1963.

Morgan, Murray. *Puget's Sound: A Narrative of Early Tacoma and the Southern Sound.* Seattle: University of Washington Press, 1979.

Morgan, Robert M. *Water and the Land: A History of American Irrigation.* Fairfax, VA: Irrigation Association, 1993.

Morris, Edmund. *Theodore Rex.* New York: Random House, 2001.

Morris, Juddi. *The Harvey Girls: The Women Who Civilized the West.* New York: Walker, 1994.

Morrison, Dorothy N. *Chief Sarah: Sarah Winnemucca's Fight for Indian Rights.* 2nd ed. Portland: Oregon Historical Society Press, 1990.

Morriss, Andrew P. "Legal Arguments in the Opinions of Montana Territorial Chief Justice Decius S. Wade." *Nevada Law Journal* 1 (Spring 2001).

Morrow, Delores. *Our Sawdust Roots: A History of the Forest Products Industry in Montana.* Helena: Montana Historical Society, n.d.

Mosher, Frederic J. "State Aid—A Challenge to California Librarians." *California Librarian* 12 (June 1951).

Moss, Pius. "The Story of the Origin of the Arapaho People." A transcript of stories told by Dr. Pius Moss, as Elder of the Arapaho Tribe on the Wind River Reservation. In *The Wyoming Companion.* Laramie, WY: High Country, 1994–2004. Available from http:// www.wyomingcompanion.com/wcwrr.html

Moynihan, Ruth Barnes. *Rebel for Rights: Abigail Scott Duniway.* New Haven, CT: Yale University Press, 1983.

Muir, John. *Letters to a Friend, Written to Mrs. Ezra S. Carr, 1866–1879.* Dunwoody, GA: Berg, 1973.

Mullen, T. *Rivers of Change–Trailing the Waterways of Lewis and Clark.* Malibu, CA: Roundwood Press, 2004. Available from http://www.riversofchange.com

Muller, Eric L. *Free to Die for Their Country: The Story of the Japanese American Draft Resisters in World War II.* Chicago: University of Chicago Press, 2001.

Murase, Ichiro Mike. *Little Tokyo: One Hundred Years in Pictures.* Los Angeles: Visual Communications/Asian American Studies Central, 1983.

Murillo, Pauline. *Living in Two Worlds.* Highland, CA: Dimples Press, 2001.

Murphy, Mary. *Mining Cultures: Men, Women, and Leisure in Butte, 1914–41.* Urbana: University of Illinois Press, 1997.

Murray, Ester Johansson. *A History of the North Fork of the Shoshone River.* Cody, WY: Lone Eagle Multi Media, 1996.

Muscatine, Doris. *Old San Francisco: The Biography of a City from Early Days to the Earthquake.* New York: G. P. Putnam's Sons, 1975.

Muscogee (Creek) Nation of Oklahoma Web Site. Available from http://www.muscogeenation-nsn.gov

Musgrave, Marilyn. "Musgrave Urges Congress to Honor Colo Voters On Gaming." Press release, June 18, 2004. Available from http://wwwc.house.gov

Myres, Sandra L., ed. *Ho for California! Women's Overland Diaries from the Huntington Library.* San Marino, CA: Huntington Library, 1980.

Nadeau, Remi A. *City Makers.* New York: Doubleday, 1948.

Nadeau, Remi A. *Los Angeles: From Mission to Modern City.* New York: Longmans, Green, 1960.

Nadeau, Remi A. *The Silver Seekers.* Santa Barbara, CA: Crest, 1999.

Nakano, Mei. *Japanese American Women: Three Generations, 1890–1990.* San Francisco: National Japanese American Historical Society, 1990.

Nash, Gerald D. *The American West Transformed: The Impact of the Second World War.* Bloomington: Indiana University Press, 1985.

Nash, Gerald D. *World War II and the West: Reshaping the Economy.* Lincoln: University of Nebraska Press, 1990.

Nation, Joseph E. *Defense Industry Transition in California.* Under Direction of the Senate Office of Research Pursuant to Rules Committee Contract Number LCB 17384. Sacramento, 1994.

National Association for the Advancement of Colored People. Archival and Manuscript Collections Records of the West Coast Region, 1946–1970. Bancroft Library, University of California, Berkeley.

National Park Service [Home page]. Available from http://www.nps.gov

National Park Service. "Sand Creek Massacre National Historic Site." Available from http://www.nps.gov/sand/sitestudy.htm

Neihardt, John G. *Black Elk Speaks: Being the Life Story of a Holy Man of the Ogalala Sioux.* New York: William Morrow, 1932.

Neils, Paul. *Julius Neils and the J. Neils Lumber Company.* Seattle: McCaffrey, 1971.

Neilson, Parker M. *The Dispossessed: Cultural Genocide of the Mixed-Blood Utes.* Norman: University of Oklahoma Press, 1998.

Nelson, Douglas W. *Heart Mountain: The History of an American Concentration Camp.* Madison: University of Wisconsin, State Historical Society of Wisconsin for the Department of History, 1976.

Nelson, Fern K. *This Was Jackson's Hole: Incidents and Profiles from the Settlement of Jackson Hole.* Glendo, WY: High Plains Press, 1994.

Nelson, Paula M. *After the West Was Won: Homesteaders and Town-Builders in Western South Dakota, 1900–1917.* Iowa City: University of Iowa Press, 1986.

Nevers, Jo Ann. *Wa She Shu: A Washo Tribal History.* Reno: Inter-Tribal Council of Nevada, 1976.

Nez Perce Tribe. *Treaties: Nez Perce Perspectives.* Lapwai: The Nez Perce Tribe of Idaho, 2003.

Nguyen, Elizabeth A.-D. Interview by Trangdai Tranguyen. July 14, 2000. West Los Angeles, California.

Nguyen, Katherine. "Herbal Healing's All the Sage." *Orange County Register,* March 9, 2002.

Nguyen, Robert N. Interview by Trangdai Tranguyen. March 15, 2000. Anaheim, California.

Nguyen, Thanh T. Interview by Trangdai Tranguyen. December 6, 1999. Santa Ana, California.

Nichols, Jeffrey. *Prostitution, Polygamy, and Power: Salt Lake City, 1847–1918.* Urbana: University of Illinois Press, 2002.

Nichols, Jeffrey D. "The Ute Trek to South Dakota in 1906 Ended in Disappointment." Available from http://historytogo.utah.gov/utah_chapters/american_indians

"Nickodemus, Kansas—A Black Pioneer Town." Available from http://www.legendsofamerica.com/OZ-Nicodemus.html

Nicolaides, Becky M. *My Blue Heaven: Life and Politics in the Working-Class Suburb of Los Angeles, 1920–1965.* Chicago: University of Chicago Press, 2002.

Niiya, Brian, ed. *Encyclopedia of Japanese-American History: An A-to-Z Reference From 1868 to Present.* New York: Facts on File, 2001.

Nimmo, William F. *Stars and Stripes across the Pacific: The United States, Japan, and the Asia/Pacific Region, 1895–1945.* Westport, CT: Praeger, 2001.

Niven, Francis. *Manhattan Omnibus.* Bozeman, MT: Francis Niven, 1984.

Noble, Bruce, and Robert Spude. "Guidelines for Identifying, Evaluating, and Registering Historic Mining Properties." *National Register Bulletin* 42 (1992).

Noble, David G., ed. *The Hohokam: Ancient People of the Desert.* Santa Fe, NM: School of American Research Press, 1991.

Noel, Thomas J. *The City and the Saloon: Denver, 1858–1916.* Boulder: University Press of Colorado, 1996.

Noel, Thomas J., Paul F. Mahoney, and Richard E. Stevens. *Historical Atlas of Colorado.* Norman: University of Oklahoma Press, 1993.

Northern Arapaho Tribal Web Site. Available from http://www.northernarapaho.com

Notarianni, Philip F., ed. *Carbon County: Eastern Utah's Industrialized Island.* Salt Lake City: Utah State Historical Society, 1981.

Notarianni, Philip F. "The Frisco Charcoal Kilns." National Register of Historic Places Nomination Form, 1981.

Notarianni, Philip F. "The Frisco Charcoal Kilns." *Utah Historical Quarterly* 50 (1982).

Nugent, Walter. *Into the West: The Story of Its People.* New York: Knopf, 1999.

Nunis, Doyce B., Jr., ed. *The Bidwell-Bartleson Party: 1841 California Emigrant Adventure, the Documents and Memoirs of the Overland Pioneers.* Santa Cruz, CA: Western Tanager Press, 1991.

O'Brien, David J., and Stephen S. Fugita. *The Japanese American Experience.* Bloomington: Indiana University Press, 1991.

O'Connor, Bryan. "Indian Historian to Realize Dream." *Billings Gazette*, September 27, 2003. Available from http://www.billingsgazette.com/index.php?id=1&display=rednews/2003/09/27/build/local/28-capture.inc

O'Dell, Scott. *Island of the Blue Dolphins.* Boston: Houghton Mifflin and Riverside Press, 1960.

Ogden, Adele. "Boston Hide Droghers along California Shores." *California Historical Society Quarterly* 8 (1929).

Ogden, Adele. "Hides and Tallow: McCulloch, Hartnell and Company 1822–1828." *California Historical Society Quarterly* 6 (1927).

Ogle, Ralph, H. *Federal Control of the Western Apaches, 1848–1886.* Albuquerque: University of New Mexico Press, 1970.

Olson, James C. *Red Cloud and the Sioux Problem.* Lincoln: University of Nebraska Press, 1965.

Olson, James C., and Ronald C. Naugle. *History of Nebraska,* 3rd ed. Lincoln: University of Nebraska Press, 1997.

Onsman, Andrys. *Defining Indigeneity in the Twenty-First Century: A Case Study of the Frisians.* Lewiston, NY: E. Mellen, 2004.

Orange County Web Site. Available from http://www.oc.ca.gov

Orange County Environmental Management Agency (OCEMA). *¡Bienvenidos al Canon de Santa Ana! A History of the Santa Ana Canyon.* Santa Ana, CA: Environmental Management Agency, 1976.

Orange County Water District Web Site. Available from http://www.ocwd.com

Orange County Water District. *A History of Orange County Water District: 1933–2003.* Fountain Valley, CA: Orange County Water District, 2003.

Ortiz, Alfonso. *Tewa World Space, Time, Being and Becoming in a Pueblo Society.* Chicago: University of Chicago Press, 1972.

Osborn, H. S., and M. W. Von Bernewitz. *Prospector's Field-Book and Guide.* New York: McGraw-Hill, 1920.

Osburn, Katherine M. B. *Southern Ute Women: Autonomy and Assimilation on the Reservation, 1887–1934.* Albuquerque: University of New Mexico Press, 1997.

Ott, John S., and Dick Malloy. *The Tacoma Public Utility Story: The First 100 Years, 1893–1993.* Tacoma, WA: Tacoma Public Utilities, 1993.

Owens, Kenneth N. *John Sutter and a Wider West.* Lincoln: University of Nebraska Press, 1994.

Oxendine, Joan. *The Luiseño Village during the Later Prehistoric Era.* Ph.D. Dissertation, University of California, Riverside, 1983.

Oyarzun, Luis. *El Oro de California y la Vida Chilena.* Santiago, Chile: Editorial Universitaria, 1967.

Pacific Northwest Library Association. *Pacific Northwest Libraries; History of Their Early Development in Washington, Oregon and British Columbia.* Seattle: University of Washington Press, 1926.

Padilla, Victoria. *Southern California Gardens.* Berkeley: University of California Press, 1961.

Page, James R. *I. N. Van Nuys: 1835–1912.* Los Angeles: Ward Ritchie Press, 1944.

Paher, Stanley W. *Las Vegas: As It Began—As It Grew.* Las Vegas: Nevada Publications, 1971.

Pala Casino Web Site. Available from http://www.palacasino.com

Pala Indians Web Site. Available from http://www.palaindians.com

Paladin, Vivian, and Jean Baucus. *Helena: An Illustrated History.* Helena: Montana Historical Society, 1996.

Papanikolas, Helen Z. "The Greek Immigrant in Utah." In *Ethnic Oral History at the American West Center*, edited by John D. Sylvester. Salt Lake City: University of Utah, 1972.

Papanikolas, Helen Z. "The Greeks of Carbon County." *Utah Historical Quarterly* 22 (1954).

Paquette, Mary Grace. *Basques to Bakersfield.* Bakersfield, CA: Kern County Historical Society, 1982.

Paquette, Mary Grace. *Lest We Forget: The History of the French in Kern County.* Fresno, CA: Valley Publishers, 1978.

Paris, Beltran, as told to William A. Douglas. *Beltran, Basque Sheepman of the American West.* Reno: University of Nevada Press, 1979.

Parker, Watson. *Gold in the Black Hills.* Norman: University of Oklahoma Press, 1966.

Parsons, Dana. "Diversity Is Pot of Gold for O. C.'s Rainbow Census." *Los Angeles Times,* May 17, 2002.

Parsons, Katherine B. *History of Fifty Years: Ladies' Literary Club, Salt Lake City, Utah, 1877–1927.* Salt Lake City, UT: Arrow Press, 1927.

Passet, Joanne E. "Bringing the Pubic Library Gospel to the American West." *Journal of the West* 30 (July 1991).

Passet, Joanne E. *Cultural Crusaders: Women Librarians in the American West, 1900–1917.* Albuquerque: University of New Mexico Press, 1994.

Pate, J'Nell L. *Livestock Legacy: The Fort Worth Stockyards, 1887–1987.* Fort Worth: Texas A&M University Press, 1988.

Pate, J'Nell L. *North of the River: A Brief History of North Fort Worth.* Fort Worth: Texas Christian University Press, 1994.

Patrick, Lucille Nichols. *Best Little Town by a Dam Site: Or Cody's First 20 Years.* Cheyenne, WY: Flintlock, 1968.

Paul, Rodman Wilson. *Mining Frontiers of the Far West, 1848–1880.* New York: Holt, Rinehart and Winston, 1963.

Paul, Rodman Wilson. *Mining Frontiers of the Far West, 1848–1880.* Rev. exp. ed., edited by Elliott West. Albuquerque: University of New Mexico Press, 2001.

Pawar, Sheelwant Bapurao. "An Environmental Study of the Development of the Utah Labor Movement: 1860–1935." Ph.D. Dissertation, University of Utah, 1968.

Payne, Judith. *Public Libraries Face California's Ethnic and Racial Diversity.* Santa Monica, CA: RAND, 1998.

Pease, Ben. "Japantowns." Available from http://www.pease press.com/Japantowns.html

Peevers, Andrea. *San Diego & Tijuana.* Oakland, CA: Lonely Planet, 2001.

Perdue, Theda, ed. *Sifters: Native American Women's Lives.* New York: Oxford University Press, 2000.

Perdue, Theda, and Michael D. Green, eds. *The Cherokee Removal: A Brief History with Documents.* Boston: Bedford St. Martin's Press, 1995.

Peterson, Charles. *Utah: A Bicentennial History.* New York: Norton, and Nashville, TN: American Association for State and Local History, 1977.

Peterson, Frank Ross. *Idaho, a Bicentennial History.* New York: Norton, 1976.

Peterson, Marie R. *Echoes of Yesterday: Summit County Centennial History.* Salt Lake City, UT: Mountain States Bindery, 1947.

Peterson del Mar, David. *Oregon's Promise: An Interpretive History.* Corvallis: Oregon State University Press, 2003.

Phan, Hieu T. "A Rare Breed of Tiger." *Orange County Register,* November 28, 1999.

Phan, Hieu T. "In Peace Together." *Orange County Register,* October 10, 1999.

Phan, Hieu T. "Music of Their Heritage." *Orange County Register,* October 8, 1999.

Phan, Hieu T. "The Verbalization of Identity." *Orange County Register,* November 25, 1999.

Phillips, Barbara A. Interview by Kathy Frazee, March 2003. Santa Ana Oral History Collection, City of Santa Ana Library, CA.

Phillips, George H. *Chiefs and Challengers.* Berkeley: University of California Press, 1975.

Phillips, George H. *Indians and Indian Agents: The Origins of the Reservation System in California, 1849–1852.* Norman: University of Oklahoma Press, 1997.

Phillips, George H. *Indians and Intruders in Central California, 1769–1849.* Norman: University of Oklahoma Press. 1993.

Philpott, William. *The Lessons of Leadville: Or, Why the Western Federation of Miners Turned Left* [Colorado Historical Society monograph no. 10]. Denver: Colorado Historical Society, 1994.

Phong, Ann. Interview by Trangdai Tranguyen. May 7, 2000. Cerritos, California.

Pigney, Joseph. *For Fear We Shall Perish.* New York: Dutton, 1961.

Piker, Joshua. *Okfuskee: A Creek Town in Colonial America.* Cambridge, MA: Harvard University Press, 2004.

Pioneer Museum vertical files. Pioneer Museum. Bozeman, MT.

Pisani, Donald. *Water and American Government: The Reclamation Bureau, National Water Policy, and the West, 1902–1935.* Berkeley: University of California Press, 2002.

Pisani, Lawrence Frank. *The Italian in America.* New York: Exposition Press, 1957.

Pitt, Leonard. *The Decline of the Californios: A Social History of the Spanish-Speaking Californians, 1846–1890.* Berkeley: University of California Press, 1966.

Pitt, Leonard. "The Midwesternization of a Cowtown." *California History* 60 (Spring 1981).

Pittman, Tarea H. "Operation of State and County Resident Requirements under the California Indigent Aid Law in Contra Costa County." M.A. Thesis, University of California, Berkeley, 1946.

Pittman, Tarea Hall. *NAACP Official and Civil Rights Worker.* Oral history conducted by Joyce Henderson, 1971–1972. Regional Oral History Office, Bancroft Library, University of California, Berkeley.

Poling-Kempes, Lesley. *The Harvey Girls: Women Who Opened the West*. New York: Marlow, 1991.

Polos, Nicolas C. *San Dimas: Preserving the Western Spirit*. San Dimas, CA: San Dimas Press, 1990.

Pomeroy, Elizabeth. *John Muir, A Naturalist in Southern California*. Pasadena, CA: Many Moons Press, 2001.

Poole, John Bruce, and Tevvy Ball. *El Pueblo: The Historic Heart of Los Angeles*. Los Angeles: Getty, 2002.

Porter, W. Kenneth. *The Negro on the American Frontier*. New York: Arno, 1971.

Pourade, Richard F. *Anza Conquers the Desert: The Anza Expeditions from Mexico to California and the Founding of San Francisco 1774 to 1776*. San Diego, CA: Copley Books, 1971.

Powell, Allan Kent, ed. *Utah History Encyclopedia*. Salt Lake City: University of Utah Press, 1994.

Powell, Lawrence Clark. *The Alchemy of Books, and Other Essays and Addresses on Books & Writers*. Los Angeles: W. Ritchie Press, 1954.

Prado, Mary S. *Mexican American Women Activists*. Philadelphia: Temple University Press, 1998.

"President Andrew Jackson's Case for The Removal Act, First Annual Message to Congress, 8 December 1830." Available from http://www.mtholyoke.edu/acad/intrel/andrew.htm

Preston, William, Jr. *Aliens and Dissenters: Federal Suppression of Radicals, 1903–1933*. Cambridge, MA: Harvard University Press, 1963.

Proceedings of the Fourth Annual Session of the Dry Farming Congress. Billings, MT: Billings Chamber of Commerce, 1909.

Proceedings of the Trans-Missouri Dry Farming Congress. Denver, CO: Denver Chamber of Commerce, 1907.

Prucha, Francis Paul. *American Indian Treaties: The History of a Political Anomaly*. Berkeley: University of California Press, 1994.

Prucha, Francis Paul. *The Great Father: The United States Government and the American Indians*. Lincoln: University of Nebraska Press, 1984.

Prucha, Francis Paul. *The Indian in American History*. New York: Holt, Rinehart and Winston, 1971.

Pryde, Philip R. *San Diego: An Introduction to the Region*. El Cajon, CA: Sunbelt, 2004.

Qoyawayma, Polingaysi. *No Turning Back: A Hopi Indian Woman's Struggle to Live in Two Worlds*. Albuquerque: University of New Mexico Press, 1964.

Quam-Wickham, Nancy. "'Another World': Home, Work, and Autonomy in Blue Collar Suburbs." In *Metropolis in the Making: Los Angeles in the 1920s*, edited by William Deverell and Tom Sitton. Berkeley: University of California Press, 2001.

Quimby, Garfield M. *History of the Potrero Ranch and Its Neighbors*. Fresno: California History Books, 1975.

Quyen, Nguyen. Interview by Trangdai Tranguyen. October 14, 2000. Redwood City, California.

Rader, Benjamin G. "The Montana Lumber Strike of 1917." *Pacific Historical Review* 36 (May 1967).

Raftery, Judith R. *Land of Fair Promise: Politics and Reform in Los Angeles Schools, 1885–1941*. Palo Alto, CA: Stanford University Press, 1992.

Rajaee, Farhang. *Iranian Perspectives on the Iran-Iraq War*. Gainesville, FL: University Press of Florida, 1997.

Ramsey, Eleanor M. "Allensworth: A Study in Social Change." Ph.D. Dissertation, University of California, Berkeley, 1977.

Ramsey, Eleanor M., and Janice S. Lewis. "Black Americans in California." *Five Views: An Ethnic Sites Survey for California*. Sacramento, CA: Office of Historic Preservation, 1988.

Ransome, F. L. *Mines of Goldfield, Bullfrog and Other Southern Nevada Districts*. Las Vegas: Nevada Publications, 1907.

Rawls, James J. *Indians of California: The Changing Image*. Norman: University of Oklahoma Press, 1984.

Rawls, James J., and Walton Bean. *California: An Interpretive History*. 8th ed. New York: McGraw-Hill, 2003.

"Record of Confederate Veterans and Their Wives, Who Were Pioneers in Orange County, California." 1938–1939 Scrapbook of Emma Sansom Chapter 449, United Daughters of the Confederacy, Santa Ana, CA.

Reed, Diane. "She Learned There Are No Limitations." *Orange County Register*, July 18, 2002.

Reese, Rina. *History of the Denver Public Library, 1860–1928*. Denver, CO: Denver Public Library, 1928.

"Rehberg Announces $5.7 Million in Grants to Montana Tribal Colleges." Press release, August 4, 2004. Available from http://www.house.gov

Reid, Hugo. *Indians of Los Angeles County*. Edited and annotated by Robert F. Heizer. Los Angeles: Southwest Museum, 1968.

Reid, John Phillip. *Law for the Elephant: Property and Social Behavior on the Overland Trail*. San Marino, CA: Huntington Library, 1980.

Reid, John Phillip. "The Layers of Western Legal History." In *Law for the Elephant, Law for the Beaver: Essays in the Legal History of North America*, edited by John McLaren, Harmar Foster, and Chet Orloff. Pasadena, CA: Ninth Judicial Circuit Historical Society, 1992.

Reid, John Philip. *Policing the Elephant: Crime, Punishment, and Social Behavior on the Overland Trail.* San Marino, CA: Huntington Library, 1997.

Reilly, Bob, Hugh Reilly, and Pegeen Reilly. *Historic Omaha: An Illustrated History of Omaha and Douglas County.* Omaha, NE: Historical Publishing Network and Douglas County Historical Society, 2003.

Reimers, David M. *Still the Golden Door: The Third World Comes to America.* New York: Columbia University Press, 1985.

Reimers, David M. *Unwelcome Strangers: American Identity and the Turn against Immigration.* New York: Columbia University Press, 1998.

Relander, Click. *Strangers on the Land: A Historiette of a Longer Story of the Yakima Indian Nation's Efforts to Survive against Great Odds.* Yakima, WA: Franklin Press, 1962.

Remini, Robert. *Andrew Jackson and His Indian Wars.* New York: Viking Press, 2001.

Remy, Jules, and Julius Brenchley. *A Journey to Great Salt Lake City.* London: W. Jeffs, 1861.

Reyes, David. "News of the World, Vietnamese Style." *Orange County Register,* February 2, 1989.

Rhode, Paul. "California in the Second World War: An Analysis of Defense Spending." In *The Way We Really Were: The Golden State in the Second Great War,* edited by Roger W. Lotchin. Urbana: University of Illinois Press, 2000.

Rhode, Paul. "The Impact of World War Two Spending on the California Economy." In *The Way We Really Were: The Golden State in the Second Great War,* edited by Roger W. Lotchin. Urbana: University of Illinois Press, 2000.

Rhode, Paul. "The Nash Thesis Revisited: An Economic Historian's View." *Pacific Historical Review* 63, no. 3 (1994).

Riccards, Michael P. *The Presidency and the Middle Kingdom: China, the United States, and Executive Leadership.* Lanham, MD: Lexington Books, 2001.

Richter, Paul, and Michael Ross. "Clinton Lifts Vietnam Embargo: Says Action Will Help Resolve Fate of MIAs." *Los Angeles Times,* February 4, 1994.

Ricketts, A. H. *American Mining Law with Forms and Precedents* [California Division of Mines and Geology Bulletin no. 98]. Sacramento: California Division of Mines and Geology, 1931.

Ricketts, A. H. *Manner of Locating and Holding Mineral Claims in California* [California Division of Mines and Geology Bulletin no. 127]. Sacramento: California Division of Mines and Geology, 1944.

Riedessel, G. A. *Arid Acres: A History of the Kimama-Minidoka Homesteaders, 1912 to 1932.* Pullman, WA: G. A. Riedessel, 1969.

Righter, Robert. *Crucible for Conservation: The Creation of Grand Teton National Park.* Boulder: Colorado Associated University Press, 1982.

RightNow Technologies Web Site. Available from http://www.rightnow.com

Riley, Glenda. *A Place to Grow: Women in the American West.* Wheeling, IL: Harlan Davidson, 1992.

Riley, Glenda. *Building and Breaking Families in the American West.* Albuquerque: University of New Mexico Press, 1996.

Riley, Glenda. *The Female Frontier: A Comparative View of Women and the Prairie and the Plains.* Lawrence: University of Kansas Press, 1988.

Riley, Glenda. *The Life and Legend of Annie Oakley.* Norman: University of Oklahoma Press, 1994.

Riley, Glenda. *Prairie Voices: Iowa's Pioneering Women.* Ames: Iowa State University Press, 1996.

Riley, Glenda. *Women and Indians on the Frontier, 1825–1915.* Albuquerque: University of New Mexico Press, 1984.

Riley, Glenda. *Women and Nature: Saving the "Wild" West.* Lincoln: University of Nebraska Press, 1999.

Riley, Glenda, and Richard W. Etulain. *By Grit & Grace: Eleven Women Who Shaped the American West.* Golden, CO: Fulcrum Press, 1997.

Ring, Daniel F. "Men of Energy and Snap: The Origins and Early Years of the Billings Public Library." *Libraries and Culture* 36, no. 3 (2001).

Ring, Daniel F. "The Origins of the Butte Public Library: Some Further Thoughts on Public Library Development in the State of Montana." *Libraries and Culture* 28 (Fall 1993).

Ringholz, R. C. *Paradise Paved: The Challenge of Growth in the New West.* Salt Lake City: University of Utah Press, 1996.

Rischin, Moses, and John Livingston. *Jews of the American West.* Detroit, MI: Wayne State University Press, 1991.

Riverside County Web Site. Available from http://www.co.riverside.ca.us

Robbins, Roy M. *Our Landed Heritage.* Lincoln: University of Nebraska Press, 1962.

Robbins, William G. *Lumberjacks and Legislators: Political Economy of the U.S. Lumber Industry, 1890–1941.* College Station: Texas A&M University Press, 1982.

Robbins, William G. "The Tarnished Dream: The Turbulent World of the Forest Products Industry in the

Northwest." *Montana: The Magazine of Western History* 37, no. 1 (Winter 1987).

Robbins, William G. "The Western Lumber Industry: A 20th Century Perspective." In *The 20th Century West: Historical Interpretations*, edited by Gerald Nash and Richard Etulain. Albuquerque: University of New Mexico Press, 1989.

Roberts, David. *Once They Moved Like the Wind: Cochise, Geronimo and the Apache Wars.* New York: Simon & Schuster, 1993.

Roberts, Richard C., and Richard W. Sadler. *History of Weber County.* Salt Lake City: Utah Historical Society, Weber County Commission, 1996.

Robertson, Frank C., and Beth Kay Harris. *Boom Towns of the Great Basin.* Denver, CO: Sage Books, 1962.

Robinson, Greg. *By Order of the President.* Cambridge, MA: Harvard University Press, 2001.

Robinson, W. John, and Bruce Risher. *The San Jacintos: The Mountain Country from Banning to Borrego.* Arcadia, CA: Big Santa Anita Historical Society, 1993.

Robinson, W. W. *Land in California: The Story of Mission Lands, Ranchos, Squatters, Mining Claims, Railroad Grants, Land Scrip, Homesteads.* Berkeley: University of California Press, 1979.

Robinson, W. W. *The Story of Riverside County.* Riverside, CA: Riverside Title, 1957.

Robinson, William W. *Land in California.* New York: Arno Press, 1979.

Robinson, William W. *The Spanish and Mexican Ranchos of the San Fernando Valley.* Highland Park, CA: Southwest Museum, 1966.

Robinson, William W. *The Story of the San Fernando Valley.* Los Angeles: Title Insurance and Trust, 1961.

Rock, Rosalind Z. "A History of Libraries in New Mexico—Spanish Origins to Statehood." *Journal of Library History* 14 (Summer 1979).

Roderick, Kevin. *The San Fernando Valley: America's Suburb.* Los Angeles: Los Angeles Times Books, 2001.

Rodnick, David. *The Fort Belknap Assiniboine of Montana: A Study in Culture Change.* Brooklyn, NY: AMS Press, 1978.

Rohe, Randall. "Gold Mining Landscapes of the West." *California Geology* 37 (October 1984).

Rolle, Andrew. *Los Angeles: From Pueblo to City of the Future.* 2nd ed. Sacramento, CA: MTL, 1995.

Rolle, Andrew F. *California: A History.* 4th ed. Arlington Heights, IL: Harlan Davidson, 1987.

Rolle, Andrew F. *California: A History.* 5th ed. Wheeling, IL: Harlan Davidson, 1998.

Rolle, Andrew F. *The Immigrant Upraised: Italian Adventures and Colonists in an Expanding America.* Norman: University of Oklahoma Press, 1968.

Rolle, Andrew F. *John Charles Fremont: Character as Destiny.* Norman: University of Oklahoma Press, 1991.

Rosales, Vicente Perez. *Oro en California.* Santiago, Chile: Editorial Nascimento, 1974.

Rosicky, Rose. *A History of Czechs (Bohemians) in Nebraska.* Omaha: Czech Historical Society of Nebraska, 1929.

Rosier, Paul C. *Rebirth of the Blackfeet Nation, 1912–1954.* Lincoln: University of Nebraska Press, 2001.

Ross, Raymond R. Interview by Barbara Oldewage, August 1995. Santa Ana Oral History Collection, City of Santa Ana Library, CA.

Rotberg, Robert I., and Theodore K. Rabb. *Climate and History: Studies in Interdisciplinary History.* Princeton, NJ: Princeton University Press, 1981.

Roug, Louise. "Little Saigon Honors Dead." *Orange County Register,* October 10, 1999.

Rowe, John. *The Hard-Rock Men: Cornish Immigrants and the North American Mining Frontier.* Liverpool, UK: Liverpool University Press, 1974.

Rowland, Donald E., John Rowland, and William Workman. *Southern California Pioneers of 1841.* Spokane, WA: Arthur H. Clark, 1999.

Royce, Josiah. *California: A Study of American Character.* Berkeley, CA: Heyday, 2002.

Rozema, Vick, ed. *Voices from the Trail of Tears.* Winston-Salem, NC: John F. Blair, 2003.

Ruoff, A. LaVonne. "Nineteenth-Century American Indian Autobiographers: William Apes, George Copway, and Sarah Winnemucca." In *The New Literary History*, edited by A. LaVonne Ruoff and Jerry Ward. New York: MLA, 1991.

Russell, Brian K. *Promise of Water: The Legacy of Pick-Sloan and the Irrigation of North Dakota.* Bismarck: North Dakota Humanities Council. Available from http://www.nd-humanities.org/html/russell.html

Russell, Dale R. *The Eighteenth Century Western Cree and their Neighbors.* Hull, Quebec: Canadian Museum of Civilization, 1991.

Russell, Jeremy. "Medicine Crow to Receive Honorary Degree from USC." *The Custer Museum Gazette,* May 10, 2003. Available from http://www.custermuseum.org/medicinecrow.htm

Rutledge, Paul. *The Vietnamese Experience in America.* Bloomington: Indiana University Press, 1992.

Rzeczkowski, Frank. "The Crow Indians and the Bozeman Trail." Available from http://www.hist.state.mt.us/education/cirguides/transrzeczkowski.asp

Sabagh, Georges, and Mehdi Bozorgmehr. "Are the Characteristics of Exiles Different from Immigrants? The Case of Iranians in Los Angeles." *Sociology and Social Research* 71 (1987).

Sachar, Howard Morley. *The Course of Modern Jewish History*. New York: Dell, 1977.

Sackman, David Cazaux. *Orange Empire: California and the Fruits of Eden*. Berkeley: University of California Press, 2005.

Salyer, Lucy E. *Laws Harsh as Tigers: Chinese Immigrants and the Shaping of Modern Immigration Law*. Chapel Hill: University of North Carolina Press, 1995.

Salyer, Lucy E. *Laws Harsh as Tigers: Chinese Immigrants and the Shaping of Modern Immigration Law*. Chapel Hill: University of North Carolina Press, 1995.

San Bernardino County Web Site. Available from http://www.co.san-bernardino.ca.us

San Gabriel Mission Registers. San Fernando, CA: Chancery Archives of the Archdiocese of Los Angeles at Mission San Fernando, various years.

Sanchez, George J. *Becoming Mexican American: Ethnicity, Culture and Identity in Chicano Los Angeles, 1900–1945*. New York: Oxford University Press, 1993.

Sanchez, George, and Arthur A. Hansen. *The Boyle Heights Oral History Project*. Los Angeles: Japanese American National Museum, 2002.

Sandmeyer, Elmer Clarence. *The Anti-Chinese Movement in California*, Urbana: University of Illinois Press, 1991.

Sando, Joe S. *The Pueblo Indians*. San Francisco: The Indian Historian Press, 1976.

Santa Ana Watershed Project Authority Web Site. Available from http://www.sawpa.org

Santino, Jack. *Miles of Smiles: Stories of Black Pullman Porters*. Urbana: University of Illinois Press, 1989.

Sarber, Mary A. "A Century of Growth: The El Paso Public Library, 1894–1994." *Password* 39 (Spring 1994).

Sato, Mike. *The Price of Taming a River: The Decline of Puget Sound's Duwamish/Green Waterway*. Seattle, WA: The Mountaineers, 1997.

Satz, Ronald N. *American Indian Policy in the Jacksonian Era*. Norman: University of Oklahoma Press, 2002.

Saunders County Historical Society. *Saunders County History*. Dallas, TX: Taylor, 1983.

Saunt, Claudio. *A New Order of Things: Property, Power, and the Transformation of the Creek Indians, 1733–1816*. New York: Cambridge University Press, 1999.

Saunt, Claudio. *Black, White, and Indian: Race and the Unmaking of an American Family*. New York: Oxford University Press, 2005.

Savage, Sherman. *Blacks in the West*. Westport, CT: Greenwood, 1976.

Saxton, Alexander. *The Indispensable Enemy: Labor and the Anti-Chinese Movement in California*. Berkeley: University of California Press, 1971.

Saylor, David J. *Jackson Hole, Wyoming: In the Shadow of the Tetons*. Norman: University of Oklahoma Press, 1970.

Schallenberger, Moses. *The Opening of the California Trail*. Berkeley: University of California Press, 1953.

Schilling, Ron. "Indians and Eagles: The Struggle over Orme Dam." *Journal of Arizona History* 41 (2000).

Schlesier, Karl H. *The Wolves of Heaven: Cheyenne Shamanism, Ceremonies, and Prehistoric Origins*. Norman: University of Oklahoma Press, 1987.

Schlissel, Lillian. *Women's Diaries of the Westward Journey*. New York: Schocken Books, 1982.

Schoenberger, Karl. "O. C. Businesses among Those Looking Eagerly at Vietnamese Markets." *Orange County Register*, February 4, 1994.

Schroeder, Albert. "A Study of Yavapai History." In *Yavapai Indians*, edited by David Horr. New York: Garland, 1974.

Schuster, Helen H. *The Yakima*. New York: Chelsea House, 1990.

Schuster, Helen H. *Yakima Indian Traditionalism: A Study in Continuity and Change*. Ph.D. Dissertation, University of Washington, 1975.

Schwantes, Carlos. *Bisbee: Urban Outpost on the Frontier*. Tucson: University of Arizona Press, 1992.

Screws, Raymond D. "Not a Melting Pot: A Comparative Study of Swedes and Czechs in Saunders County, Nebraska, 1880–1910." *Heritage of the Great Plains* 35, no. 1 (2002).

Screws, Raymond Douglas. "Retaining Their Culture and Ethnic Identity: Assimilation among Czechs and Swedes in Saunders County, Nebraska, 1880–1910." Ph.D. Dissertation, University of Nebraska–Lincoln, 2003.

Seegmiller, Jane B. *A History of Iron County*. Salt Lake City: Utah Historical Society, Iron County Commission, 1996.

Self, Robert O. *American Babylon: Race and the Struggle for Postwar Oakland*. Princeton, NJ: Princeton University Press, 2004.

Senier, Siobhan. *Voices of American Indian Assimilation and Resistance: Helen Hunt Jackson, Sarah Winnemucca and Victoria Howard.* Norman: University of Oklahoma Press, 2001.

Several, Michael. "Little Tokyo: Historical Background." Available from http://www.publicartinla.com/Downtown/Little_Tokyo/little_tokyo.html

Shaler, William. *Journal of a Voyage Between China and the North Western Coast of America, Made in 1804 by William Shaler.* Claremont, CA: Saunders Studio Press, 1935.

Shapsmeier, Edward L., and Frederick H. Shapsmeier, *Encyclopedia of American Agricultural History.* Westport, CT: Greenwood Press, 1975.

Sharette, Maxine. "Links to Poverty." *The Prevention Connection Newsletter* 5 (Fall 2001).

Sheehan, Bernard W. *The Seeds of Extinction: Jeffersonian Philanthropy and the American Indian.* Chapel Hill: University of North Carolina Press, 1973.

Shepherd, Jeffrey. "Building an American Indian Community: The Hualapai Nation in the Twentieth Century." Ph.D. Dissertation, Arizona State University, 2002.

Sherer, Lorraine M. *The Clan System of the Mojave Indians.* Los Angeles: Historical Society of Southern California, 1965.

Sheridan, Thomas E. *Arizona: A History.* Tucson: University of Arizona Press, 1995.

Sheridan, Thomas E. *Los Tucsonenses: The Mexican Community in Tucson, 1854–1941.* Tucson: University of Arizona Press, 1986.

Shinn, Charles Howard. *Mining Camps: A Study in American Frontier Government.* New York: Harper & Row, 1948.

Shipek, Florence. "Documents of San Diego History—A Unique Case—*Temecula Indians v. Holman and Seaman.*" *Journal of San Diego History* 12, no. 2 (1969).

Shipek, Florence Connolly. *Pushed into the Rocks: Southern California Indian Land Tenure, 1769–1986.* Lincoln: University of Nebraska Press, 1988.

Shipley, William. *The Maidu Indian Myths and Stories of Hanc'Ibyjim.* Berkeley, CA: Heyday Books, 1991.

Shiroishi, Julie. "Return to Little Tokyo." *Asian Week* 17, no. 37 (May 10–16, 1996). Available from http://www.asianweek.com/051096/LittleTokyo.html

"Showdown at Jackson Hole." *USA Today,* February 6, 2004.

Shukert, Elfrieda B., and Barbara S. Scibetta. *War Brides of World War II.* Novato: CA: Presidio Press, 1988.

Sides, Josh. *L.A. City Limits: African American Los Angeles from the Great Depression to the Present.* Berkeley: University of California Press, 2003.

Siems, Larry. "Loretta and the Virgin." *Aztlan* 24, no. 1 (1999).

Simmons, Leo W., ed. *Sun Chief: The Autobiography of a Hopi Indian.* Fredericksburg, VA: BookCrafters, 1970.

Simmons, Virginia M. *The Ute Indians of Utah, Colorado, and New Mexico.* Boulder: University Press of Colorado, 2000.

Simpson, R. J. "California Mineral Deposits of the San Jacinto Quadrangle, Mining in California." *California Journal of Mining and Geology* 28 (1932).

Simpson, R. J. "Historical Mineral Resources of a Portion of the Perns Block." *Journal of Mines and Geology* 31 (1935).

Singleton, Heather Valdez. "Surviving Urbanization: The Gabrielino, 1850–1928." *Wicazo SA Review* 19 (Fall 2004).

Sinke, Suzanne M. *Dutch Immigrant Women in the United States, 1880–1920.* Urbana: University of Illinois Press, 2002.

Skinner, A. E. "Books and Libraries in Early Texas." *Texas Libraries* 37 (1975).

Slickpoo, Allen P., Sr., and Deward E. Walker, Jr. *Noon Nee-Me-Poo (We, the Nez Perces): Culture and History of the Nez Perces.* vol. 1. Lapwai: The Nez Perce Tribe of Idaho, 1973.

Smith, Duane A. *Rocky Mountain West: Colorado, Wyoming, and Montana, 1859–1915.* Albuquerque: University of New Mexico Press, 1992.

Smith, Elliot B. "Vietnam America: Two Worlds Collide in a New Generation of Artists and Their Works." *Orange County Register,* December 10, 1994.

Smith, Elmer R. "Resettlement of Japanese Americans." *Far Eastern Survey* 18, no. 10 (May 18, 1949).

Smith, Jessie Carney, ed. *Notable Black American Women.* Detroit, MI: Gale Research, 1992.

Smith, Phyllis. *Bozeman and the Gallatin Valley: A History.* Helena, MT: Falcon, 1996.

Smith, Tracy A. "Uncovering a Sense of Place: The Interaction between Culture and Landscape in Santa Ana Canyon, Orange County, California." M.A. Thesis, California State University, Fullerton, 1995.

Son, Vo. Interview by Trangdai Tranguyen. March 23, 2000. Fullerton, California.

Sonnichsen, C. L. *The Mescalero Apaches.* 2nd ed. Norman: University of Oklahoma Press, 1973.

Sonnichsen, C. L. *Tucson, The Life and Times of an American City.* Norman: University of Oklahoma Press, 1982.

Sorenson, David S. *Shutting Down the Cold War: The Politics of Military Base Closure.* New York: St. Martin's Press, 1998.

Soter, Bernadette Dominique. *The Light of Learning: An Illustrated History of the Los Angeles Public Library.* Los Angeles: Library Foundation of Los Angeles, 1993.

Soule, Frank, John H. Gihon, and James Nisbet. *The Annals of San Francisco.* Berkeley, CA: D. Appleton, 1998.

Southern California Associates Committee for Economic Development. *National Defense and Southern California 1961–1970: A Statement of Policy by the Southern California CED Associates Together with a Research Report by George A. Steiner.* Los Angeles: Southern California CED Associates, 1961.

Southern California Indian Center Web Site. Available from http://www.indiancenter.org

Southern Ute Indian Tribe Web Site. Available from http://www.southern-ute.nsn.us

Sparkman, Philip Stedman. "The Culture of the Luiseno Indians." *University of California Publications in American Archaeology and Ethnology* 8, no. 4 (August 7, 1908).

Speck, Frank G. *The Creek Indians of Taskigi Town.* Washington, DC: Bureau of American Ethnology, 1904.

Spence, Clark C. *Mining Engineers and the American West: The Lace-Boot Brigade, 1849–1933.* New Haven, CT: Yale University Press, 1970.

Spence, Mark David. *Dispossessing the Wilderness: Indian Removal and the Making of the National Parks.* New York: Oxford University Press, 1999.

Spicer, Edward H. *Cycles of Conquest: The Impact of Spain, Mexico, and the United States on the Indians of the Southwest, 1533–1960.* 6th ed. Tucson: University of Arizona Press, 1976.

Spooner, Denise. "A New Perspective on the Dream: Midwestern Images of Southern California in the Post–World War Decades." *California History* 76 (Spring 1997).

Sprague, Marshall. *Money Mountain.* Lincoln: University of Nebraska Press, 1953.

Sprague, Marshall. *Newport in the Rockies: The Life and Good Times of Colorado Springs.* Rev. ed. Chicago: Sage Books, 1971.

Spring, Wilbur. Interviews by Ann Butterfield, Bozeman, MT, October 2003–January 2005.

Stafford, John Allen. *Basque Ethnohistory in Kern County, California: 1872–1934 A.D.* M.A. Thesis, Sacramento State College, 1971.

Stanley, Jerry. *I Am an American: A True Story of Japanese Interment.* New York: Crown, 1994.

Starr, Kevin. *Embattled Dreams: California in War and Peace, 1940–1950.* Oxford, UK: Oxford University Press, 2002.

Starr, Kevin. *Material Dreams: Southern California through the 1920s.* New York: Oxford University Press, 1990.

Steele, Ian K. *Warpaths: Invasions of North America.* New York: Oxford University Press, 1994.

Stegner, Wallace. *The Gathering of Zion: The Story of the Mormon Trail.* New York: McGraw-Hill, 1974.

Stein, Walter J. *California and the Dust Bowl Migration.* Westport, CT: Greenwood Press, 1973.

Steinbeck, John. *The Grapes of Wrath.* New York: Viking Press, 1939.

Steinbeck, John. *The Harvest Gypsies.* San Francisco: The San Francisco News, 1936. (Reprinted, with an introduction by Charles Wollenberg, Berkeley, CA: Heyday Books, 1988)

Steinbeck, John. *Their Blood Is Strong.* San Francisco: Simon J. Lubin Society of California, 1938.

Stephenson, Terry E. *Don Bernardo Yorba.* Los Angeles: Glen Dawson, 1941. (Reprinted Ann Arbor, MI: Edward Bros., 1963)

Stern, Jean, Janet Blake Dominik, and Harvey L. Jones. *Selections from the Irvine Museum.* Irvine, CA: Irvine Museum, 1992.

Stewart, Edgar L. *Custer's Luck.* Norman: University of Oklahoma Press, 1971.

Stewart, George R. *Donner Pass.* San Francisco: California Historical Society, 1960.

Street, S. Richard. *Organizing for Our Lives: New Voices from Rural Communities.* Troutdale, OR: NewSage Press, 1992.

Strong, Clarence C., and Clyde S. Webb. *White Pine: King of Many Waters.* Missoula, MT: Mountain Press, 1970.

Strong, Douglas H. *Tahoe: An Environmental History.* Lincoln: University of Nebraska Press, 1984.

Strong, W. D. "Aboriginal Society in Southern California." *University of California Publications in American Archaeology and Ethnology* 26 (1929).

Stroud, Hubert. *The Promise of Paradise: Recreational and Retirement Communities in the United States since 1950.* Baltimore, MD: Johns Hopkins University Press, 1995.

Sullivan, Kevin. "Vietnam War Memorial's Statue in the Place." *Orange County Register,* September 24, 2002.

Sutter, John A. *The Diary of Johann Augustus Sutter.* San Francisco: Grabhorn Press, 1932.

Sutter, John A. *Personal Reminiscences of General John Augustus Sutter.* Berkeley: University of California Press, Bancroft Library, 1876.

Sutter, John A. *Statement Regarding Early California Experiences*, edited by Allan R. Ottley. Sacramento, CA: Sacramento Book Collectors Club, 1943.

Svingen, Orlan J. *The Northern Cheyenne Indian Reservation, 1877–1900*. Niwot: University Press of Colorado, 1993.

Swartout, Robert R., Jr. "From Kwangtung to Big Sky: The Chinese Experience in Frontier Montana." *Montana: The Magazine of Western History* 38 (1988).

Sweeny, Edwin R. *Cochise: Chiricahua Apache Chief*. Norman: University of Oklahoma Press, 1995.

Swierenga, Robert P., ed. *The Dutch in America: Immigration, Settlement, and Cultural Change*. New Brunswick, NJ: Rutgers University Press, 1985.

Swindle, Lewis J. *The Fraser River Gold Rush of 1858, As Reported by the California Newspapers of 1858*. Victoria, BC: Trafford, 2001.

Tac, Pablo. *Indian Life and Customs at Mission San Luis Rey: A Record of California Mission Life by Pablo, an Indian Neophyte (1835)*. San Luis Rey, CA: Old Mission, 1958.

Takaki, Ronald. *From the Land of Morning Calm: The Koreans in America*. New York: Chelsea House, 1989.

Takaki, Ronald. *Strangers from a Different Shore: A History of Asian Americans*. Boston: Little, Brown, 1989.

Takami, David. *Executive Order 9066: Fifty Years before and Fifty Years After*. Seattle, WA: Wing Luke Asian Museum, 1992.

Takata, Roy Y. Interview with Mary McCarthy [Interview no. 127a, transcript], April 14, 1974. Fullerton: California State University Fullerton Oral History Collection.

Talanian, Debbie. "New Home for the News." *Orange County Register*, August 24, 2002.

Tall Bear, Neva. "Crank on the Crow Reservation." *AIRO (American Indian Research Opportunities) Reporter* (Summer 1999). Available from http://www.montana.edu/wwwai/imsd/rezmeth/crankoncrow.htm

Taniguchi, Nancy J. "California's 'Anti-Okie' Law: An Interpretive Biography." *Western Legal History* 8 (1995).

Taniguchi, Nancy J. "Stigmatizing Okies." In *California History: A Topical Approach*, edited by Gordon Morris Bakken. Wheeling, IL: Harlan Davidson, 2003.

Tapper, Violet, and Nellie Lolmaugh. *The Friendliest Valley: Memories of the Hemet San Jacinto Area*. Hemet, CA: Hungry Eye Books, 1979.

Tarea Hall Pittman Papers, 1951–1970. Sacramento: California State Library.

Taylor, Colin F. *The American Indian*. London: Salamander Books, 2004.

Taylor, Paul S. *Essays on Land, Water, and the Law in California*. New York: Arno Press, 1979.

Taylor, Quintard. *In Search of the Racial Frontier: African Americans in the West, 1528–1990*. New York: Norton, 1998.

Taylor, Sandra C. *Jewel of the Desert: Japanese American Internment at Topaz*. Berkeley: University of California Press, 1993.

Tebbel, John, and Keith Jennison. *The American Indian Wars*. London: Phoenix Press, 2001.

TenBroek, Jacobus, Edward N. Barnhart, and Floyd W. Matson. *Prejudice, War and the Constitution, Causes and Consequences of the Evacuation of the Japanese Americans in World War II*. Berkeley: University of California Press, 1968.

Texas State Historical Association Web Site. Available from http://www.tsha.utexas.edu

Thackeray, Lorna. "Fort Belknap Tribal College to Grow." *Billings Gazette*, November 27, 2001. Available from http://www.billingsgazette.com/index.php?section=local&display=rednews/2001/11/27/build/local/ftbelknap.inc

Thackeray, Lorna. "Thousands See Dedication of Indian Memorial at Little Bighorn." *Billings Gazette*, June 26, 2003. Available from http://www.billingsgazette.com

Thalman, Sylvia. *The Coast Miwok Indians of the Point Reyes Area*. Point Reyes, CA: Point Reyes National Seashore Association, 2001.

Thomas, Alfred B., ed. *After Coronado: Spanish Exploration Northeast of New Mexico, 1696–1727*. Norman: University of Oklahoma Press, 1935.

Thomas, June Manning, and Marsha Ritzdorf, eds. *Urban Planning and the African American Community in the Shadows*. Thousand Oaks, CA: Sage, 1997.

Thomas, Kevin. "A Look Back at a Time of Beginnings." *Los Angeles Times*, May 1, 2002.

Thompson, George A., and Fraser Buck. *Treasure Mountain Home, Park City Revisited*. Salt Lake City, UT: Dream Garden Press, 1981.

Thompson, Lucy. *To the American Indian: Reminiscences of a Yurok Woman*. Foreword by Peter Palmquist. Berkeley, CA: Heyday Books, 1991.

Thornton, Jesse Quinn. *The California Tragedy*. Oakland: California Biobooks, 1945.

Thorson, John E. *River of Promise, River of Peril: The Politics of Managing the Missouri River*. Lawrence: University Press of Kansas, 1994.

Tiller, Veronica. *The Jicarilla Apache Tribe: A History, 1846–1970*. Lincoln: University of Nebraska Press, 1983.

Todd, Helen. *Mary Musgrove: Georgia Indian Princess.* Chicago: Adams Press, 1981.

Tolnay, Stewart E., Kyle D. Crowder, and Robert M. Adelman. "Race, Regional Origin, and Residence in Northern Cities at the Beginning of the Great Migration." *American Sociological Review* 67 (June 2002).

Tonopah, Nevada, Web Site. Available from http://www.tonopahnevada.com

Torres, Luis. *Voices from the San Antonio Missions.* Lubbock: Texas Tech University Press, 1997.

"Traditions of the Creeks: Story of Their Trek from Mexico More Than Three Centuries Ago." Available from http://anpa.ualr.edu/digital_library/jrg_1/1htm

Trafzer, Clifford E. *Death Stalks the Yakama: Epidemiological Transitions and Mortality on the Yakama Indian Reservation, 1888–1964.* East Lansing: Michigan State University Press, 1997.

Trafzer, Clifford E. "European Impact on Native California Cultures." In *Early California Reflections,* edited by Nicholas M. Magalousis. San Juan Capistrano, CA: Orange County Public Library, 1987.

Trafzer, Clifford E. *Renegade Tribe: The Palouse Indians and the Invasion of the Inland Pacific Northwest.* Pullman: Washington State University Press, 1986.

Trafzer, Clifford E., and Diane Weiner, eds. *Medicine Ways: Disease, Health, and Survival among Native Americans.* Walnut Creek, CA: AltaMira Press, 2001.

Trafzer, Clifford E., and Joel R. Hyer, eds. *Exterminate Them! Written Accounts of the Murder, Rape and Enslavement of Native Americans during the Gold Rush.* East Lansing: Michigan State University Press, 1999.

Trafzer, Clifford E., and Richard D. Scheuerman. *Renegade Tribe: The Palouse Indians and the Invasion of the Inland Pacific Northwest.* Pullman: Washington State University Press, 1986.

Trafzer, Clifford E., Luke Madrigal, and Anthony Madrigal. *Chemehuevi People of the Coachella Valley.* Coachella, CA: Chemehuevi Press, 1997.

"The Trail of Tears: A Chronicle, 1830–1849." Available from http://anpa.ualr.edu/trail_of_tears/indian_removal_project/a_chronicle/a_chronicle.htm

Tran, Mai. "Hard Work Pays Off." *Orange County Register,* October 6, 1999.

Tran, Mai. "Seeking to Arrest Immigrants' Fear of Police." *Los Angeles Times,* May 17, 2002.

Tranguyen, Trangdai. *Intern Fellow's Report on Mental Health in Emerging API Sub-populations.* Baltimore, MD: Department of Health & Human Services, 2001.

Tranguyen, Trangdai. "Vietnamese American Women and ESL Classes." Unpublished paper, California State University at Fullerton, 1998.

"Tribal Packing Plant Opens Aug. 4." *Billings Gazette,* July 25, 2003. Available from http://www.billingsgazette.com/index.php?id=1&display=rednews/2003/07/25/build/local/46-packing.inc

Tribe, Patrick. "Park City, Utah: An Analysis of the Factors Causing a Decline of Mining, and of the Factors Which Have Contributed to Its Development as a Recreational Area." M.A. Thesis, Brigham Young University, 1967.

"Tribe Signs Water Compact with State." *Billings Gazette,* February 26, 2001. Available from http://www.billingsgazette.com/index.php?section=local&display=rednews/2001/02/26/build/local/tribe.inc

"Tribe Will Deal for Casino." *Fort Collins Coloradoan Online,* January 16, 2004. Available from http://www.coloradoan.com

"Tribe's Casino Delayed, but Still on Track." *Casper Star Tribune,* May 20, 2004. Available from http://www.casperstartribune.net

"Tribes Take Control of More Programs." *Billings Gazette,* October 4, 2002. Available from http://www.billingsgazette.com/index.php?id=1&display=rednews/2002/10/04/build/local/88-tribes.inc

Trimble, Marshall. *Roadside History of Arizona.* Missoula, MT: Mountain Press, 1986.

Truman, Ben C. *Semi-Tropical California.* San Francisco: A. L. Bancroft, 1874.

"Tuberculosis Outbreak on an American Indian Reservation—Montana, 2000–2001." *Montana Mortality Weekly Report* 51, no. 11.

Turan, Kenneth. "Poignant 'Scent of Green Papaya.'" *Orange County Register,* February 2, 1994.

Twitty, Eric. *Riches to Rust: A Guide to Mining in the Old West.* Montrose, CO: Western Reflections, 2002.

"Two Trainloads of Japanese at Camp." *Cody Enterprise,* August 17, 1942.

Tye, Larry. *Rising from the Rails: Pullman Porters and the Making of the Black Middle Class.* New York: Henry Holt, 2004

Tyler, Robert L. *Rebels of the Woods: The I.W.W. in the Pacific Northwest.* Eugene: University of Oregon Press, 1967.

Ubbelohde, Carl, Maxine Benson, and Duane A. Smith. *A Colorado History.* 8th ed. Boulder, CO: Pruett, 2001.

Uchida, Yoshiko. *Desert Exile: The Uprooting of a Japanese American Family.* Seattle: University of Washington Press, 1982.

Udall, Louise. *Me and Mine: The Life Story of Helen Sekaquaptewa.* Tucson: University of Arizona Press, 1969.

Ueda, Reed. *Postwar Immigrant America: A Social History.* New York: Bedford Books, 1994.

Underhill, Ruth. *Indians of Southern California.* Washington, DC: United States Department of the Interior, Bureau of Indian Affairs, 1941.

University of California Center for Water Resources Web Site. Available from http://www.waterresources.ucr.edu

University of Colorado at Boulder. "The Arapaho Project." Boulder: Colorado University Regents, 2000. Available from http://www.colorado.edu/csilw/arapahoproject/index.html

Uno, Roy. Interview with John McFarlane [Interview no. 1070, transcript], April 25, 1971. Fullerton: California State University Fullerton Oral History Collection.

Unruh, John D., Jr. *The Plains Across: The Overland Emigrants and the Trans-Mississippi West, 1840–60.* Urbana: University of Illinois Press, 1979.

Unruh, John D., Jr. *The Plains Across: The Overland Emigrants and the Trans-Mississippi West, 1840–60.* 1st unabridged paperback ed. Urbana: University of Illinois Press, 1993.

U.S. Army Corp of Engineers. *NEPA/BRAC National Environmental Policy Act Statutes, Guidance, and Information to Assist Base Realignment and Closure Activities.* Washington, DC: U.S. Army Corps of Engineers, 1993.

U.S. Bureau of Education. *Public Libraries in the United States: Their History, Condition, and Management.* Washington, DC: U.S. Government Printing Office, 1876.

U.S. Bureau of the Census. *June 1880 Federal Census.* Washington, DC.

U.S. Census Bureau. *The Native Hawaiian and Other Pacific Islander Populations: 2000.* Census 2000 Brief. Washington, DC: U.S. Census Bureau, 2001.

U.S. Census Bureau. "Table DP-1. Profile of General Demographic Characteristics: 2000." Available from http://wwwstatic.kern.org/gems/KernCOG/Bakersfield.pdf

U.S. Commission on Wartime Relocation and Internment of Civilians. *Personal Justice Denied: Report of the Commission on Wartime Relocation and Internment of Civilians.* Seattle: University of Washington Press, 1997.

U.S. Congress. House. Tolan Committee. Report no. 2124, 77th Cong., 2nd sess., 1942.

U.S. Congress. Senate. Immigration Commission. *Reports.* Vol. 1 (1911).

U.S. Department of Interior. Mission Indian Agency Allotment Schedules and Plates, Including Public Domain Allotments and Homesteads. Records of the Soboba Indian Agency, CA.

U.S. Department of Interior, War Relocation Authority. *A Quantitative Data.* Washington, DC: U.S. Government Printing Office, 1946.

U.S. Department of Interior, War Relocation Authority. *A Story of Human Conservation.* Washington, DC: U.S. Government Printing Office, 1946.

U.S. Department of Interior, War Relocation Authority. *Administrative Highlights of the WRA Program, Volume 1.* New York: AMS Press, 1975.

U.S. Department of Interior, War Relocation Authority. *Community Government in War Relocation Centers, Volume 2.* New York: AMS Press, 1975.

U.S. Department of Interior, War Relocation Authority. *Legal and Constitutional Phases of the WRA Program, Volume 4.* New York: AMS Press, 1975.

U.S. Department of Interior, War Relocation Authority. *People in Motion: The Postwar Adjustment of the Evacuated Japanese Americans.* Washington, DC: U.S. Government Printing Office, 1946.

U.S. Department of Interior, War Relocation Authority. *Relocation of Japanese Americans.* Washington, DC: U.S. Government Printing Office, 1943.

U.S. Department of Interior, War Relocation Authority. *The Relocation Program, Volume 7.* New York: AMS Press, 1975.

U.S. Department of Interior, War Relocation Authority. *Token Shipment: The Story of America's War Refugee Shelter, Volume 8.* New York: AMS Press, 1975.

U.S. Department of Interior, War Relocation Authority. *The War Time Handling of Evacuee Property, Volume 11.* New York: AMS Press, 1975.

U.S. Department of the Interior, Bureau of Land Management. *Location and Patenting of Mining Claims and Mill Sites in California.* Sacramento, CA: Bureau of Land Management, 2000.

U.S. Department of the Interior, Bureau of Land Management. *Mining Claims and Sites on Federal Land.* Washington, DC: U.S. Government Printing Office, 1996.

U.S. Department of the Interior. *The Relocation Program.* Vol. 7. Washington, DC: U.S. Government Printing Office, 1946. (Reprinted New York: AMS Press, 1975)

U.S. Department of the Interior, War Relocation Authority. *A Story of Human Conservation.* Washington, DC: U.S. Government Printing Office, 1946. (Reprinted New York: AMS Press, 1975)

U.S. Department of the Interior, War Relocation Authority. *Administrative Highlights of the WRA Program,* Vol. 1.

Washington, DC: U.S. Government Printing Office, 1946. (Reprinted New York: AMS Press, 1975)

U.S. Department of the Interior, War Relocation Authority. *Community Government in War Relocation Centers,* Vol. 2. Washington, DC: U.S. Government Printing Office, 1946. (Reprinted New York: AMS Press, 1975)

U.S. Department of the Interior, War Relocation Authority. *Legal and Constitutional Phases of the WRA Program,* Vol. 4. Washington, DC: U.S. Government Printing Office, 1946. (Reprinted New York: AMS Press, 1975)

U.S. Department of the Interior, War Relocation Authority. *The War Time Handling of Evacuee Property,* Vol. 11. Washington, DC: U.S. Government Printing Office, 1946. (Reprinted New York: AMS Press, 1975)

U.S. Department of the Interior, War Relocation Authority. *Token Shipment: The Story of America's War Refugee Shelter,* Vol. 8. Washington, DC: U.S. Government Printing Office, 1946. (Reprinted New York: AMS Press, 1975)

U.S. General Accounting Office. *Military Bases, Environmental Impact at Closing Installations: Report to Congressional Requesters.* Washington, DC: U.S. General Accounting Office, 1995.

U.S. Marine Corps. *Marine Corps Recruit Depot 2004 Biennial Report.* San Diego, CA: U.S. Marine Corps Public Affairs, 2004.

U.S. Office of the Assistant Secretary of Defense for Economic Security. *Closing Bases Right: A Commander's Handbook.* Washington, DC: U.S. Government Printing Office, 1995.

U.S. Senate. *Walapai Papers: Historical Reports, Documents, and Extracts from Publications Relating to the Walapai Indians of Arizona.* Washington, DC: U.S. Government Printing Office, 1936.

Utah History to Go Web Site. Available from http://historytogo.utah.gov

Ute Mountain Ute Tribe Web Site. Available from http://www.utemountainute.com

Utley, Robert M. *Cavalier in Buckskin.* Norman: University of Oklahoma Press, 1988.

Utley, Robert M. *The Indian Frontier of the American West 1846–1890.* Albuquerque: University of New Mexico Press, 1984.

Utley, Robert M. *The Lance and the Shield: The Life and Times of Sitting Bull.* New York: Henry Holt, 1993.

Valdes, Dionicio N. *Barrios Nortenos: St. Paul and Midwestern Mexican Communities in the Twentieth Century.* Austin: University of Texas Press, 2000.

Van Cott, John W. *Utah Place Names.* Salt Lake City: University of Utah Press, 1990.

Van Fleet, C. M., and Lucile Hooper. "The Cahuilla Indians." *American Archaeology and Ethnology* 16 (1920).

van Hinte, Jacob. *Netherlanders in America: A Study of Emigration and Settlement in the Nineteenth and Twentieth Centuries in the United States of America.* Robert P. Swierenga, gen. ed.; Adriaan de Wit, chief trans. Grand Rapids, MI: Historical Committee of the Christian Reformed Church, 2003.

Van Horn, Kurt. "Tempting Temecula: The Making and Unmaking of a Southern California Community." *Journal of San Diego History* 20, no. 1 (1974).

Van Steenwyk, Elizabeth. *Levi Strauss: The Blue Jean Man.* New York: Walker, 1988.

Van West, Carroll. *Capitalism on the Frontier.* Lincoln: University of Nebraska Press. 1993.

Vanderknyff, Rick, "Cultural Commerce Expected to Blossom." *Orange County Register,* February 4, 1994.

Varney, Philip. *Southern California's Best Ghost Towns.* Norman: University of Oklahoma Press, 1990.

Vaught, David. *Cultivating California: Growers, Specialty Crops, and Labor, 1875–1920.* Baltimore, MD: Johns Hopkins University Press, 1999.

Vichorek, Daniel N. *Montana's Homestead Era.* Helena: Montana Magazine, 1987.

Viehe, Fred W. "Black Gold Suburbs: The Influence of the Extractive Industry on the Suburbanization of Los Angeles, 1890–1930." *Journal of Urban History* 8 (November 1981).

Virden, Jenel. *Good-Bye, Piccadilly.* Urbana: University of Illinois Press, 1996.

Vizcaino, Fr. Juan. *The Sea Diary of Fr. Juan Vizcaino to Alta California 1769.* Los Angeles: Glen Dawson, 1959.

Von Bernewitz, M. V. *Handbook for Prospectors and Operators of Small Mines.* 4th ed. Revised by Harry C. Chellson. New York: McGraw-Hill, 1943.

Vose, Clement E. *Caucasians Only: The Supreme Court, the NAACP, and the Restrictive Covenant Cases.* Berkeley: University of California Press, 1959.

Voynick, Stephen M. *Climax: The History of Colorado's Climax Molybdenum Mine.* Missoula, MT: Mountain Press, 1996.

Vredenburg, Larry, Russell L. Hartill, and Gary L. Shumway. *Desert Fever: An Overview of Mining in the California Desert.* Canoga Park, CA: Living West Press, 1981.

Vredenburg, Larry, Russell L. Hartill, and Gary L. Shumway. *An Overview of the History of Mining in the California Desert.* Sacramento, CA: U.S. Bureau of Land Management, 1979.

Vu, Pham. Interview by Trangdai Tranguyen. July 11, 2000. Huntington Beach, California.

Vu, Thiennu. Interview by Trangdai Tranguyen. August 12, 2000. San Francisco, California.

Wachob, Bill, and Andrew Kennedy. "Beating B-1 Bob: How Underdog Democrat Loretta Sanchez Ended Bob Dornan's Congressional Career (Case Study)." *Campaigns & Elections* 18, no. 1 (1997).

Wagner, Henry R. *Spanish Voyages to the Northwest Coast of America in the Sixteenth Century.* 2nd ed. San Francisco: California Historical Society, 1966.

Wagoner, Jay J. *Arizona Territory, 1863–1912: A Political History.* Tucson: University of Arizona Press, 1970.

Waite, Donald E. *The Langley Story Illustrated: An Early History of the Municipality of Langley.* Altona, MB: D. W. Friesen, 1977.

Walker, Deward E., Jr. *Conflict and Schism in Nez Perce Acculturation: A Study of Religion and Politics.* Moscow: University of Idaho Press, 1985.

Walker, Don D. "Reading on the Range: The Literary Habits of the American Cowboy." *Arizona and the West* 2 (Winter 1960).

Wallace, Anthony F. C. *Jefferson and the Indians: The Tragic Fate of the First Americans.* Cambridge, MA: Harvard University Press, 1999.

Wallace, Robert. *The Miners.* Alexandria, VA: Time-Life, 1976.

War Brides in Montana Oral History Project. Interviews conducted 2001–2002 by Dr. Seena Kohl, Behavioral and Social Sciences, Webster University.

Ward, Geoffrey C. *The West.* Boston: Little, Brown, 1996.

Warren, Earl. "California's Biggest Headache." *Saturday Evening Post* 221 (August 7, 1948).

Washburn, Wilcomb E., ed. *Handbook of North American Indians, California.* Vol. 8. Washington, DC: U.S. Government Printing Office, 1978.

Wat, Eric. *The Making of a Gay Asian Community: An Oral History of Pre-AIDS Los Angeles.* Lanham, MD: Rowman & Littlefield, 2002.

Water Resources Institute Web Site. Available from http://wri.csusb.edu

Watt, Ronald G. *City of Diversity: A History of Price, Utah.* Price, UT: Price City, 2001.

Watt, Ronald G. *A History of Carbon County.* Salt Lake City: Utah Historical Society, 1997.

Weals, Frederick H. *How It Was: Some Memories by Early Settlers of the Indian Wells Valley and Vicinity.* Rev. ed. Ridgecrest, CA: Historical Society of the Upper Mojave Desert, 1994.

Weals, Frederick H. *Indian Wells Valley: How It Grew.* Ridgecrest, CA: Historical Society of the Upper Mojave Desert, 2001.

Weatherford, Jack. *Indian Givers: How the Indians of the Americas Transformed the World.* New York: Fawcett Columbine, 1988.

Weber, David J., ed. *New Spain's Far Northern Frontier.* Albuquerque: University of New Mexico Press, 1979.

Weber, Francis, ed. *King of the Missions: A Documentary History of San Luis Rey de Francia.* Los Angeles: Archdiocese of Los Angeles Archives, 1980.

Webster, Sean T. *National Patterns and Community Impacts of Major Domestic U.S. Military Base Closures, 1988–Present.* Denton: University of North Texas Press, 2004.

Weglyn, Michi. *Years of Infamy: The Untold Story of America's Concentration Camps.* New York: William Morrow, 1976.

Weglyn, Michi. *Years of Infamy: The Untold Story of America's Concentration Camps.* Updated ed. Seattle: University of Washington Press, 1996.

Weibel-Orlando, Joan. *Indian Country, L.A.: Maintaining Ethnic Community in Complex Society.* Urbana: University of Illinois Press, 1991.

Weigle, Marta, and Barbara A. Babcock. *The Great Southwest of the Fred Harvey Company and the Santa Fe Railway.* Phoenix, AZ: Heard Museum, 1996.

Wells, Merle. *Boise: An Illustrated History.* Woodland Hills, CA: Windsor, 1982.

Wells, Merle W. *Gold Camps & Silver Cities: Nineteenth Century Mining in Central and Southern Idaho.* Moscow: University of Idaho Press, 2002.

West, Elliott. "Called Out People: The Cheyennes and the Central Plains." *Montana: The Magazine of Western History* 48 (Summer 1998).

West, Elliott. *The Contested Plains: Indians, Goldseekers, and the Rush to Colorado.* Lawrence: University Press of Kansas, 1998.

West, Ray B., ed. *Rocky Mountain Cities.* New York: Norton, 1949.

Westcott, John. "A New Life in a New Land." *Orange County Register,* June 22, 2000.

Western Environmental Law Center Web Site. Available from http://www.westernlaw.org

"What Is a Ute?" Available from http://www.utefans.net/home/ancient_ute/utetribe.html

Wheeler, B. Gordon. "Allensworth: California's All-Black Community." *Wild West,* February 2000. Available from http://www.historynet.com/we/blallensworth/

Wheeler, Nik. "Bridge Too Far." *Preservation* 53, no. 4 (2001).

Whitaker, Arthur P. *The United States and the Southern Cone: Argentina, Chile, and Uruguay.* Cambridge, MA: Harvard University Press, 1976.

White, David A. *News of the Plains and Rockies, 1803–1865: Original Narratives of Overland Travel and Adventure Selected from the Wagner-Camp and Becker Bibliography of Western Americana. Vol. 2, C: Santa Fe Adventurers, 1818–1843, and D: Settlers, 1819–1865.* Spokane, WA: Arthur H. Clark, 1996.

White, Richard. *"It's Your Misfortune and None of My Own": A History of the American West.* Norman: University of Oklahoma Press, 1991.

Whiteley, Peter M. *Deliberate Acts: Changing Hopi Culture through the Oraibi Split.* Tucson: University of Arizona Press, 1988.

Whithorn, Doris. *Photo History of Livingston-Bozeman Coal Country.* Livingston, MT: Park County News, n.d.

Whitney, Mary E. *Valley, River, Mountain: Revisiting Fortune Favors the Brave: A History of Lake Hemet Water Company.* Hemet, CA: Hemet Area Museum Association, 1982.

Whittington, Roberta E. *Hemet-San Jacinto: A Geographic Survey of an Agricultural Valley.* M.A. Thesis, University of California–Los Angeles, 1987.

Widtsoe, John A. *Dry-Farming: A System of Agriculture for Countries under a Low Rainfall.* New York: Macmillan, 1911.

Wiegand, Wayne A. *"An Active Instrument for Propaganda": The American Public Library during World War I.* Westport, CT: Greenwood Press, 1989.

Wiegand, Wayne A. "Oregon's Public Libraries during the First World War." *Oregon Historical Quarterly* 90 (Spring 1989).

Wild, Mark. *Street Meeting: Multiethnic Neighborhoods in Early Twentieth-Century Los Angeles.* Berkeley: University of California Press, 2005.

Wiley, Peter Booth. *A Free Library in This City: The Illustrated History of the San Francisco Public Library.* San Francisco: Weldon Owen, 1996.

Willett, Edward. *Iran-Iraq War.* New York: Rosen, 2004.

Wilson, Benjamin D. *The Indians of Southern California in 1852: The B. D. Wilson Report and a Selection of Contemporary Comment.* Lincoln: University of Nebraska Press, 1995.

Wilson, Joseph F. *Tearing Down the Color Bar: A Documentary History and Analysis of the Brotherhood of Sleeping Car Porters.* New York: Columbia University Press, 1989.

Wissler, Clark, and D. C. Duvall. *Mythology of the Blackfoot Indians.* Lincoln: University of Nebraska Press, 1995.

Witzel, Michael. *Route 66 Remembered.* Osceola, WI: Motorbooks International, 1996.

Woehlke, Walter V. "Angels in Overalls: Being a True and Veracious Account of Workaday Life in the Angelic Region, Together with an Exposition of the Manners and Methods by Which the Inhabitants of the Angel City Boosted the Demand for Junipers and Jeans, and an Attempt to Show That Bellboys, Millionaires, Hotel Clerks and Tourists Have No Exclusive Entry into the Aforesaid Realm." *Sunset Magazine* (March 1912).

Wolfenson, Bernard J. "Festival Gives a Sense of Straddling Two Worlds." *Orange County Register,* September 7, 1999.

Wolle, Muriel Sibell. *Montana Pay Dirt: A Guide to the Mining Camps of the Treasure State.* Athens: Ohio University Press, 1983.

Women's Legal History Biography Project. "Clara Shortridge Foltz." Available from http://www.stanford.edu/group/WLHP

Wong, Kent. *Voices for Justice: Asian Pacific American Organizers and the New Labor Movement.* Los Angeles: UCLA, Center for Labor Research and Education, 2001.

Wood, Nancy. *When Buffalo Free the Mountains.* Garden City, NY: Doubleday, 1980.

Wood, Tom S. "A Brief History of the Granite Industry in San Diego County." *Journal of San Diego History* 20, no. 3 (1974).

Woods, Sister Frances J. *Mexican Ethnic Leadership in San Antonio, Texas.* New York: Arno Press, 1976.

Woodward, Grace S., Harold P. Howard, and Gae W. Canfield. *Three American Indian Women: Pocahontas, Sacajawea, and Sarah Winnemucca.* New York: MJF Books, 1997.

Woolsey, Ronald C. *Migrants West: Toward the Southern California Frontier.* Claremont, CA: Grizzly Bear, 1996.

Woolsey, Ronald C. "The Politics of a Lost Cause: 'Seceshers' and Democrats in Southern California during the Civil War." *California History* 69, no. 4 (Winter 1990–1991).

Woolsey, Ronald C. *Will Thrall and the San Gabriels, A Man to Match the Mountains.* San Diego, CA: Sunbelt, 2004.

Worcester, Donald, E. *The Apache: Eagles of the Southwest.* Norman: University of Oklahoma Press, 1979.

Wride, Nancy. "No More Looking Homeward." *Orange County Register,* April 4, 1994.

Wright, Gloria. Interviews by Leleua Loupe. January, April, and November 2001. Soboba Reservation, San Jacinto, California.

Wright, J. Leitch, Jr. *Creeks and Seminoles: The Destruction and Regeneration of the Muscogulge People.* Lincoln: University of Nebraska Press, 1986.

Wright, Muriel. *A Guide to the Indian Tribes of Oklahoma.* Norman: University of Oklahoma Press, 1951.

Wright, Willard Huntington. "Los Angeles—The Chemically Pure." In *The Smart Set Anthology,* edited by Burton

Roscoe and Geoff Couklin. New York: Reynal and Hitchcock, 1934.

Wyckoff, William. *Creating Colorado: The Making of a Western Landscape, 1860–1940.* New Haven, CT: Yale University Press, 1999.

Wyman, Mark. *Hard Rock Epic: Western Miners and the Industrial Revolution, 1860–1910.* Berkeley: University of California Press, 1979.

Yans-McLaughlin, Virginia, ed. *Immigration Reconsidered: History, Sociology, and Politics.* New York: Oxford University Press, 1990.

"Yellowtail." *Encyclopedia of North American Indians,* edited by Frederick Hoxie. New York: Houghton Mifflin, 1996.

Yi, Daniel. "Vietnamese Classes Set a New Course." *Los Angeles Times,* September 22, 2002.

Yoo, David. *Growing Up Nisei: Race, Generation, and Culture among Japanese Americans of California, 1924–49.* Champaign: University of Illinois Press, 2000.

Young, Otis E., Jr. *Black Powder and Hard Steel: Miners and Machines on the Old Western Frontier.* Norman: University of Oklahoma Press, 1976.

Young, Otis E., Jr. *Western Mining: An Informal Account of Precious-Metals Prospecting, Placering, Lode Mining, and Milling on the American Frontier from Spanish Times to 1893.* Norman: University of Oklahoma Press, 1970.

Yung, Judy. *Unbound Feet: A Social History of Chinese Women in San Francisco.* Berkeley: University of California Press, 1995.

Zanjani, Sally. *A Mine of Her Own: Woman Prospectors in the American West, 1850–1950.* Lincoln: University of Nebraska Press, 1997.

Zanjani, Sally. *Sarah Winnemucca.* Lincoln: University of Nebraska Press, 2001.

Zanjani, Sally S. "To Die in Goldfield: Mortality in the Last Boomtown on the Mining Frontier." *Western Historical Quarterly* 21 (February 1990).

Zeilbauer, Paul B. "Thinking of Tourists." *Orange County Register,* August 20, 1994.

Zhou, Min, and James Gatewood. *Contemporary Asian America: A Multidisciplinary Reader.* New York: New York University Press, 2000.

Zhu, Liping. *A Chinaman's Chance: The Chinese on the Rocky Mountain Mining Frontier.* Niwot: University Press of Colorado, 1997.

Zhu, Liping. "No Need to Rush: The Chinese, Placer Mining, and the Western Environment." *Montana: The Magazine of Western History* 49 (1999).

Zimmerman, Tom. "Paradise Promoted: Boosterism and the Los Angeles Chamber of Commerce." *California History* 64 (Winter 1985).

Zollinger, James P. "John Augustus Sutter's European Background." *California Historical Society Quarterly* 14 (1935).

Zollinger, James P. *Sutter: The Man and His Empire.* New York: Oxford University Press, 1967.